BLUE G

Please write in with your comments, suggestions and corrections for the next edition of the Blue Guide. Writers of the most helpful letters will be awarded a free Blue Guide of their choice.

BLUE GUIDE

SOUTHWEST FRANCE

Delia Gray-Durant

A&C Black • London
WW Norton • New York

First edition May 2003

Published by A & C Black Publishers Ltd
37 Soho Square, London W1D 3QZ

www.acblack.com

© Delia Gray-Durant 2003
Maps by RJS Associates, updated by Mapping Company Ltd, © A & C Black Publishers Limited.

ISBN 0–7136–5928–9

'Blue Guides' is a registered trademark.
A CIP catalogue record of this book is available from the British Library.

Published in the United States of America by
W W Norton & Company, Incorporated
500 Fifth Avenue, New York, NY 10110

Published simultaneously in Canada by
Penguin Books Canada Limited
10 Alcorn Avenue, Toronto
Ontario M4V 3BE

ISBN 0–393–32471–0 USA

The author and the publishers have done their best to ensure the accuracy of all the information in Blue Guide Southwest France; however, they can accept no responsibility for any loss, injury or inconvenience sustained by any traveller as a result of information or advice contained in the Guide.

The area covered by this book was previously featured in two separate volumes, Blue Guide South West France: Dordogne to the Pyrenees and Blue Guide Midi-Pyrénées.

Cover photographs The top photograph is of the Maison du Cadet at Beynac © Explorer; the lower image is of Limeuil in the Dordogne valley, © David Martyn Hughes. Both photographs are reproduced courtesy of Robert Harding Picture Library.
Title page Château de Bonaguil by Peter Spells.

Line drawings on pp 80, 109, 111, 163, 167, 182, 217, 261, 276, 288, 309, 323, 336, 346, 374, 408, 426, 452, 497, 542 by Peter Spells; photograph on p 524 reproduced courtesy of the CDT Ariège-Pyrénées, B. Benoit, and those on pp 199, 219, 251, 320, 529 courtesy CRT Toulouse Midi-Pyrénées.

Delia Gray-Durant's association with France began more than thirty years ago when she went to live and work in Paris. Subsequently she studied French and History of Art at University and had a home in the Midi-Pyrénées. Now she writes books and leads art history tours. She continues to spend a large part of the year in France with friends and family who live there. Delia Gray-Durant is also the author of *Blue Guide Paris and Versailles*.

A&C Black uses paper produced with elemental chlorine-free pulp, harvested from managed sustainable forests.

Printed and bound in Great Britain by Butler and Tanner Ltd, Frome and London.

Contents

Maps and plans

Introduction

Memories, prompted by some old photos, of the very first visit I made to the southwest of France conjure up a long, slow train ride to the Basque country where oxen still ploughed the fields, fishermen in St-Jean-de-Luz landed huge tuna directly onto the quay, and Biarritz had recently begun to learn about surfing. There was no *autoroute* connecting Toulouse to Bordeaux but the Château de Roquetaillade, ahead of most, was already receiving visitors. Much later I set aside an April weekend to visit Conques, seasonally draped in wisteria, and was totally hooked; fields of sweet-smelling wild narcissi in the Aubrac and my 'discovery' of the *Entombment* in Monestiés long before its restoration in 1992 simply added to the addiction.

The southwest has moved on, but much has remained timeless and anyone who samples its pleasures will surely be intoxicated. Accessibility has vastly improved with the construction of new motorways and bypasses which leave sleepy villages even sleepier, yet incorporate amazing feats of engineering such as the road bridge on stilts which spans the Viaur Valley and Norman Foster's even more ambitious project (due to open in 2004) which will carry the A75 over the Tarn Valley at Millau.

The routes that for centuries crossed France, leading the devout to the shrine of St James at Compostela in Spain, are busy again with modern-day pilgrims on foot or bicycle. These routes, with their associated churches, abbeys, bridges and hospices, stretching across the southwest from the church of Notre-Dame-de-la-Fin-des-Terres in Soulac at the tip of the Médoc to the Porte St-Jacques in St-Jean-Pied-de-Port on the threshold of Spain, have been classified UNESCO World Heritage sites. Other UNESCO designations serve to illustrate the broad sweep of cultural heritage in Aquitaine and Midi-Pyrénées: they include the Vezère Valley, sometimes described as the Valley of Man, where the unique concentration of prehistoric sites bears witness to the development and creativity of humans some 20,000 years ago; the Juridiction de St-Emilion, the eight parishes which now fall under the authority of the *jurade* whose limits were defined in 1199 by Richard the Lionheart, and which correspond to the vineyards within the St-Emilion *appellation*; and the spectacular amphitheatre formed by the Pyrenees, the Cirque de Gavarnie, an example of the great natural phenomena in Midi-Pyrénées.

Several museums have been revamped or extended since the last editions of this guide. The most important, which opened in June 2000, is the centre of modern and contemporary art in the renovated 19C slaughterhouses on the left bank of the Garonne in Toulouse. It follows the trend seen at Bordeaux's Musée d'Art Contemporain (and Tate Modern in London), of occuping former industrial buildings. The superb Musée Basque in Bayonne emerged in 2001 after a long sleep, rejuvenated and transformed into one of the most sophisticated local museums in the region. A more modern theme is tackled at the Cité de l'Espace on the outskirts of Toulouse, reflecting the region's heavy involvement in the space industry.

In the past the southwest has suffered its fair share of political upheaval and religious turmoil, but the present remains largely unhurried except at the two poles, Bordeaux in the north and Toulouse in the south, linked by the Garonne and respectively the fifth and fourth largest cities in France, which serve to anchor the layout of this book and work like magnets on the region itself.

Dynamic and prosperous but different in character, they provide a large proportion of the employment and wealth of the two administrative regions, Aquitaine and Midi-Pyrénées. Bordeaux, moulded by the success of its wine trade and of shipping, exudes an aura of calm elegance resulting from the period of urban regeneration that shaped the layout and architecture of the city during the Age of Enlightenment. Toulouse, originally an inland river port, is very much a city of the Midi, a link between the Mediterranean and the Atlantic. Its warm brick façades, Renaissance mansions and pavement life have absorbed the influences of the South of France and of Spain and reinterpreted them in a very individual manner. Each city takes advantage of its riverscapes and a massive scheme is still underway in Bordeaux to make full use of the banks of the Garonne, which were formerly made over to commercial shipping.

Between the two urban poles unroll the bucolic landscapes of this largely agricultural region watered by the Dordogne, the Lot and the Tarn. The unhurried present may account for the longevity of the inhabitants in the Gers, although they would probably ascribe it to plenty of unsaturated goose fat and good red wine. And why not? By the time you have got up on a summer's morning and have bought the croissants, everything closes and it is almost time for a siesta.

This edition of Blue Guide *Southwest France* combines two earlier titles, *South West France. Dordogne to the Pyrenees* (1994) and *Midi-Pyrénées. Albi, Toulouse, Conques, Moissac* (1995). It gathers together information on two huge regions, Aquitaine and Midi-Pyrénées, that are closely intertwined historically and geographically, to make a more comprehensive touring guide where administrative boundaries make little sense. **Aquitaine** encompasses five *départements*, Gironde, Landes, Lot-et-Garonne, Dordogne and Pyrénées-Atlantiques; the eight *départements* of **Midi-Pyrénées** are Gers, Lot, Tarn, Tarn-et-Garonne, Hautes-Pyrénées, Haute-Garonne and Ariège-Pyrénées.

Acknowledgements

I wish to thank the Comités Régionaux du Tourisme for Aquitaine and for the Midi-Pyrénées and the thirteen Comités Départementaux for their practical assistance with travel, accommodation and the organisation of visits. I would also like to thank Brittany Ferries for their help with travel to and from the region. I am personally grateful to Laurence Ibrahim-Aibo and Solenne Odon of the CRT Midi-Pyrénées and Marie-Yvonne Holley of CRT Aquitaine who have responded promptly and patiently to endless queries and requests, as have their colleagues at the Comités Départementaux. Although too numerous to mention individually, I would like to record my infinite gratitude to the staff of tourist information offices and museums, châteaux owners and church officials throughout the southwest of France who have been so forthcoming and helpful with arranging visits and providing information. I should also like to thank Alison Effeny, and Gemma Davies and Kim Teo of A & C Black for quietly keeping me on the right track. Last but not least, thanks to Will and Siân who are always there with an encouraging word.

PRACTICAL INFORMATION

 Planning your trip

When to go

The summer months, July and August, are the most crowded but also the most animated. School vacations in Europe and the French tradition of a general exodus from the cities for their annual break between 14 July and the end of August results in congestion on the roads, the necessity to book early and capacity gatherings at seaside resorts. There are also the benefits of soaring temperatures, a greater selection of activities available and longer opening times at sites, monuments and museums. At this period rental properties in the countryside are at a premium, especially those with pools because many people know that even in high season it is still possible to find peace and quiet in the rural southwest. September is busy but not as hectic as high summer and with many of the same advantages. For those with the whole year at their disposal there are unexpected pleasures to out-of-season travel, although the less-frequented sites tend to close after 1 November and do not open again until March or April.

The climate of southwest France is in general very pleasant. Temperatures range from a winter average of 10°C (50°F) to highs of 27°C (80°F) and above in July and August. This general balminess is the result of the meeting of weather patterns between the Continental mass to the northeast, the Atlantic to the west and the warm and drying wind, the *vent d'autan*, which blows in from the Mediterranean and supposedly has an unsettling effect.

But averages are averages, and there are fairly violent climate swings in certain places. **Spring** tends to be wetter than the autumn, but benefits from a wonderful range of wild flowers, which last right through to July in the mountains. **Autumn** is generally glorious to the end of October or early November (although I have known a week's non-stop rain at this time).

Midsummer is likely to be very hot, temperatures rising to the low 30s (90–95° F) and occasionally to the high 30s (95–105°F), combined with high humidity inland, when the nights are stifling. Cities such as Toulouse and Auch are unpleasantly steamy in July and August. At times the southern Atlantic coast enjoy higher temperatures than the Mediterranean, although the heat is tempered by ocean breezes. Towards the end of August heat builds up to spectacular thunder storms which do not necessarily clear the air.

Summer **rainfall** is lower than the national average, tending to drought conditions, although the Atlantic coast, the Pyrenees and the Aubrac can be pretty wet at all times. January and February are the least inspiring months, although there are exceptions and certain winter landscapes have a beautiful desolation. This is a great opportunity for a city break.

It has to be accepted that there are constant contradictions and exceptions in the weather throughout the region, aptly summed up in a favourite French comment, *'ce n'est-pas normal.'*

Meteorological information, www.meteo.fr

Passports and formalities

All British, American and Canadian travellers to France require passports but not visas. Your passport will serve as ID, which is required in France.

If you are from an EU country and intend to stay in France for more than three months, you should apply in advance for a *carte de séjour* from the nearest French consulate (see below) or, if you are already in France, at a main *préfecture de police*. Those wanting to work in France should write to the consular section of the embassy which will advise on the procedure to be followed, according to their status under EU regulations. It should be emphasised that it acts neither as an employment agency nor as an accommodation agency.

French embassies and main consulates abroad

Consult these for contact details on local consulates.

Australia   Level 26, St Martins Tower, 31 Market St, Sydney NSW 2000, ☎ 02 9261 5779, fax 02 9283 12 10, www.ambafrance-au.org

Canada   42 Promenade, Ottawa ON K1M 2C9, ☎ 613 789 1795, www.ambafrance-ca.org

Ireland   36 Ailesbury Rd, Ballsbridge, Dublin 4, ☎ 01 260 1666, fax 01 283 0178, www.ambafrance.ie

New Zealand   34–42 Manners St, PO Box 11-343, Wellington, ☎ 04 384 2555, fax 04 384 2577, www.ambafrance.net.nz

UK   58 Knightsbridge, London SW1X 7JT, ☎ 020 7201 1004, www.ambafrance.org.uk

USA   4101 Reservoir Rd NW, Washington DC 20007, ☎ 202 944 6000, fax 202 944 6166, www.info-france-usa.org

Tourist information

French Government Tourist Offices (Maisons de la France) supply general information, including how to get to France and travel within it, and suggest accommodation. They have a useful online reference guide, **www.franceguide.com**.

French Government Tourist Offices abroad

Australia   Level 20, 25 Bligh Street, Sydney NSW, ☎ 02 9231 5244, fax 02 9221 8682, email france@bigpond.net.au

Canada   1981 Ave MacGill College, Suite 490, Montreal, Quebec H3A 2W9, ☎ 514 288 4264, fax 514 845 4868, email mfrance@attcanada.net

Ireland   30 Merrion Street Upper, Dublin 2, ☎ 1 560 235 235, email frenchtouristoffice@eircom.net

New Zealand   see Australia

UK 178 Piccadilly, London W1V 9AL, ☎ 09068 244 123, fax 020 7493 6594, email info@mdlf.co.uk

USA   444 Madison Ave, 16th floor, New York, NY 10020, ☎ 410 286 8310, fax 212 838 7855, email info@francetourism.com

875 North Michigan Avenue, Suite 3214, Chicago, Illinois 60611-2819, ☎ 312 751 7800, fax 312 337 6339

9454 Wilshire Boulevard, Suite 715, Beverly Hills, Los Angeles, California 90212-2967, ☎ 310 271 6665, fax 310 276 2835, email fgto@gte.net

1–2 Biscayne Tower, Suite 1750, 2 South Biscayne Blvd, Miami, ☎ 305 373 8177, fax 305 373 5828, email webmaster@franceguide.com

Regional and Departmental Tourist Boards in France
Aquitaine
Comité Régional de Tourisme d'Aquitaine, Cité Mondiale, 23 Parvis des Chartrons, 33074 Bordeaux, ☎ 05 56 01 70 00, fax 05 56 01 70 07, email tourisme@crt.cr-aquitaine.fr, www.tourism-aquitaine.info

Comité Départemental de Tourisme de la Dordogne, 25 Rue du Président Wilson, 24009 Périgueux, ☎ 05 53 35 50 24, fax 05 53 09 51 41, email dordogne.perigord.tourisme@wanadoo.fr, www.perigord.tm.fr

Comité Départemental de Tourisme de la Gironde, Maison de Tourisme de la Gironde, 21 Cours de l'Intendence, 33000 Bordeaux, ☎ 05 56 52 61 40, fax 05 56 81 09 99. email tourisme@gironde.com, www.tourisme-gironde.cg33.fr

Comité Départemental de Tourisme des Landes, 4 Ave Aristide-Briand, BP 407, 40012 Mont-de-Marsan Cedex, ☎ 05 58 06 89 89, fax 05 58 06 90 90, email cdt.landes@wanadoo.fr, www.tourismelandes.com

Comité Départemental de Tourisme du Lot-et-Garonne, 4 Rue André-Chénier, BP 158, 47005 Agen Cedex, ☎ 05 53 66 14 14, fax 05 53 68 25 42, email cdt47@wanadoo.fr, www.lot-et-garonne.fr

Comité Départemental de Tourisme des Pyrénées-Atlantiques, 4 Allées des Platanes, BP811, 64108 Bayonne Cedex, ☎ 05 59 46 52 52, fax 05 59 46 52 46, email cdt@cg64.fr, www.tourisme64.com

Midi-Pyrénées
Comité Régional de Tourisme Midi-Pyrénées, 54 Blvd de l'Embouchure, BP 2166, 31022 Toulouse Cedex 2, ☎ 05 61 13 55 48/55, fax 05 61 47 17 16, email information@crtmp.com, www.tourisme-midi-pyrenees.com

Comité Départemental de Tourisme de l'Ariège-Pyrénées, 31 bis Ave du Gen. de Gaulle, BP 143, 09004 Foix Cedex, ☎ 05 61 02 30 70, fax 05 61 65 17 34, email tourisme.ariege.pyrenees@wanadoo.fr, www.ariegepyrenees.com

Comité Départemental de Tourisme de l'Aveyron, 17 Rue Aristide-Briand, BP 831, 12008 Rodez Cedex, ☎ 05 65 75 55 75, fax 05 65 75 55 71, email aveyron-tourisme-cdt@wanadoo.fr, www.tourisme-aveyron.com

Comité Départemental de Tourisme du Gers, 3 Blvd Roquelaure, BP 106, 32002 Auch Cedex, ☎ 05 62 05 95 95, fax 05 62 05 02 16, email cdtdugers@wanadoo.fr, www.gers-gascogne.com

Comité Départemental de Tourisme de la Haute-Garonne, 14 rue Bayard, BP 845, 31015 Toulouse Cedex 06, ☎ 05 61 99 44 00, fax 05 61 99 44 19, email bienvenue@cdt-haute-garonne.fr, www.toruisme-haute-garonne.com

Comité Départemental de Tourisme des Hautes-Pyrénées, 11 Rue Gaston Manent, BP 9502, 65950 Tarbes Cedex 09, ☎ 05 62 56 70 65, fax 05 62 56 70 66, email tourisme.hautes-pyrenees@cg65.fr, www.cg65.com

Comité Départemental de Tourisme du Lot, 107 Quai Cavaignac, BP 7, 46001 Cahors Cedex 09, ☎ 05 65 35 07 09, fax 05 65 23 92 76, email le-lot@wanadoo.fr, www.tourisme-lot.com

Comité Départemental de Tourisme du Tarn, Les Moulins Albigeois, 41 Rue Porta, BP 225, 81006 Albi Cedex, ☎ 05 63 77 32 10, fax 05 63 77 32 32, email documentation@cdt-tarn.fr, www.tourisme-tarn.com

Comité Départemental de Tourisme du Tarn-et-Garonne, 7 Blvd Midi-Pyrénées, BP534, 82005 Montauban Cedex, ☎ 05 63 21 79 09, fax 05 63 66 80 36, email cdt82@wanadoo.fr, www.tourisme82.com

Tour operators

Any accredited member of the **Association of British Travel Agents** will sell tickets and book accommodation. The numerous excellent package deals offered by agents specialising in France include cultural, sporting and other activity holidays. Watch the national press for special offers. Over 180 companies providing French holidays can be contacted through www.holidayfrance.org.uk.

Selected UK tour operators

Ace Study Tours, ☎ 01223 835 055, www.study-tours.com. Guided tour of the Dordogne.
Andante Travels, 01722 713 800, www.andantetravels.co.uk. Guided tour of the cave art of the Dordogne.
Bonnes Vacances, ☎ 01582 699 996, wwwbvdirect.co.uk. Properties to rent direct from their owners.
Brittany Ferries, ☎ 08705 143 537, www.brittanyferries.com. Specialise in *gîtes*.
Chez Nous, ☎ 08700 781 400, www.cheznous.com. Properties to rent direct from their owners.
Cycling for Softies/for Gourmets, ☎ 0161 248 8282, www.cycling-for-softies.co.uk.
France Afloat, ☎ 01905 616 428, www.franceafloat.com.
The Gascony Secret, ☎ 01284 827 253, www.gascony-secret.com. Properties to rent in the southwest.
Inntravel, ☎ 01653 629 010, www.inntravel.co.uk. Self-guided walking and cycling holidays.
Martin Randall Travel, ☎ 020 8742 3355, www.martinrandall.com. Cultural tours.
Prospect Music & Art Tours, 36 Manchester Street, London W1M 5PE, ☎ 020 7846 5704, sales@prospecttours.com. Cultural tours.
Ramblers Holidays, ☎ 01707 331 133, www.ramblersholidays.co.uk.
Something Special, ☎ 08700 270 510, fax 01279 642 890, www.somethingspecial.co.uk. Self-catering, villas and châteaux.
Vacances en Campagne, ☎ 08700 771 771, www.indiv-travellers.com. A wide range of properties to let.
VFB Cottage Holidays in France and *France à la Carte*, ☎ 01242 240 310, www.vfbholidays.co.uk. The Cottages in France offers self-catering properties, ranging from cottages to luxury villas; France à la Carte features hotel-based holidays.

Maps

The *AA Baedeker Map* of France includes main **city centre plans**. *AA Road Maps France* (1 inch:2.8 miles) is a series of 16 very clear and detailed regional maps. *Leisure Map France* (1:1,000,000 or 1cm:10km) is a new style of double-sided colour map marked with places of cultural interest, wine regions, recreation areas, and so on, from Estate Publications.

Michelin maps are always popular. The *Michelin Motoring Atlas France* (1:200,000) has a very clear format and includes 75 town plans. *Michelin Mini Atlas France* is useful for quick reference and planning your journey. The yellow Michelin Maps (1:200,000) are updated annually and easy to read and give a detailed if slightly unwieldy overview of the regions. Maps 234 (Aquitaine) and

235 (Midi-Pyrénées) cover the bulk of the southwest, 233 (Poitou-Charentes) and 240 (Languedoc-Rousillon) the extreme north and east. In the smaller, departmental, series you need maps 75, 78, 79, 80, 82, 83, 85 and 86. The *France Route Planning* map (726) gives distances, journey times, alternative routes and motorway information. The *Motorway Atlas* (914) includes toll costs, equipment at service and rest areas, distance tables and times of journeys between main towns. Maps can be ordered from the Customer Services, Michelin Travel Publications, Hannay House, 39 Clarendon Road, Watford WD17 1JA, ☎ 01923 20 52 40, www.viamichelin.com.

In conjunction with the regions, the **Institut Géographique Regional** produces *Découvertes Régionales* tourist maps (1:250,000). In the Série Rouge you need maps 110, 111, 113 and 114 for southwest France. Cyclists and hikers will find useful maps from one or more of the Série Verte (1:100,000), Série Orange (1:50,000) and Série Bleue (1:25,000).

The latest editions of these maps can be found at most good booksellers in the UK, USA and Canada and in France. *Stanfords*, 12–14 Long Acre, London WC2E 9LP, ☎ 020 7836 1321, www.stanfords.co.uk, offer a mail order service.

Health and insurance

As members of the EU, **British subjects** are entitled to use the French health services but need an E111 form. This is available from post offices and must be filled out and stamped by the post office before departure. Medical costs have to be paid in France and it is important to have the doctor sign the E111 form at the time of consultation. All receipts for consultations, treatments, prescriptions and the detachable labels on medicines (*vignettes*) must be kept in order to make a claim in France.

The average level of reimbursement of medical expenses is 70 per cent. You are strongly advised to take out **private travel insurance** to cover the cost of medical expenses and repatriation, the loss of luggage, and loss due to theft. This also applies to visitors from non-EU countries.

Pharmacies, recognisable by a green cross sign, will give first aid and medical advice. *Pharmacie du garde* open at night or at weekends; details will be listed on the door of the pharmacy and in the local press.

It is usually easy to find a doctor—consult a pharmacy, your hotel, or a telephone directory—and there is little delay getting an appointment. Not all doctors speak English. Go equipped with your insurance policy/E111 form, and remember that you will have to pay on the spot. Some doctors prescribe homeopathic remedies.

Currency

The **Euro** was introduced on 1 January 2002 and since February 2002 has been the sole currency in circulation. Central banks will exchange national banknotes up to 10 years from the time they stopped being legal tender, and national coins up to three years. The seven banknotes—in units of 5, 10, 20, 50, 100, 200 and 500—are identical throughout the Euro zone. The eight coins—1, 2, 5, 10, 20 and 50 cent, 1 and 2 Euro—have one common side which identifies the respective denomination and one side particular to the country of origin. All notes and coins are legal tender in all 12 countries that have adopted the Euro. At the time of writing, approximate conversion values are:

1 Euro = 6.56 FF	1 Euro = 1.59 CAD
1 Euro = 1 USD	1 Euro = 1.8 AUD
1 Euro = 0.67 GBP	

For more information, see www.euro.ecb.int or www.euro.gouv.fr.

Cash can be obtained from ATM machines bearing the Carte Bleue/Visa or Mastercard logo, or the Eurocard symbol, and from American Express machines. Check with your own bank about charges for using ATMs abroad. There are complicated arrangements and charges for cashing bank cheques from foreign countries. Traveller's cheques are a safe way of carrying money and can be used in some transactions, and changed at banks and *bureaux de change*, but commission is charged. *Bureaux de change* will probably be slightly more efficient than banks, which tend to be rather slow, especially in small towns. Hotels will usually change traveller's cheques but the rate tends to be less competitive. There is no advantage to taking euro traveller's cheques.

Banks tend to offer fairly similar exchange rates but the Banque Nationale de Paris has a reputation for being the most favourable. When assessing the relative rates between banks and the currency booths, check the commission; many have a flat surcharge or commisssion of about €5 for every transaction. When changing money it is likely that you will be given high denomination notes which are often awkward to use for everyday expenses. Try to ensure that you have some smaller notes and change to pay for such things as buses or taxis.

Credit cards are accepted for most transactions. French credit cards have a chip or *puce*. Cards with magnetic strips are valid but not always easily read by French machines and occasionally this can cause a problem at an ATM machine. Make sure to take your bank or card issue number with you. If your credit cards are lost or stolen, see p 40.

Disabled travellers

France is becoming increasingly aware of the needs of disabled travellers. New logos depicting four specific types of disability—physical, mental, partial sight or blindness, impaired hearing or deafness—are now displayed in airports and other public places to guide the disabled or their carers to areas where help is available. These symbols also appear in tourist literature, at public attractions and tourist sites.

Travel. For general information on transport options, see below. On Le Shuttle the disabled can stay in their vehicles. Eurostar trains are a convenient way to travel and offer disabled passengers first class travel for second class fares. When making a booking to travel on the TGV, advise your booking agent if you use a wheelchair. Most ferry companies also offer special facilities and assistance but you need to check in at least 1 hour before departure. The international blue scheme for **parking** applies in France. Reduced **tolls** on the *autoroutes* are available to vehicles fitted to accommodate the transport of the disabled. The vehicle registration must show VP or Disabled.

Accommodation. Not every hotel in France offers facilities for the disabled, although modern ones are likely to. The French Tourist Office provides brochures of hotels by region and those suitable for disabled visitors are indicated with the disabled logo.

The website www.destinationvitavie.com gives personalised advice on transport and particular destinations.

Advice in the UK

Holiday Care Information Unit, 7th Floor Sunley House, 4 Bedford Park, Croydon, Surrey CR0 2AP, 0845 124 9971, fax 0845 124 9972 www.holiday-care/org.uk. A national charity which acts a source of travel and holiday information for disabled and older people, their families and carers.

RADAR (Royal Association for Disability and Rehabilitation), 12 City Forum, 250 City Road, London EC1V 8AF, ☎ 020 7250 3222, fax 020 7250 0212, www.radar.org.uk. An organisation of and for disabled people. It provides information, campaigns for improvements and supports disability organisations.

Advice in the USA

Mobility International USA, PO Box 10767, Eugene, Oregon USA 97440, ☎ (541) 343 1284, fax (541) 343 6812, www.miusa.org. A non-profit organisation whose mission is to empower people with disabilities through international exchange, information and technical assistance.

Society for Accessible Travel and Hospitality, 347 Fifth Ave, Suite 610, NY 10016, ☎ (212) 447 7284, www.sath.org. a non-profit educational organisation that campaigns on behalf of disabled and older travellers.

Getting there

By air

From the UK

British Airways operates flights from London Gatwick and from Birmingham to Bordeaux and Toulouse.

Air France has regular flights from London Heathrow and from Birmingham to Toulouse; from Dublin to Bordeaux.

Ryanair (now including *Buzz*) offers flights from London Stansted to Bordeaux, Bergerac, Biarritz, Carcassone, Pau, Rodez, and Toulouse (not all of them all year round).

British Midland operates flights from Manchester and East Midlands to Toulouse.

BMIbaby flies from East Midlands to Toulouse.

Flybe goes from Birmingham to Toulouse.

   Connecting flights from Paris. There are frequent daily flights from Paris Orly to Bordeaux and Toulouse operated by *Air France*. *Protéus Airlines*, franchised to Air France, operates flights from Paris to Rodez (☎ 05 65 42 20 30) and Paris to Castres (☎ 05 63 70 34 77). Air-Lib runs daily flights from Paris Orly to Tarbes-Lourdes-Pyrénées.

Air France, ☎ 0845 0845 111, www.airfrance.co.uk; in France,
   ☎ 0802 802 802, information 05 56 00 40 40

Air-Lib, ☎ 08 25 09 09 09 (French number), www.airlibexpress.com

British Airways, ☎ 0845 773 3377, in France ☎ 0825 825 400,
   www.britishairways.com

Buzz, ☎ 0870 240 7070, www.buzzaway.co.uk (now part of Ryanair)

Ryanair, ☎ 0871 246 0000, www.ryanair.com

From Ireland

Aer Lingus, ☎ 0818 365 000, www.aerlingus.com, Dublin to Paris

Air France, ☎ (0)1 6050 383, www.airfrance.ie, Dublin to Bordeaux
Ryanair, ☎ 0818 30 30 30, www.ryanair.com, Dublin and Shannon to Paris

From the USA and Canada

Air Canada, ☎ 888 247 2262, www.aircanada.ca
Air France, ☎ 800 237 2747, www.airfrance.com/us
American Airlines, ☎ 800 433 7300, www.aa.com
British Airways, ☎ 800-AIRWAYS, www.britishairways.com/usa
Continental, ☎ 800 231 0856, www.continental.com
Delta, ☎ 800 241 4141, www.delta.com
Nouvelles Frontiers, ☎ 800 677 0720, ☎ 310 670 7318, www.newfrontiers.com
Northwest Airlines, 800 225 2525, www.nwa.com
United Airlines, ☎ 800 538 2929, www.ual.com

From Australia and New Zealand

Qantas, ☎ 131313, www.qantas.com
Air New Zealand, ☎ 00 649 366 2400, www.airnz.com

By sea

From the UK: car ferries

Brittany Ferries run the following **cross-Channel routes**: Portsmouth–Caen (6 hours), Poole–Cherbourg (4hrs 15mins, high-speed 2hrs 10 mins), Portsmouth–St Malo (9hrs), Plymouth–Roscoff (6hrs). An alternative route runs from **Plymouth to Santander** in northern Spain (24hrs), from where you enter southwest France via San Sebastian or through the Pyrenees.

P&O Portsmouth run Portsmouth–Le Havre (5hrs 30mins) and Portsmouth–Cherbourg (4hrs 45mins). The **Portsmouth to Bilbao** route allows entry to France via Spain, as above.

P&O Stena operates up to 35 return sailings every day Dover–Calais (1hr and 15mins to 1hr 30mins).

Hoverspeed runs two **Seacat services** per day Dover–Ostend (about 2hrs); three Superseacat services per day Newhaven–Dieppe (about 2hrs); and up to 15 Superseacat services per day during peak season Dover–Calais (just under an hour).

Sea France operates ferries Dover–Calais.

Brittany Ferries, ☎ 08705 360 360, www.brittanyferries.com
Hoverspeed, ☎ 08705 240 241, www.hoverspeed.com
P&O Portsmouth, ☎ 0870 2424 999, www.poportsmouth.com
P&O Stena, ☎ 087 0600 0600, www.pofl.com
Sea France, ☎ 08705 711 711, www.seafrance.com

From Ireland

P&O Irish Sea Rosslare–Cherbourg, Dublin–Cherbourg (both take18–19hrs), ☎ 1 800 409 049, www.poirishsea.com.

By rail

Passengers with cars can travel by Eurotunnel from Folkestone to Calais (35mins). French Motorail offers regular car-transporting trains from Calais direct to Brive and Toulouse from May to September, and from Paris to Bordeaux, Brive, Biarritz and Toulouse all year; it saves a lengthy drive but is expensive. For **foot passengers**, Eurostar is an efficient way to travel to Paris from London

Waterloo or Ashford in Kent (Waterloo to Paris Gare du Nord 3hrs).
Eurostar, ☎ 08705 186 186, www.eurostar.co.uk
Eurotunnel, ☎ 08705 353 535, www.eurotunnel.com
French Motorail, ☎ 08702 415 415, www.frenchmotorail.com
High-speed **TGV** (*Trains à Grande Vitesse*) depart from Paris Montparnasse for Bordeaux (4hrs) and Toulouse (5hrs). They also run to Agen, Arcachon (via Facture), Biarritz (4hrs 30mins), Dax, Lourdes, Montauban, Pau, Tarbes and the Spanish border at Irún/Hendaye. Corail operates regular high-speed services that are less expensive than the TGV. These depart from Paris Austerlitz to Bordeaux and Toulouse. On overnight trains *couchettes* (shared sleeping accommodation) must be reserved, which can be done up to 2 months in advance at Rail Europe or direct with the SNCF.

Rail Europe, the UK subsidiary of the French SNCF, can advise on all **rail travel in France** including Eurostar, rail passes and Motorail.
Rail Europe, 178 Piccadilly, London W1, ☎ 08705 848 848,
brochure ☎ 08705 024 000, www.raileurope.co.uk.
SNCF France for direct information/reservations in France, ☎ 08 36 35 35 35, www.sncf.com

By coach

There are very few long-distance bus companies in France, partly due to the scale and efficiency of the train service, but *Eurolines UK* (☎ 08705 143 219, www.eurolines.com) operates between Paris and the main cities of France. Tickets from most parts of Britain can be purchased through *National Express* (☎ 08705 808080, www.gobycoach.com) in France contact *Eurolines France*, ☎ 04 72 56 95 30. Coaches depart from London Victoria Coach Station. The main destinations in southwest France are Arcachon, Bayonne, Bordeaux, Cahors, Mimizan, Souillac, Tarbes and Toulouse. The main coach tours to the region are operated by firms from outside France and should therefore be booked as a complete package holiday from Britain.

Where to stay

Categories and prices

Hotels in France are officially classified by a system of stars, ranging from one to four, indicating the range of amenities offered; for example in a one-star hotel bathrooms may be shared, while two or three-star hotels are likely to offer bathrooms, televisions, lifts. Some un-starred hotels are perfectly adequate, or may be awaiting a rating. The star system is only a rough guide to **prices**, which vary considerably within each category. Prices are usually quoted per room, not per person, and do not normally include breakfast: note, however, that half- or full-board rates are quoted per person. Tariffs are generally listed outside the hotel or in the reception area, and law requires that the price is posted in the room itself. Garage parking, particularly in towns, is sometimes charged extra. The following is a very rough guide to prices which are subject to seasonal variations.

	Price per night
☆☆☆☆	€85–320
☆☆☆	€45–90
☆☆	€39–60
☆ (and no star)	€25–40

It is advisable to **book in advance** if you want rooms in July and August and during the French national holidays (*jours fériés*) in May. In the Pyrenees hotels are busy from January to March.

Other types of accommodation in France include:
Chambres d'hôte, the French equivalent of bed and breakfast
Gîtes ruraux, self-catering country cottages
Gîtes d'étape, hostels for walkers

Information outside France

The **French Government Tourist Office** in London provides the guide to *Relais & Châteaux*, free over the counter or by post for £5 from Relais & Châteaux, 35–37 Grosvenor Gardens, London SW1W 0BS, ☎ 020 7630 7667, www.relaischateaux.com. It also supplies guides to *Lôgis de France*; *Châteaux & Hôtels de France*, privately owned chateaux; *Bienvenue au Château*, stately homes welcoming paying guests; *Château Accueil*, up-market bed and breakfast; and *Grandes Etapes Françaises*, four-star hotels or 'residences of character'.

Other sources of information on hotels and restaurants are the **books** *Michelin Red Guide*, the *Gault Millau Guide France*, and the *Routiers Guide to France*, available by post from Routiers, 25 Vanston Place, London SW16 1AZ, ☎ 0207 385 6644.

Information in France

The Regional and Departmental Tourist Boards offer information on all forms of accommodation ranging from *châteaux-hotels* to campsites and will also make reservations.

Relais du Silence provide accommodation in quiet surroundings. Central booking service: Paris, ☎ 01 44 49 90 00, fax 01 44 49 79 01, www.silencehotel.com

Gîtes de France et Tourisme Vert for rental accommodation in rural France, 59 Rue St-Lazare, 75439 Paris Cedex 09, ☎ 05 49 70 75 75, fax 01 42 81 28 53, www.gites-de-france.fr

Aquitaine

The following information (unless otherwise stated) is available from the **Comité Régional de Tourisme d'Aquitaine** (CRT Aquitaine), Bureaux de la Cité Mondiale, 23 Parvis des Chartrons, F-33074 Bordeaux Cedex, ☎ 05 56 01 70 00, fax 05 56 01 70 07, email tourisme@crt.cr-aquitaine.fr

Maps

Accommodation in hotels and guesthouses

Guide des Hôtels et Résidences

'Bienvenue a la Ferme', farm accommodation including *fermes auberges* (farm inns), *fermes équestres* (farms offering horse-riding), *fermes de séjour* (holiday homes) and *camping à la ferme* (camp sites), available from the **Chambre Régionale d'Agriculture**, Cité Mondiale, 6 Parvis des Chartrons, 33075 Bordeaux Cedex, ☎ 05 56 01 33 33, fax 05 57 85 40 40, email chambragri.cra-aquitaine@wanadoo.fr

Courts séjours/short stays (2–6 days), brochure with 15 selected trips for getting to know Aquitaine

Rental accommodation

Gîtes de France, including *Gîtes Bacchus*, in a winery or in a wine-growing area; *Gîtes de Pêche*, for fishermen; *Gîtes Panda*, in conservation areas

Clévacances, label which guarantees a personalised welcome by the owner and quality accommodation (www.clevacances.com)

Thalassotherapy

Information on salt water health treatments

Campsites

Guide des Campings, Caravanning throughout Aquitaine for all categories of camp sites

Information on campsites available also from the *Fédération Régionale d'Hôtellerie de Plein Air*, BP 6, F-40600 Biscarrosse, ☎ 05 58 78 88 88

Midi-Pyrénées

Unless otherwise stated, the following information is available from the *Comité Régional du Tourisme de Midi-Pyrénées*, 54 Blvd de l'Embouchure, BP 2166, 31022 Toulouse Cedex 2, ☎ 05 61 13 55 12, fax 05 61 47 17 16, email information@crtmp.com

Reservations can be made through *MPLV (Réservations)*, 54 Blvd de l'Embouchure, BP 2166, 31022 Toulouse Cedex 2, ☎ 05 34 25 05 05, fax 05 34 25 05 09, email reservations@mplv.org or through the *French Holiday Service*, London, ☎ 0870 442 98 43, fax 0208 324 40 30, email fhs@leisuredirection.co.uk

Maps

Accommodation in hotels and guesthouses

Holiday Guide, a brochure designed for British visitors with 43 short breaks and summer holidays in hotels, châteaux, manors and mills, mountain inns or holiday homes including Toulouse en Liberté

Guide Vacances, with a selection of over 120 ideas for short breaks and weekends

Guide Art de Vivre, rental and bed & breakfast accommodation selected for unique character and quality

Guide des Hôtels, lists hotels for the whole region

Carte des Chambres et Tables d'Hôtes, a map showing accommodation and meals in guest houses and b&bs

'Bienvenue a la Ferme' Guide des Fermes-Auberges et Gouters à la Ferme, farm inns

Rental accommodation

Guide des Gîtes d'Etape et de Séjour

Gites de France Midi-Pyrénées

Clévacances, label which guarantees a personalised welcome by the owner and quality accommodation, 54 Blvd de l'Embouchure, BP 2166, F-31022 Toulouse Cedex 2, ☎ 05 61 13 55 67, fax 05 61 13 55 94, www.clevacances.com

Camping

Guide des Campings provides information throughout the Midi-Pyrénées for all categories of campsites

Also from the *Fédération Régionale d'Hôtellerie de Plein Air*, 21 Chemin du Pont de Rupé, 31200 Toulouse, ☎ 05 62 70 97 37, fax 05 61 70 17 55, www.mipycamp.com

Mountain refuges
Contact the Comités Départementaux for the Ariège, Hautes-Pyrénées and Haute-Garonne, p 13.
Spas
Guide du thermalisme gives information and special offers at spas in the region

 Food and drink

Restaurants

The cuisine of the southwest is as varied as its landscape and culture and it is possible to eat both hearty, meaty and rustic meals at reasonable prices or *haute cuisine* at correspondingly high prices. There are restaurants of all categories throughout the region and rural *fermes auberges* also offer pre-booked meals.

In this guide, restaurant **prices** denoted by Euro symbols (€) indicate a very approximate average price for lunch or dinner taking into account the variation between *à la carte* and set menus.

	Price per person
€	€25–40
€€	€40–65
€€€	€65–85
€€€€	€85 and above

Fixed-price set menus are usually good value if you are budgeting, especially at midday: you may find lunch menus from €10 upwards. Dinner is more expensive, but there are still some for around €17–20. An average price for a good meal is €25–40, although for a real gastronomic binge the sky's the limit.

Lunch is served from 12.00 to around 14.30; dinner from 19.30 to around 22.30. In small towns and rural areas the closing times may be earlier; in large towns they could be later. Restaurants are closed one day a week, often Sunday evening and/or Monday, so it is wise to check. In towns it is becoming easier to find light lunches, salads and snacks but out of town lunch is still considered the main meal of the day and snacks are hard to find. The set menu is usually good value. If buying for a picnic, don't forget that most markets and foodstores (except large supermarkets) will close between 12.00 and 14.00.

Two reliable **restaurant guides** are the *Michelin Red Guide* and the *Routiers Guide to France*. But it is also a good idea to ask locals—shopkeepers, tour guides, car park attendants and coach drivers—where they would eat. Eating is, after all, a national pastime.

Cuisine of the southwest

In general the cooking of the interior of the region is based on the fat of the land, and specifically on duck, goose and pork, while the coast abounds in good fish and oysters, but it is unwise to generalise because each *pays* has its own **specialities**. Excellent lamb is raised on the *causses* of the Quercy, in the Rouergue and around Pauillac in the Médoc; veal in the St-Gaudens area; beef in the Aubrac, the Chalosse and Bazas; and freshwater fish in the Rouergue. Not only regional, but **seasonal produce** plays an important part in the cuisine. Autumn is the time for dishes incorporating wild mushrooms, especially *cèpes* but also *girolles*, *morilles* and *pleurotes*, as well as chestnuts, walnuts and prunes; and in winter there are truffles and abundant *foie gras*, although the latter is becoming more of an all-year-round treat.

Soup *Garbure* is a hearty Pyrenean or Gascon peasant soup made mainly from vegetables (butter beans, potatoes and cabbage), with a bit of goose or duck thrown in. *Tourin* is made with onions and garlic. *Moutairol* is from the north of the region while *Le Ttoro* (pronounced Tioro) is a Basque fish soup with mussels and other fish, flavoured with onion and tomatoes.

Seafood and shellfish Oysters are available in most restaurants on the coast, especially around Arcachon. They are usually served on the half shell and consumed alive. They may be sprinkled with a little lemon juice or vinegar but in the Arcachon Basin, rather curiously, they are frequently served with *crepinettes* (grilled sausages), *foie gras* or terrine and sometimes are deep fried or served *au gratin* (browned under a grill). Oysters are perfect with a good white Graves, Entre-deux-Mers or Premières Cotes-de-Bordeaux.

Mussels may be flambéed on a bed of pine needles. *La Rouquette*, the soup of the Bassin d'Arcachon, is made from crab and loubine (local name for bass or sea-perch). *Chipirons à l'encre*—squid cooked in their ink, with various other flavourings including Armagnac, or pimentoes from Espelette and tomato—is a very popular dish on the southern Atlantic coast. In the Gironde estuary, a curious serpent-like creature called a *lamproie* (lamprey, not strictly a fish but a primitive aquatic vertebrate with a sucking mouth full of teeth) is still fished, as are the occasional sturgeon and *alose* (shad) as well as *pibales* (elvers). Freshwater fish include *brochet* (pike), *truite* (trout) and *sandre* (perch). *Le Marmitake* is a dish of the Basque coast, which was originally prepared by fishermen at sea from fresh tuna, potatoes, sweet peppers, onions, hot red peppers and white wine. *Estofinado*, a traditional dish eaten in the Lot Valley in the winter, is made from dried haddock (stockfish), potatoes, garlic and parsley; dried fish from the Baltic became a lucrative cargo carried by boats on the Lot returning from the coastal port at Bordeaux.

Meat Basic to the cooking of the southwest are poultry, duck, goose and pork. Think of the *foie gras* and *pâtés* of Gascony; the *charcuterie* (dried sausage) and *jambon cru* or *jambon de pays* (cured ham) from the Monts de Lacaune; and the best known, *jambon de Bayonne* from the Valley des Aldudes. The duck and geese fattened up for *foie gras* also produce *magrets* (breast fillets) and *gésiers* (gizzards). *Confit* is poultry or pork preserved in its own fat and eaten hot or cold. *Saucisse de Toulouse* is fresh sausage sold by the kilo.

Cassoulet is a regional dish from the Toulousain, particularly the Lauragais, and the Lot, based on white haricot beans, goose fat, goose or duck and Toulouse sausage, with local variations. *Pistache* is a variety of *cassoulet* cooked in the Pyrenees. *Sanglier* (wild boar) and *marcassin* (young boar), game and venison can be found in certain regions, and *salmis palombe* is a dish made from wood pigeon.

Peteram is tripe as it is cooked around Luchon, in the Pyrenees; in the Quercy tripe is cooked with saffron, once an important crop here; and *tripoux de Naucelles*, in the Aveyron, is tripe cooked with ham and garlic in white wine.

Vegetables White garlic produced in and around Beaumont-de-Lomagne (Tarn-et-Garonne) and pink garlic around Lautrec (Tarn) are both of a superb quality. There are also artichokes from Macau and asparagus from the Landes. Pimentoes are cultivated in Pays Basque and many dishes incorporate them, including *la Piperade*, a type of ratatouille made of onions, garlic, pimentoes, tomatoes and ham bone for flavouring; but it may also be served in a type of scrambled eggs with ham and croutons. A typical Basque dish is *Hachoa*, incorporating hot red pepper powder (preferably from Espelette peppers), with diced veal and sweet peppers, which is cooked in a pan over the heat.

Truffles are treated like gold dust: they are the ultimate complement to vegetable, egg and meat dishes and combine royally with *foie gras*. They are usually cooked, but they can be eaten raw.

Cheese One of the great regional cheeses of the southwest is the blue of Roquefort, made from the milk of sheep raised on the *causses* of the Rouergue near Millau. A totally different but equally succulent *fromage de brebis* is Ossau-Iraty, made from the milk of Basque and Bearnais ewes, and served with *cerises noires d'Itxassou* (black-cherry jam). Cow's milk is used for Laguiole, a smooth, yellow, fairly hard cheese produced in the Aubrac and mixed with potatoes and cream to become *aligot*, and also for a number of Pyrenean varieties from Bethmale and the Couserans. The best of the goats' cheeses is *cabecou* from Rocamadour in the Lot and the *rieumes* from Haute-Garonne. Note that cheese is always served before the dessert in France.

Fruit and nuts Strawberries are grown in Saint-Geniès d'Olt (Aveyron) and around Monpazier (Dordogne), the Chasselas dessert grape is special to the Moissac district, and fragrant melons are found in many areas, especially the Néracois and in the Lot. In Lot-et-Garonne and Tarn-et-Garonne peaches, nectarines, apples, pears and, more recently, kiwi fruit are cultivated as well as the plums which are transformed into the world renowned *pruneaux d'Agen*. The most exotic version of these are *pruneaux fourrés*, the stone replaced by a *crème d'Armagnac* or some other filling.

Chestnuts from the Aveyron valley are used in a number of recipes. Walnuts abound in the Dordogne and the Lot, and the chocolate-covered variety are particularly delicious.

Pastries and sweets *Croustade* is a flaky-pastry pie with a filling, usually apples; *pastis* is light-as-a-feather crisp pastry, with apples, sugar and butter and a dash of Armagnac or rum. *Gâteau à la broche*, found in the western part of the Pyrenees and in the Rouergue, is a conical cake that looks rather like a stalagmite. It has a high fat content and is cooked slowly on a revolving spit. *Fouace* is a semi-sweet cake with a little dried fruit to liven it up. *Gâteau Basque* is a light cake made with ground almonds and eggs, often cooked in a pastry base. *Macarons* are popular in the Basque country as well as St-Emilion; *mouchous* are two *macarons* attached with *crème patissière*. Bayonne is the place to wallow in pure, unadulterated **chocolate**, molten and solid.

Bread (*pain*) is usually bought at *boulangeries*; the most popular is *une baguette*, a long thin roll, sometime disappointing in the Midi. There are smaller versions made from the same dough, such as *une ficelle* and others of varying shapes. This bread does not keep—it is best to eat it straightaway. *Pain de campagne* is a larger, rustic loaf and there has been an increase in recent years of other types of bread such as *pain complet* (wholegrain), *pain aux noix* (walnut bread) and *pain de seigle* (rye bread, traditionally served with oysters). A *tartine* is buttered bread.

Food lexicon

Many French culinary terms and processes are universally known, but the following may be helpful when negotiating menus and markets.

Les potages (soups)
bouillon, broth
consommé, clear soup
crème, thick soup
potage, thick (vegetable) soup

**Hors d'oeuvre et salades
(appetisers and salads)**
aïoli, mayonnaise of vinegar, oil and pulverised garlic, often eaten with fish
croque monsieur/croque madame, toasted cheese and ham sandwich/topped with an egg
crudités, raw vegetables, usually sliced, chopped or grated
pissaladière, Provençal onion and anchovy pie
salade Niçoise, with tomato, anchovy, onions and olives
salade panachée, mixed salad
salade verte (also *salade simple* or *de saison*), green salad
tapénade, purée of black olives, capers, anchovies, from the Provençal *tapéno*, for capers

Les oeufs (eggs)
including some hot *hors d'oeuvre*
omelette aux fines herbes, savoury omelette
omelette au jambon, ham omelette, etc
oeufs durs soubise, hard-boiled eggs with a béchamel sauce with onions
à la coque, soft-boiled
durs, hard-boiled
brouillés, scrambled
en cocotte, baked in a ramekin
mollets, medium-boiled
pochés, poached
sur le plat (or *au plat*), fried

Les poissons (fish), les coquillages et crustacés (shellfish)
alose, shad
anchois, anchovy

angler, devil fish
anguille, eel
bar, freshwater bass
barbue, brill
belon, type of oyster
bigorneau, winkle
blanchaille, whitebait
brandade de morue, sort of fish pie with salt cod and potatoes
brochet, pike, often the base of *quenelles*
cabillaud, cod
calmar, squid
carpe, carp
chipiron, squid
colin, hake
coques, cockles
coquilles St-Jaques, scallops
crevettes, prawns or shrimps
cuisses de grenouilles, frogs' legs
daurade, sea bream
dorée, John Dory
écrevisse, freshwater crayfish
églefin, haddock
encornet, squid
escargot, snail
espadon, swordfish
esturgeon, sturgeon
friture, deep-fried whitebait
hareng, herring
homard, lobster
huître, oyster
lamproie, lamprey
langouste, crayfish or lobster
langoustine, Dublin Bay prawn
lieu, coley
lotte, monkfish
lotte de rivière, burbot
loup de mer, sea bass
maquereau, mackerel
merlan, whiting
mérou, grouper
morue, salt cod
moule, mussel
mulet, grey mullet
palourde, clam

poulpe, octopus
raie, skate (often served *au beurre noir*, with black butter)
rouget, mullet
rouget barbet, red mullet
rouget grondin, gurnard
st-pierre, John Dory
sandre, pikeperch
saumon, salmon
saumon fumé, smoked salmon
seiche, cuttlefish
thon, tuna
truite, trout

Les viandes (meat)

agneau, lamb
bavette/onglet, beef flank steak
bifteck, beefsteak, a franglais word in use since 1786
boeuf, beef
carré d'agneau, lamb cutlets
cassoulet, a stew of white haricot beans, goose fat, Toulouse sausage, pork and probably goose or duck
chateaubriand, fillet steak
cochon de lait, suckling pig
daube, stew
gigot d'agneau, leg of lamb
marmite, stew
mouton, mutton
porc, pork (see below)
pot-au-feu, stew
queue de boeuf, ox-tail
ris de veau, sweetbreads
rosbif, roast beef
veau, veal
viandes froides, cold meats

Meat may be ordered
bleu, very rare
saignant, rare
à point, medium
bien cuit, well done

La charcuterie (pork products, cured or cooked meats)

abats, offal
andouille, smoked chitterling sausage
andouillettes, a smaller version

boudin blanc, veal, chicken or pork sausage
boudin noir, blood sausage/black pudding
cervelle, brain
foie, liver
foie gras, goose liver
jambon, ham
jambon cuit, York ham
jambon cru, *jambon de Bayonne*, cured ham
jambon fumé, smoked ham
pieds de porc, pig's trotters
rillettes, potted shredded pork
rillons, as above, with larger pieces of pork
rognon, kidney
saucisse, sausage
saucisson, salami sausage
terrine, potted meat

Les volailles et le gibier (poultry and game)

bécasse, woodcock
caille, quail
canard, duck
canard sauvage, wild duck
caneton, duckling
cerf or *chevreuil*, venison
confit d'oie/de canard, goose/duck conserved in its own fat
dinde, female turkey
dindon, male turkey
faisan, pheasant
lapin, rabbit
lièvre, hare
marcassin, young wild boar
oie, goose
palombe, wood pigeon
perdreau or *perdrix*, partridge
pintade, guinea-fowl
poularde, capon
poulet, chicken
sanglier, wild boar

Les légumes et aromates (vegetables and herbs)

ail, garlic
aneth, dill
artichaut, globe/leaf artichoke

asperges, asparagus
basilic, basil
betterave, beetroot
blettes, chard
céleris, celery
céleri-rave, celeriac
céleri-remoulade, in mustard sauce
cèpe, wild mushroom (*boletus edulis*)
cerfeuil, chervil
champignons, mushrooms
chicorée, Belgian endive
chicorée frisée, curly chicory
chou, cabbage
chou de Bruxelles, Brussels sprout
choucroute, sauerkraut
choufleur, cauliflower
ciboulette, chive
concombre, cucumber
cornichon, gherkin
cresson, watercress
echalote, shallot
epinards, spinach
estragon, tarragon
fenouil, fennel
fève, broad bean
flageolet, flageolet bean
fonds d'artichaut, artichoke hearts
genièvre, juniper berry
girolle, chanterelle mushroom
haricot blanc, white haricot bean
haricot vert, French green bean
huile de noix, walnut oil
huile d'olive, olive oil
laitue, lettuce,
lentilles, lentils
mâche, lamb's lettuce
mesclun, mixed young salad leaves
morille, wild mushroom (morel)
navet, turnip
oignon, onion
oseille, sorrel
persil, parsley
petit pois, green pea
pissenlit, dandelion leaves
poireau, leek
pois chic, chick pea
poivre, pepper
poivron, sweet pepper
pomme de terre, potato

potiron, pumpkin
raifort, horseradish
riz, rice
romarin, rosemary
scarole, curly chicory
topinambour, Jerusalem artichoke

Dishes and styles of cooking

basquaise, with tomato and pimento
bercy, with wine and shallots
biologique, organic (becoming more popular)
bourguignonne, cooked in red wine, with bacon, mushrooms and small onions
cauchoise, with cream, calvados and apples
chasseur or *forestière*, with mushrooms
gratin dauphinois, sliced potatoes cooked in cream
gratin savoyard, similar, but with the addition of eggs and cheese
Lyonnaise, with onions
meunière, cooked slowly in butter
nivernaise, with a glazed carrot and onion garnish
Normande, with cream sauce
parmentier, with potatoes
périgourdine, with truffles and/or *foie gras*
provençale, with oil, tomatoes and garlic
quenelles, fish (often pike) or meat made into a light dumpling roll, served in a sauce
tartare, raw minced steak (occasionally tuna or salmon)

Les fromages (cheeses)

Made from cow's milk, otherwise marked (e) for ewe or (g) for goat. Only some of the more usual types are listed: there are many regional variations.

Normandy: Bondon, Boursin, Camembert, Livarot, Pont-l'Evêque

Northern France and Ile-de-France: Brie, Coulommiers, Mimolette, St-Paulin

Mayenne: Port-du-Salut

Touraine and Poitou: Chabicou (g), Ste-Maure (g), St-Paulin

Berry and Burgundy: Epoisse, St-Florentin, Valenèay (g)
Pyrenees: several cheeses, mostly cow's milk, but also ewe
Causses: Pelardon des Cévennes (g), Roquefort (e)
Auvergne: Bleu-d'Auvergne, Cantal, Fourme-d'Ambert, St-Nectaire
Alsace and Lorraine: Carré-de-l'Est, Munster, Rocollet
Franche-Comté: Bleu-de-Bresse, Comté
Savoy: Beaufort, Emmental, Reblochon, Tomme
Lyonnais and Dauphiny: Rigotte-de-Condrieu; Picodon (g) and St-Marcellin (g) are reputed

fondue Savoyarde, melted cheese (often Vacherin) with wine and kirsch
fromage blanc, a fresh white cheese often eaten with sugar

Les desserts et fruits
abricot, apricot
ananas, pineapple
banane, banana
cassis, blackcurrant
cerise, cherry
citron, lemon
coing, quince
figue, fig
fraise, strawberry
fraise des bois, wild strawberry
framboise, raspberry
groseille, red or white currant
groseille à Maquereau, gooseberry
marron, chestnut
marron glacé, candied chestnut
mendiant, mixed almonds, raisins, etc.
miel, honey
mirabelle, small yellow plum
mûre sauvage, blackberry
myrtille, bilberry
noisette, hazelnut
noix, walnut
pamplemousse, grapefruit
pêche, peach

poire, pear
pomme, apple
prune, plum
pruneau, prune
raisin, grape
raisin sec, raisin
reine-claude, greengage

bavarois, cream dessert
beignet, fritter/doughnut
cannelle, cinnamon
compote de fruits, stewed fruit
crème brulée, caramelised cream
crème caramel or *caramelisé,* caramel custard
flan, solid custard pie
glace, ice cream
ile flottante, floating island (poached meringue floating on egg custard)
liégeois, coffee or chocolate sundae
pâte d'amande, almond paste/marzipan
pâte de coings, quince jelly
pâte des prunes, plum paste
sucre, sugar
tarte Tatin, caramelised upside-down apple tart

Patisseries et confiseries (pastries, cakes and confectionery)
berlingot, pyramid-shaped hard sweet
confiture, jam
confiture d'orange, marmalade
crêpe dentelle, pancake
dragée, sugared almond
en brioche, baked in dough
galette, biscuit or pancake
gâteau sec, biscuit
gaufre, waffle
macaron, almond-paste macaroon
millefeuille, multiple layers of puff-pastry, often with jam and cream
nougatine, caramelised ground almonds
pain d'epices, spiced honey-cake or gingerbread
petit four, fancy biscuit
viennoiserie, type of bread and pastries

Wine and local drinks

A visit to the southwest of France is not complete without sampling the famous and varied wines that are produced there and which harmonise so splendidly with the cuisine. Not all are as prestigious as the magnificent *appellations contrôlées* of the Bordeaux region but many less celebrated wines of great character are produced in the smaller regions and can be purchased at reasonable prices.

Aquitaine

Some 3000 *châteaux* and about 113,000ha fall into the world-renowned category **Bordeaux** and **Bordeaux Supérieur**. Near Libourne, on the banks of the Dordogne, are the vineyards of St-Emilion, Pomerol and Fronsac, which produce rich red wines. The Médoc, north of Bordeaux on the banks of the Gironde estuary, is the Mecca of fine red wines, which develop over time an exceptionally smooth and aromatic complexity. The Graves *appellation*, stretching south of the city on the west bank of the Garonne, bears a close resemblance to the Médoc: both vineyards benefit from pebbly or gravelly soil. Elegant dry white wines are produced in the Graves region, across the Garonne in Entre-Deux-Mers and on the right bank of the Gironde around Blaye. On the slopes or *côtes* on the right bank of the Garonne and on the Dordogne a variety of soils contribute to the diversity of the wines which consist of Premières Côtes de Bordeaux, Côtes de Bourg, Premières Côtes de Blaye, Graves de Vayres, Côtes de Castillon and Côtes de Francs. These are wines which can be enjoyed when young and do not hurt the wallet. The golden sweet and semi-sweet wines such as St-Macaire, Loupiac, Barsac and Sauternes are grown on the banks of the Garonne about 40km south of Bordeaux. The region also produces rosés and *clairets*, refreshing and easy-to-drink pink wines and *crémant*—a sparkling wine and relatively recent *appellation*.

A close neighbour to the Bordelais vineyards is the **Bergerac** *appellation* in Dordogne, which consists of 12 *AOC*s covering 12,000ha and includes Bergerac, Côtes de Bergerac (red and white), Rosette (white), Pécharmant (a quality red), Montravel (dry and sweet whites), Saussignac (also sweet), and the great sweet white wine of Monbazillac.

Among lesser-known wines are the **Côtes de Duras** and **Buzet** produced in Lot-et-Garonne, and in the Landes are the vineyards of the Tursan. On the borders of Aquitaine and Midi-Pyrénées, where the departments of Hautes-Pyrénées, Gers and Landes meet, are the reds of **Madiran** and the whites of **Pacherenc-du-Vic Bilh**. In Pyrénées-Atlantiques south of Pau, towards the mountains, are the delicious white wines of the **Jurançon**, both dry and sweet. Special to Pays Basque is the **Irouleguy**, local to St-Jean-de-Luz, vineyards originally planted in the 14C by the monks of Roncevaux which have been extended over the last 20 years and produce whites and reds and obtained an *AOC* in 1970.

Midi-Pyrénées

The best-known wines of the Midi-Pyrénées come from the vineyards of Cahors and Gaillac. The so-called 'black' wines of **Cahors** are grown on the banks of the Lot to the west of Cahors and their quality, like that of the wines of Gaillac, is constantly improving. The better quality wines can be laid down for at least 10 years. The **Gaillac** *appellation* takes its name from the town on the banks of the Tarn, and covers a wide range of wines, red, white, dry, sweet, rosé and sparkling. The Frontonnais is a small region between Toulouse and Montauban producing increasingly good wines.

Other lesser wine-producing areas exist in the Aveyron, on terraced vineyards around Marcillac, as well as at Estaing and Entraygues-et-Fel in the Lot Valley. In Tarn-et-Garonne are the wines of Côtes du Brulhois, Lavilledieu-du-Temple and Côteaux du Quercy. Production in these vineyards is on a small scale—many *domaines* are family businesses and produce *appellation contrôlée* as well as table wines.

Detailed information on wines is given in the appropriate chapters of the guide, along with information on visiting *châteaux* and vineyards, especially in major regions such as Médoc, Graves and St-Emilion. **Maisons du Vin** in many wine-producing areas provide all the information you need on buying and tasting, and local tourist offices will also be happy to help. In many regions there are **wine cooperatives**. The majority of producers and distillers, private or cooperatives, will be happy to give a *dégustation* (tasting) and talk about their wines to those who have a genuine interest. This can be very time-consuming for the producer and it is advisable to make an appointment in advance. Some of the larger wineries may charge a fee but this will probably include a visit to the *chai* (cellars).

Wine vocabulary

appellation (AOC, *Appellation d'Origine Contrôlée*), legally defined area in which wines produced according to specified standards may claim a geographical name

ban des vendanges, official proclamation of the opening of the vine harvest, going back to the Middle Ages in the Bordeaux region

barrique, oak barrel used for maturing quality wine for 12–18 months. Each barrel in the Bordelais (i.e. Aquitaine) holds 225 litres

chai, a long, low cellar, generally above ground and with thick walls to ensure a cool, even temperature, where wine ages, either in vats or barrels

château, in the Gironde, this designates a wine-producing estate used to make and age wines (*domaine*, *cru* and *clos* are also used)

clairet, a red Bordeaux that spends a very short time macerating on the skins, to reach a deeper colour than a rosé

claret, the name given by the English to Bordeaux red wines in the Middle Ages

collage, 6–8 beaten egg whites put on the surface of great wines in the *barrique*. The tannins cause the whites to congeal, creating a *maillage*. Heavier than the liquid, this descends slowly to the bottom of the barrel, filtering the wine by picking up any small impurities

confréries vineuses, brotherhoods which include wine-growers, shippers and brokers in a given region or *appellation*. There are 18 *confréries* in Bordeaux, making up the *Grand Conseil du Vin de Bordeaux*

fleur de vigne, the delicate and perfumed flower of the vine which appears in June

millésime, the year the wine is gathered and made

oenologist, wine technician who carries out chemical analyses and interprets the results to perfect the making and ageing of wines

ouillage, the process of topping up wine which has evaporated in the barrel, in order to keep oxygen out

pourriture noble, the great sweet white wines (*Sauterne*, *Monbazillac*, *Jurançon*) are produced from grapes with very high sugar content, which are left on the vine to mature to the point that they are attacked by a minuscule mushroom, *Botrytis cinerea*. This results in the reduction of liquid and the grapes shrivel and look mouldy. This 'noble rot' concentrates the sugar. The grapes are harvested very late, when they are over-ripe, by hand in individual bunches.

sarments, branches cut from the vines during pruning, burned in the fireplace or on a barbecue for added flavour

soutirage, the delicate operation of transferring clear wine from one barrel to a clean one, in order to separate the sediments or impurities (*les lies*) which have fallen to the bottom. The decanting is done by hand, glass by glass, by the light of a candle, to test the clarity of the wine, every three months.

tanin, tannin, made up of organic products which exist in the pips, the skin and the stalks of the grape. It plays a part in the ageing of red wines

vendange, the grape harvest

Other drinks

Armagnac is a fiery brandy distilled in the northern part of the *département* of the Gers and the east of the Landes, around the towns of Condom and Eauze. The production of **Basque cider** (or Sagardoa) has a long history and some 70 cider brewers are in existence. It is claimed locally that the Basques taught the Normans all they know about apple wine. The small wooden stopper of the cider barrel is called a *txotx*, and this term is also used for the *cidre nouveau* celebrations beginning on the Friday following St Sebastian's day (20 January) and continuing until April.

Lillet, an aperitif created in Graves in 1887, consists of an assemblage of selected wines and fruit liqueurs aged in oak barrels for several months. Red or white, it is drunk chilled (6–8°C). **Floc** (from the Gascon for flower) is an aperitif based on either red or white wine. **Pousse rapière**, a liqueur of orange and Armagnac with a sparkling wine, is also served as an aperitif. **Pineau (des Charentes)** is made from grape juice added to Cognac, then aged in oak barrels. **Patxaran**, an alcoholic drink from the Navarre, is obtained by macerating plums in anis. The name comes from *baso aran*, the wild plum preferred in this recipe. Originally a domestic product, it is now produced industrially and is enjoyed throughout Spain.

Coffee, tea and chocolate

If you simply order *un café* you will be served an expresso. A *café crème* or *café au lait* comes with hot milk, usually in a large cup, and is served at breakfast. Some cafés (but not all) serve *un petit crème*. If you would prefer coffee with cold milk, ask for *un (grand/petit) crème avec un peu de lait froid*, or for a *noisette*. If you want a longer, less strong coffee, ask for a *café allongé* or *à l'américain*. Tea comes as a tea bag with separate hot water, and with milk (*thé au lait*), lemon (*thé citron*) or plain (*thé nature*). Hot chocolate (*chocolat chaud*) is often offered as an alternative to tea or coffee at breakfast.

Getting around

By car

Petrol prices are lower in France than in the UK, and the most competitive are offered by garages attached to supermarkets.

The main *autoroutes* (motorways) serving the southwest are listed below. Most sections are *péages* (toll roads) which are privately financed and therefore prices per km vary (e.g. Tours to Bordeaux, €25.40, Bordeaux to Hendaye, €6.20, Bordeaux to Toulouse, €14.80); credit cards accepted. For maps, see p 14.

A10: Paris–Bordeaux
A20: Chateauroux–Limoges–Brive–Cahors–Montauban
A61: Toulouse–Carcassonne–Narbonne
A62: Bordeaux–Agen–Toulouse
A63: Dax–Bayonne–St-Jean-de-Luz
A64: Toulouse–Tarbes–Pau–Bayonne
A68: Toulouse–Albi (Rodez)
A75: Clermont-Ferrand–Mende–Millau–Montpellier
E70: Bordeaux–Périgueux–Clermont-Ferrand (under construction)

Safety

The French drive on the right. Seat belts must be worn in both front and rear seats; children under 10 are not allowed to travel in the front seat except for babies up to 9 months in a rear-facing seat. Nationality stickers are compulsory; warning triangles and replacement headlight bulbs must be carried. Headlights must be adjusted for driving on the right, or converters used.

In built-up areas the *priorité à droite* (priority from the right) still applies if there is no sign to the contrary, even from a minor onto a major road, so care must be taken.

Attention should be paid at all times to car security; do not leave objects of temptation obviously visible.

Remember that weather conditions can change suddenly in mountain areas.

Documents

You must carry a passport and full valid driving licence, original vehicle registration document and motor insurance certificate. British drivers who still have the old style green driving licence are advised to obtain a European Community version (DVLA, ☎ 01792 772 134). Caravan/camper vans are advised to carry a Camping Card International.

Limits

Minimum age limit for driving is 18.

Speed limits. Autoroutes: 130kph (80mph), in wet conditions 110kph (68mph), minimum speed in fast lane 80kph (49mph);
Dual carriageways: 110kph (68mph), in wet conditions 100kph (62mph);
Outside built-up areas: 90kph (55mph), in wet conditions 80kph (49mph);
Built-up areas: 50kph (31mph).
In fog when visibility is reduced to 5m, all speeds reduced to 50kph (31mph).

Visitors who have been licensed to drive within two years must not exceed 110kph on autoroutes, 100kph on dual carriageways, and 80kph outside built-up areas.

The standard of roads and signposting is on the whole very clear, but occasionally signposts are positioned after the turnings. Driving is fairly erratic, and somewhat undisciplined at times.

The drink driving limit is 0.05 per cent and fines are on the spot.

Services

All petrol is unleaded; diesel is called *gasoil* or *gazole*; credit cards are accepted at service stations. Motorway service areas (about every 40km) are well-equipped with self-service cafés, coffee machines (frequently *jeton*-operated—buy *jeton* from the cashier), maps, 24-hour petrol stations. The numerous *aires* (lay-bys) have toilets, telephones and picnic areas. There are emergency phones every 2km.

Road and route information

AA, ☎ 09068 244 123, or www.theaa.com
RAC, ☎ 0800 550 550, www.rac.co.uk
Europ Assistance, ☎ 01444 442 442/0870 737 5777, www.europ-assistance.co.uk.
Route planner available on www.iti.fr
Motorway information on www.autoroutes.fr
Road and traffic information on www.equipement.gouv.fr
Road conditions on www.bison-fute.equipement.gouv.fr

Car hire

All the main international car-hire firms operate in France and airlines offer fly-drive arrangements. The minimum age for hiring a car in France varies from 21 to 25, and the upper age limit is on average 70.

Avis Rent A Car, ☎ 0870 6060 100, www.avis.co.uk
Budget Leisure Car, ☎ 08701 56 56 56
Europcar, ☎ 0870 607 5000, www.europcar.com
Executive Car, ☎ 0033 142 65 54 20, www.executive-car.com
Hertz, ☎ 08705 996 699, www.hertz.co.uk
National Car Rental, ☎ 08705 365 365, www.nationalcar.com
Thrifty ☎ 08705 168 238, www.thrifty.co.uk

By rail

The main train terminals are Bordeaux and Toulouse. These have links with the major centres in the region, but travelling to smaller towns and cross-country needs detailed planning. *TER* (*Transports Express Régionaux*) indicates regional express services.

Tickets

Main and larger stations have information and **booking offices** with *SNCF* (*Société Nationale de Chemin de Fer*) timetables. Most trains (including *TGVs*) offer first- and second-class travel; *TGV* seats have to be reserved. *Aller-retour* (return) tickets cost twice as much as a single ticket. Tickets may be purchased for cash or by credit card over the counter; there are also automatic ticket **vending machines** in main stations.

It is very important to **validate your ticket** (*composter*) with a date stamp at the orange machines at the entrance to the platform. If the ticket is not validated when you board the train you risk paying a fine.

SNCF **discounts** include passengers aged 12–25 years; up to four adults travelling with a child under 12 years old; and the over-60s. There are further discounts on a one-year travel pass for travellers in the above categories; for two people on a return journey together; and for a return journey of at least 200km with a Saturday night away.

Inter-Rail Pass Zone E gives you unlimited travel for 12 days, 22 days or one month throughout the rail networks of France, Belgium, Netherlands and Luxembourg with the possibility of travel on *Eurostar* and *TGV*. The **Euro Domino Pass** can be used for 3–8 consecutive days of second-class travel in a month. These passes must be purchased in the country of origin of the passenger, where they cannot be used, and cannot be purchased in the UK by overseas travellers. The passes are available as follows:

UK from *Rail Europe Travel Centre*, Victoria Station, London, *STA Travel*, some independent travel agents, or www.raileurope.co.uk

Australia and New Zealand, through travel agents

Canada ☎ 800 361 RAIL

USA 226 Westchester Ave, White Plains, NY 10604, 800 438 7245 or 800 EURAIL, www.raileurope.com

Information in Europe, UIC (International Union of Railways), www.UIC.asso.fr

By coach/bus

Coverage is patchy and services vary between *départements*. It is advisable to enquire at the main bus stations (*gares routières*); see information in relevant chapters.

Bordeaux Halte Routière de Carcan, ☎ 05 56 43 68 43 or Réseau Trans-Gironde, Allées de Chartres, ☎ 05 56 81 16 82 (for the Gironde).

Toulouse, Gare Routière, 62 Blvd Pierre-Sémard, ☎ 05 61 61 67 67.

By bicycle

Cycling is a very popular pastime among the French and the variety of terrain in the southwest offers something for very fit and less fit enthusiasts. Bicycles and mountain bikes can be hired from certain train stations, campsites and *syndicats d'initiative*. Comité Régional de Tourisme d'Aquitaine publishes a brochure, *Aquitaine à Vélo*/Aquitaine by Bike, a bilingual brochure. There is no equivalent brochure in the Midi-Pyrénées. Some of the CDTs provide bicycle route maps and information (*circuits vélos*) free of charge.

For other information and routes contact main tourist offices or:

Fédération Française de Cyclotourisme, 12 Rue Louis-Bertrand, 74207 Ivry-sur-Seine Cedex, ☎ 01 56 20 88 88, www.ffct.org

On foot

Walking and hiking are very well catered for, with marked trails of every category from the strenuous to a gentle amble. There are several *Grande Randonnée* trails, official long-distance footpaths, which cross or begin or end in the region and include two main branches of the pilgrim route to Santiago de Compostela, the GR10 and GR36. These are described in *Topoguides*, published by the

Fédération Française de Randonnée Pédestre, 14 Rue Riquet, 75019 Paris, ☎ 01 44 89 93 93, fax 01 40 35 85 67, info@ffrp.asso.fr, www.ffrp.asso.fr.

Information and maps are also published by most of the thirteen Comités Départementaux de la Randonnée Pédestre, and by **Randonnées Pyrénéennes**, Centre d'Information montagne et sentiers, 4 Rue Maye-Lane, BP 2, 65421- Ibos Cedex, ☎ 05 62 90 67 60, fax 05 62 90 67 91, www.rando-pyrenees.net. A brochure in French and German published by the two regions describes what to see along the Chemins de Saint-Jacques de Compostelle (pilgrimage route); not free.

By boat

Motorboat and houseboat hire information can be obtained from the CRT Midi-Pyrénées which publishes *La Belle Saison des Bateaux-Promenades*. CRT Aquitaine plans to bring out an inter-regional brochure (with Midi-Pyrénées and Languedoc-Roussilon) which will contain information on waterways. The CDTs of Lot-et-Garonne, Tarn-et-Garonne, Gers publish a combined brochure *Pôle Sud-Ouest* with information on boat hire, cruises and activities near or along the canals, such as cycling; the Haute-Garonne provides a map *Parcours Cyclables et Pédestres du Canal du Midi*. Further information can be found in the relevant chapters, especially in the sections on Haute-Garonne and Lot-et-Garonne.

 # Language

Increasingly the French are pleased to practise their English, but an effort to speak French is usually appreciated, especially in rural areas. The accent of the Midi can be fairly pronounced, making comprehension difficult at times.

hello/good day, *bonjour*

good morning, *bonjour*

good afternoon, *bonjour*

good evening, *bon soir*

good night (on retiring), *bonne nuit*

goodbye, *au revoir*

see you later, *à plus tard* or
    à tout à l'heure

yes, *oui*

no, *non*

OK, all right, *OK*, *d'accord* or *ça va*

please, *s'il vous plaît* (formal) or
    s'il te plaît (informal)

thank you (very much), *merci (beaucoup)*

sorry, *je m'excuse, pardon*

today, *aujourd'hui*

tomorrow, *demain*

yesterday, *hier*

now, *maintenant*

later, *plus tard*

when, *quand*

in the morning, *dans la matinée*

in the afternoon, *dans l'après-midi*

in the evening, *au soir*

at night, *dans la nuit*

a room, *une chambre*

bathroom, *une salle de bains*

breakfast, *le petit déjeuner*

cold, *froid*

hot, *chaud*

with, *avec*

without, *sans*

open, *ouvert*

closed, *fermé*

cheap, *bon marché*
expensive, *cher*
a lot, *beaucoup*
good, *bon*
bad, *mauvais*
left, *à gauche*
right, *à droite*
straight on, *tout droit*
here, *ici*
there, *là*
big, *grand*
small, *petit*

railway station, *la gare*
bus station, *la gare d'autobus* or
    la gare routière
airport, *un aéroport*
ticket, *le billet*
police station, *le commissariat de police* or
    la gendarmerie
hospital, *un hôpital*
doctor, *le médecin*
dentist, *le dentiste*
aspirin, *une aspirine*

what is your name?, *quel est votre nom?*
    quel es ton nom?
    comment vous appellez vous?
    comment t'appelles-tu?
my name is ..., *mon nom est ...*
    je m'appelle ...
I would like..., *je voudrais...*
    j'aimerais ..., je désire ...
do you have..., *avez-vous...?*
    est-ce-que vous avez...?
do you speak English?, *parlez-vous*
    anglais?
    parles-tu anglais?
I don't understand, *je ne comprends pas*
where is...?, *où est...?* or *où se trouve...?*
where are the toilets?, *où se trouvent les*
    toilettes?
what is the time?, *quelle heure est-il?*
at what time?, *à quelle heure?*
how much is it?, *ça coûte combien?*
    c'est combien?
the bill, *l'addition* or *la note*

Monday, *lundi*
Tuesday, *mardi*
Wednesday, *mercredi*
Thurday, *jeudi*
Friday, *vendredi*
Saturday, *samedi*
Sunday, *dimanche*

January, *janvier*
February, *février*
March, *mars*
April, *avril*
May, *mai*
June, *juin*
July, *juilllet*
August, *août*
September, *septembre*
October, *octobre*
November, *novembre*
December, *décembre*

Spring, *le printemps*
Summer, *l'été*
Autumn, *l'automne*
Winter, *l'hiver*

1 *un*
2 *deux*
3 *trois*
4 *quatre*
5 *cinq*
6 *six*
7 *sept*
8 *huit*
9 *neuf*
10 *dix*
11 *onze*
12 *douze*
13 *treize*
14 *quatorze*
15 *quinze*
16 *seize*
17 *dix-sept*
18 *dix-huit*
19 *dix-neuf*
20 *vingt*
21 *vingt-et-un*
22 *vingt-deux*
30 *trente*

40 *quarante*	80 *quatre-vingt*
50 *cinquante*	90 *quatre-vingt-dix*
60 *soixante*	100 *cent*
70 *soixante-dix*	

Museums, galleries and churches

Hours of admission are included in the guide for most châteaux and museums and the major churches, but these are subject to change and it is wise to check opening times by telephone or in the press, or at local tourist offices. Many châteaux and smaller museums are closed outside the tourist season, which stretches roughly from Easter to October and reaches its peak in July and August. As a general rule, the **national museums** are closed on Tuesdays and the **municipal museums** are closed on Mondays. Many shut between 12.00 and 14.00, although the large museums tend to stay open all day, especially in the summer season. Last admissions are often 30–45 minutes before closing time. During strikes or public holidays there are likely to be unscheduled closures.

The same guidelines may also apply to other monuments. Some of the smaller **churches** may be manned during the peak months, but many are locked. When a key is needed it is advisable not to interrupt the key-holder at lunchtime. It is useful to have a torch to light high places in churches.

All museums charge an **entry fee**. Children, students, and senior citizens get discounts in most museums but must be able to provide proof of status. In some cases this is reduced or entrance is free on Sundays. The quality of general catalogues of permanent collections is constantly improving, especially in the larger museums, and English versions are quite frequently available.

Entertainment

Festivals and events

Fêtes, *foires* and festivals abound in the southwest. Almost every small village has a summer fair, and throughout the year there are special markets, regional produce competitions, local crafts displays, and the celebration of local traditions, as well as religious festivals. **Carnival** is celebrated throughout much of the southwest between February and April, for example in Albi, Bayonne, Biarritz, Bordeaux, Dax, Hendaye, Mont-de-Marsan, Pau, Périgueux, St-Jean-de-Luz, Sarlat and Varaignes.

The individual Comités Départementaux or local tourist offices have up-to-date information on annual events and festivals, and on markets and fairs. The Comités Régionaux will provide a comprehensive annual list on demand. Details of local festivals and events are listed in appropriate chapters.

National events

June *Fête de la Musique*, a national day of music, all free

July *Tour de France* cycle race

September (third weekend) *Journées Nationales du Patrimoine*, open days at historic monuments, of which some are not normally accessible to the public

Regional events

June *Garonne! La Festival*, international cultural events along the Garonne river
Les Feux de Garonne, sound-and-light show and entertainment on the river banks
Opening of summer festivities in the Gironde: theatre, film, music and exhibitions, until September
Summer solstice (21 June) celebrated with great fires thoughout the Gironde

July *La Félibrée*, festival celebrating the Occitan language, music and tradition, at a different venue in Périgord each year
La Route du Sel, following the ancient salt routes to the coast across the Aveyron and other *départements*; the itinerary changes each year
Festival de Musique en Guyenne, classical concerts held in churches around Lot-et-Garonne

July–August *Festival des Hauts de Garonne*, on the banks of the Garonne in the Gironde
31 Notes d'Eté, festival of music from across the world, including classical and jazz, in various towns in Haut-Garonne

August *Festival folklorique international*, Rouergue international folklore festival

August–September *Marathon des Châteaux de Médoc et Graves*, a convivial marathon through villages and châteaux

October *Jazz sur Son 31*, jazz events in various towns in Haute-Garonne

Sport and leisure

All kinds of sporting activites are catered for in southwest France: surfing on the Atlantic coast; many golf courses; abundant tennis courts; public swimming pools, lakes and the Atlantic; skiing in the Pyrenees and the Aubrac in winter, and in the summer hiking, mountaineering and hang-gliding. The Basque sports (*pelote* and its derivations) are dealt with on p 406. There are numerous opportunities for cycling, walking and boating (see above) and information regarding horseriding can be obtained from the departmental tourist boards or local tourist offices.

 # Additional information

Banking services

Banks generally open 08.30–17.00 Monday to Friday, but are likely to be closed at lunchtime. In certain areas of the southwest they are open on Saturdays but not on Mondays. Opening times are posted outside the bank. Not every bank has a foreign exchange service, especially in small country towns.

In larger towns and cities you will find **bureaux de change** open six days a week. Some main post offices have exchange facilities and most large hotels will change cash or traveller's cheques. Arrivals terminals at main airports will also have a foreign exchange facility. You will need some form of **identification** when changing traveller's cheques.

Conversions
1 ounce = 28.35 grams, 1pound = 0.454 kilogram
1 pint = 0.56 litres, 1 quart (UK) = 1.13 litres
1 inch = 2.5 centimetres, 1 foot = 30.5 centimetres,
1 yard = 0.91 metre, 1 mile = 1.61 kilometres
2.5 acres = 1 hectare (approx.)
To approximately convert Celsius to Farenheit, multiply by 2 and add 30.

Crime and personal security
It is wise to be on your guard in southwest France as you would be anywhere else. Pickpocketing and bag-snatching do happen to the vulnerable and unwary in large towns. Do not leave bags unattended on beaches or in public areas, and hide or cover any object of value in a car. If you are the victim of any crime, **report it** to the nearest police station as soon as possible. In the case of theft it is essential to make a written statement at the police station in order to make an insurance claim.

You should carry official identification (a passport or identity card) with you at all times. It hardly needs to be mentioned that it is wise to keep a record of your passport details, traveller's cheques numbers and credit card details in a safe place.

Electric current
France runs on 220V, 50Hz AC. Most sockets take round two-pin plugs so equip yourself with a plug adaptor to use with electrical items you take with you.

Embassies and consulates
Australia Embassy, 4 Rue Jean-Rey, Paris 75724, ☎ 01 40 59 33 00/2.
Canada Consulate, 30 Blvd Strasbourg, 31000 Toulouse, ☎ 05 61 99 30 16.
Ireland Embassy, 4, Rue Rude, Paris 75116, ☎ 01 44 17 67 00.
New Zealand Embassy, 7 ter, Rue Leonard de Vinci, 75116, Paris, ☎ 01 45 01 43 43.
South Africa Embassy, 59 Quai d'Orsay, Paris 75343, ☎ 01 53 59 23 23.
UK Embassy, 35 Rue du Faubourg St-Honoré, Paris 75008, ☎ 01 44 51 31 00.
Consulates, 353 Blvd Président Wilson, 33073 Bordeaux, ☎ 05 57 22 21 10;
Victoria Centre, 20 Chemin Laporte, 31000 Toulouse, ☎ 05 61 15 02 02.
USA Embassy, 2 Ave Gabriel, 75008 Paris, 01 32 12 22 22.
Consulates, 25 Allées Jean-Jaurés, 31000 Toulouse, ☎ 05 34 41 36 50; Place Varian Fry, 13006 Marseille, ☎ 04 91 54 92 00.

Emergency telephone numbers
Ambulance, medical/accident (*SAMU: Service Ambulance Medical d'Urgence*) ☎ 15
Fire department (*pompiers*)   ☎ 18
Police hotline   ☎ 17
General emergency for non-French speakers   ☎ 112

Lost credit cards

American Express 01 47 77 72 00
Barclaycard 01604 234 234
Diners Club 0810 314 159
Mastercard 01 45 67 53 53
Visa (Fr) 01 45 67 84 84, (UK) 01383 621 166

Markets

Smaller towns and villages hold a street market for produce once a week, but in larger towns more frequently. Toulouse and Tarbes have a produce market nearly every day. Trading usually starts at about 08.00 and ends towards 13.00. There are also dozens of special markets, depending on the season or the region, and markets for things other than edibles, anything from plastic flowers to corsets. Details of market days are given in the chapters.

Newpapers

Daily regional newspapers are *Sud Ouest* in Aquitaine and *La Depêche du Midi* in Midi-Pyrénées. Weeklies include *La Semaine du Pays Basque* and *La République des Pyrénées*. An English-language newspaper called *The News* is published in Périgueux.

Opening hours

Small **shops** such as *tabacs* and *boulangeries* open around 07.00, as do many cafés. Office hours are approximately 09.00–17.30/18.00. The two-hour **lunch break** is still sacred in most of southern France: shops and banks as well as many other public places, including museums, are likely to close between 12.00 and 14.00. Most stores and shops stay open until 19.00 on weekdays and Saturdays but they may also close on Sunday and Monday. Only food stores are likely to be open on a Sunday morning. In holiday resorts opening times fluctuate seasonally.

For opening hours of banks, post offices and museums, see the relevant sections above.

Photography

There are restrictions regarding photography in some museums: these vary, from no photographs at all to no flash. In some you have to pay extra to take photographs and it is best to check on the spot.

Public holidays (jours feriés)

1 January, New Year's Day (*Jour de l'An*)
Easter Sunday and Monday (*Paques*)
1 May (*Fête de Travail*)
8 May, end of Second World War in Europe
Ascension Day (*Ascension*)
Whit Sunday and Monday (*Pentecôte*)
14 July, Bastille Day (*Fête Nationale*)
15 August, Feast of the Assumption (*Assomption*)
1 November, All Saints' Day (*Toussaint*)
11 November, Armistice Day (*le onze novembre* or *jour de l'Armistice*)
25 December, Christmas Day (*Noël*)

Public toilets

Note that the French translation is in the plural—*les toilettes* (not *la toilette*). Although the situation is gradually improving, the quality of public toilets in France still lags behind other parts of Europe and is very uneven. Some facilities have to be paid for; the amount varies. There are public toilets in car parks, which vary from really grim to okay if they have an attendant and have to be paid for; likewise in covered markets. The facilities in museums and stores are usually more reliable. The main *autoroute* service areas have good facilities but it is not a bad idea to take toilet paper with you, especially if you stop at an *autoroute aires* (lay-by) or other public places. In some towns a few coin-operated automated cabins still exist—but are so scary that you have to be desperate. You will at times still find *toilettes à la turque* (holes in the ground).

Religion

France is officially Catholic, although most people are not very devout. There is often a mass on Saturday night as well as Sunday. In the southwest, which was heavily Protestant in some places during the 16C–17C, you will still find *Temples Protestants* and other Protestant churches. There are occasional British churches, especially in the Dordogne. In large towns there are also synagogues and mosques.

Telephone and postal services

Post offices are indicated by the sign PTT. Main post offices are open 08.00–19.00 on weekdays, and until 12.00 on Saturdays. Smaller village offices may close at lunchtime. **Postage stamps** (*timbres*) are on sale at all post offices and tobacconists (*tabacs*). Letter boxes are painted yellow.

There are **phone booths** in some post offices. Public phone booths almost exclusively take phone cards (*télécartes*), which can be purchased in different denominations, or *unités*, at post offices, *tabacs* and some other stores.

☎ 12 for directory assistance. To **telephone outside France**, dial 00 followed by the country code followed by the number (omitting the initial 0 if appropriate). **Country codes** are:

Australia	61	South Africa	27
Canada	1	UK	44
Ireland	353	USA	1
New Zealand	64		

Time

France is one hour ahead of Greenwich Mean Time and remains one hour ahead of British Summer Time, changing on the same day. It is six hours ahead of Eastern Standard Time and nine hours ahead of Pacific Standard Time.

Tipping

All restaurant, café and hotel bills include a 10–15 per cent service charge but it is customary to leave an extra tip (*pourboire*), especially if the service warrants it, as a mark of appreciation. Tipping taxi drivers, porters and the attendants at public toilets is at your discretion.

BACKGROUND INFORMATION

Historical introduction

Early history

Human habitation of the southwest of France goes back thousands of years. Lower strata in the river valleys have yielded up tools and the evidence of fire, indicating the existence of *Homo erectus* in the region some 450,000 years ago. The appearance of **Neanderthal man** (*Homo neandertalensis*) is associated with the Mousterian period, identified by the production of a certain type of bifacial or two-sided flint tool. The disappearance of the Neanderthals and the emergence of our direct ancestor **Cro-Magnon man** (*Homo sapiens sapiens*), named after a site in the Périgord Noir, took place during the so-called Aurignacian period, when the earliest examples of sculpture and engraving were produced. The last Ice Age, during the Upper Palaeolithic era, lasted from around 35,000 to 10,000 years ago, during which the most important period for cave paintings and engravings was the Magdalenian, named after a cave also in the Dordogne.

Cultural periods in prehistory	
500,000–100,000 BC	Lower Palaeolitic: *Homo erectus*—Acheulean culture
100,000–35,000 BC	Middle Palaeolithic: Neanderthal Man— Mousterian culture
35,000–10,000 BC	Upper Palaeolithic: Cro-Magnon man
35,000–20,000 BC	Aurignacian culture
25,000–17,000 BC	Gravettian culture
21,000–16,000 BC	Solutrean culture
17,000–9500 BC	Magdalenian culture
9500–9000 BC	Azilian culture
9500–5000 BC	Mesolithic Age
5500–2500 BC	Neolithic Age
2000–850 BC	Bronze Age
800–50 BC	Iron Age

The **Mesolithic and Neolithic cultures** marked the evolution from simple to more sophisticated stone tools, agriculture, pottery, the primitive use of a bow and arrow, communal burials in caves, and megaliths. Towards the end of the fourth millennium BC, metallurgy was introduced into central and southwestern France and increasingly refined techniques gradually spread from the Massif Central into the Dordogne. Typical of the **Bronze Age** was the production of richly decorated weapons but, from the 8C BC, bronze was challenged by iron introduced into the Quercy and Périgord by the Hallstattians from Central Europe. The **Iron Age** was characterised not only by iron weapons, but also the establishment of hill settlements and the practice of cremation, when the ashes placed in vessels were buried under barrows or earth mounds.

The **Celts**, who descended from Northern Europe some time after the beginning of the 3C BC, subjugated or merged with the existing Hallstattians or Aquitains. These Celtic tribes, some of whom are remembered in the old regional names, included the Petrucores (Périgord), the Nitiobriges (Agenais), the Bituriges-Vivisci (Bordeaux), the Lactorates (Lectoure), the Volques Tectosages (Toulouse), the Convenes (Comminges), and the Rutenes (Rouergue).

The Romans

When the Romans arrived in the southwest of what they called **Gaul** in the 2C BC, the local Celts had already established commercial links with Roman Narbonne, founded 118 BC. By the second half of the 2C BC *Tolosa* (Toulouse), capital of the Volques Tectosages, accepted an alliance with the Romans and a garrison was established there. The foundation of *Lugdunum Convenarum* (St-Bertrand-de-Comminges) in 72 BC is attributed to Pompey and two campaigns by Julius Caesar's lieutenant, Crassus, in 56 BC resulted in the submission of the Bituriges-Vivisci people.

The **Gaulish wars** (59–51 BC) against the Romans were led by Vercingetorix (72–46 BC), the Celtic hero from the Auvergne. The last outpost of Celtic independence, Uxellodunum, *oppidum* of the Cadurci tribe which fell to Caesar in 51 BC, is thought to have been either at Puy-d'Issolud near Martel, or Capdenac-le-Haut near Figeac (both in the Lot). Following this, the **Pax Romana** lasted until the 3C AD and contributed to the development of the arts and commerce as well as urban centres such as *Burdigala* (Bordeaux), which became capital of Aquitania. *Versunna* (Périgueux), *Aginum* (Agen) and *Aquae Tarbellicae* (Dax). The Latin language was assimilated and Roman law and administration assured cohesion of the area, while Roman and local religious cults existed side by side.

By the 1C AD **wine** imports were replaced by the cultivation of vines in the region and subsequently by the export of wine to the Mediterranean, along with pottery produced in Graufesenque and Montans. A lasting reminder of the Gallo-Roman period are the many patronymic or place names identified by the suffixes -an or -ac, such as Noillan, Podensac and Fronsac.

Christian evangelisation infiltrated the region through the 3C, to be countered by persecution at the time of the Emperor Diocletian (r. 284–305), producing semi-lengendary martyrs such as St Sernin (Saturninus) in Toulouse, St Foy (Faith) in Agen, and St Front in Périgord. During the Middle Ages, the relics of these early Christians were widely venerated and attracted multitudes of pilgrims to the region. Some of the earliest recorded bishoprics in the southwest were established at Dax in the 4C, St-Bertrand-de-Comminges in the late 5C, Lescar and Oloron in the 6C.

Post-Roman divisions

The end of Roman domination was precipitated in the 3C–5C by waves of Germanic tribes such as the Alemani who swept down from the north, followed by the Vandals and Visigoths. The latter imposed a certain stability on the region. Having conquered Bordeaux in 409, in 418 they rejected it in favour of Toulouse, which became the capital of their kingdom for a century. They in turn were chased out in 507 by the **Franks**, led by Clovis (r. 481–511), who left an enduring souvenir in the present name of the former country of the Gauls, and who converted to Christianity *c* 500. In the 6C, Aquitaine was divided by factions of Clovis's dynasty, the Merovingians, and *c* 580 the Vascons or Gascons appeared from the southwest. Incursions by Arabs (also called Moors or Saracens) from Iberia northwards through the region were stemmed by Charles Martel (r. 715–41) at Poitiers in 732, although random attacks continued until the mid-8C.

Charlemagne (742–814), grandson of Charles Martel, became King of the Franks in 768. From 771, after the death of his brother, he reigned alone over a vast Christian empire covering much of Europe. Nevertheless, control of the Iberian Peninsula evaded him and the rearguard of his retreating army suffered ignominiously when ambushed at Roncesvalles (Roncevaux) in Navarre in 778. Charlemagne was crowned Emperor on Christmas Day 800 and passed on the **Kingdom of Aquitaine** to his son, Louis the Pious (r. 814–40 with interruptions), but the Carolingian Empire broke down into principalities governed by ennobled vassals. William of Orange (b. *c* 750–812), Count of Toulouse, cousin of Charlemagne, who took control of Languedoc by 793, established one of the most powerful dynasties. They were fiercely challenged by the rival Poitevin dynasty: in the mid-10C, Ebalus, Count of Poitou and distantly related to William, became the first Duke of Aquitaine (r. 927–34). The 9C was a dark period in the history of the southwest, when the **Vikings** (called Normans by the Carolingians) raided the Frankish kingdom via the main rivers and pillaged Bordeaux and Toulouse.

By the 10C the region had been divided and sub-divided by the feudal system and the French kings, in the distant north, found it almost impossible to impose their authority on the local lords. The territories of the Dukes of Aquitaine stretched from north of the Dordogne as far as Poitiers, encompassing Angoulême, the Périgord and Blaye. The Duke of Gascony's principal vassals were the Counts of Fézensac and the Viscounts of Béarn. The eastern section was dominated by the Counts of Toulouse who held sway over the Albigeois and the Quercy, and their strongest rivals were the Counts of Foix. Territorial boundaries were in constant flux and rivalries were likely to flare up at any moment. The whole of the southwest was, however, united by a common language, the *langue d'oc*. The rich dialect of the south derived from vulgar Latin, albeit with local adaptations, and is now known as **Occitan**. Modern French developed from the *langue d'oeil* spoken further north.

The 'discovery' of the tomb of St James the Great at Santiago de Compostela in northwestern Spain in the 9C and the popularity of the veneration of relics brought about a huge increase in **pilgrimage** during the 10C–11C along roads which converged on the Spanish boundary in the western Pyrenees. The needs of pilgrims, the revival of monastic life, and the acquisition of relics which attracted great wealth, led to the construction of churches along the way which were both beautiful and practical, drawing architectural and artistic influences both from the great Benedictine abbey of Cluny in Burgundy as well as from Spain. This resulted in the magnificent examples of **Romanesque architecture and carving** at St-Sernin in Toulouse, Ste-Foy in Conques and St-Pierre in Moissac.

By the late 11C, **crusades** against the Turkish 'infidels' who occupied the Holy City of Jerusalem were preached by Pope Urban II throughout France and in 1096 Raymond IV, Count of Toulouse left on the First Crusade to the Holy Land at the head of 100,000 men. The Second Crusade (1147–48) was led by Louis VII of France accompanied by his queen, Eleanor (see below), and in 1190

Richard I of England and Philippe-Auguste of France set out on the Third Crusade.

The English influence

By the 11C the Saintonge (Poitou-Charentes) and Gascony were added to the Duchy of Aquitaine. Duke William IX of Aquitaine (1071–1126), celebrated as the first troubadour to promote courtly love in the *langue d'oc*, married a woman of strong character, Philippa, widow of Sancho Ramirez of Aragon, great niece of William the Conqueror and daughter of William IV of Toulouse. William and Philippa's grand-daughter was **Eleanor of Aquitaine** (1122–1204), who was to play a role of paramount importance in the history of France, Aquitaine and England resonating over several centuries. The ancient laws of Aquitaine, inherited from the Roman period, allowed women to inherit property and Eleanor, an unusually well-educated young woman, became Duchess of Aquitaine and Countess of Poitou at the death of her father, William X, in 1137. He had made her ward of his overlord, King Louis VI (r. 1108–1137), who married her at the age of 15 to the Dauphin, the future Louis VII (r. 1137–1180). The couple had only daughters. The holy and ascetic Louis was no match for Eleanor, the ultimate feisty lady of her century, and she did not complain when the king, whom she could not stand, contrived to bring about the dissolution of their marriage on grounds of consanguinity in 1152. Her father had ensured that Eleanor's inheritance could not be absorbed into the royal domain but would pass to her heirs.

Henry Plantagenet first met Eleanor in Paris in 1151, when he was 18 and she was twenty-nine. These two spirited individuals were instantly attracted to each other. As soon as possible after her marriage to Louis was dissolved, Eleanor married Henry at Poitiers, bringing the Plantagenets the incredibly rich dowry of the Duchy of Aquitaine, encompassing territories from the Loire Valley to the Pyrenees and from the River Rhône to the Atlantic. Henry acceded to the throne of England as **Henry II** (r. 1154–89), and by 1160 the Plantagenet empire stretched from the border of Scotland to the frontier with Spain including Anjou, Maine, Lorraine and Normandy (inherited from his parents) as well as Aquitaine (Guyenne and Gascony).

For some three centuries the French kings were the notional overlords of the king-dukes of English Aquitaine. The loss of fertile and prosperous Aquitaine was, however, an untenable situation for the French. Nor was it of much financial profit to England, although the people of Aquitaine, particularly the Bordelais, were content with their lot and benefited from the trade in wine and agricultural surpluses with England. Aquitaine was administered through the English king's representatives, the seneschal in Bordeaux and vice-seneschals in the regions. Its subjects were entitled to appeal to the French, making it difficult for English officials to discharge their duties and creating tension. Every so often (1294, 1324, 1337) the French king treated the king-duke as a recalcitrant vassal and confiscated the Duchy by judicial sentence.

Eleanor also laid claim to the Toulousain through her grandmother, Philippa of Toulouse, but never managed to control this valuable link between Aquitaine and the Mediterranean, which also evaded the French for several centuries. In 1169 Eleanor handed over the control of most of Aquitaine to her favourite son, **Richard the Lion Heart**, who acceded to the English throne as Richard I (r. 1189–99). Richard was a political and military rival to Philippe-Auguste of

France (r. 1180–1223) who confiscated the territories in Aquitaine from Richard's brother and successor, King John (r. 1199–1216).

The Cathars and Albigensian Crusade

While lack of discipline in the orthodox Church gave rise to the Gregorian reforms in the 11C and pilgrimage was on the increase, the Languedoc, under the control of the Counts of Toulouse, presented a degree of religious tolerance, intellectual sophistication, and administrative confusion engendered by internecine rivalry. As such it became the refuge of the **Cathars** (from catharsis, meaning purification), also referred to as Albigensians. This breakaway fundamentalist Christian sect, which was entirely pacifist, followed a dualist doctrine based on the opposition of Good and Evil. Unlike the message of Genesis, they believed that the true God created only the invisible, spiritual kingdom, which was permanent, whereas all worldly matter was evil emanating from another Principle, the reverse of God, making man in his own likeness. The logical conclusion was that the humanity of Christ was a mere illusion and Cathars therefore rejected the events that followed. The community was divided between the majority or ordinary faithful, and ascetics or preachers known as Perfect or Goodmen, who led an exemplary life of abstinence and charity. Women had equal status. The only Cathar sacrament was the *consolamentum*, which served both in the ordination of priests and as the last rites for ordinary followers.

Although never in the majority and at first accepted in the tolerant society of the Languedoc, the Cathars through their doctrine, preaching in the vernacular, and not exacting tithes or taxes, threatened to undermine the authority, wealth and power of the orthodox church. Many attempts were made to bring the Cathars back to the orthodox faith by debate and disputation, but to no avail. The Spanish cleric, **Bernard of Clairvaux** (1090–1153), a man of intense religious conviction, founded the ultra ascetic Cistercian Order at the Abbey of Cîteaux, Burgundy in 1115. He was sent by Pope Innocent III to preach against the Cathar heritics in Toulouse and Albi in 1145, with little effect, but more successfully engendered enthusiasm for the Second Crusade to the Holy Land in 1146. An outstanding theologian, his mystical beliefs famously opposed the sceptical genius of another great Churchman and scholar of the time, Pierre Abélard (1079–1142).

Dominic de Guzman (St Dominic) settled in the Languedoc in 1206 and the order of itinerant preachers he gathered there to counteract the heresy developed into the Dominican order founded in Toulouse in 1215. Persecution was meted out to the heretics from *c* 1170 and in 1233 Pope Gregory IX confided to the most hardened Dominicans the task of the General Inquisition. In 1234 the first heretic was burned at the stake and the executions went on until well into the 14C.

The heresy also provided a handle for the French monarchy to get a grip on the Languedoc and gain the submission of the powerful Counts of Toulouse. The French king, **Philippe-Auguste**, with the support of the pope and the Cistercians, justified an attack on his own people as a religious crusade and gathered an army under the symbol of the Cross which mustered in Lyons in 1209, commanded by the papal legate, Arnaud Amaury. Thus began the Albigensian Crusade (1209–25). Following the brutal sack of Béziers, the army beseiged Carcassonne, where **Simon de Montfort** (1165–1218) emerged as leader.

Sieges and killings continued in waves until 1226 throughout the Languedoc and as far north as the Agenais and the Rouergue. Simon de Montfort died under the walls of Toulouse but the persecution and punishments continued. Eventually the Cathars took refuge in castles which were made over to them by lesser nobility sympathetic to their cause, and the last sieges were laid to the châteaux of Montségur in 1244 and Queribus in 1255. The end of major hostilities was marked by the **Treaty of Meaux** (1229) which, among many clauses, stipulated that Alphonse of Poitiers, brother of Louis IX, marry Jeanne de Toulouse, daughter of Raymond VII. These two died during the last crusade to the Holy Land, leaving no issue, and the dominions of the Counts of Toulouse reverted to France in 1271.

In the Romantic era of the 19C a popular revival of the Cathars began and their story is now exploited in the southern part of the region as a tourist attraction.

The Hundred Years War

Meanwhile, Henry III (r. 1216–72) vainly attempted to repossess the territories lost by King John. In 1259, war between Henry and Louis IX (r. 1226–70, later St Louis) resulted in the Treaty of Paris which ceded large areas of Périgord, including Périgueux, Limoges and Cahors, to the English, while Henry did homage for the Duchy to Louis. Later the French regretted their generosity, and there were local skirmishes which hotted up in the 14C during the reigns of Philippe IV of France (1285–1314) and Edward I of England (1272–1307).

The main event leading up to the Hundred Years War was the claim by **Edward III** (r. 1327–77) to the vacant French throne by right of his mother, Isabelle, daughter of Philippe IV, but he lost out to Philippe of Valois who became Philippe VI (r. 1328–50). By 1337 Edward's position had improved but ongoing tensions between the English king's representatives and local administration in Gascony reached a new crisis and Philippe declared the Duchy confiscate, escalating the quarrel from one between vassal and overlord to a power struggle between two royal dynasties. War became an almost constant feature from 1337 to 1453, in an endless cycle of siege, battle and intrigue, although few battles were fought between 1348 and 1350 when the population was severely depleted by the Black Death.

By their victory at Poitiers in 1356 Edward and his son, the **Black Prince**, obtained the Treaty of Brétigny of 1360, whereby much of southwest France reverted to the English king in return for his renunciation of the throne of France. The Duchy was elevated to a principality in 1362 and placed under the control of the Black Prince. War began again in the southwest, led by Bernard du Guesclin (*c* 1320–80), hero of the French cause. Following the English victory at Agincourt in 1415 and the Treaty of Troyes of 1420, the inheritance of the French king Charles VI (r. 1380–1422) was made over to Henry V. The Dauphin and the Armagnacs in Gascony were opposed to this and the war entered a new phase: **Joan of Arc** (1412–31) made her appearance in 1429, bringing support to the Dauphin who finally defeated the English in Normandy in 1450. Charles VII (r. 1422–61) took the spoils at the Battle of Castillon, near St-Emilion, on 17 July 1453, and the Duchy of Aquitaine was reincorporated into the domain of Royal France.

The Wars of Religion

During the 15C–16C, enormous wealth was derived in Toulouse and the Lauragais from the cultivation of **pastel** (woad), which produced a much sought-after indigo dye used in the cloth industry in Northern Europe. The *pastel* merchants of Toulouse were highly educated, rich and powerful men who built fine Renaissance mansions, introducing the new ideas in architecture emanating from Italy at the time.

By the mid-16C the tenets of humanism and the Reformation were also infiltrating the region. Protestants (known also as Calvinists or **Huguenots**) became powerful and widespread in the south of France, where they enjoyed periods of relative tolerance contrasting with moments of violent oppression. **Jeanne d'Albret** (1528–72), daughter of Henry of Navarre and Marguerite d'Angoulême, the sister of François I, imposed her Protestant faith on much of the Agenais and the Béarn and passed it on to her son, Henri III of Navarre, who was born in the Château at Pau in 1553.

During the reign of François I (1515–47), anti-Protestant feelings were already developing and intensified during the reign of Henri II (1547–59). Opposition developed between powerful Catholic families, such as the Guise clan and Anne de Montmorency, and the Protestant Bourbons, represented by the Prince de Condé (1522–88), brother of Jeanne d'Albret's husband Antoine de Bourbon, and Admiral Coligny (1519–72). Anti-Protestant feeling escalated into violence and the struggle developed into a politico-religious civil war fought during the reigns of François II (1559–60), Charles IX (1560–74) and Henri III (1574–89). Catherine de Médicis, the powerful wife of Henri II and mother of the other three, remained conciliatory until the 1570s.

The union of the Protestant Henri III of Navarre to the Catholic Marguerite de Valois did not bring an immediate solution to the religious problems and six days after the wedding in 1572 there was wholesale slaughter on the streets of Paris, known as the **St Bartholomew's Day Massacre**. A group of nobles around the Guises set up the Catholic Leagues in 1573 and 1584 to defend the faith and keep Henri of Navarre off the throne. Propaganda issued by the League increased tensions between the unpopular Henri III and the popular Guises, who gained control of Paris on 13 May 1588 (Day of the Barricades). On 23 October, Henri, Duc de Guise (1580–88) was murdered by the King's men and in January 1589, Catherine de Médicis died. Henri III was caught between the forces of the League to the north and the Union of Protestants to the south. His only ally was Henri of Navarre, who was looking to make peace. On 26 April 1589, the two Henris signed a truce, combined forces and marched on Paris. Henri of Navarre, who had a legitimate claim through his father, acceded to the throne of France in 1589 as **Henri IV** (1589–1610), the first of the Bourbon line. With the Edict of Nantes (1598), which regulated the legal rights of the Reformed Church in France, he brought about religious harmony and granted both freedom of worship and certain political and military rights to the Protestants.

The Counter-Reformation

Louis XIII (r. 1610–43), however, reunited France under the Catholic banner and exacted severe punishment on Protestant strongholds in the southwest, starting with the dismantling of fortifications at Montauban in 1621. The period 1621–24, first under Constable Luynes (1578–1621) and then with the support of Cardinal Richelieu (1585–1642), was particularly harsh and Protestants were deprived of certain privileges by the Treaty of Alès (1629). Louis established centralised royal authority by creating a body of Intendants, but upset the national budget by entering the Thirty Years War. This had little direct effect on the southwest but increasingly heavy taxes imposed on peasants in the Périgord and the Rouergue resulted in a series of insurrections among them during the 16C and 17C, known as the **Croquants revolts**.

As a result of the loss of autonomy in the southwest there was another uprising in 1629. The Governor of Languedoc, the Duc de Montmorency, who had participated in the movement in 1632, was executed in the courtyard of the Capitole in Toulouse in the presence of Louis XIII and Richelieu. This example ensured that during the series of uprisings known as **Le Fronde** (1649–53), directed against the unpopular Cardinal Mazarin and his financial demands during the minority of Louis XIV, the Midi remained faithful to Mazarin.

With great pomp and ceremony, **Louis XIV** (r. 1643–1715) married the Infanta Marie-Thérèse of Spain in St-Jean-de-Luz in 1660. He instigated major administrative and financial reforms and continued the Counter-Reformation tendencies of his father with the **Revocation of the Edict of Nantes** (1685), which resulted in a huge exodus of Protestants from France.

The driving force behind the Counter-Reformation was the **Council of Trent**, a succession of ecumenical councils held between 1545 and 1653 through which the Roman Catholic Church set about a complete revision of its discipline and a reaffirmation of essential dogmas. The physical result of this was the introduction of Classical and Baroque altarpieces found in every church in France, especially in country regions such as the Pyrenees.

Developing trade, the Revolution and Napoléon

One of the greatest engineering projects of the mid-17C was Pierre-Paul Riquet's Canal Royal du Languedoc, now called the **Canal du Midi** (1666–81), which linked Toulouse with the Mediterranean and brought great prosperity to the southern part of the region. One of the main cargoes on the canal was maize, which revolutionised agriculture in the southwest when introduced from the Americas at the beginning of the 17C.

The port of Bordeaux became the most important in the land during the 18C, due not only to wine but also to the profitable trade with the colonies in luxury goods, including sugar cane, and the authorisation for trade in slaves. Major works of **urban regeneration** and road building were undertaken by enlightened Royal Intendants such as Boucher, Tourny and Dupré de Saint Maur in Bordeaux, while in Gascony, Intendant Etigny of Auch brought a huge economic impetus to the southern part of the region with the construction of major roads.

The effect of the Revolution of 1789 was less powerful and less violent in the southwest than in Paris. Bordeaux's main involvement was through a moderate group of intellectuals, the **Girondins**, who attempted to control the more violent aspects of the Convention (the Revolutionary Assembly of 1792 to 1795) but were expelled in 1793 and executed. Toulouse, on the other hand, remained more supportive of the Convention. In 1790 most of the modern **départements** were formed, maintaining to some extent the boundaries of the old provinces they replaced. (The regional boundaries were set in 1972.)

The Concordat of July 1801, drawn up by Napoléon and Pope Pius VII, which recognised the alienation of church lands as permanent and the payment of clerical staff by the state, heralded a government-controlled religion during the First Empire.

Economic expansion of the southwest was slowed down by the Revolution, and the **Napoleonic Wars** had a particularly disastrous effect on Bordeaux, which suffered losses during the maritime wars and the embargo that prevented any British imports, or ships that had traded with Britain, coming into French-controlled ports. The British retaliated by blockading French ports. The southwest was indirectly affected by conflict when Napoléon's forces crossed the region at the start of the campaigns in Portugal (1807) and Spain (1808), and was drawn into war when the English, led by Wellington, crossed the Pyrenees in 1813 in pursuit of Marshall Soult, born near Mazamet in the Tarn. He passed through Bayonne, which refused to surrender until Orthez fell in 1814, but a small British contingent sent to occupy Bordeaux was welcomed there after the flight of the imperial authorities. On 6 April, Napoléon abdicated. This news did not reach Wellington until after his final victory over Soult near Toulouse, where the Duke was received as liberator, on 10 April 1814. Legend has it that, as they crossed the region, Wellington's officers were delighted by Pau and returned to settle there, introducing many aspects of English life.

The 19C was not the brightest for the under-populated, rural southwest and due to the lack of coal—just small open-cast mines at Carmaux and Decazeville—it was slow to participate in the **industrial revolution**. What coal there was was shipped on the Lot, and wine on the Tarn, Garonne and Dordogne. The Canal Latéral à la Garonne, the continuation of the Canal du Midi, was cut in the 1840s but almost immediately superseded by the Bordeaux to Sète railway. The rail link with Paris was established with Bordeaux in 1852, Bayonne in 1855, Toulouse in 1856, and Tarbes in 1867.

One of the major regeneration projects of the mid-19C was the creation of the **Landes forest** by the drainage and plantation of pines over some million hectares of sandy waste. The trees, which produced resin for turpentine and timber for railway-sleepers and pit-props, gave an impetus to one of the poorest regions in France. Conversely, the **phylloxera** epidemic of the 1870s wiped out entire vineyards. These were replanted mainly from Californian stock which itself had originated from France, but in some of the smaller wine-producing regions the industry was slow to recover.

Among the great 19C orators and politicians from the southwest was the ardent supporter of the Republic, Léon Gambetta (1838–82), who was born in Cahors, and the socialist campaigner Jean Jaurès (1859–1914), from Castres.

Tourism was sparked by the fashion for sea-bathing during the mid-19C and the patronage of Empress Eugénie and the court of Napoléon III (r. 1852–70), which drew visitors to the Basque coast and was accelerated by the arrival of the railway. For the same reasons Arcachon also became popular, as did certain thermal stations including Eaux-Bonnes and Eugénie-les-Bains.

The twentieth century

The main effect of the two great wars of the 20C was the severe depopulation of the region, especially in the rural communities, recorded only too clearly on memorials in every town and village. On 11 November 1942, what had been the Free Southern Zone, including Périgueux and Toulouse, was occupied by

German forces. Bordeaux was already in the Occupied Zone. The **Résistance** or *Maquis* was active in certain parts of the southwest, including the Pyrenees (the route to Spain), the Lot and the woodlands of the Périgord. The largest Jewish internment camp in the southwest was at Gurs, near Navarrenx in the Béarn.

The major positive result of wartime was the development of aviation and the **aeronautical industry** in Toulouse, which is now important for the whole of the southwest. The petro-chemical industry in Pau developed in the 1950s. De Gaulle's decision to make Toulouse the base for France's national space agency meant that by 1997, 25 per cent of European activity in astronautics took place there and 7000 jobs had been generated. In June 1993 a metro line was opened in Toulouse, and Bordeaux is now undertaking a vast project to enhance the banks of the Garonne. The **infrastructure** of the whole southwest has been improved in recent years with the construction of new autoroutes and bridges.

Despite much-needed pockets of industry and technology in the main agglomerations, the southwest remains a remarkably sparsely populated, agricultural region and is still relatively unspoilt. The British, and slightly later the Dutch, who began to purchase permanent or secondary residences here in the 1970s, particularly in the Dordogne, have contributed greatly to the revival of semi-abandoned villages and hamlets. On the whole they have integrated and are well-received by the French.

Art and architecture

On balance, architecture outweighs art in the southwest: in the medieval period it is not feasible to dissociate the two, art being integral to the architecture. There were, however, lesser-known centres of religious art in the major cities in the 17C and 18C; in the 19C art galleries were established through donations or acquisitions; and at the end of the 19C and early 20C the region had some local artists of international standing, the best known of whom was Toulouse-Lautrec.

Prehistoric to Gallo-Roman

Unique to the southwest of France is a wealth of prehistoric painting and sculpture on the walls of caves or rock shelters. Of the 173 decorated sites found in France, some 100 are in Aquitaine, 23 are in the Quercy and 27 in the Pyrenees; there are one or two in the Corrèze, and 17 further east in the Rhône delta and Provence. The period of creativity stretched over many thousands of years, between 35,000 and 10,000 BC, during the Upper Palaeolithic era. The high point, however, was the Magdalenian period, *c* 17,000–9500 BC, when such outstanding examples as those at Lascaux, Font-de-Gaume (both in the Dordogne), Pech-Merle (Lot) and Niaux (Ariège) were created. The **paintings**, frequently of animals, are without doubt the work of accomplished and practised artists and must have been of great symbolic importance, given the difficulties associated with creating them, but their *raison d'être* remains enigmatic. Pebbles, bones and horn were also engraved or carved, the oldest dating from *c* 30,000 years ago, and the earliest of the relief representations of females, described as Venuses, dates back some 20,000 years. Many of these items (or replicas of them), along with prehistoric flints and tools, are gathered at the Musée National de Préhistoire at Les Eyzies (Dordogne).

The art works of the Neolithic, Bronze and Iron Ages, 9000–50 BC, are found mainly in museums although carved monoliths or **menhirs**, dating *c* 3500–2500 BC, still stand in remote areas such as the Monts de Lacaune (Aveyron), as do the most rudimentary of Neolithic structures, the dolmen or burial chamber (Dordogne, Lot). Other artefacts of these periods are found in the Musée d'Aquitaine in Bordeaux, Musée St-Raymond in Toulouse, and at Lectoure (Gers) and Périgueux (Dordogne), and consist of vessels, coins, adornments and some fine torques. In these same museums, and at St-Bertrand-de-Comminges (Haute-Garonne), are the best of the **Roman artefacts**, of the 1C–3C AD, from various sites through the southwest. A very fine series of antique portrait busts was discovered at Villa Chiragan (now displayed in the Musée St-Raymond), and a magnificent bronze Hercules was found in Bordeaux. There are the remains of several small Gallo-Roman villas with mosaics and painted fragments at Montmaurin (Haute-Garonne), Séviac (Gers), Plassac (Gironde) and Montcaret (Dordogne). The Tour Vésone in Périgueux is the finest example of a centrally planned temple existing in France, and here as well as at Bordeaux, Toulouse, Dax (Landes), Bayonne (Pyrénées-Atlantiques), St-Bertrand-de-Comminges and Cahors (Lot) are fragments of **Roman civic constructions**—thermae or bath complexes, fortifications, amphitheatres, and so on. There was a large production of sigillated (red clay with an impressed decoration) pottery at Graufesenque, near Millau (Aveyron), and Montans, near Gaillac (Tarn).

Medieval (11th–15th centuries)

There are many outstanding examples of medieval architecture and sculpture in the region, in churches, castles and secular buildings. Various styles of **Romanesque church architecture** developed concurrently during the late 11C and 12C in this region, which was crossed by important pilgrimage routes converging on northern Spain. The best surviving examples of the classic 12C pilgrimage church in the Benedictine tradition, laid out in the shape of a Latin cross with transepts, aisles, ambulatory and galleries, are St-Sernin in Toulouse and Ste-Foy in Conques (Aveyron). Specific to the southwest are the **domed churches**, of which some 60–70 once existed, many now altered or rebuilt. Périgueux has two examples, St-Etienne, which claims to be the oldest, and St-Front, which is the largest with five domes, albeit much rebuilt. Others include those at Souillac (Lot), Moirax (Lot-et-Garonne) and Cahors, which has the largest dome in diameter. Hispano-Arabic influences, which spread across the Pyrenees to southwest France, are found in the Moorish-style cupolas on intersecting arches at St-Croix in Oloron Ste-Marie and the church of the Hôpital St-Blaise (both in Pyrénées Atlantiques), and in the decoration of some cloister capitals in Moissac (Tarn-et-Garonne).

Beautifully proportioned **Cistercian abbey churches**, although not unadulterated, can be found at Beaulieu-en-Rouergue, Loc Dieu and Sylvanès (all in the Aveyron), Cadouin (Dordogne) and Flaran (Gers). The style of the neighbouring

Saintonge spread into northern Aquitaine and is identified by the elaborately tiered and arcaded west façades of churches such as St-Pierre at Petit-Palais (Gironde). The most curious church of the period must be the monolithic church carved out of the solid rock below nearby St-Emilion; a remarkable and rare 11C belfry stands in Brantôme (Dordogne).

There is a wealth of **Romanesque sculpture** in the southwest, the output of several workshops which picked up influences travelling in both directions along the pilgrimage routes between Cluny in Burgundy and Santiago de Compostela in Spain. The most magnificent example in France of cloister capitals *in situ* is at Moissac (Tarn-et-Garonne), a Cluniac abbey which also boasts compelling sculptures around the porch. There are similarities between the work at Moissac and at St-Sernin (Toulouse), Souillac and over an area stretching from St-Alain in Lavaur (Tarn) to St-Caprais in Agen (Lot-et-Garonne). St-Sever (Landes) felt the direct influence of Cluny, but although there are some similarities in the motifs of the capitals with Conques, this last remained independent from Cluny and produced a tympanum in a style akin to that of the Massif Central. Other good examples of Romanesque carving are at Ste-Quitterie in Aire-sur-l'Adour, Hagetmau and Sorde l'Abbaye (all in the Landes), Cahors, Carennac (Lot), and the more rustic St-Lizier (Ariège). Gathered together in the Musée des Augustins in Toulouse is the largest collection anywhere of 12C sculpted capitals, saved from three cloisters demolished in the 19C. There are vestiges of 12C wall paintings, although most are later, at St-Sernin, St-Lizier and elsewhere.

Few examples of **12C secular buildings** have survived, but the so-called Hôtel de Ville at St-Antonin-Noble-Val (Tarn-et-Garonne) is distinguished by its tower, and has colonnaded openings with carvings the length of the first floor with round-headed bays above. A less ambitious example is the Pavilion d'Adelaïde at Burlats (Tarn).

Fortifications of the 12C are rare, and those remaining have been rebuilt, but part of the castle of Beynac (Dordogne) dates back to that period. **Fortified churches** of the 12C–14C are frequent in areas which were contested, especially Aquitaine during English occupation. The belfry—being the tallest building in a village or town without fortifications or a castle—served as the watchtower. At St-Amand-de-Coly is a magnificent *tour-donjon* while St-Avit-Sénieur and Beaumont-en-Périgord have tall towers and other defensive elements (all in the Dordogne); the church at Larressingle (Gers) was fortified in the 12C.

Gothic architecture in the southwest takes a particular form, and is described as meridional or **southern Gothic**. This was the style of the post-Cathar heresy, which developed as religious orders created churches adapted to preaching, and possibly from the tradition of churches without aisles already established in the region. The buttress and ribbed vaults play the same role as in northern Gothic architecture, but here the buttresses are simple and encroach heavily on the interior space to create chapels. The prototypes were the old nave of the cathedral of St-Etienne in Toulouse and the church of the Cordeliers in Toulouse, which has disappeared. The most memorable example is the severely simple brick cathedral of Ste-Cécile in Albi (Tarn), with a single-span nave which was the model for most of the parish churches in the region of Albi and Toulouse. The cathedral and the fortified 13C bishops' palace in Albi were built in the wake of the Cathar heresies, as a statement of the strength of the Catholic church. Similarly, the Dominican church of the Jacobins in Toulouse, also in brick, which is unusually divided into two equal sections by a row of tall columns down the centre, was specially designed for the teaching order that was founded to refute the heresies.

The more complicated style of **northern Gothic** with flying buttresses was imported after the integration of the Languedoc into France in 1271, when builders from the north worked on the choir of St-Etienne in Toulouse, and the cathedral of Rodez (Aveyron). The rebuilding of the cathedral of Bordeaux continued from the end of the 13C to well into the 14C and it is a mish-mash of borrowings from northern cathedrals. By contrast, Ste-Marie in Bayonne, begun in the mid-13C in the Rayonnant style of Reims or Paris, was built when the town was under English occupation.

Unsurprisingly, the major **English influence** is found in Guyenne, in the construction of castles of the mid-13C, a time when the Plantagenets were facing pressure from the armies of the French king. The local nobility, keen to hold on to the advantages they enjoyed under English dominion, were rarely refused permission to replace old feudal forts and between 1278 and 1354 about 32 authorisations were granted, along a line of defence on the banks of the Dordogne. Most of these have disappeared, are in ruins or have been profoundly altered. Typical of English *châteaux-forts* are four angle towers, one of which remains at La Réole, built by Henry III Plantagenet. Villandraut (also in the Gironde), the first of the 14C *châteaux clementines*, followed the pattern of Edward I's Welsh castles, with rounded angle towers and a square keep dominating the entrance and linked by crenellated curtain walls.

Most medieval castles grew piecemeal and some of the most romantic, ruined or intact, are in the Dordogne, including Beynac, Biron, Castlenau, and Bonaguil which was the last of its kind. The variety and evolution of great castles with towering keeps in the south of the region such as Pau, Foix and Morlanne—in which Gaston Fébus, Count of Foix in the 14C, had a hand— contrast with the small but perfect Château du Bosquet in remote Aveyron. The most complete medieval **fortified bridge**, with three towers, is the Pont Valentré which elegantly spans the Lot at Cahors and was built for defence during the Hundred Years War; similar but incomplete is the bridge at Orthez (Pyrénées-Atlantiques).

The small fortified hilltop town of Domme (Dordogne) has a magnificent gateway built in 13C bossed masonry and Cordes-sur-Ciel (Tarn) still has four early 13C gateways and part of its fortifications. Both these are **bastides** (p 262), of which there are some 300 in the southwest. Among the most perfect examples are Monpazier (Dordogne) and Sauveterre-de-Rouergue (Aveyron). High-quality medieval domestic architecture is abundant in Figeac (Lot) and also in St-Antonin-Noble-Val but there is little to match the Gothic houses in Cordes.

The cloister at Cadouin is a fine example of the **late Gothic period** in the 15C, built after the destruction wrought by the Hundred Years War, and has similarities with the very damaged cloister at Cahors. The Chartreuse de St-Sauveur at Villefranche-de-Rouergue (Aveyron), begun in the 15C, has a small decorated cloister, and another which is large but unadorned. A precious survival from this period is the delicately carved limestone choir enclosure in Albi cathedral, a veritable *tour de force*, with superb coloured sculptures representing Old Testament figures. The choir and the uniquely wonderful sculptural group of the *Entombment* at Monestiés (Tarn) were both sponsored by Bishop Louis I d'Amboise in the late 15C.

Renaissance (16th–17th centuries)

During the first half of the 16C, the late Gothic style of France and Renaissance influences direct from Italy or from the Loire merged to create the pretty early Renaissance or **First French Renaissance style**. The first decorative import were the painted vaults of Albi cathedral, and the gable on the west end of the cathedral of Rodez is straight out of Serlio's *L'Architettura*, the first book to codify the Classical orders. There are boundless examples of domestic architecture in the style—typified by four-square windows, columns and pilasters and decorated with busts and rinceaux—in the wealthier towns right across the southwest (with the exception of Bordeaux), such as Sarlat (Dordogne), Périgueux, Condom (Gers), Albi and Castres (Tarn), in the Maison Roaldès at Cahors and most especially in Toulouse, where sophisticated town houses were built by wealthy *pastel* merchants, notably the Hôtel d'Assézat. Many **châteaux** were transformed from forts to homes during the period up to the Wars of Religion, such as the Château de Pau (Pyrénées-Atlantiques), and others were built as a display of their patrons' knowledge of contemporary fashion. Examples are Puyguilhem, Monbazillac (both in the Dordogne), Assier, Montal (both in the Lot) and Bournazel (Aveyron); slightly later came the *châteaux* of Lanquais, Losse, Bannes and Bordeilles (all Dordogne), and the Hôtel d'Andurain in Mauléon (Pyrénées-Atlantiques).

In the 16C there was not such noticeable activity in the construction of churches in the southwest, although additions in the form of chapels and furnishings were made to existing churches. The cathedral of Auch (Gers) is a major example of this tendency, with a late-Renaissance west end, a very impressive group of coloured windows, typical of the period in style and technique, and a magnificent carved wooden choir enclosure. The choir of Ste-Marie at St-Bertrand-de-Comminges is also a very fine example of Renaissance wood carving, where there is also an organ of the same period. In the Pyrenees, small chapels and churches received ambitious painted décor during a period of relative wealth and security.

There was some hiatus in building between 1560 and the end of the religious strife in 1598, and by the 17C domestic architecture was becoming more Classical in style. There are fewer examples of *châteaux* in the **Second French Renaissance style**, although there are a number of *hôtels particuliers* in Bordeaux and Toulouse. Despite subsequent alterations and abuse, some of the elevations and interiors of the Château de Cadillac (Gironde) give an idea of the period, and the Château d'Hautefort (Dordogne) was updated in the 17C. The Château de Malle (Gironde) is a particularly good example, with mansard roof and rounded pediments. The Château de Gaujacq (Les Landes) unusually has definite Palladian tendencies.

Some remarkable feats of **engineering** in the 17C include the Canal du Midi, and the forts built by Vauban at Blaye (Gironde) and Bayonne.

Baroque and Neoclassical (17th–18th centuries)

Church architecture and fittings of the 17C–18C took on board the full force of the Counter-Reformation as laid down by the Council of Trent. Baroque swirls and flounces introduced high drama. Elaborate **gilded altarpieces** were installed in every church, some of the most ambitious in remote areas, and more relics were added, as at St-Sernin in Toulouse. The best 17C example on any scale is Notre-Dame in Bordeaux; Toulouse's response was St-Jérome and the Carmelite chapel. Due to the founding of secular orders (such as the Pénitents blue, white and black), small **Baroque chapels** appeared, such as the chapels of the Pénitents Noirs in Villefranche-de-Rouergue and in St-Geniez-d'Olt (Aveyron). In the Basque region the interiors of old churches were transformed in the 17C with the addition of wooden galleries, ornate retables and colourful paintwork. The 13C chapel of St-Pierre in Lachapelle (Tarn-et-Garonne) acquired Baroque décor in the 18C.

Prolific painters of religious works in the Toulousain in the 17C–18C include Antoine Rivalz (1667–1735) and his pupil Jean-Baptiste Despax (1710–73) whose work can be seen at the Carmelite chapel in Toulouse.

The **Classical revival** of the 18C, the return to the principles of Greek and Roman architecture, is nowhere better represented in the southwest than in the civic and domestic buildings of Bordeaux. Among the most active architects were the Gabriels and Victor Louis, who between them designed the elegant Place de la Bourse (1733–55), originally Place Royale, dedicated to Louis XV and embellished with Ionic columns; and the austere Grande Théâtre de l'Opéra (1773–80) in the style of the reign of Louis XVI, when orders of colossal columns became the dominant architectural feature.

The 19th and 20th centuries

The 19C introduced more practical and **industrial buildings**, typified by the simple one-storey working-class accommodation in Bordeaux known as an *échoppe bordelaise*, or by functional but grand railways stations, notably at Bordeaux. While buildings were still being destroyed and demolished there was a parallel impulse to save and restore, reflected in the creation of the **Monuments Historiques**, an agency for the protection of ancient monuments, the prime movers of which were Prosper Merimée and Eugene Viollet-le-Duc. The desire for neo-everything resulted in some magnificent follies, such as the Château d'Abbadie (Pays Basque). Unique is Viollet-le-Duc's revamp of the interior of the Château de Roquetaillade (Gironde). A range of utterly charming, if excessive, 19C domestic architecture was created in seaside resorts such as Arcachon (Gironde) and Biarritz (Pyrénées-Atlantiques), which were in full expansion right through the early 20C. Bridges include that at Bordeaux by Gustave Eiffel, and the Viaduc de Viaur (Aveyron).

Art galleries in the main towns—Bordeaux, Toulouse, Agen, Castres, Bayonne and Pau—sprang up in the 19C. They contain some excellent examples of works spanning the main periods of art in Europe from the late medieval period to the 19C. The 19C–20C collections are less eclectic. The museum in Castres is devoted almost entirely to Spanish works, with which Bayonne is also well endowed: both contain several works by Francisco Goya (1746–1828), who spent the last few years of his life in Bordeaux. Two major, but contrasting, 19C artists from the southwest, Jean-Auguste-Dominique Ingres (1780–1867) and Henri de Toulouse-Lautrec (1864–1901) have museums dedicated to them in Montauban and Albi respectively. Montauban (Tarn-et-Garonne) was the birth-place of Ingres, of the sculptor Antoine Bourdelle (1861–1929) and of the painter Marcel Lenoir (1872–1931), to whom a museum is dedicated at nearby Montricoux. At Cahors there is a collection of work by the Toulousain Impressionist, Henri Martin (1860–1943), and there are more in the Capitole in

Toulouse. Among incomers to the region were the sculptor Ossip Zadkine (1890–1967), who lived and worked at Les Arques where there is a museum dedicated to him; Jean Lurçat (1892–1966), whose works can be seen at St-Céré; and Henri Giron (b. 1914), to whom a private gallery near Gourdon is dedicated (all in the Lot). Examples of work by the three 19C–20C Bordelais artists Odilon Redon (1840–1916), André Lhote (1885–1962) and Albert Marquet (1875–1947) can be found in Bordeaux's Musée des Beaux-Arts.

Architecture at the beginning of the 20C is represented by the Théâtre Ducourneau of 1906 in Agen, and in Toulouse, the Matabiau railway station and Café Bibent. Edmond Rostand built the neo-Basque Villa Arnaga (1902) in Cambo-les-Bains (Pyrénées-Atlantiques). Bordeaux, which prides itself on the integration of good modern buildings with old, in 1926 commissioned **Le Corbusier** for the Cité Frugès (Pessac) and he also designed a *château d'eau* (water tower) at Podensac as well as at Lège-Cap-Ferret (Gironde). The development of the coastal resorts continued through the 1920s and 1930s to produce such pioneering buildings as the Sporting-Casino at Soorts-Hossegor (Landes), private houses at Arcachon and Biarritz, and the Villa Leïhorra (1926–29) in Ciboure (Pyrénées-Atlantiques). The Villa Natacha at Biarritz has an Art Nouveau interior décor, rare on the Basque coast. In contrast, the Base Sous-Marine (submarine base) was built in Bordeaux during the Second World War. Without a doubt, one of the most awesome and forbidding religious buildings in the southwest is the massive underground Basilica of Pius X of 1956–58 at Lourdes (Hautes-Pyrénées) by the architect Pierre Vao, which is designed to hold large groups of pilgrims. The development in the Meriadeck area in Bordeaux in the 1970s introduced *avant-garde* structures such as the Caisse d'Epargne (1974–80), while nearby are the Ecole Nationale de la Magistrature (1969–73) and the Tribunal de Grande Instance (1994–98) by the Richard Rogers Partnership. The transformation of industrial buildings into art galleries has been successful at Bordeaux, where the Musée de l'Art Contemporain is housed in a fine 20C adaptation of a 19C warehouse, and in Toulouse, where the old abattoirs have also become a museum of modern art.

Further reading

History
Christopher Allmand, *The Hundred Years War: England and France at war c 1300–c 1450*, Cambridge University Press, 1994
John Ardagh, *Modern France*, Penguin, 1988
Anne Curry, *The Hundred Years War*, Macmillan, 1993
Maurice Keen, *Medieval Europe*, Penguin, 1991
Malcolm Lambert, *Medieval Heresy*, Blackwells, 1994
Emmanuel Le Roy Ladurie, *Montaillou*, Penguin, 1990
Stephen O'Shea, *The Perfect Heresy. The Life and Death of the Cathars*, Profile Books, 2000
Ian Ousby, *Occupation. The Ordeal of France 1940–44*, Pimlico, 1997
Osprey Essential Histories, *The Crusades*, 1988
Alison Weir, *Eleanor of Aquitaine*, Pimlico, 2000

Art and architecture
Kenneth John Conant, *Carolingian and Romanesque Architecture 800–1200*, Yale University Press, 1993
Hayward Gallery, *Toulouse-Lautrec*, exhibition catalogue, 1991
Kathryn Horste, *Cloister Design and Monastic Reform in Toulouse. The Romanesque Sculpture of La Daurade*, Oxford University Press, 1992
Robert Rosenblum, *Jean-Auguste-Dominique Ingres*, Thames & Hudson, 1990
Meyer Schapiro, *Romanesque Art. Selected Papers*, Thames & Hudson, 1993
Juliet Wilson, *Goya's Prints*, London, 1982

Travel books in English
James Bentley, *Fort Towns of France. The Bastides of the Dordogne and Aquitaine*, Tauris Parke,1994
Michael Brown, *South to Gascony*, Hamish Hamilton, 1989
Joy Law, *The Midi*, John Murray, 1991
John Sturrock, *The French Pyrenees*, Faber, 1988 (out of print)
Freda White, *Three Rivers of France*, Pavilion, 1992

Books in French
Hachette's *Guide Bleu Midi-Pyrénées* is an extremely detailed guide to the region; the same publisher's *Guide du Routard Midi-Pyrénées* is also recommended. Three Michelin Guides cover the region: *Pyrénées–Aquitaine–Côte Basque*; *Pyrénées–Roussillon–Albigeois*; and *Dordogne–Périgord–Quercy* (the last one exists in English translation). Sud Ouest Publications publish a series of regional guides and monographs. Specially recommended in the series (in translation) are Quitterie and Daniel Cazes' *Discovering Toulouse*, 1992, and Maurice Scellès' *Visiting Moissac Abbey*, 2000. By the same publishers, Quitterie Cazes and Maurice Scellès, *Le Cloître de Moissac* (in French only).

   Editions du Rouergue publish good-quality books on the region covering all topics from art to cookery. Editions du Beffroi produce small-format guidebooks with colour photographs on specific topics or monuments in the Aveyron. Some (including that for Conques) are in English. In the series on Romanesque architecture and sculpture are *Zodiaque, la nuit des temps: Quercy Roman, Rouergue Roman, Gascogne Romane, Haut-Languedoc Roman* and *Pyrénées Romanes*. Other recommendations are:

M. Beaulieu and V. Beyer, *Dictionnaire des Sculptures français du Moyen Age*, Picard, 1992

Marcel Durliat, *La Sculpture Romane de la Route de Saint-Jacques*, CEHAG, 1990

Michel Roquebert, *Rues Tolosanes*, Privat, 1988

THE GUIDE

1 Bordeaux

Bordeaux is a stately city, prosperous and urbane, as befits the head and heart of the greatest wine-producing area in the world. With around 700,000 inhabitants, including some 50,000 students, it is the fifth city in France and administrative capital of the *région* of Aquitaine. It is also the *préfecture* of the largest *département* in France, the Gironde, a vaguely diamond-shaped chunk of land covering 10,000 sq km, which is cleft by the Garonne River. The Garonne, as it flows northwards, is swelled by the Dordogne to create the important Gironde Estuary north of the city, before emptying into the Atlantic. Bordeaux developed on the left bank of a great crescent-shaped meander in the Garonne and the combination of water and wine has been the city's *raison d'être* for many centuries. Its most outstanding feature today is the juxtaposition of the river and the magnificent buildings facing it, in an area which is undergoing a huge project of urban regeneration and landscaping to realise its full potential.

Bordeaux may not be a swinging city but it is visitor-friendly, not so large as to be intimidating but big enough to offer a variety of artistic, gastronomic and sporting activities. Its many museums include the excellent Musée de l'Aquitaine, it has an opera house, and an important wine festival, the *Fête le Vin*, is held here in June.

Practical information

Getting there and around
From the airport

An airport bus (*Jet'bus*) runs every 30 mins from Arrivals, Exit 7 to the town centre and main station, with stops at Barrière Judaïque, Pl. Gambetta, Grand Théâtre and Quai Richelieu. Taxis to the city centre cost €30–38.

Parking

There are a number of car parks in the area of the main Tourist Office (see below).

Train

The main station, Gare St-Jean, is 3km to the south of the town centre.

Bus and tram

Bus passes giving unlimited travel are available for 1 to 6 days for between €4 and €12 (*Allo Bus*, ☎ 05 57 57 88 88). A 25km tramline is due to open at the end of 2003. The main bus stations are at Halte Routière de Carcan, ☎ 05 56 43 68 43 or Réseau Trans-Gironde, Allées de Chartres, ☎ 05 56 81 16 82. From the Gare St-Jean, buses depart for coastal resorts such as Lacanau and Cap Ferret.

Traffic-free days

On the first Sunday of each month the centre of the city is closed to vehicular traffic; that day, *calèches* (horse-drawn carriages) from the Tourist Office, and *vélos* (bikes) from the Hemicycle des Quinconces, are free.

Tourist information

12 Cours du 30 Juillet, 33080 Bordeaux, ☎ 05 56 00 66 00, fax 05 56 00 66 01, www.bordeaux-tourisme.com. Open July–Aug, Mon–Sat 09.00–19.30, Sun and PH 09.30–18.30; May, June, Sept, Oct, Mon–Sat 09.00–19.00, Sun and PH 09.30–18.30; Nov–April, Mon–Sat 09.00–18.30, Sun and PH 09.45–16.30

Gare St-Jean, Arrivals. Open May–Oct, Mon–Sat 09.00–12.00, 13.00–18.00, Sun and PH 10.00–12.00 and 13.00–15.00; Nov–April, Mon–Fri 09.30–12.30, 14.00–18.00, closed Sat, Sun and PH

Visits to the Old Town

All of the following start from the main Tourist Office.

Walking tours (2 hours, bilingual) 15 April–15 Nov, 10.00 daily except Wed and Sat; 15 July–15 Aug, also at 15.00; 16 Nov–14 Apr, 10.00 daily

Coach tours 15 April–15 Nov, 10.00 Wed and Sat

Horse-drawn carriage tours 1 April–30 Sept (check times)

Thematic visits (on aspects of Bordeaux and its history, in French), 14.30 Mon, Tues, Thur and Fri

Bordeaux illuminated (by coach) July–Aug, 22.00 Thur

Bikes *Le Vélo Parlant* (the bike has a city plan and plays a recorded tour) from Bord'eaux Vélos Loisirs, Quai Louis XVIII, May–Oct 09.30–21.00 daily; Nov–April all day Wed, Sun and school holidays; Mon, Fri, Sat 14.30–18.30; closed Tues, Thur

Visits to the port and vineyards by boat depart all year round from Embarcadère des Quinconces, Quai Louis XVIII on the *Ville de Bordeaux* (☎ 05 56 52 88 88) or the *Alienor* (☎ 05 56 51 27 90),

which both offer a variety of excursions or *promenades*; or from La Bastide, on the *Burdigala* (☎ 05 56 86 64 59). All three boats have restaurants

Visits to the vineyards

Guided tours (half-day) leave from Gare St-Jean, Arrivals, 15 April–15 Nov, 13.15 daily, from the Tourist Office at 13.30; 16 Nov–14 April, Wed, Sat only at the same times. Full-day tours leave from Gare St-Jean, Arrivals, 1 May–31 Oct, 09.15 Wed, Sat, from the Tourist Office at 09.30.

Introduction to wine tasting at the Tourist Office every Thur, also Sat in July, Aug. The *Maison du Vin*, 3 Cours du 30 Juillet (opposite the Tourist Office), ☎ 05 56 00 22 88, fax 05 56 00 22 77, offers information on all the vineyards of the Bordeaux region, helps to plan visits, and runs courses at the *Ecole du Vin de Bordeaux* (School of Wine). Open Mon–Fri 09.00–17.30, closed Sat, Sun

Festivals and events

January *Salon des Antiquaires du Sud-Ouest*, South-West Antique Dealers' Trade Show

February *Le Jumping International*, International show jumping

May *Foire Internationale* of regional crafts and buildings

June *Fête le Vin* and *VINEXPO*, international trade fair for wine, in alternate years **July–August** *Musique d'Eté*, all types of music in a variety of historic venues

October alternate years, *La Fête du Vin et de la Brocante*, wine and bric-à-brac with special events

November *Festival du Film International d'Histoire*, Pessac

December *Marché du Noël*, Christmas Market

Where to stay

Hotels in Bordeaux are likely to be more expensive than in

the provinces.

☆☆☆☆ *Burdigala*, 115 Rue Georges Bonnac, ☎ 05 56 90 16 16, fax 05 56 93 15 06, www.burdigala.com. Modern hotel in an old building, good restaurant.

☆☆☆☆ *Petit Hôtel Labottière*, 14 Rue Francis Martin, ☎ 05 56 48 44 10. *Chambres d'hôte* in an 18C mansion of great charm, with two beautifully kitted-out apartments.

☆☆☆ *Bayonne/Etche-Ona*, 15 Cours de l'Intendence (4 Rue Martignac and 11 Rue Mautrec), ☎ 05 56 48 00 88, fax 05 56 48 41 60/61. Two hotels under the same management, which are pleasant and well kept. Reasonably priced.

☆☆☆ *Grand Hotel Français*, 12 Rue du Temple, ☎ 05 56 48 10 35, fax 05 56 81 76 18, www.grand-hotel-francais.com. Family-run hotel with an elegant 18C staircase.

☆☆☆ *Claret*, 18 Parvis des Chartrons, Cité Mondiale, ☎ 05 56 01 79 79, fax 05 56 01 79 00. Breakfast room on the 6th floor.

☆☆☆ *des Quatre Soeurs*, 6 Cours du 30 Juillet, ☎ 05 57 81 19 20, fax 05 56 01 04 28, email 4soeurs@mailcity.com. Centrally situated; where Wagner stayed.

☆☆☆ *Sainte-Catherine*, 27 Rue du Parlement Sainte-Catherine, ☎ 05 56 81 95 12, fax 05 56 44 50 51, www.bordeaux-hotelquality.com. Situated in the old quarter of Bordeaux. Relatively expensive.

☆☆ *Acanthe*, 12 Rue Saint-Remi, ☎ 05 56 81 66 58, fax 05 56 44 74 41, www.acanthe-hotel-bordeaux.com. Totally renovated hotel in heart of old town.

☆☆ *Continental*, 10 Rue Montesquieu, ☎ 05 56 52 66 00, fax 05 56 52 77 97, www.hotel-le-continental.com. Centrally situated and slightly higher

priced than most in this category.

☆☆ *le Chantry*, 155 Rue Georges Bonnac, ☎ 05 56 24 08 88, fax 05 56 98 91 72. Reasonable, modest hotel, in central position.

Eating out

€€€ *Didier Gélineau*, 26 Rue du Pas-St-Georges, ☎ 05 56 52 84 25. One Michelin rosette. Small and friendly, specialising in regional cooking. Try the fixed lunch menu.

€€€ *L'Estaquade*, Quai des Queries, La Bastide, ☎ 05 57 54 02 50. Terrace with views over the right bank.

€€/€€€ *La Tupina*, 6/8 Rue Porte de la Monnai, ☎ 05 56 91 56 37. Reputedly the second best bistro in the world, serving regional dishes.

€€/€€€ *Le Bar à Vins*, 20 Quai des Chartrons, ☎ 05 56 01 78 78. Smart bar restaurant with a regional menu.

€€ *Café Louis*, ☎ 05 56 44 07 00. Refurbished café of the Grand Théàtre (p 66) in 18C colours and style.

€€ *Café du Musée*, CAPC Musée de l'Art Contemporaine, ☎ 05 56 44 71 61. A very attractive restaurant and sushi bar, with terrace. Beautifully presented food and good-value lunch menu.

€€ *Chez Ducon*, 20 Allées de Tourny, ☎ 05 56 81 61 61. Animated bar/restaurant in the centre of town, with live music.

€€ *Chez Greg*, 30–31 Rue Porte de la Monnaie, ☎ 05 56 31 30 30. Small chic restaurant at the heart of the old town.

€/€€ *Café des Quatres Soeurs*, 6 Cours de 30 Juillet, ☎ 05 56 81 52 26. Simple food, good atmosphere and mid-19C décor.

€ *L'Olivier du Clavel*, 44 Rue Charles Domercq, ☎ 05 57 95 09 50. Opposite Gare St-Jean, with a good-value lunchtime menu.

History

The merits of Bordeaux's river site were first recognised by a Gallic tribe, the Bituriges-Vivisci, in the 3C BC and an important port developed, trading in Cornish tin. In 56 BC there was little resistance to the invading Roman armies of Crassus. During the subsequent *Pax Romana*, **Burdigala** developed culturally, physically and commercially to become the administrative capital of Aquitania and vines began to be cultivated locally. By AD 1 the town had a population of around 20,000 covering some 120ha laid out in a grid pattern but, undefended, it was attacked by Germanic tribes in AD 276; the defenders tore down the public monuments to build walls and Burdigala was reduced to some 32ha. The arrival of the Visigoths in AD 409 precipitated the end of the Roman Empire but they in turn were chased out by Clovis, King of the Franks, and Bordeaux was re-established under Frankish rule. By 778 the Carolingian Kingdom of Aquitaine was established, although raids by Saracens and Vikings continued in the 9C and 10C.

Christianity was introduced to Bordeaux towards the end of the 3C, and by the 7C churches and monasteries were established inside and outside the walls. By the 10C Aquitaine re-emerged as a duchy and Bordeaux became one of the principal residences of the Dukes. William IX welcomed Pope Urban II in 1096 during the latter's journey to rally support for the first crusade. When William X died on pilgrimage to Compostela in Spain his vast inheritance passed to his daughter, Eleanor, who married the Dauphin of France, the future King Louis VII, in the Cathedral of St-André in 1137. After the dissolution of that marriage in 1152 Eleanor kept her inheritance and promptly married Henry Plantagenet, the future Henry II of England. The people of Bordeaux prospered under **English domination**, benefiting from the trade, especially in wine, between the two territories belonging to the English Crown. The King-Dukes set up an efficient administrative system and installed their representatives in Bordeaux. The English connection lasted for some 300 years, during which the English developed their appreciation of claret (their name for the city's red wine), and Bordeaux grew in population and wealth. In 1206 Henry III recognised the *Jurade* (a town council consisting of aldermen and a mayor) which enjoyed a remarkable degree of freedom. By 1220 the town, with about 30,000 inhabitants, had long outgrown the Roman walls. Consequently a new enclosure was constructed to the south and even this had to be further extended between 1302 and 1327.

The **Hundred Years War** began in 1337, with the first serious attacks on the Guyenne by the French. The Bordelais remained loyal to the English throughout the war despite economic destabilisation compounded by famine and plague. Bordeaux surrendered on 12 June 1451 and, after the French victory at Castillon in 1453, the whole region returned to France. The French monarch, Charles VII, came down hard on the city, depriving it of many privileges and prohibiting trade with England. He erected defences to control rebellious Bordelais and the local economy was ruined. Under Louis XI (1461–83) there was a change for the better, commerce was reinstated with the English, and a *parlement* (law courts) was established in Bordeaux.

The **Renaissance** and the age of Humanism brought in its wake serious religious upheaval. Bordeaux, which remained staunchly Catholic, was damaged by Protestant revolts during the Wars of Religion (1568–89). From

1581 Michel de Montaigne, one of the greatest thinkers and writers of the age, was mayor of Bordeaux and certain privileges were reinstated. The 17C was marked by the **Counter-Reformation** and dominated by Archbishop Cardinal François de Sourdis, who started the trend for the redevelopment of parts of Bordeaux. After the religious wars ended the city had to face the problems of the Fronde (p 49), which had repercussions on the wine trade. Conversely there was increasing trade with America and the French West Indies, with the importation of luxury goods including sugar cane.

The **Age of Enlightenment** is still evident in Bordeaux's physical aspect. This was its golden era. It became the most important port in the kingdom and economic expansion knew no bounds. Trade with the Americas and the Caribbean increased, and from 1716 a royal decree authorising trade in slaves contributed to its wealth. This success is expressed in the grand boulevards and unified architecture introduced by the *Intendants* (representatives of the king). The Marquis de Tourny (Intendant 1743–57), changed the face of Bordeaux in the 18C with his pioneering efforts towards healthier urban living, and his work was continued by successive Intendants, Claude Boucher and Dupré de St-Maur. Lawyers and merchants built grand private residences and great patrons funded public buildings. By the time of the Revolution trade was directed primarily towards the French island territories of Martinique, Saint-Dominic and Guadeloupe. One of the major post-Revolution projects on former church land was the Place des Grands-Hommes (*c* 1792–97).

At the start of the **nineteenth century** the continental blockade on the port imposed by Napoléon I put a temporary brake on maritime trade, but once it was lifted confident urban projects were initiated. The first bridge across the Garonne, the Pont de Pierre (1822), was constructed as well as new roads and public monuments, such as that to the Girondins. The population grew to around 194,000 but a major setback was the series of devastating diseases which virtually wiped out the vineyards. Steam power took over from sail, the docks continued to thrive, and the railway came to Bordeaux in 1852.

The vineyards recovered by the **twentieth century**, but the two world wars, when the French government sought temporary refuge in Bordeaux, took their toll on the city despite there being no serious damage. In the postwar years, the town recovered and continued to expand. Jacques Chaban-Delmas (1915–2000) was mayor for 40 years from 1947. In 1973 the French mint was transferred from Paris to Pessac on the southwestern periphery of Bordeaux. In 1995 Alain Juppé, former Prime Minister, was elected mayor. Major works to the riverside and the installation of a tramway system began in 1999, and there are plans to pedestrianise Place Beyland in front of the cathedral (these works will not be completed until *c* 2007). Bordeaux also has an important share in the aeronautical and space technology, electronics and pharmaceutical industries.

The Quartier des Grand Hommes (Le Triangle)

The heart of the city of Bordeaux is Le Triangle, which is created by the three main thoroughfares, Allées de Tourny, Cours de l'Intendance and Cours Georges-Clemenceau. It is the main commercial area, with designer shops, restaurants and cafés.

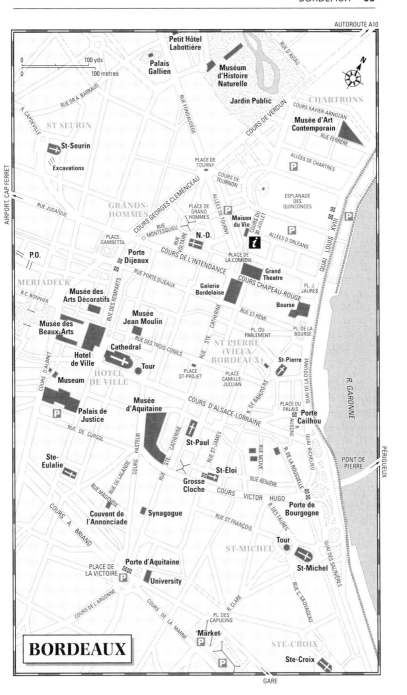

AUTOROUTE A10

RUE D'AVIAU

N

Petit Hôtel Labottière

Palais Gallien

Muséum d'Histoire Naturelle

Jardin Public

CHARTRONS

COURS XAVIER-ARNOZAN

COURS DE VERDUN

Musée d'Art Contemporain

RUE FERRÈRE

RUE DR A. BARRAUD

R. CAPDEVILLE

ST SEURIN

St-Seurin

Excavations

AIRPORT, CAP FERRET

RUE FONDAUDÈGE

ALLÉES DE CHARTRES

PLACE DE TOURNY

P

COURS DE TOURNON

RUE JUDAÏQUE

GRANDS-HOMMES

COURS GEORGES CLEMENCEAU

RUE MONTESQUIEU

PLACE DE GRAND HOMMES

ALLÉES DE TOURNY

P

Maison du Vin

ESPLANADE DES QUINCONCES

QUAI LOUIS XVIII

PLACE GAMBETTA

RUE VOLTAIRE

N.-D.

COURS DU 30 JUILLET

ALLÉES D'ORLÉANS

P

P.O.

MERIADECK

R.C. BONNIER

Musée des Arts Décoratifs

Porte Dijeaux

RUE PORTE DIJEAUX

COURS DE L'INTENDANCE

PLACE DE LA COMÉDIE

Galerie Bordelaise

Grand Theatre

COURS CHAPEAU-ROUGE

PL. J. JAURÈS

Bourse

Musée des Beaux-Arts

RUE DES REMPARTS

Musée Jean Moulin

RUE ST-RÉMI

PL DU PARLEMENT

PL DE LA BOURSE

COURS D'ALBRET

RUE STE CATHERINE

RUE DES TROIS-CONILS

Hotel de Ville

Cathedral

HOTEL DE VILLE

Tour

PLACE ST-PROJET

ST PIERRE (VIEUX BORDEAUX)

PLACE CAMILLE-JULLIAN

St-Pierre

QUAI DE LA DOUANE

R. GARONNE

Museum

Palais de Justice

Musée d'Aquitaine

COURS D'ALSACE-LORRAINE

R. DE BAHUTIERS

PLACE DU PALAIS

Porte Cailhou

QUAI RICHELIEU

RUE DE CURSOL

RUE AUSONE

Ste-Eulalie

COURS PASTEUR

RUE STE CATHERINE

St-Paul

RUE ST-JAMES

RUE NEUVE

RUE DE LA ROUSSELLE

PONT DE PIERRE

PÉRIGUEUX

RUE MARBOTIN

RUE DE LALANDE

Grosse Cloche

St-Éloi

RUE RENIÈRE

COURS VICTOR HUGO

R. DES FAURES

Porte de Bourgogne

QUAI DES SALINIÈRES

COURS A. BRIAND

Couvent de l'Annonciade

Synagogue

RUE ST-FRANÇOIS

Tour

ST-MICHEL

St-Michel

RUE C.-SAUVAGEAU

PLACE DE LA VICTOIRE

Porte d'Aquitaine

University

COURS DE L'ARGONNE

COURS DE LA MARNE

R. CLARE

PL. DES CAPUCINS

Market

P

STE-CROIX

Ste-Croix

GARE

BORDEAUX

0 — 100 yds
0 — 100 metres

The logical place to begin a town visit is outside the Tourist Office on Cours du 30 Juillet, east of Allées de Tourny, the site of the former Café Montesquieu once frequented by Stendhal. Across from it, in the wedge-shaped 18C Hôtel Gobineau built by Victor Louis (see below), is the **Maison du Vin de Bordeaux**, decorated inside with two stained-glass windows designed by R. Buthaud. Take the Allées de Tourny south towards Place de la Comédie, the Gallo-Roman site of the ancient forum where a temple dedicated to the goddess Tutellus was demolished in 1675 (fragments known as the *Piliers Tutelles* are in the Musée d'Aquitaine).

The colonnaded façade of the **Grand Théâtre** (officially known as the Théâtre de l'Opéra), begun in 1773 and inaugurated in 1780, dominates Place de la Comédie. The unpopular Governor of Guyenne, Maréchal de Richelieu, commissioned the Parisian architect Victor Louis (1731–1800) to design the theatre, diverting funds earmarked for other public buildings. It became a ballroom in the 19C, the seat of the National Assembly in 1871, and was used by the French government during both world wars. The imposing Corinthian dodecastyle portico on Place de la Comédie is decorated with twelve female figures representing Muses and goddesses. The steps were added in 1846 to raise the entrance above street level. Inside is a Doric vestibule of grandiose proportions with an innovative and monumental stairwell (20m high) decorated with niches and late 19C sculptures by Alphonse Dumilâtre, leading to a loggia covered by a cupola, with Ionic columns. This *tour de force* was Jean-Louis Garnier's model for the foyer at the Paris Opéra. The charming and elaborate Italian-style auditorium, which has over 1100 seats, was restored to its original colour scheme of blue, white and gold in 1991. The ceiling was repainted in 1917 by Maurice Roganeau. Guided visits Mon at 11.00; contact the Tourist Office, ☎ 05 56 00 66 00. On the north side of the building the elegant *Café Louis* reopened after renovations in 2000.

Cours de l'Intendance runs south of Place de la Comédie parallel with the ancient *decumanus*, Rue de la Porte Dijeaux, and roughly on the line of the Roman fortifications. As the town grew its focus shifted and Cours de l'Intendance approximately indicates the division between the medieval town and later developments. A grand and homogenous combination of 17C, 18C and 19C buildings line Cours de l'Intendance. No. 4, Hôtel du Président de Pichon, dates from 1610–14, and no. 6 has an interior courtyard. On the opposite side no. 5, with a balcony in wrought iron supported by atlantes with fishy tails, dates from 1785 whereas no. 13 and the arcade, Passage Sarget at no. 19, are 19C.

Rue Martignac and Passage Sarget both lead to Place du Chapelet and the theatrical Baroque **Eglise Notre-Dame** (1684–1707). The work of Pierre-Michel Duplessy in the style of the Counter-Reformation introduced by Vignola's Il Gesù in Rome, this was the church of the Dominican convent. On the façade is a sculpted representation of the Virgin presenting the *chapelet* (rosary) to St Dominic. The interior is showily elegant with magnificent gilded wrought ironwork, especially around the choir, by Jean Moreau (1781), a splendid marble altar and a pulpit in carved wood and marble. The nave chapels create narrow sides aisles, and have notable restored *trompe-l'oeil* décor and several early paintings by Frère André (1662–1735). The glass is by Villiets & Hurtrel (19C) and there is a magnificent organ around which is a wonderful baroque play of curves and counter-curves.

Behind the church, via a narrow passageway on the south side, is Cour Mably, the former Dominican cloisters and chapter house, used for exhibitions and concerts. The exit on the opposite side leads into the circular **Place des Grands-Hommes**, an *hommage* to the 18C philosophers who inspired the Revolution, Jean-Jacques Rousseau, Montesquieu and Voltaire. In the centre is La Grande Ronde, a modern shopping precinct built in 1992 on the site of an old market. Rues Voltaire and Montesquieu lead back to Cours de l'Intendance.

At no. 57 Cours de l'Intendance is the **Instituto Cervantes**, the Spanish Cultural Centre (no admission), where the Spanish painter Francisco Goya lived in exile from 1824 until his death in 1828. Goya was buried in Bordeaux but his body was repatriated in 1889. Set back from the main street is the former Théâtre Français (now a cinema), with a rounded peristyle. At the end of Cours de l'Intendance is **Place Gambetta**, begun 1743–70 and completed in the 19C, a busy junction around which the traffic girates and students congregate. To the south is Port Dijeaux, an archway erected at around the same time as the square, marking the start of Rue des Remparts. In this area some of the oldest *mascarons* (see box p 70) animate the façades. To the northwest is the old quartier of St-Seurin, which developed outside the walls (p 79), and southwest is the modern quarter, Mériadeck (p 80).

Cours Georges-Clemenceau links Place Gambetta to Place de Tourny, and on the third side of the Triangle is Allées de Tourny, a wide tree-lined promenade built in 1757 on the site of the first Dominican convent (1227). It is brightened up in winter with a Christmas market. At the north end of Allées de Tourny, Cours de Tournon leads to the semicircle created by the Allée de Los Angeles and a major emblem of Bordeaux, the **Monument aux Girondins**. Dedicated to the Girondins of the Revolution and to the Republic, the monument combines fountains and a 60m column topped off by an exuberant *Liberty* 'breaking the chains'. Conceived by Victor Rich and Jean Dumilâtre, the ensemble was first erected 100 years after the Revolution, between 1894 and 1902, but completed only in 1924. It was removed to be melted down in 1943 but found intact in 1945 and re-erected in 1983. The *tour de force* is the four rearing and plunging aquatic horses with webbed hooves, by Gustave Debrie. Allegorical figures represent the *Triumph of the Republic* (north) and the *Triumph of Concord* (south). The French cockerel, *Eloquence* and *History* (facing the river), are the only references to the Girondins, whose absence is symbolised by empty pedestals.

The Girondins

This group of revolutionary moderates, who gathered in 1791 under the leadership of Jacques-Pierre Brissot (1754–93), defended liberal ideals. They hailed from the educated, professional and merchant classes of Bordeaux and created a brilliant faction that included lawyers and orators such as Pierre Vergniaud (1753–93) and Armand Gensonné (1758–93). They rebelled against the Jacobin centralism of Paris and set themselves up in direct opposition to the more ruthless Montagnards. The Girondins were finally expelled from the Convention (Revolutionary government) in 1793 and eliminated. One of their heroes, Elie Guadet (1758–94), from St-Emilion, was guillotined on Place Gambetta.

Beyond the monument is the vast **Esplanade des Quinconces** (*c* 12ha), leading to the Garonne, begun in 1827 on the site of the 15C Château de Trompette. The Esplanade is a huge empty area decorated near the river by two rostral columns (1829) glorifying the maritime history of the city and huge statues of Montaigne and Montesquieu, erected in 1858. The space is animated every Thursday by the *marché bio* (organic market) near the columns; and there is an antiques fair for two weeks in November and three weeks in April.

Château Trompette

Château Trompette was built at the end of the Hundred Years War when Aquitaine reverted to the French. Charles VII was resented by the Bordelais who remained loyal to the English, and faced with deprived and rebellious citizens he built the fort to symbolise French power and as protection from possible English attack. The castle was considerably enlarged at the orders of Louis XIV in 1680 following the problems of the Fronde and a revolt against the Governor of Guyenne, and was demolished in 1816. The name has nothing to do with trumpets, but comes from *tropeyte*, a cordon thrown across the Garonne at various times from the Middle Ages until the 18C.

From the Esplanade des Quinconces, take Cours du Maréchal-Foch, or follow the river north and turn onto Rue Ferrère. On the corner with Rue Vauban is L'Entrepôt Lainé, a converted 19C warehouse which houses the **Musée d'Art Contemporain**, known locally as the Entrepôt or CAPC (Centre d'Art Plastique Contemporain). Open Tues–Sun 11.00–18.00, to 20.00 Wed, closed Mon and PH; ☎ 05 56 00 81 50, www.mairie-bordeaux.fr/musees/capc. On the terrace there is a very attractive restaurant and sushi bar, *Le Café du Musée*, and a bookshop and library on the ground floor. The architecture centre, **Arc en Rève**, in the same building, also has a bookshop and library, ☎ 05 56 52 78 36.

The Entrepôt (1822–24), typical of port architecture, was designed to store 20,000 tons of merchandise from the colonies such as coffee, cocoa, vanilla, spices and timber. The engineer/architect was Claude Deschamps, who also designed the Pont de Pierre. The building narrowly avoided demolition in the 1970s and its restoration was entrusted to Jean Pistre and Denis Vallode in 1979. It reopened in its new role in 1984.

From the exterior L' Entrepôt is an austere building with a hint of medieval Italy, whereas inside the superimposed arcades and naves create a magnificent church-like space. The building materials—local blond stone, light brick and reddish-brown Oregon pine—are all exposed, as are some old graffiti on the walls, and good use is made of the roof-terrace.

The permanent collection starts with the 1960s. Various trends or movements in contemporary art are covered: Minimalism, American Conceptualism, Italian Arte Povera, English Land Art of the 1970s, and Figuration Libre and Transavangarde of the 1980s. The work of present generations is also represented in all forms, figurative or abstract, installation or video. The majority of works are French, although Britain, Italy, Spain and the United States are well represented. Artists include Simon Hantai, Sol LeWitt, Jean-Pierre Raynaud, Claude Viallat, Christian Boltanski, Miquel Barcelo, Jose-Maria Sicilia and Susana Solano. There are a few fixed works, by Richard Long, on the terrace, and others in the café by Max Neuhaus and Niele Toroni. The collections are regularly rotated to include new acquisitions or trends, mainly in the galleries on the second floor, and sometimes in the nave or the mezzanines. Frequent important temporary exhibitions cover a variety of disciplines.

The **Jardin Public**, between the Chartrons and St-Seurin districts, was set out by Intendant Tourny in 1746. In 1856 the *jardins à la française* were enlarged and replaced by less formal English-style gardens with ponds, bridges and greenhouses. On the south side is a low colonnaded building with a statue of the Bordelaise painter, Rosa Bonheur. The Botanical Gardens were laid out in 1855 as part of the Jardin Public and contain a collection of over 3000 species of living plants. On the southwest periphery is the wonderfully old-fashioned **Musée d'Histoire Naturelle**, in a house built by R.F. Bonfin (1730–1812) at 5 Place Bardineau. Open Mon–Fri 11.00–18.00, Sat, Sun 14.00–18.00, closed Tues and PH: ☎ 05 56 48 29 86. Considerable space is given to regional fauna and palaeontology, but there are also specimens from the wider animal world, as well as minerals and fossils. The museum is due for a face-lift but the battalions of birds and animals in their 19C vitrines will stay put. There are frequent temporary exhibitions.

There are a number of elegant houses in this neighbourhood, notably the **Petit Hôtel Labottière** at 14 Rue Francis-Martin, a model 18C *hôtel particulier* by Etienne Laclotte, which has been carefully restored and furnished by its owners and has two luxury guest apartments (see p 62). Just south, surrounded by smallish houses in Rue Dr Albert-Barraud, is the **Palais Gallien**. This is no palace but the remains of the Roman amphitheatre of Burdigala, the oldest monument in Bordeaux. Destroyed by the Barbarians in AD 276, a chunk of it was removed in the 19C and only an evocative fragment of the great structure, which held 15,000 spectators, is left standing. The monumental gate and a section of the walls and arcades show the characteristic small stonework and brick coursing of Roman construction in Gaul. Open June–Sept 15.00–19.00. There is a model of the amphitheatre in the Musée d'Aquitaine.

The Quartier St-Pierre (Vieux Bordeaux)

This walk explores areas of great character in the older streets of Bordeaux. From Place de la Comédie, follow **Cours du Chapeau Rouge** which runs east to west, perpendicular to the Garonne, and was built on the site of the old city ditch outside the Gallo-Roman ramparts, in an area of marshland where houses originally had to be built on stilts. All this changed in the 16C when it became the route for royal processions. The handsome buildings lining it now are mainly 18C, although no. 40 (now a branch of the BNP), is a 17C *hôtel particulier* and no. 18 dates from the end of the 16C. The land behind the Grand Théâtre is known as *îlot Louis*, after the architect Victor Louis, who set out to develop the whole area. No. 21, the Hôtel de Saige, is typical of Louis' project. Cours du Chapeau Rouge ends at Place Jean-Jaurès and the **Quai de la Douane**, one of a succession of quays along the *Port de la Lune* (Moon Harbour), the old port of Bordeaux on the long curve in the river which is symbolised by a crescent in the city coat of arms.

Turn right at Place Jean-Jaurès to reach the magnificent ensemble, **Place de la Bourse** (1733–55), the first and most enduringly successful 18C project in Bordeaux. On the left is the old Hôtel des Fermes du Roy (customs clearance house) and its opposite number the old Palais de la Bourse (Chamber of Commerce), while the central pavilion contains the recently reinstated American

---

The quays of Bordeaux

Despite the importance of the river, the city turned its back to it until the end of the 17C, and only shops or wooden huts stood outside the city walls. Gradually, imposing mansions were built lining the river to impress visitors arriving by ship. The development was in the hands of a few wealthy local families and the principal architects were Bonfin, Chevay, Moulinié, Richefort and Alary. Alterations in the 19C did not totally destroy the over-all effect but in the mid-20C the port shifted to the right bank, leaving in its wake abandoned dockyard properties and a wide, fast-track highway. The massive project to revitalise and reanimate 4km of the waterfront between the Pont de Pierre and the Cours de la Martinique (Chartrons district) began in 1999. It includes a wide pedestrian promenade, with open spaces, trees, grass, and a cycle track; Hangar 14 will become exhibition space, and certain warehouses are earmarked for conversion into car parks, restaurants and shops. A tramway is being introduced and, as a final touch, all the old properties along the waterfront are to receive a face-lift. The total transformation is due for completion around 2007.

---

consulate. Intendant Boucher was the instigator but Jacques Gabriel and his son, Jacques-Ange, provided the architectural genius. Jacques, premier architect to Louis XV was bowled over by the potential of the site and set about demolishing a section of the old town and medieval city walls. Giant Ionic columns span the two upper storeys of the pedimented angle pavilions and the central free-standing pavilion, whereas the remaining façades have giant pilasters. The attic storey and high roofs bring a French touch to Italian Baroque, *mascarons* animate the arcaded ground floor and vases balance on the high balustrades.

The Place set the pattern for other elevations along the quayside. The bronze statue of Louis XV which once graced the Place was melted down at the Revolution and only the base has survived (in the Musée d'Aquitaine). It was replaced in 1864 by the **Three Graces** (tradition has it that these three beauties represent Queen Victoria, Empress Eugenia and the Queen of Spain!) Place de la Bourse was the first monument in the city to be illuminated at night. The **Musée des Douanes**, which retraces the history of the French Customs with the aid of documents, uniforms, weapons, models and tools of the trade, is installed in the former Hôtel des Fermes du Roy. Open April–Sept, Tues–Sun 10.00–12.00, 13.00–18.00; Oct–Mar to 17.00; closed Mon, 1 Jan, 15 Dec; ☎ 05 56 52 45 47.

Mascarons

The *mascarons* or masks (not to be confused with *macarons*; see p 100) that adorn the façades of Bordeaux were first used in Place de la Bourse and became so popular in 18C Bordeaux that some 3000 have been identified. Usually they are placed above the windows of the first floor, *l'étage noble*, although in Place de la Bourse they are above the ground-floor arcades. There is great variety within the masks, with heads ranging from beautiful to grotesque, from Christian to pagan, and from young to old. Some are original (18C–19C), others are modern remakes. The *mascherone* motif itself was imported from Renaissance Italy.

The small section of Bordeaux on the right bank, opposite Place de la Bourse, is called **La Bastide** (formerly a fort or bastion) and is also enjoying a 21C rejuvenation. It can be identified by the elongated, domed bell-tower of Ste-Marie de la Bastide, built by Paul Abadie in 1865. A cinema, restaurant and brasserie are planned, as well as new botanic gardens, and the Gare d'Orléans (19C) is being revamped. The best night view of the illuminated Place de la Bourse can be seen from the restaurant *L'Estaquade* in La Bastide.

Leading west out of Place de la Bourse are Rue St-Remi, the continuation of the old Roman road, and Rue Fernand-Philippart, formerly Rue Royale. This is lined with a series of beautiful Louis XV-style houses, notably no. 16, with an angle balcony supported by a squinch, typical of the mid-18C. At the end is the former Place du Marché Royal, now called **Place du Parlement** although the *parlement* was never on this site. A charming square (*c* 1750), it has a number of original Rococo façades still intact, a few reconstructions to maintain the overall effect, and a 19C fountain. Around the square are several eating places with terraces.

The streets beyond follow the medieval layout but the buildings are mainly 17C and 18C. The Quartier St-Pierre, renovated under the Loi Malraux (1970–75), is a real, living neighbourhood with a mixture of housing, neighbourhood shops and restaurants. Rue du Parlement St-Pierre leads to the church of **St-Pierre**, The west front (rebuilt 14C–15C) still carries a few original Flamboyant carvings but was heavily restored in the 19C when the belfry was added. High aisles light the nave in the style of a hall church, and the chancel has been restored. Behind the altar is a 17C *Pietà*. The church's dedication to the patron of fishermen is appropriate because Place St-Pierre was built over the site of the ancient Gallo-Roman port at the mouth of the Devèze River when it began to silt up in the 6C. The port was filled in completely during the 12C and reconstructed further south and the first church was erected. The town walls were extended in the 14C to contain the urban spread but the remains were demolished in the 18C. The magnificent Gallo-Roman bronze *Hercules* (2C–3C, now in the Musée d'Aquitaine) was discovered here in the 19C during excavations.

From Rue Bahutiers turn right on Rue Carcera past Square Vinet, a creation of 1975–85, and left on Rue Pas St-Georges into Place Camille-Jullian, with a monument created from fragments of antique masonry in memory of the archaeologist Jullian. Nearby is a restaurant of quality, *Didier Gélineau*. From Rue Millanges turn right, back into Rue Bahutiers where, on the angle with Rue Courcelles, are two rare 16C buildings. To the left is Place du Palais, an 18C square named after the 11C Château de l'Ombrière (from *ombre* or shade of the trees around it), a fortress-palace built against the ramparts with a tall keep, courtyards, fountains and gardens. The property of the Dukes of Aquitaine, it was occupied by the English seneschal in the 12C and was favoured by Eleanor and Henry Plantagenet during visits to Bordeaux. After the Hundred Years War, the *parlement* used the palace for their assizes. It was demolished in 1800.

Between Place du Palais and the river stands **Porte Cailhau**, which was built into the old ramparts in 1493–96 and dedicated to Charles VIII. Fortified, with high slate-clad roofs, lantern, dormer windows and Flamboyant decoration, it was both defensive gateway and triumphal arch. Bearing the King's arms on the town side, it commemorates the French conquest of Naples at Fornovo in 1495. On the river side are recarved images of Charles VIII, Cardinal d'Epinay (Bishop of Bordeaux) and St John the Baptist, patron of the *Jurade*. It was renovated in the 19C. During the summer there is a Tourist Office here and the upper floors may be visited. Open 15 June–15 Sept, daily 15.00–19.00.

From Place du Palais cross the Cours Alsace-Lorraine, built in the 19C on the site of the south section of the Roman wall to link the Garonne and Place de la Cathédrale. **Rue Ausone** was named after the Gallo-Roman poet Ausonus (*c* 310–395), who taught at the university of Burdigala and was pro-consul of the Gauls. Parallel to Rue Ausone, in Rue de la Rousselle at nos 23–25, is the birthplace of Michel de Montaigne (1553–92; p 147) and the house of Jeanne de Lartigue, wife of Montesquieu, is in Impasse de la Rue Neuve.

Take Rue Renière to Rue St-James, which runs under the Grosse Cloche or **Porte St-Eloi** into Cours Victor-Hugo. The gate, in the 13C walls, with a 13C base reworked in the 15C–18C and renovated in the 19C, is the symbol of Bordeaux. It spanned the pilgrim route to Compostela in Spain. The adjacent Hôtel de Ville burned down in 1735, but the city coat of arms representing it on the balustrade features the Grosse Cloche, a crescent and waves evoking the Garonne, the leopard of Guyenne, and a crown. The bell, which is suspended from an arch between two sturdy round towers, dates from 1775, and the present clock from 1759. Beside the gate is the former church of **St-Eloi** (11C) with a pretty 15C façade, all heavily restored, where the new magistrats of the *Jurade* gathered annually to be sworn in, and in this area Montaigne's *Essays* were printed. Around the Rue du Mirail, opposite the Grosse Cloche, the space between the 13C and 14C enceintes was occupied by the Jesuits in the 16C, and has some fine *hôtels particuliers*.

A few fragments of the city walls are still visible at nos 51–53 **Cours Victor-Hugo**, which is a busy, cosmopolitan street ending at Porte de Bourgogne, a triumphal arch built in 1755 on the quay. Beyond is Place de Bir Hakeim and the Quai des Salinières, the dock for salt used in curing fish and meat in Rue de la Rousselle. The **Pont de Pierre** (1822) was designed by Claude Deschamps, who resolved for the first time the technical difficulties of throwing a bridge across the Garonne. In the opposite direction, the Cours leads to the pedestrianised **Rue Ste-Catherine**, which links this quartier to the Triangle. It acquired its present rectilinear layout in the 18C although it probably follows the ancient *cardo* running north to south. Its name refers to the Santa-Catherina chapel in a church which no longer exists and the north end was marked until the 18C by the 12C Porta-Médoca (Médoc Gate). The equivalent of Toulouse's Rue St-Rome, it has always been a very popular commercial area where almost anything can be purchased and is at its best during the daytime. No. 36 Rue des Ayres is a good example of 17C domestic architecture. The former Jesuit church of **St-Paul** (1663–76) contains, above the main altar, a magnificent marble sculpture by Guillaume Coustou, the *Exaltation of St Francis Xavier*, installed in 1748. Alongside the church at no. 20 is the former mayoral residence with a medieval tower, where Montaigne lived when in office. Further north, at the intersection with Rue des Trois Conils, is the sad little **Place St-Projet**, where the gibbet once stood, replaced now by the tower of the church, a 15C graveyard cross and a fountain of 1738. After the intersection with Rue de la Porte Dijeaux, the ancient *decumanus*, you arrive at Place de la Comédie.

The Quartier de l'Hôtel de Ville

Musée d'Aquitaine

The Musée d'Aquitaine at 20 Cours Pasteur displays the history and archaeology of the modern region of Aquitaine (except for the Basque region, which has its own museum, see p 407). Its somewhat ambitious temporal span is from the Lower Paleolithic (*c* 700,000 years ago) to the 20C. Thematically it encompasses regional ethnography, rural and maritime activities, the wine industry, commercial life and the influence of overseas trade. The 19C building is the former Faculty of Arts and Sciences, by P.-C. Durand, built on the site of the Couvent des Feuillants. The museum, which transferred here in 1985, is attractively laid out on two floors. The **Goupil Museum**, in the same building, holds a large collection of prints and photographs from the period 1827 to 1920 published by Maison Goupil et Cie in Paris, which are used exclusively for temporary exhibitions. Open Tues–Sun 11.00–18.00, closed Mon and PH; ☎ 05 56 01 51 00/0.

The Museum begins at the beginning, with **prehistory**, condensing hundreds of thousands of years of the development of Man according to the rich finds in the southwest of France, into a few rooms. The exhibits range from primitive stone tools to the reconstruction of a rock shelter of the Middle Palaeolithic period (*c* 100,000–35,000 BC), examples of Upper Perigordian flints and the development of tools including the first needles. The progression of cave art is studied through carvings, such as the stone relief of a female figure known as the *Venus of Laussel* (25,000 years old) and small intricate carvings on bone, and the increasing sophistication of rock paintings in the Magdalenian period including a reproduction of the painting of running deer from Lascaux. Neolithic and Bronze Age objects demonstrate the progression from stone to metal, with objects used for funerary rites, in domestic life and for adornment.

Archaeological finds from the **Gallo-Roman city** of Burdigala, from 56 BC onwards, include pieces of monumental architecture and smaller objects relating to economic and social issues. Religious cults and funerary practices are represented by a number of burial urns, altars and stelae, notably that of the child Laetus (late 1C–early 2C AD). Also displayed are the magnificent bronze of *Hercules* (2C AD; see p 71), mosaics, construction materials, pottery, and treasures lifted from the Garonne riverbed. There is a modern maquette of the Roman theatre, Palais Gallien. The evolution from Roman to **early Christian Aquitaine** introduces sarcophagi, crosses and chrisms, jewellery, capitals and mosaics. Medieval expansion of the Church is addressed by displays on the pilgrimage and religious communities such as La Sauve Majeure (see p 108). There is a section dedicated to the period when **Anglo-Gascon Guyenne** was under the control of the English King-Dukes (1154–1453), with objects from daily and religious life, and from England.

The exhibits relating to Bordeaux during the **modern period** begins post 1453 with the return of Guyenne to France and the establishment of a *parlement* and stock exchange. The Renaissance period is represented by the cenotaph of the writer Michel de Montaigne and twisted columns from the chapel of the Monastery of St-Antoine-des-Feuillants (the site of this museum), where Montaigne was buried in 1592. The prosperity of the 18C is evoked by models of merchant ships and fragments of architecture such as the pedestal of the statue of Louis XV from Place de la Bourse (see p 69). The **contemporary period** is largely an enthnological display illustrating the links between rural traditions throughout modern Aquitaine as well as activities specific to certain areas, such as oyster-farming in the Arcachon Basin, the production of cheese from ewes' milk in the Béarn, and wine production in the Bordeaux region. The development of the port of Bordeaux meant the city became the gateway to other continents, and a sample of the various ethnological curiosities and collections that found their way to Bordeaux is displayed in **Cultures of the World**.

From the museum take Rue Duf.-Dubergier and in front of you are the unmistakable Tour Pey-Berland and the Cathédrale St-André.

Cathédrale St-André

Until the 18C the cathedral looked very different from today. It was built on marshy land, up against the Roman wall to the west, and the archbishops' palace was huddled up against the northwest flank. This majestic Gothic structure was begun in the 13C, added to and altered over three centuries. It was not until the mania for demolishing and rebuilding took hold in the 18C that the archbishops' residence was replaced by a new one further north and the obsolete ramparts and cloister finally disappeared. There are plans to create a pedestrian area around the cathedral.

The present cathedral superseded two earlier churches. The first was consecrated in 1096 by Urban II. Here, on 25 July 1137, Eleanor of Aquitaine married the Dauphin of France, the future Louis VII. Of that church only a fragment of the west wall, built in rubble, still stands. It was replaced by a great Romanesque cathedral, possibly domed, which can only be guessed at from the part-12C walls of the nave. That structure was, in its turn, subsumed in the next series of works which began in the 13C and led to what we now see. In c 1280 the construction of a new choir and transepts was undertaken in the Gothic or French style, inspired by northern cathedrals such as Amiens. By the mid-14C there were only two entrances, north and south. Work was speeded up in the 14C thanks to donations from Bertrand de Got, the future Pope Clement V. Anne of Austria married Louis XIII in the cathedral in 1616.

Exterior The north door (*c* 1330), always the principal entrance, has been heavily reworked, but the carvings show the *Ascension* and *Last Supper* with 10 angels, 12 Apostles and 14 Patriarchs in the intrados. The **Porte Royale** (1250), east of the north transept, was the private entrance from the medieval archbishops' residence in the northwest angle of the church. Now the door is walled up but it was used in the past by visiting royalty. The sculptures around this portal—*Last Judgement, Christ and angels*, Apostles, bishops and martyrs—owe a debt to Reims. In the 19C Eugene Viollet-le-Duc took his inspiration from the sculptures, which have not been touched, for his restorations to Notre-Dame de Paris. The south façade with a rose window is *c* 1400, although the upper part of the north façade was not finished until the 16C. Extra buttresses, mainly to the south and southwest, were added to support the vaults in the late 15C–early 16C, and the Renaissance 'Gramont' buttress, dominating Porte Royale, is *c* 1530. The west front is devoid of ornament because it originally abutted the ramparts and only in 1808 (the old Roman wall having been demolished in the 18C) was the west door opened, although Paul Abadie's project for the west façade was not carried out. The south door was damaged at the Revolution when it was enlarged to allow a cart to pass through. There were never any spires on the two south towers because of the boggy terrain, and for the same reason the belfry was built apart. There has been an intensive campaign of restoration, using a painstaking and revolutionary laser technique to clean the masonry.

Interior From the west door is a sweeping view of the vast, aisleless nave, determined by the earlier cathedral, and the Gothic crossing and chancel. When the decision was made to rebuild the cathedral *c* 1280, work started in the east end with the five radial chapels. The choir elevation was built 1310–30, and the transepts were completed in large part by *c* 1360. There are two elegant rose windows in the transepts with 14C tracery in the south and 16C in the north. The choir has typically tall pointed arcades, small blind triforium and high clerestory windows and is surrounded by a double aisle, the outer one enclosed by wrought-iron grills to create chapels. A plan to rebuild the nave was abandoned and the existing Romanesque building was amended by heightening the walls. Nevertheless, it is still slightly lower than the chancel although the large windows allow more direct light. A fragment of the Romanesque foundations is visible at the base of the north wall. Work continued on the cathedral until the 16C, including the west vaults of the nave, evident from the jump from clustered piers to a single shaft supporting the roof. The organ loft is built from the remains of a Renaissance *jubé* (rood screen, *c* 1530), dismantled in 1804, and the organ case is of 1748.

Furnishings include two Renaissance bas-reliefs under the organ loft, the pulpit (18C), tombs (19C), elegant wrought ironwork around the choir by Charlut (18C), and stalls (1690) by a member of the Tournier family from Gourdon (p 189), as well as wooden doors (18C) at the end of the choir from the church of St-Bruno. On the floor of the choir is a Roman mosaic from Hippone, Algeria, sent here by the first archbishop of Algeria after its conquest in 1830; the episcopal chairs are 19C. In the Mont Carmel chapel, north of the choir, is an alabaster statue (14C) of *Our Lady of the Nave*, typical of those imported from England at that period. The third chapel to the northeast contains the mausoleum in stone and marble (1562) of Antoine de Noailles, and two alabaster reliefs (15C), reputed to be English, of the *Assumption* and *Resurrection*. Opposite the chapel, in the ambulatory, is a polychromed English alabaster of St Martial. The axial chapel has some fine carvings of the *Life of the Virgin* and the *Childhood of Christ* in the spandrels and wood panels (17C). The southeast St-Anne chapel was found to have 15C paintings under 19C murals, and these have been restored. Opposite is the Gothic funerary niche or *enfeu* of Archbishop Arnaud de Canteloup (d. 1332). The statue of *Joan of Arc* in the ambulatory is by Antoine Bourdelle and against the choir on the south is a rather lovely *St Anne and the Virgin* (early 16C). In the St-Joseph chapel is a wooden reliquary (15C), a Spanish *Crucifixion* in ivory (15C), and a lectern in wrought iron (18C). There is little stained glass except in the south rose, which has kept its original 16C iconography, whereas the glass in the north rose has been mixed up following several restorations. There are several 17C and 18C paintings, including a *Crucifixion* by Jacob Jordaens (1593–1678) in a chapel on the south side.

The stand-alone **Tour Pey-Berland**, a Flamboyant Gothic structure (1440–46), takes its name from the archbishop at the time. It is 50m high and contains the great bell, Ferdinand-André, installed in 1869. Weighing in at 1150kg (8 tonnes), it is the fourth heaviest in France. In 1863 the over-emphatic gilded statue of *Notre-Dame d'Aquitaine* was place on the highest pinnacle. Open daily 1 June–30 Sept 10.00–18.30; 1 Oct–31 May 10.00–12.30, 14.00–17.30; closed Mon and 1 Jan, 1 May, 1 Nov, 11 Nov, 12 Dec.

Opposite the north flank of the cathedral is the **Musée Jean Moulin**, dedicated to the Resistance, the Deportation and the Free French Army, and in particular to the great hero of the Resistance, Jean Moulin, whose secret office is re-created. Open Tues–Fri 11.00–18.00, Sat, Sun 14.00–18.00, closed Mon and PH; ☎ 05 56 79 66 00.

The former archbishops' residence, Palais Rohan (1773–86), occupies a large area to the northwest of the cathedral, and was built by Archbishop Ferdinand-Maximillien Mériadeck de Rohan. Since 1835 it has been occupied by the **Hôtel de Ville**. The building work was initially financed by the sale of neighbouring land, but the project became so expensive that the Archbishop had to dig in his own pockets. The first architect was Joseph Etienne but he displeased the prelate and was replaced by Bonfin, the city architect. The main building is separated from the square by an arcaded loggia which is linked to the main façade by low buildings on both sides of the courtyard. The upper floors of the main elevation are spanned by giant Ionic pilasters on a rusticated base, and articulated by a central pavilion with rounded pediments. The rear façade has a triangular pediment and is prolonged on each side by two low pavilions with balustrades and garlands. The restrained lines and composition are undoubtedly influenced by Victor Louis, who was working on the Grand Théâtre at the time.

The interior has conserved its monumental staircase by Bonfin, a suite of grand rooms on the ground floor with wood panels carved by Cabirol, and a dining room decorated with *trompe-l'oeil* figures. Guided visits 14 June–15 Sept, Wed 14.30. More examples of elegant 18C buildings are in Rue Bouffard, Cours d'Albret (nos 91, 29, 17) and Place Pey-Berland.

Musée des Beaux-Arts

The collections of the Musée des Beaux-Arts are in the two buildings flanking the Jardin de la Mairie, 20 Cours d'Albret. The main entrance is in the south building. Open Wed–Mon 11.00–18.00, closed Tues and PH; ☎ 05 56 10 20 56, www.culture.fr./culture/bordeaux. Temporary exhibitions are held in the Galerie des Beaux-Arts, Place du Colonel Raynal, which runs off the Cours d'Albret. ☎ 05 56 96 51 60.

The Museum, which opened in 1801, was one of 14 established in France by Napoléon I, and its 3000 works (not all on exhibition at one time) constitute an excellent representative cross-section of the main currents of Western art from the Renaissance to the mid-20C, as found in most provincial museums. There is a special emphasis, however, on the work of certain Bordelais artists, especially in the modern section, with some revealing examples of work by Odilon Redon, Albert Marquet and André Lhote. The works are pleasantly and simply displayed in a series of continuous galleries.

South gallery Italian paintings from the Quattrocento to Baroque (15C–18C) include a large *Virgin and Child between Saints* by Perugino and studio (15C/16C); *Tarquin and Lucrece* by Titian (c 1571); and Veronese's *Holy Family with St Dorothy* (c 1560). Representative of followers of Caravaggio in 17C Europe are the *Lute Player* by the Dutch painter Hendrick Ter Brugghen (1624); and from France, *David holding Goliath's Head* by Aubin Vouet (17C) and *St Sebastian* by the Master of the Candle (17C). Among the varied Northern European works are Davidsz. de Heem's *Still Life with a Rose* (1636); Rubens' the *Martyrdom of St George* (c 1615); Van Dyck's portrait of *Marie de Medicis* (c 1631); and Jan 'Velvet' Bruegel's *Wedding Dance* (c 1600); and a little masterpiece of textures and surfaces by Chardin, *Still Life with Pieces of Meat* (1730). There are a number of English 18C portraits by such artists as Lawrence and Reynolds, and by Reynolds' Scottish counterpart, Allan Ramsay. Topographical engravings by Léo Drouyn record local historic monuments and moments, and a large painting by Pierre Lacour, the museum's first curator, records a view of the port and quays of Bordeaux in 1804.

North gallery The works from the 19C onwards start chronologically at the far end of the gallery. The most famous and Romantic of the five by Delacroix in the museum, *La Grèce sur les Ruines de Missolonghi* (1826), is a tribute to the heroism of the women and children who were taken hostage during the Greek battle for independence from the Ottoman Empire in 1821. Corot's *Diana Bathing* (1855) is the essence of discretion in a luminous dawn landscape whereas Henri Gervex's *Rollo*, inspired by a poem by Musset, is decidedly titillating and predictably drew the crowds when first exhibited in 1878. A small, intimate painting by Bonnard, *Les Bas Noirs* (1899), contrasts with a large and phantasmagorical painting by the Toulousain Henri Martin (see p 200), *Chacun sa Chimère* (1891), inspired by Baudelaire.

The modern collection manages to be wide ranging but at the same time draws particular attention to three local artists, Redon, Lhote and Marquet. The Symbolist Odilon Redon was influenced by Delacroix's paintings in Bordeaux, as well as by Gustave Moreau and by Darwin's theories. He produced atmospheric works, often lithographs or pastels, with a dreamlike and metaphysical tendency, as in the enigmatic *Le Chevalier Mystique* (*c* 1892). André Lhote produced a decorative version of Cubism in such works as *Baigneuses* (1935), *Pins à Arcachon* (1948) and *Entrée du Bassin à Flot de Bordeaux* (1912). Lhote played an important role in diffusing 20C developments in painting through his teaching and writing. Albert Marquet, close friend and working colleague of Matisse, Manguin and Dufy, had a brief encounter with Fauvism, *Nu à Contre Jour* (*c* 1909–11), but tended generally towards a subtler palette, understated but poetic, as in *Naples, le Voilier* (1909).

Guillaumin, Renoir, Morisot and Cassatt, the American painter of child portraits, are represented in the collection. There are also some early works by Matisse, *Belle Isle* (1896), a *Nature morte* (1898–99) and the small *Paysage Villars-sur-Ollon* (1901). Works by lesser-known adherents to the Fauve movement include *Paysage de Cagnes* (c 1910) by Louis Valtat, from Dieppe, Jean Puy's *Nu aux Bas Roses* (*c* 1924); and Othon Frièze's *Paysage—La Route* (c 1907). Picasso's portrait of his wife reading, *Olga Lisant*, is a monochrome oil of 1920, monumental and serene, characteristic of his work after the First World War. The Lithuanian, Chaim Soutine, who painted *L'Homme Bleu sur la Route* (*la Montée de Cagnes*, 1923/24), belonged to the School of Paris, and *L'Eglise Notre Dame* (1925) was painted by the Viennese artist Oskar Kokoschka, who visited France in 1925 and spent 15 days in Bordeaux. Abstraction is represented by Jean Harbin and Surrealism by André Masson.

North of the Beaux-Arts is the Hotel de Lalande, an impressive 18C mansion with a vast courtyard, built by Etienne Laclotte for the Marquis of Lalande, which now houses the **Musée des Arts Décoratifs** (entrance on Rue Bouffard). Open Wed–Mon 14.00–18.00, closed Tues; ☎ 05 56 00 72 50. The collections concentrate mainly on the decorative arts of the Bordeaux region in the 18C: furniture, ceramics, glassware, the goldsmith's art and wrought ironwork are exhibited in a series of panelled rooms on three floors. Three period rooms evoke the opulence of bourgeois interiors in Bordeaux in the 18C and 19C, and five small rooms are dedicated to a collection of Royalist souvenirs from the Jeanvrot collection. In the upper rooms are pewter, arms and locks, as well as earlier works such as enamels and 16C–17C furnishings. There are frequent temporary exhibitions (open Mon and Wed–Fri 11.00–18.00, Sat 14.00–18.00). There is also a restaurant/tea-room to the left of the entrance.

The Chartrons district

The quartier called Les Chartrons, after a 14C charterhouse (Carthusian monastery) north of the city centre, is a district now in a state of full regeneration. This was, until the 19C, the real commercial centre of the city where during the 18C English merchants, followed by other Europeans, traded. Alongside the Garonne were kilometres of wine cellars. Now the whole district is changing with the project to improve the riverside.

The gracious **Cours Xavier-Arnozan**, formerly the Pavé des Chartrons, is lined with balconied houses (1770–88) built by Etienne Laclotte, the homes of the great wine-trading families. The former English church is now Evangelical and here traffic drives on the left, supposedly an inheritance from the area's former inhabitants. The Bourse Maritime (1921–25) on the quay is a copy of the central pavilion of Place de la Bourse, and opposite is the Hôtel Fenwick, which housed the first United States consulate. Built by a rich American in 1795, it has reliefs of ships' prows on the façade. On **Quai des Chartrons** at the end of Rue Latour are the 'Dutch houses' (*c* 1680), the sole reminders of a continuous terrace of gabled houses built for a Dutch ship owner. Rue Latour leads to Rue Notre-Dame, a street of antique dealers, with the old Turkish baths at no. 29 and the Temple des Chartrons, an exemplary Neo-classical edifice (1833–35). Between Rue Notre-Dame and the quay, on the Parvis des Chartrons, is the Cité Mondiale (1992), a modern office block with the *Bar à Vins* at its base. To the right is Place Langalerie and the neo-Gothic church of St-Louis des Chartrons (1875). In the adjacent Place du Marché des Chartrons is the **Halle** or market place (1869), built in iron, stone and wood, now converted to host a variety of artistic activities. There are several cafés and restaurants in the area.

Take Rue Notre-Dame and Rue Pomme d'Or north to the **Musée des Chartrons**, 41 Rue Borie. The museum is installed in a grand *maison de négociant en vin*, a typical wine merchant's house built in 1720 by an Irish broker, Francis Burke (it is twinned with the Kinsale Wine Museum, Ireland). Complete with elegant staircase and wrought-iron balustrade and stone-vaulted cellar, the museum is installed in the upper part of the building and explains the commerce in wine through its various processes, such as bottling, labelling and shipping. Open Mon–Fri 14.00–18.00, closed Sat, Sun and PH; ☎ 05 57 87 50 60.

Moored to the bank of the Garonne is **Croiseur Colbert**, a battleship converted into a museum. Open daily June–Aug 10.00–20.00; April, May, Sept 10.00–18.00; Jan–March, Oct–Dec 13.00–18.00; closed Dec, 1 Jan, 25 Dec; ☎ 05 56 44 96 11. Just beyond the battleship is the Sunday market, **Marché Colbert**, and various restaurants and bars in the area are an opportunity for a half-dozen oysters and slurp of white wine. **Vinorama** at 12 Cour du Médoc (☎ 05 56 39 39 20) is a waxworks which retraces the history of Bordeaux wine from the Gallo-Roman period to the 19C. Cap Sciences, Hangar 16, Quai des

Chartrons (☎ 05 56 01 07 07, www.cap-sciences.net) is the window on major scientific aspects of technical innovation in research and industry. **Marinexpo** is a centre for temporary exhibitions in an old touring barge, evoking the history of Bordeaux's maritime and river life, with model boats, figureheads and other naval decoration.

The Saint-Seurin and Mériadeck districts

The basilica of **St-Seurin** is one of the earliest Christian sites in Bordeaux and an important sanctuary, second only to the cathedral, which developed *extra-muros* in the 5C. From Place Gambetta follow Rue Judaïque to Place des Martyrs de la Résistance, the heart of the ancient district which developed around the former collegiate church and still retains an atmosphere apart. From the garden to the south is the entrance to the **early Christian archaeological site** excavated in the 20C to reveal the earliest known traces of civilisation in Bordeaux. It consists of two ancient burial sites with sarcophagi, amphorae and frescoes (4C–8C) which can be visited by appointment (contact the Tourist Office). There are guided visits of the basilica, Sat 14.30–17.30.

> The first bishop of Bordeaux, Seurin, reputedly from Byzantium, is accredited with the foundation *c* 410 of a monastery outside the walls of the town on the site of the Gallo-Roman necropolis. In the 6C an oratory was built over what was probably a 4C place of worship, and as the church developed this became the crypt of the 11C church, to be refashioned again in the 16C. During the Middle Ages the Collegiate Church contained relics (St Peter's staff, Roland's horn) venerated by pilgrims *en route* to Santiago da Compostela. By the 12C much of the church was built and parts of the apse, choir, crossing, first bay of the nave and the west porch survive from this period. Henry III Plantagenet financed further work on the building in the 13C, to complete the nave and narrow aisles. The south façade is 14C, and during the 18C the belfries were raised. The neo-Romanesque west end, with statues of St Seurin and St Amand, dates mainly from 1829. This and the southwest flank have recently been restored (2001).

Behind the 19C mock-medieval west façade is a genuine Romanesque tunnel-vaulted porch with two storiated capitals, depicting the *Death of St Seurin* on the right, and opposite the *Sacrifice of Abraham*, the remaining capitals decorated with imaginary birds and beasts. A Renaissance porch protects the south portal (*c* 1200) with a central trefoil door and a multitude of figures, several restored in 1844. In the tympanum is a restored *Last Judgement* and statues in the jambs represent the Apostles, the Church on the left and the Synagogue on the right.

The interior is fairly dark with somewhat garish glass (1875–89), and evidence of several additions and rebuildings. The wide nave is supported by massive pillars which were reinforced after the vaults collapsed in 1566 and 1700, and unusually buttressed by high aisles with transverse arches spanning wide bays. The square-ended apse contains stalls with lively 15C/16C misericords and end figures. Against the north pier of the chancel is the finely chiselled stone cathedra (15C) with a decorative canopy, where the incoming prelates spent the night on the eve of their induction. Opposite is an alabaster altarpiece (*c* 1400, but re-framed) consisting of 12 scenes from the *Lives of St Martial and St Seurin*

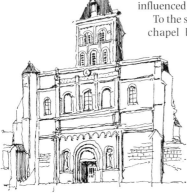

St-Seurin

and beautiful *Annunciation* and *Crucifixion* panels. It is unclear from the style and iconography whether these came from England or were made locally and influenced by English work.

To the south is a truncated transept with a small chapel but the north transept barely exists, becoming a large chapel dedicated to Notre-Dame de la Rose (1424–44), with carved pendant bosses. The chapel contains two of the treasures of the church. The English poly-chromed and gilded alabaster statue of the *Virgin of the Rose* (14C) is con-sidered one of the best of its kind in the region. A 15C retable, also alabaster, has panels depicting episodes from the *Life of the Virgin*, although the sequence was upset when they were reframed in the 19C. The complicated 15C Sacré Coeur chapel off the north aisle, with three altars, contains another 14C alabaster statue of the Virgin, known as *Notre-Dame-de-Bonne-Nouvelle*, and a stone statue of St Martial holding a staff (*c* 1500). Another statue of St Martial is in the St Etienne chapel. The baptismal font is 17C, and the organ is 18C. The entrance to the crypt is in the third bay of the nave (enquire at the Sacristy). This contains two marble Gallo-Roman or Merovingian sarcophagi, Carolingian chancel plates, and the 17C tomb of the semi-mythical St Fort.

The **Communauté Urbain Mériadeck** is a modern district south of St-Seurin and west of the Hôtel de Ville, named after Archbishop Mériadeck. An earlier prelate, Archbishop Cardinal de Sourdis, was responsible initially for draining the desolate, plague-infested marshland outside the city at the beginning of the 17C. The district remained pretty insalubrious until 1955 when the municipal-ity decided to clean it up and after 17 years of construction and reconstruction it has become the administrative and business centre of Bordeaux. This pioneer-ing exercise in mid-20C urban regeneration does not, admittedly, have much appeal to the visitor. Seven hectares is taken up by the Esplanade Charles de Gaulle, where green spaces and gardens suspended above the transport system (a similar idea to La Défense in Paris) are dotted with office buildings, but not a tower block in sight. The Caisse d'Epargne Mériadeck, on Rue Château d'Eau, is a characteristic building of the 1970s, a horizontally assembled series of curved and rectangular planes, clad in a brown stone effect.

The church of **St-Bruno** was originally the chapel of the charterhouse planned by Archbishop Cardinal Sourdis on land which was levelled and planted, pre-empting the work of the Intendants in the 18C. The church, begun in 1611, is a simple one-nave structure containing a stunning Baroque altarpiece boast-ing a painting of the *Assumption* by Philippe de Champaigne, and marble sculp-tures, of the *Virgin* and the *Archangel Gabriel* by the great Italian sculptor, Gian Lorenzo Bernini, and his father Pietro, respectively. Despite the fact that the church was ransacked at the Revolution, it kept some good choir stalls (1619–20) and panelling in the choir (1668–74). The **Cimetière de la Chartreuse** is a 19C creation with an array of tombs and sculptures and was the first resting-place of the Spanish painter, Goya.

The Saint-Michel and Sainte-Croix districts

From the eastern end of Cours Victor-Hugo, Rue des Faures or Rue de la Fusterie lead south to one of the city's great monuments, the basilica of St-Michel, from which the lively and picturesque district takes its name. On Sunday mornings, the large Place de l'Eglise is busy with a *marché à la brocante* (flea market) and on Monday and Saturday mornings, a local produce market. This was once the *quartier* of the craftsmen who worked the wood which arrived by river in *gabares*, such as carpenters (Rue Carpenteyre) and coopers (Rue de la Fusterie). The square is surrounded by North African cafés where you can sip a good mint tea. A statue by Gaston Leroux to **Ulysse Despaux** (1844–1925), a local poet who composed in the local *bordeluche* dialect, stands on the square.

Built on a hillock sloping towards the river, the church of **St-Michel** was begun in 1350, replacing an earlier one destroyed during the Hundred Years War, and took some 200 years to complete. The dominant style is Flamboyant with some early Renaissance influences. The chancel vaults collapsed in 1693, there were a number of alterations and additions in the 18C, more renovations in the 19C, and in June 1940 the church suffered from bomb damage. The Flamboyant west door (incomplete), presents the *Adoration of the Shepherds and Magi* (16C) in vertical panels which seem to be original. The north portal, considered the best of the entrances, shows the transition between late Gothic and early Renaissance in the carvings. The tympanum, divided vertically, contains the *Expulsion of Adam and Eve*, and the *Sacrifice of Abraham* (*c* 1520). There are angels in the intrados of the arches and the prophets Abraham, Isaac, Jacob and David in the niches, and a *Trinity with the Virgin and St John* above. On the south portal, reworked in the 19C, is the *Apparition of St Michael*.

The **interior** is all of the same height, giving a feeling of spaciousness similar to a hall church, with a stunning collection of modern stained glass. The choir and flat-ended apse, built in the 14C, perhaps show English influence; the transept and aisles date from the 15C, and most of the chapels were endowed by local merchants from the 16C. The vaults to the west, where there are no capitals, were completed 1553–54. Wrought-iron screens were added in the 18C to close off the chapels. The southwest chapel contains a 15C relief illustrating the legend of **St Ursula protecting her Virgins**. In the St Joseph chapel on the north, with *lierne* vaulting, is an 18C retable containing statues of the Virgin, St Catherine and St Barbara and 16C English alabasters, and on the pillar opposite this chapel is a late-15C *Pietà*, its pathos emphasised by the realistic approach. The carving of the **Descent from the Cross** or **Entombment** (1492) in the southeast is a characteristic group including the Virgin, Mary Magdalene and St John. The mahogany and marble pulpit (1753) shows St Michael overpowering the Dragon and the organ case (1760–64) is by Micot. A little 16C stained glass survived the bombing, but the bold and colourful 20C windows were created by Ingrand, Couturat, Godin and Lardeur (1962–64).

To the west of the church stands the soaring hexagonal bell tower, known locally as **La Flèche**, containing 22 bells cast in the 19C. The tower was built

1472–86, with the financial help of Louis XI, fervent devotee of St Michael, and was detached from the church due to boggy ground. Beneath it is a charnel house containing models of mummified corpses, popular but macabre curiosities. Between 1861 and 1869 Paul Abadie practically rebuilt the steeple and the tower, which unsurprisingly affords spectacular views. Open daily 15 June–15 Sept 15.00–19.00.

Rue Camille Sauvageau links St-Michel with Ste-Croix. From the 12C until 1801 there was a royal mint in this area, hence Porte de la Monnaie (1752–58) and Quai de la Monnaie. In Rue Porte de la Monnaie are two restaurants of renown, *La Tupina* and *Chez Greg*. On Quai de la Grave is part of a Neo-classical fluted column incorporated in the **Grave Fountain** (1787).

A densely populated suburb developed *extra-muros* around the 11C–12C Benedictine abbey of **Ste-Croix**, enclosed within fortified walls in the 14C. The first church was built in the 7C on a Gallo-Roman necropolis. The 12C church was influenced by the architecture of the Saintonge or Poitou, former provinces of the Dukes of Aquitaine, but the west front was subjected to the heavy hand of Paul Abadie in the 1860s, which left little of the original. The lower part, arranged like a triumphal arch, has remained essentially unchanged and the sculptures of Avarice and Lust in the intrados of the smaller arches, and the shafts and capitals, may be original. The same cannot be said for the level above, which has been drastically rearranged. The south tower is mainly 12C, but the north tower and the shorter adjacent elevation are fantasies of Abadie. The church has a tall apse and two smaller lateral chapels on a flat-ended choir.

Among surviving Romanesque decoration in the interior are several decorated capitals on the massive piers of the crossing, including three storiated ones, *Jesus among the Doctors* on the northeast, *Daniel in the Lions' Den* on the southeast and the *Sacrifice of Abraham* on the capital at the angle between the south aisle and transept; there are also eight medallions of the founders in the nave. The nave piers were adapted to carry sexpartite ribs in the 13C and there are several Gothic capitals. There are a number of objects of interest in the church including the tomb of St Mommolin (643), first abbot during the reign of Dagobert, in the northwest chapel and, in the transept, the 14C tomb of an abbot. The main altar and choir enclosure in wrought iron are 18C and the organ case has been restored and painted in green and gold.

In the 17C the monastery was affiliated to the Order of St-Maur, and a great building campaign was carried out. One of the remaining buildings now houses the Académie des Beaux-Arts. Behind the church is the Centre André Malraux and the fountain of Ste-Croix, constructed in 1735 against the 14C rampart, while 6 Place Pierre-Renaudel is the former 17C gate of the abbey. The **Musée des Métiers de l'Imprimerie** (Museum of Craft and Printing) at 10 Rue Fort Louis, contains working machinery associated with the production of books under the headings of typography, lithography and bookbinding; ☎ 05 56 91 61 17). Further south is the train station, Gare St-Jean (1888–1900).

Rue St-François leads past Place des Capucins to Place de la Victoire, with an 18C triumphal arch, **Porte d'Aquitaine**, opening onto Rue Ste-Catherine. This was the Jewish quarter, where Spanish and Portuguese refugees gathered in the 15C. The synagogue is in Rue Grand Rabin J. Cohen, off Rue Ste-Catherine. Close by, at 54 Rue Magendi, is the convent of the **Annonciade**, one of several religious houses founded around here in the 17C. Now used by the DRAC (Regional Office for Cultural Affairs), the earlier cloister (*c* 1530), and the chapel containing an *Entombment* group can be visited during office hours. Guided visits 14June–15 Sept, Wed 16.00. Rue Magendie leads to the old parish church of **Ste-Eulalie**, where pilgrims congregated before setting out to Compostela. The church contains some fine wrought iron by the master of the craft, Blaise Charlut, and a magnificent lectern.

Opposite is the Hôpital St-André (1826), and to the north, across Place de la République, is the Palais de Justice (1846) a Neo-classical building with a Doric colonnade. On the other side of this building are all that remains of the **Fort du Hâ**, two bulky towers, Tour de la Poudrière and Tour des Anglais, which Louis XI ordered built in 1456. In the 19C the fort was partly demolished to make way for the Palais de Justice and the St-André Hospital. In glaring contrast are the Ecole Nationale de la Magistrature (1972) and Richard Rogers' Tribunal de Grande Instance (1994–98).

2 Gironde: Arcachon and the Médoc

To the west and north of Bordeaux is a triangular piece of land, the Médoc Peninsula. The western part is a flat coastal plain along the Atlantic with long windswept beaches and sand dunes, tranquil inland seas and deserted pine forests, whereas on the banks of the Gironde Estuary to the east of the peninsula are well-disciplined vineyards.

ARCACHON BASIN AND CAP-FERRET

Bassin d'Arcachon

The Bassin d'Arcachon is an inland sea of 155 sq km, enjoying endlessly changing seascapes and sandscapes and remarkable luminosity. It has remained linked to the sea, unlike the lakes of Lacanau and Hourtin to the north (see p 88), because of strong currents and tides. The largest, and constantly shifting, sand deposit at the mouth of the lagoon, the Banc d'Arguin, is a wildlife reserve, as is the Ile aux Oiseaux, identified by two *cabanes tchanquées* (wooden hides on stilts). The narrow peninsula, Cap-Ferret, itself originally a sand dune, protects Arcachon from the ocean. Apart from tourism, the main industry of the basin is oyster farming. This is a determining factor on the environment and what appears as a partly submerged petrified forest in the lagoon is in fact posts (or *pignots*) marking the oyster beds. The basin is very crowded in the summer but the climate is mild in spring or autumn. The vineyards of the Médoc are only 50km away.

Practical information

Getting there and around
Car

From Bordeaux: N250 to Arcachon; D106 to Lège-Cap Ferret) all season.

Ferry and boat

There are ferries from either Arcachon le Moulleau or Port d'Arcachon to Belisaire (Lege-Cap Ferret) and other ports on the east side of Cap Ferret; to the Bank d'Arguin; and to Ports Arès, d'Andernos, de Taussat and de Cassy on the eastern side of the Basin.

Train

TER Bordeaux to Arachon via Le Teich, Gujan-Mestras, La Teste.

Bus

Citram buses from Bordeaux to Pointe du Cap Ferret via Andernos-les-Bains (☎ 05 56 43 68 43). *Autobus d'Arcachon* (from station) to Pyla, Biscarosse, etc (☎ 05 56 83 07 60).

Tram

A tramway runs between the Bélisaire jetty at Cap-Ferret and l'Horizon beach (at the southern end of Cap Ferret on the Atlantic coast) April–Sept.

Bicycle

Cycling in the Gironde. For a map of routes and details of bicycle hire companies, contact the Maison du Tourisme de la Gironde, 21 cours de l'Intendance, 33000 Bordeaux, ☎ 05 56 62 61 40, fax 05 56 81 09 99, www.tourism-gironde.cg33.fr.

Tourist information
33120 **Arcachon** Esp. Georges-Pompidou, ☎ 05 57 52 97 97, fax 05 57 52 97 77
33590 **Claouey** 1 Ave du Général-de-Gaulle, ☎ 05 56 03 94 49, fax 05 57 70 31 70
33470 **Gujan-Mestras** Ave du Maréchal-de-Lattre-de-Tassigny, ☎ 05 56 66 12 65, fax 05 56 26 19 91
33590 **Lège-Cap-Ferret** Panier Fleuri, 12 Ave de l'Océan (1 June–30 Sept), ☎ 05 56 60 63 26; and Le Canon, Place de l'Europe (1 July–30 Aug), ☎ 05 56 60 86 43

Boat trips

Boat trips may be made from most of the villages; enquire at the tourist offices

Tours

For tours of Arcachon's Winter Town, enquire at the tourist information office

Festivals and events

April *Folies*, traditional music and dance from France and overseas, Arcachon

July *Jazz en Liberté*, Andernos-les-Bains

July–August *Les Musicales*, music and tastings in oyster villages, Lège Cap-Ferret

Where to stay
Hotel prices vary widely between low and high season. Many close during winter. All the hotels named below are within easy reach of the sea or lagoon.

33120 ARCACHON

☆☆☆ *Aquamarina*, 82 Blvd de la Plage, ☎ 05 56 83 67 70, fax 05 57 52 08 26, www.hotel-aquamarina.com. Modern and bright and close to the beach.

☆☆☆ *Villa Térésa-Semiramis*, 4 Allée Rebsomen, ☎ 05 56 83 25 87, fax 05 57 52 22 41. One of the first mansions built in the Winter Town, charmingly restored.

33950 CAP-FERRET

☆☆ *La Fregate*, 34 Ave de l'Océan, ☎ 05 56 60 41 62, fax 05 56 03 76 18, www.lege-capferet.com/fregate.htm. Comfortable, good-value hotel, with a swimming pool. Open most of the year.

☆☆ *La Maison du Bassin-Le Bayonne*, 5 Rue des Pionniers, ☎ 05 56 60 60 63, fax 05 56 03 71 47. Traditional fisherman's house converted into a pretty hotel, with seven charming bedrooms, bar and good restaurant.

☆☆ **Des Pins**, 23 Rue des Fauvettes, ☎ 05 56 60 60 11, fax 05 56 60 67 41. Small hotel in an early 20C building with a garden. Open 1 April–12 Nov.

Chambres d'hôte, Mme A. Vidal, 11 Impasse des Pêcheurs, Les Jacquets, ☎ 05 56 60 80 81. On the shore; three rooms, very charming hosts. Open all year.

Chambres d'hôte, Mme M. Pulon, 2 bis Rue des Mésanges, ☎ 05 56 03 72 33. Prettily decorated, four rooms. View of the lagoon. Open all year.

3 3 9 5 0 L È G E - C A P - F E R R E T

☆☆ **Crystal**, 15 Rue des Goélands, ☎ 05 56 03 96 00, fax 05 56 03 76 20. Unfussy, practical hotel with 26 rooms. Open all year.

Chambres d'hôte, Mme F. Archambault, 2 bis Rue des Cormorans, ☎ 05 56 60 66 78, fax 05 56 03 77 52. Friendly place, with three rooms in modern chalet. Open all year.

Chambres d'hôte, Mme G. Couvidoux, 3 Rue des Pionniers, ☎ 05 56 60 66 39. Just 50m from the basin. Warm welcome.

Chambres d'hôte, Mme A. Jean, 15 Ave de l' Océan, ☎/fax 05 57 70 80 14. Very welcoming and comfortable, in attractive surroundings; two rooms.

Eating out

3 3 1 2 0 A R C A C H O N

€€ **Club House CVA**, Port de Plaisance, ☎ 05 56 83 77 10, fax 06 07 32 84 67. Between lagoon and marina. Not glamorous, but excellent seafood and views.

€€ **Le Patio**, 10 Bvld de la Plage, ☎ 05 56 83 02 72. Fish and seafood are *de rigeur* in this rustic seaside setting.

3 3 5 9 0 L È G E - C A P - F E R R E T

€€ **Le Bistrot du Bassin**, La Maison du Bassin (see above), ☎ 05 56 03 72 46. Attractive restaurant and good standard of cooking.

€€ **Chez Hortense**, Ave du Sémaphore, ☎ 05 56 60 62 56. At the Pointe du Cap with a magnificent view over the basin.

€ **L'Arrimeur**, 58 Ave de l'Océan, ☎ 05 56 60 60 60. Traditional cooking, good value.

€ **Chez Yvan le Mascaret**, 17 bis Rue des Goélands, ☎ 05 56 03 75 74. Good local dishes, good value.

€ **L'Escale**, Jetée Bélisaire, 2 Ave de l'Océan, ☎ 05 56 60 68 17.

€ **Pinasse Café**, Jetée Bélisaire, 2 bis Ave de l'Océan, ☎ 05 56 03 77 87. Both have terraces and are next to the jetty where the boats arrive from Arcachon; reasonably priced.

3 3 5 9 0 L ' H E R B E

€ **Chez Magne**, 1 Ave des Marins, ☎ 05 56 60 50 15. At the heart of the *village ostréicole* of l'Herbe.

€ **Hôtel de la Plage**. Good basic cooking in a traditional building.

Arcachon

The resort of Arcachon stands on a small peninsula southwest of the lagoon and is rather fancifully divided into four sections, each associated with a season.

In the early 19C the climate, pure sea air and the scent of pines found in this small fishing community were promoted for the rehabilitation of tuberculosis sufferers. Later in the century the vogue for sea bathing attracted more visitors, convalescents and developers. Arcachon became fashionable, receiving the royal seal of approval from Napoléon III and Eugenie in 1863, and the following year the railway chugged in. The Péreire brothers, main shareholders in the railroad, created the Ville d'Hiver (Winter Town) and visitors included the artists Toulouse-Lautrec (p 314), Cézanne and Monet. The early visitors endowed the town with some splendid examples of 19C sea-side vernacular architecture and later in the century promenades and jetties were constructed. The town's fishing industry is still active, although the modest sardine has been replaced as the main catch by rather trendier fish such as turbot, brill, monkfish and sea bass, and oysters are big business.

For an idea of Arcachon in its heyday, stroll through the **Ville d'Hiver**. The highest part of the town, it was laid out from 1862 around the Parc Mauresque, which was named after a casino inspired by the Alhambra in Granada and destroyed by fire in 1977. The Ville d'Hiver has a great variety of stylishly designed houses. The earliest are wooden, in Swiss-chalet style, with verandas and decorative eaves; outstanding among these are Villa Térésa, now the *Hôtel Semiramis*, and villas Tolédo, Montesquieur, Marguerite and Bremontier. The years 1870–1900 produced exotic, fanciful residences of Hispano-Mauresque inspiration or Belle-Epoque ostentation, featuring bow windows, stained glass, turrets and other such fancies. Villas Faust, Graigcrostan, Dumas and Vincenette are notable examples. After 1914, charming but more modest single-storey houses were favoured. The Anglican church (now the Protestant church), consecrated in 1878, has some good stained glass.

Another sector of Arcachon, the **Ville d'Eté** (Summer Town), contains the town centre and promenade. It was the first part to be developed (the neo-Renaissance Château Deganne is in fact a casino) and was unhappily redeveloped, although an effort was made in 1994 to improve the area along the Thiers Beach. Ferries to Cap-Ferret and boat trips leave from the jetties. The Ville d'Automne is the modest fishermen's district on the eastern side of town around the church of St-Ferdinand, which has a statue of the Sacred Heart on the spire. The **Ville de Printemps** (Spring Town) to the west was a younger development but harbours the 18C fishermen's church of Notre-Dame (restored in 1987), containing a marble statue of the Virgin, some good furnishings and numerous ex-votos. At Les Abatilles is the deepest still-water spring in France, exploited by Vittel, and in Le Moulleau, Notre-Dame-des-Passes is a brick and stone Byzantine/Tuscan-inspired church with some good glass.

South of Arcachon is the area's most spectacular natural phenomenon, the **Dune du Pyla**. At 105m high, 500m wide and 2.7km long, it is the largest sand dune in Europe. Its formation began in the 18C when wind carried sand from a bar in the channel, and sand continues to blow across from the Banc d'Arguin so that the great dune is shifting a staggering metre per year towards the forest. Wooden steps facilitate the climb and protect the dune.

The oyster farming at some 20 villages on the Bassin d'Arcachon has become a tourist attraction and it is possible to call in at a *cabane*, taste oysters and make a guided visit by land or water to see the *ostréiculteurs* at work. **Gujan-Mestras** is described as the oyster capital of the basin: it has seven small ports or inlets lined with the wooden huts and all the paraphernalia associated with the trade as well as traditional boats, the flat-bottomed *chalande*, the narrow-hulled *pinasse* (9–10m long), navigated by sail, oar or motor, and the *pinassotte* (a smaller version of the pinasse, with sail). The name comes from the word *pin* or pine from which they were originally built. The Maison de l'Huître at Port de Larros, Gujan-Mestras is all about oysters and the industry. Open 1 March–30 Sept daily 10.30–12.00 and 14.30–18.30, or by appointment; ☎ 05 56 66 23 71.

In the southeast corner of the basin, where the salt water is diluted by the mouth of the Leyre River, is the ornithological park of **Le Teich**. Covering 120ha of the Leyre Delta, this closely controlled natural environment has a network of dykes and locks and 6km of walks and hides to protect about 250 species of water fowl and migratory birds. The visitor centre, the Maison de la Nature, provides information on the park and its activities, including guided visits. Open 10.00–18.00, to 20.00 in summer; ☎ 05 56 22 80 93.

The largest community on the north side of the basin is **Andernos-les-Bains**, an ancient site where two prehistoric settlements have been discovered; the remains of a 4C basilica are still standing. Adjacent to the archaeological site is a small 11C–12C Romanesque church, St-Eloi.

Lège-Cap-Ferret

Lège-Cap-Ferret, the exclusive playground of Parisians and Bordelais, is a different world from commercialised Arcachon. The peninsula, usually referred to as Cap Ferret, is a narrow spit of sand stretching for 25km between the Bassin d'Arcachon and the Atlantic, with the village of Lège to the northeast and the community of Cap Ferret to the south; the tip is called La Pointe. One of the main features of the Cap are the fishing communities, or *villages ostréicoles*, where there are ample opportunities for tasting oysters. The peninsula, which is covered with maritime pines interspersed with February-flowering mimosas and small oaks, has some excellent beaches and 50km of cycle routes.

Fishermen have been coming to the peninsula since the 17C. By the mid-19C the *ostréiculteurs* began to build *cabanes* for the *tri* (sorting) of oysters at the water's edge, and these gradually became homes as well as workplaces. They huddle together near the coastline, separated only by narrow alleyways. These little villages were legally acknowledged in 1878 and are now protected *sites classés*. Building control is strictly maintained and the exclusively wooden cabins are covered in tiles and painted in bright colours. Some are still inhabited by the oyster fishermen but others are now holiday homes. From around 1830, the huge sand dune was gradually transformed over some 50 years by the introduction of deep-rooted plants and then maritime pines. The first road to Cap-Ferret was built in 1930.

Lège, at the north of the peninsula, was established in the mid-19C on a canal built to drain the vast marshes, and further developed with the introduction of the railway and then the road to Cap-Ferret. The Modernist architect Le Corbusier designed the *cité ouvrière* in 1925. Just north of Claouey, at **Jane-de-Boy**, was the small port from which pine pit-props were once exported to England.

The most northern of the picturesque *villages ostréicoles* is **Les Jacquets**, with a tiny, sheltered harbour, one of the first to be settled by the oyster farmers. Petit Piquey has smart villas and a sheltered beach, and from the dune of **Grand Piquey** is a great view of the Ile aux Oiseaux. In the 1930s the likes of Jean Cocteau, Le Corbusier, Jean Marais and André Lhote patronised the *Hôtel Chantecler*, next to the jetty. Further south are Piraillan and Le Canon (named after a cannon from the old Napoleonic fort), which were originally surrounded by sand dunes. One of the most characteristic villages is **L'Herbe** (cows once grazed here), a cluster of wooden *cabanes* close to the shore, in various states from pristine to nearly derelict. *Hôtel de la Plage*—offering good, simple fare—is typical of the large houses in Basco-Landais style, with attractive overhanging eaves and verandas. On the southern edge of the village the only reminder of the Villa Algérienne, built by Léon Lesca, engineer of the port of Algiers, and demolished in the 1960s, is the Moorish-style chapel (1865), daringly displaying both cross and crescent on the belfry. There were once vineyards around the village of **La Vigne**, planted by the Lesca brothers, but today it has a small yacht harbour replacing a fish farm and lock.

The most southerly *village ostréricole*, **Cap-Ferret**, still exists but has grown into the largest community on the cape with some fine old villas around the Bélisaire jetty. The main curiosity is the lighthouse, Le Phare (1949), 52m high with 250 steps. Guided tours daily July, Aug, weekends only June and Sept. The church of Notre-Dame des Flots (1963) cotnains many reminders of its maritime vocation. A sandy headland, Le Mimbeau, protects this shore, and from La Pointe is a marvellous view across the entrance to the Bassin d'Arcachon and the Dune du Pilat.

THE MÉDOC PENINSULA

The Médoc Peninsula is a flat land between the Atlantic and the Gironde Estuary; the name is said to derive from *media aquae* ('the middle of the waters'). To the west are sand dunes and pines and little else, but to the east is a thin strip of land dedicated almost entirely to the celebrated vineyards of the Médoc.

Some 5000 years ago, the Atlantic coast had an irregular profile, with deep inlets or harbours that were gradually cut off from the sea by banks of sand to create huge inland lakes. Now the almost unbroken strip of beaches and dunes is unprotected from the Atlantic breakers from Cap-Ferret to La Pointe de la Grave, and is part of the 270km of the Côte d'Argent (Silver Coast). Among several seaside resorts are Le Porge, Lacanau-Océan, Hourtin Plage and Montalivet and there are two huge *étangs* or lakes, Lacanau and Hourtin-Carcans (6000 ha), the largest in France. In this area a constant battle is fought against wind and tidal erosion. The population is very sparse and the area is ideal for outdoor activities; a huge network of cycle tracks criss-crosses the peninsula.

Practical information

Getting there and around
Car

D1 and N215 from Bordeaux.
Train and bus

TER Bordeaux to Pointe de la Grave via Margaux, Pauillac, Lesparre, Soulac.
Ferry
Car ferries run between Pointe de la Grave and Royan and between Blaye and Lamargque.4

 Tourist information
33680 Lacanau-Océan Pl. de l'Europe, ☎ 05 56 03 21 01, fax 05 56 03 11 89, www.lacanau.com
33123 Le-Verdon-sur-Mer Rue F.-Lebreton, 05 56 09 61 78, fax 05 56 09 61 32
33780 Soulac-sur-Mer BP2, 68 Rue de la Plage, 05 56 09 86 61, fax 05 56 73 63 78, www.soulac.com

Wine tours and tastings

See box, p 91

Festivals and events

March–April *Portes Ouvertes dans les Châteaux du Médoc*, open weekend for about 80 wineries
May *Fête de l'Agneau de Pauillac*, two days of celebration of Pauillac lamb
June *Festival de Jazz de Lesparre*
July *New Jazz and Wine*, Pauillac

Where to stay and eating out

33460 ARCINS
L'Auberge du Lion d'Or, Pl. de la République, ☎ 05 56 58 96 79. The patron of this congenial bar is a well-known character.

33250 BEYCHEVELLE
€€ *Le St-Julien*, 11 Rue St-Julien, ☎ 05 56 59 63 87. An old baker's shop turned into a very satisfying regional restaurant.

33460 LABARDE
Château Giscours, ☎ 05 57 97 09 09, fax 05 57 97 09 00, email giscours@chateau-giscours.fr. A wine-producing château in the Médoc with rooms.

33680 LACANAU OCÉAN
☆☆☆ *Golf Hotel*, Domaine de l'Ardilouse, ☎ 05 56 03 92 92, fax 05 56 26 30 57, www.lacanau.com. Situated in a park and close to the golf course. Panoramic restaurant.

33460 MARGAUX
☆☆☆ *Le Pavillon de Margaux*, Le Caire, ☎ 05 57 88 77 54, fax 05 57 88 77 73, www.paviliondemargaux.com. Hotel-restaurant with 14 rooms. Well placed for vineyards.
☆☆☆ *Le Relais de Margaux*, Chemin de l'Ile Vincent, ☎ 05 57 88 38 30, fax 05 57 88 31 73, www.relais-margaux.fr. Set in a large park with every facility. Reputed restaurant.

33460 MACAU
☆ *Ferme Auberge Chateau Guitto-Fellonneau*, ☎ 05 57 88 47 81, fax 05 57 88 09 94. On the edge of the Médoc vineyards.

33650 MARTILLAC
☆☆☆☆ *Les Sources de Caudalie*, Chemin de Smith Haut-Lafitte, ☎ 05 57 83 83 83, fax 05 57 83 83 84; spa ☎ 05 57 83 82 82, fax 05 57 83 82 81, www.sources-caudilie.com. This is a beautiful hotel set in vineyards, with fabulous food and a spa where '*vinothérapie*' is on offer.

33250 PAUILLAC
☆☆☆☆ *Château Cordeillon-Bages*, Route des Châteaux, ☎ 05 56 59 24 24, fax 05 56 59 01 89, www.relais.chateaux.fr. Ultimate in luxury and food in an elegant setting; runs wine courses.
☆☆ *France et de l'Angleterre*, 3 Aquai Labert Pichon, ☎ 05 56 59 01 20, fax 05 56 59 02 31. Attractively renovated hotel and quality restaurant where you can enjoy an initiation to wine tasting.
Chambres d'hôte, Simone & Michel Irr, 5 Pl. des Fauvettes, ☎ 05 56 59 19 62, fax 06 83 25 38 28. Pretty rooms. Near the centre of Pauillac.

33320 LE TAILLAN-MEDOC
Chambres d'hôte, Château Le Lout, Ave de la Dame Blanche, ☎ 05 56 35 46 47, fax 05 56 35 48 75. Elegantly decorated 19C mansion, in tranquil surroundings. Home-cooked food.

33340 ST-YZANS-DE-MEDOC
Château Loudenne, ☎ 05 56 73 17 80, fax 05 56 09 02 87, email chateauloudenne@wanadoo.fr. A delightful 17C charterhouse, the only château with a private port on the Gironde estuary, which offers great hospitality in a tranquil setting. *Chambres d'hôte* and Ecole du Vin.

Near the tip of the Silver Coast, between the ocean and the Gironde Estuary, is the senior town, **Soulac-sur-Mer**. Settled by the Romans, it became a staging-post for English pilgrims travelling south, and has the best medieval building in this part of the Médoc, a fine 11C–12C church, Notre-Dame-de-la-Fin-des-Terrres, supposedly founded by St Veronica. The church was almost totally enveloped in sand in the 18C and in 1859 work began to dig it out and renovate. It has three naves of equal height with a rounded apse and two chapels, a few good 12C capitals and modern glass by Chicot (1954). The resort was first developed in 1849 by Antoine Trouche and was established as a garden city by 1900. It has a splendid assortment of villas and chalets (mid-19C to 1936), fully exploiting the eclectic vocabulary of styles and decoration so beloved in seaside resorts.

For centuries the **Cordouan lighthouse** directed sailors to the entrance of the Gironde Estuary and it claims to be the oldest lighthouse in existence (there was one other on the French coast in the 15C). Cordouan, built in stone, was begun in 1584 to replace a 14C structure. In 1593 Henri IV gave his approval to elaborate on it, and royal apartments, a chapel and elegant Renaissance windows were incorporated. It was completed in the early 17C and Neo-classicised in the 18C. The lighthouse rises about 66m and is topped with a lantern dome. Electricity was connected in 1950 to light a 6000 watt lamp. Open April–Oct; ☎ 05 56 09 62 93. There are organised boat trips from Le-Verdon-sur-Mer; the crossing takes 30mins, the visit lasts 3½ hours (tourist information: ☎ 05 56 09 61 78). The seven-storey lighthouse has 310 steps.

La Pointe de Grave is the very tip of the Médoc peninsula, where sea defences against coastal erosion were erected in 1850. Tucked in on the estuary side of the headland is Le-Verdon-sur-Mer, a seaside resort and important modern harbour, built in 1976.

Médoc vineyards

The world-famous Médoc vineyards, among the most celebrated in the Bordelais, are confined to a strip about 65km long and 10–15km wide stretching along the west of the Gironde Estuary from Blanquefort, north of Bordeaux, to Lesparre. In the Médoc, *château* describes a wine-producing estate (*domaine* or *cru* are also used), not just a building. Here the mansions are mainly 18C or 19C, neo-this or neo-that, ranging from Classically elegant or Palladian practical to absurdly eclectic. A journey through this extraordinarily regimented landscape, with battalions of vines and immaculately turned-out properties, is fascinating even for non-wine buffs.

The D2 from Blanquefort (north of Bordeaux) is the main **Route des Vins**, passing many of the great *crus*. Macau, close to the estuary, where the church has an 11C belfry, is a typically simple Médoc village, as is Arsac, further inland, with a part Romanesque church. Labrede and Cantenac are in the Margaux region, and among the châteaux are several with English names: the red-and-white **Cantenac-Brown**, in English Queen Anne style (☎ 05 57 88 81 81, email infochato@cantenacbrown.com); Kirwan, which has a rose-garden; and Palmer, a pretty building not far from the estuary. The great **Château Margaux**, built by Louis Combes (1810–16), is a masterful Neo-classical pile approached by an avenue of plane trees. Visits and tastings by appointment; ☎ 05 57 88 83 83, www.chateau-margaux.com. **Château Lascombes** (near Margaux) can also be visited; ☎ 05 57 88 70 66, fax 05 57 88 72 17.

Wines of the Médoc

The temperate climate and the poor gravelly soil of the Médoc create perfect conditions for vines. The area produces only red wines, blended mainly from Cabernet-Sauvignon, Cabernet-Franc, Merlot and Petit-Verdot grape varieties. The Médoc is divided into Bas Médoc in the north and Haut Médoc in the south, both regional *appellations d'origine contrôllée*. Within Haut Médoc are six great local appellations: *St-Estèphe, Pauillac, St-Julien, Listrac, Margaux* and *Moulis*. Many châteaux receive visitors to their *chais* (cellars) and for tastings, but nearly all have to be arranged in advance.

For information on tastings and tours, contact local tourist information centres or one of the Maisons du Vin, either in Bordeaux (see p 61) or:

33460 Margaux 7 Pl. Tremoille, ☎ 05 57 88 70 82.
33180 St-Estéphe Pl. de l'Eglise, ☎ 05 56 59 30 59.
33250 Pauillac La Verrerie, ☎ 05 56 59 03 08, fax 05 56 59 23 38.
33480 Moulis 1137 Le Bourg, ☎ 05 56 58 32 74.

A *Guide Découverte* of the Médoc is published by the Conseil des Vins du Médoc, 1 Cours du XXX Juillet, 33000 Bordeaux, www.medoc-wines.com.

Around Tayac the vines peter out for a while but across the Tiquetorte river are the vineyards of **Moulis** and **Listrac** to the west of Arcins (*AOC Moulis*) including the strangely named **Château de Chasse-Spleen** (☎ 05 56 58 02 37, email infos@chasse-spleen.com) and the **Château Maucaillou**, which has a museum of wine-related arts and crafts (☎ 05 56 58 00 88, email chateau@maucaillou.com). A ferry crosses the estuary from Lamarque, which has a part 12C castle, to Blaye (see p 93). Nearby **Fort Médoc** was built in the 17C by Vauban as part of a line of defence with Blaye and Fort Pâté, to protect the estuary. Open May–Oct 09.00–20.00, Nov–April 10.00–17.00, closed Mon, ☎ 05 56 58 91 30/05 56 58 98 40. Less impressive and less restored than the citadel of Blaye, and taking a different form, the fort contains an interior courtyard with the former guardroom, bakery and powder store. From the bastion is a view over the Gironde estuary and Blaye.

The neo-Tudor **Château Lanessan** at Cussac has a museum of horsemanship *c* 1900 (☎ 05 56 58 94 80, email bouteiller@bouteiller.com). Beychevelle, at the centre of the *AOC St-Julien*, has a yachting basin on the estuary. Among the best known châteaux in this region are **Château de Beychevelle**, an attractive 18C–19C house (☎ 05 56 73 320 70, email beychevelle@beychevelle.com; Château Talbot; and **Château Leoville-Barton** (☎ 05 56 59 06 05, fax 05 56 59 14 29), originally owned by an Irish family, established here for three centuries. **Châteaux Ducru-Beaucaillou** (☎ 05 56 73 16 73, fax 05 56 59 27 37) contains a reference in its name to the stony terrain (*caillou*, stone).

The *AOC Pauillac* is named after a plain little town stretched out along the estuary. **Pauillac** has an important Maison du Vin and visitor centre with masses of information on the vineyards and châteaux. **Château Pichon-Longueville, Comtesse-de-Lalande**, overlooking the Gironde, has a collection of wine-related objects and welcomes visits by appointment (☎ 05 56 59 19 40, email pichon@pichon-lalande.com). Also falling within the Pauillac region are **Château Latour** (☎ 05 56 73 19 80, www.chateau-latour.com), with a wonderful 19C domed dovecote, and the great Rothschild châteaux, Mouton and

Lafitte, belonging to the English and French sides of the family. **Château Mouton-Rothschild** can be visited: it has video and slide shows, visits to the cellars, and a museum of wine-related art, with objects spanning 6000 years of wine production; ☎ 05 56 73 21 29, fax 05 56 73 21 28. The château is also famous for its labels, designed since 1924 by great artists, including Braque, Chagall, Baselitz, Motherwell and Balthus. The artists are paid in wine. **Château Lafite-Rothschild**, where the circular *chai* (wine store) was designed by Ricardo Boffill). Visits are strictly by appointment, ☎ 01 53 89 78 00, fax 01 53 89 78 01, www.lafite.com.

Further north are the vineyards of *AOC St-Estèphe*, one of the most eccentric mansions being **Château Cos d'Estournel**, an early 19C blending of Indian and Chinese elements, which contains a museum and exhibition room; visits by appointment ☎ 05 56 73 15 50, email estournel@estournel.com. Beyond there are oceans of vineyards, producing wine that is not quite *haute gamme* but still extremely of good quality.

3 Haute Gironde

BLAYE AND BOURG

The Garonne and the Dordogne merge at Bec d'Ambès, about 20km north of Bordeaux, to become the Gironde Estuary. Here, defences were constructed to protect Bordeaux, which was vulnerable to attack from the sea. On the right or east bank of the estuary the great fort of Blaye is surrounded by vineyards and chequerboard fields. On the border between the Saintonge (see p 560) and Aquitaine, this region was the historic boundary between the language of *oc*, in the south, and *oïl*, in the north.

Practical information

Getting there and around
Car
By A10 autoroute, Paris to Bordeaux, exit 38; RN 137 Bordeaux to Saintes, D937/D669.
Ferry
A car ferry between Blaye and Lamarque (on the Médoc side of the river) runs regularly, passing the islands of Pâté and Bouchaud-La Nouvelle (☎ 05 57 42 04 49).
Train
Bordeaux to Saintes via St-Andre de Cubzac, St-Yzan-de-Soudiac; TER Brive-la-Gaillarde to Bordeaux via Périgueux, Libourne.
Bus
Trans-Gironde network, ☎ 05 56 99 57 83.

Tourist information

33390 Blaye Allées Marines, ☎ 05 57 42 12 09, fax 05 57 42 91 94, www.blaye.net; annex inside the Citadel (summer only), ☎ 05 57 42 86 64
33710 Bourg-sur-Gironde Hôtel de la Jurade, ☎ 05 57 68 31 76, fax 05 57 68 30 25
33240 St-André-de-Cubzac 9 Allée du Champ de Foire, ☎ 05 57 43 64 80

Market days

Bourg-sur-Gironde Sunday

Festivals and events

Spring *Foire de Printemps*, flower festival, Blaye

July International show-jumping, Blaye
August–September *Festival de Théâtre les chantiers de Blaye*, in the Citadel

Where to stay

33390 BLAYE

☆☆ *La Citadelle*, Pl. d'Armes, ☎ 05 57 42 17 10, fax 05 57 42 10 34, email la.citadelle@epicuria.fr. Inside the Citadel with a view out to the estuary.
Villa Prémayac, 13 Rue Prémayac, ☎ 05 57 42 69 05, fax 05 57 42 69 09, www.villa-premayac.com. *Chambres d'hôte*; five comfortable rooms in an 18C mansion, with a Roman and a Zen garden.

Gironde Estuary

The water of the estuary is usually murky due to the mix of fresh and salt water. Particles of soil and vegetation that are suspended in fresh water clump together in salt water, creating silt on which the flora and fauna of the estuary depend. Some coastal land has been reclaimed, but there are still wetlands and wild, untamed marshes attracting thousands of birds including herons and egrets. The estuary fish include obscure species such as lamprey (*lamproie*), an eel-like creature which is in fact a parasite feeding on the blood of other fishes; eels and shad. Sturgeon, once plentiful and the mainstay of this region, is now rare and protected.

Blaye

The small town and huge citadel of Blaye, on the banks of the Gironde, are at the centre of an important wine-producing area: about 10,000ha produce *Premières Côtes-de-Blaye* and *Côtes-de-Blaye* red and white wines. There is a modern port and a nuclear power station to the north. As well as lampreys and caviar, strawberries and asparagus, another local speciality is *Praslines de Blaye* (sugar-coated almonds), named in the 17C after the Maréchal de Plesis-Praslin whose cook invented them. The new *appellation d'origine contrôlée* of Blaye was introduced in autumn 2002.

Citadelle de Blaye

The citadel is unique in Aquitaine. It covers 33ha and its 40m-high ramparts have two gateways. The area inside the fortifications covers 17ha, large enough to contain a small working community.

History

The rock dominating the estuary was an obvious place for a defensive system. Vulgrin Rudel, descendent of the Counts of Angoulême, rebuilt the existing castle (1126–37) and its remains are inside the citadel. Blaye was part of

English Aquitaine and only returned to the French in 1451 under Dunois, Comte d'Orléans (1403–68), an officer in the army of Charles VII, who fought beside Jeanne d'Arc against the English. In the 16C the town was besieged twice during the Wars of Religion, and in the 17C work was undertaken to strengthen the ramparts when the Fronde underlined Blaye's importance as the key to Bordeaux, and therefore to the whole of Aquitaine. Following a visit by Louis XIV in 1650, the construction of a larger and stronger fort was deemed necessary, to the detriment of the Rudel château, some 260 houses and eventually the church of St-Romain, yet this large undertaking was still not massive enough for the huge garrison. Two projects were submitted, by François Ferri and by Vauban (see below). Vauban's plans were realised under Ferri's supervision (1686–89). His fortifications were characterised by their angular bastions (see also Bayonne). The citadel became part of a string of fortresses across the Gironde, with Fort Pâté on the island opposite Blaye, and Fort Médoc on the west bank (see p 91). Originally called Fort Saint-Simon after the governor of the Citadelle, it was changed at the Revolution to Fort Pâté because its shape resembled a *pâté de campagne*. The citadel was in fact tested only once, by the British in 1814, in a siege lasting 14 days. In 1832 the Duchesse de Berry, Marie-Caroline of Naples, was imprisoned here after a conspiracy to topple her uncle, Louis-Philippe, from the throne of France. In 1841 the future city planner, Baron Haussmann, became *sous-Préfet* for Blaye, and the citadel continued to be used as a prison during the Second Empire (1852–70) and the First World War. It remained in the hands of the military authorities until 1954, when it was purchased by Blaye town council for the symbolic sum of 1 franc.

Enter on foot by Porte Dauphine spanning the dry moat. Stone bridges replaced wooden ones in the 18C. Inside the severe battlements is a pleasant village with around 15 residents; the garrison buildings have become workshops and boutiques for artists and craftspeople. There are also a museum and exhibition gallery, large open spaces and wonderful views. Among buildings which can be visited are the **Manutention**, a solid 17C building used for exhibitions and containing old bread ovens, and the **Pavillon de la Place**, now a small local museum, once the Duchesse de Berry's prison. The Porte Liverneuf is a relic of the time when the upper town and the esplanade were divided by walls. On the other side are the remains of the 12C **Château des Rudel**, incorporated into Vauban's fortress but reduced to ruins in the 19C. From the 12C to the 15C, the Rudel family controlled Blaye and the castle was the birthplace of the famous troubadour and author of *Amours lointains*, Jaufré Rudel, who left for Tripoli in 1147 in pursuit of his beloved Melissande, only to expire in her arms.

Commanding the estuary is the **Tour de l'Eguillette** looking across to Fort Pâté and the Médoc beyond. Further south is Place des Armes and the *Hôtel de la Citadelle* with a restaurant overlooking the Gironde. The former gunpowder store, the *Poudrière* (1687) is used by the Syndicat Viticole de Blaye and exhibitions are held in the remains of the 17C Couvent des Minimes.

Outside the citadel walls, to the east, are the foundations of the **Abbaye de St-Romain**, a site of Christian worship since the 4C. The Rudels were patrons of the abbey which was on the pilgrimage route, and legend has it that Roland, Charlemagne's chevalier, was buried here. It was badly damaged during the Wars of Religion.

Maréchal de Vauban

Born Sébastien Le Prestre, seigneur of the Château de Vauban, to a family of lesser nobility, Vauban (1633–1707) is far better known for his contributions to military architecture at the time of Louis XIV than for his genius on the field of battle or for his socio-economic activities in his native Burgundy. As an engineer, although not by training, he became Commissaire général des fortifications in 1678. While he did not invent the type of fortifications for which he is best known, he brought them to a state of perfection and is credited with the construction or repair of a network of some 150 strongholds to protect France on all fronts, ranging from massive forts such as Blaye and Bayonne to monumental gateways. He was elevated to Maréchal de France when he was 70.

Just south of Blaye at Plassac are the remains of an important **Gallo-Roman villa and museum**, a reminder of the size and luxury of Gallo-Roman rural estates. Open April and Oct daily 09.00–12.00 and 14.00–18.00; May–Sept 09.00–12.00 and 14.00–19.00; ☎ 05 57 42 84 80. The site is to the north of the church and reveals a succession of buildings erected between the 1C and 6C, each time increasing in size and complexity, eventually covering 6000m. There are some elaborate 5C mosaic floors, one covering the hypocaust and another partly hidden beneath the church. The small museum is clearly laid out and contains mosaics and some fragments of superb wall paintings in the 3rd Pompeian style (*c* AD 30–40), plans and reconstructions, as well as smaller finds such as weights, coins, pottery and jewellery.

The coastal route between Bourg and Blaye is known as the **Corniche Fleurie** (Flowered Road) because master mariners built their manors along the river. It is a viewing point for the Mascaret, or spring tidal bore (see below). Most of the dozen or so islands in the archipelago are deserted, although they were formerly inhabited, and some (Cazeau, North and Green islands), have fused as a result of the constant build-up of silt. These form the spit which protects Margaux island. The church at **Bayon** has a monumental apse on three levels with a series of superimposed blind arcades.

The Mascaret

The Mascaret is a tidal bore which occurs on the Dordogne at certain times of the year, much as on the Severn in England. It is caused when the rising tide surging up the Gironde estuary is as strong as the down current from the Dordogne, especially during extremely high tides and shallow water levels, between April and November, the optimum time being August–September. These conditions create a series of spectacularly powerful waves, spaced out over about 10m, the largest of them reaching around 2.5m in height. The phenomenon is best observed from the port of St-Pardon, west of Libourne, or from Podensac or Pont d'Arcins and its time can be precisely calculated. The Mascaret is now the only example in France of a tidal bore—the others have disappeared due to environmental changes—and is enthusiastically awaited by surfers although in the past it was extremely hazardous for navigation.

Bourg-sur-Gironde is a stunning fortified village built on a rocky outcrop surrounded by medieval ramparts and set in the vineyards of *Côtes-de-Bourg*. Picturesque narrow streets descend to the port via the sea gate, La Gouttinière, or the Escalier du Roy (King's Steps). In the centre of the *cité* is the market hall, the Hôtel de la Jurade; the citadel, built originally by the English (rebuilt in 1964); an 18C charterhouse; and a communal wash-house (1828). The Romanesque crypt of the ruined chapel of St-Saturnin-de-la-Libarde has 11C–12C carved capitals.

Among several rural Romanesque churches near Bourg-sur-Gironde, **Tauriac** has a small 12C church, with some fine relief carvings on the façade and interesting capitals inside. A 12C Templar chapel with murals has survived at **Magrigne**. There is a superb example of Romanesque at **Peujard** (D115) with a Saintonge-style portal and cupola on pendentives. In **Cubnezais**, the church has a Romanesque façade decorated with animals and figures. East of the N10 at **Marcenais**, on the D18, is a fortified Templar church.

At Prignac Marcamps, off the D669 east of Bourg, is a very important prehistoric site, the **Grotte de Pair-non-Pair**. Guided visits every 45 mins, 15 June–15 Sept 09.30–18.30; 16 Sept–14 June 09.30–12.00 and 14.00–17.30; closed 1 Jan, 1 May, 1 Nov, 11 Nov, 25 Dec; ☎ 05 57 68 33 40. It was discovered in 1881 by the local archaeologist François Daleau (b. 1845), who worked there for 15 years. The engravings found here, from the Gravettian period (25,000 years ago), are considered to be among the oldest known examples of cave art and include horses, ibex, deer, mammoths and other mammals. Bone tools and animal bones have also been found, dating the site's occupation to *c* 25,000 BC. The D669 is a pretty route with a magnificent panorama over the estuary from the terrace of the 16C **Château des Arras** (with restaurant) and a 12C church in St-Gervais.

The **Château du Bouilh** was the work of Victor Louis, author of the Grand Théâtre in Bordeaux. It was built at the orders of the Marquis de la Tour du Pin to receive Louis XVI and is set in a magnificent park overlooking the Dordogne. The park, graced with 200-year-old trees, is open most of the time. The château has a grand staircase and furnished reception rooms through which passed the Duchesse de Berry, Romantic poet Alphonse de Lamartine (1790–1869) and Maréchal MacMahon (1808–93), President of the French Republic in 1873–77. Gardens open, guided visits to interior, 1 July–30 Sept, Thur, Sat, Sun and PH 14.30–18.30; ☎ 05 57 43 01 45.

St-André-de-Cubzac on the right bank of the Dordogne was the birthplace of Commandant Jacques-Yves Cousteau, the first underwater explorer to bring the aquatic world alive to millions of people via television. He was born at 83 Rue Nationale (now a pharmacy) in 1910 and returned to his native land at the end of his life. In the town is a 13C church with a military look, having been fortified in the 14C.

The **Pont Eiffel** at Cubzac-les-Ponts has an impressive enfilade of stone piers *c* 140m long which, viewed from below, gives the effect of a Gothic cathedral. The piers support a metal road and railway bridge built by Gustave Eiffel in 1883. The lower part is open all year and freely accessible from the port.

THE LIBOURNAIS AND ST-EMILION

The Libournais is watered by the confluence of the Isle and Dordogne Rivers and is an area of intense wine-growing, notably around St-Emilion, Pomerol and Fronsac. Apart from the vineyards, the landscape is varied, and there is a wealth of châteaux and churches.

Getting there and around
Car

A10 from Paris; A89 from Bordeaux; A62/670 from Toulouse; N89 from Périgueux; D936/D670 from Bergerac/Sarlat. To St-Emilion: via the A10 from Paris; A62/D670 from Toulouse; D936 from Bergerac.

Train

To Libourne: TGV from Paris Montparnassse, and TER from Bordeaux. To St-Emilion: TGV Paris Montparnasse to Libourne; TER line Bordeaux to Salat stops at St-Emilion.

Bus

Libourne to Bordeaux, no. 302, ☎ 05 57 551 19 28. To St-Emilion: bus from Libourne, ☎ 05 57 51 19 28.

Bicycle hire

From the tourist office.

Tourist information

33330 St-Emilion Le Doyenné, Pl. des Créneaux, ☎ 05 57 55 28 28, fax 05 57 55 28 29, www.saint-emilion-tourisme.com
33500 Libourne 40 Pl. Abel Surchamp, ☎ 05 57 55 33 33, fax 05 57 55 33 76, www.libourne-tourisme.com

Market days

Libourne Tuesday, Friday and Sunday; fairs in October and November
St-Emilion Sunday

Festivals and events

April *Fête de Printemps*, a traditional festival held when the vines flower.
May *Portes Ouvertes dans les Châteaux du St-Emilion*, open day for wineries

July–August *La Bataille de Castillon*, sound-and-light re-enactment of the battle
August *Festival des Arts de la Rue*, street theatre festival, Libourne
La Dordogne en Feu, La Plage de Ste-Terre near Castillon
September/October *Ban des Vendanges*, another traditional wine festival, held at the start of the grape harvest

Where to stay

33330 ST-EMILION
Note that hotel tariffs increase when the Jurade meets in June and September.

☆☆☆☆ *Château Grand Barrail*, Route de Libourne, just outside St-Emilion, ☎ 05 57 55 37 00, fax 05 57 55 37 49, www.grand-barrail.com. A 19C château with 28 luxurious rooms and Belle-Epoque restaurant.

☆☆☆☆ *Hostellerie de Plaisance*, Pl. du Clocher, ☎ 05 57 55 07 55, fax 05 57 74 41 11. Below the belfry, a charming and beautifully presented hotel with a terrace and first-class restaurant.

☆☆☆ *Le Logis des Remparts*, 18 Rue Guadet, ☎ 05 57 24 70 43, fax 05 57 74 47 44, www.saint-emilion.org. Built against the old ramparts in the upper town, with a pretty patio, swimming pool and views of the vineyards. Comfortable.

☆☆☆ *Palais Cardinal*, Pl. du 11 Novembre 1918, ☎ 05 57 24 72 39, fax 05 57 74 47 54, www.palais-cardinal.fr. Smallish hotel within the remains of the cardinal's palace, with swimming pool, tennis courts and restaurant.

☆☆ *Auberge de la Commanderie*, Rue

des Cordeliers, ☎ 05 57 24 70 19, fax 05 57 74 44 53, www.pagesjaunes.fr. A comfortable family hotel with views over the town and vineyards.

☆☆ **Bonsaï**, Bois de l'Or, Route de Castillon, D670, ☎ 05 57 25 25 07, fax 05 57 25 26 59. A modern, functional hotel with tennis court, swimming pool and restaurant.

Chambres d'hôte, Monsieur Brieux, Château Millaud Montlabert, ☎ 05 57 24 71 85, fax 05 57 24 62 78. In the category 'Gîte Bacchus': 18C house on 4ha estate, 3km from the town.

Eating out

3 3 1 2 6 F R O N S A C

€€ **Restaurant Le Bord'eau**, Poinsonnet, ☎ 05 57 51 99 91. Have a pleasant meal virtually sitting in the Dordogne.

3 3 5 0 0 L I B O U R N E

€€ **Le Bistrot Chanzy**, 16 Rue Chanzy, ☎ 05 57 51 84 26. Simple but serious cooking, and good value fixed-price menu. Near the old train station.

3 3 3 3 0 S T - E M I L I O N

€€ **Francis Goullée**, 27 Rue Guadet, ☎ 05 57 24 70 49, fax 05 57 74 47 96. This has a good reputation for its gourmet cuisine.

€ **Amelia Canta**, Pl. du Marché, ☎ 05 57 74 48 03, fax 05 57 74 48 36. In a popular setting in the town centre, with two dining rooms and terrace, serving regional specialities.

€ **La Côte Braisée**, Rue du Tertre de la Tente, ☎ 05 57 24 79 65, fax 05 57 74 05 51. A restaurant in the rock, which gives it an authentic St-Emilion character.

€ **Chez Dominique**, Rue de la Petite Fontaine, ☎ 05 57 24 71 00, fax 05 57 74 42 96. Good regional cooking and reasonably priced menus.

€ **L'Envers du Décor**, Rue du Clocher, ☎ 05 57 74 48 31, fax 05 57 24 68 90. Attractive and lively wine bar serving local specialities.

Libourne and Fronsac

The agreeable town of **Libourne**, the second-largest in the Gironde, is strategically placed at the union of the Dordogne and the Isle.

> Edward I planned a *bastide*-port here in 1268, and it was named after Roger de Leyburn who supervised the project in 1270. English until the end of the Hundred Years War, it was protected by walls with eight fortified entrances. The advantages of the position ensured a dynamic river port shipping local wine to England and northern Europe. It suffered the usual problems in the 17C–19C, but has remained a major centre of the wine trade.

A few fragments of the ramparts still line the Isle, including the mid 14C Porte du Grand Port flanked by one complete round tower and part of another, but most of the walls have been replaced by tree-lined esplanades. The regular *bastide* layout has been maintained, and Place Abel-Surchamp at the centre is surrounded by *couverts* (arcades). This is the market place, liveliest on Sunday. The former *hôtel de ville* dates from the 15C (restored 1911–14) and houses the municipal library and the **Musée des Beaux-Arts et d'Archéologie**. Open Mon–Fri 10.00–12.00 and 14.00–18.00, closed Sat, Sun; ☎ 05 57 55 33 44. It contains paintings by Jacopo Bassano, Philippe de Champaigne, Raoul Dufy and Leonard Fujita, and has a room devoted to René Princeteau, Toulouse-Lautrec's first drawing master, and other local artists.

Between the Dordogne and Isle to the west of Libourne is **Fronsac**, which gives its name to the local *AOC*. For information visit the Maison des Vins de

Wine and vineyards of St-Emilion and the Libournais

The St-Emilion appellation covers the area between the Dordogne and the little river Barbane. The St-Emilion and St-Emilion Grand Cru *appellations d'origine contrôlées* (AOC) are spread over almost exactly the same area as the eight communes recognised in 1289 by Edward I of England and established under the ancient Jurisdiction of St-Emilion, although these communes were abolished in 1789. The vineyards then covered 7800ha, whereas the present St-Emilion *appellations* cover 5400 ha. St-Emilion produces 5.5 per cent of the total Bordeaux *AOC* red wine. The predominant grape variety in St-Emilion is Merlot combined with Cabernet Franc and Cabernet Sauvignon. In 1999 the area of the old Jurisdiction was designated a World Heritage cultural landscape by UNESCO.

There are four further St-Emilion *appellations* towards the north: Montagne Saint-Emilion, Lussac St-Emilion, Puisseguin St-Emilion and St-Georges St-Emilion, covering another 3800ha and 500 producers. The estates, therefore, are fairly small and the quality of the wines is jealously maintained. Châteaux Cheval-Blanc and Figeac are towards Pomerol. Other neighbouring *appellations* are Fronsac and Castillon. Among the 1000 or so producers of St-Emilion and St-Emilion Grand Cru, **Châteaux Ausone** and **Cheval-Blanc** have enjoyed an outstanding reputation for some 50 years. Other châteaux producing high-quality wine are Beauséjour, Bélaire, Canon, Clos-Fourtet, Figeac and La Gaffelière.

The wines of Pomerol and Fronsac abut St-Emilion. **Pomerol** is one of the smallest wine producing areas of Bordeaux along a slightly hilly plateau almost 5km long and just over 3km wide, northwest of St-Emilion. Its reds are easily recognisable for the subtle bouquet reminiscent of truffles which is accounted for by the iron oxide or 'dross' content of the soil here and the top-soil consists of gravel, more like the Gironde. These are such famous wines that they have never had to be formally classified but, like all Bordeaux wines, Pomerol is strictly monitored to guarantee the required degree of perfection. Outstanding are the wines of **Château Petrus**, but also representative are Châteaux Beauregard, le Caillou, Clos du Clocher, La Conseillante, Clos-l'Eglise, La Croix, Sergant and Borseau. Fronsac and Canon-Fronsac, the two *appellations* of the **Fronsac** area, are much sought after. The full-bodied, ruby-coloured wines are produced in about 170 wineries.

The St-Emilion tourist office advises on planning **vineyard tours and tastings**. There are daily wine tours from the tourist office: mid-May–mid-Sept, every afternoon, and twice a day in July–Aug; all visits are in English and French. For details of guided visits to vineyards by bike (2–3 hours), enquire at the tourist office. There is also a booklet, *Cellars Open to the Public*.

An **initiation wine-tasting course** is held 17 July–17 Sept at the Maison du Vin, Pl. Pierre-Meyrat, ☎ 05 57 55 50 55.

Town or vineyard visits by **petit train** from Place Poincaré are probably one of the best uses ever for a little train: 1–31 May weekends and PH only, 1 June–31 Oct 10.30–12.00, 14.00–18.30, ten departures a day; the tour lasts 35mins; ☎ 05 57 51 13 76, www.visite-saint-emilion.com.

Portes ouvertes, a weekend at the end April/beginning May, when wine châteaux open their doors.

Fronsac, Canon Fronsac; ☎ 05 57 51 80 51, fax 05 57 25 98 19. A succession of hilltop forts, or *tertres*, were built and destroyed here by Gauls, Romans, Carolingians, Vikings and the English. In 1663 the Duc de Richelieu took possession of these territories and his great nephew, Arnaud de Plessis, built a folly on the ruins. In the town is a 12C–13C church with a *clocher pignon* (gable belfry).

The church of St-Pierre at **La Lande-de-Fronsac**, on the D670/D137 north, has naïve sculptures around the south porch accompanied by an inscription. The tympanum unusually presents the ***Vision of the Apocalypse*** inspired by the text of Revelations, where Christ reveals himself to St John with 'seven stars in his right hand, with a sword coming out of his mouth'. The arches and capitals are decorated with interlacing, monsters and old bearded men. In the restored interior are archaeological excavations under glass. The square belfry has a bell dated 1347, recast in 1855.

St-Emilion

The richly endowed town of St-Emilion stands confidently on a limestone escarpment surveying the vineyards on which it depends. Beautifully turned out, it has many interesting buildings solidly built in the local cream-coloured stone, and is well organised to manage the thousands of visitors. The biggest surprise is that it is not as solid as it looks, because carved out of the rock below it is a vast network of underground galleries and a huge monolithic church. In the air there is always a hint of the wine for which it is so revered, and some 5200ha of land and 1000 vineyards of the *appellation* produce as much wine as the whole of Burgundy. Sweet specialities, *macarons* and *cannelés de Bordeaux* (small doughy cakes, coated in caramel and baked in a fluted mould), are sold all over town. The tradition of making almond biscuits or macaroons started with the Ursuline nuns who founded a community on the west of the town in 1630, although whether they made these delicacies for the poor, or whether someone benefited by selling the recipe, is unclear.

History

The 4C Roman poet and pro-consul Ausonius is connected with the vineyards, but the town took its name from Emilion (d. 767), a hermit from Brittany, who settled in a local cave and performed miracles. He was first mentioned in 12C texts, although by the end of the 11C two religious buildings already existed, dedicated to Emilion and Mary Magdalene. The large collegiate church and monastery were begun early in the 12C, as well as the fortifications. In 1199, during the period of the Anglo-Gascon alliance, the future King John granted St-Emilion the status of commune and established a body of aldermen, called the *Jurade*, to supervise the town and vineyards. Edward I granted the right of justice (independent administration of a designated area) to St-Emilion in 1289 and the region remained loyal to the English almost to the end, but the Hundred Years War and the Wars of Religion did the town no favours. The town gates and parts of the walls were demolished in the 18C–19C. The *Jurade* lost its political role with the Revolution, and the town became a place of refuge for Elie Guadet, a member of the Girondins who met his end at the guillotine in Bordeaux (p 67). As elsewhere, the wine trade suffered from mildew and phylloxera outbreaks in the 19C but in 1884 a wine syndicate was formed, and the *appellation contrôlée* was defined in 1936. In 1948 a confraternity named after the old *Jurade* was created to promote the wine.

A stroll around the perimeter of the old walls brings into focus the layout of the town and its relationship with the vineyards. The rocky outcrop forms a natural amphitheatre sloping downhill from north to south and St-Emilion is still contained within the walls erected between 1110 and 1224. Start at Place Poincaré, on the northwest of the town, near the collegiate church. The Porte des Chanoines disappeared over 200 years ago, but the wall and ditch can still be made out. Head north towards Place du Maréchal-Leclerc on the Libourne road. **Les Grandes Murailles** outside the walls are all that remains of a 13C Dominican monastery, destroyed *c* 1340. Three bays of the nave wall, a perilous 26m high by 20m, with two slender Gothic openings and fine mouldings, seem to have no business still to be standing.

Just south of the modern roundabout was the old **Porte Bourgeoise**, the main and most heavily fortified entrance to the town, but the walls and gate were demolished in the 18C–19C. Built into the walls beyond is the **Palais Cardinal**, possibly named after the first dean and cardinal. The double round-headed windows were probably part of the defences. On the corner is a section of wall with massive corbels and from here the path runs between the vineyards and the ditch. The only gate more or less in its original 12C state is the **Porte Brunet**, with later fortifications, and this and the Tour Guetteur now look out over benign battalions of vines. The path descends to Place Bouqueyre, named after the gate to the lower town; the *guérite* (lookout), a strange isolated construction, is the only fragment left of the barbican. Take Rue de la Porte Bouqueyre and turn immediately left, up a flight of steps. At the top is Rue de la Porte, leading from Porte Ste-Marie, which was walled up in the 16C. The quarries of the old Hospice de la Madeleine have become an underground pottery museum, **Poteries Populaires du Sud-Ouest** at 21 Rue André Loiseau, containing a collection of regional pottery dating from the 13C onwards. Open daily; ☎ 05 57 55 51 65.

The path runs behind the **Château du Roi**, begun *c* 1237, in which both Louis VIII and Henry III had a hand. Protected by a dry ditch, the massive, square Gascon-style keep undoubtedly played a symbolic as well as a military role. Until 1720 it was used as the town hall, and in June and September the *Jurade* adds a dash of colour when its members gather at the top in their red and white outfits to pay homage to the wines of St-Emilion. From the terrace you can see classic views over the town, uninterrupted by cables or aerials. Open May–Oct 10.00–19.00; the times can vary so check with the tourist office.

The west gate, Porte St-Martin, has completely disappeared, but the walls flanking it are still standing and in the thickness of the wall are steps which led to the *chemin de ronde* (path around the battlements). From here there is a choice between the routes outside and inside the walls. From outside you can see the best-conserved section of the ramparts (roofed over) and the rebuilt bridge. Inside the ramparts you pass the caves and entrances to the former quarries. Something like 200km of quarries, on four or five levels, provided stone to build St-Emilion, Libourne and Bordeaux. Both routes arrive near the collegiate church.

L'Eglise collégiale

The collegiate church, one of the finest in the Gironde, was established in 1110 with an independent chapter of Augustinian canons and was secularised by Bertrand de Got (see p 118) in 1306 when his nephew, Gaillard de la Motte, was installed as dean. These associations were obviously relevant to the prestige of the church. The chapter was dissolved in 1790, and it became a parish church after the Revolution.

Exterior Work began on the church before the mid-12C and continued through the 13C, and the Romanesque cloister was rebuilt in the 14C. It is an imposing but severe building, the long, low roof covered in red tiles interrupted only by the slightly truncated belfry over the narthex, and the gable and steep roof over the apse. The oldest part of the building is the nave; the west door is Romanesque with a succession of round-headed arches with a window above in the style of the Saintonge. The exterior decoration of the north door (*c* 1306) is damaged and difficult to decipher but it is just possible to make out scenes of the *Last Judgement* on the tympanum, with *Christ in Majesty*, the *Virgin and St John* and, on the lintel, the *Separation of the Righteous from the Damned*. Either side of the door, very battered, are the *Crucifixion of St Peter* and the *Martyrdom of St Paul*.

Interior The narrow, three-bay, aisleless nave is part of the original 12C building and has little decoration except for a mural (see below). The two east bays are spanned by domes on pendentives in the style of the Périgord but at some point the belfry over the west porch collapsed, bringing down the vaults (or dome) of the first bay where there is now a 13C ribbed vault. In the 13C the original transept was demolished and replaced with a Gothic construction, three bays wide and two deep, extended by a flat-ended chancel with large windows. The two chapels date from the 14C, as does the sacristy above which has a six-lobed rose window. After the Hundred Years War the Flamboyant polygonal apse with large windows was added, no doubt replacing an earlier one. The relics of St Emilion would have been conserved behind the main altar; the early 14C southeast chapel is dedicated to the saint, as well as to martyrs of the Great Wars.

There are a number of **wall paintings** but these are probably only a sample, as the remaining traces suggest a far more complete programme covering the transept and vaults. On the pilaster in the southeast of the nave is a 12C image of the *Virgin standing on the World*, and adjacent are four scenes, enclosed in circles, from the *Legend of St Catherine*. On the west wall are more murals, including a *Crucifixion*. Near the sacristy door is a 16C painted wooden statue of St Valéry, local saint and patron of wine-growers, dressed in the appropriate working outfit of the day. The late 15C–early 16C **choir stalls** have misericords with a variety of lively carvings. The pulpit is 19C, and the organ is an excellent instrument from the end of the 19C by Gabriel Cavaillé-Col, son of Aristide. There is 20C glass by Mirande.

The **cloister** is accessed from the church or from the tourist office. Of the Romanesque version, only the east and south walls remain following rebuilding at the end of the 13C or early 14C. The south wall has ten funerary niches (late 13C or early 14C) decorated with trefoil arches and dragons, whereas the east wall has a series of Romanesque niches and Gothic niches with hints of early-14C painting, restored in 1997. The cloister is used in the summer for craft markets and other activities.

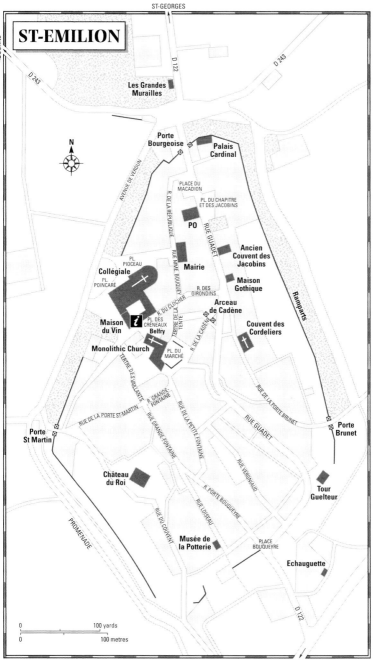

ST-GEORGES

ST-EMILION

D 122

D 243

D 243

Les Grandes Murailles

N

AVENUE DE VERDUN

Porte Bourgeoise

Palais Cardinal

PLACE DU MACADION

R. DE LA RÉPUBLIQUE

PL. DU CHAPITRE ET DES JACOBINS

PO

RUE GUADET

Ancien Couvent des Jacobins

PL. PIOCEAU

Collégiale

PL. POINCARÉ

RUE MME BOUQUEY

Mairie

Maison Gothique

R. DES GIRONDINS

R. DU CLOCHER

TERTRE DE LA TENTE

Arceau de Cadène

R. DE LA CADÈNE

Couvent des Cordeliers

Maison du Vin

PL. DES CRÉNEAUX

Belfry

Monolithic Church

PL. DU MARCHÉ

TERTRE DES VAILLANTS

Ramparts

Porte St Martin

RUE DE LA PORTE ST-MARTIN

R. GRANDE-FONTAINE

RUE GRANDE-FONTAINE

RUE DE LA PETITE FONTAINE

RUE DE LA PORTE BRUNET

RUE GUADET

Porte Brunet

Château du Roi

RUE VERGNAUD

R. PORTE BOUQUEYRE

RUE DU COUVENT

RUE LOISEAU

Tour Guelteur

Musée de la Potterie

PLACE BOUQUEYRE

PROMENADE

Echauguette

D 122

0   100 yards

0   100 metres

CASTILLON-LA-BATAILLE

The rather smart **Maison du Vin** is installed in the old Logis de l'Abbé, part of the 18C conventual buildings; note the magnificent wrought-iron staircase ramp of 1744. The Logis Malet (16C), opposite, was built into the ramparts and from across the ditch part of the *chemin de ronde* is clearly visible, below a steep gable. The façade towards the town is partly masked by an 18C building used for exhibitions. The **Doyenné** (Deanery) houses the tourist office; it has been modified considerably since the 12C but the buttresses and round-headed windows are original and the dormers are 15C–16C.

On Place des Créneaux is the great **clocher** (belfry), 133m high measured from Place du Marché below. The first two levels are 12C, the second and third 13C, and the spire was completed at the end of the 15C. In 1626 it had to be reinforced with extra buttresses. It stands directly above the monolithic church (see below) and the bell ropes originally connected with the underground building. From the top of the belfry, 187 steps above, marvellous views can be had over the town and vineyards.

From Rue du Clocher, to the east, turn right down **Tertre de la Fente**, one of four sloping *tertres* (mounds) paved with the granite which was used in the 12C as ballast on ships returning from Cornwall or Brittany after offloading their cargoes of wine. *Escalettes* (narrow stepped paths) are similar and run west to east along the contours of the hill, linking the *tertres* with steps and terraces. These were the only way of getting around until Rue Guadet was built in the 19C. At the bottom is **Place du Marché**, the hub of the town, enlivened by café tables and wine boutiques, and the entrance to the **monolithic church, catacombs, hermitage and Trinity chapel**, all in natural caves which have been modified and used since prehistoric times. Guided tours every 45mins all year round, between 10.00 and 16.15, to 17.45 April–Oct; ☎ 05 57 55 28 28.

The hermitage, Emilion's rock shelter, which was originally open to the south, is 'furnished' with a stone table and bed, and had a miraculous source of water. The Trinity chapel, built over the hermitage *c* 12C–13C, was rebuilt in 1730. In 1995 the paintings between the ribs of the early Gothic apse (13C) were discovered. The catacombs contain several sarcophagi, one with an epitaph dated 1014, and monolithic columns to support the roof, one decorated. The original entrance to the catacombs was the curious funnel-like opening with a spiral staircase supported by a dome cut into the rock. Around the base of the dome are three half-figures in relief, which seem to support the construction on their backs.

The badly damaged Gothic door of the church carries an incomplete *Last Judgement*, in the tympanum, and the *Resurrection of the Dead* on the lintel. The **monolithic church** was carved from the rock, entailing the removal of some 15,000 cubic metres of rock to enlarge an existing natural cave under Place des Créneaux. Its astounding dimensions—38m long, 20m wide and 12m high—make it the largest of its kind in Europe. The church is thought to date from the end of the 11C or beginning of the 12C. An inscription on the third pillar (south) of the nave may refer to the dedication but gives only the day and month, not the year. In April 2003 the church reopened after a lengthy programme of restoration revealing the true proportions of the beautiful simple interior of this remarkable structure. Concrete pillars (38) installed in 1990 have been removed leaving just the ten original pillars, four of which, at the base of the church tower, are reinforced with a metal corset. The floor has been returned to the medieval level by removing layers of earth that had built up over the centuries as drains became blocked; some of these drains can be seen as well as ancient stone flags. Windows have been re-opened and the lighting improved as part of the renovations thus enhancing reliefs high on the pillars and the west wall of the nave. These are mainly of animals but on the vaults are two cherubim, halo to halo, surveying the scene. The church was pillaged in 1793, and wall paintings dating from the 14C were neglected and badly damaged when saltpetre was scraped off the walls for the explosives industry in the 19C, but with the new improvements the vestiges of of these paintings are better set off. The altars are 16C and 18C.

From Place du Marché take Rue de la Cadène, passing on your left the arcaded Halle du Marché. Inside is a staircase leading to a very fine ogee and the old *hôtel de ville* upstairs. A stone archway, **Arceau de la Cadène**, is the remains of a gateway across which a *cadena* or chain was supposedly thrown to separate the upper and lower towns. The picturesque old house on the right is possibly 12C, but was messed about in the 14C and again in the 19C. Next door is the only timber-framed house (16C) still surviving in St-Emilion. Turn right and take the upper road, Rue de la Porte-Brunet, to Place du Cap-du-Pont where, on the corner, there is the so-called Templar commandery, a building with an *echauguette* (lookout) and the outlines of some pretty Romanesque windows.

Almost opposite are the overgrown ruins of the **Couvent des Cordeliers** (Franciscans) who moved inside the walls in the 14C and erected a chapel (15C), cellars and residential buildings. Already run down, it was sold in 1791. What remains of the cloisters appears to be earlier than the 14C, and was perhaps transferred from the earlier building. The walls, but not the vaults, of the chapel are still standing. In the cloisters you can enjoy a tasting of Crémant de Bordeaux and visit the wine store. Open daily March–Oct 10.30–19.30; Oct–March 14.00–18.00. Guided visits to the *chais* (cellars) in the afternoon; ☎ 05 57 24 72 07.

Retrace your steps along the 19C Rue Guadet, and nearly opposite Rue des Girondins is the **Maison Gothique** (15C–16C), with two-light windows and numerous corbels, one of the best-preserved medieval houses in St-Emilion although disfigured in the 18C. Further on is the former Couvent des Jacobins (or Dominicans), given permission to build *intra muros* on land abutting the Cordeliers convent. The gardens of the *mairie* (18C) are on the left; if they are open, see the restored wall on the right with a mixture of architectural elements. Place Mercadieu has two adjacent late-medieval buildings, one with a square tower. Rue Abbé-Bergey takes you back to Rue du Clocher and the Place des Créneaux.

The undulating countryside around St-Emilion is densely packed with strictly regimented lines of vines and the dips and hollows are described as *combes*. Small churches and villages abound.

One of the best church façades in the Gironde is that of St-Pierre at **Petit-Palais** (D21 northeast of St-Emilion), built in the late 12C and partly rebuilt in the 16C. The tiered west end, richly ornamented over the whole elevation, exhibits the influence of the Saintonge. The first level is decorated with columns and carved capitals, and the central door and side niches have multi-foil decoration which is echoed on the next level. In the spandrels of the main entrance are statues. The second level, slightly laid back, is very ornate with blind niches around the central window, clustered columns, carved capitals and arches, and in the triangular pediment are four blind arcades on double columns. The interior is late Gothic.

Across the D670, at St-Sulpice de Faleyrens, is the moated **Château Lescours** (14C–15C) to which Henri of Navarre (later Henri IV), the Duc d'Alençon and the Duc d'Epernon retreated in 1581 and 1583 during the Wars of Religion. Reputedly Henri IV took shelter in the Manoir Castellot (14C–16C) which can be visited. In the port of **Pierrefitte** close to Libourne is a 5m-high menhir, a prehistoric standing stone.

The name **Castillon-la-Bataille** gives a strong clue as to what happened here. Once a thriving town and stronghold on the Dordogne, the château and ramparts were destroyed during the Hundred Years War and the Wars of Religion, and there is not a great deal left to see.

In 1452 Castillon was controlled by the English, but Charles VII's army took Chalais and Gensac nearby, and marched on the town with 6000 men. Castillon requested help from Bordeaux. General Talbot, Count of Shrewsbury, arrived with 8000 men and met with some success but, led erroneously to believe that the French had abandoned camp, Talbot decided to continue attacking. The English army was decimated and abandoned the battle after Talbot's death, bringing the Hundred Years War and the English occupation of Aquitaine to an end. The French generals erected a chapel on the site, Notre-Dame-de-Talbot, where there is a procession during Assumption. The battle is commemorated every summer (July/Aug) on the Coly plain, ☎ 05 57 40 14 53.

4 Gironde: Entre-Deux-Mers, Graves

ENTRE-DEUX-MERS

The area called Entre-Deux-Mers is a triangular limestone plateau between the Garonne and the Dordogne where the rivers are still tidal (therefore, between two 'seas'). The region was once known as the 'bread mill of Bordeaux' and is scattered with old water mills, frequently fortified. There are many pretty rural and riverside villages in a mainly well-controlled landscape, and a multitude of small Romanesque churches. The most important château, albeit sadly mutilated, is at Cadillac, and the most important religious monument is La Sauve Majeure.

Getting there and around
Car

Créon (D936/D671), Cadillac (D10 or A62 Exit 2), Loupiac (D10/D117), Verdelais (D10/D120), Château de Malromé (D19 north of St-Macaire), St-Macaire (A62 Exit 3/N113), La Réole (A 62 Exit 4/D9 or N113), Sauveterre-de-Guynne (meeting of D672 and D670), Monségur (between Sauveterre-de-Guynne and Duras, junction of D230/D668), Blasimon (north of Sauveterre-de-Guynne, D17).

Train

Trains from Bordeaux-St-Jean to Agen stop at Portets, Podensac, Barsac, Preignac, Langon, St-Macaire, La Réole.

 Tourist information

33350 Blasimon 15 Pl. de la République, ☎ 05 56 71 59 62, fax 05 56 71 53 37

33410 Cadillac 9 Pl. de Libération, ☎ 05 56 62 12 92, fax 05 56 76 99 72

33670 Créon 7bis Rue de Docteur Fauché, ☎ 05 57 34 54 41, fax 05 57 34 54 46

33580 Monségur Office de Tourisme de l'Entre-deux-Mers, 4 Rue Issartier, ☎ 05 56 61 82 73, fax 05 56 61 89 13

33190 La Réole Pl. de la Libération, ☎ 05 56 61 13 55, fax 05 56 71 25 40

33490 St-Macaire Maison du Pays, ☎ 05 56 63 32 14; Le Prieuré (July, Aug), ☎ 05 56 63 34 52

33540 Sauveterre-de-Guyenne 2 Rue St-Roman, ☎ 05 56 71 53 45, fax 05 56 71 59 39

Market days

Cadillac Saturday
Monségur Friday
La Réole Saturday

Festivals and events

July–August *Swing de Monségur*, a jazz festival, usually first weekend of July.
Rencontres Musicales de l'Eté Girondin en Pays Foyen, musical entertainment, St Foy-la-Grande and region
Les Nuits Macariennes, medieval festival, St-Sauveur and St-Macaire

 Where to stay

33410 CADILLAC

☆☆☆ *Château de la Tour*, ☎ 05 56 76 92 00, fax 05 56 62 11 59. Next door to the château. Rather smart (though with a bit of road noise), and scrumptious food.

☆☆ *Détrée*, 22 Ave du Pont, ☎ 05 56 62 63 38. This is recommended both for the hotel and restaurant.

33670 CRÉON

☆☆☆ *Château Camiac*, Route de Branne D121, ☎ 05 56 23 20 85, fax 05 56 23 38 84. Magical castle setting with a garden and terrace restaurant.

33190 GIRONDE-SUR-DROPT
(near La Réole)

☆☆ *Les Trois Cèdres*, 92 Ave du Gen-de-Gaulle, ☎ 05 56 71 10 70, fax 05 56 71 12 10. Good basic hotel, with a restaurant.

33580 MONSÉGUR

☆☆ *Grand*, Pl. Darniche, ☎ 05 56 61 60 28, fax 05 56 61 63 89. Very reasonable, family-run hotel with good cooking.

33350 STE-RADEGONDE

☆☆☆ *Château de Sanse*, ☎ 05 57 56 41 10, fax 05 57 56 41 29, www.chateau-hotels.com. A recently converted 14C château of great charm. Rooms have terraces; pool.

33490 ST-MACAIRE

Les Feuilles d'Acanthe, 5 Rue de l'Eglise, ☎ 05 56 62 33 75, fax 05 56 76 72 02, www.feuilles-dacanthe.com. Beautifully restored Renaissance houses with spacious rooms and a pool; good-value accommodation and food. Moderate to expensive.

Les Tilleuls, 15 Allée des Tilleuls, ☎/fax 05 56 62 28 38, email tilleuls@sauternes.com. Self-catering studios rented by the night/week/ month.

33540 SAUVETERRE-DE-GUYENNE

☆ *Le Guyenne*, ☎ 05 56 71 54 92, fax 05 56 71 62 91. Simple and inexpensive.

Eating out

33410 CADILLAC

€ *L'Entrée Jardin*, 22 Rue de l'Oeuille, ☎ 05 56 76 96 96. Local cuisine served in an attractive blue-and-white setting; with a terrace. Near the château.

33190 LA RÉOLE

€ *Les Fontaines*, 24 Rue André-Benac, ☎ 05 56 61 15 25. A very pretty place with a fountain and excellent-value cooking.

33490 ST-MACAIRE

€ *L'Abricotier* (off the N113 east of St-Macaire), ☎ 05 56 76 83 63. Fresh local ingredients and personal presentation. Charming and inexpensive.

The wines of Entre-deux-Mers

These include all categories—red, rosé, dry and sweet whites—and are divided between several *appellations*. The *Premières Côtes-de-Bordeaux*, between Floirac and St-Macaire along the Garonne, produce quality reds from Merlot, Cabernet Sauvignon and Cabernet Franc grapes, combined with a small amount of Petit-Verdot, Malbec or Carmenère. The whites are produced principally from Sauvignon, Sémillon and Muscadelle. The *AOC Entre-Deux-Mers*, the major part of the region up to the Dordogne, covers exclusively dry white wines, and *Haut-Benauge*, a pocket around Langon, sweet and dry whites. *Graves-de-Vayres*, on the Dordogne, is a small *AOC* of red and sweet white. *Ste-Foy Bordeaux* in the northeast of the region produces all categories, and sweet whites are produced at Cadillac, Loupiac, Ste-Croix-du-Mont and St-Macaire, on the Garonne. For further information, contact the Maison des Vins, 4 Rue de l'Abbaye, BP 6, 33670, La Sauve, ☎ 05 57 34 32 12, fax 05 57 34 32 38.

The *bastide* of **Créon**, on the D671, was established by the English seneschal, Amaury de Craon, in 1315, in the reign of Edward II, and soon flourished at the expense of La Sauve abbey (see below). Oval in shape, it has the classic features of a *bastide*—a large central square with arcades and parallel streets—but the walls built in the 14C have long gone. Northeast of Créon are the ruins of a 14C watermill at Daignac, and another at Espiet, the 14C **Moulin Neuf** on Gallo-Roman foundations, has been converted and is inhabited.

Abbaye La Sauve Majeure

From its hilltop, the church tower beckons to the magnificent ruins of the abbey of La Sauve Majeure, one of the highlights of the Bordelais on the D671. Open June–Sept daily 10.00–18.30; Oct–May Tues–Sun 10.00–12.30, 14.30–17.30, until 18.00 Sun; closed 1 Jan, 1 May, 1 and 11 Nov, 25 Dec, ☎ 05 56 23 01 55.

Gérard, Abbot of Cluny, came to the heart of the *sylva major* (great forest) in 1079 where a simple oratory, established earlier by a hermit, stood near the ruins of a castle on the pilgrimage route to Spain. On 11 May 1080 Gérard, with Guillaume VII, Duke of Gascony, laid the first stone of the future abbey of La Sauve-Majeure. Well funded and well organised, by the time of Gérard's death in 1095 there were some 300 monks and many affiliated priories. In the safety of the shadow of the abbey, a secular community, now the village of La Sauve, developed around a parish church dedicated to St-Pierre, which was begun in 1083 by Gérard. The founder-abbot was canonised in 1197, and among those who came to venerate the relics of St Gérard were Henry II, Eleanor of Aquitaine and Thomas Becket. The abbey was attacked and badly damaged in 1179, but not repaired until 1219–31, and in 1369 it was fortified. The death knell for the abbey tolled in the 16C, when it was place *in commendam* (the tenure was passed to an absentee landlord). The Congregation of

St-Maur (founded after the Reformation and religious wars to assist religious communities that had been put *in commendam*) took it over in 1660 but ran out of funds. An earthquake caused further damage in 1759. The property was confiscated at the Revolution but the relics were saved and translated to Bordeaux. The building, used as a school, went up in flames in 1910 and was more or less neglected until 1952, when work began to consolidate the ruins.

The visit begins in a later conventual building with displays and a bookshop. The abbey was laid out in the Benedictine manner with the cloister and monastic buildings south of the church. The cloister is now just a shadow and what is left of the abbey buildings is mainly 17C. Despite all the abuse, the remains of the abbey church resonate with the beauty of the original and much good Romanesque carving has survived.

The north transept and choir are the most complete parts, and from the exterior the three parallel apses and transept chapels are remarkably intact, despite the lack of cornice and roof on the main chapel, which is divided into three by pillar buttresses. Each segment has three levels, plain base, round-headed window and blind arcade above. The side apses are much smaller and simpler. The fragments of the west façade suggest it was inspired by the Saintonge. Because the ruin is open to the sky the **belltower** (which can be climbed) is omnipresent. It stands unusually over the fourth bay of the south aisle, square in the lower level and octagonal above, the second level pierced on seven sides by large 13C twin windows with triple-moulded arches. The third level has single trefoil openings and is topped off with the remains of an open parapet, but the spire has gone. The aisled nave, open and uncovered, was higher in the central part and was no doubt enclosed to create an extended chancel, as at Albi or Auch (see pp 311 and 385). The nave was preceded by a narthex.

The eastern part of the church is the best conserved and the most decorated, and provides a pure illustration of Romanesque architecture. The large square **choir** is succeeded by a semi-circular apse. The choir vaults have disappeared, but part of the extreme eastern semi-dome has survived. The choir is on two levels. The ground level has small round-headed arcades linking the smaller side chapels to the choir and the eastern bay rests on squat but enormously powerful round pillars. The twin bays of the upper choir are repeated in the transept. The apse has three large Romanesque windows flanked by small columns with a very stylised acanthus-leaf motif extending into string courses. The mass of masonry and clear-cut shapes convey a tremendous impression of solidity and the choir, when decked out in fine funishings, must have been breathtaking. The south wall of the south arm of the transept has disappeared, but the north survives

Of the 34 **Romanesque capitals** that have survived more or less intact, the iconography is varied, including five Old and two New Testament themes, fabulous

Abbaye La Sauve Majeure

creatures and foliage. The carvings may not be as masterly as those at Moissac or Conques, but are still memorable. The most celebrated, in the last bay of the south aisle, are four scenes from the *Beheading of St John the Baptist*, including *Salome's Dance*, where in a small space below the table the dancer's body is arched seductively while she hangs on to the table edge for support. The space is used skilfully, the expression acutely observed and the scene packed with anecdotal detail. Episodes from the *Life of Samson* are on the south of the first apsidal chapel, including a nonchalant long-haired *Samson carrying One of the Gates of Gaza*, *Samson overcoming the Lion*, animal larger than man, and *Samson with Delilah*, who is wielding what look like sheep shears. Adjacent is *Daniel in the Lions' Den*, with the prophet meditating fearlessly between two snarling (or smiling) lions. On the north side of the north chapel is Adam and Eve, or *Original Sin*, a less busy composition, with the tree and serpent on the extreme right, a rather unsexy Eve tempting Adam, Eve after giving birth and Adam looking sad. In the southeast bay of the choir are scenes from the *Temptation of Christ*, including Christ emerging from a tower (more like a chimneypot) and the Devil pointing index finger downwards. The *Sacrifice of Abraham* in the last bay of the nave, south, is a more naive work, with Sarah learning that she will have a child, Abraham grasping the sword and an angel grasping his arm, and another angel arriving with the sacrifical ram. The capitals of the round pillars carry fierce combats between fabulous beasts, and in the north chapel apse are two scenes of *Ulysses and the Sirens*. There are many wondrous animals, a variety of lions, and finely chiselled plant motifs. Note also the abaci beautifully carved with decorative motifs.

The Gallo-Roman *castrum Riuncium* (built on the rock) on the banks of the Garonne south of La Sauve became the tiny medieval fortified town of **Rions**. Its fortifications were destroyed in 1295, and Edward I encouraged their rebuilding which began in 1330. By 1379 Rions was affiliated to Bordeaux as part of a defensive league with Cadillac, St-Macaire and others and by the 15C came under the control of the Albret family (see p 122). It experienced more hassle in the 16C–17C, and in 1814, when the English were returning from the Napoleonic wars in Spain under Marshall Beresford, the Rionais defended themselves from within their ramparts. Later in the 19C there was a local struggle to save the old town, and most of the 14C fortifications are still standing.

Cadillac

On the right bank of the Garonne, on the D10, Cadillac is a small *bastide* with a whacking great castle, which is the main point for going there. The town, founded in 1280 by Edward I's man, Jean de Grailly, prospered from shipping, especially of wine. Of the fortifications, begun in 1315, two of the four gates and quite a chunk of the triangular ramparts and round towers are still standing. Inside the town gates are several 15C and 16C houses, and a 19C covered market. In the church of **St-Blaise and St-Martin** is the chapel of St-Blaise which was built to contain the grandiose tomb commissioned from Pierre Biard in 1597 by Jean-Louis Nogaret de la Valette for his wife, Marguerite de Foix Candale (d. 1593). The exterior of the chapel is dated 1606, probably the date of the completion of the work, but only the white stone and black marble screen still stands following the demolition of the mausoleum in 1793. The bronze winged figure that crowned the tomb, *Renommée (Fame)* by Pierre Biard (1606), was saved at the Revolution and resides in the Louvre, with a copy in the National Gallery, London.

The **Château des Ducs d'Epernon** is now a cavernous place spoilt by many transformations, and a huge effort is needed to imagine how it was originally. Much is made of its dual role—17C palace and 19C prison. Open daily July, Aug, 09.30–13.00 and 14.00–19.00; April–June and Sept 09.30–12.30 and 14.00–18.00, closed Mon; Oct–March 10.00–12.00 and 14.00–17.30, closed Mon and 1 Jan, 1 May, 1 and 11 November, 25 December; ☎ 05 56 62 69 58.

The old feudal castle was entirely rebuilt from 1599 by the Governor of Guyenne, Jean-Louis de Nogaret de la Valette (1554–1642), Duc d'Epernon and *mignon* (favourite) of Henri III. Epernon married Marguerite de Foix-Candale, and with her came the *seigneurie* of Cadillac complete with castle (*c* 14C). Epernon's meteoric rise to power was a thorn in the flesh to Henri IV, who encouraged him to invest his considerable fortune in a grand residence distanced from Paris. Construction began in 1598, possibly to plans by Pierre Biard, although Pierre Souffron directed the work at first (1599–1603) and Gilles de La Touche until 1616, but it was not completed until *c* 1634. The new château was designed as a classic U-shaped block around a courtyard, closed by a screen wall and with a monumental gateway. The main façade, away from the courtyard, overlooked a formal flower garden. Epernon died ruined, and the second duke had no heirs, so the property passed to the Preissac family, who partly demolished the building to transform it into something more fashionable. It was eviscerated at the Revolution and turned into a women's prison and house of correction (1819–22); more structural alterations were carried out in 1865. Its doors were finally closed in 1952.

The entrance façade and lodge were rebuilt to suit the needs of the prison, and in the 19C the courtyard was planted with trees, now cleared. Around the **courtyard**, only the main building and the angle pavilions, notably the left-hand one with the tall roofs, are remotely as they were after the first building campaign. The right-hand one (*c* 1635) is more severe. The extensions were rebuilt in the 19C. The **garden façade** is the result of two building campaigns, of the late 16C and early 17C. Large pavilions which used to frame the main block were destroyed in the 18C leaving only the lower part and the stair block. The garden was restored in the 1980s.

The main block consists of series of apartments flanking the staircase on two levels. Inside, the main relics of the 17C décor are some of the 20 original **fireplaces** decorated in marble, stucco and gilt, the grandest with Michelangelesque figures. On the ground floor are the remains of beautiful 17C painted ceilings, some modern repro-

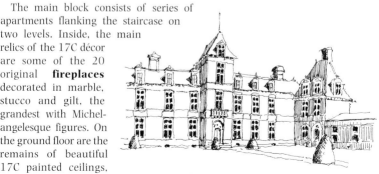

Château des Ducs d'Epernon, Cadillac

ductions of painted décor, and monumental fireplaces in the **Appartements de Madame**. The Salle de la Reine on the other side of the stairs was transformed into a chapel for the prison inmates, although again the fire surrounds have survived here and in the adjacent antechamber. **L'Appartement du Roi** on the first floor was the most sumptuous of all, but the prison and a fire in 1928 did it no favours. The best of the decorated fire surrounds, in the antechamber, sculpted in 1606 by Jean Langlois and Jean and Joseph Richier, is still partly intact and depicts Fame surrounded by trophies, with damaged stuccos with sculptures in the round of reclining and standing figures (inspired by the Pitti Palace, Florence). There is a display concerning the history of the prison. The **basements** were originally kitchens and possibly accommodated a tapestry workshop for Claude de Lapierre, who created a vast series of the life of Henri III (only two of 22 remain, one in Cadillac and one in the Louvre); they were reused as kitchens and refectory in the 19C. There is a remarkable cantilevered spiral staircase. The garden can be visited.

On the Garonne at **Loupiac**, on the D10, are interesting remains of a Gallo-Roman villa and baths (2C–5C), with mosaics. (This is private property; open Sun 14.00–18.00; at other times telephone in advance: ☎ 05 56 62 93 82/ mobile 06 07 01 64 88.) The restored Romanesque church has a three-tier west façade in the Saintonge style and a *chevet*.

Verdelais, further south, was an important centre of pilgrimage, especially for sailors. The object of veneration in the church is the *Virgin of Verdelais*, a statue (12C or 14C) in a niche in a red-marble retable (1665). The walls of the church are covered with curious naive ex-votos and plaques dating from the 17C onwards. In the churchyard at the foot of the Stations of the Cross is the tomb of Toulouse-Lautrec (see below). The **Domaine de Malagar**, on the D19 between Verdelais and St-Macaire, high in vineyards, was the country home of the novelist François Mauriac (1885–1970). Open June–Sept, Wed–Mon 10.00–12.30 and 14.00–18.00, closed Tues; Oct–Mar, Wed–Fri 14.00–17.00, Sat, Sun and PH 10.00–12.30 and 14.00–18.00; ☎ 05 57 98 17 17. A charming, simple house overlooking vineyards, it is something of a shrine and has been kept as it was in the writer's time. Mauriac enjoyed coming to Malagar and wrote *Le Noeud de Vipères* here; many of his novels are set in the landscapes of the Gironde and Landes. The visit also includes the gardens and *chais*.

A little further north, just off the D672, is the **Château de Malromé**, former home of Adèle de Toulouse-Lautrec, mother of the painter Henri de Toulouse-Lautrec. Guided visits July, Aug daily 10.00–12.00 and 14.00–18.30; April–June, Sept–Nov, Thur–Sat 15.00, 16.00, 17.00, Sun and PH 10.00–12.00 and 14.00–18.30; ☎ 05 56 76 44 92. Malromé now has no connection with the family (see p 314), but profits from the legend of Lautrec, who died here on 9 September 1901. From 1883, while his mother lived here, the painter visited regularly, while at the end of his life he lived in Bordeaux and Arcachon. Adèle owned the château until her death in 1930. Malromé, built in the 14C, stands four-square around a courtyard and was altered many times, receiving a neo-Gothic facelift in 1850. It has important wine cellars and considerable vineyards. The visit includes rooms renovated in 1996 in neo-Renaissance style emulating the 1850s–70s, with period furniture and tapestries of the type Lautrec would have known.

St-Macaire

With tightly packed houses and narrow streets, the little town of St-Macaire, set on a high point above the Garonne, is charmingly locked in a time warp. The story goes that a disciple of St Martin (d. 397), a Greek called Makarios, came to the ancient site of Ligena in the 4C–5C, but the town's real beginnings were in the 11C around the Benedictine community. Just inside the old fortified gate and town clocktower, **Porte de Benauge** (14C), is a crossroads with some fine Renaissance houses, to the left an hotel and to the right the *maison du pays* in a 16C shop. Straight ahead is Rue de l'Eglise leading to the church (see below), and the street to the right led to the château. The road to the left brings you to the narrow rectangular **Place du Mercadiou** (market place) which has not been too prettified and has kept its medieval allure, surrounded by diverse arcades and a variety of façades (13C–16C). Notable is the mansion with a tower called the *relais de poste*.

The town grew very rich during the English occupation of Aquitaine and this wealth produced two consecutive fortified *faubourgs* (13C and 14C), with the Mercadiou at the core of the earlier development. East of the *place* is the **Turon gate**, part of the 14C barbican, near which is a 19C *lavoir*. This was the route to the river port, and the water once lapped the walls, but the landscape and the fortunes of St-Macaire changed radically in the 18C when the course of the Garonne shifted, leaving the port high and dry. Rich merchants had already begun to abandon the town for Bordeaux in the 17C and by the 19C it was practically deserted, relying on cooperage and stone quarrying for its livelihood.

The **priory**, southwest of the Mercadiou, was founded in the 12C. In the little garden to the south is a 12C colonnade which is all that remains of the rectangular cloister squeezed in between the 11C ramparts and the church. Part of the refectory is also standing, with cellars beneath and monks' cells above (restored in 1968). The church of **St-Sauveur** is large and unusual and much altered since the 12C. It has a tripartite Romanesque *chevet* with a little decoration and the tower is placed against the northeast flank of the nave. The 14C west front, with a 15C rose window, is decorated with angels around the door and Christ, the Virgin and St John with the Apostles in the tympanum. Either side are saints in trefoil arcades. The nave has four square bays and is covered by 17C vaults, whereas the apses are half-domed and the crossing has massive piers as if to receive a dome. There are one or two coloured Romanesque capitals and an extensive programme of painted decoration on the east vaults, carried out in the second half of the 13C and indifferently restored in 1825. As they are now, they consist of a *Trinity* in the central mandorla, from which flows the River of Life between the Ox of St Luke and the Lion of St Mark. The left-hand mandorla contains *Celestial Jerusalem* and the right the *Lamb receiving the Book of Seven Seals* from Revelations, and the *Story of St Catherine and the Wise and Foolish Virgins*. West of the church is a section of the medieval ramparts and views of the Garonne, and further west still is the Poterne de Corne (postern gate) against the Maison Messidan, which has exceptional cellars. At the extreme west is the Porte Rendesse.

Between St-Macaire and La Réole to the east is a small church at **St-Martin-de-Sescas** with a commendable Romanesque portal and decorated *chevet*. The 12C south door has finely sculpted voussoir blocks supported by slender columns. North of La Réole on the Dropt River, via the D670 and D126, are 12 **locks and mills**, including two which are fortified, at Loubens (possibly part 11C) and Bagas (14C).

La Réole

La Réole is built on a slope which ends at a cliff high above the Garonne. At the top is the former Benedictine priory which is best viewed from the remarkable suspension bridge spanning the river, and best understood from the Esplanade du Général-de-Gaulle next to the priory at the top, where there is parking.

La Réole became Regula in the 10C after the monks who adhered to the rule of St Benedict re-established a monastery here dependent on the abbey of Fleury-sur-Loire. The town was built around the monastery and received its charter in 977. On the Franco-English border, it prospered during the English occupation of Guyenne and was enclosed in a succession of protective walls (12C–13C and 15C). A château was built by Henry III Plantagenet and it was an important river port.

The parish church of **St-Pierre** on Place Rigoulet, north of the priory, was built for the priory at the end of the 12C, underwent some rebuilding during the 13C and was knocked about by the Protestants in 1577. Renovations were carried out in 1608 and *c* 1687–90 the sexpartite vaults were introduced and the walls raised. The church was emptied out at the Revolution and many of the furnishings went to Bordelais churches, including much masterly ironwork by Blaise Charlut. The entrance is through the Flamboyant north transept door. Most of the church is Gothic, including the wide nave with no aisles and the five-sided apse with 17C alterations. Of the old church, one Romanesque capital is re-used in the south of the chancel, while the south transept chapel and the southern rose window are 15C. The *Marriage of the Virgin* (1666) is signed by the Spanish painter from Seville, Valdès-Léal.

To the west of the *place* are the remains of the important English castle (1230–45), the **Château des Quat'Sos**, meaning four sisters, a reference to the four English-style round angle towers. Beseiged many times, it was finally dismantled in 1629 and now consists of just one complete tower dominating the ravine and the stumps of two others.

The Benedictine **priory** (begun 1704) by Maurice Mazey took about 50 years to build. It is now occupied by the *services publics* and there is a library and small museum in the vaulted basement on the south side. A corridor running north to south alongside the cloister is closed at each end by very fine wrought-iron gates, the work of Charlut, who was also responsible for the balustrades on the south. The façade towards the Garonne is a fine example of Louis XIV style and is graced with a double flight of steps. Inside on the east–west corridor is a staircase with a balcony on which Instruments of the Passion are carved, and a wooden ceiling painted with *St Benedict in Ecstasy*. Another elegant monumental staircase in the east is lit by a lantern opening and there is an agreeable 17C garden court.

North of St-Pierre, at the end of Rue Peysseguin, is the most ancient building in town, the **Hotel de Ville** (11C–12C), a rare example of a civic building of this period. It was built on the orders of Richard the Lionheart and reworked in the 14C/15C. The lower part is the *halle* or market, where massive columns with robust capitals support triple arcades, and is open to the east. A staircase on the south leads up to a large open room the length of the building, empty apart from a Flamboyant gallery and a fireplace. A huge beam suggests it was once divided horizontally. It is lit by six twin-bay round-headed openings on the east side and divided by columns, while windows of a variety of designs pierce the other façades. It is due for renovation and usually open for special exhibitions. There are interesting façades in the streets on the way down to Place de la Libération such as Rue Amand-Caduc, where the metal forger, Charlut, lived at 88 Rue Bellot-de-Minière. Take Avenue du Pimpin east of the town to see parts of the ramparts.

Three English *bastides* form a triangle in the eastern part of Entre-Deux-Mers. In 1283 Edward I took the opportunity to found **Sauveterre-de-Guyenne** on the road linking the Dordogne and the Garonne. The walls were demolished in 1814, but the main gates at the four points of the compass still span the axes leading to the centre. There are houses in timber and brick as well as in stone, and wide *couverts* around the square. The church is part 13C, part 19C. There already existed a *castrum* or castle at **Pellegrue** in 1242 and the 12C church was built on the earlier foundations. In the centre of this tiny community the iron market hall dates to 1913, and the simple church, much repaired, has a 19C bell tower. **Monségur**, on the D668 northeast of La Réole, was an English *bastide* founded by Henry III's queen, Eleanor of Provence, in 1265 on a terrace above the Dropt. Protected by strong walls it nevertheless suffered badly during both the Hundred Years War and the Wars of Religion. Place du Marché is endowed with an elegant glazed *halle* (1867–97). The church is Gothic, its door 14C.

    Blasimon, north of Sauveterre on the D17, belongs to the last period (1317–22) of *bastide* building in Entre-Deux-Mers. The project was never really completed. From the neo-Gothic chapel on the edge of town, the road descends to the hidden and isolated abbey, established before the *bastide*, in 1170. This was a dependence of La Sauve Majeure. The monastic buildings are mainly in ruins, burned by the Protestants in 1587, but the church is a delight for its portal carrying high-relief decoration which, from a distance, looks as fragile as icing sugar. The west front is divided into three by tall pairs of engaged columns supporting a decorative cornice and a *clocher-pignon* (a belfry extending from the wall). The central door is framed by five colums and capitals from which spring five successive arches decorated with hunting scenes and the Vices and Virtues. Flanking the main door are two smaller blind arcades. The interior is very simple, and the remains of the cloister deserve a glance. There are two water mills near Blasimon on the Gamage River, the Moulin de Labarthe (14C with 16C tower), and Moulin de la Borie (13C) near the small lake.

GRAVES

· · · · · · · · ·

An area south of Bordeaux, 60km long by 14.5km wide, defined by the Garonne to the east and the Landes to the west, is known as the Graves. This is the oldest and arguably the most prestigious wine-producing area of the Bordelais, and includes Sauterne and Barsac. Highlights of the region are the châteaux of La Brède, Roquetaillade and Cazeneuve, the wrecked château of Villandraut, and the cathedral of Bazas.

    The birthplace of the writer, Montesquieu (see below), **Château La Brède**, reached from Junction 1 off the A62, has barely changed since the great man's time. Guided visits July–Sept, Mon, Wed–Sun 14.00–18.00, closed Tues; April–June, Sat, Sun and PH, 14.00–18.00; Oct–mid-Nov, Sat, Sun and PH 14.00–17.30; ☎ 05 56 20 20 49. An austere building, it is the result of alterations

Getting there and around
Car
The A62 runs through the Graves; D932 to Bazas; D8/D3 for Sauternes and Villandraut.
Train
Bordeaux to Langon and Bazas.

Tourist information
33430 Bazas 1 Pl. de la Cathédrale, ☎ 56 65 06 66
33210 Langon Allée Jean-Jaurès, ☎ 05 56 63 68 00, fax 05 56 63 68 09
33210 Sauternes 11 Rue Principale, ☎ 05 56 76 69 13, fax 05 56 76 63 08
33730 Villandraut Pl. du Général du Gaulle, ☎ 05 56 25 31 39, fax 05 56 25 89 33
Market days
Bazas Saturday
Langon Friday, Saturday

 Festivals and events
February/March Traditional *fêtes* including the *Boeufs gras* featuring the local Bazardais cattle, held on the Thursday before Carnival, Bazas
October Historic film festival, Pessac

Where to stay and eating out
33720 BARSAC
☆☆☆ *Château Hotel de Valmont*, 22 Rue de la Gare, ☎ 05 56 27 28 24, fax 05 56 27 17 53. Very attractive place with 12 rooms and a restaurant.

33430 BAZAS
☆☆☆ *Domaine de Fompeyre*, Rte de Mont-de-Marsan, ☎ 05 56 25 98 00, fax 05 56 25 16 25. Typical Gascon house in a large park, with pretty rooms and heated pool.
☆☆ *Hostellerie-Saint-Sauveur*, 14 Cours du Gen.-de-Gaulle, ☎ 05 56 25 12 18. Inexpensive.
€ *Ferme-Auberge Houn Barrade*, Rte de Pau (4km south of Bazas), ☎ 05 56 25 44 55. Real country atmosphere and country fare.
€ *Les Remparts*, Pl. de la Cathédrale, ☎ 05 56 25 95 24. Regional cuisine, including local Bazas beef, served on a shady terrace overlooking the ramparts.

33210 LANGON
☆☆☆ *Claude Darroze*, 95 Cours du Gen.-Leclerc, ☎ 05 56 63 00 48, fax 05 56 63 41 15. Hotel-restaurant that is three-star in every way: an 18C mansion serving wonderful food, with a terrace.
☆☆ *Horus*, 2 Rue des Bruyeres, ☎ 05 56 62 36 37, fax 05 56 63 09 99. Moderately priced rooms and food.

33210 SAUTERNES
€€ *Le Saprien*, ☎ 05 56 76 60 87. A gastronomic restaurant with an excellent reputation.
€ *L'Auberge des Vignes*, ☎ 05 56 76 60 06. Recently changed ownership but the standard remains high.

made in 1419 to a fortress dating back to the 12C. The moat reflects the remainders of an earlier fort: a 13C keep containing the library, pepper-pot towers and fortifications. Footbridges replace three drawbridges. In 1404 Pope Boniface IX authorised a new chapel. The château passed to the Montesquieu family in 1686, and the park was landscaped in the English manner by the writer in the 18C. From the entrance hall with fine wooden twisted columns, the visit takes you to the Grand Salon with portraits of Montesquieu's relatives, and memorabilia. His study bedroom contains 17C furniture, notably his four-poster bed. On the floor above is the library with an impressive chestnut ceiling and mural.

Near Portets, to the east on the N113, is the **Château de Mongenan**. Guided visits daily July–mid-Sept 10.00–19.00; rest of year 14.00–19.00, but best to check in advance; closed Jan–Feb; ☎ 05 56 67 18 11. Built in 1736, it is surrounded by unruly botanic gardens and has a small museum of traditional

Montesquieu

Charles Louis Secondat de Montesquieu, Baron de La Brède (1689–1755), deeply Gascon and a countryman at heart, is known universally as a writer and philosopher of the Age of Enlightenment. He was trained in law and appointed to the *parlement*, rising to the post of Président du Parlement in 1716. His boundless intellectual curiosity led him to carry out research at the Academy of Science, and in 1711 he began his first literary work, *Lettres persanes*, a satire on French society (completed in 1721). He was an ardent democrat, tireless traveller, frequent visitor to the court and literary salons in Paris, and especially favoured England, perhaps because the wine from his vineyards was much appreciated in the British Empire. Jeanne de Lartigue, whom he married in 1715, brought a healthy dowry and property, enabling Montesquieu to abandon his legal work in favour of his vines and writing. His *L'Esprit des Lois* (1748) was the inspiration behind the Constitution of 1791.

arts and costumes, and an 18C Masonic lodge. It is filled with reminders of Jean-Jacques Rousseau, who spent time in the Gironde *c* 1740.

The **Château de Malle** near Preignac, built at the beginning of the 17C by Jacques de Malle, a Bordelais magistrate, is a superbly elegant residence set in the midst of a park and vineyards. Guided visits daily April–end Oct, 10.00–12.00 and 14.00–19.00; ☎ 05 56 62 36 86. The main block consists of a central pavilion in the style of Louis XIV with a hipped roof and rounded pediments and low wings ending in round towers. There is a pronounced Italian influence in the

The wines of Graves

One of the best known *appellations* of Bordeaux, the region stretches from Blanquefort, north of the city, almost as far as Langon, bounded to the east by the Garonne and to the west by the Landes forests. The region prospered in the 14C as the English passion for claret (from *clairet*) developed. Graves is more diversified than Médoc, producing red and dry white wines, as well as a sweeter or medium sweet white wine. There are three distinct *AOCs*: *Graves* and *Pessac-Léognan*, which produce both red and dry white wines, and *Graves Supérieures*, reserved for sweet whites. The wine became known as Graves because of the gravelly clay soil: its surface of white quartz pebbles reflects the sun's rays, helping the ripening process. The reds are blended from Cabernets Sauvignon and Franc, Merlot, and lesser quantities of Malbec and Petit-Verdot; the white grape varieties are Sémillon, Sauvignon, and a small amount of Muscadelle. The great sweet whites of Barsac and Sauternes are produced in a small area along the valley of the Ciron River, where in autumn the early morning mists dispelled by warm sunshine are essential for producing the *pourriture noble* (noble rot, see p 31).

The Conseil des Vins de Graves, at **Maison des Vins de Graves**, produces a booklet and will provide information on visits to wine châteaux; 61 Cours du Maréchal-Foch, BP 51, 33720 Podensac; ☎ 05 56 27 09 25, fax 05 56 27 17 36. The **Maison de Sauternes**, Pl. de la Mairie, ☎ 05 56 76 69 83, the **Maison de Barsac**, Pl. de l'Eglise, Barsac, ☎ 05 56 27 15 44, and the tourist information office at Sauternes (11 Rue Principale, ☎ 05 56 76 69 13) will also provide advice.

succession of terraces leading to a small open-air theatre decorated with characters from the *commedia dell'arte*.

Langon is the main town of southern Gironde, at the highest point that the river is tidal.

The doyen among the wine châteaux of the Bordelais is **Château d'Yquem**, south of the A62, owned by the Lur-Saluces. This was the first wine to be classified as *premier cru supérieur* in 1855. With 100ha, it produces only nine hectolitres per hectare, which represents about a third or a quarter of the yield in a Médoc estate. Applications to visit the cellars (not the château) should be made in writing three weeks in advance of the intended visit; state your name, the date, the reason for the visit and the number of people (no more than 20); visits are Mon–Fri 14.00 and 15.30; wine is not sold directly but through dealers; www.chateau-Yquem.fr. The route to the château is indicated from Sauternes.

The ruined **Château de Villandraut**, further up the Ciron at the junction of the D3 and D8, was the prototype of the *châteaux Clementins*. Guided visits daily July, Aug 10.00–19.00; May–Sept 10.00–12.30 and 14.00–19.00; Oct–Apr 14.00–17.30; ☎ 05 56 25 87 57. Begun in 1306 by Pope Clement V, it combined defence and comfort and was built by English masons who had worked for Edward I in Wales. It was systematically protected by towers and arrow slits at different levels. The walls marked out a large empty interior space, without a keep, in which the pontifical palace could develop. It has not, thankfully, been renovated and the visit to the ruins includes a climb to the top of one of the six towers, conserved on three floors, and the fortified walkway. Superb fireplaces and deep vaulted cellars have also survived. The influence on Roquetaillade is obvious, but Villandraut was larger, rectangular and more refined. On the edge of Sauternes, the ruined **Château de Budos**, built *c* 1308 by Cardinal Gaillard de la Mothe, nephew of Clement V, was a refinement on Villandraut.

Bertrand de Got

Bertrand de Got (1264–1314) was born into the lesser nobility near Villandraut or Uzeste. He entered the priesthood in 1289 and rose rapidly, becoming Bishop of Comminges in 1294 (see p 492), and was appointed to the bishopric in Bordeaux in 1299. With the backing of Philippe IV he was elected pope by the Sacred College on 5 June 1305, and took the name Clement V. Due to the volatile situation in Rome, he returned to Aquitaine and in February 1306 began the château at Villandraut. He gave permission for his nephews to build châteaux in the Bazadais, known as the *châteaux Clementins*, including Castets-en-Dorthe (private), Fargues (ruins), Budos (ruins), La Trave (ruins, near Préchac, open to public) and Roquetaillade (open). Philippe IV drew Clement V into the indictment of the Templars and in 1309 the proceedings took place in Avignon, a neutral territory belonging to the Holy See. Subsequently the Pope remained in Avignon and established a papal court there. The Templars were suppressed but not condemned, their goods transferred to the Order of St John of Jerusalem. Already a sick man, Clement V started the journey back to Bordeaux in 1314, but died before reaching his destination. He was buried at Uzeste.

Château de Roquetaillade

The Château de Roquetaillade at Mazères, on the D125 from Sauternes, is a showpiece medieval castle which, for some 700 years, has been handed down through the same family. Open July, Aug daily 10.30–19.00; Easter–11 Nov afternoons only; 11 Nov–Easter afternoons on Sun, PH and school holidays; ☎ 05 56 76 14 16. Guided visits to the house in French and English.

High and visible, Roquetaillade literally means 'carved from the rock' and is two separate forts (12C–14C and 14C). It is unique because in the 19C the arch Gothicist, Viollet-le-Duc was persuaded to transform it. The grounds, which are open, consist of an English-style park and a delightful **farm museum**, with Bazardais cows, old farm equipment, and rooms typical of farmhouses in the 19C and 20C.

The old castle, part of which is still standing, was built piecemeal between the 12C and 14C. The adjacent later castle, begun in 1306 by Cardinal Gaillard de la Mothe, nephew of Pope Clement V, was conceived of as a whole and embraced innovations in fortified architecture introduced with the English, for example the central square keep, six round angle towers and crenellations. The new castle combined a degree of comfort and strong protection, and is the only complete survivor of the five Clementine fortress-palaces. The de la Mothe family supported the Anglo-Gascon alliance. In recognition, Gaillard de la Mothe received in 1313 the Archdeaconry of Oxford, but did not take it up and therefore did not receive the accompanying stipend. Lengthy proceedings over the non-payment ensued (1326–47), which ended when the French repossessed Aquitaine. The property was regularly transferred through the female line, and in 1552 Catherine de la Mothe married into the de Lansac family, who added Renaissance features. The property stayed in the family during the Revolution, and passed in 1807 to the de Mauvesin. By 1793 it was in a parlous state. The de Mauvesin, desiring a setting compatible with their status and considerable means, invited the celebrated Viollet-le-Duc to transform it. He never normally worked in the private sector but accepted in collaboration with Edmond Duthoit, and two campaigns of work followed (1866–70 and 1874–78) during which the structure was consolidated and a Gothic revivalist décor introduced. It was never completed, but detailed preparatory drawings have survived. In 1882 the last of the de Mauvesin bequeathed Roquetaillade to a cousin, Hippolyte de Baritault, whose descendants still own it.

Sections of the 12C walls and a gateway, which protected the village surrounding the castle until the end of the feudal era, still exist. The 12C **chapel** was restored and exotically decorated by Duthoit (1875–78) by combining Gothic, Arabic and Sicilian elements. The picturesque remains of the **Château Vieux** include the keep (13C), gateway tower (12C–13C) and the large hall (early 14C). Although the layout of the **Château Neuf** has not essentially altered since the 14C, the elevations were 'medievalised' in the 19C with the addition of machicolations, merlons, extra crenellations, trefoil windows and the neo-Gothic loggia on the north side bearing family coats of arms. The drop bridge over the dry moat leads through the fortified doorway in the west elevation, virtually unaltered since the 14C, with crenellations and latrines. The low arrow slits in *croix pattée* were an English innovation to accommodate crossbows. The 38m-high square keep or donjon is tall enough to survey the surrounding country, and slightly off-centre to make room for a small courtyard.

Viollet-le-Duc's designs are the highlight of the visit to the interior. His ambition to create a monumental staircase was realised in Roquetaillade's keep in 1867, when he replaced original wooden steps with a stone flight. Note the headstops over the entrance which carry the likenesses of the patrons, the architect, and Empress Eugénie. The **dining room** (1868), created from the old stables, uses metal decoratively and combines it with painted stylised trailing greenery. All the neo-Gothic furniture was designed by Viollet. The delightful bedrooms, the work of Duthoit under the supervision of Viollet, date from 1868–69, when painted décor was the height of fashion. Original fabrics in the **Chambre Rose** were replicated in Lyons a few years ago.

The **hall** has 14C vaulting and leads to the grand early 17C **Salle Synodale** with the most impressive chimneypiece of its period (19C) in southwest France, similar to two in the Château de Cadillac. This room should have been the triumph of Viollet's projects at Roquetaillade, but work was brought to a halt because in 1870 the de Mauvesin's fortunes melted away as phylloxera engulfed their vines. Other rooms include La Chambre de Tante Marthe in the style of Napoléon III (1850s), the Cabinet Viollet-le-Duc for Madame de Mauvesin, the Grand Salon with another chimneypiece of 1635, and the Chambre du Cardinal of the Renaissance era.

Eugène-Emanuel Viollet-le-Duc

Archaeologist, writer, theoretician, restorer and architect, Eugène-Emanuel Viollet-le-Duc (1814–79) began his career at 26 when he was put in charge of the restoration of the church of the Madeleine in Vézelay (Burgundy). He was given the job by Prosper Merimée (1803–70), the first *Inspecteur général des monuments historiques*, a post created in 1830 to safeguard the national heritage. Later, Viollet-le-Duc succeeded Merimée in this role. He probably did more than anyone else in the 19C to save France's heritage but, like George Gilbert Scott and others in England, he was much criticised in the 20C for his creative restorations, although the tide has now turned and his efforts are seen more favourably. Largely self-taught, his revivalist tendencies were fired by Victor Hugo and the archaeologist Arcisse de Caumont. He was involved in a number of restoration assignments in Paris and in the southwest, notably at St-Sernin in Toulouse, St-André in Bordeaux, Moissac and the Château de Roquetaillade. He published learned works on Gothic architecture, the *Dictionnaire raisonné de l'architecture française* (1854–68) and *Entretiens* (in two volumes, 1863 and 1872).

The modest village of **Uzeste** on the D222 southeast of Villandraut has an imposing collegiate church dedicated to the Virgin and selected by Pope Clement V to contain his tomb (the church is usually open but ☎ 05 56 25 87 48 to check; guided visits 15 April–15 Oct, Sat, Sun 15.00–18.00). Pilgrims had gathered here to venerate the Virgin since the 12C, but it was suitably transformed in the 14C to receive the Pope's remains. The belfry is 15C but the steeple is 19C, as are the stained-glass windows. Over the south door (entrance) is a worn image, once coloured, of the *Coronation of the Virgin*. Inside, the wide nave is flanked by alternate piers and columns, with two massive cylindrical piers at the west, and a high choir precedes a fairly shallow five-sided apse with ambulatory. The Pope's tomb, now behind the altar, was damaged and his remains burned in 1572 during the Wars of Religion. The monument, scrupulously sculpted by Jehan de Bonneval from Orléans, was completed in 1359, the *gisant* (effigy) in white Italian marble and the base in black marble from Denmark. It was originally decorated with alabaster and jasper columns.

On the D222, in the villages of Préhac (south of Uzeste) and Roaillen (north of Uzeste) are simple part-Romanesque churches.

Bazas

The attractive but quiet market town of Bazas belies an important history, although the huge cathedral is a clue; and the region is famous for its cattle of the same name.

Bazas stands on a cliff above the River Beuve, and developed into a major Roman town on an important road from Bordeaux to Toulouse. The first bishop was named in 506, and the Roman road became a pilgrimage route. Over the centuries it withstood many sieges, and was enclosed in walls in the 11C, which were extended in the 13C and had five gates. The power base gradually developed into joint control between Church and judiciary. The *présidial* (law courts) was instituted in 1551 and in the 18C the town was at the head of a vast judicial district. All this disappeared with the Revolution, and Bazas is now the modest centre of an agricultural region known for Bazadais cattle and for several traditional *fêtes*.

The focus of the town centre is the triangular Place de la Cathédrale, dominated by the west front of the cathedral to the east. To the southwest of the square is the former church of Notre-Dame-du-Mercadil (12C), and the old quarter of St-Martin. On the south side the **Hôtel du Présidial** (1730) encompasses the market-hall (1890), the *hôtel de ville* and a small museum, and nearby in Rue Servière is Hôtel Bourriot (18C), built by Pierre Bourriot, mayor of Bazas, who is credited with introducing the potato to the region. The chapter gardens on the south flank of the cathedral, overlooking the river, contain a few remains of the medieval ramparts on a Gallo-Roman base. The most eye-catching house is the **Maison de l'Astronome** (*c* 1530), on the north side, with a stepped gable and decorated with celestial bodies and an 'oriental' astronomer. Further west is the 17C Hôtel d'Andraut, with a three-level façade above three arcades. Rue Lagardère north of the cathedral leads to the only surviving fortified gateway (restored 1864), beyond which is the Hôpital St-Antoine, with an old apothecary's shop (to arrange a visit, enquire at the tourist office).

The **Cathédrale St-Jean Baptiste** was begun in 1233 to replace an 11C church, but was badly damaged by the Protestants in 1561. Remarkably the astonishing west front survived Protestant iconoclasm and is almost complete, but the body of the church was virtually rebuilt (1583–1635). The belfry on the north is part 11C (up to the openings). The three-bay lower level of the west façade has three **Gothic portals** (13C) and much of the original décor has survived. The iconography of the central door is dedicated to the *Last Judgement*, in which *Christ in Majesty* is surrounded by the Virgin, St John and angels, and

Apostles and saints occupy the voussoir blocks of the five arches. The south door has scenes from the **Life of the Virgin** and the north the **Life of St Peter**, **Adam and Eve** and **Cain and Abel**. The single-bay second level dates from a new building campaign in 1537 which introduced the Flamboyant style in the magnificent rose window with a spiral surround, the flying buttresses and crocketed pinnacles. The 17C gable collapsed and was later replaced by the Neo-classical version. After the destruction of the 16C the interior was entirely rebuilt, apart from four bays near the choir, following the same layout with a long, aisled nave, a false transept and five radiating chapels around the east.

Château de Cazeneuve

The Château de Cazeneuve is a splendid property on the edge of the Landes' pine forests, which has been owned by descendants of the illustrious Albret dynasty since the 12C, including King Henri IV and the present owners, the de Sabran-Pontevès. It is beautifully furnished and about ten rooms, the chapel and kitchens are open to the public. Guided visits to the interior, Easter–Nov, Sat, Sun and PH 14.00–18.00; 1 June–30 Sept daily 14.00–18.00; park open from 11.00; ☎ 05 56 25 48 16.

Approaching from Préchac on the D9 the Château de Cazeneuve creeps up on you unawares, and the rather severe exterior set in a seemingly flat, wooded landscape gives scant indication of the refinement and luxury of the interior. The castle is in fact on a mound descending to the valleys of the Ciron and its tributary stream, the Honburens. One solitary archway and fragments of wall remain from the medieval *enceinte* formerly protecting the medieval *cité* of Cazeneuve: the last remnant, an impressive barbican known as the Lusignan tower, disappeared in 1880.

The first fort was built here in the 11C and was enlarged towards the end of the 13C. Propitious marriages ensured that the fortunes of the family, and consequently the château, continued to grow. In 1368 Armand Amanieu VIII married Marguerite de Bourbon (one of several Marguerites associated with Cazeneuve), linking the Albret to the royal family, and the union in 1484 of Jean d'Albret with Catherine de Foix added the title of King of Navarre. Henri II d'Albret, owner of the Château de Cazeneuve in the 16C, married Marguerite d'Angoulême, sister of François I, and the title subsequently passed to their daughter, Jeanne (see p 277). Her son, Henri III de Navarre, the future Henri IV, assigned Cazeneuve in 1583 to his then estranged wife, Marguerite de France (*la Reine Margot*). Cazeneuve was a favourite hunting retreat of Henri IV but the property suffered badly during the Wars of Religion as did the King's purse, and he bequeathed it to his wealthy cousin and close friend, Raymond de Vicose. Alterations were carried out early in the 17C by de Vicose, and the medieval castle metamorphosed into an elegant and comfortable palace. In 1704 the property passed to the de Sabran-Pontevès family.

Cross the dry moat and pass through a 17C archway into the irregular five-sided courtyard, on two levels with the entrance on the right. On the ground floor are a vaulted gallery with Aubusson verdure tapestries and leather-backed chairs with the coat of arms of the the de Sabran-Pontevès family. On the same level are the **dining room**, with porcelain and earthenware pieces, a gallery of hunting trophies, and the kitchen equipped with copper pans and salt chests. In the large fireplace are a pair of firedogs—male and female versions—traditionally presented by families of the bride and groom as a wedding gift. A wide staircase leads to the first-floor gallery connecting the whole of the east wing, containing another Aubusson tapestry, paintings, a splendid clock and fine walnut chest with reliefs representing the four seasons. The luxurious **drawing room of Queen Margot** contains a magnificent marble fireplace, on which is inscribed the last two lines of verse reputedly composed by her in response to being caught *in flagrante* by her husband. The portrait of the young Louis XIV (Henri IV's grandson) was presented by the King when he stopped here on his way to Pau, and the room is furnished mainly in Louis XV style (first half of the 18C), whereas the Louis XVI bedroom is furnished in the style of that period with a bed draped *à la Polonaise* and contains souvenirs of Delphine de Sabran, beloved aunt of Chateaubriand. Also on the first floor are the bedchambers of Margot and Henri, as well as a music room. The gallery ends at the chapel with Gothic vaulting (1680), containing a painting of two saintly members of the the de Sabran family, Elzéar and Dauphine. The chapel received not only the family but also the people of the neighbourhood who entered via the *chemin de ronde* and this route now offers views over the courtyard and countryside, and leads back to the lower courtyard. The most ancient parts of the château are the vaulted caves below the yard, the well with Gallo-Roman columns, and the prison. There is also a wine cellar, and the extensive grounds leading to the Ciron Valley can be visited.

La Reine Margot

Marguerite de Valois or Marguerite de France (1553–1615), also known as La Reine Margot, was the daughter of Henri II and Catherine de Medicis, sister of kings François, Charles IX and Henri III. In 1572 she married Henri de Navarre. Delightful and outrageous, as well as beautiful, cultured and ambitious, her promiscuity was shocking even in that period of lax morals and her life was a series of barely credible episodes. Her wedding took place a few days before the appalling events of St Bartholomew's Eve (p 48). The union between these two individuals, who cared little for each other, turned out particularly ill-fated; nor did it produce an heir. In 1583, pending the annulment of their marriage, Henri installed Marguerite at Cazeneuve, which did not prevent her from continuing her amorous adventures. Her gravest and most deliberate error was to side with the Catholic League (p 48) against her husband, who consequently locked her away in the Château d'Usson in the Auvergne. She became Queen of France after Henri de Navarre's accession to the throne in 1589 as Henri IV (p 436) until 1599 when the marriage was eventually annulled. Henri finally agreed a truce, and she spent the last ten years of her life relatively happy in Paris.

5 The Dordogne: Périgord

The name Dordogne is evocative of one of the best-loved rivers in France, whose formidable waters, like the other great rivers of the southwest, for centuries created both a barrier and a major highway. The river rises in the Massif Central and flows west for 472km, receiving the Cère, the Vézère and the Isle Rivers, until uniting with the Garonne near Bordeaux.

Dordogne also designates a modern administrative *département*, which corresponds almost exactly to the former province of Périgord, and is associated with lush landscapes, intense Paleolithic activity and '1001 castles'. Those who inhabit the *département* of Dordogne are Périgordiens and the capital is Périgueux. Périgord is frequently divided into four parts, according to distinctive cultural and geological features, which are identified by colours: green, white, black (see p 148) and purple.

PÉRIGORD VERT

The northern reach of Aquitaine, and therefore of the *département* of the Dordogne, is known as Périgord Vert. It is crossed by the beautiful **Dronne River** and is well watered and densely wooded. The northeast is covered by much of the **Parc Naturel Régional du Périgord-Limousin**, which was created in 1998; it straddles the Dordogne and the Corrèze and protects 1800km sq of forest and wildlife. In the west, **La Double** is a region of forest and lakeland covering some 50,000ha. The rounded hills of the edge of the Massif Central to the east give way to a plateau about 350–400m high, into which the rivers Loue, Côle, Dronne and Bandiat are deeply incised, creating dramatic scenic contrasts. Its monuments are more modest, and it is consequently less well-known than other parts of Périgord and probably none the worse for it.

Getting there and around
Car

A20/N20 from Paris via Limoges and Brive to the east of the Dordogne. N21 Limoges to Périgueux; N89 Brive to Périgueux. N141/D675 Limoges to Nontron; N21/D707 (Thiviers) from Brive to Nontron; D675 Nontron to Brantôme; D78 Brantôme to Bourdeilles; D78/D710 Bourdeilles to Ribérac; D710 Périgueux to Ribérac.

Train

TGV Paris to Bordeaux; TER Paris Austerlitz to Périgueux; TER Périgueux to Agen line via Les Ezies, Le Bugue, Villefranche-Périgord, Penne; TER Brive-la-Gaillarde to Bordeaux, via Périgueux, Mussidan, Libourne. TER Bordeaux to Sarlat, via Begerac, Lalinde, Le Buisson; TER Limoges to Bordeaux, via Périgueux, Neuvic, Mussidan, Coutras.

Tourist information

24310 Bourdeilles Grand Rue, ☎ 05 53 03 42 96

24310 Brantôme Abbey, ☎/fax 05 53 05 80 52

24340 Mareuil Rue des Ecoles, ☎ 05 53 60 99 85

24300 Nontron Rue de Verdun, ☎ 05 53 56 25 50, fax 05 53 60 34 13

24600 Ribérac Pl. de Gaulle, ☎ 05 53 90 03 10, fax 05 53 91 35 13

24490 La Roche-Chalais Pl. du Puits-qui-Chante, ☎ 05 53 90 18 95, fax 05 53 90 33 01

24800 St-Jean-de-Côle Pl. du Château,

☎/fax 05 53 62 14 15
24320 Verteillac Ave d'Aquitaine,
☎ 05 53 90 37 78, email si-verteillac@
perigord.tm.fr
**Parc Naturel Régional Périgord-
Limousin** 24300 Abjat-sur-Bandiat,
☎ 05 53 60 34 65, fax 05 63 60 39 13
Market days
Ribérac Friday
Brantôme Friday

Festivals and events

May *Fête de St-Sicaire*, traditional fair, Brantôme
July *Festival Musiques et Paroles en Ribéracois*, classical music and jazz, Ribérac
September *Sinfonia en Périgord*, Baroque choral and instrumental music, Bourdeilles

Where to stay and eating out

24310 BOURDEILLES
✩✩✩ *Château de la Côte*, Biras on the D106, ☎ 05 63 03 70 11, fax 05 53 03 42 84. 15C/16C castle in huge park, beautifully furnished; many activities; restaurant.
✩✩ *Hostellerie Les Griffons*, Le Bourg, ☎ 05 53 45 45 35, fax 05 53 45 45 20. Lovely spot, warm welcome. Patio garden and plenty of old beams. Healthy food.

24310 BRANTÔME
✩✩✩✩ *Moulin de l'Abbaye*, 1 Rte de Bourdeilles, ☎ 05 53 05 80 22, fax 05 53 06 75 27. Stunningly picturesque water-mill setting and seriously good (expensive) food.

✩✩✩ *Chabrol*, 57 Rue Gambetta, ☎ 05 53 05 70 15, fax 05 53 05 71 85. Hotel on the river's edge, with a reputable restaurant.
✩✩ *Périgord Vert*, 6 Ave de Thiviers, ☎ 05 53 05 70 58, fax 05 53 46 71 18. Less pricey, standard hotel, with a restaurant.
€€€ *Les Frères Charbonnel*, 57 Rue Gambetta, ☎ 05 53 05 70 15. Thoughtful and fresh cooking of regional and traditional dishes. Terrace overlooking the Dronne.
€€ *Les Jardins de Brantôme*, 33/37 Rue P.-de-Mareuil, ☎ 05 53 05 88 16. Regional and traditional cooking using home-grown produce. Terrace and garden.

24350 LISLE
Le Pigeonnier de Picandine, northwest of Périgueux on the D710, ☎ 05 53 35 50 01, fax 05 53 35 50 41. *Chambres d'hôte* in an entirely renovated 17C farm; rural setting and pool.

24600 RIBÉRAC
✩✩ *France*, 3 Rue Marc-Dufraisse, ☎ 05 53 90 00 61, fax 05 53 91 06 05. 17C–18C building with antique furniture. Terrace and restaurant.

33910 SABLONS-DE-GUITRES
✩✩✩ *Le Close St-Jacques*, Brantirats, close to St-Emilion, ☎ 05 57 69 33 63. A converted post inn on the edge of the Double forest, lovingly restored; restaurant.

24800 ST-PIERRE-DE-CÔLE
Doumarias, ☎ 05 53 62 34 37. Simple but charming *chambres d'hôte*, in a house covered in Virginia creeper, with a garden and pool.

The main town of the northern part of the *département* is **Nontron**. It is an unspoilt place on the edge of the regional park in a landscape of natural beauty, pitted with lakes and ideal for hiking. Scattered over the area are local cottage industries, forges and mills, and rural museums. **La Chapelle-St-Robert**, northwest on the D75, has a handsome Romanesque church with a domed crossing; the influence of the Saintonge is evident in the west façade.

Mareuil, on the D939, was one of the baronies of the Périgord (p 169). It has a château that was rebuilt in the 15C integrating some earlier defensive elements into a more habitable Renaissance mansion. Niched in one of the towers is a Flamboyant-style chapel; the First Empire room is dedicated to an ancestor of the present owner, Maréchal Lannes, Duc de Montebello. Open in summer daily 10.00–13.00 and 14.00–18.30; out of season 10.00–12.00 and 14.00–18.00, closed Tues, Sun morning; closed Dec–Feb.

Brantôme

A tight loop in the Dronne created an island site on which the small town of Brantôme developed next to its ancient abbey, creating an unforgettable ensemble. This little town was the home of soldier-satirist Pierre de Bordeilles (1540–1614), better known under his pen name Brantôme and the author of *Les Vies des hommes illustres et des grands capitaines* and *Les Vies des dames galantes*, who was made titular abbot at the age of 16 but spent most of his time gallivanting through Europe.

The most important monument is the **abbey**, a white-and-grey collection of (17C–19C) buildings with a fine 11C belltower, now occupied by the *mairie* and the Musée Fernand-Desmoulins, of prehistoric and local art. The abbey is open July–Sept daily 10.00–19.00; April–June daily 10.00–12.30 and 14.00–18.00; Oct–March closed Tues and Jan; ☎ 05 53 05 80 63. Guided visits to belltower; closed midday. Independent visits to the troglodyte dwellings and Musée Demoulins. The abbey stands on a narrow shelf of rock between the cliff and river. To reach it, cross the Grand Jardin and the dog-leg bridge.

The abbey was founded by Wisbode, Count of Périgord, vassal of Charlemagne, in the 8C, and Charlemagne himself dedicated the relics of St Sicaire, one of Herod's slaves who converted after the Massacre of the Innocents. The abbey was destroyed by the Normans and rebuilt in the 11C.

The huge free-standing **belltower** has, beyond all the odds, survived since the 11C and is considered the oldest of its kind; it served as the model for Romanesque belfries in the Limousin. It consists of four stepped levels with a series of round-headed arches of different rhythms and sizes, with an unusual gabled element linking the third and fourth levels, and a pyramidal roof. The ground floor is domed and there is an interior staircase. The ruined 16C cloister is on the west of the church, situated there because of the constraints of the site. The **church**, basically Romanesque, has been much altered. Under the porch is a 13C relief representing the **Massacre of the Innocents**. Inside the door a Romanesque capital is used as a holy water stoup and the domes over the two bays of the tall nave and the choir were replaced by Angevin-type Gothic vaults during transformations in the 14C. The apse is flat-ended and there is a low relief of the **Baptism of Christ** in the baptistery. The church was subjected to Paul Abadie's enthusiastic attention in the 19C.

The **caverns and man-made galleries** under the belltower provided shelter to hermits who first Christianised the rock and have protected others during attacks at various times. They can be visited along the 'troglodyte trail', which has information panels in French and English. Everything is carved out of the rock, including the *chauffoir* (warming house), *lavoir* (wash house) and pigeon house and there is a spring dedicated to St Sicaire. The highlight is the cave containing a carved relief of the **Last Judgement**.

At the exit of the town on the D78 towards Thiviers there is a good example of a Neolithic tomb, the **Dolmen de la Pierre Levée**.

A pretty drive southwest along the Dronne brings you to **Bourdeilles**, another of the four medieval baronies of Périgord. The village—containing the ancient house of the seneschals, a picturesque old bridge and *bâteau moulin* (floating mill)—shelters beneath the overhanging cliff, on which stand two magnificent **châteaux**, one 13C–14C, one an elegant Renaissance pile. Guided tour, July, Aug daily 10.00–19.00; April–June, Sept–11 Oct, Christmas holidays 10.00–12.30 and 14.00–18.00, closed Tues; Feb–March, 11 Nov–Dec 10.00–12.30, 14.00–17.30; closed Tues, Fri, Sat; but times likely to vary, so ☎ 05 53 03 73 36.

In the 13C there was a family rift when the region was ceded to the English, the older generation of the Bourdeilles supporting the Plantagenets and the younger Maumonts backing the Capetians. Gérard de Maumont, supported by the French king (Philippe le Bel) took over the castle and fortified it. The property returned to the Bourdeilles at the end of the 15C and after the Wars of Religion Jacquette de Montbron, widowed sister-in-law of Brantôme (see above), decided to demolish the baronial castle and start again in the style of the day. Moreover, anticipating a visit from Catherine de Médicis, she furnished the palace accordingly. The queen never arrived, Jacquette died, and the project came to a halt.

The medieval castle, enclosed in a series of walls, has a severe 13C main block with plate-tracery windows and a wooden ceiling while the massive octagonal keep (14C) has star vaults above each floor. The Renaissance château, begun in 1598, has fairly simple two-storey elevations displaying the correct use of the orders of architecture, and is flanked by projecting pavilions. The low roof is screened by a balustrade. Inside is an extraordinary collection of 16C–17C Spanish and Burgundian furnishings, including travelling chests, tapestries and Hispano-Mauresque faïences, an *Entombment* group from Burgundy and the tomb of Jean de Chabannes (d. 1498), Chamberlain of Charles VIII. The old kitchens were transformed into a chapel. The Salon Doré, with a painted ceiling and two monumental fireplaces, was prepared for Catherine de Médicis and the bedroom of 'Charles Quint' has a heavily sculpted 16C bed. There are nice views from the terraces.

North of Bordeilles, via the D106 and D93, **Paussac** has an exceptionally fine domed 13C church, and just outside the village on the D93 is the **dolmen of Peyrelevade**.

Ribérac is a small country town typical of rural France. It has few buildings of distinction but as a main commercial centre of the region it is thronged with people on market day.

The Ribéracois, on the edge of the Forêt de la Double, is exceptionally rich in small **Romanesque churches**, typically with flat buttresses, frequently domed and often adapted for defence, with crenellations or galleries atop stout walls. There are examples at St-Martin-de-Ribérac on the D709, Siorac-de-Ribérac, altered in the 14C and 16C, and at Douchapt on the D710. Near **Tocane** is a dolmen called Margot. **Lisle**, on the D78, an unspoilt village on the Dronne, has a fortified and domed church and a market hall on columns. **Montagrier** (opposite Tocane) is a tiny village on a natural terrace above the Dronne, with a domed church with five 12C apsidal chapels with ancient re-sited sculptures including a 4C Chi-rho monogram of Christ. There is another small fortified church on a cliff at **Grande Brassac** on the D1, with an impressive crenellated belfry; a collage of sculptures, with traces of colour, above the main, north door, includes Christ, the Virgin and St John above, and in the arch the *Adoration of the Magi*. Inside, the nave has three domed bays (late 12C or early 13C).

Northwest of Ribérac, on the D709, there are more 12C gems at Allemans and St-Paul Lizonne, and fragments of wall paintings at St-Martial-Viveyrol. The church of St-Martin at Cherval, in the canton of **Verteillac**, is the finest, with three early 12C domes over the nave, a fourth, more sophisticated, of the late 12C, while the fifth is modern.

West of Ribérac, **St-Privat-des-Prés** on the D5 has an exceptionally beautiful 13C abbey church with a *chemin de ronde* (walkway) above the decorated west end. Both this church and Ste-Eulalie at St-Aulaye are influenced by the Saintonge. Close to **La Roche-Chalais** on the border with Charente, at St-Michel-de-Rivière, there is a 12C church with an arcaded two-tier façade and sculptures.

Along the valley east of Brantôme, where the Trincou and Côle Rivers unite with the Dronne, is a cluster of interesting sites. The D78 follows the Côle to the quiet village of **La-Chapelle-Faucher** gathered around a little Romanesque church with domes and carvings. High above the north bank of the river are the remains of the **Château de Lasfond**. In 1569 it suffered terribly in the hands of the Protestant leader, Gaspard de Coligny (1519–72), was besieged again in the 17C and gutted by fire in 1916, but there are still the curtain walls and postern gate, the 15C main block with towers and fortifications, and the handsome 17C stables and 18C additions. Guided visits daily 10.00–12.00 and 14.00–18.30; ☎ 05 53 54 81 48.

Lempzours has a rustic Romanesque church and from St-Pierre-de-Côle is a pretty drive along the D78 to **St-Jean-de-Côle**, in an idyllic setting. This small village with russet roofs, picturesque 12C–14C restored houses and a hump-back bridge has at its centre an extraordinary church. Built in granite the church of St-Jean-Baptiste, originally the chapel of an Augustinian priory, was begun late in the 11C under the auspices of Raymond de Thiviers, Bishop of Périgueux. On the exterior are storiated capitals, some of them sheltered by the market hall built on the east of the church, including an *Annunciation*, the *Drunkenness of Noah*, the *Creation of Man* and *Daniel in the Lions' Den*. The one-bay nave and tri-lobed chevet are the survivals of a larger church. The nave was originally covered with a dome 12m in diameter, the second largest in Périgord but, after collapsing several times, it was replaced in the 19C by a wooden ceiling. The apse has two Rayonnant chapels, and the choir was endowed in the 17C with carved stalls. Between the church and the river are the priory cloisters (16C), with large arches, included in the visit to the château. The **Château de La Marthonie** is made up of two distinct parts, one with imposing 15C–16C square towers, the other a Classical wing at right angles to the other with pilasters, mansard roofs and dormers and an elegant interior staircase. Guided visits daily July, Aug 10.00–12.00 and 14.00–19.00; ☎ 05 53 62 30 25.

The **Grottes de Villars**, west of St-Jean-de-Côle, are a double whammy: some 10km of labyrinthine galleries are not only adorned with brilliantly white stalactites and other natural formations, but also with prehistoric paintings discovered in 1958. These date back to the Aurignacian period, some 30,000 years ago, and include bison and antelope and a rare human image called 'the sorcerer'. Guided visits July, Aug daily 10.00–19.00; June, Sept daily 10.00–12.00 and 14.00–19.00; April–May, Oct, Wed–Sun 14.00–18.30, closed Mon; ☎ 05 53 54 82 36.

The **Château de Puyguilhem**, near Villars, emerges from woods covering a gently sloping valley. Guided visits July, Aug daily 10.00–19.00; March–June, Sept–Oct daily 10.00–12.30 and 13.30–19.00; Dec–Feb to 17.30, closed Mon and Jan; ☎ 05 53 54 82 18. This is a delightful example of early Renaissance architecture (completed 1530), combining an exuberant interpretation of 15C Italian detail with a charming insouciance towards the Italian Renaissance ideals of harmony and balance. Mondot de La Marthonie, president of the *parlements* in Bordeaux and Paris, built Puyguilhem on the site of an earlier redoubt. It was taken over by the state in 1939 and is furnished from the national reserves. The main building is framed by two towers, the right-hand one round and chunky with ornate machicolations, a relic of the feudal castle updated with a high conical roof and fancy dormer. Tucked in behind it is an octagonal stair-tower. The left-hand tower is taller and angled, and altogether more convincingly Renaissance, with a finely sculpted balustrade and elaborate dormers which break into the pyramidal roof. The roofs are a mixture of cool grey slate over the towers and warm red on the main building, and over the centre of the main roof is a heavily embellished chimney stack. Above the main entrance are the initials of the builder and his wife, Anne de Vernon, and inside are monumental fireplaces, one with scenes of the *Labours of Hercules*, and a fine ceiling above the main staircase.

Just outside Villars in a beautiful and isolated spot are the picturesque remains of the Cistercian **abbey of Boschaud** (built 1154–59), devastated during the Hundred Years War and Wars of Religion. A wing of the cloister with unequal arches has survived, as well as the chapter house, and the ruined church is a unique example of sober Cistercian architecture combined with a succession of characteristically Périgoridan domes.

PÉRIGORD BLANC

The White Périgord is a swathe across the middle of the *département* following the Isle River. It is described as white because of the limestone screes and numerous quarries producing typically pale masonry. Bordering the Corrèze, it is lush and green to the east but becomes increasingly industrial to the west beyond Périgueux, the ancient and modern capital of the Périgord and Dordogne.

Getting there and around
See p 124.

 Tourist information
24160 **Excideuil** Pl. du Château.
☎ 05 53 62 95 56
24700 **Montpon-Ménesterol** Pl.

Clémenceau, ☎ 05 53 82 23 77
24400 **Mussidan** Pl. de la République,
☎ 05 53 81 73 87
24190 **Neuvic** 2 Pl. de la Mairie, ☎ 05 53 81 52 11
24420 **Sorges** Ecomusée, ☎/fax 05 53 46 71 43
24110 **St-Astier** Pl. de la République,

☎ 05 53 54 13 85
24800 Thiviers Pl. du Maréchal Foch,
☎/fax 05 53 55 12 50
Market days

Excideuil Thursday
Thiviers Saturday, Tuesday organic market

 Festivals and events
January Truffle fair, Sorges
May *Foire aux Gras*, market for *foie gras*, Thiviers
September *Sinfonia en Périgord*, Baroque choral and instrumental music, Chancelade

Where to stay and eating out
24420 ANTONNE-ET-TRIGONANT
✰✰✰ *Hostellerie de l'Ecluse*, Rte de Limoges, ☎ 05 53 06 00 04, fax 05 53 06 06 39, www.finest.tm/fr/fr/dordogne.ecluse. Largish hotel, attractive veranda; excellent Périgordian cooking.
€€ *Les Chandelles*, Le Parc, ☎ 05 53 06 05 10. Good-value local cuisine in a rustic setting.
24650 CHANCELADE
✰✰✰✰ *Château des Reynats*, Ave des Reynats, ☎ 05 53 03 53 59, fax 05 53 03 44 84, www.chateau-hotel-perigord.com. Pleasantly converted 19C mansion with large rooms, pool. Serves seafood.
24160 EXCIDEUIL
✰✰ *Hostellerie du Fin Chapon*, 3 Pl. du Château, ☎ 05 53 62 42 38. Very good value accommodation and food.
24400 MUSSIDAN
✰✰✰✰ *Le Chaufourg*, Sourzac, ☎ 05 53 81 01 56, fax 05 53 82 94 87. Elegant and refined hotel, with beautiful tranquil garden and swimming pool. Expensive.
€€ *Le Clos Joli*, Beaupouyet, ☎ 05 53 81 18 01. Named after the garden enclosed in box hedges; unusual dishes add to the pleasure.
24430 RAZAC-SUR-L'ISLE
✰✰✰ *Château de Lalinde*, ☎ 05 53 54 52 30, fax 05 53 07 46 67. Tranquil setting in a wooded park, simple rooms, and gastronomic food.
24420 SORGES
✰✰✰ *L'Auberge de la Truffe*, ☎ 05 53 05 02 05, fax 05 53 05 39 27, www.auberge-de-la-truffe.com. Hotel and restaurant, garden, pool, all renovated—truffles galore.

The **Auvézère River** makes its tortuous way into the northeast of the Dordogne and flows southwest to join with the Isle about 10km east of Périgueux. There are picturesque drives or walks in the section between Sevignac-Lédrier, with a 15C forge, and Cherveix-Cubas which has a *lanterne des morts* in the cemetery similar to that in Sarlat (see p 163).

Château d'Hautefort
Just south on the D704 is the Château d'Hautefort, a grand affair shouting for attention from on high (231m), its tall slate roofs reminiscent of a Loire château. All around are commanding views and the terraces are planted with the most formal, and some of the most famous, French *parterres*. Guided visits Feb–March 14.00–18.00, April–June 10.00–12.00, 14.00–18.00, July–Aug 09.30–19.00, Sept 10.00–12.00, 14.00–18.00, Oct–Nov 14.00–18.00; ☎ 05 53 50 51 23.

The Marquis of Hautefort, Jacques-François, though a miserly man, instructed the architect Nicolas Rambourg to build the present elegant residence (1630–70) in honour of his sister, Marie, unrequited favourite of Louis XIII. This courtly love was appropriate to Hautefort whose owners in the 12C had been Constantin de Born and his troubadour brother Bertran, who dedicated verses to Eleanor of Aquitaine. Bertran managed to seize the estates of Hautefort from his elder brother, and Constantin went running to the Governor of Aquitaine, Richard the Lionheart. Bertran deployed his considerable skills in writing acerbic *sirventes* (propagandist songs) to stir up the locals against Richard and consequently lost the château. He went on to influence Richard's elder brother, the young king, Henry Court Mantel who died in 1183, elliciting an eloquent lament from Bertran, convincing Henry II to restore Hautefort to him. Bertran was eventually reconciled with Richard whom he nicknamed *Oc et No* (Yea and Nay), reflecting Richard's single-mindedness (the sobriquet Coeur de Lion only came into use later) but the unruly troubadour was relegated to the inferno by Dante.

In 1588 the fortress was modified and in the 17C the lords of Hautefort were elevated to the title of marquis. Hautefort passed to the Damas family and was finally sold in the 19C. Eugène Le Roy, author of *Jacquou le Croquant* (1899), a tale of the hardship of peasant life in the 17C, was born here. In 1929 the property was acquired and renovated by the Baron and Baroness de Bastard, but in 1968 much of it was gutted by fire; the by-then widowed Baroness, undeterred, has restored the building.

The visit to the interior is guided but the precisely trimmed box and yews of the **formal gardens** can be visited independently, as can the *parc à l'anglaise* to the west. The château is preceded by a wide esplanade and a drawbridge over the ditch, and the main entrance leads through a low building to the *cour d'honneur* with the main block to the north and open to the south. At the end of each of the flanking wings is a round tower with pepper-pot roof, the southeast tower 15C, the other a copy of 1670. The main residence has steep slate roofs, four-square windows and dormers with rounded pediments. At ground level is a gallery running the length of the building with basket-handle arches alternating with narrow rectangular bays, flanked by two forward pavilions with segmented domes and lanterns. The visit to the interior includes the chapel in the southeast tower with *trompe-l'oeil* decoration and an altarpiece made for Charles X's coronation (1830). In the main part of the building are rooms displaying tapestries and paintings; the southwest tower has a magnificent chestnut roof.

In the village, the large cruciform and domed **Hospice d'Hautefort** was founded in 1680 to give shelter to 11 old men, 11 boys and 11 young women, and contains a medical museum. Open July, Aug daily 10.00–12.30 and 14.00– 18.00; May, June, Sept, Wed, Sat, Sun 10.00–12.00 and 14.00–18.00; ☎ 05 53 51 62 98.

On the Auvézère at **Tourtoirac**, reached via the D62 and D5, are the ruins of an 11C Benedictine abbey and church; ☎ 05 53 51 12 17. The west door of the neglected remains of the church is 12C with a 14C funerary niche, and the west bay of the nave has an original barrel vault, whereas the other four bays are 19C and the crossing dome, on flat triangular pendentives, supports a belfry. There are some naive storiated capitals and fragments of wall paintings; small sections of the abbey are in the surrounding gardens. In the cemetery is a monument to a local man, Arélie-Antoine I, who became self-proclaimed king of Aurucania in Chile, in the name of France. He was eventually found out by the Chileans in 1869, and finally returned here to die in 1878 (there is a small museum dedicated to the Rois d'Araucanie at Chourgnac d'Ans).

The scenery along the valley southwest towards Périgueux is gentle and reassuring, watered by small streams. The road crosses and re-crosses the river, running past typical villages such as Le Change and Escroire. From here join the D21 for the **Château des Bories**, near Antonne. It is a typical Périgordian structure begun in the late 15C, combining medieval defensive elements with Renaissance luxury; it is privately owned. The interior is particularly splendid with a monumental stone staircase in the square tower leading to a private oratory, a guardroom vaulted from a central column, and a magnificent vaulted Gothic kitchen. The main gallery, furnished in Louis XIII style, has a fine Renaissance fireplace and Flemish tapestry, and there is a terrace overlooking the Isle. Guided visits 1 July–30 Sept daily 10.00–12.00 and 14.00–19.00; ☎ 05 53 06 00 01.

In the extreme northeast corner of the Périgord Blanc, a remote and wooded area, is Jumilhac-le-Grand, a small town dominating the river. The **Château de Jumilhac** sprouts towers and turrets of all sizes with tall slate roofs, their verticality emphasised by decorative spiky finials. Guided visits 1 July to 15 Sept 10.00–19.00, July and Aug, Tues, Thur 21.00–23.30, June and Sept Tues 21.00–23.30; mid-March–end May, Oct–mid-Nov, weekends, PH 14.00–18.30; ☎ 05 53 52 42 97. The original medieval castle was subsumed in the present 16C version by Antoine Chapelle, ultra-rich Master of the King's Forges who was ennobled by Henri IV, hence the ironwork display on the roofs. The château comprises two large 17C wings enclosing a courtyard, and inside a large staircase leads to an immense, panelled room and chimney-piece with allegorical carvings. The thick walls of the Chambre de la Fileuse (Spinner's Room) have a naive painted decoration telling the story of Louise de Hautefort, who was accused of carrying on with a local lad who, disguised as a shepherd, brought wool for her spinning wheel and managed to avoid notice by hiding under her ample pinafore. The church with an octagonal belfry was formerly the private chapel of the château. The **Musée d'Or** in the castle cellars has a display pertaining to the Gallo-Roman mines at Fouilloux. Open mid-June–mid-Sept daily 10.30–12.30 and 14.30–18.30; mid-Sept–mid-June, Sun and PH 15.00–18.00; closed Dec–Mar; ☎ 05 53 52 55 43.

Just before Thiviers on the N21, the Isle takes a southerly course through landscape which transforms from the green hills of Limousin to the limestone plateaux of the Périgord Blanc. **Thiviers** is a dynamic little market town with some picturesque old streets leading to the market square. Above the church entrance is the date 1515, and while the nave is rib vaulted (14C) the capitals indicate its Romanesque origins and that it was once domed. There is also later sculpture. Behind the church is an old, but heavily restored, fortified house, the former presbytery, and the château is much remodelled.

From Thiviers, the D76 goes across country southeast to **Excideuil** on the valley of La Loue, which is well known for its winter truffle market. The town developed at a strategic point on the old Périgord–Limousin road and vertiginous twin keeps are a reminder of the fortress built by the Viscounts of Limoges. Much renovated, the church is endowed with a Flamboyant porch thanks to Anne de Brétagne (daughter of François II, and wife of Charles VIII and Loius XII), a *pietà* and retable (both 17C), and a statue of Maréchal Bugeaud, who conquered Algeria in the mid-19C and donated a fountain to the town after his return. In Preyssac d'Excideuil there is a Romanesque church with an interesting belfry-gable and where the Loue meets the Isle, at Coulaures, is a church with 14C wall paintings.

Sorges, northeast of Périgueux, is on the map mainly for its status as an *étape gastronomique*. No detail in connection with the 'black diamond' is overlooked at the **Ecomusée de la truffe**. Open July, Aug daily 09.30–12.30 and 14.00–19.00; Sept–June, Tues–Sun 10.00–12.00 and 14.00–17.00, closed Mon; ☎ 05 53 05 90 11. Sorges has a Romanesque church whose domes were rebuilt in the 16C when a fine Renaissance doorway was added. At **Le Pey** are some 50 drystone huts or *bories de causse*, and just outside the village of Agonac, northeast of Périgueux, is the solid little fortified and domed Romanesque church of St-Martin. **Château-l'Eveque** on the D939 (☎ 05 53 04 66 84) is exactly as it sounds, the location of the former residence built for the bishops of Périgueux in the 14C–15C. Composed of two asymmetric wings, the elevation overlooking the Beauronne Valley has squared windows and machicolated towers.

Périgueux

Périgueux, in a prime position on the banks of the Isle, was made *préfecture* of the modern *département* of Dordogne in 1790. Emblematic of the city are the curious white cupolas and minaret of St-Front cathedral which stands on a knoll above the river with the medieval town clustered around it. Less conspicuous are the important Gallo-Roman remains. Périgueux is first and foremost a working town, not a tourist attraction. It is large enough to absorb visitors, has plenty to see, wonderful old streets with distinguished medieval and Renaissance buildings, excellent shops and a particularly lively twice-weekly market. In fact it is in welcome contrast to the tourist-focused Sarlat, Les Eyzies or Domme.

Practical information

Getting there and around
Air

Daily flights from Paris to Périgueux. Périgueux-Bassillac airport, ☎ 05 53 02 79 71/05 53 02 79 70.

Car

See p 124.

Train

Paris Austerlitz to Périgueux via Limoges. Bordeaux to Périgueux.

Bus

Between Périgueux and Sarlat, and Périgueux and Angoulême with CFTA, about 3 daily, Gare Routière, ☎ 05 53 08 43 13 (mainly a school bus).

Tourist information
26 Pl. Francheville, 24000, ☎ 05 53 53 10 63, fax 05 53 09 02 50, email tourisme.perigueux@perigord.tm.fr

Market days

Wednesday and Saturday; truffle market in winter

Guided tours

Guided visits in English and French from the Tourist Office (*Visites Découvertes*) June–Sept, daily except Sun, 10.30, 14.30, 16.00; includes places not usually open to the public

River cruises

Quai de l'Isle; ☎ 05 53 24 58 80, fax 05 53 73 21 20

Festivals and events
July/August *Festival Macadam Jazz*
August *Festival International du Mime*, contemporary mime; Musiques de la Nouvelle Orléans
September *Sinfonia en Périgord*, Baroque choral and instrumental music
November/December *Salon du Livre Gourmand*, every two years (next 2004)

Where to stay and eating out

24000 PÉRIGUEUX

Although more a place for eating or shopping than staying in, there is the ☆☆ *Périgord*, 74 Rue V.-Hugo, ☎ 05 53 53 33 63, fax 05 53 08 19 74. Reliable *logis de France* with courtyard-garden. €€€ *Les Berges de l'Isle*, 2 Rue P.-Magne, ☎ 05 53 09 51 50. A surprisingly good restaurant in an unpromising setting.

€€ *Le 8*, 8 Rue de la Clarté, ☎ 05 53 35 15 15. In the old town centre, pretty setting and good simple fare.

€€ *Le Roi Bleu*, 2 Rue Montaigne, ☎ 05 53 09 43 77. Rather precious food.

History

A Celtic tribe, the Petrucores, occupied the hills on the south bank of the Isle, and after the creation of Aquitania by the Romans at the end of the 1C BC, they accepted Roman domination. The territory became known as *Civitas Petrucoriorum* and the main oppidum was *Versunna* (or Versona), after a local god to whom a sacred spring was dedicated. A fine Roman town of some stature developed on the right bank, with forum, temples, basilicas, amphitheatre, thermae (public baths), aqueducts and so on, but this was attacked in the 3C by the Alemani. The inhabitants of Versona rebuilt a smaller city within the walls, using the amphitheatre as a bastion of defence, and gradually the name Versunna disappeared and this area became known as La Cité.

Legend has it that St Front brought Christianity to the Périgord, but the first bishop recorded was Paternus in 365. The relics of St Front became crucially important and were placed in the first sanctuary on the hill, or *puy*, opposite La Cité. This developed into a monastic centre around which the suburb of Puy-St-Front grew up, eventually eclipsing the Cité where traditionally the nobles lived. The bourgeois, artisans and immigrants inhabited Puy-St-Front, which came under the protection of the King of France.

By 1240 the two communities had come together as Périgueux, although unification was not necessarily harmonious. There were several attacks during the Hundred Years War, and by the Treaty of Bretigny (1360) it was subjected to English administration. Accounts vary, but either Count Archambaud V betrayed the English, or the French hero Bernard du Guesclin liberated the town in 1369. Renewal during the relatively peaceful period 1550–1650 produced the handsome Renaissance buildings which enhance the old centre. During the Reformation, Périgueux remained Catholic until taken by the Protestants (1576–81), was torn apart by the Civil Wars, and divided during the Fronde.

By the 19C, navigation on the Isle provided employment and the arrival of the railway in 1856 opened up even more opportunities. The town grew rapidly and spread beyond its medieval confines, necessitating new roads and public buildings. The start of the 20C coincided with a downturn, and the First World War and lack of employment decimated the population, although some 25,000 refugees from Alsace swelled the numbers for a while. During the Second World War there was a strong Resistance network based in Périgueux which provoked the Germans to establish a garrison here for 21 months until Liberation in August 1944. The population is now around 51,450 and the suburbs are spreading. The largest employer is the French stamp print-shops, transferred here from Paris in 1970, but Périgueux is best known as a gastronomic centre.

La Cité

Start out from Place Francheville, at the meeting point of the two old sections of the town, and head west along busy Rue de la Cité which runs along the north side of **St-Etienne-de-la-Cité**, an austere building, begun in the 11C, which was the cathedral of Périgueux until 1577.

> Originally it consisted of a succession of four domed bays, but it was damaged during the Wars of Religion and rebuilt (1625–47). Then the two domed units to the west collapsed and only the east dome was rebuilt. During the Fronde, in 1652, the Prince of Condé's men used the church as a *manège* (riding school); in 1669 the episcopal see was transferred to St-Front and at the Revolution the church was deconsecrated and used for storage until 1816. In 1979 the remains of the west bays and the belfry were cleared away.

The exterior is sober and undecorated, with high wall arcades and few windows, while the scarred west front is the 17C infill of the former internal arch of the second bay, with evidence of the lost dome at the angles. The interior is cavernous and empty and has just two bays. The oldest part is the first of these, and most impressive, with enormous Classical pendentives (9m high) that make the transition from a square of 13m to a single span dome of 15m diameter (compare Cahors 16m, St-Front 13m); the apex is 22m from the floor. The east bay, originally mid-12C, is more fancy and lighter but this dome was rebuilt in the 17C. Sombrely plain and awe-inspiring, but gloomy for lack of windows, there are lateral wall walks which seem to be left over from another construction. The sacristy was dug out in 1955 in the east bay, and one of its walls is 3C. Among the scant fittings are a *Table Pascale* dated 1168, behind the choir organ, for calculating the date of Easter up until 1253. On the north wall is the arcaded tomb of Bishop Jean d'Asside (d. 1168), with an inscription which includes the name of the stonemason, Constantine de Jarnac. The 17C Baroque altarpiece in wood features the Four Evangelists, and among the scenes on the lower part shows St Front casting the Devil off the Tour de Vésone. The Carouges organ was made in 1733 and restored several times, the last in 1993.

Rue Romaine is on the line of the old Roman town wall erected to protect *Civitas Petrucoriorum* in the 3C AD. It leads to the **Tour de Vésone** (cross the railway bridge to enter the gardens around it) which was the focal point of the Roman city, at the convergence of important roads and the market place. This is still the most imposing Roman monument in the Périgord yet consists of only the central part or cella of a 2C AD circular temple. The massive cylinder of brick, rubble and concrete is thin-walled and immensely tall (27m high and 20m in diameter), but has a dramatic rent where one side has collapsed. It stands on the remains of a circular podium and would have been surrounded by a colonnade or peristyle with an entry vestibule, but only fragments of the columns are visible. Undoubtedly once clad in marble and roofed, it has courses of large connecting blocks and narrow brick as well as brick arched openings. It was abandoned and left outside the reduced enclosure of the Roman town *c* 270. Around it are fragments of columns and statues found in digs.

To west of the Tour de Vésone a new museum is due to open in the first half of 2003. The **Musée Gallo-Romain**, designed by Jean Nouvel, will bring together the archaeological remains on site and a fine collection of Roman artefacts and objects which until now have been languishing in the Musée du Périgord. It is organised around two themes, the 'Town and Public Life' of Vesona, and 'the House and Private Life' which will incorporate the remains of the 1C Maison Gallo-Romaine.

Following Rue Romaine by the railway line you will find, on Rue Turenne, the medieval **Château Barrière**, consisting of a 15C stairtower with Renaissance windows constructed on top of the Roman wall; it was damaged in 1575. A little further on is a single Roman arch, the **Porte Normande**, one of the four original 3C town gates, damaged by Viking or Norman invaders in the 9C. Continue down Rue Turenne and turn right at the junction with Rue Chanzy to the Jardin des Arènes where the **amphitheatre** (1C AD) is disguised as a public garden. On further investigation you can make out sections of substructure including arches, vomitoria and stairs. With seating for some 20,000 it was slightly smaller than those at Arles or Nîmes. It served as an outer bastion during Goth and Vandal attacks, and as fortress and prison during the alliance between the Counts of Périgord and the English during the Hundred Years War, but much of what remained was demolished in 1391 and a convent installed there in 1640. From here return to Place Francheville.

Domed churches of Aquitaine

Of the 77 domed churches built in Aqutaine *c* 1100, some 60 remain. Périgueux is thought to be one of the most important centres for the development of this system, inspired either directly by the 6C Justinian church of the Holy Apostles in Byzantium (destroyed) or via St Mark's, Venice (1063–94). St-Etienne is often posited as the prototype domed church in the region, but some archaeologists believe that the 10C church of St-Front was already domed. The dome was, of course, already used in smaller secular buildings, and as a centralising feature it is logical at a crossing; a half dome frequently covers an apse. The use of the dome to span a nave or transept, sometimes in a file of up to four, is particular to the southwest and seems to have no precedent. These are very strong constructions, supported by solid outer walls, using pointed arches with pendentives in the transition from square to circle. Aisles were usually avoided in domed churches and there was never an ambulatory. Important examples are Cahors and Souillac.

Le Puy St-Front

The medieval *quartiers* of Le Puy St-Front are on a knoll which slopes away to the Isle on the east and is skirted on the other three sides by the modern boulevards which follow the line of the old walls. Four main streets cross the Puy from the exterior towards the cathedral: Rue Taillefer, Rue de la République, Rue Limogeanne and Rue du Plantier, through an area packed with medieval and Renaissance houses which is gradually being restored. Keep a keen eye out for details of former splendour, not as obvious as in Sarlat, such as towers, windows (many bricked up), doorways and courtyards.

From Place Francheville you see between Cours Fénelon and Rue de la Bride a sturdy round tower, **Tour Mataguerre**, the last remnant of the 28 towers and ramparts that enclosed Le Puy. This survivor, with machicolated parapet and gun loops, was rebuilt in 1477 and the more recent fleurs de lis symbolise the alliance between king and consuls of the town back in 1204. Rue de la Bride and

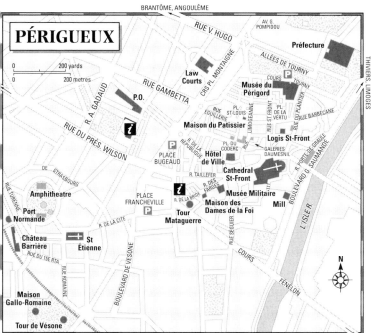

BRANTÔME, ANGOULÊME

PÉRIGUEUX

AV. G. POMPIDOU

Préfecture

RUE V. HUGO

ALLÉES DE TOURNY

THIVIERS, LIMOGES

0   200 yards
0   200 metres

Law Courts

CRS PL. MONTAIGNE

COURS TOURNY

P

Musée du Périgord

RUE GAMBETTA

P.O.

R. A. GADAUD

RUE
ÉGUILLERIE

PL. ST-LOUIS

RUE LIMOGEANNE

PL. DE LA VERTU

RUE ST PLANTIER

RUE DU BARBECANE

RUE DU PRÉS. WILSON

Maison du Patissier

Logis St-Front

R. DE LA RÉPUBLIQUE

PL. DU CODERC

GALERIES DAUMESNIL

R. PORTE DE GRAULE

BOULEVARD G. SAUMANDE

P

PLACE BUGEAUD

Hôtel de Ville

DE STRASBOURG

R. TAILLEFER

Cathedral St-Front

R. DES FARGES

RUE TURENNE

RUE DE VÉSONE

Amphitheatre

PLACE FRANCHEVILLE

R. DE LA BRIDE

Musée Militaire

Maison des Dames de la Foi

Mill

L'ISLER

Port Normande

P

Tour Mataguerre

R. DE LA CITÉ

RUE SÉGUIER

N

Château Barrière

St Étienne

RUE DU 1SE RTA

RUE ROMAINE

BOULEVARD DE VÉSONE

COURS

FENELON

Maison Gallo-Romaine

Tour de Vésone

BERGERAC, CAHORS

Rue Séguier run downhill towards the river; the ancient **Maison des Dames de la Foi** (whose mission was to bring Protestants back to the Catholic faith) at 4–6 Rue des Farges was reputedly the residence of Constable du Guesclin during the Hundred Years War. Off Rue Séguier is a small square, Place de Navarre, with renovated buildings, and beyond that on Rue Aubergerie the Hôtels Abzac de Ladouze (no. 16) and Saltgourde (no. 4–8) were fortified in the 15C. The **Musée Militaire** displays a range of military equipment. Open April–Oct 10.00–12.00 and 14.00–18.00; Oct–Dec, Jan–Mar, Wed, Sat 14.00–18.00; closed Sun, PH; ☎ 05 53 53 47 36. Passage Taillefer leads to Rue Taillefer and, leaving Place de la Clautre and the cathedral to the right, take Rue St-Silain to Place de l'Hôtel-de-Ville. This *quartier* is a commercial battleground on market days, crowded with shoppers, the brightly coloured stalls setting up vivid contrasts with the white-grey of the cathedral.

Cathédrale St-Front

St-Front (closed 12.00–14.30), on the site of an early monastic church, is one of the largest and most eye-catching cathedrals in southwest France. It results from the fusion of two Romanesque churches, one 11C and one 12C, and a radical rethink by Paul Abadie and Emile Boeswillwald between 1852 and 1901. The great bulbous pile which greets you as you cross the Isle presents a rather fanciful version of a neo-Byzantine silhouette of domes, top-knots and minaret. It is worth noting that while Abadie was working at Périgueux he was preparing to build Sacré-Coeur in Paris, and the cross-fertilisation is obvious.

The cathedral is named after the semi-legendary evangeliser and first Bishop of Périgueux around whose relics a chapel had existed since the 6C. An earlier church (10C–11C) was replaced by a larger one begun *c* 1047 and consecrated in 1077. The tower-porch led in the 11C to a domed sanctuary and high altar which contained the remarkable shrine of 1077, designed by the monk Guinamundus from La Chaise-Dieu monastery, placed under a hollow turret with dome and gables and described by Aymery Picaud in his pilgrim's guide to Santiago. The church was damaged by fire in 1120; the next version was erected east of the previous church but incorporated part of it and was completed in 1173. The shrine stayed in its original place and the church was extended beyond it, imposing a reverse orientation. Unlike the majority of domed churches in the west, St-Front was not designed with a file of domes with apse and apsidioles, but in the shape of a Greek cross.

The church was pillaged and the tomb of the saint destroyed by the Protestants in 1575. In 1669 the episcopal see was transferred to St-Front. When Abadie took over the building in the 19C it was in a poor way but served as the basis for the present cathedral although it was subjected to radical alteration. Abadie managed to accentuate its foreignness by using a very pale ashlar of a different scale and texture from the original golden rubble and red roof tiles, and by exaggerating the finials on the domes; nor was he beyond adding the odd flourish such as the top-knots on the domes.

To understand the layout of the Romanesque church enter from the west if that door is open: the modern entrance is through the porch on the north. The massive elevation to the west was originally preceded by a porch, now reduced to a single arch leading into an open forecourt or atrium formed from the nave walls after the fire in the 11C. On the lateral walls are wall arcades similar to those of St-Etienne, and great corner pylons were constructed in the 12C to sustain a dome over this space, but seemingly never completed. To the south is the cloister. The main entrance to the 12C church was beneath the extraordinary tower, one of the parts least altered by Boeswillwald in the 19C, with a succession of stepped levels decorated with pilasters, pediments and columns and topped off by a colonnaded drum with cone-shaped roof and imbrications.

From below the west tower, you pass through the narthex, covered with two sequential domes on squinches and flanked by aisles (part 11C), and to the east a doorway with original Corinthian capitals. The multi-domed **interior** is cool, spacious and gravely majestic, composed of five equal-sized domed sections, except for the little apse bumps to the east. It is also smoothly colourless and, unlike Sacré-Coeur, has no paintings or mosaics. Over the body of the church the domes, all on pendentives, are equal in size (13m in diameter and 27m high) and supported by four-part piers detached from the walls with small round-headed windows (a 19C rebuild). The space under the west dome was the site of the medieval shrine and main altar, but the traditional orientation was restored by Abadie by grafting a neo-Romanesque apse and placing the high altar in the east (the altar has now been moved to a central position). The apsidal chapels in the transepts may be 12C and in the south transept is a tiny alcove with a medieval painting on the vault; on the north and south of the chancel are medieval paintings of the *Life of St Front*.

The magnificent 17C **wooden altarpiece** with twisted columns, in the east (coin-operated light), was designed for a Jesuit chapel and transferred to the cathedral via St-Etienne. It is dedicated to the **Virgin of the Assumption**, presented by a female donor. The pulpit (*c* 1680) is also an outstanding piece with magnificent turned balusters; the stalls, also 17C, came from the abbey of Ligueux. The altar of 1762 originates from the abbey of Vauclaire. The unremarkable glass is 19C and the neo-Gothic light fittings were designed by Abadie and used at Notre-Dame in Paris for the wedding of Napoléon III.

As you leave by the north door, the 11C façade, with later gables, and transept are visible from the north, while from the garden on the southeast is a view of the 19C apse.

Head south down to the banks of the Isle via Rue de Tourville or from the Jardin du Thouin—with 16C cannons—next to the cloister and across the car park. On the quay is the old mill and the bridge provides an excellent view of the cathedral and of a group of particularly attractive houses. These are the L-shaped **Maison Lambert** (16C) in poor condition, with a wooden loggia, the **Maison des Consuls** (15C) with Flamboyant dormers and a machicolated cornice, and the high-roofed **Hôtel de Lur** (17C), also angled. Behind these buildings is Rue Porte-de-Graule, a somberly picturesque street which time does not seem to have touched. Near the end flights of steps link it with Rue Barbecane which becomes Rue Notre-Dame and leads, on the right, into the rectangular Place de la Vertu with some carefully restored Renaissance buildings. Across is Place du Musée, behind the **Musée du Périgord**. The entrance to the museum is at 22 Cours Tourny. Open 1 April–30 Sept, Mon, Wed–Fri 11.00–18.00, Sat, Sun 13.00–18.00; 1 Oct–31 March, Mon, Wed–Fri 10.00–17.00, Sat, Sun, 13.00–18.00; closed Tues and PH; ☎ 05 53 06 40 70.

This small museum has a little bit of everything, not necessarily connected with the Périgord, including some surprising exhibits. The museum took over an Augustinian monastery which was rebuilt, except for the 13C chapel, with a cloister, in 1895. The prehistoric section displays local finds. In the former there are both human remains and important engravings on stone and bone. The early Middle Ages are represented by certain religious pieces, and especially fragile masonry from the cathedral which was replicated for the restorations. Among a collection of sacred artefacts are a diptych on leather and an enamel pyx (both 13C). The museum has recently been extended to include attractive new galleries, to the right of the entrance, containing paintings and sculpture from the 15C–20C combined with furniture and other examples of the decorative arts. One of the most revered works in the museum is of the **Rialto Bridge** by Canaletto (1697–1768). There are also works reflecting local personalities and events in the context of French art and rooms have been set aside for the sculptures of Gilbert Privat and Etienne Hajdu. There are also natural history exhibits; a collection of *objets d'art* from the Limousin and Périgord; and an ethnographic collection from Africa and Oceania.

The area northwest of the cathedral is a veritable labyrinth of streets lined with wonderful boutiques of epicurean delights. Rue de la Nation, leading from Place Daumesnil, brings you to Rue de la Constitution; on the right is the **Logis St-Front**, an elegant building with late Gothic and early Renaissance features around a courtyard. Go across Rue St-Front and take a small passageway on the left into the **Galeries Daumesnil**, a series of interior courtyards between Rues de la Clarté, Limogeanne and de la Miséricord, surrounded by a group of carefully restored buildings. In Rue Limogeanne is the sophisticated **Maison Estignard** (16C) with the salamander motif of François I over the interior court-yard door. Turning north and right is another square, Place du-Marché-au-Bois. To the left, along Rue Montaigne and Puits Limogeanne is the charming Place St-Louis where there is a *marché au gras* in the winter and café tables in the summer. The *hôtel particulier* with the tower is the **Maison du Pâtissier** (1518), which has Renaissance features but is partly fortified. Rue de la Sagesse leads to Place du Coderc with the covered market (1835), leading to Place de l'Hôtel-de-Ville with the Logis Gilles-Lagrange, 18C home of the Lagrange-Chancel family. The traditional **winter truffle market** is held in Place St-Louis.

To the south of Périgueux, there is a postage stamp museum at Boulazac. **St-Laurent-sur-Manoire** has a museum dedicated to Roland Dumas (Ministre des Affaires Etrangères during François Mitterand's presidency); ☎ 05 53 04 23 16. There is a Romanesque church at **Atur** with a 12C *lanterne des morts* similar to the one in Sarlat. **Vergt** is a pretty *bastide* founded in 1285–86 by Archambaud III, Count of Périgord.

Abbaye de Chancelade

Just 6km northwest of Périgueux, west of the D939, is the abbey of Chancelade, one of the most delightful oases in Périgord. Open July, Aug 14.00–19.00; ☎ 05 53 04 86 87. Cross the village to reach the abbey, set in lush surroundings and crossed by a little stream.

The first community settled here, close to the spring, in 1096 and adopted the Augustinian rule. Construction of the abbey began in 1129 and it prospered until the Hundred Years War when the English took it over and turned it into a garrison. They were chased out by du Guesclin, but there was another hiatus during the Wars of Religion in the 16C. The abbey took off again spir-itually and physically during the time of Abbot Alain de Solminihac in the 17C.

Only the lower part of the **church** with a series of wall arches is 12C; above are Gothic-shaped windows of the 17C. Over the crossing is a square three-tier Romanesque belfry, the first two levels decorated with arches and openings but the third consisting only of short blocks supporting a roof. The 12C entry door has decorative mouldings and a cornice supports an arcaded gallery in the manner of the Saintonge, with arcades and a small window. Inside, the narrow single nave has wall arcades and the post-1629 upper level is Gothic in essence. The dome over the crossing, however, is 12C and there are wall paintings of St Christopher and St Thomas Becket, to whom an altar was dedicated in 1170. There is also a painting of **Christ Humiliated**, attributed to Georges de la Tour. Next to the church are the remaining buildings of the abbey with the bare bones of the cloister and a Gothic church. The abbot's lodgings—with a small museum of religious art—were built in the 15C and reworked in the 17C–18C. There are also a 15C wash house, stables, workshops and a fortified mill. The pure Romanesque parish church of **St-Jean**, on the other side of the road, has a lamb and cross on the west façade.

A priory was founded at **Merlande** on the D1 by monks of Chancelade in the 12C and the chapel and prior's lodgings were restored in the 20C. The chapel had two domes but one was destroyed 1170 and replaced with a barrel vault, and it was fortified in the 16C. The oldest part is the choir, decorated with arcades on small columns supporting magnificent Romanesque capitals with monsters, beasties and foliage.

Downstream, the Isle Valley broadens out towards the confluence with the Dronne, with fertile basins between the Forêt de la Double to the north and the Forêt du Landais to the south. **St-Astier** has an industrial past in lime extraction, cement and white limestone. Its old underground quarries are open in summer; ☎ 05 53 54 13 84. The square belfry (16C) of the Romanesque church dominates the small community and some good Renaissance houses surround it. In the 11C a chapel was built above the primitive sanctuary of St-Astier, the massive piers were erected in the 12C to carry the domes, and there were later additions in the 15C–16C.

Neuvic is on the banks of the Isle close to the forest. The riverside grounds of the early Renaissance-style Château Mellet (1530), with some painted rooms, have been transformed into botanical gardens. Guided visits to château, gardens independent, July, Aug 13.30–19.00; rest of year to 18.00; closed mid-Dec–mid-Jan; ☎ 05 53 80 86 65

Mussidan has had its quota of troubles. It was destroyed by Vikings in 849; it was an English stronghold during the Hundred Years War; took up the Reformation and incurred the wrath of the Catholics several times during the Religious Wars; and it was the theatre of a battle between the Resistance and German troops on 11 June 1944, resulting in the execution of 52 locals. The Musée des Arts et Traditions Populaires is a local ethnological museum in an old charterhouse. Open June to mid-Sept 09.30–12.00 and 14.00–17.00; March–May, mid-Sept–Nov, Sat, Sun, 14.00–18.00; ☎ 05 53 81 23 55.

Southeast of Mussidan by the D38 is the **Château de Montréal**, a hilltop castle built to stand guard over the road between Périgueux and Bordeaux. Guided visits, July–Sept 14.30–18.30; ☎ 05 53 81 11 03. It combines parts of a medieval feudal castle and more elegant 16C Italianate elements, with windows framed between columns and sculpted medallions. This is the Montréal which gave its name to the Canadian city: Claude de Pontbriand, lord of Montréal, was on the banks of the St Laurence with the city's founder, Jacques Cartier, on that auspicious day in 1535.

The main claims to fame of **Montpon-Ménesterol** are its museum of church organs and sturgeon hatcheries.

PÉRIGORD POURPRE

The Purple Périgord is the southwestern section of the *département* of the Dordogne. Its colour coding is somewhat contrived, having no traditional basis, but finds its justification in the purply-red wines of Bergerac. The *vin doux* of Monbazillac, on the other hand, is as gold as the sun. Bergerac is the main town of the Purple Périgord and benefits from a prime site on the banks of the Dordogne. Here the alluvial plain widens out and the limestone escarpments are less frequent than up river, creating a rolling landscape of vineyards and sunflowers, wooded towards the south. The vineyards are on both banks of the Dordogne around Bergerac; further west, towards the Bordelais, they are mainly on the right bank.

Getting there and around
Air
International and domestic flights to Bergerac airport, ☎ 05 53 22 25 25.
Car
D936 Bordeaux; N21 Périgueux to Bergerac; D25 Issigeac; D936 Ste-Foy-la-Grande and Moncaret.
Train
Bordeaux to Bergerac.

Tourist information
24100 Bergerac 97 Rue Neuve d'Argenson, ☎ 05 53 57 03 11, fax 05 53 61 11 04, www.bergerac-tourisme.com
24560 Issigeac Pl. du Château, ☎ 05 53 58 79 62
33220 Ste-Foy-la-Grande 102 Rue de la République, ☎ 05 57 46 03 00, fax 05 57 46 53 77
Market days
Bergerac Wednesday and Saturday; covered market every day
Issigeac Sunday
Ste-Foy-la-Grande Saturday
River cruises
Bergerac Departures from Quai Salvette by *Périgord Gabares*, Easter to end Oct; ☎ 05 53 24 58 80
Ste-Foy-la-Grande Boat trips from the river bank; ☎ 05 57 46 03 00

Festivals and events
July *Le Table de Cyrano*, annual food and wine festival, Bergerac
July/August *Scènes d'été*, theatre, classical music, jazz (Mercredis du Jazz)
August *Le Table de Roxanne*, biennial (2003, 2005, etc) food festival, Bergerac

Where to stay and eating out
24100 BERGERAC
☆☆☆ *Bordeaux*, 38 Pl. Gambetta, ☎ 05 53 57 12 83, fax 05 53 57 72 14. A peaceful oasis in the town; pool. Adventurous version of local food.
€€ *Côté Dordogne*, 17 Rue du Château, ☎ 05 53 57 17 57. Terrace draped with an ancient wisteria and 17C house, with excellent quality cooking.
€€/€ *L'Imparfait*, 8 Rue des Fontaines, ☎ 05 53 57 47 92. Beautiful old building and inventive dishes.
ST-JULIEN-DE-CREMPSE
☆☆☆ *Manoir le Grand Vignoble* (north of Bergerac, D107), ☎ 05 53 24 23 18, fax 05 53 24 23 18. Verdant and rural setting for a 17C manor house.
24240 MONESTIER
☆☆☆☆ *Château des Vigiers*, south of Ste-Foy on D18, ☎ 05 53 61 50 00, fax 05 53 61 50 20, www.vigiers.com. Set in a huge park with an 18-hole golf course. Pool.
33220 STE-FOY-LA-GRANDE
☆☆ *Grand Hotel*, 117–19 Rue de la République, ☎ 05 57 46 00 08, fax 05 57 46 50 70, www.grandhotelmce.com. Townhouse around inner courtyard. Simple, with restaurant.
24240 MONBAZILLAC
€€ *Le Château*, ☎ 05 53 58 38 93. Part of a château/cave complex, large and small dining rooms, and terrace. Excellent desserts and good wine.
24230 ST-MICHEL-DE-MONTAIGNE
☆☆☆ *Le Jardin d'Eyquem*, ☎ 05 53 24 89 59, 05 53 61 14 40, www.perso.wanadoo.fr/jardin-eyquem. Simple and pleasant. Large pool.

Bergerac

Bergerac, capital of Périgord until the Revolution, is now a *sous-Préfecture* and has always benefited from its position on the banks of the Dordogne. The name resonates with familiar references, notably wine and Cyrano. Wine is a flourishing industry in the region and this is a major centre for the production of tobacco with a research laboratory, the Institut du Tabac. These traditional local products are also represented at the Maison des Vins de Bergerac and the museum of tobacco. The connection between the town and Edmund Rostand's Cyrano is extremely tenuous but it is impossible to disassociate one from the other.

A great effort has been made to enhance the old part of town on the sloping north bank of the river but it is somewhat submerged by the 20C and Bergerac has no great monuments. There are picturesque narrow streets and fine buildings, reminders of the town's former importance as a river port, but the Reformation, wholeheartedly embraced here, was a mixed blessing and the majority of the older buildings date from after the Wars of Religion. A national explosives factory is the now the most important employer and the river is harnessed to produce hydro-energy.

History

The town was originally built at the foot of an old *castrum* or fort in the 11C, but by the end of the 12C it already had the advantage of a bridge, which linked upper Périgord and Bordeaux. By the beginning of the 14C, the town was protected by a brick enclosure and was at its most prosperous, then from 1345 the full fury of the Anglo-French conflict resonated through the town, bringing it three times under English control and three times under French. During the subsequent period of peace Bergerac again flourished but, around 1546, as part of the Kingdom of Navarre (see p 399), it became solidly Protestant and another ten years of struggle ensued. In 1577 Bergerac had its own Peace Treaty, signed by Henri of Navarre and representatives of Henri III. The reign of Henri IV (1589–1610) and the Edict of Nantes (1598) allowed freedom of worship to Calvinists in denominated areas, but Louis XIII's army took the town in 1620 and ordered the demolition of the ramparts. Some Calvinists stayed on until 1681, but the Revocation of the Edict of Nantes resulted in the loss in 1685 of many rich merchants and tradesmen to England and Holland. By the Revolution, Bergerac was still larger than Périgueux but the latter became the *préfecture* of the newly-formed *département* of the Dordogne in 1870.

From the Place du Port, site of the old river port northwest of the bridge, Rue du Port or Rue des Récollets lead to the old town centre, Place du Dr-Cayla. On the left is the rectangular Place de la Myrpe surrounded by pretty 17C–18C houses, some timber and brick, and the statue of *Cyrano de Bergerac* by Dorillac and Varoqueaux. The real Savinien Cyrano (1619–55), who was the basis for Rostand's character, was born in Paris, became a musketeer, adopted Gascony as his *pays*, and took the name Bergerac. He was a great duellist and also a poet, but the truth of his origins was only established in the early 20C. At the end of the square in a timbered 18C building which had been a sailors' tavern is the **Musée de la Tonnellerie et Batellerie**, of river shipping, with models and tools. Open Tues–Fri 10.00–12.00 and 14.30–17.30, Sat mornings, Sun afternoons, closed Mon; ☎ 05 53 57 80 92.

Diagonally across from Cyrano's statue are the Protestant Temple (19C) and the **Cloître des Récollets**, rebuilt in the 17C on a 12C base. This was taken over by the Pères Recollets in 1630: they had established a mission in Bergerac at the wish of Louis XIII with the express aim of bringing locals back to the Roman Catholic faith, sometimes by force. Arranged around a small, galleried courtyard it now houses the **Maison des Vins de Bergerac**, with information and exhibi-

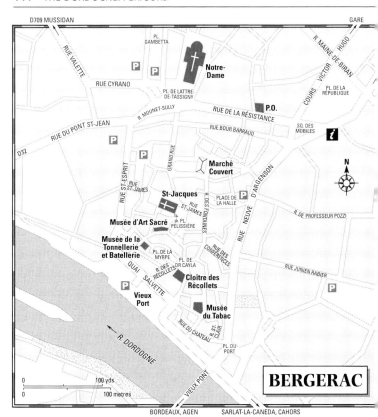

D709 MUSSIDAN

GARE

PL. GAMBETTA

RUE VALETTE

Notre-Dame

RUE CYRANO

PL. DE LATTRE-DE-TASSIGNY

R. MAINE-DE-BIRAN

COURS VICTOR HUGO

PL. DE LA RÉPUBLIQUE

R. MOUNET-SULLY

RUE DE LA RÉSISTANCE

P.O.

RUE DU PONT ST-JEAN

RUE BOUR BARRAUD

SQ. DES MOBILES

D32

RUE ST-ESPRIT

RUE ST-JAMES

GRAND RUE

Marché Couvert

St-Jacques

RUE ST-JAMES

R. DES FONTAINES

PLACE DE LA HALLE

RUE NEUVE D'ARGENSON

R. DE PROFESSEUR POZZI

Musée d'Art Sacré

PL. PELISSIÈRE

Musée de la Tonnellerie et Batellerie

PL. DE LA MYRPE

PL. DE DR CAYLA

RUE DES CONFÉRENCES

QUAI SALVETTE

R. DES RÉCOLLETS

Cloître des Récollets

RUE JUNIEN RABIER

Vieux Port

Musée du Tabac

RUE DU CHÂTEAU

R. ST. CLAIR

PL. DU PORT

R. DORDOGNE

0   100 yds
0   100 metres

VIEUX PONT

BERGERAC

BORDEAUX, AGEN   SARLAT-LA-CANEDA, CAHORS

tions concerning the *vignoble bergeracois* and its twelve *appellations*. Open June–Aug 10.00–19.00; Mar–June, Sept–Oct 10.00–12.30 and 13.30–18.00; rest of year by appointment; ☎ 05 53 63 57 55.

In the small streets to the east, on Rue de l'Ancien Pont, is the Maison Peyrarède (1604), which has a small suspended watchtower on the angle. In the 17C there were boutiques and stabling at street level. Installed here is the **Musée du Tabac**, which has a remarkable collection of pipes and other objects associated with tobacco worldwide. Open Tues–Fri 10.00–12.00 and 14.00–18.00, Sat to 17.00, Sun 14.30–18.30, closed Mon; ☎ 05 53 63 04 13.

Take Rue des Fargues and turn right onto Rue des Fontaines, passing the **Maison Doublet** where in 1577, Henry of Navarre and representatives of King Henri III met to negotiate a ceasefire during the Wars of Religion. Along Rue St-James are some fine bourgeois houses (17C–18C) and the Font-Peyre, a fountain which ran with wine during festivities when King Charles IX visited the town in August 1565. This brings you to the revamped Place Pélissière and the church of **St-Jacques**, which developed from modest chapel in the 12C to an important urban church in the 14C and where meetings were held during the Hundred Years War. Damaged then and in the 16C, it was almost totally rebuilt in 17C when the Catholics moved back. Below the church, installed in the

Catholic Mission of 1680, is the **Musée d'Art Sacré**, with 17C–18C Counter-Reformation pieces. Open July, Aug, Tues–Sun 15.30–18.00, closed Mon; rest of year Sun only 15.30–18.00; ☎ 05 53 63 40 22.

The Grand'Rue passes the covered market hall (1885), a metal structure built on the site of a Protestant church demolished in 1682. Behind it is the 15C Maison Charles IX, where the king stayed with his mother, Catherine de Médicis, in 1565. The continuation of the Grand'Rue brings you to Rue de la Résistance and the newer part of town. Opposite is the rather dull neo-Gothic church of **Notre-Dame** (1856–65), built to initial plans by Viollet-le-Duc and completed by Abadie. To the right, along Rue de la Résistance, is Place du Palais and Place de la République and the tourist office.

The **Château de Tiregand** stands at the heart of the Pécharmant vinyards east of Bergerac, on the north bank of the Dordogne (the Bergeracois) around Creysse on the D660. The château, rebuilt in the 17C, belongs to the Saint-Exupéry family (p 540) and produces a *grand cru*. The château, gardens and *chais* (wine cellars) can be visited, and tastings arranged by appointment only; ☎ 05 53 23 21 08, fax 05 53 22 58 49.

Wines of Bergerac

The Bergerac region is promoted as the 'Other Great Vineyard of Aquitaine', geographically close to and historically competing with Bordeaux. The wine has been much appreciated in the past (and the present) by the English, and from the 14C a special mark of distinction was stamped on its barrels. During the Reformation, the Netherlands was the main customer for Bergerac wine and it is now exported throughout the world. There are 12 *AOCs*, and 12,000ha under cultivation, with a production of 52 per cent red and 48 per cent white. The reds and rosés of *Bergerac*, supple and fruity, are produced from Cabernet Sauvignon, Cabernet Franc, Merlot Noir, Côt or Malbec; the dry whites are a blend of Sémillon, Sauvignon, Muscadelle, Ondenc and Chenin Blanc. *Rosette* is a sweet and subtle white wine, slightly straw-coloured. The *Côtes-de-Bergerac* produce reds, using the same grape varieties as the Bergerac red, and whites, divided between *demi-sec*, *moelleux* (mellow) and *doux*. *Montravel* is a dry white, *Haut Montravel* is *mœlleux* and *Saussignac* is another fruity sweet white. *Monbazillac* is probably the best known of the heavy *blancs liquoreux*, blending Sémillon, Sauvignon and Muscadelle which are harvested late and by hand; individual grapes are selected when they reach the correct degree of noble rot. *Pécharmant* is the most famous of the reds, its distinctive taste coming from the sand and gravel of the banks of the Dordogne which cover a deep layer of ferruginous clay, called Tran. The **Maison des Vins at Bergerac** (see above) supplies information on wines, tastings and routes.

South of Bergerac on the D31 is the **Château de Monbazillac**, built on a cliff and surrounded by vineyards. This is an opportunity for a *dégustation* in the smart Cave Coopérative, a visit to the château and a meal in the attractive restaurant (see above). Open June–Sept 10.00–19.00; July, Aug to 19.30; April–May, Oct 10.00–12.00 and 14.00–18.00; rest of year to 17.00; closed Jan; ☎ 05 53 61 52 52. Cave Coopérative; ☎ 05 53 63 65 00. The château has 3000ha of vines, the majority (2700ha) for whites—Sémillon, Sauvignon and Muscadet—

and gives its name to the sweet, strong yellow wine for which it is renowned. This is produced from grapes which are heavy in sugar and left on the vine until they arrive at a state of *pourriture noble* (rot) and produce a fungus, *botrytis cinerea*.

The château is at the end of an alley of vines and from its high terrace has stupendous views over the vineyards towards Bergerac; to the right is the restaurant. It dates from the mid-16C and is a handsome combination of military might and domestic elegance, with sturdy angle towers, decorative machicolations, steep russet roofs and four-square windows. It was a Protestant stronghold but survived the Civil Wars and the Revolution virtually unscathed. The visit takes you to three levels. In the basement kitchens is a display of bottles and a wine museum. The ground floor combines a little local ethnology with the history of local Protestantism, and rooms furnished with rustic 17C furniture. On the level above is some extraordinary 19C neo-Baroque dining-room furniture, bedrooms and old photographs of about 100 Périgordian châteaux. Cross-country to the west of Monbazillac (D17) is the **Moulin de Malfourat**, a group of wrecked windmills on a high ridge.

Southeast of here by the N21 and D14 is the higgledy-piggledy circular *bourg* of **Issigeac**. No *bastide* of straight parallel streets this. In the 17C Issigeac was much favoured by the bishops of Sarlat, in whose diocese it lay. The Gothic church, with barley-sugar arches over the porch, was built by Armand de Gontaut-Biron, Bishop of Sarlat and in the 17C, Bishop François de Salignac built a residence next to the church. This fairly formidable building with two overhanging turrets is now the *mairie*. Opposite, in the tightly packed centre, is the **Maison des Dimes**, with a tall roof covered with *lauze* and a cluster of medieval, half-timbered buildings, notably the **Maison de Têtes** on the corner of the Grande Rue, with grimacing heads carved on the timbers above the stone arcades. To the west is the Prévôté, residence of the Provost, with a *lauze*-covered porch and pigeon-tower.

The section of the Dordogne between Gardonne and Castillon-la-Bataille marks the border between the Gironde and the Périgord. On the river banks, in countryside not totally made over to vines, is the busy commercial town of **Ste-Foy-la-Grande**. Ste-Foy has one of the best markets as well as two annual fairs in March and November.

This *bastide* was built in 1255 at the orders of Alphonse de Poitiers around an existing Benedictine monastery, dedicated to Ste Foy (Faith). It became an important Protestant centre of erudite humanism where Henri de Navarre sought refuge in 1576. In the middle of the main square, Place Gambetta, is the 18C *mairie* and around it are some fairly attractive arcaded houses. The older houses are 16C or 17C, including the tourist office. Follow Rue Pasteur to the banks of the Dordogne where once there was a small harbour. In Rue des Frères-Reclus are some interesting houses, notably no. 27, and the church is a 19C remodelling of a succession of churches (13C and 17C), with only hints of its earlier life and a series of rather ugly modern windows.

West of Ste-Foy-la-Grande on the D936, at Vélines, is a romantic creation of the 1950s, the **Jardins de Sardy**. Carefully orchestrated, it has perspectives created by ornamental ponds and cypress hedges combined with a rockery and large flower beds. Open Easter to October daily 10.00–18.00; ☎ 05 53 27 51 45.

The village of **Montcaret** shelters the remains of a Gallo-Roman villa (1C and 4C). The site was excavated in 1922–39, after the village cemetery was relocated.

The remains are well conserved, partly sheltered and partly in the open, on both sides of the road and around the church that was built over the site. The museum is open daily April–June and Sept 09.30–12.30, 14.00–18.00; 1 July–31 Aug 09.30–13.00, 14.00–19.30; 1 Oct–31 March 10.00–12.30, 14.00–16.30; closed 1 Jan, 1 May, 1 Nov, 25 Dec; ☎ 05 53 58 50 18. The discoveries include some particularly fine mosaics, and reception rooms with hypocausts have been exposed although the peristyle was partly obliterated by the church. Parts of some thermae can be seen to the south of church, with the frigidarium mosaic visible. Built in Graeco-Roman style, the villa at Montcaret is similar to those at Montmaurin (p 500) and Plassac (p 95). It was probably abandoned in the 6C, and there is a leap of five centuries to the 11C Romanesque church, which incorporates some Roman elements on the exterior. Inside there are some good capitals, some recycled Gallo-Roman and some 11C, one of which shows *Daniel in the Lions' Den.*

Nearby at **St-Michel-de-Montaigne** on the edge of the Périgord is the birth-place of Michel Eyquem de Montaigne, humanist and philosopher. The château cannot be visited but Montaigne's tower can, as can the gardens from which are wonderful views. Guided visits, July, Aug daily 10.00–18.30; June, Sept–Oct, Mon, Wed–Sun 10.00–12.00 and 14.00–18.30, closed Tues; March–May, Nov–Dec, Wed–Sun 10.00–12.00 and 14.00–17.30, closed Mon, Tues; ☎ 05 53 58 63 93. The ancestral home was burned to the ground in 1885 and has been rebuilt in Renaissance style. Happily, the tower, standing apart, was spared and has remained shrine-like since Montaigne's time. On the ground floor is a small chapel, and on the floor above a bedroom linked to the chapel by a recess. On the top floor is the famous library, where the ceiling beams are decorated with maxims chosen by Montaigne to encourage meditation on the human condition. Several of Montaigne's family were buried in the village, but Montaigne is not.

Michel de Montaigne

Born Michel Eyquem (1533–92), he took the name of his birthplace. He had a Classical education and went into law, and while a member of the *parlement* in Bordeaux established a long and enduring friendship with the writer Etienne de la Boétie. Elected mayor of Bordeaux in 1581, he held office for four years. Strongly attached to his native Périgord, in 1570 he began his best-known work, *Essais,* an extraordinarily frank and modern discussion of the difficulties inherent in the search for truth, justice and tolerance, published in Bordeaux in 1580. His travels across Europe in 1580–81 were the source of his *Journal,* which served to confirm his philos-ophy. At the age of 52 he gave up his official duties to dedicate himself entirely to study and meditation in his library in the tower at Montaigne. He continued to add to the *Essais* so that by 1588 it comprised three volumes. He judged that the art of living should be based on prudent wisdom and inspired by good sense and tolerance.

Other small sites of interest in this area, known as le Gurson, include **Monpeyroux** on the D10, where the 12C church has a decorative façade. **Villefranche-de-Lonchat**, founded on the site of a priory whose 11C church was situated outside the village, was restored by monks of La Sauve Majeure in 1463, who built a crypt to compensate for the gradient of the site. The church is characteristic of the transitional stage from Romanesque to Gothic, with a simple arched doorway. There is a second church, dedicated to St Anne, inside the village. The village of **St-Martin-de-Gurson** has a 12C west front decorated in the style of the Saintonge, with arcading above the door and a variety of sculptures.

6 The Dordogne: Périgord Noir

The rather misleading description of this area, Black Périgord, derives from its woodland, especially the pine and juniper and other scrub but also the dark bark of the small variety of oak found here, which loses its leaves in spring. At the beginning of the 19C, most of this area (with the exception of the Dordogne Valley) was still covered in dense forests. In the summer it is anything but black.

The southeast corner of the Dordogne has the greatest intensity of sites and monuments in the *département*, with a remarkable concentration of prehistoric caves and rock shelters, castles and *bastides*, along the valleys of the Dordogne and the Vézère. This chapter divides the area accordingly, with an additional section on the capital of Black Périgord, Sarlat.

THE VÉZÈRE VALLEY AND PREHISTORY

The pretty and sometimes spectacular **Valley of the Vézère** revels in a wealth of prehistory. The river's course through the soft limestone created remarkable overhanging rocks and south-facing cliffs to provide prehistoric man with a profusion of *abris* (rock shelters). The pure but porous limestone also offers up numerous *grottes* (caves) and *gouffres* (caverns), some adorned by early man, some fascinating for their mineral concretions and formations. There is also a quantity of archaeological sites offering up *gisements*, the debris accumulated over the thousands of years of occupation by man. Many of the 200 or so prehistoric sites along the Vézère (which are often open to the public) are clustered around the small village of Les Eyzies, which contains the national museum of prehistory and is designated 'Capitale Mondiale de la Préhistoire'.

Getting there and around
Car

D710 from Périgueux to le Bugue; D47 to Les Ezies; D704 from N89 to Lascaux.

Train

Périgueux to Agen line via Le Bugue, Les Ezies, etc. Bordeaux or Toulouse lines, change at Le Buisson for Le Bugue, etc. Périgueux to Brive change at Condat-le-Lardin for Montignac.

Tourist information
24260 Le Bugue Pl. de l'Hôtel-de-Ville, ☎ 05 53 07 20 48, fax 05 53 54 92 30, www.perigord.com/bugue
24620 Les-Eyzies-de-Tayac 19 Ave de la République, ☎ 05 53 06 97 05, fax 05 53 06 90 79, www.perigord.tm.fr/servtourisme/otsi/eyzies
24290 Montignac Pl. Bertrand de Born, ☎ 05 53 51 82 60, fax 05 53 50 49 72

024580 **Rouffignac** Pl. de la Marie,
☎ 05 53 05 39 03
24121 **Terrasson-la-Villedieu** BP 37,
Rue Jean Rouby, ☎ 05 53 50 37 56, fax
05 53 51 01 22, www.ot-terrasson.fr

Market days

Beaumont Saturday
Beynac Monday
Le Bugue Tuesday and Saturday
Domme Thursday
Les Ezies Monday
Montignac Wednesday, Saturday
La Rogue Gagiae Friday
Terrasson-la-Villedieu Thursday

 Festivals and events
July Festival de Montignac
July–August *Festival du Périgord Noir*, classical concerts in churches and châteaux, St-Léon-sur-Vézère and other venues
Musique en Périgord, all types of music in concerts indoors and out, Le Bugue, Les Eyzies

Where to stay and eating out

24260 LE BUGUE

✩✩✩✩ *Royal Vézère*, Pl. de l'Hôtel-de-Ville, ☎ 05 53 07 20 01, fax 05 53 03 51 80, www.hotels-restau-dordogne.org/royal-vezere. Terrace overlooking the river and excellent cooking.

✩✩ *Le Château*, Campagne (4km east of Le Bugue on the D703), ☎ 05 53 07 23 50, fax 05 53 03 93 69. Quiet and attractive setting and not too expensive.

24260 LES EYZIES-DE-TAYAC-SIREUIL

✩✩ *Moulin de la Beune*, ☎ 05 53 06 93 39, fax 05 53 06 98 06. Old mill with a stream in a green setting.

✩✩ *Cro-Magnon*, ☎ 05 53 06 97 06. Hotel-restaurant in charming surroundings, thoughtful cooking.

€€€ *Le Centenaire*, Le Rocher de la Penne, ☎ 05 53 06 97 18. Inn around a courtyard with an original slant on Périgordian cooking. Rooms available.

€€ *Au Vieux Moulin*, at the Hôtel Moulin de la Beune (above). Interesting, unconventional food.

24260 MAUZENS-MIREMONT

Les Forges du Roy, north of Les Eyzies (between D710 and D470), ☎ 05 53 35 50 01, fax 05 53 35 50 41. *Chambres d'hôte* in a fine old house in woods.

24290 MONTIGNAC

✩✩✩ *Hostellerie La Roserai*, Pl. d'Armes, ☎ 05 53 50 53 92, fax 05 53 51 02 23. At the heart of the village, on the river in a charming 19C setting; pool. Reputable food.

✩✩✩ *Relais du Soleil d'Or*, 16 Rue du IV Septembre, ☎ 05 53 52 80 22, fax 05 53 50 27 54. Close to Lascaux. Gentle pace of life. Regional cooking highlighted.

24580 ROUFFIGNAC

✩✩✩ *Château de Fleurac*, ☎ 05 53 05 95 01, fax 05 53 05 98 47. A 19C pile comfortably transformed.

Prehistory in southwest France

The limestone of southwest France is riddled with caves and galleries formed by natural fissures and erosion, and by underground rivers, millions of years ago. Overland rivers carved their way through the landscape, creating deep gorges and exposing high cliffs also pitted with caves. The south-facing cliffs, especially along the rivers Veezère, Isle, Dordogne and Garonne, were populated during the last two Ice Ages (500,000–125,000 BC and 115,000–10,000 BC). The beginning of man's existence is divided into three major periods according to the implements or tools produced reflecting the progress of these early civilisations: Palaeolithic or Carved Stone Age, Mesolithic, Neolithic or Polished Stone Age, and the Metal Ages—Bronze and Iron. The Palaeolithic period which began some 450,000 years ago breaks down into Lower, Middle and Upper.

During the Upper Palaeolithic period (35,000/30,000–*c* 10,000 BC) man decorated caves whose structure has not been altered over millions of years, apart from the blockage of openings. It should be said that 'cave man' is a totally erroneous name for early man who, from the very beginning, built some kind of protection from branches and skins, and chose to be in the open in some kind of south-facing rock shelter, such as an overhanging cliff or the opening of a cave. Caves were dark, unwelcoming and soon filled with smoke. They did place their dead in caves, however, and also decorated the caves for some kind of ritualistic purpose, but exactly what that was is open to conjecture.

The first signs of *homo erectus* were during the Lower Palaeolithic period (500,000–100,000 years ago). In the Périgord, these were at La Micoque close to Les Ezies; and the oldest European skeleton (*c* 450,000 years ago) was discovered in 1971 near Tautavel in the eastern Pyrenees. These hunter-gatherers created a multi-purpose flint tool, the biface or hand axe, and there is evidence that they learned to make fire around 400,000 years ago. Neanderthal man emerged some 100,000 years ago (Middle Palaeolithic), and as well as a tool production known as Mousterian (from Le Moustier, Dordogne), they developed an appreciation for colour and buried their dead in caves (such as La Chapelle-aux-Saints in Corrèze). The only Neanderthal skeleton discovered in France, at Le Moustier in 1908, was sold to Berlin where the skull was repeatedly rebuilt, and it is now in eastern Germany.

The last and most recent category, the direct ancestor of modern man, Cro-Magnon man (*Homo sapiens sapiens*), emerged during the Upper Palaeolithic period. With the same intelligence and looks as us, they produced relatively more sophisticated tools than their predecessors, by extracting blades from a large flint core, and from animal bone and antlers. The first Cro-Magnons, the Aurignacians (*c* 32,000 to 20,000 BC), began to create figurative images as well as geometric signs—symbolic and schematised genitalia, and animals, as at Castanet and La Ferrassie in the Dordogne. (The Chauvet Cave (Ardèche), discovered in 1999, proves the existence of highly sophisticated paintings at the same period in other areas.) The Gravettian civilisation (25,000–17,000 BC) produced more recognisable images identified at Pair-non-Pair (Gironde), Gargas (Hautes Pyrénées) and Le Pataud rock shelter (Dordogne), including carvings in the round and reliefs, often fertility symbols which are known as Venuses, such as the ***Venus of Laussel*** at the Musée d'Aquitaine (p 73).

The Solutrean civilisation (*c* 21,000–18,000 BC) was relatively short but produced the skilfully knapped, extremely thin and sharp 'laurel leaf' tool as well as fine engravings, reliefs and paintings at Le Fourneau de Diable and Laugerie-Haute in the Dordogne. Hot on their heels were the Early Magdalenians (*c* 17,000 BC), named after La Madeleine (Dordogne), in the most remarkable phase of the Upper Palaeolithic era and most closely associated with cave painting, including Lascaux (Dordogne), at a time when the climate was going through a milder phase. The Magdalenians invented or made greater use of the stone tallow lamp which provided the opportunity to access deeper recesses underground and to produce imagery of the most exquisite quality. The period of the Middle Magdalenian (16,000–13,000 BC) is represented by a unique carved relief frieze of horses and other animals at the Cap Blanc rock shelter and by a mass of engravings at the cave of Les Combarelles, as well as the marvellous series of painted bisons at Font-de-

Gaume (all in Dordogne). Palaeolithic man of the Upper Magdalenian period (c 11,000–9500 BC) lived through the last cold blast of glaciation followed by increasing humidity. He developed the harpoon and left impressive examples of carved bone and ivory, as well as engravings in La Madeleine cave.

Prehistoric man developed extraordinary skills in a variety of techniques of carving, drawing and painting to create images, and had an innate ability to handle the limited palette available. He was capable of creating movement and perspective and of cleverly using the rock face to give depth and animation, which has to be imagined in the flickering light of a tallow candle. In certain caves or shelters only one technique is found, in others a combination. This work was carried out in sites which were often difficult to access, suggesting extreme dedication; the period over which the same cave was decorated might span tens of thousands of years.

The pigments for painting were limited to natural ochre—ranging from yellow to brownish red oxides obtained from iron oxides or iron ore—or black from manganese dioxide or carbon. Colour was dabbed on with the finger or some kind of rudimentary brush or with clumps of hair or moss, or applied with a 'pencil' of coloured rock. A technique of spray-painting involved projecting pigment either directly from the mouth or through a hollow bone, sometimes using a template to create a silhouette, typically the 'negatives' of hands as found in Pech Merle (Lot) and Gargas (Hautes Pyrénées), as well as to form the outline of images such as the horses at Lascaux.

The subjects are usually limited to certain animals (bison, mammoths, horses, aurochs, antelope), although there are occasional representations of fish or human figures. The paintings are described as 'mythograms', with an undecipherable symbolism, and are rarely anecdotal although occasionally some action is depicted, such as a man and an ox at Lascaux, Villars and Le Roc de Sers, mountain goats locked in combat at Lascaux, or one deer tenderly licking another at Font de Gaume.

The journey starts at **Le Bugue**, a busy and rather touristy village where the Vézère loops to create a natural amphitheatre. It has cashed in on the prehistory trail with a wide range of activities including an ornithological park, Maison de la Vie Sauvage, specialising in European species and a section devoted to palaeontology. Open July–Sept daily 10.00–13.00, 15.00–19.00; Oct–June 14.00–18.00; ☎ 05 53 08 28 10. Le Village du Bournat attempts to evoke a 19C Perigoridian village. Open May–Sept daily 10.00–19.00; Oct–Dec, Feb–April 10.00–17.00; closed Jan; ☎ 05 53 08 41 99. Le Bugue also has the Aquarium du Périgord Noir, showing freshwater fish, and the Jardins de d'Arborie (☎ 05 53 08 42 74).

Nearby caves include the **Grotte de Bara-Bahau** northwest of Le Bugue, which has engravings of the Magdalenian period on the roof. Guided visits July, Aug daily 09.00–19.00; Feb–June and Sept–Dec 10.00–12.00 and 14.00–17.00; closed Jan; ☎ 05 53 07 44 58. East of Le Bugue is the **Grotte de St-Cirq**, which also has some engravings, one entitled the *Man* or *Sorcerer of St-Cirq*, and a small museum. Guided visits Mon–Fri, Sun, June–Sept 10.00–18.00; Sept–May 12.00–16.00; closed Sat; ☎ 05 53 07 14 37. **La Ferrassie** near Savignac-de-Miremont, to the north, consists of three prehistoric sites where Neanderthal graves and Mousterian tools came to light; ☎ 05 53 06 90 80.

On the other side of the river, south of Le Bugue near the picturesque village of Audrix, is the **Gouffre de Proumeyssac**, which has no prehistoric art but some wonderful stalactites and crystalline formations. It is in a spectacular position and accessed by a man-made tunnel. Open daily May, June 09.30–18.30 July–Aug 09.00–19.00; March, April, Sept, Oct 09.30–12.00 and 14.00–17.30; Feb, Nov, Dec 14.00–17.00; ☎ 05 53 07 27 47.

Les-Eyzies-de-Tayac

Upriver is the prestigious site of Les-Eyzies-de-Tayac. The village, bounded on one side by the Vézère, creeps up the looming cliff which runs parallel to the river. Small troglodyte buildings and caves are visible on the cliff face, as well as the 13C and 16C Château des Eyzies built by the Barons of Beynac, which houses the museum of prehistory. It is pinpointed on the high terrace by a rather unfortunate sculpture, supposedly representing Neanderthal man, by Paul Dardé (1930). It was at Les Eyzies in 1868, at the Abri de Cro-Magnon, that the first remains of *Homo sapiens sapiens* were discovered. The site is near the hotel of the same name behind the station but only a commemorative plaque remains. Buried in a grave of the Aurignacian period (*c* 35,000 BC) were five skeletons, one of a man who had reached the then remarkable age of 50. Near the *abri* is the fortified church of St-Martin-de-Tayac (12C), with a *lauze*-covered keep and severe west façade.

The **Musée National de Préhistoire** housed in the château was conceived in 1913 by the prehistorian Denis Peyrony. The vast extension to the museum is due to open in the second half of 2003. Open July. Aug daily 09.30–19.00; April–June, Sept–Oct daily 09.30–12.00 and 14.00–18.00; Nov–March, Mon, Wed–Sun 09.30–12.00, 14.00–17.00, closed Tues; ☎ 05 53 06 45 45.

The museum is an essential visit for anyone interested in prehistory. It contains a fascinating treasure trove of objects from local sites (and some replicas of the more precious pieces now in the Musée d'Aquitaine in Bordeaux, and elsewhere) from some 500,000 years ago to the end of the Ice Age (*c* 10,000 BC). The collection contains a multitude of stone tools showing their morphological evolution over thousands of years. There are also replicas of a prehistoric 'hearth' of the Solutrean era, a stone-cutting workshop of the Aurignacian period and a Magdalenian dwelling.

The museum owns an important collection of engraved and sculpted stone blocks, mainly characteristic of Palaeolithic art from the end of the Würm Ice Age (*c* 20,000 BC), but some going back 50,000 years to the Neanderthal period. Palaeolithic carvings and engravings from Aurignacian to Late Périgordian (*c* 28,000 BC) include vulvas, small animals, phallic symbols and decorative contour designs on pebbles through to animals in the style of Lascaux, and towards the end of the Ice Age, a renewed interest in the female form. An outstanding and virtually unique work shows two bison moulded in red clay. There are small, transportable items such as engraved or sculpted bone or flint, usually depicting animals, including a sculpted tortoise, but also stylised humans—sometimes difficult to decipher—as well as items of personal adornment and other small domestic objects, even a whistle. Later pieces include bone harpoons and weapons. There are also moulds of famous skulls of Neanderthal and Cro-Magnon man, four graves from Combe-Capelle and the skeleton of a 5-year-old child from La Madeleine. The sepulchre from St-Germain-la-Rivière (Gironde), found in 1934, dates from the late Palaeolithic period (*c* 11,000–9000 BC), and contained the remains of a young female placed in a bent position. She was adorned with a necklace and there is evidence of some kind of stone sepulchre, important evidence of primitive burial rituals.

Downstream from the Cro-Magnon shelter is the **Musée et Site de l'Abri Pataud**. This rock shelter was inhabited by Cro-Magnon man for the entire Upper Palaeolithic period, some 15,000 years. The archaeological dig, which can be visited, is of world-wide importance for prehistory. Fourteen levels of habitation were excavated to a depth of 9.25m, mainly between 1958 and 1964, where the shelter had collapsed. The museum presents sculptures, including a beautiful relief of a mountain goat, as well as other objects found here. Guided visits; open July, Aug daily 10.00–19.00; April–June, Sept, Oct 10.00–12.30 and 13.30–19.00; Nov–March until 17.30; closed Mon, Jan; ☎ 05 53 06 92 46.

Just outside Les Eyzies on the D47 towards Sarlat is the entrance to the **Grotte de Font-de-Gaume**. It is difficult to park, and there is an uphill walk to the cave, but this is a visit not to be missed, as it is one of the last caves with original paintings still on view. Guided visits only to the cave here and to Les Combarelles (see below); visitor numbers are limited to 200 per day, so it is essential to book in advance and check the opening times; April–Sept 09.00–12.00 and 14.00–18.00; rest of the year 10.00–12.00 and 14.00–17.00 but liable to variation; closed Sat and PH; ☎ 05 53 06 86 00. There is a boutique and a bookshop. The paintings, on the sides of narrow galleries some 120m long, are quite superb. They date from 16,000–13,000 BC, in the Magdalenian period, and consist mainly of groups of bison, with some horses and other animals. Although the work has been defaced in places, it is of extremely high quality. This is a high point of cave art from the point of view of painting technique, polychromy, expressiveness and the subtle use of the contours of the rock face.

Slightly further along the same road is **Les Combarelles** (same opening hours and telephone number as Font-de-Gaume; must be booked in advance), a cave with engravings but no paintings discovered by Peyrony, Abbé Breuil and Louis Capitan in 1901. The engravings are dated from the same period as Font-de-Gaume and almost 200 have been identified. They are mainly of animals, but there is some anthropomorphic imagery as well as signs. They record the variety of fauna of the Magdalenian period, such as rhinoceros, bears, felines and wolves, but horses, bison, aurochs, bears, reindeer, mammoths and deer are favoured. The main gallery stretches for 240m and is fairly narrow, punctuated by wider sections, and has been dug out in places to make the visit easier.

Not far from Les Combarelles is the **Grotte de Bernifal**, on the left bank of the Petite Beune millstream. Open by prior booking only July, Aug 09.00–19.00; June, Sept, Oct–May 09.00–12.00 and 14.00–18.00; ☎ 05 53 29 66 39. Bernifal, discovered by Peyrony in 1902, contains both paintings and engravings of horses, bovine creatures and an ass, but the favourite animal image is the mammoth (as at Rouffignac, see below). It also contains what are known as tectiform signs, twelve engraved and one painted, unique to the Périgord. They look a bit like houses with gable roofs but their true significance remains a mystery. The cave is made up of two main galleries and a low, narrow linking corridor.

Remaining on this side of the Vézère, a small turning onto the D48 between Les Combarelles and Bernifal leads through wooded countryside to the **Abri du Cap Blanc**, where a path leads through the woods to the entrance in a building that protects the site and houses a small exhibition. Guided visits July, Aug 09.30–19.00; April–June, Sept–end Oct 10.00–12.00 and 14.00–18.00; closed Nov–March; ☎ 05 53 59 21 74. This is another extraordinary work, but different from most and unique in Périgord (there is something similar in the Vienne), in that it consists of a stunning high-relief frieze of monumental proportions, beautifully executed 16,000–13,000 years ago. The site was carelessly excavated in 1909, damaging the lower part of the frieze carved on the surface of a rock shelter which had been obscured by the collapse of the overhang. What remains is the upper part of six horses facing to the right, except for the most dominant one which is 2m long and facing the other way. The images are cleverly superimposed to give the impression of depth. There are also small bison and some other animals, more difficult to see, and traces of red ochre which suggest that the work was once coloured. A grave was discovered at the foot of the rock though this was not its original position.

Near Cap Blanc are the fairytale ruins of the **Château de Commarque**. Open April–Sept 10.00–19.00; ☎ 05 53 59 00 25. They are the remains of a fortified or 'castral' village which consisted of a Romanesque chapel, a 12C *maison tour* and lodgings, a defensive wall and ditch and a magnificent 14C keep. During the Hundred Years War it twice fell into the hands of the English and it was fought over by Protestants and Catholics in the 16C. By the early 18C the property was abandoned but a descendent of the Commarque family purchased it back in 1968, ensuring its conservation. Opposite is the restored Château de Laussel; about 500m from here is the Grand Abri where the Horned Venus was discovered (p 73).

Heading back towards Les Eyzies, at Sireuil, **Roc-de-Cazelle** is a troglodyte village in the cliff face. It takes you on a journey through prehistory with the help of models and scenes. Open July, Aug 10.00–20.00; June, Sept 10.00–19.00; March–May, Oct–Nov 10.00–18.00; Dec–Feb 11.00–17.00; ☎ 05 53 59 46 09.

There is a cluster of sites around the Gorge d'Enfer on the right bank of the Vézère on the D47 towards Périgueux. The **Musée de la Spéléologie** in the fort on the Roc du Tayac is all about the underground world of caves and potholing. Open June–Sept, Mon–Fri, Sun 11.00–18.00, closed Sat. High above the gorges with great views is the entrance to the **Grotte du Grand Roc**. This cave contains spectacular natural formations, the most special among them being the triangular crystals. Guided visits July, Aug 09.30–19.00; April–Oct 09.30–18.00; Feb, March, Nov, Dec10.00–17.00, closed Sat; closed Jan; ☎ 05 53 06 92 70, www.grandroc.com. At the **L'Abri de Laugerie-Basse** (same opening times as Grotte du Grand Roc) are prehistoric dwellings as well as modern troglodyte houses. Other sites which can be visited (book in advance, ☎ 05 53 06 90 80) include the **Abri du Poisson**, a small rock shelter with a metre-long engraving of a salmon; **Laugerie-Haute**, a vast shelter with 42 sedimentary levels; and **La Micoque**, a *gisement* which has offered up information from 450,000–100,000 BC. At little further on at Manaurie are the **Grottes de Carpe Diem** with a display of stalactites. Open July, Aug 09.30–19.00; April–June, Sept–Oct 10.00–18.00; Nov–Dec 10.00–17.00; ☎ 05 53 06 91 07.

Continue to follow the little valley of the Manaurie towards **Rouffignac**, a pleasant and tranquil village. It has a church, rebuilt after the Second World War, with a belfry-porch (*c* 1530) displaying knowledge of Renaissance vocabulary and a Flamboyant nave. The village is another important name in the annals of prehistory. Off the D32 is the **Grotte de Rouffignac** on the banks of La Binche. Guided visits in French only, April–June and Sept–Nov 10.00–11.30 and 14.00–17.00; July–Aug 09.00–11.30 and 14.00–18.00; ☎ 05 53 05 41 71, www.grottederouffignac.fr. This dry cave in a flint-rich limestone hill is described as 'the cave of a hundred mammoths'. The 226 animal images and four human representations in fact include 158 mammoths (i.e. 70 per cent of the decoration), bison, horses, ibex, and one bear, but the 11 rhinoceroses are the most unusual in general terms. The representations are drawn in black or engraved and, since no tools or other objects have been found, are dated stylistically to the Magdalenian period.

Northwest of Rouffignac on the D31 are the romantic ruins of the **Château de l'Herm** (1485–1512), built by the Calvimont family, members of the Parlement de Bordeaux. The site is identified by two robust defensive towers looming above the dark forest of Barade. A third hexagonal tower has a richly decorated Flamboyant doorway and contains a splendid spiral staircase ending in a star vault. Bizarrely superimposed monumental fireplaces decorated with the arms of the Calvimont family have been left suspended since the floors crumbled after the château was abandoned in the 17C. Open daily April–11 Nov 10.00–19.00; at other times by prior appointment; ☎ 05 53 05 46 61.

Along the Vézère

The left bank of the Vézère from Les Eyzies to Peyzac is a meandering, scenic drive through **Tursac**, which has a Romanesque domed church with a large belfry and 'scenes of prehistoric life' in a pleasant setting at the Préhistoparc; ☎ 05 53 50 73 17.

Cross the river towards Lespinasse, just beyond Tursac, for **La Madeleine**, where the 15C chapel is dedicated to Mary Magdalene, and the remains of a medieval troglodyte village probably occupied from the end of the 9C—during Viking raids—until the 19C. In 1863–64 a prehistoric *gisement* was identified close to the village. Excavations at this site prompted one of the most important phases in the study of prehistory and identified the Magdalenian culture. The prehistoric rock shelter of La Madeleine, 50m long and up to 15m wide, is at the base of the cliff at the water's edge on a particularly tight loop in the river. Open July, Aug 09.30–19.30; Sept–June 10.00–18.00; ☎ 05 53 06 92 49. In May 1864 the discovery of a large piece of mammoth tusk engraved with an image of the said animal proved that man had the living creature before his eyes. Many other works of art were also found here. Since 1872 the term Magdalenian has been applied to the most important period associated with Palaeolithic art. The large quantity of reindeer bones through the various levels excavated indicated the main diet of prehistoric man, and hundreds of decorated objects were also found. These have all been moved to museums and as there is nothing left to see here a visit is more in the form of a pilgrimage.

Dominating the left bank of the Vézère near Peyzac from a height of 80m is the most spectacular of all rock shelters, **La Roque St-Christophe**. Open July, Aug 10.00–19.00; 15 Nov–Feb 11.00–17.00; rest of year 10.00–18.00; ☎ 05 53 50 70 45, www.roque-st-christophe.com. This is a sheer cliff following the curve of the river, with five horizontal terraces and hundreds of caves which afforded protection to man from prehistoric times to the 16C. Steps are hewn into the rock to link the fourth and fifth levels some 60m above the river, and needless to say there are tremendous views over 900m of the valley along the length of the cliff. At **Peyzac-le-Moustier** is a palaeontological museum. Open July–Sept 09.00–19.30; other times by appointment; ☎ 05 53 50 81 02.

The village of **Le Moustier** on the right bank is perched on a promontory at the meeting of the Vézère and Vimont valleys. The rock shelter within the village was explored in 1863–64 and the evidence gathered in the upper shelter led to identification of the Mousterian period. The lower shelter yielded up a Neanderthal skeleton. Near the hamlet of Ruth are the shelters of Celliers, with engravings, and Pagès, which has revealed plenty of stone tools; ☎ 05 53 50 74 02. The Tour de la Vermondie (on the D45), so the legend goes, leaned over to allow the girl imprisoned in it to come closer to her lover outside. Further on up the D6 is the attractive village of **Plazac** which has a part-Romanesque church on a hill with a 12C belfry-keep and a palace built by the bishops in the 14C with a fine red sandstone doorway.

On the left bank of the Vézère, on the D65, is the village of **Sergeac**, heralded by a 15C roadside cross with images of the Virgin and St Michael. It developed around a Templar commandery and has a church that goes back to the 12C. The finds from the nine *abris* or *gisements* of **Castelmerle** (April–June 10.00–12.00 and 14.00–18.00, closed Sat; July, Aug daily 10.00–19.00; Sept–Oct 10.00–12.00 and 14.00–17.30, closed Sat; ☎ 05 53 50 74 79, www.castlemerle.com), including Labattut, Reverdit and La Souquette (☎ 05 53 50 79 70), are dispersed among various museums, but there is a small site museum in Sergeac, open all year by appointment, ☎ 05 53 50 77 45. As a respite from prehistory, back across the river at the pretty village of **St-Léon-sur-Vézère** is one of the most perfect Romanesque churches in the Périgord. A dependency of the abbey of Sarlat, it was built beside the river on the site of a Gallo-Roman villa, and has a square belfry with arcades on two levels and a *lauze* roof. Inside is a vaulted nave and domed crossing and the apsidal chapels are connected to the apse by narrow passageways. In the cemetery is a 14C chapel. The **Château de Chabans** is an elegant complex dating from the 16C–17C which has undergone considerable restoration and has a rare collection of 15C–20C stained glass. It is used for temporary exhibitions and there are gardens and parkland. Open daily May–Sept 14.30–20.00; ☎ 05 53 51 70 60.

Also on the right bank, north of Thonac along the Thonac valley, is the ravishing village of **Fanlac**. The **Château de Losse**, back on the river, is one of the most delightful smaller castles in Périgord and its position on a high rock terrace affords commanding views of the valley. Independent visits to the grounds, guided visits to interior, June–Aug 10.00–19.00; April, May, Sept 10.00–12.30 and 13.30–18.00; closed Oct–March; ☎ 05 53 50 80 08. The château began as a medieval fort with a dry moat, which was replaced in the 16C by a more gentrified version. The main L-shaped block with four-square windows has a round angle tower and crenellated walkways and machicolations under a soaring red roof. The property belonged to Jean II de Losse, preceptor of Henri IV and Governor of Guyenne. Inside there is interesting Italian and Louis XIII furniture and some good Flemish and Italian tapestries.

Le Thot Espace Cro-Magnon is an animal park and museum that has collected examples of species the same as, or similar to, those found in prehistoric imagery, including Przewalski horses (and if they do not exist they are replicated). The museum gives an overall view of Palaeolithic art and there is a fascinating film and exhibition describing the making of Lascaux II (see below) as well as the opportunity to create a cave painting. Opening hours as for Lascaux II: combined ticket available: ☎ 05 53 50 70 44; for reservations contact *Semitour Périgord*, ☎ 05 53 05 65 65.

The busy little town of **Montignac** spans the Vézère and has a ruined castle. It is the gateway to the most famous painted cave, Lascaux. Its immediate claim to fame is that the author of *Jacquou le Croquant*, Eugène Le Roy, lived in Montignac and died here in 1907. *La Paléothèque* at 59 Rue du 4 Septembre is a bookshop specialising in prehistory.

Lascaux

Lascaux, south of Montignac, is the high spot of Palaeolithic painting in France, with images of intense beauty and observation; but the cave paintings were nearly lost because of over-enthusiasm when the cave was first discovered. As a result, the cave has been closed to the public since 1968. The Grotte de Chauvet in the Ardèche which competes with, even surpasses Lascaux in quality and range of paintings, will not suffer the same fate because, for several reasons, it will never be open to the public.

Since 1983 the general public has visited a brilliant replica of the original cave called **Lascaux II**, about 200m from the real thing on the same wooded hill. During the summer, tickets must be purchased at the ticket office in Montignac run by *Semitour Périgord*. In winter they can be purchased on the spot. Timed and guided tours (some in English, about 45 minutes) July, Aug daily 09.00–20.00; April–June, Sept daily 09.30–18.30; Feb–March Tues–Sun 10.00–12.30 and 14.00–17.30; Oct–11 Nov daily 10.00–12.30 and 14.00–18.00; Nov–Dec Tues–Sun 10.00–12.00 and 14.00–17.30; closed Jan to early Feb. Confirm by telephone, *Semitour-Périgord* ☎ 05 53 05 65 65, fax 05 53 06 30 94, site ☎ 05 53 51 96 23; www.culture.fr/culture/arcnat/lascaux/en. There is a small shop with postcards and books.

The entrance to Lascaux, in a limestone hill, was blocked shortly after it was decorated by the early Magdalenians. It was not reopened until 1940 when a local boy, Marcel Ravidat, was searching for his dog. By 1948 it had been made ready for the public and the hordes who visited the limited space—the cave is only 150m long—in uncontrolled numbers did almost irrevocable damage, as did cutting a ventilation shaft to the surface. Green algae built up on the surfaces and, even worse, a deposit of opaque calcite crystals formed a coating over the paintings. By 1963 it was decided that the cave should be closed and careful monitoring of the site has brought it back almost to its original state. The cave floor had only one archaeological level but, despite careless removal in the 1940s, rich finds including the painters' tools, charcoal and pollens narrowed down the date of the works on the walls to *c* 17,000 years ago, making them among the oldest paintings of the Magdalenian period. The work is of such fine quality that it must have been executed by practised artists, indicating that the cave had a very important role in ritual or as a sanctuary.

The majority of animals depicted in Lascaux are horses, aurochs (horned bovine creatures which disappeared in the Middle Ages) and deer and the style of their execution is peculiar to Lascaux. The confidence of the line, the emotive use of colour, the manipulation of form to express movement and create depth are quite remarkable and barely surpassed in the 20C. The best known images of Lascaux are the horses, delicate creatures similar to the Przewalski horse found in Asia, with small heads and hooves and round belly; they are also described as 'Chinese' because of the black outline and delicate ochre wash. The auroch bulls are majestic and are represented in part three-quarters view, whereas most animals are in profile. The deer are delicately and gracefully drawn, the stags holding their antlers proudly erect. The animals appear in series or in friezes interspersed with a repertoire of repeated enigmatic signs, ranging from a four-part rectangle to stick-like or jagged lines. The ochre pigments, which range from deep maroon to yellow, are used in combination with outlines of black manganese dioxide.

Everything about Lascaux has been replicated as faithfully as possible, including the temperature, which is kept to an authentic 13°C. It is entered by a flight of steps leading to an outer underground cement bunker (there are no further steps inside). At the start, diagrams and displays describe the original layout, tools and pigments used in Lascaux 17,000 years ago. It is important to suspend disbelief when the doors slide back and you enter the cave. The shape and contours of the two main chambers have been precisely reproduced. The paintings are quite out-standing, in terms of both their original creation and painstaking recreation carried out by a local artist, Monique Peytral, using the same methods and materials as Palaeolithic man. Lascaux II took ten years to complete. The Hall of the Bulls is dominated by huge aurochs, which career over the walls. One, at 5.5m long, is the largest known prehistoric painting. In the narrow Axial Gallery are some of the most haunting images of horses and deer.

On the plateau some 500m from Lascaux, overlooking the Vézère Valley and Montignac, is the **Gisement du Régourdou**, a collapsed rock shelter where a Mousterian burial was found in 1957. Open July, Aug 10.00–19.00; Sept–June 11.00–18.00; ☎ 05 53 51 81 23. This site is about 60,000 years earlier than Lascaux and nearby receptacles with the remains of brown bears were found, a puzzling juxtaposition. Magdalenian man ground pigments here. There is a small museum on the site and some live bears. The Château de la Grande Filolie (no admission) on the D704 is a *manoir* of Disneyland perfection, mostly built in the 14C–15C and some in the 18C, with pointy *lauze* roofs contrasting with the local yellow limestone. The early-17C **Château de Sauveboeuf** near Aubas is in the style of Louis XIII. Open mid-May–mid-June, Sept 10.00–12.00 and 14.00–18.00; ☎ 05 53 51 89 46.

East of Montignac, off the D704 at **St-Amand-de-Coly**, the awesome fortified church towering over the village is one of the finest of its kind in the region, built in pale limestone and roofed in *lauze*. It was part of an Augustinian abbey of the late 12C that declined during the Hundred Years War and the church was transformed into a powerful fort. The towering west front has an enormously high belfry (21m) and the west door, which is flanked by slim colonettes supporting several arches, was added in the 14C. The church is very plain, in the Augustinian way, except for a few decorative features in the east and a *chemin de ronde* (walkway). The interior is simple but stunning, rising towards the east. The nave has a single-span, slightly pointed barrel vault and high windows, while the crossing is domed. Eight steps lead up to the choir which has early rib vaults, and the apse is flat with a harmonious arrangement of windows. Defensive elements were also added inside, such as a high walkway around the choir and transepts and hidden stairs.

On the border of the departments of Dordogne and Corèze is **Terrasson-la-Villedieu**, in a charming setting at the centre of a walnut- and truffle-growing region. It developed around a Benedictine abbey of which all that remains is the church, heavily restored in the late-19C in the late Gothic manner, with some good 16C glass. There are two other churches, one 12C with a Romanesque door, and another partly 15C and partly 19C with a *clocher-mur*. There is a sloping market place and at the top of the town some attractive old houses. Of the two bridges over the Vézère, one is medieval and about 100m long. **Jardins de l'Imaginaire** is a terraced garden by the river offering a journey through different geographical, cultural and temporal experiences via a range of plants, especially roses, and fountains. Open July, Aug daily 10.00–19.30; April–June, Sept –mid-Oct, Mon, Wed–Sun 10.00–13.00 and 14.00–18.45, closed Tues; ☎ 05 53 50 37 56. Just outside Beauregard-de-Terrasson, north of Terrasson-la-Villedieu, is the 17C **Château de Mellet**, with botanic gardens. Open July, Aug daily 14.30–19.00; ☎ 05 53 51 24 94.

SARLAT AND ENVIRONS

Sarlat, capital of the Black Périgord and *sous-Préfecture*, is a beguiling town which makes an excellent touring base, especially out of season, placed as it is 7km north of the Dordogne River. It has an extraordinary density of beautiful medieval and Renaissance buildings, in golden limestone combined with grey stone (*lauze*) lining attractive squares and narrow streets. Sarlat's remarkable townscape attracts some 500,000 visitors a year and as a result, there are numerous epicurian boutiques, souvenir shops and restaurants.

Sarlat

Getting there and around
Car
A20 or N20 via Souillac and D703/704.
Train
From Paris, change at Souillac for Sarlat; from Bordeaux via Bergerac; from Périgueux to Sarlat, change at Le Buisson or Libourne.

Tourist information
24590 **Salignac-Eyvigues** Pl. du 19 Mars 1962, ☎ 05 53 28 81 93
24203 **Sarlat** BP 114, Rue Tourny, ☎ 05 53 31 45 45, fax 05 53 59 19 44, www.sarlat.tourisme.com

Market days
St-Geniès Sunday
Salignac Tuesday
Sarlat Saturday and Wednesday

Festivals and events
May–June *La Ringueta*, traditional games held in alternate years, Sarlat
July/August *Festival des Jeux du Théâtre*, Sarlat
October *Festival du Film*, Sarlat

Where to stay and eating out
24200 SARLAT-LA-CANÉDA
☆☆☆ *La Madeleine*, 1 Pl. de la Petite-Rigaudie, ☎ 05 53 59 10 41, fax 05 53

31 03 62. Hotel-restaurant adjacent to the centre, tastefully revamped. Chef-owner Philippe Melot cooks with care and pride.

☆☆☆ *La Hoirie*, rue Marcel-Cerdan, ☎ 05 53 59 05 62, fax 05 53 31 13 90, www.lahoirie.com. Charming setting (with pool), efficient service and unpretentious local cooking.

☆☆ *La Mas de Castel*, south of Sarlat on D704, ☎ 05 53 59 02 59, fax 05 53 28 52 62. Quiet spot and restful rooms, pool and garden.

☆☆ *Des Récollets*, 4 Rue J.J.-Rousseau, ☎ 05 53 31 36 00, fax 05 53 30 32 62. Modest hotel on the quiet western side of town.

€€ *Le Présidial*, Rue Présidial (off Rue Fénelon), ☎ 05 53 28 92 47. Pretty setting in the old court house, in a garden. Local cooking embellished.

El Chilango, 1 rue Peyrat, ☎ 05 53 29 39 30. A tiny establishment serving Mexican food (some vegetarian) makes a refreshing change to the ubiquitous périgodenne cuisine.

24220 MEYRALS (between Sarlat and Les Eyzies.)

☆☆☆ *La Ferme de Lamy*, ☎ 05 53 29 62 46, 05 53 59 61 41, ferme-lamy@wanadoo.fr. Restful setting, in a garden with large pool. Attractively decorated rooms.

Le Vieux Moine, ☎ 05 53 35 50 01, fax 05 53 35 50 41. *Chambres d'hote* in a 15C house in the village, built on the remains of a monastery.

History

Sarlat most probably developed around a Benedictine community which settled in this remote place in the early 9C, safe from maurauding Vikings. The church was placed under the protection of St Sauveur, but at some point it received the relics of a Bishop of Limoges who had died in 720, and the dedication was changed to St Sacerdos in the 12C. The relics drew pilgrims who enriched the abbey, and until late in the 13C the abbots controlled the town, provoking dangerous rivalry. The townsfolk, already administered by consuls, struggled for emancipation from the stranglehold of the clergy and were eventually granted certain liberties by King Philippe IV in the late 13C. In 1317 Sarlat was elevated by Pope John XXII, the second pope at Avignon (1316–34), to the episcopal see of a newly formed diocese defined by the Vézère and Dordogne rivers, and the monks were replaced by canons. These developments introduced a new era of prosperity to the town and its population grew in the 15C–16C to around 6000 (today 10,650). The cathedral was rebuilt from 1505 by Bishop Armand Gontaud-Biron.

It is not known exactly when the town was enclosed, but the walls were reinforced *c* 1340–50 during the Hundred Years War. Sarlat, on the Franco-English border, was ceded to the English by the Treaty of Brétigny in 1360, but the English were chased out again in 1370 by Bernard du Guesclin (see p 47). After the Battle of Castillon (1453) Sarlat flourished for about two-and-a-half centuries. The town was granted certain royal privileges including, in 1552, the creation of the *présidial* or judiciary, and business boomed, especially in linen cloth. The wealth was displayed in buildings, and clerics, nobles and rich tradesmen vied to build the most distiguished residences. During the Wars of Religion Sarlat took a Catholic stance and was punished in 1574 by pillaging Protestants under Geoffroy de Vivans, but resisted a siege by Protestants in 1587.

During the 17C and 18C urban development slowed down although Bishop

François II de Salignac restored the episcopal palace, completed the cathedral and laid out the Plantier gardens. There was little new construction because of the lack of space inside the city until the walls were dismantled in 1750. The Intendant of Guyenne, Tourny, created a tree-lined garden on the edge of the town, the Grande Rigaudie, with a statue of Etienne de La Boétie (see below). The good times ended with the Revolution, as administrative reorganisation proved a disaster for Sarlat. It lost its clerical and legal prestige—ceasing to be a bishopric and returning to the control of Périgueux in 1790, its commercial role diminished and the railway arrived late, in 1882. The only major concession to the 19C was Rue de la République or La Traverse, which was cut straight through the old town dividing it in two. Sarlat went into a time warp until 19C disadvantages were transformed into 20C treasures. Sarlat was one of the first towns to benefit from the pioneering Malraux Law of 1962 created by André Malraux (d. 1976), France's most celebrated Minister of Culture, to safeguard historic towns. Apart from tourism Sarlat, at the centre of a rural area with a low-density population, relies mainly on agriculture, food processing (distilling, *foie gras* canneries), tobacco and the manufacture of surgical supplies.

A plan of the town shows clearly the ancient, irregular-shaped boundary around the old quarter, which is ringed by an exterior boulevard that follows the line of the old defences, fragments of which remain. Small streets creep up the slopes east and west of Place de la Liberté. Start out from **Place de la Liberté**, framed by 16C–18C houses including the 18C **Hôtel de Ville**. One Renaissance (1615) door on Rue Fénelon is all that remains of the previous *hôtel de ville*, itself on the site of a 13C *maison communale*. After a fire in 1727 the marketplace, which is at its liveliest and most mouth-watering during the Saturday morning market, was enlarged. Across from the Hôtel de Ville is the mutilated church of Ste-Marie (see below). Head south along Rue de la Liberté, passing on the right the **Hôtel de Maleville** (or Hôtel de Vienne), created from three existing buildings in the 16C. A Doric doorway leads to a stairtower, with busts in roundels, supposedly Henri IV and an unidentified female—wife or favourite, flanking 'M' for Maleville. The projecting façade next to it is early Renaissance and has a decorative gable and an original shopfront.

Next to the Maison de Maleville, Passage Henri de Ségogne leads to what were once courtyards of 13C, 15C and 17C houses, creating a maze of tiny streets around Place André-Malraux. Alternatively continue on Rue de la Liberté, with several half-timbered buildings. Both routes are very short and arrive at Place du Peyrou, between the west end of the church and **Maison de La Boétie**. This is the show house of Sarlat, built by the magistrate Antoine de La Boétie in 1525, in characteristic first French Renaissance style with mullioned windows framed with decorative pilasters and a steep crocketed gable with just enough space for a third large window. Etienne de La Boétie (1530–63), writer and friend of Montaigne, was born here. His humanist ideas were to have a long-reaching effect, especially his *Discours de la servitude volontaire*. On the opposite side of the *place* is the façade of the former bishops' palace, subjected to insensitive restoration at the beginning of the 20C, with Flamboyant Gothic windows on the lower level and above a Renaissance loggia added by Cardinal Niccolo Gaddi, Bishop from 1533. Rue Tourny leads out of Place du Peyrou, to the tourist office and Place de la Grande Rigaudie.

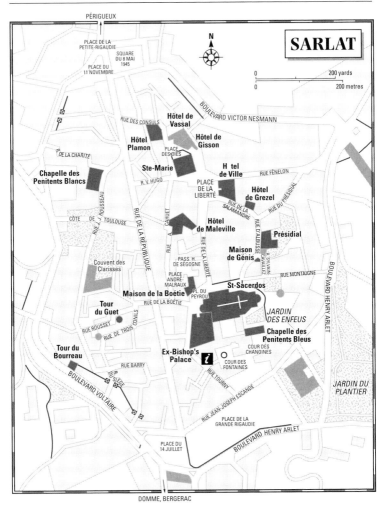

The Romanesque church of **St-Sacerdos**, originally part of the Benedictine abbey, became the cathedral when Sarlat was raised to the status of episcopal see in 1317. The present church was begun in 1504/5, during the episcopate of Bishop Armand de Gontaud-Biron, who had most of the Romanesque church demolished, but the work was not completed until 1682–85 and the result is an architectural mish-mash. Major restoration work was carried out in 2001–02.

The Romanesque tower above the west door has three levels of blind arcades, two 12C, a last level added in the 17C and an incongruous 18C bulbous top-not. Little is known about the five late Romanesque sculptures, which seem to be figures on a balcony, and the west door was altered in Classical style early in the 18C. Despite its late completion date, the majority of the exterior is Gothic. The nave (mainly 17C) has aisles and flying buttresses borrowed from northern churches, although the lateral chapels opening on aisles with interior buttresses are typically southern. The east end is the 14C cathedral of St-Sauveur, which is in the form of a Greek cross, and was absorbed into the later building. Enter through the west door into the Romanesque narthex which has a 12C corbel table on the right. The overriding impression is uninspired Gothic although it was completed in the Neo-classical period. Only the first three bays of the nave are on a straight axis, and from there the church slopes gently off to the south. The five-sided apse, adapted from the 14C church, has haphazard stellar vaulting (15C) and the chancel (completed 1686), linked to it with five arches and an ambulatory, is pentagonal. In the chancel are 17C stalls with misericords. The nave piers are early- and late-17C, some with slender spirals, and the nave was vaulted 1682–85, at the time of Bishop François II de Salignac de La Mothe-Fénelon. In the chapels are a predictable selection of 17C and 18C retables, some attributed to the Tournier workshop (p 189). The relics of St Sacerdos disappeared during the religious strife of the 16C.

South of the cathedral and accessible by the south door is the site of the **cloister**. The wall of the old chapter house (now the sacristy) to the east is decorated with arches made up of higgledy-piggledy fragments of Romanesque stonework from the old cloister. From here enter the **Cour des Fontaines**, where the first monks settled in the 9C, named after the pure spring water which gushes from three spouts. Further east is the Cour des Chanoines, closed to the south by the recently restored chapel of the **Pénitents-Bleus** or of St-Benoit (Benedict), which is pure unadorned Romanesque inside. The 15C half-timbered house opposite was the residence of the chapter. Go round the east of the chapel into the old cemetery or **Jardin des Enfeus**, with Romanesque and Gothic funeral niches cut into rock, some containing sarcophagi. Steps lead up to a tiny garden with the strangest and most inexplicable of monuments, the **Lanterne des Morts** or tower of St Bernard, resembling an elongated stone beehive. It has elicited many legends and interpretations. (There are other examples of this strange structure and conical stone roofs in the region.) From here is a view down onto the east end of the cathedral.

A small door leads into Rue Montaigne, named after La Boétie's friend (see p 147), with one of the best views of the rooftops of Sarlat and some attractive houses. Take Rue Sylvain-Cavaillez, noting the balcony on the corner, to Rue d'Albusse and the Maison de Génis (16C and 18C) with a covered balcony and balustrade. Turn right past the old **Présidial**, the 17C tribunal (now a restaurant) set in a garden, with its fancy lantern on wooden stilts to give light. Rue Landry leads to Rue du Présidial, the *quartier* of the lawyers. You then arrive just inside the old walls at the top of Rue Fénelon, its name recalling the Salignac-Fénelon family who dominated the episcopate in the 16C and 17C. On the right is a group of 15C gabled houses, and some other 16C buildings, not necessarily all restored.

Ste-Marie, now a market, Sarlat

At the bottom you are back in Place de la Liberté, opposite the church of **Ste-Marie** (1368–1507). It has a very steep stone roof and tiny dormers, and was truncated at the chancel arch in 1915. It has recently been transformed into a modern covered market by the Parisian architect Jean Nouvel. At the west end are decorative gargoyles and a rose window, and there is a tower on the north. To the right up some steps is Place du Marché-aux-Oies, the former goose market graced with three splendid bronze geese. On the right are some tall stone buildings, including the **Hôtel de Gisson** (Maison Chassaing) with plate-tracery windows (*c* 1200) and a hexagonal stairtower (16C) linking the two parts. Next to it is the **Hôtel de Vassal** (15C) with a corbelled turret and stairtower. From Place des Oies look across to the magnificent façade of the **Hôtel Selve de Plamon** or des Consuls (14C–17C) with beautiful traceried Gothic windows, built by the merchant draper, Guillaume de Plamon, who was a consul from 1330. He transformed the shop of his forebears, another floor was added in the 16C and, the family having been enobled, they had the right to add a tower. Inside is an impressive courtyard with timber staircase and galleries, under which ran a stream, no doubt used for dyeing linen or treating flax. Opposite is the vaulted Fontaine Ste-Marie.

On the angle of Rue des Consuls is an extraordinary squinch, and there are other tall buildings (15C and 17C) and some good doorways. This brings you to Rue de la République at the end of which is Place de la Petite Rigaudie (or Place du 11 Novembre). The boulevard opposite runs uphill past the remains of a town gate, following the line of the former city fortifications. The west side of Sarlat is less frequented and is still undergoing restoration. Turn down Rue de la Charité to the quarter which once belonged to the Reformed Franciscans or Pénitents Blancs. The last vestige of an important friary is the 17C chapel of the **Récollets** (closed), and the convent buildings are now a school. Rue Jean-Jacques Rousseau was the main street until the 19C and has some beautiful houses. Part of the former abbey of Ste-Claire is now a pretty hotel on a tiny square and its gardens are behind high walls on the left. The continuation of Rue J.J.-Rousseau is Rue du Siège which leads under the remains of a medieval gateway to the exterior boulevard and the **Tour du Bourreau** (Executioner's Tower). Turn back here down Rue des Trois Conils, winding down past some more freshly done-up houses back to Rue de la République. To the right is Place du 14 Juillet and Place de la Grande Rigaudie, used during the Saturday market for stalls, otherwise for parking, and beyond that is the Jardin Public du Plantier.

La Plantation de Mai

This throwback to the pagan celebration of spring is still popular in southwest France and particularly in Périgord. In the past the sacred tree of springtime was decked out in ribbons and carried by the young people of a community as a fertility symbol, much like the English maypole. Today the Mai are erected to commemorate an important event or person, such as a local election (*honneur a nos élus*), the boss of an enterprise (*honneur au patron*), or topping-out a house (*faîtage*). The tree used is usually a young pine which is stripped almost bare of branches leaving just a little tuft at the top, and decorated with the tricolour, ribbons, crêpe paper or banners. In the same way green branches, often pines or firs, are scattered with crêpe-paper bows for a wedding and placed outside the house of the bride.

North of Sarlat, off the D704, is the village of **St-Geniès**, which is all golden limestone and grey stone roofs just waiting for its picture to be painted. The whole ensemble is delightful, and includes a simple church with a Romanesque apse and a small château (15C/19C).

Northeast of Sarlat by the D704 and D60 is the hilltop town of **Salignac-Eyvigues**, gathered around a stone *halle* including the façade of the Couvent des Croisiers (13C). Rue Ste-Croix leads to the rambling, partly ruined 12C–17C château, the home of the Salignac family (see above). In places the ramparts are still standing and the main block is enlivened with towers and turrets. A Renaissance spiral staircase takes you to several rooms containing interesting 16C and 17C furniture and a portrait of Louis de Salignac (d. 1598), who became Bishop of Sarlat aged 22. Guided visits, July, Aug 10.00–12.00 and 14.00–18.00; ☎ 05 53 28 80 06.

The **Jardins d'Eyrignac**, south of Salignac off the D47, were laid out around a 17C manor house by the Marquis de la Calprenède in the 18C. Transformed in the 19C into a more informal English style as was the fashion, the formal gardens were painstakingly recreated some 40 years ago by the father of the present owner. Open June–Sept 09.30–19.00; April–May 10.00–12.30 and 14.00–19.00; Oct–Dec, March, May 10.30–12.30 and 14.30 to dusk; closed Jan, Feb; ☎ 05 53 28 99 71. The sumptuous yet controlled garden-scapes of Eyrignac are made up of evergreen walks and vistas punctuated by elaborate topiary, pools and groves with perfectly manicured lawns. The disciplined hornbeam, box, yew and cypress produce an architectonic setting articulated by variations of sunlight and shade. The **Moulin de la Tour** on the D47 east of Sarlat is driven by the waters of the Enéa and produces walnut oil. Open certain days throughout the year; ☎ 05 53 59 22 08.

West of Sarlat on the D47, the **Château de Puymartin** is a magical turreted place at the end of a steep, wooded drive. Guided visits, Mon, Wed–Sun, July, Aug 10.00–12.00 and 14.00–18.30; April–Nov 10.00–12.00 and 14.00–18.00; closed Tues; ☎ 05 53 59 29 97. Part of the château is medieval (15C–16C), but part was rebuilt in the 19C: the property has passed through the same family, which remained staunchly Catholic during the Wars of Religion. It is arranged around a three-storey central block and many furnishings and decorations have been conserved. There are several painted ceilings and fireplaces. The main bedroom is adorned with green Aubusson tapestries and the *grande salle* contains six Oudenarde tapestries depicting the Trojan War. There is 17C and 18C furniture, including a Louis XIII table and Louis XV desk, and it is possible to see the splendid timber roof structure. Two rooms are let as *chambres d'hôte*.

Just beyond Puymartin, off the D47, are the **Cabanes du Breuil**, a rare group of traditional agricultural workers huts called *cazelles* or *bories*. Built entirely in dry stone with *lauze* roofs, these little structures usually exist in isolation but here some are fused together and clustered around a small working farm. Open June–Sept 10.00–19.00; March–May, Oct–Nov 10.00–12.00 and 14.00–19.00; other times by advance booking; ☎ 05 53 29 67 15.

ALONG THE DORDOGNE VALLEY

From Sarlat to Lalinde, the Dordogne flows majestically past landscapes of walnut groves and fields of bright green tobacco, and below steep crags which have been peopled since time immemorial. Golden villages developed in the shelter of the cliffs, at the foot of the castles which protected the frontier river in medieval times, or where important river ports shipped cargo destined for Bordeaux and beyond. The *gabares* which once carried these cargoes are now replicated for use as pleasure cruises and apart from these, and the canoes and kayaks, the river is tranquil. This is a particularly popular stretch of the Dordogne as there are many sites of interest and beauty, and it is therefore best avoided in midsummer.

Getting there and around
Car

D704 and D46 from Sarlat; D710 to Belvès, and D25 off D710 to Cadouin.
Train

See above, p 159

Tourist information
24440 Beaumont Pl. Centrale, ☎ 05 53 22 39 12.
24170 Belvès 1 Rue des Filhols, ☎ 05 53 29 10 20, www.perigord.com/belves
24220 Beynac-et-Cazenac La Balme, ☎ 05 53 29 43 08, www.perigord. tm.fr
24250 Domme Pl. de la Halle, ☎ 05 53 31 71 00, www.domme-tourism.com
24510 Limeuil Le Bourg, ☎ 05 53 63 38 90, www.limeuil-perigord.com
24150 Lalinde Jardin Public, ☎ 05 53 61 08 55, fax 05 53 61 00 64, www.lalinde-perigord.com
24250 La Roque-Gageac ☎ 05 53 29 17 01
24220 St-Cyprien Pl. Charles-de-Gaulle, ☎ 05 53 30 36 09, fax 05 53 28 55 05

Market days

Beaumont Saturday
Belvès Saturday
Domme Thursday
Lalinde Thursday
St-Cyprien Sunday

River cruises

La Roque-Gageac *Gabares* depart April–end Oct 10.00–18.00, operated by *Norbert*, ☎ 05 53 29 40 44, fax 05 53 29 37 30, www.norbert.fr; or *Les Caminades*, ☎ 05 53 29 40 95, fax 05 53 59 62 51
St-Martial-de-Nabirat *Gabares de Beynac*, 05 53 28 51 15, fax 05 53 29 39 76, email kellergabares24@aol.com

Festivals and events
July *Festival Bach*, Belvès
August *Les Nuits Musicales de Beynac*

Where to stay and eating out
24480 LE BUISSON DE CADOUIN

✩✩✩ *Le Manoir de Bellerive*, Route de Siorac, ☎ 05 53 22 16 16, fax 05 53 22 09 05, www.manoir-bellerive.com. On the banks of the Dordogne, in 4ha of English-style gardens.

24220 LE COUX-ET-BIGAROQUE

Manoir de la Brunie, on the D703, north of the Dordogne, ☎ 05 53 35 50 01, fax 05 53 35 50 41. *Chambres d'hôte* in a 17C residence. Warm welcome.

24250 DOMME

€€€–€€ *L'Esplanade*, ☎ 05 53 28 81 41, email esplanade.domme@wanadoo. fr. At the heart of the *bastide*, offering panoramic views, antique furniture, carefully prepared dishes. Rooms available.

24150 LALINDE

✩✩✩ *Du Château*, 1 Rue de Verdun, ☎ 05 53 61 01 82. Hotel-restaurant in a small 13C castle with 19C updates, a pleasant stop for a moderately priced meal.

€ *La Poste*, St-Capraise-de-Lalinde, ☎ 05 53 63 43 26. A good-value, unpretentious restaurant with a pleasant ambience.

24150 LANQUAIS
Château de Lanquais, ☎ 05 53 61 24 24, fax 05 53 73 20 72. A *chambres d'hôte* in a Renaissance château.

24150 MAUZAC
La Chenaie, ☎ 05 53 35 50 01, fax 05 53 35 50 41. *Chambres d'hôte* overlooking the Dordogne at the Cingle de Tremolat. Comfortable, attractive, with a pool.

24250 LA ROQUE-GAGEAC
☆☆ *La Belle Etoile*, ☎ 05 53 29 51 44, fax 05 53 29 45 63. Modest hotel in this lovely village on the Dordogne.

☆☆ *La Plume D'Oie*, ☎ 05 53 29 57 05, fax 05 53 31 04 81. Pretty setting and good food going up-market; good-value set menu.

24510 TRÉMOLAT
☆☆☆☆ *Le Vieux Logis*, ☎ 05 53 22 80 06, fax 05 53 22 84 89, email vieuxlogis@relaischateau.fr. Classy accommodation in small buildings in a garden setting. Delicious foodie surprises.

24220 VÉZAC
€€ *Relais des Cinq Châteaux*, on the D57, ☎ 05 53 30 30 72. Regional cooking in a typical Périgordian building. Avoid Sunday crowds.

24200 VITRAC
☆☆☆☆ *Domaine de Rochebois*, Rte de Montfort, ☎ 05 53 31 52 52, fax 05 53 29 36 88. Hotel-restaurant in a superb position on the Dordogne and attractive rooms.

Heading south from Sarlat towards the Dordogne Valley on the D704 and D703 west will bring you via **Carsac**, which has a tiny domed Romanesque church (11C, restored), with naively carved capitals, recent glass, and a *chemin de croix* by Léon Zack, with texts by Paul Claudel. At **Montfort** there are dramatic views down to the Cingle de Montfort, a tight meander in the Dordogne. The nearby Château of Montfort (no admission), a mainly 19C fantasy, passed to the Turenne family who were staunch Protestants in the 16C.

La Roque-Gageac is confined between the river and the cliff, and the buildings have been forced to creep up the rock face where they glow in the afternoon sun. At each end of the village there is a castle, the neo-Gothic Château de la Malartrie to the west and the 16C Manoir Tarde to the east. A walk up the cliff brings you to troglodyte houses, the little church (16C–17C) and sub-tropical

La Roque-Gageac

gardens. River cruises on *gabares* leave from the quay, which was originally used for cargoes such as wood and wine. Fort Troglodytique at La Balme, near La Roque-Gageac, is open Easter–Nov 10.00–19.00; closed Sat except July–Aug.

Beynac and its castle

The spectacular village of **Beynac-et-Cazenac** is squeezed into a narrow space with little room to spare for motorists. The small turning in the village shoots you up (3km) to the giddy heights of the upper village and castle (there is a steep footpath if you prefer to walk). The area was on the tin route between Britain and the Mediterranean and already inhabited during the Bronze Age. As a reminder there is a 20C **Parc Archéologique**. Open July–mid-Sept, Mon–Fri, Sun 10.00–19.00, closed Sat; ☎ 05 53 29 51 28.

Château de Beynac is a magnificent fortress recognisable for miles around, glowering from its high crag above the valley, the village huddled beneath. Guided visits June–Sept 10.00–18.30; March–May 10.00–18.00; Oct–Nov 10.00–dusk; Dec–Feb, 12.00–dusk; ☎ 05 53 29 50 40.

The fortress was occupied by Richard the Lionheart for a few years in the 12C and was attacked by Simon de Montfort 1214/18 during the crusade against the Cathars of the Agenais and Périgord. De Montfort demolished only the exterior wall (whereas he demolished most of Biron). During the Hundred Years War, Beynac changed hands on several occasions. When the front line was fixed on the Dordogne, Beynac became French and Castlenaud opposite remained English, resulting in guerrilla warfare across the river. At the close of the Wars of Religion, the military role of Beynac finally ended and the fort fell into disrepair. It was sold in the 20C to the present owner who has undertaken an extraordinarily lengthy programme of restoration. Although painstakingly executed, it begs the question of when enough is enough, but the advantage is that there is a little extra to see each year. Funding is raised by visits and by its frequent use as a film set (for example, in *Jeanne d'Arc* and *Fille d'Artagnan*).

Beynac is a superb example of a medieval fortress with rare original 12C parts. It was altered in the 13C/14C and again during the Renaissance, and is now undergoing an epic 100-year recreation: the parts on display are in great part already heavily restored. Through the massive double entrance you arrive in the lower courtyard outside the castle itself, and then pass through a further entrance which leads to an interior courtyard. Inside, the stables on the right are 17C, while on the left are the 12C section of the castle and the original ramp up to the barbican and the castle door (now the exit). Another ramp leads to the terrace and panoramic views of the Dordogne and the castles of Marqueyssac, Fayrac and Castelnaud beyond. Immediately to the right is the former castle chapel, now used by the parish, with a fine *lauze* roof.

Visitors enter the building through a doorway in the gabled façade flanked by the 12C and 13C keeps, to arrive in the vast guardroom with remains of stabling for the horses at one end and a narrow spiral staircase (not accessible), which is lit only with oil lamps to maintain authentic medieval obscurity. A skilfully crafted modern wooden spiral stair leads up to the more comfortable 13C rooms with latrines and *pisé* floors. On the same level is the meeting room of the four baronies of Périgord—Beynac, Biron, Boudeilles and Mareuil—their banners hang on the walls (above the guardroom) with a slightly pointed barrel-arched vault, Renaissance chimneypiece and chapel with 15C paintings. The battlements high above the valley afford yet another staggering view, but also a rare opportunity to admire a *lauze* roof from above. A stone spiral descends to the courtyard over a 12C cistern still in use and the heavily restored kitchens and barbican.

The terraced **Jardins Suspendus de Marqueyssac** surround the château at Vézac, south of Beynac, built by Bertrand Vernet de Marqueyssac towards the end of the 17C, a great period in French formal gardens, following the example of Le Nôtre. Open July, Aug 09.00–20.00; May–June, Sept 10.00–19.00; mid-Feb–April, Oct–mid-Nov 10.00–18.00; mid-Nov to mid-Feb 14.00–17.00; ☎ 05 53 31 36 36, www.marqueyssac.com. When Julien de Cerval (1818–93) inherited the property in 1861 the gardens had been neglected but, as luck would have it, he was a keen gardener and had been much impressed by Italian gardens that he saw while serving with the Roman legion. He dedicated the latter part of his life to creating an extravaganza of box and cypress relieved by tiny winter-flowering Naples cyclamen. The sheer stone terraces, covering 22ha of the rock, take full advantage of the stunning panorama high above the Dordogne, and the 150,000 box shrubs are not restricted to straight lines and sharp edges, but disappear into the distance in undulating waves. There is a variety of small stone buildings and waterfalls, a *chemin d'eau* and a rosemary walk have been added more recently. Neglected again in the second half of the 20C, in 1996 Marqueyssac was purchased by the present owners who have returned it to its former beauty, although in 1999, 120 old trees were lost during the Christmas gales.

Château de Castelnaud

The Château de Castelnaud on the other side of the Dordogne (cross at Vézac) has developed in a different direction from its old adversary, Beynac, by exploiting its picturesque semi-ruinous state. Soaring over the confluence of the Dordogne and the Céou, the fortress has plenty of entertainment for all the family, including the Musée de la Guerre au Moyen Age with reconstructed medieval military apparatus, and the dramatic site provides more wonderful views. Open July, Aug 09.00–20.00; May–June, Sept 10.00–19.00; March, April, Oct to mid-Nov and school holidays 10.00–18.00; mid-Nov–mid-Feb 14.00–17.00; ☎ 05 53 31 30 00, www.castelnaud.com.

Castelnaud, the 'new castle', was taken from Bernard de Casnac in 1214 by Simon de Montfort, who was chased out after a year. The castle was subsequently destroyed but was ceded to the English who largely reconstructed it after the Treaty of Paris in 1259. In 1273 it reverted to the Castelnaud barons, who were a constant thorn in the flesh to Beynac, but some sort of peace held after 1317 when the pope authorised a marriage between the two families. The Hundred Years War began in 1337 with resultant hostilities across the Dordogne, especially after 1368 when the heiress of Castelnaud married into the Caumont family, loyal to the English, who took the castle in 1405. In 1442 a three-week siege by the French finally drove them out, and after the war ended, repairs were carried out to the castle. Francis de Caumont built a pleasant Renaissance house called Milandes (see below), and *c* 1520 the artillery tower was erected, more symbolic than practical. During the Reformation the castle came under the control of the feared and revered Huguenot, Geoffroy de Vivans, and such was his reputation that the castle was not attacked. It was gradually abandoned from then on, and after the Revolution deteriorated further as building stone was scavenged from the site, but a new lease of life came as a result of modern renovations (1967–98).

The ensemble is well presented with displays, audio-visuals and models; an information pack in English is available. The central part of the castle is dominated by a tall (30m) keep with a pointed roof, built by the English in the 13C. Flanking it are 15C living quarters. Between the 16C round artillery tower on the right, with cannon ports—never used—in its thick walls, and the square tower to the left as you approach is the northern wall protecting an enclosure called a *chatêlet*. The barbican (15C) inside this is the next defensive layer, designed to protect the entry to the castle at the weakest point. Beyond is the 15m-high curtain wall or *courtine* (13C), punctuated by arrow loops, linking the keep with the main building but separating the lower courtyard (bailey) from the interior courtyard. In the keep are some original wall decorations and the museum of medieval weapons, arms and armour. In the courtyard are replicas of siege equipment, including a bombard, a primitive means of projecting 100kg cannon balls, an *arbalète à tour* (fixed crossbow) and a trebuchet, a massive version of a catapult used for flinging all sorts of horrid things over high walls. The trebuchet is demonstrated on summer afternoons.

The **Château des Milandes** nearby to the west is famous as the home of Josephine Baker. Open July, Aug 09.30–19.00; mid-March–June, Sept–Oct 10.00–18.00; early Nov 10.00–17.00; closed mid-Nov–mid-March; ☎ 05 53 59 31 21, www.milandes.com.

Les Milandes was begun in 1489 by François de Caumont for his bride as an alternative to the fortress of Castelnaud, but most of the late Gothic décor was destroyed by a zealous Protestant descendent of the family. The château was reborn in the 19C as a mainly neo-Gothic structure with showy turrets. Josephine Baker (1906–75) made her name as a dancer in the Harlem cabaret *La Revue Nègre* and at the Folie Bergères in Paris in the 1920s. She worked for the French Resistance and lived at Les Milandes from 1937 to 1969 with her multi-racial group of 12 children, the 'Rainbow Tribe'.

Reminders of the old castle have survived in the shape of some fine fireplaces, panelling and stained glass. The kitchen and other rooms have been kept as they were during Josephine Baker's time, and contain memorabilia and a museum dedicated to her. The nearby private chapel, sometimes open, is in Flamboyant style but was emptied of its ornament and turned into a Protestant place of worship in the 16C. There are pleasant grounds with formal gardens and views, and falconry demonstrations.

Domme

The popular hilltop *bastide* of Domme was founded in the 13C and extended an existing 12C fortress, Domme Vieille, which has now disappeared. The shape of the hilltop resulted in an erratic layout, but there are parallel streets around a

TOWARDS LITTLE TRAIN PARK

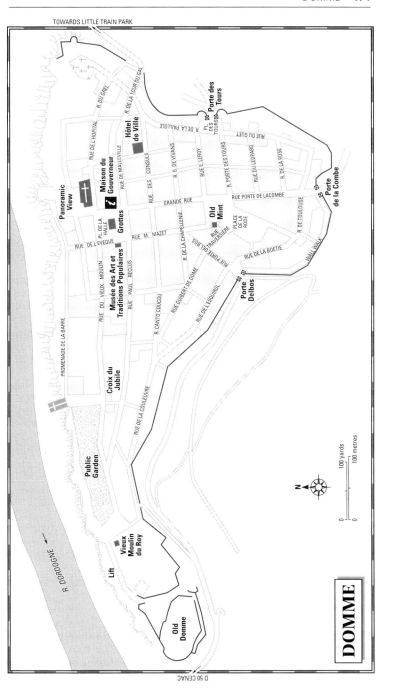

R. DU GREL

R. DE LA TOUR DU GAL

Porte des Tours

R. DE LA PAILLOLE

PL. DES TOURS

RUE DE L'HOPITAL

Hôtel de Ville

RUE DU GUET

RUE DE MALLEVILLE

RUE DES CONSULS

R. G. DE VIVANS

RUE E. LEROY

R. PORTE DES TOURS

RUE DU LEOPARD

R. DE LA ROSE

Maison du Gouverneur

Panoramic View

GRANDE RUE

RUE PORTE DE LACOMBE

Porte de la Combe

Grottes

PL. DE LA HALLE

Old Mint

R. DE TOULOUSE

RUE DE L'EVEQUE

RUE M. MAZET

R. DE LA CHAPELLENIE

PLACE DE LA RODE

RUE PORTE DELBOS

RUE TRAVERSIERE

RUE DE LA BOETIE

WALL WALK

Musée des Art et Traditions Populaires

RUE DU VIEUX MOULIN

RUE PAUL RECLUS

R. CANTO COUCOU

RUE GUIBERT DE DOMME

RUE DE L'ESQUIROL

Porte Delbos

PROMENADE DE LA BARRE

Croix du Jubile

RUE DE LA COULEUVRE

Public Garden

Vieux Moulin du Roy

Lift

R. DORDOGNE

Old Domme

N

0 — 100 yards
0 — 100 metres

DOMME

traditional covered market place. There are also sections of well-preserved ramparts and fortified gates and the pretty stone houses have been beautifully restored. Domme draws huge numbers of summer visitors, so parking is difficult. There is a little train, with commentary, from the bus-park at Le Pradal; Easter–end Oct; ☎ 06 07 02 98 66. To find it from Vitrac on the Sarlat to La Roque-Gageac road cross the Dordogne to Domme/parking.

History

Domme, founded in 1281 by Philippe III the Bold, was caught up in the Hundred Years War, changing hands several times. It came under the control of the Black Prince in 1363, and the château was loyal to the English up until 1438, but returned to the French later that year. In 1495 the town received the king's permission to hold markets and prospered until the first half of the 16C, but from 1570 the Reformation had terrible consequences and much blood was shed. Domme remained Catholic, but the Protestant Geoffroy de Vivans tried to take it, succeeding only at the third attempt in 1588, when his men climbed the undefended steep north cliff. In 1590, however, while Vivans was supporting Henri IV during the Siege of Paris, the Catholics counter-attacked and, realising the futility of maintaining it, he sold Domme in 1592. In 1594 and 1597, the *croquants* (peasants) of Domme, like those of Monpazier, joined the revolt against heavy taxes. The town was largely rebuilt in the 18C but remained isolated until the local judge and deputy, Jacques de Malleville (1741–1824), battled for improved local roads and bridges. The writer, Eugène le Roy (d. 1907), who created some of his works at Domme, famously wrote about the life of peasants in the Dordogne in *Jacquou le Croquant*.

It is the ensemble of Domme which makes it so engaging, not the individual buildings. The village is built on the slope running down from the sheer cliff on the north, and was protected by ramparts and fortified gates. Sections of the wall and three gates—Portes Delbos, de la Combe and des Tours—are still standing. Porte Delbos, to the south, leads almost immediately into Place de la Rode with, on the left, the pretty medieval mint. Leading out of the square are the busy Grand'Rue and the quieter Rue M.-Mazet. Both lead to Place de la Halle, the main square where there is a rustic 18C covered market with stone pillars supporting a wooden gallery. This stands over the entrance to the **Grottes de Domme**, caves with natural formations, stalactites and stalagmites, lit to introduce an aspect of wonder, and a few animal bones. The exit is by *ascenseur panoramic* further west. Open July, Aug 10.00–19.00; April–June, Sept 10.00–12.00 and 14.00–18.00; March, Oct 14.00–18.00; closed Nov–Feb; ☎ 05 53 31 71 00. The Maison du Gouverneur (16C), opposite, used by the tourist office, has a variety of roofs, dormers, and a huge tower with a corbelled turret.

Behind the market is the **Musée d'Arts et Traditions Populaires**. Open July, Aug 10.00–12.30 and 13.30–18.00; May–June, Sept 10.00–12.00 and 14.00–18.00; April 14.00–18.00; closed Oct–March; ☎ 05 53 31 71 00. The church is to the northeast of the market, and is a fairly severe building with a rustic belfry-gable above a sophisticated Classical west door with columns and broken pediment. Beyond the church is the shaded terrace and the Promenade de la Barre, with a bust of Jacques de Malleville and a breathtaking view over the valley and patchwork of fields and distant hills. Further west in the town are the remains of an Augustinian abbey and public gardens, and beyond them the Moulin du Roy on the emplacement of the old castle.

The *hôtel de ville* is in Rue des Consuls off the Grand'Rue. Rue Le Roy is where the writer lived. The finest individual structure is the **Porte des Tours**, a superb example of 13C fortifications, best viewed from outside the walls. The gabled archway originally had a portcullis. It is flanked by powerful twin towers, square towards the town and rounded towards the countryside, of beautifully worked masonry, with arrow slits and machicolations. Inside are graffiti carved by Templars imprisoned in 1307–18 after the suppression of the Order; guided visits available from the tourist office. Inside the gate, the road or track follows the ramparts back to Port Delbos passing Porte de la Combe, the smallest gate and the route to water.

St-Cyprien, downriver from Beynac on the D703, stands on high ground against a background of darkly wooded hills. The large church which dominates the town was part of an abbey and has retained its fortified Romanesque belfry. The rest was altered later in the Gothic period and it contains 17C furnishings including retables, pulpit, stalls and organ. Just above St-Cyprien is the partly rebuilt Château de Fages, originally 16C on 12C foundations.

At **Coux-et-Bigaroque** to the west the church has a Romanesque door. Further west by the D25 and D51, at the confluence of the Vézère and the Dordogne, is **Limeuil**. The village, which tumbles down the hill to the water, is as pretty as a picture. It was once an important fishing community. Before the construction of the bridges in 1891 the rivers were forded, preventing the heavy *gabares* from Bordeaux sailing further upriver, so merchandise had to be trans-shipped here onto lighter boats. The remains of the ramparts and fortified gates are still visible, and the handsome 16C house near the Porte du Port was the headquarters of the boatmen. The uphill walk is steep at times and runs past attractive houses and two open squares, but the medieval château has disappeared, replaced by a 1920s' house (private). On Place des Ormeaux, an iron cross is the only reminder of the Protestant Temple, and higher up is the church of Ste-Catherine, part 19C, part much older, which shelters a statue of the Virgin (14C) formerly venerated by boatmen. At the top of Limeuil is the Porte du Marquisat, beyond which is the chapel of **St-Martin** at Paunat. This sturdy little restored Romanesque chapel is dedicated to Saints Thomas, Martin and Catherine, and was jointly founded by Richard the Lionheart and Philippe Auguste as a chapel of atonement for the murder of Thomas Becket by Henry II in 1170. The exterior is very plain, with a Latin inscription over the door pleading for God's mercy, and inside there is a domed crossing and half-domed apse, a series of wall-paintings (14C/15C), and a consecration plaque on the north wall.

On the road to Le Bugue is the **Jardin Musée**, featuring old and rare varieties of plants; ☎ 05 53 63 32 06. **Trémolat** has a fortified church, and from the high white cliffs around the Cingle de Trémolat are spectacular views over the river and some of the largest walnut groves in France.

Lalinde was the first English *bastide* at the entry to the Dordogne and Vézère valleys, founded on the water's edge by Jean de la Linde for Henry III in 1267. This was a crucially important position at the ford across the Dordogne on the La Rochelle–Montpellier route. Although the regular layout has survived practically all the old town has disappeared as a result of the struggle between the

English and French in the 14C and 15C, and the Catholic versus Protestant conflicts in the 16C and 17C. The turbulence in the river here is called the Saut de Gratusse and marks the spot where a troublesome dragon, La Coul Bre, was swallowed up. Legend tells that this dragon once lived in the cliff above the town terrifying the locals. Their fears were washed away when St Front came along, faced the dragon and made the sign of the Cross. This caused the petrified monster to plunge into the river never to be seen again. The church, dedicated to St-Front-de-Coulaury, was built atop the cliff in gratitude.

South of the Dordogne on the D710, where the landscape is more wooded, **Belvès** emerges on high ground to create an attractive backdrop to the Nauze River. At the centre to the town in the Place des Armes stands the 15C *halle* on 23 wooden pillars with stone bases. Beneath it is a series of rock shelters which were inhabited by prehistoric man and during the Neolithic period, then turned into simple troglodyte dwellings and used intermittently from the 13C to 18C. The rock shelters lined the ancient city ditch, part of the medieval defences, but when the ditch was filled in they were forgotten about for some 200 years and only rediscovered by accident in 1907. The eight dwellings, which consist of just one sombre room, were excavated in 1989. Tours leave from the tourist office, 15 June–15 Sept 10.00–12.00, 15.00–18.00. In the narrow streets look out for the Maison des Consuls and the Renaissance Hôtel Bontemps. To the west of the town is the church, built 12C–13C as part of a Benedictine priory and reworked in the 15C. Some distance south by the D710 and D60, near Villefranche-de-Périgord, is **Besse**, which has a small church (end 11C–early 12C) with a remarkable porch with decoratively carved arches and capitals under a triangular pediment supported on sculpted corbels.

Cadouin

The tiny community of Cadouin to the west, on the D25, is not on the map for its delightful little 15C market hall, nor for its old quince tree, but for the magnificent **cloister** whose Flamboyant style contrasts with the plain church. There are also exceptionally good public toilets.

An abbey was founded on this site in 1114/15 by Geraud de Salles, disciple of Robert d'Arbrissel, who founded Fontevraud in the Loire. Around 1117 a cloth, said to be the *sudarium capitis*, part of the shroud that had enveloped Christ's head, came to Cadouin and around 1119 De Salles affiliated Cadouin to the Cistercian monastery of Pontigny in Burgundy. The shroud became a hugely important object of veneration and attracted pilgrims to Cadouin for eight centuries until it was de-authenticated in 1934. The monastic buildings have been greatly modified.

The abbey church (1118–54) is severe and undecorated in the Cistercian manner. It remains essentially 12C and is the most important Cistercian work in Aquitaine. The west front, looking out on what was the abbey yard, is massive and relieved only by three large round-headed windows between buttresses and a simple triple-arched doorway. A small concession to the severity is the blind arcade above, which owes a debt to the Saintonge, and a small oculus. The façade seems to lack an upper level. The unusual tower over the crossing has a stone base with a two-tier chestnut shingle roof. The interior is uncluttered and harmonious. The church is in the shape of a Latin cross and, unusually for Périgord, has nave and side aisles, although less unusual is the cupola over the crossing. The four-bay nave has slightly pointed barrel vaults. Around the east end and transepts are some carved friezes and capitals, otherwise the decoration is kept to a minimum, as are the furnishings. There is a 13C sarcophagus, a statue of the Virgin (15C), and the much-restored remains of a 15C–16C mural.

The **cloister** is a high point of Gothic art in the region, with exuberant Flamboyant tracery carved in glorious golden stone, an anachronism for a Cistercian monastery. To visit it, take the door in the large, plain elevation just south of the church. Open July, Aug daily 10.00–19.00; April–June, Sept, Mon, Wed–Sun 10.00–12.30 and 14.00–18.30; Oct–March, Mon, Wed–Sun 10.00–12.30 and 14.00–17.30; closed Tues; ☎ 05 53 63 36 28. The cloister celebrates the style of the late medieval period with an almost overwhelming array of niches, pendant bosses, corbels, tracery, lierne and tierceron vaults, curly kale, and carvings, in three galleries (north, east and south). The more sober west gallery is 16C, heavily restored in the early 20C. There are 26 bays, and the best carvings—in the north and east galleries—present scenes of monastic life, vices and virtues, scenes from the Old and New Testaments, from antiquity, and from everyday life. In the south-facing gallery against the church, therefore sunny, is the finest group around the chair of Abbot Pierre de Gaing, which is decorated with the rebus of Cadouin, a quince tree (*cadoun* in Occitan). The engaged columns either side of the chair have been wittily transformed into turrets from which figures process. On the left are monks, their abbot and a kneeling Mary Magdalene and on the opposite side are scenes from the Passion including Mary and *Christ carrying the Cross*. There is a wealth of anecdotal detail such as little figures peeping around corners. In the northeast angle are two doors, one Gothic, decorated with the Order of St Michael, and the other, partly obscured by the 15C pier, a remnant of the Romanesque cloister. On the exterior of the chapter house are scenes from the parable of Lazarus and Dives, including *Dives' Feast* and the *Death of Lazarus*, and opposite, the *Death of Dives*. The southeast door is also elaborately decorated, with a *Crucifixion*, pelican and phoenix. There are close similarities to the cloister at Cahors which fared worse during the Wars of Religion than Cadouin.

In the **chapter house** is the shroud, still described as the Saint Suaire despite overwhelming proof to the contrary. It remains an object of veneration for its quality of workmanship and age. It turns out that this superb length of cotton muslin was made by Coptic weavers in Egypt at the time of the Fatimid Empire. At each extremity there are embroidered bands in coloured silk incorporating floral patterns and Arabic script. When the text was finally deciphered in 1934, it was discovered that it sings the praises of Emir El Moustali, who reigned over Lower Egypt 1094–1101, and his powerful vizir, El Afdal. The fabric was probably acquired during the First Crusade (1096–99).

Molières, west of Cadouin on the D23, is an English *bastide* that never hit the big time. It struggled after its foundation in 1284 and was still struggling in 1365. The château is now just ruins, and never even had any walls, but it has an imposing square church tower and more greenery than most.

St Avit-Sénieur further south on the D25 is a little village on a rocky outcrop above the Couze with a mighty abbey church, severe and fortified, reminiscent of Beaumont (see below).

The relics of St Avitus, born locally *c* 487 and persecuted at the time of Clovis, were translated into a new church in 1117. The community was fortified in the 13C on the orders of Philippe III, and the abbey was ransacked and fired by the Huguenots in 1577, who demolished the great north belfry. Part of the 12C church collapsed at some point and had to be rebuilt. There have been many campaigns of restoration, in the second half of the 19C, between 1968 and 1970, and again in the 1990s.

You enter a courtyard north of the church with remnants of the old fortifications, including the *maison des gardes* (1628), on the left. Southeast of the church is the monk's dormitory, and the old sacristy and chapter house, the latter vaulted in the 12C. A porch leads to the remains of the cloister, destroyed in the 15C and used as a cemetery. The 17C presbytery on an 11C base has arrow slits, and the south wall of the cloister seems to have been constructed using Gallo-Roman techniques. There is a small museum of geology and archaeology, open in summer; ☎ 05 53 22 32 27/05 53 22 39 12. Digs have uncovered the foundations of an earlier church and monastic buildings. It is likely that domes were intended although never built. Evidence of scorch marks may date from the 13C Albigensian Crusades and the present vaults, Angevin in style, date from between the 13C and 15C. The round apse was replaced by a flat chevet in the 17C and the magnificent Gothic wall-paintings in the nave were uncovered during the last round of restorations.

Isolated in the small churchyard above the village of **Monferrand-du-Périgord** on the D26 is the tiny church of St-Christophe (11C–12C), a remnant of a larger sanctuary. The three little round-headed windows in the east are original but it was altered later. The main interest lies in the painted decoration of the interior, with a ***Christ in Majesty at the Centre of the Universe*** on the vault surrounded by the symbols of the four Evangelists (12C), and in the east an ***Annunciation*** and ***St Christopher***. The oldest, Romanesque paintings are on the north of the choir and represent a ***Miracle of St Leonard***, companion at arms of Clovis; there are some more ancient ones in the nave. On the north wall is Hell with the damned being gulped down by Leviathan.

The *bastide* of **Beaumont** (en-Périgord) on the D25/D650 was the result of a *paréage* (see p 559) between Edward I and local landowners in 1272. Lucas de Thaney, the king's lieutenant, supervised its construction and laid it out in the form of an 'H' as a tribute to Henry III. Beaumont remained English for most of the Hundred Years War, until 1442. It was attacked four times during the Religious Wars. The massive church (end 13C/early 14C) looms above the town, conscious of its medieval role of protection. There are large square twin towers at the west, and two more at the east. The west façade is fairly plain except for foliate capitals and a gallery of animal faces. The flat Gothic east end is an English touch. Inside, the cavernous single nave has a 19C vault and under the northwest tower are some good carvings. The market hall was demolished in 1864 leaving the small square rather empty, although there are arcades on three sides. Just before the village of Nojals-et-Clottes south of Beaumont is the **Dolmen de Blanc**, a splendid example of a megalith or neolithic burial chamber some 5000 years old, although much altered over the millennia.

Among a multitude of fairytale castles in the Perigord, the **Château de Bannes** is one of the most magical with a Disneyland silhouette of towers and turrets. It stands among woods on a hill above the Couze Valley, which was an important link between the Périgord and the Agenais, surrounded by English *bastides*. Badly damaged by the French in 1443, it was rebuilt by Armand de Gontaud-Biron, Bishop of Sarlat, in 1510. It is privately owned and is not open to the public.

The **Château de Lanquais**, reached via the D660 north and D37, stands in a pretty valley. Open July, Aug 10.00–19.00; May–June, Sept 10.30–12.00 and 14.30–18.30; April, Oct 14.30–18.00; closed Tues except July and Aug when open daily; ☎ 05 53 61 24 24. Grandly described by Chastel as the '*Louvre inachevé du Périgord*', this charming L-shaped building in golden stone is a text-book example of the evolution from defensive structure to comfortable residence. It demonstrates clearly at least two campaigns of building, the medieval castle (14C–15C) on the right, and a Renaissance palace (16C) on the left. In addition there is a small neo-Gothic (19C) building and chapel. There are two rooms and an apartment to rent here.

Galhiot de la Tour, the owner of Lanquais in the 16C, was cousin of Catherine de Médicis and would have had access to the best architects of the day, including Philibert de l'Orme and Pierre Lescot. Lanquais was on Protestant territory, and by extending it in 1533 in the style of the Louvre, Galhiot was using architecture to underline his Catholic and Royalist loyalties. Indeed, it provoked strong reaction from Huguenots and Henri de la Tour d'Auvergne besieged Lanquais in 1577, interrupting building works and leaving the low pavilion on the west unfinished.

The visit starts in the tall octagonal tower, built in the 15C to replace a 14C round tower; it stands on the original 12C base. The spiral staircase, acting as a spine to support the structure, which is not buttressed, ends in a sophisticated 'palm-tree' vault. The tower and 14C north block show the scars of the siege of 1577. The Renaissance angle pavilion in the style of Pierre Lescot's Cour Carrée at the Louvre was added 1561–74; the elaborate upper windows are taken from Androuet du Cerceau's *Book of Architecture*. Several rooms, including two bed-rooms, are decked out in the style of the Renaissance, with large windows and wooden bath tubs, and in Monsieur's Room, an outstanding carved fireplace and door surround (1601). The dining room was restored in the 19C by Alexis de Gourgue, while the games and music room is in the taste of 1780–90, with an English pianoforte (*c* 1840). The Grand Salon is dominated by a Renaissance chimney-piece the width of the room, altered in the 19C. The kitchens are also visited.

7 The Lot : Haut Quercy

The *département* of the Lot corresponds to much of the old province of Quercy, the name of which is derived from the Gaullish tribe, the Cadourques, who once inhabited the area. The east and centre of the Quercy has a rugged and desolate charm, in contrast to the lush valleys of the Dordogne to the north and the Lot to the south, with its tributaries the Célé and Vers. Rainfall and rivers disappear rapidly through the porous limestone plateaux called *causses*, which at their highest are only about 360m above sea-level, where caves and caverns are formed. In this stone-rich land, early man built dolmens (2500–1500 BC) with great slabs of stone, some 500 of which can be identified in the Lot; and the country is brindled with dry-stone walls and shelters called *cabanes*, *cazelles* or *gariottes*. The vegetation of the *causses* is low-key: juniper, box, or the abundant spiky blossoms of the *mimosa des causses* (cornus) that scumble the February landscape with yellow; and characteristic is the small oak among whose roots nestles the greatest culinary treasure, the magnificent truffle. The Bouriane (p 189) in the west is wooded and sandy and to the southwest is the Quercy Blanc, the chalky stone giving it its name.

Getting there and around
By car

A20 or N20 from the north, via Limoges, Brive, etc.

Train

Paris Austerlitz to Toulouse via Souillac, Gourdon, Cahors, Lalbenque, Caussade. Brive to Toulouse via Les Quartre-Routes, St-Denis-les-Martel (8km from Martel), Floirac, Rocamadour-Padirac, Gramat, Flaujac, Assier, Figeac, Capdenac.
Brive to Aurillac via Vayrac, Bétaille, Puybrun, Bretenoux, Laval-de-Cère.
Aurillac to Capdenac via Bagnac, Viazac, Figeac.

Bus

Cahors to Libos, serves the Lot valley west of Cahors; and Cahors to Capdenac for the valley east of Cahors. There are many secondary lines. Timetable is published by Conseil Général du Lot, Hôtel du Département, Pl. Chapou, BP 291, 46005 Cahors, ☎ 05 65 23 27 50, fax 05 65 23 82 18.

Tourist information

46320 Assier Pl. de l'Eglise, ☎ 05 65 40 50 60, fax 05 65 40 41 99, www.quercy.net/quercy/assier
46130 Bretenoux BP7, Ave de la Libération, ☎ 05 65 38 59 53, fax 05 65 39 72 14, email ot.bretenoux@wanadoo.fr
46110 Carennac Cour de Prieuré, ☎ 05 65 10 97 01, www.tourisme-carennac.com
46300 Gourdon 24 Rue du Majou, ☎ 05 65 27 52 50, fax 05 65 27 52 52
46240 Labastide-Murat (for Parc natural régional des Causses du Quercy), ☎ 05 65 24 20 50, fax 05 65 24 20 59
46600 Martel Pl. des Consuls, ☎ 05 65 37 43 44, fax 05 65 37 37 27, email marteltourisme@europost.org
46500 Rocamadour Hôtel de Ville, Cité Médiévale, open all year, ☎ 05 65 33 62 59, fax 05 65 33 22 01; L'Hospitalet, open during the summer, ☎ 05 65 33 22 00, fax 05 65 33 22 01, www.rocamadour.com
46400 St-Céré Pl. de la République, ☎ 05 65 38 11 85, www.quercy.net/saint-cere
46200 Souillac Blvd L.J.-Malvy, ☎ 05 65 37 81 56, fax 05 65 27 11 45, www.quercy.net/quercy

Market days

Gourdon Thursday
St-Céré Saturday; fair the first and third
Sunday of the month
Souillac Main market Friday. Also
Monday and Wednesday

 ### Festivals and events

July *Les Trétaux de la chanson
Française*, music festival,
Gourdon
Les Eclectiques de Rocamadour, festival of
just about everything.
'Sim Copans' jazz festival, Souillac
July–August *Festival du Haut Quercy*,
music festival, St-Céré and other venues
August *Rencontres Cinéma*, Gindou
(near Cazacs, Bouriane).
September *Les Montgolfiades*, European
gathering of hot-air balloons,
Rocamadour

Where to stay and eating out

46500 ALVIGNAC (D673)
☆☆/€–€€ *Hôtel/Restaurant du
Château*, Rte de Rocamadour, ☎ 05 65
33 60 14, fax 05 65 33 69 28. On the
foundations of an ancient château, this
hotel offers a flowery terrace and shady
courtyard. Friendly service.
46400 AUTOIRE
€ *La Cascade*, Le Bourg, ☎ 05 65 38
20 02, fax 05 65 10 83 66, www.
promenades-gourmandes.com. Beams
and a 16C fireplace or a terrace overlooking the village in summer, set the
scene for local produce used in imaginative combinations.
46130 BRETENOUX
☆☆/€€ **Hostellerie Belle Rive**, Port du
Gagnac, ☎ 05 65 38 50 04, fax 05 65
38 47 72. On the banks of the Cère,
pleasant individualised rooms, shady
terrace, and delicious traditional
cooking.
46350 CALÈS
☆☆/€€ *Le Petit Relais*, on D673
between A20 and Rocamadour, ☎ 05
65 37 96 09, fax 05 65 37 95 93,

www.le-petit-relais.fr. A recommended
hotel/restaurant with 15 renovated
rooms.
46110 CARENNAC
☆☆/€–€€ *Auberge du Vieux Quercy*,
☎ 05 65 10 96 59, fax 05 65 10 94
05, www.medianet.fr/vieuxquercy.
Friendly hostelry with view over the village. Popular, modern dining room and
simple bedrooms enhanced by contemporary paintings and lithographs. Good
traditional cooking.
46250 GOUJOUNAC
☆☆/€–€€ *Hostellerie de Goujounac*, Le
Bourg, ☎ 05 65 35 68 67, fax 05 65
36 60 54. On the D660; inside the
sturdy stone house is a warm welcome
and quiet comfort, with excellent food to
match.
46300 GOURDON
☆☆/€ *Hotel/Restaurant Bissonnier*, 51
Bd des Martyrs, ☎ 05 65 41 02 48, fax
05 65 41 44 67, www.promenades-
gourmandes.com. Magnificent dining
room where 7th generation chef,
Christian Bissonnier, presents his personalised and traditional recipes.
Comfortable rooms.
46240 LABASTIDE-MURAT
☆☆/€ *Hotel/Restaurant La Garissade*,
Pl. de la Mairie, ☎ 05 65 2118 80, fax
05 65 21 10 97, www.promenades-
gourmandes.com. Seductive and inventive cuisine using local produce, combined with comfortable rooms.
46240 MONTFAUCON (north of
Labastide-Murat, east of the N20)
€ *Le Cloître*, Le Bourg, ☎ 05 65 31 11
80, fax 05 65 31 11 47, www.
promenades-gourmandes.com. Prettily
presented restaurant, with terrace, and
rich and varied dishes selected according to the season and market-place.
46200 LACAVE (A62 from Souillac,
D43)
☆☆☆☆ *Château de la Treyne*, ☎ 05 65
27 60 60, fax 05 65 27 60 70, email
treyne@relaischateau.com. Medieval
château in glorious setting above the

Dordogne with luxurious accommodation and restaurant in the Louis XIII salon or on the riverside terrace.

☆☆☆/€€€ Le Pont de l'Ouysse, ☎ 05 65 37 87 04, fax 05 65 32 77 41, www.lepontdelouysse.fr. Small, family-run establishment on south bank of the Dordogne in lovely setting, with a terrace. Classy and imaginative dishes served in the restaurant (one Michelin rosette).

46600 MARTEL

☆☆☆ *Relais Ste-Anne*, Rue Pourtanel, ☎ 05 65 27 01 01, fax 05 65 27 01 02, www.relais-sainte-anne.com. Charming small hotel offers modern elegance and bright rooms in a former nuns' residence with chapel. Heated pool, sauna, walled garden. No restaurant.

Domaine de la Vaysse, Mme Christiane Gaspard, ☎ 05 65 32 49 87. *Chambres d'hôte*. Four pretty rooms with independent entrance; garden, ping-pong and pétanque on offer.

46500 PADIRAC

☆☆/€/€€ *L'Auberge de Mathieu*, Lieu-dit Mathieu, ☎/fax 05 65 33 64 68, www.promenades-gourmandes.com. This is the occasion to take your time to appreciate the cooking of Christian Pinquie who specialises in ingredients from the region, especially local lamb. Comfortable rooms, green surroundings.

46130 PRUDHOMAT

€ *Les Remparts*, 'Castelnau', ☎ 05 65 38 52 88, fax 05 65 38 44 99. At the foot of the Château de Castelnau and enjoying a magnificent view, the chef presents regional specialities in an inventive and appetising manner.

Relais du Seuil de la Dordogne, M. et Mme. de la Barrière, Vayssières, ☎ 05 65 38 50 22, fax 05 65 38 50 68, email jean.de.labarriere@wanadoo.fr. *Chambres d'hôte*. A 16C house close to Castelnau in a restful green setting, simple rooms (en suite).

46500 ROCAMADOUR

☆☆☆ *Domaine de la Rhue*, La Rhue, ☎ 05 65 33 71 50, fax 05 65 33 72 48, www.domainedelarhue.com. Set in the rolling *causse* landscape, a successful stable conversion into an elegant and well-furnished establishment with spacious rooms. No restaurant.

☆☆☆/€–€€ *Le Beau Site*, ☎ 05 65 33 63 08, fax 05 65 33 65 23, www.bw-beausite.com. Hotel and restaurant flank opposite sides of the main street at the heart of the *cité*. Pretty rooms and airy restaurant overlooking the Alzou gorges.

☆☆/€ *Sainte-Marie*, Pl des Senhals, Cité Médiévale, ☎ 05 65 33 63 07, fax 05 65 33 69 08, www.hotel-sainte-marie.fr. Terrace and all the rooms overlook the Alzou valley in quiet and restful setting. Wide choice of succulent dishes in the restaurant; brasserie for light midday meals.

☆☆ *Le Terminus des Pélérins*, Pl. de la Carretta, ☎ 05 65 33 62 14, fax 05 65 33 72 10. Situated almost opposite the steps to the sanctuaries in the old town. Reasonably priced.

☆☆ *Le Troubadour*, Belveyre (on the Padirac road/D673), ☎ 05 65 33 70 27, fax 05 65 33 71 99, email troubadour@rocamadour.com. Convenience combined with tranquillity; small and modern, with a pool.

46400 ST-CÉRÉ

☆☆☆ *La France*, 181 Ave F. de Maynard, ☎ 05 65 38 02 16, fax 05 65 38 02 98. Hotel set in gardens, with a pool, and a recommended restaurant.

☆☆☆/€–€€ *Hotel/Restaurant Ric*, Rte de Leyme, ☎ 05 65 38 04 08, fax 05 65 38 00 14, www.silencehotel.com/ hotel-ric. This oasis of calm is in a green setting above the town; pool. The owner/chef is known for his inventive cooking.

46400 ST-JEAN-LESPINASSE

☆☆☆ *Les Trois Soleils de Montal*, Montal, near St- Céré, ☎ 05 65 10 16 16, fax 05 65 38 30 66. A relatively new hotel-restaurant in leafy surroundings, very comfortable and well-equipped, with a pool.

46200 SOUILLAC

✩✩✩/€–€€ *La Vieille Auberge*, 1 Rue de Recège, ☎ 05 65 32 79 43, fax 05 65 32 65 19, www.la-vieille-auberge.com. Excellent dining in the restaurant decorated in pastel shades; comfortable but unexciting rooms, pool, sauna.

✩✩✩/€/€€ *Les Granges Vieilles*, Route de Sarlat, ☎ 05 65 37 80 92, fax 05 65 37 08 18, www.promenades-gourmandes.com. (1.5km towards Sarlat.) An old building full of character set in a 3ha park. On fine days, meals served outside near the pool. For 20 years Gérard Cayre has been concocting delights from regional produce.

46190 TEYSSIEU (near Bretenoux)

€ *La Table de la Tour*, Le Bourg, ☎ 05 65 33 82 02, www.promenades-gourmandes.com. A traditional stone and *lauze* building in the village, where you can savour carefully prepared regional dishes in one of the dining rooms or on the terrace.

46300 LE VIGAN

€ *Musée Henri Giron*, ☎ 05 65 41 33 78. Small restaurant at the museum (see below). Book in advance.

Souillac and the Causse de Martel

Southeast of Sarlat in the Périgord Noir lies the border between the *départements* of the Dordogne and the Lot. The D704 via Groléjac, which deserves a look, links Sarlat and Gourdon (see below) and the D703 follows the Dordogne upstream from Carsac (see p 167) to Souillac.

Between Sarlat and Souillac on the south of the Dordogne, accessed by the D50, is the **Château de Fénelon**, which rises out of the woods of the Bouriane on the banks of the river. Guided visits, daily July–Aug 09.30–19.00; March–June, Sept, Oct 10.00–12.00, 14.00–18.00; Jan–Feb, Nov–Dec 14.00–17.00; ☎ 05 53 29 81 45.

Fénelon

François de Salignac de la Mothe-Fénelon (1651–1715), born at the Chateau de Fénelon in the Perigord, who became Archbishop of Cambrai at the end of his life, was appointed Abbot of Carennac when the abbey was placed *in commendum*. Writer as well as prelate, he was author of *Traité de l'éducation des filles*, and came to the notice of Madame de Maintenon, influential mistress of Louis XIV who was responsible for the education of the king's children. Fénelon was appointed tutor in 1689 to the Duke of Burgundy, the Dauphin, grandson of Louis XIV, who died young. Among Fénelon's other words were *Fables*, and the more subversive *Aventures de Télémaque* (1699) in which he indirectly criticised the politics of Louis XIV which ultimately led to his disgrace. During his abbacy of Carennac, Fénelon resided at the priory, and the town claims that Fénelon returned there after he had become tutor to the prince, to work on *Télémaque*, and consequently the Ile de Calypso in the Dordogne was re-named after the island in the book (p 161).

The château was built in the 15C and 16C and altered in the 17C. It was the birthplace of François de Salignac de la Mothe-Fénelon, Archbishop of Cambrai, better known as the writer Fénelon. The family sold the property in 1780. The three defensive baileys give it a severe aspect, but the two-storey main block with 15C machicolated towers, *lauze* roofs and late-Gothic dormers adds a lighter touch. The main façade faces north and is enhanced by a fine double staircase leading to the *cour d'honneur*. Included in the visit are Fénelon's bedroom, the chapel, and the kitchen carved out of the rock. There is medieval military paraphernalia on show, as well as a variety of 17C–18C furniture, Dutch and Chinese porcelain and some good fireplaces and tapestries. Cross back to the north bank for the pretty village of **Carlux**, which has a Gothic chimney and the remains of a castle.

Souillac

Souillac is the first town of any importance on the N20 after entering the Midi-Pyrénées from the north. Situated on the Borrèze, a tributary of the Dordogne, it is a pleasant town in pale stone.

The main monument is a fine domed Romanesque church, **Ste-Marie**, part of a Benedictine abbey. Built between 1075 and the mid-12C, the church has survived although the monastic buildings of that period were destroyed in the 16C by the Protestants, and it was restored and repaired from the 17C to the 19C. The

The church of Ste-Marie, Souillac

exterior is coolly beautiful, in crisp white stone, with polygonal radiating chapels opening off the apse in a multi-tiered arrangement culminating in the *lauze*-covered cupola and lantern, one of three. To the west are the remains of the 10C belfry. The foundations of an earlier church and elements of the Carolingian chancel as well as 11C–13C sarcophagi were discovered in the crypt in 1948. Inside, the cavernous two-bay nave is covered by two cupolas on pendentives supported by massive interior buttresses, and above the crossing is a third. It is very plain but harmonious, except for some interesting carved capitals in the capacious east end. The furnishings include a 16C retable of the *Mystery of the Rosary*, a painting of *Christ's Agony on the Mount* by Chassériau (19C), and 18C choir stalls.

The most thrilling feature of the church is a group of **Romanesque reliefs** on the reverse of the west door, possibly moved here in the 17C, with many stylistic similarities to those at Moissac. The tympanum is a complicated illustration, framed by three arches, of the dream of the monk Theophilus, who, having sold his soul to the Devil, begged for the Virgin's intercession to recover it. Heavenly forces, represented by the Virgin descending from the clouds accompanied by angels, oppose the Devil, shown as half-man, half-beast. This animated scene is framed by the figures of St Peter and St Benedict. The trumeau on the north is a masterpiece of tumbling and intertwined figures, human and monsters, representing sins and their punishments on the right and centre. The left face shows the *Sacrifice of Abraham*, an extraordinarily vital composition for such a narrow space. The Prophet Isaiah on the right door jamb, a graceful figure with crossed legs, flowing beard and hair and swirling drapes which cling to his limbs, is a more vigorous version of Moissac's Jeremiah filling a larger space. The rather less wonderful figure on the opposite jamb is the patriarch Joseph or Josea.

Adjacent to the church, installed in the 17C monastic buildings in 1988 and in total contrast, is the **Musée de l'Automate**. This is a wonderland of mechanised dolls and models arranged thematically and activated in rotation to perform all sorts of acrobatics and contortions. It is the most comprehensive collection of its kind in Europe with more than 1000 pieces, dating from 1862 to 1960, and is an absolute must for children of all ages, especially on a rainy day. Open July, Aug 10.00–19.00; June, Sept 10.00–12.00 and 15.00–18.00; April, May, Oct, Tues–Sun 10.00–12.00 and 15.00–18.00, closed Mon; Jan–Mar, Nov–Dec, Wed–Sun 14.00–17.00, closed Mon, Tues; ☎ 05 65 37 07 07. The old church of **St-Martin** with a huge belfry, next to the tourist office, has been turned into an exhibition space.

The D43 along the Dordogne passes the **Château de la Treyne** and its gardens (open June–Sept, closed Mon) on the way to Belcastel and the beautiful Ouysse Valley. The **Grottes de Lacave** make a magical visit including an electric train ride, underground lakes and spectacular concretions. Open, guided visits, July, Aug 09.30–18.30; April–June, Sept–Nov 10.00–12.00 and 14.00–17.00; ☎ 05 65 37 87 03. There is stunning scenery around St-Sozy and Creysse, which has a Romanesque chapel, and there is a semi-troglodyte church at Gluges. The road follows the high cliffs overlooking the Cirque de Monvalent, a natural amphiteatre carved out by waters of the Dordogne.

Martel is the principal town on the Causse de Martel, famous for its seven towers. Its legendary founder was Charles Martel (*c* 685–741), grandfather of Charlemagne, best known for his defeat of the Arabs at Poitiers in 732. There is little basis for his association with the town and it is more likely that the name is a derivation of an Occitan word, meaning workers in stone, metal and wood which are represented by the three *marteaux* (hammers) on the coat of arms. As the ancient capital of the Viscounty of Turenne it became a free town in 1219 and has retained much of its medieval character.

The Palais de la Raymondie at the centre of the old town (13C–14C but altered later) has interesting late-Gothic windows. In the tourist office, Place des Consuls, is the Musée Gallo-Romain, a small archaeological museum, open July, Aug, Mon–Fri 10.00–12.00, 14.00–18.00. Nearby are the Hôtel de la Monnaie (13C; formerly the mint), the Tour d'Henri Court Mantel ('Short Coat')—named for the older brother of Richard the Lionheart—and the sturdy 18C covered market. South of the market is Maison Fabri (15C) with a round tower, built on the site of the house where Henri Court Mantel died of dysentery in 1183.

In Rue Droite, south of Place des Consuls, are more old *hôtels* and at the eastern end of town is the 14C church of St-Maur. The Romanesque tympanum in the porch, from an earlier church, has a *Last Judgement* with Christ surrounded by angels presenting the instruments of the Passion and sounding the trumpets of the resurrection. Inside there is a 15C *Christ on the Cross*, some 16C glass in the east end, and 18C panelling and pulpit. A walnut press, the *Moulin de Martel* at the Huilerie du Lac de Diane, can be visited at certain times (demonstrations in winter and Sat, 15.00–17.30); check times with tourist office.

Puy-d'Issolud is 14km east of Martel (D703 to Vayrac, then D119) on high ground limited by steep escarpments, where a Celtic fort was excavated during the mid-19C. In the tourist office at Vayrac (☎ 05 65 32 52 50) is the small Musée d'Uxelledunum, with finds from Puy d'Issolud.

Celtic Uxellodunum

There are three ancient *oppidi* or hill forts which contest the title of Uxellodunum on the causse de Quercy: Puy-d'Issolud, between Martel and Vayrac north of the Dordogne River; the oppidum de Murcens, on the Causse de Gramat, near Lauzes (p 212), northeast of Cahors; and Capdenac-le-Haut (p 206) on high ground above the Lot east of Figeac. Vercingetorix and the Cadurci suffered their last defeat before Caesar at Uxellodunum in 51 BC. The wall excavated at the oppidum de Murcens, made up of uncut stone and wood, corresponds to the *murus gallicus* constructed by the Celts described in Caesar's *Commentaries* and is suitably impressive, measuring some 6km. Puy-d'Issolud was fortified by earthworks and dry-stone walls, and Capdenac-le-Haut is a village perched on cliff with a commanding position above a loop in the Lot.

Carennac on the N140 and D43 is an interesting village on a backwater of the Dordogne with an ancient priory which, despite periods of abuse, has retained a certain charm. The Cluniac priory dedicated to St Peter was probably begun towards the end of the 11C. In the 15C the cloister and chapter house were rebuilt. Even before the Revolution the monastery was in a lamentable state and most of its possessions were sold soon after. The priory buildings were remodelled in the 16C and 17C and incorporate the façade facing the river known as the *château* (c 15C) which contains a museum of local history.

The Romanesque sculpted tympanum above the church porch is impressive. Protected by a deep arch and supported by a cluster of four pillars in the centre and two at each side, it is a finely chiselled but rigorous composition of great clarity, reminiscent of the north porch at Cahors (see p 194). The centre panel is filled by the hieratic figure of Christ in a mandorla, his hand raised in blessing. In the spandrels are the symbols of the four Evangelists. The space on either side is divided horizontally into two registers containing the Apostles, with small crouching figures in the extreme corners. A delicately carved vegetal rinceau outlines the composition and the narrow lintel has a regular pattern of alternating pearls and little animals.

To the east an 11C door with a double arch and four decorated capitals is signed by the mason, Girbertus. The modest 12C church has a barrel-vaulted nave and some interesting capitals. There is a shallow transept and a cupola on pendentives above the crossing and a few touches of polychromy in the vaults. The cloister has one surviving Romanesque gallery on the south whereas the rest was rebuilt in Flamboyant style in the 16C, also reminiscent of Cahors. In the restored chapter house is a 16C **Entombment**, a moving ensemble of sculptures with a hint of the original polychrome decoration. Gathered around the Christ are the life-sized figures of Nicodemus and Joseph of Arimathaea, with Mary in the centre, on her right St John, Mary Magdalene holding the ointment jar, and two other Maries.

The hamlet of Prudhomat-Castelnau, between Carennac and St-Céré on the D43, cowers in the shadow of the **Château de Castelnau-Bretenoux**. This is a truly impressive example of feudal architecture, emphasised by the blood-red colour of the ferruginous limestone of its construction and its position on a plateau overlooking the borders between the old provinces of Périgord, Limousin, Auvergne and Quercy. Open July, Aug 09.30–18.45; April–June, Sept, 09.30–12.15 and 14.00–18.15; Oct–March, Mon, Wed–Sun 10.00–12.15 and 14.00 to 17.15, closed Tues; ☎ 05 65 10 98 00, www.castelnau.com.

The Barons of Castelnau date from the 11C, and the castle remained in the hands of their descendants or a branch of the family for 38 generations until 1830. The last of the line, Albert de Luynes, was forced at the Revolution to demolish the upper part of the towers and fill in the ditches. In 1851 a fire caused extensive damage. Jean Mouliérat, a well-known member of the Opéra Comique and the castle's last private owner (1896–1932), restored it in part before donating it to the state.

The castle follows the triangular form of the plateau and has a massive tower at each angle, a semi-circular one in each side and a square keep on the southwest. The earliest section of the building is late-12C or early-13C with two-light round-arched windows. Major programmes of enlargement and fortification were carried out in the 14C and 15C assuring its defence during the Hundred Years War, but by the 16C and 17C it was transformed into a more hospitable residence. It contains among other things a collection of medieval sculpture and Jean Mouliérat's collection of religious art.

In the village the collegiate church, built in the 15C by Jean de Castelnau, still has its 16C carved wooden stalls, similar to those in the Cathedral of Auch, some fragments of Renaissance glass, several statues including a polychrome Baptism of Christ (15C) and among the treasure is a 14C reliquary, *le Bras de St Louis* (St Louis' arm).

St-Céré

St-Céré, on the D940, is a lively and cultured town and holds an important summer music festival in July and August. In the centre of town, around Rue de la République, the main street, and Rue du Mazel, are some 15C, 16C and 17C houses with medieval and Renaissance features. The Quai des Récollets, on the bank of La Bave, has pretty views onto the river, the old houses and bridges.

The artist Jean Lurçat (1892–1966) lived here for over 20 years and his work can be seen in two places. In town, off Place du Mercadial, the **Casino** combines an art gallery for temporary exhibitions, shop and café, and a permanent collection of Lurçat's tapestries and ceramics. Open 14 July–Sept 09.30–12.00 and 14.00–18.30; May–Sept, Sun 11.00–19.00; ☎ 05 65 3819 60.

The two towers high above St-Céré mark the 14C château purchased in 1945 by Lurçat, St-Laurent-les-Tours, reached via the D904. There, the **Atelier-Musée Jean Lurçat** is a fascinating insight into Lurçat's later work. Open Palm Sunday to Easter and 14 July–30 Sept daily 09.30–12.00, 14.30–18.30; ☎ 05 65 38 28 21. He started his career as a painter and was influenced by the important movements of the early 20C but he is best known as a tapestry designer, the most prolific of his generation. He began experimenting with the medium in

1917. The large rooms of St-Laurent-les-Tours, which Lurçat decorated in his own inimitable style, create a perfect setting for his highly idiosyncratic and vividly coloured tapestries. There are also tapestry cartoons, a large number of paintings, sketches, ceramics, fabrics and furniture, demonstrating the full range of Lurçat's work. Mme Simone Lurçat, the painter's widow, donated the collection to the *département*.

West of St-Céré the D673 is a pretty route with a series of interesting sites. The **Château de Montal** at St-Jean-Lespinasse is a gem of a Renaissance château with a sad story. Open from Rameau à Toussaint (Palm Sunday) to All Saints Day (1 Nov) 09.30–12.00 and 14.30–18.00, closed Sat; ☎ 05 65 38 13 72.

It was built by Jeanne de Balsac who in 1503 inherited a fortune from her father, Robert de Balsaz d'Entragues, Governor of Pisa during the French occupation of Northern Italy. Widowed in 1511, she began the construction of Montal for her son Robert but he was killed six months after his departure for Italy in 1523. Despite its present apparent composure, Montal suffered terrible degradation at the end of the 19C when it was stripped of all its decoration and sold off in job lots. It was purchased just before the First World War by a wealthy industrialist and enlightened patron, Maurice Fenaille, who, after years of patient searching, recovered many of the original pieces or commissioned copies, and Montal was made whole again. Montal was the last hiding place of the Mona Lisa during World War Two (see Loc Dieu, p 238).

This small château is characteristic of the innovations introduced into France from Italy in the early 16C and is indicative of the culture of its chatelaine. Only two wings were ever completed. The façades facing the countryside have the characteristics of a feudal fortress but the interior courtyard elevations are luxuriously decorated with an Italianate vocabulary of friezes, pilasters, candelabra, allegorical subjects, statues in niches, and high-relief busts which are memorials to Jeanne de Balsac's family. There is a very grand staircase, sculpted on the underside. In the rugged Quercy, Montal is a haven of 16C refinement.

West of Montal are the **Grottes de Presque**, one of many caves that can be visited in the region, which boast an impressive array of natural phenomena. Open July, Aug 09.00–19.00; 15 Feb–15 Nov 09.00–12.00 and 14.00–18.00; ☎ 05 65 38 07 44. Near the caves, the D38 goes through the **Cirque d'Autoire**, where a 30m waterfall cascades into the gorge. Opposite, in the sheer cliff face, are the ruins of the *château des anglais*, the description given to most rock-fortresses of this kind in the region. A little further, nestling on both banks of the valley is **Autoire**, a model Quercynois village. Gathered around a simple church (12C, 14C and 15C) and a manor house (16C), its buildings are in pale gold stone or half-timbered with hipped roofs of russet-coloured tiles. The equally alluring **Loubressac**, on the D135 just to the northwest, is a fortified village overlooking the valleys of the Bave and the Céré.

One of the most remarkable caverns in the region for its size and complexity, with probably the most famous of the underground rivers, is the **Gouffre de Padirac**. This magical visit 110m below ground is made by lift, on foot and by boat through a series of galleries and lakes and 560m of river. Open 10 July–31 Aug 08.30/09.00–18.30; April–9 July, Sept 09.00–12.00 and 14.00–18.00; 1–14 Oct 09.00–12.00 and 14.00–17.00; ☎ 05 65 33 64 56.

Rocamadour

Rocamadour, the principal attraction in this part of the Midi-Pyrénées, shelters at its heart a group of sanctuaries which have been the object of pilgrimage for hundreds of years and to which pilgrims are still drawn on the first Sunday of September. The magnetism of the place is hard to define but in the Middle Ages the challenging aspect of this inhospitable ravine and the difficulties of access probably contributed to the penance of a pilgrimage. Today the site has been fully exploited to welcome the visitor with numerous hotels, restaurants and souvenir shops. The drama of the *cité* clinging to the rock above the Alzou Valley is best viewed from the hamlet of l'Hospitalet on the plateau above.

There is **car parking** above the village, near the château: follow the road along the clifftop from l'Hospitalet and through the tunnel, then left again. The Cité Réligieuse and Grand'Rue are pedestrianised. Lifts run in two stages from the main car park to the sanctuaries and from the sanctuaries to the village, and there is a Little Train in the lower town (from Porte du Figuer) for sightseeing day and during nighttime illuminations.

The first mention of a church at 'Roc-Amadour' was in the 11C when the two Benedictine abbeys of Marcilhac and Tulle disputed the site. The monks of Tulle won the day and at this time a Marian cult associated with Rocamadour was first recorded. Its reputation was enhanced by a *Book of Miracles of Our Lady of Rocamadour* written in 1172. The pilgrimages of St Bernard (*c* 1147) and Henry II Plantagenet (1170) put the site securely on the map, and other pious notables followed in their wake. At its apogee in the 14C Rocamadour was probably as busy as today but the troubles of the Reformation started a decline until in the 19C the town was in a ruinous state. In 1829 a group of ecclesiastics instigated the physical and spiritual revival of the site and reinstated an annual pilgrimage in 1835. This is in the week beginning 8 September, and on the evening of the 14 August there is a candlelight procession.

Pilgrims would start from Porte de l'Hospitalet, where only fragments of the chapel of the old pilgrim hospital of St-Jean have survived, and would take the pilgrimage track down to the village. From here is the arduous climb up the **Grand Escalier** (216 steps) to the Sanctuaries. In the 19C a **Chemin de Croix** (Stations of the Cross, 1887), was constructed, which zig-zags up the cliff to arrive at the château. Much easier is to do the reverse, starting at the car park above the sanctuaries. There are splendid views from the ramparts of the château, originally 14C, but mainly a 19C rebuild. Of the old pilgrim hospital of St-Jean only fragments of the chapel remain, incorporated into the 19C chapel. The Grand Escalier brings you down into the village on Rue Roland le Preux through the first of five fortified medieval gateways, Porte du Figuier. There is a lift to the sanctuaries before the second and most picturesque gate, Porte Salmon. Either branch left here, passing behind the houses to arrive at Porte Basse at the far end of the village, or go straight down the main street, Rue de la Couronnerie, which has a few genuinely old buildings. Near the 15C *hôtel de ville* are the 216 steps of the Grand Escalier leading to the Cité Religieuse.

The **Cité Religieuse**, sadly lacking in spiritual warmth on non-pilgrimage days, consists of a number of sanctuaries or churches which were massively restored and rebuilt in the 19C, the best features being fragments of 12C and

15C frescoes. The churches are on different levels but all lead off a common *parvis* (forecourt) centred on the first rocky resting-place of St Amadour where, so the story goes, his body was exhumed intact in 1166, centuries after his death. Picturesque legends are associated with the saint. One proposes that he was Zacchaeus, the Jew, former tax collector of Jericho, who climbed a maple to see Christ and who, after his conversion to Christianity, distributed half his wealth to the poor (some kind of a tax rebate?). He was said to have become the servant of the Virgin, but eventually he left for Gaul and there led the life of a hermit. Another legend suggests that he and his wife, St Veronica (of the cloth with the image of Christ), sailed away up the Gironde and, after Veronica's death, Amadour lived in the caves above the Alzou. All the sanctuaries can be visited July–September; the parish church of Notre-Dame is open all year, and the basilica of St-Sauveur from Easter to Nov.

The main sanctuary, the church of **Notre-Dame**, was rebuilt after a rock fall in 1479 and damaged in the 16C. It was restored and enlarged in the 19C. To the right of the 15C portal is a fragment of a wall-painting (also 15C) of ghoulish skeletons, *The Three Dead and the Three Living*. Inside, above the altar (1889) stands the famous 12C **Black Virgin**, one of a series of enigmatic black Madonnas. The 'blackness' of this Madonna was first mentioned in the 17C. Originally a reliquary statue, it has suffered over the centuries and both Madonna and Child acquired crowns in the 19C. Rocamadour has connections with the sea, represented by ex-voto models of boats. The most phoney of all the accoutrements associated with the place has to be the replica of Roland's faithful sword Durandal, embedded in the cliff above the Notre-Dame chapel, the original of which was offered by Charlemagne's companion to Our Lady of Rocamadour. In June 1183 Henri Court Mantel (see above) and his brother Geoffrey, their allowances cut off by their father, went looting and plundering through the region, and snatched Roland's sword from Rocamadour.

On the exterior wall of the 12C chapel of **St-Michel** are some remarkable but damaged late-12C/13C frescoes of the *Annunciation* and *Visitation*, and there are more in the apse. Below the chapel was the canons' calefactory (warming room) leading to the gatehouse, which has been opened at each end to offer some good views over the village. The so-called abbey palace, mainly 19C, houses the **Musée d'Art Sacrée** dedicated to Francis Poulenc (1899–1963), who composed the *Litanies to the Black Virgin*. Although born in Paris, Poulenc came from a family who originated in neighbouring Rouergue, and experienced a religious reconversion before the Virgin of Rocamadour in 1936. It has a wide and interesting range of religious objects (11C–20C) including reliquaries, statues, stained glass and paintings, and a glass-sided lift offers great views of the valley. Open daily July, Aug 09.00–19.00; Jan–June, Sept–Dec 09.30–12.00, 14.00–18.00; ☎ 05 65 33 23 30. On the northeast side of the terrace is the largest sanctuary, the basilica of **St-Sauveur** (originally 12C), its west end built into the cliff face and supporting a wooden gallery. A rectangular space divided into equal naves by two piers with eight columns from which spring diagonal ribs, it is lit by diffused light from the five windows in the east but is confusing as it has been reorientated, with the altar in the north. Steps from St-Sauveur lead down to the church of **St-Amadour** underneath, the least altered of the medieval buildings with heavy squared ribs similar to the narthex at Moissac. The sacristy was created later from the cistern of the keep. The three further sanctuaries of

St-Blaise, St-Jean and St-Anne, containing the 17C altar from the Notre-Dame chapel, close the terrace to the east. These three sanctuaries and that of St-Amadour are only accessible during religious festivals or on guided visits between June and September and school vacations, 10.30–14.30.

To reach the **château** (built 14C, restored 19C) on top of the cliff protecting the shrines, follow the Stations of the Cross up the winding cliff walk or take the lift. Ramparts only open daily in summer 08.30–21.00; in winter 09.00–18.30.

Rocamadour offers a whole variety of tourist attractions including **La Grotte des Merveilles**, with prehistoric drawings and natural formations. Open July, Aug 09.00–19.00; April–Oct 10.00–12.00 and 14.00–18.00; ☎ 05 65 33 67 92. There is also a monkey park, the Forêt des Singes, or one can explore the Alzou Gorges.

On the D673 at Calès is the **Moulin de Cougnaguet**, a 14C fortified mill with four pairs of millstones which still grind into action. Guided visits April–Sept 10.00–12.00 and 14.00–18.00; Oct 10.30–12.00 and 14.00–17.00; ☎ 05 65 38 73 56.

Gourdon and the Bouriane

The pays between the Dordogne and Lot Valleys and the Causse of Gramat, crossed by the N20 (and A20), known as the Bouriane, has mainly wooded scenery, similar to neighbouring Périgord, with deep ochre and red soils, in contrast to the dry *causses*. Its main town is Gourdon.

West of the N20 is **Le Vigan**. This small town has a curious church, part 14C—the three bay nave—and part 15C—the complicated east end. During restoration work in 1960 Romanesque capitals from an earlier building were uncovered in the foundations.

The **Musée Henri Giron**, 3.5km from the centre of Le Vigan in a delightful rural setting, was created in 1991 around a private art collection. Open May–June, Sept–Oct 10.00–12.00 and 15.00–18.00; July, Aug 10.00–18.00; closed Mon; other times open Sun or by appointment, except Mon; ☎ 05 65 41 33 78. Henri Giron (b. 1914) was born near Lyons and now lives in Brussels. Self-taught, he almost always paints women and has developed a very distinctive figurative style. Another feature of the museum is its restaurant (see above).

The main town of the Bouriane, **Gourdon**, situated on a limestone mound typical of the landscape, is a busy little place with a music festival in July. The old town has a 13C gateway and Rue Majou (Mayor), the old main street which climbs up to the arcaded main square, has some good 13C–16C buildings. The surprisingly large but simple church of St-Pierre, which was built in the 14C, has 14C–15C and 16C stained glass and some gilded 17C works by the Tournier family, three generations (Raymond, Jean and François) of master-sculptors from Gourdon. They turned out elaborate but typically standardised, unimaginative altarpieces in line with the recommendations of the Council of Trent during the period of the Counter Reformation (1660–1720). Their work can be found over a fairly wide area. Steps behind the church lead up to the summit and an orientation table and all-round view.

The **Grottes de Cougnac** on the D704 heading north have both fantastic concretions and important prehistoric paintings of animals and human figures in black and red. Open July, Aug 09.30–18.00; 8 April–1 Nov 09.30–11.00 and 14.00–17.00; ☎ 05 65 41 47 54.

To the east of the N20 Séniergues has a cruciform Romanesque church. Further south, **Labastide-Murat** on the D10 was, as the name suggests, a *bastide*. Originally called Fortanière, in 1852 Napoléon III allowed it to be re-named after the brother-in-law of Napoléon I, Joachim Murat (1767–1815), King of Naples. He was born in the little house which is now the **Musée Murat**, created with gifts from the family. Open July–Sept 10.00–12.00 and 15.00–18.00; ☎ 05 65 21 19 23.

Southwest of Gourdon, east of the D673, at **Les Arques** is a virtually unsullied 11C Romanesque church with unique Mozarabic-inspired capitals and a crypt. The tiny village, with about 170 inhabitants, made a huge impact on the Russian sculptor, Ossip Zadkine (1890–1967), who had an on-going love affair with the Midi-Pyrénées from the 1920s and bought a house in Les Arques in 1934. Intellectual, musician and poet as well as sculptor, his arrival in this bucolic village must have caused something of a revolution. The **Musée Zadkine** opened in 1988 in his former studio, converted into a small attractive gallery. Open June–Sept, school holidays and weekends, 10.00–13.00 and 14.00–19.00; rest of year and other days, 14.00–17.00; ☎ 05 65 22 83 37. The exhibits are on loan from the Musée Zadkine in Paris but several of the large wooden sculptures were conceived in Les Arques: *Daphne* (1939), hewn from a massive trunk; *Diane* (1941) in polychromed poplar, a work he always kept in his home; and the stark, highly charged *Pietà* (1939–40) in the church. Stylistically his work owes a particularly heavy debt to Cubism and primitive sculpture but emotionally it is Expressionist. The work here shows his range including sculpture, prints, photographs and tapestries. Les Arques has the project for his first major monument, for Rotterdam, *The Destroyed City* (1947), and bronzes of his most successful work, *Orpheus* (1948), the dynamic *Arlequin Hurlant* (1956), *Arbre des Grâces* (1962) and the compact and polished *Pomone* (1960).

Zadkine participated in the restoration of the Romanesque church of St-André-des-Arques across the D45, 1km from the road, and in 1954 discovered some remarkable 15C murals which have, unfortunately, since deteriorated.

8 Cahors and the Lot Valley

The Lot River creates an extraordinarily beautiful valley which would make the basis for a pleasant tour. Less celebrated than the Dordogne Valley or Tarn Gorges it therefore attracts fewer visitors. Cahors is the linchpin between two stretches of the river which differ in character: to the east the Lot flows through countryside which is at times untamed and the population sparse, passing beneath the cliff-top village of St-Cirq-Lapopie; to the west the valley is wider and gentler, scattered with small communities and dominated by the vineyards which produce the robust red wines of Cahors.

Cahors

Cahors, situated on a peninsula protected by rocky cliffs formed by the Lot River, is the sort of small town that the French do so well, at ease with its historic past and equally comfortable in the 21C. Its major monuments, the Pont Valentré and the Cathedral of St-Etienne, deserve attention as does the medieval town, itself the focus of much careful restoration. Throughout the summer there are exhibitions, concerts and river trips. The local wine is excellent, with a cuisine to match. There are a number of good hotels in and around the town.

Practical information

Getting there and around
Train

Cahors is on the Paris to Toulouse line, and has rail links with Souillac, Gourdon and Montauban. The SNCF station is on the west of the peninsula. Bordeaux via Bergerac, Sarlat to Cahors.

Tourist trains and boats

Quercyrail runs train trips combined with rivers cruises and walks, ☎ 05 65 23 94 72 or enquire at the tourist office. July–Aug, five trips from Cahors train station:

Sat and Sun, train + boat/or Château de Cénevières
Mon, Thurs, train + Château de Cénevières
Wed, train + walk on riverbank
Mon, Wed, Thurs, train + St-Cirq-Lapopie
Tues, Fri, train + cruise
(*Quercyrail/Safaraid*)
May–Oct, Sun, train + boat/or Château de Cénevières
(see also Capdenac-Gare)

Petit Train

Town tour between the Quai-Valentré and the Cathedral, April–June, Sept, Oct, every day, 10.00–12.00, 14.00–19.00. Combined city trip and vineyard cruise July, Aug, every day except Sun and PH, 10.00–19.00 from the Pont-Valentré, ☎ 05 65 30 16 55.

Bus

Cahors to Libos, serves the Lot Valley west of Cahors; and Cahors to Capdenac for the Valley east of Cahors. There are many secondary lines. Timetable published by Conseil Général du Lot, Hôtel du Département, Pl. Chapou, BP 291, 46005 Cahors, ☎ 05 65 23 27 50, fax 05 65 23 82 18.

Festivals and events

May *Le Bon Air est dans les Caves*, wine festival in the cellars
July *Blues Festival*, Cahors
August *L'Eté musical dans la Vallée du Lot*, Cahors

Tourist information
Pl. F.-Mitterrand, ☎ 05 65 53 20 65, fax 05 65 53 20 74, www.quercy.net/quercy

Market days

The open-air market on Wednesday and Saturday is one of the best in the Lot. Flower market each Sunday morning. Daily market in the *halle*

Guided visits

June–Sept from the tourist office

River cruises

See *Quercyrail* and Petit Train above. *Bateaux Safaid* offers a variety of cruises from the Quai-Valentré, around Cahors, or as far as St-Cirq-Lapopie (see also Cajarc and Bouziès). ☎ 05 65 35 98 88 or 05 65 23 94 72

Where to stay and eating out

46000 CAHORS

☆☆☆/€€€€ *Le Terminus*, 5 Av. Charles-de-Freycinet, ☎ 05 65 53 32 00, fax 05 65 53 22 26, email terminis.balandre@wanadoo.fr. A friendly, family-run establishment, with charming rooms and exceedingly good cooking in the restaurant, *Le Balandre*. Very popular; necessary to reserve.

€€ *La Chartreuse*, Chemin de la Chartreuse, St-Georges, southwest of Cahors centre, ☎ 05 65 35 17 37. The restaurant here is good, and overlooks the river, but the building is unattractive and hotel rooms very standard.

☆☆ *L'Escargot*, 5 Blvd Gambetta, ☎ 05 65 35 07 66. Small and inexpensive hotel-restaurant that incorporates part of the old palace.

€€ *Au Fil des Douceurs*, 90 Quai de la Verrerie, ☎ 05 65 22 13 04. Floating restaurant on a barge on the Lot. Pretty views and fish dishes.

€€ *La Garenne*, St-Henri, RN 20 (direction Brive), ☎/fax 05 65 35 40 67. Just outside Cahors, this restaurant is enveloped in exotic flowers in summer. Delicate and tasty food, based on local fare.

☆☆ *Le Melchior*, Pl. de la Gare, ☎ 05 65 35 03 38, fax 05 65 23 92 75. Near the station. Good value, but basic accommodation and standard food.

€€ *Le Rendez-vous*, 49 Rue Clément Marot, ☎ 05 65 22 65 10. Good value, lovely setting and refined cooking.

€€ *La Taverne*, Pl. Escorbiac, Bvld Gambetta, ☎ 05 65 35 28 66. Next to the town hall. A long-established and slightly old-fashioned restaurant with good traditional cooking and service.

€ *Marie Colline*, 173 Rue Clémenceau, ☎ 05 65 35 59 96. A small and inexpensive vegetarian restaurant with good puds.

46090 LAMAGDALENE

€€–€€€ *Claude Marco*, ☎ 05 65 35 30 64, fax 05 65 30 31 40. To the east of Cahors, along the Lot valley in the centre of the village, this is classy cooking with a trans-European influence served in a delightfully converted vaulted winery surrounded by greenery. Also has rooms.

46090 MERCUÈS

Mas d'Azémar, M. Patrolin, ☎ 05 65 30 96 85. *Chambres d'hôte*. A charming 18C country house in the vineyards, with six high-quality rooms, terrace, garden and pool.

46090 ST-PIERRE-LAFEUILLE (8km north of Cahors on the N20)

☆☆☆/€€ *La Bergerie*, ☎ 05 65 36 82 82, fax 05 65 36 82 40, email hotel.bergerie@wanadoo.fr. Very pretty and airy restaurant and shady terrace, careful cooking and attention to vegetables.

History

The ancient city of Cahors, known by the 1C BC as *Divona* and from the 3C as *Civitas Caducorum*, was capital of the Cadurci and site of a shrine linked with the cult of water. Gallo-Roman *Divona* occupied most of the peninsula for some centuries but Frankish invasions in the 6C brought this culture to an end and barely a stone of the old city remains. Cahors was already Christianised by the 5C and the rebirth of the town is attributed to **St Didier** (bishop 630–55). In the 12C a new cathedral and cloister replaced an earlier building and when the troubles of the Cathar heresies had passed, the town expanded and in the 13C became a banking centre. In his *Divine Comedy* (1321) Dante condemned Cahors' bankers or moneylenders to hell and 'Caorsin' became synonymous with usurer.

In 1316 the town had an important boost when Jacques Duèze, from a

Caorsin family, was elected second pope at Avignon. As **John XXII** (1316–34) he bestowed many favours on his town including, in 1332, a university which enjoyed a good reputation until the 17C, and a vast programme of urban renewal was undertaken. In 1360 the Treaty of Brétigny placed Cahors, as part of Aquitaine, under English control but the town was the first to break with the Treaty after only 10 years. During the conflicts of the Reformation, extremely divisive in the Quercy, Cahors remained Catholic resulting in two attacks by the Protestants. By the 17C Cahors' zenith had passed and it was mainly a town of lawyers, magistrates and, with the foundation in 1627 of an Académie de Lettres, also of intellectuals. In 1674 the Collège des Jesuits was built, and by 1680 the town began to spread beyond the ramparts which were by then redundant and their demolition began. It was not until the 19C, when remaining ramparts were demolished and ditches filled, that the town really opened out with the construction of Allées Fénelon and Blvd Gambetta, the introduction of the railway, and erection of civic buildings such as Hôtel de Ville (1837–47), the theatre (1832–42) and the Palais de Justice (1857). Only in the 1950s did Cahors begin to spread beyond the natural confines of the peninsula.

The town is divided unequally in two by Boulevard Gambetta, a shaded avenue running north–south and lined by 19C institutions. There are four bridges crossing the Lot, Pont Louis-Philippe, Pont Cabessut, a bridge further north built in the 1990s, and the old Pont Valentré, which is pedestrianised.

Starting in the old town, this walk makes a figure of eight centering on the cathedral. The old town is crammed with interesting buildings and many courtyards which are worth investigating. Place Chapou in front of the cathedral was named after a hero of the Resistance, Jean-Jacques Chapou (1909–44), a bust of whom is outside the south door of the cathedral. The *place* was created at the beginning of the 14C, as was the former episcopal palace on the north side, but this was almost totally rebuilt and altered in the 17C and 19C and is now occupied by the *Préfecture* of the Lot.

Léon Gambetta

Born in Cahors in 1838, Gambetta was the son of an Italian grocer. He went into the legal profession before embarking on a career in politics. A vociferous defender of the French Republic, during the siege of Paris by Prussia in 1870 he fled in a hot air balloon and organised resistance from the provinces. He became President of the Chamber des Deputés in 1879 and of the Conseil de Cabinet in 1881. He died in an accident in 1882.

West of the *place* the sign *'Gambetta Jeune et Cie, bazar génois'* was discovered when the Crédit Agricole took over the premises. On Wednesday and Saturday mornings one of the best open-air **markets** in the Lot fills Place Chapou, a sensual experience of sight, taste and smell, bringing together regional and seasonal produce such as strawberries, Rocamadour goat's cheese and *cèpes*. There is a flower market on Sunday mornings and a market every day in the *halle* (1869). Two of the many heavenly delicacies found in Cahors are *pruneaux fourrés* (stuffed prunes) and *noix enrobés de chocolat* (chocolate-covered walnuts).

Cathédrale St-Etienne

A veritable textbook of architecture from the 12C to the 18C, the cathedral was begun *c* 1109–12 to replace an earlier building. Work went on almost continuously until the 13C. Major modifications were carried out at the end of the 13C and 14C, and in the cloister in the 15C. More changes were made in the 18C and restoration began in the 19C.

Exterior There are three entrances to the cathedral, two of them open. In chronological order, the first is the small south door (*c* 1130), a pretty trilobed opening under a double round-headed arch where the points of the lobes are divided and rolled. The brick arcades above are a later addition. The Romanesque **north portal**, one of the masterpieces of Romanesque sculpture in the Midi-Pyrénées, disappeared from view in the 18C. It was rediscovered in 1840 and for some time mistakenly thought to have been moved from the west. In fact, during the 12C the orientation of the streets had a different emphasis, the main north–south route through the medieval town corresponding to the present Rue Clément Marot. In the 1990s the approach to the door was lowered to return the porch to its original proportions. A deep, slightly pointed arch protects the sculpted tympanum, generally thought to date *c* 1140–50.

The main theme of the relief is the *Ascension of Christ*, but unusual emphasis is given to the patron saint of the cathedral, the protomartyr St Stephen. The work has stylistic links with that at Moissac, but although there is a serious attempt to introduce variety to the individual figures and a certain animation to the composition, the arrangement is more rigidly compartmentalised and less free-flowing. Christ, isolated in an oval mandorla, is flanked by two dancing or gesturing angels who emphasise his upright figure and form a link to the other parts of the composition. To either side of the Virgin below, her hand raised towards Christ, are the eleven Apostles present before Pentecost (when Judas was replaced by Matthias) framed in trilobed arches. It is not easy to make out the eleventh apostle who is squeezed into the left-hand corner beside the provocative back view of the tenth. Unlike Moissac, there is a striking uniformity in the size of the main protagonists.

The anecdotal scenes of St Stephen's martyrdom in the spandrels are in a different mood and tempo. On the left, Stephen professes his faith to the Sanhedrin, some of whom wear bonnets. On the opposite side, present at the stoning of Stephen is Saul, at whose feet the false witnesses place their mantles. One of Stephen's persecutors is sheltering in the foliage of the extrados. The hand of God linking the upper register to the lower is part of Stephen's vision of the Trinity. Banal scenes of hunting and aggression fill the outer arch but the cornice above the portal is peopled by a series of witty little figures whose torsos extend into the billet moulding and whose legs appear in the medallions on the underside. The rosette decoration was extended into the upper part of the portal in the early 20C.

A grand scheme of renovation and Gothicisation was undertaken from 1280 to 1324 at a propitious moment both politically and spiritually and at a time of great prosperity. It coincided with the urban reorganisation and the reaffirmation of the orthodox Church after the Cathar heresies. In a desire to harmonise the building, the cupolas were covered by a single roof and the east end was raised. The **west end** was added at the end of the 13C, its decorative features emphasised by a barely articulated surface. The elevation is divided horizontally by two moulded string courses supporting high-relief sculptures and, apart from

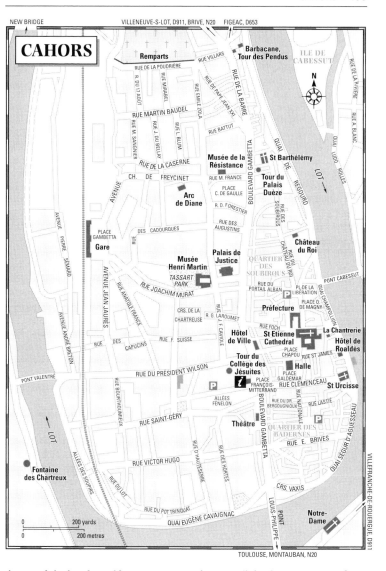

these and the hood mouldings carrying sculptures, all the decoration—made up of blind arcades organised into a square—is concentrated around the Rayonnant rose window, innovative for the period. The upper parts of the belfry-porch were completed in the 17C.

Interior The porch or narthex is linked to the nave by a descending flight of steps. Around the upper section are murals (1316–24) with twelve scenes from the *Creation* to the *Expulsion*, restored in 1988; the organ (1702–06), placed in the porch in 1722, was moved forward to its present position to expose the murals. The surprisingly vast (20m wide) aisleless **nave**, probably begun *c* 1120, was one of a group of 12C domed churches in the southwest. The cupolas at Cahors, on pendentives and carried by massive arches and six strong piers, are the most audacious, 16m in diameter and 32m above ground. In the western cupola is a rare monumental Gothic mural of the Prophets, in the corolla, and the *Martyrdom of St Stephen*, in the apex.

The walls of the east end were raised in 1280—just two Romanesque capitals survive on the north—bringing it to a height commensurate with the nave and making feasible the insertion of tall windows. The St Anthony chapel was added in 1491, and the more original **Notre-Dame** chapel (also called the Chapelle Profonde) was consecrated in 1484 by Bishop Antoine d'Alamand. The decoration introduces the Cadurcien rose motif, with *bâtons écotés* (resembling pruned branches) and suns with undulating rays. These motifs became very popular on secular buildings in and around Cahors until the beginning of the 16C. The polychrome relief panel of the *Immaculate Conception* was almost totally destroyed after the Wars of Religion but the vaults still have their original 16C painted decoration. The retable (1679–81) dedicated to the Virgin was designed by Gervais Drouet of Toulouse and made in Cahors.

Survivors from a revamp of the interior during the 18C are the main altar (1702–06) in red marble from Caunes in the Languedoc, and the red-marble north gallery (1734), which resulted in the disappearance of the north portal and the pulpit (1738). The walls were plastered in white to set off the marble. Fragments of 14C paintings discovered in the apse during restoration work in the 19C led to the repainting, or reinterpreting, of all the painted decoration. This was completed in 1874 and coincided with the installation of the new **stained glass**, commissioned in 1872 by Bishop Grimardias from Joseph Villiet of Bordeaux. The iconography is based on cycles of the lives of Christ, the Virgin and local saints as well as St Stephen. The glass is of very high quality, among the best in the Lot.

The Flamboyant **cloister**, reached by the door in the south of the choir, replaced the 12C cloister. Work began in the east gallery and continued through two building campaigns (1497–1509 and 1514–53), as is demonstrated by the complicated lierne vaults and variation in the doorways carrying the coats of arms of successive bishops, and discrepancies in the height and decoration of the arcades. A few mouth-watering samples of late Gothic sculpture survived the Reformation, notably the glorious *Virgin of the Annunciation* on the angle pillar in the northwest, with long wavy hair falling on her shoulders. The pendant boss above is decorated with Christ and angel musicians and there is more carving on the door opposite.

The **St-Gausbert** chapel off the east gallery was the former chapter house. It houses a small collection of religious artefacts and has late-15C/early-16C murals. Open June–Sept, Mon–Sat 10.00–12.30 and 15.00–18.00, closed Sun.

The southeast door leads to an enclosed courtyard with the engaging **archdeacon's house** on the south and west. Two Gothic houses around a stairwell were given a Renaissance face-lift (*c* 1520–40) with mullioned windows, rinceaux, busts in medallions, pilasters and candelabras.

Leave the cathedral precincts by a vaulted passageway leading into Rue de la Chantrerie. A complex building opposite dating from the 14C, called **La Chantrerie**, was used from the 17C by the cathedral chapter to store their wine presses or vats and was so called because of its proximity to the old residential quarters of the cathedral cantors. An exemplary restoration, the façade has two two-light windows with columns flanking a vast overhanging chimney breast above four Gothic arcades. It is a cultural centre for temporary exhibitions. Open daily 10.00–12.00 and 15.00–19.00; ☎ 05 65 36 58 28.

Turn right and right again into Rue St-James. In the courtyard at no. 27 is part of the old cathedral choir school, Le Grenier du Chapitre, a 12C–13C construction with 14C doors and windows. Maison Manhol at no. 18 is a characteristically symmetrical 17C façade with *mirandes* at the top. Just before the corner with Place Chapou is a 15C façade. Turn left at the end of Rue St-James and walk alongside the *halle*. On the left, no. 53 is worth a look.

The area south of the cathedral is known as the **Quartier des Badernes**, the lower quarter where the rich bourgeoisie built their houses. The grander houses are concentrated around the **Rue Nationale**, the old Rue Droite, which led to the Pont-Vieux. No. 116 has Cahors' most voluptuous Baroque entrance with volutes, an oculus and a heavy panelled door carved with luscious fruit and flowers. No. 128 is early 13C, with squat arcades and the outlines of a gallery with three three-light round-headed bays.

On **Rue du Dr.-Bergougnioux** is a 17C doorway; the tower on the right has damaged mullioned windows. The 16C hôtel at no. 40 is a charming if delapidated example of the arbitrary juxtaposition of successive decorative modes without regard to overall harmony: next to Cadurcien Gothic windows (1480–1500) with *bâtons écotés* is a triple bay of more Italianate design (*c* 1530) exploiting the idiom of the early Renaissance. The mid-16C back façade is altogether more disciplined and shows a better understanding of the use of the Classical orders.

Where Rue Nationale runs out of Place Rousseau are a variety of interesting details in doors and windows, and in the street elevation of the Résidence du Lavoir (no. 321) are restored 13C windows and gargoyles of a dog and a bear. If you continue to the end of the street, you arrive opposite the emplacement of the **Pont Vieux**.

Return to Rue Lastié which has a number of beautiful buildings. On the left, no. 35 has a fine 14C window with bar tracery and round the corner on Place St-Priest is a restored 17C Toulousain-style open staircase. On the right is a medieval house with the outline of a pointed gable above 14C windows. No. 117 is a particularly fine 14C jettied house with three Gothic windows above and a low 16C arch to the shop below.

There are restaurants behind several of the attractively restored 15C and 16C half-timbered façades in Place St-Urcisse. The early 13C church of **St-Urcisse** was altered in the 14C but has retained its late Romanesque door and Gothic capitals around the south door (in the garden of the neighbouring restaurant), whereas the west porch is contemporary with the west façade of the cathedral, *c* 1320, and similarly has a large rose window above the portal. On the central pillar is a standing *Virgin and Child* protected by a carved baldaquin. If you can get inside you will see storiated capitals of *Original Sin* and the *Life of Christ*.

Continue north along Rue St-Urcisse. The Romanesque house at no. 62 has a restored early 13C brick façade, and the adjacent one a timber gallery or *soleilho*. Back at Place St-James, turn right and on the right in Place Henri IV is the **Hôtel de Roaldès**, one of the best-known houses in Cahors, but heavily restored. It changed hands many times but in 1636 passed to a family of magistrates, the Roaldès. At its core is a 13C tower in brick and facing the river is a beautiful *soleilho*. The façade on Place Henri IV is richly decorated with the Quercynois idiom of the end-15C/16C, roses, *bâtons écotés* and flaming suns. Continue along the riverbank to Place Champollion where there is a colourful 19C monument to Clément Marot (1495–1544), poet, statesman and sympathiser with the Reformation, by Turcan, Denys Puech and Olivier Merson. It is worth making a detour across **Pont Cabessut** for views of the old town.

Leading out of Place Champollion is the shady Parc Olivier-de-Magny, built on the old cemetery of the church of la Daurade. The only reminders of the church and the 17C Benedictine convent attached to it are a piece of 12C nave and 15C chapels. The restored house with a tower in Rue de la Daurade dates from two campaigns of construction, *c* 1250 and late 13C–early 14C. On the corner with Rue C.-Marot stone arcades support a timber-framed upper floor with brick nogging, a 13C–14C building. Turn right into Rue C.-Marot. The 17C house at no. 12 is on the site of the birthplace of Olivier de Magny (1530–*c* 1561), lyric poet and secretary to Henri II. **Place de la Libération** has a variety of buildings—note no. 44 with three symmetrical bays (rebuilt in 1633) and a spiral staircase inside the doorway of 1642. The small streets northwest of the square are worth exploring: no. 3 Rue St-Pierre has a group of 16C/17C sculpted heads. No. 40 Rue du Portail Alban has a stairtower with a 16C door decorated with *bâtons écotés* and Neo-classical portal.

North of Place de la Libération is the **Quartier des Soubirous**, served by Rue du Château du Roi and its continuation Rue des Soubirous, leading slightly uphill. This was the upper-class *quartier*, where the principal urban palaces were built. Note the mixed styles at no. 58, and one of the few remaining exterior timber staircases in the courtyard of the 13C/14C mansion at no. 43. In Rue du Four Ste-Catherine, a narrow and picturesque impasse, is a late-15C battlemented stairtower with a splendid profusion of *bâtons écotés* around the door, one of the best examples of late-15C Cadurcien sculpture. At the back is the only remaining, and somewhat disfigured, building of the university, **Collège Pélegry**. The college, founded in 1368 by Raimond and Hugues de Pélegry for 13 poor students, survived until 1751. The **Château du Roi**, part of a modern block next door, was the temporary residence of the king's representative in the Quercy in the 15C. In the 14C it had belonged to relatives of Pope John XXII, the De Via family, who probably built it, and in the 19C it was turned into a prison.

The most remarkable medieval building in Cahors is the 14C **Palais Duèze**, attributed to Pierre Duèze, brother of John XXII. The vast urban palace was arranged around a square courtyard. What is left can best be seen from Rue Albe and Place Thiers. The tower (34m high) on Boulevard Gambetta was the tallest in the town, a certain mark of prestige, and favoured the style of the preceding century with two-light Romanesque windows. The palace was subsequently taken over by the Prince of Wales in 1364, but the main wing was demolished in 1405.

The church of **St-Barthélémy**, enclosed within the same walls as the Duèze palace, was partly rebuilt in the 14C. A rigorous building, orientated north–south, it has a monumental entrance at the base of the belfry similar in style to that of the cathedral and to St-Urcisse. The upper part of the imposing belfry-tower has blind arcades in brick. Inside is a plaque commemorating the baptism of the Pope in 1245, and some 15C murals. Return to the centre down Boulevard Gambetta or the parallel streets.

On foot or by car, follow the tree-lined Quai Cavaignac round the southern perimeter of the town to the **Pont Valentré**, the emblem of Cahors and the most famous medieval fortified bridge in France.

When the construction of the Pont Valentré began in 1308 the town already had two bridges, the Pont Vieux to the south and the Pont Neuf to the east, realised between 1254 and 1291. The slow progress of the Pont Valentré was traditionally blamed on satanic forces, but the problems were as much financial as technical despite a grant from the king in 1312. The bridge was in use by 1335 but not completed. As hostilities with the English increased in 1345 and the defences of the town were being improved and extended there was an added impetus to complete the bridge, although work continued until 1378. Restoration began in 1879 under the supervision of Paul Gout who, in tribute to the legendary diabolic intervention, sculpted a little devil clinging to the angle at the top of the central tower.

The bridge's six wide arches and the three high towers (40m above the river) are a magnificent sight. The arches at each end had a portcullis and there was a barbican on the eastern bank. The bridge is quite narrow and there are passing bays. Below the bridge a dam, which has existed since the 14C, links the lock (1808) to the 16C Périé mill downstream. Just upstream is the old pumping station (1853). Above that is the site of the ancient **Fontaine des Chartreux**, supposedly the source of the sacred fountain, Divona, around which the Gallo-Roman town developed. The fountain springs from a natural reservoir under the Causse de Limogne about 20km east. **Quai Valentré** has been pedestrianised and prettified with flowerbeds and is the departure point for a variety of river cruises on the Lot and the inevitable *petit train*.

The remaining **fortifications** are at the north of the town; they were extended in the mid-14C to protect the entire peninsula and to incorporate religious communities outside the *cité* walls. There were two fortified gates and

Pont Valentré

eleven square towers. Four survive—Tour St-Jean dominating the east bank, Tour Morlas and St-Mary in the centre, and Tour du Pal on the west. Of the gates, only the Porte St-Michel opening on to the cemetery is left and the barbican, which protected the eastern Porte de la Barre, still stands high above the river. A scrap of the antique baths (*thermae*), the **Arc de Diane**, stands in an incongruous setting on Avenue de Freycinet behind Place de Gaulle. North of the *place* in Espace Bessières is the **Musée de la Résistance**. Open daily 14.00–18.00; ☎ 05 65 22 14 25.

Moving south from the Arc de Diane, on Rue Emile Zola, is the municipal museum, **Musée Henri-Martin**, installed in the former bishops' palace in 1906. Open Mon, Wed–Sat 11.00–18.00, Sun 14.00–18.00, closed Tues; ☎ 05 65 30 15 13. It contains Gallic and Roman archaeology, pre-Romanesque, Romanesque and Gothic elements from lost buildings, and 14C, 15C and 16C religious art. The Henri Martin gallery has a collection of works given to the town by the Toulousain painter and his son, Martin Ferrères. Henri Martin (1860–1943) studied in Toulouse and Paris under J.P. Laurens and started out as a Salon painter. In 1889 he adopted neo-Impressionism and in the 1890s became known for his decorative work. The 18 paintings exhibited in Cahors are from this period when he was increasingly concerned with idealised scenes of contemporary life and idyllic pastorals. He was influenced by the work of the Italian Divisionist painter, Giovanni Segantini, and owes a debt to Pierre Puvis de Chavannes.

Behind the tourist information centre on Allées Fénelon is the pretty tower of the Jesuit college (1674) and around Place François Mitterand at the centre of town, with a large fountain and a statue of Léon Gambetta, are the public buildings of the 19C. The **Hôtel de Ville** on Boulevard Gambetta was rebuilt in 1840 but in the passageway which cuts the building (Rue Fondude) are the remains of the 17C door and 13C windows of the old residence of the seneschal.

There are two vantage points on the cliffs to the south for views over Cahors. **Mont St-Cyr** to the southeast is reached by crossing Pont Louis-Philippe; after the fountain, a footpath takes you on quite a climb past the ruins of the Hermitage of St-Cirq with a spectacular view of the whole town. It is possible to return by a path descending to the *faubourg* of Cabessut to the east of the town. By car, take the D6 from St-Georges in the direction of Lalbenque.

For a superb view of the Pont Valentré and the river, cross the bridge, and almost ahead is the route to the Croix de Magne on the Pech d'Angély (the Cross on a hill).

THE LOT VALLEY WEST OF CAHORS

Along the Lot's meandering route west of Cahors are vineyards which reach down to the water's edge and provide an opportunity to do a little wine tasting.

Leave Cahors on the D911 north to Mercuès, an ancient *bastide* entirely dominated by the **Château de Mercuès**, favourite residence of the bishops of Cahors since 1212 and now a luxury hotel and restaurant (see above). The owner, G. Vigouroux, is a wine dealer and the cellars can be visited.

Getting there and around

Bus

The Cahors to Libos bus serves the Lot Valley west of Cahors via Luzech and Puy l'Evêque.

Tourist information

46140 Luzech Maison des Consuls, ☎/fax 05 65 20 17 27

46220 Prayssac Pl. d'Istrie, ☎ 05 65 22 40 57

46700 Puy-l'Évêque Pl. de la Truffière, ☎/fax 05 65 21 37 63

Market days

Luzech Wednesday
Puy-l'Évêque Tuesday

River cruises

Navilot at Caïx, with cruises to Douelle, ☎ 05 65 20 18 19

Festivals and events

May *Le Bon Air est dans les caves*, wine festival in the cellars, Albas

Where to stay and eating out

46150 BOISSIÈRES

(D12 north of Mercuès, see above)

€ *Le Claux*, Le Bois de Claux, ☎ 05 65 21 54 10, fax 05 65 21 21 07, www.promenades-gourmandes.com. Spacious restaurant, friendly welcome, and carefully prepared seasonal fare. Rooms.

46140 DOUELLE

☆/€–€€ *L'Auberge du Vieux Douelle*, ☎ 05 65 20 02 03, fax 05 65 30 96 81, email aubergededouelle@aol.com. A popular and rustic restaurant (garden for summer eating) with a widely ranged menu in delightful river-side village. Hotel rooms are ordinary.

46140 LUZECH

€–€€ *Le Capitan*, Les Berge de Caïx, ☎ 05 65 20 18 19, www.ville-luzech.fr. On the banks of the Lot, Yves Safourcade's cooking combines the best of the Quercy and Mediterranean. There is also the possibility of a cruise on board the *Impernal*.

46700 MAUROUX (south of the Lot, southeast of Fumel D65/D5 from Touzac)

☆☆/€€ *Hôstellerie du Vert*, Le Vert, ☎ 05 65 36 51 36, fax 05 65 35 56 84, email hotellevert@aol.com. An old farmhouse comfortably converted (1 room in vaulted cellar) with a spacious terrace with views over countryside. Great care is taken in the preparation and presentation of the dishes in the restaurant.

46700 TOUZAC (south of Lot, between Grézels and Fumel)

☆☆☆/€€ *La Source Bleue*, Moulin de Leygues, ☎ 05 65 36 52 01, fax 05 65 24 65 59, www.sourcebleue.com. Medieval watermills converted into a place of total calm, with Zen gardens, pool, sauna. Restaurant *La Source Enchantée*, in an old barn with original beams, is small and intimate; evenings only; essential to book.

River transport on the Lot

The potential of transport on the Lot River was exploited as early as the 13C and became the main means for exporting overseas via the Garonne and the port of Bordeaux. The cargo most closely associated with the river was wine. By the 17C navigation had improved with numerous locks and by the 19C up to 300,000 tonnes of freight was carried each year. Then the railway took over, for 60–70 years the locks and weirs were neglected and traffic on the Lot ceased. At the end of the 20C, 70km was made navigable again and pleasure boats now offer a variety of excursions between Luzech, Cahors and St-Cirq Lapopie.

To the southwest, across the Lot on the D8, is **Douelle**, a once-important river port now used only by pleasure boats. The 15C church, heavily restored in the 19C, has a model of a boat suspended from the nave vaults and there is a modern fresco on the quay wall. On the right bank the vineyards start in earnest. At **Caillac** on the D10, the church of St-Pierre and St-Paul was built in the 11C/12C but the only Romanesque elements to survive are on the south entrance. The church was rebuilt from the beginning of the 16C and has a delicately sculpted Renaissance doorway with *Adam and Eve* on the lower right.

From the **Col de Crayssac**, reached by the D23, there is a great view down to the loop in the river encompassing the vineyards of **Parnac**, known as the capital of Cahors wine since the cooperative of the Côtes d'Olt was installed there. **Caïx**, a boating centre on the Lot, has an immaculately tended domaine belonging to the Danish royal family, a small part-12C church and a sculpted cross (1772).

Guarding a particularly tight meander in the Lot are the small town and great 12C keep of **Luzech**. After the Albigensian Crusades, both the bishops and barons of Cardaillac had a castle here, the episcopal fort on the higher ground and the seigneurial one lower down. Richard the Lionheart was overlord in the 12C. The medieval town clustered around the castle is still enclosed in part of its protective walls. In the Grande Rue, the restored 13C Maison des Consuls houses the tourist office and the small Musée Armand Viré of local archaeology (closed Sun). The village is very proud of the **Ichnospace**, which claims to be the first European museum of dinosaur footsteps and other fossilized remains (contact the tourist office for opening times). Place du Canal, now the main street, was originally a canal or moat dividing the medieval town from the *barri* (suburb), which itself has existed since the 13C. An important market is held here on Wednesdays.

Two short expeditions can be made from Luzech. The first, on foot, takes a path from the château up to the plateau above the isthmus, called the **Impernal**, a prehistoric and Gallo-Roman site which is the source of most of the exhibits in the museum. The other follows the Lot (possible by car) to the opposite extremity of the peninsula where the Flamboyant chapel, **Notre-Dame-de-l'Ile**, is submerged in vineyards. Built by Bishop Antoine de Luzech *c* 1505, in a style reminiscent of the cloisters at Cahors, it was a pilgrimage chapel for sailors and still hosts a pilgrimage in September.

Albas on the south of the Lot on the D8 is spectacularly perched on top of a cliff. This was a wine port and another favourite watering hole of the bishops of Cahors, especially in the 16C. The episcopal residence was restored by Antoine d'Alamand *c* 1485 and is decorated with Cadurcien roses. There is just one medieval gateway standing.

Across the Lot the *bastide* of **Castelfranc** is surrounded by hills: the 14C church with a splendid belfry-tower helped defend the town against the English in 1355. North on the D45, **La Masse** is a group of houses forming a square around a Romanesque church with a 15C mural. Slightly further on is the priory of Les Junies, founded for women between 1343 and 1355. The austere church of the Madeleine on the banks of the River Masse has some 14C stained glass with the figures of the founder, Gaucelme de Jean, his nephews and the family coat of arms.

Anglars-Juillac, standing in the middle of vineyards, has a restored Romanesque church (remodelled in the 16C) with a belfry-gable, and around the

Cahors wine

The Romans were cultivating wines here by the 3C and Pope John XXII took Quercynois wine-growers to Avignon where they produced Châteauneuf du Pape. The Bordelais resented the competition and did what they could to block exports but the strong dark wine of Cahors was carried to Northern Europe and became the communion wine in Russia. The final death-knell to the wine trade and river transport was phylloxera, which destroyed the vineyards in the 1880s. In 1961 new vinestock of traditional types, Auxerrois and Merlot, was planted in the valley and production and quality was gradually built up until 45 communes qualified for the *AOC* in 1971. Like many of the smaller wine-growing areas, Cahors is putting an emphasis on improving quality and it is possible to buy excellent wine at a reasonable price. Many of the vineyards offer a *dégustation*. *Le Livret du Vin de Cahors*, published by the Maison du Vin de Cahors, can be obtained from the tourist office of by post from the Maison du Vin (a professional organisation), 430 Av. Jean-Jaurès, BP 61, 46002 Cahors.

upper part of the apse is a motif special to the valley, consisting of pierced metopes. **Bélaye**, a picturesque *castrum* around a castle on a narrow spur above the river, was acquired by the bishops of Cahors *c* 1236. It has a 15C church and castle, parts of the old city walls, and stunning views towards Prayssac.

Prayssac, a lively little place on the right bank, is one of the starting points for the Dolmen Circuit—others are Castelfranc or Les Junies—a walk indicated by arrows.

On the left bank is the church of St-Pierre-ès-Liens at **Pescadoires**, a priory founded in 1037 and attached to Moissac. It has lost its apse, but is still interesting for its squat square belfry supported by a cupola and for the exterior decoration. Château Lacoste at **Grézels** was built in the 13C, rebuilt in the 16C, and restored in 1960; it is still an impressive structure built around a quadrangle with two square and two round towers. In the cellars is the Musée du Vin de Cahors. Open July–Aug, daily 15.00–18.00, or by appointment, ☎ 05 65 21 34 18. There is also a church with fine woodwork.

Puy-l'Évêque is a small, ancient town built on an escarpment on the right bank of the Lot, descending in terraces to the river where there used to be a major port. A stronghold of the bishops, it was occupied by the English during the Hundred Years War: they reinforced the defences so well that the town withstood attack during the Religious Wars. At the highest point the *donjon carré* (square keep, *c* 1230) is the only part of the episcopal fort still standing and the Esplanade de la Truffière at its base is a good vantage point. One level down, enclosed in a second *enceinte*, the Château de Bovila has a late-Gothic door with *bâtons écotés*. The 14C fortified church of St-Sauveur, on the D911, was remodelled in the late 15C by Antoine d'Alamand who added the superb porch belfry with a Flamboyant portal and above it a *Crucifixion* with the Virgin and St John.

Worth a detour north along the D28 is the Romanesque church at **Martignac**, both for the building itself and for the 15C/16C murals of *Christ in Majesty*, the *Entombment*, *Deadly Sins*, the *Virtues* symbolised by angels, and the *Saved received into Paradise by St Michael*.

One of the major Romanesque churches in the Quercy is at **Duravel** on the

D119. The church has kept many of its Romanesque elements, despite radical restoration in the 19C, and has a 15C west entrance and 14C square belfry. The lateral door is 12C and around the east end are decorated corbels and a frieze of palmettes; the pierced metope motif appears here as at Anglars-Juillac. The church was part of an important priory, founded in 1055 and affiliated to Moissac, which acquired the relics of three oriental hermits, Agathon, Poémon and Hilarion, guaranteed to attract pilgrims. Their relics are in a red sandstone sarcophagus behind the altar. There are storiated capitals with the *Martyrdom of St Peter*, reminders of Hell and the Archangel Michael, and in the nave are a Gothic holy-water stoup and a Gallo-Roman relief decorated with vines. The small, square Merovingian crypt, built to contain the relics, has four pillars and ten engaged columns supporting the groin vaults. Two of the decorated capitals are exceptional, one with a peacock, its tail spread, standing above a serpent and the other with an inscription recording the consecration of the sanctuary.

Montcabrier is a 13C *bastide* with the Gothic church of St-Louis (King Louis IX). It has a 14C Rayonnant rose window in the west, a fine doorway and a stunning belfry-gable with six arcades. Inside is a statue of a bearded St Louis. Nearby is the Château de Bonaguil (see p 275).

To the northeast on the D660 **Goujounac** is an immaculate village in golden stone with flowers and shrubs; its church has a small Romanesque tympanum with a Christ in Majesty in the south wall.

THE LOT VALLEY EAST OF CAHORS

The character of the Lot Valley east of Cahors, along the D653, is very different from downstream. Here there are very few vines, and in places this is a wide, fertile valley, lined with walnut trees and poplars, where tobacco, sunflowers and strawberries are cultivated; in other parts it is confined within high cliffs. There are a number of picturesque villages, numerous castles, and always beautiful scenery.

Getting there and around
Train

Quercyrail, July, Aug, ☎ 05 65 64 74 78. Three trips from Capdenac-Gare train station:
Tues, train + St-Pierre Toirac + boat (to St-Cirq-Lapopie)
Wed, train + St-Pierre Toirac + boat (to Cajarc)
Fri, train + boat (to Cajarc)
May–Oct, Sunday, train + boat + visit (see also Cahors)

Tourist information
46160 Cajarc Pl. du Foirail, ☎ 05 65 40 72 89, fax 05 65 40 05
46100 Capdenac-le-Haut Pl. Lucter,

☎/fax 05 65 50 01 45,
http://wanadoo.fr/capdenac-lot
46330 St-Circ-Lapopie Pl. du Sombral, ☎/fax 05 65 31 29 06, email saint-cirq.lapopie@wanadoo.fr
Market days
Cajarc Saturday afternoon
St-Cirq-Lapopie July, Aug Wednesday morning
River cruises
July–15 Oct, from Cajarc, *Le Schmilblic Bateau-promenade*, ☎ 06 03 02 08 04. Also *Bateaux Safaraid* in conjunction with *Quercyrail* (see above)

Where to stay and eating out
46160 CAJARC
☆☆/€–€€ *La Ségalière*, Rte de Cadrieu,

☎ 05 65 40 65 35, fax 05 65 40 74 92, www.pro-wanadoo.fr/ hotelsegaliere/contacts.html. The rooms have been renovated in this small hotel, and the cooking is good and tasty. **46330 ST-CIRQ-LAPOPIE** ☆☆☆ *Hotel la Pélissaria*, ☎ 05 65 31 25, 14, fax 05 65 30 25 52, email

lapelissariahotel@minitel.net. A 13C listed building, tastefully decorated, and a good, small restaurant (need to book). ☆☆ *Auberge du Sombral*, ☎ 05 65 31 26 08, fax 05 65 30 26 37. Perfectly restored house at the heart of this most picturesque of villages high above the Lot. No restaurant.

Laroque-des-Arcs was founded in the 12C to protect the Roman aqueduct, built on three levels, which carried water about 30km to Cahors. In 1370, during the Hundred Years War, the aqueduct and castle were destroyed to prevent them falling into the hands of the English and only small sections have survived. The most eye-catching of the village's four churches is the tiny chapel of St-Roch (1842). **Vers** is named after the river that cascades through the village the source of which, at St-Martin-de-Vers, provided the water for Cahors. On the banks of the Lot is the little 12C church of Notre-Dame-de-Velles.

Bouziès is divided by the river into two communities. The cliffs of the right bank have caves, the largest used as a castle by the English in the Middle Ages, and on the left is the port of **Bouziès-Haut**, from where you can catch river cruises, ☎ 05 65 30 22 84 (see also *Bateaux Safaraid*, p 204; for boat hire. *Lot Navigation*, ☎ 05 65 24 32 20). A spectacular walk to St-Cirq-Lapopie along the old towpath of Ganil (built in 1877) is carved out of the overhanging cliff in places.

The curious name **St-Cirq-Lapopie** comes from the patronymic Pompeius, which became La Popia. It is a memorably stunning sight stretched out on a ridge overlooking the Lot. This is the best-known attraction on the Lot and has developed into a well-manicured village with lots of artists, boutiques, cafés and tourists. Dominating the scene is the 16C church but it has little of interest. At the highest point, next to the church, are the remains of a feudal castle. At the extreme east is the Porte de la Pélissaria leading to the river where there were once tanneries. The attractions of St-Cirq did not go unnoticed even by the most sceptical of men, André Breton, leader of the Surrealist Movement, who purchased an old *auberge* (La Maison Breton) here in the 1950s and was joined by Foujita and Man Ray. There are also exhibitions of contemporary art at the Musée Rignault. Open mid-April–June, Sept–mid-Oct, daily except Tues 10.00–12.30 and 14.30–18.00, July, Aug open until 19.00, closed Tues; ☎ 05 65 31 23 22. The Musée de la Mémoire du Village features a wood turner's workshop. Open daily, March–May, Oct–mid-Nov 10.00–13.00 and 14.00–18.00, May–Sept open until 19.00; ☎ 05 65 31 21 51. Excursions between Cahors and St-Cirq by train and boat operate in July and August: *Quercyrail*, ☎ 05 65 35 98 88.

The **Château de Cénevières** on the D8 stands high on a cliff. Open 15 April–30 Sept, daily 10.00–12.00 and 14.00–18.00; Oct, daily 14.00–17.00; ☎ 05 65 31 27 33. Part of this charming, privately owned building is 13C, but in the 16C the fortress was transformed into a Renaissance residence. There are painted decorations on the walls of the so-called Alchemist's Room.

Across the river at **Cajarc** there is an exhibition centre for contemporary art, the Maison des Arts Georges Pompidou. Open summer daily except Sun morning 10.00–12.00 and 15.00–19.00; spring and autumn 10.00–12.00 and 14.00–18.00, closed Sun morning and Mon; check in advance, ☎ 05 65 40 63

97. Pompidou, President of France 1969–74, frequently visited the Quercy. Cajarc was also the birthplace of the writer Françoise Sagan (b. 1935). It is a pleasant old town enclosed within a circular boulevard with many interesting buildings, such as the 13C Maison de l'Hébrardie and the remains of a fortified mill. For details of river cruises see p 204.

On the right bank on the D622, **Larroque-Toirac** has an impressive château built into the rock. Guided tours, 9 July–15 Sept, daily 10.00–12.00 and 14.00–18.00; ☎ 06 12 37 48 39. **St-Pierre-Toirac** is a tumble-down place with old houses with *bolets* (terraces). At the centre is an austere 12C church with carved corbels, raised and fortified in the 14C, which contains numerous decorated capitals, many of them storiated. Merovingian sarcophagi are laid out to the south of the church. The D662 continues to Figeac via the historic and picturesque village of Faycelles.

Staying close to the Lot, which here forms the border with the *département* of the Aveyron, a pretty route ends at Capdenac Gare, a 19C conurbation whose *raison d'être* was the arrival of the railway (1856). Quickly leave Capdenac Gare for **Capdenac-le-Haut**, a beautiful village in a key defensive position high on the north bank above a kink in the river. It is optimistically promoted as the site of ancient Uxellodunum, the Celtic oppidum taken by Caesar in 51 BC and the symbol of the resistance of the Gauls (see p 43). Often besieged, it has ramparts, two Gothic gateways with a barbican, and a 14C square keep. There is a small museum, open daily 15 June–15 Sept 10.00–12.30 and 14.30–19.30, rest of year Tues–Sat 14.30–18.30; ☎ 05 65 50 01 45.

The N140 goes through Bouillac and La Roque-Bouillac. Branch off on to the D627 before the bridge, avoiding Decazeville, and wiggle your way to **St-Parthem**, a stunning village, as is **La Vinzelle** standing sentinel over the Lot valley. This is the region in which to taste *estofinado*, made from stockfish.

Near Pont de Coursavy on the D901, where the Dourdou runs into the Lot, is **Grand-Vabre**, the reputed resting place of Dadon, founder of Conques (p 218), marked by the chapel Notre-Dame-de-la-Nativité, restored in 1978. The 15C parish church has a relief with a *Pietà* with St Faith and St Catherine.

From here the Lot Valley is a pleasant drive on the D141 and D107 through a sparsely inhabited countryside, wooded with oaks, silver birch and box, to **Entraygues** (24km). The terraced slopes either side of the valley before Entraygues are reminders of the many abandoned vineyards of the Pays d'Olt, but a few have been revived between Le Fel and Espalion.

9 Figeac, Assier and the Célé Valley

Figeac

Figeac, on the north bank of the small river Célé, is the second largest town in the Lot after Cahors. It has an almost intact medieval centre with a variety of beautiful houses from the 12C onwards, combining stone, brick and timber. Although its church is less magnificent Figeac can boast a superb little museum dedicated to the Egyptologist, Champollion. It is a perfect jumping off point for exploring the Célé and the Lot valleys, as well as the Rouergue. The Célé, tributary of the Lot, rises in the Cantal and flows westwards through the Causse de Gramat, eventually to meet the Lot just south of Cabrerets. At the level of Figeac the two rivers are just under 4km apart.

 Getting there and around

Car

Shuttle bus from parking on the Forail to Pl. Champillon, Tues–Sat 08.30–12.30 every 5 mins.

Train

Paris Austerlitz to Figeac via Brive, 2 direct trains a day (one daytime, one night).
Brive to Toulouse via Figeac, Capdenac.
Aurillac to Capdenac via Figeac. Figeac railway station, ☎ 05 65 64 94 55.

Bus

For details of the limited bus services in this area enquire at the local tourist offices.

Tourist information

Hôtel de la Monnaie, Pl. Vival, 46100, ☎ 05 65 34 06 25, fax 05 65 50 04 58, www.quercy.net/quercy/figeac

Market day

Saturday

Festivals and events

March *Le Chainon Manquant*, six days of musical activities indoors and in the streets
May *Avis d'pas Sages*, festival of new music
August *L'Eté musical dans la Vallée du Lot*

 Where to stay and eating out

46100 FIGEAC

✩✩✩✩ *Château du Viguier du Roy*, 48–50 Rue Emile-Zola, ☎ 05 65 50 05 05, fax 05 65 50 06 06, www.chateau-viguier-figeac.com. In exquisitely restored medieval buildings in the town centre, with courtyard garden and pool.
€€ *La Dinée du Viguier*, 4 Rue Boutaric, ☎ 05 65 50 08 08, fax 05 65 50 09 09. Independent from the *Château du Viguier* (see above), in an adjoining building. Quality cooking in an attractive setting.
€–€€ *La Cuisine du Marché*, 15 Rue Clermont, ☎ 05 65 50 18 55. Attractive and spacious restaurant in an old house in the town centre. Carefully considered offerings include fish dishes as well as more traditional local fare. Attentive service.
✩✩/€–€€ *Hostellerie de l'Europe*, 51A, Allées Victor Hugo (across the Célé), ☎ 05 65 34 10 16, fax 05 65 50 04 57. Old coaching inn decorated in 1930s' manner. Eat well at the charming *Table de Marinette*, with an exotic interior garden.
€ *Pizzeria del Portel*, 9 Rue Orthabadial, ☎ 05 65 34 53 60. Popular with locals at lunch time for reasonably priced pizzas and huge

salads, as well as *plat du jour*.

€ *La Puce à l'Oreille*, 5–7 Rue St-Thomas, ☎/fax 05 65 34 33 08. Pretty restaurant with small courtyard in the old part of town. Traditional cooking with special attention to desserts.

46100 FAYCELLES

€ *La Forge*, Le Bourg, ☎ 05 65 34 65 09, fax 05 65 34 67 46, www.promenades-gourmandes.com.

Combination of Quercynois and Provençal recipes, and themed menus which change monthly. View over the Lot Valley from the terrace.

46100 BOUSSAC

Domaine des Villedieu, M. et Mme. M. Villedieu, ☎ 05 65 40 06 63, www.villedieu.com. *Chambres d'hôte* in the Célé Valley, near Figeac, a charming, rural location. Four ensuite rooms.

History

The town developed on the banks of the Célé River around an abbey founded in the 9C and enriched by pilgrims on their way to Rocamadour and Santiago da Compostela. On the major north–south route from Marseilles to Champagne with its medieval fairs, it grew into a huge mercantile centre with a wealthy merchant class who had trade links from the Levant to Northern Europe. The merchants grew powerful enough to challenge the abbots and town councillors were elected from among them. Their prosperity ensured a brilliant period in Figeac's architectural history from the late 12C to the mid-14C. So prestigious was the town that at the beginning of the 14C it was placed under the direct guardianship of the king through his representative, the *Viguier*. With the onset of the Hundred Years War and the plague, the town suffered a downturn from the mid-14C and did not really recover until the end of the 15C. In the following century the religious fervour of the Reformation took its toll on the the town. The Calvinists (Protestants) made the hill or Puy, their citadel and the church of Notre-Dame-du-Puy their Temple. The abbey church of St-Sauveur was wrecked by the reformers who set fire to it. Once the town was designated a Protestant place of safety in 1598 (under the terms of the Edict of Nantes), it flourished again for a short period but this came to an end with the fall of Montauban (see p 291) to the troops of Louis XIII. The Catholics took retaliatory action on Notre-Dame-du-Puy in 1622, and the citadel was dismantled in 1623. By the 17C–18C there was no more international commerce and the Figeacois turned to other trades. The town's buildings were adapted but its medieval layout barely altered. During the 19C and 20C it was not totally untouched by zealous restorers—Place Vival was opened out, the canal filled in—but since the 1980s Figeac has looked to its past with enthusiasm.

Figeac is worth many hours' exploration. There are, for example, many fine doorways in the town, from the 12C to the 20C, and the oldest door is 16C. Start out from Place Vival in the southwest, opened up in 1920. On the south side is the 13C **Hôtel de la Monnaie** containing the tourist office and the Musée du Vieux Figeac, a small museum of life in the Quercy with a collection of stone carvings including a monumental Renaissance doorway, prehistoric objects, furniture, and the 13C matrix of the town seal. It is a pretty building but disappointingly only the back elevation is authentic, and it had nothing to do with minting money; the front was reconstructed in the 1900s with windows from elsewhere. It has large arcades on the ground floor and more ornate openings on the first with two-light windows (12C) and a variety of tracery. Under the eaves is a *soleilho*.

From Rue Ortabadial, behind the Hôtel de la Monnaie, turn right on Rue Balène where the corner block is given over to the **Château de Balène**, a large urban palace built in the 14C; it was partly dismantled in 1900 but the windows with late Gothic tracery and mouldings are original. Follow it round (on the corner is a 14C arched doorway and a deep hood moulding) to arrive at **Rue Gambetta**, the main shopping street running north–south and continuing over the Célé, with many interesting façades. Characteristic of the medieval houses in Figeac are the large arches at street level, intended for storage and workshops: during the medieval period their basic shape did not change but the profiles of the arcade mouldings became more pronounced as time went on. The older, modest houses have tall, narrow doorways at the side with a staircase immediately behind, necessitating an outward-opening door. Look out for no. 13, Hôtel de Livernon, built in 1367 with the first rectangular windows (one is still in place on the tower), and also the 16C timber and brick façades at nos 28 and 27. The Crédit Lyonnais building, reconstructed in 1900, has series of Romanesque three-light windows. Nos 34–43 are a beautiful 14C *hôtel particulier* with an inner courtyard and a diversity of windows on the street façade.

Off Place aux Herbes is **Rue de Clermont** with more of the same, notably the 14C/16C Hôtel Dumont de Sournac with a corbelled chimney-breast. Turn right here to the church of **St-Sauveur**. The abbey of Figeac, rival to that at Conques (p 218), was affiliated to Cluny in 1047 and its entry into the Cluniac domain precipitated the building of a new church towards the end of the 11C. The partly completed building was consecrated in 1093 and work continued through the 12C to 14C. From 1623, after the Protestants were chased out of the town, repair and consolidation work were necessary, but during the 18C and 19C the cloisters and monastic buildings were lost. Saddest of all was the demolition of the abundantly carved west end, known as La Grotte, and its replacement by the present unspectacular west entrance in 1823. The only relics of La Grotte are the upturned capitals used as bases for holy-water stoups. The rectangular tower is 17C. There are traces of the Romanesque building on the north, juxtaposed with Gothic extensions and 17C alterations. To the south the façade is more regular and the chapter house was built in the 13C. The east end is blocked off, but there is a view of it from Rue du Monastère.

Steps lead down from the narthex into the nave, which took its present form in the 17C but has retained the general layout of a Benedictine pilgrimage church, with aisles and ambulatory. The 12C engaged columns on square piers support the 17C groin vaults of the seven-bay nave. The south elevation has a blind triforium and 14C clerestory whereas the north was rebuilt in the 17C, when the vaults were replaced, and has no triforium. The crossing vaults date from 1920 and were built after the 18C dome collapsed in 1917, but the transepts have their original 13C decorated rib vaults, some of the oldest in France, a deep cornice supported by a carved corbel table and rose windows. The mock-Gothic choir and most of the ambulatory were built in the late 17C and early 18C although the radiating chapels are late 12C, as are the carved capitals including a *Christ in Majesty* and *Martyrdom of St Stephen*. The best of the stained glass (all 19C) is in the clerestory. In the last bay of the south aisle is a wooden relief of the *Dream of St Martin*.

Opening on the south side is the 13C former **chapter house** (light switch on left by curtains) with 17C carved and painted wooden décor. The violently coloured glass dates from 1883. To the south, where the cloister once stood, is Place de la Raison, where chestnut and linden trees shade the *pétanque* arena.

Across Place Michelet in Rue Roquefort is an overhanging angle tower with an elegant base and crenellated *soleilho*, identifying the 16C town house of Galiot de Genouillac, builder of the Château d'Assier (p 213). Walk through Rue Plancat, Rue du Canal and Place Sully to **Rue Emile Zola** (formerly Rue Droite or Rue Drecha), the oldest street in Figeac, with a number of wonderful medieval houses, restored and unrestored. The whole street is worth exploring. The 14C **Château du Viguier du Roi** (see hotels) at nos 48–50 comprises a group of houses dating from the 12C, 14C and 18C around a series of courtyards and was the *Viguier's* residence from 1302 to the Revolution. The oldest part has characteristic arcades and on the *piano nobile* a magnificent Romanesque window of two-light bays divided by carved piers and subdivided by columns. Although partly reconstructed and restored, there is some original carved detail. Note also the sculpted head of a man in the 14C façade.

At the heart of the old town, the triangular **Place Champollion**, formerly the Place Haute, is surrounded by picturesque buildings. The Romanesque (12C) house at no. 4, the **Maison du Griffon**, is considered to be the oldest in Figeac. It has obscured arcades at ground level and three-light windows with sculpted elements on the first floor. South of the *place* is a restored 14C house with a series of superb traceried windows on a deep moulded course and a battlemented *soleilho*.

The little Rue des Frères Champollion, northwest of the *place*, leads to the **Musée Champollion**, a small museum of Egyptology installed in the 14C and 16C house where Jean-François Champollion was born. Open March–Oct, Tues–Sun 10.00–12.00 and 14.30–18.30; July, Aug same hours daily, Nov–Feb, Tues–Sun 14.00–18.00; closed 1 Jan, 1 May, 25 Dec; ☎ 05 65 50 31 08.

Jean-François Champollion

Champollion (1790–1832) began studying Egyptian hieroglyphics when he was at the Lycée in Grenoble. His major work was to decipher the inscriptions on the Rosetta Stone, discovered during Napoleonic expeditions in Egypt in 1799 but held in England after its capture in 1801, when the British took Alexandria. In a letter dated 27 September 1822 Champollion announced that he had solved the mystery of hieroglyphics by comparing the picture images with known scripts. The stone bears three versions—in Egyptian hieroglyphics, in Greek and in demotic script—of the same decree, drawn up by Egyptian priests at Memphis on 27 March 196 BC. Champollion did not visit Egypt itself until 1828 when he was already Curator of the Egyptology Department at the Louvre. He returned to Figeac in 1816–17, and visited for the last time in 1831.

The museum has three rooms devoted to Champollion, arranged thematically. The first contains a documented account of his life and career. The Salle des Ecritures Egyptiennes contains a cast of the Rosetta Stone given by the British Museum in the 1950s. This room is devoted to Champollion's research. The gallery contains few, but good, pieces including examples of scripts on different types of materials such as papyrus parchment, and on different supports—stelae, fragments of archiecture—and also has instruments used by scribes. The third room is concerned with the illustrations of the afterlife—pantheons, divinities, mummies and sarcophagi. There are frequent temporary exhibitions on the top floor.

The Egyptian experience does not end with the museum. The courtyard at the end of the impasse, **La Place des Ecritures**, opened in 1990 to mark the bicentenary of the birth of Champollion. It is enclosed by beautiful medieval façades and on the ground is a giant version of the Rosetta Stone, the creation of the American artist, Joseph Kosuth. The text, enlarged nearly 100 times, is engraved on black Zimbabwe granite arranged on several levels to follow the contours of the site and to symbolise the passage from one language to another. The courtyard is used for summer concerts. A French version of the hieroglyphics is engraved on the glass door of a vaulted cellar but, because of the transparent surface, is as difficult to decipher as the original.

There is an exit from the courtyard to Rue Séguier. Alternatively go up the steps through the terraced gardens, from which there is a wonderful birds-eye view of roofs. If it is open, you can leave through the 17C **Hôtel de Colomb** to see the exhibition *Portrait d'une ville, Figeac*. Open 10 July–19 Sept, daily 10.00–12.30 and 15.00–19.00; April–9 July, 20 Sept–31 Oct, Tues–Sun 14.00–18.00, closed Mon; ☎ 05 65 50 05 40.

From Rue Emile Zola, climb either Rue Boutaric or Rue Delzhens to le Puy (Mont Viguier), a commanding position over the red-tiled rooftops and beyond, and the church of **Notre-Dame-du-Puy** where restoration work is due for completion in January 2003. It stands on the site of an ancient cemetery and the first Christian sanctuary, dedicated to Notre-Dame-la-Fleurie. In 1372 the Romanesque church was destroyed by *routiers* (mercenaries) but was rebuilt and enlarged. Most of the exterior decoration, now damaged, is concentrated around the projecting west front (*c* 1345). Between the Protestants, who turned it into their temple in 1576 and the area into a citadel, and the Catholics, who took their revenge on the building when the Protestants left in 1622, there was not a great deal left. It was next repaired between 1666 and 1693, keeping as close to the original as possible. Nevertheless, the three naves were transformed into a single wide nave, only the first bay retaining the earlier nave and four aisle layout. In the east end four Romanesque storiated capitals have survived. The monumental retable, carved in walnut, was made locally in 1696, and has a profusion of columns, vines, putti, reliefs and statues and a painting of the *Assumption*. There is an 18C wooden sculpture of St James and an early 19C altar with a clothed **Virgin and Child** dedicated to Notre-Dame-la-Fleurie who, according to a legend, caused roses to open in the snow one Christmas Day.

Leave le Puy by Rue St-Jacques, a cobbled, twisting alleyway, turn left on Rue de Colomb, and right on to Rue Malleville, spanned by a vaulted passageway belonging to the 15C Hôtel de Laporte. Follow Rue St-Thomas and steps down to Rue de Crussol where the 16C/17C **Hôtel du Crussol** stands on the right, now a restaurant with an elegant galleried courtyard, external staircase and colonnaded *soleilho*. In Rue d'Aujou turn left and at the junction with Rue Séguier and Place Carnot is a notable house, the **Maison Cisteron**, which also has a colonnaded *soleilho*. The lower floor with arcades is medieval, the angle turrets are 16C, and the wrought-iron 18C. The covered market of 1900 in **Place Carnot** replaced the 13C *halle* knocked down in 1888. Around the square are *soleilhos* built from the 16C to the 19C in a variety of forms.

Rue Gambetta leads out of the southeast corner of Place Carnot, and on the narrow north façade of the building at the corner with Rue de la République is a Romanesque relief sculpture of a green man. At no. 30 Rue Caviale is the **Hôtel de Marroncles**, a fine and rare example in Figeac of an early 16C house with mullioned and transomed windows, and further along on the left is the 18C Hôtel de Salgues, the *sous-préfecture*, with an angled entrance and courtyard. From Place Barthal turn left to return to Place Vival.

The Causse de Gramat

Getting there and around
Train

Brive to Toulouse via Rocamadour-Padirac, Gramat, Flaujac, Assier, Figeac, Capdenac-Gare.

Tourist information

46320 Assier ☎ 05 65 40 50 60, fax 05 65 40 41 99, www.quercy.net/quercy/assier
46500 Gramat Pl. de la République, ☎ 05 65 38 73 60, fax 05 65 33 46 38, www.quercy.net/quercy/gramat
Market days

Gramat Tuesday, Friday

Festivals and events

August *Le Jardin dans tous ses états*, jazz in the street, Assier

Where to stay and eating out
46100 CARDAILLAC
€ *Chez Marcel*, Rue du 11 Mai 1944, ☎ 05 65 40 11 16, fax 05 65 40 49 08. Delicious regional dishes served in the village restaurant. Friendly atmosphere and small, good-value bedrooms. Picturesque village.
46210 GORSES (southeast of St-Céré/northeast of Lacapelle-Marival)
€ *Hotel-Restaurant Colombié*, Le Bourg, ☎ 05 65 40 28 02, fax 05 65 40 38 04, www.hotel-colombie.com. Friendly family-run *auberge*; inexpensive but comfortable rooms, pool, and excellent value menu.
46500 GRAMAT
☆☆/€–€€ *Le Relais des Gourmands*, 2 Av de la Gare, ☎ 05 65 38 83 92, fax 05 65 38 70 99, www.relais-des-gourmands.com. Totally refurbished hotel with pool and shady terrace. The cooking will be appreciated by lovers of good food.
€€ *Le Lion d'Or*, Pl. de la République, ☎ 05 65 38 73 18, fax 05 65 38 84 50. Great place to eat an *omelette aux truffes* on a winter's day, and generally excellent cooking at any time. (Hotel rooms not as desirable.)

Northwest of Figeac by the N140 and D18 is **Cardaillac**, a village with a glorious past and a great deal of charm, with old stone buildings lining narrow alleys. The feudal Barons of Cardaillac were one of the most powerful dynasties in the region: with 20 parishes under their control by 1300 they dominated the Haut Quercy. The original community was divided between the village and the fort to the southwest—the ruins can be visited—which existed by 1064. To the east was the priory and church of St-Julien, established by 1146, rebuilt in the 17C. Le Musée Eclaté is a guided tour of local traditions and history. Open July, Aug, Sun–Fri 15.00–18.00; Sept at 15.00 only; closed Sat; ☎ 05 65 40 10 63.

A village in a totally different vein from Cardaillac is **Assier**, on the D653 off the N140, which has a 16C church and the remains of a vast and luxurious

Renaissance château, both due to Galiot de Genouillac, Seigneur d'Assier (1465–1546).

A proud, ambitious and flamboyant soldier and administrator under three kings—Charles VIII, Louis XII and François I—Galiot became Seneschal of Quercy in 1526 and Grand Ecuyer (equerry) de France. He began to build the **Château d'Assier** in 1525 after his return from the Italian campaigns. Open July–Aug daily 09.30–12.30 and 14.00–18.45; April–June, Sept, Mon, Wed–Sun 09.30–12.15 and 14.00–18.15; Oct–Mar 10.00–12.15 and 14.00–17.15; closed Tues, 1 Jan, 1 May, 1 Nov, 11 Nov, 25 Dec; ☎ 05 65 40 40 99. The castle is more reminiscent of the Loire Valley than the Quercy, built around four sides of a vast rectangular courtyard. It was sold off piecemeal by its owners, descendants of Galiot, in 1768. The little that remains conveys the grandeur of the project and the exuberant but empirical use of knowledge acquired in Italy or in the Loire. The **church**, Gothic in essence but Renaissance in detail, was built by Galiot in 1540: his coat of arms is in the pediment. A continuous frieze around the church is concerned with military exploits and techniques, constituting a catalogue of artillery and fortifications. Inside the church is the funerary chapel Galiot built for himself, with an accomplished stellar vault and two effigies of the First Master of the Artillery, standing in armour and recumbent in court dress.

Across the N140 is the well-kept village of **Lacapelle-Marival**, built in local stone whose colour ranges from pinkish gold to grey. It has a small rectangular *halle* (15C) with a tile roof supported by stone pillars. The tall keep (15C) of the castle (13C, 15C and 18C) dominates the village and shelters a grand staircase and wall paintings. Open daily July–15 Sept 10.00–12.00 and 15.00–19.00; ☎ 05 65 40 80 24.

Nearby is the tiny *bastide* of **Rudelle** with an ancient ford and bridge, founded in 1250 on the Figeac–Rocamadour road. It is worth a visit for its unique and impressive fortified church complete with crenellations and machicolations, though the upper part owes much to 20C restoration. Other villages characteristic of the region, with houses in pale stone with wide arches and hipped or steep pointed slate roofs, are Rueyres and Aynac further north.

Gramat is at the centre of the Parc Naturel Régional des Causses du Quercy, and it has to be said that the area around has more attractions than the town itself, which is crossed by the busy N140. On the edge of the Alzou (the ruined Moulin du Saut on its banks, D677/D39), and always an important trade route which led pilgrims towards Rocamadour, today there is little of interest except the *halle*, the 16C tour de l'Horloge and old houses in Rue St- Roch. A relic of the neolithic occupation are the huge tumulus on the racecourse (D15) and the dolmen in the area, especially at Les Plassous. But Gramat is the place to stop and taste the precious truffle (see Hôtel du Lion d'Or). Nearby is the Parc Animalier with wild and domestic animals. Open daily April–Sept 09.00–19.00, Oct–April 14.00–18.00, ☎ 05 65 38 81 22).

The Valley of the Célé

This beautiful drive west of Figeac, on the D13 and D41, could be combined with an exploration of the Lot Valley (p 200). The Célé winds first through a lush, tamed landscape, these days planted with maize, sunflowers, and occasional vines and tobacco; from the 14C to the 18C saffron was a major crop. Its cliffs then close in to form a narrow defile with tiny villages clamped to the rocks or sheltering at the base.

Tourist information

46160 Marcilhac-sur-Célé ☎ 05 65 40 68 44, fax 05 65 40 61 43

Market days

Brengues Thursday evenings

Bicycle hire

Hôtel les Falaises, 46330 Bouziès, ☎ 05 65 31 26 83. *Les 4 Sabots du Mas de Saboth*, 46090 Vers, ☎ 05 65 31 20 98

Ste-Eulalie is a hamlet with prehistoric painted caves, a Romanesque chapel built into the side of the *causse* and a fountain dedicated to the saint. Further on across the river are the steep roofs of the hamlet of **Espagnac-Ste-Eulalie**, in a picturesque huddle at the foot of the cliffs. A nunnery was established here in the 13C, and despite English invasions, survived until the Revolution. The remains of the convent buildings surround the garden and what is left of the cloister. The church of Notre-Dame-de-Val-Paradis has partly disappeared, but the unusual 13C jettied half-timbered belfry is still standing, as is a section of the nave. The north door of the church opens into the 13C nave and grafted to it is the much higher 14C apse. It contains three tombs with recumbent statues (13C–14C) and an 18C gilded retable.

Brengues shelters a pre-Romanesque church with rounded corners, heavily restored in 1835. The outstanding site of the valley is **Marcilhac-sur-Célé**. Surrounded by cliffs in shades of white, grey, ochre and pink, the village runs down to the river's edge and at its heart lie the ruins of the once important **Abbaye St-Pierre**, attached to Moissac. Open April–May Wed–Sun 10.00–12.00 and 14.00–17.00; July, Aug daily 10.00–12.00 and 14.00–18.30; Sept Wed–Sun 10.00–12.00 and 14.00–18.00; ☎ 05 65 40 68 44. Dating from the 11C and 12C, it was pillaged during the Hundred Years War, and from 1461 the abbots attempted to revive and rebuild the church and the protective walls around the village. Damaged again by the Protestants in 1659, it received its final blow in the 19C, but the ruins of the church still give an idea of its former grandeur. The west portal, flanked by the bases of towers and the ruined first bays of the nave, with massive cruciform pillars, is reminiscent of Conques. Above the entrance are five primitive Romanesque reliefs, possibly re-used, of a *Christ in Majesty* flanked by the sun and the moon, and two angels, with St Peter and St Paul below. The present church, now used by the parish, incorporates the remains of the earlier one of the 15C. The chancel is protected by a narrow ambulatory and it has conserved its 17C stalls and pulpit. The best preserved Romanesque building is the late 12C **chapter house** which contains some beautiful capitals framing the door and early rectangular rib vaults. North of the chapter house are more sculpted capitals. The monastic buildings have almost entirely disappeared although two of the five defensive towers are still in place.

There are dolmens in the area. **Bellevue Caves**, open 15 June–15 Sept 10.00–18.00; ☎ 05 65 40 63 92.

The D40 leaves the lush valley for the evergreen oaks and junipers of the arid Causse de Livernon and an area of national park of about 50ha, the **Musée de Plein Air du Quercy-Cuzals**. Open June–Aug 10.00–19.00; April–1 Nov 14.00–18.00; closed Sat; ☎ 05 65 22 58 63. This is an open-air museum of rural life in the Quercy. Two complete farms have been reconstructed as well as a *pigeonnier* and a *cazelle*, and there are museums of rural crafts and animals.

Return to the D41 and **Cabrerets**, at the confluence of the Sagne and the Célé, which has a semi-troglodite castle, the Château du Diable, clinging to the cliff face opposite the bridge. An ancient stronghold of the local barons, the castle was destroyed in 1390 to prevent it falling into the hands of the English. At the other end of the village is the imposing 15C Château Gontaut-Biron (no admission).

The **Grotte de Pech-Merle** combines the A.-Lemozi prehistory museum and caves, discovered in 1922, that are some of the most interesting in the region for their natural formations and for the scope and beauty of the images they contain. Guided visits 1 Apr–1 Nov daily 09.30–12.00 and 13.30–17.00; ☎ 05 65 31 27 05/05 65 31 23 33, www.quercy.net/pechmerle; visitors to caves limited to 700 per day; booking advised July and Aug. The museum gives an introduction to the region from Paleolithic times to the Iron Age, with an audio-visual presentation. The underground visit covers some 1.2km and numerous galleries, not difficult to negotiate but sometimes damp; there are 48 steps down. The natural formations include the usual stalagmites and stalactites, but also upright calcite discs and white 'cave pearls'. Yet far and away the most awe-inspiring features are the marks left by man. The images are mainly executed in black (carbon), and red (iron oxide) and date from 20,000 to 15,000 BC, the Solutrean to the Magdalenian periods. The majority of the nearly 80 representations are of animals, the most beautiful frieze being the famous dappled horses (*c* 25,000 BC), one of several using or inspired by the natural contours of the rock.

The Causse de Limogne

If you are keen to snuffle a truffle, come to **Lalbenque** in the winter. This small town southeast of Cahors, on the D6, has the most important **truffle market** in the Midi-Pyrénées (see below); the optimum time to buy is January. Near the crossroads of D19 and D6 north, is a superb carved stone cross.

Northeast of Lalbenque by the D10 is **Aujols**, which has a *lac-lavoir*, like a village pond surrounded by washstones, and houses with verandas (*bolets*). There are more typical houses at **Concots**, east on the D10 and D911, which has an old tower called the Tour de l'Horloge. **Limogne-en-Quercy** further along the D911 is the capital of the Causse. It has a Sunday market and truffles on Fridays in the winter. There are several dolmens nearby and at **Promilhanès** there is a restored working windmill.

Laramière's windmill has no sails but the privately owned priory, next to the church with three bells, is worth a visit, although it has seen better times. Open 14.00–19.00; ☎ 05 61 85 51 48. An Augustinian priory was founded in 1148 on a rocky site above the stream. The Wars of Religion destroyed a great deal and the Jesuits altered it in the mid-17C. Despite all the abuse there are still interesting elements, including the 13C chapel, divided in two horizontally in the 17C, the Romanesque pilgrim hostel, and above all the chapter house painted with geometric designs and carved capitals representing Blanche of Castille and Louis IX.

Truffles

The slightly bitter aroma of truffles is very distinctive and the odour wafts down the street at market time. There you are likely to find them enveloped in a napkin in a small basket on trestles. The contents of a basket are sold as one lot. The price is totally dependent on supply and a kilo can fetch anything between 300 and 400 €. At Lalbenque, trading begins when a whistle is blown. The prospective purchaser writes a price on a slip of paper and if the vendor keeps it, the price is acceptable.

Truffles are a type of underground mushroom. The only variety sold is the *Tuber melanosporum* and the most surprising discovery for the uninitiated is that they are rock hard and resemble lumps of coal. The spores begin to grow in July and do best in a warm, humid season. Pigs used to snuffle them out but now the *trufficulteur* is more likely to use a dog. Since the beginning of the 20C there has been a huge decline in production, from more than 200 tonnes of truffles a year in the Lot *c* 1900 to between 5 and 20 tonnes today.

Truffle markets are held at Lalbenque (end Dec–mid-March, Tues 14.00) and Limogne-en-Quercy (Dec–end March, Fri 10.30).

10 The Aveyron-Rouergue

The modern *département* of the Aveyron, the largest in the Midi-Pyrénées, embraces the high open spaces of the limestone *causses* and the Monts d'Aubrac, the dramatic gorges of the Aveyron, Lot and Dourbie Rivers, as well as serene and green valleys. The region is often referred to by its old name, Rouergue, and its people as the Rouergats. It shelters one of the most beautiful Romanesque churches in the Midi-Pyrénées at Conques.

Getting there and around
Car
A20, exit 56 Figeac,
N140/D963/D42/D901 or
N140/D22/D901. D901 from Rodez.
Train
Paris Austerlitz to Rodez via Brive,
Capdenac (*SNCF*, ☎ 08 36 35 35 35),
Decazeville (*SNCF*, ☎ 05 65 43 12 35),
Cransac.
Clermont-Ferrand to Rodez via
Capdenac, Decazeville, Cransac.
Bus
Rodez to Conques, once daily Mon–Fri.

Tourist information
12340 Bozouls Pl. de la Mairie, ☎ 05 65 48 50 52, fax 05 65 51 28 01, www.geopole12.org/
12320 Conques Pl. de l'Abbatiale, ☎ 05 65 72 85 00/08 20 82 08 03, fax 05 65 72 87 03, www.conques.com
Market days
Bozouls Thursday
Conques July, Aug Thursday evening
Marcillac Sunday

Festivals and events
April *Film festival*, Conques
July–August *Festival de Musique*,

'*Conques La Lumière du Roman*', classical and baroque music; Concerts *l'abbatiale de Conques; Festival de Cinéma*; Conques **August** *Festival Lyrique 'Belcanto'*, song festival, Bozouls

October *Fête de Ste-Foy*, Conques

Where to stay and eating out

12340 BOZOULS

Les Brunes, Mme Philipponnat, ☎ 05 65 48 50 11/06 80 07 95 96, fax 05 65 48 83 62, www.lesbrunes.fr.st. *Chambres d'hôte.*

12320 CONQUES

☆☆☆☆ *Grand Hôtel Ste-Foy*, ☎ 05 65 69 84 03, fax 05 65 72 81 04, www.hotelsaintefoy.fr. At the heart of the village, a charming hotel with a good table.

☆☆☆ *Hostellerie de l'Abbaye*, Rue Charlemagne, ☎ 05 65 72 80 30, fax 05 65 72 82 84. In a beautiful spot close to the abbey church, overlooking the Gorges (guarded by a rather fear-some owner), with picturesque rooms.

☆☆/€€–€€€€ *Moulin de Cambelong*, Domaine de Cambelong, ☎ 05 65 72 84 77, fax 05 65 72 83 91, www. moulindecambelong.com. One of the last water mills on the Dourdou, an enchanting building with charming rooms, plus adventurous cooking.

☆☆ *Auberge St-Jacques*, ☎ 05 65 72 86 35, fax 05 65 72 86 36, www.aubergestjacques.fr. In the centre of the village with restaurant/brasserie.

€ *Au Parvis*, ☎ 05 65 72 82 81. A *salon de thé* on the forecourt (*parvis*) of the church which serves snacks, and from the window tables you can enjoy the tympanum.

12850 ONET-LE-CHÂTEAU

☆☆☆ *l'Hostellerie de Fontanges*, Rte de Conques (on the D901), ☎ 05 65 77 76 00, fax 05 65 42 82 29, www.hostel-lerie-fontanges.com. A 16C château-hotel with a superb dining room, pool, and multitude of amenities.

CONQUES AND THE DOURDOU VALLEY

Conques

Conques occupies a magnificent but isolated site, clinging to the side of a natural amphitheatre or *concha* at the confluence of the narrow Ouche gorge and the Dourdou Valley. The village, built entirely in silvery-yellow schist, its steep roofs clad in gradated fish-scale tiles, forms a protective terraced semi-circle above the Romanesque abbey church of Ste-Foy with its well-preserved sculpted tympanum. The museum holds a unique and price-less collection of religious objects. There is a centre for Romanesque studies.

Conques

Abbaye de Ste-Foy

If driving, follow the signs to park at the east of the village and walk downhill to enjoy the view down onto the apse of the abbey church of Ste-Foy.

It is said that in the 8C a hermit called Dadon settled in this place and the pious community that gathered here adopted the Benedictine Rule. The abbey's reputation was firmly secured in 866 when the relics of a young Christian, Ste Foy (St Faith), martyred in the 3C, were furtively translated from Agen to Conques. A church existed to house the relics by the end of the 10C (*c* 980) and St Faith's first miracle was in 983. Books of miracles in the 11C enhanced her reputation for curing eye problems and liberating prisoners. The cult spread throughout Europe and Conques became a major stage on the Via Podiensis to Santiago de Compostela. A larger church dedicated to St Faith was begun by Abbot Odolric (1030–65), and continued by his successors, Etienne II (1065–87), Bégon III (1087–1107) and Boniface (1107–25). The result was a very fine, albeit small, example of a pilgrimage church, and such a powerful abbey that, unlike many on the pilgrim route, it remained independent of Cluny. The abbey suffered over the centuries, however, and at the Revolution the chapter was dissolved, the property sold and most of the 12C cloister disappeared. Help was desperately sought in the 19C as the church threatened collapse. Salvation came in 1837, in the shape of Prosper Merimée, the newly appointed Inspector of Historic Monuments, who visited Conques accompanied by Stendhal. Repairs began in 1839 and have continued ever since. The Pilgrimage of St Faith is celebrated on the second Sunday in October.

Exterior A terrace above the east end of the church provides a rare view down onto the chevet, made up of abutting sections rising in a pyramid to the octagonal lantern-tower (15C and 19C). The clerestory of the choir has six blind arches supported by carved capitals and alternate windows, and superimposed engaged columns flank the windows and support the cornice. The church was begun in red sandstone in the 11C and continued in yellowish limestone with schist infill.

Steps go down to the level of the church and from here the considerable height of this satisfying building comes into perspective. The oldest door, in the north transept, has smallish, finely carved capitals with interlacing and palmettes, as does the south door. A walk around the east end reveals vaulted cavities between the chapels for tombs, the most important of which, the **tomb of Bégon III**, is in a deep recess on the south. An inscription celebrates the accomplishments of the abbot as benefactor of the cloister, and a relief panel represents Christ enthroned between the abbot and St Faith. The figures have characteristics—little ears, pierced eyes, centrally parted hair—typical of the work of the Master of the Abbot Bégon. As you climb the incline you pass on your right the Fontaine de Plô, Dadon's source of water.

The fairly severe **façade** was probably built during the abbacy of Boniface (1107–25). It is buttressed by two tall square towers culminating in the 19C belfries, and between them are an oculus, two round-headed windows and polychrome stone rose motifs. A deep arched hood protects the celebrated **tympanum**. Endearingly anecdotal, its 120 figures, in a style more Auvergnat than Languedocian, are arranged in compartments like a strip cartoon. The message is clear and numerous inscriptions reinforce it. The subject is the **Last Judgement**, based on Matthew 25, a didactic warning of reward or punishment. On the left as you face the tympanum is an orderly composition appropriate to Heaven, contrasting with the confusion of Hell. Christ enthroned at the centre is pivotal, symbolically and artistically. His hands extend beyond the mandorla, establishing a link with

Tympanum of St-Foy

mankind—with the right he shows the way to the chosen and with the left indicates the path of the damned—and at the same time orchestrating the composition. Angels above support a cross, others sound the horn and carry the instruments of the Passion, and on Christ's left four more carry the book of life and a censer and ward off evil. Opposite the blessed line up, the Virgin first, the blue of her cloak still visible, followed by St Peter and Dadon. Next is an abbot, leading Charlemagne by the hand with members of the Carolingian royal family. The last four figures with halos, one female, are not definitely identified. The three arcades below represent the abbey church and the manacles symbolise ex-voto offerings by Christian prisoners saved from the Moors by St Faith, prostrate before the hand of God. Next to her the dead rise from their earthly tombs. Framed in a series of arches in the lowest register is Abraham flanked by the Wise Virgins, martyrs and prophets, all about to be received into Paradise by way of an open door, whose hinges and lock are carved with infinite care. During the weighing of souls a sly demon is attempting, unsuccessfully, to bring the scales down on his side, watched by Archangel Michael. Juxtaposed with the Gates of Paradise are the jaws of Leviathan, into which the damned are being stuffed by a hairy demon. All the deadly sins and a few more are represented with their appropriate punishments: spiritual laxity, heresy, pride, lust, greed, gluttony, envy, anger and fornication. The scandalmonger has his tongue cut out, the poacher is roasted by a hare, and in the upper corner a money-forger, surrounded by his equipment, is forced to swallow molten metal. The inscription on the lintel reminds us: Sinners, if you do not reform your morals, know that you face a terrible judgement.

Interior When you walk inside the door you know which route you have chosen. This is a sample of Romanesque heaven. The narrow **nave** (22.1m high) is impressive yet modest, with just six bays: the total length of the church is 56m, with alternate round and square piers with attached shafts and barrel vaults. The aisles are groin vaulted. The half-barrel vaulted gallery takes the thrust of the high vault and enriches the overall design of the interior with elegant double openings divided by pairs of slender columns. Indirect light falls on the nave from the aisles and the galleries and directly from the windows in the west façade. There is one deep and one very small chapel on each arm of the ample transept. In the tradition of pilgrimage churches, it was designed with an enclosed choir where the clergy could worship undisturbed while the flocks filed past the relics.

At the **crossing** four piers rise to arches supporting the octagonal Gothic lantern (15C) which lights it. In 1982 the crossing had to be underpinned and the lantern rebuilt. A semi-circle of columns, rebuilt in the 19C, marks off the choir, presumably built on the foundations of the earlier church, from the ambulatory. Around the choir are 12C and 13C wrought-iron screens.

The sculptures in an *Annunciation* scene on the north **transept** wall are of the same period as the tympanum but it is not known where they originally stood. The Virgin, who is spinning, and the Angel Gabriel are framed in separate arches and in the angles to either side of the main group are St John the Baptist and Isaiah. There is a total of 250 carved **capitals**, 212 of them inside, most with decorative motifs and some elegantly simple. Storiated capitals are infrequent but on the fourth pier north is a *Last Supper* (south face) and the *Martyrdom of St Faith* (east face) and south of the choir is the *Sacrifice of Abraham*, a symbol of the Eucharist. The earliest storiated capitals, in the south transept, have scenes from the *Life of St Peter*. The south transept chapel dedicated to St Faith contains the only incongruous element, a 17C gilded reredos. On the south wall is a rather damaged 15C fresco of scenes from the saint's martyrdom. In 1993 new windows were installed, designed by the artist Pierre Soulages after lengthy research to perfect the manufacture of glass with varying luminosity, recalling the quality of alabaster.

On a lower level than the church, Abbot Bégon's cloister remains only in spirit, delineated by a low wall. The only relic is the beautiful serpentine stone **pool**, made at the same time as the cloister, reassembled and restored, which is skilfully decorated in miniature with 18 columns and capitals with alternate masks and atlantes. The two small arches on the east were part of the entrance to the chapter house. From the southeast corner of the cloister is the entrance to a little cemetery suspended above the Ouche gorges.

On the west side are six bays of the façade of the **refectory**. About 30 capitals of the cloister, in pale-coloured limestone from the Causse, have been conserved and reused here or exhibited in the museum. At the entrance to the gallery is an amusing capital which shows eight figures who seem to be building a wall, although one is holding a horn, and probably refers to the construction of the cloister; its opposite number has four identical armed warriors.

In the refectory gallery is the entrance to **Trésor I**, a unique collection which remarkably evaded iconoclasts and treasure seekers. Open daily July, Aug 09.00–13.00 and 14.00–19.00; Sept–June 09.00–13.00 and 14.00–18.00. The centrepiece is the reliquary statue known as *St Faith in Majesty*, a curious and disturbing work, a cult image of a type now rare but traditional in central France in the Middle Ages. It was created to contain the skull relic of the young martyr, and its chilling gaze drove pilgrims to part with money or jewels, some of the latter being added to the statue over the centuries. At its core is a basic wooden frame of two roughly sculpted pieces of wood, to which was fixed the hollow gold head from a pre-9C bust. The reliquary was assembled in the second half of the 9C and the relic was placed in the wooden body, not in the head. The wooden support was covered with embossed sheets of precious metals, filigree, precious and semi-precious stones and enamels. It contained part of the skull of the saint. A second casket reliquary of St Faith was found under a flagstone in the choir in 1875. Other reliquaries and treasures include the lantern-shaped Pepin's shrine (9C–10C); a triangular reliquary with a large rock crystal in the apex called the 'A of Charlemagne'; the portable altar of St Faith (early 12C); and

Bégon's altar (dated 26 June 1100), in porphyry with niello and silver-gilt ornament. From the goldsmiths of Villefranche-de-Rouergue are a charming small silver statue of St Faith (presented on 2 August 1497) and a magnificent processional cross (*c* 1503) which also bears an image of the child-saint which came from the silver workshops in Villefranche-de-Rouergue (p 236).

The Musée Joseph Fau or **Trésor II** is next to the tourist office. It contains Romanesque capitals, mainly from the cloister, and a collection of religious carvings, furniture and tapestries, including a series of four 16C Aubusson tapestries describe the events leading to her martyrdom.

The village of Conques is very small. The main street, Rue du Abbé Floran, runs the length of the village, east–west. Rue Charlemagne, on the lowest level, takes you under the Porte du Barry, one of the 11C gateways, past the Romanesque Fontaine du Barry, and eventually to the **Pont Romain** (not Roman but derived from the Arab word for pilgrims, *roumis*), over the Dourdou in the lower village. Just as it leaves the upper village, however, a left fork goes to the tiny 16C chapel of St-Roch where there is a beautiful view of the village.

Rue Haute (Rue Emile-Roudié), as its name suggests, runs along the top of the village above rooftops and alongside some picturesque houses. To the west of Rue Haute is Rue du Château, named after the 15C/16C **Château d'Humières**, the grandest house in the village. Round the corner, Porte de la Vinzelle, with a 17C polychrome statue of the Virgin, straddles the route the pilgrims usually took on the next stage of their journey, passing the 17C Capelette oratory.

The best place for views of Conques is across the Ouche. From the valley, take the D901 towards Rodez and turn left to the **Site de Bencarel**, immediately opposite the Pont Romain. Alternatively, cross the bridge (which is extremely narrow, not for camper vans) and climb.

There is a pretty drive south along the Gorges du Dourdou on the D901. At the end of the Gorges is the **Moulin de Sagnes**, a 17C mill built in the red sandstone of the valley. After storms, the river itself runs red. From St-Cyprien, you can cross the Causse du Comtal (see below).

The route south runs through the *vallon* or *rougier* of Marcillac, a valley washed in the purplish-red of the local sandstone. Vines, cultivated on the south-facing terraced slopes, were introduced by the monks of Conques in the 11C. The local wine can be tasted at Valady (on the D962 or D204 from Marcillac), at the *Caves des Vignerons du Vallon*.

The village of **Marcillac**, built almost entirely in red sandstone, is very picturesque, with several fine old houses grouped around the 14C–15C church to the south of the D901. A seemingly disproportionate number of them are attractively refurbished as *maisons de retraite* (retirement homes).

Salles-la-Source, in truth three villages on three levels niched in a south-facing hollow, has a 20m cascade on the higher level and various châteaux and churches lower down. Between the two levels is the Musée du Rouergue, Arts et Métiers, the local museum of industry and agriculture. Open July, Aug 10.00–12.30 and 14.00–19.00; May–June, Sept 14.00–18.00; closed Sat am July, Aug, PH and Oct–April; ☎ 05 65 67 28 96. At **Souyri** the Romanesque church was fortified in the 15C. From the terrace of the castle (14C–16C) at **Onet-le-Château**, formerly the residence of the chapter of Rodez, is a marvellous view of Rodez itself.

The remote and scenic region southeast of Conques, reached by the D901 and D46 via St-Cyprien-sur-Dourdou—which has a 15C church and belfry—is the Causse du Comtal. The **Pic du Kaymard** (707m) is the highest point in the canton of Conques. At this point the various geological strata come together: the granite of the plateau, the red sandstone of the valley, and the yellow limestone (used in the church of Ste-Foy) of the *causse*. Near Polissal is the 14C tower of a former Commandery of the Templars, and at **Villecomtal**, a 13C *bastide* in sandstone and slate, are old fortifications and a church (14C–15C) with a small polychrome *Pietà* (15C) and a finely carved altar rail and pulpit. The Château de Villecomtal which dominates the village, was built by the Counts of Rodez and offers panoramic views from the 15C keep. Open July, Aug 14.00–19.00, closed Mon; May, June, Sept–15 Oct 14.00–17.30; closed Sat, Sun and PH; ☎ 05 65 51 40 64. Follow the pretty route (D904) along the Dourdou Valley to **Muret-le-Château** with a waterfall and ancient castle (no visits).

The D68 leads to **Rodelle** (little Rodez) is perched above the left bank of the Dourdou. A Carolingian site, the church is part Romanesque, part 15C and has a very touching and unusual late Gothic polychrome *Pietà*, where Christ's head is supported by St John, and Mary Magdalene is at his feet. Just outside Rodelle is the Grotte des Meules and a modern chapel, Ste-Tarcisse (15C), with a monument to the local sculptor, Denys Puech (1854–1942), born in Bozouls.

Descend on the D20 to **Bozouls**, between the Causse du Comtal and the Lot Valley. Here the Dourdou has created a remarkable natural site, carving its route deep into the tender rock for about 700m. The newer part of town on the right bank has a small square with a monument to the war dead designed by Denys Puech for his native town. Across the bottom of the ravine is a bridge reached by Rue de l'Hospitalet, passing near two old towers, and the route climbs again on the opposite bank to the medieval village through a fragment of the old outer walls. The recently restored Romanesque church of Ste-Fauste, with Gothic chapels on the south, has some interesting storiated capitals and 15C sculptures of the Virgin, St Peter and St Anthony in the porch, and is sometimes used for concerts.

Rodez

Rodez, *préfecture* of the Aveyron, is a bustling town on a hill above the Aveyron River. The attractive old centre, concentrated around the great roseate pile of the cathedral, has been spruced up.

Getting there and around
Air

Paris to Rodez-Marcillac, *Air France*.
Lyon to Rodez-Marcillac, *Hex'air*.
Car

A20, exit 56 via Figeac/N140 via Decazeville.
A68 Toulouse to Albi and N88 via Carmaux.
A75 Clermont-Ferrand to Montpellier, exit 42, N88 via Séverac-le-Château.

Train

Paris Austerlitz to Rodez, Toulouse, Villefranche-de-Rouergue, Millau (*SNCF*, ☎ 08 36 35 35 35).
Bus

Buses to Laguiole, Entraygues/Mur-de-Barrez; Conques; Espalion, Rodez.

Tourist information
Pl. Foch, BP 511, ☎ 05 65 75 76 77, fax 05 65 68 78 15, www.grandrodez.com

Market days

Wednesday and Saturday am and pm

Festivals and events

June *Festival de Musique.*
Festival international de la vie de l'eau, in connection with the river and lakes in the vicinity
July–August *L'Estivada*, Occitan Festival, including a medieval market

Where to stay and eating out

1 2 0 0 0 RODEZ

✮✮✮ *Hôtel le Biney*, 7 Blvd Gambetta, rue Victoire-Massol, ☎ 05 65 68 01 24, fax 05 65 75 22 98, www.chateauxhotels.com. In the centre of the city, pretty modern rooms, garden, Provençal bar.
€€ *Goûts et Couleurs*, 38 Rue de Bonald, ☎ 05 65 42 75 10. Just as colourful in every way as the name suggests. This is a top quality restaurant with one Michelin rosette.
€€ *Le Saint-Amans*, 12 Rue de la Madeleine, ☎ 05 65 68 03 18. Contemporary and inventive.

Ancient *Segodunum* was called *Ruteni* by the Romans and became an important Gallo-Roman oppidum extending almost as far as the modern town until the 3C. The counts and bishops maintained a fierce rivalry lasting several centuries, and from the 13C the Comté of Rodez passed to the d'Armagnac family who made a great impact on the town. Notre-Dame was the last great cathedral begun in the Midi during the 13C and took 300 years to built under the supervision of 20 bishops.

Start from the tourist office on Place Foch, a large open square with a white marble statue, *Naïade de Vors* (1859) by Denys Puech, symbolising the Gallo-Roman supply of water from the Vors to the town. The former **Jesuit college chapel** (l'Ancien Lycée Foch) is a sober 17C Baroque building now used for concerts (open July–Sept). The attractive galleried interior has conserved the original Louis XIII painted woodwork, pink and grey stone architectural elements and rendered walls decorated with portraits of Ignatius Loyola and other leading Jesuits. To the west of Place Foch is the **Tour Maje**, the most important of the 30 fortified towers which once protected the town. Turn right into Rue Penavayre. Just before the end of the street there is a pretty Gothic courtyard with a well, in a former canonical residence.

Cathédrale Notre-Dame

The cathedral is the major monument of the town. On 25 May 1277 the first stone of a new cathedral was laid following the collapse of the belfry of the old church in 1276, which took with it the choir and part of the 10C nave. The new building, modelled on the great Gothic cathedrals of northern France, continued in fits and starts until 1562, but despite the span of some 300 years, there is little sense of hiatus in the architecture. The cathedral was brought to the state we see it today at the time of Bishop Georges d'Armagnac (1530–62).

Exterior The chevet was completed between 1277 and 1300. Five pentagonal radiating chapels are separated by large, sparsely decorated rectangular buttresses, and flying buttresses, rare in the Midi, help to take the thrust of the ambulatory vaults.

The pride of the Rouergats is the free-standing **belfry tower** (87m high) on the north flank of the cathedral. Begun in 1513 under the supervision of the master-mason Antoine Salvanh, it was completed by 1529. It is made up of three progressively more elaborate stratified octagonals and around the top are angels

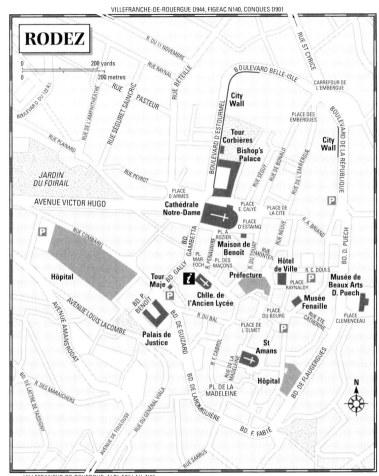

VILLEFRANCHE-DE-ROUERGUE D944, FIGEAC N140, CONQUES D901

RODEZ

VILLEFRANCHE-DE-ROUERGUE, ALBI, MILLAU, N88

with censers, saints and apostles, culminating in the figure of the Virgin of the Assumption. In 1793–94, when irreparable damage was done to the cathedral, the belfry was saved by replacing the statue of the Virgin with an allegory of Liberty, and the four Evangelists with martyrs of the Revolution, including Marat.

The Flamboyant doors on the transepts (*c* 1440–end 15C) are executed in fragile limestone and lost most of their figures during the Revolution. But the iconographic programmes seem to have been complementary: the Incarnation on the north portal and the Redemption on the south. The great west elevation, dominating the Place d'Armes, was completed *c* 1562. This part is more typical of the region—sheer and massive with little decoration, and no west door. Incorporated into the city walls, it was built towards the end of the 15C. The austerity is relieved by the elegant Rayonnant rose window, in place by 1529. Work continued on the southern tower during the episcopate of the humanist, Georges d'Armagnac (1500–85), and his secretary, Guillaume Philandrier, editor of Vitruvius, who introduced new concepts of architecture into the Rouergue. The upper part of the southwest tower is constructed in the style of a Classical temple, and above the central bay, incongruously placed between the two crocketed Gothic pinnacles, is a Renaissance gable (*c* 1562).

Interior This is a large, essentially Rayonnant cathedral, with aisles and ambulatory but very little integral ornament, typical of meridional Gothic. Whether this was dictated by financial or aesthetic considerations is debatable. The shallow undulations on the piers of the main arcades are untypical of Rayonnant Gothic except in the south, for example at Narbonne, as is the same smooth elision from the piers to the finely moulded ribs and arcade arches. Another trait of the Midi is to reduce the glazed section of the clerestory to only part of each bay. The 11 pentagonal chapels in the east were completed 1277–1300 but the Romanesque nave was still in existence until the 15C. The last bays of the nave and the façade towers brought the building near completion at the beginning of the 16C.

The plain interior is a setting for some interesting elements which survived the late 18C. The 15C Flamboyant *jubé* (rood-screen) avoided destruction at the end of the 17C but was damaged after the Revolution and lost all 38 statues. It was finally removed in the 19C but not altogether destroyed and re-sited in 1872 inside the south door. Some **choir stalls** (1478–88) were damaged when the *jubé* was removed but the elaborate episcopal throne plus 62 higher and 14 lower stalls are original. The remainder are 17C, as is the balustrade above. On the exterior of the choir enclosure a 15C mural was discovered in 1978 with scenes from the life of St Eligius (588–659). The charming late-14C statue of Notre-Dame-de-Grace has lost most of its colour and all of its precious stones. The 27 chapels contain a variety of **furnishings**. The oldest piece is the 10C marble altar table on the north wall of the axial chapel (there is a light). The main altar until 1525, it has an inscription recording that Deusdedit, the Bishop (961–1004), ordered it to be made. In 1662 it was painted with an *Annunciation* and used as a retable. In the chapel vault are 14C frescoes, probably part of a cycle originally covering the whole chapel, discovered under plaster in 1986. There are more frescoes (1340–50) in the northeast chapel of the choir which resemble stained glass: 18 of the 24 original figures are identified by their symbols or by an inscription. Others were discovered in 1994 in the southeast choir chapel.

The most important late Gothic carved **retables** are found in the two central chapels on the south of the nave. The *Mount of Olives* from the last quarter of the 15C(?) has delicately sculpted and polychromed limestone figures in a richly decorated surround. The adjacent St-Sepulchre chapel is closed by an elaborate openwork Gothic screen, but of the 12 statues only five on the interior, four sybils and an *Ecce Homo*, are original. The vast altarpiece in three registers inside the chapel (1523) introduces elements of Renaissance decoration into a late-Gothic context. The lower register contains a polychromed *Entombment* characteristic of many in the region, but in addition are three small reliefs, and crowning the ensemble is Christ stepping out of his sarcophagus. The most important painting in the cathedral is on the wall opposite—*Tobias and the Angel* (1715) by Antoine Coypel.

The entrance to the sacristy (*c* 1525) is finely sculpted, as is the screen of the

St-Raphael chapel opposite, part of the stone choir enclosure of *c* 1526–27. It contains one superb openwork panel carved with a vase, garlands and cherubs. The 16C canons' tribune is above the St-Sacrament chapel in the northwest. Relics were displayed in the chapel, which has remarkable coffered vaults. There is a very fine carved walnut organ case (1628) in the north transept.

The **Evêché** (Bishops' Palace) north of the cathedral, built in 1694 but partly reconstructed in the 19C, derives much inspiration from Fontainebleau. From inside the courtyard there is a good view of the belfry and of the 15C **Tour Corbières** in the city walls.

In the southeast corner of Place d'Estaing, east of the cathedral, a vaulted passageway leads to the best courtyard in Rodez, in the 15C **Maison de Benoît**. Typical of the transition between Gothic and Renaissance, it has a Flamboyant gallery and a tower decorated in the idiom of the early Renaissance. The old streets around the cathedral have small shops and boutiques. Rue de Bonald on the northeast leads to Place des Embergues, an imaginatively reinvented area, and Rue Cusset, south of Place d'Estaing, leads to something similar called Place des Maçons.

From Place d'Estaing, take Rue Touat, turn left into Rue Monteil, right into Rue Neuve and left into Rue Camille Douls, past Place Raynaldy, which has been given a new look, keeping parts of the old buildings.

On Place Clemenceau is the **Musée des Beaux-Arts Denys Puech**. The Aveyronnais sculptor, Denys Puech (1854–1942) came up with the idea of a museum for Aveyronnais artists and it was inaugurated in 1910. A campaign of renovation (1984–89) has created a very attractive installation in the building designed by André Boyer for the contents of Puech's studio and work by his contemporaries, including Maurice Bompard, Tristan Richard, Raymond Gayrard and Eugène Viala. The upper floor and basement have temporary exhibitions from the museum's collections. Open Wed–Fri 10.00–12.00 and 14.00–18.00; Mon, Sat–Sun 14.00–18.00; ☎ 05 65 77 89 60.

Puech's work, displayed on the ground floor, is a technical *tour de force* with a tendency towards sleek, sentimentalised and mildly erotic female or hermaphrodite nudes in mythological or allegorical guises. It is lighthearted and makes no apologies for ignoring completely any attempt at psychological insight. Works include a portrait bust of his wife, *Princesse Gargarine Stourdza* (1908) and *Mézence blessé*, which won him the Prix de Rome for sculpture in 1884. The head of the *Muse d'André Chenier* is a portrait of the singer Emma Calvé, born in Decazeville, but we are not told who was used as model for the deliciously rounded bottom and soles of the feet.

Where Rue Ste-Catherine meets Rue St-Just is the **Musée Fenaille**, in two buildings, their façades updated in the 14C and 16C. It is essentially an archaeological and history museum of ancient Rodez and the Rouergue from pre-history to the 17C. It has an exceptional collection of menhir statues, ancient standing stones (about 4000 years old) that carry rudimentary anthropomorphic carved reliefs. Open all year Tues, Thur, Fri 10.00–12.00 and 14.00–18.00; Wed, Sat 13.00–19.00; Sun 14.00–18.00; ☎ 05 65 73 84 30.

Place du Bourg, the medieval commercial centre, is framed by some interesting jettied and half-timbered houses. In the middle of the square is a bust (1900) of *A. Blazy Bou* (1778–1846) by Puech. The elegant 16C **Maison de**

l'Annonciation is named after the relief sculpted on the corner and the *Préfecture* occupies the Hôtel d'Ayssènes (1716), on Place Charles de Gaulle, more reminiscent of the châteaux of the Loire Valley than the Rouergue. A bronze plaque near the entrance was erected to the memory of Jean Moulin (1899–1944), *sous-préfet* of the Aveyron and hero of the Resistance.

Maison Trouillet is a late 15C house with some fine decoration as is the late-Gothic **Maison d'Armagnac** (1525–31) on Place de l'Olmet. A rib-vaulted passage leads to a tiny Italianate courtyard with three miniature galleries and a stairtower with Renaissance windows.

Further south is the church of **St-Amans** on the Place des Toiles, a little square with a fountain, the site of a Gallo-Roman necropolis. Reputed to be the oldest church in the Rouergue, most likely 11C or 12C, it contained the relics of St Amans, St Quintien and St Dalmas. In 1752 the decision was taken to rebuild the Romanesque church before it fell down. Much of the old building material was salvaged and reused, including the Romanesque capitals. The result is a Baroque exterior in dark pinkish-red sandstone with an impressive west façade reminiscent of Venice, in contrast with the pure Romanesque style inside. The cupola was painted by a local artist, Alexis Salinier II (*c* 1763), with scenes from the *Life of St Amans*, and 16C tapestries have the same iconography. There is a 15C **Pietà**, a curious 16C statue of the *Trinity* and a reliquary casket in Limoges enamel.

THE OLT ROUERGAT

In Occitan the Lot was known as the Olt, and Olt frequently appears in the toponymy. This section of the river across the northern Aveyron runs in part through a gorge and marks the southern boundary of the Aubrac. It was of strategic importance in the Middle Ages and a line of castles protected each crossing point.

Getting there and around
Car

A75, Paris to Montpellier via Clermont-Ferrand, exit 40, D988, or exit 42, N88/D988. D988/D920 Rodez to Espalion.

Train

Clermont-Ferrand to Toulouse via Séverac-le-Château (**SNCF**, ☎ 05 65 71 61 19) and Millau. Rodez to Séverac-le-Château via Laissac

Bus

Rodez to Mur-de-Barrez (for Entraygues, Ste-Geneviève), once daily. Rodez to Espalion three daily during term time, two daily rest of year.

Tourist information

12140 Entraygues 30 Tour de Ville, ☎ 05 65 44 56 10, fax 05 65 44 50 85, www.nord-aveyron.com
12500 Espalion 2 Rue St-Antoine, BP 52, ☎ 05 65 44 10 63, fax 05 65 44 10 39, www.ot.espalion.fr and nord-aveyron.com
12190 Estaing 24 Rue François d'Estaing, ☎/fax 05 65 44 03 22, email syndicatinitiative.estaing@wanadoo.fr
12130 St-Geniez d'Campagnac 4 rue du Cours, ☎ 05 65 70 43 42, fax 05 65 70 47 05, www.st-geniez-dolt.com or http://perso.wanadoo.fr/stgeniezdolt

Market days

Entraygues Friday and Tuesday in summer; July, August Wednesday evenings

Espalion Tuesday and Friday
Estaing July, August Thursday evenings
St-Côme-d'Olt July/August, Sunday
St-Geniez-d'Olt Saturday

Festivals and events

June–September *Son et lumière*, sound and light show at the château, Estaing
July *Musique en Pays d'Olt*, chamber music, St-Geniez, Caissac, Sevrac
Festival de la Sainte-Epine, religious festival, St-Eulalie-d'Olt
15 August *Illumination aux chandelles*, of the old town, Estaing

Where to stay and eating out

12260 BALAGUIER D'OLT
Maud Le Fur, Place de la Mairie, ☎/fax 05 65 64 42 31. *Chambres d'hôtes.*
12140 ENTRAYGUES
☆☆ **La Truyère**, 60 Av. du Pont de la Truyère, ☎ 05 65 44 51 10, fax 05 65 44 57 78. Overlooking the river, with a garden.

La Méjanassère, ☎/fax 05 65 44 54 76. *Chambres d'hôte et ferme auberge.* Comfortable place to stay and good country cooking.
12500 ESPALION
☆☆ **Moderne l'Eau Vive**, 27 Blvd de Guizard, ☎ 05 65 44 05 11, fax 05 65 48 06 94. A good place to stay and an excellent place to eat.
12190 ESTAING
Cevel, Route de Vinnac, ☎/fax 05 65 44 09 89. *Chambres d'hôte.* Comes with good recommendations; pleasant guest rooms.
12130 ST-GENIEZ D'OLT
☆☆☆ **de France**, Pl. du Général-de-Gaulle, ☎ 05 65 70 42 20, fax 05 65 47 41 38, www.hotel-circuits-france. com. Pleasant hotel with restaurant and 1km away its own *'parc de loisirs'* on the river, with pool and activities.
☆☆☆ **Hostellerie de la Poste**, Pl. du Général-de-Gaulle, ☎ 05 65 47 43 30, fax 05 65 47 42 75, www. hoteldelaposte12.com.

At the confluence of the Lot and Truyère, north of Rodez, **Entraygues-sur-Truyère** has hotels and other facilities and is a centre for exploring the rugged and off-the-beaten-track country around the Gorges de Truyère. The best part of the town is close to the 13C–14C bridge over the Truyère, restored in the 17C and claiming to be the oldest bridge in the Rouergue. Spanning the Lot is the Pont Notre-Dame. Between the two is the old town with jettied houses and covered passageways called *cantous*. Two towers of the 13C château are still standing, the remainder is 17C.

Further along the Gorges de Lot is **Estaing**, a very picturesque small town between the Lot and the Coussane, with a tall castle. The elegant 16C bridge is protected by a chapel and decorated with a wrought-iron cross and a statue of Bishop François d'Estaing (1460–1529) whose family built the castle, which now houses a religious community. The 15C church behind the château has a belfry and a pretty clocktower with a bell, and outside the Flamboyant porch are two very weathered carved crosses. Inside are sculpted bosses, some modern glass, and the usual Baroque retables and reliquaries. The narrow streets around the church are worth exploring for the fine schist houses and for the tanneries on the Coussane east of the church.

Another small town on the Lot, **Espalion**, on the old Languedoc–Auvergne route, midway between Rodez and Laguiole, is an attractive place with typical Aveyronnais red sandstone houses with slate roofs and an ancient triple-arched bridge. The Musée d'Arts et Traditions Populaires et du Scaphandre in the 15C church of St-Jean has a famous collection of holy-water stoups and one room, amazingly in such an inland location, devoted to the history of the diving suit because two Espalionais pioneered this underwater apparatus. Open May, June Wed–Sun 10.00–12.00 and 14.00–18.00; July, Aug daily 10.00–12.00 and 14.00–19.00; Sept, Oct Mon, Wed–Sun 10.00–12.00 and 14.00–18.00; Nov–March Fri–Sun 14.00–18.00; ☎ 05 65 47 01 48.

Just outside Espalion, the **Château de Calmont d'Olt** (11C and 15C) has medieval war machinery; and 1km southeast on the D556 is the church of **Perse**, all that is left of the priory of St-Hilarion. The small church in the reddish regional stone is part 11C, part 12C. It has a stunning belfry gable and a south portal of note with a sculpted tympanum representing *Pentecost*. On the lintel is an animated scene of the *Apocalypse* and the *Last Judgement* and in the west spandrel little figures represent the Three Magi and Virgin and Child.

The 15C church at **Lassouts** incorporates sculptured elements from an 11C church damaged by *routiers*, including a simply carved Romanesque tympanum with a *Christ in Majesty* and on either side six Apostles. High-relief carvings of an owl and two bulls surround the tympanum. The church has conserved some Romanesque altars and in the south chapel a very fine Romanesque piscina is embedded in the wall.

North of Espalion, off the D921, is the 12C abbey of **Bonneval**, now occupied by Trappist nuns who sell the chocolate they make (closed Sun; ☎ 05 65 44 01 22). **St-Côme d'Olt**, back on the river, is an exceptionally pretty town. The bridge, decorated with a cross, existed in the 14C but has been frequently rebuilt and the town fortifications have all but disappeared. The medieval château (now the *mairie*) opposite the church was built in the 12C inside the walled *cité*, the towers added in the 14C and restored in the 15C. There are several attractive medieval houses as well as fine 17C–18C mansions, some with pavilion roofs. The most original roof, however, is the church steeple, a tall witch's hat with a twist, intentional or otherwise, the ultimate flame on the Flamboyant church (1522–32) attributed to Antoine Salvanh, master mason of the belfry of Rodez. The carved portal has a pair of particularly splendid Renaissance doors (1523) in oak with panels containing busts, animals and linenfold; each door is studded with 365 star-shaped nails. The wooden Christ (16C) is carved in walnut, the *Pietà* is 18C, and the remainder of the furnishings are 19C. To the north the chapel of the Pénitents, the first church in St-Côme, has kept its Romanesque features although the porch was added in the 18C.

South of the river a pretty drive along the D6 and D988 leads to the beautiful village of **Ste-Eulalie d'Olt** whose 16C–17C houses were built by wealthy weavers. The 15C Château des Curières de Castelnau is well preserved, and an old mill has been transformed into a hotel-restaurant. The church has an 11C east end and a pre-Romanesque altar recording the consecration of an earlier church *c* 1000. In the 12C the church doubled up as a citadel and *c* 1530 it was enlarged by two bays to the west. Successive alterations are fairly obvious from the exterior.

St-Geniez d'Olt was an important town in the 19C and has some fine 18C and 19C *hôtels particuliers*. Whereas its former wealth was due to cloth and leather, today it is renowned for its strawberries. In Rue de l'Hôtel de Ville is the cloister of an Augustinian convent founded in the 14C and rebuilt in the 17C, now occupied by the *mairie*. The adjacent church of the Pénitents-Blancs shelters a precious small late-15C triptych, with the *Epiphany* represented by ten gilded wooden statues, and painted panels of the **Circumcision** and **Nativity**. Through the cloister and across Place de la Mairie is the tourist office, installed in the Baroque chapel of the Pénitents-Noirs. The chapel, completed in 1705, has a painted wooden ceiling and a magnificent altarpiece. On the riverbanks are the old tanners' houses; on the other side of the river, the 12C parish church of St-Geniez was transformed into a Baroque building in the early 18C, with a stately double staircase. It contains the tomb of Mgr Frassyinous (1765–1841) sculpted by M. Gayrard. The steps south of the church climb to the *Monument Talabot* by Denys Puech from where there are good views.

THE AUBRAC

The Aubrac is a beautiful high plateau at the opposite end of the region to the Pyrénées, and far less well known. Part of the southern Massif Central, it is shared between the Aveyron, the Cantal and the Lozère. Although its highest point is 1400m, there are no abrupt peaks but soft reliefs scattered with strange rock formations, smoothed and rounded in the Ice Age and eroded by time. It is particularly suited to those seeking outdoor pursuits, fishing, walking, riding, skiing in the winter, and to the plant lover in everyone.

The flora of the Aubrac

The Aubracophile will claim that it has more flower power in early summer than the Pyrenees: 1300 species of flowers have been identified here. There are fields of narcissi and daffodils; tall spiky yellow gentian; wild geraniums; *calament* or 'tea of the Aubrac', with a tiny pink flower; digitalis; euphorbia; anenomes; campanulas; German and English types of broom; and wild orchids of all varieties, some resembling bees and spiders, little spiral ones, and some that smell of goat. The most fascinating of all must be the carnivorous plant of the peat bogs, *Drosera rotundifolia*. There are also prehistoric plants called Ligulaire de Sibérie and an orchid called *Malaxis paudoas*. For those who enjoy gathering there are wild raspberries, juniper and bilberries. The pastures are occasionally interrupted by patches of woodland: beech in the northeast, at their best in autumn, chestnut to the west, and pubescent oaks in the valley.

The landscape is broken up by dry-stone walls and stone shelters called *burons* once used by the shepherds or cheese-makers, now mainly abandoned. Cattle and sheep reign supreme, but the gentle Aubrac breed of cattle is the champion. The race was revived in the 1980s and has proved its worth both for beef and milk production. When the traditional transhumance—the seasonal moving of livestock to mountain pastures—is celebrated on the Sunday nearest 25 May (St-Urbain's Day) the cattle are beribboned and garlanded and make their stately way towards the higher ground. The villages and sturdy churches are in dark granite or basalt, the roofs of the same material, sombre in winter against the snow, and there are frequent carved *croix de chemin* in the same dark stone, marking the old pilgrim route or standing outside a church.

Getting there and around
Car

A75 Clermont-Ferrand to Montpellier, exit 42, Séverac-le-Château N88, or exit 28 St-Flour, N88/D921 for Laguiole/Espalion.
D920 Espalion to Entraygues.

Bus

Rodez to Laguiole, once daily.

Tourist information
2210 **Laguiole** Pl. de l'Ancien Forail,
☎ 05 65 44 35 94, 05 65 44 35 76, www.laguiole-online.com

Guided walks

The Laguiole tourist office organises botanic walks in the Laguiole forest. Guided walks in the Aubrac M.G. Diaz, 48260 Nasbinals, ☎ 04 46 32 56 02, fax 04 66 32 56 99, www.randaubrac.com. M.D. Gourdon, 12470 St-Chély-d'Aubrac, ☎ 06 83 43 85 37, ☎/fax 05 65 44 26 81

Festivals and events
Easter *Festival des Boeufsgras de Pâques*, prize cattle, Laguiole

May (Sunday nearest to the 25) *Fête de la Transhumance*, Aubrac

Where to stay and eating out
12210 LAGUIOLE

☆☆☆☆/€€€€ **Michel Bras**, Route de l'Aubrac, ☎ 05 65 51 18 20, fax 05 65 48 47 02, www.michel-bras.fr. A modern hotel disguised as part of the landscape, with a restaurant, the **Lou Mazuc**, of the finest quality; it has three Michelin rosettes.

☆☆☆ **Grand Hôtel Auguy**, 2 Allée de l'Amicale, ☎ 05 65 44 31 11, fax 05 65 51 50 81. Family run hotel, each room in a different style, and noted for its cooking, a blend of traditional and seasonal best. One Michelin rosette.

☆☆☆ **Regis**, Pl. de la Patte d'Oie, ☎ 05 65 44 30 05, fax 05 65 48 48 44. A more down-to-earth hotel-restaurant than the above but nevertheless serving excellent food. Pool.

☆☆☆ **Le Relais de Laguiole**, Espace Les Cayres, ☎ 05 65 54 19 66, fax 05 65 54 19 49, www.relais-laguiole.com. Youthful and fresh décor, indoor pool, sauna, garden, and local speciality, *aligot*, served in restaurant.

At the centre of the Aubrac is **Laguiole**, the small but dynamic capital of the Monts d'Aubrac, held up as a shining example of the exploitation of local resources. The town's economy is built on its cattle, the Aubrac, celebrated in the marketplace (car park) by a bronze sculpture of a bull by Georges Guyot (1947); on its cheese, called Laguiole, produced since the 12C but now vigorously marketed and made into a dish called *aligot*; and on its famous knives, *couteaux de Laguiole*, with bone handles, invented by Pierre-Jean Calmels in 1829. On the corner of Place du Forail is the local history museum of the Haut-Rouergue and mountain life. Rue du Faubourg and Rue du Couvent, with a cross marking the old pilgrim route, take you up to the church, mainly rebuilt in the 17C after the Religious Wars, with scallop shells sculpted on the porch.

The **Château du Bousquet** at Montpeyroux on the D42 is privately owned by Pierre Dijols, who will probably show you round. Open all year, Tues–Sun afternoons, closed Mon; ☎ 05 65 48 41 13.

The origins of the château are uncertain, but it may have been built by the Hospitallers on the Montpeyroux family's fief to protect the oldest and most direct pilgrimage route from Le Puy-en-Velay to Conques, the Route de Godescalc. In the late 1680s this fortress became the residence of the

Roquefeuil family, who owned it until 1900, and made several alterations, notably to the windows.

The medium-sized château is everybody's dream of a medieval castle and stands on a small hill with little to interrupt the view of it. Constructed mainly in basalt, it is a remarkably well-preserved example of 14C military architecture. Solid and compact, it has four round angle towers and two square ones, the one orientated to the east enclosing a small chapel facing the rising sun; all six have high roofs. There are almost continuous machicolations and a two-level parapeted walk around the upper part. The Roquefeuils' coat of arms appears on the painted ceiling of the Gothic chapel which also contains statues and a life-size *Crucifixion* which miraculously survived the Revolution. The present staircase is 100 years old. The *grande salle* is richly furnished and the kitchen, with smoke-blackened ceiling, vast fireplace and bread oven, is a delightful part of the visit.

Southeast of Laguiole is the village of **Aubrac** (1250m), a fearsomely exposed place on a winter's day at the crossroads for the ski centres. The Dômerie d'Aubrac, a pilgrim hospice founded *c* 1120, had a battalion of knights, monks, nuns and *donats* (lay brothers) under the control of the Dom, who protected travellers, and such was its reputation that it attracted hundreds, even thousands of pilgrims. It was disbanded at the Revolution and many of the buildings demolished: still standing are the hospital, rebuilt in the 15C and now private property; part of the *enceinte* called the *tour des Anglais*; and the church of Notre-Dame, built early in the 13C, unadorned inside and out, with a belfry dating from 1457. A botanic garden of local species is situated between the church and the Tour des Anglais.

The granite village of **St-Chély-d'Aubrac** was a stage on the route to Santiago da Compostela, as the sculpted pilgrims' cross on the ancient bridge over the Boralde reminds us. On the D533 north, turn left to the **Le Neck of Belvezet**, a high volcanic peak created from a solidified lava lake which, due to erosion, resembles organ pipes.

On the D19, the small community of **Prades d'Aubrac** (925m) is built in dark basaltic stone and dominated by the silhouette of the octagonal belfry and spire of the church built in 1540. Unusually for the Rouergue the vaults have pendant bosses and shelter a 15C polychrome stone *Pietà*.

11 Along the Aveyron Valley

The Aveyron, whose source is near Séverac-le-Château in the east of the *département*, flows past Rodez and westwards towards Villefranche-de-Rouergue, sometimes visible, sometimes hidden, and then turns south-westerly to carve out lush valleys and spectacular rocky gorges. Along its banks are some of the most attractive *bastides* and towns of the Rouergue.

Getting there and around
Car

A20 Exit 59 Caussade/D926
Villefranche-de-Rouergue via Caylus.
D922 Figeac to Villefranche-de-
Rouergue via Villeneuve-d'Aveyron.
D994/D1 Rodez to Villefranche-de-
Rouergue.
D140/D922 to Villefranche-de-
Rouergue via Villeneuve-d'Aveyron.
D600/D922 Albi to Villefranche-de-
Rouergue via Cordes-sur-Ciel.
D47 Villefranche-de-Rouergue to Lexos
via Najac.
D911 Millau to Villefranche-de-
Rouergue via Baraqueville.

Train

Paris Austerlitz to Toulouse via
Caussade.
Brive to Toulouse via Capdenac,
Villefranche-de-Rouergue, Laguepie,
Lexos, Najac
and Cordes. Villefranche-de-Rouergue
station, ☎ 05 65 45 03 16.

Bus

Six a day from Rodez to Villefranche-de-
Rouergue.

 Tourist information
12390 Belcastel Mairie de
Belcastel, ☎/fax, 05 65 64
46 11, www.mairie-belcastel.fr
82800 Bruniquel Promenade de
Ravelin, ☎ 05 63 67 24 84
82160 Caylus Rue Droite, ☎/fax 05 63
67 00 28, www.caylus.com
82250 Laguepie-Varen-Verfeil Pl. du
Foirail, ☎/fax 05 63 30 20 34
82230 Monclar-de-Quercy Pl. des
Capitouls, ☎ 05 63 30 31 72, fax 05
63 30 33 19
12270 Najac Pl. du Faubourg, ☎ 05
65 29 72 05, fax 05 65 29 72 29
otsi.najac@wanadoo.fr
81140 Penne Le Bourg, ☎ 05 63 56 36 68
82140 St-Antonin-Noble-Val Pl. de la
Mairie, ☎ 05 63 30 67 01,
fax 05 63 30 66 33,

www.saint-antonin-noble-val.com
12202 Villefrance-de-Rouergue
Promenade de Guiraudet, BP 239,
☎ 05 65 45 13 18, fax 05 65 45 55
58, www.villefranche.com
12260 Villeneuve-d'Aveyron Pl. des
Conques, ☎/fax 05 65 81 79 61

Market days

Belcastel periodically in summer
Caylus Saturday in summer
Laguepie Third Tuesday of the month
Monbazens Wednesday morning
Najac 15 June–15 September Sunday
Negrepelisse Tuesday
St-Antonin-Noble-Val Sunday
Villefranche-de-Rouergue Thursday.
Also monthly fairs
Villeneuve-d'Aveyron Sunday

Guided tours

Villefranche-de-Rouergue Enquire at
the tourist office

Festivals and events

July *Festival de la chanson francophone*;
musicians from all parts of the world,
Villefrance-de-Rouergue
August *Festival en Bastides*, Villeneuve-
d'Aveyron, Villefranche, Najac. *Festival
en Bastides*, Villefranche-de-Rouergue

 *Where to stay and
eating out*
12390 BELCASTEL
☆☆☆/€€€ *Vieux Pont*, ☎ 05 65 64 52
29, fax 05 65 64 44 32, www.
hotelbelcastel.com. A small up-market
restaurant and hotel in a heavenly spot.
82140 BROUSSES
€ *La Corniche*, on the D115 bis near
Cazals, ☎ 05 63 68 26 95. Good local
fare; terrace and view.
82800 BRUNIQUEL
€ *Les Bastides*, at the foot of the village,
Route de Gaillac, ☎ 05 63 67 21 87.
Terrace with stunning view of the village; simple cooking.
€€ *Les Gorges de l'Aveyron*, Le Bugarel,
on the D115 just before Montricoux,

☎ 05 63 24 50 50, Gastronomic cooking, set in a park, with terrace.

8 2 1 4 0 C A Z A L S
€ *Restaurant du moulin*, D115 between Bruniquel and St-Antonin, ☎ 05 63 68 20 84. Enjoy local cooking on the edge of the Aveyron.

8 2 2 5 0 L A G U E P I E
€€ *Les Deux Rivières*, Av. du Puech Mignon, ☎ 05 63 31 41 41, fax 05 63 30 20 91. Offers well-cooked local recipes and specialities.

8 2 8 0 0 M O N T R I C O U X
€–€€ *Le Relais du Postillon*, Le Bugarel, on the D115 just before Montricoux, tel 05 63 67 23 58. Regional specialities, including game and fish served on a shady terrace.

1 2 2 7 0 N A J A C
☆☆ *La Belle-Rive*, Au Roc du Pont, ☎ 05 65 29 73 90, fax 05 65 29 76 88. In the valley (near the station), a family hotel with reasonable rates and food. Pool.
☆☆/€€ *Oustal del Barry*, Place du Bourg, ☎ 05 65 29 74 32, fax 05 65 29 75 32, www.oustaldelbarry.com. Popular hotel-restaurant in the village.

8 1 1 4 0 P E N N E
€ *La terrasse*, ☎ 05 63 56 35 03. Superb view of the Château de Penne; regional cuisine.

8 2 1 4 0 S T - A N T O N I N - N O B L E - V A L
☆☆ *Le Lys Bleu*, 29 Pl. de la Halle, ☎ 05 63 68 21 00/30 65 06, fax 05 63 30 62 27, email lelysbleudepayrols@wanadoo.fr. In the heart of this enchanting village, the building is rustic but the rooms very comfortable.

1 2 2 0 0 S T - R E M Y (near Villefranche-de-Rouergue)
☆☆☆ *Relais de Farrou*, Route de Figeac, at St-Remy, ☎ 05 65 45 18 11, fax 05 65 45 32 59. A charming hotel set in a park, with pool and other fitness amenities.
Mas de Jouas, M. and Mme Taillet, ☎ 05 65 81 64 72, fax 05 65 81 50 70. Pleasant and comfortable *chambres d'hôte*.

8 2 8 0 0 V A I S S A C
☆☆ *Terrassier*, Le Bourg (near Montricoux), ☎ 05 63 30 95 60, fax 05 63 30 87 40, email hotel-rest.terrassier@wanadoo.fr. A peaceful setting in a little *bourg*, with a deservedly popular restaurant using local produce. Pool

1 2 2 0 0 V I L L E F R A N C H E - D E - R O U E R G U E
€ *Restaurant Bellevue* (near the Chartreuse) ☎ 05 65 45 23 17. Unsophisticated and inexpensive.

Villeneuve-d'Aveyron on the D922 is an attractive little town north of Villefranche-de-Rouergue. It acquired the status and privileges of *bastide* in 1271 after the *sauveté* (place of refuge) that had grown around an 11C monastery had been acquired by Raymond VII, Count of Toulouse in 1231. In 1272 it was designated royal *bastide* and was fortified in 1359. Four gateways exist, the Tour Savignac or Cardaillac, built in 1359, Porte Manhanenque and Porte Isaurenque, which lost their towers in the 18C, and Porte Haute, integrated into the fortifications in 1486. Villeneuve has preserved much of interest from its past, including a number of 15C and 16C houses, with traceried or mullioned windows, notably around Place des Conques and Rue Pavie, lined with arcades. The church is made up of two parts. The centrally planned 11C chapel of St-Sépulchre has a ribbed dome centred upon an oculus and supported by four columns. It was extended by the church of St-Pierre et St-Paul—the nave and polygonal apse—in the 13C. In the north apsidiole are medieval frescoes of a *Christ in Majesty* with the symbol of the Evangelists and scenes of pilgrimage.

Peyrusse-le-Roc, on the D87 between Capdenac-Gare and Montbazens, was an important fort belonging to the Counts of Toulouse, abandoned in the 17C in favour of Villefranche-de-Rouergue. Access to what is left—12C and 13C towers and the remains of the *cité* clinging to a steep rock—is possible but not easy, but it is very picturesque. The village church has late 20C works by Hervé Vernhes, a local artist, which are lit automatically as you enter and include the altar which is in solid elm, a *Crucifixion* in walnut behind it, and a series of paintings on canvas.

Near Montbazens to the east on the D53 is the **Château de Bournazel**, a high point in the development of Renaissance architecture in the Rouergue. Two massive round towers of the medieval château mark the entrance but on the other side is a complete change of style. Presumed to have been built in 1545, the date found on the north wing, it shows a highly individual interpretation of the influences of antiquity and of Italy, with a disciplined use of the Classical orders. It was damaged by fire in 1790 and is now a retirement home. Guided visits to the village and exterior of the château only (interior closed): end Feb–early March and Easter holidays 14.00–18.00, mid-June–mid-Sept all day; closed Thurs; TI ☎ 05 65 64 16 60.

Belcastel, near Rignac, on a cliff at the edge of the Aveyron, is a bit of a sham, but a very good one. Thirty years ago the village had all but disappeared but the enthusiasm of the architect Fernand Pouillon for the castle was contagious and a concerted effort has created something rather magical. The village climbs the slope up to the château. April daily 11.00–12.30 and 14.00–17.30, May–June Sat, Sun PH 11.00–12.30 and 14.30–18.30; June–Sept daily 11.00–12.30 and 14.30–18.30; Oct–11 Nov 11.00–12.30 and 14.00–17.30; ☎ 05 65 64 42 16. A superb bridge leads to the 15C church of St-Mary-Magdalene, extended in 1891. It contains an old altar found under the flagstones, and on the left the mausoleum and tomb of Alzias de Saunhac, Seigneur de Belcastel, builder of the church. Nearby are three 15C statues, the *Virgin and Child*, St Anthony Hermit and Mary Magdalene and a 15C St Christopher with the infant Christ on his shoulders in the north transept.

Villefranche-de-Rouergue

Villefranche-de-Rouergue is a delightful market town beside the Aveyron at the centre of an important agricultural region. At its heart is a 13C *bastide* whose importance was measured by its markets and fairs which are still active. The weekly markets, held on the central square, have colourful and fragrant stalls and fairs were, and are still, held monthly outside the city walls, now replaced by leafy avenues.

History

Alphonse de Poitiers chose a strategically advantageous position at the cross-roads between Montauban, Cahors, Figeac, Rodez and Albi, to found this bastide in 1252. Privileges granted in 1256 drew peasants and rich merchants alike, and in 1342–43 the town was enclosed within walls. When, in 1369, Villefranche became the headquarters of the Sénéchaussée de Rouergue it took on the role of administrative and judiciary capital of the province, thus reducing Rodez's authority to religious and feudal capital.

Villefranche continued to prosper and develop to become, by the end of the century, one of the main bastides of the southwest and with the re-opening of the ancient bronze and silver mines in the surrounding hills, it was granted (c 1370) the right to mint coins. Handsome religious artefacts in silver were also created here (see Conques). As a result of the wealth that ensued, many buildings were refashioned in the 15C. The ideas of the Reformation pene-trated Villefranche in the mid-16C but, suppressed by Monluc, the Protestants fled to St-Antonin-Noble-Val. During the 1643, as in many regions (see Monpazier, Domme), there was short-lived peasant uprising (*révolte de croquants*) against heavy taxation and appalling conditions, but were met with harsh reprisals. With the creation of the Département de l'Aveyron at the Revolution, Villefranche lost its prestige as provincial capital.

There are three important religious monuments, the collegiate church, the chapel of the Pénitents-Noirs, and the 15C charterhouse of St-Sauveur. The tourist office is near the main bridge. From there, follow the river bank past Rue de la République at the end of the pedestrianised Pont des Consuls and turn down **Rue Polier**, lined with interesting old buildings. Turn left at Rue du Sénéchal and cross Rue de la République—to the right a view of the mighty belfry of Notre-Dame—and continue straight on to a small square with the only fountain in town, Le Griffoul (dated 1336) and the **Musée Cabrol** of archaeol-ogy and local history. Open July–15 Sept, Mon–Sat 09.00–12.00 and 14.00–18.00, closed Sun and PH; 16 Sept–June, Mon–Fri 08.30–12.00 and 13.30–18.00, closed Sat, Sun, PH. Turn right up Rue du Sergeant Bories and near the junction with Rue Marcellin Fabre there is, at the foot of a stairtower on the left, a finely carved doorway (c 1490). Turn left on Rue M. Fabre and very soon on the right is another stairtower with a splendid late Gothic door. Turn right on Rue Flassadiers/Rue Campmas to the chapel of the **Pénitents-Noirs**, begun in 1641, and one of the best Baroque churches in the Midi-Pyrénées. Open daily June–Sept 10.00–12.00 and 14.00–18.30, but enquire at tourist office. Soberly Classical from the exterior but with a curious octagonal lantern, the restored interior adds another dimension. In the shape of a quadrangle with mitred corners, its eight main ribs support the wooden lantern. The walls and timber ceiling were painted in the 17C. The ceiling, completed in 1701, includes scenes from the *Legend of the True Cross*. The overall effect was altered when the pilasters were marbled (1784) and stucco reliefs added but some of the marbling has been removed and the paintings underneath revealed. In 1709 the gilded retable was installed with *Scenes of the Passion* on four panels.

On Place St-Jacques the door marked Hôtel de la Charité is on the site of the old pilgrim *hôpital*, and in Rue St-Jacques is the façade of the 15C chapel of St-Jacques. Turn left into Rue Cabrol and right into Rue Halle, the site of the old grain market, which arrives above **Place Notre-Dame**. Among the tall arcaded houses surrounding the square is the Hôtel de Raynal on the south, an attractive early Renaissance façade with *bâton écoté* mouldings around the door and first-floor windows and carved label-stops including an *Annunciation*.

The overpoweringly huge belfry-porch of the collegiate church of **Notre-Dame** straddles the northeast corner of the square. The first stone of the church was laid in 1260, shortly after the foundation of the *bastide*; the vaults were com-pleted in 1480, and it was consecrated in 1519. The Flamboyant belfry was completed *c* 1560, although the spire was never built and it is topped off with a rather inadequate structure. It takes the traditional form of Gothic churches in the Midi, a nave without aisles and chapels, with tall windows between the buttresses. The east end of the church is Rayonnant, the west Flamboyant. The choir has heavily restored 15C glass, a gift of Charles VII. The stalls, with interesting and amusing misericords (*c* 1480) by André Sulpice, were badly damaged at some point. The pulpit is also 15C. The medallion of the altar in the north transept is attributed to Pierre Puget. The church contains paintings recovered from convents or other religious houses in Villefranche. The streets south of the church are worth exploring, notably **Rue Guillaume-de-Garrigues**, which leads back to the river.

The **Chartreuse St-Sauveur**, about 1km away on the D922, is one of the few charterhouses to have been preserved. Open June–Sept daily 10.00–12.00 and 14.00–18.30; other times enquire at tourist office.

When the charterhouse was begun in the 15C, Villefranche-de-Rouergue was a flourishing commercial town with some 8000 inhabitants. It was built with the fortune bequeathed by a rich draper, Vézian Valette, who died in Rome in 1450; his widow, Catherine Garnier, took over the task, which began in 1451. Such was the size of the donation that the church, the large cloister and the chapter house were completed in seven years, the small cloister between 1458 and 1460, and a chapel was added in 1528. Apart from a few outbuildings and the development of the agricultural annexes in the 17C, it was not altered until the community was dispersed in 1790, when it was bought by the town. It was used by the hospital until a few years ago.

The Carthusian order, founded by St Bruno in 1086, was strict but not as strict as the Cistercian rule. The monks lived according to the rules of solitude, silence and devotion while fulfilling the needs of a communal life. To accomplish this they lived in hermitages, small self-contained maisonettes on two floors with gardens, opening on to the large cloister.

The architecture and decoration is uniformly Flamboyant and has been subjected to very few restorations. The large west porch of the **church** protects carved door panels with two monks holding the coats of arms of Vézian Valette and Catherine Garnier. Inside is a simple space, the nave and polygonal choir divided by a screen. The choir contains 30 stalls (*c* 1461) with decorated armrests and misericords and beautiful carved panels, from the workshop of André Sulpice. North of the altar is a memorial to the founders and their tomb with engraved effigies; also some original glass, richly carved bosses and brackets, and a 16C chapel on the north.

The vestibule, between the church and the chapter house, has 15C glass, and the chapter house has a polygonal apse and three admirable windows with a *Nativity*, a *choir of angels*, *St George* and *St Catherine*, and carved capitals and bosses. The refectory, which has a beautiful pulpit, is usually closed. The magnificent but soberly uniform great Gothic **cloister** (60m by 40m) has remained intact. Around it are 12 hermitages, two of them original. The small cloister is more ornate and quite outstanding with 20 bays decorated with pendant bosses sculpted with the arms of the founders, 16 different adaptations of the reticulated tracery, and crocketed pinnacles and gargoyles on the piers. In the southwest, near the refectory, the lavabo has a carved relief of the **Washing of the Disciples' Feet**.

West of Villefranche-de-Rouergue on the D926 is the **Abbaye de Loc Dieu**, a former Cistercian monastery, confusing at first sight as the ancient remains are camouflaged by a 19C pastiche of a Loire château and a landscaped park. The church, chapter house and cloister of the abbey can be visited. Open July–mid-Sept 10.00–12.00 and 14.00–18.00; closed Tues; ☎ 05 65 29 51 17.

> Monks from the Limousin founded it in 1123, and a stone to the right of the church door records two dates, 1124, the beginning of the abbey, and 1159, the start of the last church, completed 30 years later. The abbey suffered the fate of most religious foundations—decline, destruction and dismember-ment—but at its lowest ebb, in 1812, it was purchased by the Cibiel family who have restored and renewed the buildings.

The pure and simple exterior of the church has been straightforwardly restored. A large part of the nave is 12C, with a shallow transept with square chapels and a pentagonal apse. The walls were heightened in the second half of the 13C and the apse *c* 1300, explaining the tall, narrow two-light plate-tracery windows and another in the west end, and the rib vaults (the aisles are barrel vaulted). Above the crossing is a square tower with three bays of two-light openings and a steep roof. It is generally free of decoration or ornament, according to the rules of St Bernard, and the drama of the interior depends greatly on the play of light and shade with an occasional carved element. The late Gothic cloisters with low wide arches and vaults springing from decorated imposts belong to the third stage of rebuilding, begun in 1470, as does the chapter house, which has three openings and three equal naves, the vaults supported by two slender clustered columns. The rest of the abbey was turned into a comfortable home in the Romantic man-ner of the 19C. In 1940, when France's art treasures were at risk, this small château in the Rouergue became the repository, for a short time, for none other than Leonardo's **Mona Lisa** and **La Belle Ferronière** (see also p 186).

The Gorges de l'Aveyron

These are less well-known than the Gorges du Tarn, and therefore much less crowded. The roads around here are narrow and winding but picturesque. The Aveyron is popular for canoeing and other water sports.

Najac, west of the D922 between Villefranche and Laguépie, stretched out pre-cariously along a clifftop ridge above a loop in the Aveyron, is a great attrac-tion.The *cité* and *bourg* developed below the castle, and were separated by a wall and gateway from the *faubourg* (or *barry*) to the east until the 18C. The Place du Faubourg is the only part that has *bastide* characteristics and is known to have existed in 1258. More a wide street than a square, it has a fountain and *couverts* on the south. The houses close in as the street descends into the *bourg*, framing a view of the castle. On the left there is an ancient fountain (1344) carved from a single block of granite.

Rue du Château marks the entrance to the *cité* and climbs up to the **château** at the west. Open daily July, Aug 10.00–13.00 and 15.00–19.00; June 10.00–12.30 and 15.00–18.30; April, May, Sept 10.00–12.30 and 15.00–17.30; closed Nov–Mar and PH, ☎ 05 65 29 71 65. Alphonse de Poitiers incorporated a 12C castle, including the Tour Carrée, into his fort of 1253, adding four linked towers and a tall keep with three floors. The castle is surrounded by a wall with a square tower and the *salle de justice* with two fine windows. Despite many periods of destruction by rival lords, Cathars, English, Protestants and *croquants* (peasants) the château was finally ruined only in the 19C when it was used as a quarry.

Further east still is the 13C church of **St-Jean-l'Evangéliste**, built after the Albigensian heresies by the Cathar community, who were forced by the Inquisition to replace the 12C church of St-Martin. Erected 1258–75, it was one of the first Gothic churches in the Rouergue. Severe but well built, it is without aisles and has a flat east end; the plate-tracery windows of 1320 have mid-19C glass. Among the furnishings are the original altar, used as a step for 150 years and returned to its rightful place in 1966, and a 15C *Crucifixion* with a 16C Virgin and St John.

It would be easy to pass through **Varen** on the D598 without noticing its treasures. The Romanesque church (second half 11C) on the main road was originally part of a Benedictine monastery dedicated to Notre-Dame-et-St-Pierre, which became the collegiate, then parish, church of **St-Serge**. The simple west entrance opens into an austere 11-bay nave with a continuous tunnel vault, flat apse and windows only on the south. There is no transept and the nave is buttressed by narrow aisles ending in semi-circular apses over crypts. The interesting capitals are concentrated around the choir and apses, inside and outside. The interlace motif in the south chapel is the oldest (*c* 1070–80). Others have vegetal and animal elements and are even storiated, including Daniel in the Lions' Den and archangels Raphael and Gabriel. The most accomplished capitals in the choir may be as late as the early 12C, and some carry traces of polychromy. Over the choir is a domical vault supporting the belfry. The flat apse is a mystery. Altered in the 14C—there are Romanesque capitals on the exterior (*St Michael and the Dragon*, *Samson and the Lion*)—it was possibly transformed from a semi-circle at some point to create access, then closed when the situation changed.

It is worth taking some time to explore the village. On the south side of the church the 15C château has been transformed into the *mairie*, and further on is a pretty fountain. Between the two, the 15C town gateway leads to the old streets, the market place and eventually a restored mill on the banks of the Aveyron.

The pretty village of **Verfeil** on the D33 has a small covered market and a Baroque altarpiece. On the same road is the **Abbaye de Beaulieu-en-Rouergue**. Open July, Aug daily 10.00–12.00 and 14.00–18.00; Apr–1 Nov, Mon, Wed–Sun 10.00–12.00 and 14.00–18.30, closed Tues; ☎ 05 63 24 50 10. Visits to the abbey are with a guide. Like all Cistercian abbeys established near water and woodland, this is a stunning place and the temporary exhibitions of contemporary art, held here since 1974 in what was the lay brothers' dormitory, are a bonus. The church is a rigorous structure, begun *c* 1275 and completed in the 14C, rhythmically articulated by tall buttresses, narrow lancets and seven plate-tracery rose windows. It has been heavily restored. The chapter house, with three open bays and traces of coloured wall paintings, is a superb piece of 13C architecture. Most of the monastic buildings were repaired and amended in the 17C and 18C.

St-Antonin-Noble-Val

To the southwest, on the north bank of the Aveyron on the D958, St-Antonin-Noble-Val is a superb and not over-prettified town, crammed with vestiges of medieval houses and a very lively market, most definitely a place to linger in. It dips its feet in the Aveyron and is overlooked by the craggy Roc d'Anglars to the south. The best place to park is north of the town at a large tree-lined junction with the D19. This is a popular site for canoeing.

A Benedictine monastery, established in Nobilis Vallis in 763, protected the relics of St Antonin, martyr of Pamiers in the Ariège. The town grew around the abbey, now replaced by the presbytery and the *école maternelle* on the southwest of the town where the little Bonnette runs into the Aveyron. The availability of water maintained a thriving leather industry in the Middle Ages and the streets bear witness to a very prosperous past, although St-Antonin, too, had its share of upheavals. There was a small spa here at the beginning of the century and now the mineral water is bottled.

St-Antonin boasts, among its many medieval houses, one of France's oldest civic buildings, on Place de la Halle, the ancient Hôtel de Ville or **Maison Romane**, also called *palais vicomtal* (Palace of the Viscounts). This is a magnificent example of Romanesque architecture, realised 1150–55. The three-bay façade abuts a tower on the south and on street level are four large archways. The main elevation has an open gallery, its full length divided by piers into three four-light bays. The piers carry some remarkable sculpture. On the right are *Adam and Eve*, and on the left a figure holding a book and a sceptre with an eagle, the *Emperor Justinian*. Justinian I, Christian emperor of Byzantium (527–65), pioneered legislative justice in his time and was considered during the Middle Ages as the first judge, the symbol of justice. This iconography suggests that the large room on this floor originally had a judicial function. Each bay is divided by paired columns with carved capitals, seven figurative representing the vices, and eleven vegetal. On the top floor are three two-light bays with round arches under a continuous moulding. Indentations in the façade once contained coloured enamelled ceramic discs (the museum has some fragments). The tower has two superimposed two-light windows; the upper trilobed opening was remade in the 19C, and the Tuscan-style campanile was added by Viollet-le-Duc in the 19C. It is used by the **Musée du Vieux St-Antonin**, with some archaeological finds from the Grotte de Bosc, but a rather dull place. Open July–Aug 10.00–13.00 and 15.00–18.00; other times by appointment; ☎ 05 63 68 23 52. The ticket also includes a visit to the Moulin de l'Huile de Noix on Pl. le Bessarel.

Opposite, the *halle* of 1840 shelters a 15C discoidal stele with a *Crucifixion* on one side and on the other the *Virgin and Child* between two bishops, one of them St Eligius. Southwest of Pl. de la Halle is the elegant **Mairie** (1751), formerly the convent of the Génovéfains. Next door is the neo-Gothic church (1862) and behind the *mairie* are some beautifully restored houses with galleries and *mirandes*. St-Antonin was a buffer town during the Hundred Years War and for a time the English had their garrison in Rue Guilhem Peyre, behind the Maison Romane, a street with many other small and interesting details. The **Roc d'Anglars** makes a scenic expedition with views over St-Antoinin and the valley. So do the **Grottes de Bosc**, northeast on the D75, with stalagmites, stalactites and *excentrique* (as opposed to concentric) formations. Open July–Aug daily 10.00–12.00 and 14.00–18.00; ☎ 05 63 30 62 91.

A 12km detour north of St-Antonin-Noble-Val on the D19 brings you to **Caylus**, in the valley of the Bonnette, its old centre hidden in a hollow beside the main road and the tall spire of the church indicating its presence. Rue Droite, which runs the length of the village from the church to the Place de la Mairie, and the quaint alleyways which intersect it have examples of Gothic or Renaissance houses, most notably the Maison des Loups (13C) with Gothic windows and high-relief carvings. In the market place is a 15C *halle* with 18 octagonal pillars protecting the old grain measures (1714). Further west on a terrace overlooking the valley is a 13C *donjon* of the ruined castle.

The church of **St-Jean-Baptiste** (14C/15C) has a stone steeple (15C) and steep slate-covered roof with tiny dormers. The entrance on the northwest is decorated with a continuous frieze, a *Virgin and Child* on the right of the door and animals on the left. The elegant seven-sided apse dates from 1470 and the tall lancets contain stained glass of the same date mixed with glass added during restoration in 1868. Hidden away, despite its monumental size, is an anguished *Christ* (1954), arms upstretched, pinned to the wall by one hand. It was carved from the trunk of an elm by Ossip Zadkine who made Caylus his home in the 1950s (p 190). There are several inscribed tombstones in the floor of the church: the most beautiful, near the Christ, is that of Coligny, Chevalier de Malte, killed at the siege of St-Antonin on 21 June 1622.

Lacapelle-Livron on the D19 north of Caylus has the remains of a Templar-Hospitaller commandery (13C–18C) with a fortified Romanesque church adjoining it (private). Just 1km south of Lacapelle is a tiny isolated Gothic chapel of Notre-Dame-des-Graces in a marvellous position on the cliff above the Bonnette (key with Abbot Jourdes).

The **Château de Cas**, south of Caylus on the D19, at Espinas, is a medieval castle transformed in the 16C into a Renaissance château. It was entirely restored in the 20C to repair damage wrought by the Revolution and the Second World War. Guided visit; open July, Aug, Tues–Sun 10.00–12.00 and 14.00–18.00, closed Mon; by appointment April–June, Sept, Oct Sat & Sun only; ☎ 01 63 67 07 04.

For a while the Aveyron runs north–south. **Penne**, perched precariously on the cliff above the road, is a village strung out along a narrow promontory with the fragile ruins of a 13C château overhanging the Aveyron valley. It has a small square and a church which has been reorientated, and beside the church an archway with a bell.

Bruniquel is an extraordinarily picturesque ensemble on a rock between the Aveyron and the Vère Rivers. On the threshhold of the Quercy, the Albigeois and the Rouergue it grew wealthy from important medieval fairs dealing in flax, hemp and saffron. The main street leading up the hill from the church (17C and 19C) passes under one of the three remaining gateways of the old ramparts and 14C–16C houses. To the left is the **Maison Payrol**, named after an important local family, a fascinating sample of civil architecture (14C–17C), built above an ancient vaulted cellar. It includes a room for receiving pilgrims or travellers, medieval wall paintings, fireplaces, a variety of windows, and a remarkable 15C sculpted ceiling over what was once a granary. There is also a collection of stone carving and documentation recording the history of the village and the château. Open April–Sept daily 10.00–18.00; ☎ 05 63 67 26 42.

At the summit are the two **Châteaux de Bruniquel**, the property of the Counts of Toulouse in the 12C and divided between two branches of the family in the 14C. Open July, Aug daily 10.00–18.00; April, June, Sept Sun and PH 10.00–18.00, other days 14.00–18.00; May, Oct, Sun and PH 10.00–18.00; ☎ 05 63 67 27 67. The Château Vieux still has its 12C keep, called the Tour de la Reine Brunehaut after the legendary Merovingian queen who reigned over the Quercy *c* 600, as well as the 13C–14C ramparts. The main part of the building was extensively altered in the 18C and 19C with the addition of an arcaded terrace looking out towards the Aveyron Valley. Changes were made in the 17C and 18C to the Château Jeune, built between 1485 and 1510.

Montricoux, to the east, is a small unspoilt town remarkable for the number of 15C–16C timber-framed houses using mud brick or wattle-and-daub infill. To the west of the village the 13C–16C church of St-Pierre was once the chapel of a Templar commandery; one of the vault bosses is carved with a tau-cross. The tall octagonal brick belfry was added *c* 1549 to a massive stone base. The church has a narrow nave and pentagonal apse decorated with a mural of the *Annunciation* by Marcel Lenoir and modern glass in the windows. The Counts of Montricoux had a funerary chapel here. Among the fittings are an ancient stoup and font, a 12C statue of St Peter, and diverse retables.

Opposite the church is a large square tower with shallow buttresses. The former keep of the Templar commandery has been integrated into an 18C château which houses the **Musée Marcel-Lenoir**. Open 1 April–15 Oct 10.00–12.30 and 14.30–18.00; ☎ 05 63 67 26 48. This is a private collection of the work of Lenoir (1872–1931), who was born in Montauban and died in Montricoux, displayed in an elegantly colourful setting. The 121 exhibits, among them many portraits, demonstrate the influence of the Nabis and Maurice Denis as well as Lenoir's interest in fresco technique and his mystic tendencies. The visit also includes the 12C Templar *salle de garde*.

Bioule, further west near Negrepelisse, is a tiny community at whose heart is the modest stone and brick Château de Cardaillac on the banks of the Aveyron. Open July, Aug 15.00–19.00; June, Sept weekends; ☎ 05 63 30 95 62. Owned for five centuries by the powerful family of Cardaillac, the château was built at the beginning of the 12C, almost entirely rebuilt in 1329, and modified in the 16C. The St-Sauveur chapel has 14C murals, and in the late 15C the *salle des preux* received its painted décor.

12 Millau and the Grands Causses

THE PLATEAU DE LÉVÉZOU AND MILLAU

The Lévézou is a high plateau separating the two main towns of the Aveyron, Rodez and Millau, and dividing the wetter, wooded western Rouergue from the dryer and more Mediterranean east. At 1000m above sea-level it is exposed but its numerous artificial lakes are a big attraction to visitors looking for outdoor pursuits such as windsurfing, sailing, canoeing and fishing.

Getting there and around
Car

A75/N9, Clermont-Ferrand to Millau.
D911 Rodez to Millau.
Train

Paris Austerlitz to Béziers via Sévérac-le-Château, Millau (*SNCF*, ☎ 05 65 60 34 02).
Clermont-Ferrand to Toulouse via Sévérac-le-Château (*SNCF*, ☎ 05 65 71 61 19) and Millau.
Rodez to Séverac-le-Château via Laissac.
Bus

Regular services from Millau to St-Affrique, St-Jean-du-Bruel, and Montpellier l'Hospitalet du Larzac.
In summer, Gorges du Tarn via Aguessac, Rivière-sur-Tarn, Le Rozier.

 Tourist information
12103 Millau 1 Pl. du Beffroi, BP 331, ☎ 05 65 60 02 42, fax 05 65 60 95 08, www.ot-millau.fr
12290 Pont-de-Salars Pl. de la Mairie, ☎ 05 65 46 89 90, fax 05 65 46 81 16
12410 Salles-Curan-Pareloup Pl. de la Vierge, ☎ 05 65 46 31 73
12150 Séverac-le-Château 5 rue des Douves, ☎ 05 65 47 67 31, fax 05 65 47 65 94, www.severaclechateau.com
Market days

Millau Wednesday and Friday
Pont-de-Salars July, August, Saturday morning, Wednesday evening
Séverac-le-Château Thursday and July–August Friday evening
Sales-Curan Saturday and July–August Tuesday evening
Guided tours

July, Aug guided visits around Millau old town; enquire at tourist office.
Activities

On and around the lakes of Lévézou are facilities for sailing, windsurfing, dinghy sailing and canoeing.

Festivals and events

July *Millau sur Scene*, dance festival.
Millau en Jazz
July/Aug *Festival Européen de l'Espace*, Millau
August *Festival Folkorique international du Rouergue*, Pont-de-Salars
Mémoire de Sévérac, history of the village in sound and light, Sévérac-le-Château

 Where to stay and eating out
12700 LOUPIAC
☆☆☆ *Le Mûrier de Viels*, close to Sévérac-le-Château, ☎ 05 65 80 89 82, fax 05 65 80 12 20, www.murierdeviels.fr.st. Set in 6ha grounds with pool and other activities, embellished with modern sculpture, this hotel has just eight impeccably presented bedrooms.
12103 MILLAU
☆☆☆ *La Musardière*, 34 Av. de la République, 05 65 60 20 63, fax 05 65 59 78 13, email hotel-lamusardiere@wanadoo.fr. Elegant 14 bedroom stately

home in centre of Millau, with restaurant.
☆☆ *Château de Creissels*, Rte de St-
Affrique, Creissels, on D922, ☎ 05 65
60 16 59, fax 05 65 61 24 63,
www.chateau-de-cressels.com.
Set in a park, with a restaurant
in a vaulted cellar.

1 2 4 1 0 S A L L E S - C U R A N
☆☆ *Hostellerie du Lévézou*, Rue du
Château, ☎ 05 65 46 34 16, fax 05 65
46 01 19, www.hostelleriedulevezou.
com. Fairly inexpensive, in green
surroundings.

East of Rodez there is an impressive little fortified church at **Ste-Radegonde**
with an arcaded belfry with a pointed roof on top of the machicolated tower.
Another similar fortified church at the charming village of **Inières** further south
protects a superb *Annunciation* group (*c* 1470), which probably comes from the
cathedral at Rodez.

Pont-de-Salars is on a smallish lake but to the south is the vast **Lac de
Pareloup** (1300ha), into which a thousand streams pour their contents to
supply the hydro-electric stations on the Tarn River. **Salles-Curan** is a strange
mixture of old and new. It has become an important centre for tourism, benefiting from the lake, but the town has narrow streets and old houses, and a bit of
19C kitsch in the form of a polychromed statue of the Virgin with a rakish starry
halo, of which the bishops of Rodez, who resided here in the 15C, may or may
not have approved. The 15C church has some fine carved choir stalls adorned
with a whole range of beasts and vegetal motifs. The human figures have fared
less well. There is some restored 15C glass. The bishops' residence, also 15C, is
now a hotel. The Renaissance house below the church with an angle window is
where the *dimes* (tithes) were collected.

Les Canabières, to the southeast on the D44, is a severe schist hilltop village
which seems to consist entirely of farms, if the aromas are anything to go by. The
first Templar commandery in the Rouergue was established here and the church
made over to the Knights in 1120. Unlike the village, the church porch is in pinkish sandstone, and the tympanum has carved reliefs. The low, narrow church
has a few carvings inside and an upturned capital used as a holy water stoup.

Montjaux, further southeast on the D993, is the most stunning of this series
of villages, clinging, as the best always do, to the side of a high escarpment and
looking out over the Grands Causses and the Muze Valley towards Roquefort.
Washed in red, the houses are arranged in tiers stretching out along the hillside,
with a stocky Romanesque church at the far end. The ruins of an old château,
supposedly on the site of a temple dedicated to Jupiter, look down on it, and there
is a 'newer' château (16C–17C) below. The delightful church, in pink sandstone
with blue-grey slate roofs, was originally part of a priory attached to Chaise Dieu
(Auvergne) and shows the stylistic influence of that region. It is mainly 12C,
with some 15C parts and a façade and belfry rebuilt in 1856. Over the crossing
is a domed lantern on pendentives. It has a number of capitals with large simple
carvings of animals and birds, monsters in combat and other fantastic beasts.

North of Montjoux, **Castelnau-Pégayrolles** is a sensational red sandstone
village, a tiny place among the chestnuts and oaks, magnificent in the autumn.
It is a little neglected, with interesting windows and the odd sculpted cornice.
There is a cluster of 15C–16C houses around the château, one of the oldest in
the Rouergue. Open June, July 14.30–18.30, closed Tues; April–Nov open to
groups by appointment only; ☎ 05 65 52 00 94/out of season ☎ 01 46 33 72

73. The village, above the Muze, is fortress-like, with two churches, both dating from the 11C. The larger, the parish church of St-Michel, was begun in the 11C but was subsequently modified in the 13C and 15C. The older church of Notre-Dame (11C–12C) in the cemetery has some wall paintings.

St-Beauzély on the D30 is a high fortified village with a 16C castle that is part of the Musée de Rouergue de la Vie Rurale and exhibits some 2500 objects associated with agriculture, rural life and stone working. Open July, Aug daily 10.30–12.30 and 14.30–18.30; May, June, Sept 14.30–18.30; ☎ 05 65 52 03 90. The 12C priory of Combéroumal, on the D171 west of the village, was an austere Grandmontain monastery.

At **St-Léons**, the village where the eminent entomologist Jean-Henri Fabre was born, is **Micropolis**, 'city of insects'. Open daily July, Aug 10.00–19.00; June, Sept 10.00–18.00, closed Mon; March–May, Oct–Dec 11.00–17.00, closed Mon; ☎ 05 65 58 50 50, www.micropolis-cite-des-insectes.tm.fr. Somewhere between a museum and a theme park, this is presented as a voyage into the world of insects in their natural environment. There are 13 themed interactive exhibitions, state-of-the-art models, giant beehives, a butterfly house and vivaria for observing insect life in close to natural conditions. Multi-lingual audioguides are available. It is impressive, educational and fun.

Jean-Henri Fabre (1823–1915) started out as a mathematician and scientist, but his interest in the natural world developed from 1851 in Corsica. He was a born teacher, his studies wide-ranging, and he acquired great academic honours. His numerous writings and theses ranged from hunter wasps to agricultural chemistry, hymenopteras and a book of stories.

Vezins has a 12C/17C château. Open June–Sept, 10.00–12.00 and 14.00–19.00; ☎ 05 65 61 87 02.

Sévérac-le-Château is the point of entry to the Rouergue on the A75, midway between Rodez and Millau, and is handy for the Causses and the Aubrac. The medieval town is entered through a fortified gate and dominated by the ruins of a large feudal castle. The château shows the signs of wear and tear resulting from frequent conflicts and subsequent restorations. Open July, Aug daily 09.00–19.00, 15–30 June, Sept daily 10.00–12.30 and 14.30–18.00; May–15 June Sat, Sun PH 10.00–12.00 and 14.30–18.00.

Millau

Millau is a vibrant and active *sous-préfecture* of the Aveyron, at the eastern extremity of the Midi-Pyrénées. Although not as obviously eye-catching as Rodez or Albi, Millau stands at the centre of spectacular landscapes, on the right bank of the Tarn near the confluence with the Dourbie, and is surrounded by the omnipresent Grands Causses, limestone plateaux on the edge of the Cevennes. It is in an excellent position for exploring the wonderful rugged countryside and some unusual sites, such as Templar commanderies and Roman potteries, and is well placed for a visit to the gorges which are part of Languedoc-Roussillon. The A75, a new *autoroute* linking Clermont-Ferrand with Montpellier, passes by Millau. The last link in this major project (due for completion in 2005) is the construction of a massive viaduct 2460m long, designed by Norman Foster, to span the Tarn Valley at a height of 343m in places.

History

Ancient civilisations (*c* 2500–1500 BC) inhabited the caves in the region and erected dolmens and menhirs, but it was not until *c* 2C BC that people came down from the hills. The Celtic tribe, the Rutenes, called their settlement *Condatomagos*, 'market-town on the confluence'. The Romans established an important pottery manufactory here from 10 BC to AD 150, and throughout the Middle Ages it was a major commercial centre, trading leather, cloth and copper with goods from the Languedoc seaports. By the 8C the town was known as *Amiliavum*, and Millau achieved autonomous rule in the 12C by an oligarchy of consuls, but lost its independence in 1361 when it came under English domination. It picked itself up again during the period of peace following the Hundred Years War, then, unlike most of the Rouergue, embraced the Reformation in the 16C.

The leather trade, and especially glove-making using the pelts of lambs sacrificed to assure sufficient milk for cheese production, was already well established and expanded with the town through the 18C and 19C and flourished until the 1930s—everyone wore gloves in Millau. There are still *gantiers* (glovers) at work in Millau, among them *Maison Fabre*, 18–20 Boulevard Gambetta. The two traditional industries, pottery and glove-making, are also represented at the museum. Most of the medieval buildings were destroyed at the Reformation but the town has retained its medieval layout.

At the centre of Millau is **Place du Mandarous**, a half-circle where four large boulevards meet. The tourist office is to the northwest, off Boulevard de la République, and the old town is to the south, enclosed by boulevards forming an oval, which replaced the city walls. Take the narrow Rue du Mandarous and turn left on to **Rue Droite**, the former main street, parallel with the river, a pleasant pedestrian street of small shops. This brings you to **Le Beffroi** (13C–17C) which is the leitmotif of Millau, towering 42m over the old town. To visit, ☎ 05 65 59 50 32. The lower square section is all that remains of the 12C tower which was part of the city defences and represented seigneurial power. It was bought by the town in 1613 and subsequently became a symbol of municipal authority; the upper octagonal section was built to contain a bell and the town clock.

The vast **Place Emma Calvé** is named after an Aveyronnaise opera singer (1858–1942), heralded locally as *notre Carmen*, a role she sang 1389 times. After the Beffroi turn left to the large covered **market**, a huge metal-and-brick construction with cellars, which was erected in 1899 and renovated in 1984–85, when Boulevard Sadi-Carnot and Rue Coussergues were created.

Return to Rue Droite and carry on to **Place Grégoire**, with interesting 17C façades, doorways and a corbelled angle tower. This in turn leads to **Place du Maréchal-Foch**, the prettiest, and the oldest, square in Millau and the only public space in the old town. Along one side are arcades with a colonnade of cylindrical piers which, according to popular tradition, come from cloisters destroyed during the Religious Wars. However, the capital above the stone table in the northwest, possibly part of the old pillory, has an inscription in Occitan '*gara que faras enant que comences*', the salutary message that you should give a thought to what you are about to do before you begin. The oldest houses on the north are 15C–16C; in the centre is a cool fountain (1835); and the old grain market of 1836 is now occupied by a school.

North of the square is the church of **Notre-Dame-de-l'Espinasse**, mainly post-Reformation. From the time it reopened in 1646 until 1828 it was the only parish church in Millau. Little remains of the church consecrated in 1095 except perhaps the lower walls of the heavily buttressed east end and the base of the belfry (also 17C), which is Toulousain in style. The west façade is pure Baroque. The interior space is straightforward, without aisles but with the addition of a gallery on three sides, and a seven-sided apse with murals by Jean Bernard (1940); the glass, blues to the north and pinks to the south, was made by Claude Baillon (1984).

On the southeast side of Place Foch is the **Musée de Millau** in the 18C Hôtel de Pégayrolles. Open May–June, Sept daily 10.00–12.00 and 14.00–18.00; July, Aug daily 10.00–18.00; Oct–March Mon–Sat 10.00–12.00 and 14.00–18.00; ☎ 05 65 59 01 08. Sober but genteel, the building is arranged around a U-shaped courtyard and has a fine staircase inside. The museum is divided between archaeology to the left and gloves to the right. The archaeological section has an area devoted to local palaeontology with the fossilised footprint of a dinosaur. The Bronze Age is also represented. The Gallo-Roman period (1C–4C) is made up mainly of objects from the site of Graufesenque (see below) and includes lamps, fibulae (brooches), money, figurines in white and in terracotta pottery, bronze statuettes, mosaics and some glass, and pots as far as the eye can see. The potters of Graufesenque were expert in sigillated pottery (red with an embossed decoration) and the techniques, stages and periods of production from 10 BC to AD 250 are explained. Ceramics from Graufesenque were exported as far as Scotland, North Africa, even India. There is a room devoted to Millau from the 10C to the 18C and another to a week in the life of an everyday Rutene.

Up the stairs on the right of the entrance is a pretty octagonal room with a coffered vault and gloves of all kinds—long, short, coloured, flashy, sporting, old, new, and some from Buffalo Bill's last show in Paris. There is all you ever wanted to know about glove-making here, from tanning the skins (*megisserie*) to glove design. There is also an exhibition of dolls, which may or may not appeal to children (the dinosaur footprints will probably fare better), with ... mini gloves.

Turn left out of the museum, through the covered passageway, right on Rue Guilhem-Estève and left on to Rue Haute to the **Quartier du Voultre**. The Dominican convent was destroyed by the Calvinists who took over the 16C church, and eventually a new Protestant Temple was built in 1869. The Porte du Voultre was probably part of the old fortifications and gave its name to the leather-workers' quarter. Rue du Voultre comes out into Boulevard de l'Ayrolle, built on the old city ditches. To the left is the Tarn and the Rue de la Tannerie will bring you to **Pont Lerouge** (1821), next to which are two arches of the 12C bridge and a 15C mill.

If you turn right at the end of Rue du Voultre you will find along on the left a small elegant colonnaded building, the grandest **lavoir** ever, in which citizens could wash their linen in public. Built in 1749 as part of an urbanisation scheme. it takes the form of a Neo-classical semi-circular pavilion with arcades.

Return to the old quarter down Rue St-Martin. Rue Peyroliers has interesting façades and leads back to Rue Droite. The church of **St-Martin**, on the south side of Place E.-Calvé, is a small simple church with a large Baroque painting of the *Descent from the Cross* attributed to the 17C Flemish painter Gaspar de Crayer.

The site of **Graufesenque** is across the Tarn via the Pont du Larzac, a short walk for the energetic or a five-minute car drive. On the plain where the Tarn and the Dourbie converge, the settlement covered some 10ha of which 4000m sq have been excavated. The site is well maintained and the visits are accompanied. Open 09.00–12.00 and 14.00–18.30; ☎ 05 65 60 11 37.

Excavations from 1973 to 1981 uncovered traces of three successive periods of habitation. In the Celtic and early Gallo-Roman period (2C–1C BC) there was intense commercial activity with the Mediterranean. From the 1C AD to the first half of the 2C, the workshops of Gallo-Roman potters attest to a massive production of pots for export. Later, 150–300 AD, there was a marked deterioration in the quality of the dwellings. The variety of buildings demonstrates the organisation of the community, and includes the modest homes of the potters and others, as well as two sanctuaries. There are also roads, gutters, drains, baths and hypocausts, to support the domestic side of life. The most fascinating are the buildings related to the enormous production of pottery—workshops, wells, clay-storage areas, and of course kilns. Three kilns have been uncovered: the largest (6.8m by 11.3m) could have held between 10,000 and 40,000 vessels at one firing. The industry was run on the lines of a cooperative, with a multitude of support activities, and at the height of its production there were about 500 potters working at Graufesenque.

THE CAUSSE NOIR, DOURBIE AND LARZAC

The Dourbie, having carved a route through the Causse Noir and the Causse du Larzac, unites with the Tarn at Millau. The landscape through which it flows is varied, from the valley, brindled with Romanesque churches and justly described as the Garden of the Rouergue to the barren and spectacular Causse du Larzac and its Templar villages.

Getting there and around
Bus
Millau regular service to St-Jean-du-Bruel, via La Mona, La Roque, Ste-Marguerite.
Millau to Montpellier regular service via La Cavalerie, l'Hospitalet du Larzac, le Caylar.

 Tourist information
12250 Roquefort-sur-Soulzon Av. de Lauras, ☎ 05 65 58 56 00, fax 05 65 58 56 01, www.roquefort.com
12230 Ste-Eulalie-de-Cernon Mairie, Le Bourg, ☎ 05 65 62 72 99
12400 St-Affrique Blvd de Verdun, ☎ 05 65 98 12 40, fax 05 65 98 12 41, email info.st-affrique@ roquefort.com

 Festivals and events
July–August *Les Festivals du Larzac*, medieval-style events in the Templar sites of the Larzan

 Where to stay and eating out
12230 ST-JEAN-DU-BRUEL
☆☆/€–€€ *Du Midi*, ☎ 05 65 62 26 04, fax 05 65 62 112 97.
L'Oustal, ☎ 05 65 62 29 87. Restaurant recommended.
12230 STE-EULALIE-DE-CERNON
Auberge la Cardabelle, ☎ 05 65 62 74 64.

East of Millau, the D991 almost immediately penetrates a deep and magnificent rift between the limestone cliffs. **Massebiau** is on a tight loop in the Dourbie and there are remains of castles which protected the access to the Causse Noir. The scenery becomes more rugged and the villages scattered along the valley are the inheritors of medieval forts defending the territory. **La Roque-Ste-Marguerite** is a small community with a château (rebuilt in the 17C) and church (11C and 18C) picturesquely clamped to the cliff. The extraordinary natural phenomena of **Montpellier le Vieux** (open April–Sept, 09.30–19.00) and **Roquesaltes** consist of groups of rocks resembling ruined and deserted villages. The **Grottes de Dargilan**, the pink grotto. Guided visits April, May, June, Sept 10.00–12.00 and 13.30–17.30; July, Aug 10.00–18.30; Oct 10.00–12.00 and 14.00–16.30; ☎ 04 66 45 60 20.

Beyond Ste-Marguerite the road crosses the Dourbie, and high above are tiny villages, some abandoned, such as **St-Véran** and **Cantobre**, in a vertiginously spectacular spot where the dolomitic rock and buildings merge into one craggy mass.

The valley now widens out, becomes gentler, and fulfils its description as the *Jardin du Rouergue*. On the edge of the route is the church of **Notre-Dame-des-Cuns**, the most complete Romanesque church in the valley. Built in golden limestone, it is compact and sturdy, with a polygonal apse, the only addition being a chapel in the 15C. Like many Romanesque churches in this vicinity with similar characteristics, it was affiliated to St-Victor at Marseille.

Nant is a village all the more charming in that a visit entails no climbing. On the banks of the Dourbie, it has a graceful 14C bridge, an arcaded 16C market with huge stone pillars and vaults (no longer used), and a *mairie* in an elegant 18C building with staircase and stucco. There is also a notable church with a massive, fortified west end. Once part of an important Benedictine abbey, the church of St-Pierre is all that remains. The pentagonal east end has conserved many of its 12C elements but the Romanesque narthex was amended two centuries later with the addition of a Gothic door and tower. The nave chapels are 14C and 19C, and the windows 19C. The interior is impressive and subtly lit. The nave has pointed barrel vaults supported by pairs of engaged columns and the short transept has apsidal chapels. The crossing is domed and the apse is semi-circular from the interior with three windows and simple decorations. There are 121 sculpted capitals altogether, mainly cubic in form, with stylised vegetal or geometric designs; they seem to be the work of several sculptors and some probably came from an earlier church.

Beyond Nant, on the edge of the Cévennes at St-Jean-de-Bruel, is **Noria**, an exhibition all about water in a restored 13C watermill on the banks of the Dourbie. A series of rooms and exhibitions explains the crucial role of water in the past, present, and the future. Open May, June, Sept 10.00–18.00, closed Mon; July, Aug daily 10.00–19.00; Oct–Dec 10.00–16.00, closed Mon; ☎ 05 65 62 20 32, www.noria-espacedeleau.com.

The desolate **Plateau du Larzac** is a vast territory of some 1000km sq, grazed by huge flocks of sheep.

It was once covered in forest but, cleared for agricultural purposes over many centuries, it evolved into its present grassland state in the 18C. Donations of land in the Rouergue were made to the Templars from the mid-12C, but the acquisition of the church of Ste-Eulalie in 1151 was the watershed. Gradually, by fair means or foul, they became the principal landowners of the Larzac, at times coming into conflict with their neighbours. The Larzac provided an important link between the Mediterranean and the Massif Central, and there was land aplenty for crops and horses. When the Templars were disbanded in 1312 their property was transferred to the Knights Hospitaller, who added fortifications to the settlements.

The Templar *cité* of **La Cavalerie** is submerged in a small town on the edge of the N9 and A75 so that it has much less appeal than St-Eulalie or La Couvertoirade. Nevertheless, more than half the 15C fortifications are still there, punctuated by three huge towers at the corners and over the main gateway. Along the old streets inside the walls are 15C–17C houses. The church, begun in the 12C, was almost entirely rebuilt 1760–61, but inside some fragments of the old building can still be seen.

Ste-Eulalie-de-Cernon is unmistakable, with five defensive towers and belfry standing proud above the red roofs. The Grande Rue leads up to a large open square with a 17C fountain. This was the cemetery until 1641 and marks the divide between the fortified town, enclosed in walls by the Hospitallers in the 15C, and the earlier Templar castle. A church here, on the site of the present one, was made over to the Templars in 1151. The present church is sober with little ornament and was reorientated in 1648. A new main door, with broken pediment and statue of the Virgin, was constructed in the former apse, to either side of which are the only old chapels (13C). The belfry was rebuilt in 1842 and the remainder of the chapels were opened out in the 19C. The château was built (1187–1249) around a courtyard but has suffered many vicissitudes and alterations. The oldest part is the façade facing the square, and only one of four original square towers remains. A wing was added in 1648 to provide an upper floor with a grand staircase, murals and mullioned windows.

La Couvertoirade on the D55 is probably the best known of the Templar towns. It is truly impressive, enclosed in 15C walls and isolated in a hollow in the rugged *causse*. The only entrance is through the Porte du Haut (the Porte du Bas collapsed in 1917). It is likely that the Templars took control of an existing community here some time towards the end of the 12C and by 1249 they had built the castle. La Couvertoirade remained a dependence of the commandery of Ste-Eulalie until made over to the Hospitallers in the 14C.

The series of fortified towers and curtain walls follows the irregular shape of the rock on which it is built, and from the ramparts is an overall view of the village. The 17C/18C Hôtel de la Scipione contains a permanent exhibition but the castle, incorporated into the *enceinte* in 1439, is now a ruin. The church opposite, a simple vaulted building with a tall tower that looks little different from the military buildings, was built by the Hospitallers in the 14C. Near the church is the communal oven, and below the flight of steps is a public reservoir, Les Conques, supplied by rainwater from the church roof. There are a number of delightful houses particularly along Rue Droite on the south, which formerly linked the two entrances, lined with 16C and 17C buildings with exterior steps up to the doors and vaulted cellars beneath.

From **Viala-du-Pas-de-Jaux** there is a stunning view over Ste-Eulalie. A massive fortified barn built here in the 15C by the Hospitallers is being restored.

Another pretty village, **St-Jean-d'Alcas**, has fortifications with four towers which are in good order.

Probably the most familiar name associated with the Aveyron is **Roquefort-sur-Soulzon**, famous for its blue cheese, which is the explanation for all those sheep on the *causse*.

Roquefort

Milk from some 800,000 sheep owned by 2500 farmers produce the cheese to which *Penicillium Roqueforti* is introduced. It is then wrapped and left to mature in cold, damp and draughty natural caves on long trestles—row upon row of silver discs—to acquire its blue veining and distinctive flavour. Only around the end of March is there a great deal of activity in the cellars, otherwise, except for being turned regularly, the cheeses are left to their own devices.

Three producers offer visits to the cellars or caves where the cheese matures: ***Roquefort Société***, ☎ 05 65 59 93 30, www.roquefort-societe.com; ***Roquefort Papillon***, ☎ 05 65 58 50 08, www.roquefort-papillon.com; ***Roquefort Gabriel Coulet***, Pl. de l'Eglise, ☎ 05 65 59 90 21, www.gabriel-coulet.fr

THE TARN VALLEY, FROM MILLAU TO ALBI

The Tarn Valley is a quieter alternative to the Gorges du Tarn. It is very different from upriver, much wilder and dryer, with formidable villages untamed and untouched by the urge to prettify, picturesque castles and stunning river scenery.

Getting there and around
Car
D999 from Millau or Albi. D25 from Rodez.
Train
Millau to St-Affrique.
Bus
Millau to St-Affrique, regular service via St-Rome-du-Tarn, St-Rome-de-Cernon.

Tourist information
81160 St-Juery Plateau du Saut-du-Tarn, 26 Rue Germain-Téqui, ☎ 05 63 45 97 07

River cruises
Departures from Mas de la Nauc, June–Sept daily; April–Nov check times; ☎ 05 65 62 59 12 or 05 65 62 52 49

Festival and events
July *Festival du court-métrage*, short-film festival, St-Affrique
July–August *Festival de la Vallée et les Gorges du Tarn*, concerts

Where to stay and eating out
8 1 4 3 0   A M B I A L E T
☆☆ ***Du Pont***, La Moulinquié, ☎ 05 63

55 32 07, fax 05 63 55 37 21. A tried and trusted hotel-restaurant overlooking the Tarn.
Fabas, ☎ 05 63 79 54 02. Farmhouse offering *chambres d'hôte* in three pretty rooms and home cooking, including homemade croissants.

12480 BROUSSE-LE-CHÂTEAU
✲✲ *Relays du Chasteau*, ☎ 05 65 99 40 15, fax 05 65 99 40 15. On the banks of the Tarn at the foot of the castle.

12520 COMPEYRE
Ferme auberge de Quiers, ☎ 05 65 59 85 10, www.ifrance.com/quiers. *Chambres d'hôte* in a quiet and remote spot.

12720 MOSTUÉJOULS
✲✲✲ *La Muse et du Rozier*, ☎ 05 65 62 60 01, fax 05 65 62 63 88, www.hotel-delamuse.com

12720 PEYRELEAU
L'Ermitage, M. and Mme Gars, ☎ 05 65 62 61 91. A quality *chambres d'hôte* in a quiet and remote spot.

12550 PLAISANCE
€€ *Les Magnolias*, ☎ 05 65 99 48 70, fax 05 65 99 48 71. Delightful building in a pretty setting and good fare.

12380 ST-SERNIN-SUR-RANCE
✲✲ *Carayon*, Pl. du Fort, ☎ 05 65 98 19 19, fax 05 65 99 69 26, www.hotelcarayon.com. Hotel-restaurant set in a park with a pool, offers numerous activities.

Le Rozier, upstream from Millau, is a pretty village where the Gorges du Tarn and the Gorges de la Jonte converge. From there to Millau is a scenic drive between strange rocky outcrops. In the field beside the river near **Mostuéjouls** is the little church of Notre-Dame-des-Champs, with a *clocher-peigne* (a comb-like belfry). At **Peyrelade** are the ruins of one of the most important castles in the Rouergue, currently under restoration. Open July, Aug daily 10.00–12.30 and 15.00–19.30; ☎ 05 65 59 80 74. **Compeyre** is a crafts village, with wood and leather workers, ceramicists, jewellery makers, and artists.

Peyrac and Comprégnac were once wine-producing villages but the terraced slopes surrounding them now show little sign of cultivation. Around **Candas**, however, there are a few vines among the woods and a view of Montjaux looking down from its rocky nest (p 244).

St-Rome-de-Tarn, on the left bank of the Tarn on the southbound D993, is an attractive village surrounded by old vineyards. For a boat trip on the Rasps, an idyllic section where the river flows through steep wooded cliffs, depart from **Mas de la Nauc** on the right bank and D73 (see above). This is hydro-electric country and the Le Pouget plant at Le Truel can be visited; ☎ 05 65 46 65 00.

On the south bank close to where the Dourdou meets the Tarn are some beautiful *pigeonniers*. **St-Izaire** on the D25 is an impressive site that was chosen by the bishops of Vabres for their episcopal château, towering above the reddish-stone houses arranged in terraces above the valley. A large square building, built between the 14C and 17C, it has a little look-out tower on the angle towards the village and a variety of fenestration. Inside is a chapel with 14C frescoes and a marquetry ceiling. Open May–Sept Tues–Sat 10.00–12.00 and 14.00–19.00; closed Mon, Sun, PH; Jan–April daily 14.00–18.00; Oct–Dec Tues–Sat 14.00–18.00; ☎ 05 65 99 42 27. **Broquiès**, on the north of the river, has old houses and views.

Brousse-le-Château, further west on the D54, is first and foremost a formidable castle with ramparts and towers clinging to a high rocky spur between the Tarn and the Alrance Rivers. It is also a pretty village on a hill with tall houses lining the bank of the Alrance, linked to the road by an ancient humpbacked stone bridge reputedly dating from 1366. Over the pedestrianised bridge and up a winding path is the castle. Open July, Aug 10.00–19.00; Sept–Dec and Feb–June 14.00–18.00; closed Jan; ☎ 05 65 99 45 40. Brousse was first mentioned in the 10C and the considerable fortifications have been consolidated and restored. Inside the 13C gateway is a grassy area, and the whole is enclosed in a 15C *enceinte* incorporating earlier constructions. Almost totally intact, the ramparts follow the contours of the rock to make an irregular polygon, narrower at the southeast than the northwest, with a multitude of openings for a variety of weapons. The highest tower in the region, La Picardie, was dismantled in the 17C and only the base is left as a reminder; the oldest complete tower, built towards the village, is 14C. Some of the towers were used as lodgings or for confinement. The château remained in the hands of the d'Arpajon family from the 13C until 1700, and some time after the 15C they converted the main lodgings into something more habitable. These buildings contain the well, a bread oven (restored in the 19C), stables, large rooms with fireplaces and a 17C staircase. There is a little museum of tools and pieces of masonry, part of a menhir, stucco and furniture. The early Gothic church in the village and its cemetery replaced the chapel inside the fortified enclosure. A little rustic edifice, it has a small belfry and a very simple plate-tracery rose window. A tiny house adjoins the east end.

Another imposing castle, on high ground south of the river on the D33 at **Coupiac**, has been restored. Open July, Aug, 10.00–19.00; Sept–June 09.00–12.00 and 14.00–18.00; ☎ 05 65 99 79 45. Different in character from Brousse-le-Château, it was built in the 15C on a rock in the middle of the village; three high round towers bear down on it. The châtelain, Louis de Panat, was forced to dismantle a quarter of his castle by Louis XI after partipating in a local revolt in 1465; the section between the north towers was rebuilt in the 16C and amendments continued until the 18C. Part fortification, part luxury residence, it has arrow slits, cannon holes, a *chemin de ronde* and machicolations for defence, ogee and mullioned windows, Renaissance dooways, fireplaces, two spiral staircases, a vaulted kitchen and latrines for comfort. It is furnished with local objects. For something like five centuries Coupiac has owned an authentic relic of the *Saint-Voile* (Holy Veil), hidden during the Wars of Religion and forgotten until it happened to be uncovered by a bull. In 1968 an oratory was built behind the castle to display the relic, which is still venerated, and there is a pilgrimage at Assumption. The neo-Byzantine décor of the oratory was painted by the Estonian-born Nicolas Greschny (b. 1912), who made his home in the Tarn. Another relic is the beautiful 11C tympanum from the first church, Notre-Dame-de-Massiliergues, now under the archway west of the 19C parish church. It is semi-circular and has a monogram of Christ, or chrism, very unusual in the Rouergue, with a cabled outline inscribed in a tilted square. On either side are angels and small flowers or stars.

The charming village of **Plaisance** has a little hotel-restaurant in the 14C house where Paul Valéry once lived (see above). At the top of the hill in the village is a small church (part 12C, part 15C/16C). Steps lead up to an entrance with deep roll-mouldings and bulbous capitals and bases. The exterior of the apse is also decorated, and above the south transept door is an ancient re-used tympanum with a chrism similar to that at Coupiac, flanked by two lions and daisies. Inside are storiated capitals, including *Daniel in the Lions' Den* at the crossing and leaping lions in the northwest transept. The crossing is covered by a lantern on pendentives supporting the chunky belfry.

St-Sernin-sur-Rance, on a spur high above the confluence of the Rance and the Merdanson, has a fine 16C/17C bridge and was an important medieval stronghold. In the older part of town to the south are the 15C *hôtel de ville* and church, with a square rustic belfry and a small bell. In the south wall above a sundial is a pretty stone rose window. Inside the church is a lierne-vaulted chapel with Christ and the four Evangelists on the bosses, carved brackets and varied window tracery.

St-Sernin is the world centre for *gimblettes*, a small hard cake with caraway seed. Its other claim to fame is the statue, on Place du Fort, of the wild boy of the Aveyron, who is thought to have been raised by wolves. He first came to light in the district of Lacaune in 1798, and in 1800 he spent a few days at a house in St-Sernin-sur-Rance. François Truffaut made a film about him.

Alban is not particularly inspiring but the modern church of Notre-Dame has an interesting mixture of decoration and fittings. The west façade has modern abstract coloured glass by Bruno Schmeltz and an old balustrade. The door is late 18C in style and the interior is decorated with murals (1957/58 and 1967) by Nicolas Greschny. A crowned *Madonna and Child*, possibly 16C, stand on the main altar and against the north wall is the most outstanding piece, a 16C wayside cross sculpted on three sides with *Scenes of the Passion*. It was found in the old cemetery in 1927, and is considered the best of its kind in the Tarn.

On the approach to **Ambialet** from the D53 there is an excellent view of the dramatic site where the Tarn forces its way through high cliffs to form a tight loop and a narrow isthmus. On the cliff above is a priory. There is a small hydro-electric plant and the weir is the other side of an archway next to the 19C Electricité de France building. When the river is not in flood this is a pleasant walk. The priory on the cliff can be reached on foot by following the Stations of the Cross up a path which starts near the car park, or by road. At the summit is a wide terrace with spectacular views and a long flight of steps leading up to the west end of the little 11C church of Notre-Dame-de-l'Oder. There is still a religious community in the priory but the much-restored church can be visited. The deep porch has four carved capitals supporting a square belfry and the interior is very plain and simple with huge square pillars and exposed stone. The three-bay nave is barrel vaulted and the aisles have half-barrel vaults. There are shallow transepts and a trilobed east end.

On the approach to Albi from the east along the D172 stands **St-Juery**. Its bridge across the Tarn overlooks the Saut du Sabo, an 18m cascade in the river creating hydro-electric power. The **Musée du Saut-du-Tarn** is a former hydro-electric plant, where 200 years of industrial history are retraced through animated models. Guided tours May–Sept daily 14.00–19.00; Oct–April Wed, Sun, PH 14.00–18.00; ☎ 05 63 45 91 01.

Lescure, east of the N88, has a 12C church, St-Michel-de-Lescure. Open July, Aug afternoons or during exhibitions; ☎ 05 63 60 76 73. Once part of a Benedictine abbey, it has the best **Romanesque sculptures** in the Albigeois. The west door has a wealth of sculpted decoration including four elaborately carved archivolts, mouldings, corbels and cornice, and capitals reminiscent of the Porte des Comtes at St-Sernin in Toulouse. The inner capitals have eagles and lions, and the outer ones the **Sacrifice of Abraham**, the **Temptation of Adam and Eve**, **Lazarus and Dives**, and the sinful receiving punishment. The east end is also richly decorated. The nave has three bays with cruciform pillars and aisles. The nave, aisles and crossing are covered by a wooden roof. The belfry collapsed at some point, bringing down the cupola, and was rebuilt, as was the apse. There are a number of carved capitals of varying degrees of sophistication: at the entrance to the choir are two storiated capitals, **Jacob and Esau** and **Daniel in the Lions' Den**; at the crossing, a rare floral motif, eagles, and lions rampant, all influenced by Moissac. Several of the nave capitals are of a more traditional design, and include dragons with crossed tails and the **Sacrifice of Abraham**.

THE ROUGIER DE CAMARÈS AND LACAUNE

The area between the *causses* of the southern Aveyron and the Monts de Lacaune further south, at the eastern end of the Tarn, is more scenic than monumental, although there are a number of dolmens and menhirs in the region as well as the Cistercian abbey of Sylvanès. The Rougier de Camarès is an area of dark red soil, a mixture of sandstone and marl, where the villages are built in the local warm red sandstone. The Lacaune is famous for *charcuterie* and *salaisons* (sausage, cured and dried meats) and for the bottled water of Mont Roucous.

Getting there and around
Car
D999 St-Affrique to Albi, D607 to Lacaune.

Tourist information

81230 Lacaune Pl. Général-de-Gaulle, ☎ 05 63 37 04 98, fax 05 63 37 03 01,
www.pageloisirs.com/ot-lacaune

Market days
Lacaune Sunday
Murat-sur-Vèbre Saturday

Festivals and events

July–August *Festival International de Musique Sacrée*, Sylvanès
August *Festival de Théâtre*, Château de Montaigut

Where to stay and eating out
81230 LACAUNE LES BAINS
☆☆☆ *Central Hôtel Fusiès*, Rue de la République, 05 63 37 04 98, fax 05 63 37 10 98, email hotelfusies@grandsud.fr. A traditional French hotel owned by the same family for 300 years, with a highly recommended restaurant.
☆☆☆ *Fusiès*, Rue de la République, ☎ 05 63 37 02 03, fax 05 63 37 10 98, email hotelfusies@wanadoo.fr. In the town centre, a traditional French hotel-restaurant owned by the same family for 300 years, with a highly recommended restaurant.
12260 GISSAC
☆☆☆ *Château de Gissac*, near Sylvanès, ☎ 05 65 98 14 60, fax 05 65 98 14 61, www.sylvanes.com. Splendid château converted to an elegant hotel, with a vaulted dining room, courtyard, formal gardens and pool.

The boundary of the *départements* of the Tarn and the Aveyron is wooded country with great views: the most spectacular panorama is at **Roquecézière** (900m), dominated by a monumental statue of the Virgin. There is a small folk museum at **St-Crépin**, containing examples of menhir statues from the St-Sernin region. Open all year, ☎ 05 65 99 61 43/68 66.

Notre-Dame-d'Orient, to the north on the D33 and D91, is a beautiful hidden hamlet around a large red sandstone church. The austere and unadorned exterior has the date 1666 on the southwest gable above a huge sundial, and a disproportionately small belfry on the east. At the beginning of the 17C, after the Religious Wars, Franciscan friars re-established a community here and built a model Counter-Reformation church. The uncomplicated interior space is crammed with Baroque busyness on a predominantly blue background. The walls are covered with *trompe l'oeil* pilasters, candelabra, rinceaux and, behind the retable, draperies. The curved ceiling is the most original part, covered in wood panels in a sort of herringbone design. The altar is decorated with paintings in medallions and the retable is quite splendidly over-the-top with a *Virgin and Child*, crowned in gold, in the centre. The central section is set off by pairs of Corinthian columns and flanking it are statues of St Francis and St Clare, and the whole thing is liberally sprinkled with angels. The polychromed relief medallions portray saints important to the Franciscan order. There are more Baroque altarpieces in the chapels of the nave and the Ste-Marguerite chapel has a very fine worked leather antependium.

The Rance River, followed by the D91, runs through gentle pastures, tiny villages and deserted farmsteads before arriving at **Combret-sur-Rance**, a typical once-fortified medieval village of the southern Aveyron in an impressive site. It has an old *halle de justice* and a restored church with a fine porch.

An old bridge spans the river outside **Belmont-sur-Rance**, which stands on a hill above and dominates the countryside with its celebrated crocketed spire (75m tall), contemporary with the spire of Rodez cathedral and in similar red sandstone. It stands over the west end of the Gothic collegiate church (1515–24) at the top of the village which has a fussy Flamboyant tympanum and Renaissance and Gothic fenestration in the tower. The houses near the church have some nice Renaissance details and the steep streets serve as gutters.

To reach the **Château de Montaigut** from here, take the D999 and D12 and go through Montlaur, then take the D101, cross the Grauzou, and there it is on the right atop a conical hill. The views over the Rougier de Camarès and the Grauzou Valley are marvellous from here, and sometimes stretch as far as the Monts de Lacaune. Open April–June, Sept–1 Nov 10.00–12.00 and 14.30–18.00; July, Aug 10.00–18.30; ☎ 05 65 99 81 50. The château, which has retained its early medieval layout, possibly 11C, originally controlled the route between St-Affrique to the north and Camarès (see below) and has been saved by a long programme of restoration. The huge château-keep, a massive but simple construction, is protected to the south by an *enceinte* around a courtyard with stables and outhouses. In the lower vaulted rooms are a deep cistern and cellar carved out of the rock—safeguards against siege. The transformation from severe fortress to comfortable and decorative residence began in the 15C with the addition of a large fireplace and ogee doorway, and was carried further in the 17C with the insertion of large windows, more fireplaces and sophisticated decoration in stucco (*gypseries*). The plaster, or gypsum, used for the stucco was quarried and milled to the northwest of Montaigut and these sites can be visited on foot; ask for the pamphlet *Sentier du Plâtre*. There are small exhibitions of stucco, archaeological finds and military architecture. At the end of the track to the château is a small farmhouse which has been turned into a museum with geological exhibitions and a reconstructed farm interior of 1914 on the upper floor, with commentary. There is also a tiny church.

The D101 between Montaigut castle and **Gissac** follows an amazingly empty, furrowed valley, typical of the Rougier, with dark red soil and bright green vegetation.

Further south, a sinuous route follows the Rance gorges west of **Camarès**. The *ville haute* and the lower town are divided by the Rance which is spanned by a picturesque bridge with one very high and two smaller arches. This is a popular tourism centre.

From Camarès northeast on the D10 is the **Abbaye de Sylvanès** is in the green and wooded valley of the Cabot. Today Sylvanès is an important cultural centre where courses are held nearly all year round. Open July, Aug daily 09.00–12.30 and 14.00–18.00, guided visits 10.30, 14.30, 16.00, 17.00; ☎ 05 65 98 20 20.

The abbey was founded in 1132 by a repentant brigand of noble birth, Pons de Léras, and four years later adopted the rule of Cîteaux. It was the first Cistercian abbey in the Rouergue and the church, begun *c* 1151, is a good example of the style. Its construction lasted nearly a century, resulting in an interesting juxtaposition of Romanesque and Gothic building techniques. The church was left almost untouched by the Calvinists and at the Revolution, although the monastic buildings fared less well. The west end is plain with just two small doors (for the dead to the north and the lay brothers to the south), and a Rayonnant window with glass from the end of the 13C to early 14C and a small arcaded belfry over the crossing. The exterior of the east end is more inspiring, the flat chevet pierced with four rose and three lancet windows, and a cornice of small arcades running around the exterior. Some of the wrought iron is 12C. Even more uplifting is the interior, with the play of light from the many windows and uncluttered, beautifully proportioned elevations. The five-bay Cistercian-style nave is a paradigm for aisleless Gothic churches in the Midi. Nave, transepts and choir have pointed barrel vaults, whereas primitive rib vaults are introduced at the crossing and in the first bay of the nave. A door in the nave opened into the cloister and two doors in the south transept gave access to the monastic buildings.

Of these only the east wing has survived, plus an incomplete gallery of the cloister, probably built later, towards the end of the 13C. The rectangular sacristy with a low vault has a decorated tympanum over the door to the cloister and the chapter house has one single bay of vaulting with rectangular ribs springing from carved imposts in the angles. The walls were stuccoed in the 18C. Finest of all is the monks' room or scriptorium, saved from near ruin by an important programme of restoration, and used as a refectory or for concerts. Four central columns divide it into ten vaulted bays with rounded ribs similar to the chapter houses at Escaladieu and Flaran (pp 375), although it probably pre-dates either of these, being built *c* 1160–80.

The mineral waters of **Bains-de-Sylvanès** were exploited in the 17C and 18C, and Thomas Becket stayed in Brusque.

Murat-sur-Vèbre is a typical town of the Lacaune where the houses, huddled together shoulder-to-shoulder, are not only roofed in slate but have overlapping slate shingles on exposed walls. There is an 11C church and all around are magnificent beech forests, glorious until late autumn. Either side of the D622, between Murat and Lacaune, are **menhirs**, some signposted. There are two off the D169 north, more around Moulin-Mage, one at Rieuviel, one in the middle of a farmyard at Haute-Vergne, and a huge one in a field on the left of the D622 not far before the junction with the D607. The best view around is from **Mont Barre** (990m), on the D62 north of Moulin-Mage.

> ### Statue-menhirs
>
> In the region of the Monts de Lacaune are a number of menhirs, monolithic blocks of flat stone, frequently carved on one face with rudimentary male or female features. They were created at the end of the Stone Age (*c* 3500–2500 BC) by peoples who lived in the Lacaune mountains (see also p 52). Their symbolism and significance are still wreathed in mystery and they take some seeking out.

Lacaune is a small unpretentious spa nestling under slate roofs on the edge of the Monts de Lacaune in the Haut Languedoc regional park, midway between Albi, Millau and Béziers and between *causses* to the north and forests and lakes to the south. At an altitude of 800m, it is dominated by the peak of Montalet (1260m). The town's main monument is the Fontaine des Pisseurs in Place du Griffoul, erected in 1559 by four consuls, a reminder perhaps of the diuretic properties of the waters; or maybe symbolic of the consuls .... In the same square is the Musée du Vieux Lacaune, a small museum of local pre-1940 history, the spa in the 19C; it also has a Salle de l'Enfant Sauvage (p 254). Open 15–30 June, July, August, 1–mid-Sept daily 10.00–12.00 and 14.00–18.00; April–14 June, mid-Sept–Oct 14.00–18.00, closed Mon; ☎ 05 63 37 25 38. The church, built in 1668, has modern windows and a new organ which is used for recitals in the summer. There is a statue-menhir outside the tourist office, where you should ask for more information on menhirs and maps of their whereabouts. The Maison de la Charcuterie is a very professional exhibition of the business of making the sausages so important to this region. Open 15 June–15 Sept daily 10.00– 12.00 and 15.00–18.30; ☎ 05 63 37 46 31.

The large lakes to the south of Lacaune offer beautiful scenery, water sports, and another chance to go menhir hunting. The **Lac de Laouzas** has a beach, reached by the D162 which continues on around the lake, through the village of Villelongue, to the dam at the south. **Salvetat-sur-Agout**, in the *département* of the Hérault, is an important tourist centre on the cliffs beside the Agout. Although it is categorised as one of the *plus beaux villages de France*—with its tall, austere slate-clad houses catching the sunlight—it is no run-of-the-mill picturesque village. Nearby are plenty of water-based activities on the **Lac de la Ravière**, which has a beach at the west.

13 Guyenne: Lot-et-Garonne

The mighty Garonne was, for several centuries, the frontier between French Gascony to the south and English Guyenne to the north. **Guyenne**, thought to be a popular phonetic deformation of Aquitaine, was the name given to the English province of Aquitaine from the mid-13C until the end of the Hundred Years War in 1453. Until the 15C it was a vague area of fluctuating boundaries, determined more by natural constraints, language and religion than by administrative concerns: it stretched from the Gironde estuary along the Garonne, incorporating the dioceses of Bordeaux and Agen, to Valence d'Agen and north to Monpazier and the Périgord. It ended north of the Dordogne, at the frontier with Limousin and Charente, and to the east at the Quercy. It was absorbed into the modern *département* of Lot-et-Garonne. The main town, **Agen**, on the banks of the Garonne, is mid-way between Bordeaux and Toulouse and borrows a little from each.

The Garonne is swelled by the Lot arriving from the east and by two lesser tributaries, the Baïse and the Dropt. To the east of the *département* these rivers flow through rolling hills and gentle valleys, a landscape of lush pastures and plum orchards. To the west the landscape drifts away into the flat and sombre pine forests of the Landes. The tumultuous history of this region has left a liberal scattering of castles, austere little churches and *bastides*. Shipping on the rivers was dangerous and the volatile Garonne was finally supplanted in 1856 by the more controllable **Canal latéral à la Garonne**.

BASTIDES IN THE DROPT VALLEY

The Dropt River rises near Monpazier (Dordogne) and flows some 120km, linking the Périgord with the Guyenne, until it meets the Garonne west of La Réole. In the 13C this was the boundary between English Guyenne and French Agenais, and to protect their territories both sides built *bastides* (p 262). The rolling countryside is unsensational but pretty, a patchwork of vineyards, woodland and fields of maize, and is dotted in places with the remains of windmills, and a number of small, simple Romanesque churches and old *lavoirs* in the villages.

Getting there and around
Car

From Bergerac N21/D933, D1/D668.
From Bordeaux N10/D668.
Train

See Marmande, p 266.

Tourist information
47800 **Allemans-du-Dropt**
Pl. de la Liberté, ☎ 05 53 20 25 59, fax 05 53 20 68 91
47330 **Castillonnès** Pl. des Cornières, ☎/fax 05 53 36 87 44, email office-tourism-castillonnes@wandoo.fr

47120 **Duras** Blvd Jean-Brisseau, ☎/fax 05 53 93 71 18; also ☎ 05 53 83 63 06, fax 05 53 83 65 45, email otsi.duras@wanadoo.fr
24500 **Eymet** Pl. Gambetta, ☎ 05 53 23 74 95, fax 05 53 27 98 76, email ot.eymet@perigord.tm.fr
47410 **Lauzun** Rue Taillefer, ☎ 05 53 20 10 07, fax 05 53 94 49 20
47800 **Miramont-de-Guyenne** 1 Rue Pasteur, ☎ 05 53 93 38 94, fax 05 53 93 49 56, www.ville-miramont-deguyenne.fr
24540 **Monpazier** Pl. des Cornières, ☎ 05 53 22 68 59, fax 05 53 74 30

08, email ot.monpazier@perigord.tm.fr
47120 Pays de Duras Blvd Jean
Brisseau, ☎ 05 53 93 71 18, fax 05 53
93 96 20, www.paysdeduras.com
47210 Villeréal Pl. de la Halle, ☎ 05
53 36 09 65, fax 05 53 36 63 58, email
ot.villereal@wandoo.fr

Market days

Biron Wednesday in summer farmers'
market
Castillonnès Tuesday
Duras Monday; evenings in July
Eymet Thursday; Tuesday evenings
July, August
Lauzun Wednesday
Monpazier Thursday
Villeréal Saturday; Monday evenings
July, August

Festivals and events

July *Evocation Historique*, re-enactment
of town history, Duras

Where to stay and eating out

47800 AGNAC
Château de Péchalbet (west of Eymet),
☎/fax 05 53 83 04 70. On the borders
of the Lot-et-Garonne and the
Dordogne, *chambres d'hôte* in a 17C
mansion in rural surroundings.

47330 CASTILLONNÈS
✩✩✩ *Les Ramparts*, 26/28 Rue de la
Paix, ☎ 05 53 49 55 85, fax 05 53 49
55 89, www.logis-de-france-47.com.
Small hotel-restaurant in a charming
18C setting, with courtyard and garden.
Quality cooking at reasonable prices.

47120 DURAS
✩✩ *L'Hostellerie des Ducs*, Blvd Jean-
Brisseau, ☎ 05 53 83 74 58, fax 05 53
83 75 03, www.hostellerieducs-
duras.com. An oasis of calm in an old
monastery, with pool. Home cooking.

24540 MONPAZIER
✩✩✩ *Edward Premier*, 5 Rue St-Pierre,
☎ 05 53 22 44 00, fax 05 53 22 57
99. This little castle has nicely appointed
rooms.
€–€€ *La Bastide*, 52 Rue St-Jacques,
☎ 05 53 22 60 59. Enthusiastic and
skilful cooking, with generous helpings.

Duras

Duras is a popular little *bastide* built on a ridge overlooking the Dropt and
surrounded by the vineyards of Côtes-de-Duras abutting those of Bordeaux.
Duras claims the oldest AOC in the Guyenne (compared to Côtes-de-Buzet and
Côtes-de-Marmandais) and produces the whole *gamme* (whites, reds and rosé) to
a good quality. At its western extremity is the elegant 17C château, much
restored, and often used for theatrical performances. The writer, Marguerite
Duras, née Donnadieu (1914–96), adopted her professional name from the area
where her father owned a property.

Protecting the **Château de Duras** is a medieval fortified gateway and on the
left is the 18C *petit château*. Open daily July, Aug 10.00–19.00; June, Sept 10.00–
12.30 and 14.00–19.00; April–May, Oct and winter hols 10.00–12.00 and
14.00–18.00; Nov–March 14.00–18.00; ☎ 05 53 83 77 32.

The first castle was begun in the 12C but rebuilt in 1308 by Bertrand de Got,
a member of one of the most powerful local families and nephew of Pope
Clement V (another Bertrand de Got) from Villandraut (p 118). In 1324, the
strongly fortified property with eight towers passed to the Durfort family who
fought with the English during the Hundred Years War and remained stead-
fastly English until Charles V made an all-out bid to regain the Guyenne in
1376. A powerful army led by Bernard du Guesclin laid siege to Duras, which
capitulated after eight days; all therein were executed. After the English defeat

at Castillon in 1453, the lords of Duras fled to England. By 1689 the Durfort became Dukes of Duras for services rendered to Louis XIV and built the prestigious 17C residence we see now. After the Revolution all the towers but the largest were truncated, the place was sold and left to deteriorate until the commune took over and began restoration in 1973.

Inside is a large courtyard with a double flight of steps to the entrance, which leads into the vast Salle des Maréchaux and the adjacent Chambre de la Duchesse on the ground floor. Beyond is an inner courtyard with Italianate peristyle on the east and view of the park to the west. On the next floor is the Salle de la Charpente with a fine wooden ceiling; originally there were 11 fireplaces. From here you gain access to the large south tower—a bit of a climb but a rewarding 360 degree view. The visit continues through various exhibitions and down to the two lower levels of vaulted cellars with a close-up of the remarkable great well of the house. Most of the basement rooms are used to house a small museum of local archaeology and culture. There are more rooms, corridors and dungeons, some 32 in all, on upper levels.

The main street, Rue Jauffret, leads from the Place du Marché, with a few arcades, past the former 17C Protestant Temple. This reverted to the Catholic Church in 1685 and has been known as the church of the Madeleine ever since. The interior was given a decorative work-over in 1932 by Giovanni Mazutti. At the end of the street is the only remaining ancient town gate. At Rue des Eyzins is the **Musée du Parchemin et de l'Enluminure**, with reconstructions of medieval workshops demonstrating the making of parchment and illuminations. Open April–June, Sept 15.00–19.00; July, Aug 11.00–13.00 and 15.00–19.00; ☎ 05 53 20 75 55, www.museeduparchemin.com.

A few kilometres northwest of Duras at **Esclottes** is one of the oldest Romanesque churches (11C, rebuilt in the 13C) in the region, with sculpted capitals representing *Christ in Glory*, the four Evangelists, the *Adoration of the Magi* and *Tobias and the Fish*. There are also Romanesque churches at Savignac-de-Duras and, east of Esclottes, at Loubès.

On a high bluff at **Monteton**, south of Duras on the D668 and D423, is the movingly simple Romanesque church of Notre-Dame with a gable belfry, and a view from the terrace of 13 other belfries. The interior is equally uncomplicated, the buttresses linked by arches and the *Hand of God blessing the World* on the altar. At neighbouring **Allemans-du-Drop** the church of Ste-Eutrope is basically 12C and was decorated in the 15C with an extraordinary group of murals, discovered in the 20C. (There is a light switch on the pillar near the door.) Over the chancel is a horseshoe arch in Mozarab style.

The paintings include the *Last Supper* on the north wall, and in the chancel the *Carrying of the Cross*, *Crucifixion*, *Entombment* and the *Resurrection*. In *Christ in Judgement*, a spirited St Michael overcomes demons and the condemned are carried off to Hell like eggs in a basket. Behind the altar are the coat of arms of the lords of

Monteton

Allemans and St-Martin. There is an old *halle* behind the church, and another 16C *halle aux prunes* nearby.

Bastides

These were the planned towns of the Middle Ages, of which some 300 still exist in southwest France between Bordeaux and the Pyrenees. New towns were not exclusive to southwest France but their density and the word *bastide* (from Occitan *bastir* (*bâtir*), to build) are. Their creation was in part a response to overall demographic and commercial expansion in Europe in the 12C, and in part for geopolitical reasons. They were a means to administer the domains of the ruling factions, the Counts of Toulouse (crucial following the Albigensian Crusades) and of Aquitaine. From 1154, the Dukes of Aquitaine were also the Plantagenet kings of England, and as tension increased between them and the French Capetians, *bastides* were a means of establishing administrative supremacy and, later, military domination. During some 300 years of struggle between the English and the French, the Haut-Agenais (Lot-et-Garonne and Dordogne) was the frontier zone between territories, accounting for the high number of *bastides* here.

The *bastides* date mainly from the beginning of the 13C to *c* 1370. There are five main groups according to founder: the Counts of Toulouse; Alphonse de Poitiers (1249–71), who inherited land in the southwest through his wife, Jeanne de Toulouse; the Kings of England; and the Kings of France from 1281 onwards. The last category was foundation by *paréage*, a joint arrangement between a founding authority (the overlord) and the ecclesiastical or secular owner of the land, when the deeds of foundation were drawn up defining the rights and benefits of each of the signatories. A *chartre des coutumes*, crucial to the inhabitants, set out civil and political liberties or constraints, legal obligations and economic objectives, the most important privilege being the status of freeman.

The following general principles apply to the majority of *bastides*, although inevitably there are slight variations. Some *bastides* were built on virgin territory, others on or near a pre-existing community. Sites were chosen for their natural advantages, on top of a hill or in proximity to a main route or junction, a ford, or good agricultural land. The overall shape was regular (square or rectangular) as far as topography allowed: one of the major characteristics is the rectilinear grid plan with a large open *place centrale* for trading. The land was divided into equally sized *îlots* or building plots, usually long and narrow, which were allocated to prospective inhabitants. The church was nearly always set back diagonally from the centre. The community would be granted the right to hold markets and to build market halls (*halles*) which sometimes incorporated weights and measures and communal bread ovens. Adminstration was controlled by consuls whose *maison commune*, or meeting place, was in certain instances built in or over the *halle*. The main streets are called *charretières*, the minor ones *carrerots*, and *androne* are the narrow spaces separating the houses for drainage or firebreaks. The arcades around the central square were not part of the original construction but were added when permission was granted to extend façades over the public walkway. *Bastides* were not necessarily fortified from the outset, and many acquired ramparts and gates later on.

On the road towards Monségur is a very handsome 17C hexagonal *pigeonnier* on pillars and an old *lavoir*. The church of St-Gervaise at **La Sauvetat-du-Dropt** boasts a fine 12C choir, but was damaged by a cyclone in 1242 (see the inscription). Rebuilt in the 16C, the choir and portal are flamboyantly decorated. An old bridge over the Dropt has a series of round arches followed by a series of 13C arches.

One of the best-preserved *bastides* in the Dropt Valley is **Eymet** on the D933, founded in 1270 by Alphonse de Poitiers as part of a line of French defences on the southern boundary of the Périgord.

The site has been occupied since the dawn of time: standing stones point to Bronze Age activity nearby, traces of Roman villas have been discovered, and a priory was established here by Moissac *c* 1000. This was near the junction of two Roman roads and the castle remains are built on the 11C *castrum*. In 1279 it came under the control of the Plantagenets who added fortifications *c* 1320 (destroyed in 1830). Eymet's history was tumultuous but it remained mainly English despite a particularly bloody battle in 1377 against du Guesclin's men. When the siege was over, the southern gate had to be partly demolished because a huge war machine got stuck there, and has been called the Porte de l'Engin ever since. The town supported the Protestant Jeanne of Navarre and Henri of Navarre frequently passed through Eymet.

It has retained its attractive *place*, surrounded typically by a variety of arcades and façades, and a 13C keep which is part of the old château and houses a small museum of archaeology. Open July, Aug, Mon–Sat 15.00–18.30, also Thur, 10.00–12.00. Just outside the *bastide* is a 'Roman' bridge and the huge lake of Lescourroux.

South of the Dropt on the D1, **Lauzun** is a quaint little place with some surprises. It was the birthplace in 1632 of Antoine Nompar de Caumont, favourite of Louis XIV, who became Maréchal de France and, scandalously, the lover of the Grande Demoiselle, niece of the king. The home of the Dukes of Lauzun was the château (now a hotel and restaurant) begun in the 13C although the main building, which sports an octagonal tower, is 15C–16C. The two parts are linked by a domed pavilion built by the Maréchal in the 17C (and 19C). The little church is mainly Gothic although a tiny part of the west front is Romanesque and it contains some good furnishings including the 17C altar, retable and carved panels. In the neighbourhood, but they take some searching, are some tiny examples of Romanesque churches at Queyssel, Maurillac and St-Colombe.

Spread out along a ridge above the Dropt valley, **Castillonnès** was founded in 1259 as a result of a *paréage* between Alphonse de Poitiers and the abbey of Cadouin (p 174). The pretty Place Centrale had only narrow passages at the corners until the 19C when the arcades were removed to allow vehicular access. The *mairie*, which has an attractive courtyard, originally belonged to the abbey and tithes were gathered here. It passed to Henri IV's military governor in the 17C and was renovated in 1984 when the commune took it over. The main interest of the church, built *c* 1265 but much altered, is the modern stained glass (1968), designed by Czechoslovak artists. The iconography was taken from Genesis I and represents *Water*, *Fire*, the *Holy Spirit*, *Earth* and *Air*.

The small community of **Villeréal** further east, overlooking the right bank of the Dropt, is an Alphonsine *bastide* founded in 1269 with a wonderful covered market on 14C wooden piers with a 16C–17C second floor, and a fortified church.

Monpazier

The ultimate *bastide* in the southwest is Monpazier, which has conserved much of its original character. It is a rectangle 400m by 220m, with sections of the walls still standing and the four gateways virtually intact.

A contract to found this town was entered into between Edward I and Pierre de Gontaut-Biron in 1284. Strategically placed between the Agenais and Périgord, it completed a chain of English defence and colonisation which had begun in 1267. But this peaceful little town was not always so. It fell to the French, returned to the English in 1316, and during Anglo-French hostilities changed hands several times between 1360 and 1453. In 1574 it was taken by the Protestants. Serious peasant revolts broke out in the region in 1594 and 1637 and the leader of the latter, Buffarot, was horribly executed on a wheel in the square.

The main streets arrive at the corners of the large *place* which is empty except for the covered *halle*, a forest of chestnut timbers. In it are the old grain measures. Jostling for room around the square and abutting awkwardly at the corners, the old houses adhere strictly to the original uniform dimensions but that is all that is uniform. Each façade and roofline expresses a total independence of style developed over the centuries, as do the variety of cool arcades spanning the walkways, flooded with pools of light and shade on a bright day. The church, off the main square, was begun at the same time as the town but modified in the 15C and 16C. The sculpted portal was remade in the 16C, and on it is a Jacobin proclamation: *Le peuple français reconnaît l'existence de l'être suprême et de l'immortalité de l'âme* ('The French believe in the existence of a supreme being and the immortality of the soul'). Inside are some rustic Romanesque capitals and some very fine 14C choir stalls with carvings. Opposite the church is the 14C Maison du Chapitre on three floors with Gothic bays, where tithes were collected.

This is a big strawberry-growing area—the late local fruit are utterly delicious—and also produces tobacco and the ubiquitous maize. The source of the Dropt is at Capdrot, to the east of Monpazier, and to the south is the Château de Biron.

Château de Biron

The awe-inspiring silhouette of the Château de Biron greets you from its lofty position, with a cluster of houses at the foot of the knoll. The château is the product of several stages of construction determined by the vagaries of history and the fortunes of the Gontaut-Biron family, who owned it for some 800 years. Guided visits daily July, Aug 10.00–19.00; May, June 10.00–12.30 and 14.00–18.30; March, April, Sept–Dec 10.00–12.30 and 14.00–17.30; closed Mon in March, Oct–Dec; closed Jan, Feb; ☎ 05 53 63 13 39.

Biron was the seat of one of the four great baronies of Périgord (the others were Beynac, Bourdeilles ane Mareiul). The first baron, Gaston de Gontaut, a very distant ancestor of Lord Byron, built a fort in the 12C to protect his territory from the neighbouring Agenais. A later baron with Cathar sympathies felt the wrath of Simon de Montfort and the consequent destruction of much of Biron in 1212. It was besieged during the Hundred Years War. In the late 15C Pons de Biron, one of many soldiers who returned from campaigns in Italy with money to spend and new ideas of comfort and elegance, remodelled his castle in a style akin to those of the Loire valley. More changes were affected by Baron Armand de Gontaut (1524–92), Maréchal de France, who fought with Henri IV against the Catholics. His son Charles was elevated to duke in the 1598 by the king, but soon fell from grace and was beheaded at the Bastille in 1602. After the Religious Wars the moats were filled in. The family fortunes revived in the 18C with the inheritance of Lauzun and more alterations were made, and Viollet-le-Duc got his hands on the castle in the 19C.

The château is on several levels, irregular in shape, and arranged around a large outer or lower courtyard and a more compact upper *cour d'honneur*. The visit begins in the **lower court**, dominated by the main part of the château to the west and a church opposite. There is some Renaissance detail in the 16C loggia. The surprisingly large **chapel**, one of the masterpieces of Biron, was built in the early 16C and displays late-Gothic and early Renaissance characteristics. It consists of two superimposed naves, the upper one opening into the courtyard for the use of the nobility, and the lower serving as the parish church accessed from the village. The upper chapel originally contained a superb group of sculptures, of which two tombs are still in place; although damaged, their quality is obvious. The tomb nearest the altar is that of Pons de Gontaut (d. 1524) and has scenes from the *Life of Christ* and of Lazarus. The other tomb commemorates the Bishop of Sarlat, Armand de Gontaut (d. 1531), who built the chapel, and is decorated with the *Three Virtues*. The chapel has stellar vaults and pendant bosses. The missing works, a very fine *Pietà*, and an *Entombment* comprising eight figures in a wooden frame, were sold in 1907 and are now in the Metropolitan Museum of Art, New York.

Around the main courtyard or **cour d'honneur** are the remains of the 12C fort, including the keep and the main living quarters redesigned in the 15C with mullioned windows. The large Classical-style building (17C), built by the Maréchal de Biron before his disgrace, contains the council chamber of the Etats Généraux, which dates from pre-revolutionary France and was convened by the king to treat important matters of state. Inside is a huge kitchen, some fine fireplaces and precious parquets. The water supply, as in most castles, was from a cistern under the courtyard. At the end of the courtyard, an arcade and peristyle with 18C columns form a loggia with views over Périgord Noir.

MARMANDE AND THE GARONNE VALLEY

The **Marmandais**, surrounded by the Dropt, the Garonne and the Lot, was traditionally given over to market gardening, although now cereals and vineyards are cultivated. The Marmande tomato, plump and tasty, was perfected at the end of the 19C, and tobacco was introduced in the 18C: there are a few surviving wooden tobacco-drying sheds. The vineyards of the little-known Côtes-du-Marmandais extend over both banks of the Garonne, around Seches, Cocument and Beaupuy.

Getting there and around
Train

TER from Paris Montparnasse to Agen, via Bordeaux, stops at Marmande, Tonneins, Aiguillon.

Bus

Marmande to Mont-de-Marsan.

 ## Tourist information

47000 Agen 107 Blvd Carnot, ☎ 05 53 47 36 09, fax 05 53 47 29 98

47190 Aiguillon Pl. 14 Juillet, ☎ 05 53 79 62 58, fax 05 53 84 41 17, email tourisme.aiguilon@wanadoo.fr.

47160 Damazan ☎ 05 53 88 26 36, fax 05 53 79 26 92, email mairiedamazan@wanadoo.fr

47200 Marmande Blvd Gambetta, ☎ 05 53 64 44 44, fax 05 53 20 17 19, wwwmairie-marmande.fr

47430 Mas d'Agenais Pl. de l'Eglise, ☎ 05 53 89 50 58, fax 05 53 20 17 51, email communedumasdagenais. 47@wanadoo.fr

47180 Meilhan-sur-Garonne Mairie, tel 05 53 94 30 04, fx 05 53 94 31 27, email communedemeilhan.47@ wanadoo.fr

47400 Tonneins 3 Blvd Charles-de-Gaulle, ☎ 05 53 79 22 79, fax 05 53 79 39 94, email office-tourisme-tonneins@wanadoo.fr

47370 Tournon d'Agenais Pl. de l'Hôtel-de-Ville, ☎ 05 53 40 75 82, fax 05 53 40 76 98

47200 Val de Garonne (Fourques-sur-Garonne) Pont-des-Sables, ☎ 05 53 89 25 59, fax 05 53 93 28 03, www. cc-val-de-garonne.fr

Market days

Aiguillon Tuesday and Friday
Damazan Thursday; Tuesday evening in July and August
Marmande Tuesday, Thursday and Saturday
Tonneins Wed, Fri, Sat; farmers' market Wednesday evening July and August

River cruises and boating
Boat trips

47320 Clairac *Lot Evasion*, l'Epervier, ☎ 05 53 84 34 48

47200 Fourques-sur-Garonne *La Gabarre Val-de-Garonne*, Pont-des-Sables (no ☎, see below)

47500 Fumel *La Gabarre Fuméloise*, Office du Tourisme, Pl. G. Escande, BP 56, ☎ 05 53 71 13 70, fax 05 53 71 40 91

47400 Lagruère *Halte nautique de Lagruère*, ☎ 05 53 89 58 12

47180 Meilhan-sur-Garonne *Croisière l'Escapade*, Lees Jardins, ☎ 05 53 94 36 82 or 05 56 63 06 45, fax 05 56 76 19 36 The tourist offices at Agen and Val de Garonne also have details of boat trips.

Motorboat/houseboat hire

47160 Buzet-sur-Baïse *Aquitaine Navigation*, ☎ 05 53 84 72 50, fax 05 53 84 03 33, www.aquitaine-navigation.com

47160 Damazan *Compagnie Nautic*, Quai Canal, ☎ 05 53 79 59 39, fax 05 53 79 34 49

47200 Fourques-sur-Garonne *Emeraude navigation*, Pont de Sables, ☎ 05 53 64 46 86 or 06 13 45 44 85, fax 05 53 64 58 53

47430 Le Mas d'Agenais *Crown Blue Line*, 44 Rue de l'Ecluse, ☎ 05 53 89 50 80, fax 05 53 89 51 13

47140 Penne d'Agenais *Babou Marine*, Port de Penne, ☎ 05 65 30 08 99, fax 05 65 23 92 59, www. baboumarine.fr

Acitivies in Lot-et-Garonne

Infomation from CDT de la Randonée Pédestre, www.cdrp47.asso.fr

 ## Festivals and events

July *Festival de Jazz de la Vallée de Lot*, Aiguillon

August *Les Nuits Lyriques en Marmandais*, opera, operetta and other musical events at various venues, Marmande

Where to stay and eating out

A central reservation service for Lot-et-Garonne is offered at www.resinfrance.com

47190 AIGUILLON

☆☆ *La Terrasse de l'Etoile*, 8 rue Alsace-Lorraine, ☎ 05 53 79 64 64, fax 05 53 79 46 48. Unsophisticated and inexpensive, with a restaurant and terrace with pool. In the town centre.

Le Clos Muneau, 28 Rue Victor Hugo, ☎ 05 53 79 58 84, fax 05 53 79 59 83. *Chambres d'hôte* in a spacious *maison de maitre* in the town centre; garden gives the impression of being in the countryside. Three rooms.

47000 MARMANDE

☆☆ *Auberge de l'Escale*, Pont des Sables, Fourques-sur-Garonne (south on D933), ☎ 05 53 93 60 11. Shady terrace beside the Canal with quality cooking.

€–€€ *Glycines et Gourmandises*, at Coussan (south on the D933), ☎ 05 53 93 61 10. Good local dishes served in an attractive setting on the Garonne; pool.

47400 TONNEINS

☆☆☆/€€€ *Côté Garonne*, 36, 38 Cours de l'Yser, ☎ 05 53 84 34 34, fax 05 53 84 31 31, www.cotegaronne.com. A combination of the best of the southwest with a hint of the exotic, served in a beautiful setting overlooking the Garonne. Also 5 charming rooms.

47200 VIRAZEIL

€–€€ *Le Moulin d'Ané*, Rte de Gontaud (D933 east), ☎ 05 53 20 18 25. An old watermill deep in the countryside on the banks of the Trec is the foil for fine food.

Marmande

Marmande, also known as 'Marmande la jolie', an accolade awarded by 1940s' mayor, M. Grassot, depended for centuries on the Garonne for its living. Not richly endowed in monuments, its main claims to fame are its *chartre des coutumes*, granted by Richard the Lionheart in 1182, and tomatoes. The bronze statue *La Pomme d'Amour*, which has become the emblem of the town, is of a young girl with a tomato, a reference to the legendary properties (erotic, exotic, aphrodisiac) of the fruit. It sits in the rather heartless Place Clemenceau, with the *hôtel de ville* on the south. Close by is the **Musée Municipal Albert-Marzelles** of local history. Open Tues–Fri 15.00–18.00, Sun 10.00–12.00 and 15.00–18.00; ☎ 05 53 64 42 04. The town's ancient source of fresh water is remembered by the nine fountains (19C) on Place des Fontaines. Rue L.-Faye leads to the church of **Notre-Dame** (13C–17C), whose redeeming feature is its Renaissance cloister. Of the original building begun in 1275 (partly rebuilt 14C–15C), only the main façade and porch and the last bays of the aisles survived following a fire and explosion in 1648, when choir and tower had to be rebuilt. The central vault boss has six fleurs-de-lis which suggests a date prior to the reign of Charles V (1354–80) who replaced multiple fleur-de-lis on the royal coat of arms with three as symbol of the Trinity, the object of royal devotion. Below the rose window with trefoil tracery is a tribune and one of the best Cavaillé-Col organs in Aquitaine. There is a 17C *Entombment* in wood. The cloister (1545) on the south was desecrated during the Religious Wars and contains the late 16C doorway of the Caillade chapel. In 1950 the cloister and adjoining land were transformed into a classical French garden, with box topiary and lindens.

West of Notre-Dame is the Place du Marché and further west, in **Rue Labat**, are some of the best old façades (15C–16C) in Marmande. On the banks of the Garonne is the Lavoir des Cinq Cannelles, the *chemin de ronde* and a wall-mosaic depicting historic moments in the town's history. The château terrace, Place du Moulin, was built onto the old walls.

Just northwest of Marmande and giving views over the town is **Beaupuy**, a hilltop village with a wine co-operative. **Castelnau-sur-Gupie**, further up the D708, was a 13C English *bastide* dominating the valley, as **St-Pierre-de-Londres** (east on the D933 near Puymiclan) should have been, but only the church was built and most of that was demolished in the 18C; there are a few storiated capitals in the porch. **Seyches**, further up the same road, has a tower-gateway and was an English possession. The Dukes of Biron hailed from the village of **Gontaud-de-Nogaret**, southeast on the D641, which has an exceptionally pretty church with 13C façade and 12C transept and apse. Nearby is the painstakingly restored 18C Gibra windmill (☎ 05 53 83 47 78).

The now modest village of **Mas d'Agenais** on the south bank of the Garonne started out as Roman *Velenum Pompejacum* and here, in 1877, the fine marble statue of Venus (now in Agen's museum) was uncovered by a farmer in his field. There is a solid little market hall with 17C timbers and attractive restored houses. The Fontaine Galiane (along Rue Galiane) is also under a timber structure. South of the main square, via the Roman gate, is a view over the Garonne and the Canal.

The main attraction of Mas is a *bonafide* painting by Rembrandt in the church of **St-Vincent** (buy *jetons* from the tourist office or shops to illuminate the work), but the church itself comes a very close second. The church is a gem, one of the best in the region, such was the importance of Mas during the Middle Ages. It was begun in 1085 after the destruction of a 6C church, and completed about 40 years later. Viollet-le-Duc and Abadie rebuilt the west front in 1862, and the wooden spire was taken down in 1873, resulting in a somewhat severe exterior. There is much to delight inside, however. Enter through the south transept. The layout is Benedictine, similar to Moirax (p 287), with a barrel-vaulted nave and aisles, barely projecting transepts, and tripartite east end. The crossing was rebuilt in the 16C as was the five-sided chapel. The richly carved capitals are worth close investigation. To the left of the entrance is a Merovingian (7C) capital, to the right the *Sacrifice of Abraham*, and opposite on the southeast pier, *Daniel in the Lions' Den*. Between the southeast chapel and the apse is an arcade with three decorative capitals; the windows around the east end are carved. In the east are an *Annunciation* and *Visitation*, *Supper at Emmaus*, *St Michael slaying the Dragon* and *Martyrdom of St Vincent*. In the south aisle, near the Gothic Sacré-Coeur chapel are *David and Goliath* and, opposite, *Samson and the Lion*. Furnishings include an early Christian (4C–5C) marble sarcophagus in the southwest aisle, 17C stalls by Jean Tournier from Gourdon (Lot) in the apse and, most importantly, Rembrandt's painting in the north chapel. This is a stark but powerful rendition of *Christ on the Cross* (1631), part of a group of seven Stations of the Cross commissioned by a Dutchman. The Dufour family, who originated from Mas d'Agenais, purchased the work and donated it to the town in 1804. Its authenticity was confirmed in 1960; the rest of the cycle is in Munich.

Small river or canal-side towns include **Tonneins**, on a rocky promontory from which there is an excellent vista of the Garonne. It used to be an important cigarette-producing town. The story of the Garonne, shipping and tobacco is told at the Espace Exhibition Garonna at the Quai de la Barre. Open July, Aug daily

15.00–17.00; March–June, Sept, Oct by appointment only; ☎ 05 53 79 22 79. The classic *bastide* of **Damazan** (13C), southwest of Tonneins on the Canal latéral, has a central square with arcades and *halle* with *mairie* atop. **Buzet-sur-Baïse**, to the south, lies in a watery flatland where the Canal, the Baïse and the Garonne meet, with multiple locks, a river marina, canal walk and boat rides (see above). Buzet wine has improved in quality due to the efforts of the co-operative. About 80 per cent is red, a blend of Merlot and Cabinet matured in oak casks. The fortified 11C church at **St-Pierre-de-Buzet** has some interesting features. The south door leads to a sub-belfry chamber with longitudinal barrel vaults and the three-bay nave ends in a deep choir and apse.

Aiguillon has a prime site where the Baïse and the Lot join the Garonne, and is central to the *département*, but its past is more impressive than its present. A Roman encampment, then a French *bastide* founded in 1300 by Philippe le Bel, it became the residence of the notorious and decadent Duc d'Aiguillon, who received Madame du Barry, the mistress of Louis XV, here in the 18C. The Neo-classical Château des Ducs, begun in 1765 (no admission), surveys the river from its clifftop. There are old houses in the medieval quarter, and Rue Sabathier brings you to the 12C Château de Lunac. The locks and weirs on the Garonne were neglected in the 20C, and only 4.5km between St-Léger and Nicole, close to Aiguillon, linking the Baïse and the Lot, are now navigable.

Also on the Garonne, **Porte Ste-Marie** has three churches: a 13C Templar church, St-Julien and Notre-Dame (16C), where sailors came on pilgrimage to pray for protection on the journey downstream to Bordeaux. From its heights above the Garonne, **Clermont-Dessous** kept a watch on river traffic. All here is designed for protection—ramparts, fortified gateway, 11C fortified church and a *chemin de ronde*.

ALONG THE VALLEYS OF THE LOT AND LEDE

The Lot rises in the Cévennes and is one of the longest and most beautiful rivers in France (see also p 200). During the English occupation of Guyenne it was border territory, hence the intense concentration of *bastides*, founded for defence by both the French and the English. It is also plum country, where the famous *pruneaux d'Agen* are produced. The most splendid of several castles along the valley is the secluded and anachronistic Château de Bonaguil.

Getting there and around
Train

TER Périgueux to Agen via Villefranche-du-Périgord, Monsempron-Libos (for Fumel), Trentels-Ladignac, Penne-d'Agenais and Pont-du-Casse.

Bus
Bus to Villeneuve-sur-Lot.

Tourist information
47290 Cancon Route National 21, ☎ 05 53 01 09 89, fax 05 53 01 60 24, email mairie.cancon@wanadoo.fr

47440 Casseneuil Les Promenades, ☎ 05 53 41 13 33, fax 05 53 41 14 13

47250 Castelmoron-sur-Lot Connoisseur, Port Lalande, Rte de Fongrave, ☎ 05 53 79 58 17, fax 05 53 79 56 20, www.connoisseur.fr

47320 Clairac 16 Pl. Viçose, ☎/fax 05 53 88 71 59, www.clairac.com

47500 Fumel Pl. Georges-Escandes, BP 56, ☎ 05 53 71 13 70, fax 05 53 71 40 91, www.fumel.fr

47260 Granges-sur-Lot Mairie, ☎ 05 53 79 11 66, fax 05 53 88 73 30, email tourisme-granges@worldonline.fr

47150 Monflanquin Pl. des Arcades, ☎ 05 53 36 40 19, fax 05 53 36 42 91, www.patrimoinemonflanquin.ifrance.com

47140 Penne d'Agenais Rue du 14 Juillet, ☎ 05 53 41 37 80, fax 05 53 41 40 86

47300 Pujols Pl. St-Nicolas, ☎ 05 53 36 78 69, fax 05 53 36 78 70, email mairie-de-pujols@wanadoo.fr

47110 Le Temple-sur-Lot Pl. des Templiers, ☎ 05 53 40 64 55, fax 05 53 01 10 98

47304 Villeneuve-sur-Lot 47 Rue de Paris, ☎ 05 53 36 17 30, fax 05 53 49 42 98, www.ville-villeneuve-sur-lot.fr

Market days

Casseneuil Wednesday

Fumel Tuesday, Friday, Sunday

Monflanquin Thursday

Penne d'Agenais Sunday

Pujols Sunday, March–November

Villeneuve-sur-Lot Tuesday and Saturday; farmers' market Wednesday; Christmas market second half of December

 ## Festivals and events

July *Festival du Rire*, Villeneuve-sur-Lot *Festival de Jazz de la Vallée de Lot*, Villeneuve-sur-Lot. *Foire à la tourtière*, celebrating local pastry, Penne d'Agenais

July–August *Semaine Musicale de Clairac*

August *Fêtes Médiévales*, medieval fair with street entertainment, Monflanquin *Festival des Arts de la Rue*, circus, music, dance, marionettes, Miramont-de-Guyenne *Festival du Théâtre*, Château de Bonaguil and Fumel *Festival des Blues'rie*, Tombebœuf

August–September *Festival de Musique en Pays de Serres*, Penne d'Agenais, Tournon

 # Where to stay and eating out

47500 BONAGUIL

Le Cellier, ☎ 05 53 71 23 50. At the foot of the château, with a shady terrace, serving local cuisine.

47140 PENNE D'AGENAIS

L'Air du Temps, Mounet, ☎ 05 53 41 41 34. Pleasant and tastefully arranged *chambres d'hôte*.

€–€€ *La Maison sur la Place*, ☎ 05 53 01 29 18. Traditional cooking of a rare quality and with a touch of originality, in a charming setting in the village centre.

47300 PUJOLS

✩✩✩ *Des Chênes*, ☎ 05 53 49 04 55, fax 05 53 49 22 74, www.hoteldeschenes.com. On the side of the valley opposite Pujols, a small hotel shaded by oaks with pool and terrace.

47210 STE-EUTROPE-DE-BORN

Le Moulin de Labique, west of the D676 between Villeréal and Monflanquin, ☎ 05 53 01 63 90, fax 05 53 01 73 17. *Chambres d'hôte* with five charming rooms, friendly atmosphere and pleasant setting. Regional cooking and terrace dining. Pool.

47140 ST-SYLVESTRE-SUR-LOT

✩✩✩✩ *Château Lalande*, ☎ 05 53 36 15 15, fax 05 53 36 15 16, www.chateau-lalande.com. A dreamy hotel-restaurant with pools arranged like Roman thermae and exceptional gastronomy.

47110 LE TEMPLE-SUR-LOT

✩✩✩ *Les Rives du Plantié*, Rte de Castelmonon, ☎ 05 53 79 86 86, fax 05 53 79 86 85, www.rivesduplantie.fr.st. A 19C house offering a restful and tasty break on the banks of the Lot.

€–€€ *La Commanderie*, Pl. des Templiers, ☎ 05 53 01 30 66. Local cuisine in the superb setting of a 12C Templar commandery.

47304 VILLENEUVE-SUR-LOT
€€–€€€ *La Toque Blanche*, Pujols,
☎ 05 53 49 00 30, fax 05 53 70 49
49, www.la-toque-blanche.com. A long-
established reputation combined with a
perfect hilltop village setting. Cuisine
using local produce and wines.
€€ *Lou Calel*, Pujols, ☎ 05 53 70 46
14, fax 05 53 70 49 49. Annex of the
above, with two terraces, serving a
combination of traditional and modern
cooking.

Clairac, situated on the right bank of the Lot northeast of Aiguillon, is a little town steeped in history. It began life around a Benedictine abbey in the 8C. The monks are credited with the introduction of the *prune d'Ente*, the particular type of plum used in the production of prunes, and of tobacco, and the region has benefited ever since. Clairac should be pretty, and from the river it is but, despite a few good half-timbered 15C/16C houses, overall it is rather disappointing. The original abbey was all but razed during the Wars of Religion but the later brick and stone buildings are attractively restored.

There are three museums, two of which are aimed at children, La Fôret Magique and Le Musée du Train. The life of the abbey lives on in the third, the **Musée des Automates**. Open April–Oct daily 10.00–18.00; Nov–March, Wed, Sat, Sun 10.00–18.00; ☎ 05 53 79 34 81. The museum consists of tableaux with automated models of rather daft but benign monks doing monkish things and amusingly conveys a quantity of information (French commentary, English text) on monastery life and the history of Aquitaine. It also introduces celebrated personalities associated with the town, such as Montesquieu, who wrote *Lettres persanes* (1721), a satirical description of French society, at Clairac.

Plums and prunes

The succulent *pruneaux d'Agen* are quite the best prunes in the world and the Lot-et-Garonne is responsible for 65 per cent of national production. It all began when the Templars brought the plum from Damascus in the 11C but it was not until the 15C/16C that the transformation of plums into prunes began seriously. From 1815 the fruit of the *prunier d'Ente* (from Old French *enter*, to graft) was the main variety. The prunes originally received the stamp of the port of Agen when shipped out on the Garonne, and the label has stuck. The plums are harvested between 15 August and 25 September. In 1856 Pierre Pellier took plum scions embedded in potatoes to his brother in California where they grafted the first plums and so began the prune industry on the US west coast. However, nothing beats veritable *pruneaux d'Agen*. A remarkable number of *prumandises* have been devised including creams, juices and concentrates, prunes in syrup, in Armagnac, in *eau de vie*, and preparations which include chocolate. The most exotic are *pruneaux fourrés*, the stone replaced by a *crème d'Armagnac* or some other filling. But the top-quality prunes are best eaten simply as they are.

The countryside is densely cultivated with vines, plums and maize all along the valley to Granges-sur-Lot and the **Au Pruneau Gourmand, Atelier-Musée**. Open Mon–Sat 09.00–12.00 and 14.00–19.00, Sun and PH 15.00–19.00; Nov–March closes 18.30; closed last 2 weeks of Jan; ☎ 05 53 84 00 69. This museum is well presented and offers not only all sorts of historic details about the life and times of the prune, including an audio-visual display, but also the opportunity to sample and buy the remarkable number of *prumandises* that have been devised. On the other side of the Lot is **Laparade**, a fortified *bastide perché*, founded by the French in 1269.

At **Le Temple-sur-Lot** are the handsome remains of a Templar commandery and chapel founded in the 12C and rebuilt in brick in the 15C by the Knights of Malta, with round towers and mullioned windows. Nearby off the D911 is the water-lily garden of **Latour-Marliac**, the oldest waterlily nursery in the world, founded in 1875. Open May–Sept 10.00–17.00; ☎ 05 53 01 08 05. Hardy varieties were developed here by Joseph Bory Latour-Marliac and the fame of his work was such that Claude Monet purchased the lilies for his own garden at Giverny from here. There are some 100 varieties of waterlilies and other water plants, mainly in outdoor tanks, as well as gardens with a statue of the founder, and a small museum.

The church at **Fongrave** north of the river was once part of a priory dependent on the abbey of Fontevraud in the Loire, from which it acquired an elaborate wooden retable, an excessive but magnificent piece in Counter-Reformation style, with twisted columns framing a painting of the *Adoration of the Magi*. There are several *bastides*, most on hilltops along the valley, such as **Monclar d'Agenais**, 187m above the valley. Founded by Alphonse de Poitiers in 1256, it has a large Gothic church (15C–16C). **Ste-Livrade-sur-Lot** was founded by the English, whose church was once part of a priory. The chevet is a Romanesque classic, decorated with arcades, storiated capitals and billet mouldings. The rest is rather a botched job, rebuilt (15C) in brick. Inside, the apse is covered in a half-dome and there is a recumbent marble statue of a bishop, finely carved but damaged.

Casseneuil, between the Lot and the Lède, was a little river port and has pretty riverside façades, and a 12C–16C brick church with a series of early 16C murals in the east. (Get the key at the tourist office.) **St-Pastour**, an Alphonsine foundation of 1259, unusually does not have a central *place* but it does have an old wooden *halle*.

On a hill covered with fruit orchards above the Lot, **Pujols** is one of those French villages of heart-rending perfection.

Such a strategic position has understandably been occupied since time immemorial and a Roman *castrum* protected the route between the Pyrenees and the Landes forest, called La Ténarèze. It became one of the most important fortifications in the Agenais by the 7C and later a fiefdom of Raymond VI of Toulouse. It was not besieged during the Albigensian crusades but following the Treaty of Meaux in 1228 (p 47) the stronghold was razed and the inhabitants moved to Villeneuve in the valley. Later in the 13C the hill was substantially re-fortified with ramparts, towers, deep ditches and a castle enveloping the community. During the Religious Wars and the Fronde, Royalist Pujols stood firm against rebellious Villeneuve but suffered badly. After the Revolution the fortifications were abandoned, the ramparts demolished, and the château sold for its building materials.

Some of the 13C ramparts are still in place and a chunky round tower to the east is a reminder of the castle. The entrance to the village is under the church belfry and leads to the Place du Marché with a wooden *halle* (1860). The 15C church of St-Nicolas is Gothic Flamboyant going on Renaissance, and inside are tribunes equipped with fireplaces where the baronial families kept warm during mass. There are one or two good furnishings, including the holy water stoup, painted wooden statues, an 18C *Crucifixion* and reliquaries, and five Renaissance funerary panels. The other church, Ste-Foy-La-Jeune (15C) to the south of the town, is now an exhibition space and contains some splendid murals (end 15C), including the *Martyrdom of St Faith* (p 282), in three bays of the nave and choir.

The small town of **Villeneuve-sur-Lot** originated in another *bastide* founded by Alphonse after the Albigensian crusade in 1264. Place Lafayette is a bit of a let-down compared with other *bastide* squares, but in general the market town is bustling and lively. The remains of the old defences consist in the Porte de Pujols to the southwest and the Porte de Paris to the northeast of the river, each with a stone base, brick above and steep roof. These demarcate the extent of the old town. Linking the old gates is the 13C Pont Vieux, built by the English (part rebuilt in 1642) and from it are views of picturesquely dilapidated houses lining the river. On the north of the bridge is the chapel of Notre-Dame-du-Bout-du-Pont (rebuilt in the 16C) curiously suspended over the river and containing ex-votos. Villeneuve has two churches. Ste-Catherine is a neo-Romano-Byzantine pile by Corroyer, begun in 1898, of appalling starkness in bright red brick, white stone and granite, with a tall octagonal belfry. The interior is reminiscent of Westminster Cathedral, with mosaics representing different St Catherines (of Alexandria, Bologna, Siena, Sweden etc). In the chapels are 23 precious stained-glass windows (15C to early 16C) saved from the Gothic church and similar to those in Auch Cathedral (p 383) but without the sophistication. St-Etienne on the south bank is Gothic redesigned in the 17C with furnishings of the latter period.

The Moulin de Gajac in Villeneuve houses the Musée de la Vallée du Lot (open for temporary exhibitions only; ☎ 05 53 40 48 00) and at Eysses (direction Monflanquin) is the archaeological site of the 1C AD Gallo-Roman settlement, Excisum (guided visit, July, Aug, 14.30–18.30, ☎ 05 53 70 65 19).

Monflanquin

The meandering valley of the Lède River, followed by the D676, leads to Monflanquin, an important *bastide* which follows the shape of the hilltop to form an uneven oval.

Alphonse de Poitiers acquired the 'mountain of Monflanquin' in 1252, and the *bastide* received its charter in 1256. When the Agenais passed to Edward I, Monflanquin, on border territory, was fortified with ramparts and towers; seconded by the French in 1346, it went back to the English again ten years later. The Château de Roquefère (13C–16C) to the north was part of the defensive system. Monflanquin was an active Protestant town from 1562 and its fortifications played a part during the Reformation and Catholic attacks. It was subsequently recognised as a Protestant place of safety in 1598. After the accession of Louis XIII the ramparts were dismantled and in their place is the exterior boulevard.

The **Place des Arcades** at the centre, is defined by the two parallel streets, Ste-Marie and St-Pierre, and enhanced by harmonious but not uniform *cornières* (arcades). A 13C house has a timber-and-brick façade supported by one main beam: the pillars of a 15C house supported the grain measures; and the so-called Black Prince's house (14C) is distinguished by its height, the quality masonry and window tracery. The tourist office houses the **Musée des Bastides**, a comprehensive exhibition and explanation of the history and creation of the planned towns, using models, sculptures, audio-visual and scenographic displays (English translations). Open July, Aug daily 10.00–12.30 and 14.30–19.00; rest of year Mon–Sat 10.00–12.30 and 14.30–18.30, Sun 15.00–17.00; closed 1 Jan, 1 May, 25 Dec. The smaller streets, or *carrerots*, which sub-divide the space are occasionally spanned by bridge-like *pontets* built in timber with brick or cob infill. Between the Carrerots Cabannes and Augustins is the former Protestant Temple and the library. If the latter is open, take advantage of the terrace for a panorama of the rooftops and beyond. The church of Notre-Dame, on a diagonal with the main square, dates from the same time as the *bastide* but by the end of the 17C was in a parlous state; it was rebuilt in the 18C and more radically altered in the 19C, but some of the 13C base survives. The glass for the upper windows comes from Bordeaux and for the three lower ones from the Benedictine abbey of En Calcat in the Tarn (p 339). The west front had hardly been completed when it was struck by lightning, and the Toulousain-style open belfry dates from 1923.

Still on the free-spirited valley of the Lède is **Montagnac**, with a fortified church and old mill, the Moulin de Cros (open July, Aug, Tues and Thurs 15.00–18.00; ☎ 05 53 36 44 78). Further upstream, a huge six-storey keep rises out of the vertical cliff overhanging a narrow gorge. This is the only substantial reminder of the 11C–13C **Château of Gavaudun**. Guided tours in French or English, June–Sept daily 10.00–18.00; ☎ 05 53 95 62 04. At **St-Avit** is the **Musée Bernard Palissy**, dedicated to the Renaissance ceramicist, scholar and writer (1510–89/90), who was born here. Open May–Aug 10.00–12.00 and 15.00–19.00; Sept–Oct 15.00–18.00, closed Tues; Nov–April Sun only 15.00–18.00; ☎ 05 53 40 98 22. He perfected his art at Saintes, where he researched the technique of enamelled pottery. His strange, rustic ceramics decorated with high-relief flora and fauna brought him fame at court, but he was persecuted for his Protestant beliefs and died in the Bastille. The museum also holds temporary exhibitions.

Back on the Lot, the next star attraction, way above the valley, is **Penne d'Agenais**, its steep sided streets and high-quality medieval houses remininsicent of Provence. When Richard Lionheart became Duke of Guyenne in 1169 he fortified the small fort of Penne which had probably existed since the 11C. The fortress became a focus for siege and military operations at the time of the Albigensian Crusades in the 13C, again in the 14C during the Hundred Years War, and during the Wars of the Religion in the 16C. A pilgrimage to Penne was encouraged by the Pope in 1373 who offered indulgences to those who visited the existing chapel and helped with repairs, and it has been a pilgrimage site ever since. The most recent in a succession of churches (1897–1947) is a rather unfortunate white neo-Byzantine basilica at the summit recalling St-Front at Périgueux.

Lustrac has a 13C fortified mill and, southeast, **Tournon d'Agenais** is a high *bastide* fortified by Edward I. It has some delightful half-timbered buildings including the 13C Maison de l'Abescat, arcades, and a clocktower with sundial. The *chemin de ronde* looks out over gentle countryside.

On the north of the Lot, looking down into the valley, **Monsempron-Libos** has a sturdy church with a square tower, built 11C–12C on the site of a temple dedicated to Cybele, ancient Phrygian earth goddess; a large choir was added in the 16C. It is decorated with pierced metopes on the exterior, and the nave vaults and domed crossing are Romanesque. **Fumel** is an industrial town on the north bank of the Lot, but at its heart is a handsome 18C château housing the *mairie* and attractive river frontage. Gardens and guided tour of the château daily June 10.00–12.00 and 14.00–17.00; July, Aug 10.00–17.45; Feb–Nov 10.00–12.00 and 14.30–16.30; closed Jan. There are marvellous views from the terrace and an interesting collection of trees and shrubs in the gardens.

Château de Bonaguil

The route (D673 from Fumel, then left on D158) to the magnificent Château de Bonaguil twists and turns through lush countryside, but suddenly it towers before you. On the edge of the region of 1001 châteaux, it was the last of the great fortified castles to be built in France. It is everything that a castle should be, standing on a rocky promontory with 13 towers and turrets, 350m of perimeter walls, and military architecture ranging from the 13C to the 18C. Open daily July, Aug 10.00–17.45; June 10.00–12.00 and 14.00–17.00; Feb–May, Sept–Nov 10.30–12.00 and 14.30–16.30; Dec hols 14.30–16.30; closed Jan; ☎ 05 53 71 13 70. Guided visits in English in July, Aug.

The beginnings of Bonaguil remain wreathed in mystery but it is known that a château existed here in the 13C on land belonging to Jeanne de Toulouse. At her death in 1271 it became the property of the king, Philippe III, and some time later it passed to the powerful house of Roquefeuil. Jean de Roquefeuil reconstructed it in the 15C but the present version, which incorporates some earlier elements, dates between 1480 and 1520, the work of the remarkably long-lived Béranger de Roquefeuil (1448–1530). He vowed to build a castle which neither his 'brutish subjects, nor the English if they had the cheek to return, nor even the most powerful soldiers of the King of France, could seize'. Béranger's stronghold was somewhat of an anachronism at the beginning of the 16C, a time when most *chatelains* were building luxury palaces not feudal forts, but adapted to contemporary advances in military technology. There is no documented evidence of attacks, although there is evidence of damage during the Wars of Religion. Its downfall came at the Revolution when the château was declared a national property and was partly demolished. Bonaguil changed hands several times after that, until taken over by the commune of Fumel in 1860. Restoration work was carried out in the late 19C, 1949–50 and 1977, sometimes brutally.

Bonaguil spans the style of military architecture of the end of the Middle Ages and the beginning of the Renaissance. It is organised concentrically, with a very strong exterior enclosure including bastions and barbican. The interior enclosure has five towers, one with exceptionally thick walls, and at the very centre is the superb keep topped with a slender look-out tower. Between the first and second enclosures were dry ditches which allowed men and arms to circulate outside, or through an underground gallery, part natural and part man-made.

The entrance is through the massive semicircular **barbican** on the vulnerable northern side, which leads into a courtyard overlooked by the prow of the vast

central donjon to the left and great tower, huge but truncated, to the right. Between the barbican and the inner enclosure there was originally a drawbridge, now a fixed one, leading to the **main entrance**, to either side of which are *cannonières* (cannon loops). The slope to the left leads past the dovecote to the **lower courtyard** (La Cour Basse) in the shadow of the keep, from

Château de Bonaguil

where it is obvious how its shape was determined by the rock that it stands on. On the lower level are the remains of outbuildings and beyond are the curtain walls of the outer enclosure. The entrance to the underground gallery is to the right, ending close to the **great tower** (La Grosse Tour), originally 40m high (now 29m). Within its huge walls was a self-contained living unit and defences (similar to towers at Aigues Mortes and Carcassonne). The remains of the *chemin de ronde* are supported by corbels in the shape of inverted pyramids and pierced with round machicolations. The esplanade to the south is 18C and ends in a *chicane* or carefully designed trap. The square tower (La Tour Carrée) had its own drawbridge, and beyond is the red tower (La Tour Rouge); both have cannon loops. The square tower leads to the **main courtyard** (La Cour d'Honneur), with a well and the main apartments (Le Logis Seigneurial) including the great room. The doorway to the main living area has an elegant ogee arch and inside are rooms with monumental fireplaces (late 15C) and graffiti (16C–18C). A steep flight of 22 steps and a spiral staircase of 68 steps in the look-out turret climbs to the terrace on top of the keep. Eighteen more steps take you up the turret. In the keep two rooms are set up as a small museum.

THE PAYS D'ALBRET

The area between the Garonne and the forests of the Landes de Gascogne, known as the Pays d'Albret or Néracais, was associated with the powerful Albret dynasty from the 11C. Its capital is Nérac, where the greatest of them all, Henri III of Navarre (1553–1610) who became King Henri IV, and his queen resided for some years, gathering around them a court to rival that at the Louvre. The gently undulating fields and woodland are crossed by numerous small rivers, notably the Baïse and the Avance, and punctuated by *bastides*, castles, fortified churches, *pigeonniers* (dovecotes) and mills.

Getting there and around
Train

Agen is the nearest station.
Bus

Agen to Mont-de-Marsan via Nérac.

Tourist information
47230 Barbaste Pl. de la Mairie, ☎ 05 53 64 84 85, fax 05 53 97 18 36, email mairie.barbaste@wanadoo.fr
47700 Casteljaloux Pl. du Roy, ☎ 05

53 93 00 00, fax 05 53 20 74 32, email
office.tourisme@casteljaloux.com
47230 Lavardac Ave du Général-de-
Gaulle, ☎/fax 05 53 65 94 69, email
mairie.lavardac@wanadoo.fr
47170 Mezin Pl. Armand Fallières,
☎ 05 53 65 77 46, fax 05 53 65 33 03,
47600 Nérac 7 Ave. Mondenard, ☎ 05
53 65 27 75, fax 05 53 65 97 48,
www.mezintourisme.com
47230 Vianne Pl. des Marrionniers,
☎ 05 53 65 29 54, fax 05 53 97 08 07

Market days

Casteljaloux Tuesday and Saturday
Nérac Saturday, Tuesday evenings,
June–September
Vianne Friday evenings
June–September, 21–23 December

River cruises and boat hire

47600 Nérac *Croisière du Prince
Henry*, Quai de la Baïse, ☎ 05 53 65 66
66, fax 05 53 65 06 44

Festivals and events

February *Festival de Guitare*,
jazz, country, blues from
around the world, Nérac
July–August *Festival de Musique en
Albret*, Nérac
August *Festival International des
Menteurs*, celebrating the art

of lying, Moncrabeau
Festival de la Baïse au Missipi in Pays
d'Albret, country, blues, cajun, French
and international music

Where to stay and eating out

47230 BARBASTE
€ *La Table du Meunier*, Moulin des
Tours, ☎ 05 53 97 06 60. In an old
underground mill near the magnificent
Moulin des Tours, a choice of regional
cooking or Gascon *crêpes*.

47700 CASTELJALOUX
☆☆☆ *Château de Hautelande Ruffiac*,
Ruffiac, ☎ 05 53 93 18 63, fax 05 53
89 67 93, www.hautelanderuffiac.com.
This 14C clergyman's residence in a
green and pleasant site has 20 rooms;
pool.
€–€€ *La Vieille Auberge*, 11 Rue
Posterne, ☎ 05 53 93 01 19. In a small
street at the heart of the town, this
restaurant offers refined local cooking;
3 rooms.

47600 FRANCESCAS
Relais de la Hire, 11 Rue Porte-Neuve,
☎ 05 53 65 41 59. An 18C mansion
serving top-quality cuisine using fresh
local produce.

Protestantism and the Albrets

In 1527 Marguerite d'Angoulême, sister of François I and author of *The
Heptameron*, married Henri d'Albret, King of Navarre. A cultured woman,
Marguerite introduced the humanist ideas of the Renaissance to Nérac and
the great thinkers of the day were drawn to her court. Marguerite's daughter, Jeanne d'Albret, converted to the Protestant faith under the influence of
Théodore de Bèze (1519–1605), a disciple of Jean Calvin (1509–64), both
of whom visited Nérac. She took with her much of the Agenais and ordered
the complete substitution of the Protestant faith in the Béarn (p 48), with
far-reaching consequences. The first active centres of Protestantism were
Nérac and Oloron, followed by Ste-Foy, Bergerac and Agen. Jeanne created
the Protestant Academy of Orthez. She made her son, Henri III of Navarre
(who alternated between Catholicism and Protestantism six times for various reasons), head of the Protestants when the Religious Wars broke out.

Casteljaloux is a small sleepy town, linked to the Garonne by the Avance River at the gateway to the Landes. From the 11C it was an important centre in the north of the Albret territories and Henri of Navarre had a hunting lodge here, for sporting and amorous pursuits. Much is made locally of the Romantic association with Edmond Rostand's Cyrano de Bergerac and the Cadets de Gascogne (p 431). There is not a great deal left of Casteljaloux's past. The old town is centred on Place du Roy, and streets around it have some attractive jettied 15C–16C houses and the former Cordeliers convent (14C–15C), now a retirement home. The church of Notre-Dame, southeast of the *place*, was totally destroyed in 1568 by Protestant troops and in 1635 Louis XIII donated materials from the demolished Albret château to its reconstruction (1682–1711), in the proscribed royalist but dull Neo-classical style. The inscription on the pediment, however, is the battle cry of the Republic, *Liberté, Egalité, Fraternité*. Behind the east end of the church runs the Avance, and scant remains of the castle are surrounded by the municipal park. To the south, **Durance** is a tiny 13C *bastide* in the Landes, still with a few sections of its walls, where the princes of Navarre had a hunting lodge.

To the east of Casteljaloux, **Villefranche-du-Queyran** was an English *bastide*. Just outside, towards Damazan, there is a little Romanesque church, St-Savin. **Xaintrailles** is a hilltop village on the old Roman way, La Ténarèze. The château, rebuilt in the 15C, was the birthplace of Joan of Arc's companion in arms, Jean Poton de Xaintrailles. **Mongaillard** is a circular bastion with walls and fortified gate intact but the imposing 12C–14C castle in ruins.

The *bastide* of **Vianne**, to the east on the D642, is special from the exterior because it has an almost perfectly preserved set of ramparts, towers and fortified gateways. Within the walls is less interesting, although the chequerboard layout has been respected. It was founded as Villelongue in 1284 by Edward I's seneschal, Jourdain de l'Isle, lord of Mongaillard, and was later named after de l'Isle's aunt. In the medieval cemetery near the north gate is a tiny Romanesque church with a fortified belltower and large west door. The barrel-vaulted interior has some surprisingly lively carved capitals. The village has had a tradition of glassmaking since the 1920s. On Friday evenings in summer there is an open-air market with regional products and alfresco eating.

Lavardac to the south was a French *bastide*, founded in 1256 on the banks of the Baïse, and a major river port for shipping Armagnac. Nearby, on the Gélise River at **Barbaste**, is an extraordinary and unique fortified mill, the **Moulin-des-Tours**. The mill and the old bridge are 13C. The mill became the property of the Albrets in 1308 and Henri of Navarre took pleasure in the title *Meunier de Barbaste*. The milling was limited to the core of the building, while the four towers, the tallest of which is 29m high, were reserved for defence. It was used as a mill until the mid-19C, but the mill wheels were ripped out when it was taken over by a cork manufacture, and it was badly damaged by fire in 1937. Open June–Sept 10.30–12.00, 13.00–19.30; Oct–Dec, Sun 14.00–18.00; Feb–March, Wed–Sun 14.00–18.00; closed Jan; ☎ 05 53 65 09 37. The 19C Maison Aunac on the river adjacent to the Moulin-des-Tours, has been brought back to life, if in a rather fey manner, as Le Château Imaginaire. This magical fairyland enlists the help of interactive installations, holographs, mirrors and sculptures, and was concocted by 25 artists. Open July–Sept 10.00–19.00 and Tues, Wed 21.00–23.00; April–June 10.00–13.00, 14.00–18.00; Oct and PH 14.00–18.00; ☎ 05 53 97 25 15, www.chateau-imaginaire.com.

Nérac

The old buildings clustered around the remains of Henri IV's château on the left bank of the Baïse at Nérac create a picturesque ensemble. This town draws the crowds for its historic associations with France's favourite monarch, although in reality the remains of the Château of Nérac are modest. The river carves a fairly substantial course here on its way north and is spanned by two bridges, new and old.

The Albret family inherited the property from the abbey of Condom in the 11C. Their astute politics, judicious marriages and successful wars resulted in great power and wealth until the Gascon princes dominated a kingdom extending as far as Pau (p 436). In 1572, when he was 19 years old, Henri of Navarre married Marguerite de Valois (*la Reine Margot*). In 1576 Henri based himself in Nérac where he spent some of his best years enjoying the good life and firmly establishing his reputation as the *Vert Galant* (Old Charmer). In 1578 with the arrival of his wife and his mother-in-law, Catherine de Médicis, the provincial court of Nérac became as showy as that of the Louvre but Nérac was abandoned for ever in favour of Paris when Henri acceded to the French throne in 1589. After the Wars of Religion, during Counter-Reformation fervour, Louis XIII had the citadel of Nérac destroyed. The Pays d'Albret settled down to relative peace in the 18C and had a thriving agricultural economy exporting wheat, wine, flax and linen. The rivers were a vital means of transport until the 19C but the locks were destroyed by terrible flooding in December 1952 and the Baïse was declared non-navigable until the 1990s, when repairs began.

The **Château** contains an exhibition dedicated to the Albret family and a museum of local archaeology. Open June–Sept 10.00–12.00 and 14.00–19.00; Oct–May to 18.00; closed Mon; ☎ 05 53 62 21 11. The year after Henri IV's death in 1610, the château burned down with the loss of the archives. Originally it consisted of a four-square building around a courtyard with towers at each angle, dry ditches and a fortified entrance. All that remains is one wing and what you see was originally an internal façade onto the courtyard, a pretty example of 15C–16C transitional architecture, between the late-Gothic and early-Renaissance. It is possible that this wing contained Henri's apartments and, at the river end, doorways and a fireplace hang suspended where once there was a corner pavilion. The building is just one storey high and dominated by a steeply raked roof with red tiles. Along the length of the façade is a loggia with basket-handle arches supported by carved capitals; the twisted columns appear to continue through the cornice below to culminate in sculpted bosses. There is little of architectural interest inside; the ground floor displays local archaeological finds; the exhibition on the first floor gives a detailed account of the court of Nérac and its political and cultural importance.

St-Nicholas was rebuilt 1759–87 in sober Neo-classical style on the site of an earlier church consecrated in 1096. It received two steeples in 1855. Most of the furnishings are 19C, including the organ and the stained glass with Old and New Testament scenes. In streets behind the church are some 16C houses and the 17C *hotel de ville* (with a fine Gallo-Roman mosaic floor), while near the Pont Vieux in Petit Nérac is the 16C Maison de Sully. At the end of the Pont Neuf is **La Garenne**, a park created by Jeanne d'Albret's husband, Antoine de Bourbon, on the river bank. There is a fragment of Gallo-Roman mosaic near the entrance as well as a fragment of the Roman villa, and several fountains in the park. Notable is a positively flesh-creeping 19C statue, *Fleurette noyée* by Daniel Champagne, in memory of Fleurette, the first of Henri of Navarre's many conquests who drowned herself in despair when abandoned by her royal lover. The king of Navarre's park is the setting for Shakespeare's *Love's Labour's Lost*.

In a landscape of pines and vines a 'Roman' bridge and an old mill adorn the banks of the Gélise near **Mézin**, southwest of Nérac on the D656, a former Cluniac-sponsored halt on the pilgrimage route to Spain. The large church has a Romanesque chevet with a 13C nave and 14C west front. There is a flourishing cork industry here, as demonstrated at the Musée du Liège et Bouchon. Open Feb–May, Oct 14.00–18.30, closed Mon; June–Sept 10.00–12.30 and 14.00–19.00, closed Sun, Mon mornings; ☎ 05 53 65 68 16. The Italianate **Château de Poudenas** dominates the village of the same name just to the west. On 13C foundations, it was extended in the 16C–17C and is famous for the proliferation of windows. Guided visits, mid-July to end Aug; ☎ 05 53 65 78 86.

AGEN AND THE AGENAIS

Agen

Agen, *préfecture* of the *département* of Lot-et-Garonne, is an attractive if not thrilling town of some 30,000 inhabitants on the banks of the Garonne. The old centre has some interesting half-timbered domestic buildings and the highlight is the excellent fine art museum. Agen is probably best known as the guarantee of quality of French prunes and has the remarkable accolade (from a poll by L'Express magazine) of *ville la plus heureuse de France*. Close to the A62, and at the intersection of the Canal latéral à la Garonne with the river, it is a convenient stopping or starting point.

Getting there and around
Air

Agen airport, ☎ 05 53 77 00 88
Car

Autoroute A62 from Bordeaux or Toulouse, exit 7. N113 from Langon/Marmande (N) and from Moisaac/Toulouse (S).
Train

TGV Paris Montparnasse to Agen
TER Bordeaux to Agen
TER Bordeaux to Toulouse via Agen, Moissac, Montauban
TER Périgueux to Agen
Agens tation is to the north of the town on Blvd Sylvanin Dumon

Bus

SNCF bus from train station to Pau via Aire-sur-Adour; Mont-de-Marsan via Nérac;
Villeneuve-sur-Lot.

 Tourist information
47000 Agen 107 Blvd Carnot, BP 237, ☎ 05 53 47 36 09, fax 05 53 47 29 98, email otsi.agen@wanadoo.fr
47220 Astaffort Pl. de la Nation, ☎ 05 53 67 13 33, fax 05 53 67 10 06, www.astaffort.com
82340 Auvillar Pl. de la Halle, ☎/fax 05 63 39 89 92, www.webpan.com/auvillar

47470 Beauville Le Bourg, ☎ 05 53 47 63 06, fax 05 53 66 72 63, email office-tourism-beauville@wanadoo.fr

47240 Bon-Encontre 55 Rue de la République, ☎ 05 53 96 14 85, fax 05 53 48 29 93

47390 Layrac Rue du Dr Ollier, ☎/fax 05 53 66 51 53, email ot.layrac@wandoo.fr

47310 Moirax Mairie, Le Bourg, ☎ 05 53 87 13 73, fax 05 53 67 55 60

47270 Puymirol 7 Pl. Maréchal Leclerc, ☎ 05 53 95 32 30, fax 05 53 95 32 38, www.mairie-puymirol.fr

Market days

Agen Wednesday and Sunday, Saturday on the Esplanade du Gravier
Auvillar Sunday farmers' market
Layrac Friday
Puymirol Sunday May to December
Prayssas Sunday

Boat trips

47000 Agen

Bateau l'Agenais, Quai de Dunkerque, ☎ 05 53 87 51 95 or 06 11 48 97 45, fax 05 53 87 27 42, http://perso.wanadoo.fr/l.agenais
The Office du Tourisme also has details.
Locaboat Plaisance, Quai de Dunkerque, ☎ 05 53 66 00 74, fax 05 53 68 26 23. For motorboats or houseboats

Festivals and events

May *Festival International d'Ongues de Babarie*, biennial (04, 06 etc) festival of barrel organ and mechanised music, Agen
June *Festival de Dance*, Agen
June–July *Festival des Bouts d'Choux*, entertainment for children, Agen
July *Festival de Théâtre*, Agen
August *Foire aux Fruits*, festival of produce from France's largest orchard, Prayssas
August–September *Festival de Musique en Pays de Serre*, Madaillan

Where to stay and eating out
47000 AGEN

Rue Voltaire at the centre of the town is called *la rue des restaurants* and has a friendly atmosphere and affordable prices. Closed to traffic Thursday–Saturday evenings in summer.

☆☆☆☆ *Hôtel-Château des Jacobins*, 1 Pl. des Jacobins, 2 Rue Jacob, ☎ 05 53 47 03 31, fax 05 53 47 02 80, www.chateauxhotels.com/jacobins. Smallish château set in a garden in the centre.

€€€ *Le Mariottat*, 25 Rue Louis-Vivent, ☎ 05 53 77 99 77, fax 05 53 77 99 79. Garden and terrace make a beautiful, tranquil setting for gourmet cooking.

€–€€ *La Bohème*, 14 Rue Emile-Sentini, ☎ 05 53 68 31 00. Popular spot with good value menus and local dishes.

47550 BOÉ

☆☆☆☆ *Château St-Marcel*, ☎ 05 53 96 61 30, fax 05 53 96 94 33, www.chateau-saint-marcel.com. An impressive 17C château set in woodland. The decoration is refined and cooking creative; pool.

47310 BRAX

☆☆ *Le Colombier du Touron*, 187 Rte des Landes, ☎ 05 53 87 87 91, fax 05 53 87 82 37, www.logis-de-france-47.com. Ten charming rooms in a pleasant and quiet setting near Agen (6km).

47470 PUYMIROL

☆☆☆☆ *Les Loges de l'Aubergade*, 52 Rue Royale, ☎ 05 53 95 31 46, fax 05 53 95 33 80, www.aubergade.com. A hotel created in a very personal manner by Michel and Maryse Trama in a former property of the Counts of Toulouse, around a courtyard with pool.

47310 SÉRIGNAC-SUR-GARONNE

☆☆☆ *Le Prince Noir*, Rte de Mont-de-Marsan (D119 west of Agen), ☎ 05 53 68 74 30, fax 05 53 68 71 93, www.le-prince-noir.com. A former convent near the Garonne, with restaurant, pool, tennis court.

History

The city of the Nitiobriges people became a Roman administrative district, *civitas Agennensium*, which developed as the prosperous city of Aginnum with its own theatre and amphitheatre in the 1C–2C AD on the heights above present-day Agen. By the 4C the town had relocated to the banks of the Garonne and some of its people had embraced Christianity: one of the most revered local martyrs, St Faith (see p 273) was persecuted here. In common with the rest of the southwest, the area was overrun by Visigoths, Vascons and Normans, and by the 5C there was a small protected enclosure around the cathedral, on the site of the present covered market.

The town developed during the 11C–12C under the control of the Church but by the 13C the commune was strong enough to proclaim a degree of independence from the prelates. With the accession of Henry Plantagenet in 1154, Agen found itself in the position of border town between the territories of England and France, so that between the end of the 12C and 1370 the town changed hands no fewer than 11 times. Nevertheless it continued to prosper despite, or because of, its position during the Hundred Years Wars. The Renaissance period was a brilliant one for the Agenais. The area received a series of Italian bishops, encouraging an influx of Italian scholars and artists, including the humanist Giulio-Cesare Scaliger (1484–1558). His son, the Protestant philosopher Joseph-Juste Scaliger (1540–1609), was born in Agen. Gradually the town burst through its walls and a new, extended enclosure was built incorporating the church of St-Caprais. The town was affected by the religious upheavals of the 16C and 17C but in the following century Agen built boulevards, gardens and grand mansions. After the Revolution the former collegiate church of St-Caprais became the cathedral. The river port on the Garonne, and in the 19C the Canal, were great assets until the introduction of the railway, and contributed to a flourishing fabrics industry from the 17C until the Continental blockade after the Revolution. One of its main industries today is fruit packing and wholesaling.

From the Esplanade du Gravier on the east bank of the Garonne, take Rue Filomet and Rue R. Coeur-de-Lion to pass the great brick church of the **Jacobins**. The Dominican order was established here in Agen in 1249 and although the monastery buildings have disappeared the church still stands and is open for exhibitions. Laid out on similar lines to the church of the Jacobins in Toulouse (p 545), the large empty interior designed for preaching is divided by central columns supporting 'palm' vaults, but unlike Toulouse, Agen's church has a flat apse. It is decorated with Gothic *trompe l'oeil* designs and has 14C windows with trefoil tracery.

From here, continue past Hôtel Montesquieu-Suffolk at no. 55, a sophisticated 18C house. **Rue Beauville** on the right leads to a cluster of remarkable half-timbered houses grouped on an island plot. These picturesque properties, sensitively restored, have intricate timber designs, brick nogging, deep overhanging jetties and fine windows. **Place Dr Pierre-Esquirol** (named after a local mayor) was the site of the Gallo-Roman town whose walls were absorbed by the buildings now containing the museum. Other buildings on the *place* are the 17C *hôtel de ville* and the Théâtre Ducourneau by Guillaume Tronchet (begun 1906), the first theatre in France to use reinforced concrete.

Musée des Beaux-Arts

The Musée des Beaux-Arts ranks among the best of the provincial galleries in the southwest. It occupies a series of four 16C–17C *hôtels particuliers* of rich interest in themselves, with elegant staircases and panelled décor. The entrance is in the **Hôtel d'Estrades** (*c* 1600 and 19C), of alternate brick and stone under a steep roof. It belonged to the Count d'Estrades (1607–86), ambassador and Maréchal de France during the reigns of Louis XIII and XIV. The **Hôtel de Vaurs** has an Italianate façade on the Rue des Juifs and played host to Scaliger and Nostradamus. The Hôtel de Vergès has an interior courtyard and Hôtel de Monluc was the town house of the Catholic leader Blaise de Monluc during the Wars of Religion.

The space in this somewhat labyrinthine but charming setting is well used and the exhibits are presented with care. The collection includes items from prehistory through to the 20C and is presented chronologically. Like the museums at Bayonne and Castres, it is remarkably well endowed with Spanish paintings. Open May–Sept 10.00–18.00; Oct–April 10.00–17.00; closed Tues, 1 Jan, 1 May, 1 Nov, 25 Dec: ☎ 05 53 69 47 23.

Archaeological and historical collections These contain objects discovered during excavations in Lot-et-Garonne since the end of the 19C. Iron Age finds include a superb bronze helmet and a stunning *Horse's Head* in bronze (5C BC). Among **Roman works** are the 1C BC marble *Venus* from Mas-d'Agenais, in the style of the Greek sculptor Praxiteles; the smaller alabaster *Venus of Tayrac* (2C AD); a bronze *Horse* (2C AD) discovered at Aubiac; and two early Christian sarcophagi (6C) in white Pyrenean marble. Prehistoric finds are shown in the basement and include tools, engraved bones and other objects from the Palaeolithic to Neolithic periods. The medieval room contains capitals from the lost Romanesque cloister of St-Caprais and from the Augustinian monastery founded in 1287, both of which disappeared during the Revolution. There are gold and silverwork, enamels, and a reconstructed Romanesque fireplace.

Paintings On display on the upper floors are some 100 out of a diverse group of 600 paintings acquired mainly through donation or bequest. Works of the 16C works include a Flemish triptych of the *Crucifixion*; five portraits of men by Corneille de Lyon; and a painting of *Rinaldo and Armida* illustrating Tasso's epic poem *Gerusalemme Liberata*, restored in 1997 and attributed to Tintoretto. Representative of 17C French paintings are a *Madonna and Child* and *Portrait of Etienne Delafons*, both by Philippe de Champaigne; and the Classical-style *Daedalus and Pasiphaë* from the Cretan myth of the minotaur. Among the lush still lifes are Jan Davidsz de Heem's *Still Life with Fruit* (1650) and *Still Life with Apricots and Plums* by Pierre Dupuis, both making good mileage from the artists' skill in evoking contrasting textures.

The 18C paintings are dominated by the pictures confiscated from the estate of the Dukes of Aiguillon at the Revolution. They include works by J.-F. de Troy, F.-H. Drouais, Jean-Baptiste Oudry, François Jouvenet, and small gouaches of the *Aiguillon Château at Veretz* (1771) by H.-J. van Blarenberghe, crammed with topographical details. **Spanish art** centres on five fine works by Goya: *Self-Portrait* (1783), a confident statement of the artist as young man; *The Balloon* (1792), showing a hot-air balloon floating above a milling group of people, demonstrating Goya's extraordinarily varied technique; also *Sketch for the Equestrian Portrait of Ferdinand VII* (1808), *Capricho* (1818–19), which echoes his engravings of the same title, and *The Churching* (*c* 1819).

The museum has a rich collection of **19C paintings**. From the earlier part of the century they include paintings by Millet, Corot and Boudin. Later works include a delightful pastel by Gustave Caillebotte of *The Diver* (1877); bursts of colour in Alfred Sisley's *September Morning* (1888); and Francis Picabia's *Banks of the Loing at Moret* (1904). The Romanian artist, Nicolae Grigorescu, who regularly visited France between 1862 and 1887, is represented by two utterly charming portraits of young women. The 20C collection focuses on a small group of artists: there are about 38 works by a local painter, Roger Bissière (1886–1964), born in Villeréal, who was influenced by Cubism and Abstraction, but also designed stained glass; and sculptures by François-Xavier and Claude Lalanne.

Decorative arts There are collections of sculpture, faïence, porcelain, crystal and tapestries from France and elsewhere. Among them is a sample of the ceramic creations of Bernard Palissy, born at St-Avit (p 274) near Agen. There are also collections of Middle Eastern art and Asian sculpture.

From the museum take Rue Chaudordy past a Renaissance courtyard and across Rue Montesquieu into Rue Droits-de-l'Homme, to arrive at a small space in front of the little 13C church of **Notre-Dame-du-Bourg**. The church is a mixture of brick and stone, and over the porch is a tower with an open belfry. Damaged by Protestants, the interior is devoid of decoration, and has simple lancet windows. Rue de Raymond leads to modern Boulevard Carnot with shops and banks and the tourist office on the left. Rue Marché au Blé (at the junction of Rues de Raymond and Droits-de-l'Homme), leads to Place Durand and Rue Lagrille, which leads into Ruelle des Juifs, the narrowest alley in town, where the money-lenders hung out until the end of the 14C. This opens into the **Place des Laitiers** which, until Boulevard de la République sliced the town in two, led straight into **Rue des Cornières**, the main commercial district since the 13C. Both the *place* and the street are lined with arcades (*cornières*) of various designs which have undergone steady renovation.

Rue des Cornières leads towards the cathedral, passing the oldest monument in Agen, the 11C **Tour Chapelet**, built on Roman foundations and incorporated into the first medieval fortifications. The twin towers are later, and the 16C–17C monastery was rebuilt in the 19C. At the end of Rue Arago turn right to the **Cathédrale St-Caprais**. It was built originally as a collegiate church to receive St Caprais' relics in the 6C, and was elevated to cathedral only in 1803. The building was begun in the 12C, but badly damaged by the Huguenots in 1591 and the cloister was destroyed during the Revolution. A major rebuild in the 19C resulted in the construction of the belfry. The best part of the church is the Romanesque east end with apse and radiating chapels, sculpted corbels and capitals; the west door is Gothic. Enter by the south door. The interior is unremarkable. It was left unfinished in the Romanesque period and the large square piers with restored capitals suggest that a dome was originally intended. The shallow transept was vaulted in the 13C and the nave completed in the 16C. The decoration is out-landishly 19C. The chapter house contains the best surviving Romanesque work and the relics of Agen's martyrs. For guided visits, enquire at the tourist office.

In Rue des Martyrs behind the cathedral the 18C **Martrou** is the purported resting place of St Caprais, beheaded in the 3C at the time of Diocletian. The site of the chapel dedicated to the girl saint, Faith (p 218), who was martyred at the same time as Caprais, is marked by a 19C tower at the end of Boulevard Carnot.

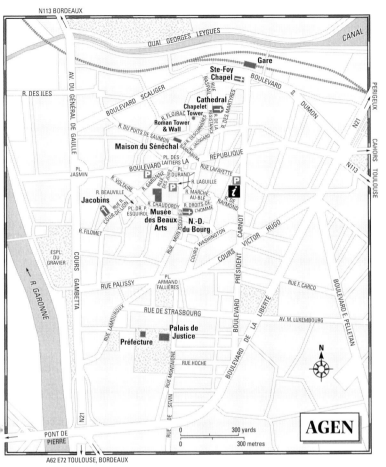

Return to Rue des Cornières and turn into **Rue Floirac** for some good 16C–19C doorways, and the severely Classical Hôtel Amblard (1773), built by the local banking brothers Pélissier. Rue Puits de Saumon has one of the best examples of medieval domestic architecture in Agen, the 14C **Maison du Sénéchal**, with pointed arches on the ground floor and an open loggia above with trefoil tracery.

Return to Place des Laitiers and descend towards Place Jasmin and the Garonne, passing on the left Rue Voltaire, which is packed with eating places. The **Esplanade du Gravier** was created in the 19C from an island in the river, and the footbridge was built (1833–40) at the spot where piers were erected at the time of Richard the Lionheart. South is the Pont de Pierre, begun in 1812 following a visit by Napoléon I in 1808, and to the north the **Pont Canal** spectacularly carries the Canal latéral à la Garonne on 23 arches over the river. There are ample opportunities for water tourism here.

In the southern part of the town on the vast **Place Armand-Fallières**, the *préfecture*, claiming to be one of the finest in France, is housed in the 18C bishops' palace built by Leroy in grand Neo-classical style. The Palais de Justice was built in 1869 during the Second Empire by Juste Lich, who was responsible for the Elysée Palace in Paris.

The area northwest of Agen, between the Garonne and the Lot (and between the N21, D118 and N113), is known as the **Pays de Serres**, a jagged rocky landscape that is difficult to cultivate, though there are plum orchards, vines, wheat and maize. It harbours small delights in the shape of isolated churches, tiny *bastides*, and caves with remarkable natural formations as at **Fontirou** in Castella. Open July, Aug daily 10.00–12.00 and 14.00–18.00; May–mid-June Sun and PH only 14.00–17.30; 15–30 June and 1–15 Sept daily 14.00–17.30; ☎ 05 53 41 73 97. Also **Lastournelle** at Ste-Colombe-de-Villeneuve. Open July, Aug 10.00–12.00 and 14.00–18.30; rest of year Sun or by appointment; ☎ 05 53 40 08 09.

Further west, in an area where the sweet Chasselas grape is cultivated, **Prayssas** is a circular 13C *bastide* with four gates and a 12C chancel and tower on the church. To find the **Château de Madaillan** (13C–15C) follow signs from the D118 between Villeneuve and Prayssas. It is a stronghold which resisted several sieges by Blaise de Monluc against the Protestants who had taken it over in 1575. Guided visits, Aug daily; for other times, ☎ 05 53 87 56 23. **Monpezat d'Agenais** on the D13 was the only English *bastide* in this region and the last Huguenot stronghold in the Agenais to surrender at the accession of Henri IV. A footpath leads to the churches of St-Jean de la Balerme, St-Vincent-de-Pérignac, St-Médard and Floirac.

Northeast of Agen by the D656 and D310 are some attractive little places such as **Laroque-Timbaut**, with a 12C *halle* (restored). In the valley is a church and a fountain which, legend has it, cured Roland's army of a contagious illness. **Hautefage-la-Tour** has a Renaissance tower and a 15C church under which is a spring that supposedly cures sterility in women—Anne de Neaujeu, daughter of Louis XI, visited and conceived a daughter. **Frespech** is a minuscule fortified village of much charm within the remains of 11C/14C walls, boasting an 11C chapel and a museum of foie gras. True to its name, **Beauville** further east is a pretty *bastide* set high above the Séoune Valley.

Puymirol, east of Agen by the N113 and D16, was the first *bastide* in the Agenais. It was established in 1246 by Raymond VII, Count of Toulouse, on a ridge overlooking the valley at a strategic point close to the Clermont–Agen route which had already been occupied in Roman times. It was strongly fortified and supposedly impregnable yet, by whatever means, the Protestants took it in 1574 and remained until 1589. As a consequence in the 17C the town received the usual treatment by Louis XIII, destruction of much of the ramparts although worse was to come at the end of the 19C and early 20C when the inhabitants used the stone from the walls to build their houses. Its main *place* is embellished with arcades, an old well, a restored *halle aux grains*, and a 13C church with an impressively deep porch. In the town centre an 18C house has been transformed into an unusual and elegant hotel-restaurant (see above).

The peaceful village of **St-Maurin** owes its existence to a Cluniac abbey, daughter-house of Moissac (p 298), founded in 1097 and wrecked in 1802. The village is very attractive, with half-timbered houses roofed with round tiles and a timber market *halle* in the square. Of the abbey, announced by square towers, there are only fragments. The tall stone tower, now the *mairie*, was part of the abbot's house which abutted the west of the abbey. The nave has gone but there are some vaults, a few walls, and the tower above a chapel is in fact the south transept. The painted apse carries a half dome and contains some naïve Romanesque capitals. The 16C chapter house was north of the now non-existent nave and cloister. There is also a kitchen with a monumental fireplace and some 15C and 17C buildings. A model of the Gothic church is displayed in the Musée de l'Abbaye de St-Maurin, an ethnological museum specialising in customs and regional trades. Open July, Aug 15.00–19.00; closed Tues; ☎ 05 53 95 31 25.

Agen to Auvillar

The area south of Agen is rich in Romanesque churches. The tiny community of **Aubiac** on the D931 nestles at the foot of sloping vineyards in the shelter of the sturdy fortified church of Ste-Marie (12C), its west façade flanked by two square towers and a round turret. To the east, around the apse roofed in stepped *lauze* stone tiles, are carved corbels. The west door is round-headed and inside is a single nave with barrel vaults and a narrow apse with two chapels. There is a square lantern dome on crossed arches, in Carolingian style, with billet mouldings and palmettes, and some indifferent paintings added later. Adjacent is an 18C château, with cellars and old grain stores where exhibitions are held, and nearby are windmills.

The reason behind **Moirax** was a Cluniac priory, founded in 1045 by Guillaume-Arnaud de Moirax. The little town, huddled around the church, still has remnants of the walled enclosure and a tower. The abbey church (*c* 1070–1140) is the Romanesque high spot in the Agenais and introduces local characteristics to the Cluniac formula. The harmonious tripartite west façade (restored) has a large decorated door, echoed by a round-headed window above inscribed in an arch, and arcades and windows either side. Above is a small belfry with a disproportionately large roof. The exterior of the nave and transepts is sober, but the choir has a scallop design and three high windows, and the apse is enlivened with much-restored carvings. The conical dome is topped off with a mini campanile and pepper-pot roof.

The interior is breathtaking, with a rhythmical pattern of columns and arches dividing up the space, and some 100 carved capitals, 17 of them with a lion motif and 13 storiated. The church is built on a basilical plan, the nave covered with slightly pointed barrel vaults (remade in the 19C) and flanked by aisles. There is no tribune as in Toulouse or Conques, but the transition from the nave to chancel is made with massive piers supporting an arch which encompasses both the aisle entry and a twin-arched opening above, suggesting a tribune was originally intended. The square crossing has capitals with primitive carvings, including *Adam and Eve* and *Daniel in the Lions' Den*, some with touches of colour. The transepts are rib-vaulted (15C) and the chapels are decorated with capitals and wall arches which interconnect. Above the chancel is a cupola supported by squinches, rebuilt in the 17C. In the north and south walls are three round-headed bays above wall arcades, all with capitals. The apse is covered by a half-dome. In the nave are late-17C walnut stalls, which have acquired a subtle patina, and carved panels by Jean Tournier.

The Romans chose to settle on the bluff near the confluence of the Gers and the Garonne which is now occupied by **Layrac**, standing out impressively on approach. In the village centre is a pleasant square with arcades and a 17C *fontaine-lavoir*. This town, like Moirax, developed around a Cluniac priory, a dependent of Moissac, consecrated by Pope Urban II in 1096. The priory church is the focal point of a visit. The west end is partly obscured by later cladding, and in the style of the Saintonge the portal is flanked by two blind arcades. Blind arcades also articulate the exterior of the nave and the large apse and there are damaged Romanesque capitals on the south transept chapel. Over the crossing is a huge cupola. The large entrance opens into a wonderfully luminous interior (ignoring the 19C paintings). The aisleless nave has a pointed barrel vault and transverse arches on half-shafts and the crossing is domed (18C). There are Romanesque carved capitals on the crossing piers and the barrel vault of the chancel continues without a hiatus into the half-domed apse decorated with foliate capitals. The transept chapels have little space, and on the west walls of the transept are large blind arcades with windows set unevenly. In the chancel are 12C mosaics representing the *Triumph of Samson*, and there is an over-the-top Neo-classical altarpiece.

During Antiquity, **Astaffort** to the south commanded the route from St-Bertrand-de-Comminges to Lectoure and Agen. Here the hills become more rounded in comparison with the Serres, and the houses tend to brick rather than stone. Astaffort was the arena of the defeat of the Prince de Condé during the Fronde (p 49) but there is little to see except the former church of Ste-Geneviève, now a cultural centre, which has some good Romanesque capitals.

Moving east, **Caudecoste** is a little circular 13C *bastide* with arcades and half-timbered houses. At **Donzac** there is a small museum of rural life. Open July, Aug daily 09.30–12.00 and 14.00–19.00, Sept–Dec and Feb–June 14.00–18.00; closed Mon and Jan; ☎ 05 63 29 21 96.

Auvillar is a small brick town of great charm built on an escarpment above the Garonne. The attractive Porte de l'Horloge, the old city gate with a clocktower rebuilt in brick and stone in the 17C, is all that is left of the city defences demolished in 1572. In the town centre is a small triangular arcaded *place* surrounded by fairly grand 17C and 18C brick houses and one 16C building. The justly famous circular *halle*, its roof radiating out from a small central drum to rest on a sturdy Tuscan colonnade, was built in 1825 and under its skirts are ancient grain measures. Auvillar reached its commercial high-point in the 18C, thanks to its port on the Garonne, now a *base de loisirs*, and to the manufacture of pottery. There is a collection of faïence in the Musée du Vieil-Auvillar.

The château, north of the marketplace, disappeared in the 16C but the Place du Château offers a tremendous vantage-point over the vast Garonne Valley and as far as the slopes of

Auvillar

the Quercy. The church of St-Pierre has an extraordinary ruined west tower, with two turrets and a belfry, built in the 16C but almost entirely demolished in 1794, and then restored in 1862. The church has a curiously disjointed exterior, the result of damage and rebuilds during the Hundred Years War and the Wars of Religion. It is strikingly large (43m long), the older parts in stone while the rest is in brick. The north apsidal chapel is all that is left of the earlier (11C–12C) church, with some carved capitals of that period. The apse is Flamboyant and the nave dates from the 15C and 17C. There is a Counter-Reformation retable behind the main altar.

14 Montauban and the Garonne Valley

The *Département du Tarn et Garonne* was created only in 1808, as opposed to 1790 for the majority, with its *Préfecture* at Montauban. It encompasses the Bas Quercy, part of the Lomagne (which it shares with the Agenais and Gascony) and a slice of the Rouergue and benefits not only from a rich picking of monuments but also a diversity of landscapes. It takes its name from the major rivers which run almost parallel across but just north of Montauban the Tarn, swelled by the Aveyron, then turns west to meet the Garonne between St-Nicolas-de-la-Grave and Moissac. This was a wide and dangerous confluence in the Middle Ages but is now transformed into a tranquil boating lake.

MONTAUBAN

Montauban, a pink brick town on the banks of the Tarn, is an attractive, lively, and slightly dusty place with a number of museums and gardens and big markets. At the heart of the town is the old Place Nationale and there is an important museum dedicated to the painter Ingres.

Getting there and around
Car

A62, Bordeaux to Toulouse via junction 10 and A20/N20 to Montauban. A20/N20 Limoges to Montauban via Cahors. D927, N113/D927 from Agen via Moissac. D999 from Albi. N124/D928 from Auch via Beaumont-de-Lomagne. D926 from Caylus via Caussade. D115 from St-Antonin-Noble-Val via Bruniquel, Montricoux. **Parking** on the banks of the Tarn close to the Pont Vieux on Rue Alphonse Jordain with lift up to Place Desnoyer

and the museum. Also parking on Rue de la Monnaie when no market.
Train

TGV Paris Montparnasse to Toulouse stops at Montauban. TER Paris Austerlitz to Toulouse via Montauban; to Agen via Moissac; to Cahors via Caussade. Montauban station, ☎ 06 63 35 35 35.
Bus

Montauban has town buses. Buses between Montpezat-de-Quercy and Caussade, Mon only, ☎ 05 63 22 55 00.

Tourist information

8200 Montauban Pl. Prax-Paris, ☎ 05 63 63 60 60, fax 05 63 63 65 12
82700 Monech 1bis, Pl. de la Mairie, ☎ 05 63 64 83 90

Market days

Montauban Wednesday and Saturday. Evening market in July–August
Montech Tuesday; farmers' market Sunday

Canal cruises

Cruises depart from Montech on the barge *Ville Montech*, ☎ 05 63 04 48 28

Festivals and events

May *Alors chante!*, French song festival
July *Jazz à Montauban*, in several venues around town, some free
August *Fête du Goût et des Saveurs*, appreciation of local produce sold under the label '*Bienvenue à la Ferme*'; a regional event. *Fêtes des 400 coups* in memory of the siege of Montauban in 1621.
September (4th weekend) *Châteaux chantants en Tarn-et-Garonne*, classical music in the most beautiful châteaux of Tarn-et-Garonne during the *journées du Patrimonie*.

Where to stay and eating out

82710 BRESSOLS

☆☆ *L'Hexagone*, 225 Impasse Fontanilles, ☎ 05 63 02 11 44, fax 05 63 02 90 90. A place to relax in green surroundings beside two large pools.

82170 GRISOLLES

☆☆ *Le Relais des Garrigues*, N20 south of Montauban (20km), ☎ 05 63 67 31 59, fax 05 63 64 13 76, email fred.calandra@wanadoo.fr. A friendly and welcoming base for excursions, close to the canal.

82000 MONTAUBAN

☆☆☆ *Mercure*, 12 Rue Notre-Dame, ☎ 05 63 63 17 23, fax 05 63 66 43 66, email mercure.montauban@wanadoo.fr. The hotel occupies an entirely renovated 18C mansion in the heart of the old town.

☆☆ *D'Orsay*, 31 Rue Salengro (opposite the train station), ☎ 05 63 66 06 66, fax 05 63 66 19 39. Recommended for one of the best family-run restaurants in the Tarn-et-Garonne, *La cuisine d'Alain*, email cuisinedalain@wandoo.fr. Some rooms sound-proofed and air-conditioned.

82290 MONTBETON

☆☆☆ *Hostellerie des Coulandrières*, Rte de Castelsarrasin, ☎ 05 63 67 47 47, fax 05 63 67 46 45. Warm welcome, quality food and spacious rooms in a large park with pool and mini-golf.

History

Always a major town in the southwest, Montauban lost its status as *chef-lieu* (main town) of a huge *généralité* (adminstrative district) in 1790 and became part of the Lot, but some negotiating during a visit by Napoléon in 1808 resulted in its reinstatement at the head of the *département* of Tarn-et-Garonne, which acquired choice parts of Quercy, Gascony, Rouergue and Languedoc. It is famous as the second Protestant stronghold in France after La Rochelle but, in common with most Protestant towns in the southwest, it has few pre-Reformation buildings. Less obvious in the hurly-burly of today's activities is that Montauban was one of the first *bastides* in the region, founded in 1144 by the Count of Toulouse, Alphonse Jourdain. The town enjoyed tremendous prosperity as a commercial centre after the Albigensian crisis, benefiting from its position between two navigable rivers, the Tarn and the Aveyron. Access and defence were improved by the Pont-Vieux across the Tarn, erected 1304–35, and during the Hundred Years War the town, taken by Captain John Chandos in the name of the Black Prince, became the last frontier between Guyenne and the Languedoc until 1368.

The recovery of the town's commercial status at the end of the 15C engendered a brilliant cultural life in the early 16C and resulted in the establishment of numerous schools which were a breeding ground for humanist ideas and the support of Calvinism. The first of the Wars of Religion had a profound effect on the town: Protestant zealots set fire to the cathedral on 20 December 1561 and destroyed all churches except St-Jacques, which became their temple. Montauban was already a Protestant place of safety in 1570, following the Peace of St-Germain, reconfirmed by the Edict of Nantes in 1598. This situation lasted until 1621 when Louis XIII and his constable, de Luynes, marched on Montauban with an army of 25,000 and held the siege for three months (18 August to 12 November), but despite terrible damage the locals held. However, after the fall of La Rochelle in 1629, Richelieu achieved politically where the king had failed.

As a powerful administrative centre Montauban continued to trade and prosper, particularly with the construction of major roads across the southwest. This wealth was converted into elegant, brick townhouses. The most obvious symbol of the Counter-Reformation is the Neo-classical cathedral built partly in stone. Prior to the Revolution the economy slowed down and the few new buildings followed the pattern of the 18C, resulting in an extraordinarily unified architecture. Montauban was the birthplace of two eminent artists, the painter Ingres and the sculptor Antoine Bourdelle.

Montauban is on a plateau overlooking the Tarn, and the two levels can be confusing. Park in Place Desnoyer alongside the Tarn south of the Pont-Vieux; steps or a lift go up to the Musée Ingres. At the head of the bridge is Bourdelle's epic **Monument to the Dead of 1870** (1893–1902), at first considered too controversial for a public monument (see below).

Musée Ingres

The Musée Ingres is installed in the former episcopal palace, a brick building of 1664, on the site of Alphonse Jourdain's castle. In 1360 the English started to build their garrison here, and it was incorporated in the defences during the Wars of Religion: the English guardroom is the lower basement of the museum. The wide-ranging collection, with items from the 4C to the 20C, occupies most of the five floors. Open July, Aug daily 09.30–12.00 and 13.30–18.00; other times Tues–Sun 10.00–12.00 and 14.00–18.00, closed Mon; also closed Sun am 15 Oct–Palm Sunday; ☎ 05 63 22 12 91.

Ingres' work is exhibited in six elegant rooms on the first floor with ceilings painted in 1868. His art is a constant balancing act between Classicism and Romanticism and the works at Montauban, if not his greatest or best known, demonstrate his range. Two small landscapes, rare in Ingres' repertoire, were probably painted in Rome before summer 1807. Among the best of the portraits is that of his friend, the Italian sculptor **Lorenzo Bartolini** (1806), who persuaded him to move to Florence between 1820 and 1824, and the **Portrait of Madame Gonse** (1840s), the sort of accomplished work for which the painter is best known. The **Dream of Ossian** (1812–13 and 1835), as Romantic a work as you could wish for, was commissioned by Napoléon for the ceiling of his bedroom

Jean-Auguste-Dominique Ingres

Jean-Auguste-Dominique Ingres was born in Montauban in 1780. He studied in Toulouse, then in Paris in 1797 at Jacques-Louis David's studio. He won the Grand Prix de Rome in 1801 but only went to Italy in 1806, where he remained for 18 years and where he studied the Italian masters who had a profound influence on his work, especially Raphael. During the early years there he painted his first large turbanned nude, *Bather of Valpinçon* (1806–10) and established the portrait style for which he was acclaimed. The *Vow of Louis XIII* (see below) was well received at the Salon of 1824 which proved a turning point; he went on to open an extremely well-patronised studio in Paris and by 1826 was Director of Museums of France. A consummate draughtsman, he maintained that 'drawing is the property of art' and Montauban regularly mounts exhibitions of his drawings. Ingres' idiomatic linear style, combined with formal composition, gives an immediate impression of calm yet belies a disturbing underlying tension. He returned frequently to the same subject or even the same painting. He barely modified his style during his successful career which spanned a period when decisive changes were taking place in French art. In 1851 Ingres donated 54 paintings and antique vases to the museum, and at his death in 1867 more than 4000 drawings, his personal collection of paintings and memorabilia. His pupil Armand Cambon was the first curator, and there are some charming works by him.

at the Quirinale Palace which he never got around to sleeping in. This curious painting, based on the greatest literary hoax of the 18C, was originally oval but Ingres repurchased it and squared it up with the help of assistants. The Gobelins tapestry version of the most classical of subjects, the *Apotheosis of Homer* (1867), is based on a commission for a ceiling decoration at the Louvre of 1826. *Roger freeing Angelica* is one of four paintings of this subject (the others are in Paris, London and Detroit); the Montauban version of hard metal and yielding flesh was painted in 1841. There are a number of works and studies which demonstrate Ingres' great debt to Raphael. Among his possessions are a delightful little painting of *Ingres' Studio in Rome* (1818) by Alaux and the *Portrait of a Spanish Girl* by Claudio Coello. The huge collection of drawings is rotated thematically. There are also paintings by Ingres' followers Hippolyte Flandrin and Théodore Chassériau, and on the top floor are French and European paintings from the 15C to the 18C, including a number of fine Italian works donated by Ingres.

Antoine Bourdelle was born in Montauban in 1861 and died at Le Vésinet in 1929. Works by him were donated by his daughter and are displayed on the ground floor. Bourdelle was from a poor background and studied first at Toulouse. At 18 he experienced a close identification with Beethoven and the museum owns a bronze head by him of the composer. In Paris, Bourdelle studied with Jules Dalou, then worked in Rodin's studio between 1893 and 1906. His career divides into two phases, the first described as Dionysian, with works of explosive, unrestrained nature, as in the *Monument to the Dead of 1870* (1895). The dynamic *Hercules the Archer* (1909) is a pivotal work, before he moved to the synthetic approach expressed in the *Head of Apollo* (c 1900), bringing him into line with the early 20C. His constant concern was the relationship of sculpture to architec-

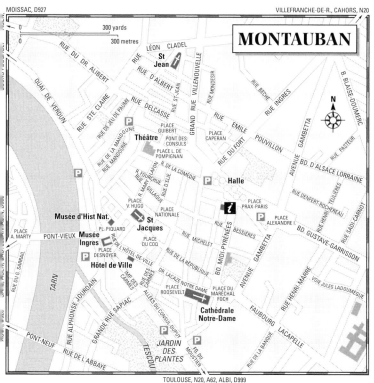

MOISSAC, D927

VILLEFRANCHE-DE-R., CAHORS, N20

MONTAUBAN

0   300 yards
0   300 metres

N

RUE DU DR ALIBERT
LÉON CLADEL
St Jean
RUE D'ALBERT
RUE DELCASSE
RUE DU JEU DE PAUME
RUE STE CLAIRE
QUAI DE VERDUN
RUE DE LA MANDOUNE
RUE MANDOUNE
GRAND RUE VILLENOUVELLE
RUE ST-JEAN
RUE MONDESIR
RUE BECHE
RUE INGRES
RUE EMILE
RUE
PLACE GUIBERT
Théâtre
PONT DES CONSULS
PLACE L. DE POMPIGNAN
PLACE CAPERAN
POUVILLON
RUE DU FORT
AVENUE BD. D'ALSACE LORRAINE
B. BLAISE-DOUMERC
RUE PASTEUR
GAMBETTA
R. DE LA COMÉDIE
R. FOURCHUE
RUE MAGILLAGUE
RUE D'ELIE
PLACE V. HUGO
PLACE NATIONALE
Halle
PLACE PRAX-PARIS
i
PLACE ALEXANDRE I
RUE DENFERT-ROCHEREAU
RUE HENRI FEULIERES
BD. GUSTAVE-GARRISSON
RUE SADI-CARNOT
Musée d'Hist Nat.
PL. PIQUARD
St Jacques
PLACE DU COQ
RUE BESSIÈRES
RUE MICHELET
BD. MIDI-PYRÉNÉES
PLACE A. MARTY
PONT-VIEUX
Musée Ingres
PLACE DESNOYER
Hôtel de Ville
RUE DE L'HÔTEL-DE-VILLE
RUE DE LA RÉPUBLIQUE
DR. LACAZE
AVENUE GAMBETTA
VOIE JULES LADOUMEGUE
RUE HENRI-MARRE
RUE DE G. SARRAIL
TARN
RUE ALPHONSE JOURDAIN
GRANDE RUE SAPIAC
IMPTES CARMES
RUE DES CARMES
PLACE NOTRE DAME
PLACE ROOSEVELT
PLACE DU MARÉCHAL FOCH
Cathédrale Notre-Dame
FAUBOURG LACAPELLE
RUE DE LA BANDE
PONT-NEUF
RUE DE L'ABBAYE
RUE DU MOUSTIER
ALLÉES DU CONSUL-DUPUY
JARDIN DES PLANTES
TESCOU

TOULOUSE, N20, A62, ALBI, D999

ture and in 1911 he worked on the reliefs for the Théâtre des Champs-Elysées. Montauban is graced with several fine examples of his work. Other local painters represented are François Desnoyer, a Fauve, Marcel Lenoir and Lucien Andrieu.

In the lower basement are local Gallo-Roman and medieval exhibits. The main room of the first basement, with particularly beautiful brick vaults, is used for temporary exhibitions and has a collection of 18C and 19C regional ceramics.

From the museum, turn right on Rue de l'Hôtel de Ville. The grandiose bleached face of the Neo-classical **Cathédrale Notre-Dame** makes precisely the contrast with the rest of the town that was intended. Louis XIV's architects conceived a church which would symbolise the Counter-Reformation and celebrate the power of the monarchy. Its design and materials played an important psychological role. It was begun in 1692 to plans by François d'Orbay, son-in-law of Le Vau, modified by Robert de Cotte, and was consecrated on 1 November 1739.

The façade has a Doric peristyle of four columns and the Ionic order above. The interior is imposing and austere, taking the form of a Greek cross with 16 arcades; it is 87m long in total, the nave barely longer than the choir, the Doric order used throughout. The pitted originals of statues of the four Evangelists (1719) made by Marc Arcis for the façade have been brought inside and replaced by reproductions. The pendentives of the dome are decorated with the *Four Virtues*. The most important work is Ingres' painting of the *Vow of Louis XIII*

(1824); there is a timer light switch on the wall left of the altar. It was commissioned in 1820 and carried out in Florence. It shows Louis XIII placing France under the protection of the Virgin of the Assumption. The result is an eclectic work which bears out the duality of the theme. Ingres borrowed heavily from Raphael for the Virgin, but she is a wordly creature, imperious and sensuous, bathed in a diffused light and framed by drapes held back by voluptuous angels. The king, with up-stretched arms, is painted in harsher tones and in direct light. Also worthy of note is some fine late-18C–19C wrought iron, a monumental candlestick with dolphins and a vast lectern and 18C choir stalls. A 15C console with Bruniquel marble is used as an altar with a 16C statue placed on it. The organ, built in 1675, came from St-Jacques (see below) and has kept its original case. In one of the chapels on the left of the choir are gilded stucco sacred ornaments by Ingres *père*.

Northwest of the cathedral, between Rue de l'Hôtel-de-Ville and Boulevard Midi-Pyrénées, is the old town. At the end of Boulevard Midi-Pyrénées is the tourist office in the former Jesuit College, a large 17C brick building with *mirandes*. Outside, Bourdelle's graceful bronze statue of **Penelope** (1912) overlooks **Place Prax-Paris** where the markets are held. Rue de la Comédie, behind the tourist office, leads to Place L. de Pompignan in front of the theatre, and another Bourdelle sculpture, *Sappho* (1925). From the *place*, the Pont des Consuls flies over the Vallon de la Mandoune.

Take Rue d'Elie to **Place Nationale** in which, in keeping with the rest of the town but unusual in the realms of *bastides*, the buildings around the square are entirely in brick, of different types and qualities incorporated with great subtlety, some parts possibly designed to be plastered over, some purely decorative. Also unusual is a double arcade following the layout of the original *place*, with arches at each angle. Two sides were destroyed by fire in 1614. Plans were drawn up by Pierre Levesville and were carried out; then, in 1649, the two remaining sides were consumed by flames and a new campaign of building was led by Charles Pacot following Levesville's plans. Some houses were not completed until 1708.

West of Place Nationale is the church of **St-Jacques**, the only church spared by the Calvinists. It was built as a parish church dedicated to St James of Compostela; the fortified west end is 13C, but after the Hundred Years War major repairs were carried out and the chevet dates from 1481. The octagonal Toulousain-style belfry has three levels of openings and was restored in the 18C. It still carries scars inflicted by royalist bullets during the siege of 1621—it is a pity no one has taken a pot-shot at the repellent ceramic reproduction of Raphael's **Vision of Ezekiel** above the west door. The characteristic aisleless nave with chapels was extended in the 15C and revaulted in the 18C. Sad and sombre with peeling paint, the chapel of St-Jacques (south) has gilded stucco work by Ingres *père*.

South of St-Jacques is the municipal library in a grand building overlooking Rue du Général-Piquart, with Bourdelle's **Dying Centaur** (1914). Lower down on the right is the **Musée d'Histoire Naturelle** on Place A.-Bourdelle. Open Tues–Sat 10.00–12.00 and 14.00–18.00, closed Mon and Sun am; ☎ 05 63 22 13 85. In the same building is the very small Musée du Terroir (local history), open 10.00–12.00 and 14.00–18.00; closed Mon, Sun; ☎ 05 63 66 46 34.

The **Pont-Vieux**, a very strong construction in brick and stone and originally fortified, was begun in 1304. Straight rather than hump-backed, because of the difference in the levels of the two banks, it has seven high arches. The extremity of each triangular cutwater is in stone as are the bases of the piers, which helped it withstand the exceptional floods of 1441, 1766 and 1930.

Return to the banks of the Tarn via the steps or lift next to the Ingres museum. There is a memorial to Ingres by Antoine Etex (1868), in the square on the left, and further along the Impasse des Carmes and Rue Sapiac is the refreshing **Jardin des Plantes**, created in 1860, where the Tescou meets the Tarn. There is a bust of *Auguste Quercy*, a local poet who wrote in Occitan (d. 1899), by Bourdelle (1911).

To the north, on the banks of the Tarn in Cours Foucault, laid out in the late 17C by Intendant Foucault, is Bourdelle's great memorial to the dead of the First World War, *France watching over her Dead*, a contrast in style to his Franco-Prussian war monument (see above).

THE QUERCY BLANC

The white chalky plateaux which charactertise the Quercy Blanc, the most southerly part of the Quercy, and stretch into the Pays de Serres in the Lot-et-Garonne (p 286), are eroded by several small rivers creating fertile valleys which peter out in the Garonne. The landscape is punctuated by white or grey villages, and scattered with windmills, fountains and *pigeonniers*.

Getting there and around
Train
Cahors to Montauban via Montpezat de Quercy, occasional trains (station 5km from village).

Tourist information
82300 Caussade 11 Rue de la République, ☎/fax 05 63 26 04 04

46170 Castelnau-Montratier 27 Rue Clémenceau, ☎ 05 65 21 84 39, fax 05 65 21 84 56, www.castelnau-montraiter.com

82110 Lauzerte Pl. des Cornières, ☎ 05 63 94 61 94, fax 05 63 94 61 93, www.quercy.blanc.net

82150 Montaigu-de-Quercy Pl. du Mercadiel, ☎ 05 63 94 48 50, fax 05 63 94 35 05

82270 Montpezat-de-Quercy Blvd des Fossés, ☎ 05 63 02 05 55

Market days
Caussade Monday; *foie gras* November–March; truffles December–March; evening market

July, August
Lauzerte Saturday; farmers' market Wednesday
Montaigu-de-Quercy Saturday
Valence-d-Agen Tuesday; farmers' market Tuesday; evening market August

Festivals and events
July *Festival Art Vivant*, performing arts, Lauzerte
Music festival, Quercy Blanc
Estivales du chapeau de Caussade et Septfonds, celebrating all types of hats
August *Festival du Quercy Blanc*, classical music at Lauzerte, Montpezat-de-Quercy and Cazes-Modenard
Castelsarras' in Louisane New Orleans, Cajun and jazz in the streets of Castelsarrasin
Au fil de l'eau ... une histoire An epic tale of the waterways at Valence d'Agen

Where to stay and eating out
82300 CAUSSADE
☆☆ *Hôtel Larroque*, Ave du 8 Mai, ☎ 05 63 65 11 77, fax 05 63 65 12 04, email

hotel.larroque@worldonline.fr. An agreeable and comfortable family hotel with open-air barbecue and traditional Quercynoise cuisine.

8 2 1 1 0 C A Z E S - M O N D E N A R D
(east of Lauzerte D34)

☆☆ *L'Atre*, Pl. de l'Hôtel-de-Ville, ☎ 05 63 95 81 61, fax 05 63 95 87 22. In the heart of a village, with a charming rustic restaurant.

8 2 1 3 0 L A F R A N C A I S E
☆☆ *Au Fin Gourmet Hôtel Belvédère*, 16 Rue Mary Lafon, ☎ 05 63 65 89 55, fax 05 63 65 80 18, email fingourmet@oreka.com. Excellent cooking with local produce, and comfortable, pretty rooms.

8 2 1 1 0 L A U Z E R T E
☆ *Le Luzerta*, at Vignals near Lauzerte, ☎ 05 63 94 64 43/06 83 03 54 62, fax 05 63 94 66 67. Close to a pretty village on the Barguelone, it consists of five chalets around a pool.

8 2 1 5 0 S T - B E A U Z E I L
☆☆ *Château de l'Hoste*, l'Hoste, near Monagu-de-Quercy, ☎ 05 63 95 25 61, fax 05 63 95 25 50, email chataudelhoste@wanadoo.fr. Built in typical white limestone of the region, in a beautiful setting, serving quality food.

Northeast of Montauban on the N20.D926 is **Caussade** is a funny old place that feels lived in and is famous for its straw hats and markets (see above). Further north, on the D17, is **Puylaroque**, a village of great character, undoubtedly an important agricultural centre in the 13C and 14C. The old narrow streets fan out from Place E.-Capin to climb the ridge which drops sheer at the southwest. At the start of Rue de la République is the most complete of several Gothic houses, with large arcades and geometric tracery in the three upper windows, reminiscent of Cordes or Lauzerte. The church, which shows evidence of many periods of alteration and restoration, has fragments of Romanesque sculpture. The streets all converge on Place de la Citadelle with the remains of the château.

Just west of the N20, northwest of Caussade, is Montpezat-de-Quercy, a lovely medieval stone and timber village with Gothic and Renaissance houses, a small arcaded square closed at one end by the *hôtel de ville*, a 14C town gateway, and 16C tapestries in the church of St-Martin. The town's great benefactors were the family des Près, who numbered several prelates among them. The church, completed by 1339 and consecrated in 1343, was designed by an architect from the papal court at Avignon. Harmonious, sober, clean and white, it is built into a hollow in the slope of the hill to the east of the town centre. The church adheres to the Gothic style of the south, with a simple nave and no aisles, and with one rose window. Behind the church is a marvellous group of timber-framed houses, the old canons' college or living quarters built in the mid-14C. Go armed with some coins for lighting.

The main interest of the church is its furnishings and fittings. In the choir are the famous made-to-measure tapestries, of Flemish origin, which have been here since 1520 when Jean IV des Près presented them to the church on the occasion of his elevation to Bishop of Montauban. They are stitched, not woven, and are made up of five panels with 15 scenes of the *Legend of St Martin of Tours*. Above each scene is an explanatory octosyllabic quatrain in Old French verse. Note the animated compositions, the architectural detail and the shimmering colours. They read from left to right. The first panel shows St Martin in the town of Amiens, about to share his cloak with a beggar. Then follow other, less well-known, episodes in Martin's life—his dream, his journey across the Alps when he is stopped by robbers, his ordination as Bishop of Tours and chasing away pagan beliefs. He is shown effecting conversions and cures in Germany. The last tapestries change emphasis and are concerned with the battle between good and evil. Finally there is a reminder to attend mass.

Left and right of the entrance to the choir are two funerary effigies of the benefactors, Cardinal Pierre des Près (1288–1361) in Carrara marble and his nephew Jean, Bishop of Coïmbra in Portugal then of Castres (1338–53) in Quercy stone, formerly polychromed. The painting (16C) above the dean's stall represents Jacques des Près (d. 1589), the last bishop in the family. The 26 stalls are 15C and have carved misericords. Other worthy objects include **Notre-Dame de-Pitié-de-Montpezat** (1475), sculpted in sandstone in Villefranche-de-Rouergue and polychromed in the 19C, in the first chapel south. It was an object of veneration in the 16C and there is still a pilgrimage on the third Sunday in September. In the next chapel is an alabaster diptych (15C/16C), made in Nottingham, with scenes of the *Nativity*, the *Resurrection* and the *Ascension*, and in the third chapel is a headless *St Anne and the Virgin* (13C). In the second chapel on the north is an English alabaster *Virgin with Doves* (14C). There are two 14C reliquary caskets in the last chapel.

For a detour (about 5km) to the little chapel of **Notre-Dame-de-Saux** travel via the D20 in the direction of Cahors, turn left to Saux and at the crossroad straight on, then follow the signs. The charming little rural church with a belfry is in the middle of woods and is the frame for some precious 14C murals. Ask for the key at the presbytery or at the *hôtel de ville*, Montpezat.

Lauzerte, northwest of Montauban, on the D927, justly deserves its reputation as one of the most beautiful villages in France. Clinging to a rock dominating the Cahors–Moissac road and the land from which it derived its wealth, it has a profusion of fine old houses that have been lovingly restored, an arcaded square, the Place du Marché, and an interesting Gothic church enlarged in the 17C containing some outstanding Baroque retables. Another church at the bottom of the hill also contains a fine 17C retable. It is the sort of place that attracts artists and craftsmen.

Castelnau-Montratier between Lauzerte and the N20 is a pretty village perched above the Barguelone and the Lutte Rivers, at the centre of a fruit-growing region. It is overlooked by three windmills on the Cahors road, one still working. The village is arranged around a triangular *place*, with chestnut and linden trees and some old houses.

MOISSAC

Moissac is a modest town but contains one of the major Romanesque sites of France, the abbey church of St-Pierre. The breathtakingly beautiful cloisters are open all year, and early November is the best time to photograph the celebrated tympanum of the church.

Moissac draws crowds but never seems crowded. It is convenient for the A62, Montauban, Toulouse and Agen; has the advantage of rivers and the Canal latéral à la Garonne; and is situated in a fertile valley, the market garden of the region, producing some 200,000 tonnes of fruit, including kiwis and the unique Chasselas, a small sweet dessert grape with an *appellation contrôlée* label.

Getting there and around
Car
A62, Bordeaux to Toulouse via junction 9 and N113. **Parking** on Pl. des Récollets when no market.
Train
TER Agen to Montauban via Moissac. Station is west of town centre.

Tourist information
82200 Moissac 6 Pl. Durand-de-Bredon, ☎ 05 63 04 01 85, fax 05 63 04 27 10, www.frenchcom.com/moissac
82210 St-Nicholas-de-la-Grave Pl. du Château, ☎/fax 05 63 94 82 81
Market days
Saturday and Sunday

Festivals and events
April *Fête des Arts*, local activities and displays of arts and crafts
July *Les Vibrations de la Voix*, tales, musical concerts and choral work

September (third weekend) *Fête des Fruits et des Legumes*, celebration of the Chasselas grape and other fruits

Where to stay and eating out
82200 MOISSAC
☆☆ *Le Chapon Fin*, 3 Pl. des Récollets, ☎ 05 63 04 04 22, fax 05 63 04 58 44. A comfortable hotel in the town centre which offers a warm welcome.
☆☆ *Le Pont Napoléon*, 2 Allées Montebello, ☎ 05 63 04 01 55, fax 05 63 04 34 44. Refined cooking of repute, and comfortable accommodation. View over the Tarn.
€€ *Bistrot du Cloître*, Pl. Durand-de-Bredon, ☎ 05 63 04 37 50. Tucked away in the corner of this pretty *place*, this restaurant is recommended.
82400 POMMEVIC
☆☆☆☆ *La Bonne Auberge*, on the N113 west of Moissac, ☎ 05 63 39 56 69, fax 05 63 39 70 93. Very comfortable, quiet rooms, and friendly atmosphere.

The approach to the abbey church is most dramatic along Rue de la République from the market place, **Place des Récollets**. In the pretty Place Durand-de-Bredon, west of the church, are the tourist office, exhibition hall and entrance to the cloisters.

Church and cloister of the Abbaye St-Pierre

History
Legend attributes the foundation at Moissac to Clovis in 506 but the Benedictine monastery was most probably founded by Bishop Didier of Cahors (630–655) at the time of Clovis II (639–657). It received gifts of land from rich benefactors, Nizezius and Ermintrude, in 680, and more gifts arrived in the 9C from the Carolingian monarchs and the bishops of Cahors. Moissac suffered incursions from all sides from the 8C to the 10C and, as the power of the Carolingians diminished the abbey came under the protection of the Counts of Toulouse, who found it a valuable source of revenue. Its consequent decline was recorded in the chronicles of Abbot Aymeric de Peyrac (1377–1406). By 1030 part of the church had collapsed and in 1042 a fire put paid to the rest. There was no choice but to enlist the help of Cluny, then in full expansion. Abbot Odilon was only too happy to add Moissac to Cluny's chain of staging-posts on the Via Podiensis to Santiago, and Moissac became part of a spiritual network woven across northern Spain and southwest France carrying artistic influences in both directions.

A Cluniac monk, Durand de Bredons, was named Abbot of Moissac on 29 June 1048 and St-Pierre maintained its abbey status despite subordination to Cluny. Out of the ashes grew one of the richest, most influential abbeys in France with sculpture that transcends any other of the period. De Bredons (1048–71) and Hunaud de Gavaret (1072–85) re-established the scriptorium and its illuminated manuscripts were undoubtedly a source of iconographic and stylistic inspiration to the sculptors. Durand de Bredons became Bishop of Toulouse from 1059 and through him Moissac played a leading role in Gregorian reforms in the 11C.

A Romanesque church, constructed on the apse of the earlier Carolingian building, was consecrated on 6 November 1063 and the monastic buildings were blessed by Urban II in 1096. The cloister, completed in 1100, was created during the time of Abbot Ansquitil (1085–1115) who also added the massive porch and belfry at the west end of the church. Ansquitil's successor, Abbot Roger de Sorèze (1115–31) fortified the west end and was responsible for the famous monumental doorway. Attacked by Simon de Montfort during the Albigensian crusades in 1212, the cloisters and church suffered. A long period of stagnation was interrupted by the abbacy of Bertrand de Montaigut (1260–95) who restored the cloisters. Aymeric de Roquemaurel (1431–49) and Pierre and Antoine de Carmaing (1449–1501) repaired the monastery after the Hundred Years War when the church was reconstructed in Gothic style and the brick part of the belfry was added. The church as we now see it dates from this period.

Pierre de Carmaing placed the abbey *in commendam* in 1466. In 1626 secular canons replaced the monks, plunging it into decline, and the library of some 120 manuscripts, already neglected, was sold to Louis XIV's chief minister, Jean-Baptiste Colbert. In 1767 some monastic buildings were demolished and others were sold and damaged at the Revolution. A small seminary was installed in a building to the north, but was returned to the parish at the beginning of the 19C and now houses the Centre d'Art Roman Marcel Durliat. Disastrously, however, *c* 1845 the refectory was replaced by a section of the Bordeaux–Sète railway, even though the church and cloister had been classified historic monuments in 1840 and restoration work on the cloister had begun in 1838–42. In the 1850s Viollet-le-Duc and Théodore Olivier worked on the porch and belfry.

Exterior The famous tympanum over the south entrance of the abbey church is simultaneously enthralling and profoundly moving and its impact never diminishes. The church, however, is a hotch potch of Romanesque and Gothic, a testament to successive building campaigns which transformed the late 11C–12C stone church into a 15C Gothic church of brick. The Romanesque bays, identified from the windows, were arbitrarily divided and submerged by the buttresses to support the higher levels. The belfry was amended in the 15C and 17C. In 1985 the paving immediately in front of the portal was dug out to counteract damp problems, revealing a paving of brick and pebbles dated 1611, and below that the two 12C steps flanking the entrance were uncovered. Thus the portal was finally restored to its original proportions.

On the engaged column on the east of the porch is the effigy of Abbot Roger de Sorèze (1115–31); his opposite number is unidentified. Note the horn player on one of the merlons. The remarkable south door was executed between 1120 and 1125; the influence of Cluny is found in the vaulting of the narthex, the cusping of the jambs and the plate drapery of the sculptures. Hints of colour suggest that it was originally polychromed. The whole ensemble presents a developing theme, part narrative and moralising, part visionary and inspirational, from the Incarnation to the Last Judgement, climaxing with the Christ of the Parousia (the Second Coming). It is impossible to take in the whole programme at one glance.

The famous semi-circular tympanum is composed of 31 figures on separate blocks and presents an apocalyptic vision based on the text of Revelations 4: 2–11. The image of *Christ in Majesty*, enthroned, with one hand raised in blessing and the other on a book, dominates and focuses the composition. On his head is a crown surrounded by a large, richly decorated cruciform halo. His gaze is immobile and his beard and hair highly stylised The rest of the composition fluctuates and flows around him, infinitely restless. Swooping in and out are the four *Apocalpytic beasts*, symbols of the four Evangelists (Rev. 4: 7), and flanking them are two seraphim. Around the throne are the *Four and Twenty Elders* (Rev. 4: 4), each crowned and carrying a musical instrument (rebec or viol), goblet or perfume flask, who represent the twelve prophets of the Old Testament and the twelve Apostles of the New Testament. There is repetition but no monotony; the figures are meticulously detailed and in varied poses, craning their necks as they listen attentively. The horizontal lines which structure the composition lose their rigidity behind the undulations which evoke the 'sea of glass like unto crystal' (Rev. 4: 6) and around the outer edge a beautifully carved ribbon ornament adds to the mobility of the composition. The conceptual originality of this creation is matched only by the skill and subtlety of its execution by an unknown individual of unique creative genius. The tympanum rests on a lintel decorated with eight large thistles and foliage spewing out of the mouths of beasts at each end (this is a block of reused marble with an earlier frieze on the under edge).

Three pairs of lions and lionesses on a floral background appear to move restlessly on the supporting trumeau. Unseen when facing the portal straight on is the *Prophet Jeremiah*, on the right face of the trumeau. This is the single most moving figure at Moissac. Head inclined, hair and beard flowing, attenuated to blend with the narrow space, he exudes gentleness and sorrow rather than doom and gloom, but there is also a suppressed dynamism and tension in the crossed legs and floating drapery. His opposite number on the west face is *St Paul*, presenting the same plastic virtues as Jeremiah but a different character, more tense and alert but acquiescent and receptive, his open hand contrasting with Jeremiah's closed around a scroll. On the left jamb is a strangely contorted *St Peter*, with a diabolic animal at his feet, old but vigorous, with the key of the Holy Kingdom. The only works that come near these are at Souillac (p 182).

The left (west) side of the porch carries the parable of *Lazarus and Dives*. In the top register, Dives the rich man is at his table while, at his gate, Lazarus lies dying, the dogs licking his sores. An angel gathers up Lazarus's soul, represented by a little nude body (only the feet remain), and delivers it into the bosom of Abraham. St Luke, seated on the left, unrolls the text of his gospel. Below is the *Death of Dives*, whose soul is shown departing with demons (the angel arrived too late) and mourned by his widow, and in the lower register are almost illegible punishments for lust and avarice.

On the right-hand jamb the figure of the *Prophet Isaiah* balances that of

St Peter, and like Jeremiah he carries his prophesy on a scroll. To his left his prophesy is confirmed in an *Annunciation* (badly worn, the angel poorly remade in the 19C) and *Visitation* (also a copy) and above, scenes of the *Nativity* and *Epiphany*, the Virgin seated on her bed holding Jesus, Joseph standing behind, and an ox munching disinterestedly. The frieze above contains animated scenes, from right to left, of the *Presentation at the Temple*, in which Jesus is held by Simeon while the Virgin offers two doves; and the *Flight into Egypt*, with the Virgin tenderly embracing her child as the false idols fall from the temple at the arrival of the true God.

Interior Enter the square, dark narthex (*c* 1110–15), where everything is on a massive scale to support the belfry tower. From solid pillars with engaged columns spring heavy primitive square ribs. Some of the huge capitals have foliate or decorative motifs, and the others show *Samson slaying the Lion* and lambs in the jaws of wolves.

As can be surmised from the exterior alterations, there is little of the Romanesque structure obvious in the interior. But the surprise is the overall painted decor in luminous yellow on the walls and ochres on the vaults, a modern (1963) restoration of its 15C appearance. The decor distracts from the sometimes clumsy later transformations which turn it into a typically aisleless southern Gothic church. The mid-12C project, after the completion of the west-work, seems to have been to create a domed church similar to Cahors. Romanesque walls and massive piers exist in the west bay, but the second bay was rebuilt towards the end of the 13C and the polygonal, straight-sided east end dates from the 15C, when it replaced the apse of 1063. The rib vaults were completed later in the 15C. There are shallow chapels between the buttresses.

Among the **furnishings** are a wooden *Christ on the Cross* (1130–40), contemporary with the portal sculptures and very close stylistically, but the cross itself is probably 13C. There are three Gothic polychromed groups: a *Flight into Egypt* in wood (15C, the figure of Joseph is 17C); a stone *Pietà* flanked by Mary Magdalene and St John (1476), with donor figures; and an *Entombment* (15C, restored in 1985) in walnut with eight figures arranged around the body of Christ. An ancient marble sarcophagus (possibly 4C) was used as the tomb of Raymond de Montpezat (d. 1245). The organ case (mid-17C) carries the arms of Cardinal de Mazarin, Commendatory Abbot (1644–61), who paid for it with a fine for neglecting his duties; the instrument was remade by the Cavaillé-Col family *c* 1865. The early-16C choir enclosure was once gilded and polychromed but has been reversed and lost its original statuary. Through the screen on the left on the north wall can be seen the plaque recording the dedication of the church of 1063. The carved wooden altar rail and stalls are 17C as are the two panels representing the martyrdom of St Ferreolus.

Cloister The entrance to the cloister is via the tourist office on Place Durand-de-Bredon. Open July, Aug 09.00–19.00; 16 March–30 June, Sept–14 Oct 09.00– 12.00 and 14.00–18.00; 15 Oct–15 March 09.00–12.00 and 14.00–17.00; closed 1 Jan, 25 Dec; ☎ 05 63 04 01 85.

The almost square cloister on the north side of the church is on a grand scale (40m by 37.5m), and only one dark shady cedar planted about 160 years ago encroaches on the regularity. On a continuous low wall stand 116 slender columns, alternately paired and single, supporting capitals of a dramatic form

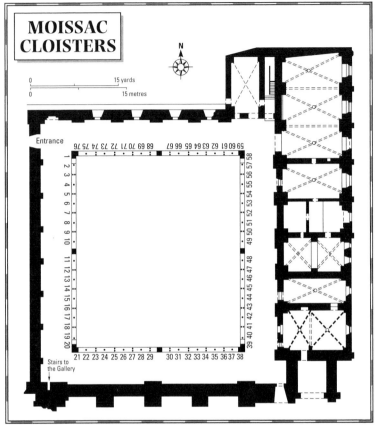

which widen out from a narrow base like an inverted pyramid or a flower, emphasised by a deep cut-away abacus above. All the faces of the capitals and the impost blocks are carved. This is the oldest and largest collection of Romanesque carved capitals which are still in their original place and represents a defining moment in Romanesque art. The date of the original cloister, 1100, is recorded on the central pillar of the west gallery. Although the capitals are all original the arcades were remodelled in moulded brick in the 13C.

In the southwest corner is the stairway to the **gallery** above the narthex, with a domed vault supported by 12 heavy ribs centred on a compression ring, overlooking the church and the forecourt. In the chapter house and chapels on the east of the cloisters are sculpted elements from earlier buildings and from the south door.

The **angle pillars** have carved reliefs on reused Pyrenean marble sarcophagi representing eight of the Apostles, each identified by an inscription. Durand de Bredons, Abbot of Moissac and Bishop of Toulouse, is on the central east pier. The forms are stylised and static, the figures full frontal and the heads in near profile, similar to the ambulatory reliefs at St-Sernin in Toulouse. All are dressed in tunics and cloaks except James, who wears a chasuble.

The **capitals** have been damaged but a remarkable amount is still intact. The drum and the abacii are carved on all faces and each part is worth close examination for the artistic and anecdotal detail. Some 46 of the 76 capitals have narrative themes with inscriptions and were intended as contemplative visual aids designed to affirm faith. The iconography is based on both the Old and New Testament. Particularly important are episodes from the life of Christ, from the Incarnation to the Last Supper, and to these are added apocalyptic scenes concerning the Second Coming, selected martyrdoms, parables and miracles, but no scenes of the Passion. The capital (no. 40 on the plan, p 302), at the southeast corner, in a prominent position between the church and the chapter house, portrays the *Martyrdom of St Peter*, patron of the abbey, and the *Martyrdom of St Paul*, with an inscription in mock Kufic script; until 1793 a tiny cavity in the column contained a minuscule shrine with relics of the two saints. The exquisite decorative and foliate capitals have a pure and immaterial beauty, with deeply incised palmettes or entwined stems, some inspired by Mozarab work. The angel, the holy messenger, is the most frequent motif appearing in both the Old and New Testament scenes.

A list of pillar reliefs and capitals

This list starts opposite the entrance to the cloister in the northwest corner and continues anti-clockwise.

Western Gallery
Northwest pillar (west face), St Philip
1. Sacrifice of Abraham
2. Glorification of the Cross
3. Acanthus leaves
4. Birds and lions
5. Daniel in the Lions' Den/ Christ's Birth announced to the Shepherds
6. Acanthus leaves
7. The Devil Unleashed
8. Raising of Lazarus
9. Palm leaves
10. Fantastic figures and animals
Central pillar inscribed: 'In the year 1100 of the Incarnation of the Lord Eternal, this cloister was constructed, at the time of Dom Ansquitil, Abbot. Amen.' St-Simon on the east face
11. David anointed by the Prophet Samuel
12. Vegetal design
13. Birds and animals
14. Acanthus leaves
15. Eight Beatitudes from the Sermon on the Mount
16. Lions rampant
17. Cain and Abel
18. Vegetal design

19. Ascension of Alexander
20. David's Victory over Goliath
Southwest pillar (west face), St Bartholomew

Southern Gallery
Southwest pillar (south face), St Matthew
21. Herod's Feast
22. Birds among plants
23. City of Babylon
24. Birds
25. Dream of Nebuchadnezzar
26. Martyrdom of St Stephen
27. Acanthus leaves
28. David and his Musicians
29. Holy City of Jerusalem
Central pillar, red marble panel, with no decoration
30. The Well of the Abyss
31. Symbols of the four Evangelists
32. Canaanite Woman and the Centurion
33. Good Samaritan
34. Temptation of Christ in the Desert
35. Revelation of St John at Patmos
36. Transfiguration
37. Imprisonment and release of St Peter

38. Baptism of Christ
Southeast pillar (south face), St Paul

Eastern Gallery
Southeast pillar (east face), St Peter
39. Samson wrestling with the Lion
40. Two Martyrdoms: St Peter and
 St Paul
41. Vegetal design
42. Adam and Eve and the Fall
43. Acanthus leaves
44. Martyrdom of St Laurence
45. Christ washing the Disciples' Feet
46. Palm leaves
47. Lazarus and Dives
48. Eight eagles or dragons and human
 heads
Central pillar, Durand de Bredons,
Abbot of Moissac (1047–71), Bishop of
Toulouse (1059–71)
49. Four figures seizing eagles by the
 neck
50. Wedding at Cana
51. Vegetal design
52. Epiphany/Massacre of the
 Innocents/Herod at the Gates of
 Jerusalem
53. Palmettes and animals' muzzles
54. Acanthus leaves
55. Martyrdom of St Saturnin
56. Acanthus leaves
57. Martyrdoms of St Fructuosus,
 St Augurious and St Euologius

58. Annunciation and Visitation
Northeast pillar (east face), St James

Northern Gallery
Northeast pillar (north face), St John
59. Angels wrestling with Dragons
60. Eagles
61. Vegetal design
62. Two Miracles of St Benedict
63. Birds
64. St Peter healing the Paralytic
65. Vegetal design
66. Celestial Kingdom
67. Miraculous Draught of Fishes
Central pillar with grey marble slab decorated with wavy lines and imbrications
68. Daniel in Prayer in the Lions'
 Den/Prophet Habakkuk bringing
 Food to Daniel
69. Procession, possibly the crusade to
 Jerusalem
70. Vegetal design of Mozarabic
 influence
71. Symbols of the four Evangelists
72. Birds
73. Meshach, Shadrach and Abednego
 in the Fiery Furnace
74. Scenes from the Life of St Martin
75. Scrolling design of Mozarabic
 influence
76. Jesus and the Good Samaritan
Northwest pillar (north face),
 St Andrew

The town has no surviving medieval buildings and very few from the 16C or 17C. The attractive abbot's residence, east of the church, houses the **Musée Moissagais**, a museum of folk and popular art (combined ticket with the cloister). It was frequently rebuilt; the oldest part of the building is an 11C chapel in the south tower with 12C paintings on the vault; the rest is 17C and 18C.

At the end of Rue de la République is the market place, built on the site of an old convent, with the *halle* (1895) and Halle de Paris (1930). Cross the canal by the Pont St-Jacques, a swivel bridge, to the banks of the Tarn. Until the 18C the river was very busy, with navigation and many mills, but all this had to be rebuilt after the floods of 1930.

A section of the Canal latéral à la Garonne, cut between 1843 and 1847, is carried over the Tarn by a magnificent **aqueduct**. To reach it, cross the Tarn in the direction of Castelsarrasin, turn left towards the campsite and follow the road for about 1km. The usefulness of the canal was short-lived as it was superseded by the railway in 1856.

On the N113 west, just after the railway station, is a church dedicated to **St-Martin**. This is the oldest sanctuary in Moissac, built on the site of a Gallo-Roman hypocaust. Incorporated into the chancel is the old church with a flat east end, dating from the end of the 6C or early 7C. It was extended to the west in the 10C using an already existing wall with large rounded buttresses. More repairs and alterations were carried out from the 13C–15C and it was saved from destruction in 1922.

St-Nicolas-de-la-Grave is a small town to the southwest of Moissac (N113, D15). Its most famous son was Antoine Laumet de Lamothe-Cadillac (b. 1658), coloniser and founder of Louisiana and Detroit (1701), whose name was selected by General Motors to mark their luxury range of cars. His birthplace, now the Musée de Lamothe-Cadillac, is in a small street of the same name near the *halle*. Open all year but times vary; enquire at the tourist office. St-Nicolas is close to the great confluence of the Tarn and the Garonne, where medieval pilgrims crossed by ferry. It is spanned by a mighty 19C suspension bridge and a 400ha lake has been created with a *base de loisirs* (☎ 05 63 95 50 00), for boating and swimming (pool), with a campsite.

The former **Abbaye de Belleperche** south of Moissac (N113, D45 at Castelsarrasin and D26), founded *c* 1143–44 and largely rebuilt in the 13C, was one of the largest and richest Cistercian monasteries in the south. Open July, Aug 10.00–18.00, June, Sept 10.00–12.00 and 14.00–18.00; closed Mon; also closed Sun am June and Sept; Oct–May by appointment only, ☎ 05 63 95 62 75/05 63 95 68 34. The vast church with a belfry recalling that of St-Sernin in Toulouse, dates from 1230–63. The Protestants set fire to the abbey in 1572, it was restored in the 17C and altered again in the 18C when the pillars and vaults of the 13C *grand cloître* (38 x 45m) were reconstructed (1720–30). Closed at the Revolution, a large part was demolished in the 19C. The revival of the abbey began in 1993 and despite on-going work there is nevertheless a fair bit to see including the 13C infirmary, the only one surviving in the southwest, and the spacious brick cloister (13C and 18C). The passage between the large and the small cloister is the only section that is medieval (13C) in its entirety. There are several other buildings and rooms, mainly 18C, and an exhibition.

15 Albi and the northern Tarn

The *département* of the Tarn is a land of transition between the Massif Central and the Midi Toulousain and holds many surprises. The rugged Ségala in the northwest gives way to fertile valleys in the central north to south corridor of the *département*, and to the southeast are the great forests of La Montagne Noire. The Tarn River carves a wide and, in most places, peaceful valley across the *département* which has taken its name, and was for several centuries crucial for carrying wine from the Gaillac vineyards to Bordeaux via the Garonne. On its banks is the elegant brick town of Albi, *préfecture* of the Tarn, dominated by the picturesque

The Albigensian Crusades

The problem of the heretics or Cathars (p 46) in the southwest had been rumbling for some time before forcible repression was first suggested by the Church in 1177. The Counts of Toulouse were either ineffectual or reluctant to be heavy handed and Church-organised preaching missions met with little success in stemming the heretical tide. The incident that triggered the first crusade against a Christian country was the assassination in 1208 of the Papal Legate, Peter of Castelnau, in Languedoc, by a servant of the Count of Toulouse, Raymond VII. This gave the Church (Pope Innocent III, backed by the Cistercians) the excuse to encourage the French barons, with the promise of plenary indulgences, to appropriate the land of the Counts of Toulouse. It also gave the French king, Philippe-Auguste, the opportunity to gain control over evasive Languedoc.

In June 1209 the crusading army gathered at Lyon, first besieging Béziers and Carcassonne. It was at the latter that Simon de Montfort took command. By 1210 the crusaders had spread into the Albigeois and Toulouse was attacked for the first time in 1211. There was an important battle at Muret in 1213 and fighting went on intermittently, spreading across the Quercy, Rouergue, Périgord and Agenais in 1214, when King John became involved. Simon de Montfort died in 1218 during another siege of Toulouse. The need for peace was not recognised until much later. On 12 April 1229 the Treaty of Paris was signed: Raymond VII undertook, among many things, to marry his daughter Jeanne to Alphonse de Poitiers, brother of Louis IX. Paris had got its hold on the Languedoc, but the heresies were not subdued. Pope Gregory IX ordered the Inquisition in southern France in 1233 and entrusted the task to the Dominicans. Persecution was severe throughout the 1240s.

It is unclear why the name Albigensian was adopted for this episode in history, but it is possibly because the Albigeois (the present *département* of the Tarn) was the scene of attempts at reconciliation between the Church and the 'heretics', or because there were intense military operations here early in the crusades. It was only in the 1960s that the term Cathar began to be widely used.

ensemble of Gothic cathedral and bishops' palace, while Castres on the Agout is built mainly in stone and has the advantage of being the main industrial centre of the southern Tarn. The Tarn also boasts one of the most celebrated *bastides* in the southwest, Cordes-sur-Ciel which, since the 13C, has gradually encased the hill of Mordagne to the west of Albi.

ALBI

Albi is the best-known and most decorative of the brick towns of the Tarn and Garonne valleys, eliciting many comparisons with Tuscany and much pink prose. Yet the ochres, roses, reds and purples do not disappoint. The cathedral, on a spur above the Tarn, dominates and protects the town beneath it. Albi's most famous son was Henri-Marie-Raymond de Toulouse-Lautrec Monfa whose work is represented in the museum installed in the former bishops' palace (Palais de la Berbie).

Practical information

Getting there and around
Car

From Paris A6, A10, A20, N20.
From Bordeaux, A62, A20, A68, N88.
From Toulouse, A68.

Train

TER to Toulouse to Rodez via Albi.
Albi Ville station on Blvd Stalingrad.

Bus

Montauban to Albi.
Gare routière (bus station), Pl. Jean
Jaurès, ☎ 05 63 54 58 61.

Tourist information

81000 Albi Pl. Ste-Cécile, ☎
05 63 49 48 80, fax 05 63
49 48 98, www.tourisme.fr/albi

Market days

Saturday; flea market on Saturday in
Place du Castelviel

River cruises

River trips on a replica *gabare* depart
from Quai Choiseul: *Toulouse
Croisières*, mid-June–end Sept; ☎ 06
77 13 29 60/05 65 35 98 88, fax 05
65 35 98 89, email bateaux-safaraid@
clubinternet.fr-toulouse-croisiers.com

Festivals and events

May *Jazz en Balade*, all types
of jazz

June, July *Festival du Théâtre
Les Bâtisseurs de Ste-Cécile*, sound-and-
light show

July–August *Un été à Albi*, classical
music performed at various prestigious
sites

September *Grand Prix Automobile*,
motor racing, Albi.

Where to stay and eat-
ing out

81000 ALBI

✩✩✩✩ *Hostellerie St-Antoine*, 17 Rue
St-Antoine, ☎ 05 63 54 04 04, fax 05

63 47 10 47. Near the town centre,
with pretty rooms and a small garden.

✩✩✩✩ *La Réserve*, Rte de Cordes-
Fontvialane, ☎ 05 63 60 80 80, fax 05
63 47 63 60. A luxury hotel-restaurant
on outskirts of Albi in a lovely setting
beside the Tarn.

✩✩✩ *Le Chiffre*, Rue Séré-de-Rivières,
☎ 05 63 48 58 48, fax 05 63 477 20
61. Unfussy but attractive, with the
pleasant *Restaurant Bâteau Ivre*;
centrally placed.

✩✩✩ *Grand Hôtel d'Orléans*, Pl.
Stalingrad, ☎ 05 63 54 16 56, fax 05
63 54 43 41. A family-run hotel opposite the station; excellent value in the
Restaurant Le Goulu. Pool.

✩✩✩ *Mercure Albi-Bastides*, 41 Rue
Porta, ☎ 05 63 47 66 66, fax 05 63 46
18 40, www.mercure.com. A comfortable, modern hotel installed in a old mill
of 1770 with impressive views over the
Tarn and the old town.

✩✩ *St-Clair*, 8 Rue St-Clair, ☎ 05 63
54 25 66, fax 05 63 54 96 75. Small
hotel in the middle of the old town.

€€ *Esprit du Vin*, 11 Quai Choiseul,
☎ 05 3 54 60 44. Below the bishops'
palace, a small restaurant with quality
cooking.

€€ *Moulin de Lamothe*, ☎ 05 63 60
38 15, fax 05 63 60 38 15. Gorgeous
setting on the banks of the Tarn to the
southwest of the town centre. Delicious
food.

€€ *La Table du Sommelier*, 20 Rue
Porta, ☎/fax 05 63 46 20 10. Popular
and modern-style restaurant concentrating on local fresh produce and local
dishes with a lighter touch. €25 menu
designed around 3 different wines
(wines sold by the glass). Must reserve.

€–€€ *Le Lautrec*, 13–15 Rue H. de
Toulouse-Lautrec, ☎/fax 05 63 54 86
55. A pretty restaurant in the heart of
the old town with a varied menu.

History

Settled by the 4C BC, *Civitas Albigensium* was mentioned for the first time *c* 400 and was head of a diocese in the 5C. By the 7C the *cité* was taking shape under the shared power of the Church and the nobility. At the break-up of the Carolingian Empire the Counts of Albi became vassals of the infamous Trencavel dynasty, self-styled Counts of Béziers, Carcassonne and Albi, and protectors of Cathars, rivalled them in the 13C until the Albigensian Crusade. Some half-century after the Crusade, the orthodox bishops undertook the rebuilding of the cathedral as a symbol of their sovereignty. Despite the usual problems of the Middle Ages, the town's prosperity increased during the late 15C and 16C thanks largely to *pastel* (p 331). At about the same time two bishops of Albi, uncle and nephew Louis I (1474–1503) and Louis II (1504–10) of Amboise, great patrons of the arts, decorated the interior of the cathedral. The metallurgical, mining and glass industries, which developed in the 19C, have mainly disappeared.

Place du Vigan, created in the 18C, marks the divide between the medieval quarter to the west and the modern town, and was recently renovated and an underground car park created.

At no. 14 Rue Timbal, northwest of the *place*, is the **Hôtel de Reynès** (*c* 1520), built by a rich *pastel* merchant. The small Italianate courtyard is the most sophisticated of the period in Albi, combining a stairtower in the tradition of Gothic buildings with the elegance of a Renaissance loggia. On the south façade are two busts in medallions, reputedly of François I and probably his second queen, Eléonore. Almost opposite, on the corner of Rue des Pénitents, is the 16C Maison Enjalbert or **Pharmacie des Pénitents**, an outstanding timber-framed house using the vocabulary of the Renaissance, triangular pediments and Ionic and Corinthian pilasters. Turn left into Rue Mariès. The massive south flank of the cathedral looms into focus as you descend the street.

On the left is the slightly run-down Place du Cloître at the east end of the collegiate church of **St-Salvy**. Salvy was made Bishop in the late 6C and in 943 his relics were translated to this site. The cult of St Salvy was widely venerated in this region during the early Middle Ages. The lower part of the church, with one 12C chapel, is built in stone, with a thrusting 15C brick structure above. Follow the passageway through to the modest and secret cloistral remains, with just one gallery left, Romanesque-going-on-Gothic (begun 1270). The tomb of Vidal de Malvési, creator of the cloister, and his brother, is against the church. Enter the church from the cloister. Despite successive modifications from the 12C to the 18C, the interior is quite harmonious, if gloomy. The lower parts of the four east bays (completed *c* 1100) are heavily restored. Lateral chapels were added during the 14C and 15C and the chancel and two preceding bays, rebuilt in the 15C, are Flamboyant. Louis d'Amboise consecrated a new altar in 1490. The clerestory was added in the 18C, as was the rose window. The early 16C organ was transferred from the cathedral in 1737 by master carpenter Christophe Moucherel, and subsequently was used for concerts. Behind a wrought-iron screen (light switch on the right) is a group of polychrome figures (*c* 15C), an *Ecce Homo* and the *Sanhedrin*. A replica of the 12C wooden image of St Salvy stands behind the ornate Baroque altar with a baldaquin (1721). Leave by the north door, originally Romanesque but almost obliterated by a pedimented version although the sculpted capitals are still in place. The three-tiered belfry, the **Tour de la Gâche**, on the right is a textbook example of changing styles and proves that Albi was once more white than red. The Romanesque base (*c* 1080) with Lombard-style blind arches and the second stage (*c* 1220–40), both in white stone, are topped off with a late-14C brick crown and watchtower.

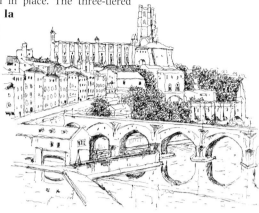

Albi

Turn left into **Place Ste-Cécile**. On the far right are the bishops' palace and the tourist office.

Cathédrale Ste-Cécile

The austere and inscrutable fortress of faith, the cathedral of Ste-Cécile, totally dominates the square. It has stood isolated like a beached ship since the houses that surrounded it were cleared away in the 18C–19C and a small market square transformed into a huge car park (the market is still held here). (Work is due to be carried out in the square in 2003.) Open June–Sept 09.00–18.30; Oct–May 09.00–12.00 and 14.00–18.30; ☎ 05 63 43 23 43. Buy tickets to enter the choir from the postcard stall.

The cathedral took about 100 years to build, replacing a more modest Romanesque church, at a time of spiritual renewal and pecuniary rigour between 1282 and 1383. Basically a skeletal structure supported by buttressing with non load-bearing walls, its originality is due both to the brick, a cheaper and faster means of building, and to the massive rounded buttresses which echo, and were probably inspired by, the fortifications of the adjacent bishops' palace. Its seriousness reflects the objective of its main champion, Chief Inquisitor Bernard de Castanet, Bishop of Albi (1277–1307), to reaffirm the authority of the Roman Catholic Church following the subversive Cathar heresies in the 12C with a church that resembles a fort.

A great undulating pile of brick that looks as if it were tipped all of a piece from a celestial mould, it epitomises southern or meridional Gothic, having none of the fractured restlessness of the High Gothic of northern France. There are no walls of glass, simply modest lancets; the lower windows were added in the 15C. The silhouette of the cathedral was altered in the 19C during work to solve the problem of water infiltration when the roof, which originally had wide overhanging eaves and rested directly on the vaults, was raised by the architect César Daly, a disciple of Viollet-le-Duc. The 19C work is demarcated by the gargoyles and the lighter brick. Daly began prettifying the roofline with small belfries to match one already existing, but local disapproval led to their demolition. The 78m tiered cathedral **belfry** was built between 1355 and 1366. The tower is articulated by quarter-circle relieving arches between great rounded buttresses but the rhythm changes to octagonal in the upper level (1485–92).

The main entrance to the cathedral is on the south, approached from Place Ste-Cécile through the archway built by Bishop Dominique de Florence (1397–1410), which incorporates a round tower that was part of the fortifications of the episcopal city. Climb up to the ornate entrance under the early 16C crocketed Flamboyant baldaquin and filigree tympanum. The sculptures of the entrance were remade by Daly between 1865 and 1870, when the baldaquin vaults were filled in.

Interior The Flamboyant vestibule (*c* 1510–20) offers a hint of what is inside but nothing quite prepares you for the contrast between the severe exterior and the excesses of the interior. The cathedral was transformed in the calm years of nascent humanism before the Reformation. In a basically simple, unified space, without aisles, where the interior buttresses form the lateral chapels and support a rib vault rising to a height of 30m. The coherence of this space was disrupted before the end of the 15C by the elaborate choir enclosure. Two bishops, Louis I and Louis II of Amboise, were responsible for the metamorphosis—powerful men from a great family of prelates and ambassadors, they had access to the latest artistic trends in the Loire, in Burgundy and in Italy. There is no written documentation extant relating to the work as all the archives were destroyed during the Revolution. The all-over *trompe-l'oeil* pattern of the chapels and walls, conceived *c* 1509–20, has been subjected to numerous restorations, especially in the 19C.

The *Last Judgement* on the west wall is thought to date from the time of Louis I, whose gold and red heraldic colours fill the lower space. This is the largest surviving wall painting of the period in France and was probably executed by Franco-Flemish artists contemporaneous with Hieronymus Bosch. Applied directly to the brick, it covers some 200 square metres. The composition is organised according to tradition but there is one disturbing omission: the key figure of Christ in Judgement. In the 17C different priorities permitted the piercing of an opening through the wall to the chapel where the relics of St Clair, first Bishop of Albi, lie and consequently the work is arranged around a void.

The composition is divided vertically, the blessed on your left, lined up in orderly fashion on a calm blue ground, and opposite, a murky hell in all its confusion. It is also divided horizontally into three main registers: Heaven is subdivided into three hierarchies, of angels, the 12 Apostles, and a line-up of the saved with St Louis, Charlemagne and others now unidentifiable. Below is the theatre of the Resurrection where those mortals already judged hold the Book of Life open on their chests. Opposite them sinners are thrown back to the underworld. The bottom register is Hell, depicted in as much horror as the artists could muster and compartmentalised into scenes representing each of the seven deadly sins, which are annotated in Old French: from left to right, pride, envy, anger or wrath, avarice or greed, gluttony and lust (sloth is missing), each with the appropriately grisly punishments.

In quite a different artistic timbre, high above this didactic message, is the splendidly Baroque Moucherel **organ** (1734–36) supported by two muscular atlantes. The carved case is mainly in oak, and the figures, including St Cecilia holding her small organ with tin pipes and the joyful angel musicians, are in lime. Restored in 1981, it is one of the best instruments in France and frequently used for recitals.

To meet a need to accommodate large congregations in the 19C after the destruction of several parish churches at the Revolution, and to avoid having to dismantle the precious Gothic choir enclosure, the **main altar** was placed at the west. The black marble altar with enamels was made by two Parisian artists, Jean-Paul Froidevaux and his wife, Marie-Josephe Tournon-Froidevaux (1980).

The magnificent Flamboyant **jubé** (roodscreen, *c* 1474–84) that divides the nave from the chancel, a profusion of ogees and lacework, pinnacles and broccoli leaves, was carved in tender limestone which has hardened over the centuries. The cutting and undercutting of this scintillating work is a tribute to the technical virtuosity of French stonecarvers. The original 75 statues in the niches have disappeared; those present are replacements.

The **choir** is the most spectacular part of this amazing building. The entrance to the ambulatory is in the south section of the screen. Inside, around the outside of the choir screen, is a procession of magnificent **polychromed statues** (*c* 1480). They represent Old Testament prophets, priests and kings, those who have not yet seen the light but predict or prefigure the Coming of Christ. Above the entrance is a very sweet, long-haired *Virgin of the Annunciation*, her hand on the Bible, as she receives the message of the Angel Gabriel to her left (on the choir screen). Of the 48 large-format sculptures over 30 are around the ambulatory and are in excellent condition; it is not known if their colour is original and, if not, the date of the repainting. The figures stand in ornate niches, most carry a banderole and several are identified by name. The image-makers, who undoubtedly included Flemish masters, had a penchant for the anecdotal and descriptive use of costume and fashion, but also the expressive quality of each individual. Note *Isaiah*, presented as a prosperous bourgeois merchant, and *Jeremiah*, appropriately grave. *Simeon*, the High Priest of the Temple, at the axis, is the linchpin between the Ancient and the New Law. His importance places him on the opposite side of the screen from the Virgin and Child. (Below Simeon is a plaque commemorating the quick action of a local official to save many of the 254 original carvings from destruction at the Revolution.) The only female Old Testament figures are *Esther* and *Judith*, the latter wearing a rich red brocade dress hanging in heavy folds and a bejewelled headdress. The two great Christian Emperors, *Charlemagne* and *Constantine*, stand sentinel opposite each other over the north and south entrances to the choir. Inside the choir (entrance on north) are the Apostles, those who have seen the light, but they are less glorious artistically. At the west, on the reverse of the roodscreen, is a small but voluptuous *St Cecilia* with her attributes, a crown of roses and lilies, a portative organ and a martyr's palm. All around the western part of the chancel, above the 120 oak stalls, are 70 delicately sculpted child angels, each holding a musical instrument or scroll, and above them are the arms of Louis of Amboise. The canopy of the **episcopal throne** is a *tour de force* of undercutting, whereas the modern altar table of white marble is a refreshingly simple piece.

What little medieval **glass** (*c* 1320–25) there is, is in the high windows at the east. Works in the chapels include a fresco of the *Resurrection* and the *Legend of the True Cross* (*c* 1460–70), both heavily restored. In the east chapel are four paintings sent from Rome by Cardinal de Bernis in the 18C.

The **vaults** were painted between 1509 and 1512 by Bolognese artists who

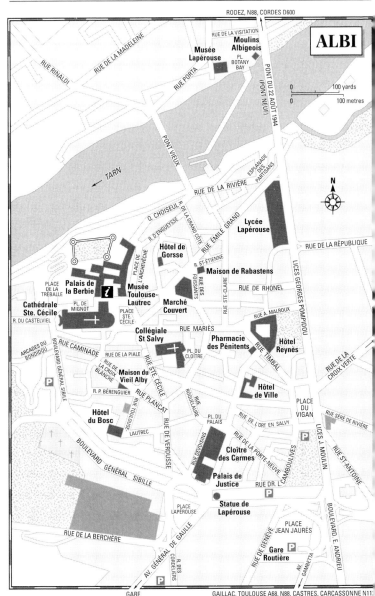

worked suspended in baskets. The iconographic programme, like the chancel statues, unites the Old and New Testaments. The New Testament figures are painted in gold, the others in silver, on a deep blue ground, and have hardly been touched since they were painted. The scenes are arranged in the form of a triumphal procession from west to east with St Cecilia in the centre, and tell of the return of man to God under the guidance of the Church, culminating in the *Christ of the Second Coming* surrounded by the symbols of the four Evangelists. On the boss nearest to the organ are the multiple fleur-de-lis of France as they appeared before the mid-14C (see also Marmande, p 267). Among the scenes most easily recognisable are, reading from west to east, the *Last Supper*, the *Transfiguration*, the *Coronation of the Virgin*, *St Cecilia and Valerian*, the *Annunciation*, then Cecilia and Valerian again at each extremity of the next bay, the parable of the *Wise and Foolish Virgins*, the *Coronation of the Virgin* again, and the *Tree of Life*. *Adam and Eve* are easy to recognise in the east bay. This significant work was the first major example of Italian Renaissance art in the Midi, and compares very closely to the decoration of churches near Pavia in Northern Italy.

The **Chapelle du Rosaire**, northwest of the nave, contains a 14C **Sienese polyptych**, and further east is a chapel containing a highly sentimental statue of St Cecilia, copied from the Trastevere, Rome, showing the saint as she was reputedly found in her tomb in 1599.

On leaving the cathedral, follow the south flank of the cathedral along Rue du Parvis Ste-Cécile built over the Bondidou River, which now runs underground but precluded a west entrance. Immediately west of the cathedral is Place du Château and the very ancient quarter of **Castelviel** with its minuscule *places*. Rue du Castelviel is overwhelmed by the belfry. From Place de la Tréballe there are steps down to the *berges du Tarn* (riverbank). Follow the north flank of the cathedral past the small door and down Rue de la Temporalité, into the light of Place Ste-Cécile.

One of the loveliest places in Albi is the **garden of the bishops' palace**. Descend the steps towards the Toulouse-Lautrec museum entrance, and at the bottom turn left and follow the path which brings you out on to a terrace high above the Tarn. From here there is a marvellous view of the river, spanned by the old and newer bridges to the right, and beyond the brick façades of the old suburb of La Madeleine. On the horizon what appears to be a miniature of the cathedral is the 19C church of Notre-Dame-de-la-Drèche (p 322). The fomal garden below you was installed by Archbishop Hyacinthe Serroni (1678–87), who was also responsible for the vine-shaded walk on the old ramparts, reached via the steps in the southwest corner. The statues in the alcoves are 18C.

On the right is the great mass of the **Palais de la Berbie**, the name derived the from the old Occitan word *bisbia*, meaning bishops' palace. The Berbie fortress-palace is a powerful building of disparate parts, begun in the second half of the 13C by Bishop Durand de Beaucaire and completed by Bishop Bernard de Castanet *c* 1277, to protect their authority over Albi and as part of the town's defences. Built entirely in brick, tamed and modified over the centuries, its architecture complements the cathedral. The oldest part is the Tour Notre-Dame on the east overlooking Place de l'Archevêché. The mighty Tour St-Michel on the west was completed by 1277, and only a stump is left of the largest tower. Ste-Catherine, built facing the river before 1300 and dismantled in the early 17C. The bastions along the Tarn were probably constructed during the Hundred Years War. The Bishops of Amboise amended the east wing and Bishop Gaspard Daillon de Lude added the *salon doré* and the monumental staircase in the style of the Loire. By 1790 the building was taken over by the state although the episcopal see was reinstated in 1823.

Musée Toulouse-Lautrec

The main function of the Berbie since 1922 has been to house the largest single collection of works by Toulouse-Lautrec, some 1000 items, including paintings, drawings, lithographs and posters. The majority were donated by his mother, Countesse Adèle, encouraged by Lautrec's oldest friend and supporter, the art dealer Maurice Joyant. It also has an eclectic collection including local archaeology, two superb authenticated paintings by Georges de la Tour, one by Francesco Guardi, and a vast group of 19C and 20C works by local artists and such notables as Corot, the Pont-Aven Group, Vuillard, Bonnard, Matisse and Dufy and sculptures by Rodin, Bourdelle and Maillol. There are frequent temporary exhibitions.

Open July, Aug daily 09.00–18.00; June, Sept daily 09.00–12.00 and 14.00–18.00; April, May daily 10.00–12.00 and 14.00–18.00; March, Oct 10.00–12.00 and 14.00–17.30; Nov–Feb 10.00–12.00 and 14.00–17.00; March, Oct–Feb closed Tues; ☎ 05 63 49 48 70, www.musee-toulouse-lautrec.com.

Henri de Toulouse-Lautrec

Lautrec (1864–1901) is a legendary figure, a direct descendant of one of the oldest and most prestigious dynasties in southwest France, the Counts of Toulouse, but through a tragic quirk of fate also misshapen and ugly. Most importantly he was a dedicated painter caught up in the social debates of his time. He was also revered and protected by his family.

He was born within sight of the cathedral, to Adèle Tapié de Celeyran and her first cousin Alphonse de Toulouse-Lautrec. The main occupation of the eccentric count and his family was hunting, but they all had a gift for drawing. In 1878, at the age of 14, Henri slipped on the polished parquet in Albi and fractured a leg; the following year, he broke the other leg. The bones did not knit and he remained just over five feet tall, so he took up drawing instead of riding. Until 1881, when he went to Paris to become a professional artist, his time was divided between the different family estates in the southwest. In 1882 he moved to Léon Bonnat's studio and then to Fernand Cormon in Montmartre. By 1884 he was established there and pursuing his profession among the Parisian avant-garde. He evoked the sub-culture of Montmartre in all its gaiety and squalor. He travelled prodigiously but not far; he knew Van Gogh, the Pont-Aven Group, and Degas, whose work he admired most; he also knew Oscar Wilde, James Whistler and Aubrey Beardsley and was heavily influenced by Japanese prints; he made use of the effects of theatrical lighting; he assimilated Art Nouveau tendencies; and the popular illustrations of the 1880s were possibly the single most tangible influence on his art. Lautrec's *annus mirabilis* was 1892, when he produced his first colour posters. They brought fame to him and to the people he portrayed and were his main contribution to 20C art, but in fact he only made 32 lithographs for posters in the last ten years of his life. He died in 1901 at the Château de Malromé, near Bordeaux (p 112).

The **permanent exhibitions** occupy the first, second and third floors (there is a lift.) (At the time of writing the archaeology and the 19C–20C sections were closed.) Off the staircase is a small, brick vaulted gallery dedicated to archaeology, and the Chapelle Notre-Dame (13C), the oldest part of the palace. The first of the main galleries, the Salon Doré, with an elegant 17C ceiling *à la française*, contains two magnificent works by Georges de la Tour (1593–1652) of *St Jude and St James Minor*, commissioned for the cathedral, and *Notre-Dame de la Salute*, Venice, by Francesco Guardi (1712–93). Fourteen galleries are dedicated to Toulouse-Lautrec, with paintings by his family, paintings of him by his friends, including Vuillard (1898), and self-portraits. The paintings are arranged thematically rather than chronologically, although at the beginning these coincide. Lautrec's earlier paintings reflect the influence of his first teacher, René Princeteau (1839–1914), and his aristocractic milieu. There is a tiny, rather inept, portrait of *c* 1879 of his father on horseback, dressed as a Caucasian, his falcon on his wrist. A form of diluted Impressionist landscapes gives way to linear studies of figures and interiors in the long corridor. By 1885 his work was becoming far more experimental and his social conscience was stirred. The small circular room contains *La Buveuse* or *Gueule de bois* (1889), for which his mistress Suzanne Valadon posed shortly before they separated, is a comment on isolation and self-destruction. Compare this dejection with the quiet dignity of the two portraits of another woman seated and alone, his mother, *Comtesse Adèle de Toulouse-Lautrec* (*c* 1881 and 1887). In the same room is a large painting of *Maurice Joyant en baie de Somme* (1900), dressed in yellow oilskins and sou'wester that Lautrec had acquired from the USA and wanted to paint, took 75 sittings. There are dandies and women with complicated coiffures, in a style he developed after 1889, in thin oils on board with a breathtaking fluidity and economy of line.

Doubleback through the long gallery and then turn right for the hard-core Montmartre works. In these—sensual, erotic, funny, tender or wickedly satirical, with a straightforward realism that was considered outrageous at the time—Lautrec's critical observation and technical prowess come together. Representative of his work are the two famous versions of *Au Salon de la Rue des Moulins* (1894), one a pastel study in preparation for the oil painting. A studied and carefully orchestrated piece in large format (111.5 x 132.5cm), it is the culmination of his studies and sketches of *maisons closes* (brothels) and their occupants, made from 1891 to 1895. In these galleries are all the music-hall stars found in the posters, Yvette Guilbert, Jane Avril, La Goulue and Loïe Fuller (1893), a swirl of veils and graceful arabesques.

The second floor contains original **lithograph stones**, which Lautrec prepared himself, and the posters. Lautrec's earlier work and experiments are synthesised in this flattened decorative formula which projected the art of the poster into the 20C. He was a man with a foot in two camps, the establishment and Parisian sub-culture and this dichotomy is brought into perspective in this museum.

The 19C–20C collection is on the third floor. This is an eclectic group of works from Corot to Cubism, not exhibited to best advantage but worth the effort as a background to the influences on Lautrec, and an added bonus are the views over the river and gardens. Many major painters are represented by just one work. There is a Degas pastel *Man in an Opera Hat*, a Matisse, a Vlaminick, a Marquet and a Dufy. There are paintings by members of the Pont Aven group, Emile Bernard and Paul Sérusier, and some small bronzes by Gauguin. Intimisme is represented by Bonnard, Félix Valloton and Edouard Vuillard, Cubism by André Lhote and Expressionism by Georges Rouault. Yves Brayer is the most important of the group of local artists, and there are sculptures by Rodin, Bourdelle, Aristide Maillol and Paul Belmondo (father of Jean-Paul).

North and east of the cathedral

The **quartier de la rivière** on the slopes of the Tarn has many beautiful old buildings, the majority thoughtfully renewed. Set out from Place de l'Archeveché, noting the 16C slate roofs and dormers, on the southeast of the Berbie. Rue d'Engueysse has some jettied houses with open galleries or *soleilhos* (sometimes called *galetas*), originally used for drying crops, including *pastel*.

The pointed arches indicate the oldest part (*c* 1220) of the much-modified **Pont-Vieux** and the brick sections indicate the enlargements made after 1820 to allow carts carrying coal and glass to pass. River trips on a replica *gabare* depart from Quai Choiseul (see above).

Across the river is the Faubourg du Bout-du-Pont which developed in the 11C, and on the right in Rue Porta is a terrace overlooking the river. Just after the fork with Rue Porta enter Square Botany Bay. The **Musée Lapérouse** is devoted to the life and times of Jean-François Galaup de Lapérouse (1741–88), a sailor and explorer born near Albi, who was active at Hudson Bay against the English during the American Wars of Independence. Open Mon, Wed–Sun April–Oct 09.00–12.00 and 14.00–18.00; Nov–March 10.00–12.00 and 14.00–17.00; closed Tues; ☎ 05 63 46 01 87. The old mills of Albi were below here.

Return across the river by Rue de la Visitation and the Pont Neuf (1866), renamed **Pont-du-22-août-1944** to commemorate a combat between members of the Resistance and a German column. On the west side of Lices Georges Pompidou is the 19C **Lycée Lapérouse** where Jean Jaurès, the local socialist hero, taught philosophy from 1881 to 1883. He played a key role in encouraging local glassmakers to form the Verrerie Ouvrière d'Albi in 1896, one of the first worker-managed enterprises in France.

Between Esplanade des Partisans, the river and Rue Emile-Grand is a tangle of narrow streets. Rue de la Grand'Côte was one of the most important before the 18C. At the end of Rue Emile-Grand on the left is the **Maison Pierre-Raimond de Rabastens**, the remains of the oldest house in Albi (12C), built in stone. Quite a contrast is the spruce, brick and steel *marché couvert* (covered market, 1901–02). It functions every day but positively bustles with activity on Saturdays. The best house nearby is the 16C **Hôtel de Gorsse**, in a courtyard at the top of the steps north of the market. Return to Place Ste-Cécile along Rue St-Julien, where no. 16 has a *soleilho*.

South of the cathedral

South of the cathedral is a mainly pedestrian and up-market quarter, with restaurants and chic boutiques among the carefully restored medieval, Renaissance, 18C and 19C houses. From the southeast corner of Place Ste-Cécile, take Rue Ste-Cécile. Where Rue Puech-Bérenguier and Rue de la Croix-Blanche meet is the pretty **Maison du Viel Alby**, used for regional exhibitions. Open Mon–Sat 15.00–19.00, closed Sun and PH; ☎ 05 63 54 96 38. The *Artisan Pastellier*, a boutique/workshop, has objects dyed with the blue of *pastel* (p 331). In Rue Toulouse-Lautrec, no. 10 has an attractively restored late-Renaissance courtyard. Further along on the right are the home of Lapérouse (see above) at no. 14, and the **Hôtel du Bosc**, where Toulouse-Lautrec was born and where, in 1878, he broke his leg.

Continue to Rue de Verdusse and turn right to **Place Lapérouse** with a large monument to the explorer by Nicolas Bernard Raggi (erected 1853). Rue

Devoisins opens into Place du Palais where the **Palais de Justice** occupies the former Carmelite convent, an early 17C brick building around a small cloister. Take the street opposite to join **Rue de l'Hôtel-de-Ville**. This once most prestigious street is lined with some of the best noble houses, the most outstanding at nos 13, 14 and 17, and no. 16, the *hôtel de ville* since the 18C. Above the doorway of the restored 17C façade is the coat of arms of Albi and inside is a very attractive brick courtyard. Rue de l'Hôtel-de-Ville leads back to Place du Vigan.

THE ALBIGEOIS

This area in the northwest of the Tarn is crossed by the little valley of the Cérou, a tributary of the Aveyron, which flows through beautiful fertile landscapes scattered with particulaly fine hilltop towns and bastides, including Cordes-sur-Ciel, and in nearby Monestiés is a unique group of Gothic sculptures.

Cordes-sur-Ciel

Cordes-sur-Ciel, described locally as the *perle des bastides*, is the showpiece of the northern Tarn. One of the oldest and most picturesque *bastides* in the region, its charter was granted by Raymond VII of Toulouse in 1222. The suffix sur-Ciel ('in the sky') was officially recognised in 1990 to distinguish it from Gordes in the Vaucluse, and is not such a fantasy as it seems. Just after dawn on a clear autumn day, the mists are likely to gather in the Cérou Valley and swirl around the base of the hill on which it stands. Apart from the spectacular site, it is graced with a unique group of Gothic houses. Unsurprisingly, Cordes has attracted a number of artists and artisans and there are some classy shops as well as a few trashy ones.

The best way to get to the top of the hill is to walk, not as daunting as it looks. There is some parking at the top, or in the lower town car park to the west off the D600. A shuttle bus from the foot of the hill stops outside the upper walls.

Getting there and around
Car

D600 Albi to Cordes.
Train

TER Brive to Toulouse via Vindrac-Cordes (night train from Paris Austerlitz stops at Vindrac-Cordes). Station about 6km out of Cordes and taxis scarce.

Tourist information
81170 Cordes-sur-Ciel
Maison Fontpeyrouse, Grande Rue (at the top of the hill), ☎ 05 63 56 00 52, fax 05 63 56 19 52, www.cordes-sur-ciel.org
81640 Monestiés Pl. de la Mairie, ☎ 05 63 76 19 17, fax 05 63 76 19

86, www.monesties.com
Market day

Cordes-sur-Ciel Saturday

Festivals and events
July *Fête du Grand Fauconnier*, traditional medieval fair, Cordes
July *Musique sur Ciel*, music festival, Cordes-sur-Ciel. *Les samedis gourmands*, gastronomic festivals, Cordes-sur-Ciel. *Festival Pause Guitar*, French and international guitar music and song, Monestiés

Where to stay and eating out
81170 CORDES
✵✵✵✵ *Le Grand Ecuyer*, 79 Grande Rue

Raymond VII, ☎ 05 63 53 79 50, fax 05 63 56 18 83, www.thuries.fr. Hotel established in a beautiful Gothic house, with chef Yves Thriès' top-quality restaurant.

✩✩✩ *Vieux-Cordes*, Rue St-Michel, ☎ 05 63 53 79 20, fax 05 63 56 05 47. Hotel-restaurant in a charming setting in old Cordes, with a wisteria-covered courtyard.

✩✩ *La Cité*, Rue de la République, ☎ 05 63 56 03 53, fax 05 63 56 02 47. Small hotel in the *bastide*, around a courtyard.

€–€€ *Hostellerie du Parc*, Les Cabannes (west of Cordes on DD600), ☎ 05 63 56 02 59, fax 05 63 56 18 03, www.cuisineries-gourmandes.com. A reliable and generous table, reasonably priced, served in a rustic setting. Terrace.

81140 CAHUZAC-SUR-VÈRE
✩✩✩ *Château de Salettes*, ☎ 05 63 33 60 60, fax 05 63 33 60 61. www.chateau-de-salette.fr. A hotel of character and charm among the vineyards between Cordes and Gaillac.

Cordes is made up of four concentric enclosures, the first two dating from the *bastide* built in 1222, the others later. The suburb of La Boutellerie on the eastern side remained outside the protected perimeter. From Place de la Boutellerie take the no-entry to cars road, past the chapel of the old Hôpital St-Jacques, to the junction with the **Escalier du Pater-Noster** on your left—with as many steps as there are words in the Lord's Prayer. On the right is the Porte de l'Horloge, with a clock and a round tower. This was the eastern entrance to the fourth *enceinte*, built in the 16C to enclose the four *faubourgs* that had surrounded the medieval fort since the 14C. It gets steeper here.

There was never a feudal castle at Cordes, but around the next bend the mighty **barbican** looms up on a cliff-like base which was part of the third enclosure, built at a time of great prosperity and population explosion at the end of the 13C or early in the 14C, when the earlier enclosures were outgrown. The road bends to arrive at Porte du Planol (1222–29), parallel with the wall, with a semicircular tower, engulfed by the buildings around it. Opposite is the late 15C Maison Gorsse, with early Renaissance windows.

The road then turns left to pass through the barely altered **Portail Peint** (13C), which originally had two portcullises and a wooden door, to the heart of the upper town. Immediately on the right is the entrance to the **Musée Charles Portal**, a private museum of local archaeology and history with a remarkable and eclectic collection. Open July, Aug daily 11.00–12.30 and 15.00–18.30; Easter–June, Sept, Oct, Sun and PH only 15.00–18.00; ☎ 05 63 56 00 52.

On the **Grand Rue** are the best of the remarkable group of Gothic houses. The first Gothic house on the left is the **Maison Carrié-Boyer**, considered to be among the earliest built (1295–1320). On three floors, the façade aggressively altered, it remains an example of how most of the houses were left in the 19C. Next door is **Maison Prunet**, of about the same date, with three arcades on the ground floor and three two-light windows with a circular oculus outlined in deep mouldings, and carvings at the apex. It houses the Férie de l'Art du Sucre, with sugar fantasies conjured up by local restaurateur Yves Thuriès. Open daily July, Aug 10.00–19.00; Feb–June, Sept–Dec 10.00–12.00 and 14.30–18.30. The next house, **Maison du Grand Fauconnier**, is one of the three masterpieces, probably dating from the first half of the 14C. Two of the original birds of prey from the façade are in the Portal Museum. This is one of the most carefully

Gothic houses of Cordes

This unique group of *hôtels particuliers* was begun nearly a century after the foundation of the *bastide* with fortunes made from linen and leather. At that time the population could have been around 5000. The best are to the south, built into the hill, with an average of three floors on the town side but up to five or six facing out. On the ground floor are large arches of varying size giving access to the courtyard, stables or boutiques. The first floor is the most ornate, corresponding to a large room the width of the building lit by a series of sophisticated traceried windows. The sculpted decoration is usually concentrated around the windows and on the string courses linking the bays. The rhythm of the bays and the carvings are slightly different for each house. As the population decreased the occupants moved to the lower floors, partitioned the interior, blocked doors and windows (especially when windows were taxed in the 17C), and sliced off the relief carvings to hang shutters, but left the upper floors unmolested. When the time came to restore the houses, the second floor often served as a model for the lower one. The names are an invention of the 19C, inspired by nothing more than the decoration on the façade.

executed façades, with five arcades at ground level and series of traceried windows on the first and second floors, arranged in different rhythms with high-relief carvings.

The **Yves Brayer Museum**, with 17 paintings donated by the artist, best known for his landscapes of Provence but who lived here 1940–42, is on the first floor of the Grand Fauconnier: go through the courtyard and up the spiral stair-case. Open daily 10.30–12.30 and 14.00–18.00; closed Jan; ☎ 05 63 56 14 79. Below is a permanent exhibition of lace-making, an important industry in Cordes at the beginning of the 20C. Opposite is **Place de la Bride**, where an open square with chestnut trees and a terrace overlooking the countryside have replaced the former public buildings of the *bastide*. Look over the terrace wall to see steep steps connecting the different levels.

Take the steps next to the Hôtel de la Bride down to the **halle**, where the two major streets converge. There was probably a market here in 1276, but it was rebuilt in 1358. The 24 octagonal pillars have been frequently repaired and the chestnut roof timbers were replaced in the 19C. The depth of the well (85m) indicates that it was only used for emergencies; in any case there were other wells and cisterns.

The rather severe church of **St-Michel** lower down was built 1263–87 when the community outgrew the earlier church outside the village. The nave was enlarged in 1345, and again between 1460 and 1485. The constant amend-ments are only too clear at the west end, a model of asymmetry: the belfry (1369–74) on the north side, square at the base and octagonal above, doubled as a look-out post; it is supported by a relieving arch containing a rose window. Filling the rest of the façade is a walled-up Flamboyant portal suspended high and dry above the present level of the small *place*. Note the polychrome wooden sculpture of the Virgin above the south door. The interior is typical of Gothic churches in the Midi, with little of the original building left. The organ came from Notre-Dame in Paris in 1849 and is used frequently for concerts. Near the church is the **Maison du Violon** which demonstrates the stages in the construction of the violin and has a collection of old instruments. Open daily July, Aug 15.00–18.00; May, June, Sept weekends and PH only 15.00–18.00

The **Maison du Grand Veneur** on the Grande Rue is named after the huntsman in the narrative frieze running across the façade. It is the only house with the third floor still intact and is similar to the Grand Fauconnier but without the rhythmical arrangement of the bays. The first-floor windows are a reconstruction modelled on the second floor. Its special charm is the anecdotal nature of the high-relief carvings. Birds perch, dogs play and crouching figures inhabit the mouldings. The figures of the huntsmen, their hounds and their prey fill the spandrels on the second floor. The **Maison Fontpeyrouse**, on the opposite corner, houses the tourist office and cultural centre. Heavily restored, it is arranged around a large courtyard with a wooden staircase and galleries serving

A café in Cordes-sur-Ciel

the floors. The **Maison du Grand Ecuyer** (Great Equerry), now synonymous with its restaurant (see above), has a most accomplished façade, with simpler tracery, heavily foliate capitals and discreet carvings in the deep recesses of the window mouldings.

Follow one of the cobbled streets down to the **Porte des Ormeaux** on the west. Two semi-circular bastions flank the gate but the upper parts of the archway and towers were rebuilt at a very early stage. Turn right to Porte de la Jane, also between two semi-circular towers, but badly damaged during the Wars of Religion. There is more to explore on the lower levels and from here it is an easy route to the lower town.

Continue down the hill towards the town centre: on the left is the **Jardin des Paradis**, an intimate garden with some unusual concepts in landscaping. Open July–mid-Sept daily 10.30–18.30; May,

June mid-Sept–mid-Oct weekends only 11.00–18.00; ☎ 05 63 56 29 77.

The Cérou, followed by the D91, cuts its dainty way through a valley between Cordes and Carmaux. The pretty village of **Salles**, famous for its stone quarries in the Middle Ages, has a part Romanesque, part Gothic church containing four 16C painted wooden statues.

Monestiés

Monestiés is another charming village which shelters a group of magnificent late-Gothic sculptures, the *Entombment* (*Mise au Tombeau*), housed in the little chapel of **St-Jacques** on Le Barry, the street across the main road from the fountain. In 1992 the sculptures were restored (perhaps too vigorously, reducing the original quite strong colours to very delicate, even faded, shades) and rearranged. The chapel was renovated at the same time. Open July, Aug 10.00–

13.00 and 14.00–19.00; 16–30 March, Sept, Oct 10.00–12.00, 14.00–18.00; Nov–14 March 14.00–17.00; ☎ 05 63 76 41 63.

The chapel is the perfect foil for this deeply moving group of polychromed stone statues, which has been here for two centuries. The work was originally commissioned *c* 1490 by the Bishop of Albi, Louis I of Amboise, for the chapel of the bishops' residence, the 13C Château of Combefa 3km south of Monestiés. It was designed, unusually, as the retable of the main altar. The plastic and expressive qualities of the carving compare with the finest produced in France at the end of the 15C, marking the transition between Gothic spirituality and humanist naturalism.

This monumental work represents three episodes of the Passion, *Crucifixion*, *Pietà* and *Entombment*, in a vast triangular composition. At the apex is the Crucifixion whose Christ who has passed through suffering to a state of compassion and below is the Pietà, a rare iconography where the five Maries and St John accompany the Virgin. The Entombment, forming the base of the triangle, which expands on the Pietà group with additional figures, is a masterpiece of medieval art conveying a deep sense of tenderness and grief. Notice also the minute attention to detail. This is another unique arrangement, with five male and five female figures spread out either side of the tomb to include the donor prelate, Louis I of Amboise, who holds the shroud at Christ's head thus displacing Joseph of Arimathaea. Next is St James, holding a book, a rare participant an Entombment scene, followed by St John and finally the 'weeping woman'. On the opposite side, behind Nicodemus, are the Virgin Mary, Mary Cleophas, Mary Magdalene and the 'praying woman'. The chapel also contains the stalls and some floor tiles recovered from Combefa and recent glass in the windows.

Monestiés is a pretty village and merits a stroll around the centre past the medieval houses, the old market place, the church of St-Pierre and particularly the old bridge. The **Centre Bajén-Vega** on Place de la Mairie exhibits the work of two Spanish painters who took up residence in the Albieois, Francisco Bajén and Martine Véga; ☎ 05 63 76 19 17.

THE SÉGALA AND THE VALLEY DU VIAUR

The *ségala* is a generic name applied to regions where the soil was poor and only *sèigle* (rye) and chestnuts would grow, until lime dressing was brought to the region by the newly built railway in the 19C. The term applies to the area north of Albi. The Viaur Valley is dramatic and fairly inaccessible.

Getting there and around
Car
N88 Albi to Rodez via Carmaux.
Train
TER Rodez to Toulouse via Naucelle-Gare, Tanus, Carmaux.

Tourist information
81400 Carmaux Pl. Gambetta, BP9,
☎ 05 63 76 76 67, fax 05 63 36 84 51
12800 Naucelle Pl. St-Martin, ☎ 05 65 47 04 32, fax 05 65 72 03 03
12800 Sauveterre-de-Rouergue Pl. des Arcades, ☎ 05 65 72 02 52
81190 Tanus Mairie, Av. Bodin, ☎ 05 63 76 36 71, fax 05 63 55 76 17

Market days
Carmaux Friday (Thursday if Friday a PH)

Naucelle Saturday in July, August
Sauveterre-de-Rouergue July, August,
Friday evening

 Festivals
July *Summer Rock Festival*,
Blaye-les-Mines
October *Fête de la Châtaigne et du Cidre
doux*, chestnut and cider fair,
Sauveterre-de-Rouergue

Where to stay and eating out
81130 CAGNAC-LES-MINES
Las Campagnès, ☎ 05 63 53 92 97, fax
05 63 53 92 97. *Chambres et table
d'hôte* between Cordes-sur-Ciel and the
site Cap'Découverte, Valérie et Didier
Jolly-Valentin welcome you to their
market-garden property which is cosily
and orignally decorated.
**12800 SAUVETERRE-DE-
ROUERGUE**
✬✬✬ *Auberge le Sénéchal*, ☎ 05 65 71
29 00, fax 05 65 71 29 09, www.
senechal.net. This is a small, nicely
appointed hotel in the beautiful *bastide*,
with an indoor pool and a gourmet
restaurant. One Michelin rosette.

Five kilometres outside Albi is the mainly 19C brick church of **Notre-Dame-de-la-Drèche** (follow the N88 north, then the D90), which, from a distance, echoes Albi Cathedral although close-up the form is very different. On the site of a 13C church, it comprises an octagonal rotunda (19.5m high and equally wide) over a nave with six chapels begun in 1861; the old east end is encased in a brick carapace. An ancient place of pilgrimage, the sanctuary shelters the 12C statue of the *Madonna of La Drèche* and the interior has a series of 81 murals completed in 1894 on the theme of Our Lady. In the spandrels she is represented by 16 women of the Old Testament; higher, flanking the windows, are 14 scenes of the Life of the Virgin Mary; and on the vault of the nave against a background of blue with gold stars is *Mary Glorified by the Saints*. The four paintings of the choir record events associated with the statue of the Madonna, including St Dominic's homage to it.

Further north, the relics of open cast-mines have been conserved at the **Musée de la Mine**, Cagnac-les-Mines. Open daily May–Sept 10.00–12.00 and 14.00–18.00, Sun to 19.00; Oct–April 10.00–12.00 and 14.00–17.00, Sun to 18.00, closed Mon; ☎ 05 63 53 91 70. **Carmaux** is a former mining town with a museum of the glass industry, the Musée du Verre. Open June–Aug Mon–Fri 09.00–12.00 and 14.00–18.00; Sept–May Mon–Fri 09.00–12.00 and 14.00–18.00; Sun and PH 15.00–18.00; ☎ 05 63 36 30 83.

The road continues on and up. In the woods above the Viaur Gorges, just south of Tanus the D53 peters out and there is a track to the magical site of **Las Planques**, where the only relic of a ruined village is the stark and dramatic 11C church built in dark gneiss (collect key from *syndicat d'initiative*, at the *mairie*, at Tanus). Just north of Tanus the new road spans the Viaur ravine, the boundary between the *départements* of Tarn and Aveyron, on a dramatic new road bridge (2000) on stilts high above the valley. It dwarfs the elegant **Viaduc de Viaur** (1902), a railway bridge on the Carmaux–Rodez line slightly further upstream. To view it, take the old road down into the valley and up again; there is a parking area on the right. The old viaduct was no mean feat at the time and is still one of the most impressive constructions of its kind in France, built by a local engineer, Paul Bodin, who won the competition held in 1887.

At Naucelle turn right on to the D10 and follow the signs to the **Château du Bosc**, one of the properties still belonging to descendants of the family of

Toulouse-Lautrec and where the painter spent much of his childhood. Guided visits all year; ☎ 05 65 69 20 83, fax 05 65 72 00 19. Quite apart from this connection, it is salutary to spend an hour or so in a property that has not been sold since the 12C and in a setting that epitomises *la France profonde*. The visit takes you through the library, dining room, private chapel and drawing room as well as the bedroom of Adèle, Countess Toulouse-Lautrec, the painter's mother, with the English books, crayons and Punch and Judy that belonged to little Henri. A visit to the Bosc offers an important insight to Toulouse-Lautrec's background and the family's attitude to him, and complements a visit to the museum in Albi.

Not far from the Bosc via the D10, D83 and D617 is the 13C–14C **Château de Taurines**, worth a visit mainly because it is being restored with such enthusiasm by local people and holds interesting exhibitions of contemporary art; for opening times, ☎ 05 65 74 28 47.

To the west of the N88 is **Naucelle**, a busy little town with a tiny arcaded square and a restored church with Flamboyant decoration inside the porch. **Sauveterre-de-Rouergue** is an excellent *bastide* with a rectangular plan, founded in 1281. The large central *place* is overlooked by a variety of well-restored 15C and 16C houses, shoulder to shoulder and extended to form continuous *couverts*. When Rouergue was under English domination between 1362 and 1369, Sauveterre was one of their most resistant strongholds.

Sauveterre de Rouergue

BETWEEN CORDES, GAILLAC AND RABASTENS

The forest (Forêt de la Grésigne), on a knoll (300–500m) between the high plateaux of Quercy and the Albigeois, was an ancient possession of the Counts of Toulouse which passed to the royal domain in 1271. Its oaks were used for shipbuilding in the 17C and until the mid-19C this was an important glass-producing area. The forest now covers some 3500 hectares.

There are several towns of rustic pink brick on the banks of the Tarn southwest of Albi in a landscape that has been patchworked with vineyards for about a thousand years. Towns such as Gaillac, Lisle-sur-Tarn and Rabastens are linked by the old road, D988, from Albi to Toulouse, which follows the Tarn until St-Sulpice.

Getting there and around
Car
D922 between Cordes and Gaillac. D15/D964 southeast from Vaour.

Train
TER Rodez to Toulouse via Marssac, Gaillac, Lisle-sur-Tarn, Rabastens-Couffouleux.
TER Brive to Toulouse via Vindrac-

Cordes, Gaillac, Lisle-sur-Tarn, Rabastens-Couffouleux, St-Sulpice-Tarn. TER Toulouse to St-Sulpice-Tarn. TER Clermont-Ferrand to Toulouse via Gaillac.

Bus

Montauban station to Albi via Gaillac and Marssac-Tarn
TER Toulouse to Mazamet via St-Sulpice-Tarn.

 Tourist information

81140 Castelnau-de-Montmiral Pl. des Arcades, ☎ 05 63 33 15 11, fax 05 63 33 17 60, email tourisme.bastide.castelnaugresigne@wanadoo.fr
81600 Gaillac Abbaye St-Michel, ☎ 05 63 57 14 65, fax 05 63 57 61 37
81310 Lisle-sur-Tarn Pl. Paul Saissac, ☎ 05 63 40 31 85, fax 05 63 33 36 18, www.ville-lisle-sur-tarn.fr.
81140 Puycelsi Chapel of St-Roch, ☎/fax 05 63 33 19 25, email office-de-tourisme-puycelsi@wanadoo.fr
81140 Pays de Vaour Le Bourg, Penne-du-Tarn, ☎ 05 63 56 36 68, fax 05 63 56 01 79, email ot.paysdevaour@libertysurf.fr
81800 Rabastens 12 bis Rue du Pont de Pâ, ☎/fax 05 63 33 56 90

Market days

Castelnau-de-Montmiral Tuesday
Gaillac Thursday, Friday and Sunday
Rabastens Tuesday and Saturday
Vaour Thursday

Wine tastings

Maison de la Vigne et du Vin, Abbaye de St-Michel (also Tourist Office), in Gaillac, ☎ 05 63 57 70 60, email civg@vins-gaillac.com, will provide information on local wines and tastings
Cooperatives *Cave de Técou*, Técou (5km from Gaillac direction Graulhet), ☎ 05 63 33 00 80, www.cave-de-tecou.fr; *Cave de Labastide-de-Lévis*, 81150 Labastide-de-Lévis, ☎ 05 63 53 73 63; *Cave de Rabastens*, 81800

Rabastens, ☎ 05 63 33 73 80

Festivals and events

July *Les Musicales*, music festival, Castelnau-de-Montmiral. *Son et lumière Roche d'Oc*, sound and light, Penne
August *Fête du Vin*, Gaillac. *L'été de Vaour*, international comedy festival, Vaour

 Where to stay and eating out

81140 CASTELNAU-DE-MONTMIRAL

☆☆ *Les Consuls*, Le Bourg, ☎ 05 63 33 17 44, fax 05 63 33 61 30. At the heart of this charming and peaceful medieval *bastide* is a small hotel in a 17C building.

81600 GAILLAC

☆☆ *La Verrerie*, 1 Rue de l'Égalité, ☎ 05 63 57 32 77, 05 63 57 32 27, email verrerie@club-internet.fr. A *Logis de France* in a town not well-endowed with hotels.

Le Mas de Sudre, Philippa Richmond-Brown, ☎/fax 05 63 41 01 32, email masdesudre@wanadoo.fr. *Chambres d'hôte*. This English-owned large *maison de maître* is set in a peaceful location at the heart of the Gaillac vineyards.

€ *La Table du Sommelier*, Pl. Thiers, ☎/fax 05 63 41 20 10 (see Table du Sommelier, Albi).

81140 LARROQUE

€ *Les Chênes at Les Abriols*, ☎ 05 63 33 10 92. Traditional cooking and panoramic views of the Forêt de Grésigne at this *ferme auberge*. By reservation only.

81140 PUYCELSI

☆☆☆ *L'Ancienne Auberge*, Pl. de l'Eglise, ☎ 05 63 33 65 90, fax 05 63 33 21 12. A classy hotel-restaurant in a medieval house in this most beautiful of hilltop towns.

81140 VAOUR

Serene, ☎/fax 05 63 56 39 34, email francis.bessieres@freesbee.fr. *Chambres et table d'hôte* between *bastides* and forest, peacefully situated in beautiful rural surroundings. Brigitte and Francis Bessières open their farmhouse which goes back to Templar times.

The D91 winds south from the Aveyron River along the perimeter of the vineyards and the Forêt de Grésigne. At a high point between the D91 and D15 near **Vaour** are a dolmen with panoramic views of the Quercy and, on the D33, ruins of a Templar commandery.

Between Bruniquel and Gaillac, on the D964, **Larroque** is a mainly 17C village built into the cliffs below the Grésigne forest which has been much restored in the last few years. **Puycelsi** is an impressive sight as you drive up to the plateau. Just beside the car park by the war memorial, on a terrace which was the site of the old château, is the tiny Baroque chapel of **St-Roch** (now used by the tourist office). Built in 1703, it contains a vine-entwined gilded retable. The village is still enclosed within the boundaries of its 15C walls. Beyond the chapel is a fortified gate, Porte d'Irrissou, the 15C Château du Petit St-Roch, and various other fortifications, including a 17C tower and the prison tower. In Place de la Mairie are the old *maison commune* and good 15C and 16C façades. The church of St-Corneille, part 14C, part 15C with an 18C belfry, is a simple structure with one or two amusing carvings around the porch. There are a few craftsmen working in Puycelsi and a restaurant.

Castelnau-de-Montmiral is a veritable *bastide* in miniature, also on a hill, founded at the same time as Cordes. There is a car park at the top. On the south side of the tiny arcaded square is a plaque commemorating a visit by Jean-Paul Sartre and Simone de Beauvoir; there is a pillary on the northwest side. The tourist office is also on the *place*. The church contains (behind bars in the northeast, with a light) a remarkable 13C wooden reliquary cross, 96cm tall, covered in silver and gilt, decorated with filigree and studded with semi-precious stones, containing a relic of the True Cross.

The **Château du Caylar** at Andillac, near Vieux, reached via the D922 and D115a, a 14C and 18C house, was the birthplace of the Romantic writers Eugénie de Guérin (1805–48) and her poet brother Maurice (1810–39). Open May–Sept 10.00–12.00 and 14.00–18.00, closed Tues; Oct–April 14.00–18.00, closed Mon, Tues; ☎ 05 63 33 90 30. East of the D922 at Senouillac, near Cahuzac-sur-Vère, is the **Château de Mauriac**, a severe military fortress domesticated during the Renaissance, which belongs to the painter Bernard Bistes (b. 1941). Many years of dedicated renovation, including several murals and ceiling paintings by the painter and his wife, have turned it into a beautiful setting for Bistes' works. Open May–Sept daily 15.00–18.00; Oct–April Sun and PH only 15.00–18.00; ☎ 05 63 41 71 18.

Gaillac

The town which gives its name to the vineyards is at first glance rather dusty and drab but on further investigation reveals some interesting brick buildings in the old town south of the D988 and an attractive riverscape. Its history is similar to most towns in the area, and although it came through the Albigensian crusades fairly unscathed the Wars of Religion were a bloody period. The economy of this small town has revolved around the wine trade despite the crises of the 19C, and is at its liveliest at the beginning of August during *La Fête des Vins de Gaillac*.

From the shady Place de la Libération take Rue Portal past the old church of

The wines of Gaillac

Gaillac is promoted, like most wine-producing areas, as one of the oldest in France; the cultivation of vines on the banks of the Tarn is thought to go back to the 6C BC. The Benedictine monks of the abbey of St-Michel, who settled here in 972, were the prime movers in the development and perfection of viticulture and vinification and as early as 1271 a charter was granted guaranteeing the quality of Gaillac wine. The wine was carried via the Tarn and the Garonne to Bordeaux, and shipped to northern Europe. In the 1920s there was a strong revival after the phylloxera epidemics of the 1870s, and by 1938 the Gaillac whites received an *appellation contrôlée* label, followed in 1970 by the reds.

There are 400 producers and three cooperatives over an area of more than 2000 hectares between Cordes, Rabastens, Graulhet and Castelnau-de-Levis on the banks of the parallel valleys of the Tarn and the Vère, where the micro-climate and soils are suited to vines. The local grape varieties are Mauzac and Len de l'El plus Sauvignon and Muscadelle for whites; the basis of the red *appellation* is Duras and Braucol complemented by Syrah, Gamay, Merlot and Cabernet. The cooperatives are at Labastide-de-Levis, Rabastens and Técou, the latter producing an excellent and typical red provocatively named *Passion* (see wine tastings, p *324*). The characteristic of the Gaillac reds is a flavour of blackcurrants or raspberries and the whites are slightly appley. Most of the 400 producers and the cooperatives are happy to give a tasting.

St-Pierre with a 13C doorway. **Hôtel de Brens**, just off Rue Portal on the right, is a pretty 13C–15C building in timber and brick with two overhanging turrets and a pentagonal gallery. At the end of Rue Portal is Place Thiers with arcades and Le Griffoul fountain in the middle. This is the heart of the old town.

Leave the square by the southeast corner to arrive in Place St-Michel, in front of the sheer brick face of the old abbey church of **St-Michel**. The gabled west end is flanked by a tower (13C and 14C) and the portal was added in 1847. The single vessel of the nave, typical of the Midi, is huge (47.5m by 17m) and was painted in *trompe l'oeil* in the 19C. The oldest part of the church is the 13C east end, profoundly modified in 1869 when pillars and arcades were substituted for a semi-circular wall around the choir. Between the interior buttresses are chapels, except on the third and fourth bays south where the abbey abuts the church. The chapel in the second bay on the north, with decorated capitals, was built in the late 14C, possibly as a funerary chapel, by Abbot Roger de Latour whose coat of arms is on the boss. There are some fittings and furnishings of note, including a polychromed wooden statue of the *Virgin and Child* (early 14C); a holy water stoup (13C?) on the left of the entrance, decorated with birds and flowers; a Baroque retable with a painting by Antoine Rivalz; and on the wall of the southeast chapel a high-relief panel of the *Resurrected Christ appearing to Mary Magdalene* (15C). The main altar is of 1785–90 and the elaborate pulpit was made in 1883–85. The organ above the west door was made by Dominique Cavaillé-Col, from the dynasty of organ-builders who originated from Gaillac.

Beside the bridge is the very attractive **Maison des Vins**, with a wealth of information on the local wines, and the tourist office. In the same building, the Musée de l'Abbaye, which shows archaeology, navigation, wine and local history. Open 10.00–12.00 and 14.00–18.00, closed PH; ☎ 05 63 41 03 81.

East of the church are the park and **Château de Foucaud**, built in 1647 on the edge of the Tarn. The building shows its most elegant face to the river, with double flights of steps leading to a formal garden and terraces to the river bank. In the château is the fine arts museum, with works by regional artists. Open May–Oct, Mon, Wed–Sun 10.00–12.00 and 14.00–18.00, closed Tues; Nov–April, Fri, Sat and Sun; ☎ 05 63 57 18 25.

Southwest of Gaillac on the D87 is **Montans**, today a tiny community of about 200 inhabitants, but once the site of a huge Gallo-Roman pottery works. It has a fascinating museum of local finds, the **Archéosite**, with a 'Gallo-Roman street' and exhibitions. The display of the techniques, tools and periods of production from 100 BC to the early 4C is very comprehensive. Open June–Sept 10.00–12.00 and 14.00–18.00; Oct–May, Sat, Sun and PH 14.00–18.00; ☎ 05 63 57 59 16.

Occupied since the Iron Age (c 700 BC), the village developed on the edge of a small ravine above the confluence of the Rieutort and the Tarn. With all the raw materials on hand, pots were produced here before the arrival of the Romans, who introduced skilled potters from Arezzo with more sophisticated techniques and decoration. The best and most creative period was AD 20–75, after which production became more utilitarian. Much of the work is signed. At the height of production there could have been as many as 40 or 50 kilns at one time and only a part of the huge area used by the potteries has been excavated. In 1992 an important find of 40 gold pieces was made here.

Lisle-sur-Tarn on the N88, on the north bank of the river among vineyards, is a warm and sleepy brick *bastide* founded in the 13C. It has the largest square in the southwest, surrounded by *cornières* and *couverts* and a variety of façades, some half-timbered, some rebuilt from the 17C–19C entirely in brick. The narrow streets behind the square are lined with brick and timber houses in different states of repair, six with *pontets*. The church of Notre-Dame-de-la-Jonquière is a 14C southern Gothic aisleless brick building with a 13C Romanesque-style porch on the north with sculpted capitals and arches. The porch at the west supports a two-tier octagonal belfry. Most of the interior furnishings are 17C and 18C. The Musée Raymond Lafage has drawings and engravings by the local 17C artist, who spent time in Rome, and local glass and archaeology. Open June–Oct, Mon, Wed–Fri 10.00–12.00 and 14.00–18.00, Sat, Sun 14.00–18.00, closed Tues; Oct–May Thurs, Fri 10.00–12.00 and 14.00–18.00 or by appointment; ☎ 05 63 40 45 45.

Rabastens

Rabastens, like Lisle-sur-Tarn, overlooks the Tarn River. Towards the middle of the 12C Moissac founded a priory here where the old Roman road crossed theriver and it became an important stage for medieval pilgrims between Rodez and Toulouse, partly because until the end of the 18C Rabastens possessed numerous relics, including some of St James.

The priory church of **Notre-Dame-du-Bourg** (☎ 05 63 33 56 90) is at the west of the town, on the D12. At the end of the Albigensian period the church was rebuilt. Eight capitals (1190–1200) with their slender marble columns were re-used in the recessed west porch. The capitals have scenes from the *Childhood of Christ* and the *Temptation in the Wilderness*. The new church, conceived in the Gothic style of the southwest, has a cliff-like, angular west end pierced by a small rose window and two turrets flanking a rectangular gable belfry, the upper part completed in the 19C. The interior is rather gloomy and heavily ornate, reminiscent of Albi, with an unaisled nave. The 13C church was built with a flat east end, but in the 14C this was opened and extended to make a large choir and polygonal chevet with chapels between the buttresses and an unusual Romanesque-style arcaded triforium was built above. The remodelled east end was consecrated in 1318. The vaults, walls and most of the chapels have **painted decoration** from different periods which disappeared under plaster after the Reformation. With few exceptions they were rediscovered *c* 1859 and almost entirely repainted 1860–63 by Joseph Engalières.

The murals on the vaults of the nave are thought to originate from the second half of the 13C, and include St James on the first crossing arch and St Christopher on the second, and knights, possibly participating in a pilgrimage or in a crusade. On the walls of the nave are two cycles: on the south scenes from the *Childhood of Christ*, but in the fourth bay the original mural was replaced by the *Expulsion of Adam and Eve* in the 15C; on the north are the *Resurrection*, *Crucifixion* and *Ascension*. Five chapels were built between the nave buttresses between 1374 and the end of the 15C. The chapel of St-Roch on the north was painted in 1520–30, but only discovered in 1972 and subsequently restored. The choir vaults up to the triforium were painted with a geometric design and quadrilobe medallions with the busts of Christ, the Virgin, Apostles and saints (*c* 1320). Only the choir chapels of St-Martin and St-Jacques on the north, and St-Augustin on the south, have conserved their 14C paintings, with episodes of the life of the respective saint. Late in the 14C or early in the 15C, another cycle of the *Childhood of Christ* was painted in the spandrels on the high walls of the choir. St James appears again on the transverse rib of the chancel arch (14C) and on the east side of the arch are Christ and the four Evangelists.

In a narrow street opposite the church is the **Musée du Pays Rabastinois** in Hôtel de la Fite, a fine end 17C–18C mansion. The museum has a collection ranging from a Gallo-Roman mosaic to *haute-couture* embroidery and also shows temporary exhibitions. Open May–Sept, Tues–Sat 10.00–12.00 and 15.00–18.00; Feb–April, Oct–15 Dec, Wed–Sun 14.30–17.30; ☎ 05 63 40 65 65.

Overlooking the Promenades along the D988 is the former 15C/16C priory building, significantly altered in 1830 but retaining the elegant 16C tower giving access to the church. The Hôtel de Rolland de Combettes, further west, is a 15C building that was entirely renovated and embellished in the 19C. The view from the bridge over the Tarn is impressive.

16 Castres and the southern Tarn

The Agout, a tributary of the Tarn, crosses the southern part of the *département* linking the towns of Lavaur and Castres. The the vineyards of Gaillac give way, south of the Tarn river, to arable crops of maize, sunflowers and, around Lautrec and Réalmont, garlic. In the 14C and 15C this region was famous for the production of *pastel* (p 331), but this is no longer cultivated.

LAVAUR AND LAUTREC

Getting there and around
Car

D87 from Gaillac to Lavaur. D631/D83 Lavaur to Lautrec via Graulhet. N112/D631/D92 from Albi. D83/D112 from Castres.

Train

TER Toulouse to Mazamet via St-Sulpice, Lavaur, Castres. Albi to Castres via Lautrec.

Tourist information

81300 Graulhet 1 Sq. Foch, ☎/fax 05 63 34 75 09, email graulhet.ot@ wanadoo.fr
81140 Lautrec Rue du Mercadial, ☎ 05 63 75 31 40, fax 05 63 75 32 90, http://lautrec.fre.fr
81500 Lavaur Tour des Rondes, ☎ 05 63 58 02 00, fax 05 63 41 42 89
81700 Puylaurens 2 Rue de la Mairie, ☎ 05 63 75 28 98, fax 05 63 75 29 00

Market days

Lautrec Friday
Lavaur Saturday
Puy Laurens Wednesday

Festivals and events

August *Festival de l'ail rose*, celebration of pink garlic, Lautrec

Where to stay and eating out

81470 CUQ-TOULZA
Cuz-en-Terrasse, Cuq-le-Château, ☎ 05 63 82 54 00, fax 05 63 82 54 11. Hotel-restaurant in an old house on a west-facing ridge, stunningly restored and presented, with garden terrace. Great food.
€–€€ *Chez Alain*, Route de Castres, ☎ 05 63 75 70 35, fax 05 63 75 76 08. A reliable restaurant with outdoor eating in summer. Rooms.
81300 LABESSIÈRE-CANDEIL
€–€€ *Le Pigeonnie*, La Ginestarié, 3km north of Graulhet, ☎ 05 63 4 08 04. An old *pigeonnier* is the setting for inventive and varied dishes based on good local produce.

Between Gaillac and Lautrec is **Graulhet** (D964 or D83), which at one time was an important leather-producing centre. This industry is recalled at the **Maison des Métiers du Cuir**. Guided visit and temporary exhibitions; open May–Oct and school hols, 10.00–18.30, ☎ 05 63 42 16 04. Further east, **Réalmont** is a 13C *bastide* with an arcaded square half-way between Albi and Castres on the N112. To the northeast at **Teillet** D86/D81, is the curiously romantic vision of the ruins of the Château de Grandval (☎ 05 63 55 74 45), semi-submerged when the Rassise dam was constructed. Occupied by the *maquis* (local Resistance) it had already been damaged by fire in 1944 by German troops.

Lavaur is a small but active town, built in brick and still smartening itself up. It has one of the major markets in the area. Its most outstanding monument is the Gothic cathedral on a sheer cliff above the Agout, surrounded by pleasant gardens and a high terrace overlooking the river and the old port. This was a Cathar stronghold and felt the wrath of the crusaders in the 12C.

The **Cathédrale St-Alain** (open 09.00–18.00) replaces a church all but destroyed by Simon de Montfort. In 1255 the city fathers, in the presence of the Inquisitors, undertook to build a new one and five bays of the new church had been completed in 1317 when the town was elevated to episcopal see. The exterior walls between the buttresses were added in the 14C and the two south-east chapels in 1450. The massive west end closely resembles Albi cathedral, but is more squared off, and it has a truncated octagonal tower added at the end of the 15C. The rather too small east end, sheer above the river, has two silly little turrets. On the small south belfry is a *jacquemart*, who hits his bell with a hammer every hour. There has been one here since 1604, but the present oak figure dates from 1922, the bell from 1523.

The simple interior has a single nave with shallow chapels on the north and extended on the south in the 15C. It was damaged at the Revolution and restored 1843–47 when the *grisaille* and coloured *trompe l'oeil* decoration was added by Italian painters, the Ceroni. The cathedral has salvaged the 12C altar table, a relic of the first church, sculpted with a eucharistic theme on the chamfer, notably similar to the altar table at St-Sernin in Toulouse and the capitals of Moissac. Also from the first church is the Romanesque porch, conserved in the first chapel on the right; the carved capitals have scenes from the **Childhood of Christ** (the first and last are 19C plaster replicas). An organ was installed in 1523 and the magnificent organ case was recently restored. When the instrument was remade by Aristide Cavaillé-Col in 1874, certain elements, notably the volutes, vases and balustrade, were added as well as a coating of dark varnish, which has been removed to reveal the original 16C colours. Other fittings include the mausoleum of Bishop Simon de Beausoleil (d. 1531); a wooden painted and gilded *Pietà* (17C); six paintings of **Scenes of the Passsion** (18C), attributed to Pierre Subleyras; the main altar in polychrome marble; the wrought-iron lectern signed by Bernard Ortet (1778), who worked at the cathedral of St-Etienne in Toulouse; and the 19C pulpit. The stained glass of the choir is dated 1853–54.

From the handsome *mairie*, take Rue Villeneuve past **Le Plô**, the site of the old castle which fell to Simon de Montfort in 1211. Wiggle through the small streets beside the Maison Occitane on Rue Père-Colin and left across Place du Vieux Marché, which brings you out at the **Tour des Rondes**, a sturdy brick and stone bastion of the old fortifications now housing the tourist office. (The new market *halle* is on the edge of the old town south of the Tour des Rondes.) Return to the Grand' Rue via Rue Viel and the church of St-François, the church of the Cordeliers, dedicated to St Francis, built in the 14C and restored in the 19C. The Cordeliers were one of the first groups of Francsicans to settle in France (1226).

Giroussens, northeast of Lavaur (D87), by the D12, started in the 12C as a fort defending the castle of the Viscounts of Albi in a strategic position overlooking the Agout. It was granted the privileges of a *bastide* in the 13C, and was a pottery town. Ceramicists are still working here, at the *Maison de la Céramique Contemporaine*. Exhibitions and sales; ☎ 05 63 41 68 22. The 15C church was repaired and amended in the 17C, and contains two 17C retables; and the main retable in wood (18C), sumptuously decorated and gilded, has a painting of the *Crucifixion*.

Off the D12, at St-Lieux-les-Lavaur, is the **Petit Train Touristique** with steam and diesel engines. Trips (7km round trip) Easter–Oct Sun and PH; 14–31 July, 16–31 Aug, Sat, Sun, Mon PH; 1–15 Aug daily; trains leave every 30 mins from 14.30; ☎ 05 61 47 44 52. Virtually next door are the **Jardins des Martels** featuring water plants, especially lotus and waterlilies. Open May–Aug daily 10.00–19.00; Sept–April Sat, Sun and PH 10.00–19.00; ☎ 05 63 41 61 42.

Southwest of St-Paul-Cap-de-Joux, close to the D112, is the Renaissance **Château de Magrin**, at the heart of the Pays de Cocagne (see below), with a museum of the history of *pastel*, its cultivation, production and use. Musée du Pastel open Easter–Oct and by appointment; château July, Aug, Sun; ☎ 05 63 70 63 82.

Pastel

Isatis tinctoria L. (also known as Persian blue or Dyer's woad, and in French as *pastel*) is a cruciferous plant producing a very high-quality blue or indigo dye. From the 15C it was cultivated intensively in the damp valleys of the Lauragais, east of Toulouse. Its use was extremely labour intensive and involved picking the leaves, not the yellow flowers, of the plant, which were harvested twice a year. They were reduced to a pulp, dried, and compressed into balls called *coques* (which gave rise to the expression in this region *le pays de cocagne* or 'land of plenty'). It could remain drying in this form for up to a year and then the cycle continued, with crushing, reduction, and fermentation for another 4–5 months. The raw material was exported all over Northern Europe for the dyeing trade and was in such demand that it brought enormous wealth to the region until the mid-16C. The combination of a market crash in London and Anvers in 1561, the Wars of Religion, and the importation of indigo, caused the bottom to fall out of the *pastel* industry by the end of the 16C. (To find articles made using the *pastel* dye visit l'Artisan Pastellier, 5 Puech Bénenguier in Albi old town.)

The **Château de Roquevidal** on the D12 is a medieval château transformed in the late 16C–17C, and owned in the 17C–18C by Protestant families. Open Aug, Sun 10.00–12.00 and 15.00–19.00; ☎ 05 63 41 32 32.

The fame of **Puylaurens**, to the east on the D184 and N126, rests on the fact that it claims to be the cradle of Marianne, symbol of the French Republic. The poet, Guillaume Lavabre, gave this name to the Republic and composed a song called *La Garison de Marianne*. There is a stunning view of the hilltop village of **Lautrec** from the D92—which approaches from the south off the D112 between Lavaur and Castres—and panoramas on all sides including the Montagne Noire to the south. Is there also a hint of garlic on the air? The region's 380 producers grow pink garlic with an *appellation contrôlée* at the rate of 4000 tonnes a year from 1000ha, one-tenth of the production of France. Kept in a cool place it will last up to a year.

Lautrec itself is a charming medieval village on a hill with some well-maintained 16C and 17C timber-framed houses with jetties or arcades. Still intact on the east side of the town are part of the old ramparts and one of the eight original gateways, Porte de la Caussade. The church of St-Rémy was begun in the

15C, vaulted in 1769, and has lots of 19C *trompe l'oeil* and false marbling. Behind the church in Rue de St-Esprit, off the Grande Rue, are the steps up to the greatest attraction of Lautrec, the still-turning 17C **Moulin à vent de la Salette**. Open July, Aug 14.30–19.00 and Sept–June, Sun, PH only 15.00–17.00; ☎ 05 63 75 31 40.

CASTRES AND THE SIDOBRE

This part of the *département* of the Tarn is under the spell of the Montagne Noire and encompasses part of the Parc Régional du Haut Languedoc and the strange rocky outcrop of the Sidobre. It is as close as the Midi-Pyrénées gets to the Mediterranean; Carcassonne is just over the mountains. There are no vineyards here but there are relics of the metal, leather and granite industries. The main town, Castres, vies with Albi for importance in the Tarn, and enjoys a buoyant economy with more industry between here and Mazamet than in the rest of the *département*.

Getting there and around
Air
Paris to Castres/Mazamet, ☎ 05 63 70 32 62.
Car
N126 Toulouse to Castres.
N20 Limoges to Montauban, exit 66 (D930/D630) via Lavaur to Castres.
N112 Albi to Castres and Mazamet.
D118/N112 Carcassone to Castres.
Train
TER Toulouse to Mazamet via St-Sulpice, Lavaur, Castres.
Bus
Rodez to Carcassone via Castres and Revel.
Toulouse to Mazamet via Castres.
Mazamet to St-Pons.
Sorèze to Castelnaudary (Aude) via Revel.
Gare routière, Pl. Soult, Castres, ☎ 05 63 53 37 31.

Tourist information
81100 Castres Rue Milhau-Ducommun, ☎ 05 63 62 63 62, fax 05 63 62 63 60, email ot.castres@free.fr
81110 Dourgne Pl. Jean Bugis, ☎/fax 05 63 74 27 19, www.paysdedourgne-tourisme.com

811290 Labruguière Rue Jean Jaurès, ☎/fax 05 63 50 17 21
81200 Mazamet Rue des Casernes, ☎ 05 63 61 27 07, fax 05 63 61 31 35, email officedetourisme.mazamet@wanadoo.fr
81260 Sidobre Paysage Sculpté, Maison du Sidobre, Vialavert, Le Bez, ☎ 05 63 74 63 38, fax 05 63 73 04 57
81540 Sorèze 7 Pl. Dom Devic, ☎/fax 05 63 74 16 28, www.ville-soreze.fr
81330 Vabre Rue Vieille, ☎ 05 63 50 48 12, fax 05 63 74 40 64

Market days
Castres Tuesday, Thursday, Friday and Saturday
Mazamet Tuesday, Saturday, Sunday

River cruises
From Castres, short trips on *le Miredames* depart opposite the Quai des Jacobins (across the Pont Vieux), May–Oct; ☎ 05 63 71 56 58

Festivals and events
July *Extravadance*, a wide range of music and dance, Castres
Fanfares sans Frontières, music, marches and festivities, Mazamet
July, August Histoires d'un Soir,

evening street festival, stories and theatre with a historic theme, Castres and Mazamet (and Albi)

August *Festival Couleurs du Monde*, international festival of the arts, Castres

All year *Cabarets Nomades*, readings, theatre, poetry, song, dance, in several towns of the southern Tarn (Mazamet, Labruguière, etc)

 Where to stay and eating out

81700 BLAN

Les Abélias, Lamothe, ☎/fax 05 63 75 75 14, www.revel-lauragais.com/abelias.html. *Chambres d'hôte* in a hamlet in the Pays de Cocagne, near La Montagne. Two rooms in an old building full of character belonging to Christian Barbier.

81100 BURLATS

Le Castel de Burlats, 8 Pl. du 8-Mai-1945, ☎ 05 63 35 29 20, fax 05 63 51 14 69. Set in a 3ha park, this small 14C château is delightfully presented and the rooms tastefully furnished.

81100 CASTRES

☆☆☆ *L'Europe*, 5 Rue Victor-Hugo, ☎ 05 63 59 00 33, fax 05 63 59 21 38, www.france.resa.com. An Italian Renaissance-style hotel-restaurant with patio and very comfortable, attractive modern rooms.

☆☆☆ *L'Occitan*, 201 Av. Charles-de-Gaulle, ☎ 05 63 35 34 20, fax 05 63 35 70 32, www.hotel-restaurant-l-occitan.fr. In a quiet setting surrounded by a park with simple, modern and well-appointed rooms.

☆☆☆ *Le Renaissance*, 17 Rue Victor-Hugo, ☎ 05 63 59 30 42, fax 05 63 72 11 57. Hotel-restaurant in an 18C building with beams and exposed brick, with beautifully furnished rooms. Conveniently placed close to the town centre.

€€ *La Table du Sommelier*, 6 Pl. Pélisson, ☎/fax 05 63 82 20 10. (See *La Table du Sommelier*, Albi, p 307.)

81110 DOURGNE

€–€€ *Hostellerie de la Montagne Noire*, 15 Pl. des Promenades, ☎ 05 63 50 31 12. At the centre of this little town, well-prepared local dishes. Terrace under the plane trees.

81240 LACABARÈDE

☆☆☆ *La Demeure de Flore*, 106 Rte Nationale (N112 between Mazamet and Labastide-Rouairoux, ☎ 05 63 98 32 32, fax 05 63 98 47 56, www.hotelrama.com/flore. Set in a park, with garden and pool.

81090 LAGARRIGUE

☆☆☆ *Best Western Montagne Noire*, 29 Av. de Castres, ☎ 05 63 35 52 00, fax 05 63 35 25 59, www.lamontagnenoire.com. Modern hotel with restaurant which uses fresh local produce, fitness facilities and indoor pool.

81660 PONT-DE-L'ARN

Château de Montlédier, Rte d'Anglès, ☎ 05 63 61 20 54, fax 05 63 98 22 51, www.montledier.com. Close to Mazamet, a medieval castle with pretty rooms and vaulted restaurant serving gourmet meals and local wines.

Marican, ☎/fax 05 63 98 16 60, www.marican.com. *Chambres et table d'hôte* in the Parc Régional du Haut Languedoc. This *maison de maître*, belonging to Kate and John Orr, is set in extensive grounds with views over Mazamet and the Montagne Noire. Pool.

81110 ST-AVIT

€–€€ *Les Saveurs de Saint Avit*, La Baraque (north of Dourgne), ☎ 05 63 50 11 45. An old farm disguises an ultra modern restaurant with Surrealist paintings, where the English born chef and his French wife offer colourful and inventive international dishes.

81540 SORÈZE

☆☆☆ *Le Logis des Pères* and the ☆☆ *Pavillon des Hôtes* have combined under the same management, *l'Hotellerie de l'Abbaye-Ecole*, 18 Rue Lacordaire, ☎ 05 63 74 44 80, fax 05

63 74 44 89, www.hotelfp-soreze.com. Freshly and attractive renovations to both buildings, the *logis* (18 rooms) is installed in the former convent with interior courtyard overlooking the park and village, and the Pavillon (52 rooms) in the former Dominican monastery overlooks the main courtyard, park and cloisters.

€–€€ *Les Collets Rouges* (see l'Hotellerie de l'Abbaye-Ecole, above), is tastefully decorated in the style of old refectories and offers the flavours and sensations of the southwest.

Castres

Castres is a pleasant, leafy, prosperous town built mainly in stone on the banks of the Agout River. Comparable in size to Albi, it is less exciting visually but has a charm and character of its own and a friendly market. The town owns an important collection of Spanish art exhibited in the Goya museum. An international arts festival is held here during August.

History

An important stage on the Via Tolosane to Santiago, holding relics of St Vincent of Saragossa in an 11C basilica, Castres had a major Cathar community at the end of the 12C. It avoided major damage during the Albigensian crusades by submitting to the crusading armies. The town came under the control of the de Montforts in 1229. It was elevated to a bishopric by Pope John XXII in 1317, a status it maintained until 1801. The town enthusiastically embraced Calvinism to become a Protestant place of safety second only in the region to Montauban. In 1576 Henri IV helped the peaceful return of the Catholics with the institution of the Chambre de l'Edit to legislate over sectarian disputes. Between the Edict of Alès (1629) and the Revocation of the Edict of Nantes (1685) Castres enjoyed its most brilliant period: the population increased, monasteries were reinstated and most of the town was rebuilt. Architects from the Ile de France were introduced to build a new episcopal palace and design a garden typical of the Grand Siècle. Castres was the birthplace of the politician and pacifist, Jean Jaurès (see below).

The former **bishops' palace** is used by the hôtel de ville and the Goya museum. Jules Hardouin-Mansart drew up the plans for this soberly Classical building, inaugurated in 1675. Around three sides of a courtyard with a monumental staircase, the unadorned façade serves as a backdrop to the dark greens of the yew trees and box hedges of the **formal garden** designed by Louis XIV's gardener, André Le Nôtre (1613–1700). Planted on the site of the southern ramparts and ditch, the garden began to take shape in 1696. The knot-gardens nearest the palace have box hedges trimmed into a fleur-de-lis pattern and the yews have a variety of designs. The avenue of limes along the river had to be replanted to replace the originals a few years ago; the chestnuts are some 90 years old.

Musée Goya

On the first floor of the bishops' palace, this is a very pleasant, quiet museum with an excellent collection of Spanish works. Open 09.00–12.00 and 14.00–17.00; April–Sept to 18.00; Sun and PH opens 10.00; closed Mon except July–Aug; ☎ 05 63 71 59 30, www.ville-castres.fr. Inspired by the donation in

1893 of three paintings and complete sets of etchings by Goya which had belonged to the local painter Marcel Briguiboul (1837–92), the museum has concentrated on Spanish works since 1947. Regional funding since 1972 has helped to make this one of the most important Spanish collections in France and the museum often holds temporary exhibitions with a Spanish bias.

Works by the **Spanish primitives** (14C–15C) are among some of the most beautiful in the museum, and testify to a variety of influences. Among them are *La Crucifixion et la Transfiguration de Christ au Mont Tabor entre Moïse et Elie* showing the Flemish influence is attributed to Juan Rexach, who worked in Valencia 1431–84; in the style of International Gothic is *La Flagellation du Christ*, attributed to Luis Borassa; a strange little work, *St Jean l'Evangeliste dans l'île de Patmos* is a panel from a triptych (the central panel is in the Thyssen collection in Madrid) by Juan Mates; and a later painting *L'Adoration des Rois Mages* by Alejo Fernandez, a more sophisticated painting compared to the others which shows the influence of northern Europe. However, a large part of the collection represents the 'Golden Age' of Spanish painting in the 17C, and includes a replica of the Prado *Portrait of Philip IV* (1634–36) attributed to Velázquez, a sweetly gentle *Virgin Mary with a Rosary* (c 1650) by Murillo, and Zurbaran, Francisco de's *Carthusian Martyr* (c 1636), as well as a large work by Francisco Pacheco, *Christ Served by the Angels in the Desert* (1615–16). There are also works by Claudio Coello, Juan de Valdés and Alonso Cano.

The room dedicated to **Goya** has three of his works and paintings inspired by him. The masterpiece is the calm, self-assured *Self-Portrait with Glasses* (c 1797–1800), painted some years after the illness that left him deaf (see Bayonne, p 408); the second portrait is of *Don Francisco del Mazo* (c 1815). Filling the whole of the end wall of the gallery is the huge *Session of the Royal Company of the Philippines* (1815), an atmospheric work with a veiled criticism of bureaucracy. The museum also owns original prints by Goya from his series *Los Capricos*, the *Disasters of War*, and *Los Proverbios*, as well as the *Tauromaquia*.

Among the modern Spanish works is a token Picasso. The museum frequently mounts exhibitions with Spanish themes.

The **municipal theatre**, close to the museum, opened in 1904 and is an imposing Belle-Epoque building designed by Joseph Galinier of Toulouse, a pupil of Garnier, designer of the Paris Opéra; it was restored in 1982.

Cross the courtyard to the **Tour St-Benoit** (c 1100) on the northwest side, the last remaining fragment of the abbey of St-Benoit, with a 17C roof. Opposite is the large and ordered south flank of the Baroque **Cathédrale St-Benoit**. Begun in 1678 and consecrated in 1718, the project was never completed to the specifications originally envisaged by the architect Guillaume Caillau. The interior is rather dreary in spite of the *trompe l'oeil*, but there is some nice woodwork and a number of large paintings by local artists, François Cammas, Le Chevalier de Rivalz, and Jean-Baptiste Despax. The coloured marble altar of 1763 is covered by a grandiose baldaquin made in 1768 by the Cailhive workshop.

At the east end of the cathedral the space is enhanced by an elegant 19C colonnade made from columns salvaged from the old abbey and a small square, **Place du 8-Mai-1945**, the only sizeable square in the town centre before the Revolution. Passage St-Vincent opens into one of the main commercial streets, Rue Alquier-Bouffand, which was almost entirely rebuilt after a fire in 1724.

Turn right to the **Pont Neuf** to see the colourful timber craftsmen's houses on

Castres, houses on the Agout

the banks of the Agout, the most original and emblematic feature of the town in a region where the economy was based on leather and textiles. They stand on large arcaded stone cellars (perhaps 14C) opening directly into the river. These houses were once the homes and workshops of tanners, weavers and dyers and their restoration began in 1979. The Quai des Jacobins offers another good view of them, and there are short boat rides from across the Pont Vieux.

The market is held on **Place Jean-Jaurès**, a tree-lined square created in the medieval heart of Castres in 1872, graced with a pretty fountain with angels at one end and a statue of Jaurès at the other.

Take Rue Emile-Zola from the west of Place Jean-Jaurès and turn right into Rue Frédérick-Thomas. **Hôtel de Nayrac** (now a Société Générale) on the left was built in 1620 by a wealthy draper, Jean Oulès, using brick and stone, in the manner of the Renaissance mansions of Toulouse or Albi. The three linked façades have elegantly decorated dormers, and the main entrance, flanked by paired Doric pilasters with a huge coat of arms, is on the right. There used to be boutiques under the arcades on the street. The plaster has been removed from the 17C façades of no. 14 uncovering the timber frame, known in Castres as *corondat*.

Place Pélisson is a small smart junction decorated with a fountain and contains the **Musée Jean-Jaurès**, attractively installed in an old printing works since 1988. The museum has a permanent exhibition, documentation centre, and holds temporary exhibitions. Open 09.00–12.00 and 14.00–17.00; April–Sept to 18.00; closed Mon except July, Aug; ☎ 05 63 72 01 01.

Jean Jaurès (1859–1914), socialist leader, parliamentary orator, journalist and historian, was born in Castres on 3 September 1859. Republican Deputy (member of the Chambres des Députés, now the Assemblée Nationale) for the Tarn in 1885, in 1889–93 he turned to socialism and championed causes such as the miners' strikes in Carmaux, the independence of the glassworkers in Albi, and Alfred Dreyfus, falsely accused of spying for Germany in 1894. He was described as the apostle of peace but his pacifist ideals led to his assassination on the eve of the First World War, on 31 July 1914.

Turn left on Rue Sabaterie, and left again to **Rue des Boursiers** where there is a string of 16C and 17C façades between nos 4 and 14; no. 1 has a late Gothic doorway. Turn left into Rue Emile-Zola and right into Rue Tuboeuf. Rue de l'Hôtel-de-Ville runs parallel with Rue E.-Zola. Linking them is another old street, Rue Victor-Hugo, with Castres' second religious monument, the **Eglise de la Platé**, rebuilt in 1743 by the Jesuits. The accomplished Italianate façade on Rue

Victor-Hugo superimposes Doric and Ionic orders and the Florentine-style campanile can best be seen from Rue de la Platé. The Baroque interior has a grandiose main altar flanked by six red marble columns supporting a canopy and the retable in Carrara marble of an *Assumption of the Virgin* by Italian artists (1754). There are paintings by the ubiquitous Despax, of the *Visitation* and *Annunciation*. The superb organ, with a sumptuous gilded case supported by atlantes and adorned with angel musicians, was installed in 1764 and decorated by a local artist called Chabbert. It was restored in 1980 and is used for concerts.

Opposite, in Rue de la Chambre de l'Edit, is the **Hôtel de Viviès** (1585), considered one of the best pieces of late Renaissance architecture in the town, but corrupted with Baroque additions. Nevertheless it has been brought into the 21C by the **Centre d'Art Contemporain**, which holds resolutely modern exhibitions. Open July, Aug daily 10.00–12.00 and 14.00–18.00, Tues to 19.00; Sept– June, Tues–Fri 10.00–12.00 and 14.00–17.30, Tues to 19.00, Sat, Sun, Mon 15.00–18.00; clsoed PH ☎ 05 63 62 80 23.

Rue Tolosane, at the west end of Rue de la Chambre-de-l'Edit, is flanked by two piers of the old Porte Tolosane. **Hôtel de Poncet** in Rue Gabriel-Guy is an elegant building with a balustraded terrace supported by caryatids and a loggia with Ionic columns reached by a monumental cantilevered staircase.

On the eastern edge of town, in the Lardaille district (direction Sidobre) on Blvd Giraud, is the church of **Notre-Dame de l'Esperance**, which contains a monumental modern work of the *Apocalypse of St John at Patmos* by Gaston-Louis Marchal, follower of Ossip Zadkine, in 84 panels executed in pen and ink and watercolour crayons.

The Sidobre

Immediately northeast of Castres is the granite plateau of the Sidobre (600–700m), on the edge of the Massif Central. Wooded in places, with scrubby moorland or marshes elsewhere, its attractions are scenic. Its main curiosities are the strange biomorphic rock formations: giant granite boulders, smoothed and rounded by time, isolated or in a tumbled confusion called a *chaos*, have acquired descriptive names, Roc de l'Oie (Goose Rock), Trois Fromages, Chapeau du Curé, etc. The natural phenomena of the Sidobre are best seen along the D30 and D58. This is an area for walks and picnics, beside the Lac du Merle or the valleys and gorges of the Agout.

Burlats

The most significant architectural site in the Sidobre is the small village of Burlats on the D89 and D58 from Castres, in woods beside the Agout. The church of **St-Pierre** was part of a large Benedictine priory founded *c* 1160 but was wrecked during the Wars of Religion. The sacristy on the north is occupied by the *mairie* and the remains of the Romanesque cloisters are now the schoolyard. The east end of the Romanesque church is mainly intact, as is the north transept door in the form of a triumphal arch with the remains of two carved capitals, one with birds, the other peopled. The west door has a similar but more elaborate arrangement with a triple portal and seven vigorously sculpted capitals. The skeletal ruin of the nave is separated from the chancel by a double transverse arch and some of the capitals, decorated with heads and volutes, have survived.

Standing isolated near the river is the ravishing **Pavillon de Adélaïde**, a rare masterpiece of Romanesque secular architecture, named after a legendary lady remembered in the songs of troubadours. Open by appointment; ☎ 05 63 35 07 83. A simple rectangular stone building, it has been carefully restored and its outstanding features are the beautiful two-light windows on the upper floor—four on the south façade and one on the west—carved with a variety of motifs. The floors are divided by string courses on which the upper windows rest. The first floor has large and small openings, and at ground level are three arched openings (as found at Figeac or Cordes).

The **Bistoure tower** to the east was part of the Gothic ramparts, and near the bridge is the 12C Maison d'Adam with the outlines of one Romanesque window. Its carved elements found their way to the USA.

Cross the river and turn left and left again to take the D4 to **Roquecourbe**, an old textile town on the Agout with overhanging houses around the square. From here the D55 follows the winding route of the Agout through wooded gorges for 21km to the little schist town of **Vabre** overlooking the Gijou, once an important textile centre, its medieval bridge revised in the 19C.

A few kilometres along the D53 is the château at **Ferrières**, the grandiose home of the Calvinist leader, Guillaume Guilhot, governor of Castres in 1562. The medieval castle was revamped over several centuries and brought up-to-date in the early Renaissance, but has seen better times. Opposite is the **Musée du Protestantisme en Haut-Languedoc** which follows the history of the Huguenots in the Haut Languedoc. Open July, Aug daily 11.00–13.00 and 14.00–19.00; April–Nov, Sun and PH afternoons; ☎ 05 63 74 05 49. The road continues around the Sidobre to **Brassac**, another schist and slate town on the Agout with a Gothic cobbled bridge and a 17C château at each end. It is close to the Forêt de Castelnau and on the route to the lakes (p 258).

Mazamet, the Montagne Noire and Sorèze

This is the gateway to the **Parc Régionale du Haut-Languedoc**, 145,000ha of natural beauty—flowers, beech, conifers and wildlife—and a walking centre *par excellence* with 1800km of signposted paths. The Pic de Nore (1210m) is the highest peak of the Montagne Noire from where you can see the Monts de Lacaune and the Pyrenees.

The main town southeast of Castres is **Mazamet**, enclosed by the Montagne Noire. An essentially modern town and gastronomic centre at an important junction, it revolves around the Place de l'Hôtel-de-Ville. It still has a Protestant community: the Protestant Temple is indicated by the medieval tower of St-Jacques. The Catholic church of St-Sauveur was built in 1740. In Maison Fuzier is the local history and archaeological museum, Musée Mémoire de la Terre et Horizons Cathares, concentrating on regional burial rites; ☎ 05 63 98 99 76.

The D118 and then D54 climb steeply out of Mazamet into the forest to **Hautpoul**, a village vertiginously perched above the Arnette Valley. A Cathar stronghold fortified by Pierre Raymond d'Hautpoul in the 12C, it was besieged by Simon de Montfort in 1212, then ravaged during the Wars of Religion; parts have since been salvaged. See the Maison du Bois et du Jouet, a collection of wooden games and toys; ☎ 05 63 61 42 70.

Labruguière, an industrial centre northwest of Mazamet on the D621, has an ancient town at its heart, built in concentric circles. It also has the Musée Arthur Batut, dedicated to the inventor of aerial photography (in 1888) who was born in Castres in 1846. Open Wed–Sat 15.00–18.30, Mon, Sun 15.00–18.00, closed Tues; ☎ 05 63 50 22 18.

Massaguel, to the southwest on the D85, is a charming village with a church with modern glass and a mural (1960) by Dom Robert (see below). Just beyond Massaguel is **Dourgne**, a small town with a large fountain and arcades. A winding route, on the D12, goes up into the forested slopes around the little mountain village of **Arfons** (660m) on the ancient pilgrimage route. On the northern side of Dourgne are the Benedictine abbeys of **Ste-Scholastique** (1895 and 1927) and **St-Benoît-d'En-Calcat** (1890–1936). The brotherhood publishes religious books and has a shop selling these and other crafts they produce. A member of the community was Dom Robert (1907–97), who designed tapestries and murals.

Sorèze, enclosed within avenues of plane trees, is a most attractive and well-to-do small town with jettied houses. The Collège de Sorèze was a private school from 1682 to 1991. June–Sept, Mon–Fri 10.00–12.00 and 14.00–18.00, Sat, Sun 15.00–17.00, closed Tues; Oct–May 10.00–12.00 and 14.00–17.00, clsoed Tues; guided visits other times; ☎ 05 63 50 86 38. On the site of a Benedictine abbey founded early in the 9C and affiliated to Moissac in 1119, but totally destroyed during the Wars of Religion, the Congregation of St-Maur rebuilt the abbey in 1637 and later opened the school for the sons of impecunious gentlefolk. In 1776 it was elevated to royal military establishment. One of its most famous pupils was the future South American statesman Simon Bolivar (1783–1830). Père Lacordaire, from Paris, took over in 1854 and maintained the institution's reputation.

The crenellated tower and octagonal belfry of St-Martin, towering above the college and the village, are all that remains of the 15C parish church. The remains of the apse below the tower are open and unprotected since the church disappeared, exposing the Flamboyant decoration in the interior. The Maison du Parc is an archaeological museum and temporary exhibition space. Open summer 14.30–18.30, closed Tues; rest of year Sat, sun PH 14.00–18.00; ☎ 63 74 11 58.

The minuscule but remarkably active 'copper' village of **Durfort** has several shops and a small copper museum, Musée du Cuivre. Open July.Aug 15.00–19.00, closed Mon; June and Sept 14.00–18.00, closed Tues, Wed, Sun; ☎ 05 63 74 22 77. There are lakes at **Cammazes** and **St-Ferréol** which supply water to the Canal du Midi, and provide a refreshing summer interlude.

17 Les Landes

The *département* of Les Landes, the second largest in France, takes its name from a landscape of uncultivated moorland and marshes known as *landes* or *lannes*, which has been transformed into one of regimented pine forests and undulating sand dunes, with dead-straight roads and a scattered population. This ends at the silver beaches of the Atlantic on the Landais coast and gives way to oaks, maize and vines in the Sud Adour, between the River Adour and the Gave de Pau. To the east of the department is Armagnac Landais, the smallest geographic region of the Landes, historically and geographically part of Gascony. The main towns are Mont-de-Marsan, Dax and Aire-sur-l'Adour. The Landes has several fine abbey churches and two good museums of rural life.

THE LANDAIS COAST AND FOREST

The western part of the Landes has a long straight shoreline, the **Côte d'Argent**, extending over 106km of sandy beaches which attract many French visitors in the summer. (The only hiatus is the military zone between Biscarrosse-Plage and Mimizan-Plage, with no public access.) The landscape—which extends north into the Gironde and south to the Basque coast—is punctuated by lakes and criss-crossed by small rivers, but permanent communities are small and scattered. The main attractions are outdoors and the historic monuments are few and far between, but the Coastal Way follows part of a secondary pilgrimage route.

Getting there and around
Train

TER Bordeaux to Tarbes via Sanguinet, Biscarrosse (bus station), Parentis-en-Born, Morcenx, Dax and Puyoô (some stations served by bus).
TER Bordeaux to Hendaye via Morcenx, Dax, St-Vincent-de-Tyrosse, Labenne, Boucau, Bayonne.

Bus

Marmande to Mont-de-Marsan via Gabarret, Barbotan-le-Thermes, Cazaubon, Villeneuve-de-Marsan.
Agen to Mont-de-Marsan via Gabarret, Barbotan-le-Thermes, Cazaubon, Villeneuve-de-Marsan.

Cycling and hiking

Information from the CDT Landes or from local tourist information centres.

Tourist information
40600 Biscarrosse-Plage 55 Pl. du G. Dufau, BP 1, ☎ 05 58 78 20 96, fax 05 58 78 23 65, www.biscarosse.com
40130 Capbreton Ave G. Pompidou, ☎ 05 58 72 12 11, fax 05 58 41 00 29, www.tourisme.fr/capbreton
40150 Hossegor Place des Halles, BP 6, ☎ 05 58 41 79 00, fax 05 58 41 79 09, www.ville-soonts-hossegon.fr
40170 Lit-et-Mixe 23 Rue de l'Eglise, BP 3, ☎ 05 58 42 72 47, fax 05 58 42 43 02, www.tourisme.fr/lit-et-mixe
40202 Mimizan-Plage 38 Av. Maurice Martin, BP 11, ☎ 05 58 09 11 20, fax 05 58 09 40 31, www.mimizan.com
40660 Moliets-et-Maa Rue du Général Caunègre, ☎ 05 58 48 56 58, fax 05 58 48 52 93, www.moliets.com
40460 Sanguinet 1 Pl. de la Mairie, BP 13, ☎ 05 58 78 67 72, fax 05 58 78 67 26, www.sanguinet.com.
40510 Seignosse Av. des Lacs, BP 11, ☎ 05 58 43 32 15, fax 05 58 43 32 66, www.seignosse.com
40141 Soustons Grange de Labouyrie, BP 53, ☎ 05 58 41 52 62, fax 05 58

41 30 63, www.mairie-soustons.fr
40480 Vieux-Boucau 11 Promenade du Mail, ☎ 05 58 48 13 47, fax 05 58 48 15 37, www.ot-vieux-boucau.fr

Market days

Biscarrosse Friday in July and August
Hossegor-Capbreton Monday to Wednesday; Sunday Whitsun to end September
Mimizan Friday, and Thursday from 15 June to 15 September

Boat trips

Léon Popular boat trip on the Courant d'Huchet; book on ☎ 05 58 48 75 39

Festivals and events

July *Festival du Conte*, story-telling (in French), Capbreton.
La nuit des bandas, major celebration with marching bands, Parentis-en-Born.
Festival de jazz, jazz, Latin and blues music, Sanguinet.
August *Musicalarue*, three days of all kinds of theatre and music, Luxey.
Déferlantes francophones, French music from North America, Capbreton.
Rip Curl Pro Surf championships, Hossegor.
Festival de contrebasses, double bass as classical and jazz instrument, Capbreton

Where to stay and eating out

40600 BISCAROSSE-PLAGE

☆☆ *La Caravelle*, 5314 Rte des Lacs, Lac Nond Ispe, ☎ 05 58 09 82 67, fax 05 58 09 82 18, www.lacaravelle.fr. A quiet hotel near golf course and ocean.

40130 CAPBRETON

€ *Pizza Marine*, ☎ 05 58 72 13 42. On the port, serving pizzas and seafood, patronised by the locals.

€ *La Pecherie*, chez Ducamps on port. Good food, very popular.

40150 HOSSEGOR

☆☆☆☆ *Les Hortensias du Lac*, 1578 Ave du Tour-du-Lac, ☎ 05 58 43 99 00, fax 05 58 43 42 81, www.hortensias-du-lac.com. An authentic *basco-landais* lakeside house, with beautifully presented rooms and apartments.

☆☆☆ *Le Pavillon Bleu*, 1053 Ave du Touring-Club-de-France, ☎ 05 58 43 49 48, fax 05 58 43 49 49. A modernised hotel with very comfortable rooms in excellent position by the lake.

€€/€ *Les Huitrières du Lac*, 1187 Ave du Touring-Club-de-France, ☎ 05 58 43 51 48, fax 05 58 41 73 11. Seafood and oysters plus local cuisine. Views over the lake.

40140 MAGESCQ

☆☆☆ *Relais de la Poste*, off the N10 and D116, ☎ 05 58 47 70 25, fax 05 58 47 76 17. Family-run establishment in the pine forests of the Côtes-Sud serving high-class Landes cuisine.

40202 MIMIZAN

☆☆/☆☆☆ *Au Bon Coin du Lac*, 34 Ave du Lac, ☎ 05 58 09 01 55, fax 05 58 09 40 84. Indeed a good corner: hotel-restaurant in a rustic setting, with lake views. Food uses local ingredients.

40630 SABRES

☆☆☆ *Auberge des Pins*, ☎ 05 58 08 30 00, fax 05 58 07 56 74, www.auberge-des-pins.com. A Landais farmhouse in a peaceful setting with attractive rooms and high-class restaurant.

40510 SEIGNOSSE

Chambres d'hôte, Mme Annic Noëllie, 1 Ave Hilton Head, ☎ 05 58 41 64 29, fax 05 58 41 64 29, www.perso.wanadoo.fr/tygias. Villa on the gulf with garden and pool.

40140

Chambres d'hôte, Mme Bertrand, La Renardière, Quartier Hardy, ☎ 05 58 41 37 43, email soniabertrand@mageos.com. Accommodation for four people.

Sanguinet, on the eastern extension of the Etang de Cazaux-Sanguinet, has a small museum of archaeology, the Musée des Sites Lacustres. Open July, Aug 10.00–12.30 and 14.30–19.00; ☎ 05 58 82 13 32. **Biscarrosse** enjoys a magnificent position between two large lakes, Cazaux-Sanguinet and the Etang de Biscarrosse-Parentis. Its long association with pioneering aviation is celebrated in the Musée de l'Hydraviation. Open July, Aug 10.00–19.00; rest of year 14.00–18.00; closed Tues and PH; ☎ 05 58 78 00 65. The church at **Parentis-en-Born**, despite its medieval fortified belfry, is mainly Flamboyant Gothic. Houses here are often built in red brick, but **Pontenx-les-Forges**, to the south on the D46, is a picturesque village built in *garluche*, the local stone; it has a 15C church. There is a little Romanesque church at **Bouricos** just east.

Mimizan, where Gallo-Roman and medieval settlements were engulfed by the sand, now offers floral walks around the Etang d'Aureilhan and a richly sculpted Gothic doorway at the former abbey church. The belltower was a symbol of encouragement to pilgrims. Nearby is the local history museum, the Musée du Vieux Bourg. Open mid-June–mid-Sept, Mon–Sat 10.30–19.00, closed Sun; rest of year by appointment; ☎ 05 58 09 00 61.

The village of **Lit-et-Mixe** developed on the old Roman coastal road. To the east, the typical Landais village of **Lévignacq** has an outstanding church, fortified in the 13C–14C, with a curious curved spire. The church contains 15C and 18C painted decoration. The 13C church at **Saint-Girons** to the south is one of the oldest on the coast. A popular excursion from the Etang de Léon to **Moliets-Plage** is the trip on a *galupe* or *barque* (flat-bottomed boat) on the Courant d'Huchet (departures at 10.00, 14.30, by reservation only; ☎ 05 58 48 75 39). This is the only way to see the Huchet, the most significant of the small rivers or *courants* typical of the Landes which run directly to the sea, and an opportunity to enjoy the lush vegetation along its banks, including wild orchids.

The **Landes Côte Sud**, from Moliets to the Adour Estuary, is more densely populated and set up to receive larger numbers of visitors. The fortunes of the small fishing ports on this part of the coast were deeply affected by changes in the course of the Adour. Until the early 14C the river ran into the Atlantic at Capbreton, but the port silted up forcing the river to flow further north to meet the ocean at **Vieux-Boucau** (which means old mouth of the river). This lasted until 1578, when the present estuary was created west of Bayonne.

Hossegor-Capbreton

The most popular seaside resort in this part is Hossegor-Capbreton, two small ports either side of an estuary which have merged into one community.

Hossegor is typical of the Landes coast with sand dunes, pines and seafront, numerous hotels and sports and leisure activities, including golf. Its development as a resort began early in the 20C and, while not on the scale of Arcachon or Biarritz, it has enormous appeal and character. A major asset is the saltwater lake, which began as a freshwater pond created when the Adour was redirected in the 16C. The construction of a canal linking it to the ocean in the 19C—an attempt to prevent the build-up of silt in the channel—transformed it into a tidal saltwater lake. The fight goes on and the channel is constantly dredged mechanically.

The main building in Hossegor centre is the **Sporting-Casino** (1930), adjacent to the *fronton*, a wall against which to play the Basque game *pelota*; there is an indoor *jai alaï* hall, a *fronton* with three walls (1956) (p 406). Very special to the town are the colourful façades (*c* 1925) on the seafront around the semicircular Place des Landais, and houses of similar style (*c* 1920–40) are repeated along the wide promenade looking out towards the Bay of Biscay. There is a pleasant 6km walk all around the lake. One of the first hotels on the east bank, the Hôtel du Parc, is now the post office, and among the pine trees on the west bank are villas of the 1920s and '30s, often in *basco-landais* style, the most beautiful of which is the **Villa Julia**.

The port at the confluence of the Bourret and Boudigau rivers divides Hossegor from the older **Capbreton**, the only fishing village between Arcachon and Anglet. In the Middle Ages this was the largest community on the Landais coast and the 17C engineer Vauban considered expanding the port into a naval base. At the western extremity is l'Estacade, a rebuilt mid-19C wooden jetty, with great views of the coastline and Pyrenees. The fishing port, marina and the fish market are across the Boudigau and around the Port de Pêche are some lively restaurants. In the old centre the church of **St-Nicolas** offers a panoramic view from the tower. Inside the church is an interesting series of engraved plaques in memory of ships' captains and crews, a 14C figure of Christ and a fine 15C *Pietà*, both carved in wood. Near the church are a few jettied houses, the best in Rue Jan-Lartigau.

Soorts a little way inland still has some 19C farmhouses, as well as one of the oldest golf courses in France, created in 1930. The environment is carefully protected and at **Seignosse-Bourg** around the Etang Noir there is a 50ha nature reserve (guided tours June to September; ☎ 05 58 72 85 76). The inland village of **Tosse** has a pretty 12C restored church and Landais farmhouses in timber and brick. The Etang Blanc is a favourite place for fishing and walking, and at **St-Vincent-de-Tyrosse** is a Romanesque church (11C–12C), restored in 1926 in a curious Romano-Byzantine style.

The **Marais d'Orx** is a marshy terrain close to **Labenne** (N10) which was dried out in the 19C but has been allowed to return to its natural state since it became a protected nature reserve in 1989. On one of the most important migration corridors of Europe some 250 migrant birds collect here annually. Open July–Sept, Mon–Sun 10.00–13.00 and 14.00–19.00; Oct–March, weekdays 09.00–12.00 and 14.00–17.00, weekends 14.00–17.00; April–June to 18.00; ☎ 05 59 45 42 46.

Forêt de Landes

The Landes forest is a vast triangular swathe of land extending over nearly 11,000 km sq across much of the *département* of Les Landes and part of Gironde. Before the 19C the centre of the Landes was mainly open moorland (*lande*), essentially flat and sandy, with numerous small rivers and shallow wells, with patches of marsh as well as small woods with both broad-leafed and evergreen trees. Dominating the landscape were endless stretches of poor grass grazed by sheep, watched over by shepherds who walked on stilts 1.5m tall in order to cover long distances rapidly and to watch over distant flocks.

In the 19C maritime pines were planted to improve and stabilise the land and in 50 years the countryside was transformed. This relatively young forest is the largest in Western Europe and is covered with a network of hiking tracks and cycle routes through the enfilades of trees where green ferns and violet heather flourish. **Note** When driving through the forest of the Landes, you are advised to keep your headlights on.

Parc Naturel Régional des Landes de Gascogne

The park was created in 1970 to maintain the balance between tourism and the natural environment. At its heart is the **Ecomusée de la Grande Lande** at Marquèze, near Sabres on the junction of the N134 and D44. It reconstructs traditional life in the *landes* before the wholesale planting of pines. Access is by train from Sabres station (10min); it is important to check departure times. Open April–Nov, trains approximately 40min intervals, June–Sept, starting at 10.00–12.00 and 14.00–17.20; March–May, Sept–Nov, Mon–Sat 14.00–16.40, Sun and PH 10.10 until 16.40; ☎ 05 58 08 31 31, www.parc-landes-de-gascogne.fr.

The train takes you to the heart of the museum, which offers guided tours, restaurants and a picnic area, and frequent special exhibitions, demonstrations and displays. It is laid out as a pre-1850s *airial*, an isolated, self-sufficient rural community of peasants who grouped together on grassy areas of common land. The museum has preserved a number of typical rural buildings; the dwellings are painted white and the others are farm buildings, including a *poulailler perché* (raised chicken coop). There is also livestock. Exhibits relate to the main occupations of the Landais peasant, shepherding, farming, milling and tapping for resin. The finest house is the *maison de maître* (*c* 1900), a low, timber building that was inhabited by the ploughman, anchorman of the community, and his family. The precious oxen were part of the family and a place was reserved for them inside the house. Sheep were considered more lowly but were far more numerous, and had many uses. By the river is a working mill, and in the pine woods resin is tapped for turpentine, an industry which developed with the growth of the forest.

Other aspects of traditional life in the Haute Lande can be explored at the Maison des Artisans in Pissos, at the Musée du Patrimoine Religieux et des Croyances Populaires (popular beliefs) at Moustey, in the L'Atelier des Produits Résineux (pine resin workshops) and the Maison de l'Estupe Huc, Gascon for *eteins le feu* (fire-fighting in the forest), both at Luxey, and the Vieux Forges in Brocas.

ARMAGNAC LANDAIS

The most easterly part of Les Landes is an area of contrasting landscapes, where the forest of the Landes and the farmland and vineyards of Armagnac overlap. Its vulnerable position between the territories of France and England in the Middle Ages made it a battle ground, and *bastides* were founded at strategic points by both sides.

Getting there and around
Train

Mont-de-Marsan has connections with Bordeaux and Bayonne, changing at Dax or Morcenx.

 Tourist information
40240 Labastide d'Armagnac Pl. Royale, ☎ 05 58 44 67 56, fax 05 58 44 84 15, www.labastide-d-armagnac.com
40011 Mont-de-Marsan 6 Pl. du Général-Leclerc, BP 305, ☎ 05 58 05 87 37, fax 05 58 05 87 36, www.mont-de-marsan.org
40240 St-Justin Pl. des Tilleuls, ☎/fax 05 58 44 86 06

Market days

Labastide d'Armagnac Monday
Mont-de-Marsan Tuesday and Saturday

Festivals and events

February–March *Carnaval*, weekend festivities with costumed cavalcade, Mont-de-Marsan

June *Jeu de Quille*, old-fashioned local version of skittles, St-Justin

July *Festival d'Art Flamenco*, Spanish dancers and guitarists give performances and classes, Mont-de-Marsan
Fêtes de la Madeleine, traditional *féria* or festival lasting about 5 days, with bull-fights, *courses landaises*, cavalcades and concerts, Mont-de-Marsan

August *Les peinters dans la rue*, street painters, local and national artists exhibit in the street, antiques market, Labastide d'Armagnac

October *Championnat de France d'Equitation*, specialist horse-riding, Tartas

November *La Flamme de l'Armagnac*, after the harvest, Armagnac producers open their cellars. Armagnac region of Landes and Lot-et-Garonne

Where to stay and eating out

40240 BETBEZER
Chambres d'hôte, Mme Darzacq,
Domaine de Paguy (outside Labastide d'Armagnac), ☎ 05 58 44 81 57, fax 05 58 44 68 09. 16C property over-looking vineyards in quiet surround-ings, with pool.

40310 GABARRET
☆☆☆ *Château de Buros*, off the D656 3.5km northeast of Gabarret, ☎ 05 58 44 34 30, fax 05 58 44 36 53, www.chateaudeburos.com. Converted 19C château with courtyard restaurant and pool.

40240 LABASTIDE D'ARMAGNAC
La Citadelle, Chemin de Broustet, Créon d'Armagnac, ☎ 05 58 44 85 39/06 86 11 89 65. *Chambres d'hôte* close to the pretty village, set in a garden with terrace.

40000 MONT-DE-MARSAN
☆☆☆ *Le Renaissance*, Rte de Villeneuve, ☎ 05 58 51 51 51, fax 05 58 75 29 07. Regional food in a modern setting.

40240 ST-JUSTIN
☆☆/☆ *France*, Pl. des Tilleuls, ☎ 05 58 44 83 61, fax 05 58 44 83 89. A simple bistrot with good, local fare served under the arcades in summer.

The most attractive *bastide* in the Armagnac Landais is **Labastide d'Armagnac**, east of Mont-de-Marsan by the D933 and D626. It was founded in 1291 by Bernard IV d'Armagnac to defend his territory against troublesome neighbours in the Marsan, and its charter was ratified by Edward I in 1294. Labastide lost its walls and gates in the 17C but has retained much of its medieval character and has not been over-prettified. Place Royale is large and empty, enclosed by attrac-tive façades and continuous arcades combining stone with brick and timber. Unusually for a *bastide* the church opens onto the square with a towering belfry porch (15C), thought originally to be part of the fortifications; the interior is painted with 19C *trompe l'oeil* and contains a 15C–16C polychrome wood Pietà. Adjacent to the church is the *mairie*, above the old *halle* which still has a grain measure. Reputedly the view over the square from the Maison Malartic opposite the church, which was visited several times by Henri IV, was the inspiration for Place des Vosges in Paris. Labastide was an important Protestant centre for the region and suffered the consequences. Maison Clave on Rue Castay contains murals which appear to date from the Protestant period, and near the west exit to the village is a simple building dated 1607, described as *Le Temple extra-muros*, or Protestant church, which has been turned into an exhibition centre for *bastides* in Gascony; enquire at the tourist office for opening times. The French national sport of cycling is honoured at the chapel **Notre-Dame-des-Cyclistes** at Geoü, 2km east of Labastide d'Armagnac, on the site of a 4C Roman villa. A

Labastide d'Armagnac

tiny, restored 11C Romanesque building has been completely given over to cycling memorabilia. Open July, Aug 10.00–12.00 and 15.00–19.00, Sun and May–Sept 15.00–19.00.

A few kilometres west is the slightly busier **Saint-Justin**, which was granted *bastide* status in 1280 as a result of a *paréage* (agreement) between the Hospitallers of St John of Jerusalem and the Vicomtesse de Marsan. The town was badly knocked about by the English in 1359, by the Protestants in 1569, and was considered destroyed by 1654 following the problems of the Fronde. Nevertheless, a section of the ramparts with two octagonal towers and an attractive arcaded square shaded with lindens have survived along with some good buildings, including a fine Renaissance timber-framed house.

The privately owned **Château de Fondat**, outside St-Justin, is a deliciously Romantic concoction which began as a large farm estate built in 1607 by a Scotsman, Lord Argelouse. Heavily remodelled in the 19C, it is set in interesting gardens with old trees and a dovecote on stilts. For guided visits, enquire at the tourist office in Labastide or St-Justin.

Mont-de-Marsan

Situated where the Douze and Midou unite to become the Midouze, Mont-de-Marsan is known as the town of three rivers. The centre of what appears at first to be a rather dull modern administrative town of some 30,000 inhabitants turns out to have some good points and at its core there are reminders of its history. Crowds gather for the Fêtes de la Madeleine in July, and for *férias* and *courses landaises* at the arena at Plumaçon.

History

The town which developed around the *castelnau* (fortified settlement) established by the Viscount of Marsan between the Douze and Midou *c* 1133 became an important stage on the pilgrimage route because of the Benedictine priory of La Madeleine. The town was strongly defended with ramparts on both banks and the Porte de Roquefort and Château de Nolibos, possibly built by Gaston Fébus (p 521) in 1344, to the east. The château was demolished in the 17C. A suburb soon developed on the opposite bank of the Midouze at the river port from where grain and wine were transported to Bayonne, and during the Hundred Years War the walls were extended around it. In the 18C trade picked up, rich families built grand mansions and the town was cleaned up and opened out. Mont-de-Marsan became capital of the *département* of Les Landes created in 1790, and was endowed with administrative buildings.

Just east of Place du Général-Leclerc, where the tourist office is located, two foot-bridges cross the Midou to the old part of town. The further one, Passerelle des Douves, leads past gardens to a terrace below the old castle. The other, Passerelle des Musées, brings you down to Rue Lacataye and the **Musée Despiau-Wlérick** in the 14C Lacataye keep. Open 10.00–12.00 and 14.00–18.00, closed Tues and PH; ☎ 05 58 75 00 45. The museum has a unique and rich collection of early 20C sculpture, including works by Bourdelle and Rodin, and of two local sculptors, Charles Despiau (1874–1946) and Robert Wlérick (1882–1944). Some of the sculptures have overflowed out of the museum galleries into the gardens and streets of the town. From the top of the building is a good view over the town.

Beyond the museum are sections of the old ramparts, and along Rue Victor-Hugo are the 19C Neo-classical buildings of local administration, including the Préfecture, the Hôtel du Département, the Palais de Justice and the old Gendarmerie and prison. The church of **La Madeleine**, rebuilt 1825–30 by D.-F. Panay to harmonise with the other public buildings, contains a main altar (18C) by the Mazetti brothers from Avignon whose work is in several Landais churches (see Aire-sur-l'Adour and Dax, below).

Behind the Préfecture in Rue Maubec are two stone houses described as Romanesque, but probably 13C. Rue G. de Gourgues south of the church brings you to Place de Général-de-Gaulle, once the site of the 12C castle but now replaced by the theatre and market. Cross the Pont de l'Hôtel-de-Ville at the confluence of the Douze and Midou, and turn west to the Pont de Commerce, the area of the old port and of the Cales, or quays, of the Midouze. The houses around Place Joseph-Pancaut were built by wealthy merchants in the 18C.

The village of **Bascons**, southeast of Mont-de-Marsan, has a simple 13C rural chapel, Notre-Dame-de-la-Course-Landaise, and a museum dedicated to the sport of that name. Open May–Oct 14.30–18.30. Meanwhile **Pomarez**, in the south of the region, is considered the Mecca of the *courses landaises*.

Basco-landais sports and festivals

Courses landaises have been practised at least since the 13C. This bloodless teasing of a bovine is the main event of village fêtes in the Landes and took its present form c 1830/40 when certain rules were established and oxen were gradually replaced by feisty cows weighing around 300–400kg. The performance takes place in an arena, the objective being to provoke the animal and the art to avoid its charges gracefully. To the mainly Spanish terms employed are added the French *l'écart*, *la feinte* and *le saut* (swerve, false swerve and leap). The *saut* is perhaps the least important but most spectacular and has different versions, such as *le saut les pieds dans le béret*. *Courses landaises* are followed most enthusiastically in the Chalosse, the Tursan, Armagnac, in northern Béarn and the Bigorre where they are enacted in some 80 arenas from May to September. The *corrida*, introduced into the southwest during the Second Empire by Empress Eugénie, is a bull fight in the Spanish tradition, with matadors and *novilleros* who exhaust the animal before killing it. A *ganaderia* is where the bulls or cows for fighting are bred. *La fête* in the Landes and Gascony combines *courses landaises* with a colourful summer street celebration when *bandas* (brass bands) animate the streets at night. The *féria* is an annual festival with bull-fighting.

The **Château de Ravignan** to the east, at **Perquie** near Villeneuve-de-Marsan on the D934, is one of the best in the Landes. It was begun in the 17C and completed in the 19C. The elegant Classical building is set in a *parc à la française* and contains good furniture and *objets d'art* and a collection of men's costumes from the court of Louis XVI; ☎ 05 58 45 22 04 or 05 58 45 26 44.

THE SUD ADOUR: THE CHALOSSE AND TURSAN

South of the Adour the pine forests of the Landes de Gascogne are replaced by gentle hills and fields of maize similar to the neighbouring *departement* of Gers, old Gascony. The main towns here are St-Sever, Aire-sur-l'Adour and Dax. The region around Montfort is still described by its old name, La Chalosse, and in the southeast, centred on Geaune, is the Tursan, which differs from the Chalosse by virtue of its vineyards. The old name of the land south of Dax, of which Peyrehorade was the capital, is the Pays d'Orthe.

Getting there and around
Car
From Bordeaux, A62 exit 5, and D9333.
From Toulouse, N124 via Auch to Nogaro, D6 and D30.
From Tarbes, D935 to Aire-sur-l'Adour, and N124.
From Bayonne via Dax, N10/N124.
Train
TER Bordeaux to Bayonne/Hendaye via Dax, St-Vincent-de-Tyrosse.
TER Bordeaux to Pau/Tarbes via Dax.
Bus
Agen to Pau via Aire-sur-l'Adour.
Dax to Tarbes via Grenade-sur-l'Adour, Mazères-sur-l'Adour, and Aire-sur-l'Adour.
Mont-de-Marsan to Agen via Villeneuve-de-Marsan, St-Justin, Labastide d'Armagnac, Cauzabon.
Mont-de-Marsan to Hagetmau via St-Sever.
Mont-de-Marsan to Marmande via Cazaubon.
Mont-de-Marsan to Pau via Aire-sur-l'Adour.

Tourist information
40801 Aire-sur-l'Adour Pl. du Général-du-Gaulle, BP 155, ☎/fax 05 58 71 64 70, email otsi.aire@wanadoo.fr
40104 Dax Pl. Thiers, BP 177, ☎ 05 58 56 86 86, fax 05 58 56 86 80, www.dax.fr
40320 Eugénie-les-Bains 147 Rue R. Vielle, ☎ 05 58 51 13 16, fax 05 58 51 12 02, www.ville-eugenie-les-bains.fr
40320 Geaune 4 Pl. de l'Hôtel-de-Ville, ☎ 05 58 44 50 01, fax 05 58 44 40 03, email communes.tursan@wanadoo.fr
40705 Hagetmau Canton d'Hagetmau, Pl. de la République, BP 56, ☎ 05 58 79 38 26, fax 05 58 79 47 27, email tourisme.hagetmau@wanadoo.fr
40380 Montfort-en-Chalosse Pays de Montfort, 25 Pl. Foch, ☎ 05 58 98 58 50, fax 05 58 98 58 01, email ot.montfort.chaloose@wanadoo.fr
40300 Peyrehorade Pays d'Orthe, 147 Quai du Sablot, ☎ 05 58 73 00 52, fax 05 58 73 16 53, email ot-peyrehorade@wanadoo.fr
40993 St-Paul-Lès-Dax 68 Av. de la Résistance, BP 100, ☎ 05 58 91 60 01, fax 05 58 91 97 44, www.ot-saint-paullesdax.fr
40500 St-Sever Pl. du Tour de Sol, ☎ 05 58 76 34 64, fax 05 58 76 00 10
Market days
Aire-sur-l'Adour Tuesday; evening

markets in summer

Dax Saturday and Sunday; evening markets in summer

Montfort-en-Chalosse Wednesday

Peyrehorade Wednesday

St-Sever Saturday

Guided walks

Dax Themed walks from the tourist office.

Festivals and events

February–March *Carnaval*, weekend festivities with costumed cavalcade, Dax

April *Festival Art et Courage*, celebration of *courses landaises*, Pomarez

June *Festival des Abbayes*, promotion of religious buildings through classical concerts, Pays d'Orthe and Chalosse. *Fête patronale*, local festivities, Aine-sur-l'Adour. *Fête patronale*, St-Sever

July *Music d'Arts*, music festival in a small village, Brassempouy

July–August *Féria*, festival lasting about 5 days, with bullfights, *course landaise*, cavalcades and concerts, Dax

August *Festival Paso Passion*, three-day Spanish music festival with *bandas* (bands), Dax

August–September *Festival Musiques Croisées*, music festival, St-Sever

September *Toros y Salsa*, bullfighting and dance, Spanish/Mexican food, Dax

October *Festival d'Art Sacré*, Dax

Where to stay and eating out

40380 CASSEN

☆☆☆ *Equiland*, Rte de Gamarde, ☎ 05 58 98 98 98, fax 05 58 98 98 99, www.domaine.equiland.com. Hotel and sporting complex set in 17ha of parkland. **40100 DAX**

☆☆☆ *Le Richelieu*, 13 Ave Victor-Hugo, ☎ 05 58 90 49 49, fax 05 58 90 80 86, www.le-richelieu.fr. Comfortable, centrally placed hotel with patio restaurant.

40320 EUGÉNIE-LES-BAINS

☆☆☆☆ *Les Prés d'Eugénie*, a luxury hotel in a colonial-style building close to the thermal spa. The restaurant *Michel Guérard* is virtually unbeatable.

☆☆☆ *Les Logis de la Ferme Grives*, a charming hotel with a restaurant serving local wines and dishes cooked to perfection in a rustic setting.

☆☆☆ *Le Couvent des Herbes*, an 18C dwelling with high quality accommodation.

Michel and Christine Guérard own these three establishments and restaurants which are so famous and of such quality that they attract visitors from far and wide. For all reservations, ☎ 05 58 05 06 07, fax 05 58 51 10 10, www.michelguerard.com, email michelguerard@relaischateaux.fr.

40207 GRENADE-SUR-L'ADOUR

☆☆☆ *Pain Adour et Fantasie*, Pl. des Tilleuls, ☎ 05 58 45 18 80, fax 05 58 45 16 57, www.chateauxhotels. com/fantasie. In a 17C building on the Adour, mouth-watering food and a good-value set-price menu.

40700 HAGETMAU

☆☆☆ *Les Lacs d'Halco*, Rte de Cazalis, 3km south of Hagetmau on D349, ☎ 05 58 79 30 79, fax 05 58 79 36 15. A modern, well-appointed hotel-restaurant with indoor pool in a peaceful setting on the edge of a small lake.

40300 PORT DE LANNE

☆☆☆ *La Vieille Auberge*, 66 Pl. de l'Eglise, on the D117 west of Peyrehorade, ☎ 05 58 89 16 29, fax 05 58 89 12 89. 18C Gascon inn at the centre of the village. Pool set in a shady park.

40990 ST-PAUL-LÈS-DAX

☆☆☆ *Caliceo*, Lac de Christus, ☎ 05 58 90 66 00, fax 05 58 90 68 68, www.caliceo.com. Modern hotel with large indoor pool; fitness programmes.

€€ *Moulin de Poustagnacq*, ☎ 05 58 91 31 03, fax 05 58 91 37 97. A lively place where imaginative cooking meets musical accompaniment.

40500 ST-SEVER
€€ *Patio des Jacobins*, 11 Pl. Verdun,
☎ 05 58 76 32 04, fax 05 58 76 38

84. A small, reasonable and popular eating place with original dishes carefully prepared.

Saint-Sever

Saint-Sever is the first town in the Sud Adour, and in the Middle Ages was a major halt for pilgrims on the road between Bordeaux and the Pyrenees. The important **church** is the theatre of a magnificent group of 11C–12C sculpted capitals. The town is sheltered by the Belvédère de Morlanne, a natural balcony of rock commanding the river valley and the sea of pines beyond.

History

The Romans occupied the *oppidum* on the hill of Morlanne, but the town is named after Severus, a Christian from Eastern Europe, who was sent by the pope to evangelise the area. He was successful in his mission, but early in the 5C was beheaded by Vandals and, predictably, took up his head and walked. A spring gushed forth and the area became a site of pilgrimage. Guillaume Sanche, Duke of Gascony, fulfilled his vow that if successful in battle he would rebuild the sanctuary dedicated to Severus. Late in the 10C he purchased land and the abbey was founded. Around 1025 the first church was built, with a vast apse, two apsidal chapels and probably a timber roof. In the 11C abbey a precious illuminated manuscript, the *Béatus* (or Apocalypse) of Saint-Sever, was compiled at the abbey.

Grégoire de Montaner (Abbot 1028–72), of noble birth and trained at Cluny, assured a privileged position for St-Sever. When in 1060 the monastery was ravaged by fire, Grégoire initiated an ambitious project of rebuilding inspired by the particular brand of architecture and decoration established by the Cluniac Benedictines. Shortly before his death, the main altar was consecrated and by the 12C much of the structure of the church was in place. The abbey was not, however, left in peace: an earthquake in 1372, the Hundred Years War and the Wars of Religion left it desperately scarred. It came under the auspices of the Congregation of Saint-Maur in the 17C, who carried out major repairs and alterations. The Revolution did further damage and 19C restorers left their decisive mark on it. It is now the parish church.

The **exterior** of the church is something of a hotchpotch, in poor shape in places, rebuilt in others, but essentially Romanesque. The nave is short in relation to the unusually long chevet, and the tall apse with a domed roof was remodelled in the 17C. The 19C restorers created the neo-Romanesque west end to replace a 17C Classical doorway and reopened the small door in the north transept; the belfry on the northern transept dates from 1930. The tympanum in the north door is Romanesque, albeit badly damaged, and reuses two Roman capitals from Morlanne.

The **interior** is a shady forest of columns and pillars, but the carvings, some coloured, are important and warrant close inspection. The chevet is orchestrated by six apsidal chapels in echelon, three each side, which increase in size and height to culminate at the east in a deep apse, the same layout used at the second abbey church of Cluny (Burgundy) in the 10C. The walls between the chapels are pierced to form arcades linking one to the next. This is a rare arrangement for southwest France and the result is an exceptionally large two-bay choir which, along with the choir and transepts, has 12C barrel vaults. Each transept has an elegant gallery above the chapel which gives access to the upper part of the choir chapels, a system usually associated with northern France. The southern gallery is closed by a screen. The main altar and baldaquin are pure Baroque eye-candy but under the wooden floor of the apse are fragments of mosaics, part of the extraordinarily rich decorative programme in the Romanesque period. A variety of materials indicate different building campaigns or alterations. The three round pillars in the southwest, the rib vaults of the aisles (except for the south-east bay) and the Rayonnant tracery are the result of building campaigns in the 14C–15C, while the barrel-vaulting of the short nave is 17C–18C.

The **carved capitals**, some 150, are a magnificent testament to the impor-tance of Saint-Sever in the 11C–12C. Those of the chevet, completed by the end of the 11C, place the abbey church among the major creative centres of the first wave of Romanesque sculpture, and show certain similarities with those at St-Sernin in Toulouse and Conques. The second wave of construction and decoration began in the early 12C. Some of the capitals appear disproportion-ately large, and many were repainted in the 19C, hopefully re-creating the medieval colours. Recycled Roman elements include a number of marble columns and one capital in the middle chapel north of the choir.

The earliest capitals on the north of the chevet demonstrate a free interpreta-tion of antique models with vigorous variations on the acanthus or smooth leaf designs. The form of the capital and abacus adapts according to the role or position, and there are different techniques used in the carving. Balls and lions start to appear in the north and are expanded on and added to on the south of the chevet, suggesting the same workshop. Complicated designs incorporating interlacing appear, and more lions, including two particularly elegant ones on the south of the middle chapel; another, with a figure between two lions, may be a reference to *Daniel in the Lions' Den*. Birds of increasing complexity include a deeply cut image where the feet of two birds meet above a man's head. The stori-ated capitals are from a later period, and include a *Christ in Majesty with St Peter*, on the angle of the north transept and aisle and, near the west door, are (north) an enigmatic painted scene in which four figures help four more to scramble up through foliage; and opposite, easily decipherable, *Herod's Feast* and the *Beheading of John the Baptist* on three faces of the capital. The organ was renovated by the Cavaillé-Col workshops in the 19C; there is a gilded wooden altar (17C) from the Jacobins (see below) in the north aisle. From the sacristy there is access to the **cloister**, built in the 17C and restored.

From the cloister take Rue du Général-Durrieu, with some good 18C–19C houses; no. 21 is 16C. Turn left on Rue Lamarque to arrive at the convent of the **Jacobins** or Dominicans (*c* 1280), which contains the small and dusty Musée de la Ville, usually open in the afternoon; check times at the tourist office. The convent was established under the patronage of Eleanor of Castile, Edward I's queen, outside the town walls. In the 14C the walls were extended to encompass the convent and at this time the first repairs were carried out. It was again exten-sively repaired and rebuilt *c* 1660 following Protestant attacks. The cloister (open between 08.30 to around 20.00) had only two wings in the 14C, but was replaced by the present irregular four-sided one in the 17C. To the east it is linked by three arcades with the chapter house, in which murals have survived. You enter the large brick church from the cloister. Recently restored, it is unadorned and impressively spacious, its main asset being the splendid timber roof.

The small **museum** is on the west of the cloister, through a small door and upstairs. It may be a bit dusty and forgotton but it contains a fascinating collection of Gallo-Roman finds from Morlanne (4C–8C), the Gallo-Roman villa at Augreilh (4C), fragments of the 11C–12C abbey church and from the Jacobins. In the tourist office there is an exhibition dedicated to the remarkable 11C manuscript known as the *Apocalypse of Saint-Sever* or the *Beatus*. The town owns one of only three reproductions (original in Bibliothèque Nationale in Paris) which was produced in the abbey by Brother Stéphane Garcia de Castile at the time of Abbot Grégoire. It consists of an illuminated transcript in French of the text of the Apocalypse of St John, and originally included the commentary of Béatus de Libiena (*c* 786), who instigated the cult of St James at Compostela. The colours of the illuminations, the work of several artists, are particularly brilliant. The illuminations are presented in slide form with commentary. Open July, Aug, Mon–Sat 09.30–12.00 and 14.00–17.30, Sun and PH 10.30–12.30; rest of year Mon–Fri 09.30–12.00 and 14.00–17.30, Sat 09.30–12.00.

Further east along the river at **Larrivière**, near Grenade sur-l'Adour on the N124, is another Romanesque church with a sporty dedication, **Notre-Dame-de-Rugby**, crammed with ex-voto tributes to the oval ball, including the stained glass. Open every day, morning and evening; ☎ 05 58 45 91 14.

To the south, **Eugénie-les-Bains**, a commune established in 1861, has become a green oasis on the edge of the desert of the Landes. This spa town is heralded as both *premier village minceur de France* and gastronomic centre. On one hand, the spa waters aid the treatment of obesity; on the other, since 1975 the chef Michel Guérard has pioneered *cuisine minceur*, proving that good food can be part of a calorie-controlled diet. The hotels and restaurants are dominated by the Guérard dynasty, and the thermal centre is the smart place for celebrities to destress. Empress Eugénie beneficently offered her patronage to the town after reputedly sheltering there during a storm in 1859.

Around Eugenie-les-Bains are some pretty villages such as Buanes and Vielle-Tursan, which has a part-Romanesque church. The 14C Tour Maubourguet at **St-Loubouer** is where Gaston IV of Foix (1436–72) brought together the Estates of Lannes (Tursan, Chalosse and Dax) and made them swear allegiance to Charles VII. There is also a Romanesque church with a fortified belfry and 12C sculptures.

Aire-sur-L'Adour

The bustling market town of Aire-sur-L'Adour is on two levels, the lower part on the banks of the Adour, and the *quartier du Mas* on rising ground to the south-west. Aire is at the heart of an agricultural region where the economy depends largely on the production of geese and ducks, and the *marché au gras* (foie gras market) is one of the most important in France. In June the town is animated by the local *fête*. Aire boasts two important religious buildings, the cathedral and Ste-Quitterie-du-Mas.

The tourist office is on the banks of the Adour east of the bridge. The old bridge was washed away by serious flooding in 1743 and 1795, and rebuilt only in

1834 thanks to Madame de Berry, for whose visit six years earlier a wooden bridge had been hastily erected. Further along the river is the arena where the *courses landaises* are held during the traditional festivities in June. From the tourist office, Rue Maubec takes you past a working Carmelite convent with a 19C chapel, on the site of the 12C episcopal mills. Beyond is the former **Cathédrale St-Jean** (the bishopric transferred to Dax in 1933). It was begun in 1092, but a bay was demolished during the Hundred Years War and in 1569 Protestants attacked the church and massacred the prelates. The severe west façade combines stone and brick, relieved only by the undecorated door and a plain oculus, and the slate-roofed belfry is set slightly back. Inside, the nave is vast and dark with extensive painted décor of 1860. Of the Romanesque building, relatively intact until the 18C, only the brick choir, transepts and some capitals have survived. The north transept is barrel-vaulted, but the south is ribbed. In 1766 the apse was replaced by a huge rotunda and the stalls, woodwork and main altar in coloured marble are also 18C. The nave was radically altered in the 19C when the arches were punched through and aisles added. The 1750s' organ was restored in the 1990s. There are occasional visits to the tower and to the sacristy. In the latter, which has Romanesque openings and 14C ribbed vaults supported by a central column, chasubles and church treasures are on display.

South of the cathedral is the former episcopal palace, rebuilt in 1647, which now houses the **Hôtel de Ville**. It has a fine stone staircase, panelled Salle du Conseil, and a small museum of Gallo-Roman mosaics. Across from here on Rue Labeyrie is the large early 20C covered market with the *marché au gras* next door. The commercial centre is along the two parallel main streets, Gambetta and Carnot, and the present Crédit Agricole in Rue Gambetta was the *halle aux ceréales*. At the corner of Rues Labeyrie and Libération is the restored 14C **Maison de l'Officialité**, with Gothic and Renaissance windows, where local magistrates used to meet. The canal belonging to the cathedral chapter was dug in the 16C to provide water for the mills and the bishops' palace and linked Aire with Barcelonne-du-Gers to the east. One somewhat dilapidated mill still survives and is due for restoration. The **Halle aux Grains**, on Avenue de Verdun, is a seriously elegant octagonal market built in 1855, with an arcaded peristyle and magnificent roof timbers, restored in 1991.

Ste-Quitterie

From Rue Labeyrie head south and uphill along Rue Felix-Despagnet to the *quartier du Mas* and the Romanesque church of Ste-Quitterie. It is a fair walk; by car, head in the direction of Pau. Despite many vicissitudes and consequent repair and alteration, the ancient pile stands dignified and impressive. Guided visits; ☎ 05 58 71 79 78 or enquire at tourist office.

The Mas was inhabited from Gallo-Roman times onwards. An early Christian sanctuary was established here, and in 1092 the existing abbey was taken over by Benedictine monks. The church, dedicated to St Peter, was begun in the 11C and incorporated a 4C mausoleum sheltering the venerated relics of a young Christian girl identified as Quitterie, a Christian Visigoth princess. She refused to abandon her faith to marry a high-ranking pagan Visigoth, Euric, was pursued, took refuge in Aire, and was beheaded there on 22 May 476, at the foot of the hill of Mas where a spring gushed forth water. Quitterie gathered her head in her hands and carried it up the hill to the site where the church now stands. The area around the abbey developed into a veritable cultural centre protected by walls, ditches and a château.

The oldest part of the church visible from the exterior is the east end (11C–12C). A walk gives an understanding of the site and there are sarcophagi from an ancient Christian burial ground to the north. The north wall has a stone base (11C–12C) but the upper part was rebuilt in the 14C in brick following a fire during a local revolt in 1288. The massive **west front**, also part stone (13C), is enhanced by two levels of continuous arcades. The brick section, including the square **belfry**, with recycled Gallo-Roman columns on the two lower levels, was also part of the 14C alterations, although the last stage of the belfry is 18C. The Gothic porch was attacked by the Protestants in 1569 when fire scorched the stone, and angels, apostles and prophets on the arches were destroyed; the figure of St Peter on the central trumeau survived until the 18C. The carvings on the tympanum represent the *Last Judgement* with *Christ in Majesty*, the Virgin and St John, framed by the instruments of the Passion. Below are the *Expulsion of Adam and Eve from Paradise*, and Hell, with the damned in cauldrons, or led by chains attached at the neck through the jaws of Leviathan. Traces of colour are faintly discernible in places.

Interior Immediately inside the door are holy water stoups, the one on the right supported on an old nave boss carrying the arms of Foix, and the other a Roman capital in marble on a Visigoth stone sculpture. The **nave**, with Classical pillars erected after the Wars of Religion in the 17C, is a bit disappointing. When the Romanesque nave was rebuilt in the 14C, the floor was raised to the level of the choir, which had to be high enough to accommodate the roof of the crypt. At the same time a large window was opened in the north transept. More light was shed on the nave in the 16C by four new openings. The transept floor was raised to the height of the choir in the 17C.

The **choir** gives an idea of the grandeur and beauty of the original church. In 1886, stalls and panelling were removed to expose 12 damaged Romanesque capitals supporting arcading lavishly decorated with delicate friezes and interlacing. Two capitals near the altar represent scenes from the Old Testament including *Balaam on his Ass* and the *Song of Songs*. Four capitals carry scenes of the vices and the appropriate punishments, and the six others carry foliate designs and animals. Some of the arcading was removed when the choir was attacked by an elaborate Baroque décor of coloured marble and stucco, the work of the Mazetti brothers in 1771. The centrepiece of the altar is *Ste Quitterie in Glory*. The end of the apse is still concealed beneath 18C decoration but the northeast chapel was dedicated to St Philibert in the 19C, when it was entirely restored. Here are eight 12C capitals, one carrying a *Visitation* and scenes of vice, animals or monsters. Before descending to the crypt, note the waiting area between the apse and apsidal chapel created in the 14C, where the insane were retained (or restrained, there is still evidence of the manacles), leaving their families free to descend to the crypt and pray for sanity to be restored.

Stairs lead down to the original 4C–6C mausoleum or **crypt**, built around a spring which was no doubt the site of an ancient cult; the floor is scattered with Gallo-Roman fragments. Here lies the splendid early Christian (4C) **sarcophagus of St Quitterie** in white Pyrenean marble. The relics have disappeared but the iconography of the reliefs on the sarcophagus is important proof of the early existence of Christianity in this region. The carvings on the lid show the ***Sacrifice of Abraham***, the ***Healing of the Paralytic***, ***Jonah and the Whale*** (a monster in early Christianity), and ***Tobias and the Giant Fish***. On the main face from left to right are the ***Raising of Lazarus***, ***Daniel in the Lions' Den***, the ***Good Shepherd carrying the Lamb*** between the Church, with St Quitterie in her arms, and a veiled female representing the Synagogue, ***Adam and Eve with the Serpent***, and what might be the ***Creation of Man*** or the ***Baptism of Christ***. Jonah features again on the end faces. In the 11C chapel of St-Désiré opposite are 14C paintings with the coats of arms of the great Gascon families, and the ***Annunciation***, ***Nativity*** and ***Adoration of the Magi***. Speak aloud to the altar and your voice will echo around the crypt.

The miraculous fountain whose water was considered to have healing properties, site of Quitterie's martyrdom, is on Rue du Château below the church.

There are a number of picturesque villages and sites in the neighbourhood of Aire-sur-l'Adour which are worth a glimpse, such as the small 15C/19C **Château du Lau** at Duhort-Bachen on the D39. Open in summer Mon–Fri by appointment; ☎ 05 58 71 51 89, email lelau@wanadoo.fr. There is a fine pulpit in the 15C church at Renung, further on.

The capital of the old region of Tursan, **Geaune**, southwest of Aire on the D2, was a *bastide* established by the English in 1318. **Pimbo** due south on the D111 was a pilgrimage halt on the journey from Le Puy to Compostela: the 12C collegiate church of St-Barthélémy provided shelter. It is mainly 14C, with a few fragments of Romanesque sculpture. Guided visits; ☎ 05 58 44 49 18. Pimbo was the oldest *bastide* in the Landes, jointly founded in 1268 by the Canons of Pimbo and the representative of Henry III. It also has a botanic garden.

Samadet, west of Geaune, is a little town of pretty coloured façades stretched out along a ridge which produced faience (glazed earthenware) in the 18C. Earthenware, which had appeared in France in the mid-16C, gained in popularity because of restrictions on silverware at the time of Louis XIV. A Manufacture Royale was established in 1732–1838 thanks to the Marquis de Roquepine, Abbot and Baron of Samadet. The **Musée de la Faïence et des Arts de la Table** has an excellent collection of faïence from Asia and traces the evolution of tableware in France from the Middle Ages to the 19C. Open April–Oct 10.00–12.00 and 14.00–19.00; Nov–March 14.00–18.00; closed Mon, 1 Jan, 1 May, 1 Nov, 11 Nov, 25 Dec; ☎ 05 58 79 11 56.

The small town of **Hagetmau** south of St-Sever has a well-kept centre with a complicated one-way system. On the outskirts, just off the D933 ring road, is the Romanesque **Crypte St-Girons**, a tiny vestige of a once-important abbey dedicated to the 4C saint. The crypt was the traditional burial place of Girons and contains a remarkable group of sculptures. The abbey survived until 1904, when it was demolished leaving just the present low building. It was restored 1905–08, but little work has been done since. Open July, Aug 15.00–18.00, or check with the *mairie*; ☎ 05 58 05 77 77. Steps descend into a marvellous space which is an extended polygon with a Gothic ribbed vault. The saint's tomb was placed at the centre of the crypt, framed by four free-standing antique marble columns. The 14 capitals of these columns plus the two engaged columns and eight stone wall piers are 12C. The capitals carry sculptures which are deeply cut and display a variety of figures, birds, lions and imaginary beasts. Of the free-standing capitals, one has confused scenes of damnation, another a vigorous image of a man and birds, and the third is clearly recognisable as the parable of *Lazarus and Dives*. The engaged capital on the south wall carries the *Deliverance of St Peter from Prison*.

Just off the D18 at **Maylis** is an Olivetian abbey (a branch of the Benedictine order) dedicated to Notre-Dame, which is famous for the Gregorian chant sung regularly at mass, and for the *tisane* produced here; ☎ 05 58 97 72 81. The village is on a ridge with views over the Chalosse, and the church is a very creamily restored neo-Gothic pile with a statue of Our Lady. A short distance to the south is a beautifully simple 14C chapel in dark stone restored by the monks.

This corner of France is rich in prehistory and near St-Cricq-en-Chalosse, south of Maylis on the D2, a flowery village with a tiny arena, is **Le Chemin de la Préhistoire**. Open July, Aug, Mon, Tues, Thur–Sun 10.00–12.00 and 14.30–18.30, closed Wed; ☎ 05 58 79 86 99. This ambitious journey through prehistory starts in the Neolithic period (*c* 5000 years ago) and travels as far back as the mid-Paleolithic (*c* 60,000 years ago). Those who like to get mucky (in French) can experience hands-on practice in prehistoric skills such as making flints, producing fire and throwing pots.

A celebrated site in the annals of prehistory is the village of **Brassempouy**, further south on the D58. Here, in the Grotte du Pape 3km from the village, an ivory carving known as the *Venus of Brassempouy* or the *Lady with the Hood* came to light in 1894 (now in the Musée des Antiquités Nationales at St-Germain-en-Laye). This beautiful little head (36.5mm long) was carved from mammoth tusk *c* 21,000 BC and is considered one of the oldest carvings ever found. The Musée de la Préhistoire specialises in female representations in prehistory and describes excavations during the 19C. Open daily June–Sept 10.00–12.00 and 14.30–18.30; Oct–mid-Dec 14.00–18.00; March–May 14.00–18.00; ☎ 05 58 89 21 73. There are visits to the caves during digs. Also in the village is the part-Romanesque church of St-Sernin, built on an ancient castle mound.

The charming **Château de Gaujacq** and Plantarium lie on the D58 between Brassempouy and Bastennes. House open mid-Feb to mid-Nov, guided visits at 15.00, 16.00, 17.00; June also 18.00; July, Aug also 11.00, 14.00. Garden open 14.30–18.30; both closed Wed; ☎ 05 58 89 01 01. This beautiful site was occupied in the Gallo-Roman and medieval periods. The present château was built in 1693 by the Marquis de Sourdis, godson of Henri IV and brother of Cardinal François de Sourdis, Archbishop of Bordeaux (pp 64, 80). The house, very Palladian and quite unusual in France, is single storey arranged around four sides of a rectangular garden court, with a continuous Ionic arcade of 44 arches. The gardens of the court are laid out fairly informally and some magnificent 150-year-old *Magnolia grandiflora* shade the house.

The visitor entrance is on the northwest, and the visit includes a large part of the privately owned and still inhabited château. The apartments for the numerous domestic staff in the 18C—concierge, surgeon and gardener—are used for exhibitions. The main reception rooms on the southeast, with views towards the Pyrenees and the Luy Valley, have conserved their 17C and18C décor and furnishings, and some floors of Pyrenean marble. Louis XIV played billiards in what is now the large dining room and the small apartments of the Marquis de Sourdis have 17C panelling, some painted. One room is arranged as a memorial to Cardinal Sourdis, who died in Gaujacq in 1707. Throughout the house there is an interesting collection of furniture and *objets d'art*. The botanic gardens or **Plantarium** behind the house, created in 1986, are a delight. They contain, in eight main flower beds, a large collection of shrubs and perennials planted to combine English informality with French structure.

The **Château d'Amou** near the D158, an excellent example of 17C Classicism built in 1678 by Léonard de Caupenne, Governor of Bayonne and Marquis of Amou, is still in the same family. Guided visits 15.00, 16.00, 17.00; closed Mon in July and second half of August; ☎ 05 58 89 00 08. There is also a Romanesque church in Amou.

The main town at the heart of the Chalosse, a fertile and sometimes lush region watered by the River Louts and renowned for beef cattle and *foie gras*, is **Montfort-en-Chalosse** on the D32 between St-Sever and Dax. The church goes back to the 11C, with a Romanesque nave and Gothic additions.

Local rural traditions and the tranquillity of this part of the Landes are reflected in the **Musée de la Chalosse** on the outskirts of Montfort, a part open-air museum which is not at all dusty or fusty (it includes a multimedia library). Open April–Oct, Tues–Fri 10.00–12.00 and 14.00–18.30, Sat, Sun and PH 14.00–18.30; Nov–March, Tues–Fri 14.00–18.00, closed Mon and 15–31 Dec; ☎ 05 58 98 69 27. To the right of the courtyard is the reception building and space for temporary exhibitions. Opposite is the beautifully restored *maison de maître* (1649), a substantial gabled farmhouse which typically has one long and one short roof and deep overhanging eaves. The stone surrounds of openings are left exposed and the doors and shutters painted in *bleu de Chalosse*. Inside the farmhouse the rooms—kitchen, dining room, bedrooms—are furnished in the style of a well-to-do 19C farming family and there is a display of *quilles de neuf*, a version of skittles played in the Landes and the Béarn. An arched two-storey building leads to the farmyard where you will find a bread oven and cellar, an ancient local breed of pig, and a pair of Chalosse oxen named Yoan and Martin; there are also a vegetable garden and vines.

For aficionados of Romanesque there are examples, or partial examples, of churches in the Chalosse going back to the 6C in Nerbis, Montaut, and St-Cricq Chalosse; to the 11C foundations in Bergouey, Doazit, Larbey, Caupenne; and 11C–12C at Laurede, Baigts and St-Aubin.

Dax

The spa town of Dax on the south bank of the Adour is the second largest in the *département*. The long exploitation of the hot, muddy, mineral-laden water for which it is famous, used in the treatment of rheumatism and other complaints, has led to Dax's rank of *première station thermale de France*. Therefore hotels and shops are plentiful, and it is surrounded by parks and gardens. The town combines a certain towelling-robed gentility with a tendency to scruffiness and it is not immediately obvious why non-cure visitors should gather here.

History

Roman *Aquae Tarbellicae* was established on an island and the city built on wooden piles. As the community spread onto the mainland the lake was filled in and by the 4C an area of some 8ha was enclosed in walls 1465m long. Christianity was introduced in the 4C by Vincent de Xaintes, bishop and martyr, whose relics were translated in the 11C to the site of the present cathedral. A castle built in the Middle Ages, reputedly by Richard the Lionheart, was demolished in the 19C, as were the Roman and medieval walls which had survived virtually intact until then, leaving some 300m standing. At this point Dax began to expand beyond its Roman confines and the spa facilities were modernised. Dax now boasts 18 thermal treatment centres which attract around 55,000 *curistes* a year.

Across Place Thiers from the tourist office is **Parc Borda**, bounded to the south by the surviving fragments of Gallo-Roman walls. In the park is the arena built in 1913 for the summer *férias*. Many of the thermal baths and spa hotels are strung out along the river to the west, beyond which, in the Bois de Boulogne, is the Trou des Pauvres, an ancient public baths. The principal monument of a town somewhat lacking in them is the **Fontaine Chaude** or Source de la Nèhe. The hot springs are contained in a rectangular pool enclosed in iron railings and a three-arched Doric portico, an early 19C successor to several Roman and medieval versions. The pool is fed by water at a temperature of between 60–64°C, which forces its way through more than 2000m of rock to arrive at the surface totally unpolluted but rich in minerals. It can be sampled from taps disguised as lion-heads decorating the fountain.

South of Rue Fontaine-Chaude are pedestrianised streets leading to the cathedral (see below). Behind the elegant wrought-iron gate of the Hôtel St-Martin-d'Agès (1650), in Rue Cazade, is the local archaeology museum, the **Musée Borda**, named after the mathematician and sailor Jean-Charles de Borda, born in Dax in 1733. He explored new techniques in shipbuilding and created new navigational instruments. Open Tues–Sat 14.00–18.00, closed Mon, Sun and PH; ☎ 05 58 74 12 91. It houses Gallo-Roman and medieval finds, including 1C AD bronzes found in Dax in 1982, mosaics, ceramics and sculpture. There are also 18C–19C paintings and a room dedicated to Borda. In the **Musée Georgette Dupouy** at the same address (☎ 05 58 56 04 34) is a collection of works by this 20C artist. The **crypte archéologique** at 27 Rue Cazade is all that remains of a 2C Gallo-Roman temple, part of which can be seen from the street. To visit, enquire at the Borda museum.

A statue in Place de la Cathédrale refers to the legend that the properties of the muddy water of Dax were recognised when a Roman centurion's ailing dog was cured after falling into a warm spring. The **Cathédrale Notre-Dame** is a rather bland, Neo-classical affair (rebuilt 1683–1719), but it does have an interesting Gothic portal inside.

A cathedral existed here from 1102. The Romanesque church apparently suffered badly at the hands of the English in 1295, as a Gothic version was begun in the second half of the 13C. This building survived until Huguenots desecrated it in the 17C and, with the exception of the façade and sacristy, the ruins were demolished. The post-Reformation cathedral, designed by Pierre

Battut, was inspired by the 17C domed church of St-Paul-St-Louis in Paris. It was consecrated in 1755. The Gothic sacristy was demolished in 1890, and in 1894 the Gothic doorway of the Apostles was moved to its present location.

The interior is an imposing mixture of Classical and Baroque with giant orders which have Rococo-type friezes. The 13C **Apostles portal**, which makes the visit worthwhile, is in the north transept. On the central trumeau is a modern figure of Christ flanked by the 12 Apostles with their attributes, and on the tympanum above is the traditional iconography of a *Last Judgement*, including the figures of Christ, the Virgin and St John, the separation of the saved from the damned, and the appropriate punishments for the latter. The grandiose main altar (1751) of coloured marble is the work of the Mazetti brothers, the authors of many altarpieces in the region, as is the altar of the Virgin (1765). The fine choir stalls with sculptures and misericords are 16C–17C, the pulpit is 18C, and the organ case dates from 1786 onwards.

On the edge of the town, at the end of Boulevard Carnot, is the mediocre 19C church dedicated to **St-Vincent-de-Xaintes**, the site of the cathedral before 1055. Many Merovingian sarcophagi were found nearby as well as a 3C mosaic which was restored and placed in the present church. **Parc du Sarrat** was created in the 19C (restored in 1995), and has themed gardens containing rare plants and a house, redesigned in 1959, in the style of Frank Lloyd Wright.

Tucked away in the modern town of **St-Paul-Lès-Dax** is a tiny, part-Romanesque church. By car, cross the Adour and head north to the N124, then west towards Bayonne and follow the signs. The main interest of the church is the exterior of the chevet which is decorated with 14 carved capitals in white and coloured marble and 11 inset plaques of hard white marble. The sculptures, somewhat reminiscent of St-Sernin in Toulouse, include an *Angel at Christ's Tomb* and the *Holy Women*, bearded men on thrones, the *Last Supper*, which is the most celebrated, *Judas' Betrayal*, the *Crucifixion*, *Samson*, *St Veronica*, and the *Resurrection*. Two capitals stand out: one is carved with animals which have horses' heads and talons for feet and a figure with two bodies but one head; and another with an acrobat and musicians. The Gothic nave disappeared in the restorations of 1857, but the east is fairly intact with a barrel-vault over the chancel and an apse with 11 niches.

St-Vincent-de-Paul, east of St-Paul-Lès-Dax, originally called Pouy, took the name of the saint who was born there in 1581. Monsieur Vincent dedicated his life to working with the poor and suffering, founded charitable and educational institutions, and was active in the reform of the Catholic Church. He died in 1660 and was canonised in 1737.

Various routes converge on the north bank of the Gaves Réunis at **Peyrehorade**. The town has a particularly good market and is one of the few places where *pibales* (elvers) are still fished in the winter. Of monuments it has few, just a bit of the 16C Château Montréal built by the Viscounts of Orthez and the keep of the Château d'Apremont, but nearby are two interesting abbeys, d'Arthous and Sorde.

Abbaye d'Arthous

Between Hastingues and Peyrehorade, in what was originally a remote wooded valley, is the former abbey of Arthous, founded *c* 1167 by Premonstratensian friars from Case-Dieu in the Gers. Although seriously desecrated over the centuries, substantial and lengthy restorations have been carried out recently and the abbey is well worth a visit. The church is open March–Oct 09.00–12.00 and 14.00–18.00; check winter opening times; ☎ 05 58 73 03 89.

The Premonstratensians were dedicated to preaching, poverty and work. Essentially they were cattle breeders but their abbey grew rich from donations of land and animals and the reception of pilgrims. In the late 13C during the English occupation of Aquitaine, the abbot and Edward I signed a *paréage* to found Hastingues (see below) on abbey lands. The abbey was hardly touched by the Hundred Years War but was badly damaged in 1523 during the war between François I and Charles I of Spain (Emperor Charles V), and again in 1571 by Protestant iconoclasts. There were phases of rebuilding in the 17C and 18C, but by the time of the Revolution the monastery was much depleted and only three canons remained. Used as a farm after 1791, the abbey continued to deteriorate until it passed to the Conseil Général of the Landes in 1964. It is now a heritage education centre.

The first thing you come to is the exterior of the **chevet**, the highlight of the church. Double engaged columns run the entire height of the apse, and the three small windows are framed by smaller columns and capitals. The decorations include billet mouldings, carved corbels with a variety of decorative motifs, and sculpted capitals. One capital on the southeastern side of the apse represents the *Flight into Egypt*.

Beyond, gates lead into a courtyard, enclosed by the church to the south, and to the north and west by 17C buildings in fairly good condition, although little remains on the east. A new museum, partly archaeological, partly local history, **Musée de l'Histoire du Pays d'Orthe**, is planned for autumn 2003 in conjunction with the Centre Départemental du Patrimoine, a study centre in the abbey which opened in 2002.

The **church**, dedicated to Notre-Dame, was probably begun soon after the foundation of the abbey and spans the transition from Romanesque to Gothic. The vast, aisleless nave was divided in two in 1727 and the damaged western part acquired a secular use. The east end is tripartite and the transept arms do not extend beyond the chapels. The vaults over the apse and north apsidal chapel are Romanesque, whereas the south chapel has early rib vaults and the transept slightly pointed barrel vaults. The ribs of the crossing are 14C, and the nave originally had a wooden ceiling supported by diaphragm arches springing from capitals; it was vaulted much later. The capitals in the apse have similar foliate designs to those on the exterior but are technically more confident. The capitals in the south transept are more evolved, although damaged, and include one with stylised vegetation from which a centaur shoots an arrow. In the south nave is a rare surviving example of interlacing and flowers. Carving on the old tympanum of the west door represents, on the right, the *Virgin and Child*, with Joseph and a star, and on the left two Magi, but the central part has disappeared.

The tiny *bastide* of **Hastingues**, perched on a promontory commanding the valley of the Gaves Réunis, was named after John Hastings, the English Governor of Gascony, when founded in 1289 by Edward I. Of the fortifications added in 1303, just one gateway and a section of wall remain. It was attacked in the 16C and 17C, but several 15C and 16C houses have survived on the square and main street, the most notable among them being the *mairie*. Disappointingly the church is 17C–19C. The **Aire d'Hastingues** (motorway service area) on the A64 (between Pau and Bayonne) has made a feature of the fact that it is a few kilometres from the crossroads of three of the four major pilgrimage routes to Santiago de Compostela in northwestern Spain (for the French, St-Jacques-de-Compostelle). The exhibition building was inspired by the scallop shell, symbol of the pilgrimage, and the visitor is led through a very well-presented exhibition along symbolic routes which develop the historic, spiritual and practical themes of the pilgrimage.

Sorde l'Abbaye

To the southeast of Peyrehorade on the D29, the village of **Sorde l'Abbaye** is strung out between the foot of a cliff and the lush banks of the Gave d'Oloron. Its *raison d'être* was a powerful Benedictine abbey situated near a ford where a Roman villa had once existed. A toll bridge was built in 1289 and two years later the village acquired *bastide* status. Some remnants of the protective walls of the old town survive and the main street, Rue Laville, runs past what is left of the west gate and leads to the square on the north flank of the abbey. At right angles to the main street is a road running past the west front of the church to the river and the old abbey mill (*c* 1100), transformed into a small hydro-electric generating station in 1923. A salmon ladder is a reminder of how important these fish were to the abbey in the Middle Ages but now the numbers have declined, and salmon have been replaced as a major source of income by kiwi fruit cultivated on the islands in the Gave. Four of the five medieval dykes still exist and, further west along the river bank, is the Bourgneuf fountain and communal washhouse, used until 1960. In the village are a few examples of typical farmhouses of the Pays d'Orthe.

Since prehistoric times man has lived here where the river was fordable and the cliffs provided shelter. In the Gallo-Roman period it developed into a staging post on the Bordeaux–Pamplona road. The abbey, first mentioned in a document of 975, grew rich and powerful from donations and pilgrims who stopped here before crossing the Gave d'Oloron, the last major obstacle before the Col de Roncevaux (p 427). Sorde abbey was marked by the French–Spanish conflict in 1523, by the Wars of Religion in 1569 and in 1665, in common with many important abbeys, it came under the control of the Congregation of St-Maur, who restored and rebuilt it. At the Revolution this all ended, the abbey buildings were confiscated and sold, and the church passed to the parish. The owners of the abbey gave the property to the abbey of Belloc (near Bayonne) in 1980, and they returned it to the commune in 1995. The abbot's house is still privately owned.

The church of **St-Jean-de-Sorde** was begun at the end of the 11C, and despite inevitable damage and rebuilds is still a handsome structure. It has retained its overall Romanesque outline, but only in the east end has the 11C structure survived in the shape of a large main apse flanked by transept chapels which appear to have been heightened in the Gothic period. The north transept (12C), in an attractive combination of stone and brick, with scorch marks, is unusually flanked by a square tower on the northwest. The surround of the transept door flows over onto the base of the tower and, despite damage, it is an interesting example of Romanesque art. The seven consecutive arches, supported by columns and capitals, show versions of the *Wise and Foolish Virgins*, the months of the year and the signs of the zodiac. An image of *Christ in Majesty* on the tympanum is just recognisable. Gothic elements were added to the upper part of the transept, including a *chemin de ronde* (walkway), blind tracery, a pointed arch framing a simple rose window, and a pendant over the door. The south transept also has a rose window and a little *clocher-mur* (belfry).

The cavernous interior bears witness to many alterations and there is little evidence of the original church except in the east. The southwest pillar of the transept still carries its old capitals and, despite major restoration to the apse in the 19C, the capitals at the entrance to each of the transept chapels are apparently original. They present episodes from the *Life of Christ*, with north, *Daniel in the Lions' Den* and *Christ's Arrest in the Garden of Gethsemane*, and south, the *Virgin and Child* and *Presentation at the Temple*. The greatest surprise, however, is the magnificent 11C **mosaics** behind the main altar, possibly inspired by the Roman mosaics in the abbot's lodgings, and decorated with geometric patterns, intersecting spheres, animals and birds. The main altar is an elaborate affair in 10 different marbles produced by the Swiss-Italian brothers Mazetti in 1784. The five-bay nave, on a bit of a slant, has always been aisled. It was remodelled in the late 13C or early 14C and re-vaulted in the 17C, leaving the 12C vault responds with no function. In the nave is a model of the church in the 18C.

The entrance to the **monastic buildings** is behind the east end of the church. Guided visits every 30mins in summer, some in English; April–mid-Nov 10.30–12.00 and 14.30–18.30, closed Mon; mid-Oct–March, Mon–Fri 09.00–12.00 and 13.30–16.30; ☎ 05 58 73 09 62. The conventual buildings south of the church leading down to the river were badly damaged in the 13C and those still standing date mainly from the 17C–18C. The visit starts with the physic garden, chapter house and cloister, which can only be guessed at and are rather uninteresting. But it livens up when you reach the terrace overlooking the Gave in front of the vast main wing of the abbey, because beneath the terrace is a unique underground gallery or cryptoporticus, built *c* 1710. Steps lead down to a long passageway with arcades along its length on the river side and a series of 14 cells, some with their original doors, where supplies were kept. Below this level is a dock and fish tank, where salmon were landed and prepared for the kitchen. (The only other of its kind in France is at Haute-Combe in Savoie.)

The 16C **abbot's house**, with a stairtower and mullioned windows (closed at the time of writing) was built over medieval lodgings which in turn had been constructed on the remains of a Roman villa. Much of the villa (3C and 4C) has been excavated revealing the thermae, hypocaust and about 15 Roman mosaics.

In the extreme south of the Department of the Landes, west of Peyrehorade on the north bank of the Adour, is about 110ha of marshland known as the **Barthes de l'Adour**, rich in regional flora and fauna (250 species of migrant birds collect here annually) which has been protected since 1984. Open all year, raised hides; information from the reception at Pontonx or ☎ 05 58 90 18 69.

18 The Gers: Gascony

The heart of old Gascony, the land of swashbuckling swordsmen and musketeers, virtually coincides with the *département* of Gers (the 's' is pronounced). The Gers, the most westerly of the eight *départements* of the Midi-Pyrénées, turns historically and culturally to Aquitaine rather than to the Languedoc but the Gascon language, still sometimes heard in a market place, is a local version of Occitan.

The Duchy of Gascony was formed in 852, defined by the wide arc of the Garonne to north and east and the Pyrenees to the south. Gascony was joined to Aquitaine in 1036, and was subjected to English domination in the 12C, resolved only in the 15C at the end of the Hundred Years War. The proliferation of *castelnaux* (communities protected by castle walls), *sauvetés* (protected by the Church) and *bastides* (planned towns with economic and political advantages) between the 11C and 14C are an integral part of the Gers.

As time went on, Gascony was controlled by three main feudal dynasties: Foix-Béarn, Armagnac, and Albret, and in 1527 Henri II d'Albret inherited the House of Armagnac through his marriage to Marguerite d'Angoulème. Their daughter Jeanne d'Albret inherited all three great Gascon domains and at her death in 1572 these passed to her son, Henri of Navarre (p 436). These territories were reunited with France on his accession as King of France in 1589.

The landscape is characterised by shallow valleys and softly undulating ridges determined by the Gers and other small rivers which rise in the foothills of the Pyrenees and fan out on their way north. These days 37 per cent of the sparse population of the *département* is concerned with agriculture. Vines are cultivated on the slopes in the north and west, while sweeping fields of wheat and maize cover the plains. The Gers may not have the sharp contrasts of landscape of the other departments of the Midi-Pyrénées but it does offer such varied experiences as *corridas* (bullfights), motor racing and jazz. It is also synonymous with Armagnac brandy and a hearty rustic gastronomy, with dishes based on goose fat.

LECTOURE, FLEURANCE AND THE LOMAGNE

Between the Rivers Gers and Garonne is the Lomagne, the name of a former duchy of Gascony, which sits astride the meeting point of the three departments, Gers, Tarn-et-Garonne and Lot-et-Garonne. This is an important agricultural area especially famed for the production of white garlic. Of particular interest is Lectoure, in the Gers, the main town of the Lomagne.

Getting there and around
Car

Autoroute A62 between Toulouse and Bordeaux: exit 7 and N21 to Lectoure/Fleurance/Auch; exit 8 and D 40 to St-Clar;
exit 9, and N113/D928 to Beaumont-de-Lomagne.

Bus

Agen to Auch via Lectoure, Fleurance.

Tourist information

82500 Beaumont-de-Lomagne 3 Rue Fermat, ☎/fax 05 63 65 51 17
32500 Fleurance 1121 bis Rue de la République, ☎ 05 62 64 00 00, fax 05 62 06 27 80, email

tourismefleurance@free.fr

32700 Lectoure Pl. du Général-de-Gaulle, ☎ 05 62 68 76 98, fax 05 62 68 79 30, email ot.lectoure@wanadoo.fr

32380 St-Clar Pl. de la Mairie, ☎ 05 62 66 34 45, fax 05 62 66 32 17, www.saint-clar-de-lomagne.com

Market days

Beaumont-de-Lomagne Saturday and small-scale wholesale garlic market Tuesday and Saturday, June–September

Lectoure Friday

St-Clar Thursday and very small-scale wholesale garlic market Thursday, July–Oct

Canal cruises

Bateau mouche trips depart from Montech: ☎ 05 63 04 48 28

Festivals and events

July *Ail de Lomagne en Fête*, celebration of white garlic, Beaumont-de-Lomagne

August *Au fil de l'eau—une Histoire*, on the canal port, a great sound and light show, Valence-d'Agen

Festival du ciel et de l'espace, astronomy and astrology, Fleurance

Where to stay and eating out

82500 BEAUMONT-DE-LOMAGNE

☆☆/€–€€ *Le Commerce*, 58 Ave du Maréchal-Foch, ☎ 05 63 02 31 02, fax 05 63 65 26 22. Great value food and comfortable rooms.

32000 FLEURANCE

☆☆☆ *Le Fleurance*, Rte d'Agen, ☎ 05 62 06 14 85, fax 05 62 64 05 12, www.occitania.com/lefleurance. A relaxing setting, some rooms with balconies or private gardens, and high-quality cooking.

32700 LECTOURE

☆☆/€€ *Le Bastard*, Rue Lagrange, ☎ 05 62 68 82 44, fax 05 62 68 76 81. An excellent restaurant and well-appointed hotel in an elegant late-18C town house.

32340 MIRADOUX

Chambres d'hôte, Lou Casau, ☎ 05 62 28 73 58, fax 05 62 28 73 17. A warm welcome and attractive surroundings on offer at this 19C house at the heart of the *bastide*; pool and terrace.

Chambres d'hôte, André and Béatrice Lanusse-Cazale, Lou Casâu, 5 Pl. de la Halle, ☎ 05 62 28 73 58, fax 05 62 28 73 17. The owners make you welcome in their 18C house in this small village. Pool, garden and terrace.

32380 ST-CLAR

La Garlande, ☎ 05 62 66 47 31, fax 05 62 66 47 70, email nicole.cournot@wanadoo.fr. An arcaded house in this delightful *bastide*, with enclosed garden and three ensuite *chambres d'hôtes*.

Chambres d'hôte, Jean-François and Nicole Cournot, La Garlande, Pl. de la Mairie, ☎ 05 62 66 47 31, fax 05 62 66 47 70, email nicole.cournot@wanadoo.fr. Rooms in a large house which is part of the 13C market place of the village.

Lectoure

Lectoure is a town that appears *bien dans sa peau*, confident in its ancient if turbulent past, at ease behind its refined and genteel Neo-classical façades, and solid as the rock it is built on despite the narrowness of the ridge. The three main monuments in Lectoure, the cathedral, the museum and the fountain of Diana, are at the east end of the town which has one main street running one-way, east–west. The tourist office is next to the church.

History

Lectoure, capital of the Lomagne, was the site of an *oppidum* occupied by a Gallic tribe, the Lactorates, who circumspectly surrendered to the Roman invaders c 120 BC. Subsequently the Gallo-Roman city, capital of Novempopulania, flourished on the plain at a crossroads. The high ground was reserved for the temples dedicated to Jupiter and, more importantly, to Cybele, ancient Phrygian earth goddess, in whose cult the ritual sacrifice of the bull and ram, symbols of strength and fertility, was important. A remarkable find of altars decorated with bull's heads (now on display in the museum) was made in 1540 when the city wall was demolished east of the cathedral.

In the Middle Ages Lectoure was the main residence of the Viscounts of Lomagne and then became the headquarters of the powerful Counts of Armagnac until the siege of Lectoure, between November 1472 and March 1473, when Louis XI's troops invaded and ransacked the town and murdered Count Jean V. Soon afterwards the town was reborn as a royal seneschalcy, only to suffer again during the Wars of Religion.

In the 13C Bishop Giraud de Monlezun took a pledge of allegiance to Edward I of England, and built an episcopal residence and repaired the cathedral. The **Cathédrale St-Gervais-et-St-Protais** is a fairly complex structure which has suffered the horrors of war and the caprices of individuals. The plain west façade was erected in the 15C and has been subjected to many modifications and obvious restoration. Supported by two angle buttresses, the low arch of the entrance is a 19C replacement and the series of ten niches above the door has almost melted away, such is the fragility of the limestone. The fenestration is modest, with only a three-light window and a small oculus. The belfry on the north is impressive but not as impressive as it once was. The original version was demolished by Louis XI's army during the siege of Lectoure when the cathedral was part of the city defences. A tall spire was erected in the 15C, but had to be demolished, along with the upper level of the belfry, in the 18C. The five stepped levels, more ornate towards the top, are supported by angle buttresses which lost their statues in the Revolution. A tall isolated gabled buttress on the north flank of the cathedral indicates the incomplete rebuild of the choir in the 16C. The east and south sides of the cathedral can be seen from the adjacent Jardins des Marronniers and the courtyard of the Hôtel de Ville respectively.

Inside, a choir with apse and ambulatory in the style of the north of France was grafted to the single nave and the transition from nave to chancel is effected by an awkward triumphal arch partly obstructing the view of the high choir vaults. The two square bays of the nave are defined by six massive piers, the cores of which are Romanesque and were designed to carry domes in the manner of Cahors or Souillac; perhaps this plan was never completed, because at the end of the 12C the nave was vaulted. Repairs to the nave were carried out in 1480, and at the beginning of the 16C vaulted chapels were inserted and more alterations followed in the 17C and 18C. The reconstruction of the chancel and apse began in the 16C, at which time the five square chapels in the east were completed with massive triangular sections of masonry between them. Only in 1600 were the ten cylindrical piers introduced to create the ambulatory. The choir vaults have three polychromed pendant bosses and the carved early 17C choir stalls were placed here in the 19C. The chapel to the left of the choir has an 18C altar and elegant wrought iron, as well as a white marble statue of the *Assumption of the Virgin*, probably Italian. The Sacré-Coeur chapel has a series of 17C easel paintings of the *Passion*, and in two chapels are carved oak communion rails. The former baptistery contains a museum of sacred art.

The **Hôtel de Ville** (1676–82), contiguous with the cathedral, was originally the episcopal palace. A majestically regular but unadorned building with numerous windows, its brick vaulted kitchen and cellars have been transformed into a fascinating **Musée Archéologique de Lectoure**, opened in 1972. The building does not always appear to be open when in fact it is; tickets are sold by the concièrge, on the left as you enter. The entrance to the museum is to the right, below the magnificent cantilevered staircase set off by the scrolling outlines of the wrought-iron balustrade. Open 10.00–12.00 and 14.00–18.00; closed Tues; ☎ 05 62 68 70 22.

The seven rooms of the museum are arranged chronologically, the first part dedicated to local palaeontology. The Gallic era is represented by burial pits of the second half of the 1C BC, sculptures, pottery—including huge amphorae for wine—and coins. The showpiece, **20 pagan altars** from the 2C and 3C, are mainly in Pyrenean marble and decorated with the head of a bull (*taurobole*) or a ram (*criobole*). The engraved inscription on each stone records the date of the initiation ceremony involving the sacrifice of a bull or ram, and the name of the receiver of the rites. This unique collection of altars was always recognised as exceptional, yet in 1591 they were re-used at the base of the pillars of the *halle aux grains* where they stayed until 1842; by 1874 they were in the *mairie*. There are other pagan and Christian funerary monuments, sarcophagi, and mosaics exhibited in an attractive vaulted chamber dated 1680, one with an awesome portrayal of the god Oceanus.

On leaving the Hôtel de Ville turn left and left again down to the bottom of Rue Fontelié to the **Fontaine de Diane**, a spring and pool covered by a 13C vaulted construction with a double-arched opening and 15C iron grille. Water from this spring was used at the **royal tannery**, further down the street, now the Maison d'Ydrone retirement home. This important workshop (built 1752–54) was one of the most advanced in its day and employed over 100 people. A double flight of steps leads down into the yard, and above the industrial building is a pretty ironwork gable which once contained the works' clock.

Turn left up the Chemin de Ste-Clair which follows the old city walls enclosing public gardens, cross the main road and continue on to the northwest side of town and the former home of the executioner, the 14C **Tour du Bourreau**, part of the old town walls. Wind your way back through the old streets past the **Hôtel de Castaing-Bastard** in Rue Lagrange, now converted to a hotel-restaurant (see above), an elegant building with fine stucco and fireplaces inside. Back on Rue Nationale, just after the corner with Rue des Frères Danzas is the 13C **Tour d'Albinhac**. To the west of the town is Cours d'Armagnac and, on the site of the castle of the Counts of Armagnac, is the hospital, begun in 1760 and completed in 1809–12. Behind the hospital on Allées Montmorency are the remains of the castle where the Duc de Montmorency was imprisoned after the battle of Castelnaudary (Aude) before being executed in Toulouse in 1632 for opposing Richelieu (p 49). Complete the amble along Boulevard Jean Jaurès, built on the southern ramparts.

Fleurance

Fleurance, situated on the Gers River, south of Lectoure, and conveniently located on the N21 between Agen and Auch, is one of the best-known *bastides* and one of the main commercial centres of the Gers today, but it is not quite as impressive as its Tuscan namesake. The co-founder, Eustache de Beaumarchais, was instrumental in the creation of many *bastides* in Gascony and the Toulousain and had a penchant for naming his foundations after foreign towns (e.g. Pampelonne, Grenade, Cologne).

The buildings that surround the 60m sq arcaded *place* are 18C but were undoubtedly laid out to the plan of the original *bastide*, founded *c* 1272. The houses on the west and east are the best conserved and many have good wrought iron. The wonderful Neo-classical *halle* (1834–37) is a serious work on two floors designed by an architect from Auch called Ardenne. At its exterior angles are fountains with graceful statues in bronze, by A. Durenne, representing the four seasons.

The amply proportioned church of **Notre-Dame et St-Jean-Baptiste** was begun during the last third of the 13C. Three successive campaigns of building from the 14C to the 16C, and a difference in the level of the site from west to east of about 4m, contributed to the mixture of materials and the unevenness of the exterior elevations as well as to the varying heights and arrangement of the roofs. To absorb the thrust of the high nave, small flying buttresses in brick were used for the first time in the region. The west elevation, entirely in stone, was deprived of much of its decoration during attacks on the town by the Huguenots. Twelve corbels above the portal signify the existence at one time of a covered gallery, and the outline of arches on the north are all that remain of a chapel. The lower part of the belfry is said to be an ancient Gallo-Roman tower and the octagonal Toulousain-style belfry, in stone, was completed at the beginning of the 15C.

The interior is dark as there are only small clerestory windows and, typical of the Midi, there is little integral decoration. The three earlier east bays of the nave have quadripartite vaults and the west bays tierceron ribs. The discrepancy in floor levels was dealt with in the 18C, resulting in the disappearance of the bases of the eastern piers under the floor. The showpiece of the church is undoubtedly the three **windows** of the east end with Rayonnant tracery and stained glass by Arnaud de Moles and his workshop. They are thought to have been executed between 1506 and 1520. On the left in the main panels are St Laurence, Mary Magdalene and St Augustine; above is a *Pietà* and below the *Martyrdom of St Laurence*, *Noli me Tangere*, and *St Augustine's Conversion*. The central window has a large Trinity flanked by *Christ Resurrected* and the Virgin, with a choir of angels, and the *Crucifixion*. The third is a Jesse window crowned by the Virgin enthroned in a large flower. Among the furnishings is a 15C statue of the Virgin and Child—*Notre-Dame-de-Fleurance*—in the St-Jean chapel, the source of numerous miracles during the Wars of Religion, and three paintings by J.-B. Smets, of a family of Flemish painters living in Auch in the 18C. The 19C organ has been restored and is used for concerts during the summer.

The 13C Château de Miramont-Latour (south of Fleurance on the D241) has a collection of agricultural tools and objects. Open July, Aug, Thurs–Sun 15.00–19.00, ☎ 05 62 62 27 90.

Northeast of Lectoure by the D23 is the oldest *bastide* in the Gers, **Miradoux**, founded in 1253. It has an imposing but battered church, with a bare west end except for one rose and a pedimented Renaissance doorway. Across from the church is the *hôtel de ville* and built up against it a 16C *halle*.

Flamarens, further northeast up the D953, is a tiny place with a château (13C–15C) with one wing and a round machicolated tower looking out over the countryside. It was badly damaged by fire in 1943 and is under restoration but can be visited. Open July, Aug, Mon, Wed–Sun 10.00–12.00 and 1500–19.00, closed Tues. The Grossolles family owned the château from 1466 to 1882 and the arms of Hérard de Grossoles, Bishop of Condom (1521–43), with the date 1541, are above the door of the spectacularly ruined church. To the west of the village is the rather tired **Ecomusée de la Lomagne**, a museum of rural life centred around a typical 19C farm. Open daily 09.00–12.00 and 14.00–18.40; ☎ 05 62 28 64 13.

At the heart of the village of **Lachapelle**, east of the D40, resides a miniature rustic Baroque gem which offers a respite from medieval *bastides* and castles. The little church of St-Pierre (13C), attached to the château and originally its private chapel, became the parish church. The main interest lies inside. Open May–Oct, Mon, Wed–Sun 10.00–12.00 and 15.00–18.00, closed Tues; rest of year, Sat, Sun and PH 14.00–17.00; ☎ 05 63 94 12 28. Tiny though it is, the interior was entirely decked out in 1776 by a craftsman called Muraignon Champagne with an all-encompassing scheme of gilded and painted woodwork, panels, pilasters and mouldings. Around the nave a superimposed series of arcades and loggias imitates the interior of a theatre. Apart from the dusty aspidistras, there are furnishings of a similar quality to the woodwork, including a pulpit and altars of the same date, a 16C statue of Ste-Quitterie, some late 16C–early 17C choir stalls with carved misericords, a 17C *Virgin and Child*, a relic of St Prosper (born in Aquitaine *c* 390) that came from Rome in 1777, and a two-eagle lectern presented by Napoléon III. There was some damage at the Revolution and the church was reworked to a certain extent in the 19C, but during more recent restoration a ceiling was removed to reveal the original gilded vault above the altar.

Due east of Lectoure by the D40 is the part Gothic, part Renaissance **Château de Gramont**, an excellently restored castle beside the river Arratz, the ancient frontier between Gascony and Languedoc (now the frontier between Tarn-et-Garonne and Gers). Guided visits, May–Oct 10.00–12.00 and 14.00–19.00; rest of year 14.00–18.00; closed PH; ☎ 05 63 94 05 26.

It was first mentioned in 1215 when Simon de Montfort made it over to Eudes de Montaut; as a reminder of this the tower on the south is called Tour Simon de Montfort. The château was staunchly defended during the Hundred Years War by its *châtelain*, the Chevalier de Barbazan, who killed single-handed six soldiers of the English army and for this act of heroism was permitted not only to use the coat of arms of France but in 1432 was buried with the royals at St-Denis. Gramont was inherited in 1491 by a member of the Voisins family, one of whom, Aymeric, was inspired to transform the medieval castle into a sumptuous Renaissance palace. From 1642 it passed through several hands and was more or less abandoned until purchased in the 1960s, restored, and bequeathed to the state.

The visitors' entrance is through the Simon de Montfort tower opposite the church, where there is a small exhibition. The château is composed essentially of two unequal wings. The smaller, known as the Châtelet, abutting the Simon de Montfort tower, is the older, dating from the time of the Montaut family, and incorporates elements of the 13C, 14C and 15C. The monumental main entrance, with the arms of the Montaut family above, was erected in the 17C. The upper part of the tower was removed and the arrow slits and cross windows are 19C fantasies. Inside is a large courtyard with the later and much larger wing (*c* 1535–40), in bluish-grey limestone, on the north; here the Corinthian and Ionic orders are used casually. Steps lead up to the two doorways on the elevated ground-floor level. The garden façade, flanked by pavilions, is slightly more ordered, with pedimented smaller windows and larger ones with entablatures. Inside the main entrance on the north, also reached by an exterior platform, is a staircase with late-Gothic vaults with heavily moulded ribs.

The interior proportions and décor have been restored as far as possible, and the Grande Salle has a particularly fine monumental Renaissance fireplace. The upper floor of the Châtelet has been refurbished for exhibitions and concerts, which are held regularly at the château.

This is an important garlic-producing area and at certain seasons a slight whiff of garlic mingles with the scents of wild flowers. **St-Clar** south of Gramont is a *bastide* on a hill, founded jointly in 1289 by Edward I of England and the Bishop of Lectoure, Géraud de Monlezun, on the site of an earlier *sauveté*; this resulted in two arcaded squares corresponding to the different periods of development. The older area, the Castelviel, is now partly restored but its old church (12C and 14C) is in a poor state and cannot be visited. The later *bastide* has retained its original orthogonal layout around the main square with a covered *halle*, which consists of a simple roof supported by timber posts, contiguous with the rebuilt *maison commune* (19C). The church is a dull 19C neo-Gothic affair.

Just outside St-Clar is the **Château d'Avezan**, a severe 13C château on a bluff, with 15C and 17C additions. Open Apr–Oct 15.00–18.00; ☎ 05 62 66 45 93.

Beaumont-de-Lomagne is a pleasant *bourgade* with a mighty 14C covered market supported by a veritable forest of timbers. In the square is a statue of the mathematician Pierre Fermat (1601–65), who was born here. Beaumont, like St-Clar, has important markets for the high-quality white garlic grown in the Lomagne. The markets are not, unfortunately, held under the beautiful *halle* but at the *marché au forail* on Tuesdays and Saturdays from about June to September.

On the Canal latéral de la Garonne to the east, just north of **Montech**, is a unique *pente d'eau*, a system devised in 1984 to by-pass five locks by means of a mechanised structure that straddles the by-pass canal and scoops up both boat and water.

CONDOM AND THE TÉNARÈZE

This section covers a small area on the edge of the Landes forest with three major but contrasting sites and an opportunity to visit Armagnac distilleries.

Getting there and around
Car
Autoroute A62, exit 7 Agen, D931. D930 from Auch.
Bus
Agen to Pau via Condom; Bordeaux to Auch via Condom.
Condom to Auch via Valence-sur-Baïse; Condom to Mont-de-Marsan via Nogaro, Barcelonne-du-Gers; Condom to Barbotan-les-Thermes via Eauze; Condom to Lectoure and Fleurance.

Tourist information
32100 Condom Pl. Bossuet, ☎ 05 62 28 00 80, fax 05 62 28 45 46, email otsi@condom.org
32250 Fourcès Mairie, ☎ 05 62 29 50 96, fax 05 62 29 47 44, email si.fources@wanadoo.fr
32250 Montréal-du-Gers Pl. de la Mairie, ☎ 05 62 29 42 85, fax 05 62 29 42 46, email otsi.montrealdugers@wanadoo.fr

Market days
Condom Wednesday, also *marché aux gras* Oct–April
Fleurance Tuesday, also *marché aux gras*
Montréal Friday
Valence-sur-Baïse Wednesday

River cruises
Condom and Valence-sur-Baïse Cruises on the Baïse in summer operated by *Gascogne Navigations*, Quai de la Barquerie; ☎ 05 62 28 46 46

Festivals and events
April *Marché aux fleurs*, flower market, Fourcès
May *Festival International de Bandas y Peñas*, colourful spectacle with a Spanish flavour, Condom

July *Les Théâtrales*, Condom
Nuits Musicales en Armagnac, Condom, Flaran, Lectoure
Fête Mediévale, sound and light, Larressingle

Where to stay and eating out
32100 CONDOM
☆☆ *Le Logis des Cordeliers*, Rue de la Paix, ☎ 05 62 28 03 68, fax 05 62 68 23 71, www.logisdescordeliers.com. Pleasant hotel in a tranquil setting (*Relais de Silence*). Pool.

32250 FOURCÈS
☆☆☆/€€ *Château/Restaurant de Fourcès*, ☎ 05 62 29 49 53, fax 05 62 29 50 59, www.chateau-fources.com. The château, which dates back to the 12C, has been sumptuously restored and offers a delightful pool and other activities.
Château du Garros, 5min walk from centre of village, ☎/fax 05 62 29 47 89, www.chateaudugarros.com. *Chambres d'hôte* in a large early 19C Gascon house with garden. Three spacious and charming double rooms.
Chambres d'hôte, Anne Carter, Château du Garros, ☎/fax 05 62 29 47 89, email perso.wanadoo.fr/chateaudugarros. A spacious and charming house surrounded by private grounds. Three rooms (7 people).

32310 VALENCE-SUR-BAÏSE
☆☆ *La Ferme de Flaran*, at Maignaut-Tauzia, ☎ 05 62 28 58 22, fax 05 62 28 56 89, email fermdeflaran@minitel.net. Set in undulating country-side. The 14 rooms have been entirely renovated; excellent meals in a rustic dining room; pool.

Condom

Condom is the major town of the Gers and capital of the Ténarèze, the central section of the *département*, named after a line of hills between the Adour and the Garonne. Since time immemorial this has been the north–south corridor linking the Garonne and the Pyrenees. Refreshed by the Baïse River, used in the 19C for transporting valuable cargo of Armagnac to Bordeaux, the town is still one of the three main brandy centres, with Auch and Eauze. It has handsome 17C and 18C white stone *hôtels particuliers* reminiscent of Bordeaux, and is variously described as the town of seven churches or of a hundred towers (supposedly 100 fortified residences were built by 100 noble families). The number of churches has been whittled back and the most important now is the former cathedral of St-Pierre.

The etymology of the town's unforgettable name is either a synthesis of *condate* and *dum*, meaning a hill at a confluence, or is derived from *condominium*, a jointly controlled stronghold, as it was when the Vascon people from the Iberian peninsula, ancestors of the Gascons and the Basques, settled here *c* 721.

History

Condom is little mentioned until the 11C when a Benedictine abbey was established and it became a stage on the Via Podiensis. It suffered the usual tribulations and political strife of the Middle Ages—the backlash of the Albigensian Crusades (p 46) in Languedoc and problems with the English in Aquitaine. It was elevated to episcopal see in the 14C but the Hundred Years War caused havoc until 1453. Just over a century later, having adhered to the Reformation, it was the theatre of more unrest during the Wars of Religion and the cathedral was ransacked in 1569. Peace was restored with the Edict of Nantes in 1598 and the rebirth of the town dates from the 17C. Its most celebrated bishop was the great orator Jacques Bénigne Bossuet (1627–1704), named Bishop in 1670, but his contribution to the diocese was somewhat ephemeral as he was always busy elsewhere—he was tutor to the son of Louis XIV and spent most of his time at Court.

The town centre is Place St-Pierre, dominated to the north by the **Cathédrale St-Pierre**, opening to the east into Rue Gambetta, and with elegant houses on the south.

The Benedictine abbey dedicated to St Peter, an important centre of learning, reached its apogee in the early 14C, and on 13 August 1317 Pope John XXII elevated Condom to bishopric with 130 parishes, a status it kept until the Revolution. The present cathedral was designed at the end of the 15C by Jean Marre (d. 1521), who rose through the ranks from prior at Eauze and Nérac to confessor to the king, before becoming Bishop of Condom. By 1511 work on the cathedral was already at an advanced stage and by 1521 the only parts still to be finished were the choir stalls and the roof. Bishop Hérard de Grossoles completed the work in 1524 and the cathedral was consecrated in October 1531.

The rather gloomy south flank of the cathedral faces the square. The exterior is generally in a rather sorry state and the south door very run-down despite some recent restoration. It was built in a transitional style between Flamboyant and Renaissance. The best of the sculpture on the south is in the archivolts; the deep, ornate niches are empty. Above the entrance are the arms of Jean Marre. It is solidly buttressed all round and there is a 40m square tower over the west end.

The large aisleless 16C building without an extended transept is tacked on to the 14C Ste-Marie chapel at the east and the two parts are not exactly aligned. The wide nave with tiercerons has no triforium gallery but is lit by the clerestory windows with *grisaille* glass. The nave piers have clustered shafts and carved capitals but the lierne-vaulted choir is surrounded by undecorated cylindrical columns. The stone *jubé* (roodscreen) is the third version, made in 1844 by the Virebent workshop in Toulouse, and forms a pseudo-ambulatory. The stained glass of the choir was made in a local workshop in 1861. A little light relief is added by an interesting group of vault bosses repainted in 1841, among them, above the choir, St Sauveur, dedicatee of the first church, and St Peter, the present patron in pontifical dress with the keys; Jean Marre is represented by a sheep (*marrou* is Gascon for ram). Angel musicians evoke the celestial choir as well as the sumptuous liturgy of the 16C cathedral famed for its organ and counter-tenor chants and above the nave is the royal coat of arms of Anne of Brittany, a portrait of Louis XII, and the fleur de lis.

The original, late-Gothic-to-Renaissance pulpit, with an openwork baldaquin, is still in place. Of the large chapels on the north, the first contains the tombs of Bishops Marre and Milon and the third a carved walnut altar of 1704 salvaged at the Revolution from the pilgrim chapel, Notre-Dame-de-Piétat. A monument to Bishop de Grossoles stands in the sixth chapel. In the west tribune is the 17C organ built locally by Daumassens.

The west door opens into Place Bossuet with a worked metal cross of 1824. The tourist office is on the left. North of the cathedral is the **cloister**, built by Bishop Grossoles in the 16C in a similar style to the cathedral. There are double arcades on the east and west, somewhat excessive for the space, and in the northeast corner a doorway with Italianate decoration. The upper level has been occupied since 1861 by the *hôtel de ville*, and the cloister serves as a public thoroughfare. On the north, between the old episcopal palace and the cloister, is the episcopal chapel, now part of the entrance to the **Palais de Justice**, also built in the first half of the 16C. An imposing Renaissance door links the chapel with the **Hôtel de la Sous-Préfecture**, the old episcopal palace begun in 1764 by the last bishop.

The magnificent U-shaped stables with timbered ceilings have been converted to house the **Musée de l'Armagnac**. Created in 1954, it retraces the history of the *eau-de-vie* and explains its production. Open April–Oct 10.00–12.00 and 15.00–18.00, Nov–March 15.00–17.00; closed Tues; ☎ 05 62 28 31 41.

Round the corner at 21 Rue Jules-Ferry is the grandiose **Hôtel de Polignac** (1780–85), now a school, with colonnades and wrought iron, built by the Abbot Marie Dorlan de Polignac, Prior of Layrac, on the ruins of the old citadel. The west façade overlooking the river is equally impressive. Further down the street is the former 18C seminary of Bishop de Milon, now the Lycée Bossuet.

Rue des Eclosettes leads back via Rue des Jacobins to the covered market and from the southeast corner of the square the narrow Rue Voutée leads into **Rue**

Armagnac

Armagnac brandy is probably France's oldest distillate of wine, certainly older than cognac or calvados. When it was first produced in the 15C it was taken for medicinal purposes only but during the 16C it started to acquire a different status. Production peaked in the 19C, stemmed by the phylloxera epidemic in 1878.

The area which comes within the Armagnac *appellation* was defined in 1909 and covers nearly 13,000ha, mainly in the Gers but also in neighbouring Landes. The *appellation* is divided into three areas according to soil type: **Bas-Armagnac**, or Armagnac-Noir, to the west on the edge of the Landes, is the largest area (7548ha), with acidic, predominantly sandy soil which produces perfect grapes for distillation; the limestone of **Haut-Armagnac** to the east and south (157ha) has grapes better suited to wines; the central region of **Ténarèze** (5127ha) has a mixture of clay and chalk with sand. White wine, low in alcohol and high in acidity, is produced for distillation from three main grape varieties, Folle blanche, Ugni blanc and Colombard. Distillation has to take place by 31 March following the harvest and the alembic, or distilling vessel, is particular to the region. The wine is heated twice but distilled only once (whereas cognac is distilled twice), and maturation is in oak casks and not in the bottle, which gives it a particular bouquet of prune and violet. Depending on the number of years left to age in wood, Armagnac is sold under the *appellations* XXX (less than two years), VSOP (four years) and Napoleon (five years or more). Aperitifs based on Armagnac are the sweet Floc de Gascogne, red or rosé; and La Belle-Sandrine, made with passion fruit.

Gambetta, a lively, pedestrian street with the post office in the old Neo-classical Hôtel de Ville and the pretty 17C Hôtel de Lagarde (now the *Trois Lys* hotel, see above).

In **Allée Général de Gaulle** (Rue Jean-Jaurès) are stately 18C residences built on the line of the old fortifications, such as the Hôtel du Bouzet de Roquepine (1763) with *oeil de boeuf* windows. The adjacent Hôtel de Cugnac is laid out around three sides of a courtyard and closed to the street with formidable railings. It is occupied by an Armagnac distillery, *Maison Ryst-Dupeyron*, and can be visited; ☎ 05 62 28 08 08. Opposite, at the angle with Rue des Cordeliers, is Hôtel de Cadignan (1775).

From Place de la Liberté turn right into Rue Cauzabon where on the left is the Louis XV-style Hôtel de Galardon with a pilastered portico and *mascaron* (mask) motif. Place du Lion d'Or and Rue Charron, which lead back to Place St-Pierre, also have some pretty houses. Rues Ichon and des Armuriers run down to the banks of the Baïse and **Pont des Carmes**, south of which are gardens and a leisure area.

From a distance, the bluff mass of the walls and battlemented towers of **Larressingle**, on the D15 west of Condom, is a stunning sight and as described locally suggests a pocket-sized Carcassonne (☎ 05 62 28 26 25). The church was fortified in the 12C and later a 270m rampart was thrown around the church and castle, surrounded by a ditch. Recognised by the popes in the 13C as the property of the abbeys of Agen and Condom, it became the official residence

of the bishops of Condom until the end of the 16C when they moved to Cassaigne, taking most of the transportable timber elements with them.

The barrel-vaulted fortified entrance on the west, where there was once a draw-bridge, is very narrow and the protection afforded by the walls and towers to the houses huddled up against them gives the enclosure a rather cosy feel inside. Opposite the entrance is the semi-ruined, massive castle keep on four floors, with signs of later alterations and additions to make it more habitable. Nestling behind that is the little 12C church of St-Sigismond; its west façade has a porch with Romanesque capitals and the *Lamb of God* in the tympanum. The half-dome of the 12C church was pierced when a two-bay extension was added to the east end in the 13C. The route to Santiago passed this way, and the other road from Larressingle (between the cemetery and the *mairie*) will take you down to the old pilgrim bridge, the Pont d'Artigues. The Cité des Machines du Moyen Age (Larressingle), displays copies of medieval siege equipment, Easter–Nov 11.00–17.00; ☎ 05 62 68 33 30.

Larressingle

One of the most enchanting *bastides* in the Gers is the little circular village of **Fourcès** (pronounce the 's'), on the D29 and D114 north of Montréal. A bridge over the Auzoue leads into the centre under the watchful eye of the 16C château. This tiny community has only about 350 inhabitants but is decked out in blooms during the flower festival on the last weekend of April. The village probably developed around a primitive fortification, long disappeared, and was later enclosed in an all-embracing wall, fragments of which remain, as does the pretty belltower astride the lane on the west. The old houses, some with arcades and others half-timbered, link to enclose the plane-shaded *place*.

Montréal, built on an escarpment, was one of the first *bastides* founded in Gascony, in 1256. By the time it was finished in 1289 it was already under English domination. It has the typical regular layout with a central square, arcades and a large church off-centre, with aisles and primitive capitals and corbels in the east, bearing the scars of Protestant iconoclasm, particularly around the south door. At the tourist office is a two-room **Musée des Fouilles de Séviac** crammed with items found at Séviac since 1868. Open March–Nov 10.00–12.00 and 14.00–18.00.

Séviac, just southwest of Montréal, off the D29, has a low-key setting that belies the importance of the archaeological site, one of the largest in Gascony covering 2ha. Open July, Aug 10.00–19.00; March–June, Sept–Nov 10.00–12.00 and 14.00–18.00; ☎ 05 62 29 48 57. Excavations in 1959 uncovered a classic Gallo-Roman villa with peristyle which dates from the 2C to the 5C. A large interior courtyard 35m square is itself bordered by a gallery 4m wide; the living quarters consist of mainly rectangular rooms and, around them, another gallery. On the east is a large building with an apse heated by a hypocaust and to the south, separated from the villa by an interior courtyard in which marble columns have been found, are vast thermae (bath complex) with white and green marble slabs and mosaics still in place in the piscina.

Séviac has some remarkable and well made 4C and 5C **mosaics**. Of around 30 surviving pieces of varying size, some are surprisingly complete. The background colour is a creamy white and the designs are picked out in terracotta red, pink, olive green, dark blue and yellow ochre. Nearly all are geometric repeat patterns but a few have stylised fruit and vegetal designs. During the Merovingian era (6C and 7C) the villa was divided into smaller dwellings with transverse walls. On the southeast are traces of Merovingian Christian sanctuaries with a baptistery and necropolis.

Mouchan, southwest of Condom on the D931, has a small but satisfying 12C church in the typical yellowish-orange stone of the region with a square tower, all that remains of the former Cluniac priory of St-Austrigile. Open May–Sept afternoons. There are simple carvings on the exterior and inside are 31 decorated capitals, mainly with a stiff leaf design similar to that seen at Flaran (see below), but also interlacings, and five with figures or animals. One of particular note, in the east end of the church, is carved on three faces with little scenes inscribed in arches.

Also southwest of Condom, on the D208, is the **Château de Cassaigne**. Set in 27ha of vines, it attracts 40,000 visitors a year, both to visit the building and to sample the Armagnac. Open every day; ☎ 05 62 28 04 02, www.chateau decassaigne.com. The 13C castle became the summer palace of the bishops of Condom at the end of the 16C. It was remodelled in the stylish comfort of the Renaissance by Bishops Jehan de Monluc and Jean Duchemin, who were both very attached to it and died here. Their work forms the core of the building, but it was restyled during the time of Bishop Louis de Milon (1693–1734), who was responsible for the restrained elegance of the present west entrance façade. Work continued on the gardens in the 18C. The Faget family, descendants of the Intendant of the last bishop, have owned the property since 1827. A visit to the château includes the kitchen with a beautiful brick vault, likened to an outsize bread oven; an audio-visual presentation in English and French; and a tasting.

Just south of Cassaigne on the D229, the **Château of Busca Maniban** (1649) in a marvellous setting above the vineyards offers a visit to the house and the distillery. Open Easter–15 Nov 14.00–19.00, closed Mon; ☎ 05 62 28 40 38. There is a typical Gascon *pigeonnier* nearby.

Flaran and La Romieu

Abbaye de Flaran

On the banks of the Baïse between Condom and Auch, on the D930, is the abbey of Flaran. The best-preserved Cistercian edifice in the Gers, it is a handsome group of 12C and 17C–18C buildings which were carefully restored after a fire in 1970. Apart from their architectural merit, they are used as a centre for cultural events and for information on the pilgrimage routes. Open July, Aug 09.30–19.00; Feb–June, Sept–Dec 10.00–12.30 and 14.00–18.00; closed 3 weeks in Jan, 1 Jan, 1 May, 25 Dec; ☎ 05 62 28 50 19.

Flaran was founded in 1151 and donations of land and property during the second half of the 12C enabled the construction of an important and very beautiful monastery. The upheavals of the 14C and 15C took their toll, and placed in the hands of secular abbots at the end of the 15C it continued to decline. In 1569 the abbey suffered devastating attacks by the Protestants, but in 1573 Abbot Jean de Boyer started restoration work on the church and repairs to other buildings were carried out through to 1603. In the 18C a general remodelling of the abbey was effected, particularly the guest quarters.

The entrance to the abbey is across the great courtyard with the church to the east and stables and outhouses to the west, and through the former *quartier d'hôte*, the **prior's residence**, conceived on the lines of a small Gascon château in 1759 with a grand staircase and stucco decoration.

At the heart of the abbey is the beautiful church of **Notre-Dame** (begun *c* 1170), a rare example in the southwest of quintessential Cistercian architecture with minimal decoration and maximum light. It has a wide transept, square chancel and semicircular main apse with two apsidal chapels on either side decorated on the exterior with a band of small arcades. These disappeared from the central apse when a brick-and-timber rising was added, possibly in the 17C. The crossing is vaulted with rectangular ribs and the three-bay nave (raised *c* 1220) received a pointed barrel arch. A small rose window was inserted in the west. The south aisle is barrel-vaulted but the north is ribbed. The numerous capitals all have stylised foliate, geometric or interlace motifs, and over the door from the cloister is a simple chrism. The west door has geometric friezes and reused marble columns.

Abutting the north transept are the 12C monastic buidings, the *armarium* (library), sacristy and the very gracious **chapter house**, which has nine ribbed bays supported by four coloured marble columns and simple capitals. It opens on to the **cloister** with three richly moulded recessed bays supported by capitals on short marble shafts. The rooms to the north and west are used for exhibitions. The cloister has been rebuilt twice since the 12C. All that remains of the 14C reconstruction is the west gallery, with rectangular piers subdivided by paired columns and capitals with vegetal motifs or hybrid animals and figures. The remaining galleries are very simple constructions with timber and tile roofs, and an upper floor on the north.

Above the chapter house was the **dormitory**, communicating directly with the church. The variety in the fenestration indicates alterations in the 15C and the 17C, and in the 18C it was extended when individual and more comfortable rooms replaced the dormitory, an ironic decadence of the original Cistercian ethos.

A passageway in the northeast of the cloister leads to a traditional **monastic garden** with aromatic and medicinal plants and an excellent view of the east end of the church. The garden façade was embellished by a monumental gateway in the 18C. The refectory on the north of the cloister was reduced in size at some point and adorned with elegant stuccowork (*c* 1730–80). The kitchen and the warming house, either side of the refectory, were altered in the 18C. On the walls of the upper gallery, originally closed, are 18C mural paintings.

The **Madeleine farm**, restored in 1988, can also be visited: a section is used for exhibitions.

Nearby **Valence-sur-Baïse** is a 13C *bastide* with a 14C church. The D142 and D42 bring you east to **St-Puy**, a charming village on the site of an ancient *oppidum*. This was the land of Blaise de Monluc (1500–77), Maréchal de France, whose *Commentaires* were written partly in response to the reputation he acquired for his harsh treatment of the Protestants during the Wars of Religion, when he was attempting to quell disturbances in Guyenne. At the many-times rebuilt **Château de Monluc** you can discover more about wine, Armagnac and the Armagnac-based liqueur, *pousse-rapière*, a wickedly potent aperitif, in its beautiful vaulted cellars. Open all year Mon–Sat 10.00–12.00 and 15.00–19.00 ☎ 05 62 28 94 00.

Between the D654 and D7 are **Pouy-Petit** and **St-Orens**, two of the many fortified sites in the Gers. Further east, **Terraube** is a little village with a stunningly dramatic château, property of the Galard family since the 10C.

La Romieu

The two towers of the church high above the countryside signal La Romieu, a walled village of just over 540 inhabitants on the site of a Benedictine abbey founded, so it is said, by two monks returning from Rome *c* 1062. The **Collégiale de St-Pierre** is an unexpected and interesting example of Gothic architecture. Open daily June–Sept 10.00–12.00 and 14.00–19.00; Oct–May to 18.00, closed Jan and Sun morning; ☎ 05 62 28 86 33.

The village's name, from the Latin *romaeus* meaning pilgrims, was first mentioned in 1082. It was granted *bastide* status in the 14C at the wish of its great benefactor, Arnaud d'Aux—cousin of Bernard de Got, first pope at Avignon—who was born at La Romieu *c* 1260. The village was English from 1279 to 1453. After an illustrious career, Arnaud was made cardinal in 1312 and that year envisaged the construction of his funerary monument, composed of collegiate church, cloister and residence. It was inaugurated on 30 July 1318.

The church is approached through the 14C cloister which originally had two, possibly three levels. The Rayonnant bays, with two trefoil and one polyfoil opening in each, are divided by slender columns. Despite the degradations inflicted by the Protestant troops of Gabriel Montgomery (*c* 1530–74) and at the Revolution, it still maintains an aura of peace and grace. The aisleless church, supported by massive buttresses, has a five-bay nave with the four tombs of the Cardinal and his nephews, also damaged. Below the octagonal tower on the east is the sacristy, entirely decorated with some remarkable 14C murals. The eight walls are covered with octagonal medallions containing portraits of founders, biblical figures or geometric patterns and the vaults with a variety of angel musicians and censer angels. The other, square, tower is all that is left of the Cardinal's palace.

BAS ARMAGNAC AND MADIRAN

Getting there and around
Car
D6/N124 from Mont-de-Marsan. D935 from Tarbes. D931 from Condom.
Bus
Between Tarbes and Mont-de-Marsan.

Tourist information
32290 Aignan Pl. Colonel Parisot, ☎ 05 62 09 22 57, fax 05 62 09 22 46, email si.aignan@wanadoo.fr
32800 Eauze Pl. d'Armagnac, ☎ 05 62 09 85 62, fax 05 62 08 11 22, email office.tourisme.eauze@wanadoo.fr
32360 Lavardens Coeur de Gascogne, ☎/fax 05 62 58 10 62, email info@coeur-gascogne.com
32110 Nogaro 81 Rue Nationale, ☎ 05 62 09 13 30, fax 05 62 08 88 21, email ot-nogaro@wanadoo.fr
32400 Riscle 6 Pl. du Foirail, ☎ 05 62 69 74 01, fax 05 62 69 86 07, email canton.riscle@wanadoo.fr
32190 Vic-Fézensac 22 Pl. Julie-St-Avit, BP 28, ☎/fax 05 62 64 44 33, www.vic-fezensac.com
Market days
Aignan Monday
Eauze Thursday, also *marché aux gras*
Nogaro Wednesday and Saturday
Riscle Friday
Vic-Fézensac Friday; nocturnal markets alternate Wednesdays July–August
Wineries
32290 Aignan Cave d'Aignan, Av. d'Armagnac, ☎ 05 62 09 24 06
65700 Madiran Cooperative winery: Maison du Vin du Madiran et Pacherenc, Le Prieuré, ☎ 05 62 31 90 67, fax 05 62 31 90 79
32400 St-Mont Union des Producteurs Plaimont, Caves des Producteurs Plaimont, ☎ 05 62 69 62 87, fax 05 62 69 61 68

32110 Nogaro Cave des Producteurs Réunis, Rte d'Aire, ☎ 05 62 09 01 79. Armagnac, Croix de Salle, ☎ 05 62 09 03 01

Festivals and events
April *Coupes de Pâques*, motor racing, Nogaro
May *Foire aux Grandes Eaux-de-Vie d'Armagnac*, festival of brandy, Eauze
Féria de Vic, bullfighting, Vic-Fézensac
July *Festival Tempo Latino*, Latin American music and dance, especially salsa, in the arena and streets, Vic-Fézensac
September *Grand Prix*, motor racing, Nogaro

Where to stay and eating out
32290 BOUZON-GELLENAVE
Chambres d'hôte, Elisabeth and Florent Poinsot, Château de Bascou, 5km west of Aignan (via D48), ☎ 05 62 69 04 12, fax 05 62 69 06 09. A wine-producing domain of the Cotes de St-Mont area, with 3 tastefully decorated rooms.
32400 PROJAN
Château de Projan, near Aire sur l'Adour, on the D946, ☎ 05 62 09 46 21, fax 05 62 09 44 08, email chateaudeprojan@libertesurf.fr.
Chambres d'hôte in the south of the Gers in a tranquil setting surrounded by forest, with a lake and views towards the Pyrenees.
32400 SARRAGACHIES
Domaine de la Buscasse, ☎ 05 62 69 76 07, fax 05 62 69 79 17. A handsome 17C/19C house among the vineyards of Côtes-de-St-Mont opposite the Pyrenean chain. *Chambres d'hôte* accommodation in three double rooms.
Chambres d'hôte, Fabienne and Jean-Michel Abadie, Domaine de la Buscasse,

15km west of Aignan, north of Riscle), ☎ 05 62 69 76 07, fax 05 62 69 79 17, email Buscasse@aol.com. Calm surroundings with wonderful views, the 18C house is in the middle of an agricultural and winemaking concern; pool.

The Bas Armagnac, also known as Armagnac Noir, is the western side of the Gers and the heartland of Armagnac brandy (p 373), where vast stretches of vines overlap with forests.

Eauze

Eauze, southwest of Condom on the D931, was the ancient city of the Elusates people. Elusa became one of the three main political, administrative and commercial centres, with Auch and Lectoure, during Roman occupation of Novempopulanie. The busy commercial town was created by Charles IX in the 16C when he granted the right to hold a market. Now the Armagnac capital, Eauze holds an Armagnac fair in Ascension week and is one of several towns in Bas Armagnac which hold *corridas*.

Roman buildings and treasure have been excavated and in 1985 an extraordinary collection of jewels and 28,000 coins was discovered dating from 3C–4C. This, along with some 50 precious objects (4C), is on display in the **Musée du Trésor d'Eauze** on Place de la Liberté. Open June–Sept 10.00–12.30 and 14.00–18.00; Feb 14.00–17.00; ☎ 05 62 09 71 38. The town's most famous house, on the central arcaded square, Place d'Armagnac, is the timber-framed **Maison Jeanne d'Albret**. Jeanne's son, Henri of Navarre, was taken ill here on 15 June 1579 and was cared for by his queen Marguerite de Valois (Margot) for 17 days. There are small streets with timber-framed houses in varying degrees of dilapidation. The octagonal belfry tower, in stone and yellowish brick with a distinctive roof, indicates the 15C–16C church of **St-Luperc**. Long, narrow and aisleless with a three-sided apse, the interior is enlivened by the fact that the walls are not rendered, adding colour and texture to an otherwise plain church (except for the 1977 murals in the apse) with little fenestration. The painted bosses contain the coats of arms of France and Eauze and of Jean Marre, prior of Luperc and Bishop of Condom in the 16C.

Further southwest on the N124, **Nogaro** is the small rural capital of Bas Armagnac. It has two particular attractions: motor racing in April and September, at the Circuit Paul-Armagnac, and an interesting church. It is a village with plenty of half-timbered houses and the oldest Armagnac distillery; and the *courses landaises* (see p 347) championships are held here every three years.

This was a *sauveté* (place of refuge) on the pilgrimage route to Spain created by the Archbishop of Auch in 1060 and has one of the largest Romanesque churches in the Gers, although it was much modified in the 17C, and again in the 19C. There are Romanesque elements around the north door, including Christ and the symbols of the Evangelists. The vault of the three-bay nave was rebuilt in brick in the 17C but the arches with ovolo moulding between the nave and aisles date from the end of the 11C. The capitals in the east end are sculpted with, from left to right: acanthus leaves; a centaur between two horsemen; *Daniel in the Lions' Den*; musicians; *Christ with Zacchaeus*, who climbed a sycamore tree the better to see Jesus; and *Jesus in a Boat with the Two Sinners*. The sacristy was a 16C addition. The collegiate buildings which, with the church, once contributed to the protection of the town now shelter what is left of the cloister, transformed into a garden. Just one bay of the outer wall of the old cloister gives a clue to the beauty of the original carvings.

Wines of the Madiran

Madiran is a small wine-producing region between the towns of Riscle and Maubourguet and Lembeye further south, straddling the border between the Midi-Pyrénées and Aquitaine, along the valleys of small rivers which flow north into the Adour. Although its history is long, the region went into crisis at the beginning of the 20C and was reduced to only 6ha in 1953, but vines again cover over 1000ha and the wines are gaining recognition. The wine, introduced and perfected by the Benedictines of the abbey at Madiran in the 11C and 12C, was used for communion and was appreciated by pilgrims on the Santiago road. It was awarded *appellation contrôlée* status in 1948 but its first official recognition were the *lettres de noblesse* (letters patent) issued by François I and the court of England in the 16C. The wines used in the production of the exclusively red wines of Madiran are the Tannat, a local variety of black grape, Cabernet Franc and a small amount of Cabernet Sauvignon. The most recently conferred *appellation* in the region was the *Côtes-de-St-Mont* in 1981. *Pacherenc*, the delicious white wine of the Vic-Bilh, the old name of the region around St-Mont, is produced from local grape varieties with curious names—Arrufiac, Gros Manseng, Courbu and Petit Manseng—plus a little Sémillon and Sauvignon. Maison du Madiran et Pacherenc, Le Prieuré, 65700 Madiran, ☎/fax 05 62 31 90 79.

Riscle on the D935 is busy on Fridays, market day, but probably not at any other time. The name is derived from *risclo*, meaning a row of stones in the river arranged to catch fish. It has tidy 17C/18C houses and a church with a Flamboyant portal overlooking the main square.

Go 5.5km west on the D946. **St-Mont** is the most interesting village of the Madiran, with a cooperative winery, the *Union des Producteurs Plaimont*; ☎ 05 62 69 62 87, fax 05 62 69 61 68. As its name suggests the village is perched on a hill and overlooks the Adour Valley. There are pretty pebble and brick houses lining the street up to the tall but sturdy stone church at the summit, which has conserved a small number of remarkable Romanesque capitals. (The key is at the house just below the church.) The area in front of the church is landscaped but next to it are the abandoned buildings of the 18C priory.

The abbey of St-Mont, dedicated to St John the Baptist, was founded in 1045 by Bernard II of Armagnac, who had the unlikely name of Tumapaler, and was attached to Cluny in 1055. The abbey's history is obscure but it was ransacked by the Protestant troops of Montgomery in 1569 and then rebuilt. After the Revolution all the buildings except the church were sold.

The interior is wonderfully light and spacious; the aisleless nave is not quite lined up with the apse. All that remains of the 11C building are the south transept and apse and part of the south wall of the nave. The vaults were added and the north side of the church altered at a later date, around the late 12C or early 13C. The oldest and finest capitals from the first building campaign at the entrance to the south apsidiole—vegetal on the left and lions in tendrils on the right—show an affinity to the work at St-Gaudens in the Collegiate church (p 498). There are stylistic similarities to Jaca (Spain) in the next two, slightly later capitals on the southwest, one with a double Corinthian motif, and the other with the theme of *David and his Musicians*, as well as a reused capital in the southeast of the main apse with the story of *Balaam's Ass*. There are more carved capitals in the south transept and on the south side of the nave.

East of Riscle by the D3 and D48, **Termes d'Armagnac** is not difficult to track down because of the splendidly massive 13C keep towering over the Adour Valley, the only part still intact of the castle built on the border (*terminis*) between the ancient territories of Armagnac and Béarn. This was the château of Tibault d'Armagnac who, alongside several hundred other Gascons, fought with Joan of Arc. The spectacular vantage point of this lofty edifice (36m) will be appreciated by those who can cope both with the climb to the top up a spiral staircase and the six levels of reconstructed history in the form of thematic tableaux called the Musée du Panache Gascogne. Open June–Sept 10.00–19.30; Oct–May 14.00–18.00; ☎ 05 62 69 25 12. The church next door, with a belfry-porch and distinctive roof, has been subjected to many alterations but proudly displays a magnificent 18C gilded retable.

A drive through rolling countryside on the D20 brings **Aignan**, the first residence of the counts and therefore first capital of Armagnac with traditional house, and an arcaded square. Now an important commercial centre for brandy with a cooperative *chai* which can be visited. Aignan suffered badly at the hands of the English in 1355 but the church has conserved several 12C carved elements around the portal and some good capitals inside around the two apses. It was modified in the late 13C when the massive square belfry was topped by a distinctive roof and lantern.

Close to Aignan by the D48 is the attractive village of **Sabazan**, with a 17C *château-domaine* producing Armagnac and a miniature church with an 11C–12C apse, simple carvings and an overhanging timber gallery on the tower, added in the 13C.

Lupiac to the east is a modest village with a large square and timber arcades, described as the cradle or *berceau d'Artagnan*. The villages in this district, around here called the Pays d'Artagnan, have been able to capitalise on Alexandre Dumas' hero because the real man behind the myth, Charles de Batz-Castelmore, was born between 1610 and 1620 at the Château of Castelmore (privately owned) about 4km north of Lupiac on the D102. Although Dumas tidied up the facts, Charles de Batz, who adopted his mother's name, did have an illustrious career in the service of Louis XIV. He died during the siege of Maastricht in 1673 and legend has it that he is buried at Lupiac, but of this there is no proof. The St-James chapel (or Notre-Dame-de-la-Pitié) was founded by Charles de Batz, uncle of the musketeer, in 1605 (p 431). The Centre d'Artagnan explores the real story of the musketeer. Open July, Aug daily 10.30–19.00; Sept–June 14.00–18.00, closed Mon; ☎ 05 62 09 24 09.

On the Osse River in the centre of Gascony is the small town of **Vic-Fézensac**, a popular centre for tourism and best known for the Whitsun *corrida* (bullfight). The medieval town was divided between the Counts of Armagnac and the archbishops of Auch, causing constant tension. In the 18C the town was physically cut in two when Baron d'Etigny drove the main road through the middle of the old *place*. The *halle* was destroyed in 1866.

The most interesting part of the church, founded in 1190 by the bishops, is the Romanesque chevet with some of its original decoration and some 15C paintings in the south. The 15C nave was repaired and covered with a timber roof in the 17C. The altar and font are 18C and the octagonal belfry is a 19C confection. The 15C tower of the canons' residence and the 14C–15C square tower of the former Cordeliers convent, founded by Count Jean III d'Armagnac in 1382, are original, but most of the convent had to be rebuilt after the Reformation.

Off the D930 north of Auch, **Jegun** is an attractively restored *village perché* strung out along the ridge, with a variety of 15C and 16C houses and an *halle* with a Neo-classical building above it. The church of Ste-Candide, part 12C, was altered in the 15C and two aisles were added in the 19C to support the nave.

Lavardens, a picturesque Gascon village clinging to a rocky bluff, was a stronghold of the Counts of Armagnac in the 13C and was inherited in 1496 by Marguerite d'Angoulême. The streets are too narrow and steep for motor vehicles, but who would want to drive through it anyway? Five of the old towers of the *enceinte* still survive but the huge château which dominates the village was dismantled by Henri of Navarre's troops in 1577. Rebuilding began in 1620 under the direction of the architect Pierre de Levesville but was interrupted by a plague epidemic in 1653. It changed hands twice in the 18C and after 1820 it was more or less abandoned until 1970, when restoration work was undertaken. The west part of the château is the most elegant, standing proud above the valley. It can be visited; although it has few rooms there are some quite outstanding tiled floors. Open July, Aug 10.00–19.00; enquire for other times; ☎ 05 62 64 51 20.

19 Southern Gers

AUCH
• • • • • •

Auch, Préfecture of the Gers, is centrally placed in the *département* and midway between Aquitaine and Langedoc. If arriving on the N21, you will benefit from the view of the mass of the cathedral rearing against the sky in the *ville haute* or old town, where narrow medieval lanes contrast with the elegant 18C Allées d'Etigny. Monumental steps lead down to the River Gers and the new town on the plain, which has a modernised train/bus station.

History
The first settlers of the *oppidum* Elimberris were a Celtic tribe, the Auscii. Defeated by the Romans in 56 BC, *Augusta Auscorum*, one of the main cities of Roman Aquitaine, developed on the right bank of the river. From the 9C the

population returned to the hill and built a simple oratory, the core of the medieval *cité*. As the town of Auch expanded it came under the shared authority of the consuls of Auch, the Count of Armagnac, the Archbishop of Auch and the Prior of Saint-Orens.

Between 1715 and 1768 Auch became a separate *généralité* or administrative centre, covering a huge territory between the Garonne and the crest of the Pyrenees. The 18C was the high point for Auch, largely due to its Intendant from 1731 to 1767, Baron Antoine Megret d'Etigny, who invigorated the economy of the town and the region with a huge road-building programme linking Auch with the mountains and the Canal du Midi. The Province of Gascony disappeared in 1789 and the larger part of it became the Gers.

Getting there and around
Car

A62 Exit 7 Agen, N21 to Auch and Auch to Tarbes; N124 Toulouse to Auch and Auch to Aire-sur-l'Adour.

Train

Auch to Toulouse via Gimont, L'Isle-Jourdain.
Train station, ☎ 08 36 35 35 35.

Bus

Auch to Bordeaux via Condom.
Auch to Agen via Fleurance.
Auch to Montauban via Mauvezin.
Auch to Mont-de-Marsan via Vic-Fézensac, Nogaro, Aire-sur-l'Adour.
Auch to Mont-de-Marsan via Marciac, Plaisance-du-Gers, Riscle.
Auch to Tarbes via Mirande, Miélan.
Auch to Lannemezan via Masseube.
Auch to Toulouse via Gimont, l'Isle-Jourdain.
For more information on bus routes in the area, ☎ 05 62 67 42 73.

Bus station, ☎ 05 62 05 76 37.

 Tourist information
32003 Auch 1 Rue Dessoles, BP 174, ☎ 05 62 05 22 89, fax 05 62 05 92 04, www.gers-gascogne.com

Market days

Thursday and Saturday

 Festivals and events
June Music festival
October Festival of Cinema

 Where to stay and eating out
32000 AUCH

☆☆☆/€€ *France*, 5 Pl. de la Libération, BP 124, ☎ 05 62 61 71 71, fax 05 62 61 71 81, email auchgarreau@intelcom.fr. Opposite the cathedral, this comfortable hotel has a very high-class restaurant, *Le Jardin des Saveurs*.

Start your visit from Place de la République, the market place in front of the cathedral. The tourist office is in the pretty timber-framed **Maison Fedel** on the north side of the *place*.

Cathédrale Sainte-Marie

The cathedral (closed midday) was one of the last Gothic cathedrals in the south-west, begun at the end of the 15C, just after Albi cathedral was completed. It replaced a Romanesque church consecrated in 1121. At about the same time a canons' residence had appeared on the south and an episcopal residence on the north while to the east was a steep escarpment. Despite the restrictions, the cathedral, designed by Jean Marre, bishop and architect of Condom cathedral, extended to the south as well as to the east where it was supported by a crypt built into the rock. The first stone was laid on 4 July 1489 and the unfinished building was consecrated in 1548. It was not fully completed until 1680.

Exterior The exterior more than the interior shows the evolution of styles over the 200 years of construction. Viewed from the north or south, it appears to be a fairly standard Flamboyant building with flying buttresses and a shallow transept. It is impossible to walk around the east end and, therefore, the only view of the chevet is distant.

The three entrances, begun in 1560, were the work of the architect Jean de Beaujeu. The north and south portals and the four buttress-towers flanking them had risen to the height of the aisles by 1567 and were completed *c* 1635. Above each portal is a Flamboyant rose window beneath a triangular pediment. The decoration of each doorway is transitional, juxtaposing Flamboyant aedicules with pinnacles and crockets and delicately carved Italianate friezes. The massive but elegant west elevation, completed by 1680, uses an exclusively Classical idiom. The three round-arched entrances correspond to the nave and aisles and lead to an open portico, closed by railings in the 18C. The square towers above are on two levels and the Corinthian order is applied throughout. The niches have always been empty.

Interior The interior is regular and harmonious, unencumbered by integral ornament, an intrinsic feature of southern Gothic architecture. The simple quadripartite vaults and transverse arches are emphatically outlined but spring from shafts which are pared down to the minimum, while sharply profiled aisle arches spring directly from the smooth round piers without the hint of a capital. The blind triforium under low basket arches is more like a Renaissance balcony. Five pentagonal radiating chapels surround the apse while the rest of the 21 chapels are square. This very plain interior is the foil to two great treasures: the stained-glass windows and the magnificent carved choir enclosure. Both were installed by the time the cathedral was consecrated in 1548, when the chapels and ambulatory were vaulted, although the choir had a temporary timber roof and the nave was still a skeleton.

The series of 18 Renaissance **stained-glass windows** (1507–13) were made by Arnaud de Moles for the ambulatory chapels. To produce the intense reds, blues, greens and golds, used here in large areas and to great effect, he took advantage of new advances in glass-making and in the techniques of abrasion and annealing. The iconographic programme brings together monumental figures from the Old and the New Testament, a line-up of prophets, patriarchs, sibyls, saints and apostles, with small scenes relevant to their prophesies or lives. The themes were probably furnished by the incumbent archbishop and donor of the stained glass, Clermont de Lodève (1507–38), a member of the great Amboise family. There are three key storiated windows. The *Creation* cycle in the first chapel north has figures of *Adam and Eve* and small scenes above and below of the Creation and the Fall. The three windows in the main apse dealing with the theme of the *Crucifixion* have magnificent fleur de lis in the upper register. In the central bay is *Christ on the Cross* with the Virgin, St John and Mary Magdalene. The window in the left bay contains Isaiah, the Apostle Philip and prophet Micah, and on the right King David, James the Great as a pilgrim, and a prophet. The *Resurrection* window, on the southwest, combines Christ's apparition to Mary Magdalene, *Noli me Tangere*, in the central bay, and the *Incredulity of St Thomas* with a small scene of the *Supper at Emmaus*. At the top Auch is represented by its coat of arms, and above the main figures are Claude de France, daughter of Louis XII, and her betrothed, the future François I, representing the two branches of the Crown, the Valois and the Orléans. At the base are more prophets and apostles and the arms of Clermont de Lodève.

The visit to the **choir enclosure** (entrance fee), intended as it was to separate worshipping clerics from *hoi polloi*, takes you into a world apart. It is a totally enclosed area, one of three in the Midi-Pyrénées—with Albi and St-Bertrand-de-Comminges—to survive church reforms in the 17C. The 113 choir stalls that line three sides are an extraordinary *tour de force*. Carved from heart of oak, richly patinated, the sanctuary contrasts in texture and abundance with the plain stone and the radiant stained glass. The enclosure was probably completed *c* 1552–54 but there is no recorded date for the start of the work, calculated at *c* 1510–20. Gothic in essence, with late Flamboyant-style baldaquins, the iconography of the age of humanism brings together biblical and mythological figures.

The **choir stalls** are on two levels. The carved reliefs of the high backs of the upper 69 develop the theme of the Creation, starting with Adam and Eve in the northwest. Proceeding anti-clockwise, the male-female alternation is maintained with figures representing the Old Law, including Moses; sibyls and prophets juxtaposed with the Evangelists, Apostles and allegories of virtue; David in several scenes leading up to his accession as King; sibyls and prophets representing fidelity and infidelity, and fortune and misfortune; Babylon and the tests of exile in the shape of more sibyls and prophets. The programme culminates with Saints Peter and Paul, the joint founders of the Christian Church, and above the entrance to the choir are St Jerome, St Augustine and the Virgin. The lower stalls carry scenes from the life of Christ from the Annunciation to the Crucifixion in high-relief panels on the end stalls. The **misericords** are decorated with lively and sometimes provocative anecdotes and the armrests with weird and chimerical beasts and demons. Barely a surface is left decorated.

Closing the choir to the east is a monumental **retable** (*c* 1609) by a local sculptor, Pierre Souffron II, with pilasters and columns in Pyrenean marble and two stone ambones. The four statues were salvaged in 1860 when the old *jubé* (roodscreen), sculpted in 1671 by Gervais Drouet, was dismantled. The mosaics in front of the altar were placed here in 1860.

The **crypt**, built to support the east end, has five undecorated radiating chapels corresponding to the main chapels. The 7C sarcophagus of the Bishop-Saint Léothade, from the former Benedictine abbey of St-Orens d'Auch, is the most interesting piece. The cathedral treasure is in the former sacristy. The **St-Sépulchre chapel**, in the southeast where the first stone was laid, is the only chapel of the apse without glass because it is against the canonical buildings. Its contains an important sculpted group enacting the *Entombment* (*c* 1500), with the usual line-up of life-sized participants in rigid postures: Joseph of Arimathaea and Nicodemus at the head and feet of the body of Jesus as he is lowered into the tomb, the Virgin carrying the crown of thorns, St John, Mary Magdalene and Maries Salome and Cleophas. This particular group is flanked by four soldiers and covered by a gilded baldaquin with a Trinity and numerous angels. All ten chapels of the nave were dedicated to Our Lady when the sculptor Jean Douillé was commissioned in 1662 to make 13 retables. Just two retables have survived complete, and part of another. The most noteworthy, in the chapel of the Assumption on the right of the west door, was restored in 1964.

Among other furnishings are the early 16C ciborium above the 19C altar in the St-Sacrament chapel; a reconstruction (1803) of the mausoleum of Baron d'Etigny, originally at St-Orens d'Auch but demolished at the Revolution; and the 18C pulpit.

The 17C *jubé*, at the west of the choir, elements of which are now scattered around the cathedral, was replaced in 1860 by a new ensemble with painted décor, stalls and altar of white marble. This arrangement was itself altered in 1970 when the altar was moved forward. The **choir organ** above the west end of the enclosure was given by Emperor Napoléon III and Empress Eugénie; an instrument designed for French Romantic music, it is signed Aristide Cavaillé-Col. The **main organ** in the west end below the rose window is one of the finest in the region and is used for concerts during the summer music festival. Built by Jean de Joyeuse, its installation was completed in 1694. The case is carved in chestnut and is decorated with caryatids, eagles and angel musicians, with Our Lady in the centre and reliefs of King David and St Cecilia on the lower part.

South of the cathedral **Place Salinis**, created *c* 1863, is shaded by *micocouliers* (nettle) trees, typical of the Midi. Towering 40m above it is the 14C **Tour d'Armagnac** against the former canons' residence, originally built as a prison with a cell on each level.

East of Place Salinis the famous **Escalier monumental**, built *c* 1863 to the detriment of the old fortifications, descends to the banks of the Gers and the lower town via six flights of steps and three terraces. Covering the central section of the top terrace (from where, in favourable conditions, you might see the Pyrenees) is a vast horizontal relief of words wrought in iron, called *L'Observatoire*. Conceived in 1991 by a Catalan artist, Jaume Plensa, and designed to be walked over—a strange sensation in thin-soled shoes, unwise in high heels—it is engraved with the biblical text of the Flood and recalls the disaster of 1977 when the Gers burst its banks. Its other half, the *Faux Refuge*, is on the opposite bank across the footbridge. Firmin Michelet's bronze statue of **D'Artagnan** (p 381), erected in 1931 on the level below, is far from *avant garde*.

The top terrace of the monumental steps leads to the **Pousterles**, ancient steep lanes with names such as Coulomates (*colombes*) and las Houmettos (*ormeaux*), linking the lower and upper towns, and to the old town gate, the **Porte d'Arton**.

At the end of Rue de la Convention (off Rue Vieille Pousterle) on Place Garibaldi is the former pilgrim **Hôpital de St-Jacques**, rebuilt in 1765. Turn right into Rue d'Espagne. In the tiny courtyard is a splendid staircase. Rue de Valmy leads to Place des Carmélites with a wrought-iron cross and Place Salustre-du-Bartas, named after a Gascon poet (1544–90) born near Cologne (Gers), whose statue is in the square. The municipal library is installed in the former 17C Carmelite chapel and can be visited.

The large Place de la Libération with a circular fountain was one of Intendant d'Etigny's creations, and overlooking it is the **Hôtel de Ville** (1777) which has a room with portraits of illustrious Gersois and a small theatre. At the end of the shady Allées d'Etigny, a statue of the great man, erected in 1817, surveys his work.

North of Place de la Libération on Rue Gambetta the **Maison de Gascogne**, the restored 19C grain market, is now used for shows and the post office opposite has taken over the former Hôtel de l'Intendance (1759). Cut through to **Rue**

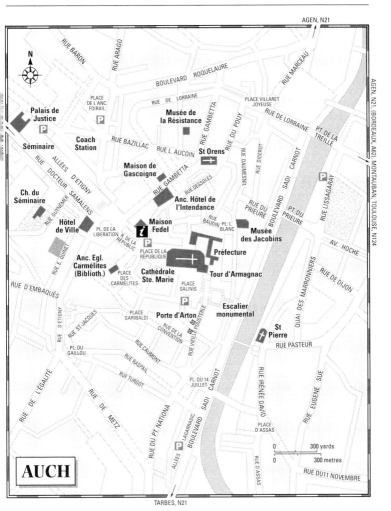

AGEN, N21

BOULEVARD ROQUELAURE

RUE MARCEAU

AGEN, N21 (BORDEAUX, A62) MONTAUBAN, TOULOUSE, N124

N

RUE BARON

RUE ARAGO

PLACE
DE L'ANC.
FOIRAIL

RUE DE LORRAINE

PLACE VILLARET
JOYEUSE

RUE DE LORRAINE

PT. DE LA
TREILLE

Palais de
Justice

Musée de
la Résistance

RUE GAMBETTA

RUE DU POUY

RUE DE LORRAINE

Séminaire

Coach
Station

RUE BAZILLAC

RUE L. AUCOIN

St Orens

RUE DIDEROT

RUE DALIMESNIL

BOULEVARD SADI CARNOT

ALLÉES D'ETIGNY

Maison de
Gascoigne

RUE GAMBETTA

RUE DESSOLES

PT. DU
PRIEURE

RUE LISSAGARAY

Ch. du
Séminaire

RUE DOCTEUR SAMALENS

RUE GUYNEMER

Anc. Hôtel de
l'Intendance

RUE DU
PRIEURE

AV. HOCHE

Hôtel
de Ville

PL. DE LA
LIBERATION

Maison
Fedel

R. DE LA
REPUBLIQUE

RUE
BAUDIN

PL. L.
BLANC

Musée
des Jacobins

Anc. Egl.
Carmélites
(Biblioth.)

RUE E. QUINET

PLACE DE LA
RÉPUBLIQUE

Préfecture

PLACE
DES
CARMELITES

Cathédrale
Ste. Marie

PLACE
SALINIS

Tour d'Armagnac

QUAI DES MARRONNIERS

RUE DE DIJON

RUE D'EMBAQUÉS

RUE D'ETIGNY

RUE ST-JACQUES

PLACE
GARIBALDI

Porte d'Arton

RUE VIEILLE FUSTERIE

Escalier
monumental

RUE DE LA
CONVENTION

St
Pierre

RUE PASTEUR

PL. DU
GAILLOU

RUE CAUMONT

RUE EUGENE SUE

RUE DE L'ÉGALITÉ

RUE RASPAIL

RUE TURGOT

RUE DE METZ

PL. DU 14
JUILLET

RUE SADI CARNOT

RUE IRÉNÉE DAVID

PLACE
D'ASSAS

RUE DU PT. NATIONA

ALLÉES LAGARRABSIC

BOULEVARD SADI CARNOT

RUE D'ASSAS

RUE DU 11 NOVEMBRE

0   300 yards
0   300 metres

AUCH

TARBES, N21

Dessoles, a lively, pedestrianised street (the old Camin Dret) with the 19C Classical-style church of St-Orens at the north end and some notable restorations of *hôtels particuliers* at nos 40 and 45. Should you pass this way in Whit week, you will see on sale at **R. Boiziot**, the butcher on the corner of Rue Bazeilles, the much sought-after quality beef from the bulls killed at the *corrida* at Vic-Fézensac (p 381). The street leads back uphill to the tourist office. The former 18C episcopal palace is now occupied by the *Préfecture*.

To reach the **Musée des Jacobins** in the old Jacobins convent, take the road past the Préfecture, north of the cathedral, and follow the signs. The 15C convent, radically modified in the 17C, was acquired and restored by the town in 1976. Open April–Oct 10.00–12.00 and 14.00–18.00; Nov–March 10.00–12.00 and 14.00; closed Mon, PH; ☎ 05 62 05 74 79.

The museum has some fine Gallo-Roman exhibits displayed, with the medieval items, in an attractive gallery looking out on the garden. It contains some brightly coloured Gallo-Roman frescoes (between 20 BC and 1C AD) found in 1962 at Villa la Sioutat, 9km from Auch. Among the funerary objects is a touching epitaph to a dog called Myia, and a beautiful perfume flask (after 2C AD) found intact in a sepulchre at la Hourre, Auch. There are also medieval carvings, examples of 18C decorative arts, ceramics, 18C and 19C paintings, and a regional ethnological collection of the 19C and 20C. The biggest surprise is the very rich Latin American section donated by Guillaume Pujos in 1921 of Pre-Colombian Mexican and colonial art.

MIRANDE AND THE BASTIDES OF THE ASTARAC

This area has a good sample of the many Gascon *bastides* south and west of Mirande, as well as a couple of small, rustic churches.

Getting there and around
Car
N21to Mirande from Tarbes or Auch.
Bus
Auch to Mont-de-Marsan via Marciac, Plaisance-du-Gers, Riscle.
Auch to Tarbes via Mirande.

 Tourist information
32320 Bassoues Au Donjon, Mairie, ☎ 05 62 70 97 34, fax 05 62 70 90 47
32300 L'Isle-de-Noë (Canton de Montesquiou), ☎ 05 62 70 91 42, fax 05 62 70 95 25
32230 Marciac Bastides et Vallons du Gers, Pl. du Chevaliers d'Antras, ☎ 05 62 09 30 55, fax 05 62 09 31 88, email ot.marciac@wanadoo.fr
32140 Masseube Val de Gers et Hautes Vallées, 14 Ave E. Duffréchou, ☎ 05 62 66 12 22, fax 05 62 66 96 20, email otmasseube@wanadoo.fr
32170 Miélan Pl. du 8 Mai, ☎ 05 62 67 52 26
32300 Mirande 13 Rue de l'Evêché, ☎ 05 62 66 68 10, fax 05 62 66 78 89, email bienvenue@ot-mirande.com
Market days
Bassoues Sunday
Beaumarachais Saturday
Marciac Wednesday
Miélan Thursday
Mirande Monday; *foie gras* market Monday in winter
Seissan Friday, also *marché au gras* October to April

 Festivals and events
July *Festival de Country Music*, Mirande
(third Saturday) *La Madeleine*, important cattle fair, Montesquiou
August *Jazz in Marciac*, the most important jazz festival in southwest France, Marciac, www.marciac.com

 Where to stay and eating out
32300 MIRANDE
☆☆/€€ *Les Pyrénées*, 5 Ave d'Etigny, ☎ 05 62 66 51 16, fax 05 62 66 79 96, email hotel-des-pyrenees@wanadoo.fr. In the heart of Gascony, this hotel is set in a shady park with pool and has a good restaurant.
32300 ST-MAUR
Domaine de Lorantel, ☎ 05 62 66 51 55, fax 05 62 66 78 58. Set in a vast park with cedars and plane trees, this is an elegant and spacious 19C residence with *chambres d'hôte*.

Mirande

Mirande on the banks of the Baïse is one of the largest and best-preserved of the *bastides* of southern Gers.

It was conceived in 1281 as a *paréage* (agreement) between the Counts and the Abbots of Berdoues, and was the old capital of the Astarac, a small medieval fiefdom between Armagnac, Fézensac and Bigorre, between the 10C and 15C. Mirande was a garrison town and Alain-Fournier (1886–1914), author of *Le Grand Meaulnes*, did his officer training here.

The town's outstanding feature is the massive porch-tower of the church, straddling the street. The large square is surrounded by arcades in warm yellowish stone and has a pretty bandstand in the middle. The small but well-presented **Musée des Beaux-Arts et Arts Décoratifs**, in a purpose-built gallery of 1983, contains 15C–19C Italian, Flemish and French paintings, including a number of charming portraits and works attributed to Nicolas Largillière and J.B. van Loo; among the landscapes are one or two from the School of Barbizon. There is an important group of faïence from the main French producers and from the south-west and a few pieces of medieval sculpture. Open Mon–Sat 10.00–12.00 and 15.00–18.00; closed Sun and PH; ☎ 05 62 66 68 10.

The aspiration that Mirande would be raised to the status of episcopal see accounts for the grandiose proportions of the church of **Ste-Marie**, begun in 1409. The most original part of the building, which had to be fitted into an area surrounded by already existing streets and houses, is the west tower and porch. The road runs under the porch, above which flying buttresses support the four-level belfry with turrets and a complex roof. Flying buttresses are used on the north and south elevations, unusual in this part of the world, and although the church gives an impression of homogeneity, only the openings on the southern façade are original. In each façade is an identical portal with a statue of St Anthony on the north and St John the Baptist on the south. The Flamboyant west portal, now closed, was heavily restored in 1877–80. The St-Sacrament chapel contains some 15C glass, the *Virgin and Child* and *St Michael slaying the Dragon*, with the arms of the town. The remainder of the glass was made by Thibault of Clermont-Ferrand in 1860–61.

South of Mirande, isolated in a field between Berdoues and Belloc, is the tiny rustic chapel of **St-Clamens**. The key is held at the farm opposite. This remarkably unaltered 11C chapel was built on the foundations of a Gallo-Roman temple and, to prove it, under the makeshift porch on the south is a white marble pagan funerary monument, discovered in 1886, decorated with reliefs and an inscription to Arulianus, possibly the owner of a Gallo-Roman villa. The minuscule windows of the apse are flanked inside and out by 8C or 9C capitals and columns and inside are 12C and 16C wall paintings in a perilous state. In front of the altar is an outstandingly beautiful white antique marble **sarcophagus** (probably 4C), found on the site *c* 1820. The carving on the lid is a possible allegory of the passing of life represented by a wheel pushed by four winged figures, with a winged head at each corner. The base is more deeply engraved with a portrait of the defunct in a medallion supported by four figures, and either side of it are scenes representing the seasons. The weather-beaten Gothic font was formerly kept outside, and there are two 18C statues.

Take the D939 and the D127 east at St-Michel, and turn right at the sign to seek out the remote 16C chapel of **Theux**, principally for its marvellous site on a ridge between the Baïsole and the Petite Baïse. There are some superb farm buildings around here, built in chequerboard patterns using adobe bricks (sun-baked bricks) and pebbles.

Miélan is a fairly attractive *bastide* founded in 1284, destroyed by the English in 1362, on the 18C route from Paris to Bagnères-de-Bigorre. Between Miélan and Rabastens-de-Bigorre, on the N21, the range of the Pyrenees unfolds before you on a clear day from the **Puntous de Laguian**. At 320m it is one of the highest points in the Gers.

Tillac, north of Miélan on the D3, is an absolute gem of a 13C *castelnau* with a narrow arcaded street bordered with timber-framed houses, two ancient town gateways with towers, and a 14C church with, if you are unwise enough to press the button, a recorded message and guided visit. The church (*c* 1334) was badly damaged by fire in the 19C, destroying the 17C timber roof. The choir stalls on the left are 18C but the rest are neo-Gothic. There is a gilded retable (1741) from the famous Ferrère workshop in the Asté (Pyrenees) and behind it a ciborium with Renaissance decoration.

Marciac

One of the best-known villages in the region is Marciac, a conventional, sleepy 13C *bastide* where, unlikely as it may seem, the population of around 1200 has been swelled beyond all proportion every August since 1979 for the annual jazz festival. The main concerts are held under a zebra-striped marquee on the rugby pitch, and the effervescence bubbles over into the arcaded *place* and streets during the day. The idea is contagious and other towns in the Midi-Pyrénées have their jazzy moments. The exhibition **Territoire du Jazz** is a musical journey through jazz from its origins to the present. Open daily April–Sept 09.30–12.30 and 14.30–18.30; Oct–March, Sun–Fri, closed Sat and PH; ☎ 05 62 09 30 18

The crocketed spire of **Notre-Dame-de-Marciac** marks one of the loveliest churches in the Gers, built in yellow stone in the 14C to the east of the main square. The spire, which stands on a square tower, was completed in 1865 to a height of approximately 90m, making it the highest in the *département*. There are matching early Flamboyant portals on the north and south and a narthex was added in the 15C and closed by a wrought-iron grille in the 18C. The entrance is through the south door. The church has a four-bay nave with aisles with large screened chapels flanking the choir. There is a shallow pentagonal apse and two smaller chapels in the east. The western part of the nave was partly rebuilt after suffering at the hands of Protestant iconoclasts in the 16C when the original octagonal piers and pointed arches were replaced by cylindrical pillars and round arches. The church was vaulted in 1869 when some restoration was accomplished. The nave is lit by a series of rose windows in the clerestory.

There is some rich and interesting **sculpture** in the east of the church which shows a curious nostalgia for the archaic forms and iconography of Romanesque art. The capitals at the entrance to the main apse present *Daniel in the Lions' Den* and *Samson and the Lion*, and in the south apsidal chapel are various episodes from the *Life of St Eligius*, patron saint of blacksmiths. Note also the carvings at the bases of the clustered shafts in the choir. The Flamboyant west porch, enclosed in the 15C when the two chapels either side were added, has some decorative sculpture of varying quality; there are also large sculpted bosses in the narthex.

East of Marciac by the D943, at **St-Christaud**, there is a great Gothic pile in brick with diamond openings, built *c* 1250 on a knoll to watch over the pilgrim route. To the north on the D3 and D946, perched up high, is the pretty little village of **Beaumarchés**. A *bastide* created in 1292, it was named after its founder Eustache de Beaumarchais and is dominated by a Flamboyant church with a massive west porch supporting an incomplete belfry.

The D946 follows an east–west ridge with some good views. The D102 (between Lupiac and Bassoues) leads to the villages of **Baccarisse**, with a 17C church and six-level belfry, **Gazax** with a part-13C church and house in adobe, and **Peyrusse-Grande** which has a part-Romanesque, part-16C church with some fine carvings.

The massive keep (*donjon*) of the village of **Bassoues** on the D943 signals a *bastide* well worth visiting. It was founded by the Archbishops of Auch in 1279 not far from a monastery they acquired in the 13C. The huge square tower with angle buttresses and machicolations (1368) is a magnificent piece of military architecture completing the fortifications to protect the community. It contains a permanent exhibition on *sauvetés, castelnaux* and *bastides* in Gascony. Open daily April–May 10.00–12.00 and 14.00–18.00, June–Oct 10.00–19.00, Nov–March 14.00–17.00; ☎ 05 62 70 97 34. Next to the keep is the former archbishops' residence, which was altered in the 16C and 17C. The other major curiosity is the beautiful 16C timber-framed *halle* which straddles the road, similar to the one at Gimont (see below), with some pretty houses either side. The 15C parish church—aisleless Gothic, rather empty—near the market is built into the slope of the hill. In the cemetery on the western edge of the village, past the keep, is the 15C/19C basilica containing the tomb of the local hero St Fris, nephew of Charles Martel, who died in mortal combat against the infidels near Bassoues in the 8C. The legend of his death is remembered over the south and west doors.

Montesquiou, a picturesque village further east on the D943, with an aristocratic name and home of the maternal family of d'Artagnan, is a small *castelnau* on a hill with a medieval fortified gate. There are prehistoric sites in the neighbourhood, a 12C belfry on the church, and every July there is an important cattle fair here called La Madeleine. **St-Arailles**, north on the D34, is also a picturesque village.

Back on the D943, **Barran** is a well-kept *bastide*—perhaps because it is close to Auch—with golden stone houses and a good market square. It also has a strangely contorted church spire covered in grey slate which, although very celebrated, is slightly unsatisfying as it twists irregularly and looks suspiciously like a case of warped timbers.

THE VALLEYS OF THE SAVE AND THE GIMONE

The villages of the two almost parallel valleys of the Save and Gimone Rivers, southeast of Auch, show the influence of the Toulousain in the predominantly brick buildings, which include the impressive fortified church of Simorre. This region is renowned for its production of *foie-gras*.

Getting there and around
Car

N124 from Auch or Toulouse, and
south on D634 and D632.

Train

Toulouse to Auch via L'Isle Jourdain,
Gimont.

Bus

Toulouse to Auch via L'Isle Jourdain,
Gimont. Montauban to Auch via
Mauvezin. Toulouse to St-Plancard via
Samatan, Lombez.

Tourist information

32430 Cologne 12 Pl. de la
Halle, ☎ 05 62 06 99 30 fx
05 62 06 77 30, email domisyndicat@
wanadoo.fr

32200 Gimont 83 Rue Nationale,
☎ 05 62 67 77 87, fax 05 62 67 93
61, email contact@ot-gimont.com

31230 L'Isle-en-Dodon ☎ 05 61 94
53 56, fax 05 61 94 53 50, email
mairie.social@wanadoo.fr

32600 L'Isle-Jourdain Maison du
Tourisme, Rte de Mauvezin, ☎ 05 62
07 25 57, fax 05 62 07 24 81 email ot-
isle-jourdain@wanadoo.fr

32120 Mauvezin Pl. de la Libération,
☎ 05 62 06 79 47, fax 05 62 06 90
74, email officedetourismedemauvezin@
wanadoo.fr

32130 Samatan 3 Rue du Chamoine
Dieuzaide, ☎ 05 62 62 55 40, fax 05
62 62 50 26, email ot.samatan@
wanadoo.fr

32450 Saramon Mairie, Grande Rue,
☎ 05 62 65 49 71, fax 05 62 65 42
45, email mairie-saramon@free.fr

32420 Simorre Rue de la Mairie,
☎/fax 05 62 65 36 34, email
si.simorre@wanadoo.fr

Market days

Cologne Thursday

Gimont Wednesday; *marché au gras* during the winter

L'Isle-Jourdain Saturday

Lombez Saturday

Mauvezin Monday

Samatan Monday; *marché au gras*

Festivals and events

May *Courses landaises*, cattle running,
Gimont

Where to stay and eating out

32220 GIMONT

✩✩✩ *Château de Larroque*, Rte de
Toulouse, ☎ 05 62 67 77 44, fax 05 62
67 88 90, www.chateau-larroque.com.
Romantically elegant château-hôtel set
in a park; swimming pool, tennis court.

32200 JUILLES

Au Soulan de Laurange, Chemin de la
Devèze, ☎/fax 05 62 67 76 62.
Chambres d'hôte accommodation for up
to 10 guests in this charming 18C *mai-
son de maître* with views towards the
Pyrenees.

Chambres d'hôte, Gérard Crochet and
Alain Petit, Au Soulan de Laurange,
Chemin de la Devèze, 5km southwest of
Gimont (D12), ☎/fax 05 62 67 76 62.
An 18C Tuscan style home, with a flow-
ery terrace, wonderful views over the
côteaux de Gers; *table d'hôte* by reserva-
tion on certain days; pool.

32490 MONFERRAN SAVES

Chambres d'hôte, Anne-Marie and Jean-
Raymond Lannes, Le Meillon, ☎ 05 62
07 83 34, fax 05 62 07 83 57. A farmhouse with a huge garden, pool and
panoramic views. *Table d'hôte* most days.

32600 PUJAUDRAN

Le Puits St-Jacques, Pl. de la Mairie,
☎ 05 62 07 47 11, fax 05 62 07 44
09. In a former pilgrimage staging post,
this is a gastronomic restaurant serving
imaginative dishes based on regional
produce.

32300 ST-MAUR

Chambres d'hôte, Jean and Marie
Nedellec, Domain de Loran, ☎ 05 62 66
51 55, fax 05 62 66 78 58. Warm welcome offered at this handsome Gascon
house with garden and games room.

L'Isle-Jourdain

L'Isle-Jourdain, on the N124 towards Toulouse, is a fairly important town of around 5000 people.

It was the capital of the lands belonging to the de l'Isle family. Count Raymond de l'Isle and his countess accompanied Raymond IV, Count of Toulouse and de l'Isle's cousin, on the First Crusade (1096–99) and while in Palestine the countess gave birth to a son. His baptism in the waters of the Jordan was remembered in the name of the town. Raymond's brother, Bertrand de l'Isle (1044–1124), became Bishop of Comminges (p 492) and was canonised in the 13C. The dynasty died out in the 15C and the county was sold in 1421 to Jean IV, Count of Armagnac.

The town has two squares. The older, Place Gambetta—called the *marcadieu*—with arcades on two sides, is on the edge of the route built by the Intendant of Auch, d'Etigny. The other square contains the late-18C *hôtel de ville*, a sophisticated Italianate building in brick with a rusticated ground floor and wrought-iron balconies above. Adjacent is the Neo-classical brick **halle** (1819), with a mass of elegant octagonal pillars, converted to house the Musée Européen d'art campanaire, which presents the six stages involved in making bells and chimes. Open June–Sept 10.00–12.00 and 14.30–18.00; Oct–May to 17.30; closed Tues; ☎ 05 62 07 30 01. L'Isle-Jourdain was the birthplace of Claude Augé (1854–1924), the creator of the *Dictionnaire complet illustré* (1889), which became the *Petit Larousse Illustré* in 1906, and the building opposite is named after him.

L'Isle adhered to Calvinism and, in common with most Protestant towns, the majority of its pre-17C monuments (castle, fortifications, church) were destroyed. The only fragment of medieval architecture remaining, against the northeast of the church, is the brick **keep** of the château dismantled by Richelieu in 1621. The church was raised to collegiate status in 1318 by Pope Jean XXII. In the late 18C it was replaced by the severely Neo-classical church of **St-Martin**, designed in 1785 by Jean-Arnaud Raymond, which takes the form of two superimposed Greek crosses using the giant Doric order. The interior was entirely decorated in the 19C, the vaults by Engalières (*c* 1879) and the walls by Terral (*c* 1889). The reliquary chapel on the south contains the relics of St Bertrand-de-L'Isle, Bishop of Comminges (1040–1123) and of St Odo, second Abbot of Cluny (879–942), plus a relic of the True Cross.

Alongside the N124 between L'Isle and Toulouse is one of the most impressive *pigeonniers* of a type found frequently in Gascon; there are more along the D634 running southwest.

Gimont

Closer to Auch on the N124 is Gimont, the only town in France where a *route nationale* runs not only straight through the middle but through the covered market straddling it (thankfully there is a by-pass for heavy vehicles). Founded by the Cistercian abbey of Planselve (see below) in 1266, as a *paréage* with Alphonse de Poitiers, Gimont clings to a narrow promontory above the Gimone River, hence the restricted layout.

Originally surrounded by arcades, the massive **halle** has 28 octagonal piers supporting a timber roof, and was heightened and rebuilt in the 19C—there are two dates, 1331 and 1825, on pillars east and west. The *foie gras* markets are not in the old *halle* but in the *marché aux grains* down the hill to the north. In the road-straddling market during May there are *courses landaises*—not the moment to choose to drive through.

The church of **Notre-Dame**, northeast of the *halle*, was planned in 1292 but the date above the porch is 1331. It is mainly in brick: the later belfry is built over the vaulted stone sacristy with a Flamboyant window on the north, whereas the upper brick part is 16C or early 17C. The church contains some interesting items, including a 15C pulpit, an 18C altar in Caunes marble, and a small 15C *Virgin*. The most famous work is a 16C triptych of the *Crucifixion* from nearby Planselve which, according to Flemish tradition, has a painted central panel and carved wings. There are relief sculptures of the Virgin, St Lazarus and an Angel of the Last Judgement, and Mary Magdalene and St Martha on the outside.

Close to Gimont on the D12 is all that remains of the **abbey of Planselve**. Divided between two privately owned properties, it was opened to the public in 1992 and can be visited with a guide; for details contact the tourist information offices.

This was an important Cistercian abbey whose origins in 1142 are well documented. It maintained a hospice and chapel for pilgrims on the edge of the property and prospered until 1557 but deteriorated at the hands of absentee abbots, during the Wars of Religon and the Revolution, until in 1802 demolition began. The buildings are almost entirely in brick. The little that is left is unusual and interesting. The property was enclosed in a long brick wall, and the entrance is through the 14C gate-house which contains a model of the monastery in 1737. There are two beautiful *pigeonniers* near the Gimone.

South of the N124, along the Save Valley (D634), is the **Château de Caumont**, on high ground with a spectacular view of the Pyrenean range. The main body of the château is screened by neo-Gothic outbuildings. Guided visits, July, Aug daily 15.00–18.00; May–June, Sept–Oct, Sat, Sun and PH 15.00–18.00; ☎ 05 62 07 94 20, email chcaumont@aol.com.

The present residence, was begun *c* 1535 on the site of a medieval fortress by Pierre de Nogaret la Valette, who had accompanied François I on his campaigns in Italy. He endowed his property with elements of Renaissance elegance and comfort without altering the basic medieval structure. The defences were dismantled after the Wars of Religion and the château was damaged by fire in the 17C.

When James MacMahon, an Irish mercenary, married Pauline de Montgaillard la Valette in the late 18C, he chose to adapt the château to the then highly fashionable *style troubadour* (early Gothic revival), ruining much of the property and himself. He also made an unsuccessful bid to breed merino sheep.

The main building, alternating brick and poor-quality stone from Auch, is arranged around three sides of a courtyard whose level was raised by MacMahon and lowered by the present owners, who have restored most of the windows. At the exterior angles are square towers with steeply pitched roofs, and between these flanking the north entrance (16C) are two stairtowers with pepper-pot roofs. The east façade has a gallery supported by huge stone corbels, the west (17C) has a rusticated loggia on the ground floor, and the south is also 17C.

Throughout the interior there are examples of MacMahon's Romantic intentions, including the vast hall or Salon Troubadour painted in neo-medieval *trompe l'oeil*. The second salon (1840), is in *style Pompéien* or Malmaison style. Also open to view are the library behind the door in the tower, the kitchen and the cellars, the first-floor corridor transformed by MacMahon and the bedroom known as La Chambre du Roi where, legend has it, Henri IV slept. Most moving is the little chapel created by MacMahon and his son-in-law the Marquis de Castelbajac, one of Napoléon's generals and Ambassador to Napoléon III, for Caroline MacMahon, Marquise de Castelbajac who died at 18 in childbirth.

The small town of **Samatan** is the location for the most famous of all the *marchés au gras* (*foie gras* markets) in the region. Although not for the squeamish, these are reassuring indications of the ritualistic importance that the French still put on the production, selection and purchase of food. At Samatan the markets are held on Mondays on the edge of the town in three huge sheds beside the car park. The *foies* (livers), weighing anything from 400 to 900g, are set out on long trestles in one of the three sheds and the trading is done rapidly by barter. There are three markets: the first for *foie gras* itself, at about 09.45; at 10.45 the poultry carcasses are sold; and at 11.30 is the *marché de volailles*, live poultry and other animals. Not surprisingly, Samatan has the Musée du fois gras et des traditions populaires, open July, Aug, 10.00–12.00 and 15.00–17.00; ☎ 05 62 62 55 40; see also www.foie-gras-gers.com.

Foie gras

This is a major product of the southwest of France, especially Gascony and the Périgord and is a by-product of both geese and ducks. The Egyptians reputedly noticed that migrating geese naturally overfeed thus extending their livers before long flights. This knowledge was passed on to the Jews of eastern Europe, but the production of foie gras in Gaul was promoted by the Romans who fed the geese on figs. From *jecur ficatum* (*la foie due au figue*, liver thanks to figs) came, *figuido* (8C), *fedie, feie* and finally *foie*. Although geese and ducks virtually disappeared from the southwest with the Romans, they were known to be present in the Béarn in the 14C/15C. The turning point came in the mid-16C with the introduction of maize from the Americas, which proved to be an ideal foodstuff for poultry. About the same time it was known that the Jews of eastern Europe had inherited Egyptian knowhow for producing *foie gras*. It was made a fashionable delicacy by Louis XVI.

There are more ducks (over 4,000,000) than geese (130,000) reared in the Gers, and this imbalance is general throughout the *foie gras* producing areas. The ducks (Mulard ducks are used, a cross between the Barbary and common Pekin duck) and geese are reared free-range, once they have their adult plumage, until they are brought into the feeding sheds for the last two or three weeks of their lives where *gavage* or feeding takes place two or three times a day, depending on species. In the Gers, good quality white maize is used. The fattened liver is not diseased and will return to normal if the bird is released and the process is not painful or harmful. As one farmer explained ' to 'ave good fois gras you 'ave to 'ave 'appy ducks'. The products associated with duck and geese are high in polyunsaturates and therefore contribute to the low incidence of heart disease in the southwest (along with the red wine of course).

The fashionable drink to serve with *foie gras* is a high-quality sweet white wine—Sauternes, Monbazillac or Jurançon for example—but this is not to everyone's taste. There is a confusing range of *foie gras*; the goose variety is considered slightly more delicate and sweeter than the duck. Fresh, the liver can be cooked (fried) in slices at a high temperature as a main course or starter. *Foie gras mi-cuit*, is 100 per cent *foie gras*, cooked and pasturised and available in jars or tins. Most traditional is the *foie entier* (whole), in its sterilised form, conserved in jars or tins and served cold as a starter. There are also mixes: *mass* is 100 per cent *foie gras* but reconstituted; *parfait* is miniumum 75 per cent; *mousse, galantines* or *pâtés*, are minimum 50 per cent *foie gras* mixed with pork or another meat. Sometimes the *foie gras* is flavoured with *truffes* (truffles). These products can be bought at the specialist markets (*marchés aux gras*), in general markets, in stores, and directly from the producers.

Lombez

The nearby community of Lombez is gathered around the **Cathédrale Ste-Marie**. The diocese, founded in 1317, was one of several in the region created by Pope John XXII and lists 32 bishops until its suppression by Pius V in 1801. A plaque to the right of the west entrance records the visit of the Italian poet Petrarch in 1330, arranged by Bishop Jacques Colonna (1328–41), himself of Italian extraction, who made Petrarch an honorary canon in 1335. The old Tribunal (now the *mairie*) has a permanent exhibition dedicated to the poet.

The rather severe exterior of the brick church is characteristic of the Midi Toulousain with tall buttresses around the chevet, *mirandes* (ventilation holes) below the roof, and a five-tiered octagonal belfry with mitred bays. The foundations, belfry and first bay were constructed *c* 1346 and the west end has the typical blank face of meridional Gothic relieved only by a small roundel and the Flamboyant entrance in stone.

The interior is divided into two by an enfilade of pillars, similar to the Jacobins church in Toulouse, but the north section is smaller than the south. Beside the first pillar on the left is a trap door which opens to reveal the floor level before it was raised as protection against flooding. The restored 12C baptistery in the northwest, below the tower, was part of an earlier church. It has an eight-rib vault and contains a remarkable collection of treasures. Outstanding is the lead **baptismal font** referred to by Eugène Viollet-le-Duc in his *Dictionnaire Raisonné*: it is made of two separate pieces, the lower decorated with religious figures in medallions in the style of the 13C and the upper part with a frieze of profane scenes of antique design. It was possibly made up of two disparate pieces stored in the workshop. The stopper in the base suggests it was used for total immersion which was practised until the 9C. Other items worth noting are a late-15C sculpture of the **Dead Christ**; 17C choir stalls in walnut, less grandly carved than those of Auch but with some splendid atlantes on the episcopal throne; the altar in Carrara marble was consecrated in 1753, and has a bas-relief by François Lucas; the wooden balustrade from the chancel (1671–1710); some quality 18C ironwork by G. Bertin; and the 18C organ. The brilliantly coloured 15C–16C glass by the followers of Arnaud de Moles, restored in the 19C, illustrates scenes from the *Life of Christ* and from the *Passion*.

The church shares the square with a fine **covered market** with brick pillars, and its walls with the houses to the south.

L'Isle-en-Dodon, further south on the Save by the D17, is a classic *bastide* with a central square surrounded by arcades; a Neo-classical brick *hôtel de ville/halle*, and several timber-framed houses. The 14C church has a fortified east end with battlemented towers and an octagonal belfry over the west porch. A Gallo-Roman stone altar is embedded in the east wall and the vivid 16C stained glass expresses a debt to the work of Arnaud de Moles.

Between Gaujan, on the Gimone valley (D12), and Meilhan, the courage of the Resistance during the Second World War is commemorated by a tall carved columnar monument marking the site where 84 members of the *Maquis* (the underground French resistance movement) died on 7 July 1944.

The formidable brick church of **Simorre** now stands in a large empty square but was once part of a Benedictine community, its abbey documented since the 9C.

After it was destroyed by fire *c* 1140, the present site was chosen to start again. Some 600m of walls and a ditch protected the religious as well as the secular community, both under the control of the abbots. A cloister was built in 1240 and the new brick church, begun in 1292, was blessed in 1309 when a long drawn-out feud between the abbots and the Counts of Astarac was coming to an end. The octagonal belfry and sacristy were added in 1350, and from 1442 the church was lengthened towards the west, using stone, while in the 15C the abbey buildings were embellished. With many changes during the 16C, fire damage in the 17C and repairs and demolition from 1756 until the Revolution, the monastic buildings were lost. In 1843 Simorre's historic and architectural importance was recognised and Viollet-le-Duc stepped in to restore and modify the church between 1844 and 1858. Further restoration was carried out in 1960.

A sturdy version of Toulousain Gothic with shallow articulation of the elevations, it has a military appearance emphasised by the continuous crenellations added (or extended) in the 19C. The 14C stone façade was originally preceded by a porch with a Flamboyant doorway and you can see the gable embedded in the southwest wall. On each of the short transept arms is a small belltower. The striking exposed brick nave was entirely rib-vaulted in the 14C. Over the crossing is an octagonal lantern on pendentives and ribs, with mitred openings. Although the west end is blank, the fenestration is surprisingly rich in the east part, with fine 14C tracery and a variety of stained glass, the oldest (1357) in the upper part of the square east end. Five windows of the choir and south transept have stained glass dated 1482, and one 1519. The stained glass opposite the south door is 1525, and there is a 19C imitation of the original style in the north transept window. The very fine carved choir stalls, sadly mutilated in parts, were a gift in 1517 from Jean Marre, a monk of Simorre who became Bishop of Condom. In the north transept there is an interesting 15C *Pietà* with several figures. The sacristy has murals of 1380; for opening times and guided visits, ☎ 05 62 65 36 34. There are some pretty houses in the village.

North of Simorre, near Saramon, which has Renaissance houses, is **Boulaur**, a serene and appropriately *bon locus* for the only active Cistercian community of nuns in the Gers who some years ago took over a long-abandoned Fontrevist house founded in 1142. Visits are possible outside the hours of mass: contact the tourist office. Note the barns to the left with wooden latticework typical of southern Gascony. The 13C–14C abbey church with *mirandes* and a watchtower was restored in the late 20C. The spacious interior has painted décor in the manner of the Jacobins in Toulouse. Most of the buildings and the fine wrought iron of the church are 18C.

On the Arrats river to the west, on the D40, **Castelnau-Barbarens** is arranged in terraces around a castle which was razed in the 19C to make way for a parish church. It is worth stopping to investigate the 17C Notre-Dame-de-la-Pitié, the arcaded streets and steep flight of steps, and the views.

In the direction of Auch is **Pessan**, which once had a small abbey whose origins in the 8C place it among the oldest in the Gers. The church of St-Michel is all that remains, with elements from the 11C to the 19C. The 11C church was damaged in 1250 although the transept survived. The east end, elegantly rebuilt *c* 1252, is dominated by a little square tower and slate spire. There are some 15C choir stalls.

To the north of the N124, on the D12, is **Mauvezin**, a village on a hill between the Arratz and the Gimone rivers. It was once an important stronghold but in the 17C the castle was divided up and the fortifications dismantled. It is laid out around a vast empty square surrounded by mainly 18C whitish limestone houses, with the 14C *halle* on stone piers to one side. The post office is in a 16C building, and the *hôtel de ville* is 17C.

Solomiac is a late *bastide* (13C) on the Gimone with a 14C *halle* and 15C and 16C *couverts* (arcades) around it. Curious and picturesque **Sarrant** is a circular village arranged around its church, with a 14C tower over the old town gateway.

East of Mauvezin, on the D654, is arguably one of the prettiest *bastide* squares and covered markets, at **Cologne**. Wide-open and spacious, it is surrounded by houses harmoniously combining brick, stone and timber, all well restored, the oldest on the north and south. The *halle* itself is 14C. This is a simple structure, with a small square building in the centre (used for exhibitions) from which the roof radiates out, supported by stone piers at the angles and wooden pillars elsewhere, the whole thing topped by a small belfry. There are still 15C grain measures under the *halle*.

20 Pyrénées-Atlantiques: Pays Basque

The Basque region of France, Pays Basque, is part of the modern *département* of the Pyrénées-Atlantiques in the southwesternmost tip of France. A small world of its own, it encompasses the old provinces of Labourd, Basse-Navarre and Soule and its limits are the Adour River to the north, the Gave de Mauléon to the east, Spain to the south and, to the west, the ocean. The Pays Basque is linked historically, geographically and linguistically to the Spanish Basque region, but as part of French Aquitaine it also has many differences.

With the benefit of both the Atlantic coast and the Pyrenees, there is a stunning variety of scenery and the climate is mild, especially on the coast; the mountain weather is notoriously variable. The main towns, Bayonne and Biarritz, are close geographically but poles apart in character. Different again are the old coastal port of St-Jean-de-Luz and St-Jean-Pied-de-Port in the foothills of the Pyrenees. The domestic architecture is very specific to the region, as are the post-Reformation galleried churches. The Basque people proudly defend many of the region's characteristics and customs, including the language, Euskara, and sports, notably variations of *pelote*.

History

The Basques have populated this part of Europe since time immemorial and have retained their identity despite being infiltrated and fought over. In the 9C the semi-legendary Inigo Arista founded the dynasty of Navarre and made Pamplona his capital. Two centuries later, Sanche III le Grand (1000–35) annexed many Spanish territories, giving him control of the passes through the Pyrenees used by pilgrims. Navarre passed to the Kingdom of Aragon in 1076, then recovered its independence until the 13C when, for one reason or another, it passed back and forth between French and Spanish dynastic houses. It became French in 1285 and returned to Aragon in 1425. In 1484 the title King of Navarre passed to the house of Albret through the marriage of Jean d'Albret to Catherine de Foix. This provoked Ferdinand of Aragon to annex the Navarre peninsula in 1512 and split it. Jeanne III d'Albret inherited only Basse-Navarre, a tiny province north of the Pyrenees (the area around St-Jean-Pied-de-Port), and from her it passed to her son, the future Henri IV of France. It was absorbed into France finally in 1620.

The Labourd, on the coastal region, which had existed since 1023, and the Soule, on the border with the Béarn (see p 432), were indistinct parts of the Duchy of Gascony and became loosely attached to English Aquitaine. Soule reverted to the House of Foix in 1449 and both ceded to France in 1451. The Treaty of the Pyrenees, which definitively laid down the frontier territories of Spain and France, was signed in 1659 and gave both sides the security to confirm local liberties or customs, such as the authority of human justice, *fors* in France, *fueros* in Spain. At the Revolution these local privileges were suppressed and the Pays Basque experienced a harsh period with a decline in the fishing industry and the burden of war with Spain. In 1813 the war spread into Labourd as the Imperial army retreated across it, and there were battles there between generals Wellington and Soult. The city of Bayonne held out until the French defeat at Orthez (see p 448).

The start of the fight for Basque liberty began in 1895 with the founding of the Basque Nationalist Party (*Partido nacionalista vasco*), whose objective was to unite the seven Basque provinces of France and Spain. Its founder, Sabino Arana Goiri (1865–1903) created the word *Euzkadi* (Basque Country), adopted by the Basque community and introduced the *ikurrina*, the red flag with a green and a white cross. Autonomy was granted to the Spanish Basque regions in 1936 but General Franco's regime rescinded this, resulting in the birth of *ETA* (*Euzkadi ta Azktasuna*, Freedom for the Basques) in 1959. The French nationalist movement *Embata*, created in 1960, was much less active.

BAYONNE

Bayonne is a busy city at the confluence of the Nive and Adour with elegant and colourful river frontages and a uniquely confident charm. It is just 7km from the Atlantic coast, spans the Basque–Gascon frontier, and is the capital and main commercial centre of the Pays Basque. As the second largest urban centre in the *département* of the Pyrénées-Atlantiques, with 42,000 inhabitants, it is a close rival in attractions to Pau. For culture lovers it offers two excellent museums, the Musée Bonnat and the Musée Basque, and there are chocolate houses to satisfy the most decadent chocoholics. If you think that the name of the city has a familiar ring, this is probably due to the fact that it gave its name to the bayonet (*baïonette*). *Les Fêtes de Bayonne*, an important festival inspired by that of St Firmin in Pamplona, is held during the first week of August. Bayonne was the first French city to formalise the *corrida*.

History

The Romans had a fortified encampment above the estuary in the 4C, called *Lapurdum* (the origin of the province of Labourd). The name Bayonne appeared only in the 11C. Part of the Duchy of Aquitaine, in 1125 it received a charter of emancipation and came under English domination between 1151 and 1452. Richard the Lionheart separated the city from the Labourd in 1174 and as a result Bayonne went from strength to strength. Fortifications were built and a new cathedral begun in the mid-13C. Bayonne became a shipbuilding and naval outpost for the English, whom it supported during the Hundred Years War, but in 1451 it returned to France. Around this time, sand blocked the mouth of the Adour estuary at Capbreton, causing disastrous flooding and altering the course of the river to run into the ocean some 30km further north.

A period in the doldrums was followed by a revival in the 16C due to the city's strategic position *vis-à-vis* Spain, and because in 1578 Charles IX's engineer, Louis de Foix, redirected the Adour to create a new mouth, Boucau-Neuf, 6km to the west of the city. Bayonne was protected by its girdle of defences during the Wars of Religion and the Fronde, but Louis XIV instructed his engineer Vauban to construct more fortifications and a citadel as protection against Spain. The maritime trade with Europe and the West Indies, cod and whale fishing in the New World, and shipbuilding secured the prosperity of the town in the 18C. It was declared a free port in 1784, by which time maritime activity had moved further downstream. In 1814,

Bayonne held out until the French defeat at Orthez (see p 448), proving its motto *Nunquam Polluta* ('Never Defiled'). The railway came in 1854 and the town expanded beyond its cordon of fortifications to spread westwards along the Adour, leaving the old centre largely unaltered. Continuing restoration is re-enhancing the magnificent houses, with woodwork painted crisply in *sang de boeuf* red, greens and blues against white walls. The important docks at Boucau and Anglet make Bayonne the ninth river port in France, handling 4,500,000 tonnes of shipping—industrial, military, pleasure and fishing.

Practical information

Getting there and around
Airport
Biarritz/Bayonne International Airport, ☎ 05 59 43 83 83, www.biarritz. aeroport.fr
Shuttle bus (*navette*) to Biarritz centre, Anglet-Plage and Bayonne; also to St-Jean-de-Luz; and to Hendaye. By taxi, 5mins to Biarritz, 10mins to Bayonne.
Car
From Paris, Autoroute A10 and N10. From Toulouse, N117 and A64. From Spain (Bilbao) A8, A63.
Train
TGV Atlantique from Paris Montparnasse (4h 36min), and TGV from Lille.
TER Bordeaux to Hendaye via Bayonne, Biarritz, Guéthary, St-Jean-de-Luz-Ciboure.
TER Toulouse to Bayonne.
TER Bayonne to St-Jean-Pied-de-Port. Station 3km from centre of Bayonne, ☎ 05 59 50 83 07, www.sncf.fr
Bus
Bayonne to Biarritz and Anglet-Plage. Bayonne to Irun via Biarritz, Bidart, Guéthary, St-Jean-de-Luz, Ciboure, Urrugne, Béhobie, Hendaye.
From train station, buses to Capbreton, Hossegor, Seignosse.

Tourist information
64108 Bayonne Pl. des Basques, BP 819, ☎ 05 59 46 01 46, fax 05 59 59 37 55, www.bayonne-tourisme.com
Agence de Tourisme du Pays Basque, 1 Rue de Donzac, BP 811, 64108 Bayonne Cedex, ☎ 05 59 46 46 64, fax 05 59 46 46 60, www.tourisme64.com
64600 Anglet 1 Av. de la Chambre d'Amour, ☎ 05 59 03 77 01, fax 05 59 03 55 91, www.anglet-tourisme.com

Market days
Bayonne Monday to Saturday (all day Friday) in the covered market; Wednesday, Pl. des Gascons; Friday, Pl. de la République and Polo Beyris; Tuesday, Thursday, Saturday, clothes, Carreau des Halles and produce, Quais de la Nive; Friday, flea market, Pl. Paul Bert and first Saturday of month, Remparts Lachepaillet
Anglet Thursday and Sunday
Ustaritz Saturday

Guided walks
Themed 2hr walks from the tourist office Oct–July, Sat 15.00

Boat trips
Boat *Le Bayonne*, from *Allées Bouffleurs* (left bank), Adour and tributaries, ☎ 06 8074 21 51
Les pays du Val d'Adour (from Hastingues, Urt, Lahonce and from Landes bank), *Balades en Couralins*, river cruises and, reservations at least 24hours in advance, ☎ 05 58 73 16 08 or 05 59 56 88 15

Festivals and events
April *Foire aux Jambons*, ham fair

May *Journées du Chocolat*, celebration of the product and visits to producers
July *Jazz aux Remparts. Marché Médiéval*, Pl. Montaut, medieval market
August *Les Fêtes de Bayonne*, five-day festival with dancing, traditional sports (e.g. *pelote*) and *corridas* (the latter continue till September)
October *Festival du Théâtre Franco-Ibérique et Latino-Americain*, festival of theatre.

Where to stay and eating out
6 4 1 0 0 B A Y O N N E

☆☆☆ *Loustau*, 1 Pl. de la République, ☎ 05 59 55 08 08, fax 05 59 55 69 36. Recently renovated and in a central position.
☆☆☆ *La Patoula*, at Ustaritz, about 12km south on D932, ☎ 05 59 93 00 56, fax 05 59 93 16 56. Hotel-restaurant set in a park on the banks of the Nive.

Central Bayonne has three old *quartiers* based on commercial and military traditions. Vieux (Grand) Bayonne lies around the cathedral on the west bank of the Nive, and Petit Bayonne on the east bank, while St-Esprit is on the north bank of the Adour.

Start the visit to **Vieux (Grand) Bayonne** from the *hôtel de ville* and municipal theatre (1842), Pl. de la Liberté, on the banks of the Nive, with a mosaic in the forecourt of the arms and motto of the town. This was a busy commercial centre from the very beginning and several of the street names still refer to local trades or guilds. Just beyond the *hôtel de ville*, at the end of Rue Victor-Hugo, **Hôtel de Brethous** (1732), was occupied by the young Hugo when he accompanied his father, a General of the Empire, to the acceptance by Napoléon of the surrender of Spain in 1808. Rue Victor-Hugo is aligned with the bridges that span the Nive and Adour in an area that was originally marshland, with houses propped on timber supports. Until the end of the Middle Ages the streets perpendicular to the river were canals where cargoes were off-loaded, lined with arcades with living quarters above. Wooden bridges were eventually erected, **Pont Mayou** (Main Bridge) being the first. By the 17C–18C quays for receiving merchandise had been built to replace the canals.

Rue du Port-de-Castets, opposite Pont Marengo, leads to the **Carrefour des Cinq Cantons**, the site of the Roman east gate and of the first stock exchanges in France. This was the medieval gathering-place for tradespeople between the upper and lower towns. At the heart of the pedestrian area is an impressive variety of old buildings, notably the grand **Maison Sorhaindo** on Rue Orbe, where Louis XIV stayed before his marriage to the Infanta Maria-Theresa (see p 417). **Rue du Port-Neuf** (off Rue Orbe) was a canal lined with arcades—now mainly rebuilt—and is famous for its *chocolatiers*, descendents of the first chocolate houses in France. The dark ambrosia can be sampled at *Cazenave*, whose reputation rests on drinking chocolate, or *Daranats*, best known for chocolate bars.

Three of the typical tall and narrow Bayonnais buildings in **Rue de Salie** have been rehabilitated, the façades conserved and the original colour schemes strictly adhered to. As you walk up Rue Argenterie and Rue du Pilori towards the highest part of Bayonne, the tall apse of the cathedral comes into sight on **Place Pasteur**. This was important in the Middle Ages as the site of the gallows and of the old *maison de vesiau* or *hôtel de ville*, which became the Palais de Justice in the 19C.

Bayonne's chocolate houses

Bayonne was the first city in France to manufacture chocolate. Cacao beans and cocoa were discovered by Cortez in Mexico in 1518 and were carried from the New World to Spain in 1585, but did not reach France until the early 17C. The introduction of the chocolate trade to Bayonne was attributed to Sephardic Jews, expelled from Spain and Portugal at the time of Ferdinand and Isabella and the Inquisition. Around 1619 they settled in the St-Esprit *quartier* outside the main part of Bayonne. The cocoa merchants among them traded directly with the Americas and the word 'chocolate' was documented in Bayonne for the first time in 1670. The trade thrived so that by the mid-19C there were some 33 chocolate producers. After a downturn in the 20C, the Académie du chocolat was established in 1993 and there are once more several chocolate houses in Vieux Bayonne, as well as a chocolate museum in Biarritz (see below).

Cathédrale Ste-Marie

Ste-Marie is the exception to the rule of most Gothic churches in this region because it was almost entirely modelled on the cathedrals of northern France. Open Mon–Sat 07.30–12.00 and 15.00–19.00, Sun 15.30–18.30; no visits during services. It was begun in 1258 to replace a Romanesque structure destroyed by fire, and was therefore built during English occupation of Aquitaine. It was completed in the 15C. There were additions in the 16C but the 18C, unsympathetic to Gothic architecture, did it no favours, while the Revolutionary period wrought more havoc. Restoration work began in the 19C under the supervision of Emile Boeswillwald.

Exterior From Place Pasteur there is an uninterrupted view of the very fine 13C **east end**, with radiating chapels between pinnacled buttresses and double lancet windows with oculi reminiscent of Reims. The balustrade was restored in the 19C. By the time the transepts, nave and aisles were constructed in the 14C the Rayonnant style of Gothic architecture had taken over and flying buttresses introduced. The north porch, with two polygonal turrets, lost its sculptures during the Revolution and was clumsily restored, but a magnificent bronze **door-knocker** (15C–16C) has survived. At the beginning of the 16C, a Flamboyant sacristy and chapter house were added. At the west there was already a south tower (end 15C or 16C), and in the 19C a north tower was begun to balance it. This was completed only in the 20C—the white stone is 19C and the yellow 20C—and both towers were topped off with matching spires. The gable between carries a copy of the original *Pietà*, and the balustrade above the rose window is a restoration. The restored porch is a mixture of Rayonnant and Flamboyant, its statuary destroyed in 1793–94.

Interior The relatively narrow 13C choir is surrounded by an ambulatory and chapels; the seven-bay nave was built in the 14C. Typical of Rayonnant architecture are the fine responds and mullion shafts, thin vault ribs, triforium and clerestory, giving an impression of height (26m) and lightness. Rib **bosses** in the east bring together the leopards of England and the fleurs de lis of France; brightly painted in the south transept vaults are the arms of Bayonne complete with sailboat, castle and five sailors surrounded by the four Evangelists. The glass in the upper part of the nave dates from the 16C and 17C, restored in the 19C and 20C, and represents the ***Creation*** (south) and the ***Nativity*** and scenes from the New Testament (north), whereas the rose window in the west is 20C. In the south aisle is a rose window with mouchette tracery and 15C glass; the most celebrated window (1531) in the second chapel on the north shows the story of the ***Canaanite Woman*** with donor figures. It is worth trying to find someone to open the 16C Flamboyant-style **sacristy** which protects an almost intact 13C double portal. Influenced by Reims, it carries the ***Adoration of the Virgin*** and ***Virgin and Child*** on the left, and a ***Last Judgement*** on the other side. The main altar is 19C, with a ciborium in gilded wood designed by Boeswillwald; the Baroque pulpit sculpted in mahogany from the Canaries and the organ case are both 18C.

The splendid **cloister** (open June–Sept 09.30–18.00; Oct–May 09.30–12.30 and 14.00–17.00), on the south side, was built in the 12C–13C and reworked in the 15C–16C. It has three surviving wings: the north was demolished in the 19C. It is particularly spacious and unusual in that it starts at the level of the third bay of the nave and encompasses the transept. The west aisle, which has delicate tracery of four lancets and three oculi, is the oldest and may in parts survive from the earlier construction. The south tracery has slight variations, and the east gallery has similar tracery and vault bosses to the south, although the ribs spring from corbels sculpted from large pieces of limestone. The cloister was originally used as a cemetery and there are the remains of tombs and tombstones; it was also used for guild meetings.

The former bishops' palace, opposite the west door of the cathedral, is now the municipal library and behind it is the **Château Vieux** (no admission), a low, heavy building with four towers and curtain walls, begun at the time of the Viscounts of Labourd in the 11C–12C but much altered. The keep was demolished in the 17C when Vauban was extending the fortifications. It was used by the English seneschal 1154–1451 and occupied by the Black Prince who imprisoned Bernard du Guesclin, hero of the French and thorn in English flesh, here in 1367. And it was from here that, after François I's defeat at Pavia in 1525, the Duc de Montmorency sent a ransom of 2000 *écus* to free the royal children held hostage. This district, the highest part of Bayonne, is riddled with about 200 **vaulted cellars**, constructed from the 13C to 18C to protect merchandise from fire and used as shops and stores. Visits are organised by the tourist office.

West of the Château Vieux, alongside Rue du Rempart-Lachepaillet, is the **Passage de la Pusterle**, through ramparts built by Vauban in the 17C, with a gateway decorated in antique style to the glory of Hercules. On the other side of the ramparts is a small **botanic garden** with Japanese overtones, and some 1000 species.

Rue des Faures was the blacksmiths' street where the first *baïonnette* was forged in the 16C, and is now a neighbourhood of antique shops. Here, too, there is one of the last craftsmen making *makilas*, the traditional Basque walking-stick ideal for pilgrimages and hiking. The wood used is from the medlar: it is initially carved while still attached to the tree, cut six months later and dried over several years, and secreted in the handle is a fine steel blade.

At the end of Rue d'Espagne is **Porte de l'Espagne** where the three successive building campaigns of the fortifications can be distinguished: the Gallo-Roman section and the bases of semi-circular medieval towers; a section of the 16C wall; and Vauban's construction. Follow Rue Tour-du-Sault. (On the left is a little

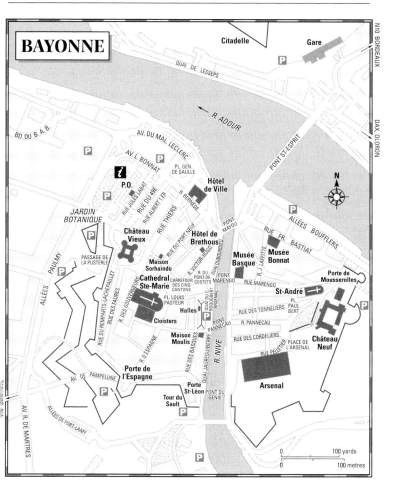

square, **La Plachotte**, with a fragment of the Gallo-Roman walls and a fine Renaissance tower.) At the end, facing the Nive, is the **Tour du Sault**, a section of the old barrier protecting the port. In the gardens south of the old tower is a fountain dedicated to St Léon, patron saint of Bayonne who, after spreading the gospel in the north of Spain, returned to Bayonne but was beheaded for his troubles by Norman pirates. Where his head fell a spring gushed forth; the martyr picked up his head (as they do) and ran 300 steps to this place where first a tomb, and then a chapel, were erected.

Rue des Basques, parallel with the river, has conserved its 13C layout and is lined with jettied houses sporting wrought-iron balconies. From Quai Jaureguiberry is a classic view of the elevations and quays of Petit Bayonne, and at the Pont Pannecau end stands the very splendid 17C timbered **Maison Moulis**, altered in the 19C, which appears to be three houses, but is in fact one, with three *corps-de-logis*. It was originally painted in ox-blood to protect the timbers from damp. It overlooks the *halle*, rebuilt in the 1990s in 19C style, which has small restaurants inside. The buildings around the square are mainly 18C–19C.

Pont Marengo and Pont Pannecau link Quai du Commandant-Roquebert with **Petit Bayonne**, the 'new borough' or Borc Nau established on the marshes in the 12C and then populated by important religious communities. Now the picturesque narrow streets and regular façades shelter the town's two major museums. In times gone by, female miscreants were punished by being dipped in the river from **Pont Pannecau** and the Basque museum owns a replica of the type of cage used. The large complex of buildings to the south of Pont Pannecau is the refurbished Arsenal. Rue des Tonneliers, to the north, home to the coopers' guild and base for corsairs, was originally an arcaded canal. This street leads to **Trinquet St-André**, one of the oldest enclosed *pelote* courts in the Pays Basques where Louis XIV reputedly played *jeu de paume*. Check the sporting calendar at the tourist office for games. Next door is the neo-Gothic church of St-André which contains a painting of ***The Assumption*** by Léon Bonnat (see below).

Pelote Basque

Traditional to the Pays Basque and Béarn, *pelote* (meaning 'ball') is a game played out-of-doors against a *fronton* (wall) by two teams of three players or *pelotaris*. The name comes from the Roman handball game *pila*, which evolved into *jeu de paume* (real tennis) in France and fives at Eton College in England. *Pelote Basque* falls into three basic categories—*main nue*, played with the bare hand; *chistera*, using a wicker basket; and *pala*, played with a wooden racquet—but there are something like 21 variations on these themes. The *chistera* is a long curved wicker basket attached to a leather glove, worn like an extension to the player's arm to throw and catch the ball. It developed first in Spain out of a need to protect the players' hands, and spread to the Labourd. Today there is only one *chistera*-maker in France, based in Anglet. *Cesta punta* is a more modern and spectacular version of *pelota main nue*, played in a covered court with three walls (*jaï alaï*); it was introduced some 30 years ago and is reputed to be the fastest ball game in the world. Matches and tournaments are advertised locally. Each Basque or Béarnais community has its *fronton* or *trinquet* and it is not unusual to find a game of *pelote* underway in a village on a summer's evening.

Place Paul-Bert is the centrepiece for the annual *Fêtes de Bayonne* and the *courses de vaches* (see p 402). The **Château-Neuf**, with two enormous round towers, was built on the orders of Louis XI after Bayonne was attached to France. Completed in 1498, it faces towards the town to keep an eye on the troublesome Bayonnais, and has 17C and 19C additions. It is now used for temporary exhibitions in conjunction with the Basque museum (see below). In the fortifications behind the Château-Neuf, reinforced by Vauban in the 17C, is the **Porte de Mousserolles**, which still has its drawbridge. Further west, just off Place de l'Arsenal at 41 Rue des Cordeliers, is **Ibaïalde**, a traditional producer of *jambon de Bayonne*. Here you can watch the curing process and taste the famous regional ham which was originally shipped through Europe via the port of Bayonne. The top-quality ham carries the *Ibaïona* label and has an *appellation contrôlée*.

Musée Basque

Opposite Pont Marengo is the Musée Basque et de l'histoire de Bayonne, housed in both the Maison Dagourette at 37 Quai des Corsaires and the Château-Neuf. Open Tues–Sun May–Oct 10.00–18.30; Nov–April 10.00–12.30 and 14.00–18.00; closed Mon and PH; ☎ 05 59 46 61 90, www.musee-basque.com.

The 17C Maison Dagourette, one of the buildings which house the collection, was heavily disfigured, especially in the 20C, but some of the original façade survived hidden, and restoration began in 1991. The entirely renovated and revitalised museum re-opened in 2001. Its objective is to develop an understanding of Basque culture in the seven provinces of the Pays Basque, both French and Spanish. The presentation has been attractively adapted to the revamped interior by using traditional materials and simple vitrines. It is designed to encourage a fresh look at ethnography and makes use of sound, moving images, works of art, documents, models, photographs, and costumes to give an overall image of the Basque culture. The annotations are in French, Basque and Spanish, on discreet transparent panels which, unfortunately, are difficult to decipher.

The visit is arranged thematically under the usual ethnological headings: 'Agro-Pasturalism', 'Architecture of the House', 'Vessels and Furniture' (note the *zuzulu*, a handy bench-table for fireside meals), and 'Clothing' (with clogs and berets). Canalisation and the port of Bayonne are examined in 'Maritime and River Activity'; 'Economic and Financial Activities' covers the money exchange and mint in Bayonne in the 17C to 19C. 'Games, Sports and the Arts' includes *pelote Basque* and *quilles* (skittles) as well as rugby and bull-fighting and 'Music, Dance and the Theatre' illustrates various festivals. 'Popular Religion', 'The Cathedral' and 'Bereavement in Pays Basque' include architecture along the pilgrimage route, 18C woodwork from the choir of Bayonne cathedral, and the superstitions associated with death. More specifically Basque are the sections on 'Religious and Literary History', showing that the birth of a Basque conscience started to evolve with the first translation of the Bible into Basque in the 16C–17C; it also covers the integration of Jews in the 16C–17C and the 'Rediscovery of Pays Basque', which looks at the Basque indentity as it developed in the Romantic era (19C–early 20C) under the influence of philosophers, linguists, writers and artists, culminating in the creation of the Basque museum in 1922. The section on 'Neo-Basque' is the continuation of this history through to the creation of a new mythology of the Basques in the 20C.

Musée Bonnat

From the Basque museum take Rue Marengo and turn east on Rue Jacques-Lafitte to the Musée Bonnat. This art gallery houses works of surprising variety and quality in a specially designed building of 1901, and is an enduring tribute to Léon Bonnat. Open Mon, Wed–Sun, May–Oct 10.00–18.30; Nov–April 10.00–12.30 and 14.00–18.00; closed Tues and PH; ☎ 05 59 59 08 52, fax 05 59 59 53 26.

Bonnat was born in Bayonne in 1833, was brought up in Spain and trained as an artist in Madrid, and travelled to Rome. Back in France he became a successful, if rather dull, portraitist but was sufficiently wealthy to fund his avid acquisition of paintings, *objets d'art* and above all drawings, from all periods. He donated his collection and many of his own works to Bayonne in

1891, making this one of the best provincial museums in France. Frequent temporary exhibitions are themed around the numerous works in reserve.

The **entrance** is arranged around an arcaded atrium with wrought-iron arches painted a fresh viridian. The large triptych by Bonnat's most notable pupil, Henri-Achille Zo, shows *Bonnat and his Basque and Bearnais Pupils*, with Bayonne in the background. Space is devoted to the drawings and engravings of Paul Helleu (1859–1927), a sensitive draftsman and portraitist who served as the model for Elstir in Proust's *A la Recherche du Temps Perdu*. Bonnat's extensive collection of Egyptian, Greek and Roman antiquities is in the Salle des Antiques on the lower-ground floor.

On the **first floor** are most of the paintings, subject to reorganisation from time to time. Numerous works by Bonnat himself include the powerful and unrelenting portrait of *Mme Léopold Stern* (c 1863) and *Job* (1880), a tribute to Spanish painting. The museum owns portraits by Degas of *Léon Bonnat* and of his brother-in-law *Enrique Melida*. Predictably, French 19C painters are well represented, and the collection includes finished and unfinished studies by Girodet, Géricault, Delacroix and Corot and works by the great animal sculptor, Antoine-Louis Bayre. There are also paintings by Courbet. The preponderance of works by Ingres includes one of his most enticing small paintings, *The Bather*, using the odalisque formula of smooth flesh, twisted scarf and plaited hair to stunning effect. A large decorative panel of *Le Doux Pays* (1882) by Puvis de Chavannes emulates Florentine fresco painting and proposes an idealism that was admired by the Symbolists. Other European works include sketches by Rembrandt, Rubens and Van Dyck and there are drawings and preparatory works by Giovanni Bellini, Leonardo da Vinci, Michelangelo, Raphael and Titian. There is a sensitively observed *Head of a Stag* (c 1503) and other drawings by Dürer. English painters are represented by Reynolds' *Study of Colonel Tarleton*, c 1782, and by a fine portrait of *Henry Fuseli* by Sir Thomas Lawrence.

Bonnat greatly admired Spanish painting and consequently the collection of Spanish works (15C–19C) is particularly rich, with a beautiful *Adoration of the Magi* (15C) from the School of Valencia, and works by El Greco, Murillo and Ribera among others. There are three major works by Goya, *Self Portrait* (1800), a preparatory study for the Castres version (p 335), *Last Communion of St José de Calasanz* (1819), and the large portrait of the *Duc d'Osuna* (1816), reading a letter. There is a 14C statue of *Christ*, once part of a group now in the Augustine museum in Toulouse (see p 551) and among the *objets d'art* is a 15C Florentine painted chest.

Bayonne waterfront

Cross the Adour to the *quartier* of **St-Esprit** and Vauban's citadel, with four bastions. Of the Gothic collegiate church of St-Esprit, dedicated by Louis XI, all that remains now is the wide central nave and narrow aisles, but it contains a beautiful polychromed wooden group representing the *Flight into Egypt*. It was in this *quartier* that the Sephardic Jews from Spain—who introduced chocolate to Bayonne—settled in the 17C (see above).

Euskara: the Basque language

A mystery surrounds the language spoken in this corner of Europe, yet it is the most important unifying element of the region. It does not have the Indo-European roots of other European languages and it preceded the Roman conquest. Its closest similarities are with the languages of the southern Caucasus. It is sophisticated and complicated grammatically, but it never had its own written language and in the Middle Ages took on Latin characters. It is pronounced phonetically. The vowels are as in other European languages, but the consonants vary: for example, 'z' is pronounced as the 'ss' in French, 'x' as 'ch', and 'tx' as 'tch'. It is likely that some form of Euskara was spoken all through southern France from Aquitaine to the Mediterranean in pre-Roman times. There are now four recognisable dialects across the whole Basque region. It is spoken by 21 per cent of Basques and used by more than half of those living in Basse-Navarre and the Soule. In 1919, the Academy of the Basque Language, Euskalzaindia, was formed; since 1960, some primary and secondary schools have taught in Euskara; and in 1984 a university syllabus in Basque was introduced.

BIARRITZ

Biarritz, the Atlantic coast's answer to Nice, is a town of some 30,000 inhabitants which sprawls along a dramatically craggy coastline indented with coves and softened by *hortensias* (hydrangeas) and tamarisks. As a fashionable resort from the mid-19C to the Second World War, it had elegant or eccentric mansions, more Deauville than Pays Basque, bestowed on it by glitzy residents and visitors. It acquired a particularly racy reputation in the 1920s and is now the playground of surfers. Since the 1990s the town has had a new lease of life and its fun and trendy seaside image has returned. This has done nothing, of course, to alleviate problems of crowding during the summer. Nevertheless it is the gateway to the Pays Basque and its countless hotels and other facilities, as well as the mild climate, make it an excellent off-season centre. The town also offers a wealth of festivals and entertainment and even its own ballet company.

History

Under English sovereignty in the 12C, whaling was the main industry of the small, protected port of Beiarrids, and since 1351 a whale has featured on the town's coat of arms. The creatures were beached at high tide and every part was used—the tongue being a particular delicacy. By the end of the 17C the whales had moved on and men were forced to hunt them as far away as Newfoundland and, as in St-Jean-de-Luz, corsairs or privateers took over. The pleasures of sea-bathing were already appreciated locally and by the mid-18C had received official approbation in the interests of health.

Eugénie de Montijo launched Biarritz on the international scene in 1854 when she returned to the site of her childhood holidays, bringing her husband, Napoléon III. Charmed by the place, he built Villa Eugénie for their summer visits and they came regularly until 1868. In the wake of the Imperial couple followed crowned heads and aristocrats from most European countries, including Queen Victoria in 1889. From then on, through the Belle Epoque, Biarritz glittered with thousands of visitors annually, all anxious to be seen. In 1918 Picasso arrived with his wife, the dancer Olga Kokhlova, and the roaring '20s saw the likes of Cocteau and Hemingway as well as the Windsors, Frank Sinatra and Rita Heyworth in the 1950s who all joined in the fun after the Second World War. Over the period flamboyant and stylish villas appeared alongside hotels and casinos. The English were responsible for the first golf course at Biarritz. The town suffered from German occupation and Allied bombing in 1944.

Despite the introduction of surfing by the film director, Peter Viertel, in 1957, the town suffered a marked downturn in popularity in the 1970s and '80s. Then in 1991 the town began to host an international surfing competition every July. This sparked off the rejuvenation of Biarritz, when Mayor Borotra and his cohorts took action to conserve the architectural heritage, and now some 800 buildings from the 1860s to 1950s are protected. The town has acquired a business and a sporting image, the main activities being surf, golf (there are now 10 courses), and *pelote Basque*.

Practical information

Getting there and around
See Bayonne, p 401.

Tourist information
64200 Biarritz 1 Square d'Ixelles,
☎ 05 59 22 37 10, fax 05 59 24 97 80, www.biarritz.tm.fr
64210 Bidart Rue d'Erretegia, ☎ 05 59 54 93 85, fax 05 59 54 70 51, www.bidarttourisme.com
64210 Guéthary Rue Comte de Swiecinsky, ☎ 05 59 26 56 60, fax 05 59 54 92 67, wwwguetary-france.com

Market days
Daily in the covered market (*halles*) on Pl. Clémenceau. Saturday, Bidart

Guided walks
Guided walks of town and seaside at 10.00 on Monday, 18.00 on Friday, July and August

Festivals and events
March *Bi Harriz Lau Xori*, Basque festival of song, cinema, theatre and poetry. *Carnaval*
April *Fêtes musicales*, classical music festival
May *Terre d'Images*, international festival of travel photography
June *Fête des Casetas*, the bars and 'bodegas' set up shop on the Côte des Basques beach
July *Courses de trot à l'Hippodrome des Fleurs*, trotting races
Cesta Punta Basque et Pelota, Biarritz Masters Jaï Alaï Tournament
Biarritz Surf Festival, big names in surfing come to Biarritz
August *Gant d'Or*, the Golden Glove professional Pelota Tournament
Féria Andalouse, Andalousian festival
September *Le Temps d'Aimer*, ballet season including classical and contemporary works

Cesta Punta Super Champions Trophy, the best players of the season (see p 406)
September–October *La CITA, festival des Cinémas et Cultures d'Amérique Latine*, huge gathering addressing educational, social and economic events in Latin America as well as culture
October *Pro-am International des Makilas*, golf tournament

Where to stay and eating out

64210 ARBONNE

✩✩✩ *Les Laminak*, close to Biarritz on the D255, ☎ 05 59 41 95 40, fax 05 59 41 87 65. Ten tastefully turned-out rooms in a 17C farmhouse.

64200 BIARRITZ

✩✩✩✩ *Palais*, 1 Ave de l'Impératrice, ☎ 05 59 41 64 00, fax 05 59 41 67 99. Napoléon and Eugenie's 1850s summer residence overlooking the ocean, rebuilt and extended in 1903 as luxury hotel. If nothing else, take tea here.

✩✩✩ *Château du Clair de Lune*, 48 Av. Alan-Seeger, Rte d'Arbonne, ☎ 05 59 41 53 20, fax 05 59 41 53 29. Romantic lodge set in mimosas; try for a room in the château rather than the new annexe.

✩✩✩ *Maison Garnier*, 29 Rue Gambetta, ☎ 05 59 01 60 70, fax 05 59 01 60 80. A small hotel in a pretty, *fin-de-siècle* mansion with attention to detail.

✩✩✩ *Plaza*, 10 Av. Edouard-VII, ☎ 05 59 24 74 00, fax 05 59 22 22 01. The listed Art Deco exterior by Boileau has been conserved and the interior partly renovated.

✩✩ *Beaulieu*, 3 Esplanade du Port-Vieux, ☎ 05 59 24 23 59, fax 05 59 24 93 69. A small hotel on the south side of the bay, overlooking the Virgin rocks.

✩✩ *Maïtagarria*, 34 Av. Carnot, ☎ 05 59 24 26 65, fax 05 59 24 27 37. A reasonable and pleasant hotel near the public gardens and town centre.

✩✩ *Le Petit*, 11 Rue Gardères, ☎ 05 59 24 87 00, fax 05 59 24 32 34. This is a recently renovated, centrally placed and friendly hotel with 12 rooms.

€€ *Chez Albert*, Port des Pêcheurs, ☎ 05 59 24 43 84, fax 05 59 24 20 13. Lively atmosphere, specialising in fish and seafood.

€€ *Le Clos Basque*, 12 Rue Louis Barthou, ☎ 05 59 24 24 96. Shaded terrace and charming surroundings plus refined Basque cuisine.

€€ *Le Galion*, 17 Blvd du Général-de-Gaulle, ☎ 05 59 24 20 32. Large bay windows ensure great sea views. Specialising in southwestern dishes and seafood.

€–€€ *L'Auberge*, 22bis Rue Harispe, ☎ 05 59 41 01 41. Regional cuisine and décor, a touch of the country in town.

€ *Le Bar Jean*, 5 Rue des Halles, ☎ 05 59 24 80 38. Typical *tapas* bar brings Spain a tad closer.

€ *Bar Le Royalty*, 11–13 Pl. Clémenceau, ☎ 05 59 24 01 34. An English-style bar close to the beach, with terrace, a great meeting place.

64210 BIDART

✩✩✩ *La Hacienda*, Rte d'Ahetze, ☎ 05 59 54 92 82, fax 05 59 26 52 73. A touch of Provence in Pays Basque, in this hotel-restaurant with bright coloured décor and display of arty, crafty collections. Cuisine part Basque, part Provençal.

✩✩✩ *Villa L'Arche*, Rue Camboenea, ☎ 05 59 51 65 95, fax 05 59 51 65 99. Superb building with just eight spacious and dreamy rooms overlooking the ocean, two steps from the beach.

€–€€ *Le Blue Cargo*, Pl. d'Ilbarritz, ☎ 05 59 23 54 87. Trendy place for lunch on the beach, with two bars.

64210 GUÉTHARY

Mariéna, Ave Mgr Mugabure, ☎ 05 59 26 51 04. This small and unpretentious hotel is extremely popular and very inexpensive.

The **Pointe St-Martin** to the north of the town, on the coast, is a good starting-place for a view of the whole bay across to the Atalaye plateau and the Virgin rock. For an even better view, climb up the 248 steps of the **lighthouse** on Av. de l'Impératrice (built 1831–32). Open July, Aug 10.00–12.00 and 15.00–19.00, clsoed Mon; other times from 15 April, school holidays, Sat, Sun 15.00–19.00. At 73m above sea-level, the layout of this part of Biarritz comes into focus, with the golf course established in 1888. Initially Biarritz developed in two distinct areas, around the church of St-Martin towards the interior and around the old port behind the Atalaye plateau. As this coastline became fashionable, the land around the old *quartiers* was divided into numerous *lotissements* (building plots) linked by a complex system of avenues and streets.

> ### *Biarritz Eclecticism*
> The style, or non-style, of a type of domestic architecture found in coastal resorts from around 1830 up until the Second World War is described as *eclectisme*, an expression coined by the philosopher, Victor Cousin. Nowhere is this better demonstrated than in Biarritz's gloriously idiosyncratic private villas. Eclecticism borrows from all styles and periods in a totally pragmatic way, to produce neo-Gothic, neo-Louis XIII and neo-Classical hybrids; Hispano-Mauresque rubs shoulders with neo-Basque or Norman-urban-seaside, which slot in between Belle Epoque, Art Nouveau and Art Deco. In Biarritz materials are varied: brick is often used, as is stone from the nearby quarries of Bidache, or wood and plaster, and later reinforced concrete; there are multiple roofs, gables, turrets, verandas, balconies, bay windows and columns; and decorations include glazed brick and tiles, wrought iron, ceramics, terracotta mouldings, stained glass, and polychromy of all kinds.

The most important estate, the Lotissement Impérial, owned 15ha between Pointe St-Martin and the Hôtel du Palais until 1880, when it was sold and divided up into 270 plots. Typical of the fashionable residences that appeared are Villa Etchepherdia (Green House) at 7 Rue d'Haitzart (1900) as well as 1 Av. Mac Croskey; and Le Manoir at 2 Av. Mac Croskey, which belonged to Bolo Pacha, a colourful character who was shot for spying in 1918. **Avenue de l'Impératrice** offers many lively examples of eclectic architecture, such as nos 54, 36, 18, 17 and 15. The domed **Russian Orthodox church** (1890–92) dedicated to St Alexander Nevsky is the work of Oscar Tisnes. The unmistakable **Hôtel du Palais** (1904–05), with glorious ocean views, replaced the Villa Eugénie which was sold in 1881 to became the Palais Biarritz, hotel and casino; that opened in 1894 but burned down in 1903. The present Belle-Epoque building by Niermans, architect of the Negresco in Nice, combined the existing ground floor and added a wing using reinforced concrete camouflaged as brick. *La Rotonde* restaurant, designed by Alfred Laulhé, is worth a peek, and this last word in luxury hotels serves a very good cup of tea in its gracious lounge.

Behind the Hôtel du Palais on Rue des Cent-Gardes is the **Imperial chapel**. Open mid-July–mid-Sept, Mon–Sat 15.00–19.00; mid-April–mid-July, mid-Sept to mid-Oct, Tues, Thur, Sat 15.00–19.00; mid-Oct–Dec, Thur 15.00–17.00; ☎ 05 59 22 37 10. Built in 1864–65 for Eugénie, a devout Catholic, the chapel is the epitome of Eclecticism and the only remaining imperial relic. Designed by Boeswillwald, with the advice of Merimée, it is a simple shape with a porch and semi-circular apsidiole, using stone and glazed brick. The interior is colourfully decorated in a busy combination of Romano-Byzantine and Hispano-Mauresque motifs, floral and geometric, and *azulejos* (glazed tiles). The chapel, which was consecrated at the time of the war in Mexico, is dedicated to Notre-Dame-de-Guadalupe whose image, painted by Louis Steinheil, is on the ceiling above the altar.

Some of the hotels (most converted to apartment blocks) in **Avenue de la Reine-Victoria** are worth studying, such as the Continental (1881–89) at no. 2, by Pierre Louis, similar to the Louis XIII style of Eugénie's original villa and one of the first buildings erected after the sale of the imperial estate; the Hotel Carlton (1910) by Cazalis; and the Majestic (1913, adapted in 1925) by Godbarge. The pretty Hostellerie Victoria (no. 12) is a Deauville-type villa, and no. 11, Etche Handia (Great House, *c* 1908), was built by Alfred Laulhé for himself in brick and stone with pretty details. There is more of the same in the adjacent streets.

In comparison with the *lotissement*, the town centre has a greater mix of commercial buildings, casinos, palaces, modest houses, squares and public gardens. The years 1924–29 were a period of expansion when most of the buildings along the sea front were rebuilt. Gracing the Esplanade du Général-de-Gaulle overlooking the Grande Plage is the splendid Art Deco **municipal casino** (1929) by Laulhé, on the site of the Moorish-style baths of 1858. The casino was about to be replaced by a hotel complex but was saved and renovated in 1994; along with the gaming tables and slot machines there is a large restaurant with sea views. Around the corner at 4 Rue Gardères is one of the earliest Art Deco buildings (1926) in this area. Villa Larralde at nos 3–9 was the property of an English banker during the mid-19C and was praised by Viollet-le-Duc as an example of modern stone architecture; Coco Chanel lived and worked here for a while. Avenue Edouard VII is a busy commercial street with the most outstanding Art Deco building in Biarritz, the **Hôtel Plaza** (1926–28), notable for its mosaics, glass and wrought iron, designed by L.-H. Boileau and Paul Perrotte, as was the old Au Bon Marché (1928–29), transformed into the *mairie*. East of here on Square d'Ixelles is the tourist office.

At the western end of the **Grande Plage** is the touristy Place Bellevue, dominated by the large **Espace Bellevue** (1858), the first hotel-casino on the Basque coast but altered many times and turned into a convention centre in 1999. Place Bellevue opens into Place Georges-Clémenceau with the Grand Hôtel (1860). Not far away is the **Musée historique**, in the former Anglican church on Rue Broquedis. It retraces Biarritz's history, from its beginnings around small fishing and agricultural communities to its blossoming as a fashionable resort, with reference to paintings, costumes, artefacts and documents. Open Tues–Sat 10.00–12.00 and 14.30–18.30, closed Sun, Mon; ☎ 05 59 24 86 28.

Where Rue Gambetta meets Rue Mazagran is the former workshop of the couturier, Jean Patou, designed by Louis Süe (1925), while at no. 4 is the old **Hotel d'Angleterre** by Tisnes, architect of the Russian church, begun pre-1870, with additions in 1878 by Pierre Louis and by Laulhé in 1929.

Beyond Place Bellevue is Place Eugénie, a church, gardens and a cliff walk to the **Plateau d'Atalaye**, with more views and the little port. The **Port des Pêcheurs**, protected by the Basta rock, was created in 1870 and is a fun place for a drink or seafood meal. The unmistakable villa **Le Goéland** was transformed and embellished *c* 1903–04 to benefit from its position on the plateau. It looks out towards the **Rocher de la Vièrge**, named after the statue of the Virgin erected in 1865 on the headland lashed by breakers: it can be reached via a metal footbridge made in Eiffel's workshops.

Opposite the Virgin rock is the **Musée de la Mer**. The museum, built in 1932, shows its age. Nevertheless, it has over 150 species of fish and invertebrates native to the Bay of Biscay, a shark grotto and seal tank (feeding at 10.30 and 17.00), and exhibits of local interest in connection with fishing and whale hunting, the history of sea-bathing, geology and ornithology. There is a café on the terrace with ocean views. Open July, Aug 09.30–24.00; other times 09.30–12.30 and 14.00–18.00; closed morning of 1 Jan, second and third week of Jan, 25 Dec; ☎ 05 59 22 75 40.

Until the 17C, the main activity of the sheltered **Port Vieux** was whaling. In the 19C it was recognised as ideal for sea-bathing and a bathing station was built *c* 1858; the present one dates to 1951–52. South of the cove, on a rocky headland, is one of the most symbolic buildings in Biarritz, **Villa Belza**, an extraordinary pile with terraces and outcrops, towers and turrets, named after the West Indian governess who saved the Dubreuil children during the Revolution.

Above Boulevard du Prince de Galles is a tamarisk-covered walk with views of the Côte des Basques, the beach at the foot of the Falaise d'Hurlade where surfers gather. Take the upper route, along the **Perspective de la Côte des Basques**, to admire a number of grand houses. If you wish to visit the chocolate museum, continue south from Carrefour d'Hélianthe. The **Musée du Chocolat** at 14–16 Avenue Beaurivage offers a video history of chocolate, which was introduced to France during the reign of Louis XIV (p 403), as well as sculpture in chocolate. Open Tues–Sat 10.00–12.00 and 14.30–18.00; daily July, Aug until 19.00; ☎ 05 59 41 54 64. Alternatively, turn inland along Rue Gambetta, cross Avenue Carnot, and turn left into Rue de la Fontaine where nos 6–8 belonged to Queen Natalie de Serbie in 1905. Take a right into Rue Peyreloubilh and continue downhill along the Passage du Chapeau-Rouge past a pretty Andalucian-style house. Left and right brings you back onto the Plateau d'Atalaye.

Further inland, down Avenue Foch, is the Gare du Midi, transformed into a modern theatre, and behind it, at 1 Rue Guy-Petit, is **Asiatica**, the museum of Oriental art. This has a remarkably rich collection of some 1000 high-quality works from India, Nepal, Tibet and China. Open Tues–Sat 10.00–12.30 and 14.30–19.00, until 22.00 on Sat; Sun 14.30–19.00; ☎ 05 59 22 78 78.

In Rue St-Martin is the church of **St-Martin**, the oldest church in Biarritz, first mentioned in the 12C. It has been subject to several transformations, including in the 16C; the porch was rebuilt in 1844. The nearby **Château Gramont** was built by Mayor Jules Labat in 1866 because he wanted to replace his existing villa with something grander and more fashionable, although both Napoléon I and Napoléon III had stayed in the original residence.

Bidart and Guéthary occupy the gap on the coast between Biarritz and St-Jean-de-Luz. Follow the Corniche into **Bidart** from the N10 to arrive at the chapel of Ste-Madeleine (rebuilt 1820) and views from the clifftop. **Guéthary** is the smallest community on the Basque coast, with a *fronton-mairie*, museum and tiny port and the prettiest clifftop railway station. The **Ecomusée de la Tradition**

Basque, on the RN10 just north of St-Jean-de-Luz, is a good introduction to Basque life, history and culture and complements the Basque museum in Bayonne. Open July, Aug daily 10.00–20.00; Sept–June, Mon–Sat 09.00–19.00, closed Sun; ☎ 05 59 51 06 06. The exhibits are painstakingly presented in an old Basque farmhouse and include traditional crafts, smuggling, Basque sports, festivals and dances, and the symbolism of the white, red and green Basque flag and Basque cross. Outside are rustic buildings.

SAINT-JEAN-DE-LUZ TO THE SPANISH BORDER

The seaside resort and small historic town of St-Jean-de-Luz, in the lee of the western Pyrenees, is undoubtedly the most attractive on this coast. A remarkable church, narrow streets lined with 17C–19C houses, fishing boats and a pretty beach in an oval bay, as well as a wide choice of hotels and restaurants, make for a holiday atmosphere but also for congestion in the summer. The Pyrenees and the valley of the Nivelle, Bayonne and the Atlantic coast are on the doorstep.

History

The name of the town is misleading; it has nothing to do with light, but is a contraction from the Basque, *Donibane Lohitzun*, in French *St-Jean-de-Marais*, a town on the marshes where houses were supported on chestnut props. St-Jean-de-Luz has the only fishing port of any importance on this part of the coast and depended on whaling from the 11C, first locally but later off the American coast. With the loss of the New World fishing territories in 1713, Luzien fishermen turned to cod and sardine, although tuna became king fish around the 1950s, and today anchovy, hake and conger eel are also landed. The town's seafaring history includes piracy and the more legal form, privateering, for which the Corsaires Basques required a *lettre de marque* from the admiralty granting royal approval to arm their ships as protection against the Spanish and English. Many an astute Luzien shipowner made his fortune from these privileges by using his vessel in 'commercial' ventures. St-Jean prospered in the 16C–17C and enjoyed its greatest moment of glory on 9 June 1660, when it hosted the marriage of Louis XIV and the Infanta Maria-Theresa, according to the Treaty of the Pyrenees (see below). Terrible storms and high tides wiped out part of the old town in the 17C and 18C, leading to the construction of protective breakwaters in the 19C, and by the end of the 19C tourism had already taken a strong hold.

Getting there and around

Car

From Biarritz/Bayonne A64 or N10. From St-Jean-Pied-de-Port D932/D918. From Spain (Santander/Bilbao) A8, A63.

Train

See Bayonne, p 401. TER to Hendaye and to Guethary, Biarritz and Bayonne.

Bus

To Sart/Grottes de Sare via Ascain, Col de St-Ignae, Petit Train de la Rhune.

 Tourist information

64500 Ciboure 4 Pl. du Fronton, ☎ 05 59 47 64 56, fax 05 59 47 64 55, email cibourne.tourisme@etxc.fr

64700 Hendaye 12 Rue des Aubépines,

BP 18, ☎ 05 59 20 00 34, fax 05 59 20 79 17, www.hendaye.com
64502 St-Jean-de-Luz Pl. du Maréchal-Foch, BP 265, ☎ 05 59 26 03 16, fax 05 59 26 21 47, www.saint-jean-de-luz.com
64122 Urrugne Maison Posta, Pl. René Soubelet, ☎ 05 59 54 60 80, fax 05 59 54 63 49, www.urrugne.com

Market days

Ciboure Sunday
Hendaye Saturday (Port de Plaisance) and Wednesday (Pl. de la République); evening market in July, August, Blvd de la Mer
St-Jean-de-Luz Tuesday and Friday; Saturday in July and August
Urrugne Thursday

Boat trips

Ciboure-St-Jean-de-Luz April–Oct, from Digue aux Chevaux, Port de Larraldenia, Port de Socoa, *Navette Maritime San Antonio*, ☎ 06 11 69 56 93
Hendaye from the port, *Goelette Haut Couthelain*, sea trips as far as Spain, ☎ 06 16 70 89 33. *Navette Maritime* (sea crossing) to Fontarrabie: all year, *Bateau Marie Louise*, from Port de Plaisance, ☎ 06 07 02 55 09
St-Jean-de-Luz April–Sept, from the quay (Embarcadère) near the tourist office, morning fishing, afternoon (30mins/1 or 2hr) sightseeing. *Nivelle III* (☎ 06 09 73 61 81) or *Marie Rose* (☎ 06 08 25 49 74)

Festivals and events

February *Carnaval St-Jean-de-Luz*
April *Récitals de Printemps de l'Académie Ravel*, spring concerts, St-Jean-de-Luz
May *Udaberria Dantzan*, dances from the seven Basque provinces, St-Jean-de-Luz.
Festival Andalou, Spanish-style festival with flamenco and parades, Whitsun, St-Jean-de-Luz

June–August *Pelote Basque à Cesta Punta*, pelota/jaï alaï (see p 406) championships, St-Jean-de-Luz
August–September *Musique en Côte Basque*, music on the Basque coast, St-Jean-de-Luz
September *Académie Maurice Ravel*, Ravel Academy music festival, St-Jean-de-Luz.
October *Festival des Jeunes Réalisateurs*, festival of young film-makers

Where to stay and eating out

64500 ST-JEAN-DE-LUZ

✩✩✩✩ *Le Grand*, 43 Blvd Thiers, ☎ 05 59 26 35 36, fax 05 59 51 99 84, www.luzgrandhotel.fr. Re-opened in 2001, this is grandeur and luxury right on the beach, with a reputable restaurant, *La Coupole*.
✩✩✩✩ *Parc Victoria*, 5 Rue Cépé, ☎ 05 59 26 78 78, fax 05 59 26 78 08. This magnificent Art Deco mansion is discreetly tucked away in beautiful gardens with a swimming pool.
✩✩✩ *La Réserve*, Rond-point Ste-Barbe, ☎ 05 59 51 32 00, fax 05 59 26 11 74. In a superb position overlooking the ocean. Some bedrooms decorated with *azulejos* (Spanish tiles). Pool, tennis.
✩✩ *Maria-Christina*, 13 Rue Paul Gélos, ☎ 05 59 26 81 70, fax 05 59 26 36 04. Fairly simple hotel with pretty entrance and courtyard, 5min from the beach.
✩✩ *Ohartzia*, 28 Rue Garat, ☎ 05 59 26 00 06, fax 05 59 26 74 75. Absolutely central, close to the beach, yet quiet hotel with garden, reasonably priced.
€€ *Pil Pil Enea*, 3 Rue Sallagoiti, ☎ 05 59 51 20 80. Terrific fish and seafood.
€–€€ *Kaïku*, 17 Rue de la République, ☎ 05 59 26 13 20. Impressively situated in the oldest house in town, good-quality cooking, serving late.
€ *La Peita*, 21 Rue Tourasse, ☎ 05 59 26 86 66. Pretty tavern

with simple cooking.

€ *La Taverne Basque*, 5 Rue de la République, ☎ 05 59 26 01 26. In this street of many restaurants, this one can be counted on for classic Basque cooking.

6 4 1 2 2   U R R U G N E
☆☆☆ *Château d'Urtubie*, on the N10, ☎ 05 59 54 31 15, fax 05 59 54 62 51, www.chateaudurtubie.fr. This attractive historic house has nine rooms; possibility of dining in the château.

Close to the Nivelle and west of the tourist office is the busy, tree-lined **Place Louis XIV**, with a bandstand. This is the heart of the old town and focal point for many activities especially in the summer. The **Maison Louis XIV**, on the corner of the Place and Rue de la République, was used by the young King on the occasion of his marriage to the Spanish Infanta Maria-Theresa, and from here he reputedly threw celebratory gold coins to the crowd below. Guided visits June–Sept 10.30–12.00 and 14.30–17.30; July, Aug 10.30–12.30 and 14.30–18.30; closed Sun mornings and PH; ☎ 05 59 26 01 56. The house was built in 1643 by a shipowner, Johanis de Lohobiague, and has passed down through his family. Many of the rooms were altered by later generations but there is some good furniture, many mirrors, and rediscovered painted beams. In the royal bedroom is a portrait of the king aged 22, in the year he married his bride (also 22), and a bed specially installed here at the time. The Infanta stayed for five days after the union which, by court convention, should have been consummated publicly; but Anne of Austria tactfully closed the drapes. From the south-facing gallery is a view of the port and the convent (1650) on the Ile des Récollets where Louis XIV attended mass every day. Rather more sombrely, the alleyway alongside the house contained the guillotine in the 18C. The adjacent building is the *Erriko Etxea* or *mairie*, built in 1654, with an equestrian statue of *Louis XIV* by Bouchardon.

Visitors gravitate towards the port where huge tunas were once landed in vast quantities. The colourful fishing boats still sail from here, but most of the fish is whisked away to the processing plants on the other side of the river at Ciboure, and the *vent à la criée* (fish auction) on the quay is reduced to a whisper. On a clear day the peak of La Rhune is seen to preside over the town. On the quay is the unmistakable **Maison de l'Infante** or Joanoenia (1640). A pretty Italianate building in brick and stone, with superimposed loggias flanked by square towers on the main façade, it is mainly used for temporary exhibitions. Open mid-June–mid-Oct 11.00–12.30 and 14.00–18.30, closed Sun and Mon mornings; to check times, ☎ 05 59 26 36 82. The house belonged to the ennobled whaling family of de Haraneder, who provided Louis XIII with two ships to take supplies to French troops during the siege of the Ile de Ré at the time of the Wars of Religion. There are one or two interesting elements inside, such as the Renaissance fireplace with a coat of arms and some fine painted ceilings.

Next door is the **Musée Grevin**, a waxworks museum of major historic events. Open 10.00–12.00 and 14.00–18.00; July, Aug to 20.00. Down Rue Mazarin is the pretty red-and-white **Maison Grangia Baïta**, Wellington's headquarters in 1813. This street leads to the entrance to the port and the lighthouse, at the southern end of the beach. Across the harbour entrance is the Fort de Socoa (see Ciboure).

The houses along the seafront of St-Jean-de-Luz date mainly from the 1920s and are connected to the beach by footbridges spanning the 19C seawall, built to prevent the town from becoming one big sandcastle. (The sand, however, was washed away naturally some 50 years ago.) Apart from one nasty 1970s' high-rise block, the bay is lined with attractive small houses and hotels, and closed at the far end by the Sainte-Barbe headland.

In Rue de la République, at no. 17, the **Maison Eskerrénéa** (16C) is one of the few houses that resisted the maurauding Spanish in 1558 and consequent conflagrations. This narrow pedestrian street is jam-packed with jostling holi-daymakers in the summer, as is Rue Gambetta, where numerous restaurants offer local dishes. Along both are shops and boutiques selling Basque linens, espadrilles and berets, Basque macaroons (made with butter), *mouchous* (maca-roons with cream), *turons* (almond confectionery) and fudge, not to mention *gateaux Basques* and a whole range of sauces and spices based on the famous Basque *piments d'Espelette* (see below). And right in the middle of all these worldly assaults on the senses is the church.

St-Jean-Baptiste, a sombre affair from the outside, was completed in the 17C having been reconstructed piecemeal from the 15C onwards to replace a church which burned down in 1419; the belfry was truncated in the 18C by lightning. The building was incomplete when Louis XIV and Maria-Theresa were married here in 1660, and it is possible that the king donated money for the church, the only one in a town with a population of about 22,000. The entrance used by the royal couple was later walled up and replaced by another further west in 1664. This in its turn was embellished in 1868 with Flamboyant-style décor and a statue of St John the Baptist.

The plain stone exterior gives way to wood, gilding and colour inside with a timber roof, likened to a ship's hull, over a simple but vast single space (49m by 21m). Wooden galleries on three levels were added at the end of the 17C. Uniquely, St-Jean-Baptiste remained independent from the Bishopric of Bayonne, enabling it to keep for itself all funds raised, and only baptisms (not deaths) were recorded here. Much of the interior decoration has a strong Spanish character, especially the dressed statues and the sumptuously gilded Baroque retable, which fills the whole of the apse. It was made in Bidache and installed after the royal wedding: the light switch is behind the last column on the right. Arranged on three levels, it presents a multitude of gilded saints and is topped off with God the Father and a pelican, symbol of Christ's sacrifice. In the centre of the upper level is the *Assumption of the Virgin* and, below, St John the Baptist. To the right of the altar is a painting of the *Adoration of the Magi* (1727) by Jean Restout, a ref-erence to the traditional celebration of the Epiphany in St-Jean. The large ex-voto boat was presented by Empress Eugeenie in 1856 in thanks for a lucky escape when her ship was wrecked off the coast, when all but one rescuer were saved. The great organ of 1656, made by Gérard de Rodez, counterbalances the altar-piece; the decorative pulpit dates from 1878.

At 20 Rue Gambetta is the **Maison Goritienea**, a typical house of the Labourd, built by the Corsaire Labrouche. It was used by Maréchal Soult prior to Wellington's arrival. Rue Garat leads back to the seafront.

Across the Nivelle stands **Ciboure**, in Basque Ziburu, from *zubiburu* ('head of the bridge'). On the island in the Nivelle is the former Récollets convent; it is now offices but the fine 17C cloister has survived. The Dutch-style building on the bank of the Nivelle (opposite the Maison de l'Infante) was the birthplace of the composer Maurice Ravel on 7 March 1875. Ravel (d. 1937) lived most of his life in Paris but returned to the area where he found inspiration for the famous *Boléro* suite. Henri IV planned the **Fort de Socoa** to protect the town from the Spanish, but it did not get built until the 17C; it is now a centre for young people.

Several Art Deco villas were built here in the 1920s: one of the most classic and complete examples is Villa Leïhorra at 1 Impasse Muskoa (1926–29), built by the architect Joseph Hiriart. Arranged around a patio decorated with mosaics, it has stained glass by Gruber and decorations by Daum and Schwartz. Guided visits some afternoons; to check times, ☎ 05 59 47 07 09.

On higher ground at **Urrugne** an octagonal tower, the Tour Bordagain, is the only remains of a 12C fortified church. On the N10 the **Château d'Urtubie** (see Where to stay) was originally a keep authorised in 1341 by Edward III, which was added to until the 18C. It has remained in the same family since its construction, and both Wellington and Soult were received here during the Napoleonic Wars. Guided visits April–Oct 11.00, 14.00–19.00; ☎ 05 59 54 31 15. Further west is the **Parc Florénia**, a pleasant botanic and flower garden covering 16ha.

The Route de la Corniche, the D912, follows a relatively unspoilt coastline with views of Spain and Mont Jaizkibel (500m) at the end of the Pyrenean chain. The route brings you to the last town in the southwest corner of France, **Hendaye**, a holiday resort with a good sandy beach on the Atlantic coast and a marina on the Bidassoa River. Opposite is the Spanish town of Fontarabie. The river marks the frontier between France and Spain and the Île des Faisans (or Île de la Conférence), now reduced by the flood tides to a narrow wooded bar, was regularly used for exchanges between the two countries. In 1469 Louis XI of France and Henri IV of Castile met here; François I was released nearby after his capture in Pavia in 1525, in exchange for his two sons; in 1615 two more royal marriages were agreed; and in 1659 the Treaty of the Pyrenees was signed here. East of the bay, on the Pointe Sainte-Anne, the **Domaine Abbadia** is a nature reserve of 64ha, mainly for the protection of some 30 species of birds as well as other flora and fauna.

Treaty of the Pyrenees

This treaty settled endless frontier disputes between Spain and France. After three months of negotiation, Cardinal Mazarin for France and Don Luis de Haro for Spain signed the treaty on 7 November 1659, on the Île de la Conférance (or des Faisans) near Hendaye. Spain ceded certain territories to France, notably Roussillon, the Artois and several strongholds to the north. It was agreed that Louis XIV would marry the Infanta Maria-Theresa, daughter of Philip IV of Spain, who would renounce her rights to the Crown of Spain, in return for a payment of 500,000 gold *écus*. In 1861 Queen Isabella of Spain and Napoléon III inaugurated a monument to this important agreement.

There are magnificent views over Urrugne and La Rhune from the churchyard of **Notre-Dame-de-Soccori**, a former pilgrimage site, although the 14C church was rebuilt in the 19C.

Higher on the headland by the D912 is the idiosyncratic **Château d'Antoine d'Abbadie**, a remarkable neo-Gothic confection built between 1857 and 1879 by Antoine Thomson d'Abbadie (1810–97), explorer, scientist, astronomer and polyglot who was born in Ireland of a devout Catholic family from the Basque region. Educated in France, he travelled widely in Europe, the Middle East and North Africa, but Ethiopia, whose languages he studied, held a particular fascination for him. Open daily June–mid-Sept 10.00–14.00, guided tours 15.00–17.30, Sun 14.00–18.00; Feb–May and mid-Sept–mid-Dec, Mon–Fri 10.00–12.00, guided tours 15.00–16.00; closed mid-Dec–Jan; ☎ 05 59 20 04 51.

In the course of building his castle, Abbadie fell out with two architects before calling for advice on the master of Gothic revivalism, Eugène Viollet-le-Duc, in 1864. Viollet drew up the overall plans for the pile from afar, being occupied with Roquetaillade in the 1860s and 1870s (p 119), and put his collaborator Edmond Duthoit to the task. Externally the château epitomises the neo-medieval tendencies of the period, with asymmetric plan and elevations, giving the effect of a random agglomeration of parts over the centuries that was sought in 19C England. The château has three distinct wings, one for working, one for living, and one for devotions. The interior is very much Duthoit's domain but adapted to the particular tastes of his patron. The *horror vacui* décor wavers between neo-Gothic and Art Nouveau, with a particular colour scheme for each room, including black for the entrance hall and red for the Salon Arabe. Scattered around are references to Abbadie's eclecticism, such as Irish shamrocks, a neo-medieval fireplace, a quotation from the poet Robert Buchanan, Kufic inscriptions, family mottos and so on. The furnishings range from late-Gothic style chairs to fashionable divans, Oriental drapes and a *porte-torchère* (lampstand) modelled on a young Ethiopian, Abdullah.

As well as the observatory, built to catalogue the stars, one of the most curious installations in a house of curiosities is a small tunnel bored through its walls. Antoine intended to study the refraction of light by focusing his telescope onto the highest point of the horizon, the summit of the Rhune. Unfortunately the rest of the house got in the way, hence the hole through it. The experiment turned out to be a total flop but the exit of the tunnel, next to the main entrance, is marked with a stone surround with the inscription *ez i kusi, es i kasi* ('I have seen nothing, I have learned nothing').

THE LABOURD AND BASSE-NAVARRE

Some of the prettiest villages, often with the *fronton, mairie* and church assembled around the centre and set in idyllic scenery, are scattered through the foothills of the Pyrenees and the countryside of the Labourd.

Getting there and around
Car
See Bayonne/St-Jean-de-Luz (pp 401, 415)

A64/N117/D933 Toulouse to via St-Palais, St-Jean-Pied-de-Port and the Spanish border.
D932/D918 Biarritz/Bayonne to St-Jean-Pied-de-Port.
D918 St-Jean-de-Luz to St-Pée, Espelette.

Train
See Bayonne/St-Jean-de-Luz, pp 401, 415.
TER Bayonne to St-Jean-Pied-de-Port.
Bus
St-Jean-de-Luz to Grottes de Sare, via Ascain, Col de St-Ignace, Petit Train de la Rhune, Sare.
St-Jean-Pied-de-Port to St-Etienne-de-Baïgorry.

Dax to Mauléon via St-Palais.
Cambo-les-Bains to Bayonne.
Bayonne to St-Palais, St-Jean-Pied-de-
Port to St-Etienne-de-Baïgorry.

Tourist information

64250 Aïnhoa Mairie, ☎ 05
59 29 92 60, fax 05 59 29
86 31
64310 Ascain Le Bourg, ☎ 05 59 54
00 84, fax 05 59 54 68 34
64780 Bidarray Barbastenea, ☎/fax
05 59 37 74 60
64250 Cambo-les-Bain BP15, ☎ 05 59
29 70 25, fax 05 59 29 90 77, email
cambo.les.bains.tourisme@wanadoo.fr
64250 Espelette Château des Barons
d'Ezpeleta, ☎ 05 59 93 95 02, fax 05
59 93 89 71, www.espelette.com
64240 Labastide Clairence Maison
Darrieux, ☎/fax 05 59 29 65 05,
www.labastideclairence.com
64120 St-Palais Office de Tourisme de
Basse Navarre, Pl. Charles-de-Gaulle,
☎ 05 59 65 71 78, fax 05 59 65 69
15, email office.tourisme.stpalais@
wanadoo.fr
64310 St-Pée-sur-Nivelle Pl. de la
Poste, ☎ 05 59 54 11 69, fax 05 59 54
17 81, www.saint-pee-sur-nivelle.com
64310 Sare Herriko Etxea, BP 16,
☎ 05 59 54 20 14, fax 05 59 54 29
15.
64430 St-Etienne-de-Baïgorry
Elizondea, ☎ 05 59 37 47 28, fax 05
59 37 49 58
64220 St-Jean-Pied-de-Port 4 Pl.
Charles-de-Gaulle, ☎ 05 59 37 03 57,
fax 05 59 37 34 91

Market days

Ascain Saturday
Cambo-les-Bains Friday
Espelette Wednesday; Saturday in July,
August
Hasparren alternate Tuesday in winter,
every Tuesday in summer
St-Jean-Pied-de-Port Monday (Tuesday
when Monday a PH), all day

Festivals and events

January Pottok fair, tradi-
tional Basque event around
the local horse fair, Espelette
February *Carnaval*, St-Palais and St-Pée-
sur-Nivelle
March *Carnaval*, Sare, Cambo-les-
Bains, Baïgorry
June *Biennale des arts plastiques en
Navarre*, visual arts, street activities,
music, St-Jean-Pied-de-Port
Arnaga Côté Jardins, top-quality crafts
and garden fair, Cambo-les-Bains
July *Fête de la danse*, dance festival, Sare
Fêtes du village, village festivities,
Labastide Clairence
July–August *Expo-vente de produits gas-
tronomiques et artisanaux au marché cou-
vert*, gastronomy and crafts St-Jean-
Pied-de-Port
August *Fêtes locales*, local festivities,
Cambo-les-Bains
Concours d'Irrintzina (cri Basque), long
rallying call used in Basque mountains,
Hasparren
Festival de Théâtre d'Arnaga, theatre festi-
val, Cambo-les-Bains
Festival Musical de Basse Navarre, music
festival, St-Etienne-de-Baïgorry
Fêtes locales, local festivities, St-Jean-
Pied-de-Port
Festival de Force Basque, a competition of
physical strength, St-Palais
September *Fêtes locales*, local festivities
Sare
October *Fête du Piment*, Pimento fair
Espelette

Where to stay and eat-
ing out
64250 AÏNHOA

✯✯✯ *Ithurria*, Rue Principale, ☎ 05 59
29 92 11, fax 05 59 29 81 28. Typical
17C house of the Labourd in this beautiful 13C *bastide*. Gardens and pool.
64240 LABASTIDE-CLAIRENCE
Maison Marchand, ☎ 05 59 29 18 27,
fax 05 59 29 14 97, http://perso.wanadoo.
fr/maison.marchand. *Chambres d'hôte*.

Rooms are pretty and well equipped; very congenial atmosphere especially on evenings when *table d'hôte* is on offer.

64430 ST-ETIENNE-DE-BAÏGORRY

✮✮✮ *Arcé*, follow the signs through the village past the church, ☎ 05 59 37 40 14, fax 05 59 37 40 27. A hotel of great charm, on the banks of a small river in an attractive village near the Spanish border, where the food is excellent.

Château d'Etchauz, directions as for Hotel Arce, ☎ 05 59 37 45 58, fax 05 59 59 01 90. *Chambres d'hôte*. Completely restored in the 1990s, this imposing residence has five delightful and individually styled rooms.

64220 ST-JEAN-PIED-DE-PORT

✮✮✮ *Les Pyrénées*, ☎ 05 59 37 01 01, fax 05 59 37 18 97. A former post house with an interior garden and pool, and some of the best traditional cooking in the Basque country.

€ *Pecoïtz*, at Ancillé (southwest on D933, D18), ☎ 05 59 37 11 88. Large hotel-restaurant in a Basque country house with hearty, family cooking. Rooms.

€ *Cidrerie Aldakurria*, at Lasse (west by the D918 and D403), ☎ 05 59 37 13 13. Rustic setting and Spanish-style cooking.

€ *Arbillaga*, 8 Rue de l'Eglise, under the ramparts, ☎ 05 59 37 06 44. This restaurant is always reliable.

64310 SARE

✮✮✮ *Arraya*, ☎ 05 59 54 20 46, fax 05 59 54 27 04, www.arraya.com. A delightful hotel in an ancient pilgrimage hospice at the heart of the village; recommended restaurant.

The valley of the Nivelle (followed by the D918) links St-Jean-de-Luz and **Ascain**, where a 'Roman' bridge—in fact 16C—crosses the river. There are attractive old buildings as well as Notre-Dame-de-l'Assomption, typical of medieval Basque churches enlarged in the 16C–17C, with a massive porch-tower. The interior is brighter than the church of St-Jean-de-Luz, with painted corbels, ceiling and chancel arch. Galleries on three sides are supported by stone columns and the pulpit is suspended from the first level. There is some good quality carving, and an 18C altarpiece above the raised altar.

Basque churches

Basque churches, as found in the Labourd or Navarre but not in the Soule, are generally sober from the exterior, heavy and strong like a fortress, with sturdy stone walls. Many were damaged during the Wars of Religion in the 16C and rebuilt after the Council of Trent (1556) and mainly in the 17C. A large porch, often incorporated into a west tower, provides shelter from the vagaries of the climate. Inside is a large, single space, covered by a wooden roof, flat or arched and usually painted. Wooden galleries on the side walls, possibly added later, are polished and sometimes carved. The men sat in the galleries, the women in the nave. A small pulpit, often highly decorated, is usually attached to the north gallery. The main altar, by contrast, is often a joyous overkill of Baroque motifs, colour and gilding, expressing the strength of local belief in scenes, statues, twisted columns, swags and vines. In the churchyards are many discoidal stelae, reminiscent of Celtic crosses.

St-Pée-sur-Nivelle (St-Pierre) although rather overrun and bustling, has some good 17C and 18C houses along the main street, notably the Maison Altzola (1676), where the timbers of the two upper floors are painted in traditional ox-blood red and rest on a stone base. The plain entrance of the church, restored in 1606, opens to reveal a magnificent altarpiece under a shell-like vault, filling the whole of the apse, with numerous gilded statues arranged around St Peter. Only a romantic ivy-clad ruin remains of the **Château d'Ibarron** (15C and 17C) to the west, which burned down in 1793.

The most emblematic of French Basque mountains, **La Rhune**, rises to 905m above the village of Sare on the D4, and on its slopes are the remains of cromlechs and fortifications. Excursions may be made up La Rhune on a little wooden milk train dating from 1924. *Le Petit Train de la Rhune* leaves from the Col de St-Ignace mid-March–mid-November at 08.30 in summer, 09.00 in winter, depending on weather; ☎ 05 59 54 20 26. There is a bus connection from St-Jean-de-Luz. The journey to the summit, the frontier with Spain, takes about 30 minutes. Small wild horses, or pottoks, a recognised breed related to pit ponies, graze on the mountain. One kilometre from the station is a traditional 17C timber-framed Basque farmhouse, **Ortillopitz**. Open April–August 10.00–18.00; Sept 11.00–17.00; Oct 14.00–17.00; ☎ 05 59 85 91 92.

Sare itself is a gem of a village deep in the countryside, with remarkably beautiful old houses, a museum of the *gâteau Basque* and a cider press. The belfry-gable of the parish church of St-Martin carries a rather sobering 17C inscription, and under the west porch is a modern *Pietà*. Inside are galleries and a raised altar with five retables and painted chancel arch. The village was appreciated by Napoléon III and Eugénie, to the extent that in 1867 Sare dedicated the chapel of Ste-Catherine to the Empress, and small oratories around the village were built from the 17C onwards at the behest of local fishermen. The series of vast **Grottes de Sare** are open all year round and give an audio-visual presentation but sadly the prehistoric traces were damaged in the 20C. Open July, Aug 10.00–19.00, Easter–June, Sept 10.00–18.00, Oct–mid-Nov 10.00–17.00, carnival to Easter 14.00–17.00; ☎ 05 59 54 21 88.

The star of the Labourd is **Ainhoa**, founded in the 13C by the Premonstratensian friars on the route to Santiago, with a battalion of perfect Basque houses with wide central doorways along its one main street. Most were rebuilt in the 17C–18C after the village was ransacked by the Spanish in 1629 and the façades, under gable roofs, make satisfying geometric patterns of green and red on white. The houses traditionally face east and some carry decorative friezes, dates or inscriptions. At the end of the lane beside the *mairie* is a 19C chapel dedicated to Notre-Dame-de-l'Aubépine. The church, at the end of the village, has an unusual octagonal lantern and slate-covered spire on a square base. The rounded east end is 14C, while the remainder is a plain building of the 17C/18C. Inside is the usual arrangement of galleries, but here the walls are painted white to show off the woodwork and the gilded altarpiece, which is under a blue and gold dome. Immediately behind the church is the *fronton*.

The red-and-white façades of **Espelette**, further east on the D20 and D918, are adorned in the summer and autumn with strings of red pimentos (small hot peppers) hung out to dry. Successfully grown here for generations, the moderately piquant *capsicum annuum* was introduced from the Americas in the 17C to flavour chocolate and is now sold fresh, dried, as powder or paste, and flavours many Basque recipes.

Espelette is a pretty place on two levels, with typical 16C–18C Basque houses, and an old château. The modest 17C church in the lower part of the village is

The Basque house

The Basque house (*etche* or *extxea*) is particularly attractive yet functional, well adapted to the needs of an extended family and to local climate and materials. Generally wide, low and large, the timber-framed structure stands on a stone base, with the beams painted red or green to create striking geometric patterns. The red-tiled gable roofs are typically long and shallow with deep eaves like Swiss chalets; sometimes the pitch is uneven because the house has been extended in one direction to accommodate a growing family. The buildings are carefully orientated against bad weather, their backs turned to the west or northwest, windows and balconies facing the rising sun. The wide doorways were designed to allow loaded carts through, and the ground-floor space was divided between the animals on the north, to provide warmth, and the family. In some cases the family rooms were on the floor above. The attic, sometimes with triangular openings, where crops were dried also acted as insulation. Some of the most striking examples of this type of Basque house are in the Labourd, in villages such as Sare, Aïnhoa and St-Pée-sur-Nivelle but there are slight regional variations and differences in materials. The less colourful style of the Basse-Navarre is typified at Baïgorry, and further east, in the Soule, the houses are still more sombre, and roofed in flat tiles or slate. Such was the importance of a house that many a description—*etcheverry* ('new house'), *etchegaray* ('house on the hill'), *etchegorri* ('red house')—was adopted as the family name.

crammed with carved wooden galleries and turned balusters, a painted wooden ceiling and 17C gilded altarpiece.

The upper town of **Cambo-les-Bains** is grouped around the typical, perfectly maintained, Labourdine single-nave church, with galleries and ubiquitous Baroque retable. It stands on a plateau overlooking the Nive Valley, where the spa developed in the 19C around two hotwater springs.

On the edge of the town, surrounded by woodland, is the former house of Edmond Rostand (1868–1918), author of *Cyrano de Bergerac* (1897). This house, which he called **Arnaga**, is now a shrine to the poet. Guided visits April–Sept 10.00–12.30 and 14.30–18.30; Oct–mid-Nov afternoons only; Feb, March, Sat, Sun afternoons; ☎ 05 59 29 70 57. Rostand first came to Cambo in 1900 to recuperate from pleurisy and made such a good recovery that he decided to establish a base there; the building of a neo-Basque house set in large formal gardens began in 1903. The project was closely supervised by Rostand and most of the rooms have their original décor, incorporating wood panelling, painted decoration, *trompe-l'oeil* and coloured glass, while some are themed (Chinese, Empire). A small bedroom was reserved for Rostand's creativity and its walls are now papered with documents referring to his origins. The gardens frame views of the mountains around Itxassou and contain a pergola inspired by the Gloriette at Schönbrun in Vienna.

In the deeply green and lush Nive Valley is the village of **Itxassou**, reached by the D918 and D349. It is in two parts, around a square with *fronton* and *mairie*, and around the simple but impressive 17C church, which is painted white with a red roof and square tower and stands in a graveyard where there are a number of discoidal stelae. The interior was endowed with a Spanish-style retable and galleries in the 18C, and there are wooden statues including a 17C Virgin carved in wood.

From Itxassou follow the Nive by the D938 to **Louhossoa**, a typical Labourdin village, and **Bidarray**, perched on a plateau above the valley. It has a minute but solid 12C church with a 17C façade and belfry gable, built in the distinctive sandstone of the Basse-Navarre.

Ossès further south boasts a church with a tall white-and-pink octagonal belfry unlike anything else in Pays Basque, built with help from Antoine de Bourbon and Jeanne d'Albret. Inside is a sumptuous red-and-gold retable liberally scattered with cherubs and foliage, set in a pink sandstone sunburst. On the Irissarry road is the remarkable **Maison Sastriarena**, with a massive carved lintel bearing the date of its restoration, 1628.

Stretched out along the Nive in the Vallée des Aldudes, **St-Etienne-de-Baïgorry** is a fairly typical Basque village with houses with carved lintels. Follow through to a pretty bridge spanning the Nive des Aldudes, which at times runs red with mountain mud (*ibaï gorri* means 'red river'). Nearby is the church of St-Etienne, and under the 18C tower is an entrance reputedly reserved for the *cagots* (untouchables). A main door opens into a typical Basque church with galleries and altarpiece, as well as some pre-renovation elements including a few Romanesque capitals. The most unusual feature is the Baroque organ in the manner of southern Germany. A festival of music is held here in summer. The charming little **Château d'Etchauz** (11C and 16C), former seat of the Viscounts of Baïgorry, has two round towers and two Renaissance watchtowers and offers *chambres d'hôte* accommodation. Open July–Sept 10.00–12.00 and 14.30–17.30, closed Mon; ☎ 05 59 37 48 58. The narrow wooded valley leading to the Col d'Urquiaga is typical of the Basque landscape.

Going west from St-Etienne-de-Baïgorry to the Col d'Ispegu along the D949 is a tortuous but spectacular drive through land where France and Spain share the grazing rights. The local wine from the vineyards around Baïgorry, Anhaux and Irouléguy has the deliciously evocative *appellation* Irouléguy.

St-Jean-Pied-de-Port

In a hollow surrounded by mountains is the picturesque *bastide* of St-Jean-Pied-de-Port ('at the foot of the pass'). The old capital of Basse-Navarre, it controlled the ancient and busy route to Spain over the Col d'Ibañeta via Roncevaux; the border is 8km away. The attractive houses overhanging the Nive, the old city wall and gateways (17C), markets and festivities are designed to draw the crowds, but it is a good base for exploring the eastern Pays Basque.

History

St-Jean-Pied-de-Port has always served as a resting-place for travellers, merchants and armies on the road to Spain through Roncevaux, protected until 1178 by the fortress of St-Jean-le-Vieux, destroyed by Richard the Lionheart. From the 10C it became a major route for pilgrims flocking to Santiago de Compostela, and with the revival of interest in this footslog, modern pilgrims now gather here, sometimes in large groups. The fortress was replaced at the end of the 12C by the present *bastide*, founded by the Aragonais kings of Navarre, and it became the capital of Basse-Navarre. The commercial success of St-Jean-Pied-de-Port was assured and a flourishing leather industry developed. The marriage in 1484 of Jean d'Albret with Catherine de Foix added King of Navarre to the family's already illustrious titles but the War of Navarre (1512–30) between the Aragonais and the Bourbons-Albrets resulted in the division of the territory. Only the small segment, Basse-Navarre, was retained by the Albret. With the accession of Henri IV to the throne in 1589, St-Jean reverted to France and was used as a frontier garrison town during the Franco-Spanish War in the 17C. Its military role was revived in the 19C as a base for expeditions against Spain.

Starting out from Place Charles-de-Gaulle, opposite the elegant 17C *hôtel de ville*, head south to the bridge over the Nive for the classic postcard view of balconied Navarrais houses standing in the river, the old bridge and the church against a backdrop of wooded slopes. From Place Floquet turn left on Rue Urhart to the **Rue d'Espagne** leading south to the Porte d'Espagne and the road to Spain. This is a touristy street, traditionally the commercial area, lined with handsome 17C–18C stone houses with overhanging roofs and carved joists. Turn north to cross the old bridge and pass under the fortified belfry tower, **Porte Notre-Dame**, complete with studded doors and portcullis. Stone seats were provided for the poor waiting for the hospice to open. In the 14C there was a wooden bridge which could be raised, but until the 11C the only crossing was a ford. The river-bank alongside the church takes you to the Eyheraberry or 'Roman' bridge, the first built in stone: it is probably no earlier than the 13C, and was rebuilt in 1634. The church was part of the fortifications, and steep steps behind it climb up to the *chemin de ronde* (circuit) and the citadel.

The church of **Notre-Dame-du-Bout-du-Pont** is a severe affair although the violet tints of the stone add warmth. The lower parts of the walls are Gothic (14C), but the rest is 17C–19C. The bare interior with nave and aisles is unlike the Basque churches of the Labourd, with just two galleries in the west and two windows in the east presenting the arms of the town and of the province. Rue de l'Eglise, opposite the church, is spanned by the 13C **Porte de Navarre** in the old fortifications, and steps again climb to the *chemin de ronde*. There are some fine jettied houses and stone lintels carved with dates, names and professions are characteristic of houses in the old streets.

Rue de la Citadelle climbs steeply between 17C–18C houses, and one 16C timber-and-brick house. The **Prison des Evêques** (1584) was a prison only in the 18C. Adjoining is the Maison des Evêques, a reminder that there was an episcopal see here during the Great Schism (14–15C). Rue de France leads to another gate with steps in the walls, and no. 39 is the pilgrim hostel. The street is straddled by the **Porte St-Jacques**. Pilgrims from different parts of Europe converged on Ostabat about 20km northeast and arrived in St-Jean-Pied-de-Port this way. The present hiking routes, the GR10 and GR65, follow the old pilgrimage routes.

St-Jean-Pied-de-Port

A right bend takes you up to the

plateau of the **citadel**, attributed to Vauban although his involvement was minimal. It is now occupied by a school; to visit, enquire at the tourist office. The views from here towards the town, the Pays de Cize and the Cols of Ibañeta and Bentarte are glorious. The citadel replaced a castle damaged by the Spanish in the 16C, and *c* 1644 the present fort, after plans by Deville, began to take shape. Additions suggested by Vauban, including covered paths, and further alterations in the 18C made this a highly modern defensive system and St-Jean-Pied-de-Port the main stronghold between Pamplona and Bayonne during a period of almost permanent conflict between France and Spain.

There is a short but beautiful excursion into the Basque countryside along the mountain-valley road, the D301, to St-Michel and the village of **Esterunçuby**. For enthusiasts of the *Chanson de Roland* or pilgrimage history, the N135 over the Col d'Ibañeta drops down to the vast plateau of Roncevaux, a monastery going back to the 12C, and the Gothic collegiate church with the tomb of Sanche VII. Open 10.00–14.00 and 16.00–20.00.

Battle of Roncevaux

The route via Roncevaux (Roncevalles) has been known since time immemorial as a relatively easy way through the Pyrenees, but was lifted into the realms of legend by the attack on Charlemagne's army on 15 August 778. While returning from the siege of Saragossa to put down a revolt in France, the rearguard under the command of Roland was ambushed by the Vascons in the narrow Col de Bentarte. The exhausted Frankish battalion, impeded by the military hardware and supplies they were moving, were slaughtered to a man. The event, Roland's heroic death, even his sword Durandel, were immortalised in the medieval epic poem *La Chanson de Roland*. Following this battle, Charlemagne created the Kingdom of Aquitaine.

St-Palais northeast of St-Jean was a new town founded in the 13C at the confluence of the Bidouze and the Joyeuse, which became the capital of Basse-Navarre in the 16C. In a fertile region, it is an important agricultural centre where maize has been cultivated since the 16C. There is a small museum of the history of Basse-Navarre and the roads to Santiago de Compostela in the interior courtyard of the *mairie*. Open July, Aug, Mon–Sat 09.30–13.00 and 14.00–19.00, Sept–June, Mon–Sat 09.30–12.30 and 14.00–18.00; ☎ 05 59 65 71 78. The most famous house is the Maison des Têtes, opposite the church of St-Paul, with images of the Albret dynasty. Just 3km south on Mont St-Sauveur is the **Stèle of Gibraltar**, marking the convergence of the pilgrimage routes from Le Puy, Paris and Tours, and Vézelay (although another tradition cites Ostabat).

At Saint-Martin-d'Arberoue, between Hasparren and St-Palais, are the superimposed **Grottes d'Isturitz et d'Oxocelhaya**, which have impressive natural formations and were frequented and decorated by prehistoric man from the Mousterian to Magdalenian periods. A number of objects were found, and there are copies in a small local museum. Guided visits July, Aug 10.00–12.00 and 13.00–18.00; March, April, May, Oct, Nov at 11.00, 12.00, 14.00, 17.00; ☎ 05 59 29 64 72.

Further north, in the town of **Bidache** on the D936, D11 and D10, on the old boundary between France, Navarre and the Béarn, are the striking ruins of the

Château de Gramont silhouetted on a cliff above the little Bidouze River. In 1320 this territory came under the control of the Dukes of Gramont who still own the property, mainly 16C–17C, which was set on fire during the Revolution. What remains is skeletal in places.

The main Classical pedimented entrance is wedged between two round 14C towers, and a substantial amount remains of the north wing with Renaissance elements. There are similarities inside with Cadillac (p 110). A wing of *c* 1600 and a chunky medieval tower have also survived.

Labastide-Clairence is a proud little village where Gascon and Basque influences blend harmoniously. It was founded on the banks of the Joyeuse, a tributary of the Adour, in 1312 by Louis le Hutin, King of Navarre with the objective of reconnecting Navarre, which had just lost its coastal territories, with the outside world via the Adour. The town was populated by immigrants from the Bigorre in Gascony, and the layout—along straight, parallel arcaded streets around a central square—is more typically Gascon than Basque, although the colourfully decorated half-timbered houses are not.

The impeccable main street, with a number of artisans' workshops, runs uphill to the church, built in the 14C, the only stone building until the 17C. Surrounding the church is an unusual *couvert* paved with tombstones which was, and still is, the burial place for local people. Until the end of the 18C, the Etats Généraux of Navarre held their meetings here, and the graveyard of a Jewish community has been preserved nearby. There are rustic carvings on the church porch and the interior is arranged in a typically Basque manner.

THE PAYS DE SOULE AND THE BARÉTOUS

This is the meeting point of Pays Basque and the Béarn in the south of the Pyrénées-Atlantiques. The Pays de Soule is the most rugged part of the Pays Basque, and the Barétous is the most western valley of the Béarn cleft by the Gave de Mauléon.

The smallest of the three French Basque provinces, the Pays de Soule was ceded at the end of the 15C by Louis XI to his nephew, François-Phébus de Foix, King of Navarre. A year after the death of the king, Soule was detached from the Béarn and returned to the Crown of France. Nevertheless, it continued to be part of the diocese of Oloron, which came under the King of Navarre. The Soule remained staunchly Catholic at the Reformation but the churches were ruined by the Protestants.

The foothills are green and lush, but the scenery becomes more dramatic towards the Spanish border. The area is crossed by spectacular mountain routes over the high pass of Col Bargargui (1327m) or the Col d'Aphanize (1055m) and there are two passes into Spain at the Port de Larrau and Pierre-St-Martin.

Getting there and around
Car
From autoroute A64 junction 7 (Salles-de-Béarn) and D933/D918 to St-Palais.

From Oloron-Ste-Marie, D919/918 to Mauléon.

From St-Jean-Pied-de-Port, various route across the high passes (advisable only in fair weather), or D933/D918 to Mauléon.

Train

TER Pau to Oloron-Ste-Marie.

Bus

Pau to Mauléon (until July 2003).
Dax to Mauléon.

Tourist information

64560 Larrau Mairie, ☎ 05 59 28 62 80
64130 Mauléon-Licharre 10 Rue B.-Heugas, ☎ 05 59 28 02 37
64470 Tardets Pl. Central, ☎ 05 59 28 51 28, fax 05 59 28 52 46, email office-tourisme-tardets@wanadoo.fr

Market days

Mauléon Tuesday all day, Haute Ville; Saturday all day, Pl. des Allées
St-Palais Friday
Tardets alternate Mondays all day in winter, every Monday in summer

Festivals and events

April *Spectacle de chants et de danses de la culture basque,* Mauléon
July *Junte de Roncal,* ceremony held on the 13th in connection with an ancient treaty with Spain, Col de la Pierre St-Martin (D132)
Foire gastronomique et artisanale, gastronomy and crafts, Tardets
Foire aux produits fermiers, evening market, Mauléon
August *Foire transfrontalière Soule/Navarre,* cross-border fair, Mauléon
Fête de l'Espadrille, celebration of the espadrille (shoe), Mauléon

Fêtes locales, local festivities, Tardets
Foire aux fromage, cheese fair, Tardets

Where to stay

64130 MAULÉON
☆☆ *Bidegain,* ☎ 05 59 28 16 05, fax 05 59 19 10 26. An old staging post with original features conserved with well turned-out rooms and excellent cooking.

64130 BARCUS
☆☆☆ *Chilo,* D24 southeast of Mauleonm, ☎ 05 59 28 90 79, fax 05 59 28 93 10, www.hotel-chilo.com. A 'gourmet' *auberge* whose owner is one of the best cooks in Pays Basque. The little hotel is a delight. Pool.

64470 ABENSE DE HAUT
☆ *Le Pont d'Abense,* D57 just south of Tardets, ☎ 05 59 28 54 60, fax 05 59 28 75 91. Pretty rooms, guest-house style. Delicious breakfast served on the terrace as soon as the sun comes up.

64560 LARRAU
☆☆ *Etchémaïte,* on the D26 south of Tardets, ☎ 05 59 28 61 45, fax 05 59 28 72 71, www.hotel-etchemaite.fr. Not far from the Pic d'Orhy, in a rural setting, a small family-run hotel renovated with simplicity and charm. Some rooms with mountain views. Quality traditional food.

64470 MONTORY
☆☆☆ *L'Auberge l'Etable,* D918 east of Tardets, ☎ 05 59 28 69 69 fax 05 59 28 69 78. Simple but comfortable hotel with pool. The owner is passionate about 4-wheel drives, handy for the local terrain.

Three routes across the Soule link St-Jean-Pied-de-Port (p 425) and the Gave de Mauléon. The highest and most spectacular, the D18 across the Haute Soule, goes through the **Forêt d'Iraty** to Col Bargargui. Tucked under the highest peak hereabouts, the Pic d'Orhy (2017m), is the sombre mountain village of **Larrau**, which grew around a pilgrim hospice and church, the latter restored in 1656 with its Romanesque apse still intact. In a landscape of ravines, the most accessible is the **Holzarté crevasse** (Holçarté), a relatively easy walk (best in spring or autumn) on the GR10 from the D26. At the end of the world on the D113 is a tiny Romanesque church, **Ste-Engrâce** (☎ 05 59 28 60 83), which shelters some carved and polychromed capitals of *Solomon and the Queen of Sheba*, *Salome's Dance*, the *Virgin and Child* and the *Epiphany*, and a superbly over-the-top Baroque altarpiece. South of Ste-Engrâce are the truly spectacular **Gorges de Kakouetta** and **Gorges d'Ehujarre**; access mid-March–mid-Nov 08.00–nightfall.

The lower route, the D417, branches off at **Mendive**, with panoramic views just off the D117 at the Col d'Aphanize. Certain of the rugged mountain churches contain elaborate Baroque altarpieces, and at **Aussurucq** on the D147 is a typical triple belfry gable (*clocher pignon trinitaire*). The **Château de Trois-Villes** (Elicabia) on the D918 is a small 17C château built by the Comte de Tréville, Captain of the King's Musketeers. Guided visits Jan–March, Oct–Dec Sat, Sun 14.30–18.30; April–May, July, Sept, Sat, Sun, Mon 14.30–18.30; closed June, Aug; ☎ 05 59 28 54 01.

The third route into the Soule is the D918 via the Col d'Osquich where, in October during the migration season, the hunting of wood pigeons (*palombes*) is still permitted by the traditional, but frankly distressing, method of trapping them in nets. In the pretty village of **Ordiarp** is a 12C church with a gable-belfry.

Mauléon-Licharre on the Gave is the main town of the Soule. Mauléon was the *bastide* around the medieval castle on the hill and Licharre, below, was formerly an independent commune and is a major centre for the manufacture of *espadrilles* (linen and twisted cord sandals). The castle was built in the 12C and was held by the English in 1307; in 1449 it was handed over to the Counts of Foix. It is possible to walk around the ramparts. Inside is an exhibition of its history; to visit, contact the tourist office.

On the main square is the **Château d'Andurain** (Château de Maytie), a very handsome example of late-Renaissance architecture. Guided visits July–mid-Sept 11.00–12.00 and 15.00–18.00; closed Thur, Sun mornings and PH; ☎ 05 59 28 04 18. It was built at the end of the 16C by Pierre de Maytie in open countryside. His son, Arnaud de Maytie, Bishop of Oloron, restored the Catholic faith to the diocese and two other members of the family were bishops of Oloron in the 17C. The most impressive feature of the exterior is the enormously high roof, partly covered in wooden shingles (*bardeau*). The façade is asymmetrical and flanked by angle pavilions which were heightened in the 18C; the mullioned windows have broken pediments on the ground floor; and in the roof are three elaborate dormers decorated with masks. There is a corbelled balcony over the main entrance. Enter by the left-hand pavilion. The house is privately owned and the alterations made by successive occupants are part of its charm. The visit includes the main reception rooms, including the dining room altered to 19C tastes and the salon with a 17C monumental Italian-style fireplace; a precious 16C patchwork and appliqué bedspread given to the household by Jeanne d'Albret; and Louis XV style chairs with their original yellow tapestry fabric. Straight flights of stairs of a sophisticated construction lead to the apartments of the three bishops and another magnificent fireplace. There is a prayer book presented by Louis XIII and a remarkable collection of 16C–17C rare books.

Between the Pays Basque and the Hautes Pyrénées is Le Barétous, an agricultural region and the territory of the characters who inspired Dumas' *Three Musketeers*. High in the mountainous frontier, **La Pierre St-Martin** (1640m) is a centre for excursions and winter sports and famous for an ancient frontier treaty, La Junte de Roncal (1375), which is celebrated every year on 13 July at the Col de la Pierre St-Martin on the Spanish border (D132). The ceremony died out in the 19C but since the road was constucted from Arette to the Col (D132) in 1950, it has become an annual tourist attraction. It is considered the oldest peace treaty still in effect in Europe and was drawn up following a violent frontier dispute to allow cattle from the Barétous the right to graze on the Spanish side of the mountains. There are similar agreements in the Pyrenees but this is the only one where the ceremony is still performed.

All that remains of **L'Hôpital St-Blaise**, the commandery established on the pilgrimage route by the Knights of Malta, is the remarkable little church which has undergone a 10-year restoration. Audio guide and light show April–Nov 10.00–19.00; ☎ 05 59 66 11 12. Squat and rustic, in the form of a Greek cross, a central octagonal belfry was added later; the roof is of wooden shingle. Despite its simplicity, the architecture combines severe 12C Romanesque with exuberant Hispano-Mauresque. The west door has been recarved, and on the tympanum is Christ in a mandorla surrounded by the symbols of the four Evangelists. Inside is very simple, the four naves covered by slightly pointed vaults and enhanced by the restoration and lighting and a few Baroque additions. The most exciting feature is the eight-pointed star vault of the cupola, created by intersecting ribs springing from corbels and supported by squinches, reminiscent of the cupola at Ste-Croix in Oloron. Other Moorish touches are the narrow plate-tracery windows decorated with simple shapes.

On the other side of the D936 is the **Château d'Aren** (15C–17C). It has been restored by the present owner and contains a mural of 1450. Open June–Sept 14.00–19.00; ☎ 06 89 60 01 06/06 88 69 90 45.

Between Navarrenx and l'Hôpital St-Blaise, at **Gurs**, is the grim reminder of the largest internment camp in the south of France, through which 18,500 people—mainly Spanish Republicans, then German and foreign Jews—passed between 1939 and 1944. It was built in 42 days in 1939 and it is marked with a monument by an Israeli artist, Dani Karavan.

The **Château de Mongaston** at Charre off the D23 north of Mauléon is a 13C keep with a 14C stairtower, entirely restored in 1999, on a hill overlooking the Vallée du Saison (Gave de Mauléon). Inside is a local history museum with models. Open May–Oct 14.30–18.00, closed Tues; ☎ 05 59 38 65 92.

The Three Musketeers

With the accession of Henri IV to the throne, many *cadets* or younger sons took advantage of the opportunities that opened to the Béarnais to seek their fortune and adventure in Paris. Immortalised by Alexandre Dumas, the Three Musketeers, *cadets de Gascogne et du Béarn*, were based on real characters. D'Artagnan came from the Lupiac (p 381) in Gascony, whereas the others were Béarnais. The character of Aramis was based on a lay abbot from Aramits in the Barétous; Porthos was born in 1617 in Pau and legend claims he owned a château at Lanne in the Barétous; Athos, in reality Armand de Sillègue, came from a village near Sauveterre which inspired his fictional name. Monsieur de Tréville, captain of the Musketeers, was in fact Arnaud Jean du Peyrer, born in Oloron in 1598, and builder of the Château de Trois-Villes, near Tardets.

21 Pyrénées-Atlantiques: the Béarn

The **Béarn** covers the eastern part of the *département* of the Pyrénées-Atlantiques, stretching from the plains of Gascony, across the fertile foothills of the Pyrenees, to culminate at the Spanish border at the Cols de Somport and Portalet. The Béarn presents a distinctive character and its traditions, language and local industries are fiercely protected. The arms of Béarn feature two gold cows, symbolic of the active pastoral life of the region where sheep and cattle are moved to the mountains in the summer during transhumance (see p 457). Local products include cotton and linen textiles, espadrilles, golden Jurançon wine and the famous Basque beret, which has Béarnais origins. The main town is Pau; other centres are the towns of Oloron-Ste-Marie and Orthez and the magnificent valleys of the Aspe and Ossau. The Parc National des Pyrénées (see p 465) also overflows into the Béarn.

The **Béarnais language** is a form of Occitan, derived from Latin, the same root as Provençal or Toulousain. It remained the official language of the Béarn from the 13C to the Revolution, and can still be heard. *Calendretas* are primary schools set up to teach in Béarnais. *Syndicats de communes*, by which all the land in the valleys is communally owned, were created about 50 years after the Revolution. Property passes to the eldest in a family, male or female.

History

The Béarn was an independent province until 1589 and it was wholly united with France only in 1620. Its name orginates from a people called the Venarni who crossed the Pyrenees and settled near Lescar. By the early 11C local viscounts are mentioned, and between the 11C and 13C they became vassals of the Aragonais kings. In 1188, Count Gaston VI of Moncade (1173–1214) established the *Droit Béarnais*, a throwback to Roman times, with a unique set of laws and liberties including the right to transfer a title or inheritance through female descendants. In the 13C, Gaston VII of Moncade (1229–90) reorganised the legal system and divided the Béarn into *vics* (districts). The link with Spain weakened in the early 13C and Gaston VII, forced to stand firm against the opportunist English, threw up fortifications and moved his capital to Orthez. Around this time the Béarnais language took over from Latin.

Gaston III Fébus, Count of Foix and Viscount of the Béarn (1343–91), inherited the territory through his mother (see p 521) and established his capital at Pau. Gaston IV (1436–72), another warrior, took the French side, regained the territory lost to the English, and married Eléonore of Navarre. The viscounts acceded to the crown of Navarre in 1481 but in 1512 the Spanish, angered by the Béarnais' support of the French, split the territory. They kept Haute Navarre, and Basse-Navarre became part of the Béarn, bringing to Henri d'Albret (1517–55) and his descendants the title King of Navarre. Under Jeanne d'Albret, his daughter, the province wholeheartedly embraced the Protestant faith, which resulted in terrible destruction of lives and buildings, especially in 1569: Jeanne and her son, Henri III of Navarre, in La Rochelle at the head of the Protestant armies, were taken prisoner by Charles IX who order the Catholic Terride to take the Béarn. When Henri acceded to the French throne as Henri IV in 1589 he famously declared, *'Je donne la France au Béarn'* ('I give France to the Béarn'). After Henri IV's death, reunification was brought about by Louis XIII. The province was forced to relinquish many of its traditional privileges at the Revolution, and in 1790 the Béarn was absorbed into the *département* of the Pyrénées-Atlantiques.

PAU, THE JURANÇON AND GAVE DE PAU

The capital of the Béarn, **Pau** is a largish town between the plain and the mountains, in a stunning position on a ridge high above the Gave de Pau, and with a pleasantly mild climate. On a clear day, there is a heady view of the Pyrenean range to the south from the famous Boulevard des Pyrénées. The town's reputation and its most prestigious monument, the château, owe much to the two golden boys of the southwest, Gaston Fébus, who built the medieval castle in the 14C, and Henri IV, who was born there in the 16C. Pau became very fashionable with English and American expatriates in the 19C: they left their mark on the town in the shape of elegant villas and luxurious gardens, rugby, and the oldest golf course in France. The Musée des Beaux-Arts was built in the 1930s to conserve one of the best collections in Aquitaine.

Practical information

Getting there and around
Air

Pau-Pyrénées international airport, ☎ 05 59 33 33 00, www.pau.aeroport. fr. Shuttle bus (*navette*) to town, ☎ 05 62 37 67 67.

Car

From Bordeaux, autoroute A62, exit 3 Langon, D932/D934 (Aire-sur-l'Adour) N124; or A63/N10, exit St Gours, D17 to Peyrehorade, A64 via Orthez. From Toulouse or Bayonne, autoroute A64, exit 11, Soumoulou, N117. For Jurançon N134 south from Pau, and D24 or D934. D938 from Pau to the Gave de Pau.

Train

TGV Paris Montparnasse to Pau. TER Paris Austerlitz to Pau. TER Toulouse to Bayonne via Pau. TER Bordeaux to Tarbes via Pau. TER Pau to Oloron-Ste-Marie via Gan, Buzy. A free funicular links the train station, directly below the Boulevard des Pyrénées, to the town centre.

Bus

Agen to Pau via Sarrou, Carlin, Auriac, Sauvagnon. Mont-de-Marsan to Pau via Aire sur l'Adour, Sarron, Garlin. Buzy to Artouste via Bielle, Béost, Laruns. Oloron-Ste-Marie to Canfranc (frontier) via Sarrance, Bedous, Accous.

Tourist information

Agence Touristique de Béarn, Maison du Tourisme, 22ter Rue J.J. de Monaix, 64000 Pau, ☎ 05 59 30 01 30, fax 05 59 84 14, www. tourisme64.com
64360 Monein 58 Rue du Commerce, ☎ 05 59 21 29 28, fax 05 59 21 27 01.
64800 Nay Maison Carrée, Pl. de la République, ☎ 05 59 61 34 61, fax 05 59 61 34 61, www.ot-nay.fr
6400 Pau Pl. Royale, ☎ 05 59 27 27 08, fax 05 59 27 03 21, www.ville-pau.fr

Market days

Billière Saturday

Monein Monday

Gan Monday, Wednesday

Nay Main market Tuesday, local produce Saturday

Pau Every day except Sunday and PH, Halles and Pl. de la République; Saturday, Sunday, Monday, bric à brac, Pl. du Foirail; Wednesday, Saturday, organic produce, Pl. du Foirail; Sunday, flowers and books, Pl. Gramont. December, Christmas market, Pl. Clémenceau

Guided walks

Pau From the Tourist Office, July, Aug, at 10.30 and 16.30, themed walking tours: the heart of the royal city, parks and gardens, etc. All year, at 13.15, visit to historic centre with recorded information and map

Festivals and events

February–March *Le Carnaval Biarnès de Pau*, traditional winter celebrations in the Béarn, Pau

March *Pyrénéa Triathlon*, running, biking, skiing, Pau/Gourette

March–April *Le Festival de Danse Plurielles*, dance festival, Pau

April *Fête des Fleurs*, flower festival, gardens of the Château de Momas, Pau

June *Grand Prix de l'Automobile*, formula 3 motor racing, Pau

Festival de théâtre, theatre, dance and music festival, Pau

June–July *Festival de Pau*, professional and outstanding young performers of theatre dance and music at various venus, Pau

July *Fête de Monein*, crowds turn to taste wine and fruit, Monein. *Fêtes de Nay*, folklore and fireworks, Nay

October *Concours Complet International d'Equitation*, international horse trials, Pau

Festival International de Pau, guitar, jazz and flamenco music throughout the city, Pau

November Festival Acces(s), multi-disciplinary festival of creative art and thought—exhibitions, concerts, films, projects, lectures, workshops, Pau

December *La clôture des vendanges*, wine harvest festival, Jurançon

Where to stay and eating out

64290 BOSDARROS

Chambres d'hôte, Mme C. Bordes, Maison Trille, Chemin de Labau, 64290, ☎ 05 59 21 79 51, fax 05 59 21 57 54. Charming rooms in an 18C Bearnais house around a courtyard.

€-€€ *Auberge Labarthe*, Rue Pierre-Bidau, ☎ 05 59 21 50 13, fax 05 59 21 68 55. Highly recommended cooking—desserts a speciality—in a delightful setting.

64290 GAN (south of Pau)

✰✰✰ *Hostellerie l'Horizon*, Chemin Mesplet, ☎ 05 59 21 58 93, fax 05 59 21 71 80, www.hostellerie-horizon. com. In a pleasant wooded setting on the edge of the village, with a terrace. Restaurant recommended.

64110 JURANÇON (south of Pau)

✰✰✰ *Castel du Pont d'Oly*, 2 Ave Rauski, ☎ 05 59 06 13 40, fax 05 59 06 10 53. A prettily restored mansion with a swimming pool. The chef is talented and the menu is good value.

€€€ *Chez Ruffet*, 3 Ave Charles-Touzet, ☎ 05 59 06 25 13, fax 05 59 06 52 18. Top-quality restaurant serving the best regional products beautifully.

64110 LAROIN (southwest of Pau)

Chambres d'hôte, Mme A.-M. Marque, Maison Miragou, Chemin de Halet, ☎ 05 59 83 01 19. Three quiet *chambres d'hôtes* in a restored farmhouse with a large garden, near Jurançon vineyards.

64290 LASSEUBE

Chambres d'hôtes, Mme I. Browne, Quartier Rey, Maison Rances, ☎ 05 59 04 26 37. Beautiful Béarnais farmhouse with swimming pool. Mountain and vineyard views.

64800 LESTELLE-BETHARRAM

☆☆☆ *Le Vieux Logis*, Route des Grottes, ☎ 05 59 71 94 87, fax 05 59 71 96 75. Hotel-restaurant well placed between Pau and Lourdes, with a swimming pool.

64000 PAU

☆☆☆ *Le Roncevaux*, 25 Rue Louis-Barthou, ☎ 05 59 27 08 44, fax 05 59 82 92 79, www.hotel-roncevaux.fr. Centrally situated hotel.

€€ *Chez Pierre*, 16 Rue Louis-Barthou,

☎ 05 59 27 76 86, fax 05 59 27 08 14. The décor refers to the former Englishness of Pau but the cooking is totally Béarnais.

€-€€ *Casino de Pau*, Allée Alfred-de-Musset, ☎ 05 59 27 06 92. Pleasant restaurant and bar in the renovated Casino in the Parc Beaumont.

€-€€ *Le Bistrot*, 2 Pl. Gramont, ☎/fax 05 59 83 86 37. Parisian-style setting and quality cooking with some novel ideas.

Central reservation service for *chambres d'hôtes*, ☎ 05 59 80 19 13.

History

The town derived its name from the wooden palisades (in Béarnais, *paù*) erected to protect the cattle and trade routes. It grew in importance around the château of Gaston Fébus, when Pau became the administrative capital of Foix-Béarn. Pau's old churches were razed during the religious turmoil of the 16C but following the reunification of the Béarn with France in 1620 Roman Catholicism was re-imposed on the region and a parlement established in Pau. It had the dual role of justice and administration, but honoured Béarnais law. A period of prosperity ensued, which is reflected in the elegant buildings in the town centre.

In the 18C foreigners, particularly British, were drawn to the Pyrenees (pp 410, 496); Napoléon passed through Pau in 1808, and Wellington in 1815. Gradually the fashion for Pyrénéisme combined with the promotion—by a Scotsman, Dr Alexander Taylor—of the curative properties of the gentle air of Pau made the town a smart resort for foreign visitors. Over time the British visitors became residents, built villas set in English-style gardens, and gave a singularly Anglo-Saxon character to the urban centre, which still exists. The foreigners also introduced mains drainage, street lighting and the first golf course, and St Andrew's, one of the few English parish churches still active in France. The Boulevard des Pyrénées was built and lined with elegant hotels and residences.

Since 1908–14, when the Wright brothers patronised the local school of aviation, Pau has been associated with the aeronautical industry and, after natural gas was discovered in the 1950s, Elf Petroleum based its headquarters here. The University of Pau, founded in the 1960s, now has some 15,000 students.

The visit to Pau is determined by the **Boulevard des Pyrénées**, which stretches 1800m from the château at the west (the older section, constructed in the 1850s) to Parc Beaumont at the east (completed by 1900). Almost in the middle is Place Royal, tree-lined and graced with a statue of *Henri IV* (1843) by Raggi, erected on the instructions of Louis-Philippe to replace an effigy of Louis XIV destroyed at the Revolution. North of Place Royal is the tourist office. Rue Henri IV and its extension, Rue Louis-Barthou, are lined with smart boutiques. Take Boulevard des Pyrénées west to the Château de Pau.

Henri III of Navarre, Henri IV of France

Henri III, King of Navarre, was born in the Château de Pau on 13 December 1553 to Antoine de Bourbon and Jeanne d'Albret. Through his mother he inherited his title and his Protestant persuasion; through his father he inherited the crown of France. In 1572 Henri married Marguerite de Valois, daughter of Henri II, and narrowly escaped the St Bartholomew's Day massacre of Protestants in Paris by temporarily rejecting the doctrines of the Reformation and escaping to Nérac (see p 279). Recognised by Henri III as the legitimate successor to the throne of France, he took the name Henri IV in 1589, then had to conquer his kingdom, winning battles at Arques (1589) and at Ivry (1590). He had to renounce his Protestant beliefs again in 1593—he is famously quoted as saying '*Paris vaut bien une messe*' ('Paris is well worth a Mass')—and made his entry into the capital in 1594.

Although Henri spent very little time in Pau he is referred to locally as '*Noste Gran Henric*', and generally as the *Vert Galant* (Old Charmer). Despite the religious problems of his reign and his reputation with the ladies, he is remembered as a good and popular king. He was a man of his time, and he was also courageous, diplomatic and tolerant. By the Edict of Nantes (1598) he ended the Wars of Religion that had raged since 1562, and established interior religious stability. By the Peace of Vervins (1598) he made peace outside the kingdom. He undertook the work of restoring royal authority, reorganising France and improving communications helped by the Protestants, Sully and de Serres, and the Catholics, d'Ossat and Jeannin. Finances were rapidly cleaned up, agriculture was encouraged, and the cloth and silk industries were revived. The King extended the eastern boundary of France by forcing the Duke of Savoy to make over some of his territories (1601) and Quebec was founded (1608). Henri IV united his fiefdoms with the Crown of France (1607), with the exception of Basse-Navarre and the Béarn (incorporated in 1620). He was assassinated by Ravaillac in 1610 and his son, from his second marriage to Marie de Médicis in 1600, was Louis XIII.

Château de Pau

The château, a combination of medieval citadel and Renaissance palace, with 19C makeovers during the Restoration and Second Empire, stands defiantly above the Gave de Pau. It contains a fine collection of furniture, paintings and tapestries. Open for guided tours only, in French, mid-June–mid-Sept 09.30–12.15 and 13.30–17.45; April–mid-June and mid-Sept to Oct 09.30–11.45 and 14.00–17.00; Nov–March 09.30–11.45 and 14.00–16.15; closed 1 Jan, 1 May, 25 December; ☎ 05 59 82 38 19, www.musee-chateau-pau.fr.

A 12C fort with three towers standing guard over the valley was transformed by Gaston III Fébus into one of the most important citadels protecting his territories. Between 1372 and 1379 he added the great brick *donjon carré* (33 m high), a watchtower (the Tour de la Monnaie), and raised the existing main wing (*corps de logis*) by a level. More changes had been made by the mid-15C but, more importantly, after the marriage of Henri d'Albret to Marguerite d'Angoulême in 1527 the latest influences from the Loire Valley were introduced, and between 1529 and 1535 the medieval castle was transformed into a Renaissance palace with large mullioned windows and a grand staircase with straight flights, a step ahead of the Louvre. The sumptuous gardens Henri and Marguerite created on the west and north have disappeared, although the formal garden on the south terrace has been replicated.

The birth in Pau in 1553 of the future Henri IV, first of the Bourbons, secured the reputation of the château and sealed the fate of the Béarn. Henri in fact favoured Nérac, came rarely to Pau and made no alterations to the building. His last visit was in 1587 and his sister, Catherine de Bourbon, lived here until 1592. When the Béarn returned to the French crown, the château was used as a prison or barracks and fell into neglect.

With the return of the Bourbons after the Revolution an attempt at consolidation was made and the great restorer, Louis-Philippe (King of the French, 1830–48), who saw some political advantage in resurrecting Henri's IV's birthplace, employed Lefranc, a pupil of Fontaine who created the Empire style. The Tour Louis-Philippe was erected to match and balance the existing Tour Mazères, creating the classic view of the Château de Pau from the west. The décor of the royal apartments is a unique example of the period 1838–48. From *c* 1853, Second Empire craftsmen completed Louis-Philippe's work for Napoléon III and Eugénie, for whom Pau was a convenient stopover on the way south. The 14C tower was renovated, the north wing made habitable, and the old buildings to the east were demolished and replaced in 1862 by a neo-Renaissance portico, along with a high tower imitating the 15C buildings of the north wing; between 1864 and 1872 considerable work was carried out on the exterior of the south wing. 15C buildings of the north wing; between 1864 and 1872 considerable work was carried out on the exterior of the south wing, the interior of the grand staircase and the chapel, under the direction of Auguste Lafollye. The statue in Pyrenean marble of Gaston Fébus in the costume of a bear hunter, by Henri de Triqueti, was placed in the park facing the Pyrenees. The park is in the process of being completely re-landscaped.

The château stands on a motte which was consolidated with a stone glacis in the 14C, restored in the 19C. The entrance is on the right of the courtyard through the neo-Renaissance portico. Gaston Fébus's massive brick tower is to the left, and next to it is access to the south terrace. The visit includes rooms in the west and south of the château on three floors. In the 16C rib-vaulted kitchen is a model of the pre-16C château. The **Salle aux Cent Couverts** contains an immense oak table lage enough to seat 100, dating from the time of Louis-Philippe (1841), and the statue of Henri IV (1605) wearing the orders of Saint-Michel and Saint-Esprit, in Carrara marble by Pierre de Franqueville. Louis XIII signed the Act of Union (Edict de l'Union) of Béarn and Navarre and supremacy of the Catholic Faith in this room on 20 October 1620. The Salle aux Cent Couverts leads to the grand staircase (1528–35), with a coffered ceiling, decorated with Henri and Marguerite's intertwined initials, but extended and altered in the 19C.

On the first floor of the south wing is a sequence of reception rooms from the 14C, which were panelled and decorated at the time of Louis-Philippe. The **Salon de Famille**, originally Jeanne d'Albret's bedroom and possibly the true birthplace of Henri IV, was later decorated entirely in the style of Napoléon III. In the west wing are the more intimate rooms of the private Appartements de l'Empereur et de l'Impératrice, including the **Appartement de l'Impératrice Eugénie** with 15C fireplace and doorway. The **Chambre du Roi**, Henri IV's birthplace, is on the second floor, its décor dating from 1845–47. Also on this floor are the apartment where Abd al-Qadir was imprisoned in 1848 after France's victory over Algeria, and the **Salle des Peintures**.

The magnificent **tapestries**, displayed throughout the apartments, were chosen by Louis-Philippe from the royal reserves and are a special feature of the château. They include some 100 hangings from 10 series woven at the Gobelins manufactory in Paris and in Brussels between the 16C and 18C. The styles and iconography vary widely, although they represent predominantly mythological scenes (*Story of Psyche, Marriage of Flora and Zephyr, Arabesque Months*), as well as aristocratic activities such as *Maximilian's Hunts* (Gobelins, 1685, the remainder in the Louvre), after designs by Bernard van Orley, or outdoor scenes (*Child Gardeners*).

In the Chambre du Roi, the focus of attention is the **tortoiseshell cradle**. Such a shell was inventoried in the *cabinet de curiosités* of Pau and Nérac belonging to the Albrets in 1561–62. In 1582 a new shell had been acquired and by the 17C, ambiguous references were made to the cradle of Henri IV, although nothing points to it being more than a simple wooden one. Gradually, the two objects merged into one. By the 18C the shell had virtually acquired the status of relic and attracted 'pilgrims'; its veneration developed into the custom of carrying the tortoiseshell in procession through the town. This led to its association with the Béarnaise identity and it became the centrepiece for some elaborate festivities in the 18C, when Henri IV was definitely in vogue. By 1793 attitudes had obviously changed and the precious shell was burned or, so the story goes, replaced by another in the nick of time. From 1822 the tortoiseshell cradle was presented in a setting of lances, banners and a white-plumed helmet.

Throughout the apartments there is a wide range of furniture and rare objects from the 16C to the 19C, from a superb Renaissance bed (1562) to a Boulle clock and 18C copies of Japanese vases. Among the finely crafted 19C furniture are unique pieces made for Pau as well as items purchased during the period. Memorabilia includes Henri IV's jewel case (1607), in black walnut and mother of pearl, and a beautiful inlaid backgammon board (*c* 1600).

Paintings, engravings, sculptures and decorated porcelain also celebrate good King Henri, such as Bosio's well-known statue of *Henri as a Child* (1822) and Sèvres vases with scenes of his reign; paintings include the *Adoration of Henri IV's Cradle by the Inhabitants of the Ossau Valley* by H.P. Poublan and *The Birth of Henri IV* (1827) by E. Devéria. Ingres' *Don Pedro of Toledo kissing the Sword of Henri IV* is one of four versions painted 1814–21. Also in the collection is a magnificent portrait of Henri's father, *Antoine de Bourbon* (1557) from the studio of François Clouet. Access to the terrace gardens, which replicate the 16C formal flowerbeds, is between the large *donjon* and the main building.

The house opposite the château belonged to Duc de Sully, Maximilien de Béthune (1560–1641), Henri IV's Protestant Superintendent of Finances. Rue du Château leads into Rue du Maréchal-Joffre, formerly the Grande Rue, lined with 17C and 18C mansions. The medieval town was surrounded by walls, extending from the level of the arcaded **Place Reine-Marguerite**, site of markets and the scaffold in the Middle Ages, to the present Rue Foch. From the *place*, the narrow Rue Fournets brings you into the **Quartier du Hédas**, built over a stream which became a covered drain in the 19C. The district of Pont des Cordeliers and Passages du Hédas and Parentoy is worth exploring for its medieval *chaume*.

To the east of Rue Fournets, on Rue Tran, is the **Musée Bernadotte**, birthplace in 1763 of the cooper's son, Jean Baptiste Jules, who joined the revolutionary army, became Maréchal de France under Napoléon I, and was elected heir to the Swedish throne in 1810. As Charles XIV, he was the first of the present Swedish dynasty. Open Tues–Sun 10.00–12.00 and 14.00–18.00, closed Mon; ☎ 05 59 27 48 42.

Follow the street to Place des Sept-Cantons, and turn left onto Rue Montpensier, where there are reminders of the Englishness of Pau in the 19C, including the church of St Andrew in Rue Planté. Return to Rue Joffre, cross Place G.-Clemenceau, and follow Rue Foch to Rue Mathieu-Lalanne on the right, and the fine arts museum.

Musée des Beaux-Arts

This important collection consists mainly of paintings, a varied but rich selection of Spanish, Italian and Northern European works (mainly 17C–18C) and French works with a heavy local emphasis (mainly 19C–early 20C). The star of the collection is an early work by Degas. Open Mon, Wed–Sun 10.00–12.00 and 14.00–18.00, closed Tues; ☎ 05 59 27 33 02.

The venture was inaugurated in 1864, with 25 paintings, and was expanded by the La Caze donation and helped by a financial bequest from Emile Noulibos (d. 1875), who made his money from textiles. It moved into the present building in 1931, although it was forced to close between 1942 and 1953. Some rooms have recently undergone much needed renovation and reorganisation.

A Cotton Exchange in New Orleans (1873) was painted by Edgar Degas during a visit with his brother to the family business in New Orleans. His brother is engrossed in the *Daily Picayune*, which announced the liquidation of the family company that year. The palette is subtle and limited to the contrast of white cotton, newspaper and sleeves with black business suits. The space is defined by diagonals and uses the abrupt cut-off point which is a characteristic of Degas' style. The painter planned to sell the work to a Lancashire cotton magnate, but instead it ended up in Pau in 1876, and was purchased by the museum with money from the Noulibos bequest. This was the first work by Degas to enter a museum, during his lifetime.

Among the Spanish works are 15C religious paintings from Aragon, one of several versions of **St Francis receiving the Stigmata** (*c* 1595) by El Greco, and a moving painting of **St Jerome** (1633) by José de Ribera. Italian paintings include works by Ghislandi (Fra Galgario), Piazzetta and Giuseppe Ricci, whose *At the Station* (*c* 1890) is a beautifully observed and delicately executed yet puzzling scene in the waiting room of a maritime station. There are works from Northern Europe by Jan Brueghel the Elder, Jacob Jordaens, and two by Rubens. Among the paintings from Holland is Nicolas Berchem's **Return of Tobias** (1670–80); and English works include portraits by George Romney and Sir David Wilkie.

There is the mandatory landscape by Corot, *Fontainebleau, the Gorges d'Apremont* (1834). The majority of the French works are 19C–20C including several examples of Orientalism, by Benouville, Guillaumet, Cormon and others. The Belle Epoque is represented by Léon Bonnat (see p 407) with a portrait of **Madame Maurice Pascale and her Dog, Tiny** (1905), Ernest Bordes, Henri Zo and so on. There are a number of landscapes by local artists and a Turneresque watercolour, *Le Cirque de Gavarnie* (1882), by a non-local, Gustave Doré.

There is a good group of works by painters on the peripheries of Impressionism and Fauvism, such as Carolus-Duran; a somewhat Symbolist work by Fantin-Latour, *Dances* (1891); Guillaumin's *Creuse landscape* (*c* 1900), a Fauve-influenced landscape; and two by the Bordelais painter, André Lhote, including *14 July, Avignon* (1923); Albert Marquet; Berthe Morisot's *Pasie sewing* (1881), a delicate painting of soft greens and violets; and Jean-François Raffaelli. There are also works by Kees van Dongen and Edouard Vuillard, a pastel, *Demolition, Rue de Calais* (1927); and a small collection of later 20C works.

Out of the museum, turn right and right again to the Triangle, a popular café area. Southeast of the museum, at the end of Boulevard des Pyrénées, is **Parc Beaumont**, carrying on the tradition of horticulture, and the Palais Beaumont, a casino and conference centre, which has a pleasant restaurant. Opposite the casino is the former Jesuit College, established during the Counter-Reformation and now part of the *lycée*.

The Jurançon

The Jurançon is the area west of Pau, between the Gaves de Pau, the d'Ossau and d'Oloron. It is famous for its white wines, favourite of Henri IV. The landscape consists of small narrow valleys and hills with stunning panoramas of the Pyrenees, and large 17C–18C Bearnais farmhouses, sober but diginified, with marble lintels, roofs covered in flat tiles and decorated with a double *génoise* moulding under the eaves.

> ### Wines of the Jurançon
> The vineyards cover some 1000ha over about 40km along the steep slopes of the Gave de Pau, facing the Pyrenees. The vines thrive in pebbly ground and a mild climate that combines rain carried from the west and the sunshine of the south. The vineyards are mainly small and sometimes perilously steep, planted at an average of 300m above sea-level to avoid spring frosts. The delicious white wines, dry and *moelleux*, are produced from regional grape varieties, Gros Manseng, Petit Manseng, and small amounts of Courbu, Camaralet and Lauzet. The **Maison des Vins** in the Commanderie du Jurançon, Lacommande, promotes wine from a selection of independent producers in the region and offers tastings. Open Mon–Sat 14.00–18.00, Sun 14.00–18.30; ☎ 05 59 82 70 30, fax 05 59 82 74 64.

The pretty village of **Lacommande**, on the D34, developed around a hospice built on the pilgrim route to Santiago. The mainly 12C church of St-Blaise was restored in 1970, as was the hospice at right angles to it, now the *mairie*. The interior is particularly fine with carved capitals of the *Adoration of the Magi* on the high arch of the chancel, and around the apse arcades, *Daniel in the Lions'*

Den, *Salome's Dance*, and the *Flight into Egypt*. In the old cemetery south of the church are a number of discoidal stelae. **Lasseube**, further south on the same road, is a pretty village with some fine examples of Béarnais houses.

West on the D9 is the thriving town of **Monein**, set in a fertile plain. It flourished from the mid-15C to the 17C and was resolutely Calvinist during the Reformation. The church of **St-Girons** (1464–1530) is the largest of the period in the Béarn and is famous for its roof timbers. It has a hugely tall tower (40m) like a land-locked lighthouse, supported by massive angle buttresses and a stair-tower. The 60m-long church is constructed in stone, pebble and brick and the steep roof is covered in slate which replaced the original wooden shingles in 1964. Although powerful, it was never a fortified church and owes its scale to the wealth of the town. Inside the porch is the surprisingly ornate Renaissance entrance to the nave. The double arch is decorated with foliage and angels carrying the instruments of the Passion, and the jambs are also carved. To the right is the Flamboyant door leading to the belfry and roof space. Inside, the nave has simple vaulting, and one aisle half its width and the same height on the north. The window tracery is Flamboyant, the latest glass installed in the 16C, and the apse six-sided. A restoration begun in 1999 uncovered painted décor of fleur de lis, which is being reproduced. Behind the main altar is an early 18C Counter-Reformation retable made in the town, with the symbol of the four Evangelists, including a goose-like eagle. The church was Protestant for 60 years but was not damaged, simply cleared of its ornament.

A climb to the **roof** is well worthwhile and the visit is presented as a *son-et-lumière* show. Guided visits from the tourist office July, Aug, Mon–Sat at 11.00, 15.00, 16.00, 17.00; Sun and PH 16.00, 17.00, Sept–June, Sun–Fri 16.00, 17.00. This magnificent structure (50m long, 18m high, 20m wide) used 1000 hearts of oak and took three years to assemble. The purpose of the huge tower is to protect and support the *charpente* (wooden roof frame) which is in two parts, one covering the nave and the other the north aisle. It is mighty impressive although the sound-and-light show drags on a bit.

The Gave de Pau

Nay

Strategically placed on the Gave de Pau is the *bastide* of Nay, centred on the vast arcaded Place de la République, which has a very busy market. The original *halle* has disappeared and been replaced by the arcades under the 19C *mairie*. The most prestigious building on the square is the Maison Carrée, and Nay prides itself on perpetuating certain traditional craft industries such as the manufacture of berets and cattle bells.

Nay was founded in 1302 by Marguerite of Moncade, in conjunction with the Augustine monastery in Gabas, where a community already existed close to the bridge built in the 12C on the vital route linking France and Spain. The local cotton, linen and woollen industries go back a long way, and the force of the river torrents was harnessed to power the mills. The town had its fair share of disasters and raids, did not escape the effects of the Hundred Years War, and many buildings were lost during a fire in 1543.

The church of **St-Vincent** was rebuilt after that fire. The massive stepped belfry tower, originally integral with the 14C walls, ends in a curious octagonal structure added in the 19C. The door next to the tower is a survival of the 13C, but the window tracery is Flamboyant, as is the very fine south door with a decoration of *choux frisés* (curly kale). The interior arrangement is typical of the southwest, with a single nave and interior buttresses, particularly massive in the west. The vaults are brick, with lierne and tierceron vaulting over the east. On a vault boss is the image of *St Vincent of Zaragoza and his Book* with the crow that protected him. The sacristy doorway is worth noting. The holy-water stoup near the entrance is 16C, the pulpit Flamboyant, and the organ case 17C.

The **Maison Carrée** (*c* 1550) is a stunning example of Renaissance domestic architecture, influenced by Italy and adapted to France, as in Toulouse and Lyon. Open July, Aug, Tues–Sun 10.00–12.00 and 15.00–19.00, closed Mon, Fri–Lyon; May–June, Sept, Oct, Tues–Sat 10.00–12.00 and 14.00–18.00, closed Mon, Sun; Nov–April, Sat only 10.00–12.00, 14.00–18.00; ☎ 05 59 61 34 61.

The builder was a Spaniard, Pedro Sacaze, who had made his fortune in the cloth trade and in *pastel* (see p 331). After many years of neglect, the Maison Carrée was painstakingly renovated in the 1990s and a museum installed. The street façade has mullioned windows above arcades, and dormers in the steep roof. The surprise comes when you enter. The house is composed of two main wings, north and south, linked by galleries which enclose a courtyard. There is a garden behind the south wing. The west gallery consists of a sophisticated two-tier loggia above the arcades, using the Classical orders in their established sequence, and an attic storey. Only one column is fluted: the project was interrupted by the Wars of Religion. There are reliefs of the proprietor and his wife on the north façade. Pedro Sacaze's son-in-law, François de Béarn, Captain Bonasse, a staunch Catholic, continued the work but was killed by Protestant troops during the siege of Tarbes and Jeanne d'Albret confiscated the house. Consequently the matching east gallery was never completed and a simpler wooden version links the two wings, which is perhaps less elegant but nevertheless fascinating, as some of the wooden panels which enclose it are original 16C examples. The museum contains a collection of Béarnais furniture (17C–19C) and local ethnology as well as a model of Nay in the 16C.

It may come as quite a shock—hold on to your hats—but the famous *béret Basque* originated in the Béarn. A film and exhibits explain it all at the **Musée du Béret** on Place St-Roch. Open July, Aug daily 10.00–12.00 and 14.00–19.00, April–June, Sept–mid-Nov, Tues–Sat 10.00–12.00 and 14.00–18.00, Dec daily 10.00–12.00; ☎ 05 59 61 91 70, fax 05 59 61 29 05.

The museum is in an attractively restored 19C building and has a shop. Mystery surrounds the evolution of this quintessentially French rural head-covering, but there is local evidence that it goes back a long way. Adaptable and comfortable, the beret is now enjoying a revival, since fashion icons such as Julia Roberts have been recorded sporting one. Another traditional activity may be witnessed at the *Fabrique de Sonnailles* at 24 Rue des Pyrénées, one of the only two workshops where sheep bells, each with its own particular sound, are made. Open by appointment only Mon, Sat 14.00–17.00; ☎ 05 59 61 00 41.

The nearby village of **Lestelle-Bétharram**, a site of pilgrimage for 700 or 800 years and dedicated, like Lourdes, to the Virgin, was frequently visited by Bernadette Soubirous (p 474).

The chapel was badly damaged by Protestant troops in 1569 and rebuilt between 1614 and 1710 at a period when an increasing number of miracles revitalised the site. The exterior is of grey marble decorated with white marble statues of the *Virgin and Child* and the four Evangelists. In contrast the interior is heavily ornate, every surface decorated with gilt and paintings (1690–1710). On the front panels of the tribune above the west entrance are scenes of the early miracles performed in the chapel, and below are depictions of the ancestors of Christ. The organ case is dated 1710 but the organ itself was replaced by Napoléon III after the original was damaged in 1793. The 19C statue of *Our Lady of Beau-Rameau* by Alexandre Renoir on the main altar evokes the miracle of a drowning girl saved by the Virgin, who holds a branch out to her. Another apparition of the Virgin to local shepherds is the subject of the retable (1620–30) in the south aisle chapel. In contrast to all the Baroque flamboyance is the Second Empire mausoleum of St Michel Garicoïts, Bernadette Soubirous' mentor. Covered by a glass dome, it was designed by the architect Gabriel Andral and consecrated in 1928.

There is also a small local history museum, and on the hill outside a Calvary (1840–45). The old bridge near the chapel is dated 1687. The D226 alongside is a twisting drive through woods and open countryside to join the D126.

The **Grottes de Bétharram** are a spectacular five-level network of caverns, visited partly by boat and partly by little train. Open April–July, Sept–Oct daily 09.00–12.00 and 13.30–17.30; Aug 09.00–18.00; Feb–March at 14.30; ☎ 05 62 41 80 04. **St-Pé**, further down the D937, has a pretty square with arcades and the remains of a Romanesque abbey incorporated into the parish church.

BÉARN-ADOUR

The region on the border with Gascony, north of Pau and Tarbes and the A64, is described variously as the Béarn-Adour or the Vic-Bilh Montánérès (*vic-bilh* meaning 'old country') and embraces part of the vineyards of Madiran and Pacherenc (see p 380). In this rolling countryside with fields of maize the villages are often grouped around Romanesque chapels and 16C manor houses.

Getting there and around

See details for Pau, p 433.

Tourist information

64160 Morlaàs Pl. Ste-Foy,
☎ 05 59 33 62 25, fax 05 59 33 62 25, email
morlaas.tourisme@wanadoo.fr
64350 Lembeye Pl. du Marché, ☎ 05 59 68 28 78, fax 05 59 04 81 30

Market days

Morlàas Friday (fortnightly); local produce Saturday
Lembeye Thursday
Garlin Wednesday
Soumoulou Friday (fortnightly)

Festivals and events

April *Fête des fleurs*, spring flower show, Château de Momas
August *Fêtes des Vins de Madiran*, wine festival, Crouseilles

Where to stay and eating out

64350 ARROSES
(between Pau and Tarbes)
Chambres d'hôte, M. J. Labat, 64350 Arroses, ☎/fax 05 59 68 16 01.
Comfortable rooms in an old farm in

Madiran vineyards, with a swimming pool. Excellent cooking.
64370 MORLANNE
Chambres d'hôte, Mme R.-M. Jehle-Leconte, Manoir d'Argelès, ☎ 05 59 81 44 07, fax 05 59 81 42 47, www.manoir-d'argeles.bellerose.com. Artist's home on the edge of a charming village, with views and swimming pool. Good food.

From *c* 1070 until the 13C, **Morlaàs** was the capital of the Béarn, and the viscounts granted to its inhabitants important privileges called the *for de Morlaàs*, the impetus behind the town's development in the 12C. On the edge of a plateau dominating the plain, the site is not unlike that of Lescar (see below), and is now a rural suburb of Pau with a few picturesque old houses and a market. Its church of **Ste-Foy** has (or had) one of the best sculpted portals in the Béarn.

It benefited from large donations from Count Centulle V, in expiation for his marriage to a blood relative, and came under the protection of the abbey of Cluny from 1079. The church was built in the 12C and heightened in the 14C; fire damaged the west façade in 1520 and 1569, the belfry collapsed in 1617, and there was another collapse in the 18C, damaging the roof. It was pillaged at the Revolution but work began to rebuild and restore in 1840, and was completed early in the 20C.

The west front remains of interest despite a total rebuild (1857–1903) and there are many references in iconography and layout to Ste-Marie at Oloron (see below). The recarved central trumeau has atlantes in chains and above the door the **Massacre of the Innocents**, the **Flight into Egypt**, **Christ in Majesty**, St Matthew and St John are depicted. The successive arches framing the tympanum are decorated with ducks, and the **Twenty-four Elders of the Apocalypse**; among the souls of the saved is Boeswillwald, Inspector of Historic Monuments. The statues of the 12 Apostles in the door jambs are also 19C. The interior of the church has a mainly 14C and 17C nave with false wooden nave vaults and 19C aisles, the chancel is barrel vaulted and the east apse has Romanesque capitals painted in the 19C, including the **Martyrdom of St Faith**, who appears again on a south window capital.

Nearer Tarbes, by the N117, D63 and D27, is a fort built by Gaston Fébus, the **Château de Montaner**. Built to protect his territory from the English, in the 14C it was decked out as a palace. Open July, Aug, daily 10.00–19.00; April–June and Sept–Oct, Wed–Mon 14.00–19.00, closed Tues; ☎ 05 59 81 98 29. The great brick *donjon*, one of the most remarkable in the southwest, stands on a mound guarding the entrance and the circular enclosure. The church of St-Michel at the foot of the hill was rebuilt in the 14C–15C in brick and pebbles, and inside are interesting murals (*c* 1490–1530), restored in the 1980s.

The church at **Lembeye**, further north on the D943, has Flamboyant Gothic doors and a 14C fortified gate. At **Castéra-Loubix** on the D202 is a Romanesque church (11C, 15C and 18C) with murals (end 15C–16C) of the **Passion** and **Last Judgement**.

Château de Mascaraàs-Haron is near Garlin, north of Pau on the D104. A pretty building overlooking the Vic-Bilh, it was used as a hunting lodge by Jeanne d'Albret, and altered in the 17C–18C. It boasts one of the most important decorative ensembles in this part of the Pyrénées-Atlantiques, with 16C–18C works of art and an old library. Guided visits mid-May–mid-Sept, Wed–Mon 10.00–12.00 and 15.00–18.00, closed Tues; ☎ 05 59 04 92 60. **Sévignacq**, north of Morlaàs by the D943 and D42, has a mainly 12C church with a fine sculpted doorway in sandstone and limestone.

West of the N134, the **Château de Momas**, privately owned but open to the public, has restored gardens where rare species of plants and ancient vegetables are cultivated. Open for guided visits April–Oct, Sat, Sun afternoons, or by appointment; ☎ 05 59 77 14 71. Northwest again on the D946 is **Morlanne**, a pretty village associated with Gaston Fébus. The church of St-Laurent was built in the 13C and fortified in the 14C to defend Gaston's territories. The exterior towers, two with pointed roofs, and the stairtower are relics of that period, but larger windows were opened in the 16C and the west door is an 18C addition. At the Reformation it became a Protestant temple. The asymmetrical aisleless Gothic nave has chapels along the north side, the first with a 14C circular window; light floods in from the west and apse windows. Two vault bosses are carved, one with an angel and phylactery, the other with the patron saint and his grid-iron, and there are pretty 14C capitals in the apse. The lectern and candlesticks are 17C, and the Baroque pulpit 18C.

Opposite the church is a former 15C *abbaye laïque* (lay abbey, the property of a layman with certain ecclesiastical rights) with mullioned windows. The road alongside, lined with well-kept 16C–17C tile-roofed houses, brings the **Château de Morlanne** into view. A truly magnificent sight with immaculate brickwork, perfect crenellations and pleasantly landscaped, it is almost too good to be true; which in fact it is, having been extensively restored in the 1970s in the spirit of the 14C by its last owners, Raymond and Hélène Ritter. From the car park take the path to the left of the château and keep going around it to the gateway on the north. Open July, Aug daily 10.00–19.00; March–June, Sept–Oct, Wed–Mon 14.00–19.00, closed Tues; ☎ 05 59 81 60 27.

Gaston Fébus purchased the land in 1373 to defend his western territories. From the 15C the castle changed hands several times, eventually falling into disrepair, and was subjected to injudicious alterations in the 19C. By the time of its rescue in 1969 by the historian and writer, Raymond Ritter, it was in an appalling state with the *donjon* only half its present height. The Ritters decided not just to consolidate but, with infinite care and huge expense, went for a wholesale restoration, using other Fébusian fortresses as models, notably Montaner.

Typically Fébusian, the castle is built on a motte with a towering *donjon*. It has five sides around a courtyard, is built in brick and the main buildings are on the west. The interior is the showcase for the Ritters' collection of antiques and paintings, the rooms displayed thematically or chronologically: Romanesque, Medieval, 16C, Louis XVI, 18C, Rococo, Empire, Second Empire, and so on. Among the wealth of objects displayed is a 12C ***Christ in Majesty*** from the Toulousain, Louis XV commodes, furniture by Georges Jacob, a Dutch roll-top writing desk, an elaborate Italian jewel cabinet, an Empire period Egyptian-style bed, and furniture from Alsace, M. Ritter's birthplace. There are also tapestries and sculptures, porcelain and pottery, engravings and watercolours. The fine collection of paintings includes works by Canaletto, Fragonard and Pannini, as well as a room devoted to René Morère, a local painter much admired by M. Ritter.

Medieval pilgrims used **Arzacq**, east of Morlanne on the D946, as a staging-post to Santiago. Now it boasts *La Maison du Jambon de Bayonne*, dedicated to the drying and curing of the famous local ham which was exported from the port of Bayonne. Open July, Aug 10.00–12.00 and 14.00–17.00; Sept–June closed Sun morning, Mon; ☎ 05 59 04 49 35. In the other direction from Morlanne, the tiny chapel at **Caubin** near Arthez-de-Béarn is the only remnant of a pilgrimage hospice founded in the 12C by the Knights of St John.

THE BÉARN DES GAVES

Closely linked with the history of the Béarn are the old capitals of Lescar and Orthez, the cathedral of Lescar and the castles built along the Gaves de Pau and Oloron to defend the Béarn.

Getting there and around
Car
N117 Pau to Orthez; D933 south to Sauveterre-de-Béarn. Navarrenx by the D936, D947 or D111.
Train
Pau to Orthez.

Tourist information
64230 Lescar La Cité, ☎ 05 59 81 15 98, fax 05 59 81 12 54

64190 Navarrenx 17 rue St-Germain, ☎ 05 59 66 14 93, fax 05 59 66 54 80, email otc.navarrenx@wanadoo.fr

64300 Orthez Maison Jeanne d'Albret Rue du Bourg-Vieux, ☎ 05 59 69 02 75, fax 05 59 69 12 00, email tourisme. orthez@wanadoo.fr

64270 Salies-de-Béarn Rue des Bains, ☎ 05 59 38 00 33, fax 05 59 38 02 95

64390 Sauveterre-de-Béarn Pl. Royale, ☎ 05 59 38 58 65, fax 05 59 38 94 82, www.bearn-gaves.com

Market days
Anzacq Saturday (fortnightly)
Mourenx Wednesday, Saturday
Orthez Tuesday; *marché au gras* Nov–March
Sales-de-Béarn Thursday; organic Saturday

Guided walks
July, Aug 10.00 Thurs, walking tours from the tourist office

Festivals and events
Easter *Foire artisanale*, craft fair with Béarnais furniture, decorative objects, pottery, etc, Navarrenx

May *Musique de la Transhumance Atlantique/Transmusicales de Las*, concerts, evening events, Laàs

July *Salies à peindre*, amateur and professional painters erect their easels and compete for the best picture of the town, Salies-de-Béarn

Fête d'Orthez, five days of *féria*—bull-fighting, berets and *bandas*, Orthez

August *La Piperadère Béarnaise*, *piperade* competition (local dish made of eggs, tomatoes, hot peppers and onions), Salies-de-Béarn

September *Fête du Sel* (La Heste de la Saü), with salt carrying and ham rolling, craft market, concerts, parade, Salies-de-Béarn

October *Octobre à Lescar*, music festival, Lescar

Where to stay and eat
64270 CASTAGNÈDE
☆☆ *La Belle Auberge*, ☎ 05 59 38 15

28, fax 05 59 65 03 57. Quiet country hotel with swimming pool and good local cooking.

64190 NAVARRENX

☆☆ *Commerce*, Pl. des Casernes, ☎ 05 59 66 50 16, fax 05 59 66 52 67, www.hotel-commerce.fr. Time stands still in this old house with large fireplaces and delicious food.

64300 ORTHEZ

☆☆ *Au Temps de la Reine Jeanne*, 44 Rue Bourg-Vieux, ☎ 05 59 67 00 76, fax 05 59 69 09 63. Attractive rooms in the centre of the town with a pretty interior garden and quality restaurant.

€–€€ *Auberge Saint Loup*, 20 Rue Pont-Vieux, ☎ 05 59 69 15 40, fax 05 59 67 13 19. Old pilgrimage hospice with fireplace, terrace, innovative cuisine and friendly reception.

64270 SALIES-DE-BÉARN

☆☆ *Golf*, Domaine Jelios, Route d'Orthez, ☎ 05 59 65 02 10, fax 05 59

38 16 41. Hotel-restaurant in a verdant setting, with swimming pool and tennis court.

Chambres d'hôte, Mme M.-C. Potiron, La Closerie du Guilhat, Quartier de Guilhat, ☎/fax 05 59 38 08 80. Traditional *maison de maître* in an oasis of greenery. Good local cooking.

€ *La Terrasse*, ☎ 05 59 38 09 83, fax 05 59 38 10 95. Beautiful woodwork, old fireplaces. Specialities: meat cooked on the grill, dishes using salt from Salies.

64270 SALIES-DE-BÉARN

Parc, ☎ 05 59 38 31 31, fax 05 59 38 31 32, email salies@europe-casinos. com. The hotel is under restoration, but its splendid building, brasseries and casino are open.

€–€€ *Auberge des Platanes*, ☎ 05 59 67 50 15, fax 05 59 67 55 77. Elegant restaurant with stylish presentation of traditional dishes.

Lescar

Lescar, just west of Pau on the N117 and D509, is now a pleasant residential town with a magnificent 12C cathedral. At the foot of the escarpment dominating the Gave de Pau was the site of ancient *Beneharnum*, a Gallo-Roman *oppidum* and, from 506, the seat of a diocese. Virtually wiped out by the Normans in 840, it re-emerged on the hill in the 10C as Lescar and in 1125 the cathedral was begun on the site of a monastery. Lescar became one of the main religious centres of the Béarn, containing the relics of St Galactoire, the first bishop, and the mausoleum of the Kings of Navarre.

The cathedral stands just beyond a terrace on the remains of the 16C ramparts. The tourist office is in the 16C tower of the old presbytery. To the north of the cathedral are two 17C city gates and to the west, on Place de l'Evêché, are the two surviving towers of the bishops' palace, in pebble with brick coursing. A **Musée Art et Culture** on Rue de la Cité presents the history of Lescar, beginning in 2000 BC; a Roman mosaic floor (4C AD); and the discovery of the tombs of the Kings of Navarre in the 1930s. Open April–Oct, Wed–Mon 10.00–12.00 and 14.30–18.30, closed Tues; ☎ 05 59 81 31 91.

Cathédrale Ste-Marie

Despite a turbulent history and unfortunate restoration in the 19C, the cathedral remains a magnificent building. A recent clean-up has accentuated the glorious reds and ochres of the exterior brick and stonework.

It was begun by Bishop Guido (Guy de Lons) in 1125, was damaged by fire in the 14C, and the furnishings were wrecked in 1563 on the orders of Jeanne d'Albret, after which it became a Protestant church. Further destruction ensued in 1569 when Huguenot troops under Montgomery ransacked the town and cathedral, and chased out the Catholics. When the Catholics returned in 1620 the building was in a parlous state, and essential rebuilding of the vaults was carried out. At the Revolution there was more sacrilege and the cathedral became a Temple of Reason. With the Concordat in 1802, Lescar lost its status as cathedral and from 1843 parts of it were demolished or disappeared under cement and plaster.

The **south wall** reveals the diverse stages of construction: evidence includes walled-up Romanesque doorways and Gothic windows. Set in a stone frame near the south door is the tombstone of the founder, Bishop Guido, above an inscription recording that it was placed here by Bishop Jean de Salettes in 1620. The **east end**—best viewed from the cemetery—is Romanesque and highly decorated with carved corbels and billet moulding, some restored. The neo-Romanesque west end and the door in the north wall date from the 17C.

Enter from the south. The **interior** is light and spacious, with a four-bay barrel-vaulted nave supported by mighty pillars, and in the aisles are transverse barrel vaults abutting the nave. The crossing was rebuilt in the 17C and the 12C apse and side chapels have semi-domes. There are some good 12C **storiated capitals** (some may be copies). In the south aisle and around the transept they include *Adam and Eve*, *Cain and Abel*, and scenes from the *Life of Daniel*, the *Sacrifice of Abraham* and *Herod's Feast*. There is also the *Birth of Christ*, the *Flight into Egypt*, and a *Christ in Majesty* in the apse. On the floor of the apse is an unusual **mosaic** (12C, discovered and restored in the 19C) depicting a hunt, with lions and wild boar as well as birds and a donkey, which pursue or are being pursued by two huntsmen, each with an oliphant (ivory horn). One is dressed in a 12C tunic and the other, described as Moorish, seems to have one good leg while the other is a wooden peg. The Latin inscription records that Bishop Guido commissioned the work. The site of the former sepulchre of the Kings of Navarre, whose remains were discovered in 1929, is indicated by a bronze plaque before the altar. In the crossing are some 17C wooden stalls with low-relief carvings of Christ, Apostles, the Virgin and local saints. There is a large gilded 18C altarpiece dedicated to the Virgin in the north aisle and the organ case is also 18C.

Orthez

The Gave de Pau flows northwest, through the historic market town of Orthez. On the N117 and close to the A64 it makes a convenient touring base between Gascony and the Pyrenees. The capital of the Béarn for 200 years, its more recent claim to fame is the Orthez-Pau basketball team, and its best monuments are the 13C fortified bridge and the Tour Moncade.

The town developed on a major crossroads where a bridge already existed and became an important halt for pilgrims on the Vézelay–Santiago road in the 12C. Gaston VII of Moncade built a fortified stone bridge, the church and the château and made Orthez his capital. Gaston Fébus altered the bridge and gave the town its motto '*tourqey si gaouses*', loosely translated as 'take us if you dare'. In the 16C Orthez was the main Protestant town in the region and suffered the consequences in 1569 during the Wars of Religion when the Protestants threw the Catholic priests into the *gave* from the bridge. Orthez then settled down to a period of prosperity when the Protestant Academy, established in the former Jacobin Convent, was raised to the status of university in 1583, but with the re-establishment of the Catholic Church and the final absorption of the Béarn into France in 1620, its moment of glory was over. In 1814 Wellington won a victory over the Napoleonic army of General Soult here.

The tourist office is in Rue du Bourg-Vieux, installed in the **Maison de Jeanne d'Albret**, a pretty building (15C–17C) with mullioned windows and stairtower which Jeanne accepted in exchange for granting its owner a title of nobility. It can neither be proved nor disproved that Jeanne stayed here: she might have preferred the château. Behind it are a 17C *colombier* (dovecote) on tall, stilt-like columns typical of the region, and a small formal garden. Examples of the traditional pewter, copper and wood industries and fabrics are on display in the tourist office. The **Musée du Protestantisme** on the second floor of the house gives a fascinating account of Protestantism in the Béarn and Pays d'Adour in the 18C and 19C with the aid of documents, ecclesiastical furnishings and engravings. Open Mon–Sat 10.00–12.00 and 14.00–18.00, closed Sun and PH; ☎ 05 59 69 14 03.

The Maison is situated between the *bourg vieux*, which developed in the 12C near the bridge, and the *bourg neuf*, which dates from the Renaissance. Take **Rue Bourg-Vieux** (its extension is Rue de l'Horloge), lined mainly by 18C houses with large entrances and sombre façades masking courtyards. Turn right into Rue des Aiguilletiers, which runs parallel with the *gave* and the railway line. In front is the tower of the **Pont-Vieux**, one of the few surviving bridges with medieval defences. Built in the 13C when Orthez became the capital of Béarn, probably with two towers and removable wooden sections at each end, it was altered in the 14C and took on its present form, with one main arch over the *gave* and three to take the flood water; one is now under the railway. The 2m-high parapets were damaged in 1814 when the French were retreating before Wellington, and the tower was restored in the 19C by Boeswillwald. Pilgrims used to make a halt on the route to Santiago on the other side of the bridge at the Hospice St-Loup. Near the Pont-Vieux are old houses characteristic of the region with steep, tiled roofs; *génoise* mouldings (cornice of Roman-style tiles) are found on the richer houses. They are being renovated. Facing the *gave* at 22 Rue des Aiguilletiers is the workshop of M. Guy Pendanx, one of the champion metalworkers of France; and on the corner is a little tower where the ladies sat to watch the world go by.

Turn right, past the Salle de la Moutète, 'temple' to the famous basketball team, and the covered market. Opposite, in Rue Lasserre, is the **Maison Badcave**, a heavily restored 15C–17C house, part timber-framed, with wattle and daub infill, steep roof, dormers and a balcony.

Rue de la Moutète brings you to the church of **St-Pierre**, which was part of the defence system of the town outside the walls. It was begun towards the end of the 13C, completed about a century later, and turned over to the Protestants after the Wars of Religion. There were several campaigns of rebuilding and the neo-Gothic belfry and porch, which protects the original entrance, are 19C. The 14C nave is narrower and higher than the apse and transepts, the chancel is 13C Gothic, and the brick vaults have carved bosses. The rose window and décor are also 19C, and in 1865 a Cavaillé Col organ was installed. Above the door is a work by Bonnat, the *Beheading of St Denis*.

From Place Marcadieu follow Chemin Gaston-Fébus, along the line of the town wall which was also the outer defence of the château, towards **Tour Moncade**. To the left, where the road bends to meet Rue Moncade, are vines planted in 1991 to commemorate the death of Gaston Fébus 600 years earlier. Open May to September, for times enquire of the tourist office; ☎ 05 59 69 37 50.

The château, about 100m above the old town, was begun by Gaston VII of Moncade with money received for fighting for Henry III of England against Louis IX. The fort took some 20 years to build and consisted of a *corps de logis* leading directly to a keep, which was a prison on the lower level and a guard room above. A *bourg* or *quartier* grew up around it protected by a wall, and this wall along with two further ramparts and a masonry ditch formed a formidable outer defence. Gaston Fébus made the castle his headquarters and added three extra levels to the tower, raising it to 45m. He installed the court of Orthez here in relative comfort. It was here that Gaston Fébus dictated his *Livre de la Chasse* ('Book of the Hunt'). When the viscounts moved to Pau in 1464, the glorious days of Château Moncade were over and the castle fell into decay; it was finally sold off at the Revolution to a demolition company who did their work.

The little that survived was purchased by the town in 1845 and now all that remains is the truncated tower, fixed at 33m, with false crenellations, and the outline of the *corps de logis*. An entrance has been created and there is an exhibition in the tower. After a climb up a narrow spiral staircase, the views from the top are deservedly rewarding.

Return via Rue Moncade and Rue de l'Horloge, where at no. 14 is the late medieval Hôtel de la Lune. The **Maison Chrestia** at 7 Avenue F.-Jammes was the home of the poet and novelist Francis Jammes (1868–1938) for some of the 33 years he lived in Orthez. Open July, Aug, Mon–Fri 10.00–12.30 and 15.00–17.30; otherwise Mon–Fri 08.45–12.45; ☎ 05 59 69 11 24

West of Orthez, above the Gave de Pau on the N117, are the romantic ruins of the castle at **Bellocq**, built by Gaston VII of Moncade as a defensive outpost in the 13C, probably remodelled by Gaston Fébus in the 14C. Open July, Aug 09.00–12.00 and 14.00–19.00; ☎ 05 59 65 20 66. Following Protestant occupation, the fortress was almost entirely dismantled in 1621 on the orders of Louis XIII, leaving only the stumps of the seven towers. Gaston VII also founded the little *bastide* in 1281, the oldest and one of the best-designed in the Béarn. The 13C church, altered in the 15C–16C, is of minor interest except for the carvings around the doors, especially the west, where there is a figure wearing a beret, notorious as proof of the long existence of this headgear.

To the south of Bellocq by the D430 or D933, **Salies-de-Béarn** is a picturesque village and spa on the Saleys River whose existence depends on salt deposits.

The discovery of the salt here is traditionally due to huntsmen who found a wild boar that had escaped them, lying dead in boggy ground, its wounds covered in salt crystals. In reality, the salt spring was already exploited during the Bronze Age and the town grew around the spring, in the present Place du

Bayaà. Salt was such a precious commodity that by 1587 a corporation had been established and tight regulations laid down for the collection of salt water, allowing each family who lived in the town the right to collect a certain volume in a certain length of time. Salt is essential for the production of *jambon de Bayonne* and during the second weekend in September this is re-enacted at the Fête du Sel.

The locals had the right to sell salt in the Béarn and Bigorre along the old salt routes, but when the 16C exemption from salt tax ended, the town exploited the curative properties of the mineral instead. By the 19C, salt-water baths were considered to cure a variety of problems. The modern spa offers general fitness programmes lasting for just an hour to a week: the water is so salty that you have to be weighted down in the tub.

The tourist office, in the 1930s' casino building, stands between the old salt town and the **spa**. For the latter, turn left down Rue des Bains, for the baths (built in 1857 and rebuilt since), in a vaguely Moorish style, the gardens and bandstand. The vast Hotel du Parc and Casino (built in 1893), with a timber-galleried atrium, is being renovated.

From the tourist office, straight ahead across Pont d'Andioque is the higgledy-piggledy town centre where the houses have flowered balconies and steep tile roofs. Narrow alleys linking the streets were short cuts for carrying salt water from spring to home in a limited time, each family taking its turn. Beneath **Place du Bayaà** at the heart of the old town is the celebrated spring, commemorated by a fountain with a wild boar (1927), but the pool was covered in 1867.

The **Musée des Arts et Traditions Béarnais** is in a 16C house on the *place*. Open mid-May to mid-Oct, Tues–Sat 15.00–18.00, closed Mon, Sun; ☎ 05 59 38 00 33. The *mairie*, opposite, was built in 1810. The **Musée du Sel** in Rue des Puits Salants (same hours as above) is a small museum of the history of salt extraction. In the wall outside is a reconstruction of a *coulédé*, where the salt water was poured and stored; there is a genuine example at 8 Rue Pont Mayou. The houses on stilts in the river near Pont de la Lune are a particular feature of Salies, and beyond is the church of St-Vincent, begun in the 11C, with a huge tower.

Sauveterre-de-Béarn

The former prestige of Sauveterre-de-Béarn—in a stunning position on a cliff above a loop in the Gave d'Oloron, reached by the D933 and D936—can be deduced from the relics of its past, a large church, fortified bridge, and the ruins of the castle where Gaston VII of Moncade wrote his last will and testament and Gaston Fébus died. But its fortunes changed in the 16C and neglect set in. A pleasant walk from the church down to the old bridge takes in the extent of the medieval town.

This *sauveté*, or place of safety, was founded by the Bishops of Dax and Oloron in 1071. In the 12C, when Orthez, Salies-de-Béarn and Sauveterre were snatched from the control of the Viscounts of Dax and became part of the Béarn, and Gascony passed to the English, the strategic importance of this site was undisputed. Gaston VII of Moncade fortified Sauveterre, and Gaston Fébus completed the defences in the 14C to make it one of the most important towns in the region during the Middle Ages, at the centre of the Kingdom of

Béarn-Navarre. This came to an end with the loss of the Haute Navarre, and the increased importance of Navarrenx (see below).

Place Royale (18C) and the elegant *hôtel de ville* (16C) that now houses the tourist office were outside the town walls. The old east gate, Porte de Miqueu, was at the start of Rue St-André, on the pilgrimage road; adjacent is the Esplanade, high above the valley. The church of **St-André**, Romanesque and chunky, has a massive fortified belfry over the crossing which was part of the town defences. Built at a period of transition (late 12C to early 13C), the layout is indeed Romanesque with aisles, transept and apses covered in half-domes, whereas the west door and the vaults of the nave and aisles are Gothic. Major work was carried out *c* 1869. The small north door is simply decorated with a chrism but the later west doorway, heavily restored, has an arrangement similar to Oloron, with twin sub-tympana spanned by an arch, but a central pendant boss instead of a trumeau. It is decorated with Christ in a mandorla and the symbols of the Evangelists, the sun and the moon, two angels sqeezed in at the extremities and more angels in the voussoirs. The height of the interior is surprising, and in the east are some 12C capitals of note including a *Nativity* on the eastern respond of the north aisle, and on the northeast crossing, *Gluttony and Slander*.

West of the church is the shell of Gaston of Moncade's 33m-high **Tour Montréal**, sheer with the cliff face. Descend the steps from here to the foot of the tower and follow the banks of the *gave*, past some of the six fountains of Sauveterre, the arcades of the Maison du Sénéchal de l'Hôpital and the chapel of St-Joan. The picturesque half-bridge, the **Pont Fortifié**, also known as Pont de la Légende, dates from the time of the two Gastons and was the entry to and exit

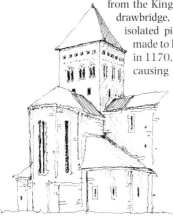

from the Kingdom of Navarre. It originally had a wooden drawbridge, allowing access to the Île de la Glère, and the isolated pier dates from 1732 when an attempt was made to lengthen it. Attached to the bridge is a legend: in 1170, Sancie, the wife of Gaston V, was suspected of causing the death of her deformed baby and was thrown into the river, but survived. A foot-bridge further west crosses to the island.

Return to the town along Rue Pont de la Légende, uphill from the bridge, with the Maison and Fontaine du Sénéchal on the right, and pass through the remains of the southern gate, Porte de Lester, into **Rue Pléguignou**, which is lined with typical Béarnais or Navarrais houses. Higher up, off to the left, is the old west gate, **Porte du Datter**. On the right are the remains of the Château Vicomtal (13C and 14C; no admission), where Gaston Fébus spent the last few hours before his death in 1391. At the end of Rue des Innocents, turn right on Rue Bérard to return to Place de l'Eglise.

Sauveterre-de-Béarn

East of Sauveterre by the D936 and D27 is the **Domaine de Laàs**, a 17C château set in a 12ha park. It contains a superb collection of furniture, tapestries and paintings brought together by Louis Serbat, former President of the French

National Society of Antiquaries, who purchased the property in 1946. There is a Flemish slant to the paintings, but also works by Fragonard and Vigée-Lebrun. The park and gardens overlook the Gave d'Oloron, and there are various exhibitions including a museum of maize and a maize labyrinth. Open July, Aug daily 10.00–20.00; April 14.00–19.00 and June, Sept, Oct, Wed–Mon 10.00–19.00, closed Tues; ☎ 05 59 38 91 53.

East again on the D933 and D111 is **Navarrenx**, which played a major role in the history of the Béarn. This small *bastide* overlooking the Gave d'Oloron was founded in 1316 but was not fortified until the 16C as part of Henri II d'Albret's ambition to reconquer the Spanish part of Navarre, including Pamplona, following the reduction of his territory to a small corner north of the Pyrenees. The fort, virtually the first of its kind in France, was designed by an Italian engineer, Fabrici Siciliano, and built 1538–47 with forward angle bastions, a century before Vauban's career was launched (see p 95). The efficacy of the structure was tested, not against the Spanish but the French, in 1569 during the Wars of Religion. It held out as a safe place for Protestants for two months against a Catholic siege led by Terride, followed by a harrowing massacre meted out by the defendants.

The town fell gradually into decline but has been carefully restored and today the fortifications make a pleasant walk. From the bridge on the south (13C, enlarged 18C and 19C), enter through the well-preserved Porte St-Antoine, protected by a fine *echauguette* (watchtower) and a bastion called La Cloche. This leads to an open square surrounded by the severe garrison accommodation, where a plaque publicises the amorous adventure of Franz Liszt and Caroline de Saint-Cricq at Navarrenx. A flight of steps leads up to the ramparts and ends at a complex of defensive structures with underground galleries. The walls to the east were demolished for the Oloron road, but on the north side much survives. The Gothic church of St-Germain dates from 1551–62 and 19C, and la fontaine du Siège was restored in 1989.

OLORON-SAINTE-MARIE

Oloron-Ste-Marie stands in the foothills of the Pyrenees, where the Gave d'Aspe and the Gave d'Ossau meet, and is therefore a perfect spot from which to explore the southern part of the Béarn and the Pyrenees. The formerly rather sombre town is now looking infinitely more cheerful with fresh paint and flowers. The rearing of sheep and cattle (*les Blonds des Pyrénées*) forms an important part of the local economy, as do the linen and cotton industries, which originated in the production of linen cloth to protect working oxen from heat and insects. Traditional fabrics are woven at **Tissages Lartigue**, Avenue Georges Messier, ☎ 05 59 39 50 11.

The present medium-sized town was built on the site of an Iberian, then a Roman settlement, *Iluro*. It was destroyed in the 9C but revived at the end of the 11C by Centulle V, Viscount of Béarn and Count of Bigorre, who granted a charter of privileges establishing a staging-post on the pilgrimage route to Spain. Two distinct areas evolved: a fortified town on the cliff between the two *gaves*; and the episcopal city around the cathedral to the west. Only in 1858 were the two reunited as Oloron-Ste-Marie.

Getting there and around
Car
D936 from Navarrenx and N134 from Pau.
Train
TER links Oloron with Pau. Station is on Av. de la Gare.

 ## Tourist information
64400 Oloron-Ste-Marie Pl. de la Résistance, ☎ 05 59 39 98 00, fax 05 59 39 43 97, www.ot-oloron-ste-marie.fr
Market day
Friday; evening markets in July, August
Guided walks
Walking tours of the town and visits to certain industries from the tourist office

Festivals and events
May *Foire Traditional*, traditional fair
July *Festival du Jazz*; *Fêtes*, local festivities
September *Foire du Terroir*, fair in celebration of the local produce;
La Garburade, celebration of the traditional soup

Where to stay and eating out
64400 OLORON-STE-MARIE
☆☆☆ *Alysson*, Blvd des Pyrénées, ☎ 05 59 39 70 70, fax 05 59 39 24 47, www.alysson-hotel.fr. Hotel-restaurant with swimming pool.
64660 LURBE-SAINT-CHRISTAU
☆☆ *Au Bon Coin*, south of Oloron, ☎ 05 59 34 40 12, fax 05 59 34 46 40. Hotel-restaurant with pleasant rooms and outstanding cooking. Swimming pool.
64290 ESTIALESCQ (northeast of Oloron)
Chambres d'hôte, Mme J. Pericou, Maison Naba, ☎ 05 59 39 99 11, fax 05 59 36 14 92. In a delightful farmhouse surrounded by a shady park, close to valleys of Aspe and Ossau.

From **Place de la Résistance**, the market place with the Fontaine Henri (19C), cross Place A.-Gabe, leaving the 19C church of Notre-Dame behind you. After Pont Ste-Claire spanning the Gave d'Ossau, turn left into Rue de la Filature—its name a reference to spinning—through an archway and climb up the winding Rue des Chevaux to the Biscondau and a view of the ramparts. Slightly out of breath you arrive in **Place St-Pierre**, surrounded by 17C–18C houses and the 18C church of St-Pierre, now deconsecrated.

Eglise de Ste-Croix
Rue Centulle leads up to the top of the **Ville Haut**, or Old Town, built on the ancient *oppidum* and gathered around the Romanesque church of Ste-Croix, the oldest monument in Oloron. Open 08.00–19.00; ☎ 05 59 39 01 70.

It stands on the site of a 6C sanctuary dedicated to the first bishop, Gratus. It was destroyed by the Normans in the 9C and reputedly the first stone of the present building was laid in 1070 by Bishop Amat. Under the orders of Jeanne d'Albret, Ste-Croix became a Protestant church between 1569 and 1621. In 1640 the east end was damaged when the château to the east, containing explosives, blew up. Although listed as a historic monument in 1841, Boeswillwald considered it hardly worth saving and the responsibility fell to Abbot Menjoulet. He saved the church in the 1850s, but went a bit over the top by adding an extension to the west with a statue of the Virgin. In 1960, the 19C porch was demolished, the statue placed in front of the cemetery, and the west front returned to its primitive state.

The exterior is impressive and austere with a massive off-centre belfry, formerly part of the fortifications, a tall cupola, heavily restored apse, and rustic west front. The Romanesque **south door** has marble columns and pillars supporting a suite of six round arches and two badly damaged capitals representing *Damnation*, a woman attacked by griffins, on the left, and opposite, *Life Eternal*, a dove and chalice.

The interior of the church is gloomy: a coin-operated box in the north transept will activate lights and commentary. The nave vaults are supported by cruciform pillars on decorated plinths, and capitals with flat palm-leaf or ball-flower carvings although on the south are atlantes in a supporting role. The most unexpected structure in the building is the **cupola**, an 18m-wide octagon supported on a round drum with four false pendentives, painted in *trompe-l'oeil* to look like scallop shells. The arches intersect to create a very Moorish looking eight-pointed star similar to, although older than, the cupola of the Hôpital St-Blaise (p 431) and following the pattern of those in the mosque in Cordoba, Spain. Significantly the Béarn came under the control of Aragon in the late 11C. The Romanesque **capitals** are more ornate towards the east end. On the high arches of the chancel, though difficult to see, are the *Adoration of the Magi*; the *Baptism of Christ*, *St John the Baptist in Prison*, *Herod's Feast* with Salome performing acrobatic feats, and the *Temptation in the Desert*, with Christ richly dressed and the demon depicted twice. A console in the south chapel carries a curious representation of the Trinity as a head in triplicate. The smaller capitals of the blind arcades in the apse are easier to see; they show *Adam and Eve*, *Cain and Abel* and the *Sacrifice of Isaac*. In the north transept is a dusty Baroque altarpiece (*c* 1704) made by a local sculptor, Dartiganave; the pulpit and stalls are *c* 1717.

Opposite the church are delapidated medieval houses with arcades. In Rue Dalmais are the 14C **Tour de Grède** and the **Maison du Patrimoine**, a small private museum of local history housed in the gracious 17C Maison Marque, with a fine staircase and panelling. Open July–Sept, Tues–Sun 10.00–12.30 and 15.00–19.00, closed Mon; ☎ 05 59 39 10 63. As well as local ethnography, there is documentation regarding the internment camp at Gurs (p 431). From Place Manjoulet to the west of the church, next to the cemetery, you reach the **Promenade Bellevue** with a view over the town and the *gave*.

Go down the steps to Rue L.-Barthou, an attractive shopping street, turn left over the bridge crossing the Gave d'Aspe and go across Place de Jaca for a view towards the Pyrenees. A short detour left down Rue Adoue, the road to Spain built in 1751, brings you to a small bridge, Pont de Forbeig, with some more views of the *gave*.

Cathédrale Ste-Marie

From Place de Jaca take Rue de Révol to the cathedral. Open 08.00–20.00; ☎ 05 59 39 04 15.

The cathedral of Ste-Marie was built at the time of Gaston IV and Bishop Roger de Sentis between 1102 and *c* 1150 but was damaged over the centuries, *c* 1212 by *routiers* and in 1302 by a storm, after which the apse and part of the nave were rebuilt in Gothic style with flying buttresses. It was converted to the Protestant faith, subjected to wholesale iconoclasm in 1569, and a major renovation was begun in 1602. The Revolution brought more havoc, and when it was returned to Christian worship in 1801, the cathedral had lost its status and become a parish church. About 1860 Viollet-le-Duc visited and restoration, albeit criticised, was begun.

The cathedral can be seen from all sides and its **exterior** is fairly forbidding. The apse is 14C, with radiating chapels. There is a crenellated tower on the south, and another at the west above the porch protecting the most celebrated part of the cathedral, the Romanesque **west door** (restored in the 19C and again in 2001), the only obvious survival of the 12C church. The carvings are endearing and lively, enhanced by the use of contrasting materials, yellowish limestone and white marble. The tympanum is composed of marble slabs—which may prove to be recycled Gallo-Roman stelae—carved with the *Descent from the Cross*, unusual in this position, showing the Virgin, St John and others present at the entombment of Christ, as well as the Sun and the Moon represented as small figures. Beneath Christ is a chrism and bull's head and above the doorway, divided by a central marble trumeau (19C) representing two captives in chains, are sub-tympana. On these are heavily restored images of *Christ in Glory* between two lions, and a figure holding two monsters by the throat. To either side are high reliefs: on the left, a grizzly scene of a demonic beast devouring his victim; and on the right, a horseman, suggesting the punishment of evil and the Church triumphant. In the outer arch of the entrance are the *Four and Twenty Elders of the Apocalypse*, each holding a viol, lute or rebec, or a long-necked phial. On the inside arch is a busy scene of the preparations for the *Marriage at Cana*, exactly as if this were the prelude to a 12C wedding in the Béarn. The wooden doors were given to the cathedral by Henri IV after his marriage to Marie de Médicis, when the Catholic religion was reinstated.

The **interior** is a less interesting hotchpotch, rebuilt almost entirely in the 14C, the apse with five chapels and the only ambulatory in the Béarn. One Romanesque pillar on the south of the choir has survived as well as four 13C piers of the nave, but the vaulting is 14C, the transept chapels 15C, and the side chapels, endowed with Counter-Reformation altarpieces, were added in 1749. The wooden pulpit of 1523 comes from Mauléon (see p 430) and its painted and gilded decoration, restored in the 17C, includes a depiction of St Charles Borromeo, an outstanding Catholic reformer. The most interesting object in the cathedral is the 17C **crèche** in the sacristy on the north. It is accredited as one of the oldest of its kind and, as well as the set-piece Nativity, has an unusual group of seven freestanding figures dressed in regional costume, one sporting a beret. These figures are only brought out at Christmas; to see them, ask a church attendant.

Opposite the west end of the cathedral, at 13 Place de la Cathédrale, is the food store *Arts et Délices*, specialising in regional delicacies, where you can buy an excellent snack or take-away; ☎ 05 59 36 02 17.

Returning to Place de Jaca, turn left to Place Mendes-France, and take the path along the *gave* leading to Rue de la Poste, from which there is a footbridge back to Rue Barthou. Alternatively, stay on the footpath as far as Place Gen-de-Gaulle and Pont Ste-Claire, which brings you back to Place Mendiondou, and Rue Justice back to Place de la Résistance. The road opposite the tourist office leads to

Place G.-Clemenceau and the 19C *halle-marie*; Rue Camou to the right brings you to a fork with Rue des Fontaines to the left, and here is the old *lavoir* (wash house).

THE VALLEYS OF OSSAU AND ASPE

The Vallée d'Ossau is southeast of Oloron-Ste-Marie and is followed by the D9 34. The Vallée d'Aspe is directly south of Oloron and shadowed by the N1 34. Both are ancient pilgrimage routes, crossing the border into the Spanish state of Aragon at Col du Portalet and Col du Somport respectively, and the two valleys are linked by the D294 across the Plateau du Bénou and the Col Marie-Blanque. The scenery is spectacular, and the houses and barns are mainly simple but solid stone buildings with steep, slate-covered roofs and the occasional grand entrance with a grey marble surround or sculpted dormer window. There are some small Romanesque churches but more usually the churches are 16C and, typical of the mountain region, contain a proliferation of 17C and 18C fittings. The pastoral traditions of the mountains are carefully monitored and the cheeses produced there are such an important part of the economy that from here to the Atlantic coast is the Route de Fromage Ossau-Iraty (the cheese route) indicating places where you can sample *pur-brebis*, the delicious local sheep's milk cheese with an AOC.

Getting there and around
Car

N1 34 south of Oloron-St-Marie and D1 34 south of Pau.

Train

Gave d'Aspe: Oloron to Lanfranc. Oloron to Arudy.

 ## Tourist information

Vallée d'Aspe 64490 Bedous, Pl. Sanmaillé, BP 11, ☎ 05 59 34 71 48, fax 05 59 34 52 51
Vallée de Barétous 64570 Arette, Pl. de la Victoire, ☎ 05 59 88 95 38, fax 05 59 88 95 41
64440 Artouste-Fabrèges Maison de Fabrèges, ☎ 05 59 05 34 00, fax 05 59 05 37 55, email artouste.tourisme@wanadoo.fr
64260 Arudy Pl. de l'Hôtel de Ville, ☎ 05 59 05 77 11, fax 05 59 05 80 31, email office.de.tourisme.darudy@wanadoo.fr
64440 Eaux-Bonnes ☎ 05 59 05 33 08 , fax 05 59 05 12 56, www.ot-eaux-bonnes-gourette.fr

64440 Laruns Maison de la Vallée d'Ossau, ☎ 05 59 05 31 41, fax 05 59 05 35 49, email ossau.tourisme@wanadoo.fr
64440 Gourette (Route Thermale), ☎ 05 59 05 12 17, fax 05 59 05 12 56

Market days

Aramits Sunday
Arundy Tuesday, Saturday
Bedous Thursday
Estaut Thursday evening in July, August
Laruns Saturday

 ## Festivals and events

May *Fête de la montagne*, mountain festival with special hikes and mountains music, Laruns
June/July Transhumance, movement of sheep and cattle to the mountains, valleys of Aspe and Ossau
July *Fête du fromage*, Etsaut
August *Fête d'été*, traditional festival with local costmes and music, Laruns
September *Marché a l'ancienne et foire aux fromage*, traditional market and cheese fair, Laruns

Where to stay and eating out

64260 BIELLE

☆☆ *L'Ayguelade*, south of Arudy, in the Ossau Valley close to the D934, ☎ 05 59 82 60 06, fax 05 59 82 61 17. Hotel-restaurant with good value, slightly old-fashioned rooms and excellent cooking.

64440 GABAS

☆☆ *Le Biscau*, south of Laruns, ☎ 05 95 05 31 37, fax 05 59 05 43 23

☆ *Hotel Vignau*, ☎ 05 59 05 34 06. Rustic and simple with country cooking. Both these *auberges* produce some of the best cheese in the region.

64260 SÉVIGNACQ-MEYRACQ

€–€€ *Les Bains de Secours*, south of Pau, ☎ 05 59 05 62 11, fax 05 59 05 76 56. Tucked away in an isolated part of the Ossau Valley. Cooking of a wonderfully subtle nature. Rooms available.

The Gave d'Ossau tumbles down from the high Pyrenees through the stunning mountain scenery of the **Vallée d'Ossau**, which starts at Sévignac-Meyracq where there is a 16C chateau (no admission). The lower valley as far as Laruns is wide, open and fertile, supporting small communities, but the valley narrows further south and is more enclosed as it climbs towards Gabas and beyond, with the Pic du Midi d'Ossau (2884m) ever looming in the background.

Arudy is a small town with old houses, a *lavoir*, and a church rebuilt in the 16C. Behind the church the Maison d'Ossau, a 17C building with a slate roof and sculpted pediment, contains the local history and ethnography museum and a permanent exhibition on the Parc National des Pyrénées. Open July, Aug daily 10.00–12.00 and 15.00–18.00; Sept–June, Tues–Fri 14.00–17.00, Sun 15.00–18.00, closed Mon, Sat; ☎ 05 59 05 61 71.

Bielle is the ancient capital of the valley and mountain pastures owned collectively are still administered from here. There are some good 16C houses, an 18C château, and the church is 16C with a late Gothic doorway typical of the Béarn. This marks the start of the D294 over the Col de Marie-Blanque to the Aspe Valley.

South of Bielle is **Laruns**, a busy little town at the start of the high valley which is animated by traditional summer celebrations in mid-August and a cheese fair in October. Insensitive updating of old and rather sombre façades has not totally obliterated interesting fragments of sculpture, some from the parish church which was destroyed by flooding in 1801. Its replacement of 1892 is dull. The *Fromagerie Pardou* offers a guided visit to cheese cellars and a tasting; ☎ 05 59 82 60 77.

Across the *gave*, strung out on the ridge opposite Laruns, is a series of small villages overlooking the valley. The main attraction at Aste-Béon is the **Falaise aux Vautours**, where vultures and other birds of prey can be observed live on film via a camera installed in a cliff. Open daily June–Aug 10.30–12.30 and 14.00–18.30; May, Sept 14.30–18.30; school holidays 14.30–17.30; ☎ 05 59 82 65 49.

At the centre of the little community of **Béost** is a pretty ensemble of a church with a fortified house to the east and the medieval *abbaye laïque* to the west (altered in the 16C and 18C), described as the Château d'Aramits, of musketeering fame (see p 431). To visit, ☎ 05 59 05 30 99. The church has conserved its Romanesque apse and around the south door (14C) are some re-sited Romanesque elements including marble reliefs of Christ teaching and resurrected, with Apostles and angels. The rest, including the tall belfry, is 15C. Inside are some carved capitals and a marble *Pietà* (15C). On the corner opposite the church is a primary school where only the Béarnais language is used, and there are some attractive houses with inscriptions and dates as well as a superb *lavoir* in need of restoration.

At the top of the village of **Assouste** is a tiny, recently restored 12C church, one of the oldest in the valley, with carved corbels and a chrism supported by angels over the door, flanked by old tombs, two carved capitals and marble columns. The interior is very simple but the church is usually locked; ask for the key locally. Among the houses, strung out along the mountain face to catch the sun, are 18C and 19C marble door frames, courtyards, cowsheds and wooden balconies.

The old communities of Béost, Assouste and, higher still, Aas, barely more than a hamlet, are older than the now more important spa town of **Eaux-Bonnes**. The curative properties of its waters were first tested in the 16C when François I came to recover from injuries sustained in battle in Northern Italy. In 1800 Napoléon had a road constructed so that he could send his wounded soldiers for treatment, and in 1809 what is now the *mairie* was built to house them. During the heyday of the spa it was visited by well-known artists such as Devéria and Delacroix. The town is built on a narrow ledge between the *gave* and tree-covered cliffs, and the tall and sombre houses are huddled together in the confined space.

The road from Laruns winds up through sequoia trees planted more than 100 years ago by the Empress Eugénie, who first came here as a young woman in 1840. She was also responsible for the *promenade horizontal*, for improving the English garden and, more ambitiously, for the **Route Thermale**, the D918—running through two high passes, the Col d'Aubisque (1709m) and the Col du Soulor (1474m)—linking Eaux-Bonnes with Argelès-Gazost (p 475). People come here now not to cure battle wounds but for the treatment of bronchitis and asthma.

To the south, the road runs through Eaux-Chaudes before reaching **Gabas** (1000m), the last village before the Spanish border and the night stop during the transhumance of cattle in the summer. The two *gaves*, d'Ossau and de Brousset, meet here, on the edge of the national park, making it an excellent starting-point for excursions to the Lac de Bious-Artigues and the *petit train* described below. This small village handles about 80 per cent of the local production of ewes' milk cheese, some 10,000 cheeses, which are refined here in salting cellars. The tiny chapel with a porch (1121) was one of the last stops on the pilgrimage route before crossing the Pyrenees into Spain, and inside is a typical Baroque retable; the key is kept at the Bar Turon opposite.

Southeast of Gabas the cable car from **Artouste-Fabrèges**, which has restaurants and shops, will take you up to the **Train Touristique du Lac d'Artouste**. Operates end May–Sept; ☎ 05 59 05 34 00. Allow at least three hours for the 10km train journey there and back and one hour at the top at an altitude of about 2000m. There is a café/restaurant. This gives you time to enjoy the marvellous scenery, the short walk to Lac d'Artouste where a huge dam was built in the 1920s as part of a hydro-electric scheme, or longer hikes. There is also a hiking route down to the bottom. If you would like to learn more about the Pyrenees and local customs it is possible to spend a day with a shepherd. For more information, enquire at the tourist office in Artouste.

> ### *Fromage de brebis*
> The shepherd milks the ewes by hand in the mountains twice a day during the summer and begins the process of transforming the milk into cheese. This involves heating the milk, churning, moulding, separating and salting it. The cheeses are sent to a *saloir* in the valley to complete the maturing process. Each cheese is individually processed (wiped, salted and turned) each day and stored on wooden slats. The cheeses may remain in the *saloir* for up to 18 months, but most are sold after six. Twenty-five litres of milk is needed for each 5kg cheese. The shepherd has the right to one out of every 12 cheeses he makes. Side products are the *grueil* or *petit-lait* (whey), sold at the markets and flavoured with sugar and coffee, and *caillé* (curd), sold only by specialists. The Route du Fromage Ossau-Iraty-Brebis-Pyrénées across the Béarn and Basque regions has 46 locations where you can sample and buy local cheeses. A map showing the route is available at tourist offices.

The **Vallée d'Aspe** runs parallel with the Ossau Valley to the Spanish border, but the scenery is very different. For about 45km from Escot the *gave* runs through a steep and wooded valley, sometimes narrowing into a gorge, sometimes slightly wider to create a fertile plain. The villages are small and isolated, turned in on themselves, yet they line the most direct route from Bordeaux to Saragossa, followed by Roman armies, thousands of 12C pilgrims, and medieval tradesmen. The modern route into Spain takes you through tunnels and under the Col de Somport (1632m). The Reformation took a strong hold in the valley and there are still some Protestants here. As in the Ossau Valley, the main livelihood outside tourism is based on cattle and cheese production. As an introduction to local history and rural life the four parts of the **Ecomusée de la Vallée d'Aspe** are indispensable: they are situated in locations relevant to their subject, at Sarrance, Accous, Lourdios-Ichère and Borce.

From Oloron the D238 or N134 follow the *gave* between wooded cliffs before it widens slightly at **Sarrance**. Turn right from the N134 immediately as you arrive at the village. At the centre is the small Place de l'Eglise enclosed by the church, the *lavoir*, a monumental fountain, and 17C–18C façades.

> The history of Notre-Dame began in 1345 when Premonstratensian friars founded a monastery, which drew pilgrims in ever increasing numbers to the statue of the Virgin, including Louis XI in 1461. Although the cult of relics was incompatible with her reforming ideals, Marguerite of Navarre mentioned Sarrance, where she withdrew to write, in *The Heptameron*. The monastery was destroyed in 1569 by the Protestant forces of Jeanne d'Albret and later sold, but the monks returned in 1605 and rebuilt the chapel and hostel although the pilgrimage never regained the momentum of the 15C and was eclipsed by Bétharram (see below).

The present church of 1609 has a curvilinear façade and an imposing octagonal belfry with concave faces and statues, topped with an arcaded cupola covered in slate. The inside is far more rustic and gaudily decorated, with pendant bosses over the nave, and has chapels on the north. The gilding has spread all over, and on the walls are coloured reliefs. The sanctuary was entirely restored in 1865 and on the gilded half-dome is a *Tree of Jesse*. Immediately behind the altar is an ungainly statue of the *Virgin and Child* made up of disparate elements and placed here in 1888. The chapel dedicated to St Norbert, founder of the Premonstratensian order, contains a retable with another gilded *Virgin and Child* (18C) and reliefs which probably come from the 18C Calvary, and depict the *Agony in the Garden* and the *Sleeping Apostles*, with an embossed leather antependium. The St-Martin chapel contains a replica head of the Black Virgin attached to a dressed statue in an ornate niche, and naive coloured reliefs (18C) recount the legend of the Virgin of Sarrance—note the ox. The pulpit is 18C and the organ case is 17C, restored in 1985. Against the south wall is an unusual two-tier cloister, much restored, and in the gardens off the cloister is a walk uphill along the route of the Calvary that existed in the 18C.

The legend of the Virgin of Sarrance

In times gone by, when only a few cowherds and cattle frequented the valley, a herdsman noticed that one of his oxen regularly disappeared, to return looking fitter and stronger each time. He decided to investigate and discovered the beast beside the *gave*, kneeling on a large stone in front of a little statue of the Virgin which emerged from a mountain spring that became known as the Source du Taureau. The Bishop of Oloron took the statue to his cathedral, but it soon went missing, only to reappear again at its original site. An oratory was subsequently erected there but, removed a second time by vandals and chucked into the deepest part of the *gave*, the statue again miraculously returned to its rightful place.

Below the church is the **Ecomusée Notre-Dame-de-la-Pierre**, where the legend of the Virgin of Sarrance, the church, the village and the reintroduction of the pilgrimage in the 1930s are delightfully recreated using audio-visual displays, commentary, music, sculptures and reliefs, and a model of the valley. The original head of the statue of the Virgin, simply and roughly carved in dark stone, is part of the collection of local religious artefacts. The chapel on the main road marks the location of the miraculous discovery. Open July–Sept daily 10.00–12.00 and 14.00–19.00; Oct–June, Sat, Sun and PH 14.00–18.00; ☎ 05 59 34 55 51.

At **Lourdios-Ichère**, on the D241 between Sarrance and Bedous, is another part of the Ecomusée. **Un Village se Raconte** is the story of a once isolated village based on a 19C document written by the school teacher. Interiors of the period are reconstructed and the exhibition traces the dependence of village life on livestock and the rhythm of the seasons. It constitutes an excellent introduction to the valley and rural customs, such as the *meule de fougère* (stacks of bracken used in place of straw). A video explains the rest. Outside, about 100m to the left of the museum, the exhibit continues along a *sentier de découverte* (discovery trail). Same opening times as Notre-Dame-de-la-Pierre; ☎ 05 59 34 44 84.

Further south on the N134 is the Plaine d'Accous, sprinkled with villages on the eastern side of the *gave*. **Bedous** is the most active of these, with streets lined with 16C–18C houses, the 19C Place de la Mairie and church of St-Michel with a Classical pediment of 1691, mainly rebuilt after a Protestant raid in 1569. A pretty winding route from here towards Aydius brings you to the picturesque hamlet of **Orcun**, huddled close to the hillside around a tiny chapel, quite plain on the outside. The interior is something else, transformed in the 17C into a miniature stage set, with every surface painted and every statue gilded. It was renovated a few years ago. Open daily 15.00–16.00, although someone might unlock it at other times on request.

Stay on the small routes through higgledy-piggledy villages where cattle sheds are attached to the houses, the shutters are gaily painted and there are water troughs and *lavoirs*. Then follow the road to Accous, on the old pilgrimage route, passing the oldest church in the valley at **Jouers**, which has some striking corbels around the exterior of the apse. In the narrow streets of **Accous** are some notable houses and a monumental *mairie* on the square. The **Fermiers Basco-Béarnais**, part of the Ecomusée, is a cheese-producing co-operative with three *saloirs* where you can learn all you need to know about cheese production in the valley. Open July–mid-Sept daily 09.30–13.00 and 14.00–19.00; mid-Sept–June, Mon–Sat 09.30–12.00 and 14.00–18.00, closed Sat, Sun; ☎ 05 59 34 76 06.

South of Accous the N134 runs through another narrow gorge with a hydro-electric centre near the bridge. The road to the right at l'Estanguet takes you up to the **Cirque de Lescun**, one of the most beautiful landscapes of the Pyrenees, looking towards the Billare range, habitat of the rare native bear, whom you are unlikely to meet.

The N134 continues on to Etsaut and Borce and the last of the quartet of museums, **Hospital St-Jacques de Compostelle, Borce**. The exhibition, in an old pilgrim hospice with a 12C chapel, explores the origin of the pilgrimage to Compostella and the conditions of the journey. For opening times, ☎ 06 81 32 58 32. The **Clos aux Ours de Borce**, is a small museum-park concerned with the survival of the remaining indigenous bears (there are seven) in the Pyrenees. It is close to the Maison du Parc National at the village of Etsaut and opens mid-June–mid-Sept 10.00–12.00 and 14.00–19.00. The last community before the border is Urdos, on the edge of the Parc National des Pyrénées (p 465).

22 Hautes-Pyrénées: the Bigorre

The Département des Hautes-Pyrénées, often referred to as the Bigorre, the old province to which it roughly corresponds, benefits from a wondrous variety of landscapes. The mountain peaks of the central Pyrenean range in the south rise to over 3000m and include one of the best known, the Pic du Midi-de-Bigorre (2865m), while the natural amphitheatre, the Cirque de Gavarnie, is among the most spectacular of many natural sites of great beauty. The natural assets of the mountains are protected by the Parc National des Pyrénées in the southwest along the Spanish border. The *département* stretches north through the foothills of the Pyrenees with picturesque mountain villages, to the gentle slopes of the Madiran between Gascony (Gers) and the Béarn (Pyrénées-Atlantiques). Mountain torrents are known here as *gaves* or *nestes*, the main ones being the

Gave de Pau, which flows north and west, through Lourdes, an important site of pilgrimage; the Grande Neste, which marks the eastern border of the Bigorre; and the Adour which waters the main town, Tarbes, and the plain beyond. The D935 now follows the Adour valley which has been the main route to the mountains since ancient times.

The Pyrenees

The Pyrenees, which form a huge natural barrier between France and the Iberian Peninsula, are in fact two ranges running more or less east–west with a tiny break in the middle, the Vallée d'Aran, south of Luchon in the Central Pyrenees. The highest peak in the French Pyrenees is Vignemale (3298m) south of Cauterets, and many other peaks are over 3000m; the highest of all, the Pic d'Aneto (3404m), is in Spain. Although the peaks in the Pyrenees are not as high as in the Alps, there are Pyrenean valleys at a higher altitude than Alpine ones. The highest section overall is in the central-west Pyrenees, covered by the *départements* of the Hautes-Pyrénées, Haute-Garonne and Ariège-Pyrénées. A multitude of rivers, including the Garonne, rise in the mountains and flow towards the north, carving out valleys and gorges. It is an area of varied and breathtaking natural beauty offering a great choice of outdoor activities.

As in all mountain regions, the weather is very changeable, even in the summer when mist or rain can suddenly descend; snow can close the high passes from November to March. There are cultural and scenic differences across the length (about 150km) of the Pyrenees. The west is greener, more lush, influenced climatically by the Atlantic and culturally by Gascony and Aquitaine, while the eastern part is more Mediterranean and arid, and is historically part of the Languedoc. There are also distinct cultural, climatic and geographic differences on either side of the divide. The southern slopes, turned towards the Iberian peninsula and Africa, can guarantee more hours of sunshine, while the French Pyrenees, which rise more suddenly and steeply from the plain, have more dramatic panoramas and a greater variety of landscape. Conversely there are cultural similarities binding all the mountain people together. The Basque country is a case in point; the people here are often closer to their Spanish than their French neighbours (p 399).

 ### Tourist information

The **head office** of the Parc National des Pyrénées is at 59 Route du Pau, 65000 Tarbes, ☎ 05 62 44 36 60, fax 05 62 44 36 70, www.parc-pyrenees.com, email pyrenees.parc.national@especes-naturels.fr, and supplies all information regarding hiking, routes, weather, refuges, etc.

Maisons du Parc, Pyrénées Atlantiques
Vallée d'Apse, 64490 Etsaut ☎ 05 59 34 88 30 or 05 59 34 70 87

Vallée d'Ossau, 64440 Laruns Bureau d'Acceuil, Gabas, ☎ 05 59 05 32 13

Maisons du Parc, Hautes-Pyrénées
Vallée d'Azun, 65400 Arrens-Marsous Argelès-Gazost, ☎ 05 62 97 43 13
Vallée de Cauterets, 65110 Cauterets ☎ 05 62 92 52 56
Vallée de Luz, 65120 Luz-St-Sauveur ☎ 05 62 92 38 38
Gavarnie, 65120 Luz-St-Sauveur ☎ 05 62 92 49 10
Vallée d'Aure, 65170 St-Lary ☎ 05 62 39 40 91

Where to stay

There is no accommodation in the park, only refuges designed for overnight stays for hikers. These have dormitory accommodation and minimal facilities. Space must be booked at least 48 hours in advance. Contact the Parc National des Pyrénées (see above). No camping is allowed in the park, only one night bivouacing with tent. For accommodation in *gîtes/chambres d'hôtes* near the Park (including **Gîtes Panda** in the Park periphery and specially equipped to observe nature) contact: **Gîtes Ruraux des Hautes-Pyrénées**, 22 Pl. du Forail, 65000 Tarbes, ☎ 05 62 34 31 50, fax 05 02 34 37 95, www.gites-france-65.com. Also **Maison des Gîtes de France et du Tourisme Vert**, 59 Rue St-Lazare, 75439 Paris, ☎ 05 49 70 75 75, www.gites-de-France.fr

History

By the 5C Iberian tribes had settled as far north as the Garonne, and after the Romans crossed the mountains and colonised the region at the beginning of the last millennium, the local people were described as Bigerri or Bigerriones by Julius Caesar. During the Gallo-Roman era the mineral water spas, as well as the marble quarries, were an important natural resource. The Visigoth and Carolingian empires extended either side of the Pyrenean range, as did the Kingdom of Aragon, and the word Bigorre appeared in the 6C AD as the name of a diocese. The frontier between France and Spain, which runs more or less along the crests, was determined by the Treaty of the Pyrenees in 1659 (see p 419). Both licit and illicit trade across the border continued for centuries. The Pyrenees thrived during the 18C but suffered hugely in the 19C when local industries such as mineral extraction, marble quarrying, farming, forestry and weaving went into severe decline, precipitating huge depopulation which left many of the more remote villages with only tiny permanent communities. Closer to the present, during the Spanish Wars and the Occupation of France in the Second World War, the mountains provided refuge to many.

The main **industry** today, apart from tourism, is *la houille blanche*, hydro-electric power generated by seven power stations. The energy potential of mountain torrents was recognised by Aristide Bergès (1833–1904), born near St-Lizier, and first harnessed in 1869. Iron ore is still extracted in the Ariège, where there is also a talc quarry, a cigarette paper works and the only tungsten mine in France. There are plenty of cattle and sheep, and cheese is made in the mountains, but the major industry today is summer and winter tourism.

The **spas** are the oldest resorts and of the 17 spa towns in the Midi-Pyrénées region, 13 are in the Pyrenees. The water acquires its curative properties by rumbling around underground, picking up minerals, and sometimes heat, for anything between a few to several hundred or even millions of years. Different spas offer different *cures*—the range is astounding. Some spas double as **ski resorts**, of which there are 21 in total; many cable-cars and lifts also operate in summer enabling walkers and non-walkers to reach the higher slopes. Tourist centres have a vast range of information on **walking**, categorising different levels from very easy walks taking up to three hours (*promenades*) to hikes taking several days (*randonnées*), with details of guides and lists of mountain refuges. A series entitled *Les Sentiers d'Emilie*, published by Milan, has easy walks for children of all ages in various parts of the region.

Parc National des Pyrénées

The Parc National des Pyrénées was created in 1967 in order to conserve a stunningly beautiful landscape as nearly as possible in its natural state, without barriers or fences, cars or dogs, litter or noise, yet intensively monitored. It aims to be a haven for wildlife and a heaven for hikers. The park stretches along the length of the Pyrenees from the upper valley of the Aspe in the west (Pyrénées-Atlantiques) to the upper valley of the Aure in the east, covering 45,700ha along the Spanish border, from an altitude of 1067m to its highest point, the Pic du Vignemale (3298m). On the other side of the national border is its Spanish equivalent, the **Parque Nacional de Ordesa** (15,000ha), reached on foot through the Brèche de Roland at Gavarnie. There are 118 lakes, many rivers and torrents, and no habitation, although 50 per cent of its area is used for grazing. Around the central zone is an outer area of 206,352ha where life goes on, but complements the objectives of the park. Within this is a special area, the **Réserve Naturelle de Néouville** (2300ha), which also comes under the protection of the national park, and south of Gavarnie is its Spanish continuation, the **Parque Nacional de Ordesa y Monte Perdido**.

The flora and fauna of the whole park are protected. The abundant **flora** includes valerian, orchid, fritillary, asphodel, gentian, saxifrage, edelweiss, *rhododendron ramondia des Pyrénées, jacinthe sauvage* (wild hyacinth) and *lys des Pryénées* (lily of the valley): 150 species are endemic to the Pyrenees. **Fauna** includes two indigenous species of butterfly and a curious little animal that has survived in small numbers, the desman, a sort of aquatic mole with an extended snout; also the *izard* (a Pyrenean antelope), marmot, and many varieties of raptors, tetrax and game. Tragically, the Pyrenean brown bear is an endangered species, having been hunted to near extinction; half a dozen were identified in 1999. Solitary and nocturnal, it can reach 200kg in weight and measure 2m in height. The Maison du Parc at Etsaut has an exhibition on the Pyrenean bear. Bears from Eastern Europe have been introduced in some parts of the Pyrenees.

Much of the park can be driven through, and there are 350km of paths, refuges for long-distance walkers and picnic areas. Campsites and *gîtes* are confined to the periphery, as is skiing. The limits of the park are marked by *balises* (marked posts) representing the head of an izard. The park is safeguarded by *garde-moniteurs* who welcome the public and have expertise in all aspects of the mountains.

Maisons du Parc are open during the holiday period to provide information and documentation on every aspect of the national park, including hiking, fishing and themed guided walks, and put on films and exhibitions. There are five Maisons du Parc in Hautes-Pyrénées and two in Pyrénées-Atlantiques.

TARBES AND EAST

Tarbes is the capital of the Bigorre (see p 462), the second largest agglomeration in the Midi-Pyrénées and the main town of the *département* of the Hautes-Pyrénées. It is a somewhat characterless garrison town relieved by fountains and green areas. A Roman settlement developed here in the Adour Valley on the important Bayonne–Toulouse route. After the usual changes of fortune, it is now the most dynamic industrial centre in the region. The market is particularly lively and the parks are worth a visit, the best being Jardin Massey, as is the Haras National (National Stud) founded in the 18C.

Practical information

Getting there and around
Air

Tarbes-Lourdes-Pyrenees, ☎ 05 62 32 92 22, www.tarbes-lourdes.aeroport.fr Shuttle buses to Tarbes and Lourdes, ☎ 05 62 94 20 96.

Car

Autoroute A64 or N112 from Toulouse to Bayonne.
N21 from Auch.
A935 from Aire-sur-l'Adour.

Train

TGV from Paris Montparnasse (about 6hrs) to Lourdes.
TER Paris to Tarbes.
TER Toulouse to Bayonne via Tarbes, Lourdes, Pau.
Shuttle service from Lourdes and Tarbes to ski resorts.

Bus

Tarbes to St-Lary-Soulan via Lannemezan, Arreau, Ancizan, Vielle-Aure.
Tarbes to Bagnères-de-Bigorre/ La-Mongie via Vielle-Adour, Montgaillard, Ste-Marie-de-Campan.
Tarbes to Mont-de-Marsan via Vic-Bigorre, Maubouguet, Riscle.
Tarbes to Auch via Rabastens-de-Bigorre, Miélan.
Tarbes to Trie-sur-Baïse.
Tarbes to St-Lary via Lannemezan, La-Barthe-de-Neste, Sarrancolin, Arreau.
Tarbes to Barèges via Argelès-Gazost, Luz-St-Sauveur.

Tourist Information
65130 Capvern-les-Bains Rue des Thermes, ☎ 05 62 39 00 46, fax 05 62 39 08 14, email otcapvern@wanadoo.fr
65230 Cizos Maison du Magnoac, BP 23, ☎ 05 62 39 86 61, fax 05 62 39 81 60, email maison.du.magnoac@wanadoo.fr
65300 Lannemezan 73 Rue Jean-Jacques Rousseau, ☎ 05 62 98 08 31, fax 05 62 40 21 50, www.lannemezan. com
65700 Maubourguet 30 Rue Maréchal Joffre, ☎ 05 62 96 39 09, fax 05 62 31 71 45, email otmaubourguet@hotmail. com
65140 Rabastens-de-Bigorre ☎ 05 62 96 65 67, fax 05 62 96 66 51
65000 Tarbes 3 Cours Gambetta, ☎ 05 6251 30 31, fax 05 62 44 17 63, www.ville-tarbes.fr
65220 Trie-sur-Baïse Maison du Pays de Trie, 31 Pl. de la Mairie, ☎/fax 05 62 35 50 88, email pays-e-trie@wanadoo.fr
65190 Tournay 8 Pl. d'Astarac, ☎ 05 62 34 79 67, fax 05 62 34 79 68

Market days

Capvern-les-Bains Tuesday (May–October)
Castelnau-Magnoac Saturday
Lannemezan sheep market Wednesday
Tarbes Thursday, Saturday, Sunday
Trie-sur-Baïse pork market Tuesday (pork products, eggs and poultry)

Festivals and events
April *Les Pic d'Or*, French song festival, Tarbes
La Hestayade, gathering of Occitan choirs, Ibos (near Tarbes)
June *Nuits Musicales*, concerts performed in the Monastère des Carmes

Trie-sur-Baïse
Les Nuits du Mont Ares, variety of dramatic and visual arts using the 'Théâtre de Verdure' to the full, Nestier
July   *Equestria*, festival of the horse, Tarbes
Lou Grant Macat, recreation of traditional markets, Rabastens-de-Bigorre
August   *La Pourcailhade*, pig festival and pig-noise championship, Trie-sur-Baïse
Les Rencontres de Maubourguet, meeting of artists and sports-people who experiment in front of an easle, Maubourguet
Festival de Musique et Chants d'Amérique Latine, Latin American festival with music, legend and dance, Capvern-les-Bains
Guitares en Concert, Tournay
Festival de Tango Argentin, tango from beginning to end, Tarbes
Fête du Vin à Madiran, colourful wine festival, Madiran
September   *Fête du Haricot Tarbais*, ways of presenting the modest bean, Tarbes
November   *Festival Ibéro-Andalou*, Spanish dancing, Tarbes

Where to stay and eating out
6 5 3 2 0   B O R D È R E S - S U R - E C H E Z
Chambres d'hôte, Marthe Fontan, 18 rue Pasteur (D7 north of Tarbes), ☎ 05 62 36 42 61. One room of great character (for 2–3 people) with antique furniture.
6 5 8 0 0   C H I S
Chambres d'hôte, Jacques Dalat, Ferme St-Féréol 'le Buron', 1 Chemin du Camparces (N21 north of Tarbes), ☎ 05 62 36 21 12. Three rooms in a well-restored old farmhouse; various activities available.
6 5 3 6 0   M O M È R E S
Chambres d'hôte, Arlette Cabalou, 32 Rte de Tarbes (D935 south of Tarbes), ☎ 05 62 45 99 34 or 06 07 96 31 04, fax 05 62 45 31 57. This local farm-*auberge* has 6 rooms, with garden, terrace, lake, and offers guiding in the mountains.
6 5 0 0 0   T A R B E S
☆☆ *Des Tourists*, 38 Rue du IV-Septembre, ☎ 05 62 93 15 26, fax 05 62 93 57 42. Reasonably priced accommodation with restaurant and parking on the south side of town between the Haras and the Forail.

Start out from **Place de Verdun** (north of the tourist office), where there is parking, and turn left on Rue Abbé Torné. The characteristic building material of the Tarbes plain is smooth round pebbles, with stone or brick courses, often arranged in a herring-bone pattern. The **Cathédrale de la Sède**, begun at the end of the 12C or early 13C, and extensively restored, is an interesting combination of brick, stone and pebble in a mixture of styles, from Romanesque at the east, with a massive octagonal belfry, to Neo-classical at the west. On the south flank are the remains of a Romanesque cloister. The interior décor is predominantly 18C, its main features the wooden stalls and panelling, the wrought iron, chequered floor, and the altar and baldaquin by Marc Arcis, using coloured Pyrenean marble. Above the crossing is an octagonal lantern on pendentives. The restoration of the 17C organ was completed in 1993.

One block north of Rue Abbé Torné at 2 Rue de la Victoire is the birthplace of Field-Marshall Foch (1851–1929), Commander of the Allied Forces in 1918, now a museum, the Maison Natale du Maréchal Foch. Open May–Sept 09.00–12.00 and 14.00–18.30, Oct–April 10.00–12.00 and 14.00–17.00, closed Tues, Wed, 1 Jan, 1 May, 1 Nov, 25 Dec; ☎ 05 62 93 19 02.

North of Place de Verdun up Rue Massey is the **Jardin Massey**, a 14ha green oasis bequeathed to the town by Placide Massey (1777–1853), naturalist and director of the Orangerie at Versailles. The park has a collection of exotic trees and several sculptures, including busts of the writer Théophile Gautier

(1811–72), born in Tarbes, by his daughter Judith, and of the poet Jules Laforgue (1860–87) by Michelet. It also contains four galleries of a 14C **cloister** salvaged from the former Benedictine abbey of St-Sever-de-Rustan (see below). The iconography of the capitals includes scenes from the Old Testament, the *Creation of Adam and Eve* and original sin, the *Birth of Christ*, the *Passion* and martyrdoms, as well as allegorical themes and foliate capitals.

The **Musée Massey et des Beaux-Arts** is installed in Massey's former house, designed by Jean-Jacques Latour. It was begun in 1852 at a time when Hispanic styles were in vogue, and is now a museum with two distinct sections. Open 10.00–12.00 and 14.00–17.00 (in 2003 only during the first week of month); closed Sat; ☎ 05 62 36 12 83. The **fine arts museum**, a rather dusty affair, has an archaeological display in the first room with a remarkable Bronze Age mask of the local god Ergé. The collection of European paintings from the 16C to the present is arranged by school and chronologically, with pride of place being given to a painting by Utrillo, *The Préfecture of the Hautes-Pyrénées at Tarbes in 1935*. Also of note are an *Adoration of the Magi* by the School of Jan Scorel, some pleasing 16C/17C Dutch and French portraits, and landscapes by William Didier-Pouget. The other collection, the **Musée des Hussards**—a dashing array of arms, uniforms and models which conveys the glamour of this élite regiment—is closed for renovations.

The main commercial quarter of Tarbes is east of Place de Verdun. **Rue Brauhauban** is a presentable pedestrian street lined with some good 18C and 19C houses, among them Gautier's birthplace at no. 2. The collegiate church of St-Jean was first mentioned in 1268 but the church as it stands dates from the 15C, with a massive tower built later and 19C additions. Place Montault, at the end of rue Brauhauban, has an imposing fountain (1874). Turn right to **Place du Marcadieu**, dominated by the grand Duvignau fountain (1896) evoking the four valleys of Bigorre—Aure, Bagnères, Argelès and Tarbes—is at the heart of the market quarter with its splendid **halle**, a typical construction of the 1880s in iron.

The **Haras National** is southwest of Place de Verdun, the entrance on the south side. Guided visits Mon–Fri 10.00–12.00 and 14.00–17.00; ☎ 05 62 56 30 80. The cavalry stud was established in Tarbes at the order of Napoléon I. This is a refreshing place even if you are not an equine devotee as it is graced with a beautiful group of Empire buildings designed by the architects Devèze, Larrieu and Ratouin in 1881. The light and airy stables, for pampered horses, have been restored using original materials: pebbles and cobblestones for the floor, marble for the troughs, loose-boxes (some of the first examples) in solid oak, and a curved ceiling in chestnut, with false marbling reproduced inside and out. Equestrian events are held here regularly.

The area to the east of Tarbes is known as the **Lannemezan**, around the town of the same name which itself is of little interest. Take the D21 through countryside which is gently hilly (up to 600m), but unsensational, far from the madding crowds at any time, with superb examples of rural architecture in traditional building materials. In the summer it is green and peaceful but in the winter, when the fields have been ploughed, the pebble walls and farm buildings of mud-brick and plaster become one again with the raw siennas and ochres of the soil. In fascinating contrast is the wholehearted enthusiasm for paint and gilt in post-Reformation church décor.

At the hamlet of **Moulédous**, south on the D20, resides a Baroque retable of

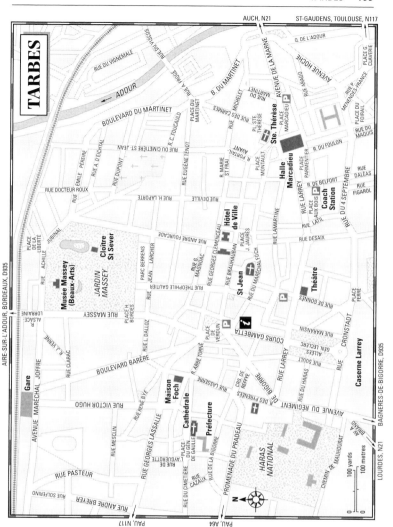

traditional style, returned to its original glitzy splendour in 1982–86. It may have come from either or both the workshops of two families of artists from Asté (south of Bagnères), the Ferrère and the Soustre. The central panel represents the *Assumption of the Virgin* with a saint-bishop and St John the Baptist, with God the Father above flanked by St John and St Matthew. If the church is locked, enquire at the house opposite or at the café; ☎ 05 62 35 73 19.

To the north, where the D14 and D632 cross at **Chelle-Debat**, are examples of rough-textured pebble walls and wooden lattice-work haylofts. On the D14 between Chelle and the N21 is the former **Abbaye de St-Sever-de-Rustan** on the banks of the Arros. Guided visits in season daily 14.00–18.00; out of season, Fri–Sun; ☎ 05 62 96 63 93.

A Benedictine community existed here early in the 11C and seems to have flourished until the 14C, when it was overtaken by the Hundred Years War, then abused by secular abbots, and finally overrun by Protestant troops in 1573. The restoration was begun in 1646 by the Congregation of St-Maur, and in the 18C the abbey received secular decoration typical of the period and of the St-Maur abbots; but the Revolution brought everything to a halt and parts of the abbey were sold off.

The cloister ended up in the Jardin Massey in Tarbes and the organ in the church of Castelnau-Magnoac (see below), but the church, the sacristy and monastic buildings can still be visited. The Romanesque portal in the south wall of the abbey church has been in this position since the 18C. Part of the nave is also Romanesque, with a round-arched window curiously inserted in the south buttress. The carved capitals, like the storiated capitals of the nave, have stylistic links with the late 11C carvings at St-Sernin, Toulouse. A Gothic-style east end seems to have been hastily and clumsily added during rebuilding in the 16C, and the church bears the traces of several stages of modification or adaptation. The major legacies of the 18C are the monastic buildings, some beautiful wood panelling in the sacristy, the monumental staircase in the southwest of the former cloister and some fine stucco-work.

To the southeast, at the junction of the D17, D939 and D632, is **Trie-sur-Baïse**, notorious for the largest pork markets in France and for the annual competition to find the person who can utter a sound most like a pig! This *bastide* was founded in 1323 by Jean de Trie and has kept its original layout despite pillage by the English in 1356 and destruction in 1569 during the Wars of Religion. The cloister of the oldest church in Trie belonging to a Carmelite monastery has been reconstructed in the Cloisters Museum, New York. The very large central square has a graceful 19C iron *halle* encompassing the stone *mairie*. On the south side, the parish church of Notre-Dame-des-Neiges was begun in 1444, the date of the peace treaty between the English and the Counts of Foix and Bigorre. The massive porch-belfry of the church has a stairtower with arrow slits, part of the town defences, a Flamboyant doorway on the north, and a 19C spire.

Look out for examples of buildings using sun-dried or mud brick, sometimes in conjunction with fired brick or pebbles, around **Castelnau-Magnoac** further east on the D632 and D929, an appealing market town with half-timbered houses and a Gothic collegiate church. In the church (light switch in the choir) the 18C wooden stalls with carved ends and misericords have acquired a rich patina; the 18C organ is from St-Sever-de-Rustan. It also contains a rare late-15C sculpture of the Virgin suckling the Infant Jesus.

On the D9, just off the D929 going south, is **Monléon-Magnoac**, where against the wall of the church stands one of the old town gates; inside the church are wood carvings from Notre-Dame de Garaison. South of here on the D9 is the sanctuary of **Notre-Dame de Garaison** (usually open; ☎ 05 62 99 43 22).

This belongs to the long tradition of Marian devotion practised throughout the Pyrenees, notably along the pilgrim route from Notre-Dame-de-Rocamadour in the Lot to Montserrat in Catalonia, passing St-Savin, Aragnouet, Luz, Bourisp and Gavarnie. Garaison was the site of a cult dedicated to Our Lady of September in the Middle Ages. In 1515 a young shepherdess, Anglèze de Sagasan, received visions of the Virgin near the fountain of Garaison telling her to create a new chapel (and anticipating by some 200 years the apparitions of the Virgin to Bernadette de Soubirous at Lourdes); this was undertaken in the 16C (the chapel was restored in the 17C) and became an important centre of veneration in the 18C and 19C.

The Gothic-style sanctuary, built in brick with rib vaults, is entirely decorated with 16C and 17C murals and has furnishings from the 15C to the 18C. It is part of a stunning group of buildings—now used as a Catholic boys' school—built around a semi-formal garden. The 17C main door, graciously painted in shades of blue, is a foretaste of the unusual but colourful decoration of the church. The narthex has paintings dated 1699 inspired by a popular book about Garaison published in 1646, and naive paintings recounting the appearance of the Virgin, dressed in white, to Anglèze. There are also scenes of the history of the sanctuary including a file of the devout across the ribs of the vault, and medallions added in the 18C. The tempera ex-voto paintings on the walls of the nave are reminders of some of the many miracles and cures associated with the site; represented on the vaults is the local martyr, St Sabin. The paintings in the chapels (c 1560–80) represent St John the Baptist and St Catherine, and on the vault of the first chapel north are medallions of the prophets including Isaiah and Ezekiel. The sacristy, through the door to the left of the choir (there is a light switch on the right before the steps), is also completely covered with paintings in tempera. It was built c 1612, and the paintings were carried out in 1618.

LOURDES AND THE LAVEDAN VALLEY

The wide valley of the Gave de Pau (p 441) flows through one of the most beautiful and thriving areas of the Pyrenees, the **Lavedan**, in the western part of the Bigorre between Lourdes and the Spanish border. The Lavedan consists of seven valleys: Barèges is the largest; there are four on the left bank of the Gave de Pau, Cauterets, Estrem-de-Salles, Bats-Surguère and Azun; and two lesser valleys, the Néez and Davant-Aygue, on the right bank. The lower Lavedan is pleasantly green, with pastures and broad-leafed trees, but further into the higher terrain after Soulom, where the valley divides, the scenery becomes more rugged, the vegetation changes and there are spectacular waterfalls, culminating in the best known natural site in the whole range, the Cirque de Gavarnie (p 483).

Practical information

Getting there and around
Air
See Tarbes, p 466.
Train
See Tarbes, p 466.
Train station, Av. de la Gare, northeast of Sanctuaries.

Bus
Lourdes to Cauterets via Argelès-Gazost, Pierrefitte-Nestalas, Luz-St-Sauveur, Barèges.
Lourdes to Pau via Saint-Pé, Lestelle-Bétharram.
Lourdes to Bagnères-de-Bigorre.

Tourist information

65400 Argelès-Gazost 15 Pl. de la République, ☎ 05 62 97 00 25, fax 05 62 97 50 60, www.argeles-gazost.com

65400 Arrens-Marsous Maison du Val d'Azun, ☎ 05 62 97 49 49, fax 05 62 97 49 45, email val.dazun@wanadoo.fr

65110 Cauterets Pl. Foch, BP 79, ☎ 05 62 92 50 27, fax 05 62 92 59 12, www.cauterets.com

65100 Lourdes Pl. Peyramale, ☎ 05 62 42 77 40, fax 05 62 94 60 95, www.lourdes-infotourisme.com (general), www.lourdes-france.org (pilgrimage)

65260 Pierrefitte-Nestalas 45 Av. Jean Moulin, ☎/fax 05 62 92 71 31, www.pierrefitte-nestalas.com

65270 St-Pé-de-Bigorre ☎ 05 62 41 88 10, fax 05 62 41 87 70, www.ot-saint-pe-de-bigorre.fr

65100 Ségus Vallee de Batsurguère, ☎ 05 62 34 10 95, fax 05 62 94 10 95, www.escbatsurguere.free.fr

Market days

Argelès-Gazost Tuesday, Saturday
Arrens-Marsous July–August
Cauterets Thursday (June–September), Friday fair
Lourdes Thursday (every two weeks), Saturday
St-Pé-de-Bigorre Wednesday

Festivals and eating out

All year *Pacques Animations* Lourdes, a variety of festivals, Lourdes

11 Feburary *Anniversaire de la Première Apparition*, anniversary of the first apparition to Bernardette Soubirous, Lourdes

April *Festival International de Musique Sacrée*, classics and lesser-known pieces, Lourdes

June *Confreriales de Bigorre*, festival of gourmet goods and crafts, parades, Argelès-Gazost

July *Festival des Montgolfieres*, hot air balloons, Argelès-Gazost

Théâtrale de Bigorre, a series of plays, Argelès-Gazost

August *Le Défi Pyrénéen*, bike race between Argelès-Gazost and Bagnères-de-Bigorre

8 December *Fête de l'Immaculée Conception*, Festival of the Immaculate Conception, Lourdes

Where to stay and eating out

65100 ARCIZAC-EZ-ANGLES (D937 east of Lourdes) *Chambres d'hôte*, Amélie Tarbes, ☎/fax 05 62 42 92 63. In a well situated house arranged around a grassy courtyard, three good standard rooms in the owner's house.

65400 ARGELES-GAZOST
☆☆ *Beau Site*, 10 Rue du Capitaine Digoy, ☎ 05 62 97 08 63, fax 05 62 97 06 01, email hotel.beausite@wanadoo.fr. Set in the heart of a charming little Pyrenean spa with views all around; hotel of charm with good accommodation and reasonably priced.

☆☆ *Les Cimes*, 1 Pl. d'Ourout, ☎ 05 62 97 00 10, fax 05 62 97 10 19. www.hotel-lescimes.com. Comfort and calm, covered pool, pretty bedrooms and attractive restaurant.

☆☆☆ *Le Miramont*, 44 Av. des Pyrénées, ☎ 05 62 97 01 26, fax 05 62 97 56 67, www.hotelmiramont.com. Extremely charming, with restaurant for unhurried enjoyment of dishes made with local specialities; *Les Jardins du Miramont*, separate garden annex with 8 rooms.

65100 ARTIGUES (off D7 southeast of Lourdes) *Chambres d'hôte*, Colette Capdevielle, ☎ 05 62 42 92 42, www.pyrenees-online/Capdevielle. Three well appointed ground-floor rooms, two with independent entrance, in a converted farmhouse and barn.

65100 ASPIN-EN-LAVEDAN
(4km south of Lourdes)
Chambres d'hôte, famille Boyrie-
Lamarque, Ferme Mongeat, 1 Chemin
du Touroun Débat, ☎ 05 62 94 38 87
or 06 81 35 53 01, http://perso.
libertysurf.fr/boyrie. A variety of rooms,
accommodating 18 altogether, in
farmer's house. Also *ferme auberge* for
meals.

65100 BARTRÈS (D3 northwest of
Lourdes)
Chambres d'hôte, Daniel Laurens, Ferme
Laurens, 3 Rte d'Adé, ☎ 05 62 42 34
96, fax 05 62 94 58 06. A farm at the
heart of the village, five comfortable
rooms, enclosed grounds and restaurant
at 80m.

65110 CAUTERETS
✩✩ *Lion d'Or*, 12 Rue Richelieu, ☎ 05
62 92 52 87, fax 05 62 92 03 67.
www.perso.wanadoo.fr/hotel.lion.dor.
Sweetly old-fashioned in a 19C building,
rooms renovated, all different, closed to
the spa, to the cable car and town
centre.

65100 JUNCALAS (D26 southeast
of Lourdes)
Chambres d'hôte, Arlette and Robert
Assouère, Maison Mgr Laurence, ☎ 05
62 42 02 04, fax 05 62 94 13 91.
Attractive accommodation (4 rooms) in
an 18C house of character, birthplace of
the Bishop of Lourdes. Garden with
stream.
Chambres d'hôte, Daniel Coumes, 31 Rue
de Castelloubon, ☎ 05 62 94 76 26.
Three pleasant and well appointed
rooms in an old house with garden and
interior courtyard.

65100 LOUBAJAC
Chambres d'hôte, Jean-Marc and Nadine
Vives, 28 route de Bartres (D940 northwest of Lourdes), ☎ 05 62 94 44 17,
fax 05 62 42 38 58, www.anousta.
com. Typical Bigourdan house with
large garden and good accommodation.

65101 LOURDES
There are more hotels in Lourdes than
any other town in France after Paris,
with something like 18,000 rooms in
350 hotels and guesthouses, ranging
from very reasonable to luxurious, plus
30 camp sites.
✩✩✩✩ *Impérial*, 3 Av. du Paradis, ☎ 05
62 94 06 30, fax 05 62 94 48 04,
www.sudfr.com/hotel-imperial. Situated
on the banks of the Gave, close to the
sanctuaries, with elegant rooms, garden
and solarium.
✩✩✩ *Beau Séjour*, 16 Av. de la Gare,
☎ 05 62 94 38 18, fax 05 62 94 96
20, www.hotel-beausejour.com. Turn of
the 20C charm on the wide avenue
opposite the station with great views,
spacious bedrooms, attractive public
areas, brasserie and restaurant.
✩✩✩ *Du Christ Roi*, 9 Rue Mgr
Rodhain, ☎ 05 62 94 24 98, fax 05 62
94 17 65. Largish good quality hotel
situated to the west of the town on the
route to Le Béout above the Gave.

65120 VISCOS
Les Campanules and *Granges aux
Marmottes*, ☎ 05 62 92 88 88, fax 05
62 92 93 75. In a magical village, a
family-run hotel and restaurant,
beautiful views, garden and pool.

Lourdes

Lourdes is one of the prime places of pilgrimage in Europe, the product of an
intense veneration of the Virgin in the Pyrenees and of an impressive promo-
tional exercise, much the same as that which elevated Santiago de Compostela in
Spain to the most important European shrine in the Middle Ages.

History

The history of Lourdes began on the limestone promontory dominating the Gave de Pau, where in the 11C the Counts of Bigorre built a stronghold. It was subsequently occupied by the English and then by Gaston Fébus, Count of Foix, before the region reverted to the French by the Treaty of the Pyrenees in 1659. Lourdes would probably have remained a fairly insignificant town but in 1858 its fortunes were completely reversed when **Bernadette Soubirous** (1844–79), a poor and devout child of 14, received 18 visions of the Virgin of the Immaculate Conception in the Massabielle grotto beside the *gave*. The statistics concerning Lourdes since then are, to say the least, miraculous. Over five million people, many sick or disabled pilgrims, from 130 countries pour into the valley from the Sunday before Easter to mid-October, by plane (to Tarbes), by specially adapted trains, or by road.

Even the sheer organisation of such numbers is quite a feat. The extent of the facilities makes Lourdes an excellent base; conversely, it can be a difficult place for the non-pilgrim observer. The material exploitation, from the tacky souvenir shops to the risk of pickpocketing, is probably little different from pilgrimage towns through the ages, although the McDonald's and the waxworks add a purely 21C dimension, as does the recently opened Aquarium des Pyrénées. Nevertheless, even a non-participating observer can find the experience of the youth Mass on a Saturday evening, or the torchlight procession every evening at 20.45, and the overwhelming atmosphere of solidarity of people with a common cause, contagiously moving.

Old town

The town is divided by the Gave de Pau. The Marian City, built around the Massabielle grotto, is to the west. A visit to the old town, to the east, is centred around the castle and the sites connected with the Soubirous family. The latter include the 19C parish church of Sacré-Coeur in Rue Lafitte, which shelters the Romanesque font used for Bernadette's baptism on 9 January 1844; the **Cachot de Bernadette**, Rue des Petits-Fossés, where she was living when she had her first vision in 1858; in Rue Bernadette-Soubirous the **Moulin de Boly**, birthplace of the saint on 7 January 1844 and her home from 1858 until she entered the Convent of St-Gildard at Nevers in 1866; and also the **Moulin Lacadé**, which her father ran, and which Bernadette used to visit. She died in Nevers in 1879 and was canonised in 1933.

The **Château-Fort de Lourdes**, on the opposite side of the *gave*, dates from after 1407 and was modified in 1590. It subsequently became a prison and was damaged at the beginning of the 19C but restoration work began in 1828 and the museum (see below) was installed in 1922. Entrances are on Rue du Bourg and Rue le Bondidier, the latter with a lift. Open April–Sept 09.00–12.00 and 13.30–18.30; Oct–March 09.00–12.00 and 14.00–18.00, Fri 14.00–17.00; closed Tues, PH; ☎ 05 62 42 37 37. From the terrace of the château the whole of the Marian City is clearly laid out before you with the fast-moving *gave* below.

The château is home to the **Musée Pyrénéen** (open April–Sept daily 09.00–12.00 and 13.30–18.30; Oct–March 09.00–12.00 and 14.00–18.00; Fri 14.00–17.00; ☎ 05 62 42 37 37, an interesting resumé of the prehistory and palaeontology of the Pyrenees, its natural history and local traditions, and a good introduction to mountain culture. It is an eclectic collection in 18 rooms around a courtyard attractively laid out with a rock garden and models of regional houses. The Ramon de Carbonnières room is dedicated to Pyreneeists who conquered the high peaks from 1796 to 1956, including Count Henry Russell who made 33 ascents of Vignemale between 1861 and 1904. The rural life section has curious *cires de deuil*, spaghetti-like coiled candles still used in some villages at funerals to represent the dead and protect the living; and there are elements of medieval architecture.

Marian city

The **Boulevard de la Grotte** is the main route to the sanctuaries. To accommodate the vast numbers who gather here, the **Esplanade des Processions** was built in 1875 and divides into sweeping walkways leading to the two superimposed basilicas at the apex. The neo-Gothic Basilique de l'Immaculée Conception, designed by Hippolyte Durand, consecrated in 1871, is built immediately above the **Grotte de Massabielle** where the Virgin of the Immaculate Conception appeared to Bernadette. On the lower level is the neo-Byzantine Baislique du Rosaire, designed by Léopold Hardy (1883–89), which holds 1500 people. In the grotto a sentimental 19C marble statue of the Virgin by Carrate watches over the continuous file of the faithful. Two further basilicas, cavernous, concrete, and functional were designed in the 20C to accommodate thousands of worshippers, wheelchairs and stretchers. The oval underground **Basilique de St Pius X**, consecrated in 1958 by Cardinal Roncalli, later Pope John XXIII, resembles a vast fallout shelter and can hold nearly 30,000 pilgrims. The impasto stained-glass decorations by Jean-Paul and Germaine Sala-Malherbe make a desultory attempt to cheer it up. More recent is the church of St-Bernadette opposite the grotto, inaugurated in 1988, made up of two adjacent amphitheatres.

Probably worse than seeing Lourdes heaving with pilgrims, helpers and the merely curious, is to see it empty. Without the emotional content it is very jaded indeed. One way to distance yourself from Lourdes without using a car is to take the funicular, from Av. F. Lagardère, to the **Pic du Jer** (948m), on the N21 south of Lourdes.

Argelès-Gazost, *sub-préfecture* of the Hautes-Pyrénées, is south of Lourdes at the junction of three valleys. It capitalised on its potential as a spa in the late 19C and is crowded on market day. The old town, built on the flank of the hill, has some interesting streets and 16C and 17C houses, and near the 17C Tour Mendaigne (next to the tourist office) is a sunny terrace overlooking the Gave de Pau, with a *table d'orientation*.

If you take the D918 from Argelès, you will find at **Arcizans-dessus** an extraordinary concentration of tiny, rustic mills, some restored and fitted out. Moulin Musée open July, Aug 15.00–18.00; rest of year by appointment; ☎ 05 62 97 52 54.

At **Aucun** is the Musée Montagnard du Lavedan of local history, customs and trades. Open daily during school holidays, other times by appointment; ☎ 05 62 97 12 03. Next to the museum is the little church of St-Félix, part 11C and part Gothic. Above the south door is an 11C monogram of Christ with a bird and a lamb, possibly relocated when the church was altered in the 15C. The apse, with a billeted cornice and simple carvings, is also 11C. On the west is the entrance to the old cemetery and a porch used by the *coussous* (municipal authorities) for meetings, and the doorway and font once reserved for the *cagots*—medieval marginals who participated at Mass only from a distance. On the north are two baptismal vats used for the immersion of ailing newborn babies. The most interesting pieces are the 16C baptismal font and holy-water stoup, both in granite. The former is decorated with curious mundane scenes, such as a goat chewing a tree, and an acrobat on his hands; the latter has even stranger primitive carvings of animals and figures.

The much-modified 12C–13C church of **Marsous** contains a large 16C polychrome *Christ on the Cross*, some 17C and 18C woodwork, retables and paintings. Spectacular, but tricky to find as it is surrounded by buildings on a hillock at the junction with the D105, 800m south of the village, is the 18C chapel of **Notre-Dame-de-Pouey-Laün**. It was erected on the site of a pilgrim hospice built into the solid granite of the hill. The exterior of the domed chapel is soberly Classical, but the interior is something else. Not surprisingly, it is known as the *chapelle dorée* (gilded chapel) because of the abundance of gold leaf used on the ornate Baroque interior, the work of the Ferrère brothers from Asté. The retable of the main altar is resplendent with vine-entwined cabled columns and an *Assumption* on the pediment above a statue of *Our Lady of Pouey-Laün*. The retables of the chapels, dedicated to St Anne and St Joseph, are slightly less emphatic but nevertheless very splendid. The overall effect, including the woodwork of the choir and other furnishings, is joyously over-the-top.

The D105 follows the Arrens valley, entering the Parc National des Pyrénées at **Porte d'Arrens**, a region of romantic mountain lakes where in springtime the valley becomes a multi-coloured flowered carpet. The D918 continues to the village of **Arrens** where the church of St-Pierre probably dates from the 13C, the end of the Romanesque period in this region. The porch has a Romanesque tympanum with Christ surrounded by the symbols of the four Evangelists and some Gothic decoration. In the graveyard wall to the right of the entrance are the remains of a Gothic window protecting the *bénitier des cagots*, a font or stoup used by medieval outcasts. Also in the surrounding wall is an elegant Renaissance window. The church furnishings include a large polychromed wooden statue of Christ (possibly 13C) above the Romanesque altar in the north chapel, and a Renaissance consuls' bench.

Above Arrens is the **Col du Soulor** (1474m), a favourite stopping-place with wonderful wide mountain panoramas, weather permitting, a rustic chalet-café and local cheese for sale. The safe road is the D126 to Nay and Pau but for the more adventurous, the continuation of the D918 climbs even higher to the **Col d'Aubisque** (1709m) on a road with restricted access that descends to the Gave d'Ossau (p 458).

Saint-Savin

On the D921, the alternative route south of Argelès, is St-Savin, where well-kept houses, *embans* or *couverts* (arcades) and three hotels around the irregular square look down to the valley some 580m below. The abbey was a victim of the Revolution but the comfortably solid Romanesque (1140–60) **church** dedicated to St Savin, a 6C hermit who lived at Pouey-Aspé, still stands guard at the north, although it was never a fortress. Open daily April–Sept 14.30–18.30; ☎ 05 62 97 02 23. Built 1140–60, its proportions were altered in the 14C when the walls and belfry were raised, making it more elegant, less squat. It is enlivened by the play of light and shade on the *mirandes*, the buttresses and the octagonal drum of the belfry, with the distinctive candle-snuffer spire. In the shape of a regular Latin cross with a main apse and two apsidal chapels, sturdy pillars and buttresses, it is covered with a timber and slate roof (14C). On the **tympanum** of the main west doorway is a rare image of *Christ in Majesty* dressed in priestly garments, surrounded by the symbols of the four Evangelists. The south door (19C) is decorated with a Romanesque chrism, and on the cornice of the south apsidal is a tetramorph.

The church has a remarkable number of interesting **furnishings**. Inside the west door is a ten-sided Aragonese stoup (1140) and font (10C and 18C). Further into the nave, opposite the pulpit (17C), is an impressive Spanish-style *Crucifixion* (14C), carved in wood and polychromed. The nave is dominated by the Renaissance organ (1557) with 16C and 18C decoration including three mechanised wooden masks below it activated by the organ pedals. In the south transept is a Romanesque font called the *bénitier des cagots*, carved in granite and supported by two little figures back to back. The St-Catherine chapel has a 12C table and Renaissance retable of the *Descent from the Cross*, and in the chapel of St-Pierre there are an 8C table and 19C tabernacle. The main altar is the 11C black marble tomb of St Savin and behind it stands part of a 14C gilded Tower of the Eucharist. Either side of the choir are two large 15C panels with paintings on wood of scenes from the *Life of St Savin* and his miracles. The 28 choir stalls are walnut, and the arms of Mgr de Foix (Abbot 1540–1606) are on the officiate's stall. There are also 15C and 17C paintings. The north apsidal chapel, dedicated to the Virgin, has two Renaissance retables and a *Virgin and Child* in wood; the altar and paintings are all 17C, and the frescoes are 19C.

A door from the north transept leads to the sacristy and the 12C **chapter house**, the only part of the monastic buildings still intact, with simply carved capitals and bases. The window capitals have shallow reliefs of bearded heads facing inwards and masks towards the cloister, and a variety of symbolic images. There is a small museum of treasures including a 15C reliquary in the form of a château with turrets at the angles, three outstanding 12C statues of the *Virgin and Child* and masonry from the former cloister. What remains of the cloister and other monastic buildings are mainly reconstructions providing rooms and offices for the *mairie*.

South of St-Savin on the D13 is the **Chapelle de Piétat** (11C–14C and 18C), which contains a 15C painted wooden statue of *Our Lady of Hope*, fragments of 14C murals, and 18C murals, the *Garden of the Virgin*.

The D13 drops down into **Pierrefitte-Nestalas** where the road divides. The left fork, the D921, continues to Luz-St-Sauveur and the Vallée de Barèges (p 483). The right, the D920, leads to **Cauterets**, the best-known spa town in the Pyrenees for many centuries with a formidable array of thermal springs. It can also claim the longest list of illustrious visitors.

Jeanne de Navarre and Gaston Fébus came here in the 14C; Rabelais in the 16C; and Marguerite de Navarre, sister of François I, reputedly wrote part of her *Heptameron* (1559) here. A new influx of the great, including J.-J. Rousseau, benefited from a new road in 1763; but the town's finest era was the 19C when Romantic fervour for nature and the picturesque, combined with the patronage of King Louis of Holland and Queen Hortense, drew about 25,000 *curistes* a year, helped by improved transport, monumental hotels and the exploitation of further thermal springs. Victor Hugo wrote about Cauterets in 1843. By 1882 the community had reached nearly 2000 and the first tarmac road in France was built between the Raillère Baths and the Griffons Baths in 1903. Baudelaire, Tennyson, Chateaubriand, George Sand, Edward VII, Gabriel Fauré and Claude Debussy all came. After a decline the town is again thriving. A ski resort was established in 1964 in the Cirque du Lys (1850–1250m), reached from Cauterets by cable car.

At 1000m above sea-level and on the river, this is a bright and lively centre. The old train station, a delightful wooden building (1897) in a combination of alpine and American western styles, can be visited but no longer functions. The Musée 1900 is a local ethnological museum with displays of elegant costumes (1850–1925), less elegant articles to do with mountaineering, and a kitchen *de l'epoque*. Closed 15 Nov–15 Dec; ☎ 05 62 92 02 02. There are numerous public gardens, the most famous of them the Esplanade des Oeufs; many thermal baths; a memorial to Marguerite de Navarre near the Neo-classical gold-and-grey Thermes de César in the older part of town; Belle Epoque grandeur on Boulevard Latapie-Flurin; and to top it all, the Russian Princess Galitzine's villa in Avenue du Mamelon-Vert.

There is a vast choice of walks either from the centre of Cauterets or using the cable-cars, and more, further up the D920. Eight kilometres, several hairpin bends, and numerous cascades later, through alpine scenery and rocks highlighted by masses of wild flowers, is **Pont d'Espagne**, the start of more walks in the national park and the country of the Lac de Gaube (1728m) and also of Henry Russell, the 19C Irish mountaineer, known in France as '*pionnier du pyrénéisme*'.

BAGNÈRES-DE-BIGORRE AND ESCALADIEU

Bagnères-de-Bigorre is a pleasant watering-hole in the wide Campan Valley on the banks of the Adour, with all the characteristics of a spa town. Its mineral waters are used in the treatment of rheumatoid, psychosomatic and respiratory problems. The proximity of the mountains and numerous hotels and campsites in the surrounding area make Bagnères a popular French family holiday centre.

Getting there and around
Train
From Lourdes or Tarbes.
Bus
Bagnères-de-Bigorre to La-Mongie via Ste-Marie-de-Campan.
Bagnères-de-Bigorre to Montgaillard, Tarbes, Vielle-Adour.
Bagnères-de-Bigorre to Lourdes via Montgaillard.

Tourist information
65202 Bagnères-de-Bigorre
3 Allées Tournefort, BP 226,
☎ 05 62 95 50 71; La Mongie, ☎ 05 62 91 94 15, fax 05 62 95 33 12,
www.bagneresdebigorre-lamongie.com
65130 Sarlabous Maison des Baronnies, ☎ 05 62 40 93 01, fax 05 62 40 93 00

Market days
Bagnères-de-Bigorre Saturday

Festivals and events

August *Festival Europe et Théâtre de Rue*, street entertainment
Défi Pyrénéen, bicycle race between Argelès-Gazost and Bagnères-de-Bigorre; *Fête des Fleurs*, musical entertainment, decorated floats, Bagnères-de-Bigorre

Where to stay

65200 BAGNÈRES-DE-BIGORRE

☆☆☆ **Pyrénées Sports**, Rte des Cols, Gerde (D8 south of Bagnères), ☎/fax 05 62 95 53 11, email citecycle@ wanadoo.fr. Just outside the spa in a beautiful setting, with garden, restaurant, opportunity to take advantage of all that is on offer in the Pyrenees.
☆☆ **de la Paix**, 9 Rue de la République, ☎ 05 62 95 20 60, fax 05 62 91 09 88, www.hotel.paix.free.fr. Hotel with garden and solarium.
☆ **Thermal Bellevue La Reine**, Pl. des Thermes, ☎ 05 62 91 09 09, fax 05 62 95 51 90. Smallish hotel in the centre of the town; reasonably priced.

65200 MONTGAILLARD (D935 12km north of Bagnères)
Chambres d'hôte, Jean-Louis and Jo Cazaux, Maison Buret, 65 le Cap-de-la-Vielle, ☎ 05 62 91 54 29 or 06 11 77 87 74, fax 05 62 91 52 42. A pretty manor house with gables and shutters, with 3 rooms (one with fireplace), with private grounds. Meals available.

The old town is bordered to the east by Allées des Coustous, site of the bustling market, and Place des Thermes to the southwest. Conserved in a small garden at the angle of Rue des Thermes and Rue St-Jean are the Gothic portal of the church of St-Jean, and the remains of the cloister of the Jacobins convent destroyed at the Revolution. Also in the area are the 15C tower of the Jacobins, Tour de l'Horloge, and the Maison de Jeanne-d'Albret (1539). The church of **St-Vincent** (c 1366), northeast of the old quarter, has a 14C belfry gable and the remains of a fine Renaissance porch (1557), but the belfry and lateral chapels to the choir were not added until the 19C. There is a Baroque pulpit, and 20C scenes of the *Passion* decorate the east end. The organ, rebuilt in 1708, has been entirely restored.

The extensive gardens on the slope on the west side of Place des Thermes colourfully frame the spa buildings, which consist of the Neo-classical marble façade of the thermal baths of 1823 with additions of 1860, and the **Musée Salies**, built in 1930. The museum contains a modest collection of paintings organised thematically with works by Daubigny, Chassériau, Isabey and Jongkind, the Orientalists against a bright-red background. There are also floral works by a local painter, Blanche Odin (1865–1957), and ceramics and sculptures. Look out for the open-work wooden balconies, typical of the domestic architecture of Bagnères known as *style thermal*.

Abbaye d'Escaladieu

East of Bagnères, defined by the D938 to the north, are the **Baronnies**, an unspoilt section of the foothills of the Pyrenees spanning the area between the Adour and Nestes valleys. A Daedalian confusion of narrow routes links small communities built on the wooded slopes along the valleys of the Arros and the Luz.

The point where these two rivers meet, 10km northeast of Bagnères on the D938, was the site chosen c 1140 by Cistercian monks, originally from Morimond in Burgundy, for the abbey of Escaladieu. Although wilfully damaged and laid waste from the 14C to the 16C and again in the late 18C, it still evokes the majestic tranquillity of all Cistercian abbeys. The restored buildings are used for concerts, conferences and exhibitions. Open May–Sept daily 10.00–12.00 and 14.00–19.00; Oct–April 10.00–12.00 and 14.00–17.00, closed Tues; ☎ 05 62 39 16 97.

Enter through the 17C gatehouse to the west of the church. All that remains of the **cloister**, partly enclosed by buildings but completely devoid of galleries, is the ghost of its physical presence and an aura of claustral peace enhanced by swallows, a catalpa tree, some fragments of masonry and an 18C fountain.

To the south, bordering the road, the impressively simple **abbey church** (1143–63) has also retained its grace and harmony despite mutilation. A Latin cross 44m long, the nave was reduced to six bays in the 14C when the apse was also destroyed. The nave has pointed barrel-vaults and is flanked by interconnecting chapels which form rhythmically satisfying aisles when viewed along their length. The truncated east end was closed by a flat wall in the 16C and two flat-ended chapels were built into each transept. In the 17C the south transept received the distinctive octagonal belfry which dominates the street elevation of the church. The pillars of the nave show traces of the original 12C stone stalls which were replaced by wooden ones at the end of the 16C. Immediately next to the north door are the three round-arched bays of the *armarium claustri* (cloister library), and the sacristy, its original doorway and window almost intact. The layout of the **chapter house** is unusual, comprising six full and three half bays. The ribbed vaults are supported by four marble columns while a stone bench runs round the edge. It opens onto the cloister through a triple-arched round-headed doorway flanked by double windows. On the floor above, the narrow lancets with brick surrounds indicate the monks' dormitory, and under the blocked-off staircase leading to it is the 14C prison.

After the *auditorium* (parlour) is a corridor to the garden bounded by the river. A doorway in the north wing opens into an entrance with a 17C/18C staircase leading to the 17C rooms now used for exhibitions. The *scriptorium* (common room) below is very attractive. West of the entrance is the warming room, with a marvellous flagstone floor, the only room with a fireplace.

The ruins of the **Château de Mauvezin**, 2.5km east, are very different. This grassy hillock, the site of an ancient *oppidum* and a Roman *castrum* above the village of Mauvezin, dominates the Arros Valley, the Baronnies and the Tarbes–Toulouse route. The strategic advantages of the castle were not lost on the Counts of Bigorre in the 12C, nor on the English when Aquitaine, including the Bigorre, came under the control of the Black Prince in 1360. After a long siege in 1373, the fortress capitulated. The golden boy of Foix, Gaston Fébus (p 521), took advantage of his power and the weakened circumstances of others to buy the estate in 1377 and rebuilt the château as a link in the chain of forts controlling traffic across the Midi.

The castle is a classic medieval stronghold with a square keep (34m high) in the south side and a square courtyard (30m square) with powerfully buttressed walls enclosing a 12C cistern. It is now the headquarters of the *Escole Gastou Fébus*, a Gascon language society which saved Mauvezin from complete desuetude. It is an interesting site for the medieval fortification enthusiast, and has a magnificent view from the top of the keep for everybody.

At the small spa town of **Capvern-les-Bains** (west of the N117) is the Musée

Christhi, open mid-April–mid-Oct 10.00–12.00, 15.00–19.00; mid-Oct–mid-April 15.00–19.00; closed Mon; ☎ 05 62 40 91 13, which has a unique collection of coloured advertising cut-outs and other paper imagery for popular brand names between 1870 and 1920.

Also in the Baronnies, by the D929 south and D26, is the **Gouffre d'Esparros**, caverns with interesting natural formations. Open Sat, Sun and holidays, 10.00–12.00 and 13.00–18.00; ☎ 05 62 39 11 80.

THE ADOUR VALLEY AND GAVARNIE

The Adour Valley runs south of Bagnères, tracked by the D935.

Getting there and around
Train
From Lourdes or Tarbes.
Bus
Barèges to Tarbes via Luz-St-Sauveur, Pierrefitte-Nestalas, Argelès-Gazost, Lourdes.
Luz-St-Sauveur to Gavarnie via Gèdre (July, Aug).

Tourist information
65120 Barèges Pl. Urbain-Cazaux, ☎ 05 62 92 16 00, fax 05 62 92 69 13, www.bareges.com
65710 Campan Quartier Bourg, ☎ 05 62 91 70 36; Beaudéan, ☎ 05 62 91 79 92, fax 05 62 91 61 26, www.campan-pyrenees.com
65120 Gavarnie ☎ 05 62 92 49 10, fax 05 62 92 42 47, www.gavarnie.com
65120 Gèdre ☎ 05 62 92 48 05, fax 05 62 92 46 12, email ot.gedre@gavarnie.com
65120 Luz-St-Sauveur Pl. du 8 Mai, ☎ 05 62 92 30 30, fax 05 62 92 87 19, www.luz.org

Market days
Barèges Wednesday (summer)
Campan Sunday
Luz-St-Sauveur Monday
Pierrfitte-Nestalas Saturday
Ste-Marie-de-Campan Wednesday (summer)

Festivals and events
March *Les Etoiles du Tourmalet*, week of astronomy, Barèges and La Mouqie
Easter *Pâqu 'à Luz'*, music festival, Luz-St-Sauveur
July *Le Festival de Gavarnie*, great open-air spectacle of theatre, music and dance, Gavarnie
Festival du Jazz, day-long jazz, indoors and out, Luz-St-Sauveur
Festival Pianos aux Pyrénées, piano recitals, Barèges
August *Festival du Théâtre Haut Adour*, open-air music and theatre, Beaudéan
September *Moutonades*, Fêtes des Cotelettes, return of sheep from the mountains, Luz-St-Sauveur

Where to stay
65710 BEAUDÉAN (near Bagnères)
☆☆ *Le Catala*, Rue Larrey, ☎ 05 62 91 75 20, 05 62 91 79 72. Comfortable and reasonably priced hotel with a good restaurant, though the décor is somewhat idiosyncratic.
65710 CAMPAN
☆☆ *Domaine de Ramonjuan*, Lesponne, west of Campan on the D29, ☎ 05 62 91 75 75, fax 05 62 91 74 54. Fifteen apartments set in a park, with evening entertainment, pool and numerous sports facilities.
65120 GAVARNIE
☆☆ *Le Marboré*, ☎ 05 62 92 40 40, fax

05 62 92 40 30, www.lemarbore.com. Hotel of character in wonderful mountain setting, with excellent food, fitness centre, pub, and friendly atmosphere.

The **Grottes de Médous** are rich in exotic stalactites and stalagmites. The visit includes 200m by boat on an underground section of the Adour. Open July, Aug 09.00–12.00 and 14.00–18.00; April–June, Sept, Oct 08.30–11.30 and 14.00–17.30; ☎ 05 62 91 78 46.

Beaudéan was the birthplace of Baron Dominique Larrey (1766–1842), surgeon to Napoléon and the Grande Armée, who invented the mobile hospital otherwise known as an ambulance. His birthplace, Maison Larrey, is open to the public: 10.00–12.00 and 14.00–18.00; closed Mon in May–June, Sept, Mon and Tues Oct–April; ☎ 05 62 91 68 96. On the banks of a tributary of the Adour, the village is dominated by the 16C church with a distinctive slate-covered spire with pinnacles, typical of the region, and near the river is an old *lavoir*.

Campan is a pleasant village on the D935 with a fine 16C covered market and fountain, and a 16C/17C church. A pretty valley, with occasional houses with stepped gables, opens out as it climbs up to **St-Marie-de-Campan** (857m) at the foot of the Col du Tourmalet, well-known to participants in the Tour de France cycle race. A left fork crosses the Col d'Aspin and the ski resort of Payolle, dropping into the Aure Valley.

The right fork, the D918, takes you over the Col de Tourmalet linking the valley of Haut Adour with the Gaves Valley. The distant views are, as one would expect, spectacular and the pastures in the foreground are inhabited by grazing cattle and sheep, and a profusion of flowers including, in July, vast patches of dark-blue Pyrenean iris. **La Mongie**, on the very edge of the road, is a graceless modern ski resort with all the ironmongery and criss-crossing cables that the sport necessitates. The bright colours of the drifting parachutes of numerous parascenders and hang-gliders are far more acceptable. After 17km you reach the **Col du Tourmalet** (2115m). The **Pic du Midi-de-Bigorre** (2865m) dominates the landscape for miles around and is easily recognisable by the **observatory** at its summit. This was rendered more accessible in 2001 with a new cable-car and can now be visited up to Level 6 (2877m). Apart from a glazed viewing gallery, a maquette of the site, and images of the solar system, it contains the Coelostat, an instrument which projects the image of the sun in order to study its surface. In addition there is a large animated model of the 2m telescope of astronomer Bernard Lyot. For information, ☎ 05 62 56 70 65.

Barèges (1250m) is a small, essentially modern, resort with plenty of modest hotels. It is the highest spa town in France and the oldest winter sports centre in the Pyrenees, established as such in 1921. Until the 18C it was difficult to reach because of poor roads but by the 18C Colbert was able to exploit the potential of the spa waters for treating the military. The route over the Col was improved in 1730 and some years later the route through the gorges was built. The thermal baths, in an elegant building in shades of grey, were built in 1861. Barèges is in the Toy Valley. The **Jardins botanique du Tourmalet** here have a wondrous collection of flowers of the Pyrenees in their natural surroundings. Open mid-May–mid-Sept 09.00–19.00; ☎ 05 62 92 18 06.

Continuing west, the villages of **Betpouey** (*pouey*, meaning viewpoint, derives from the Toy patois) and **Viey** have picturesque churches. At **Viella**, the part-Romanesque church of St-Michel has a recently restored retable, dated 1730, executed by Soustre father and son, sculptor-carpenters from Asté. Incorporating a profusion of putti and gilded grapevines, it is one of the richest in the Hautes-Pyrénées, with no space left undecorated. If the church is locked ask for the key at the *auberge*.

The main town in the Barèges Valley is **Luz-St-Sauveur** (711m), made up of Luz and the spa of St-Sauveur to the south, which benefited from the patronage of Napoléon III. He and the Empress Eugénie both suffered bad health, and spent some months at St-Sauveur. They endowed the town with a spectacular bridge completed in 1861, its single arch suspended 65m above the Gave de Pau. Luz is a charming medieval town, with houses embellished with pearl-grey marble and slate roofs around the remarkable fortified church of **St-André**. A primitive sanctuary, built here at the end of the 11C by the St-André family, was handed over to the Hospitallers of St John of Jerusalem in the 14C. The Hospitallers fortified the church and dug a ditch around it to protect the inhabitants of the town from the *Miquelets*, Aragonese bandits.

Amazingly this little church has retained many of its medieval characteristics including the battlemented wall completely surrounding the church and its graveyard, each merlon protected by a piece of schist held down with a large stone. The arsenal tower to the north was built to defend the original entrance and in the vault of the passageway is a 14C fresco restored in 1867. The stepped gable-belfry is typical of the Luz Valley, with two open arcades containing the bells, and at the angle of the nave and right transept is the high clocktower. Over the south porch is a high relief of Christ surrounded by the four Evangelists, badly damaged in 1793, with a monogram of Christ surmounted by a painted Hand of God; the capitals and bases of the columns supporting the tympanum are also decorated. The mainly Romanesque church was tampered with during the 19C when a new church was mooted but the work never really got under way due to lack of funds. The most interesting things inside are the 12C font with a cover, the splendid 18C pulpit, and confessionals not dissimilar to good-quality wardrobes. To the left of the entrance to the St-Joseph chapel a 13C child's tomb was for a long time used as a holy-water stoup. The 17C chapel of Notre-Dame-de-la-Pitié contains a collection of paintings and sculptures including a 12C *Virgin and Child* and a 15C *Pietà*.

Luz still commemorates the traditional transhumance of sheep from the high summer pastures with a colourful festival, the *Foire aux Cotelettes*, in September.

Follow the D921 south of Luz: the road bifurcates at the village of **Gèdre** (1000m). After passing the rocky disorder of the Chaos de Coumély, the right fork continues climbing to **Gavarnie**, at 1365m the highest village in the Pyrenees. Its deservedly famous **Cirque de Gavarnie** (now a UNESCO Heritage site) is a sheer wall of snow-capped rock, a vast natural amphitheatre averaging 1676m in depth, 890m wide at the base and fanning out in three stages to stretch 11km between Pic de Pinède and Pics Gabiétous. It was created some 20,000 years ago when an immense glacier slid down the valley towards Lourdes, scooping out the fragile limestone rocks. Its crest is the border between Spain and France. Around it are a group of peaks over 3000m and across the border in Spain is **Mont Perdu** (3355m).

The village developed at the time of the pilgrimages to Santiago when a commandery was established for the protection of travellers. The mainly 14C church, originally the hospice chapel, stands on the old pilgrim route. The village, also a ski resort, has eight hotels and two campsites and was an important centre for Pyrénéisme in the 18C and 19C. It is an easy walk from the village to the *Hostellerie du Cirque* (1570m)—there is alternative transport on donkey or horseback—to view at closer quarters the amphitheatre and the **Grande Cascade**, the highest waterfall in Europe, crashing out from the back of the cirque to drop some 423m. There is a vast choice of walks, some more demanding than others, and a ten-hour trek into Spain and back through the gap known as the Brèche de Roland, supposedly carved out of the rock by Roland's faithful sword Durandal.

ARREAU AND THE NESTES

The central Pyrenees are dependent on their celebrated mountain scenery, the properties of the waters and the Pyrenean national park, to attract both summer and winter visitors. The area takes its name from the ancient name for mountain streams and rivers, and strictly speaking marks the old boundary of the province of Bigorre. This is an area where there are no major monuments but many small ones of great charm. Rural communities, built in schist and slate, have ancient but modest churches, decorated with murals or frescoes from the 12C through to the 16C. They are not always easy to locate, and are frequently closed for protection, but visits are arranged through the local tourist offices and are well worth the effort.

Getting there and around
Train

Toulouse to Tarbes via Lannemezan.
Bus

Lannemezan to St-Lary-Soulan via La-Barthe-de-Neste, Sarrancolin, Arreau. Tarbes to St-Lary-Soulan via Lannemezan, Arreau, Guchen, Vielle-Aure.

Tourist information

65170 Aragnouet Piau Engaly, ☎ 05 62 39 61 69, fax 05 62 39 61 19, www.piau-engaly.com
65240 Arreau Château des Nestes, ☎ 05 62 98 63 15, fax 05 62 40 12 32, www.vallee-aure.com
65590 Bordères-Louron ☎ 05 62 99 92 00, fax 05 62 99 92 09, email vallee-du-louron@wanadoo.fr
65250 La Barthe-de-Neste Neste Barronnies, ☎ 05 62 98 87 02, fax 05 62 98 88 07, www.ot-neste-baronnies.com
65510 Loudenvielle Maison de Peyragudes, ☎ 05 62 99 69 99, fax 05 62 99 65 85, www.peyragudes.com
65170 St-Lary-Soulan 37 Rue Vincent Mir, ☎ 05 62 39 50 81, fax 05 62 39 50 06, www.saint-lary.com
65150 St-Laurent-de-Nestes Pl. de la Mairie, ☎/fax 05 62 39 74 34
65170 Vielle-Aure ☎ 05 62 39 50 00, fax 05 62 40 00 04, www.vielleaure.com

Guided visits

Visits to Romanesque chapels in the Neste de Louron arranged by the tourist office at Bordères-Louron.

Market days

Arreau Thursday
Bordères-Louron Sunday in summer
La Barthe-de-Neste Sunday (May–October)
Loudenvielle farmers' market Tuesday

evening, July–August
St-Lary-Soulan Saturday
Sarrancolin Tuesday, Saturday
Vielle-Aure Tuesday (July, August)

Festivals and events

June–October *Spectacles Lyriques*, choral music and song festival, Aure and Louron valleys
August *Sur les Chemins de St-Jacques-de-Compostelle*, festivities along the pilgrimage route, Sarrancolin, Arreau, Antignan, Guchen, Vielle-Aure, St-Lary, Aragnouet, all in the Aure Valley

Where to stay

65240 ARREAU
☆☆ *Angleterre*, on the Luchon road, ☎ 05 62 98 63 30, fax 05 62 98 63 30. Boasts a long tradition and a mention by the English mountaineer, Henry Russell, in *Souvenirs d'un montagnard* (1889).

65240 CADÉAC
☆☆ *Hostellerie du Val d'Aure*, Rte de St-Lary, ☎ 05 62 98 60 63, fax 05 62 98 68 99. With a swimming pool and tennis courts in a park.

65170 ST-LARY-SOULAN
☆☆☆ *Mercure Crystal Park*, Jardin des Thermes, Rte de Soulan, ☎ 05 62 99 50 00, fax 05 62 99 50 10. Recommended hotel with garden, in great situation for the mountains.
☆☆ *La Pergola*, Rue Principale, ☎ 05 62 39 40 46, fax 05 62 40 06 55, email jeanpierre.mir@wanadoo.fr. Delightful small hotel.

65170 VIELLE-AURE
☆☆ *Aurelia*, BP 23, close to St-Lary-Soulan, ☎ 05 62 39 56 90, fax 05 62 39 43 75, www.hotel-aurelia.com. Small and charming family hotel.

Arreau

Arreau (730m) has the typical steep slate roofs with attic windows and subdued silver-grey colours of all the mountain towns. It used to be the capital of the Four Valleys—Aure, Magnoac, Barousse and Neste—and is well placed between the mountains, the plain, and Spain (via the Tunnel de Bielsa). A visit to the town, built between the Neste d'Aure (Robinson Crusoe's route through the Pyrenees) and the Neste de Louron, is accompanied by the sound of water rushing into the valley.

Park on the right bank near the cream-and-grey **Château des Nestes** on the water's edge which was a commandery protecting the sanctuary of St-Exupère in the 11C, a judiciary building in the 17C, a mill and grand residence in the 18C, and now shelters the Musée de l'Histoire Locale; ☎ 05 62 98 63 15. The chapel of **St-Exupère** opposite is dedicated to the 5C Bishop of Toulouse who was born in Arreau. His story is told on one of the six archaically decorated Romanesque capitals of the portal which is flanked by pink marble columns and outlined by three carved voussoirs. On the tympanum is a chrism typical of the high valleys of the Nestes and Bigorre; the octagonal tower has triple windows. Inside the porch is a wooden coffer for offerings. Most of the chapel is in Flamboyant Gothic style and a 16C wrought-iron screen protects a Romanesque stoup. Next door is the fine building known as the **Maison St-Exupère** (1554), and overhanging the river is the balcony of the Maison de la Molie (18C) with marble columns.

On the other side of the bridge are the covered market with a little belfry and the famous **Maison aux Lys** (16C), on Grande Rue, its façade timbers carved in a fleur-de-lis pattern as a reminder of the moment when, at the end of the 14C, the inhabitants opted for allegiance to Louis XI and the Crown of France rather than to the successor of the Count of Armagnac, Jean V. Note the rounded, flower-like swastika of the Pyrenees, used liberally to decorate doors and façades.

Further up the slope, on the left bank (the same side as the market) in the old quarter, is the parish church of Notre-Dame, basically Romanesque with Gothic aisles and a 16C tower with two-light bays.

The tiny hill village of **Jézeau**, 2km east of Arreau on the D112, has a proportionally tiny church, basically Romanesque with Gothic extensions, and a monogram of Christ from the portal is reused in the cemetery wall. Its east end, painted white and gold, looks positively anthropomorphic from the cemetery gate. Inside are Renaissance (16C) paintings on wood.

South from Arreau the D929 takes you through **Cadéac**, which has a 16C church and the chapel of Pène-Tailhade straddling the road, past Guchen and Ancizan, their slate roofs glinting in the sun, to the neat silver-grey village of **Vielle-Aure**. In a beautiful setting, its pleasant 16C, 17C and 18C buildings are in striking contrast to the jarringly modern ski resort of Soulan above it. Just off-centre, the small church of St-Barthélemy has a Lombardy-style east end, massive piers and a Romanesque altar, but has been modified since the 12C. Murals were added in the 15C and a Flamboyant door in the 17C. Scallop shells and a statue of St James testify to this alternative pilgrimage route into Spain via the Rioumajou Valley.

Vielle-Aure's more dynamic neighbour, **St-Lary-Soulan** (836m), whose much-restored 12C church of Ste-Marie to the north of the town near the baths, was on the same route. Two Romanesque carvings, a Christ and a chrism, are reused on the exterior and the church preserves an eyecatching Baroque retable from the now-demolished church of St-Hilaire. St-Lary-Soulan is a buzzing little centre for walkers and skiers, a mixture of old and new, with a number of hotels. One of the six gateways to the national park, the Maison du Parc is in a 16C building (p 464). The **Maison de l'Ours** is dedicated to safeguarding three bears and unravels the facts and myths attached to this unfortunate creature in the Pyrenees. Open school holidays, 10.00–12.00 and 14.00–18.00; other times to 17.00; closed Nov; ☎ 05 62 39 50 83.

St-Lary is on the doorstep of the 2300ha **Réserve Naturelle du Néouvielle**, containing the Lac d'Orédon. This is a wondrous Garden of Eden with carmine wild roses and lilac asters, thistles, dianthus, saxifrages in all varieties, dark-blue gentians, and so on. Some 1250 flowering plants have been identified, above all in June and July: not much appears before May but many plants flower through August and September. The 15 lakes of the reserve also have an exceptional number of animals and vegetation. The road, quite winding in places, is closed in the winter.

The last monument this side of the Spanish border is in the **Plan d'Aragnouet**, on the right of the D118. The so-called Templar chapel is a little gem, its two stages of belfry wall silhouetted against the mountains.

Neste de Louron

Along the D618 southeast from Arreau is a series of **Romanesque chapels** (at Autist, Bourisp, Cadéac, Gouaux, Guchen, Jézeau, Loubajac, Ourde, Samuran and those described below) with 16C murals, on the old pilgrim route. To protect these fragile works, visits are arranged from the Maison du Tourisme at Bordères-

Louron. The Renaissance decorations, either tempera on wood or fresco on plaster, were added to these simple structures after the Council of Trent in 1563, coinciding with increased prosperity in the valley resulting from a growth in trade with Spain, particularly in wool, following the discovery of the New World in 1492, and from the integration of the region into France.

At **Vielle-Louron** on the D25 the plain exterior of St-Mercurial gives no clue to the stunning interior decoration painted in intense colours. Several themes cover the walls: an *Annunciation*; a vivid *Last Supper*; scenes from the *Passion*, from the *Flagellation* to the *Entombment*; and *St-Mercurial fighting the Infidels*. On the vaults are the *Tree of Jesse*, a tetramorph, and Christ surrounded by the Apostles. In the lateral chapel, now the sacristy, is a *Last Judgement* with a very explicit image of the jaws of Leviathan.

The **Vallée de Louron** is beautiful, gentle and restful, perhaps too much so for its own good: the once tiny and remote community of **Génos** (about 150 residents), with a ruined château, lake, swimming pool, hotels, two ski resorts, and in recent years a thermal baths, Balnea, attracts 30,000 visitors in the summer.

St-Blaise at **Estarvielle**, back on the D618, is a Romanesque church remodelled in the 16C, with a Baroque retable which partly obscures the paintings. On the north side is *Christ carrying the Cross*, and on the south a *Descent from the Cross*. Framed by the central part of the retable is a *Crucifixion* representing the moment when Christ's side was pierced by Longinus's lance and the soldiers playing cards on Christ's tunic.

After the junction with the D25, at **Mont**, the church of St-Barthélemy is exceptional as some of the painted decoration is outside. In an oratory in the cemetery are frescoes relating to the *Life of St Catherine of Alexandria*, signed by Bona. Under the church porch is a *Crucifixion* and there is a large *Last Judgement* on the wall between the buttresses. The nave paintings, dated 1574 and attributed to Melchior Rodigis, have scenes from the Passion, *Christ before Pilate* and *Christ with the four Evangelists* as well as *Isaiah announcing the Birth of Christ*. The north chapel contains scenes from the *Life of John the Baptist* and a *Visitation*, *Annunciation* and *Nativity*. The two painters' styles are quite distinctive, but both use contemporary dress for their figures.

The **Col de Peyresourde** (1569m) marks the departmental boundary with the Hautes-Garonne, after which the road drops down towards the Luchon Valley.

Neste d'Aure

North of Arreau by the D929, on the Neste at **Sarrancolin**, is an interesting and original church in the shape of a Greek cross. It is crowned by an admirable belfry with triple round arches on small columns on the upper level and a candle-snuffer spire with spirelets. The first church was built here by Benedictines from Simorre in 952 and was replaced in the 12C and 13C. It is dedicated to a local martyr, St Ebons, and by some miracle the superb 13C reliquary made to contain the saintly remains is still in the church despite being thrown in the Neste at the time of the Revolution and being carried off by thieves in 1911. It is a wooden casket covered with gilded and enamelled copper and is one of the finest in France. On one face are Christ, a king (possibly St Louis), St Ebons, Apostles and saints; on the other scenes from the *Birth of Christ*; and on the gables at each end are St Peter and St Paul. Following a fire *c* 1570, the choir was enclosed by a wrought-iron screen and contains the late 16C choir stalls and misericords and the altar and retable of 1651. In the north transept is a 17C gilded polychrome relief with the *Annunciation*, *Visitation*, *Martyrdom of St Lawrence* and *Jesus preaching at the Synagogue*.

In the village, all that is left of the protective walls is the old door called the Tour de la Prison and there are some fine 15C and 16C jettied houses. Red marble was extracted here from antiquity until an earthquake in 1749 caused the collapse of the quarry.

East of La Barth-de-Nest by the D938 and D26 at **Nestier** is La Calvaire du Mont-Arès, a curious enfilade of 11 bare stone oratories and a chapel, the first one more-or-less underground, built up the grassy slope of Mont Ares. Constructed in stages during the mid-19C they had almost disappeared under the brambles until a clean-up operation was embarked on in 1984. At the summit is a simple altar in the ruins of a chapel. During the summer open-air plays are performed in the small modern amphitheatre outside the restored monastery.

Further along the D26 are the **Grottes de Gargas** at Aventignan. While these caves do not have the overall appeal of Pech-Merle, nor paintings as outstanding as at Font de Gaume, they do have a baffling series of more than 200 hands represented in silhouette, other prehistoric decorations and geological concretions. Guided visits July, Aug 09.30–12.00 and 14.00–19.00; other times by appointment only; ☎ 05 62 39 72 39, 05 62 39 75 07.

Prehistoric man used the caves over a long period during the last Ice Age, but the decoration is the work of late-Palaeolithic man, between 25,000 and 30,000 years ago. The hands, mainly in red or black, are in ten clusters of up to 43 silhouettes in the first gallery of the lower cave, and there are others further on, including in the Sanctuaire des Mains. The silhouettes were created by projecting pigment from the mouth, but their intention and interpretation have no definitive explanation. A frequent feature of the hands is that one, sometimes two, fingers are incomplete although the thumb always features.

In different parts of the caves are the 148 animal images, probably executed over a long period, but due to difficulty of access and their fragility only a few can be seen and the visitor has to make do with a number of reproductions. Some of the drawings, the majority of which represent oxen, bison and horses, are easy to decipher, whereas others are unfinished or piled up on each other like a tangled skein of thread.

23 Haute Garonne: the Comminges

The *Département d'Haute-Garonne* is determined by the Garonne River which rises in the Pic d'Aneto in Spain to flow north into France, turns northwest towards Toulouse then north again. The different areas or *pays* encompassed in Haute-Garonne include the Comminges and Central Pyrenees, the Volvestre and Lauragais, and the Toulousain, which offer an extraordinary diversity of scenery, architecture and a wealth of historic sites.

Modern Comminges is an administrative subdivison of the *département*, which loosely follows the boundaries of a medieval province of the same name spanning the Garonne Valley, between the plains of Gascony and the central Pyrenean chain. St-Gaudens is the major administrative centre in the Comminges, with St-Bertrand-de-Comminges the most important historic site. Bagnères-de-Luchon (or simply Luchon) in the Central Pyrenees south of the Comminges, is a popular mountain spa resort.

The **Comminges** was a semi-independent province in the Middle Ages, reaching the extent of its power towards the end of the 12C or early 13C under the first four counts (of Comminges), all called Bernard. Evidence of prehistoric, Iron Age and Celtic man has been found in this *pays* which, according to a 4C text by St Jerome, was annexed by Pompey in 72 BC on his return from the Iberian Peninsula, although this is not confirmed. The people who gathered here were known as the Convenes and by 15 BC their city, *Lugdunum Convenarum*, had become the capital of part of the province of Aquitania. Christianity was probably introduced by 250 AD and Lugdunum, an episcopal city in the 4C, flourished until the arrival of the Visigoths *c* 408–409. By the 6C the town was known as *Convenae*. In 585, during the Frankish invasions, it was reputedly devastated. Then it faded into obscurity until the 11C when Bertrand de l'Isle, the future St Bertrand, put it back on the map. Comminges was absorbed into the kingdom of France in 1456, and pilgrimage to St Bertrand's relics was in full swing by the 17C and this was revived after the Revolution around 1805.

Getting there and around
Car

St-Bertrand is easily accessible from the A64 Toulouse to Bayonne (exit 17) and on the N117/N125. Bagnères-de-Luchon is further south on the D125.

Train

TGV Paris Montparnasse to Toulouse (5hrs).
TER Toulouse to Montréjeau via Muret, Carbonne, Cazères-sur-Garonne, Martres-Tolosane, Boussens, St-Martory, St-Gaudens.

Bus

Montréjeau to Luchon via Loures-Barbazan, Cierp, Lège.
St-Gaudens to Luchon, via Bordes-de-Rivière, Gourdan-Polignac, Valcabrère, Cierp, St-Béat, Luchon.
St-Béat to Fos.
Muret to St-Sulpice-sur-Lèze.
Boussens to St-Girons via Salies-du-Salat, Mauvezin.

Tourist information
31420 Aurignac ☎ 05 61 98 70 06, fax 05 61 98 90 08, www.aurignac.fr
31110 Bagnères-de-Luchon 18 Allée d'Etigny, ☎ 05 61 79 21 21, fax 05 61 79 11 23

31510 Barbazan ☎/fax 05 61 88 35 64, email office-tourisme-barbazan@ wanadoo.fr
31219 Montréjeau 22 Pl. Valentin Abeille, BP 6, ☎ 05 61 95 80 22, fax 05 61 95 37 39
31440 St-Béat Mairie, Ave de la Gerle, ☎ 05 61 79 45 98, fax 05 61 79 57 07
31510 St-Bertrand-de-Comminges Les Olivetains, Parvis de la Cathédrale, ☎ 05 61 95 44 44, fax 05 61 95 44 95, email olivetains@wanadoo.fr
31800 St-Gaudens 2 Rue Thiers, ☎ 05 61 94 77 61, fax 05 61 94 77 50, www.stgaudens.com
31260 Salies-du-Salat Blvd Jean-Jaurès, ☎ 05 61 90 53 93, fax 05 61 90 49 39, www.salinea.free.fr/salies-salat

Market days

Aurignac Tuesday
Bagnères-de-Luchon Wednesday
Montréjeau Monday
St-Gaudens Thursday, Saturday
Salies-du-Salat Monday

Festivals and events

July–August *Festival du Comminges*, outstanding musical event, St-Bertrand-de-Comminges and St-Just-Valcabrère
August *Fête des Fleurs*, flower festival created by Edmond Rostand, Bagnères de Luchon

Where to stay and eating out

31420 ALAN

Gîtes Hôpital Notre-Dame-de-Lorette, from Le Frechet (D635) follow the signs, ☎/fax 05 62 98 98 94, www.notredamedelorette.com. Two peaceful apartments onto the cloister, high level accommodation with handcrafted furnishings.

65370 AVEUX (south of St-Bertrand on D925)

☆☆ *Moulin d'Aveux*, Rte de Mauléon-Barousse, ☎ 05 62 99 20 68, 05 62 99

79 27. Hotel set in a park.

31110 BAGNÈRES-DE-LUCHON

☆☆☆ *Corneille*, 6 Av. A.-Dumas, ☎ 05 61 79 36 22, fax 05 61 79 81 11. A hotel-restaurant of quality and charm.
☆☆ *Dardenne*, 2 Blvd Dardenne, ☎ 05 61 94 66 70, fax 05 61 79 62 00. Hotel in a residential quarter close to the centre, with a view of the Pyrenees from the restaurant. Reasonable.
☆☆ *Etigny*, ☎ 05 61 79 01 42, fax 05 61 79 80 64. Hotel-restaurant in a charming 19C mansion opposite the baths, with a large garden. Good service.

31510 BARBAZAN

☆☆☆ *L'Aristou*, Rte de Sauveterre-de-Comminges, ☎ 05 61 88 30 67, 05 61 95 55 66. Just 6 comfortable rooms in a hotel-restaurant with a garden, in the foothills of the Pyrenees.

31110 CASTILLON-DE-LARBOUST

☆☆ *L'Esquérade*, D618, just west of Luchon, ☎ 05 61 79 19 64, fax 05 61 79 26 29. Traditional Pyrenean hotel, warm and friendly.

31510 ST-BERTRAND-DE-COMMINGES

☆☆ *Comminges*, Pl. Parvis, upper town, opposite the cathedral, ☎ 05 61 88 31 43, fax 05 61 94 98 22. Hotel in a wisteria-draped old family house, entirely renovated.
☆☆ *L'Oppidum*, Rue de la Poste, ☎ 05 61 88 33 50, fax 05 61 95 94 04. Hotel of character and ambience in the upper town.

31800 ST-GAUDENS

☆☆ *Commerce*, 2 Pl. du Foirail, ☎ 05 61 89 44 77, fax 05 61 98 06 96. Pleasant hotel and restaurant in the centre of town.

31510 SAUVETERRE-DE-COMMINGES

☆☆☆ *Sept-Molles*, off the D9/D26, ☎ 05 61 88 30 87, 05 61 88 36 42. Hotel-restaurant in a beautiful rural

setting, spacious and comfortable with enjoyable food.
3 1 5 1 0 VALCABRÈRE
€€ *Le Lugdunum*, north of St-Bertrand

on the N125, ☎ 05 61 94 52 05. A restaurant recreating the gastronomy of ancient Rome.

SOUTH OF THE GARONNE

St-Bertrand-de-Comminges

St-Bertrand-de-Comminges is a major showpiece, and the whole ensemble is spectacular. A wooded cliff provides the backdrop to the Gothic cathedral which rises in overwhelming proportions above a medieval walled village set on a small mound. At its feet are more medieval buildings, Gallo-Roman sites and the Romanesque church of St-Just-de-Valcabrère, and in the distance are the mountains. Wherever you look, Gallo-Roman elements are reused, or medieval stone is recycled. Despite its tiny population (about 250), St-Bertrand welcomes some 200,000 visitors a year but, like most small towns, it is unlikely to be busy at either end of the day so it is best to stay nearby. There is an annual festival in July and August with concerts in the cathedral, at St-Just and at St-Gaudens.

To the northeast, below the hill and on either side of the D26, are the remains of successive archaeological sites from the **Gallo-Roman** to early Christian periods. The site is open all year for guided visits and exhibitions. The vestiges revealed by the excavations date from *c* 20 BC up to the 6C. When the settlement was elevated to the status of colony in the 2C it expanded to cover some 30ha stretching from the foot of the hill to the banks of the Garonne and as far as the Romanesque church of St-Just (see below). The multitude of inscriptions, sculptures, domestic objects, artefacts, sarcophagi and the buildings themselves reveal the sophistication of this civilisation.

The temple of the **forum** and its enclosure, west of the D26, were built during the reign of Augustus (27 BC–14 AD) and abandoned by the 4C or 5C. The adjacent **thermae**, of the same period, were rebuilt on a larger scale with hot and cold baths, piscina and hypocaust. A partial reconstruction of this site is underway. Part of the cardo (the north–south axis) divided this from the vast **macellum** (market), east of the D26 on the site of an earlier basilica. The market had three monumental entrances and a large open space in the middle bordered by a double row of stalls to the south and one row to the north. A large porticoed square was a later addition to the market complex. Between it and the forum a small round monument has been reconstructed: its precise function has not been identified but it may have marked the intersection of the Roman ways to Dax and to Toulouse. The late 2C **northern thermae**, northwest of the forum are the most complete, with easily identifiable piscina, natatio, frigidarium, tepidarium, praefurium, caldarium and so on. Parts of just three terraces of the early 1C **theatre** are visible on the hill behind the car park; the rest disappeared when the road was built in the 18C.

In the attractive lower town, near the little parish church of St-Julien, is the overgrown site of an early **Christian basilica** (5C); marble sarcophagi scattered around indicate its use as a burial ground. Take note of the magnificent example of a Comminges barn near the basilica, with hooped or semi-circular timbers in the upper part.

There are three entrances to the hill village which is still confined within the medieval ramparts: on foot through Porte Cabirole (east) and Porte Majou (north), or by car via Porte Hyrisson and car park (west). A little train runs from the car park to Porte Hyrisson. Enter by **Porte Cabirole**, which has Roman inscriptions on the outer wall. The little building opposite was built on to the remains of the barbican and reuses some medieval masonry. A short way up the street on the left is the half-timbered **Maison Bridaut** (rebuilt 1577) with a Renaissance tower. Turn left at the *Hôtel Oppidum*—there is a 15C house with medallions under the eaves on the right—then right and past an 18C fountain to arrive at the centre of the *cité*. Suddenly, there is the great looming west front of the cathedral. On the left of the forecourt is the neo-Gothic church of **Les Olivetains**, part of a former monastery attached to the Sienese branch of the Benedictine order established here in the 19C. The buildings are occupied by the tourist office, bookshop, library, museum and art gallery. Open daily mid-July, Aug 10.00–19.00; April, May, June, Sept, Oct 10.00–18.00; rest of year 10.00–17.00; closed Jan. The 19C chapel is used to exhibit an ensemble of statues and sculptures known as the *Trophy* (*c* 24 BC), an allegory of Augustus' conquest of Gaul and Spain. Some 115 fragments were discovered in 1926 and 1931 in ditches near the temple and have been pieced together. Opposite is a small covered market.

Cathédrale Ste-Marie

Open every day. No visits Sunday morning; ☎ 05 61 89 04 91.

Bertrand de L'Isle, great Church reformer and builder, Bishop of Comminges from 1083 to 1123, was responsible for the first cathedral, consecrated in 1200. In 1218 Bertrand was canonised and in tribute Lugdunum Convenarum became St-Bertrand-de-Comminges. Such was the veneration of St Bertrand that Bertrand de Got, Bishop 1294–99 and later Pope Clement V (see p 118), initiated, supervised and financed, through his intermediary Canon Adhémar de St-Pastou, the transformation of the cathedral to accommodate the influx of pilgrims. The building was completed at the time of Bishop Hugues de Châtillon (1336–52).

Exterior Work started *c* 1307 at the east, with the chevet. The Romanesque nave was incorporated into an aisleless Gothic structure and 14 gabled and pinnacled buttresses support the walls which were extended upwards. At the west, under the Gothic carapace, elements of the old church are visible in the narthex and the first three bays with simple lancets. The austere façade was enlarged and the belfry raised in the 14C. The **west portal**, approached by marble steps and submerged in a deep recess, has richly sculpted décor. On the marble Romanesque tympanum is the theme of the *Epiphany* watched by St Bertrand, and the lintel carries a relief of the twelve Apostles. The five capitals of the porch carry figures and animal motifs with stylistic similarities to the west porch of St-Sernin in Toulouse.

Interior The massive **narthex** conserves capitals and half-barrel vaults from the 11C–12C church. Built in silvery-grey local stone, the fairly small cathedral

(55m by 16m and 28m high), with five radiating chapels and no transept, has simple quadripartite vaults and little integral decoration except painted bosses bearing the coats of arms of the bishop-builders. The beautiful calm greyness of the Gothic church is disrupted by the heavily ornate 16C choir enclosure of burnished oak, the **jubé** (roodscreen) of which is at the level of the second bay of the nave. This consists of a gallery with pendant bosses and above are 20 figures including God the Father, an *Ecce Homo*, Apostles and virgins, and on the two lower panels are polychromed statues including St Bertrand, St Roch and St Sebastian.

Placed on the diagonal on the north of the first bay, to serve both the choir and the nave, is the equally ornate three-tiered **Renaissance organ**, supported on a coffered platform by five fluted columns, which was donated by Bishop Jean de Mauléon (1523–55). Stripped of its lead pipes at the Revolution, it has undergone three restorations and was returned to its original configuration in 1975. Incorporated in it is the 16C pulpit which faces the parish altar in the **St-Sacrement chapel**, added in 1621. The chapel contains the famous crocodile ex-voto.

The closed partitions of the wooden church-within-a-church separate the **choir enclosure** from the body of the cathedral. The bequest of Jean de Mauléon, inaugurated at Christmas 1535, this is one of the rare complete choir enclosures left in France, and one of three in the Midi-Pyrénées, with Albi and Auch. The enclosure provided an area where the clergy could perform Mass unobserved and undisturbed by the public who would, nevertheless, hear it from the ambulatory. The exterior is relatively sober, the full glory of the carved oak being reserved for the inner sanctum. Arranged in two tiers around three sides of the choir are the 66 stalls assigned, according to status, to canons and church dignitaries—the 38 in the upper row, with sculpted backs and canopies, were reserved for higher ranks. The tribune, on the reverse of the *jubé*, has at its centre the ambo from where the deacon read aloud the Epistle and Gospel.

The iconographic programme leads the faithful, via saints, prophets, sibyls, virtues and various biblical characters, towards salvation. The carving is profuse and harmonious, using a variety of woodcarving and marquetry techniques: the large figures on the back of the upper stalls are in relief; on the stall ends the images are carved in the round and take the form of little scenes such as the *Tree of Jesse*, the *Temptation of Adam and Eve*, the *Virgin and Child*, the *Four Evangelists*, and the *Temptation of Christ in the Desert*; and marquetry is used on the episcopal throne as well as the seats of the celebrant and his acolytes for the images of St Bertrand, St John the Baptist and St John the Evangelist. Added to the religious, mythological and allegorical mix typical of the 16C are animal motifs, on the carved armrests, and the traditionally mundane and profane subjects of the famous misericords, which are executed with exuberance and humour. Throughout the carvings of the choirstalls are versions of foliate heads or 'green men'.

The decorative wooden retable, which received a garish coating of paint and gilt in the 18C, has an extraordinary frieze of 27 animated paintings of the *Life of Christ and the Virgin*. The main altar, in Sarrancolin marble, dates from 1737 and the lectern is 18C. At the east end of the choir enclosure is the 15C stone **mausoleum of St Bertrand** in the form of a large casket. The side facing east is covered with scenes of the life of the saint painted in the 17C, with a silver reliquary bust containing St Bertrand's head on the altar. The other side forms a small passageway and in the central cavity is the large silver and ebony casket containing the body of the saint.

Of the 15 windows of the cathedral, three in the east contain 16C **stained glass**. In the central window is the kneeling figure of the donor, Jean de Mauléon, with scenes of the *Nativity* and the *Baptism of Christ*; in the north the *Annunciation*, and in the south the *Presentation at the Temple*. The Flamboyant Notre-Dame chapel (late 14C–15C) contains the 15C marble tomb of Hugues de Châtillon who was responsible for its construction.

The Ste-Marguerite chapel, or Chapelle Haute, was built above the north gallery of the cloister in the 14C and has the entrance to the chapter house and **treasury** which contains, among other things, two medieval embroidered copes, with scenes of the *Passion* and the *Virgin and Child*, given by Clement V to celebrate the translation of St Bertrand's relics on 16 January 1309, and brilliant *opus anglicanum* embroideries produced by workshops in London.

On the south flank of the cathedral is the Romanesque **cloister**, albeit much remodelled. Since the 19C the south gallery arcades, built above the ramparts, have been open towards the countryside, bringing a garden-like gaiety to what is normally an enclosed contemplative space. The layout is unavoidably lopsided with three 12C aisles, west, south and east, with eight, twelve and five bays respectively. Pairs of slender columns and double capitals support round arches and a light timber-and-tile roof. The central western pier is made from the drum of a Roman column carved with the four Evangelists, heavily inspired by antiquity; on the capital above are the *Labours of the Months* and the *Signs of the Zodiac*. The best capitals are on the west and include an elegant foliate design, *Adam and Eve*, *Cain and Abel* and four with decorative motifs. The only indication of the former monastic buildings is the trefoil entrance and walled-up Gothic window of the chapter house. The cloister served for a time as a burial place, and in recesses in the vaulted late-Gothic north gallery, known as the **Galerie des Tombeaux**, there are sarcophagi with epitaphs of seven canons and benefactors.

Leave the village by the **Porte Majou**, the main entrance to the medieval town, which was rebuilt in the 18C and used as a prison. On the inside is a Roman funerary stele and, outside, the arms of Cardinal de Foix (15C).

St-Just-de-Valcabrère

Leave St-Bertrand by the D26 to reach Valcabrère 1.5km away and turn right in the village. The basilica of St-Just-de-Valcabrère is an outstanding Romanesque building in a pastoral setting. To enjoy the famous view of St-Just surrounded by cypresses, with the casket-like cathedral in the distance, take the narrow road before the church, park on the incline and take the unmade track on the right-hand side. A fee is payable. Open daily July–Sept 09.00–19.00; May–June 09.00–12.00 and 14.00–19.00; April, Oct 10.00–12.00 and 14.00–18.00; in winter, Sat, Sun, and school holidays 14.00–17.00; ☎ 05 61 95 49 06.

The exact dates of the basilica are not known, but it seems likely that a church was begun in the 11C, slightly before the first church at St-Bertrand, on the site of an early Christian necropolis near the ruins of the Gallo-Roman town plundered for its stone. Numerous antique carvings and early Christian funerary monuments were used in its construction.

The church has a simple, well-proportioned belfry. Incorporated in the gateway are 1C inscriptions and a medieval chrism. On the tympanum of the 12C north entrance is a relief of **Christ Enthroned**, framed in a mandorla, with two censer angels and four chubby Evangelists. Either side of the entrance are marble **statue-columns** with traces of colour, similar to the Evangelists' pillar in the cathedral cloister. A little scene on each capital identifies the main figure, from left to right: the **Decapitation of St Just**; the **Stoning of St Stephen**; a man inviting a woman—probably St Helen—to mount a horse watched by an angel, a possible allusion to the pilgrimage of the mother of Constantine; and the **Arrest and Flagellation of St Pasteur**. On the south side of the church are fragments of pre-Romanesque walls and of a Romanesque cloister, and embedded in the wall of the church is an engaging antique carving of a theatrical mask. The splendid east end is a complex structure progressing from rectangle to polygon via a round arch and squinches.

The variety of textures and colours in the **interior** is very beautiful. It consists of four uneven barrel-vaulted bays, half-barrel vaults in the aisles, and a trilobed east end less complicated inside than out. Massive pillars separate nave and aisles. Behind the basin-shaped table covering the altar is a facsimile of a document found in 1886 recording the dedication of the altar to St Stephen (Etienne), St Just and St Pasteur in October 1200. A sarcophagus supported on a vaulted passage behind the altar contained the relics of St Just and St Pasteur, and pilgrims could either pray below it or climb the steps to touch it. The richest decoration in the east bay includes paired marble columns standing against the piers on antique bases, and two inverted antique friezes as well as a frieze of acanthus leaves. On the south wall a tombstone dated 347, and another in the pier to the right of the entrance, testify to the introduction of Christianity by the 4C. Two hollowed-out Roman capitals standing on columns against the two northwest pillars are used as holy-water stoups.

On the other side of the Garonne from St-Bertrand is the attractive spa of **Barbazan** where the waters were taken as a cure for malaria during the colonial era but are now used to combat stress. Like all spas, it has gardens and a small thermal establishment. Between St-Gaudens and Barbazan on the D9, in a pretty wooded area, is Sauveterre-de-Comminges (see above). The *bastide* of **Valentine** on the D8 was built near the site of a large 4C Gallo-Roman villa. Several Christian churches were built on the ruins of a 4C temple, the last becoming part of a Benedictine priory in the 13C, destroyed in the 18C by the Protestants. In the 19C the town was famous for its blue faïence, now to be seen in the museum in St-Gaudens.

Central Pyrénées: Bagnères-de-Luchon

Enclosed in a deep wooded valley about as far south as one can go in France (not quite as southerly as Ax-les-Thermes in the Ariège), Luchon is sometimes described as La Reine des Pyrénées. The town's official name is **Bagnères-de-Luchon** and in a minor way it is the region's answer to a coastal resort, a typically bourgeois spa town with some 60 hotels, the third largest thermal station in France in summer, while in the winter there is skiing.

Luchon is the former Gallo-Roman city of *Ilixon*. The properties of its sulphurous waters were already recognised in 25 BC and appreciated for six centuries until it returned to obscurity between the 5C and 10C. Its rebirth in the 18C was due mainly to Baron d'Etigny, the King's Intendant at Auch, who visited the town for the first time in 1759. He was responsible for a new access route from Montréjeau and for instigating a programme of works to link the old town with the baths, a radical exercise in Haussmanism before its time. By 1827 the town owned 78 springs and this heralded the beginning of a fashionable period for the spa, which was patronised by the rich and famous from all over Europe—Flaubert, Mata Hari, Lamartine, Alexander Dumas *fils*, Bismarck and Leopold II of Belgium—until the beginning of the 20C. Both Luchon and St-Béat claim the balcony that inspired the duplicitous scenes in *Cyrano de Bergerac*.

In 1993, a cable-car was opened from the centre of town to the ski-resort of Superbagnères (1797m), and there are plans afoot to bottle the local mineral water.

To learn more about Luchon, visit the 10 rooms of the **Musée du Pays de Luchon**, which cover such subjects as local archaeology, the mountains, winter sports, local history and architecture. Open daily 09.00–12.00 and 14.00–18.00; closed Nov, Wed, Fri, Sat, PH; ☎ 05 61 79 29 87. The grander buildings along the dead-straight Allées d'Etigny date from the mid-19C and near the end of this lin-den-lined avenue there is the faint but distinct aroma of sulphur. The Parc des Quinconces, with its catalpas and tulip trees, bandstand, pond, pony rides, and a statue of d'Etigny by G. Crauk (1889) surveying it all, was created in 1849 after the Etablissement Chambert was built in 1848 to replace baths destroyed by fire in 1841. Its elegant colonnade is of St-Béat marble. The Pavillon du Prince Impérial was built in 1960 and in 1970 the glass, steel and grey-marble Vaporarium, with natural saunas, was the first in Europe. To the east of Allées d'Etigny is the casino, surrounded by another park of 4ha with pond, grotto and exotic plants, but the casino only has croupiers of the one-armed variety.

In the vicinity of Luchon are 31 **Romanesque churches**, but to protect precious furnishings and decoration the only way to see the interiors is through visits organised by the *Bibliothèque Pour Tous*, 9 Avenue Jean-Boularan, Luchon (no telephone). So integrated are these little mountain churches with the land-scape that most views are enhanced simply by the fact that they are there, their characteristic rusticity set off by belltowers with slate spires.

The **Vallée d'Oueil** to the west, reached by the D618 and D51, is a pastoral valley running north–south and leads to two rural 12C churches built in schist, **Benque-Dessus** and **Benque-Dessous**—the latter has slightly better-conserved Romanesque characteristics while the former has Gothic murals. The little church at **St-Paul d'Oueil** has a sculpted tympanum, and the quite minuscule St-Barthélemy at **Saccourvielle** is endowed with one of the loveli-est belltowers in the area.

St Aventin

St-Aventin, back on the D618 at the start of the Vallée de Larboust, has the most outstanding of the area's small churches, the presence of venerated relics of the local saint accounting for its importance. Park at the bottom and walk up the 100m slope.

The structure is typical of the first Romanesque style in the Midi (early 11C): bare walls, small windows and a blind arcade around the east end. The easternmost of the two towers is the older, and a simple gable was replaced by a taller tower with double, triple and quadruple openings in ascending order above the stepped west façade. Apart from some Gallo-Roman stones embedded in the south wall, most of the **sculptures** date from the second half of the 12C. Above the porch, Christ, in a mandorla supported by angels, is surrounded by the four Evangelists holding their symbols. On the capital to the right is the *Martyrdom of St Aventin*, who reputedly met his death at the hands of Muslims, and on the left the *Massacre of the Innocents* and *Mary Magdalene anointing Christ's Feet*. A pillar

St-Aventin-de-Larboust

faced in marble east of the portal is carved with a somewhat chunky *Virgin and Child*, Mary's hair centrally parted, with animals around her and under her feet, and on the east face is Isaiah, stylistically similar to the sculptures at St-Just at Valcabrère (see p 495). On the buttress to the right is a relief showing the legend of St Aventin's relics being discovered by a bull.

The pilasters in the nave and aisles are proof that the original building was designed to be vaulted, but not the vaults we see now. The surprisingly high nave is flanked by narrow aisles and the interior is decorated with a series of **paintings** from the end of the 12C through to the end of the 13C or 14C. Some are faded and difficult to decipher as they were hidden under plaster until the end of the 19C. On the apse walls St Sernin and St Aventin are in the place of honour, their names written in the banderoles. In the dome are visions of glory, with a cycle of the *Life of Christ* in the upper register. In the nave Christ's image is represented in a medallion supported by six angels, and the Hand of God between *Cain and Abel* framed in another, while on the intrados of the large arcades are *Adam and Eve*, probably painted in the 14C. There are several Romanesque pieces such as a holy-water stoup carved out of a capital, another stoup with strange reliefs, a wrought-iron screen and a crudely executed marble crucifix.

A further kilometre west on the D618 another valley runs south along the **Neste d'Oô** leading to a series of natural lakes at 1504m or more, reached only on foot. Almost opposite this turning is the little church at **Billière** with an apse at each end. The 11C church of **Cazaux-de-Larboust** has a typical belltower but its main attractions are the 15C frescoes, which include *Christ in Majesty* and the four Evangelists, Mary and the Apostles, *Adam and Eve*, the *Birth of Eve*, the *Temptation* and the *Expulsion from Eden*, and the *Last Judgement*.

Another 2km west on the D618 is a charming little 9C–10C church isolated in the middle of a field at the foot of the Col de Peyresourde, with a multitude of names, **St-Pé-de-la-Moraine**, Moraine de Garin, Sants-Tristous, or other variations on these themes. It has a simple belfry-wall with antique bells, a staircase to the roof, and tiny windows, and a number of Gallo-Roman marbles with pagan imagery incorporated into the construction both inside and out. It also has a mosaic stone floor with a rare early representation of the Christian sign, the fish. Somewhat anachronistic but not unusual is an 18C retable with wooden statuettes of Christ, St Peter and St James.

Between Luchon and St-Béat, northeast on the D44, are the marble quarries at Marignac and the Lac de Géry. **St-Béat**, built on both banks of the still narrow defile of the Garonne in the southern part of the old province of Comminges (p 489), is grandly called the Key to France, a title it acquired in the Middle Ages because of its position close to the Spanish border, yet it is a modest town. It is famous for the marble quarried here during Roman times and used extensively in the southwest, although there was a break in production during the Middle Ages. The quarries were reactivated when fashions changed in the late 17C and 18C and the marble was used in such prestigious palaces as Versailles as well as in many more modest locations, including the houses of St-Béat itself, and for many a Baroque altarpiece in the region.

North of the town are the ruins of an 11C château with 12C and 15C walls; its keep, rebuilt in the 19C, stands sentinel over the valley. The church was built in 1132 and has been tastefully restored. On the tympanum is a fairly standard *Christ in Majesty* and the symbols of the four Evangelists and the four decorated capitals include an *Annunciation* and *Visitation*. It has a collection of mainly 16C–18C furnishings. Also of note is the Consuls House (1553). Maréchal Galliéni (1849–1916), minister for war and military governor of Paris from 1914, was born in St-Béat.

NORTH OF THE GARONNE: ST-GAUDENS

St-Gaudens is sub-*préfecture* of Haute-Garonne, the main industrial centre in the Comminges and an important market town. The farmers' market on Thursdays has been held on the same site for 700 years and there are numerous fairs and a large cattle market serving a region famous for its veal. St-Gaudens stands on a high ridge above the Garonne with what would be a marvellous panorama of the Pyrenees if it were not marred by the unfortunate situation of the steaming factories of Cellulose du Rhône et d'Aquitaine in the valley below. Medieval pilgrimage routes to Santiago from St-Giles, St-Girons and St-Bertrand once converged here; today the N117 carries traffic between Toulouse and Tarbes.

Collégiale
St-Gaudens is not a place to linger very long, but the collegiate church is of interest.

The story goes back to persecution of a Christian community in this region *c* 5C–6C. It is traditionally associated with La Caoue, on the Luchon road, where a tiny oratory was erected and rebuilt in the 20C. According to legend, the decapitated Gaudens set off with his head under his arm to the site of the present church. The cult was officially recognised and drew numerous pilgrims in the Middle Ages and the Bishop of St-Bertrand established a chapter of canons here until the Revolution. A church was begun during the period of ecclesiastical reform between 1056 and 1063 by Bishop Bernard II, of the family of the Counts of Toulouse. At the end of the 11C and beginning of the 12C—the time of the great pilgrimages and of the chapter's increasing fortune—a grander church was begun, inspired by St-Sernin in Toulouse. Bernard II's unfinished church was incorporated into the new one, and for a short period stone-carvers of remarkable skill worked in the collegiate church.

Part of the 11C building is conserved in the walls of the three east bays and a large portion forms the lower part of the apse, but much of the decoration was lost in the 19C when the building was profoundly altered. The cloister on the south, begun towards the end of the 12C, was destroyed *c* 1810 but has been re-created in golden stone. Here the new capitals, modelled on seven originals, prove the influence of the Toulousain cloister workshop. The 13C **chapter house** contains a small museum of religious art from the Comminges. The west door of the church is 19C as are the belfry (1874) and the two-level roof (1887). The north entrance is 17C although the marble relief in the tympanum was probably salvaged from the 12C doorway portal destroyed in the 16C. This is an elaborate and elegant version of a chrism in a circle decorated with lozenges and supported by four angels emerging from clouds.

The **interior** is rather dark: there is a lighting box at the west end. The barrel-vaulted nave has five unequal bays with galleries in the two east bays. When the decision was taken in the late 11C to build a church with a gallery, the east bay was already complete. To minimise disruption to worship, work began in the second bay with the construction of a tribune or gallery, after which an adjacent tribune was built and the existing vault was raised. Lack of funds then put paid to the ambitious scheme for a galleried nave and the remainder of the church is closer to the one envisaged by Bernard II.

From this brief period date the eight finest **capitals** (once attributed to the 19C) influenced by the Spanish workshops on the pilgrimage road. The iconography of the capitals principally addresses morality and original sin. Their execution is vigorous and the carving crisp. On the capitals of the north pier are lions in foliage (west) and monkeys in obscene positions, attached with ropes around their necks to men who seem to be leading them (east); on the south pier, a man is devoured by a lion while his companions try to save him (south) while Adam and Eve flank the serpent (east), and the west capital has a man leading an animal by a rope. The oldest capital in the south chapel has a horseman among foliage and interlacings. The tribune carvings, including the scene of a baptism, were carried out slightly later and do not show the same virtuosity as the Spanish-influenced ones. Virtually all the Romanesque décor of the chevet has been replaced by 19C paintings by Lamothe (1858) of the religious history of Comminges. The stalls are 17C but were damaged during the Revolution. In the aisles are late-18C Aubusson tapestries of the *Triumph of Faith* and the *Transfiguration*. In the background of the tapestry of the *Martyrdom of St Gaudens*, made for the church, is a panorama of the town *c* 1760. The 17C organ was restored in 1981.

To the east of Place Jean-Jaurès is the tourist office, and in Place du Mas-St-Pierre the **museum** of local history and traditions which has a collection of blue porcelain from Valentine. The town has a number of parks and gardens and west of the old town, on Bd. E.-Azémar, in the public gardens, is part of the cloister of the abbey of Bonnefont (see below).

Montmaurin and Aurignac

Hidden among cypresses in the cemetery just outside the village of **St-Plancard**, on the Save River and D633, is the delightful 11C chapel of St-Jean-des-Vignes. The key is held at the café/*tabac*. It has a perfectly simple shape, with an apse each end and one chapel on the south; the roof timbers rest directly on the walls, which are pierced by three small windows in the east, and the walls carry some precious 11C murals discovered in 1943. The features are stylised, the colours delicate and images faint, but it is possible to decipher a *Christ in Majesty* surrounded by the Evangelists, and a *Crucifixion* on the east wall; and in the south chapel, Christ enclosed in a double mandorla surrounded by numerous figures, with the Hand of God above and the *Temptation of Adam and Eve* to the right. On the arch of the chapel is a decorative frieze.

At the southern end of the Gorges de la Save is the important archaeological site of **Montmaurin**, the largest excavated Roman villa in France. Open daily April–Sept 09.30–12.00 and 14.00–18.00; Oct–March to 17.00; ☎ 05 61 88 74 73.

> The ancient routes from Agen to Lugdunum Convenarum (Comminges) and Toulouse to Spain crossed this pleasant alluvial plain, where in the mid-1C a large villa was constructed at the centre of cultivated land. The site was abandoned towards the end of the 2C or early 3C, when the Save burst its banks, until the mid-3C. Around 330 AD the main building of the earlier construction was transformed into a luxurious residence, and *c* 350 more buildings were added, arranged around successive inner spaces to create a unified architectural ensemble of great beauty. Although it was consumed by fires in the 4C, the parts excavated evoke the harmonious layout of the villa. The setting is enhanced by well-maintained hedges and a scattering of dark cypress trees.

Begin at the point furthest away from the public entrance, at the hemispherical main courtyard that was the ancient entrance and reception area. Contained within the hemisphere is a temple. Following on is a large courtyard with peristyle flanked by living accommodation on the northwest—the southeast has not been excavated—and beyond is a second courtyard with fishponds surrounded by the summer quarters, with some fragments of mosaic still in place. To the northwest of the large courtyard is the thermal wing, the most complete section, comprising nymphaeum, piscina, hypocaust, hot and cold baths, a garden surrounded by slender columns, and a pergola facing out towards the landscape.

In the village, the very modest **museum** of Montmaurin next to the *mairie* is devoted to the prehistory and Gallo-Roman history of the area which includes the 30,000-year-old Mandibule de Montmaurin, the jawbone of a Palaeolithic man of the Aurignacian period found near Aurignac in 1949.

Towards Toulouse, south of junction 20 on the A64, is **Monsaunès**, the site of an important Templar commandery founded in 1156. The Romanesque chapel in stone and brick still stands, its west doorway decorated with scenes of the *Crucifixion of St Peter*, the *Stoning of St Stephen*, the *Raising of Lazarus* and *Christ and the Apostles*, and inside are murals of the same period. Nearby **Salies-du-Salat** is the second most important spa town in the Comminges.

To visit what little remains *in situ* of the former abbey of Notre-Dame at **Bonnefont-en-Comminges**, turn off the motorway onto the D81 heading north and follow the signs. An effort is being made to revitalise the abbey in this remote place. Founded in 1136, it was the most important Cistercian abbey in the Comminges and became the burial place of the Counts of Comminges. Still standing is the wing reserved for the lay brothers.

St-Martory, nearby on the D117, spans the Garonne at the crossroads between St-Lizier and St-Bertrand. It once used its natural resources to manufacture paper. St-Martory was the birthplace of Norbert Casteret (1897–1987), speleologist and co-pioneer of pot-holing in France. In 1931 he confirmed the source of the Garonne as the Pic d'Aneto in Spain. Among his important discoveries in the vicinity, an area riddled with grottoes, were drawings and the oldest statues in the world at Montespan, southwest of St-Martory (closed to the public), in 1923. The church on the north of the river is difficult to visit because traffic hurtles through on the main road, so park on the south and cross the three-arched bridge, built in 1724, which has preserved its monumental toll gate decorated with the French cockerel and Louis XIV's sun emblem. A menhir and Gallo-Roman funerary stele are erected near the remodelled church of 1387, which has a 12C marble font, a Romanesque door from Bonnefont and a 16C terracotta *Pietà*.

Aurignac, to the north by the N117 and D635, is a pretty village on the ridge of a hill. Over the town gate is a Flamboyant belfry and the 15C church porch has rare cabled columns from the Crucifix chapel demolished in 1791. The capitals are cubic inside and hexagonal outside. Discoveries of bones and other objects in nearby caves, 1.2km away on the D635, were made in 1860–61 by Edouard Lartet and marked an important advance in research on Cro-Magnon man. The Aurignacian period (30–27,000 BC) saw the appearance of figurative art and the Musée de la Préhistoire devotes a section to the subject and includes a copy of the small (14.7cm) but curvaceous Venus of Lespugue. Open July, Aug 09.30–12.00 and 14.00–18.00; rest of year Mon–Fri 09.00–12.00 and 14.00–18.00; ☎ 05 61 98 90 08.

A sign on the road between Aurignac and Alan to the east leads you to the unique sight of an extraordinarily well-conserved **Gallo-Roman piscina** in a bucolic farmyard. Call at the farm house.

Alan, on the D10 midway between St-Bertrand-de-Comminges and Toulouse, was the excellent choice in 1270 of the Bishops of Comminges as the site of a residence. Successive bishops left their mark on the buildings over five centuries, and time has taken its toll, but there are some reminders of past glories. Open mid-June–mid-Oct 10.00–12.00 and 15.00–19.00; ☎ 05 61 98 71 12. Jean-Baptiste de Foix-Grailly, elected in 1470, undertook major revisions including a monumental Flamboyant porch adorned with the Béarn cow from his coat of arms. The palace was saved in 1969 by the opera singer Richard Gaillan, and is used for concerts and exhibitions. On the large square in the village is a 13C–15C church and the *halle*, which has been restored.

A kilometre south of Alan, the **Hôpital Notre-Dame de Lorette** was built by Bishop du Bouchet in 1734 to care for the sick. Privately owned and lovingly restored, the pharmacy, cloister and chapel can be visited on Sunday afternoons. It is also an unusual place to stay in a *gite* (see Where to stay, p 490); ☎ 05 61 98 98 84.

THE VOLVESTRE AND THE LAURAGAIS

The Volvestre derives its name from a Celtic tribe, the Volques, who settled around Toulouse about 2000 years ago, and refers to the valleyed region southwest of Toulouse, lying midway between the plain and the mountains. The Garonne flows northeast through to the Toulousain and, on and off between 1259 and 1453, marked the border between Languedoc and English Guyenne.

The Lauragais, east of Toulouse, follows the corridor between the Pyrenees and the Montagne Noire (Black Mountains) and the route to the Mediterranean, and is crossed by the Canal du Midi. It is an undulating and fertile land with a particular windswept charm. The wide, exposed valley is frequently buffeted by the *vent d'autan*, the southwesterly wind which dries the land and reputedly drives its people mad. The wind was once harnessed and put to work through windmills, most now abandoned, usually sail-less, often headless, and sometimes just skeletons. The Lauragais had many Cathar communities in the 12C and 13C. In the next centuries, *pastel* (woad) was intensively cultivated in the valley; it brought wealth to the region generally and huge fortunes to some individuals (see p 331). By the mid-16C imported indigo took the place of *pastel*, and by the 17C maize was extensively grown in the Lauragais.

Getting there and around
Car
From Toulouse, follow N117 southwest or N113 southeast.
Train
Toulouse to Carcassonne, via Bram, Castelnaudary, Avignonet.
Bus
Castelnaudary to Sorèze via Revel.

 ## Tourist information
31290 Avignonet-Lauragais Place de la République, ☎ 05 61 81 63 67, fax 05 61 81 15 83
31390 Carbonne 3 Rue Jean-Jaurès, ☎ 05 61 87 59 03, fax 05 61 87 47 51
31220 Cazères-sur-Garonne 13 Rue de la Case, ☎ 05 61 90 06 81, fax 05 61 90 16 43
31220 Martres-Tolosane Blvd du Nord, ☎ 05 61 98 66 41, fax 05 61 98 59 29, email matres@libertysurf.fr
31600 Muret 48 Rue Clément-Ades, ☎/fax 05 62 23 05 03, www.ot-muret.com.
31310 Montesquieu-Volvestre 20 Pl. de la Halle, ☎ 05 61 90 19 55, fax 05 61 90 19 55

31310 Rieux-Volvestre 9 Rue de l'Evêche, ☎/fax 05 61 87 63 33, http://tourisme-volvestre.com

Market days
Caraman Thursday
Carbonne Thursday, Saturday
Cazères Saturday
Montesquieu-Volvestre Tuesday
Muret Tuesday, Saturday
Nailloux Wednesday
Revel Saturday
Rieux-Volvestre Tuesday
Saint-Martory Friday
Villefranche-de-Lauragais Friday

Cruises on the Canal du Midi
31290 Avignonet-Lauragais *Bateau Lucie*, ☎ 05 68 60 15 98, pleasure cruises
31290 Gardouch *Les Croisières en Douce*, le Surcouf, ☎ 05 61 27 14 77 pleasure cruises/restaurant
31450 Montesquieu Lauragais *Locaboat Plaisance*, Ecluse de Négra, ☎ 05 61 81 36 40, houseboats for hire
31250 Revel Pl. Centrale, Pl. Philippe VI-de-Valois, ☎ 05 34 55 67 68, fax 05 34 66 67 67, www.revel-lauragais.com
31540 St-Félix-Lauragais Pl. G.-de-

Nogaret, ☎ 05 62 18 96 99, fax 05 62 18 90 84

31170 Tournefeuille *Société Sunshine Cruisers*, 20 Rue des Martinets, ☎ 06 10 28 88 08. Boat hire

31290 Villefranche-de-Lauragais Sq. Charles-de-Gaulle, ☎/fax 05 61 27 20 94

 Festivals and events

April *Foîre à la cocagne*, tribute to the pastel industry, St-Félix-Lauragais

May *Fêtes du Papogay*, traditional competition to shoot down a wooden bird, Rieux-Volvestre

June *Foîre de Messidor*, includes the eating of a giant *cassoulet*, Nailloux

July *Regates*, regatta, Cazères-sur-Garonne

 Where to stay and eating out

31410 NOÉ

☆☆ *L'Arche de Noé*, 2 Pl. de la Bascule, ☎ 05 61 87 40 12, 05 61 87 06 67. A little haven of greenery and peace close to A64.

41310 ST-SULPICE-SUR-LÈZE

€€ *La Commanderie*, 11 Pl. de la Mairie, ☎ 05 61 97 33 61. Attractive and highly recommended.

31250 REVEL

☆☆ *Midi*, 34 Blvd Gambetta, ☎ 05 61 83 50 50, fax 05 61 83 34 74. Hotel-restaurant in an early 19C building with garden. Seasonal local cooking.

31290 VILLEFRANCHE-DE-LAURAGAIS

☆☆/€ *Hotel de France*, 106 Rue de la République, ☎ 05 61 81 62 17, fax 05 61 88 66 04. Particularly recommended as a place to sample a really good *cassoulet*.

09230 FABAS

Chambres d'hôte, Margit Honné and Hans Georg, Château de Poudelay (5km from ste-Croix Volvestre), ☎ 05 61 66 88 86, fax 05 61 66 89 07, www.ifrance.com/poudelay. An absolutely stunning château where Napoléon III frequently stayed, with views and beautiful surroundings.

The Volvestre: Garonne and Lèze valleys

Muret, on the west bank of the Garonne, is now virtually part of greater Toulouse but was once the administrative capital of the Comminges (see p 489).

A decisive battle was fought here during the Albigensian Crusades between the combined forces of Raymond VI, Count of Toulouse and his opportunist brother-in-law Peter II of Aragon, against the crusading army of Simon de Montfort, representing the French king and the pope. On 12 September 1213 the defending army suffered a crushing defeat and Peter of Aragon was killed, giving de Montfort the opportunity to enter Toulouse.

Muret was an important stage on the pilgrim route to Santiago, but the 12C church of St-Jacques was remodelled in brick in the 14C and 16C and endowed with a two-tier Toulousain-style octagonal belfry. It has preserved the 12C chapel of the Rosary where St Dominic is said to have meditated on the eve of the battle of Muret, and it also contains some good furnishings. The aviation pioneer, Clement Ader (1841–1925), was born in Muret and there is a museum dedicated to him in the *mairie*. When the weather is clear there are fantastic views of the Pyrenees as you head south.

The D4 and D919 follows the Lèze Valley. **St-Sulpice-sur-Lèze** was one of many *bastides* founded by Alphonse de Poitiers. This stunning little town is built entirely in brick, and the Place de l'Hôtel-de-Ville is one of the most impressive of its kind, surrounded by arcades and timber-framed houses. A block from the square is the former church of the Hospitallers (1450–80), more interesting outside than in, with an elaborate octagonal belfry with mitred two-bay windows and a crocketed brick spire. The interior is reached by a long covered corridor running along the north wall. The southwest chapel off the aisleless nave does, however, have the remains of a late 15C/early 16C fresco of the *Last Judgement*.

Crossing into the Département d'Ariège, **Lézat-sur-Lèze** further south is also a pleasant market-town with a small brick *halle*, 14C–16C timber-framed houses and a church with a weatherbeaten Romanesque west porch and some 15C and 16C frescoes.

On a ridge between the Lèze and Arize valleys southeast of Montesquieu-Volvestre is **Carla-Bayle**, a tidy little town with a wide view. The medieval stronghold became a Huguenot bastion and suffered heavily during the Wars of Religion. In the 18C the community of Carla-le-Comte actively supported the Revolution and became Carla-le-Peuple, acquiring its present suffix in 1879 in tribute to its most famous son, Pierre Bayle. Bayle's birthplace houses the Musée Pierre Bayle, an excellent little museum retracing his life and work, and one of the best Protestant museums in the region. The house is arranged around an interior courtyard and the collection includes documents, engravings and acerbic cartoons. It also reconstructs Pierre Bayle's study and a kitchen of the period. Open mid-June–mid-Sept 10.00–12.00 and 15.00–19.00; mid-Sept–mid-June by appointment 14.00–18.00; ☎ 05 61 68 51 32.

Pierre Bayle

Bayle (1647–1706) was a Protestant philosopher and the author of *Pensées sur la comète* and *Dictionnaire historique et critique* (1696–97). He was the victim of anti-Protestant persecution and settled with a French community in Rotterdam, where he published his works, in October 1681. His self-imposed exile saved him but not his brother, who was imprisoned and executed because of Bayle's publications. His famous plea for freedom of conscience—'*C'est donc la tolérance qui est la source de la paix et l'intolérance qui est la source de la confusion et du grabuge*' ('It is tolerance that is the source of peace and intolerance that is the source of confusion and mayhem')—pre-empted John Locke's ideas and announced the spirit of the 18C, but his liberalism also led to conflict with fellow Protestants.

Round the corner from the museum is the Protestant Temple which can be visited; ask at the museum. Indistinguishable from the other houses from outside, it is a simple galleried hall with two spiral staircases, benches, an ancient stove, a piano and a wooden table. The pulpit in the centre is inscribed *Gij zijt Gods tempel, I Cor. 3.16* (Ye are the Temple of God). The date over the porch of the Catholic church is 1687; the date of the Revocation of the Edict of Nantes was 1685.

In the Montagnes de Plantaurel on the winding D119 (off the D919) is **Mas d'Azil**, a pleasant *bastide* with a small museum of prehistory next to the church (18C). Open July, Aug 10.00–18.00; April–June, Sept 10.00–12.00 and 14.00–18.00; ☎ 61 69 97 22. In the vicinity are dolmens and megaliths.

The site is most famous, however, for the vast natural tunnel carved through the limestone range of the Plantaurel by the Arize, the **Grotte du Mas d'Azil**, where primeval man, Cathars and Calvinists all apparently took refuge. Now the D119 disappears into the yawning black hole in the side of the hill: this is particularly disconcerting if you are arriving from the south. The caverns were inhabited by a succession of groups of early man who left reminders of their occupation—some of these are on display as part of the visit. There are tools and bones of the Magdalenian period and harpoons and coloured pebbles of Azilien man, named after the location. The vast, dark, dry cavern, on three levels, is itself less interesting than the artefacts, as it has no fantastic mineral formations. Nevertheless the landscape is green and undulating.

Back in the Haute Garonne, where the Arize meets the Garonne, is the *bastide* of **Carbonne**, founded *c* 1256 by Alphonse de Toulouse in *paréage* with the abbey of Bonnefont (p 499). The principal monument is the 14C church of St-Laurent east of the town near the Garonne, restored in the 19C, with a three-stage belfry and a huge porch with crocketed gable sheltering a fine 14C portal: it is usually closed. Near the church is the former home of sculptor André Abbal, whose works are exhibited in the very attractive gardens as well as inside. Open in summer Tues–Sun 10.00–12.00 and 15.00–19.00; in winter also closed Sat, Sun 14.00–18.00.

Rieux-Volvestre

The most attractive of the brick towns of the Volvestre, bordering the meandering Arize, is Rieux-Volvestre. Rieux was given a diocese in 1317 by the beneficent Cadurcien Pope John XXII, and the Franciscan bishop Jean Tissendier rebuilt the **Cathédrale Ste-Marie** in brick in the second quarter of the 14C, incorporating the nave and chancel of earlier edifices. The refined, almost stark, elevations are mitigated by the use of brick and the surrounding water and greenery. The roof, resting on the *mirandes*, has a wide overhang to protect the walls. The sophisticated octagonal belfry, the pride and joy of Rieux, is a variation on the theme of the Jacobins church in Toulouse, its tall lower level composed of blind arches surmounted with stone quatrefoils. Each angle of the octagon is outlined by an engaged column in pink marble, the three upper stages each set back from the level below, with traditional two-light bays under mitred arches, the whole crowned with a balustrade but no spire. There is a Flamboyant entrance portal on the south with the wooden Renaissance door still in place.

The interior gives a feeling of space and has an unusual arrangement with three large chapels on the north and none on the south. The nave and choir of the older church were incorporated and more modifications were carried out in the 17C during the time of the three bishops Bertier, when two chapels and the choir were rebuilt. There are some good carved choir stalls (17C), a gilded Virgin (15C), St Sebastian carved in stone (16C), and a polychrome marble retable (18C).

The most important treasure of Ste-Marie is the unique 17C **reliquary bust of St Cizi**. This effigy of the Roman fighter of Sarrasins and patron of the town was made in 1671/2 by Pierre Desnos of Toulouse, in wood plated with 5kg of silver. The treasury also contains other reliquaries including a bust of St Sebastian and a vast collection of richly embroidered chasubles in desperate need of restoration. Guided visits only to church and treasures, July, Aug daily

10.30, 15.00, 17.00, except Wed evening and Sun morning; mid-Nov–mid-April Mon–Sat 10.30, 14.30, 15.45; other times daily except Sun 10.30, 14.30, 16.15.

Rieux has celebrated the festival of Papogay ('Parrot') with an archery competition since the 14C (see above). Its patron, predictably, is St Sebastian. The village has a number of old streets and timber-framed houses as well as a covered market and is worth an extended visit. The **Musée de Papogay**, is a small museum (enter via tourist office) of local history and traditions including a room dedicated to the Tir au Papogay. Open July, Aug daily 10.00–12.00 and 14.00–19.00 (closed Sun morning); Nov–April, Mon–Sat 10.00–13.00 and 14.00–17.00; other times to 18.00.

Montesquieu-Volvestre, to the south on the D627, is a *bastide* of 1246, founded by the counts of Toulouse near an existing château on the banks of the Arize. Protected by the verdant slopes of the Plantaurel range, it has been the most important town of the Volvestre since 1317. A brick town with a regular layout, its best features are the covered market on 20 octagonal pillars and the Gothic (14C–16C) church opposite, dedicated to St Victor, whose relics it once claimed to own. This has a massive, gabled west elevation and a tall belfry that is a 15C interpretation of the usual 13C/14C Toulousain model, on the south side. The tempo is doubled, so that it has 16 rather than the usual eight sides, each face with a narrow lancet window. The grand Renaissance portal in stone (1552), inset into the blind central arch, is flanked by fluted Corinthian columns. Inside are a number of interesting pieces, including an *Entombment* group (16C) in painted stone, a wooden *Crucifixion* (15C) and, in the northeast, an *Adoration of the Shepherds and the Magi* (16C) painted on wood. There is a Baroque pulpit and a painting by Despax of the *Martyrdom of St Victor* (18C). The crypt was rediscovered in 1983 and restored; there is a light on the left pillar. It was built *c* 1390 and blocked up in 1747, and contains four reliquary busts.

Cazères-sur-Garonne

Back on the Garonne, Cazères-sur-Garonne is a cheerful town on a wide expanse of the river in the foothills of the Pyrenees.

The Gallo-Roman town of St-Cizy developed on the road linking Toulouse and Dax. It belonged to the Comminges in the 12C before coming under the control of the Counts of Toulouse and benefited from the rights of passage to traders and pilgrims across the river between Languedoc and Foix, and from a long tradition of shipping.

From the D10 you arrive north of the old town, which is on a promontory above the left bank of the river, enclosed in modern boulevards. The tourist office is to the northwest of the old centre, installed in **La Case de Montserrat**, a timber-framed house built in 1547. Purchased by the Benedictine abbey of Montserrat in Spain, it was used by the Procurer General of Montserrat who travelled in France and beyond collecting donations to cover the costs, for three months, of pilgrims on the road to Montserrat and Santiago.

The church of **Notre-Dame-de-Cazères** was built in the 14C and until 1795 had a very different west end from the one it has now; the upper part was demolished by order of the Convention and the present unusual façade dates from 1885–96. The church has a long history as the centre of a Marian cult associated with a spring on the banks of the Garonne. It has a large and varied collection of furnishings and religious art, most of them exhibited in the Baptistery room. Most notable are the Romanesque font in stone, on a Gothic base, a superb 17C retable from the Capuchin monastery, with a *Pietà* attributed to François Lucas, and a number of reliquaries. The Notre-Dame chapel contains a large retable with 18C paintings.

Opposite the church is the metal *halle* of 1904 with statues (1905) at either end by Frédéric Tourte, an assistant to Bourdelle, symbolising the principal agricultural activities of the region at the time. The road alongside the church, Rue Ste-Quitterie, marks the primitive *cité* and crosses the Hourride, where there is a fountain of 1562, to bring you via Rue Massenet to the Promenade du Campet overlooking the Garonne. At the foot of the church is the **Grotte de Notre-Dame-de-Cazères**, an oratory erected in 1630 following a plague epidemic. To the south, next to the bridge, is the old wooden boathouse. Cazères had an important boat-building industry, especially at the end of the 19C, and the last boat, a trawler, left this workshop in 1948 to go to Sète on the Mediterranean. The very attractive 19C bridge, rebuilt after the floods in 1875, has recently been restored. Follow Boulevard P.-Gouzy away from the bridge. In Rue des Capucins is the **Capuchin monastery** (1612–19) with a cloister of 1717, which can be visited.

From Cazères the D10 passes southwest, under an arch of the ramparts of the 16C château (no admission) in the 13C *bastide* of **Palaminy**.

Martres-Tolosane is a small town with a circular centre and houses with bulging old pebbly walls. It is best known for its *faïenceries d'art* (hand-painted earthenware), and for six local Gallo-Roman villas which have offered up the best antique statuary in the region, most of which is at the Musée St-Raymond in Toulouse. Martres has a Musée Archéologique in the 13C keep in Rue du Donjon, although many of its exhibits are copies of those in Toulouse. Open July–Sept daily 10.00–12.30 and 14.30–18.00.

The priory (*c* 1000) was replaced by the brick church of St-Vidian or Notre-Dame-des-Martyrs, consecrated in 1309; the belfry was rebuilt in 1865. There are a number of pieces of ancient stone and marble re-employed in the walls, and two sarcophagi in Pyrenean marble at the west end of the nave. The portal from the Romanesque church is incorporated into the chapel of St-Vidian, inside which are a Flamboyant altar and the saint's relics. A colourful reminder of the battle between the Christians and the infidels, when virtuous Vidian was slain, is a re-enactment on the first Sunday after Whitsun. There is plenty of pottery on sale in the town and at its seven workshops; *Association des Faïenciers*, 15 Rue de Matet; ☎ 05 61 98 81 30.

The Lauragais and the Canal du Midi

The N20 runs south of Toulouse following the Ariège Valley. At **Vernet**, which has a pretty church with a belfry gable in regional style, cross the river on the D74. Of the Romanesque Benedictine abbey-church of St-Pierre in **Venerque**, only a part of the east end has survived. It was enlarged in brick in the 14C–15C to accommodate pilgrims who came to venerate the shrine of St Phébarde and it has a 12C reliquary. The belfry was gradually transformed into a defensive tower or keep, and at the end of the 19C the upper part of the church was heavily restored and battlemented. There are some Romanesque capitals, but the lower sections of those of the St-Phébarde chapel and around the entrance are faithful 19C copies of the west door of St-Sernin in Toulouse. It is possible that the wrought iron around the font was originally part of the 18C screen dividing the choir and nave.

The eating of a giant *cassoulet* (see p 508) is part of the Foîre de Messidor, held annually at **Nailloux** between the Ariège and the Canal on the D622. In the town is a Gothic church in brick with a belfry gable of five bays between two polygonal towers; in the centre of the town is a windmill.

Montgeard just to the south is a small *bastide* founded in 1319 on a slope dominating the plains of the Lauragais. A *pastel* baron, Durand de Montgeard, was the principal benefactor of the brick church which was modelled on St-Cécile in Albi. The west tower with rounded buttresses was built in 1561, although the upper part is modern and the narthex has sculpted stone inserts. The interior is rendered and painted in splendid *trompe l'oeil* on a blue background, the ribs, tiercerons and bosses in gold, red and green. The elegant alabaster font is dated 1516, and there are four Renaissance alabaster reliefs—on the southwest wall, in the two chapels near the altar and above the pulpit—of the **Assumption**, St Catherine, the **Coronation of the Virgin** and the **Mystical Throne**. In the village a small 16C château was built by the same Durand, who bought his seigneurial rights from Catherine de Médicis, Countess of Lauragais. Open April–Oct, Sat, Sun, and PH 10.30–18.30; rest of year check times; ☎ 05 61 81 52 75. A watchtower of the same period, on the angle of a wall at the end of a path alongside the grounds of a 17C house, was built to survey the precious fields of *pastel*.

The main, or only, reason to stop in **Villefranche-de-Lauragais**, further east across the canal, would be to eat *cassoulet*.

The fame of **Avignonet-Lauragais** on the N113, standing sentinel over the valley, rests on an incident on 28 May 1242, when a group of about 60 armed men commanded by Pierre-Roger de Mirepoix descended from the Cathar stronghold of Montségur (p 515). Aided and abetted by the locals, they avenged the persecution of heretics by slaughtering all the members of the recently installed Inquisition, including Inquisitors Guillaume Arnaud and Etienne de Saint Thibery. As a consequence the fate of Montségur, the last Cathar sanctuary, was sealed and early in 1243 the Council of Béziers decided to destroy it. A small, severe church (end 14C) in yellowy-pink stone dominates the little town. Its rectangular tower supports an octagonal belfry with simple two-light windows topped off by a small crocketed spire. There are fragments of the 13C and 15C ramparts, so-called Cathar crosses, and the narrow Tour de Ravelin (1352), originally a prison, with the statue of a warrior.

At the intersection of the autoroute and the canal, at **Port-Lauragais**, the motorway service area contains the Centre Pierre-Paul Riquet, with a permanent exhibition and information on the Canal. Southeast of Port-Lauragais on the D80a is the obelisk which indicates the highest point on the canal, the **Col de Naurouze** (189m).

The Canal du Midi

Although an overland trade route had crossed the valley for more than 1000 years, carrying goods from the Mediterranean to Toulouse and on to the Atlantic via the Garonne, the problem of transporting increasing quantities of grain from the Toulousain to the Languedoc arose in the 17C. It was solved by Pierre-Paul Riquet's great engineering feat, the Canal Royal du Languedoc, now called the Canal du Midi. Louis XIV's minister Colbert obtained royal approval for Riquet's scheme in 1666 and work began in 1667. In less than 14 years, 240km of canal was dug by a workforce of 12,000 head (three women equalled two heads). Over 60 locks, single, double and multiple, coped with the considerable slopes, and water was channeled from a reservoir at St-Ferréol in the Montagne Noire to Naurouze, the highest point, from where the canal flowed downhill in each direction. Riquet died, exhausted and penniless, in 1680, a year before the canal's completion. In 1856 the Canal Latéral à la Garonne (see p 259) was realised and canal barges could make the entire journey to Bordeaux, instead of off-loading at Toulouse on to river craft. Shortly afterwards rail transport replaced the canal and in the 20C the Autoroute de Deux Mers (A61) was built to follow the same route.

On a high vantage-point on the D622, north of the N113, the 13C *bastide* of **St-Félix-Lauragais** offers a splendid view east to the Montagne Noire and south to the Pyrenees. In the manner of most *bastides*, the focal point of the town is the central marketplace and it still possesses an *halle* with a belltower. Around the square are timbered houses and in front of the tourist office is a rare specimen of a *pastel* plant. The importance of the *pastel* tradition is celebrated around Easter (see above). The 14C–19C church has a Flamboyant porch and an 18C organ. Next to it is the former canons' house with a sculpted door and four-square windows and further along, opposite the market, is the 17C–19C house where the composer Déodate de Séverac (1873–1921) was born. On the north of the village, overlooking the plain, is the château dating from the 12C to the 18C, which hosted the first Cathar synod in 1167 in the presence of the Cathar Bishop Nicétas.

Les Cassés, south of St-Felix, stands above the *rigole*, the channel which brings water from the dam at St-Ferréol to the Naurouze basin to feed the Canal. Like so many isolated villages in the region, Les Cassés harboured Cathars, 50 of whom were burned at the stake by Simon de Montfort in 1211.

The largest town in the Lauragais is **Revel**, east of St-Félix on the D622, a *bastide* founded in 1342 by Philippe VI who laid down in the charter the dimensions of the houses and the length of time allowed to erect them. The huge 14C *halle* (now housing the tourist office) in Place Philippe VI-de-Valois has ancient roof timbers around a central stone building with Serlian windows and a lantern belfry. The houses that surround the *place* are mainly 18C and 19C, and the result of constant remodelling. The *bastide* was originally contained within hexagonal walls but these were demolished in 1629, and the exterior boulevards follow the same pattern.

Revel has been the capital of quality reproduction furniture, marquetry and all associated crafts since 1888 when a specialist cabinetmaker from Versailles,

Alexandre Monoury, settled here and opened a school. The Conservatoire des Métiers du Bois in Rue Moulin is an exhibition which follows the process from tree to *objet d'art*; check opening times at the tourist office. Samples of modern cabinetmaking can be seen at Espace Art et Meuble on the Castres road.

St-Julia, on the D1 west of Revel, is also known as Gras-Capou ('Fat Chick'), a reference to the capons reared here since time immemorial and sold on the Sunday before Christmas. Part of the fortifications still stand with a 16C gateway. The 14C church, restored by Marguerite de Valois, has a beautfiul *clocher-pignon* (a belfry that extends from a gable) with five arcades containing the oldest bell (1396) in Haute-Garonne. Perched on an escarpment protecting the border with the Albigeois, the little *cité* of **Caraman** further west on the D1 is the ancient capital of the *pays de Cocagne*. Southwest of Caraman, on the D11 at Caragoudes, are windmills.

Northeast of Caraman, near the N126, the pretty village of **Loubens-Lauragais**, has an interesting château and park which has been owned by the same family since 1096 and was remodelled in the 16C. Open May, June, Sun and PH; July, first and last Sun; Aug, Thurs, Fri, Sat and Sun; Sept–mid-Nov, Sun and PH 14.30–18.30; ☎ 05 61 83 12 08.

24 Ariège-Pyrénées

The Ariège-Pyrénées is a rugged and sparsely populated land, which catches the winds and the sun of the Mediterranean and the imagination with its decorated caves, tales of large and tenacious Cathar communities and ancient châteaux. It benefits from the natural advantages of mineral water springs and an abundance of wildlife, shelters rustic Romanesque churches, and is the home of hydro-electricity. There are endless opportunities for exploration on foot, by bike or on horseback. A new autoroute links Toulouse to Pamiers and the high-speed N20 runs to to Foix, Ax-le-Thermes and the border with Andorra and Spain via the Puymorens tunnel.

BASSE ARIÈGE: VALS, MIREPOIX, MONTSÉGUR

The valley of the Hers in the Basse Ariège crosses the Pré-Pyrénées, a lower (1000m), parallel range to the Pyrenees proper, consisting of the Plantaurel hills and the Monts d'Olmes. Without the obvious attractions of the high ranges, it still provides many vistas of great beauty enhanced by fields of golden sunflowers in July, and a number of interesting towns and villages. There were numerous Cathar hideouts in this area, close to Carcassonne, the most famous of which is Montségur.

Getting there and around

Car

From Toulouse, A61 and A66 to Mazères; or the N20 to Saverdun. Carcassonne to Mirepoix, A61 exit 22; Pamiers to Mirepoix, D119.

Train

TER from Toulouse to Latour-de-Carol via Pamiers and Foix.

Bus

Lavalenet to Foix, Chalabre, Saverdun; Mazères to Pamiers, Les Pujols.

 Tourist information

09300 Bélesta ☎ 05 61 01 60 02, fax 05 61 03 50 40
09500 Camon ☎ 05 61 68 88 26, fax 05 61 68 12 07, http://mairiecamon. ifrance.com
09300 Lavalenet Maison de Lavalevet, BP 89, ☎ 05 61 01 22 20, fax 05 61 03 55 09, email lavalet.tourisme@ wanadoo.fr
09270 Mazères Vallée d l'Hers, Mairie, ☎ 05 61 69 31 02, fax 05 61 69 37 97
09500 Mirepoix Pl. du Maréchal Leclerc, ☎ 05 61 68 83 76, fax 05 61 58 89 48, www.ot-mirepoix.fr
09300 Montségur ☎ 05 61 03 03 03, www.monsegur.org

Market days

Bélesta Tuesday
Lavalenet Wednesday (small), Friday
Mazères Thursday
Mirepoix Monday; Thursday farmers' market
Monségur Sunday pm July, August

Festivals and events

June Summer solstice, Montségur

July–August *Festival International de la Marionette*, Mirepoix
Au Pays de Martin Guerre ... Garils le Gros, open-air theatre, Gabre
August *Médievales de Mazères*, the town rediscovers its medieval past in colourful and animated celebration, Mazères
November *Jazz'Velanet*, Lavelanet

 Where to stay and eating out
09500 MIREPOIX

✳✳✳ *La Maison des Consuls*, ☎ 05 61 68 81 81, fax 05 61 58 81 15. Small hotel with modern rooms in a 14C house.
09700 MONTAUD
Chambres d'hôte, M. et Mme Maes, Domaine de Pégulier (3.5km from Saverdun), ☎/fax 05 61 68 30 65, www.ifrance.com/pegulier. Chill out and relax in an elegant 18C mansion with exceptional surroundings; heated pool.
09300 MONTFERRIER
€€ *Le Castrum*, ☎ 05 61 01 35 24. Top-quality restaurant serving variations on tradtional regional cooking and fish dishes.
09500 RIEUCROS
Chambres d'hôte, Magali Bagros, Domaine de Marlas, ☎ 05 61 69 29 88. Five rooms decorated very prettily in this vast property with pool.
Chambres d'hôte, Alain and Nicole Meunier, Les Volets Bleus, ☎/fax 05 61 96 68 55, www.ariege.com/ lesvoletsbleus. You will receive a warm welcome at this house set in the middle of a luxuriant garden; two rooms available.

Southeast of Toulouse, and north of Pamiers on the D11, is **Mazères**, founded in 1253 by the neighbouring abbey of Boulbonne. It was one of the main *bastides* in the Basse Ariège, in the territory of the medieval Counts of Foix, powerful vassals of and rivals to the Counts of Toulouse. The château of Mazères was the favourite residence of Gaston Fébus, the legendary Count of Foix (see below), where he grandiosely entertained the French King Charles VI in 1390. Palace and abbey were destroyed by the Protestants during the Wars of Religion in the

16C. Consequently Mazères presents a post-Reformation face, its 17C and 18C houses and market influenced by the brick buildings of Toulouse. The one notable exception is the Renaissance Hôtel d'Ardouin, built *c* 1580 for a *pastel* merchant and now transformed into the Musée de Vieux Mazères, the history of *pastel* and Gaston Fébus, among other things. Open Sunday mid-June–mid-Sept 15.00–18.00; ☎ 05 61 69 42 04. The Gothic church has a Neo-classical façade.

The D525 southwest of Belpech takes you past the mainly 17C Château de Gaudiès and close to **St-Félix-de-Tournegat**, a fortified village whose rebuilt Romanesque church (part 11C–12C) has an extraordinary *clocher-peigne*.

South of St-Félix on the D40 is the tiny hamlet of **Vals**, in a rural setting, with a small but sensational *église rupestre* (church hewn out of the rock). One of the most ancient churches in the Midi, **Sainte-Marie** was erected at the site of a Celtic *oppidum* and pagan temple and is built into a small mound of pudding-stone. At the west end the tower-keep stands proud above ground. Adding to the drama, the entrance to the sanctuary is through a natural cleft in the rock into which 23 steps are carved, leading up to the crypt-like nave of a 10C sanctuary, part-natural, part-manmade. To the east, on a slightly higher level, is the flat-ended barrel-vaulted 11C apse. This is decorated with 12C paintings discovered in 1956; there is a light switch left of the steps. Influenced stylistically by Catalonia, the paintings are executed primarily in red and black pigment, complemented by grey, yellow and white. The theme of Christ's birth is represented in the east bay by the **Annunciation**, the **Nativity** (where the Virgin is covered by a cloth decorated with circular medallions), the **Bathing of Jesus** and, in a fragment on the east wall, the **Adoration of the Magi**. In the vaults is the Christ of the **Last Judgement**, accompanied by the tetramorph and the Apostles two-by-two. On the north is the figure of Christ, his hand raised in blessing. The next level of the church has been much modified and has 19C plastered vaults. On the third level is a 12C chapel dedicated to St Michael which was transformed into a tower in the 14C. The large arch was opened later. Outside on the north wall is a discoidal cross, probably from the cemetery. An upper floor of one of the houses in the village has become a small archaeological museum of the area from prehistory to the 20C, exhibiting finds from the immediate vicinity. Church and museum open mid-May–mid-Sept; ☎ 05 61 68 88 26.

Mirepoix

The main town in the Pays d'Olmes, Mirepoix is a *bastide* with some exceptional characteristics. True to *bastide* format, it is laid out on a grid system around a central *place*, unusually planted with grass and rose bushes. This is just the spot to relax with a glass of Blanquette de Limoux, sparkling wine from neighbouring Aude.

The first *bastide* was founded in 1207 by Raymond-Roger of Foix, but it harboured a great many Cathars and two years later was taken by Simon de Montfort, who dispossessed Pierre-Roger de Mirepoix and installed his own man, Guy de Lévis. In 1229 Guy became the King's representative for the region, a sensitive area between Toulouse and pockets of Cathar resistance in the mountains. The original *bastide* was on the right bank of the Hers: it was obviously too close to the river because in 1279, when the dam broke at Puivert 28km upstream, the village was completely washed away. Ten years later, a project to rebuild in a safer place on the left bank, near the castle and Benedictine chapel was decided and carried out by Jean, son of Guy. The layout of the town centre has not altered since the 13C, although a fire in 1380 destroyed many buildings and the houses date from the 14C onwards.

The first floors of houses extend over the public right of way around the square, supported by timber posts and lintels creating a *couvert* (arcade); several are decorated. Outstanding is the 15C or 16C **Maison des Consuls** on the north, its 25 joists sculpted at the extremities with a variety of strange animals and human heads. To the south side of the square is the covered market, an elegant turn-of-the-20th-century wrought-iron construction on slender columns.

The **Cathédrale St-Maurice**, in a large, shady square created in the 15C, is the third church on the site. The originality of the Gothic cathedral is its enormously wide nave, the second widest Gothic nave in Europe after Gerona in Spain. The problem of vaulting the 22m span was not resolved until the 19C when the church was finally completed.

The post-flood town encompassed a small Benedictine chapel which was rebuilt as a parish church in 1298, itself considered too modest when the Cadurcien Pope, John XXII, raised the status of Mirepoix to diocese in 1317. The first two bishops raised funds to build the chevet (1343–49), determining the ambitious dimensions of the nave, but work was interrupted from the mid-14C by the Hundred Years War. Building started again with the eighth bishop, Guillaume de Puy (1394–1433), and surged ahead from 1493 during the episcopate of Philippe de Lévis, who was responsible for four main constructions: the octagonal belfry with its crocketed spire; the episcopal palace contiguous with the church; the new west wall; and the Renaissance door on the south. He also built the episcopal chapel above the north entrance dedicated to St Agatha, and opened the three Flamboyant windows. When Philippe de Lévis died in 1537, activity ground to a halt until a long time after the suppression of the diocese. Only in 1858 were the walls of the chevet raised and the choir vaulted. Viollet-le-Duc advised on the second campaign of work (1861–67), when the chapels were pushed back to enlarge the nave by about 3.3m in order to line it up with the choir, and the later walls were raised.

The strange arrangement of gables above each face of the apse, as well as the flying buttresses and slate roof—both atypical of the region—are all 19C. The Flamboyant north entrance has sculpted capitals but has lost its statues. The wide aisleless nave is disproportionate to the height (24m) and length (48m), making the vaults appear to bear down on the space. The interior décor is mainly neo-Gothic and little is left of the earlier furnishings with the exception of a funerary statue of Constance de Foix, wife of Jean de Lévis; the 14C bosses of the choir chapels sculpted by the Master of Rieux; and a 14C polychrome wooden crucifix of Catalan origin. The pulpit is all that remains of the 15C wooden fittings made locally. Next to it is a gilded retable presenting the fifteen mysteries of the Rosary. The *Crucifixion*, by the Flemish painter Larivière Viscontius, in the St-Maurice chapel is the only surviving example from a series of seven works by this painter, heavily influenced by Velázquez. The episcopal chapel above the porch has a fine painted tile floor of 1530, the most precious part being the labyrinth, which the faithful followed on their knees, the last to be placed on the floor of a Western church. The cabled columns, part of the altar of this chapel, have been moved to the chapel of the Virgin. The glass is 19C, as is the organ.

On the west of the town is the **Porte d'Arval**, the last gate of the city defences left standing. There is a pleasant walk along Les Cours, a tree-lined avenue on the old city ditch filled with water from the Cantirrou, and a magnificent 18C bridge over the Hers.

The ruined **Château de Lagarde**, southeast via the D626 and D28, is a picturesque ruin evocative of its past splendour. The property passed to the Lévis family in 1215 and was rebuilt in 1330 by François de Lévis. Their descendants, the Lévis-Mirepoix, made frequent modifications as fashion or need dictated, but its fate was sealed at the Revolution when it was confiscated and badly damaged. To visit, ☎ 05 61 68 24 86.

Camon, south on the D7, is a golden and peaceful village in the green valley of the Hers on the Mediterranean side of the Ariège.

As so often, legend attributes the beginnings of the village to Charlemagne. More certain is that a Benedictine abbey existed here in 923, coming under the protection of the abbey of Lagrasse in the Aude in 943, and designated priory in 1068. The village developed as a *sauveté* or refuge around the abbey but this gave it no protection against devastation by the flood of 1279. It was rebuilt as a fortress at the end of the 13C, and was enclosed in fortifications (1360–85) during the Hundred Years War, although in 1494 the abbey and church were again destroyed. The village took its present form between 1503 and 1535 when the Bishop of Mirepoix, Philippe de Lévis, began another campaign of reconstruction, improving the living quarters in the great rectangular tower, which then became known as the château, and enclosing the village in an *enceinte*. The defences were amended (1560–70) during the Wars of Religion by Cardinal Georges d'Armagnac, Prior of Camon, but with the dissolution of the priory at the end of the 18C the château became private property.

The entrance to the village is through an elegant archway of 1684 with a clock, and an ancient bronze bell (1342) placed above it. The abbey, rebuilt in 1526, has a cloister, frescoed chapel and rooms with painted ceilings *à la française*. Open July, Aug 09.00–12.00 and 14.00–18.00. The château has a restaurant and snack bar and is used for temporary exhibitions. In the small garden is a medieval well and a 14C cross sculpted on both sides. The interior has some good features such as 16C tiles, 16C murals of mythological scenes in the former prelate's study, and a bedroom with 20C painted décor by a local artist, Mady de la Giraudière. The church was rebuilt by Philippe de Lévis and its embellishment was continued by successive priors in the 17C and 18C.

South of Camon between Léran and Montbel is a vast **lake**, covering 570ha, a welcome oasis in the summer for visitors and for migratory birds; ☎ 05 61 01 34 94. Just over the border in the *département* of Aude, southeast of Camon on the D12 from Chalabre, is the ruined **Château de Puivert**, beseiged by the Crusaders in 1210. On flat ground, this is one of the most accessible Cathar castles, with parts of its defences and the keep still standing.

To the west, **Lavalenet** has a curious museum of horn combs and textiles, traditional industries in the region. Open June–Sept 14.00–18.00; closed Sun and PH; ☎ 05 61 03 01 34. Further west by the D117 and D9 is the very ruined château of **Roquefixade**, which stands on a rocky outcrop above the valley. Argued over by the Counts of Toulouse and Foix, it became a French garrison only to be dismantled in 1632 after the Wars of Religion. It is possible to visit the little that is left; ☎ 05 61 01 55 02. The church of the *bastide* below has a notable gilded Baroque altarpiece (1727).

Montségur

The D109 and D9 run south of Lavalenet (or from Bélesta) through the village of Montferrier, with a local history museum, to the most celebrated of all the Cathar citadels, Montségur. Vertiginously perched at 1207m on a granite outcrop in the St-Barthélemy range it is visible from all around and is at its most impressively forbidding in winter. The site is one of the most stunning and the story the most legendary and moving of the whole saga of Cathar persecution

For about 40 years the rock had an exclusively Cathar population. The Cathars, who were never builders, had persuaded Raymond de Péreille, a local member of the lesser nobility sympathetic to their cause, to rebuild his ruined château *c* 1204. During the Albigensian Crusade (1209–29) Péreille's family occupied the keep and the Cathar population lived there in safety. With the annexation of Languedoc by France at the end of the Crusades, the region was put under the protection of a French governor, Guy de Lévis. In 1232 Guilhabert de Castres, the Cathar bishop, chose Montségur as a place of safety, bringing with him the elders of the Cathar Church and consequently elevating the site to the spiritual centre of the Cathar faith. The community grew to about 400 to 500 people, grouped around the château in a terraced village clinging to the rocky outcrop, probably with a complicated and extensive defensive system.

The site was not challenged until after 1240, when Raymond VII of Toulouse, reminded by the king of his undertaking to fight the Cathars, made a derisory attempt to take Montségur. The task was then assigned to the more resolute Seneschal of Carcassonne, Hugues des Arcis. The mounting crisis was compounded when, in 1242, Cathar knights slaughtered the Inquisitors at Avignonet in the Lauragais (see p 508). The fate of Montségur was sealed. In 1243 an army of some 1500 men was raised and, with the blessing of the Archbishop of Narbonne, Pierre Amiel, laid siege to Montségur in May. The defence of the refuge was commanded by Pierre-Roger de Mirepoix, one of Raymond de Péreille's henchmen. The defenders, supported by their faith, by a continuous stream of supplies made possible by weaknesses in the blockade, and above all by the difficulties posed by the steep mountain, held out for ten months. Gradually, however, conditions deteriorated for the Cathars and by Wednesday, 2 March 1244, a surrender was agreed and a 15-day truce negotiated, giving the faithful time to prepare for death by taking the *consolamentum* or last rites. On 16 March the château was evacuated and over 200 who refused to convert to Catholicism were burned at the stake for their heretical beliefs.

Guy II de Lévis became seigneur of the fiefdom of Montségur sometime after July 1245 and rebuilt most of the fortress, where a small garrison was installed until the end of the 15C. The village on the hill was demolished or left to decay. Mentioned once in 1510, the château and its story lay forgotten until in 1862 the ruins were classified as an historic monument and Napoléon Peyrat published his *Histoire des Albigeois* (1872), a romanticised version of the drama embellishing the legends of the site. A monument to those who were massacred was erected in 1960 at the foot of the mountain, and today the site attracts a huge number of visitors.

There is a car park at the foot of the hill. The climb to the top by a well-trodden track takes about half an hour and is not too difficult, though fairly steep in places. The **château** is an irregular shape, the longest of the five sides on the north, with the main entrance on the southwest and a smaller one opposite. Open daily May–Aug 09.00–19.30; Sept to 18.00; April and Oct 09.30–18.00; March and Nov 10.00–17.00; Feb 10.00–16.00; closed Jan; guided visits at peak periods; ☎ 05 61 01 06 94/05 61 01 10 27; www.montsegur.org.

The interior space, about 700 square metres, is enclosed by high walls built into the natural rock with no openings, only regularly spaced hollows to receive wooden building supports. There are three flights of stone steps up to the *chemin de ronde* and at the northwest extremity the keep, originally accessed from the upper floor by a wooden ladder, has a spiral stair in the southeast angle to the lower level. There are a few signs of rudimentary comfort, such as a fireplace, vaulted ceilings and windows, and in the western part of the ground floor was the cistern. The east wall is very thick, about 4.2m, with grooves made to contain beams to support the platform of a catapult.

The **village** is southeast of the citadel. The streets are very narrow; use the car park. It has a hotel and some eating places as well as the small **Musée de Montségur**. This contains explanations and information about the site, a model of Montségur at the time of the Cathars, and some of the best archaeological finds from local sites plus plenty of literature. Open daily May–Sept 10.30–12.00 and 14.00–18.00; Sept to 18.00; Oct–April, afternoons; ☎ 05 61 01 06 94.

Between Montségur and Bélesta, on the D9/D5, is the waterfall of **Fontestorbes**, an eccentric torrent with the singularly fascinating habit of gushing for 35mins (if there is enough water) then, once the reserve is empty, slowing down to a trickle for 25mins.

The universally famous but almost abandoned village of **Montaillou**, with just 12 residents, is to the south off the D613. The Cathar community established here in the Middle Ages was the subject of Emmanuel Le Roy Ladurie's book *Montaillou*, based on information contained in the Inquisition register of Jacques Fournier, Bishop of Pamiers, kept in the Vatican archives. A few houses, a rebuilt church and the ruined medieval château are, sadly, all that is left. The road climbs up over the Col de Chioula to Ax-les-Thermes (see below).

THE ARIÈGE VALLEY: PAMIERS, FOIX, NIAUX

The Ariège, in the southeast corner of the Midi-Pyrénées region, is the river from which the *département* takes its name. It flows northwards from its source in Andorra to join the Garonne south of Toulouse. The N20 follows this wide valley connecting the Toulousain with the Pyrenees, Andorra and Catalonia, with a tunnel under Puymorens. Here the climate is influenced by the Mediterranean and the landscape is of extremes.

Getting there and around
Car
Due south of Toulouse on the N20 or the E80/A61.
Train
TER from Paris Austerlitz and Toulouse to Foix.
TER from Toulouse to Latour-de-Carol via Pamiers and Foix.
Foix station, across the river from the town centre. Pamiers station is to the east of the town centre.
Bus
Toulouse to L'Hospitalet via Pamiers, Varilhes, Foix, Tarascon-sur-Ariège, Ax-les-Thermes, Mérens-les-Vals.
Between Foix and St-Girons; Serres-sur-Arget; Tarascon; Lavalenet; Pamiers and Auzat.

Tourist information
09000 Foix 29 Rue Delcassé, ☎ 05 61 65 12 12, fax 05 61 65 64 63, www.mairie-foix.fr
09103 Pamiers Blvd Delcassé, BP 95, ☎ 05 61 67 52 52, fax 05 61 67 22 40, www.ot.pamiers.free.fr
Market days
Foix alternate Mondays, Fridays; craft and farmers' markets during July and August
Pamiers Tuesday, Thursday and Saturday

Festivals and events
July *Fiesta* and international festival of theatre, Pamiers. *Festival International de Films-Résistances*, film debate, and associated activities on the theme of Resistance, Foix
July–August *Il était une Foix, histoire et legende de l'Ariège*, local legends acted out at the foot of the castle, Foix; Medieval fair, Foix

Where to stay and eating out
09000 FOIX
☆☆☆ *Audoye Lons*, 6 Pl. George-Dutilh, ☎ 05 61 65 52 44, fax 05 61 02 68 18. A charming hotel in the small capital of the Ariège, with a restaurant.
09100 LUDIES
Chambres d'hôte, Laure Bogulinski, Le Château (6km east of Pamiers, D129), ☎ 05 61 69 67 45, fax 05 61 67 39 26. Six rooms available in this beautifully restored house which has kept original features and character; pool; *table d' hôte*.
09100 PAMIERS
☆☆☆ *de France*, 11 Rue de l'Hospice, ☎ 05 61 60 20 88, fax 05 61 67 29 48. Small, cosy and very welcoming hotel with pretty rooms.

Pamiers

Pamiers, on the N20, built mainly in brick like the towns of the Toulousain, is the largest town of the *département* of the Ariège but not the *préfecture*; that honour went to Foix in 1790. Although not an immediately appealing town, it probably has fewer tourists and as many facilities as Foix.

An abbey, first mentioned in 961, was built at the site of the martyrdom in 507 of Antonin, Christian grandson of the Visigoth King Theodoric I. In 1111 the Counts of Foix came to a partnership agreement with the powerful abbots when Roger II, Count of Foix, returning from the First Crusade, built a château here named Apamie after a town in Asia Minor. During the Cathar crisis in the 12C–13C the town remained orthodox and was rewarded for its constancy by elevation to episcopal see in 1295. Jacques Fournier, Bishop of Pamiers and of Mirepoix (1318–25), became third pope at Avignon, as Benedict XII (1334–42). Most of Pamiers' medieval buildings were destroyed during the Wars of Religion in the 16C.

The Ariège was navigable from Pamiers to the Garonne during the Middle Ages, when canals were created for the dual purpose of defence and to run the mills, and a **canal** still delineates the old town. On its banks is a small public garden around a former mansion, now the municipal library, and the tourist office on Boulevard Delcassé. West of the gardens, in Rue du Collège, is a **Carmelite chapel**, founded in 1648 and rebuilt in the 18C, arranged internally to corre-spond to a mystical ascension by successive levels to a high altar. The square tower outside was built as a keep by Count Roger-Bernard III in 1285.

The cathedral stands in the middle of **Place Mercadal**, the old town centre at the foot of the hill where the Counts' castle stood. The **Cathédrale St-Antonin** was formerly the parish church of Notre-Dame du Mercadal and was rededicated when it became the cathedral in the 16C. Apart from the octagonal belfry, modelled on the Jacobins church in Toulouse in the 14C, which served as a watchtower, the building was demolished by the Protestants in 1577 and was reconstructed 1657–89. Only the badly mutilated Romanesque portal has survived from the earlier church. The already crude carvings of the capitals have suffered with time but it is just possible to make out a *Martyrdom of St John the Baptist*, *Adam and Eve*, *Cain and Abel*, *Daniel in the Lions' Den*, *Samson slay-ing the Lion* and, opposite the door, a *Martyrdom of St John the Evangelist*, the two St Johns being the patron saints of the very first church. The furnishings include a 16C wooden statue of Mary Magadalene and five 19C paintings of the legend of St Antonin.

On the perimeter of the square are the 18C Palais de Justice, the 17C seminary, now the *lycée*, and the *mairie* in the 17C episcopal palace; the present Bishops' Palace is on the south. Near the *mairie*, on the west, the **Porte de Nerviau** is a fragment of the fortified enclosure separating two quarters, altered in the 15C. In the gardens at the foot of the *castella* plateau there is a bust of the composer Gabriel Fauré (1845–1924), who was born in Pamiers.

The **Tour de la Monnaie** on Rue Charles-de-Gaulle was originally adjacent to a building of 1419 in which Count Jean I of Foix established a mint to make copper coins called Guilhems, to pay the troops who fought against William of Orange. This street leads to the present lively commercial centre and the church of Notre-Dame-du-Camp, rebuilt in the 17C except for the massive 14C rectan-gular façade flanked by two small towers. The portal was rebuilt in 1870 and the gloomy interior has nothing to detain the visitor. Further north is the belfry of the old Cordeliers church (1512).

About 6km north of Foix, where the N20 and D919 converge, the small, carefully restored Romanesque church of **St-Jean-de-Verges** was part of a priory attached to the abbey of Foix, and is one of the most sophisticated in the Ariège. Built *c* 1100–1110, it was inspired by the Toulousain except for the sim-ple belfry, which stands in place of a tower never built. Here the Counts of Foix took up the Crusade in 1229 and in 1272 swore an oath of allegiance to King

Philippe III the Bold. The quality of the materials and the decoration around the windows as well as on the capitals both inside and out are reminiscent of the transept of St-Sernin in Toulouse.

The **Rivière Souterraine de Labouiche** on the D1, southwest of St-Jean-de-Verges at Vernajoul, is the opportunity for a sensational 1500m underground boat trip. Open daily July, Aug 09.30–17.15; May, Sept 10.00–11.15 and 14.00–17.15; Whitsun week Mon–Fri 14.00–17.15; April, Oct, Nov Sat, Sun and PH, school holidays 10.00–11.15 and 14.00–16.30; ☎ 05 61 65 04 11.

Foix

Foix, mid-way between Toulouse and Spain, with a population of 10,000, is one of the smallest *préfectures* in France and is the ancient headquarters of the Counts of Foix. The main landmark is the castle on a rocky outcrop above the old town, inextricably bound up with its Counts and the history of the region.

The first Count of Foix, in the 11C, was Bernard, the second son of the Count of Carcassonne; the dynasty, which established a *paréage* with the abbots of St-Volusien in 1168, ended in 1391 with Gaston Fébus (see below). The Counts were neighbours of the Counts of Toulouse, whose dominance they challenged, and showed Cathar sympathies during the Albigensian crisis. After the annexation of Languedoc to France in 1229, they extended their domain southwards to Andorra and in 1290, when Roger Bernard III inherited the Viscounty of Béarn, the most splendid period in their history began.

Begin the visit from behind the *hôtel de ville*, built where the old pilgrimage hostel of St-James had stood. **Place Parmentier**, the potato market in the 19C, has some 16C half-timbered houses. Take the old streets Rues Lazema, des Grand-Ducs and Rocher de Foix up to the **Château des Comtes de Foix**, high above the town, with three towers linked by battlemented walls silhouetted against the mountains. In the rock beneath the castle are caves which were inhabited in prehistoric times. Open July, Aug 09.45–18.30; Aprily–June, Sept–Oct 09.45–12.00 and 14.00–18.00; Nov–March 10.30–12.00 and 14.00–17.30; closed Mon and Tues; ☎ 05 61 65 65 05.

Nothing is known about the first fort on the site, mentioned in the 11C. The castle was besieged by Simon de Montfort during the Albigensian Crusade—but was finally occupied by cunning rather than force in 1214—and it was taken by the King of France, Philippe III the Bold, in 1272. Gaston Fébus frequently stayed here at the beginning of his reign but after 1364 more rarely, preferring Mazères. The square towers linked by a two-storey building seem to have been built by the end of the 13C, the Arget tower to the north probably the oldest; and the round Fébus tower was added in the 15C. The castle was saved in the 17C when many others were destroyed at Richelieu's orders, and was used as a prison until 1862. The castle was given its 19C look during restoration and modification between 1885 and 1897 by Paul Boeswillwald, pupil of Viollet-le-Duc, including the belltower of the Arget tower.

Six rooms in the castle are devoted to the Musée de l'Ariège, which has exhibits ranging from local archaeological finds to displays of rural life and 19C building

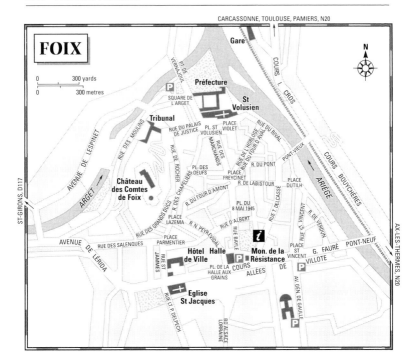

materials. It also has seven Romanesque capitals from the abbey cloisters, one recalling the persecution of St Volusien in 507 (see below), a collection of armoury and a Henri IV bed (16C).

In the 10C–11C the town grew at the foot of the castle in the quarter around Rue du Palais de Justice and the ancient church of St-Nazaire. The house at 30 Rue des Chapeliers was that of Monsieur de Tréville, a descendant of the Captain of the Musketeers at the time of Louis XIII.

The **Préfecture**, opposite the church, has a grandiose but crumbling 19C stone-and-brick façade with caryatids. The church of **St-Volusien** once sheltered the saint's relics. Volusien, the 7th Bishop of Tours, found sanctuary in the Ariège Valley following victimisation by the Visigoths at the end of the 5C and died a natural death here. The only relic of the 12C sanctuary which was rebuilt two centuries later, then damaged during the Wars of Religion, is the Romanesque portal with four sculpted capitals. The belfry was rebuilt in the 16C and the choir raised and vaulted in the 17C. The church was restored in the 1960s. Inside there is a band of Gothic-style polychrome carvings around the choir and a 16C polychromed terracotta *Entombment*; the stalls (*c* 1670) are from St-Sernin in Toulouse. In the Romanesque crypt is a 14C polygonal chapel.

Place St-Volusien was the ancient commercial centre of Foix. Rue des Marchands, leading out of it, was one of the grandest of the old city, containing the buildings of government and administration of the former province of Foix.

East of the church, 37 Rue du Rival has a fine door dated 1617, and at the end of this street is the old bridge over the Ariège. There are several small squares with fountains in the old town, Place Dutilh, Place St-Vincent, and Place de Labistour, where one of the old city bastions stood; in Place du 8 Mai 1845 is an 18C portal.

Allées de Villotte, a wide tree-lined avenue at right angles to the river and built on the old ramparts outside the medieval *enceinte*, is now the main road of the town and has a large grain market built in 1870. The hospital opposite the town hall was the former Capuchin church of St-Jacques. To the west of the roundabout there is a fine view of the castle from Pont de St-Girons.

At Montgailhard, south of Foix, are the **Forges de Pyrène**, devoted to 120 ancient trades on a 5ha site. Open daily June–Sept 10.00–18.00; Oct–May, Tues–Fri 13.30–18.00, weekends 10.00–18.00; closed Mon and Jan; ☎ 05 34 09 30 60. Further south, the **Pont du Diable** at Ginabat is a fortified bridge with two arcades, built in the 13C. Like other medieval bridges, it is associated with a legend involving the Devil. Off the D618 is **Mercus**, where the church of St-Louis, a possession of St-Sernin in Toulouse in the 11C, has a low, rustic porch (12C) with carvings.

Gaston Fébus

The legendary blond warrior Gaston III (1331–91), a consummate self-publicist, poetically chose the name Fébus (Occitan for Phoebus, the sun god). He inherited the Béarn in 1343 through his mother and dominated the Bigorre, although he did not govern it. His aim was to link his territories across the south with a chain of castles from Mazères to Pau, thus controlling an important east–west route between the Mediterranean and Bayonne. He made Pau his capital when he became Prince of Navarre and it was a regular port of call. Unsurprisingly, his vast inheritance was fraught with political and military problems but he defended it on all sides: against the English in Aquitaine, the French in the east and against the armies of Armagnac to the northwest. He was a man of many talents, and in his castle at Orthez he wrote a book on hunting, the *Livre de la Chasse*. In 1380 he took solitary refuge in the great donjon of Pau after murdering his only son, who had tried to poison him, and there he wrote his *Livre des oraisons* (Book of Prayers). He maintained independence until 5 January 1390 when, inexplicably, he surrendered to Charles VI by the Treaty of Toulouse, which named the King of France as his successor, but could not be applied as no conquest had taken place. The line of the Counts of Foix ended with his death in 1391. The Bigorre was added to the huge county of Foix-Béarn in 1425 under Jean I, and passed eventually to Henri III of Foix-Béarn, King of Navarre, who acceded to the throne of France as Henri IV in 1589 (see p 436).

Route des Corniches

The D20 from Bompas is a winding route above the valley that runs parallel with the N20 and avoids the hurly burly of the main road. Strung out along it are several Romanesque churches and a château. Just outside **Arnave** is the pre-Romanesque pilgrimage church of St-Paul, undoubtedly built on a pagan site, reached by a half-hour walk up a narrow footpath into the hills. Further along the D20, the D120 leads to **Verdun** and the little church of St-Blaise, with belfry-porch and gable, the only building to survive a flood that destroyed the village in 1875.

On the D20 again at **Axiat**, overlooking the valley, is the small 12C church of St-Blaise, with a sturdy square belfry of superimposed triple and quadruple bays. The date of the portal is contested but could be as early as 1075, and the structure is built in superb ashlar, but unfortunately the interior decoration has been badly messed up. Structural changes were made at the end of the 17C when the nave was lengthened.

Lordat (900m) is a small village dominated by the proud ruins of what was one of the largest medieval castles in the County of Foix, possibly built in the 10C. The 10min walk up is worthwhile for the splendid views, explained by three *tables d'orientation*, as well as for the military architecture. Three successive elliptical *enceintes* defended the castle keep from the east and south. One wall of the keep is perhaps from the first construction, but this is difficult to confirm as the castle was rebuilt in 1295 and because of subsequent deterioration. It served as refuge to Cathars after the fall of Montségur in 1244 and was dismantled in 1582.

A more prosaic curiosity 12km north is the great white talc quarry at **Trimouns** (1800m). It can be visited; book in advance. Open mid-May–mid-Oct, Mon–Sat; ☎ 05 61 64 60 60.

There is a discreet little Romanesque chapel at **Vernaux** (11C? and 16C), but one of the best churches on this route is **St-Martin d'Unac** on the D2, about 4km southwest of Bestiac. Built at the end of the 11C at the time of Roger II of Foix, it was a dependency of the abbey of Foix. Part of the nave and the 24m high belfry, with double openings on three levels, are survivors of the first church, which was enlarged in the 12C when the three apses were added. Its main features are the decorations inside and out: the three east windows—outlined with billets, zig-zags, rosettes and stars—have columns and capitals in marble. Inside, around the choir, are some marvellous capitals whose quality suggests a link to the workshop of St-Sernin in Toulouse. On the south wall is a 15C mural depicting St Michael in the role of a knight, a pilgrim kneeling before him, an open book in his hands.

THE VALLEYS OF THE SOUTHERN ARIÈGE

Deep into the Pyrenees close to the Spanish border, the mountain torrents such as the Vicdessos, the Saurat, the Aston and the Oriège carve their way through some of the highest and wildest places of the *département*. This is the country of winter sports and spa towns and of the Grotte de Niaux, the most celebrated of the decorated caves in the department, where visits are limited and must be booked in advance.

Getting there and around
Car
N20 from Foix; N22 from Andorra.
Train
TER Toulouse to Latour-de-Carol via Tarascon-sur-Ariège, Ax-les-Thermes, Mérens-les-Vals, L'Hospitalet.
Bus
Toulouse to L'Hospitalet via Tarascon-sur-Ariège, Ax-les-Thermes, Mérens-les-Vals.

Between Tarascon and Foix; Saurat and Tarascon; Ax-les-Thermes and Saverdun.

Tourist information

09400 Tarascon-sur-Ariège Ave des Pyrénées, BP 33, ☎ 05 61 05 94 94, fax 05 61 05 57 79, email pays.de.tarascon@wanadoo.fr
09220 Pays d'Auzat-Vicdessos Auzat, Rue des Pyrénées, ☎ 05 61 64 87 53, fax 05 61 64 89 59, email otauzat@club-internet.fr
09110 Vallées d'Ax Ax-les-Thermes, La Résidence, 6 Av. T. Declassé, ☎ 05 61 64 60 60, fax 05 61 64 68 18, www.vallees-ax.com

Market days

Ax-les-Thermes mid-June to mid-September, Tuesday, Thursday, Saturday; mid-September to mid-June, Tuesday, Saturday

Tarascon Wednesday, Saturday
Vicdessos Thursday

Festivals and events

June *Festival of St-Jean,* Ax-les-Thermes
July *Festival de l'Art et de la Culture Latino-Américain,* Tarascon-sur-Ariège
September *Festival des Saveurs,* restaurateurs and producers join forces in a discovery of the tastes of Ariégois products

Where to stay and eating out

09110 AX-LES-THERMES
☆☆ *Le Grillon,* Rue St-Udaut, ☎ 05 61 64 31 64/05 61 64 25 48, www.hotel-le-grillon.com. A quiet and pleasant hotel, whose owner is also mountain guide, and weekly outings are organised. Vegetarian dishes on the menu.

Tarascon-sur-Ariège is strategically situated where five valleys converge in the southern Ariège. It was once an important town but there are only a few reminders of its illustrious past. The château was demolished in 1632 but relics of the old town on the hill, destroyed by a conflagration in 1702, are the Tour de l'Horloge, Place Garrigou, the 14C St-Michel tower and one of the town gates, the Porte d'Espagne. The 16C church of La Daurade has rich and dramatic décor.

From Tarascon the **Vallée de Saurat** and the D618 run west via the Col de Port from the bare slopes of the Ariège to the greener valleys of the Couserans. At the head of the valley are the **Bédeilhac Caves**. Open July, Aug 10.00–18.00; April–June, Sept–Oct and school holidays 14.30–16.15; ☎ 05 61 05 95 06, www.grotte-de-bedeilhac.org. These vast caves, of both geological and prehistoric interest, were requisitioned during the Second World War by the French army, then by the Germans, who contemplated using them as an aircraft factory and even as an underground runway! Remarkably, Magdalenian paintings, engravings and animals modelled in clay are still in place. The main village, **Saurat**, is stretched out along the old road and the valley offers a variety of scenic walks and has a rare sandstone quarry worked entirely by hand; ☎ 05 61 05 92 54.

At the junction of the N20 and the D8, the Romanesque church of **Notre-Dame-de-Sabart** has an unmistakably 19C face; its façade, designed by Viollet-le-Duc, was rebuilt in 1842. The church was badly damaged during the Wars of Religion but the 11C pillars and arches survived. The Black Virgin dates from the Renaissance, but only the hands and head are carved, the rest of the figure being dressed like a doll. There is some 13C glass—rare for the region—with an image of St Peter. The rest of the decoration is 17C or later.

Grotte de Niaux

The Midi-Pyrénées region has innumerable caves and grottoes, caverns and underground rivers, all different, fascinating and tremendously popular, but for the sheer beauty of their prehistoric paintings the caves of Niaux are singled out. The entrance is up a winding road off the D8. Numbers are strictly limited for conservation reasons and visits have to be booked in advance. The visit is a round trip of 1.5km over broken ground so good walking shoes and a warm sweater are recommended; lamps are supplied. Open all year but visits strictly by prior reservation (see Parc de la Préhistoire); ☎ 05 61 05 10 10/05 61 05 88 37, www. niaux.net.

Grotte de Niaux

The first tourists came here in the 17C but, undisciplined and unsupervised, they carried off pieces of the calcite formations as souvenirs and left graffiti in exchange. The majority of the paintings accessible to the public are concentrated in what is called the **Salon Noir**, a huge cavern about 700m into the cave. They date from the Magdalenian period some 12,850–13,850 years ago, the last and most brilliant era, in creative terms, of the Upper Paleolithic. In 1925 a new gallery with a number of paintings was found beyond an underground lake, and discoveries continued to be made up to 1975. In total there are **104 animal paintings**, three-quarters in the Salon Noir, most frequently of bison but also of horses, ibex, and a few aurochs, fish and deer, and many undeciphered signs and symbols. The animals are always represented in profile and the majority are painted, either in red pigment (iron ore) or black (manganese oxide or finely ground charcoal) over an outline sketch drawn first in charcoal or occasionally engraved. The motivation for these inspired creations can only be hypothesised. The effect of the paintings, especially in lamplight, is quite magical. They are profoundly moving, skilfully executed, sensitive to individual characteristics of texture and expression, yet drawn with an economy of line that has no temporal boundaries.

The Salon Noir and other galleries of Niaux are faithfully replicated at the **Parc de la Préhistoire** near Tarascon-sur-Ariège. The park covers 13ha and offers numerous exhibitions, demonstrations and hands-on experiences relating to prehistory. Open July, Aug daily 10.00–20.00; April–June, Sept–Oct, Mon–Fri 10.00–18.00, Sat, Sun 10.00–19.00; ☎ 05 61 05 01 10.

At **Alliat**, in the valley almost opposite Niaux, are the smallest of the caves in the region open to the public, La Vache, which have paintings as well as carved objects of the Magdalenian era and archaeological debris from the Neolithic period. Visits July, Aug 10.00–18.00; April–June, Sept–Oct and school holidays 14.30–16.15; ☎ 05 61 05 95 06. The Musée Pyrénéen is a collection of over 3000 objects which reflect life in the Ariège from prehistoric times to the end of the 19C.

The Renaissance house at **Siguer**, a charming village on the D24, was the hunting lodge of the Counts of Foix. Slate was mined here at one time, but there are still red-tiled roofs as far south as Tarascon; the iron ore mines at Rancié closed in 1929. Tourism and skiing have now taken over. Les Mines du Rancie offer a discovery tour around the site and museum. Open July, Aug 10.00–12.00, 15.00–18.00; ☎ 05 61 64 87 53.

The **Vallée de Vicdessos**, southwest of Tarascon and followed by the D8, closes in on the river and leads to the village of Vicdessos and the multitude of lakes which are the beauty of this part of the high Pyrenees, most of them accessible only on foot. Little more than a pile of stones marks the former **Château de Montréal-de-Sos** and village of Olbier, near Auzat, an important outpost of the Counts of Foix in the 13C but long abandoned. It is a wonderful place nevertheless. The D18 continues through the wild and rugged scenery of the Vicdessos region—dominated by the Montcalm (3078m), Canalbonne (2914m) and La Rouge (2902m) peaks, the landscape becoming even more lunaresque over the Port de Lers (1517m)—to the popular lake, the **Etang de Lers**.

Ussat-les-Bains is a small spa on the banks of the Ariège with a shady park, where the waters are used to treat psychosomatic and neurological problems. The Grotte de Lombrives is reputedly the largest underground grotto in the European Union. A panoramic ride in a little train takes visitors up to the entrance at 640m. There are plenty of concretions and some of the best stalagmites in fairy-like grottoes. Visits every 20mins July, Aug 10.00–17.00; for other times, ☎ 05 61 05 98 40.

Running south from Les Cabannes on the N20, the **Vallée d'Aston** is considered one of the most beautiful, and has a cross-country ski centre at Plateau de Beille. At Luzenac the N20 links up with the Route des Corniches (see above).

Ax-les-Thermes (720m), the last town of any significance before Andorra, is as its name would imply, a spa town. Archaeological evidence suggests that the curative properties of the waters were appreciated even before the Romans arrived. Three valleys, the Ariège, the Lauze and the Oriège meet here, and it has more facilities than most other centres in the Ariège, catering both for those in their dressing-gowns coming for a cure, and for the more hardy specimens in their boots, intent on an outdoor activity holiday or skiing at Ax Bonascre.

The most entertaining and novel feature of Ax is the Bassin des Ladres in the town centre, where anyone can strip off his or her boots or shoes and dangle aching, or even non-aching, feet in the hot (77°C) sulphurous water. According to tradition, St Louis (Louis IX) founded the neighbouring hospital to treat leprous soldiers returning from the Crusades. Of the medieval town there is only one gate, the Porte d'Espagne to the south.

Three major routes lead out of Ax. One is the N20, which climbs up to **l'Hospitalet** (1436m) at the border with Andorra, passing through the Mérens valley, which boasts the oldest Romanesque church of the Haute Ariège (10C–11C), the delightful remains comprised only of the Catalan-style belfry with three levels of double openings, the walls of the apse and one apsidal chapel. This beautiful valley is also famous for its small black horses, descendants of those captured in the paintings of Niaux, well-adapted to mountainous terrain.

The second option is the D22 which follows the **Vallé d'Orlu** on the Oriège through Orgeix with its lake, and Orlu, crosses the Réserve Nationale d'Orlu, inhabited by herds of izard, and after less than 10km finally peters out to become a footpath with walks up to the lakes at around 2000m.

The third option is the D613 and D25 via **Ascou**, with a ski centre at Pailhères, and the valley of the Lauze, a route running alongside the Lac de

Goulours and over the Col de Pailhères (2002m), rich in woodland and flowers, to the ruined castle of **Usson**. The 18C stable has become a museum, open July, Aug daily 10.00–13.00 and 15.00–19.00; May–mid-Oct, Sat, Sun 14.00–18.00; mid-Oct–June check times; ☎ 04 68 20 41 37. **Quérigut**, with another castle, is in the canton of Donezan, a high plateau surrounded by summits of over 2000m, the last outpost of the Ariège on the border with the Aude.

THE COUSERANS: ST-LIZIER AND ST-GIRONS

The Couserans was an ancient viscounty, tucked in between the land of the Counts of Foix and the province of Bigorre, ruled by vassals of the Counts of Comminges. The designation is still used to describe part of the *département* of the Ariège. Despite the barrier formed by the Pyrenees, there were close links between the Couserans and Catalonia and Aragon during the Middle Ages. The Spanish participated in pilgrimages to Notre-Dame-du-Marsan, near St-Lizier, and St-Lizier was a stage on the route to Santiago crossing the Pyrenees at the Col d'Aula. There is, however, no modern route from the Couserans into Spain.

Many rivers rise in the mountains, forming a network of valleys which divide and sub-divide and divide again, making 18 in all. The main valleys are those of Bellongue, Biros and Bethmale, and three which join the Haut-Salat, the Ustou, Garbet and Arac. The smaller valleys can be entered by car but often just peter out in a track leading to the border. This is a walkers' paradise, with well indicated and documented routes with an abundance of sub-alpine and alpine flowers above the forest line, as well as animals. St-Lizier and St-Girons, twin towns that complement each other, are the main centres in the Couserans.

Getting there and around

Car

Toulouse to St-Girons/St-Lizier A64, exit 20 D117. Foix to St-Girons D117.

Bus

Boussens to St-Girons via Lorp, St-Lizier. Between St-Girons and La Bastide-de-Desplas; Aulus; Foix; Massat; St-Lary; Seintein, Ustou.

Tourist information

09140 Aulus-les-Bains Centre Ville, ☎ 05 61 96 00 01, fax 05 61 96 52 90, www.haut-couserans.com
09800 Castillon ☎ 05 61 96 72 64, email otcastil@club-interenet.fr
09320 Massat 1 Rte du Col de Port, ☎/fax 05 61 96 92 76, www.ariege.com/massat
09190 St-Lizier Pl. de la Cathédrale, ☎ 05 61 96 77 77, fax 05 61 96 08 01, www.ariege.com/st-lizier

09800 Sentein ☎ 05 61 96 10 90, fax 05 61 66 96 92
09200 Pays de Couserans St-Girons, Pl. Alphonse Sentein, ☎ 05 61 96 26 60, fax 05 61 96 26 69, www.ville-st-girons.fr
09240 Seronais La Bastide-de-Serou, ☎ 05 61 64 53 53, fax 05 61 64 50 48, www.seronais.com
09140 Pays de Haut-Couserans Seix, ☎ 05 61 96 00 01, fax 05 61 96 52 90, www.haut-couserans.com

Market days

Aulus-les-Bains July, August Sunday
Castillon 3rd Tuesday of month; July, August Tuesday
Masset 2nd and 4th Tuesday of month; July, August Sunday
Sentein July, August Friday
St-Girons Saturday

Guided visits

For visits to the small Romanesque

churches of the Couserans at Moulis, Arrout, Oujout and Sentein, ☎ 05 61 96 26 60. Fridays at 14.00–18.30 must make reservation

Festivals and events

May *Festival d'Art Sacré*, religious art in all its forms (music, painting, drama), St-Girons and St-Lizier

June *San Joan Beth e Gran*, festival of St John, valley of the Couserans and St-Girons

July *Festival Rite*, dance, song and music from around the world, St-Girons

August *Festival de St-Lizier*, classical music in the cathedral, St-Lizier. *Marché d'ature fois le Couserans*, old-fashioned market, St-Girons

Where to stay and eating out

09800 AUDRESSEIN

☆ *L'Auberge d'Audressein*, Castillon, ☎ 05 61 96 11 80, fax 05 61 96 82 96. An unassuming but charming inn, recommended for imaginative cuisine incorporating traditional recipes and local produce.

09200 ST-GIRONS

☆☆☆ *Eychenne*, 8 Ave Paul-Laffont, ☎ 05 61 04 04 50, fax 05 61 96 07 20. This long-established family-run hotel is in an old coaching inn. The swimming pool is a modern innovation. Authentic cuisine served in the restaurant.

☆☆ *Horizon*, Lorp Sentaraille, on the D117 north of St-Girons, ☎ 05 61 66 26 80. Hotel with an excellent restaurant.

☆☆/€–€€ *La Clairière*, Av. de la Résistance, ☎ 05 61 66 66 66, fax 05 34 14 30 30, www.ariege.com/la-clairiere. Light and airy building with attractive restaurant and excellent cooking; near town centre; terrace and pool.

Relais d'Encausse, from the D117 south of St-Girons take the tiny Rte de Saudech; signposted, ☎ 05 61 66 05 80. *Chambres d'hôte* in a peaceful setting near the town, with a warm welcome and a good *table d'hôte*.

09140 SEIX

☆☆☆ *La Terrasse*, Aulus les-Bains, ☎ 05 61 96 00 98, fax 05 61 96 01 42. A welcoming, family hotel-restaurant with a riverside location. State-of-the-art cuisine.

St-Lizier

On a hill beside the Salat, St-Lizier is the architectural high-spot of the Couserans. It is small but has the distinction of having co-cathedrals, both founded in the 11C, in the two separate quarters of the town. Notre-Dame-de-la-Sède, inside the *cité* walls, was the original. The sanctuary in the *bourg* is known today as the cathedral of St-Lizier. One of the oldest and most prestigious music festivals in the region takes place at St-Lizier in July and August, when concerts are performed in the cathedral.

The *cité* of the ancient Consorani people and capital of the Couserans, *Lugdunum Consonanum*, founded by the Romans, was elevated to episcopal see in the 5C and maintained this status until 1801. Bishop Glycerius, of Spanish or Portuguese origin, who died *c* 540, was reputed to have defended his city from Visigoths and Vandals. When canonised he became St Lizier.

From the D117 a 16C **bridge** leads to the base of the town; it descends in tiers and protects three old mills. There is parking at the top in the square by the cathedral.

Cathédrale St-Lizier

The cathedral, built by Bishop Jourdain I in the late 11C, probably on the site of a sepulchre, was consecrated in 1117 by St Raymond, Bishop of Barbastro in Spain. Open 09.00–12.00 and 14.00–19.00. Treasury and pharmacy guided visits only, contact the tourist office; ☎ 05 61 96 77 77.

The many stages of reconstruction are evident from the **exterior**, the only remaining part of the 11C building being the south wall of the nave, visible from the cloister. The church was extended east with a transept and five-sided apse before the consecration. Gallo-Roman friezes and columns were haphazardly incorporated into the ashlar and a little later the walls were raised to take vaults. The apse with its heavy cornice dwarfs the two earlier chapels that flank it, low, undecorated and with hugely thick walls. The church was badly damaged in the 12C when the Counts of Comminges attempted to take control of St-Lizier and the nave was enlarged and modified in the 14C. Above the crossing are two levels of a Toulousain-style octagonal belfry (*c* 1300) in brick with mitred bays, crowned by ugly modern crenellations. The 15C entrance on the north has recessed brick arches and marble columns. On the right-hand wall is the scallop-shell symbol of St James.

The stylistic juxtapositions and strangely irregular shape of the **interior** are quite endearing. The north wall of the aisleless nave is not straight so that the pillars, heightened in the 15C when the nave was rib-vaulted, are not opposite each other. The nave is out of alignment with the choir, and the transept, enlarged in the 14C, is also uneven. The most ancient parts are the massive walls of the apsidal chapels, the rest taking its basic form at the end of the 11C or beginning of the 12C when two large, semi-engaged columns were added to support the chancel arch. While the exterior of the main apse is angled, the interior is semi-circular.

The greatest glory of the cathedral is the **Romanesque murals**. The paintings in the choir, discovered in 1960, are on two levels and date from two different periods. The walls, erected and painted in the late 11C, were tampered with when the choir vaults were reconstructed in the 12C. Part of the original decorative scheme, in muted colours, has survived in the bays either side of the windows. This consists of friezes, heads and, framed by the painted architectural setting of blind arcades, pairs of standing figures, the Apostles in the apse and Kings and Prophets to the side. Below are images of the ***Three Magi in the House of Herod***, the ***Adoration of the Magi***, the ***Annunciation***, ***Visitation*** and ***Nativity***. The elongated figures are strikingly beautiful, the most moving being those in the ***Visitation***, where Elizabeth and Mary are cheek-to-cheek, their haloes fused. The work is attributed to a 12C painter who worked in the Catalonian Pyrenees and in the Val d'Aran, identified as the Master of Pedret. The vault paintings, containing the arms of Bishop Auger de Montfaucon, which place them at the end of the 13C or early 14C, are in a rather less eloquent style, and a rosy-cheeked ***Christ in Majesty***, surrounded by the symbols of the Evangelists, beams down.

The 12C murals in the north chapel, discovered in 1980 under a thick layer of plaster, are interesting for their unusual iconography based on the Revelation of St John at Patmos. Two groups of three figures with haloes stand before the six gates of Heavenly Jerusalem, their arms outstretched towards the kings of the earth who carry treasures. Beneath them are the symbols of the Evangelists and the figure of St John at the moment he receives his vision from an angel. The words *Sanctus Andreas* can be deciphered on the north, and the east wall has a

Virgin suckling the Infant Jesus (*c* 1300). The shadow of an inscription below the Virgin indicates that there was also an image of St John in the east end.

The large capitals of the transept have sober decoration, but delightfully the bases of the **columns** have a motif of human feet, both bare and shod. A vaulted recess in the south transept, discovered in 1958, was the sepulchre of the bishops, including St Lizier before his relics were placed under the altar. It now contains a sarcophagus with the relics of 13C and 14C bishops. The stalls are 17C and the 18C black marble altar incorporates part of the original altar. The Gothic painted décor of the nave was uncovered during restoration in 1978–83 and in the window opposite the door is 15C stained glass. There are a number of post-Reformation pieces in the nave, including the 17C organ with rather curious little angels at the top, restored in 1983.

The other major feature of St-Lizier is the fine Romanesque **cloister**, the only one in the Ariège, which is the result of two building campaigns, the first 1150–80 and the second in the 13C, accounting for a variety of styles of capitals and different types of vaulting. In the 14C the cloister was shortened by two bays when the transept was built, and the upper level was added in the 16C. The 32 bays are supported by alternate single and double marble columns, with a cluster of four in the west gallery. The capitals are decorated with allegorical, geometric

Cloister of Cathédrale St-Lizier

and vegetal designs, the most accomplished in the north gallery. The rare figurative images include *Adam and Eve*, in the north gallery, and *Daniel in the Lions' Den* with Habbakuk in the east. Round the cloisters are several medieval tombs.

The **treasury**—in the sacristy off the cloister—contains a remarkable collection of treasures from the 11C to the 19C of diverse origins, the finest being the elegant Renaissance reliquary bust of St Lizier, made by Antoine Favier of Toulouse, in embossed and gilded silver studded with gems. The **pharmacy** of the hospice in the Hôtel Dieu, built in 1771 adjacent to the cathedral cloister, is complete with wooden cabinets and locally made jars, an operating table and a dictionary of pharmaceutical prescriptions.

On foot, take the road to the east of the square which takes a sinuous route up to the old **cité** at the top of the hill, enclosed in about 740m of ramparts. Gallo-Roman walls erected in the late 3C or early 4C, punctuated by six semi-circular towers and two gates, have been rebuilt. Inside it is strangely empty except for the square tower and the episcopal buildings. This part of St-Lizier is lifted above the gardens and tiled roofs of the houses clustered around the cathedral, carrying the eye beyond the fields and wooded slopes of the St-Gironnais to the distant Pyrenees and the dome of Mont Valier (2838m). The **Cathédrale de Notre-Dame-de-la-Sède** (from *la Séda*, Occitan for episcopal see), of fairly modest proportions, was begun in the 11C adjacent to the south ramparts and there is not a great deal left to visit. The apse, of the late 11C, is the oldest part, and in the Romanesque chevet are reused Roman friezes; the three-bay nave dates from the late 15C. The choir stalls and altars are 17C and the wood-panelling is late 18C. There is nothing left of the cloister to the north, but the 13C chapter house with brick vaults has survived.

To the west is the bishops' palace, built *c* 1660 into the Roman constructions, a sober building with towers at each extremity. It has been transformed into a **museum** of local ethnology with a well-displayed collection from the valley of Bethmale. Open July, Aug daily 10.00–12.30 and 14.00–18.30; April–June, Sept–Oct 14.00–17.30, closed Mon; ☎ 05 61 04 81 86. Return by the Porte de l'Horloge west of the bishops' palace.

The picturesque village of **Tourtouse** north of St-Lizier dates back to 1195 and has the remains of the ramparts, St-Barbe chapel and bishops' palace (1626) with a 12C keep; ☎ 05 61 66 27 98.

St-Girons is the largest town in this part of the Ariège and *sous-préfecture*. Apart from being a small dynamic commercial centre with a lively market, it is not of any particular architectural interest. Originally called Bourg-sous-Vic or Bourg-sous-Ville, in acknowledgement of its subordinate role to St-Lizier, it was called St-Girons when the remains of the Christian martyr Gerontius were brought here after the sack of St-Lizier by the Counts of Comminges in 1130.

The advantages of its position in the wide valley where the three rivers Salat, Baup and Lez converge are obvious and the riverbanks are still St-Girons' strong point, with tree-lined walks and pleasant gardens surrounding the remodelled château of the Viscounts of the Couserans, now municipal offices. The parish church, rebuilt in the 19C, has conserved its 15C belfry, and in the southeast of the town, the much-restored 12C church of St-Vallier still has its Romanesque portal.

Mongauch, on the D33 west of St-Girons, has a massive church built in the 11C and heightened in the 12C, the main interest of which lies in the fine wall paintings inside, including a *Christ in Majesty* with the symbols of the Apostles and archangels.

To the east, the **Abbaye de Combelongue** (12C–18C) at Rimont, between La Bastide-de-Sérou and St-Girons, is a rare Premonstratensian abbey founded in 1138. Unusually, the Romanesque building shows the influence of the Spanish *mudéjar* style. Open Aug daily 15.00–18.00; July, Sept, Sat, Sun 15.00–18.00; ☎ 05 61 95 37 33.

The D618 on the left bank of the Salat runs through the enclosed and densely wooded Gorges de Ribaouto. **Massat**, between the Col de Port and the Gorges de l'Arac, was the medieval capital of the Viscounts of the Couserans. Hints of 18C affluence are evident in doorways and wrought-iron balconies, particularly of the *hôtel de ville*. The Baroque façade of the collegiate church (1700–50) is surprisingly splendid for such a small place: it replaced the church of 1290 destroyed and pillaged in the 16C by the Huguenots of Mas d'Azil. Standing free beside it is the 15C octagonal belfry tower, in yellow-gold stone, the tallest in the Couserans. All that was salvaged from the 13C church is a statue of a nude child draped with the shawl of Abraham, on the baldaquin of the pulpit. Otherwise, 18C and 19C statues and paintings, including a copy of Leonardo's *Last Supper* (1849) signed Scurruité and two paintings given by Napoléon III in 1866, adorn the interior. The widespread veneration of the Virgin in these mountain communities is exemplified by the simple chapel dedicated to her at the west of the town. The 18C mill on the banks of the Arac can be visited. Open

July, Aug, Sat, Sun 17.00–19.00, or by appointment; ☎ 05 61 96 96 66.

Roads lead out of Massat to the Col de Port and to the Etang de Lers, through bucolic mountain landscapes with scattered buildings in traditional style, their roofs covered with beautiful silver schist cut in fishscale shapes.

From Massat the D17 is a narrow road with a few tiny hamlets, at first running through chestnuts and acacias, then beech forests, to the **Col de Saraillé** (942m), where the scenery changes and the trees are mainly silver birch. Gradually the landscape expands into a wide deforested valley, in the summer scattered with harebells, clover, candytuft and some modest cottages. Especially precious are the rare examples of shepherds' huts with stepped gables (*à pas d'oiseau*) designed to withstand winter snow, originally thatched but many now sadly patched up with corrugated iron.

Aulus-les-Bains, on the D32 to the south, is arguably the most out-of-the-way spa town in the whole of France, at 780m at the bottom of the Garbet valley.

The church at **Oust**, west of Massat, has a strange bulbous belfry and Counter-Reformation retable while **Vic d'Oust** has an 11C church with a gable belfry (closed). This has been a cheese-producing region since Roman times. Nearby **Seix** on the D3 is the most important village of the Haut-Salat. Above the village is the Château du Roi and houses with wooden balconies overhang the river; it is a veritable mountain torrent at this point and Seix is a popular centre for canoeists. The Baroque church has a strange neo-Romanesque belfry (1897); inserted in the façade buttress and base of the belfry are carvings from an older building.

The D17 from Sentenac d'Oust follows the **Vallée de Bethmale**, considered the most beautiful of all the Couserans valleys, scattered with the purples, pinks, mauves and blues of meadow flowers—wild orchids, wild thyme and bilberries—on the way up to the Col de la Core (1395m). This is such a popular place for walkers and motorists (and hang-gliders, who add a dash of primary colour) that it is almost crowded in the summer. On the descent from the col is the equally popular—because so accessible and beautiful—Lac de Bethmale, in a glade abundant with bees, berries and butterflies, raspberries and wild strawberries. There are small communities, with several old *lavoirs* (wash houses), strung out along the valley but they have suffered poverty and abandon.

In **Samortein** there is a *sabotier* who makes wooden clogs with long, curved and pointed toes which look quite impossible to wear but are part of the traditional costume of Bethmale; ☎ 05 61 95 78 84. **Borde-sur-Lez** has a lovely old bridge leading to the hamlet of Ourjout and the 12C church of St-Pierre (see below) as well as the chapel of Aulignac. The wooded **Vallée de Biros** begins here, tracked by the D4, and at Sentein is the grandest of several little churches in this remote region, with a reddish sandstone belfry, the third highest in the Couserans. The octagonal section of the belfry is 14C and the spire was added in 1749. Its Romanesque base is the baptistery, the entrance to which has an unusual arrangement of simple capitals on the outside supporting the arch and four columns inside. The body of the church was amended in the 14C and has late 15C to early 16C paintings in the east bay of the nave of Apostles, Prophets and Doctors of the Church, and in the west bay 12 figures in contemporary dress. The choir paintings are 18C and in the south chapel is a 12C chrism. Two very rustic towers with witches' hat roofs were part of the fortifications.

At **Castillon**, above Bordes on the D4, the chapel of St-Pierre, perched above the village with an impressive belfry and a statue of St Peter, originally belonged to the château demolished in 1632. From here, D618 follows the **Vallée de la Bellongue**, crosses the Col de Portet d'Aspet (1069m) and drops down into the Comminges. **Audressein** is a pretty village at the start of the valley with a lovely 14C church, Notre-Dame-de-Tramesaygues, beside the river. Open Sundays 09.00–18.00. The deep porch has a series of ex-voto scenes in true fresco technique (restored 1987–88). The large figures of angels, St James and St John the Baptist are more sophisticated than the anecdoctal scenes presenting individuals in some sort of trouble or danger—sick, imprisoned, tumbling from a tree, departing on a crusade—who are all subsequently saved and are shown giving thanks to Our Lady. There is a *sabotier* in this village. Deeper into the valley, at **Galey**, the church shelters a wooden Renaissance retable with 13 painted panels.

25 Toulouse

Toulouse, the fourth city in France, is the capital of the vast Midi-Pyrénées region. Typical of the Midi and within easy reach of the Pyrenees, it is a melting-pot of many cultures and is distinguished by its mellow brick buildings and panoramas across the Garonne, which have inspired many comparisons with Tuscany or Spain. The motorway network makes it all too easy to drive past but, for lovers of bustling cities, Toulouse's treasures are manifold.

The aeronautical and space industries contribute in large part to the modern prosperity of the metropolis and the surrounding area, while the 110,000 students of the university, the second largest after Paris, add a youthful dynamism. Toulouse is one of the rare places where crystallised violets are still confected and sold, after a revival of the industry in the late 20C.

Practical information

Getting there and around
Air
Toulouse-Blagnac airport lies to the west of the city, ☎ 05 61 42 44 00, www.toulouse.aeroport.fr. An airport bus runs every 20 mins 05.20–23.30 to the town centre and bus station (see below); ☎ 05 34 60 64 00, www.navetteria-toulouse.com. For airport taxis, ☎ 05 61 30 02 54.

Car
Around Toulouse is a ring road (*rocade*) which the Autoroutes link into.
A62 Montauban/Bordeaux, A68

Albi/Rodez, A61 Carcassonne/Montpellier, A64 St-Gaudens/Tarbes/Bayonne, A602/N124 Auch, and Toulouse-Blagnac Airport, A601.

Train
TGV Paris Montparnasse to Toulouse (5hrs).
TER Paris Austerlitz to Toulouse via Brive, Cahors, Montauban.
The main station, Gare Matabiau, is northeast of the centre on Blvd P.-Sémard, ☎ 08 91 67 68 69 (times), or ☎ 08 92 35 35 35 (information/sales).

Regional buses

Depart from the *gare routière*, 68–70 Blvd P.-Sémard (next to the train station, at the end of Allées Jean-Jaurès), ☎ 05 61 61 67 67 or 05 61 61 67 59; also **Eurolines**, ☎ 08 36 95 52 52 or 05 61 26 40 04, www.eurolines.fr; and *Intercar*, ☎ 05 61 58 14 53, www.intercars.fr

Metro and city bus

At present Toulouse has one metro line, with fully-automated, no-driver trains. The line runs northeast–southwest between Jolimont and Basso Cambo. Of the 15 stations, the most central are St-Cyprien-République, Esquirol, Capitole, Jean-Jaurès.

Single fare ticket can be purchased and used both on city buses and metro. For all information concerning city buses and metro, *Allo Semvat*, ☎ 05 61 41 70 70.

Parking

Toulouse is a very congested city, especially the centre, and the driving haphazard. Public transport is recommended.

Central parking at Pl. du Capitole, Pl. Victor Hugo, Pl. Occitaine, Pl. Esquirol, Pl. St-Etienne, Pl. des Carmes, Blvd Carnot, Pl. Jeanne-d'Arc, St-Georges (3 entrances) and Gare-Matabiau.

Tourist information

Donjon de Capitole, 31000 Toulouse, ☎ 05 61 11 02 22, fax 05 61 22 03 63, www.ot-toulouse.fr. Open May–Sept, Mon–Sat 09.00–19.00, Sun and PH 10.00–13.00 and 14.00–18.30; Oct–April, Mon–Fri 09.00–18.00, Sat 09.00–12.30 and 14.00–18.00, Sun and PH 10.00–12.30 and 14.00–18.00

Market days

All markets function only in the morning, from around 08.00 to 13.00.
Produce Blvd de Strasbourg, Pl. Béteille, Pl. du Marché aux Cochons, Pl.

Saint-Georges, Pl. Arnaud-Bernard, every morning except Monday; Pl. Salin, Tuesday and Saturday; St-Aubin, Sunday; Pl. du Ravelin (St-Cyprien), Friday
Covered markets Victor-Hugo, St-Cyprien, and Les Carmes (about to change) are open every day except Monday
Organic market (*marché bio*) Pl. du Capitole, Tuesday, Saturday
Books (*bouquinistes*) Pl. Arnaud-Bernard, Thursday; Pl. St-Etienne, Saturday
Clothing and soft goods Wednesday, Pl. du Capitole
Flea markets (*brocante*) Allées Jules-Guesde, first Friday/Saturday/Sunday of each month; Pl. St-Sernin, Saturday and Sunday morning

Organised tours

Themed walking tours leave from the tourist office every Saturday at 15.00, and on Wednesdays in June and during school holidays. They take about 2 hours. (In English for groups only by prior arrangement.)

Boat trips

On the Garonne **Toulouse Croisières**, from Quai de la Daurade, ☎ 05 61 257 257
Garonne and Canal **Péniche Baladine**, ☎ 05 61 80 22 26, www.bateaux-toulousains.com. restaurant and cruise boat.
Garonne and Canal **L'Occitania**, ☎ 05 61 63 06 06, www.loccitania.com. restaurant and cruise boat.
On the Canal **Rosa Croisières**, ☎ 05 61 51 03 59, www.rosa-croisieres.com. Hotel boat, for canal excursions

Boat hire

Canal du Midi and Canal Lateral **Navicanal**, ☎ 05 61 55 10 91, www.navicanal.com

Festivals and events

March *Cinémas d'Amérique Latine*, Latin

American film of all kinds

Printemps du Rire, festival of European humour

May *Fête des Berges*, discover the banks of the Garonne by bike or on foot

June *Fête du Grand Fénétra*, celebration of Fronton wine and folklore in Place du Capitole

July *Festival Garonne Toulouse*, music festival and songs by the river

July–August *Musique d'Eté*, all types of music performed at different historic sites, Jacobins cloisters, La Daurade and the opera house

September *Piano aux Jacobins*, recitals in the cloisters

Printemps de Septembre, photography and video, dialogue between the arts

September–October *Toulouse les Orgues*, organ festival taking advantage of the wealth of instruments in the town

October *Cinespaña*, special viewings of Spanish films in the original version, sub-titled in French

November–December (bi-annually, even years) *Marionnettissimo*, puppet festival

 ### Where to stay

✩✩✩✩ *Grand Hôtel de l'Opéra*, 1 Pl. du Capitole, ☎ 05 61 21 82 66, fax 05 61 23 41 04. Hotel and restaurant, *Les Jardins de l'Opéra*, of great charm, discreetly tucked away in a courtyard next to Place du Capitole; ultra-refined cuisine and impeccable service.

✩✩✩ *Beaux-Arts*, 1 Pl. du Pont-Neuf, ☎ 05 34 45 42 42, email contact@ hotelsdesbeauxarts.com, restaurant ☎ 05 61 21 12 12. Close to the river and the old centre, with attractive Art Nouveau décor. Reliable food including shellfish.

✩✩✩ *Brienne*, Blvd M.-Leclerc, ☎ 05 61 23 60 60, fax 05 62 23 18 94. A comfortable modern hotel near the Canal de Brienne.

✩✩✩ *Holiday Inn-Capoul*, 13 Pl. Wilson, ☎ 05 61 10 70 70, fax 05 61 21 96 70. A largish, modern hotel at the heart of Toulouse.

✩✩✩ *Mermoz*, 50 Rue Matabiau, ☎ 05 61 63 04 04, fax 05 61 63 15 64, www.hotel-mermoz.com. Nicely appointed hotel between the station and city centre.

 ### Eating out

€€–€€€ *Pastel*, 237 Rte St-Simon (St-Cyprien), ☎ 05 62 87 84 30 or 05 61 40 59 01, fax 05 61 44 29 22. The chef makes excellent use of regional products for a truly wonderful experience from the beginning to the mouthwatering desserts. One Michelin rosette.

€€–€€€ *Michel Sarran*, 31 Blvd A. Duportal, ☎ 05 61 12 32 32, fax 05 61 12 32 33. One of the great Toulouse restaurants

€€ *Au Gré du Vin*, 19 Rue de la Fleau, ☎ 05 61 25 03 51. Opposite the Paul Dupuy museum.

€€ *Benjamin*, 7 Rue des Gestes, ☎ 05 61 22 92 66. Reasonably priced menus and modern dishes. In the old part of town.

€€ *Chez Carmen*, 97 Allée Charles-de-Fitte, ☎ 05 61 42 04 95. Across the Pont-Neuf, an extremely popular brasserie (must reserve) for fresh, simple and fragrant food.

€€ *Chez Jambier*, 8 Ave Maurice-Hauriou, ☎ 05 61 14 05 67. Cosy and convivial, but designed for serious eating.

€€ *Edelweiss*, 19 Rue Castellane, ☎ 05 61 34 70 19. Smartish place deservedly popular for its careful attention to ingredients and cooking.

€€ *Le Grand Café de l'Opéra*, 1 Pl. du Capitole, ☎ 05 61 21 37 03. A smart café-brasserie for light and lively meals.

€€ *Le Mange-Tout*, 29 Rue de la Chaine, ☎ 05 62 30 02 35. To the west of St-Sernin, a charming bistrot where the dishes combine the Mediterranean and the Toulousain.

€€ *Orsi*, 13 Rue de l'Industrie, ☎ 05 61 62 97 43. A 1930s' brasserie in the style of a 'Bouchon Lyonnais' with hearty dishes and good ambience.

€-€€ *Brasserie Capoul*, 13 Pl. Wilson, ☎ 05 61 21 08 27. Sit at pavement tables or in the mirrored interior. A good, classic brasserie on this attractive square.

€-€€ *Café Bibent*, 5 Pl. du Capitole, ☎ 05 61 23 89 03. The most famous café on the *place*, with Belle Epoque décor.

€-€€ *7 Place St-Sernin*, 7 Pl. St-Sernin, ☎ 05 62 30 05 30. An elegant little place with food to match. Small terrace.

€ *Les Caves de la Maréchale*, 3 Rue J. Chalande, ☎ 05 61 23 89 88. Beyond a small courtyard. The décor uses typical brick vaults to advantage. Traditional cooking.

€ *Saveur Bio*, 22 Rue M. Fonvieille, ☎ 05 61 12 15 15. A rare vegetarian restaurant.

History

The advantageous position of the fertile Garonne valley between the Atlantic, the Mediterranean and the Iberian Peninsula attracted Celtic settlers, the Tectosages, in 3C BC, followed about a century later by the Romans. Ancient **Tolosa** grew wealthy from the importation of wine, so that by the 2C AD it had acquired the status of colony, with 20,000 inhabitants. Only fragments of the 1C city walls remain in place, although the site of the ancient temple or Capitolium was discovered in 1992 during excavation work under Place Esquirol. The Capitolium was crucial to the history of the early Christian era and the martyrdom, in 250, of **St Sernin** (Saturninus), the first Bishop of Toulouse, who refused to worship pagan idols and died after being roped to a half-crazed sacrificial bull by crowds assembled on the steps of the Capitolium.

For a century from 418 the Visigoths made Toulouse their capital, after which came incursions by the Franks, Arabs and Normans. The history of the town and surrounding area as an almost autonomous principality began in the 8C with the creation by Charlemagne of the **county of Toulouse**. In the feudal hierarchy this was part of the Kingdom of Aquitaine belonging to the French monarchy, but allegiance to the French diminished to a purely nominal status as the Counts' power increased, until they had dominion directly or indirectly over a vast territory where the language of Oc was spoken. By the 12C, the boundary of the Languedoc covered an area loosely contained by the Dordogne, Gascony, the Montagne Noire, the Mediterranean and the Pyrenees, but was constantly in flux. The power of the princes and the Church developed side by side through the 11C and 12C, economic prosperity and civil liberties stimulating urban growth and the Gregorian reforms (p 558) adding to the authority of the ecclesiastics. A new cathedral was begun in the 11C, in 1096 the altar table of the unfinished church of St-Sernin was consecrated and in the same year Raymond IV of Toulouse led the First Crusade. In spite of this activity in the orthodox Church, a breakaway fundamentalist Christian movement, described then as a heresy and now as Catharism, took root in the Languedoc. It resulted in the only crusade by the French against their own people, beginning in 1209, and was popularly known as the **Albigensian Crusade** (see p 306). The foundation of the university in 1229 was a bid to counteract heretical beliefs through the teaching of theology and canon law.

The architectural style of the counter-heresy, generally referred to as southern or meridional Gothic, developed as religious orders created churches adapted to the liturgy and to preaching to the masses, with one vast aisleless rib-vaulted space. The earliest extant model is the 13C nave of the cathedral of St-Etienne (see below). The scarcity of stone in the alluvial basin of the Garonne contributed to the tradition of building in the elongated Roman-style brick which has become the hallmark of **Toulousain archi-tecture**. Five serious conflagrations destroyed much of the town between 1463 and 1551 and in 1555 precise regulations were imposed forbidding reconstruction in wood and stipulating brick or stone. The golden era of many towns in the region, not least Toulouse, began during a period of peace after the Hundred Years War (1337–1453) and ended with the start of the Wars of Religion in 1560.

A variety of factors contributed to the prosperity of Toulouse and the Toulousain: one was the definitive establishment in 1443 of the *parlement*, a judicial and legislative institution, the second most important in France, elevating the town to the status of provincial capital; another was the com-merce in indigo or *pastel* (see p 331). The *pasteliers* were a merchant élite of about a dozen families whose members often rose to eminent positions in the municipal hierarchy and built Renaissance mansions. **Renaissance Toulouse** had close links with the humanists of Bologna University and also with the printing trade in Lyons, and from 1476 became the fourth town in France to have presses, although until the beginning of the 16C documents were printed exclusively in Latin and Occitan. The introduction of maize to the region in the 17C and the means of transporting it by canal brought an era of renewed prosperity, and in the 18C municipal schemes included the realisation of dykes, ports, bridges and a canal. Hand in hand with this came the demolition of medieval buildings, including the once-great church of Notre-Dame-de-la-Daurade. Toulouse, unlike other large towns in the Midi, adhered to the **Revolution** but after the suppression of the *parlement* in 1790 became simply *chef-lieu* (county town) of the *département* of Haute-Garonne, created in 1790. Napoléon's popularity gradually waned—largely because of the decline in corn prices due to the blockading of ports and war in Spain— to the point where French troops under Marshall Soult, retreating before Wellington's army, were not welcomed by the inhabitants of the town. On 10 April 1814 Soult was defeated and the Duke was received as liberator of Toulouse, a pointless exercise, happening four days after Napoléon's abdication.

The end of the 18C and 19C brought the destruction of many religious buildings and parts of the old *cité*, to be replaced with new boulevards and public buildings. By the beginning of the Second Empire (1852) the popula-tion had increased to 100,000 but the industrial revolution had hardly touched this part of France. The building of the **railway** in 1856 linked Toulouse to the metropolitan north of France and helped to improve the economy but, until the eve of the First World War Toulouse's largest factory was the state-owned tobacco factory on the banks of the Garonne. The leap into the 20C was due, in the end, to its distance from the hub of activity and therefore of battle during the 1914–18 war, combined with plentiful supplies of manpower and energy (coal from Carmaux, hydro-electricity from the Pyrenees). The father of aviation, Clement Ader from Muret, made a primitive flying machine, *Eole*, which lifted off the ground in 1890, and is also credited with the invention of the word *avion* (aeroplane). Pierre Latécoère's boiler-making factory near Toulouse was converted to produce Salmson observation aircraft in 1917, and following the First World War Latécoère launched **Aéropostale**, with which the aviators St-Exupéry and Mermoz were both associated. Fighter planes were pioneered in the workshops of Emile Dewoitine; Concorde made its first flight in Toulouse in 1969; and Airbus Industrie is now an important employer in the region. In June 1993 a metro opened and the town has restored many monuments and created new centres for the study of art and of space. Toulouse is now the French Cité de l'Espace. It still provides the pulse that reverberates around a region whose furthest point north is some 200km away.

Place du Capitole and St-Sernin

The hub of Toulouse is the huge **Place du Capitole**. The square is a vast semi-pedestrianised area (created 1811–52) with pavement cafés and covering an underground car park. It springs to life on Wednesdays with a colourful market.

The space is dominated by the brick-and-marble façade of the **Capitole** building (1750–60). The entrance is in the northeast corner of the courtyard. Galeries du Capitole open Mon–Fri 08.30–17.00, closed Sat afternoon and Sun, except PH; ☎ 05 61 11 34 12.

Capitole is an unusual title for what anywhere else in France would be known as the *hôtel de ville* (town hall) and stems from an historical and etymological mutation. By the 11C the elected council or chapter of the municipality—*capitulum* in Latin and *capitol* in Occitan—enjoyed considerable autonomy. *Capitulum*, *capitol* and *capitolium* (the name of the ancient temple) fused to become Capitole, denoting both the chapter and the *maison commune*, and its officers were known as *capitouls*. The *maison commune* was established here in the 12C, deliberately distanced from the Counts' palace at the other end of town, now Place du Salin.

The present façade—designed by Guillaume Cammas—was intended as a monumental screen for a disparate group of buildings which existed until 1873, when most were indiscriminately demolished. It now masks the town hall and the Théâtre du Capitole. The central pedimented portico is emphasised by eight columns in candy-pink marble from the Montagne Noire—to symbolise the eight *capitouls*—and there are large sculptures above the central portico by Marc Arcis, François Lucas and Louis Parant. The central archway leads to Cour Henri IV (1602–06) with a monumental gateway begun in 1546 by Nicolas Bachelier (d. 1556/57), the most original and talented Toulousain architect of the Renaissance. Above the arch is a statue in polychrome marble of Henri IV (1607). A marble plaque in the paving commemorates the execution of the Duke of Montmorency, Maréchal de France, Governor of Languedoc and godson of Henri IV, on 30 October 1632, for opposing Richelieu.

The **Galeries du Capitole** on the first floor include the Salle des Mariages with light-hearted décor dedicated to themes of love (*c* 1916) by Paul Gervais. The next room has Impressionist-style murals by the local painter Henri Martin (see p 200), including a frieze-like composition of a group strolling on the banks

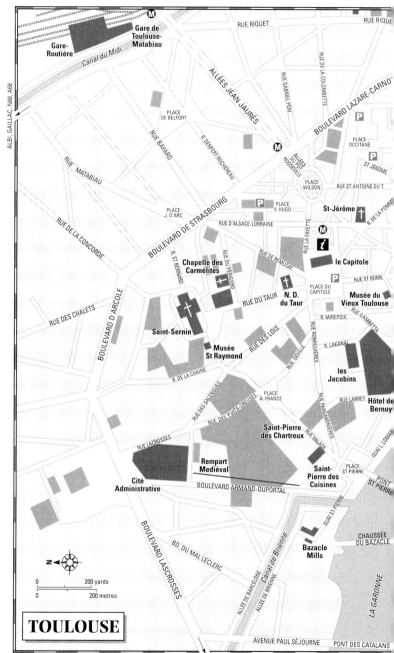

ALBI; GAILLAC; N88, A68

RUE RIQUET

RUE RIQU

Gare de Toulouse-Matabiau

M

Gare-Routière

Canal du Midi

RUE DE LA COLOMBETTE

RUE GABRIEL PÉRI

ALLÉES JEAN JAURÈS

BOULEVARD LAZARE-CARNOT

P

PLACE OCCITANE

PLACE DE BELFORT

R. DENFERT-ROCHEREAU

M

ALLÉES DU PDT ROOSEVELT

P

ST-JÉRÔME

RUE MATABIAU

RUE BAYARD

PLACE WILSON

RUE ST ANTOINE DU T.

RUE DE LA CONCORDE

PLACE J. D'ARC

BOULEVARD DE STRASBOURG

P

PLACE V. HUGO

RUE D'ALSACE-LORRAINE

RUE DE RÉMUSAT

RUE LA FAYETTE

St-Jérôme

T

R. DE LA POMM

M

i

Chapelle des Carmélites

R. ST BERNARD

RUE DU PÉRIGORD

le Capitole

P

RUE ST ROME

PLACE DU CAPITOLE

Musée du Vieux Toulouse

RUE DES CHALETS

BOULEVARD D'ARCOLE

RUE DU TAUR

N. D. du Taur

R. MIREPOIX

RUE GAMBETTA

Saint-Sernin

Musée St Raymond

RUE DES LOIS

RUE DÉVILLE

RUE ROMIGUIÈRES

R. LAKANAL

les Jacobins

R. DE LA CHAINE

RUE DES SALENQUES

RUE DES PUITS-CREUSES

PLACE A. FRANCE

RUE PARGAMINIÈRES

RUE LARREY

Hôtel de Bernuy

RUE LACROSSES

Saint-Pierre des Chartreux

RUE VALADE

QUAI L'LOMA

Rempart Mediéval

PLACE ST PIERRE

PONT ST PIERRE

Cité Administrative

BOULEVARD ARMAND-DUPORTAL

Saint-Pierre des Cuisines

QUAI ST-PIERRE

CHAUSSÉE DU BAZACLE

BOULEVARD LASCROSSES

BD. DU MAL LECLERC

CANAL DE BRIENNE

Bazacle Mills

LA GARONNE

N

0   200 yards

0   200 metres

ALLÉE DE BARCELONE

ALLÉE DE BRIENNE

AVENUE PAUL SÉJOURNE

PONT DES CATALANS

TOULOUSE

MONTAUBAN, N20, A62, AIRPORT

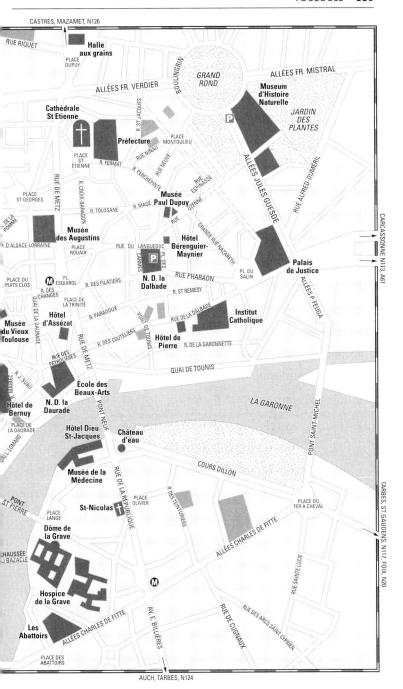

CASTRES, MAZAMET, N126

RUE RIQUET

Halle
aux grains

PLACE
DUPUY

GRAND
ROND

ALLÉES FR. MISTRAL

ALLÉES FR. VERDIER

Museum
d'Histoire
Naturelle

BOULINGRIN

JARDIN
DES
PLANTES

Cathédrale
St Etienne

R. ST JACQUES

Préfecture

PLACE
MONTOULIEU

PLACE
ST
ÉTIENNE

R. FERMAT

RUE NINAU

RUE NEUVE

R. PERCHEPINTE

RUE
ESPINASSE

ALLÉES JULES GUESDE

RUE ALFRED DUMÉRIL

PLACE
ST GEORGES

RUE DE METZ

R. CROIX-BARAGNON

R. TOLOSANE

RUE MAGE

R. UZENNE

Musée
Paul Dupuy

DE LA
POMME

R. D'ALSACE-LORRAINE

Musée
des Augustins

PLACE
ROUAIX

RUE DU LANGUEDOC

RUE
CARMES

PL. DES

Hôtel
Bérenguier-
Maynier

GRANDE RUE NAZARETH

PL. DU
SALIN

Palais
de Justice

CARCASSONNE N113, A61

PLACE DU
PUITS CLOS

ESQUIROL

R. DES CHANGES

R. DES FILATIERS

N. D. la
Dalbade

RUE PHARAON

R. ST REMESY

ALLÉES P. FEUGA

PLACE DE
LA TRINITÉ

R. PARADOUX

RUE DE LA DALBADE

Institut
Catholique

Hôtel
d'Assézat

QUAI DE LA DAURADE

R. DES COUTELIERS

PONT DE TOUNIS

Musée
du Vieux
Toulouse

RUE DE METZ

Hôtel de
Pierre

R. DE LA GARONNETTE

RUE DES
PEYROLIÈRES

QUAI DE TOUNIS

R. J. SUAU

École des
Beaux-Arts

LA GARONNE

PONT SAINT-MICHEL

R. MALBEC

Hôtel de
Bernuy

N. D. la
Daurade

PONT NEUF

PLACE DE
LA DAURADE

ALL. LOMARD

Hôtel Dieu
St-Jacques

Château
d'eau

COURS DILLON

PONT
ST PIERRE

Musée de la
Médecine

RUE DE LA RÉPUBLIQUE

PLACE
LANGE

St-Nicolas

PLACE
OLIVIER

R. DES TEINTURIERS

PLACE DU
FER A CHEVAL

TARBES, ST GAUDENS, N117, FOIX, N20

CHAUSSÉE
J BAZACLE

Dôme de
la Grave

ALLÉES CHARLES DE FITTE

RUE SAINTE LUCIE

Hospice
de la Grave

AV. E. BILLIÈRES

RUE DE CUGNAUX

RUE DES ARCS SAINT CYPRIEN

Les
Abattoirs

ALLÉES CHARLES DE FITTE

PLACE DES
ABATTOIRS

AUCH, TARBES, N124

of the Garonne, among them Jean Jaurès, the socialist politician who came from the Tarn (see p 336). The stuccoed and gilded gallery overlooking the Place du Capitole, the Salle des Illustres (1892–98), inspired by the Villa Farnese in Rome and combined with turn-of-the-century excess, was the creation of Paul Pujol. The statues represent illustrious citizens while the walls and ceiling carry historical and allegorical paintings of the great moments in the history of Toulouse.

The opposite side of the building from Place du Capitole is **Place Charles de Gaulle**, a public garden with fountains. The back of the Capitole building is an 1883–84 replica of the west elevation. The tourist office is housed in a building called the **Tour des Archives** (1525–30), the only surviving part of the old Capitole. Since its restoration in 1873 by Eugène-Emmanuel Viollet-le-Duc, chief architect of the Monuments Historiques (see p 56), it is more reminiscent of buildings of the Loire Valley than the Midi.

On the northwest of Place du Capitole, at the angle of Rue des Lois and Rue Romiguières, is the **Hôtel du Grand Balcon**, a modest establishment haunted by the memory of aviation pioneers such as Antoine de Saint-Exupéry (author of *The Little Prince*) and Jean Mérmoz.

Take **Rue du Taur**, the old north–south route that served the *bourg* of St-Sernin. To the right above the rooftops appears the *clocher mur* (belfry gable), characteristic of the Toulousain, on the 14C brick church of **Notre-Dame-du-Taur** (begun *c* 1300). According to legend, the church of Notre-Dame stands on the site of St Sernin's first resting-place. On the south wall of the rather dingy interior of the aisleless building is a mural showing the genealogy of Jacob, with 38 figures.

The area west of Rue du Taur was the heart of the **medieval university**: Rue des Pénitents-Gris leads to Rue du Collège de Foix where, behind a wall, stands the former college founded in the 15C by Cardinal Pierre de Foix; and in the same street are the steeple and the gateway, all that remain of the great 13C/14C convent of the Cordeliers.

On the east side of Rue du Taur, at the intersection with Rue du Périgord, is **Tour Maurand**, a fragment of the oldest secular building in Toulouse. In Rue du Périgord, behind the pink façade and green door on the left, is the small Counter-Reformation **Carmelite chapel**. Between 1741 and 1751 the walls and ceiling of this simple building were decorated by the painters Jean-Pierre Rivalz and Jean-Baptiste Despax with themes of theological and monastic virtues mixed with Old Testament prophets, scenes from the New Testament and the *Glorification of St Theresa*. The chapel's exceptional acoustics, due to the wooden roof, make it a perfect venue for musical performances. Open May–Sept 09.30–12.30 and 14.30–18.00; Oct–April 09.45–12.30 and 14.00–17.30; closed Mon and PH; ☎ 05 61 21 27 60.

At 69 Rue du Taur is the monumental doorway designed by Nicolas Bachelier (*c* 1555) for the Collège de l'Esquile, now the **Cinémathèque**; for programme information, ☎ 05 62 30 30 11.

Basilique de St-Sernin

Rue du Taur leads to Place St-Sernin and the south flank of the most celebrated building in Toulouse, the basilica of St-Sernin, the largest conserved Romanesque church in Europe. Open July–Sept, Mon–Sat 08.30–18.15, Sun 08.30–19.30; Oct–June, Mon–Sat 08.30–11.45 and 14.00–17.45, Sun 08.30–

12.30 and 14.00–19.30. Apse and crypt open July–Sept Mon–Fri 10.00–18.00, Sun 11.30–18.00; Oct–June Mon–Fri 10.00–11.30 and 14.30–17.00, Sun 14.30–17.00; ☎ 05 61 21 70 18. Take binoculars to see the carved capitals inside.

Small green gardens and mature trees soften its surroundings but most of the oval *place*, created in the 19C to the detriment of the monastic buildings, is littered with cars. (At weekends the stalls of a flea market form a barricade around the basilica but no barrier to pickpockets.) Built in a combination of brick and stone, St-Sernin underwent a huge programme of repair, consolidation and derestoration at the end of the 20C to secure, clean and return it to its putative profile of 1860/1872, before Viollet-le-Duc. The restoration work inside and out was completed *c* 2000.

The first shrine on this site was planned by Bishop Silve but built by Bishop Exupère *c* 400 to shelter St Sernin's relics, translated in 402 or 403 from Bishop Hilaire's modest wooden oratory to the south. By the end of the 11C a larger building was needed—and a more beautiful one desirable—to accommodate hordes of pious travellers *en route* for Santiago de Compostela, and for the needs of the resident clergy. The chapter was in funds as a result of the Gregorian disciplinary reforms, and the new church was begun in the third quarter of the 11C in the form of a Latin cross, with double aisles flanking the nave and radiating chapels around the apse and on the east side of the transepts. The altar table is inscribed with the date of its consecration by Pope Urban II, 24 May 1096, and is signed by the stonecarver, Bernard Gilduin. Raymond Gayrard, saintly canon and former builder of bridges, took charge of the building works at the end of the 11C when the chevet and the transept were already complete. By the time of his death in 1118 the three east bays of the nave had been vaulted and the body of the church was finished up to the level of the tribune windows, the part in stone and brick visible from the exterior. The collegiate church was elevated to abbey in 1117 and attention then turned to the construction of the cloisters and the monastic buildings, leaving the church unfinished, although there was a surge of activity in the 13C under Abbot Bernard de Gensac (1243–64).

Exterior The **east end** of the basilica is the most beautiful part of the building. The five semi-circular radiating chapels clustered around the apse and the four chapels of the transepts create an undulating rhythm, with a secondary rhythm of colour contrasts set up by the use of brick for the mass and stone for the structural elements. All the elements are repeated in different tempos, resulting in a finely orchestrated yet powerful structure culminating in the 65m-high octagonal **belfry**. At the end of the 20C restoration of the upper part, where there is an obvious lack of stone, reinstated the *mirandes* under the eaves. The belfry was built in four stages: the first stage with blind arcades covers the crossing dome, then come two levels with twin round-headed open bays surmounted by two stages with mitred bays built in the second half of the 13C. The stone spire was added in 1478.

On each transept is a portal in the form of a triumphal arch, but both are now closed, and only the **Porte des Comtes** (*c* 1082–83) on the south transept has kept its sculpted décor. Members of the leading family of nobles were buried in the small funerary recess on the left in sarcophagi from the early Christian

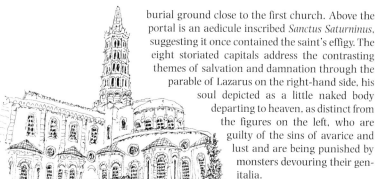

St-Sernin

burial ground close to the first church. Above the portal is an aedicule inscribed *Sanctus Saturninus*, suggesting it once contained the saint's effigy. The eight storiated capitals address the contrasting themes of salvation and damnation through the parable of Lazarus on the right-hand side, his soul depicted as a little naked body departing to heaven, as distinct from the figures on the left, who are guilty of the sins of avarice and lust and are being punished by monsters devouring their genitalia.

The delicately sculpted Renaissance archway, formerly part of the 16C enclosing walls, stands before the south door which is known as the **Porte Miègeville** (*c* 1110–15), which used to run through the town centre, *mièja vila*. A projecting bay with a single arch and heavily sculpted cornice protects the all-important carved tympanum, one of the first examples of its kind. The iconography deals in a literal manner with the theme of the *Ascension*: Christ is assisted by angels who lift him physically by his waist. On the lintel below, the 12 Apostles contemplate the scene, flanked by the two men cited by the Acts who explain that Christ will return. The stylised twisted postures emphasise the awe of the scene, just as the deep carving of the folds stresses the solidity of the bodies and the upward fluid movement of the whole composition. There are stylistic similarities with the altar-table carvings by Gilduin in St-Sernin, and by the master of Jaca, Spain.

Three of the four capitals flanking the door are storiated. On the right is the **Expulsion from the Garden of Eden**; its counterpart on the left depicts the *Annunciation*, the antithesis to the Fall. Note that the Angel Gabriel has his legs crossed, one of the earliest appearances in sculpture in the Languedoc of the convention for expressing movement. On the side face is a *Visitation* and the outer left capital graphically describes the *Massacre of the Innocents*. The fourth capital, with two lions imprisoned in tendrils, suggests the influence of the sculpture at Santiago. Carved consoles support the lintel: on the left is King David, the musician ancestor of Christ, between two lions; on the right, two round-faced figures wearing Phyrgian bonnets sit astride lions, one foot bare and the other shod, an unexplained motif. In the right spandrel is St Peter holding the keys of heaven. The panel above, with two angels, was placed or replaced here in the 19C, whereas the panel below, representing Simon the Magician, has never been moved. In the left spandrel St James is framed between bare tree-trunks, his name engraved in his halo, as it is at Santiago. Below him is a panel with two women astride lions flanking a male figure.

The **west portal**, begun after the Porte Miègeville (*c* 1115–18), although unfinished, shows a progression from the others in quality and wealth of decoration. Eight capitals are deeply and vigorously carved with intricate vegetal forms twined around human figures and animals which cling on to the astragals with fingers or claws. Sculpted reliefs from this portal are in the Musée des Augustins. Above the double doorway is a gallery of five arches surmounted by a large rose window with no tracery. The narthex was not tampered with during the 19C and still has its original *mirandes*. The two incomplete towers were brought to their present state in 1929.

Interior The interior is reassuringly harmonious and tranquil, unified by the regularity of the eleven bays of the nave and soft light from the aisles and the tribune. The barrel-vaulted nave is 21m high, divided by transverse arches springing from engaged columns supported by square pillars. The double aisles take the thrust of the high nave and also create beautiful diagonal views. The elegant tribune around the nave and transepts consists of a series of double openings, each pair divided by twin columns. The floor was lowered in the 19C.

In the 1970s, when the 19C plaster and paint were removed to reveal the alternating brick and masonry, several **medieval wall paintings** were discovered in the north transept. Among these, on the last pillars of the north aisle, are an angel seated on clouds and a *Noli me Tangere*. The largest fresco is on the west wall of the north transept (c 1180), using the arches to frame five scenes from the *Resurrection*, culminating with the Lamb of God in the vaults. There are other fragments in the north transept and 14C murals in the south transept chapel dedicated to the Virgin. The 12C *Christ on the Cross* in wood and gilt was heavily restored in the 19C.

The finely carved choir stalls (1670–74) have similarities with those at the cathedral of St-Etienne. The famous **altar table** by Bernard Gilduin, carved on the chamfered edge, can be glimpsed through the 18C choir enclosure; there is a replica in the north transept. The crossing has been subjected to many structural alterations and decorative additions. It received painted decoration (recently restored) in the 16C and a reredos carved by Marc Arcis in 1720. The final resting-place of St Sernin is beneath the ostentatious Baroque baldaquin (1718–58), behind the altar. Etienne Rossat's sculpture of St Sernin was added in 1759.

The **capitals** are quite remarkable for their quality and quantity (some 268). Many are in the tribunes, and while the majority have vegetal designs of great skill, variety and beauty, some are storiated. They date from c 1080 in the east to c 1118 in the west. Many of them are difficult to see, and a full description would take another book, so it is a good idea to take binoculars.

Enter the **apse** from the north transept. The oldest storiated capital is of Daniel between some rather benevolent lions, on the east capital of the southeast apsidal chapel. On the inner wall of the ambulatory are seven late 11C marble reliefs recalling carved ivories or metalwork on a monumental scale. The three smaller panels in the centre, attributed to Bernard Gilduin, may have been part of an altarpiece and are known to have been in this position since the 19C. The central panel portrays a fleshy, heavy-jowled but dignified Christ framed in a mandorla and surrounded by the symbols of the four Evangelists. On his right is a cherub, on his left a seraph. Flanking these are two angels and two Apostles, in a larger format and possibly later. In 1258 the relics of St Sernin were raised from the crypt and placed under a heavy canopy in the church, and the **crypt** was then rib-vaulted. The lower crypt was vaulted in the 14C and its central pier is reputed to be the only surviving fragment of the previous church. There are a number of reliquaries on display but the most valuable have been transferred to the Musée Paul Dupuy.

In the 17C the **ambulatory** became the Tour des Corps Saints (Circuit of the Holy Relics), where carved and gilded shrines of the Counter-Reformation were placed in the chapels and aedicules, demanding some considerable aesthetic adjustment. These were ripped out and dumped in the tribunes in the 19C but restored and replaced in 1980. There is also a 16C post-plague ex-voto offering suspended above the north ambulatory, and an altar table designed by Viollet-le-Duc in the main chapel. Sections of the organ case date from the 17C and the instrumental part was replaced in 1888 by an organ from the workshop of Aristide Cavaillé-Col, adapted to the size of the building and to the sounds of the late 19C and early 20C using many of the earlier pipes.

West of St-Sernin is the **Musée St-Raymond**, an important archaeological museum housed in the former Collège St-Raymond, an attractive brick building of 1523. A go-ahead place, extended and renovated a few years ago, it has a wide-ranging collection from the Bronze Age to the early Middle Ages. Open daily 10.00–18.00; June–Aug to 19.00; closed 1 Jan, 1 May, 25 Dec; ☎ 05 61 22 31 44. Finds made in the Midi include Iron Age (3C–2C BC) jewellery such as the splendid gold torques and bracelets from Lasgraïsses (Tarn) and from Fenouillet, near Toulouse; and from Toulouse come mosaics, trinkets, small bronzes and coins. The highlights of the collection are the antique sculptures discovered in the Villa Chiragan at Martres-Tolosane, notably the largest find of portrait busts in France. The museum also owns such treasures as a replica by a Roman sculptor of Praxiteles' *Venus of Cnidus*, copies of Myron's *Discobolus* and *Athena*, and a series of vigorously sculpted reliefs of the *Labours of Hercules*.

From Rue St-Bernard is a great view of the chevet of the basilica, best in winter when the trees are bare. The *faubourg* of St-Sernin was incorporated within the *cité* walls when they were rebuilt in 1346 at the time of the Hundred Years War. Turn right into Boulevard de Strasbourg, on the line of the medieval defences, where the produce market is held.

At the junction with Rue de Remusat is a department store built in 1908, now occupied by *Galeries Lafayette*, a vaguely Art Nouveau structure in exposed metal and yellow brick. The main north–south thoroughfare, **Rue d'Alsace-Lorraine**, was carved through the medieval town in the late 19C. Rue Rivals leads to **Place Victor-Hugo** and the combined car park (above) and *halles* (below).

Southwest of the market is **Place Wilson**, a 19C oval space with a garden, fountain, specimen trees and statue of Pierre Godolin (1580–1649), the most celebrated Occitan poet of the 17C, by Alexandre Falguière. Around the square are cinemas and pavement cafés. Off the *place*, in Rue Pierre-Baudis, is the **Théâtre de la Cité**, a nice mixture of modern and ancient architecture, with a fragment of the Roman ramparts in the basement. After a recent revamp, it is an interesting exercise in the use of space, with a large foyer and café. It offers a variety of entertainment; ☎ 05 34 45 05 00, fax 05 34 45 05 10.

Place Wilson, with Allées du President Roosevelt and Allées Jean-Jaurès, was part of a grand scheme opening out towards the **Canal du Midi**. Traces of *céruse* (distemper) in pale *café-au-lait* or other pastel shades can still be seen on many 19C buildings. This was not simply frivolous camouflage but an attempt to brighten the streets at night and so increase the safety of the public, following an order of 1783 by the city fathers.

The building on the corner of Rue d'Alsace-Lorraine and Rue La Fayette was the first department store in Toulouse, *Bazar Labit*, which was replaced in 1877 by another store, the Maison Universelle, for which the present building was constructed.

The Jacobins and the quays of the Garonne

Southwest of Place du Capitole, between the right bank of the Garonne and Rue St-Rome, is the former Dominican monastery of the Jacobins, the second most celebrated religious building of Toulouse.

Eglise des Jacobins

From Rue Gambetta, with a colourful Art Nouveau building, turn right into Rue Lakanal to be confronted by the cliff-like apse of the church of the Jacobins. Open daily 09.00–19.00; ☎ 05 61 22 21 92. Fee payable to visit cloisters.

Dominic de Guzman (1170–1221), a Spaniard, settled in the southwest in 1206 with the express intention of turning people away from their so-called heretical beliefs, and in 1215 he founded an order of preaching friars avowed to poverty. Recognised in 1217 by Pope Honorius III, the brotherhood developed and eventually moved in 1229 to the present site, where the building of the first church began in 1230. Dominic left Toulouse after less than six months but his followers grew ever more powerful and resolute, to the extent that in 1233 Pope Gregory IX confided to the Dominicans the task of the General Inquisition. The prior, Pons de Saint-Gilles, and four brothers were named Inquisitors. On 4 August 1234 the church was consecrated and in the same year the Inquisition began its persecution. Subsequently the Dominican Inquisitors lived and worked from Place du Salin while the rest lived a monastic life at the Jacobins convent. The name Jacobins was acquired from their Parisian community in Rue St-Jacques. The church was requisitioned by the artillery after the Revolution, altered and desecrated; in the 1840s the army deemed the building unworthy of attention. It survived thanks to Prosper Merimée and a lengthy programme of restoration but before this could begin some 5000 cubic metres of soil, which had been used to raise the floor to street-level, had to be removed.

Exterior The church was built not to receive pilgrims but to preach to the masses. Its simple volumes, almost devoid of decoration, are a sober reminder of its predicative function and the avowed poverty of the Dominican order. Constructed entirely in warm russet-coloured brick and tiles, the exterior is articulated by tall angular buttress piers and narrow lancet windows in recesses, creating a rhythm of deep shadows. The only vestige of the church of 1234 are the late Romanesque-style arch and early Gothic capitals of the **west façade**, hidden until 1964 by 18C remodelling. A new campaign of building began in 1244 and continued for more than a century. The octagonal belfry of 1298, built to receive the great bell of the university, was undoubtedly inspired by the upper levels of the belfry of St-Sernin.

Interior The entrance on the south is mainly a reconstruction of the 14C entrance with the coat of arms of Cardinal Godin, who bequeathed 4000 florins to the church in the 14C, in the vault. The exterior does not totally prepare you for the unusual arrangement of the interior, which is divided lengthwise by an enfilade of tall slender columns creating two equal sections, the south destined for the public, the north reserved for the clergy. On the ground in the first five bays, black marble slabs indicate the extent of the earlier building, which was extended eastwards with a five-sided apse (1244–53). This was later raised and vaulted (1275–92), and the first mass was celebrated on 2 February 1292 in the main chapel dedicated to the Virgin. The rest of the church was raised to the same height between 1324 and 1326 thanks to Cardinal Godin's bequest. The glory of the Jacobins church is the elegant **column** at the east from which spring 22 ribs, like the branches of a palm tree, to support the vaults 28m above ground. The effect is enhanced by the use of alternate red and green to outline the ribs.

From the beginning this simple and austere edifice was held in such high esteem that in 1368 Pope Urban V, penultimate pope at Avignon and former student of Toulouse, selected it as the resting-place for the **relics of St Thomas Aquinas** (d. 1274), who was canonised in 1323. Returned in 1974 to their original 13C position at the centre of the north nave, the relics of the saint lie in a gilded wooden casket (1827) beneath the main altar, a simple marble table.

Of the 11 chapels, the four eastern ones were enlarged in the 16C, and in 1609 the axial chapel was converted into a rectangular shape with a four-sided brick dome and lantern. The painted wall and vault decoration, discovered under plaster, dates from the end of the 13C and early 14C, and is claimed to be 60 per cent original. Most of the medieval stained glass disappeared in the 19C. The present windows in the chevet were installed between 1923 and 1930 while the modern glass in the nave was designed by Max Ingrand in 1951.

In the northwest corner of the nave a small door leads to the **cloisters**, a dark green oasis of box hedges and cypresses in the red-brick frame of the monastic buildings. The cloister, with brick arcades supported by 80 pairs of slender marble colonnettes and grey St-Béat marble capitals with foliate designs, took shape between 1306 and 1310. It was dreadfully damaged in the 19C to allow the horses which were stabled here to circulate, and original elements were scattered throughout the region, but some were recovered and used in 1965–70 to return the cloister to its original form. The central well has a new coping and in the northeast corner is the cover of the remains of the lavabo.

The **chapter house** (1299–1301) has two slim hexagonal marble columns supporting the vaults on intersecting ribs, and traces of 17C mural paintings. The floor has been reconstituted from fragments of old tiles and tombstones. The St-Antonin chapel, wedged between the chapter house and refectory in the northeast angle, was built 1337–41 by the Dominican Bishop of Pamiers as a chantry chapel and burial place, and is dedicated to the patron of his diocese. Irreparable damage was inflicted in the 19C when it was transformed into the veterinary hospital for the artillery, although the rich 14C painted décor of the *Second Coming* and the *Legend of St Antonin* has survived on the upper walls and vault. The great **refectory**, which replaced an earlier, smaller one in 1303, was damaged in the 15C by the earthquake. It now houses exhibitions of modern and contemporary art. The entrance to the gallery is on Rue Pargaminières.

South of the Jacobins, the Lycée Fermat on Rue Lakanal was founded by three *capitouls* in 1566 as a Jesuit college and named after the mathematician Pierre Fermat (1601–65). The great entrance gate on the diagonal dates from 1606. It occupies a building begun *c* 1502 by Jean de Bernuy, a Castillian who came to

Toulouse to make his fortune in *pastel*. The **Hôtel de Bernuy** is a complete and delightful example of an early Renaissance *hôtel particulier*. The flat brick façade on Rue Gambetta has a late Gothic doorway sculpted by Aymeric Cayla (1504), concealing an early 16C courtyard which can be visited during the academic year. The return of the façade and the right side of the courtyard (1530) are the work of Louis Privat. In this small space is an abundance of Italianate motifs—busts in medallions, candelabra, deep cornices and a pierced balustrade. A perilously low coffered basket arch and vaulted passageway in the northwest lead to a second courtyard with a *tour capitulaire*, also by Cayla, with angle windows and busts. Jean de Bernuy, who guaranteed François I's ransom after his defeat at Pavia (Italy) in 1525, is said to have died in his own palace in 1556 during a mini-*corrida* to celebrate the arrival of his nephew.

Rue J. Suau, named after the painter born at no. 8, has one of the rare Art Nouveau houses in Toulouse at no. 4. The street opens out into the Place de la Daurade and garden beside the river.

The area to the west is worth exploring, and includes the churches of St-Pierre-des-Chartreux, Rue Valade and **St-Pierre-des-Cuisines**. The latter, which has been renovated, is used by the Conservatoire de Musique as an auditorium. The Gothic church in brick was built over the fragments of a 5C funerary basilica which can be seen in the archaeological crypt. Open mid-July–Aug daily 14.00–19.00; Sept–June, Mon 09.00–12.30; ☎ 05 61 22 31 44. The banks of the Garonne (quai St-Pierre) bring you to the **Canal de Brienne**, built in 1768, and the mills of Bazacle, established in the 12C, which brought their shareholders enormous profit. A hydro-electric plant was installed in 1889 and put an end to milling. The **Bazacle** can be visited and has an exhibition space. Reopening September 2003; ☎ 05 62 30 16 00.

The riverbank, once the site of the gardens of the Benedictine monastery of La Daurade, was pulled into shape in 1766–77 at the time of Lomenie de Brienne (Archbishop of Toulouse 1762–88), to create the Quai and the **Port de la Daurade**. The loss of the gardens is regrettable, but even more so the gilded sanctuary called La Dorée, which stood on the site of the parish church of **Notre-Dame-de-la-Daurade** until 1759.

The origins of this sacred precinct are a subject of debate but are usually cited as being of the 5C. Negligible documentation exists to record the splendour of the polygonal domed structure covered with gold leaf and mosaics illustrating the *Life of the Virgin*. It became a Benedictine priory in the 11C under the auspices of Cluny when a cloister was built. By 1759–61 the church was so insecure that it had to be demolished. The cloister disappeared in 1811 but some of the magnificent 11C capitals were gathered up and are conserved in the Musée des Augustins.

The present grandiose building was begun in 1772 and consecrated in 1838. The Marian tradition associated with this site is perpetuated in the *Black Virgin and Child*, a copy (1807) from memory of a 14C wood statue burned in 1799, venerated by pregnant women. The gloomy Neo-classical interior is decorated with a series of seven episodes from the *Life of the Virgin* by J. Roques, and a late-19C enamelled ceramic composition by Gaston Virebent provides the background to the Black Virgin.

Immediately adjacent to the church of La Daurade is the jollier *fin-de-siècle* **Ecole des Beaux-Arts** by Pierre Esquié, inaugurated in 1895. The Quai de la Daurade provides a shady green walk on a hot dusty day. The **Pont Neuf** was begun in 1544, in use by 1603 and completed in 1632. The seven low arches are almost semi-circular and gill-like openings outlined in stone pierce the massive brick piers, a practical embellishment to allow floodwater to flow through. Now the oldest bridge across the Garonne, it once linked Languedoc, on the right bank, with Gascony on the left. From it there is a view of the dignified brick elevation of the **Hôtel-Dieu St-Jacques**, containing a museum of the history of medicine (open Wed–Sun; ☎ 05 61 77 84 25) and to the west the dome of the **Hospice de la Grave**, the successors to the plague hospitals and hospices for the poor founded in the suburb of St-Cyprien during the Middle Ages. Sheltering at the base of the Hôtel-Dieu is the last remnant of the old 15C Pont Couvert, at the narrowest part of the river.

Once across the Garonne you have a wonderful view back to the city. In a brick tower at the end of the bridge there is a photographic gallery, the **Château d'Eau**. Open Tues–Sun 13.00–19.00, closed Mon and PH; ☎ 05 61 77 09 40. Built in 1822, the year that Nicéphore Niepce pioneered photography, it is probably the only gallery anywhere installed in a circular water tower. Worth visiting simply for the building, it has excellent temporary exhibitions. Certain parts of the Hôtel-Dieu St-Jacques opposite can be visited, and nearby is the 14C church of **St-Nicolas** with a reredos designed by J.-B. Despax (1768), one of the finest in Toulouse. South of the Château d'Eau is Cours Dillon and a grassy area beside the river.

Still on the left bank, but further north at the end of Pont des Catalans, is **Les Abattoirs**, the centre for modern and contemporary art. This is an exciting new venue bringing Toulouse's art scene into the 21C. Open Tues–Sun 12.00–20.00, closed Mon; ☎ 05 62 48 58 00, www.lesabattoirs.org. The nearest metro is St-Cyprien-République.

Brick abattoirs built in 1827 by Urbain Vitry, who became chief architect of the town, have been inventively transformed into an art gallery which consists of a large central hall, two levels of smaller galleries on either side (a Musée d'Orsay in miniature), and a basement. The centre also has a café, bookshop and multi-media library. The collection comprises some 2000 works from the second half of the 20C, by 667 artists from 44 countries (not all on show at once), made up from donations and national collections. It is particularly focused on artists of the 1950s–70s and there are representative samples of the major movements of the period from Europe, the United States and Japan, such as Art Informel, Cobra, Gutai, Arte Povera, Trans-avantgarde, and so on. Artists represented include Robert Mapplethorpe, Robert Rauschenberg, Victor Vasarély, Marcel Duchamp, Jean Dubuffet, Hans Bellmer, Lucio Fontana, Sam Francis, Jean-Paul Riopelle, Antonio Tàpies, Armand-Pierre Arman, Brassaï, César, Combas and Hans Hartung. There are installations, interactions, videos and temporary exhibitions. One work that does not fit the general requirements is a large stage backdrop designed by Picasso with Luis Fernandez for Romain Rolland's ballet *Le Quartoze Juillet* (1936), which is exhibited alternately with other works in the basement space.

The *quartier* has picked up with the new focus on Les Abattoirs. Nearby is the

Centre Municipal de l'Affiche which presents three exhibitions a year on a particular theme. Open Mon–Fri 09.00–12.00 and 14.00–18.00; ☎ 05 61 59 24 64. The area along the river between the gallery and the Hospice de la Grave has been landscaped.

Back on the right bank, **Rue de Metz** was built in the 19C to join the Garonne to the canal and bypass the ancient east–west route. During construction work the site of the Roman theatre was uncovered at the junction with Rue Peyrolières.

From the Pont Neuf, follow the river along the **Quai de Tounis**, originally important commercial wharves but now a ship-shape recreation area. On the left is a street called Pont de Tounis because it was originally a bridge. It leads to Rue de la Dalbade and the eclectic west façade of the church of **Notre-Dame-de-la Dalbade**. The brick mass of the 16C façade has a Flamboyant rose window above a stone portal with Renaissance motifs. In the tympanum is Virbent's eye-catching pastel-tinted ceramic copy of Fra Angelico's *Coronation of the Virgin* (1874). The church, the fourth on this spot, takes its name from the first, Notre-Dame de l'Eglise Blanche, and was built *c* 1480–1550. Inside is a 17C polychromed processional statue of *St Peter walking on the Water*, as the patron of the *Confrérie des bateliers et pêcheurs de Tounis*.

The long and narrow **Rue de Dalbade** leading to Place du Parlement was the obvious place for wealthy parliamentarians to live. A discreet exploration of courtyards is often rewarding. Next to the church at no. 32 is the Hôtel des Chevaliers de Saint-Jean de Jerusalem, built in the 17C by Jean-Pierre Rivalz, inspired by the Chigi Palace in Rome. The **Hôtel de Pierre** at no. 25, built in 1538 for Jean de Bagis, is the most famous in the street. It bears the hallmarks of Bachelier's work in the arrangement of the window reveals around the courtyard as well as the powerful atlantes supporting the pediment of the west doorway. François de Clary added antique marbles recovered from the river bed in 1613 to the east and west wings of the courtyard and created the overpowering façade from stone originally intended for the Pont Neuf, to which were added huge sculpted motifs in 1857. Equally extravagant is the portal dated 1556 at no. 22, ironically bearing the motto '*sustine et abstine*', which marks the entrance to the fairly modest Hôtel Gaspard Moliner. Towards Place du Parlement, at 31 Rue de la Fonderie on the old Roman ramparts, is the **Institut Catholique**, with a small museum dedicated to archaeology, iron casting (cannons) and 19C agricultural tools. For opening times, ☎ 05 61 36 81 00.

From the church of La Dalbade, cut through from Square de Gorsse to **Rue Filatiers**, where linen spinners and tailors worked. Here are several timber-framed houses, some sympathetically modified, some negligently modernised. The triangular **Place de la Trinité**, refreshed by a fountain inaugurated in 1826, was one of the first of many projects designed by Urbain Vitry. No. 57 is a Neo-classical delight with a balcony, full-length statues and busts in niches. Rue des Marchands has a specially fine selection of the many caryatids which prop up parts of Toulouse, the best at no. 28, made by Auguste Virebent in 1840. The Virebent dynasty capitalised on the properties of clay and new manufacturing techniques to produce for this stone-poor city every kind of decorative element in terracotta.

Cross Place d'Assézat to the **Hôtel d'Assézat**, the most famous of the *pastel* palaces and the finest Renaissance *hôtel particulier* in Toulouse. Pierre d'Assézat, seduced by the lure of the *pastel* industry, quit his native Rouergue, became a *capitoul* in 1552 and in 1555 engaged the eminent architect, Nicolas Bachelier, to build his mansion. Bachelier, who designed the north and west wings of the courtyard, came up with a very personal interpretation of the Classical idiom using brick and stone. Pairs of superimposed orders on the façades isolate the windows. At the junction of the two wings is a square stairtower with a monumental entrance at the base. The tower extends upwards into a *tour capitulaire* topped with an elegant lantern. Pierre d'Assézat never saw the completion of his *hôtel*. In 1561 his election as *capitoul* for the second time coincided with the collapse of the *pastel* industry and his exile because of his Protestant convictions. Bachelier's son, Antoine, completed the screen wall to the street *c* 1571. The extension to the east was never carried out and some of the original fenestration was altered in 1761.

The building became the home of the **Académie des Jeux Floraux**, ancestor of the Académie Française, founded in 1323 to safeguard the language and poetry of Oc and organise an annual competition. In the 16C the story got about that the funds originated from a rich beauty, Dame Clémence, as the flowers distributed to the laureates were made of silver. In the portico on the reverse of the south façade is a statue supposedly of this semi-mythical patroness, Clémence Isaure; it is, in fact, the remodelled tomb statue of Bertrande Ysalguier (d. 1348). On 3 May each year, the winners of the competition are presented with flowers blessed on the altar of the Black Virgin of La Daurade; among those honoured by the society have been Ronsard, Chateaubriand and Victor Hugo.

The Hôtel d'Assézat now houses the very fine collection of the **Fondation Bemberg**. This is a permanent display including over 40 European works, predominantly from the 16C and 17C, among which are paintings by Lucas Cranach, Jean Clouet and Pieter de Hooch; and more than 80 French paintings from the late 19C and 20C, of which 35 are by Pierre Bonnard, and others by Edouard Manet, Camille Pissaro, and the Fauves. Open Tues–Sun 10.00–12.30 and 13.30–18.00, Thur to 21.00, closed Mon, 1 Jan, 25 Dec; ☎ 05 62 27 11 50.

In Rue de la Bourse is the elegant 18C Hôtel de Nupces and, almost opposite, the 15C **Maison Pierre Delfau**, also built by a *pastel* merchant, one of the few remaining houses of the late Middle Ages. Further along Rue du Metz is **Place Esquirol**, a large square where the recent discovery of the Roman Capitolium was made. Close by is the Musée des Augustins (see below).

To return to Place du Capitole, turn left into **Rue des Changes**. This street, with Rue des Filatiers and Rue St-Rome, was the main artery between the Capitole and the *parlement* in medieval times. While the layout of the street and the plots have hardly changed, the fire of 1463 destroyed most of the buildings which were almost totally rebuilt by rich merchant families and *pastel* magnates. A lively, pedestrian street, since the beginning it has been full of boutiques, small tradesmen and general commerce. Look up at the variety of buildings huddled together, with an occasional *tour capitulaire* showing above the façades. Parts of 15C–16C houses remain at nos 16 and 19.

Rue St-Rome—named after the church of St-Romain, the very first Dominican monastery given by Bishop Foulques to Dominic de Guzman in 1216—starts at the junction with Rue Peyras. At one time the street was named after the fishmarket, Bancs Majous, where no. 14 now stands; it closed in 1550 but the aroma lingers on and on ... No. 3 is one of the most beautiful Henri IV-style buildings in Toulouse, in alternating stone and brick with sculpted mullions, bossed door and arched boutiques partly uncovered; the courtyard, opening on to Rue Tripière, was remarkably restored in 1974.

Tucked away in **Rue Tripière** are two interesting houses, built by *capitouls* in 1529 and 1617, acquired in 1898 by the journeymen carpenters and now the Musée des Compagnons. Open Wed 14.30–17.30. In Rue du May, the **Musée du Vieux Toulouse** is installed in the 16C house of Antoine Dumay, doctor to Marguerite de Navarre, restored by Dr Simeon Durand in 1914. In the dark rooms around an attractive courtyard are many objects relating to the history of Toulouse. Open daily mid-May–mid-Oct 14.00–18.00; ☎ 05 61 13 97 24.

Rue Saint-Rome leads back to Place du Capitole.

The Musée des Augustins and Cathédrale St-Etienne

Set off from Place du Capitole at the corner between the theatre and the *Grand Hôtel de l'Opéra*, the site of the 14C Collège St-Martial which became a convent in the 17C. South of Rue Poids de l'Huile, sandwiched between Rue St-Rome and Rue d'Alsace, is a tangle of small streets radiating out from **Place Salengro**, created in 1849, with a pretty fountain and some well-restored façades. Place des Puits Clos has four pink marble columns saved from the retable of the church of La Dalbade.

Turn east and cross Rue d'Alsace to Rue Lt.-Col. Pélissier. In 1576 the secular order of the Pénitents-Bleus made their base in this street and, in 1622, commissioned Pierre Levesville to build their church, **St-Jérôme**. This curious building exudes a secular atmosphere because the narthex is a passageway with display cabinets and is often used as a short-cut by shoppers. The church, all curves, stucco and small loggias, decorated in the 18C by the painter J.-P. Rivalz and sculptor Marc Arcis, resembles a Baroque theatre. The corridor comes out into Rue de la Pomme, a pleasant shopping street which brings you to the most congenial square in Toulouse, **Place St-Georges**, with a small garden, pretty façades and a host of inviting restaurants and pavement cafés. Its ambience undoubtedly derives from the fact that it is one of the oldest squares and was the main market for centuries.

Musée des Augustins

Rue des Arts runs alongside the church and chapter house of the former Couvent des Grands Augustins, begun in 1309, now the Musée des Augustins, the rich and wide-ranging municipal fine art collection in an unexpectedly delightful setting. Open Mon, Thur–Sun 10.00–18.00, Wed 10.00–21.00, closed Tues, 1 Jan, 1 May, 25 Dec; ☎ 05 61 22 21 82, www.augustins.org.

> The religious community of the monastery was disbanded at the Revolution and part of the premises was occupied by the Ecole des Arts in 1804. It was partly demolished in the 19C, then given its definitive and dignified role as museum and art gallery. Viollet-le-Duc's project for the museum in 1873 was carried out by his pupil, Denis Darcy, who built the western galleries between 1880 and 1896.

Enter from Rue de Metz: a short flight of steps leads down to the large cloister completed in 1396, where a **cloister garden** has been created. On the left is a welcoming choir of upturned gargoyles from the old Cordeliers church. There are sarcophagi in the cloister aisles, and engraved medieval inscriptions (11C–16C) in a small gallery on the west. The museum has the most important collection of **Romanesque sculpture** anywhere in the world. The 350 pieces include capitals and other sculptures rescued from the cloisters of La Daurade, St-Sernin and St-Etienne. The eight oldest capitals (c 1100) are from the first workshop of La Daurade and show a great affinity to the Moissac cloister capitals but include themes not found there. Two famous and enigmatic sculptures from the west façade of St-Sernin, the signs of Leo and Aries (first quarter of the 12C) are iconographically unique in Christian art. The St-Sernin cloister capitals (1118–25) show an advance in technical skill to create fluent carvings, mainly of animal and vegetal motifs. The cutting is deeper, more subtle, the detail more delicate and the plastic qualities of the carving enhanced. The group of capitals from the second Daurade workshop place greater emphasis on narrative dynamism than the first. One of the most celebrated capitals from St-Etienne, *Herod's Feast* (c 1120–40), portrays an overtly seductive Salome. Also from the cathedral are the very fine reliefs by Gilabertus of St Andrew and St Thomas and others from the same workshop.

   Gothic sculpture is presented on the east of the cloister in the former sacristy, the chapel of Notre-Dame-de-Pitié (1341) and chapter house (14C–15C). These include funerary objects such as the remarkable 14C recumbent statue of Guillaume Durant, 16 statues from the Chapelle de Rieux, including Bishop Jean Tissendier presenting the chapel which was part of the Cordeliers church, and the exquisitely moving 15C *Notre-Dame-de-Grasse*. The youthful Virgin and her infant face outwards, away from each other, suggesting they were originally part of a larger group. The 14C/15C church is used for a collection of **religious paintings** by local artists such as Antoine Rivalz and Nicolas Tournier. Other European paintings include an early Murillo, one of three versions of the *Legend of St Anthony of Padua* (c 1627–32) by van Dyck, Rubens' highly dramatic *Christ between the Two Thieves* (c 1635), and a Perugino. The Bachelier reliefs (1544–45) made for La Dalbade are also here. A wide range of 17C–19C **secular paintings** are exhibited in the upper galleries of the west wing, rebuilt in the 19C. Local painters such as Chalette and Roques are represented among others. Outstanding is the charming portrait of *La Baronne de Crussol* by Vigée-Lebrun. The 19C is splendidly evoked by the Salon Rouge where *pompier* works are hung in the manner of the Salons, one atop the other against a red brocaded wall. Delacroix, Ingres and Toulouse-Lautrec are also represented. Overtly narcissistic are the 19C plasters, echoed by duplicates on the staircase in the southwest corner.

Cross Rue de Metz at the junction with Rue d'Alsace-Lorraine and walk along Rue de Languedoc as far as Place Rouaix, so named since before 1180. Since 1913 the chamber of commerce has occupied the 18C Hôtel de Fumel at the start of **Rue Croix-Baragnon**, originally the residence of the presidents of the *parlement*. An agreeably well-maintained street with some expensive boutiques, Croix-Baragnon is representative of the smart residential area this side of town. no. 15, called the Romanesque house (c 1300), is considered the oldest in Toulouse. Typical of the 18C, the Hôtel de Castellane is in brick and terracotta painted to imitate stone. Pause at the junction with Rue des Arts for an impressive double view which will help you understand the geography of the town: towards the north is the belfry of the Augustins and, at the end of Rue Croix-Baragnon to the east, the strangely asymmetrical west front of the cathedral of St-Etienne. No. 1 Rue des Arts is a rare example of a timbered house from before the blaze of 1463. Inside 22 Rue Croix-Baragnon are the tastefully reused and replicated arcades from the 16C Hôtel Jean des Pins, demolished at the beginning of the 20C. At no. 41 is one of the best early Louis XVI façades, with superb ironwork by Bernard Ortet, who worked at the Capitole and the cathedral in the 18C.

The spacious triangular **Place St-Etienne**, the result of 19C and 20C remodeling, has many 17C and 18C houses. The Griffoul fountain in the centre of the square is the oldest in Toulouse. On the octagonal lower basin (1549) are spaces still awaiting the coats of arms of *capitouls*. Four columns support another basin, from the former provosts' dwelling, and the obelisk (1593) by Antoine Bachelier incorporates four little figures spouting water, re-cast from four *mannikin pis* considered slightly improper in such a holy situation.

Cathédrale St-Etienne

The cathedral is set off to advantage by the *place* but the building lacks the coherence of St-Sernin. The decidedly disturbing effect of the façade is due to a succession of modifications made since the 11C. The cathedral in fact consists of two incomplete churches, one dating from the early 13C and the other begun *c* 1272.

The first documented reference to a cathedral dedicated to St Etienne (St Stephen) is 844. At the time of Gregorian reform, Bishop Isarn, who was elected in 1071, stimulated moral and physical improvements including the rebuilding of the cathedral. The Romanesque church, transformed during the episcopates of a Cistercian, Foulques de Marseille (1205–31), and a Dominican, Raimond du Fauga (1232–70), is a prototype of the aisleless, rib-vaulted meridional Gothic church. When Bertrand de l'Isle-Jourdain was elected to the episcopate he planned to build a cathedral twice as large as the previous one to the east and north of the earlier nave. (When work began in 1272, the Rayonnant cathedral of Narbonne was under way; de l'Isle had been involved in settling a dispute in Narbonne over the site of the new cathedral, and was undoubtedly influenced by the work going on there.) After his death in 1286 the work was further slowed down when Pope John XXII reduced the size of the diocese, and it came to a halt at the end of the 14C due to lack of funds. By this time the choir, up to the level of the triforium, and 15 chapels had been completed and were protected by a provisional wooden roof. Work did not take off again seriously for over a century, and it was not until a fire in 1609 devoured the timber roof and all the choir furnishings that the stone vault was begun in 1611 by Pierre Levesville, with money donated by Cardinal de Joyeuse. The work was not completed until the 20C when the north door was built.

Exterior The earlier church seems to lean against the brick belfry but is in fact supported by two enormous brick buttresses at right angles to the façade. Between these, under a slightly pointed relieving arch, is a large rose window inserted when the façade was almost complete. The Flamboyant portal, inserted *c* 1450, is decidedly off-centre because the architect, Martin Baudry, was at pains to save the baptismal chapel north of the entrance. The **belfry** is composed of a Gothic portion on Romanesque foundations, capped by the 16C gable belfry. From the gardens on the north you can see the large rectangular buttresses of the later Rayonnant building. Continue round the chevet to the south courtyard where, until 1811, the Romanesque cloister and monastic buildings stood. The south buttresses are more elaborate than on the north. Enter by the south door and you are midway between the two different structures.

Interior   The effect of the interior is as disconcerting as the exterior because the two sections are not on the same axis and juxtapose two styles of Gothic architecture. They were separated by a wall until the beginning of the 16C when Archbishop Jean d'Orléans attempted to begin the transept by building the massive round pillar now standing incongruously between the two parts. On it is a memorial to Pierre-Paul Riquet, designer of the Canal du Midi (see p 509). Only three bays of the early 13C church remain and anything that previously existed further to the east has been consumed by the great late 13C choir. To the west is the rather dark and cavernous section known as **Raymond VI's nave** because of the east boss, carved with 12 pearls in the shape of the Cross of Toulouse. A vast single space with wide rounded vaults, it is supported by powerful rectangular ribs which spring from Romanesque capitals salvaged from the 11C church. The only light falls from the rose window, containing some original glass. This part of the building was nearing completion during one of Simon de Montfort's sieges of Toulouse, in either 1211 or 1217–18. On the walls are tapestries woven in Toulouse in the 17C recounting the story of the Bishops of Toulouse.

The vast proportions of the five-bay **choir**, with ambulatory and radiating chapels, dwarf the older nave. The shafts are little more than undulations on the surfaces of the cylindrical cores, and the capitals minimal, but the triforium is ornate. The height of the vaults at 28m is considerably lower than the planned 40m and the ribs spring from just above the triforium. Of the 15 chapels, the oldest date from 1279–86, but the majority were completed during the 14C accounting for some interesting carved bosses, such as *St Louis Enthroned* (*c* 1300) in the St-Joseph chapel. The first chapel on the south, built in the 15C by Archbishop Bernard du Rosier, is almost a church within a church. The majority of the **stained glass** is 19C, but there is some earlier, including panels from the end of the 13C in the St-Vincent de Paul chapel. This is the oldest stained glass in Toulouse, created from windows salvaged from the Jacobins, and depicts a Bishop and St Stephen, St Michael and the Virgin and Child. The glass in the St-Augustin chapel is also 14C, and that in the St-Louis chapel is 15C with portraits of Charles VII, King of France and the Dauphin, the future Louis XI. There is some 17C glass which shows a similarity with the work of Arnaud de Mole in Auch.

The **furnishings** offer a series of interesting works, especially the double range of choir stalls carved in walnut between 1610 and 1613 by Pierre Monge of Narbonne. Their decoration includes pagan and mythological subjects which contrast with the little statue of the Virgin under the triumphal arch at the top of the episcopal throne. Also carved at the same time was the walnut case of the organ, perched some 17m above the floor. Restored in 1868 by Cavaillé-Col and again in 1976, it is often used for concerts. The tapestry hanging (*c* 1609) by Jean du Mazet, from Castillon near Lombez, has scenes from the life of

St Stephen. The rather hectic Baroque retable of the main altar was designed by Pierre Mercier, and Gervais Drouet sculpted the central panel of the ***Stoning of St Stephen*** (1667). The four Evangelists carved by Marc Arcis were added at the beginning of the 18C. The polychrome marble is from the Carcassonne region, carried to Toulouse on the Canal du Midi. The more restrained ironwork of the choir enclosure (1766) is the work of Bernard Ortet, and the medallions were originally gilded. There are paintings by H. Pader and Nicolas Bollery (17C) and by Despax (18C), who delighted in the use of pastel colours. The 19C episopal throne is by Auguste Virebent.

From the west door of St-Etienne you pass in front of the **Préfecture**, housed since 1800 in the former archepiscopal palace (17C). The area southwest of the cathedral is the posh end of Toulouse, where the wealthy professionals and *haute bourgeoisie* have their homes. Most visitors do not get this far, but the old narrow streets lined with grand *hôtels particuliers* with courtyards and gardens make a very pleasant afternoon's wander.

Rue Fermat is a street rich in Louis XVI façades and elegant ironwork; the tiny Place Stes-Scarbes has a modern fountain composed of six columns and a rather fine 18C balcony at no. 6. Rue St-Jacques leads to a fragment of the 1C Gallo-Roman enclosure, uncovered in 1962, and the vast Palais du Maréchal-Niel, built in the 19C for Napoléon III's war minister in the style of a Parisian palace. Rue Ninau contains the charming **Hôtel Ulmo**, purchased in 1526 by Jean d'Ulmo, first president of the *parlement*, who had the house enlarged and embellished with a unique design for the main entrance consisting of a double flight of steps to a *perron* (platform) under a baldaquin.

Either Rue Ninau or Rue St-Jacques will take you to the green and pleasant spaces of the Grand Rond and the **Jardins des Plantes**. A former Carmelite property was used for the natural history collections forming the basis of the Jardin des Plantes and the science faculty, later to become the medical school. In 1865 the **Musée d'Histoire Naturelle** opened its doors to the public. It boasts the second largest collection of stuffed monkeys in France, as well as the first Prehistoric gallery, thanks to historians E. Cartailhac and Abbot Breuil. Closed until 2005 for renovations; ☎ 05 61 52 00 14. Simon de Montfort met his death near here, killed by a missile from a catapult on the city walls on 25 June 1218. In Avenue F. Mistral is the **monument to the Résistance** (1971). Open Mon–Fri 10.00–12.00 and 14.00–17.00, closed Sat, Sun and PH. Not far from the Jardin des Plantes is the Musée Georges Labit, with non-European art and artefacts, at 43 Rue des Martyrs de la Libération. Open Mon, Wed–Sun June–Sept 10.00–18.00; Oct–May to 17.00; closed Tues and PH; ☎ 05 61 22 21 84. The Musée de la Résistance et de la Déportation is at 52 Allée des Demoiselles. Open Mon–Fri 09.30–12.00 and 14.00–18.00, Sat 14.00–17.00; ☎ 05 61 14 80 40.

Leading off Place St-Scarbes is **Rue Perchepinte**, originally the main street of this aristocratic neighbourhood. The houses are modest but the overall effect is agreeably attractive with some pretty details and plenty of good ironwork. Where Place Perchepinte meets Rue Espinasse is what remains of the superb **Hôtel de Mansencal** (1527–47), combining Gothic form with Renaissance decorative elements.

The **Musée Paul Dupuy** is housed in the former Hôtel de Besson at 13 Rue de la Pleau, restored in a manner befitting this important decorative arts museum.

Open Mon, Wed–Sun June–Sept 10.00–18.00; Oct–May to 17.00; closed Tues and PH; ☎: 05 61 14 65 59. Paul Dupuy, wealthy owner of the Toulousain department store **Bon Marché**, collected the items that others rejected and installed them here after purchasing the building in 1905. On the ground floor is the complete interior of the 17C pharmacy of the Jesuit college with its jars and bottles. The museum contains a variety of religious artefacts and the famous *cor de Roland*, an 11C carved ivory oliphant from southern Italy described in the 15C as belonging to Roland, the legendary nephew of Charlemagne. Charmingly displayed on the first floor are porcelain and *faïence*, 17C Venetian glass and 19C and 20C glass by Baccarat and Emile Gallé. The Salon de Musique has mainly 18C and 19C instruments, and a marvellous pink room displays an exotic automaton called La Leçon de Chant, signed Robert Houdin, Paris 1844. The museum is probably most famous for its exceptional collection of clocks and watches of all kinds donated by Edouard Gelis, and it has recently added to this a series of magic lanterns and cinema apparatus. There are regular temporary exhibitions.

On Rue Ozenne is the Renaissance tower erected in 1533 by Guillaume de Tournoer or Tournier. When Rue de Languedoc was cut in the late 19C, **Hôtel Vieux-Raisin** or Bérenguier-Maynier was spared, and after many years of neglect it has been totally restored. The Gothic wall on Rue d'Aussargues was endowed with Renaissance windows after the *capitoul* Bérenguier-Maynier, a man of his time, acquired the house in 1515. He also added two wings to the principal dwelling. Jean Burnet became the owner in 1547 and, influenced by the work of architects such as Bachelier, built the front courtyard facing the Rue de Languedoc with a portico linking the two wings. All the façades are heavily adorned with caryatids, atlantes and fauns. Where Rue de Languedoc and Rue d'Ozenne meet is a classy confectioner and pastry shop, **R. Pillon**, selling a speciality cake called Le Fénétra, found only in Haute-Garonne and made with lemon and almonds.

Further along Rue de Languedoc is one early 16C façade of the sober **Hôtel de Pins**, the house of Jean de Pins, Bishop of Pamiers and Rieux, scholar of Bologna and Italian ambassador to François I, who was condemned for his friendship with Erasmus. Rue d'Alsace-Lorraine will take you back to Place Charles de Gaulle, and Rue des Changes to Place du Capitole.

The **Cité de l'Espace**, a sophisticated and informative theme park on the edge of Toulouse, opened in 1999. It is designed to give as much back up as possible to Toulouse's designation as 'City of Space' and the scope of the exhibits ranges from a fragment of moon rock to the Ariane 5 rocket. Take the Périphérique east and Exit 17 or 18. Open July, Aug, Sat, Sun, school holidays and PH 09.30–19.00; other times to 18.00; ☎ 05 62 71 48 71.

The **Roman amphitheatre** (1C AD) at Purpan-Ancely, northwest of Toulouse, is a vestige of antique Toulouse which has largely disappeared, a few remains of the vomitoria and some building blocks remain, but it mainly has to be imagined. Remains of the thermae were discovered under a neighbouring building and these can also be visited. Open Sat, Sun, May–Oct 14.00–18.00; July, Aug 15.00–19.00; ☎ 05 61 12 06 89.

Glossary

-eost, -ac suffixes denoting a Gallo-Roman origin

abacus horizontal element above a capital

abbaye laïque specific to the Béarn from late Middle Ages to the Revolution; describes the property (house) of a 'lay abbot' or layman, a member of the lesser nobility, with certain associations with the church such as collecting the *dîme* (taxes paid to the clergy) and the right to propose a curate for nomination by the bishop

abrasion a technique used in stained glass: the surface of an outer coloured layer of glass is ground away to reveal white glass beneath

abri rock shelter as used by prehistoric man

ambo an early version of the pulpit, where the Epistle and Gospel were read aloud

annealing a technique used in stained glass: the insertion of a jewel-like piece of glass into a larger context without using leads

apsidiole small apsidal chapel

astragal a small semi-circular moulding found at the top of a column, etc

atlante supports in the form of sculpted male figures

basket-handle arch low almost semi-circular arch, late medieval/Renaissance

bastide planned town of the Middle Ages

bat a valley (Pyrenees)

bateau moulin floating mill

bâtons écotés a moulding resembling a branch whose off-shoots have been pruned

bolet an upper terrace or veranda reached by exterior steps leading to the entrance (Quercy)

borie a stone hut

bourg town or village

cabane hut or log cabin

cagots marginals or outcasts in the Middle Ages, of unknown origin, who lived and worshipped on the edge of the community or church

caldarium hot room

Calvinist most French Protestants (Huguenots) adhered to the doctrine of John Calvin

capital a conical or pyramidal block, frequently with decorative carvings, between a column or pier and a horizontal block; it is made up of the drum (main block), the abacus (flat slab above the drum), and astragal (the moulding below the drum)

capitoul the name given to municipal administrators of Toulouse until the Revolution

cardo Latin name for the main street running north–south

castlenau a community coming under the jurisdiction of, and protected by, a new castle and walls

causse a limestone plateau

cazelle a rural stone refuge (Quercy)

chauffoir warming house

chai(s) a wine and spirit storeroom, wine cellar

charterhouse/chartreuse a Carthusian monastery

chartre de coutumes medieval charter stipulating laws and privileges (usually in connection with a *bastide*)

chauffoir heated room in a monastery

chemin de ronde a walkway around the battlements of a castle

chevet a French word to describe the east end of a church, including the apse and ambulatory

chrism the chi-rho monogram of Christ, from the first two letters of the Greek word *Christos*

cirque steep-sided hollow or natural amphitheatre

cité the oldest part of certain towns

clocher peigne a gable belfry divided vertically into two or three sections, something like a comb

clocher pignon/clocher mur a church belfry that is a flat extension of the gable or wall

collégiale collegiate church, i.e. with chapter of canons

in commendam where the tenure of a religious establishment was given to a cleric or layman, often an absentee landlord, who benefited from the revenues

commune the smallest administrative division in France, each with a mayor

concordat an agreement reached between the Holy See of Rome and Napoléon in 1802 regulating the connection between Church and State

Congregation of St-Maur created in 1621 after the Reformation and Religious wars to assist religious communities that had been put *in commendam*.

corps-de-logis main building

corrida a bull fight (Spanish)

courses landaises cattle running, when cows (rather than bulls) from the Landes are chased but not killed

couvert the arcades or covered walk around the centre of a *bastide*

croix pattée an arrow slit to accommodate a crossbow, introduced by the English

decumanus Latin name for the main street running east–west

département an administrative division in which the main executive is the *préfet*; most were created in 1790

dodecastyle portico with 12 columns

dolmen a megalithic tomb of large flat stones

donjon a castle keep or tower above ground

echaugette a suspended watchtower, often on the angle of a wall or fortification

enceinte enclosure

enfeu niche

enfilade a line, series, suite of columns, windows, doors, etc

ex-voto an offering given in fulfilment of a vow

faïence glazed earthernware

faubourg close suburbs or outskirts of a town

Flamboyant late medieval style of French decoration and architecture (equivalent period to Perpendicular in England)

four banal a communal oven

frigidarium cold room

fronton a wall against which the Basque ball game *pelote* and its variations are played

fronton-mairie town hall with a wall that doubles as a *fronton*

gabarre a traditional flat-bottomed river boat used on the Dordogne

gariotte a little stone hut (Quercy)

gave a mountain torrent (Pyrenees)

généralité administrative district from 1633 until 1789, at the head of which was an *intendant*, agent of the king

génoise mouldings a cornice of superimposed Roman-style tiles

gisant recumbent statue

gisement mineral deposit in the ground

glacis a defensive arrangement at the foot of the wall consisting of a gentle slope; contemporary with the introduction of cannons

Gregorian reforms Gregory VII (St Hildebrand), Pope 1073–85, great spiritual leader of the medieval period, gave his name to ecclesiastical discipline and reform which had begun in the mid-11C under his predecessors. The reforms addressed such issues as the marriage of priests, simony (by which holy office is obtained for money), and the investiture of ecclesiastics by laymen, which was settled only in 1122.

griotte type of bitter cherry (morello)

Guyenne the part of Aquitaine owned by the English in the 12C–15C

gypseries a composition like stucco, made from lime (gypsum) with powdered marble or plaster, which can be modelled

halle couverte a covered marketplace

hôtel particulier a private town mansion

Huguenot French Calvinists or Protestants: by association with the name of a burgomaster from Geneva, Hugues Besançon, and a Swiss-German word meaning 'confederate'

hypocaust underfloor heating comprising hollow space

intendant steward

intrados inner curve of an arch

jacquemart a mechanical figure which strikes the hour with a hammer

Jacobin Dominican churches; from the Dominican community in Rue St-Jacques in Paris. Also a political group at the time of the Revolution

jubé the rood screen or altar screen in a church

jurade medieval term used in connection with wine confraternities

label-stop an ornamental boss at the end of a hood-mould (ie the moulding around an arch, doorway or window)

labyrinth found in some medieval churches whose route the faithful followed on their knees in penance or supplication

lanterne des morts an expression used for a comical stone structure found in Périgord, often in cemeteries

lauze traditional stone roof cladding in the Périgord and Rouergue. In Périgord the *lauze* is rectangular and held in place on steeply racked timbers by the sheer weight of the superimposed stones; in Rouergue the *lauze*, sometimes shaped like a fishscale, is pegged to the timbers with a single nail.

lavoir a public wash house, usually roofed but open at the sides

lierne vaulting tertiary rib in late Gothic vaulting which is decorative, not load bearing

mandorla an oval shape, usually framing images of Christ (from Italian, almond)

marché au gras a market for specialities produced from duck or geese, particularly foie gras

mascaron decorative grotesque masque ornamenting a façade

merlon raised portion of a battlement (or crenellation)

mirande small openings immediately under the roof to ventilate the timbers, which are found in many buildings in the Midi from the 13C, sometimes incorporated into a *chemin-de-ronde*

narthex the vestibule of western part of a church between the entrance and the nave

natatio swimming pool

neste a pre-Celtic word for river (Pyrenees)

Occitan the modern name for the language of Oc, spoken in the southwest

paréage the foundation of a *bastide* by agreement between local nobility, a representative of the King (seneschal) and the Church (abbeys or monasteries)

parlement law courts equivalent to an assizes

parvis open space in front or around a church

pastel dyers' woad, the leaves producing a high-quality blue dye, cultivated in large quantities in parts of the Languedoc from the 14C to the 16C

pech, puech, puy old word for hill or mound (Occitan)

pelican a Christian symbol representing the Eucharist

pendentive a concave spandrel leading from the angle of two walls to the base of a circular dome; a means of effecting the transition from square or polygon to circle

Pénitents members of secular confraternities who practised piety and charity and wore a hooded costume coloured (blue, white or black) according to the order

perron an exterior platform with steps

phoenix a Christian symbol of the Resurrection

pigeonnier a dovecote either integral with the farmhouse or freestanding, in a variety of forms (Gascony and the Quercy). Pigeons were an important source of food and fertiliser until the 19C, and the size of the pigeonnier was a measure of the property of the owner

piscina bathing pool; in a church, a container or basin that holds holy water

pisé a floor made out of *lauze* stones laid upright in a clay bed

plate tracery decorative openings cut out of a solid piece of stone (12C–13C)

pompier *style pomier* from the French for fireman, refers to pompous and frigid academic paintings, reputedly derived from such works as David's Sabine Women (1799) where male nudes in firemen's helmets posed as classical Greek heroes.

pontet or **pountet**   a construction joining two buildings, often spanning a public right-of-way

préfecture   the main town in a *département*

présidial   a high-level tribunal or magistrates court (but lower than *parlement*) instituted by Henri III in 1552

Rayonnant   Gothic style *c* 1230–*c* 1350, named after the pattern of radiating lights in rose windows

région   the largest administrative division in France, made up of several *départements*; created in 1972

retable   a freestanding decoration, painted or carved, behind the altar

rinceau   a low-relief frieze with a foliate or floral motif

routier   a hired mercenary (or a sort of highwayman)

Saintonge   an old province (capital at Saintes), included in present-day Poitou-Charentes, where a distinctive style of church architecture featuring a very decorative, multi-tiered west end developed in the Romanesque period

sauveté/sauveterre   a place of refuge or safety under the protection of the Church

seneschal   an agent of the king in charge of administrative or judiciary functions; suppressed in 1191 but the title remained to describe royal officers who had the power of bailiffs

Serlian window   window with three openings, the central one arched and wider than the others; so-called because first illustrated in Serlio's *Architettura* (also known as Palladian or Venetian)

sigillated pottery   clay pots with impressed patterns applied with stamps or moulds, decorated with red slip and fired at a high temperature

soleilho   an open gallery on the top floor of a house, often used for drying crops

souillarde voûtée   an outside scullery (Quercy)

spandrel   a triangular surface between an arch, the horizontal drawn from the level of its apex, and the vertical from its springing; also the area between two arches in an arcade; or the surface of a vault between adjacent ribs

squinch   an arch placed diagonally at the angle of a square tower—often in a system of concentrically wider and gradually projecting arches—to effect the transition to a polygonal or round superstructure

star vault   (also stella) vaulting where the liernes and tiercerons are arranged in the shape of a star

stela   a standing block, sometimes engraved or sculpted

talus   the slope at the foot of a fortified wall

tepidarium   warm room

tertre   slightly raised on elevated ground

tetramorph   the apocalyptic beasts each with the face of a man as seen in a vision by Ezekiel which became the symbol of the Four Evangelists

thermae   bath complex, usually public

torchis   wattle and daub

tour capitulaire   an extended stairtower which is a symbol of status and wealth incorporated into the houses of Toulousain *capitouls* or *parlementaires*

transhumance   the transfer of sheep and cattle from the valleys to summer pastures in the mountains

trumeau   the central pier supporting the lintel of a monumental doorway

vic   a subdivision or group of several villages (Pyrenees)

vielle   the old word used as a suffix and prefix to mean commune or rural district (Pyrenees, expecially the Louron district); further north replaced by the suffix *ac*

viguier   the magistrate and representative of the king, who meted out justice in certain provinces until 1789

Index

To find abbeys, caves (*grottes*), châteaux, rivers and valleys, please see under the relevant subject headings. Birth and death dates are provided for artists and architects.

T